ECOL

BOOK CATALOG

Environmental Conservation Library

Minneapolis Public Library

AMERICAN LIBRARY ASSOCIATION

Chicago 1974

Library of Congress Cataloging in Publication Data

Minneapolis. Public Library. Environmental Conservation Library.
    Book catalog of the Environmental Conservation Library, Minneapolis Public Library.
    At head of title: ECOL.
    1. Man—Influence on nature—Bibliography—Catalogs. 2. Environmental protection—Bibliography—Catalogs. 3. Minneapolis. Public Library. Environmental Conservation Library. I. Title.
Z5861.M56 1974   301.31   73-21865
ISBN 0-8389-0173-5

International Standard Book Number 0-8389-0173-5 (1974)

Copyright © 1974 by the Minneapolis Public Library

All rights reserved. No part of this publication may be reproduced in any form without permission in writing from the publisher, except by a reviewer who may quote brief passages in a review.

Printed in the United States of America.

Contents

Introduction	v
Environmental Reference Tools	vii
Author and Main Entry Catalog	1
Subject Catalog	83
Title Catalog	149
Appendix 1. Pamphlet File Subject Headings	193
Appendix 2. Periodical List	197

Introduction

BACKGROUND

This catalog represents the collection of the Environmental Conservation Library of Minnesota (ECOL) as of September 10, 1973, when it contained over 2,800 titles of books and government documents, augmented by periodicals and substantial numbers of pamphlets, papers, brochures and related materials.

ECOL was launched as a public department of the Minneapolis Public Library in April, 1972. Before its formal opening, the collection was funded by $50,000 in private contributions. In 1971 the Minnesota Legislature appropriated money for its support and designated it a statewide environmental information center, thereby making it a cooperative enterprise of the State and the Minneapolis Public Library. ECOL now lends books and provides information services without charge to any person or organization in Minnesota. Further, this collection is available to users nationwide under the usual interlibrary loan conditions.

SCOPE OF THE COLLECTION

ECOL attempts to bring together publications from all subject fields which relate to man's physical environment and his impact upon it. The collection includes writings on such diverse subjects as resource management, environmental policy, law, pollution, conservation, population, forestry, wildlife, energy, and environmental education. These publications come not only from trade publishers but also from professional associations, industries, citizen organizations, and agencies of federal, regional, state and local governments.

Because it cuts across the traditional subject divisions of library collections and of academic disciplines, ECOL possesses a special vitality that derives from its being a coherent body of information that might otherwise be diffused in a general collection.

The collection contains works ranging in sophistication from introductory books for children to highly technical reports on minute aspects of single subjects. From this description the user can readily perceive the wide sweep of problems ECOL covers. Its scope insures that any particular information he may seek will almost surely be found somewhere in the collection.

Although the books and documents here cataloged have been selected with particular attention to the concerns of Minnesota and those contiguous areas circumscribed by a five-hundred mile radius from Minneapolis (an area proudly dubbed the "golden circle" by Minnesota's dean of conservationists, Sigurd Olson), the collection is sufficiently general to serve as a guide and model for any other library. Only in part can ECOL be said to have a regional emphasis, for only in part are environmental problems amenable to regional solutions. The regionalism of ECOL—and its wider range of application—is manifest in two fundamental respects. First, because it has a definite geographic focus, ECOL seeks to cover intensively all environmental and ecological situations that occur within its domain. For example, ECOL has excellent coverage of the ecology of wetlands. Obviously this strong segment of its collection will be of lesser interest to those who live and work in arid or semiarid sections of the country. However, ECOL's regional coverage of the ecology of wetlands will undoubtedly be of great value to those in other wetlands regions who must also deal intensively with this aspect of ecology.

Secondly, ECOL's regionalism is reflected in its exhaustive coverage of the publications of governmental and private agencies, such as agricultural experiment stations, located within its domain. Here again, the work is regional only in part. Broader use may be made of ECOL by adapting this list to the requirements of libraries in other regions, with librarians substituting their own regional materials for the Minnesota materials represented here.

FUTURE EDITIONS

Since the ECOL collection will continue to grow, supplements and new editions of the catalog are projected. Titles added between editions will be reflected in

Introduction

the card catalog in the Environmental Conservation Library.

USES OF THE CATALOG

As the systematic bibliographic record of a coherent collection, the ECOL catalog serves as a guide to the selection and acquisition of environmental materials by other libraries. Its complete author, title and subject approaches make it an effective tool for the bibliographic verification of titles cited in other sources. It may be used as a basis for ordering books on interlibrary loan, a service which ECOL is pleased to render outside Minnesota under the usual conditions, to the extent such service does not deprive its primary clientele. And finally, it is the primary tool for access by ECOL's major clients—the citizens of Minnesota. From the catalog they may identify materials for borrowing, and if those users are not conveniently located to pick up the desired materials themselves, ECOL will mail to any point in the state.

COMPUTER PREPARATION

The catalog has been prepared by computer. It conforms as nearly as possible to Library of Congress cataloging, classification and subject headings. Because the collection is relatively small, an elaborate system of cross-referencing has been provided to improve its serviceability for the reader who may not be highly sophisticated in the ways of libraries. Filing is basically that of the American Library Association's rules for filing catalog cards, but modified in this case for computer processing. Proofreading was performed as part of the computer operation.

ORGANIZATION

In the *author and main entry* catalog, the author may be an individual, a firm, a government agency, an institution, a conference, or some other organization. In cases where neither an individual nor a corporate author is identified, the main entry is under the title. If an author may be identified in more than one way, suitable cross-references are supplied to lead the inquirer to the correct entry.

The *subject* catalog will lead the reader to works which deal entirely or in part with a given topic. Subjects are arranged alphabetically. Subdivisions of a subject which follow dashes precede all other extensions of the subject, such as inverted and phrase headings. Many cross-references are provided in this part of the catalog.

The *title* catalog will aid the reader who knows the title of a book sought for. Initial articles such as "a," "an," or "the" are ignored in alphabetizing, as are their equivalents in foreign languages.

The *call number* is printed in bold type at the end of each entry and it appears as a single line (e.g., **QH541.13.W34**). It is the device which brings together books on a subject for shelving in the library, and is an important piece of information to provide when requesting books.

REF before a call number means that the book is for use only in the ECOL library and cannot be sent out or borrowed.

f before a call number means that the book is larger than normal and may be shelved in a separate section.

Fiction without a call number means that the work is a novel, not a factual treatment of the subject.

ECOL at the end of each call number distinguishes ECOL books from the rest of the Minneapolis Public Library collection.

Full instructions for borrowing books from ECOL are provided on a separate sheet distributed to Minnesota recipients of this catalog. Out-of-state users should consult their community librarians or write directly to ECOL at the following address: Environmental Conservation Library, Minneapolis Public Library, 300 Nicollet Mall, Minneapolis, Minnesota 55401, (612) 372-6609.

PAMPHLET FILE SUBJECT HEADINGS AND PERIODICAL LIST

Appended to the basic file is a subject heading list which gives an indication of the scope of the pamphlet collection. This list, compiled from many sources and revised continually, will serve as a tool for research in ECOL and other collections, as well as a model for replication or adaptation by other libraries.

It should be observed also that the basic author-subject-title catalog records only books and government documents. Therefore, also appended to the ECOL catalog is a list of periodicals which includes subscription information for libraries or for clients who may wish to initiate their own subscriptions.

NEW TOOLS IN ENVIRONMENTAL SCIENCE

Beginning in 1970, several major new indexing and abstracting services in environmental science have been launched. Since they are expensive and relatively little known, a special annotated list of the most important of these services is included in the following preliminary pages.

Environmental Reference Tools

Because of the interdisciplinary nature of environmental studies, almost every indexing and abstracting service from the *Readers Guide* to *Science Citation Index* provides access to some environmental material. Particular aspects of environmental subjects can be traced through such traditional library tools as *Chemical Abstracts, Applied Science and Technology Index,* and the *Art Index*. But since environmental information crosses traditional disciplinary lines, none of these indexes covers all aspects of any particular environmental problem.

Since 1970 several new environmental reference tools have appeared. Used in conjunction with established indexes, abstracts and information services, they can lighten the task of the environmental researcher.

The following brief guide to selected new tools lists only those of general interest, useful chiefly in public and college libraries. More sophisticated and technical abstracts appropriate for research collections are omitted.

ABSTRACTS AND INDEXES

Environment Information ACCESS. Environment Information Center, Inc., 124 East 39th St., New York, NY 10016, 1971– . Biweekly. $125/year. *Environment Index,* annual, $75.

This biweekly journal abstracts and indexes environmental information from scientific and general periodicals, newspapers, government documents, corporate reports, conference papers and proceedings, and studies by citizen groups. Its broad coverage includes technical and socioeconomic aspects of environmental problems and programs. The abstracts usually provide enough information to determine whether the full text is needed, and sometimes will answer specific questions in themselves.

Abstracts are grouped in 21 subject categories, making it possible for the reader to skim the abstracts of recent publications in his field of interest. However, the categories often overlap (for example, Land Use and Misuse and Renewable Resources—Terrestrial), so it is advisable to peruse all possible categories as well as the subject index.

A separate section summarizes significant environmental entries from the *Federal Register,* and a calendar of conferences appears in most issues. Each issue includes a table of standard abbreviations and a list of keywords used in that issue's subject index.

Three indexes are provided: subject, industry, and author. The subject index uses a mixture of narrow and rather broad terms, so that very specific subjects may be difficult to locate. For example, articles on particular endangered species are listed under the heading Endangered Species but not under the species name. The alphabetical industry index includes Standard Industrial Classification numbers and indexes materials of interest to persons in particular industries and to those studying them.

The indexes are cumulated annually into *The Environment Index,* which may be purchased separately from ACCESS. It provides the full indexing and complete citations, but no abstracts. In addition, it summarizes the year's environmental legislation and major events, and lists pertinent U.S. patents, films and books.

These two publications index information from throughout the world, including extensive coverage of United Nations activities, but the emphasis remains on United States publications.

Pollution Abstracts. Pollution Abstracts, Inc., PO Box 2369, La Jolla, CA 92037, 1970– . Bimonthly. $80/year ($65 to high schools, junior colleges and municipally funded public libraries. Index extra.).

This journal serves as a key to the world's literature on all aspects of pollution control and pollution research, resulting in about 8,000 abstracts each year. Sources include journals, books, reports, newspapers, government documents, and conference proceedings. Concise abstracts attempt to summarize the conclusions reported in the original documents. The division of

Environmental Reference Tools

abstracts into technical and non-technical sections avoids retrieval of inappropriate material. The permuted keyterm index provides quick identification of materials on specific subjects, and an author index is also provided.

The first issue each year includes a master list of the publications cited, with additions listed in each subsequent issue. Each issue also includes a list of acronyms and of abbreviations, prefixes and symbols, as well as a calendar of coming meetings, symposia and exhibits. The indexes are cumulated annually into a separate volume.

CURRENT INFORMATION SERVICES

Energy Management. Commerce Clearing House, Inc., 420 Lexington Ave., New York, NY 10017, 1973– . Updated weekly. $144/year.

This loose-leaf volume covers federal actions relating to the U.S. supply of energy and its regulation. Basic federal documents are reproduced, including presidential messages and proclamations. The federal agencies whose actions have an impact on the nation's energy system are listed and their relationships explained. Energy-related bills in the House and Senate are summarized as they are introduced, and their status is reported each week.

The New Developments section alerts users to proposed actions and recent activities, and includes notice of state actions, recent studies, and energy-related environmental impact statements.

The Topical Index, which is continually revised, provides access to the whole volume. Some subject headings are quite broad, so the user must be persistent in searching broad subject areas for the most useful term.

Environment Reporter. Bureau of National Affairs, Inc., 1231 25th St., NW, Washington, DC 20037, 1971– . Updated weekly. $340/year.

A weekly environmental reference service in ten loose-leaf volumes, this set provides comprehensive coverage of current developments in environmental management and pollution control. The texts of laws, regulations and administrative actions on the federal and state levels are included, as well as directories of environmental agencies and officials.

The Current Developments volume provides a weekly update of activities in research and industry as well as government. The Journal section of Current Developments lists the week's highlights in Congress and the states, as well as noting upcoming meetings.

The Decisions binder covers all Supreme Court decisions and other significant actions of federal and state courts involving environmental issues, providing full texts of opinions as well as digests and indexes. Decisions are bound into permanent volumes annually.

Several indexes provide access to the information in this set. The Master Index in the Federal Laws binder covers the volumes of Federal Laws, Federal Regulations, and Monographs. Tables of contents are provided for the volumes of State Air Laws, State Water Laws, and State Solid Waste—Land Use. Each volume of Decisions contains a Topical Index; a Classification Guide to points of law; an Index Digest summarizing legal subjects covered in the opinions; a Table of Cases listing cases by name; and a Table of Cases by Jurisdiction. Topical indexes to the Current Developments weekly reports are provided at intervals of several weeks, and are cumulated quarterly.

Environmental Law Reporter. Environmental Law Institute, Suite 614, 1346 Connecticut Ave. NW, Washington, DC 20036, 1971– . Monthly. $75/year.

This legal reference tool covers environmental litigation in federal and state courts, as well as related administrative and statutory activities. The full text is provided for decisions in environmental cases, and summaries of the new cases which are added are provided each month. Federal statutes, agency guidelines, and rulings of federal, state and local bodies are included. Special articles expand upon the implications of particular actions for environmental law. Pending litigation and legislation is summarized, with lists of related documents which may be ordered from the Environmental Law Institute.

This service includes three indexes. The first, by case name, lists all of the cases reproduced in the *Reporter* as well as all cases cited in the reported proceedings. The Statutory Index lists all constitutions, statutes, administrative materials and international agreements which are included or cited. The General Index provides access to all parts of the *Reporter* by subject.

Author and Main Entry Catalog

A

ABBE, E. C.
Forbes, Alexander.
Northernmost Labrador. 1938. **F1136.F67 ECOL**

ABBEY, EDWARD, 1927-
Cactus country, by Edward Abbey and the editors of Time-Life Books. Time-Life Books 1973 (American wilderness) **QH88.A2 ECOL**
Slickrock; the canyon country of southeast Utah. Words by Edward Abbey, photos. and commentary by Philip Hyde. Sierra Club 1971 (The Sierra Club exhibit format series) **fF830.A62 ECOL**

ABBOTT, HENRY E.
Century Research Corporation.
Social aspects of urban water conservation. 1972. **fTD388.5.C4 ECOL**

ABBOTT, JACOB BATES, illus.
Henry, Marguerite.
Birds at Home. 1972 **fQL676.H52 1972 ECOL**

ABKIN, JOSEPH D.
Legal control of water pollution. 1969 **KF3786.A32L4 ECOL**

ABRAHAMSON, DEAN E., comp.
Environmental cost of electric power compiled by Dean E. Abrahamson. Scientists' Institute for Public Information, 1970 (A Scientists' Institute for Public Information workbook) **fTK1005.A26 ECOL**

ABT ASSOCIATES.
Factors affecting pollution referenda. Prepared for the Environmental Protection Agency. Washington Environmental Protection Agency, Water Quality Office; for sale by the Supt. of Docs. U.S. Govt. Print. Off., 1971. (Water pollution control research series) **fGH4952.A6 ECOL**

ABUL-HAJJ, Y. jt. auth.
Su, K. Lee.
Aquatic plants from Minnesota part 3—antimicrobial effects. 1972. **GB701.M554no.48 ECOL**

ACKERMANN, WILLIAM C.
Illinois. Water Survey.
Research needs on waste heat transfer from large sources into the environment. 1971. **fTD427.H4I4 ECOL**

ACS SYMPOSIUM ON DETERMINATION OF AIR QUALITY, LOS ANGELES, 1971.
Determination of air quality; proceedings. Edited by Gleb Mamantov and W. D. Shults. Plenum Press, 1972. **TD890.A2 1971 ECOL**

ADAMS, ALEXANDER B.
Eleventh hour; a hard look at conservation and the future by Alexander B. Adams. Putnam 1970 **S936.A3 ECOL**
Eternal quest: the story of the great naturalists, by Alexander B. Adams. Putnam 1969 **QH26.A3 ECOL**

ADAMS, ANSEL EASTON, 1902-
This is the American earth by Ansel Adams and Nancy Newhall. Sierra Club 1960 **fHC103.7.A68 ECOL**

ADAMS, ANSEL EASTON, 1902- illus.
Brower, David Ross.
Not man apart. 1969 **F869.B63B7 1969 ECOL**

ADAMS, JAMES TRUSLOW, 1878-
American Geographical Society of New York
New England's prospect: 1933. 1933. **HC107.A11A82 ECOL**

ADAMS, RUTH, 1923-
Say no! Rodale Press 1971 **HC110.E5A63 ECOL**

ADELSTEIN, MICHAEL E., comp.
Ecocide and population. Michael E. Adelstein and Jean G. Pival, editors. St. Martin's Press 1971, c1972 (Perspectives) **GF75.A35 ECOL**

ADLER, IRVING.
Air by Irving and Ruth Adler. Rev. ed. John Day Co. c1972 (The Reason why series) **PZ10.A3A12 ECOL**

ADLER, IRVING, 1913-
Rocks and minerals and the stories they tell, by Robert Irving [pseud.] illus. by Ida Scheib and with photographs. Knopf, 1956. **QE432.A35 ECOL**

ADLER, RUTH, jt. auth.
Adler, Irving.
Air. Rev. ed. c1972 **PZ10.A3A12 ECOL**

ADVANCED WASTE TREATMENT RESEARCH LABORATORY.
Aerojet-General Corporation. Environmental Systems Division.
Reverse osmosis renovation of municipal wastewater. 1970 **fTD754.A35 ECOL**

ADVANCES IN ENVIRONMENTAL SCIENCES. V.1-
Wiley-Interscience 1969- v. **REF TD180.A38 ECOL**

ADVENTURE IN ENVIRONMENT; national environment education development, a National Park Foundation program produced with the cooperation of the National Park Service.
Silver Burdett Co. 1971 **QH48.A25 ECOL**

ADVENTURE IN ENVIRONMENT: NATIONAL ENVIRONMENTAL EDUCATION DEVELOPMENT, a National Park Foundation program produced with the cooperation of the National Park service.
Silver Burdett Co. c1971 **fQH48.A24 ECOL**
Silver Burdett Co. 1971 **fQH48.A23 ECOL**

ADVERSE EFFECTS OF COMMON ENVIRONMENTAL POLLUTANTS;.
papers by Kingsley Kay, M. M. Hipskind, M. Schafer, et al. MSS Information Corp. 1972 **RA1270.P4A32 ECOL**

ADVISORY COMMITTEE TO THE DEPARTMENT OF HOUSING AND URBAN DEVELOPMENT. LAND USE SUBCOMMITTEE.
Urban growth and land development; the land conversion process; report. National Academy of Sciences, 1972. **HD205 1972 .A35 ECOL**

AEROJET-GENERAL CORPORATION. ENVIRONMENTAL SYSTEMS DIVISION.
Reverse osmosis renovation of municipal wastewater. Advanced Waste Treatment Research Laboratory; for sale by the Supt. of Docs., U.S. Govt. Print. Off., 1970 (Water pollution control research series) **fTD754.A35 ECOL**

AGASSIZ, LOUIS, 1807-1873.
Lake Superior. With a narrative of the tour, by J. Elliot Cabot. Arno 1970, c1850 (American environmental studies) **QH104.5.G7A35 1970 ECOL**

AGNEW, ROBERT W.
A free floating endless belt oil skimmer. Prepared for Office of Research and Monitoring, U.S. Environmental Protection Agency. U.S. Govt. Print. Office 1972. (Environmental protection technology series) **TD899.P4A3 ECOL**

AGNEW, WILLIAM G., ed.
Symposium on Emissions from Continuous Combustion Systems, General Motors Research Laboratories, 1971.
Emissions from continuous combustion systems. 1972. **TD881.S86 1971 ECOL**

AGRICULTURAL PRACTICES AND WATER QUALITY.
Ed. by Ted L. Willrich and George E. Smith. Iowa State Univ. Press 1971,c1970 **TD420.A33 ECOL**

AGRICULTURAL SCIENCES INFORMATION NETWORK.
Directory of information resources in agriculture and biology. Beltsville, Md., National Agricultural Library; for sale by the Supt. of Docs., U. S. Govt. Print. Off., 1971. **REF QH321.A37 ECOL**

AIR POLLUTION.
by Allen A.[sic] Nadler and others. Scientists' Institute for Public Information, 1970(A Scientists' Institute for Public Information workbook) **fTD883.A47 ECOL**

AIR POLLUTION CONTROL.
Edited by Werner Strauss. Wiley-Interscience v. (Environmental science and technology) **TD883.A474 ECOL**
School of Law, Duke Univ., 1968.(Law and contemporary problems, v.33, no.2) **KF3812.A75A35 1968 ECOL**
Clark C. Havighurst: editor. Oceana Publications, 1969. (Library of law and contemporary problems) **KF3812.A75A35 ECOL**

AIR POLLUTION CONTROL ASSOCIATION.
Directory of governmental air pollution agencies. 1970- **TD882.D5 ECOL**
Proceedings digest of the annual meeting. 62nd-1969- v. **REF TD884.A55 ECOL**
Technical manual no.1- 1963- v. **REF fTD881.A4 ECOL**
Toxicologic and epidemiologic bases for air quality criteria. 1969 **REF fTD890.T6 ECOL**

AIR POLLUTION TECHNICAL INFORMATION CENTER.
Air pollution aspects of emission sources: a bibliography with abstracts. Research Triangle Park, N.C., Environmental Protection Agency, Air Pollution Control Office, U.S. Govt. Print. Off., 1971- (Air Pollution Control Office publication no.AP-92-) **Z7173.A4A5 ECOL**
Air pollution translations: a bibliography with abstracts. Compiled by Office of Technical Information and Publications, Air Pollution Technical Information Center. U.S. National Air Pollution Control Administration, 1969- **REF TD881.U55no.AP-56 ECOL**

Chlorine and air pollution: an annotated bibliography. Research Triangle Park, N. C., Environmental Protection Agency, Office of Air Programs; for sale by the Supt. of Docs., U. S. Govt. Print. Off., 1971. (Office of Air Programs publication no.AP-99) **Z7173.A4A513 ECOL**

Hydrochloric acid and air pollution: an annotated bibliography by Office of Technical Information and Publications, Air Pollution Technical Information Center. Research Triangle Park, N. C., Environmental Protection Agency, Office of Air Programs; for sale by the Supt. of Docs., U. S. Govt. Print. Off., 1971. (Office of Air Programs publication no.AP-100) **Z7173.A4A52 ECOL**

Photochemical oxidants and air pollution: an annotated bibliography by Office of Technical Information and Publications, Air Pollution Technical Information Center. Research Triangle Park, N. C., U. S. Environmental Protection Agency, Air Pollution Control Office; for sale by the Supt. of Docs., U. S. Govt. Print. Off., 1971. 2 v. **REF Z7173.A4A53 ECOL**

AIRPORT OPERATORS COUNCIL INTERNATIONAL.
United States. Federal Aviation Administration.
Planning the metropolitan airport system. 1970. **TL725.3.P5U525 ECOL**

AL-KHAFAJI, AMIR, ed.
Workshop on Hydrologic and Hydraulic Aspects of Flood Plain Construction, Madison, Wisc., 1968.
Proceedings. 1968? **fGB1225.W6W6 1968 ECOL**

ALAMO AREA COUNCIL OF GOVERNMENTS.
Basin management for water reuse. Prepared for the Office of Research and Monitoring, Environmental Protection Agency. Author: Louis Koenig. Wash., U.S. Environmental Protection Agency U. S. Govt. Print. Off., 1972. (Water pollution control research series) **fTD225.S225A65 ECOL**

ALASKA SCIENCE CONFERENCE, 20TH, UNIVERSITY OF ALASKA, 1969.
Change in Alaska; people, petroleum, and politics. Edited by George W. Rogers. University of Alaska Press 1970 **HD9567.A4A64 1969 ECOL**

ALASKA. UNIV. INSTITUTE OF WATER RESOURCES.
International Symposium on Water Pollution Control in Cold Climates, University of Alaska, Fairbanks, 1970.
Papers Held at the University of Alaska, July 22-24, 1970. 1972 **TD423.I5 ECOL**

ALASKA. UNIVERSITY. INSTITUTE OF SOCIAL, ECONOMIC AND GOVERNMENT RESEARCH.
Alaska Science Conference, 20th, University of Alaska, 1969.
Change in Alaska. 1970 **HD9567.A4A64 1969 ECOL**

ALBERTA, A NATURAL HISTORY;.
editor-in-chief: W. G. Hardy. 1st ed. Alberta, M. G. Hurtig c1967 **fQH106.A54 ECOL**

ALEXANDER, PETER, 1922-
Atomic radiation and life. Completely Rev. ed. Penguin Books 1965 (Pelican books, A399) **QH652.A6 1965 ECOL**

ALEXANDER, ROBERT M.
Social aspects of environmental pollution. Corvallis, Air Resources Center, Water Resources Research Inst., Oregon State Univ. 1971. (Oregon. State University, Corvallis. Water Resources Research Institute. WRRI-7.) **fTD177.A4 ECOL**

ALEXANDER, WILFRID BACKHOUSE, 1885-
Birds of the ocean, a handbook for voyagers containing descriptions of all the sea-birds of the world, with notes on their habits and guides to their identification...with 140 illus. Putnam, 1928. **QL673.A37 ECOL**

ALFORD, ANN L.
Southeast Water Laboratory.
Catalog of pesticide NMR spectra. 1971. **fSB951.S64 ECOL**

ALGAE, MAN, AND THE ENVIRONMENT;
proceedings of an international symposium held at Syracuse University June 18-30, 1967.
Ed. by Daniel F. Jackson. Syracuse University Press c1968 **QK564.5.A4 ECOL**

ALLAN, GEORGE GRAHAM, 1930-
Washington (State). University. Institute of Forest Products.
Pollution abatement by fiber modification. 1971. **fTD899.W65W38 ECOL**

1

ALLAN, J. DAVID.
Recycle this book! Ecology, society, and man. Edited by J. David Allan and Arthur J. Hanson. Wadsworth Pub. Co. 1972 **GF8.A4 ECOL**

ALLAN, LESLIE.
Council on Economic Priorities.
Paper profits: pollution in the pulp and paper industry. c1972 **TD899.W65C65 1972 ECOL**

Council on Economic Priorities.
Paper profits: pollution in the pulp and paper industry. 1971 **REF fTD888.P8C6 ECOL**

ALLEE, WARDER CLYDE, 1885-
Principles of animal ecology, by W. C. Allee and others Saunders Co. 1949 **QL751.A616 ECOL**

ALLEN, DURWARD LEON, 1910-
The life of prairies and plains by Durward L. Allen. Published in cooperation with the World book encyclopedia. McGraw-Hill 1967 (Our living world of nature) **QH541.5.P7A4 ECOL**

Our wildlife legacy. Rev. ed. Funk & Wagnalls 1962 **SK361.A66 1962 ECOL**

ALLEN, GERTRUDE E.
Everyday animals. Houghton, 1961. **PZ10.A478Ev ECOL**

ALLEN, HERBERT ELLIS, 1939-
Nutrients in natural waters, edited by Herbert E. Allen and James R. Kramer. Wiley 1972 (Environmental science and technology) **QH96.A48 ECOL**

ALLEN, RICHARD H., comp.
A glossary of coastal engineering terms. U.S. Army, Corps of Engineers, Coastal Engineering Research Center, 1972. (U.S. Coastal Engineering Research Center. Miscellaneous paper 2-72) **REF TC1645.A4 ECOL**

ALLEN, ROBERT PORTER.
On the trail of vanishing birds. McGraw 1957 **QL696.G8A4 ECOL**

The whooping crane. National Audubon Society, 1952. (Research report of the National Audubon Society, no.3) **QL696.G8A43 ECOL**

ALLEN, SHIRLEY WALTER, 1883-
Conserving natural resources; principles and practice in a democracy by Shirley Walter Allen and Justin Wilkinson Leonard. 3d ed. McGraw-Hill c1966 **HC103.7.A7 1966 ECOL**

ALLISON, ANTHONY.
Population control, edited by Anthony Allison. Penguin Books 1970 **QL752.A58 ECOL**

ALLMAN, GRADY.
American Enka Corporation. Central Engineering Dept.
Zinc precipitation and recovery from viscose rayon waste water. 1971. **fTD899.T4A44 ECOL**

ALLRED, E. R.
Continuation of studies on the hydrology of ponds and small lakes. 1971. **fGB1825.M6C6 ECOL**

ALLRED, E. R., jt. auth.
Manson, Philip W.
Some aspects of the hydrology of ponds and small lakes. 1968. **fGB1825.M6M35 ECOL**

ALLSOPP, BRUCE.
The garden Earth; the case for ecological morality. Morrow 1972 **GF80.A4 1972b ECOL**

ALPINE GEOPHYSICAL ASSOCIATES.
Oil pollution incident, platform Charlie, Main Pass block 41 field, Louisiana. Prepared for the Water Quality Office, Environmental Protection Agency. Washington, Environmental Protection Agency, Water Quality Office; for sale by the Supt. of Docs., U. S. Govt. Print. Off., 1971. (Water pollution control research series) **fGC1221.A4 ECOL**

ALTMAN, HAROLD, jt. comp.
Troost, Cornelius J.
Environmental education: a sourcebook. 1972 **QH541.2.T76 ECOL**

AMADON, DEAN, jt. auth.
Murphy, Robert Cushman.
Land birds of America. 1953 **fQL681.M85 ECOL**

AMERICAN ACADEMY OF ARTS AND SCIENCES, BOSTON. COMMISSION ON THE YEAR 2000.
Toward the year 2000; work in progress. Ed. by Daniel Bell. Beacon Press 1970,c1968 (Beacon paperback no.318) **E169.1.A47192 1970 ECOL**

AMERICAN ASSEMBLY.
The population dilemma. 2d ed. Prentice-Hall 1969 (A Spectrum book: The American Assembly series) **HB851.A4 1969 ECOL**

Uses of the seas. 1968 **GC1015.U8 ECOL**

AMERICAN ASSOCIATION FOR THE ADVANCEMENT OF SCIENCE.
Environmental education 1970. 1970 **fS946.E55 ECOL**

Indicators of environmental quality. 1972. **TD172.5.I5 1972 ECOL**

Is there an optimum level of population? 1971 **HB851.I8 ECOL**

Science and the future of man. c1970 **CB151.S37 ECOL**

Symposium on the Global Effects of Environmental Pollution, Dallas, 1968.
Global effects of environmental pollution. 1970 **REF TD172.5.S95 1968 ECOL**

AMERICAN ASSOCIATION FOR THE ADVANCEMENT OF SCIENCE. AAAS MISCELLANEOUS PUBLICATION 72-13.
Bausum, Howard T.
Science for society: a bibliography. 3d ed. 1972. **fZ7401.B3 1972 ECOL**

AMERICAN ASSOCIATION FOR THE ADVANCEMENT OF SCIENCE. COMMISSION ON SCIENCE EDUCATION.
Bausum, Howard T.
Science for society: a bibliography. 3d ed. 1972. **fZ7401.B3 1972 ECOL**

Moore, John A.
Science for society: a bibliography. 2nd ed. 1971 **fZ7401.M6 1971 ECOL**

AMERICAN ASSOCIATION FOR THE ADVANCEMENT OF SCIENCE. COMMITTEE ON SCIENCE IN THE PROMOTION OF HUMAN WELFARE. AIR CONSERVATION COMMISSION.
Air conservation; ... report. 1965. (Publication of American Association for the Advancement of Science, no. 80) **TD883.2.A65 ECOL**

AMERICAN ASSOCIATION OF PETROLEUM GEOLOGISTS.
Symposium on Underground Waste Management and Environmental Implications, Houston, Tex., 1971.
Underground waste management and environmental implications; proceedings. 1972. **TD761.S95 1971 ECOL**

AMERICAN CHEMICAL SOCIETY.
ACS Symposium on Determination of Air Quality, Los Angeles, 1971.
Determination of air quality. 1972. **TD890.A2 1971 ECOL**

Chemicals controlling insect behavior. 1970. **QL461.S88 1969 ECOL**

Environmental Science & Technology.
Pollution control directory. 1971/72- **REF fTD180.E52 ECOL**

Organic pesticides in the environment; a symposium. Aaron A. Rosen and H. F. Kraybill, symposium chairmen. American Chemical Society, 1966. (Advances in chemistry series, 60) **SB951.A4 ECOL**

AMERICAN CHEMICAL SOCIETY. COMMITTEE ON CHEMISTRY AND PUBLIC WELFARE. SUBCOMMITTEE ON ENVIRONMENTAL IMPROVEMENT.
Cleaning our environment: the chemical basis for action; a report. 1969. **TD180.A4 ECOL**

AMERICAN CHEMICAL SOCIETY. DIVISION OF AGRICULTURAL AND FOOD CHEMISTRY. PESTICIDE SUBDIVISION.
American Chemical Society.
Organic pesticides in the environment; a symposium. 1966. **SB951.A4 ECOL**

AMERICAN CHEMICAL SOCIETY. DIVISION OF WATER, AIR, AND WASTE CHEMISTRY.
American Chemical Society.
Organic pesticides in the environment; a symposium. 1966. **SB951.A4 ECOL**

THE AMERICAN COAST.
Introd. by Jean Stafford. Scribner 1971 **fE169.02.A648 ECOL**

AMERICAN ENKA CORPORATION. CENTRAL ENGINEERING DEPT.
Zinc precipitation and recovery from viscose rayon waste water. Authors: David M. Rock and Grady Allman. Prepared for the Environmental Protection Agency, Water Quality Office. U. S. Govt. Print. Off., 1971. (Water pollution control research series) **fTD899.T4A44 ECOL**

AMERICAN FOUNDATION FOR CONTINUING EDUCATION.
Young, Louise B.
Evolution of man. 1970. **QH368.Y68 ECOL**

AMERICAN FOUNDRYMEN'S SOCIETY. WATER POLLUTION COMMITTEE.
Water pollution from foundry wastes. 1st ed. American Foundrymen's Society, 1967. **fTD899.A45 ECOL**

AMERICAN GEOGRAPHICAL SOCIETY OF NEW YORK.
New England's prospect: 1933, by James Truslow Adams, Henry S. Graves, Edward A. Filene... and others American Geographical Society, 1933. (its Special publication no.16) **HC107.A11A82 ECOL**

Pioneer settlement; cooperative studies by twenty-six authors. American Geographical Society, 1932. **GF51.A5 ECOL**

Problems of polar research; a series of papers by thirty-one authors. American Geographical Society, 1928. (American Geographical Society. Special publication no.7, ed. by W. L. G. Joerg) **G576.A6 ECOL**

AMERICAN GEOLOGICAL INSTITUTE.
Environmental studies. Rev. ed.? 1971,c1970 **LB1027.E6 1971 ECOL**

AMERICAN HERITAGE.
The American heritage book of natural wonders, by the editors of American heritage, the magazine of history. Editor in charge: Alvin M. Josephy. Chapters by Peter Matthiessen and others. American Heritage Pub. Co. c1972,1963 **fE169.A496 1972 ECOL**

AMERICAN INSTITUTE OF ARCHITECTS.
McCue, Gerald M.
Creating the human environment. 1970 **HN59.M22 ECOL**

AMERICAN INSTITUTE OF BIOLOGICAL SCIENCES.
Casarett, Alison P.
Radiation biology. 1968 **QH652.C3 ECOL**

AMERICAN INSTITUTE OF CROP ECOLOGY. AIR POLLUTION SECTION.
Nuttonson, Michael Y.
Air pollution in relation to certain atmospheric and meteorological conditions and some of the methods employed in the survey and analysis of air pollutants. 1971. **fTD883.7.R9N87 ECOL**

Nuttonson, Michael Y.
Measurements of dispersal and concentration, identification, and sanitary evaluation of various air pollutants. 1971. **fTD883.7.R9N873 ECOL**

AMERICAN INSTITUTE OF MINING, METALLURGICAL, AND PETROLEUM ENGINEERS.
Environmental Control Symposium, San Francisco, 1972.
Environmental control. 1972 **TD888.M4E58 1972 ECOL**

AMERICAN INSTITUTE OF PLANNERS.
Environment and change. 1970, c1968 **HT167.E46 ECOL**

Environment and policy. 1968 **HT167.E48 ECOL**

Environment for man. 1967 **HT167.E5 1967 ECOL**

AMERICAN INSTITUTE OF PLANT ENGINEERS.
Western Plant Engineering and Maintenance Conference, San Francisco, 1970 Proceedings. 1970. **fTS184.W4**

AMERICAN MANAGEMENT ASSOCIATION.
Buggie, Frederick D.
Toward effective and equitable pollution control regulation. 1972 **fHC110.P55B8 ECOL**

AMERICAN MUSEUM OF NATURAL HISTORY, NEW YORK.
Atkinson, Justin Brooks.
This bright land. 1st ed. 1972. **GF503.A8 ECOL**

Edlin, Herbert Leeson.
Plants and man. 1969, c1967 **S519.E3 ECOL**

Joffe, Joyce.
Conservation. 1970,c1969 **S940.J64 ECOL**

Lauwerys, Joseph Albert.
Man's impact on nature. 1970,c1969 **QH368.L38 ECOL**

Laycock, George.
Wild refuge. 1969 **S962.L39 ECOL**

McHarg, Ian L.
Design with nature. 1st ed. 1969. **fHC110.E5M33 ECOL**

Mech, L. David.
The wolf: the ecology and behavior of an endangered species. 1970 **QL737.C22M4 ECOL**

Reid, Keith.
Nature's network. 1970, c1969 **QH541.14.R43 ECOL**

Schwartz, George I.
Life in a log. 1972 QH541.5.F6S39 ECOL
Vayda, Andrew Peter.
Environment and cultural behavior. 1969.
GF51.V35 ECOL

AMERICAN NATIONAL STANDARDS INSTITUTE.
American national standard leakage-rate testing of containment structures for nuclear reactors. Sponsor: American Nuclear Society. Approved March 16, 1972. 1972 REF fTK9211.A4 ECOL

AMERICAN NUCLEAR SOCIETY.
American National Standards Institute.
American national standard leakage-rate testing of containment structures for nuclear reactors. 1972
REF fTK9211.A4 ECOL
Nuclear methods in environmental research; proceedings of American Nuclear Society Topical Meeting, University of Missouri-Columbia, Aug. 23-24, 1971 Edited by James R. Vogt, Thomas F. Parkinson, Robert L. Carter. University of Missouri 1971
fTD172.5.A4 ECOL

Nuclear news buyers guide. 1972-
REF fTK9012.N82 ECOL

AMERICAN ORNITHOLOGISTS' UNION.
Check-list of North American birds, prepared by a Committee of the American Ornithologists' Union. 4th ed., constituting the "Systema avium" for North America north of Mexico. American Ornithologists' Union, 1931. REF QL677.A52 1932 ECOL

AMERICAN PETROLEUM INSTITUTE.
Joint Conference on Prevention and Control of Oil Spills, Washington, D.C., 1971.
Proceedings of Joint Conference on Prevention and Control of Oil Spills held June 15-17, 1971 at the Sheraton Park Hotel. 1971? fGC1080.J6 ECOL
Robinson, Elmer.
Sources, abundance, and fate of gaseous atmospheric pollutants. 1968. fTD885.R6 ECOL
Robinson, Elmer.
Sources, abundance, and fate of gaseous atmospheric pollutants: supplement. 1969. fTD885.R62 ECOL

AMERICAN PROCESS EQUIPMENT CORPORATION.
Ultrasonic filtration of combined sewer overflows. Prepared for the Environmental Protection Agency, Water Quality Office. U.S. Govt. Print. Off., 1970. (Water pollution control research series)
fTD753.A6 ECOL

AMERICAN PUBLIC HEALTH ASSOCIATION.
Glossary: water and wastewater control engineering. 1969. TD9.G55 ECOL
Standard methods for the examination of water and waste water, including bottom sediments and sludges. Prepared and published jointly by American Public Health Association, American Water Works Association, Water Pollution Control Federation. Ed. 13. c1971 REF QD142.A5 1971 ECOL

AMERICAN PUBLIC WORKS ASSOCIATION.
Combined sewer regulator overflow facilities; report. Prepared for the Federal Water Quality Administration, Dept. of the Interior, and twenty-five local governmental jurisdictions. U.S. Govt. Print. Off., 1970. (Water pollution control research series)
fTD662.A42 ECOL
Feasibility of computer control of wastewater treatment. Prepared for the Environmental Protection Agency, Water Quality Office. Washington Environmental Protection Agency, Water Quality Office; for sale by the Supt. of Docs., U.S. Govt. Print. Off., 1970. (Water pollution control research series)
fTD746.A43 ECOL
Midwest Regional Seminar on Horizons in Resource Recovery, University of Chicago, 1972.
Horizons in resource recovery: presentations and discussions of a seminar held Feb. 23, 1972. 1972.
fTP995.A1M5 1972 ECOL
Prevention and correction of excessive infiltration and inflow into sewer systems; manual of practice. Washington Environmental Protection Agency, Water Quality Office; for sale by the Supt. of Docs., U.S. Govt. Print. Off., 1971. (Water pollution control research series) fTD678.A44 ECOL
United States. Environmental Protection Agency. Office of Research and Monitoring.
The swirl concentrator as a combined sewer overflow regulator facility. 1972. TD662.U5 ECOL
Water pollution aspects of urban runoff. 1969. (Water pollution control research series) TD420.A4 ECOL

AMERICAN PUBLIC WORKS ASSOCIATION. INSTITUTE FOR SOLID WASTES.
Municipal refuse disposal. Assistance provided by the Bureau of Solid Waste Management, U.S. Dept. of Health, Education and Welfare. 3d ed. Public Administration Servide 1970
TD795.A45 1970 ECOL

AMERICAN SOCIETY OF CIVIL ENGINEERS.
McPherson, M. B.
Hydrologic effects of urbanization in the United States. 1972. fGB665.M3 ECOL
McPherson, M. B.
Urban runoff. 1972. fGB665.M35 ECOL
McPherson, Murray Burns.
Feasibility of the metropolitan water intelligence system concept (Integrated automatic operational control). 1971. fTD211.M3 ECOL
McPherson, Murray Burns.
Management problems in metropolitan water resource operations. 1971. fTD353.M3 ECOL
Tucker, L. Scott.
Metropolitan industrial water use. 1972.
fTD223.T8 ECOL

AMERICAN SOCIETY OF CIVIL ENGINEERS. URBAN WATER RESOURCES COUNCIL.
McPherson, Murray Burns.
Prospects for metropolitan water management. 1970. fTD353.M32 ECOL

AMERICAN SOCIETY OF INTERNATIONAL LAW.
Conference on Legal and Institutional Responses to Problems of the Global Evnirenment, Arden House, 1971.
Law, institutions, and the global environment. 1972.
KF3775.A75C6 1971 ECOL

AMERICAN SOCIETY OF LANDSCAPE ARCHITECTS.
Robinette, Gary O.
Plants/people/environmental quality. 1972
QK901.R6 ECOL

AMERICAN SOCIETY OF LIMNOLOGY AND OCEANOGRAPHY.
Remote sensing in ecology. 1969
QH541.15.R4R4 ECOL

AMERICAN UNIVERSITY, WASHINGTON, D.C.
Wolozin, Harold.
The economics of air pollution. c1966
HC110.A4W6 ECOL

AMERICAN WATER WORKS ASSOCIATION.
Water quality and treatment; a handbook of public water supplies. 3d ed. McGraw-Hill 1971
TD430.A6 1971 ECOL

AMERICAN WATER WORKS ASSOCIATION RESEARCH FOUNDATION, NEW YORK.
Information resource: water pollution control in the water utility industry. Authors: Faber, H. A., and Nardozzi, A. D. Environmental Protection Agency, 1971. REF fTD429.A4 ECOL

AMERICA'S CHANGING ENVIRONMENT.
Edited by Roger Revelle and Hans H. Landsberg. Houghton Mifflin, 1970.(The Daedalus library, v. 15)
HC110.E5A56 ECOL

AMOS, WILLIAM HOPKINS.
The infinite river; a biologist's vision of the world of water. Random House 1971,c1970 QH90.A59 ECOL
The life of the pond by William H. Amos. McGraw-Hill 1967 (Our living world of nature)
QH541.5.F7A45 ECOL

ANACAPA SCIENCES, INC.
Harris, Douglas H.
Assessment of turbidity, color and odor in water. 1972. fTD380.H3 ECOL

ANDERSON, DAVID A., jt. auth.
Thorud, David B.
Freezing in forest soil as influenced by soil properties, litter, and snow. 1969. GB701.M554no.10 ECOL

ANDERSON, PAUL K., 1927- comp.
Omega; murder of the ecosystem and suicide of man by Paul K. Anderson. W. C. Brown Co. 1971
QH541.A5 ECOL

ANDERSON, WALT, 1933- comp.
Politics and environment: a reader in ecological crisis. Goodyear Pub. Co. 1974 HC110.E5A67 ECOL

ANDERSON, WENDELL R.
Minnesota. Governor, 1971-
Securing a quality environment in Minnesota. 1973?
REF fHC107.M6A35 ECOL

ANDREWARTHA, HERBERT GEORGE, 1907-
Introduction to the study of animal populations by H. G. Andrewartha. 2nd ed. Univ. of Chicago Press 1971
QL752.A63 1971 ECOL

ANDREWS, DAVID, illus.
Ardley, Neil.
How birds behave. 1971 fQL785.5.B6A7 ECOL

ANDREWS, WILLIAM A., 1930-
A guide to the study of environmental pollution. Contributing authors: William A. Andrews, Donna K. Moore and Alex LeRoy. Editor: William A. Andrews. Prentice-Hall 1972 (Contours: Studies of the environment) TD174.A53 ECOL
A guide to the study of freshwater ecology. Editor: William A. Andrews. Contributing authors: Daniel G. Stoker and others. Prentice-Hall 1972 (Contours: studies of the environment) QH541.5.F7A48 ECOL

ANGIER, BRADFORD.
One acre and security-how to live off the earth without ruining it. Illustrated by Arthur J. Anderson. Stackpole Books 1972 S561.A574 ECOL
Survival with style. Stackpole Books, 1972.
SK606.A54 ECOL

ANIMAL LIFE SERIES (NEW YORK).
Barber, Carolyn.
Animals at war. 1st U.S. ed. c1971
QL758.5.B37 1971 ECOL
Long, Tony.
Mountain animals. 1st U.S. ed. c1971
QL113.L66 1971 ECOL
Maddock, Alison.
Animals at peace. 1st U.S. ed. c1971
QL751.M216 1971 ECOL
Tate, Ro.
Desert animals. 1st U.S. ed. c1971
QL116.T37 1971 ECOL

ANTEVS, ERNST, 1888-
Rainfall and tree growth in the Great basin... Ed. by J. K. Wright. Carnegie Institution of Washington and the American Geographical Society of New York, 1938. (Carnegie Institution of Washington, Publication, no.469) QC925.1.U35 1938 ECOL

ANTEVS, ERNST, 1888- tr.
Nordenskjold, Otto.
The geography of the polar regions, consisting of a general characterization of polar nature. 1928.
G587.N6 ECOL

ANTONIOU, JIM.
Environmental management planning for traffic. McGraw-Hill c1971 fHE333.A57 ECOL

APPLEMAN, PHILIP, 1926-
The silent explosion. With a foreword by Julian Huxley. Beacon Press 1965 HB851.A48 ECOL

APPLEYARD, DONALD.
The urban environment: selected bibliography. Council of Planning Librarians, 1972. (Council of Planning Librarians. Exchange Bibliography, 291)
REF fZ7164.U7A6 ECOL

ARBIB, ROBERT S.
The hungry bird book by Robert Arbib and Tony Soper. Illus. by Don Gillmor. Taplinger Pub. Co. 1971 QL676.5.A7 1971 ECOL
The Lord's Woods by Robert Arbib. 1st ed. Norton 1971 QH76.5.N7A72 ECOL

ARCHER, SELLERS GAMBRELL, 1908-
Rain, rivers, and reservoirs; the challenge of running water. Coward-McCann c1968,c1963 (Challenge books) GB671.A7 ECOL
Soil conservation. Univ. of Oklahoma Press 1969
S624.A1A7 1969 ECOL

ARDLEY, NEIL.
How birds behave. Illustrated by David Andrews. Grosset & Dunlap 1971 (The Knowledge library)
fQL785.5.B6A7 ECOL

ARE OUR DESCENDANTS DOOMED?
Technological change and population growth. Edited by Harrison Brown and Edward Hutchings, Jr. Viking Press 1972 HB849.A74 1972 ECOL

AREY, DAVID G., jt. auth.
Russell, Clifford S.
Drought and water supply. 1970
TD223.R88 ECOL

ARID LANDS IN PERSPECTIVE; including AAAS papers on Water importation into arid lands.
Editors: Wm. G. McGinnies and B. J. Goldman. Washington, American Association for the Advancement of Science; Tucson, Univ. of Arizona Press 1969 fS613.A7 ECOL

ARMCO STEEL CORPORATION.
Limestone treatment of rinse waters from hydrochloric acid pickling of steel. Prepared for the Water Quality Office, Environmental Protection Agency. Environmental Protection Agency, Water Quality Office; for sale by the Supt. of Docs., U. S. Govt. Print. Off. 1971. (Water pollution control research series) fTD899.M45A75 ECOL
Treatment of waste water-waste oil mixtures. Report to the Federal Water Pollution Control Administration, Dept. of the Interior, by Armco Steel Corp. U.S. Dept. of the Interior, Federal Water Pollution Control Administration 1970. (Water pollution control research series) fTD455.A7 ECOL

ARMSTRONG, GEORGE R., jt. auth.
Guthrie, John Alexander.
Western forest industry. 1961 **HD9755.G8 ECOL**

ARMSTRONG, TERRY R., 1946- comp.
Why do we still have an ecological crisis? Edited by Terry R. Armstrong. Prentice-Hall 1972 (A Specturm book, S-287) **TD174.A75 ECOL**

ARNY, MARY (TRAVIS).
Ecology: a writer's handbook. With a full glossary of ecological terms by Mary Travis Arny and Christopher R. Reaske. 1st ed. Random House 1972
QH541.A72 ECOL

ARONOW, SAUL, ed.
The fallen sky; medical consequences of thermonuclear war. Ed. for Physicians for Social Responsibility by Saul Aronow, Frank R. Ervin, and Victor W. Sidel. Hill and Wang 1963
RA569.A7 ECOL

ARTHUR JAMES F.
California. Dept. of Water Resources.
Removal of nitrate by an algal system, phase II. 1971. **fTD475.C342 ECOL**

ARTZ, ROBERT M., ed.
National Recreation and Park Association.
Guide to new approaches to financing parks & recreation. 1970 **SB482.A4N38 ECOL**

ARVILL, ROBERT.
Man and environment: crisis and the strategy of choice. Revised ed. Penguin 1970,c1969 (Pelican books, A889) **HC253.5.A7 1970 ECOL**

ARYA, LALIT MOHAN.
Water flow in soil in presence of soybean root sinks. University of Minn., Water Resources Research Center, 1973. (Minnesota. University. Water Resources Research Center. WRRC bulletin 60)
GB701.M554no.60 ECOL

AS WE LIVE AND BREATH; the challenge of our environment.
Foreword by Gilbert M. Grosvenor. Prepared by the Special Publications Division, National Geographic Society. National Geographic Society, 1971
GF75.A8 ECOL

ASHBAUGH, BYRON L.
Trail planning and layout, by Byron L. Ashbaugh and Raymond J. Kordish. National Audubon Society, Nature Center Planning Division 1971
QH58.A8 ECOL

ASHBAUGH, BYRON L., jt. auth.
Shomon, Joseph James.
Wildlife habitat improvement. 2d print., rev. 1969
SK361.S52 1969 ECOL

ASIMOV, ISAAC, 1920-
ABC's of ecology. Walker c1972
fQH541.14.A85 ECOL

The genetic effects of radiation by Isaac Asimov and Theodosius Dobzhansky. U.S. Atomic Energy Commission, Division of Technical Information c1966 (Understanding the atom) **QH652.5.A8 ECOL**

ASSESSMENT OF THE EFFECTIVENESS AND EFFECTS OF LAND DISPOSAL METHODOLOGIES OF WASTE WATER MANAGEMENT,.
by Charles H. Driver and others. Dept. of the Army, Corps of Engineers 1972.(Wastewater management report 72-1) **fTD760.A86 ECOL**

ASSOCIATION OF AMERICAN GEOGRAPHERS.
Environmental perception and behavior. 1967.
GF51.E5 ECOL

ASSOCIATION OF ENGINEERING GEOLOGISTS.
Symposium on Engineering Geology in the Urban Environment, San Francisco, 1969.
Environmental planning and geology. 1971
TA705.S95 1969 ECOL

ASSOCIATION OF METROPOLITAN SOIL AND WATER CONSERVATION DISTRICTS.
Land in Transition Symposium, 1971, St. Paul, Minn. 1971 **fS623.L3 1971 ECOL**

ASSOCIATION OF THE BAR OF THE CITY OF NEW YORK. SPECIAL COMMITTEE ON ELECTRIC POWER AND THE ENVIRONMENT.
Electricity and the environment: the reform of legal institutions; report. West Pub. Co., 1972.
KF2125.A97 ECOL

ATKINS, PATRICK R.
The pesticide manufacturing industry—current waste treatment and disposal practices. Prepared for the Office of Research and Monitoring Environmental Protection Agency. U.S. Govt. Print. Office, 1972. (Water pollution control research series)
fTD899.C5A8 ECOL

ATKINS, PETER F., jt. auth.
Barnes, Robert A.
Ammonia removal in a physical-chemical wastewater treatment process. 1972. **TD462.B3 ECOL**

ATKINSON, JUSTIN BROOKS, 1894-
This bright land; a personal view by Brooks Atkinson. Drawings by Earl Thollander. 1st ed. Published for the American Museum of Natural History by Natural History Press, 1972. **GF503.A8 ECOL**

ATKISSON, ARTHUR A., jt. auth.
Faith, William Lawrence.
Air pollution. 2d ed. 1972
TD883.F23 1972 ECOL

ATKISSON, JEAN.
Evaluated bibliography of free and inexpensive conservation publications, prepared by Jean Atkisson and Rudolph J. H. Schafer. State Dept. of Education 1972 **REF fZ7164.N3A8 ECOL**

ATLANTIC COUNCIL OF THE UNITED STATES.
Managing the environment: international economic cooperation for pollution control. 1971
HC79.E5M35 1971 ECOL

ATWOOD, ANN.
The kingdom of the forest. Text and photos. by Ann Atwood. Scribner 1972 **QH541.5.F6A88 ECOL**

AUBURN UNIVERSITY.
Fuller, Richard Buckminster.
Approaching the benign environment. 1970
Q171.F96 ECOL

AUDUBON SOCIETY OF MASSACHUSETTS. URBAN ENVIRONMENTAL EDUCATION PROJECT.
Dickey, Miriam E.
Beyond the classroom: using the urban environment as an instructional medium. 1972.
fQH541.2.D52 ECOL

AUGENSTINE, LEROY GEORGE, 1928-
Come, let us play God by Leroy Augenstein. Harper 1969 **R724.A83 ECOL**

AULD, D. A. L., comp.
Economic thinking and pollution problems, edited by D. A. L. Auld. University of Toronto Press 1972
HC120.P55A84 ECOL

AULICIEMS, ANDRIS.
The atmospheric environment; a study of comfort and performance. Pub. for the Univ. of Toronto, Dept. of Geography, by the Univ. of Toronto Press, 1972
QP82.2.T4A9 ECOL

AUSTIN, TEXAS.
Design guides for biological wastewater treatment processes, by the City of Austin, Texas, and Center for Research in Water Resources and Environmental Health Engineering Research Laboratory, Civil Engineering Dept., Univ. of Texas, Austin. Authors: Joseph F. Malina, and others. U.S. Environmental Protection Agency. U.S. Govt. Print. Off., 1971 i.e.1972 (Water pollution control research series)
fTD755.A87 ECOL

AYERS, JOHN C.
Lake Michigan environmental survey: final report. Univ. of Michigan, Great Lakes Research Division, 1970. (Michigan. University. Great Lakes Research Division. Special report no.49)
REF fQH543.6.A9 ECOL

AYLESWORTH, THOMAS G.
This vital air, this vital water: man's environment crisis. Rand McNally 1968 **TD180.A9 ECOL**

AYMAR, GORDON CHRISTIAN, 1893-
Bird flight, written & designed by Gordon C. Aymar; a collection of 200 action photographs. Dodd, 1935.
QL698.A9 ECOL

AYRES, ROBERT U.
Alternatives to the internal combustion engine; impacts on environmental quality, by Robert U. Ayres and Richard P. McKenna. Published for Resources for the Future by the Johns Hopkins University Press 1972
TL210.A96 ECOL

Technological forecasting and long-range planning by Robert U. Ayres. McGraw-Hill 1969 **T174.A9 ECOL**

AYRES, ROBERT U., jt. auth.
Kneese, Allen V.
Economics and the environment. 1970
HC68.K57 ECOL

B

BABCOCK, RICHARD F.
The zoning game; municipal practices and policies by Richard F. Babcock. Univ. of Wisconsin Press, 1966.
KF5698.B3 ECOL

BACH, WILFRID.
Atmospheric pollution. McGraw-Hill 1971, c1972 (McGraw-Hill problems series in geography)
TD883.B24 ECOL

BACHERT, RUSSEL E., JR., comp.
Directory of degree programs, related to conservation, ecology, environmental education, environmental science, outdoor education & natural resources. Interstate Printers & Publishers, 1971 (Conservation Education Association. Education: key to conservation, no.7) **fS946.B3 ECOL**

BAIER, KURT.
Values and the future; the impact of technological change on American values. Ed. by Kurt Baier and Nicholas Rescher. Free Press 1969
HM221.B27 ECOL

BAILEY, ALFRED MARSHALL, 1894-
Birds of Colorado, by Alfred M. Bailey and Robert J. Niedrach. Denver Museum of Natural History, 1965. 2 v. **REF fQL684.C6B3 ECOL**

BAKER, BILL, 1942- jt. auth.
Kotsonis, Helen Hoch.
Modern lesson plans in environmental science. 1972
QH541.2.K68 ECOL

BAKER, DONALD G.
Snow cover and winter soil temperatures at St. Paul, Minn. Water Resources Research Center, Univ. of Minn. Graduate School, 1971. (WRRC bulletin, no.37)
GB701.M554no.37 ECOL

BAKER, DONALD G., jt. auth.
Pabst, Arthur F.
Flood forecasting in the Upper Midwest: data assembly and preliminary analysis. 1972.
fGB678.P32 ECOL

BAKER, JERRY.
Jerry Baker's Back to nature almanac. 1973-
Nash Pub. v. **SB455.B257 ECOL**

BAKER, KENNETH FRANK, 1908- ed.
International Symposium on Factors Determining the Behavior of Plant Pathogens in Soil, Berkeley, Calif., 1963.
Ecology of soil-borne plant pathogens.
fQR111.I55 1963 ECOL

BAKER, MARY, 1897- illus.
Bridges, William.
Wild animals of the world. 1948
fQL706.B89 ECOL

BAKER, P. S., tr.
United States. Atomic Energy Commission. Division of Technical Information.
Safety manual for use of operators dealing with radiography and industrial gammagraphy. 1968?
TA417.25.U5 ECOL

BAKER, PHILIP SCHAFFNER, 1916-
Radioisotopes in industry by Philip S. Baker and others. U.S. Atomic Energy Commission, Division of Technical Information c1965 (Understanding the atom)
TK9400.B3 ECOL

BAKKER, ELNA S.
An island called California; an ecological introduction to its natural communities by Elna S. Bakker. Figures by Gerhard Bakker, Jr. Photos. by Philip Hyde. University of California Press, 1971.
QH105.C2B3 ECOL

BALAKRISHNAN, S.
State of the art review on sludge incineration practice, by S. Balakrishnan, D. E. Williamson and R. W. Okey, for the Federal Water Quality Administration, Dept. of the Interior. U. S. Federal Water Quality Administration; for sale by the Supt. of Docs., U. S. Govt. Print. Off. 1970. (Water pollution control research series) **fTD803.B36 ECOL**

BALARAT CENTER FOR ENVIRONMENTAL STUDIES.
Denver Urban environmental studies for grades kindergarten—six. 1971. 1v. **QH541.2.B25 ECOL**

BALDWIN, DONALD N., 1923-1972.
The quiet revolution: grass roots of today's wilderness preservation movement by Donald N. Baldwin. With an introd. by Orville L. Freeman. 1st ed. Pruett Pub. Co. c1972 **QH76.B35 ECOL**

BALDWIN, FLETCHER N., 1933- jt. auth.
Maloney, Frank Edward.
Water law and administration. 1972.
REF KFF446.M3 ECOL

BALDWIN, FRANK B., 1939- ed.
Legal control of water pollution. 1969
KF3786.A32L4 ECOL

BALDWIN, MALCOLM F., 1940- ed.
Law and the environment. 1970
KF5505.A75L38 ECOL

BALLANTINE, RICHARD, jt. auth.
Griffiths, Joel.
Silent slaughter. 1972   **RA1231.R2G74 ECOL**

BANFF CONFERENCE ON POLLUTION, 1ST, 1968.
Man and his environment; proceedings. Edited by M. A. Ward. 1st ed. Pergamon Press 1970-   v.
   TD172.5.B3 1968 ECOL

BANKER, R. F., jt. auth.
Patterson, W. L.
Estimating costs and manpower requirements for conventional wastewater treatment facilities. 1971 i.e. 1972   **fTD743.P36 ECOL**

BANKS, M. E.
New chemical concepts for utilization of waste plastics, prepared by M. E. Banks, W. D. Lusk and R. S. Ottinger for the Federal Solid Waste Management Program. United States. Environmental Protection Agency. Solid Waste Management Office 1971. (Solid waste management series)   **TP156.R38B3 ECOL**

BANNISTER ENGINEERING CO., ST. PAUL, MINN.
Report on reducing untreated combined wastewater overflows to the St. Croix River. St. Paul, 1970.
   fTD525.S7B3 ECOL

BANNON, EILEEN, ed.
Ulrich, Stanley.
Superior pollutor: a saga of the struggle to stop pollution of the largest fresh water lake in the world by its most egregious polluter—the Reserve Mining Company. 1972.   **TD224.M6U6 ECOL**

BANSAL, I. K., jt. auth.
Wiley, Averill J.
Reverse osmosis concentration of dilute pulp and paper effluents. 1972.   **fTD899.W65W5 ECOL**

BARBER, CAROLYN.
Animals at war. 1st U.S. ed. Harper & Row c1971 (Animal life series)   **QL758.5.B37 1971 ECOL**

BARBOUR, IAN G., comp.
Western man and environmental ethics; attitudes toward nature and technology. Edited by Ian G. Barbour. Addison-Wesley Pub. Co. 1973 (Addison-Wesley series in history) **GF80.B37 ECOL**

BARBOUR, IAN G., ed.
Earth might be fair. 1972   **GF80.E15 ECOL**

BARKALOW, FREDERICK SCHENCK, 1914-
The world of the gray squirrel by Frederick S. Barkalow, Jr., and Monica Shorten. Illus. with photos. Lippincott 1973 (Living world books)
   QL737.R68B37 ECOL

BARKER, CAROL M.
Classified files: the yellowing pages; a report on scholars' access to government documents, by Carol M. Barker and Matthew H. Fox. Twentieth Century Fund, 1972.   **JK468.S4B35ECOL**

BARKER, WILL.
Familiar animals of America. Drawings by Carl Burger. Foreword by Alastair MacBain. Harper 1956
   QL715.B25 ECOL
Wildlife in America's history. Illustrated by Howard Jerome Smith. R. B. Luce 1962   **QL155.B3 ECOL**

BARNES, CYRIL H., jt. auth.
Glysson, Eugene A.
The problem of solid-waste disposal. 1972.
   TD791.G5 ECOL

BARNES, ROBERT A.
Ammonia removal in a physical-chemical wastewater treatment process, by Robert A. Barnes, Peter F. Atkins and Dale A. Scherger. Prepared for Office of Research and Monitoring, U.S. Environmental Protection Agency. U.S. Govt. Print. Off., 1972. (Environmental Protection technology series)   **TD462.B3 ECOL**

BARNETT, HAROLD J.
Scarcity and growth; the economics of natural resource availability, by Harold J. Barnett and Chandler Morse. Published for Resources for the Future by Johns Hopkins Press, Baltimore 1963   **HC55.B3 ECOL**

BARNETTE, HENLEE H.
The church and the ecological crisis, by Henlee H. Barnette. Eerdmans 1972   **BT695.5.B37 ECOL**

BARNHART, E. L., jt. auth.
Manufacturing Chemists' Association.
The effect of chlorination on selected organic chemicals. 1972.   **fTD462.M3 ECOL**

BARON, NORMAN J.
A survey of attitudes towards the Mississippi River as a total resource in Minnesota. Written by Norman J. Baron, E. James Cecil and Philip L. Tideman. Ed. by James P. Ludwig. Univ. of Minn., Water Resources Research Center, 1972. (Minnesota. University. Water Resources Research Center. WRRC bulletin 55)
   GB701.M554no.55 ECOL

BARON, ROBERT ALEX.
The tyranny of noise. St. Martin's Press 1970
   TD892.B37 ECOL

BARON, WILLIAM MICHAEL MUIR.
Nature conservation; a practical handbook by W. M. M. Baron. Methuen Educational 1971 (Methuen studies in science)   **QH77.G7B28 ECOL**

BARR, DOUGLAS W.
Over-all plan for Nine Mile Creek Watershed District. 1961. v.   **fTC424.M6B36 ECOL**
Feasibility study: Mt. Normandale Lake and Marsh Lake, for City of Bloomington and Nine Mile Creek Watershed District. 1967. v.   **fTC424.M6B32 ECOL**
Feasibility study of Mud Lake improvement; report to the Village of Edina and Nine Mile Creek Watershed District. 1966. v.   **fTC424.M6B322 ECOL**

BARR ENGINEERING COMPANY.
The drainage plan for Burnsville, Minnesota. 1966.
   fTD525.B8B3 ECOL
Harza Engineering Company.
A program for preserving the quality of Lake Minnetonka. 1971   **fTD225.M63H3 ECOL**
Hydrological study of Hyland-Bush-Anderson lakes, for Nine Mile Creek Watershed District, Hennepin County Park Reserve District, City of Bloomington. 1971.   **fTC424.M6B326 ECOL**
Mud Lake hydrologic study. Prepared for the Village of Edina and Nine Mile Creek Watershed District. 1972.   **fTC424.M6B34 ECOL**
Nine Mile Creek Watershed District; proposed rules and regulations and model ordinances. 1973.
   fTC424.M6B35 ECOL
Report to the Board of Managers, Nine Mile Creek Watershed District; engineer's annual report, 1964-
v.   **fTC424.M6B3 ECOL**

BARR, JOHN, 1926-
The assaults on our senses. Methuen, 1970.
   QH77.G7B29 ECOL

BARROW, GEORGE.
Your world in motion; the story of energy. Illus. by Mildred Waltrip. Harcourt 1956   **QC25.B23 ECOL**

BARRY, JAMES P.
The fate of the lakes; a portrait of the Great Lakes. Text and photos. by James P. Barry. Baker Book House 1972   **F551.B37 ECOL**

BARTLETT, MARGARET FARRINGTON.
Down the mountain; a book about the ever-changing soil. With illus. by Rhys Caparn. Young Scott Books, c1963.   **PZ10.B1748Do ECOL**

BARTLETT, RICHARD A., ed.
Chittenden, Hiram Martin.
The Yellowstone National Park. 1964
   F722.C54 1964 ECOL

BARTLEY, THOMAS R., jt. auth.
Otto, Norman E.
Aquatic pests on irrigation systems: identification guide. 1972,1965   **QH96.O88 1972 ECOL**

BARTON, JAMES R., jt. auth.
Fuhriman, Dean K.
Ground water pollution in Arizona, California, Nevada & Utah. 1971 i.e. 1972
   fTD223.9.F85 ECOL

BARTSCH, A. F.
Role of phosphorus in eutrophication. National Environmental Research Center, Office of Research and Monitoring, U.S. Environmental Protection Agency, 1972. (Ecological research series)
   QH96.8.E9B3 ECOL

THE BASIC BOOK OF ORGANIC GARDENING.
Edited by Robert Rodale. Compiled by Glenn F. Johns. Ballantine Book, 1971   **S605.5.B37 ECOL**

BASILE, ROBERT M., 1916-
Smith, Guy Harold.
Conservation of natural resources. 4th ed. 1971
   S938.S58 1971 ECOL

BATES, DAVID B.
A citizen's guide to air pollution. McGill-Queen's Univ. Press, 1972.   **TD883.B23 ECOL**

BATES, MARSTON, 1906-
The forest and the sea; a look at the economy of nature and the ecology of man. Random House 1960
   QH541.B3 ECOL

BATTAN, LOUIS J.
The unclean sky; a meteorologist looks at air pollution by Louis J. Battan. Illus. by the author and D. C. Perceny. Anchor Books, 1966. (Science study series, S46)   **TD883.B3 ECOL**

BATTELLE MEMORIAL INSTITUTE, COLUMBUS, OHIO.
Corrosion potential of NTA in detergent formulations by Peter J. Moreland and others. Prepared for the Water Quality Office, Environmental Protection Agency. U.S. Govt. Print. Off., 1971. (Water pollution control research series)   **fTP992.5.B3 ECOL**
Managing the environment: international economic cooperation for pollution control. 1971
   HC79.E5M35 1971 ECOL
Sweet, David C.
The economic and social importance of estuaries. 1971.   **GB454.E8S95 ECOL**

BATTELLE MEMORIAL INSTITUTE, COLUMBUS, OHIO. COLUMBUS LABORATORIES.
Drobny, N. L.
Recovery and utilization of municipal solid waste: a summary of available cost and performance characteristics of unit processes and systems. 1971.
   TD793.D76 ECOL
An investigation of techniques for removal of chromium from electroplating wastes. Environmental Protection Agency, 1971. (Water pollution control research series)   **fTD899.M45B3ECOL**
An investigation of techniques for removal of cyanide from electroplating wastes. U. S. Environmental Protection Agency; for sale by the Supt. of Docs., U. S. Govt. Print. Off. 1971 i.e. 1972 (Water pollution control research series)   **fTD899.M45B32 ECOL**
Multidirectional turbulence probe development. Phase I: Unidirectional turbulence sensor development, by Battelle Columbus Laboratories for the Environmental Protection Agency. U.S. Environmental Protection Agency (Water pollution control research series)   **fTC177.B3 ECOL**
Solid Waste Resources Conference, Columbus, Ohio, 1971.
Design of consumer containers for re-use or disposal. 1972.   **TD785.S6 1971 ECOL**
A state-of-the-art review of metal finishing waste treatment. U.S. Federal Water Quality Administration; for sale by the Supt. of Docs., U.S. Govt. Print. Off. 1968 i.e.1970 (Water pollution control research series)
   fTD899.M45B33 ECOL

BATTELLE MEMORIAL INSTITUTE, COLUMBUS, OHIO. PACIFIC NORTHWEST LABORATORY, RICHLAND, WASH.
Concept development of a hydraulic skimmer system for recovery of floating oil. Prepared for the Environmental Protection Agency, Water Quality Office by John R. Blacklaw. Environmental Protection Agency, Water Quality Office; for sale by the Supt. of Docs., U.S. Govt. Print. Off. 1971. (Water pollution control research series)   **fTD427.P4B29 ECOL**

BATTELLE-NORTHWEST.
Inorganic fertilizer and phosphate mining industries—water pollution and control. Prepared by Battelle Memorial Institute, Richland, Washington for the Environmental Protection Agency, Research and Monitoring; for sale by the Supt. of Docs., U.S. Govt. Print. Off., 1971. (Water pollution control research series)
   fTD899.F47B38 ECOL

BATTEN, JAMES W., 1919-   jt. auth.
Gibson, J. Sullivan.
Soils: their nature, classes, distribution, uses, and care. 1970   **S591.G52 ECOL**

BAUFLE, JEAN MARIE.
Photographing wildlife by Jean-Marie Baufle and Jean-Philippe Varin. Translated from the French by Carel V. Amerongen. Oxford University Press, 1972.
   fTR727.B2813 ECOL

BAUM, BERNARD, jt. auth.
Warner, Arthur J.
Plastics solid waste disposal by incineration or landfill. c1972, 1971.   **fTD798.W36 ECOL**

BAUMANN, DONALD J.
Beefland International, Inc.
Elimination of water pollution by packing-house animal paunch and blood. 1971.
   fTD899.M4B4 ECOL

BAUSUM, HOWARD T.
Science for society: a bibliography. Prepared by Howard T. Bausum for the Commission on Science Education, American Association for the Advancement of Science. 3d ed. AAAS Commission on Science Education, 1972. (AAAS miscellaneous publication 72-13)   **fZ7401.B3 1972 ECOL**

BAY LAUREL, ALICIA.
Living on the earth; celebrations, storm warnings, formulas, recipes, rumors & country dances. Vintage Books 1971, c1970   **fS605.5.B3 ECOL**

BAYER, T. N.
Hogberg, Rudolph K.
Guide to the caves of Minnesota. 1967
   GB605.M5H6 ECOL

BAYNES, ERNEST HAROLD, 1868-
Wild bird guests; how to entertain them; with chapters on the destruction of birds, their economic and aesthetic values, suggestions for dealing with their enemies, and on the organization and management of bird clubs, by Ernest Harold Baynes; with 50 photogravure illus. from photographs. Dutton, 1915.

SK353.B4 ECOL

BEAR, FIRMAN EDWARD, 1884-
Earth, the stuff of life. Univ. of Oklahoma Press 1962
S591.B33 ECOL

BEASLEY, ROBERT PATRICK.
Erosion and sediment pollution control by R. P. Beasley. 1st ed. Iowa State University Press 1972
S623.B33 ECOL

BECCHETTI, DON, jt. auth.
Dooley, David.
Summer school guide for education for an improved environment. 1971. **fQH541.2.D6 Suppl. ECOL**

BECKER, BURTON C., jt. auth.
Maryland. Dept. of Water Resources.
Guidelines for erosion and sediment control, planning and implementation. 1972. **fS624.A1M3 ECOL**

BECKERS, CHARLES V.
Quantitative methods for preliminary design of water quality surveillance systems, by C. V. Beckers, Stanley G. Chamberlain and G. Paul Grimsrud. Prepared for Office of Research and Monitoring, U.S. Environmental Protection Agency. U.S. Govt. Print. Off., 1972. (Socioeconomic environmental studies series)
TD365.B4 ECOL

BEEBE, CHARLES WILLIAM, 1877-1962.
Galapagos, world's end, by William Beebe ...with 24 coloured illus. by Isabel Cooper, and 83 photographs, mostly by John Tee-Van. Putnam, 1924.
QH123.B4 ECOL

Pheasants; their lives and homes. Published under the auspices of the New York Zoological Society by Doubleday, 1926. 2v. **REF QL969.G2B26 ECOL**

BEEFLAND INTERNATIONAL, INC.
Elimination of water pollution by packing-house animal paunch and blood. Author: Donald J. Baumann Environmental Protection Agency, Office of Research and Monitoring, 1971. (Water pollution control research series) **fTD899.M4B4 ECOL**

BEER, FRANCIS A.
Growing against ourselves: the energy-environment tangle. 1972. **TD195.E4G76 ECOL**

BEER, STAFFORD.
The Teilhard Review.
Change or decay: a symposium on the Blueprint for survival. 1972. **HC68.T4 ECOL**

BEET SUGAR DEVELOPMENT FOUNDATION, FORT COLLINS, COLO.
State-of-art, sugarbeet processing waste treatment. U.S. Environmental Protection Agency U.S. Govt. Print. Off., 1971. (Water pollution control research series), 1971. **fTD899.S8B43 ECOL**

BEHNKE, FRANCES L.
The changing world of living things. Illus. with photos. Holt c1972 (Changing world book)
QH541.14.B47 ECOL

BEISER, ARTHUR, jt. auth.
Krauskopf, Konrad Bates.
Fundamentals of physical science. 6th ed. 1971
Q160.2.K7 1971 ECOL

BELL, DANIEL, ed.
American Academy of Arts and Sciences, Boston.
Commission on the Year 2000
Toward the year 2000. 1970,c1968
E169.1.A47192 1970 ECOL

BELL, DERWIN, illus.
Dorr, John A.
Geology of Michigan. c1970
REF fQE125.D6 ECOL

BEMIDJI STATE COLLEGE. CENTER FOR ENVIRONMENTAL STUDIES.
Wanek, Wallace J.
A study of the impact of snowmobiling on northern Minnesota ecology. 1971 **fTL234.W3 ECOL**

BENARDE, MELVIN A.
Our precarious habitat by Melvin A. Benarde. 1st ed. Norton 1970 **TD180.B45 ECOL**

BENDER, DAVID L., jt. ed.
McCuen, Gary E.
The ecology controversy: opposing viewpoints. 1971
QH541.M3 ECOL

BENNETT, DEAN B.
Guidelines for planning and implementing a comprehensive community environmental inventory. Prepared by: Dean B. Bennett and Richard H. MacGown. Rev. ed. Maine Environmental Education Project, 1972. **fQH541.2.B38 1972 ECOL**

BENNETT, DEAN B., jt. auth.
MacGown, Richard H.
The school site in environmental education. Rev. ed. 1972. **.fLB3220.M3 1972 ECOL**

BENSON, FERRIS B.
Indoor-outdoor air pollution relationships: a literature review by Ferris B. Benson, John J. Henderson and D. E. Caldwell. Research Triangle Park, N.C., Environmental Protection Agency, National Environmental Research Center, 1972. (Publication no. AP-112) **TD890.B4 ECOL**

BENSTOCK, MARCY, jt. auth.
Zwick, David.
Water wasteland. 1971. **TD223.Z86 1971ECOL**

BENTHALL, JONATHAN, ed.
Ecology in theory and practice. Viking Press 1973,c1972 **QH541.B4 1973 ECOL**

BENTON, ALLEN H.
Field biology and ecology by Allen H. Benton and William E. Werner, Jr. 2d ed. McGraw-Hill 1966
QH318.5.B4 1966 ECOL

Manual of field biology and ecology, by Allen H. Benton and W. E. Werner. 4th ed. Burgess c1965
QH307.B3 1965 ECOL

BERG, BENGT MAGNUS KRISTOFFER, 1885-
Tavlor av Svenska faglar. Norstedt c1925 1v.
REF fQL690.S5B46 ECOL

To Africa with the migratory birds; with 75 illus. Putnam, 1930. **QL692.B4 ECOL**

BERG, GEORGE G., 1919-   comp.
Water pollution compiled by George G. Berg. Scientists' Institute for Public Information, 1970 (A Scientists' Institute for Public Information workbook)
fTD420.B46 ECOL

BERG, GEORGE G., 1919-   ed.
Chemical fallout. 1969 **SB959.C45 ECOL**

BERG, RICHARD HAROLD, 1937-
Washington (State). University.
The oxygen uptake demand of resuspended bottom sediments. 1970. **fGC380.W3 ECOL**

BERG, TIMOTHY J., jt. auth.
Ulrich, Stanley.
Superior pollutor: a saga of the struggle to stop pollution of the largest fresh water lake in the world by its most egregious polluter—the Reserve Mining Company. 1972. **TD224.M6U6 ECOL**

BERGER, ANDREW JOHN, 1915-
Bird study, by Andrew J. Berger. Dover Publications 1971,c1961 **QL673.B47 1971 ECOL**

BERGER, CARL F.
Science Curriculum Improvement Study.
Subsystems and variables. 1971,c1970
LB1585.S38 1971 ECOL

BERGER, HAROLD.
Nondestructive testing. U.S. Atomic Energy Commission, Division of Technical Information 1965 (Understanding the atom) **TA417.2.B4 ECOL**

BERGER, KERMIT CARL, 1910-
Sun, soil, and survival; an introduction to soils by Kermit C. Berger. University of Oklahoma Press 1972
S591.B45 1972 ECOL

BERGLUND, BERNDT, 1920-
Wilderness survival; A complete handbook and guide for survival in the North American wilds. Scribner 1972
SK606.B47 ECOL

BERKAU, E. E., jt. auth.
Martin, G. B.
Effects of fuel additives on air pollutant emissions from distillate-oil-fired furnaces. 1971.
TP355.M29 ECOL

BERLIN, G. LENNIS.
The urban environment: a climatological anomaly. Council of Planning Librarians 1972 (Council of Planning Librarians. Exchange bibliography, no. 292)
REF fQC981.7.U7B47 ECOL

BERLIN, ROISMAN & KESSLER.
Law and taxation; a guide for conservation and other nonprofit organizations. Prepared for the Conservation Foundation. Conservation Foundation 1970
KF6449.Z9B4 ECOL

BERMONT, HUBERT INGRAM, ed.
National Recreation and Park Association.
Guide to new approaches to financing parks & recreation. 1970 **SB482.A4N38 ECOL**

BERNAL (J. D.) PEACE LIBRARY.
Conference on Chemical and Biological Warfare, London, 1968.
CBW: chemical and biological warfare. 1969,c1968
UG447.C655 1968 ECOL

BEROZA, MORTON, 1917-   ed.
Chemicals controlling insect behavior. 1970.
QL461.S88 1969 ECOL

BERRILL, JACQUELYN.
Wonders of animal migration. Illus. by the author. Dodd 1964 **QL754.B4 ECOL**

BERRILL, NORMAN JOHN, 1903-
Inherit the earth; man on an aging planet by N. J. Berrill. Dodd, Mead 1966 **Q162.B56 ECOL**

The life of the ocean by N. J. Berrill. McGraw-Hill c1966 (Our living world of nature)
QH91.15.B4 ECOL

BERRY, MARCIA.
Environment study; an ecology-based science outline. Prepared by Marcia Berry and others. Edina Public Schools, 1971. **QH541.2.B4 ECOL**

BERTRAND, ANSON RABB, 1923-   jt. auth.
Kohnke, Helmut.
Soil conservation. 1959. **S623.K56 ECOL**

BESSELIEVRE, EDMUND BULKLEY, 1887-
The treatment of industrial wastes by Edmund B. Besselievre. McGraw-Hill 1968,c1969
REF TD897.B38 ECOL

BEST'S ENVIRONMENTAL CONTROL AND SAFETY DIRECTORY; safety-security-pollution control products.
13th ed.-   1971/72-   A. M. Best Co. v.
REF fT55.B4 ECOL

BEVILACQUA, CARLO, 1924-   illus.
De Michele, Vincenzo.
The world of minerals. 1972
QE372.D3413 ECOL

BIANCARDI, F. R.
United Aircraft Corporation. Research Laboratories, East Hartford, Conn.
Advanced nonthermally polluting gas turbines in utility applications. 1971. **fTJ778.U5 ECOL**

BIEGING, JAMES K., jt. auth.
United States. Environmental Protection Agency. Office of Research and Monitoring.
Storage and treatment of combined sewer overflows. 1972. **fTD662.U54 ECOL**

BIG GAME IN MINNESOTA.
by Bernard A. Fashingbauer and others ed. by John B. Moyle. Dept. of Conservation, Division of Game and Fish, Section of Research and Planning, 1965.(Minnesota Dept. of Conservation. Division of Game and Fish. Technical bulletin no.9)
SH11.M64no.9 ECOL

BILLINGS, WILLIAM DWIGHT, 1910-
Plants, man, and the ecosystem by W. D. Billings. 2d ed. Wadsworth Pub. Co. 1970 (Fundamentals of botany series) **QK901.B5 1970 ECOL**

BILLINGTON, ELIZABETH T.
Understanding ecology by Elizabeth T. Billington. Illus. by Robert Galster. F. Warne 1971
QH541.14.B5 1971 ECOL

BINGHAM, TAYLER H.
The beverage container problem; analysis and recommendations, by Tayler H. Bingham and Paul F. Mulligan. Prepared for the Office of Research and Monitoring, U.S. Environmental Protection Agency. U.S. Govt. Print. Off., 1972. (Environmental protection technology series) **TD793.B5 ECOL**

BIOLOGY AND ETHICS; proceedings of a symposium held at the Royal Geographical Society, London, on 26 and 27 September 1968;. edited by F. J. Ebling. Published for the Institute of Biology by Academic Press, 1969.(Institute of Biology. Symposia, no. 18) **HM216.B48 ECOL**

BIOLOGY AND THE FUTURE OF MAN.
Edited by Philip Handler. Oxford University Press, 1970. **QH307.2.B56 ECOL**

BIOSPHERICS INCORPORATED.
Biomass determination—a new technique for activated sludge control. Prepared for the Office of Research and Monitoring, Environmental Protection Agency. U.S. Govt. Print. Off., 1972. (Water pollution control research series) **fTD756.B5 ECOL**

BISHOP, A. BRUCE.
Analysis of water reuse alternatives in an integrated urban and agricultural area, by A. Bruce Bishop and David W. Hendricks. Utah Water Research Laboratory, College of Engineering, Utah State Univ., 1972.
fTD429.B5 ECOL

BISHOP, RICHARD EVETT, 1887-   illus.
Williams, Eugene Russell.
The ways of wildfowl. 1971
REF fQL696.A5W48 ECOL

BITUMINOUS COAL FACTS. 1970-
National Coal Assoc. v.
REF fHD9544.B47 ECOL

BITUMINOUS COAL RESEARCH, INC.
The economics of generating clean fuel gas from coal using an air-blown two-stage gasifier, based on a study sponsored jointly by Bituminous Coal Research, Inc. and the Office of Coal Research, U.S., Dept. of the Interior. Bituminous Coal Research, Inc., 1971.
fTP759.B5 ECOL

BIXBY, WILLIAM.
Of animals and men; a comparison of human and animals behavior. McKay Co., 1968.
QL751.B53 ECOL

BLACK, A. P., jt. auth.
Gainesville, Fla. Dept. of Public Utilities.
Magnesium carbonate, a recycled coagulant for water treatment. 1971. **fTD433.G3 ECOL**

BLACK & VEATCH, KANSAS CITY, MO.
Environmental report; Sherburne County Generating Plant. Northern States Power Co., 1971- 1v.
fTK1331.N6B7 ECOL

Metropolitan sewer board; location and cost study, interceptors and treatment works, metropolitan sewer service region. 1970. v. **fTD525.T9B5 ECOL**

Process design manual for phosphorus removal, by Black & Veatch, Consulting Engineers, for U.S. Environmental Protection Agency, Technology Transfer. U.S. Govt. Off. 1971. 1v.
REF fTD745.B5 ECOL

BLACK, IRMA (SIMONTON) 1906-
Busy water. Words by Irma Simonton Black. Pictures by Jane Castle. Holiday House, c1958.
PZ10.B29525Bu ECOL

BLACK, JOHN DAVID, 1908-
Biological conservation, with particular emphasis on wildlife. Blakiston c1954 **SK361.B55 ECOL**

BLACK, JOHN N.
The dominion of man; the search for ecological responsibility by John Black. Univ. Press, 1970.
GF80.B55 ECOL

BLACK, SIVALLS AND BRYSON, INC., KANSAS CITY, MO. APPLIED TECHNOLOGY DIVISION.
Evaluation of a new acid mine drainage treatment process. Prepared for the Environmental Protection Agency, Water Quality Office. Authors: Paul J. LaRosa, James A. Karnavas, and Eugene A. Pelczarski Water Quality Office. Environmental Protection Agency; for sale by the Supt. of Docs., U. S. Govt. Print. Off., 1971. (Water pollution control research series)
fTD899.M5B55 ECOL

Study of sulfur recovery from coal refuse, by Black, Sivalls & Bryson. Inc., Applied Technology. Authors: Paul J. LaRosa and H. James Michaels. Prepared for the Environmental Protection Agency. U. S. Environmental Protection Agency. Water Quality Office; for sale by the Supt. of Docs., U. S. Govt. Print. Off., 1971. (Water pollution control research series)
fTN890.B57 ECOL

BLACKLAW, JOHN R.
Battelle Memorial Institute, Columbus; Ohio. Pacific Northwest Laboratory, Richland, Wash.
Concept development of a hydraulic skimmer system for recovery of floating oil. 1971.
fTD427.P4B29 ECOL

BLACKMORE, MICHAEL, 1916-
Your book of watching wild life. With drawings by Eileen Hill. Faber and Faber ltd., 1971. (The Your books series) **QL60.B55 ECOL**

BLACKWOOD, PAUL EVERETT, 1913-
Push and pull; the story of energy. Illus. by William D. Hayes. Rev. ed. McGraw 1966
TJ147.B52 1966 ECOL

BLAKE, PETER, 1920-
God's own junkyard; the planned deterioration of America's landscape. Holt 1964
HF5843.5.B55 ECOL

BLOMBERG, KARIN.
Direct experience teaching in the out-of-doors. 1967.
fLB1047.B56 ECOL

BLOOME, ENID.
The air we breathe! Doubleday, 1971.
TD883.13.B56 ECOL

The water we drink! Doubleday, 1971.
PZ10.B29545Wat ECOL

BLOUGH, GLENN ORLANDO.
Discovering plants, by Glenn O. Blough. Pictures by Jeanne Bendick. McGraw-Hill 1966
PZ10.B29553Dk ECOL

BLUEPRINT FOR SURVIVAL,.
by the editors of the Ecologist: Edward Goldsmith and others. Houghton, 1972. **S936.B5 1972 ECOL**

BLUMENFELD, HANS.
The modern metropolis; its origins, growth, characteristics, and planning. Edited by Paul D. Spreiregen. Massachusetts Institute of Technology 1968,c1967 **HT166.B54 ECOL**

BLUMENSTOCK, DAVID IRVING, 1913-
The Ocean of air. Rutgers Univ. Press, 1959.
QC863.B55 ECOL

BOATWRIGHT, MODY COGGIN, 1896-
Folklore of the oil industry. With illus. by William D. Wittliff. Southern Methodist University Press c1963
TN872.A5B6 ECOL

BOCK, ALAN.
The ecology action guide. Nash Publishing c1971
GF75.B6 ECOL

BOCKRIS, JOHN O'M., ed.
Electrochemistry of cleaner environments. 1972.
TP256.E43 1972 ECOL

BODSWORTH, FRED, 1918-
Last of the curlews; illus. by T. M. Shortt. Dodd, 1955. **QL696.L7B6 ECOL**

BODWITCH, WILLIAM P., jt. auth.
Powell, Mel D.
Community action guidebook for soil erosion and sediment control. 1970 **fS624.A1P68 ECOL**

BOEN, DOYLE F.
Study of reutilization of wastewater recycled through groundwater, by D. F. Boen, J. H. Bunts and R. J. Currie of the Eastern Municipal Water District, Hemet, Calif. Prepared for the Office of Research and Monitoring, Environmental Protection Agency. U.S. Govt. Ptg. Off., 1971. v.1- (Water pollution control research series)
fTD429.B6 ECOL

BOESEN, VICTOR.
They said it couldn't be done: the incredible story of Bill Lear. 1st ed. Doubleday, 1971.
TL540.L364B64 ECOL

BOETTCHER, R. A.
Air classification of solid wastes; performance of experimental units and potential applications for solid waste reclamation. Environmental Protection Agency, 1972. **TD796.7.B64 ECOL**

BOLD, HAROLD CHARLES, 1909-
The plant kingdom by Harold C. Bold. 3d ed. Prentice-Hall c1970 (Prentice-Hall foundations of modern biology series) **QK48.B59 1970 ECOL**

BOLLENS, JOHN CONSTANTINUS, 1920-
The metropolis; its people, politics, and economic life by John C. Bollens and Henry J. Schmandt. 2d ed. Harper & Row 1970 **JS422.B6 1970 ECOL**

BOLT, BERANEK, AND NEWMAN, INC.
Noise from construction equipment and operations, building equipment, and home appliances. U.S. Environmental Protection Agency 1971 i.e. 1972
fTD893.B63 ECOL

BONBRIGHT, JAMES CUMMINGS, 1891-
Public utilities and the national power policies, by James C. Bonbright. Da Capo Press, 1972, c1940 (Franklin D. Roosevelt and the era of the New Deal)
HD2766.B57 1972

BOND, RICHARD G.
Gibson, Ulric P.
Integrating water quality management into total water resources management in Minnesota. 1970.
GB701.M554no.23 ECOL

BONEM, GILBERT W., jt. auth.
Wollman, Nathaniel.
The outlook for water. 1971
REF fTD223.W6 ECOL

BONESTROO, ROSENE, ANDERLIK AND ASSOCIATES, INC., ST. PAUL, MINN.
Report on sanitary sewerage facilities Airlake Industrial Park for Lakeville, Minnesota. 1967.
fTD525.L3B6 ECOL

BONGERS, LEONARD H.
Sand and gravel overlay for control of mercury in sediments, by Leonard H. Bongers and Mohammed N. Khattak. Prepared for the Office of Research and Monitoring, Environmental Protection Agency. U.S. Govt. Print. Off., 1972. (Water pollution control research series) **fTD427.M4B6 ECOL**

BONNER, JOHN TYLER.
Chemical ecology. 1970. **QH345.C435 ECOL**

BONVIE, CAROLYN.
Art & design in the environment. Written by: Carolyn Bonvie, V. Eugene Vivian and Karen Ambry Miller. Ed. by Norma T. Vivian. Conservation & Environmental Studies Center 1971 **fLB1047.B6 ECOL**

BOOTH, ERNEST SHELDON, 1915-
How to know the mammals by Ernest S. Booth. 3d ed. W. C. Brown Co. 1972, c1971 (Pictured-key nature series) **QL715.B66 1972 ECOL**

BORCHERT, JOHN R.
Minnesota. Lakeshore Development Study.
Minnesota's lakeshore. 1970-
REF GB459.5.M5M5 ECOL

Minnesota settlement and land use 1985, by J. R. Borchert and Donald C. Carroll. Minnesota State Planning Agency, 1970. **HD111.B6 ECOL**

BORG-WARNER CORPORATION.
Jennings, Burgess Hill.
Interactions of man and his environment. 1966.
TD180.J4 ECOL

BORGSTROM, GEORGE, 1912-
Harvesting the earth. Abelard-Schuman 1973
HD9000.5.B56 1973 ECOL

The hungry planet; the modern world at the edge of famine. Rev. ed. Collier Books 1967
HD9000.5.B54 1967 ECOL

The hungry planet; the modern world at the edge of famine. 2nd rev. ed. Collier Books 1972
HD9000.5.B54 1972 ECOL

BORGWARDT, R. H.
Selected studies on alkaline additives for sulfur dioxide control. 1971. **TD885.5.S8S4 ECOL**

BOROS, JOSEPH A.
Troy, Joseph C.
Oxidation of pyrites in chlorinated solvents. 1972.
TD899.M5T7 ECOL

BORRELLI, PETER.
California Institute of Technology, Pasadena. Environmental Quality Laboratory.
People, power and pollution: environmental and public interest aspects of electric power plant siting. 1971. **fTK1193.U5C3 ECOL**

BOSTON COLLEGE, BOSTON, MASS.
Science and the future of man. c1970
CB151.S37 ECOL

BOSTON COLLEGE INDUSTRIAL AND COMMERCIAL LAW REVIEW.
Recent developments in environmental law. March 1971- Boston College Law School. v.
KF3775.A75B6 ECOL

BOSTON COLLEGE LAW SCHOOL, BRIGHTON, MASS.
Boston College industrial and commercial law review. Recent developments in environmental law. March 1971- **KF3775.A75B6 ECOL**

BOUGHEY, ARTHUR S.
Ecology of populations by Arthur S. Boughey. Macmillan 1968 (Current concepts in biology)
QH541.B67 ECOL

Man and the environment; an introduction to human ecology and evolution by Arthur S. Boughey. Macmillan 1971 **GF43.B68 ECOL**

Population and environmental biology by Arthur S. Boughey. Dickenson Pub. Co. 1967 (Dickenson series on contemporary thought in biological science)
QH83.B68 ECOL

BOULDING, KENNETH EWART, 1910-
Resources for the Future.
Environmental quality in a growing economy. 1968,c1966 **HC103.7.R39 ECOL**

BOUNDARY WATERS CANOE AREA, MINNESOTA.
Ohmann, Lewis F.
Wilderness ecology, virgin plant communities of the Boundary Waters Canoe Area. 1971.
SD11.A45476no.63 ECOL

BOURLIERE, FRANCOIS, 1913-
The natural history of mammals. Tr. from the French by H. M. Parshley. 1st American ed. Knopf, 1954.
QL751.B663 ECOL

BOURNE, ARTHUR G.
Pollute and be damned. Dent, 1972.
TD175.B68 ECOL

BOUWER, HERMAN.
Renovating secondary sewage by ground water recharge with infiltration basins, by Herman Bouwer, R. C. Rice, and E. D. Escarcega. Prepared for the Office of Research and Monitoring, Environmental Protection Agency. U.S. Govt. Print. Off., 1972. (Water pollution control research series) **fTD765.B6 ECOL**

BOVEY, MARTIN KOON.
Saga of the waterfowl. Drawings by F. L. Jaques. Wildlife Management Institute, 1949.
REF SK331.B6 ECOL

BOWEN, EZRA.
The high Sierra, by Ezra Bowen and the editors of Time-Life Books. Time-Life Books 1972 (The American wilderness) **F868.S5B6 ECOL**

BOWER, BLAIR T., ed.
Resources for the Future.
Environmental quality analysis. 1972
HC79.E5R46 ECOL

BOWER, BLAIR T., jt. auth.
Kneese, Allen V.
Managing water quality: economics, technology, institution. 1968 **TD423.K52 ECOL**

BOWERS, C. EDWARD.
Computer program for statistical analysis of annual flood data by the log-Pearson Type III method, by C. E. Bowers, Arthur F. Pabst, and Stephen P. Larson. Water Resources Research Center, Univ. of Minn. Graduate School, 1971. (WRRC bulletin, no.39)
GB701.M554no.39 ECOL

Computer programs in hydrology, by C. E. Bowers, A. F. Pabst and S. P. Larson. Water Resources Research Center, University of Minnesota, 1972. (WRRC bulletin no.44)
GB665.B6 ECOL

Review and analysis of rainfall and runoff data for selected watersheds in Minnesota; by C. Edward Bowers and Arthur F. Pabst. Water Resources Research Center, University of Minnesota, 1968. (WRRC bulletin no.8)
GB701.M554no.8 ECOL

BOWERS, C. EDWARD, jt. auth.
Larson, Curtis L.
Numerical routing of flood hydrographs through open channel junctions. 1971.
GB701.M554no.40 ECOL

Pabst, Arthur F.
Flood forecasting in the Upper Midwest: data assembly and preliminary analysis. 1972.
fGB678.P32 ECOL

BOWKER (R. R.) COMPANY, NEW YORK.
Publishers' trade list annual.
Books in print. **REF Z1215.P972 ECOL**

Publishers' trade list annual.
Books in print supplement: authors, titles, subjects. 1972/73- **REF fZ1215.P972 Suppl. ECOL**

BOWMAN, ISAIAH, 1878-
The pioneer fringe. American Geographical Society, 1931. (American Geographical Society. Special publication no.13) **GF51.B6 ECOL**

BOYCE THOMPSON INSTITUTE FOR PLANT RESEARCH, YONKERS, N.Y.
Interaction of herbicides and soil microorganisms. U.S. Environmental Protection Agency, U.S. Govt. Print. Off., 1971. (Water pollution control research series) **fSB951.4.B68 ECOL**

BOYD, GAIL B.
Methods of predicting solid waste characteristics, by Gail B. Boyd and Myron B. Hawkins U.S. Environmental Protection Agency; for sale by the Supt. of Docs., U.S. Govt. Print. Off. 1971.
TD793.7.B68 ECOL

BOYD, GAIL B., jt. auth.
Sartor, James D.
Water pollution aspects of street surface contaminants. 1972. **fTD665.S2 ECOL**

BOYD, LOUISE ARNER, 1887-
Polish countrysides; photographs and narrative by L. A. Boyd; with a contribution by Stanislaw Gorzuchowski. American Geographical Society, 1937. (American Geographical Society. Special publication no.20) **DK407.B6 ECOL**

BOYLE, ROBERT H.
The Hudson River; a natural and unnatural history by Robert H. Boyle. 1st ed. Norton 1969
QH105.N7B68 ECOL

The water hustlers by Robert H. Boyle, John Graves and T. H. Watkins. Sierra Club 1971
HD1694.A5B58 ECOL

BRADFORD, ALBERT.
Nuclear explosives in peacetime. 1970
fQC792.N8 ECOL

BRADY, NYLE C., jt. auth.
Buckman, Harry Oliver.
The nature and properties of soils. 7th ed. 1969
S591.B88 1969 ECOL

BRAGDON, CLIFFORD R.
Noise pollution: the unquiet crisis by Clifford R. Bragdon. University of Pennsylvania Press c1971
TD892.B69 ECOL

BRAINERD, JOHN W., 1918-
Nature study for conservation; a handbook for environmental education by John W. Brainerd. Macmillan 1971 **S946.B68 ECOL**

BRAMER, HENRY C., 1921-
Synectics Corporation.
A system for industrial waste treatment RD&D project priority assignment. 1971.
fTD897.5.S9 ECOL

BRANDWEIN, PAUL FRANZ, 1912-
The world of living things by Paul F. Brandwein and others. Editorial collaborators: Jerome J. Notkin, Clifford R. Nelson and Herbert Drapkin. Harcourt, Brace & World 1964 (Harcourt, Brace & World science program) **QH308.5.B7 1964 ECOL**

BRANDWEIN, PAUL FRANZ, 1912- jt. auth.
Morholt, Evelyn.
A sourcebook for the biological sciences. 2d ed. 1966
QH53.M67 1966 ECOL

BRANLEY, FRANKLYN MANSFIELD, 1915-
Air is all around you. Illus. by Robert Galster. Crowell 1962 (Let's-read-and-find-out science book)
PZ10.B65Ai ECOL

BRAUER AND ASSOCIATES, INC., EDINA, MINN.
A study of parks and recreation for the village of New Brighton. 1967 **fGV54.M6B7 ECOL**

BRAUN, ERNEST.
Living water. Photos. by Ernest Braun. Words by David Cavagnaro. American West Pub. Co. 1971
fQH46.B7 ECOL

BRECHER, JOSEPH J., 1941-
Environmental law handbook by Joseph J. Brecher and Manuel E. Nestle. California Continuing Education of the Bar 1970 **REF KF3775.B7 ECOL**

BREGMAN, J. I.
The pollution paradox by J. I. Bregman and Sergei Lenormand. Books c1966 **TD180.B7 ECOL**

BREIDENBACH, ANDREW W.
Composting of municipal solid wastes in the United States. 1971. **TD796.5.C64 ECOL**

BRENNEMAN, DONALD R.
Troy, Joseph C.
Oxidation of pyrites in chlorinated solvents. 1972.
TD899.M5T7 ECOL

BRESLER, JACK BARRY, 1923- ed.
Human ecology; collected readings. Jack B. Bresler, editor. Addison-Wesley 1966 (Addison-Wesley series in the life sciences) **GF31.B65 ECOL**

BRICE, WILLIAM C.
Possible environmental impact of base metal mining in Minnesota. State of Minnesota, Dept. of Natural Resources, Division of Waters, Soils and Minerals 1972
fTN24.M6B7 ECOL

BRIDGE, RAYMOND.
The complete snow camper's guide. Scribner 1973
SK602.6.B74 ECOL

BRIDGES, EDWIN MICHAEL.
World soils by E. M. Bridges. Cambridge U.P., 1970.
S591.B85 ECOL

BRIDGES, WILLIAM, 1901-
Wild animals of the world. Animal portraits by Mary Baker. Introd. by Roy Chapman Andrews. Garden City Pub. Co. 1948 **fQL706.B89 ECOL**

BRIGGS, PETER.
Water: the vital essence. Harper c1967
GC21.B83 ECOL

BRINGS, LAWRENCE MARTIN, 1897- ed.
Outdoor horizons; a book about American wildlife for sportsmen and those who love the outdoors. With special articles by eminent outdoor writers. 12 paintings and 24 drawings by Roger E. Preuss. Denison c1957
fSK33.B83 ECOL

BRINKHURST, RALPH O.
The role of sludge worms in eutrophication. Prepared for Office of Research and Monitoring, U.S. Environmental Protection Agency. U.S. Govt. Print. Office 1972. (Ecological research series)
QH96.8.E9B7 ECOL

BRITISH ECOLOGICAL SOCIETY.
Conservation and productivity of natural waters. 1972. **QL1.Z733no.29 ECOL**

Goodman, Gordon T.
Ecology and the industrial society. 1965
TD180.G6 ECOL

BRITTIN, WESLEY EMIL, comp.
Air and water pollution; proceedings of the summer workshop, August 3 to August 15, 1970, University of Colorado. Edited by Wesley E. Brittin, Ronald West and Robert Williams. Colorado Associated University Press 1972 **TD881.B75 ECOL**

BRITTON, PAUL W., jt. auth.
Muhich, Anton J.
Preliminary data analysis. 1968.
TD795.M82 ECOL

BROCK, THOMAS D.
Principles of microbial ecology by Thomas D. Brock. Prentice-Hall 1966 (Prentice-Hall biological science series) **QR41.B72 ECOL**

BROCKMAN, CHRISTIAN FRANK, 1902-
Recreational use of wild lands. McGraw-Hill, 1959. (The American forestry series) **SB481.B66 ECOL**

Trees of North America; a field guide to the major native and introduced species north of Mexico. Illus. by Rebecca Merrilees. Under the editorship of Herbert S. Zim. Golden Press 1968 (Golden field guide)
QK481.B864 ECOL

BRODEUR, PAUL.
Asbestos and enzymes. Introd. by Rene Dubos. Ballantine Books 1972 (A Ballantine Walden edition)
RA1231.A8B76 ECOL

BRODINE, VIRGINIA.
Nuclear explosives in peacetime. 1970
fQC792.N8 ECOL

BRONSON, WILLIAM.
How to kill a Golden State. Doubleday, 1968.
F866.2.B7 ECOL

BROOK, ALAN J.
The phytoplankton of Minnesota lakes—a preliminary survey. Water Resources Research Center, University of Minnesota Graduate School, 1971. (WRRC bulletin, no.36) **GB701.M554no.36 ECOL**

BROOKINGS INSTITUTION, WASHINGTON, D.C. INSTITUTE FOR GOVERNMENT RESEARCH. STUDIES IN ADMINISTRATION, NO. 19.
Cameron, Jenks.
The development of governmental forest control in the United States. 1972. **SD565.C3 1972 ECOL**

BROOKS, ALLAN, 1869- illus.
Hoffmann, Ralph.
Birds of the Pacific states. 1927.
Ref QL683.H65 ECOL

Phillips, John Charles.
American waterfowl. 1930. **QL696.A5P45 ECOL**

BROOKS, DAVID B.
Low-grade and nonconventional sources of manganese, by David B. Brooks. Washington, Resources for the Future; distributed by Johns Hopkins Press, Baltimore 1966 **REF TN490.M3B85 ECOL**

Peaceful use of nuclear explosives; some economic aspects, by David B. Brooks and John V. Krutilla. Resources for the Future; dist. by the Johns Hopkins Press, Baltimore 1969 **HD9698.U52B7 ECOL**

Supply and competition in minor metals, by David B. Brooks. Resources for the Future; dist. by Johns Hopkins Press, Baltimore c1965
REF HD9506.U62B7 ECOL

BROOKS, MAURICE GRAHAM, 1900-
The life of the mountains by Maurice Brooks. McGraw-Hill 1967 (Our living world of nature)
QH541.5.M65B7 ECOL

BROOKS, PAUL.
The house of life: Rachel Carson at work; with selections from her writings published and unpublished. Houghton, Mifflin, 1972. **QH31.C33B7 ECOL**

The pursuit of wilderness. Houghton, 1971.
QH75.B73 ECOL

Roadless area. Drawings by the author. Knopf, 1971,c1964. **QH75.B74 ECOL**

BROROWSKY, GEORGE.
Yellow pages of learning resources. 1972.
Ref fLC215.Y45 ECOL

BROWER, DAVID ROSS, 1912-
McPhee, John A.
Encounters with the archdruid. 1971
S942.M26 ECOL

The Sierra Club wilderness handbook, ed. by David Brower. 2nd rev. ed. Ballantine Books c1971 (A Sierra Club-Ballantine book, U6095)
SK601.B845 1971 ECOL

BROWER, DAVID ROSS, 1912- ed.
Muir, John.
Gentle wilderness. Rev. ed. 1971c1968
F868.S5M88 1971 ECOL

Not man apart; lines from Robinson Jeffers. Photos. of the Big Sur Coast, by Ansel Adams and others. Edited by David Brower. Sierra Club 1969 (A Sierra Club-Ballantine book) **F869.B63B7 1969 ECOL**

Only a little planet. 1972
fPS3553.O4749O5 ECOL

Porter, Eliot.
The place no one knew: Glen Canyon on the Colorado. 1963 **fF832.C7P6 ECOL**

BROWER, KENNETH, 1944- ed.
Hay, John.
The primal alliance: earth and ocean. 1971.
fQH95.7.H32 ECOL

BROWN, ALISON LEADLEY.
Ecology of fresh water. Harvard University Press, 1971. **QH541.5.F7B7 1971b ECOL**

BROWN, DALE.
Wild Alaska, by Dale Brown and the editors of Time-Life Books. Time-Life Books 1972 (The American wilderness) **QH105.A4B7 ECOL**

BROWN, EDWARD DUNCAN.
The legal regime of hydrospace, by E. D. Brown. Stevens for the London Institute of World Affairs, 1971. (The Library of world affairs, no. 70)
JX4411.B73 ECOL

BROWN, GEORGE W.
An improved temperature prediction model for small streams. Water Resources Research Institute, Dept. of Forest Engineering, Oregon State Univ. 1972
fQC909.B7 ECOL

BROWN, HARLEY P.
Aquatic dryopoid beetles (Coleoptera) of the United States. Environmental Protection Agency, 1972. (Biota of freshwater ecosystems, Identification manual, no.6.)
fQH96.A2B5no.6 ECOL

BROWN, HARRISON SCOTT, 1917-
The next hundred years: man's natural and technological resources; a discussion prepared for leaders of American industry, by Harrison Brown, James Bonner and John Weir. Viking Press 1970,c1963
HC55.B7 1970 ECOL

BROWN, HARRISON SCOTT, 1917- ed.
Are our descendants doomed? 1972
HB849.A74 1972 ECOL

BROWN, JAMES C.
An investigation of curricula materials and methodology for training operators of wastewater treatment plants. Water Resources Research Institute, North Carolina State University 1972. (North Carolina. University. Water Resources Research Institute. Report no. 74)
fHD1694.N8N6no.74 ECOL

BROWN, KEITH CATES, 1933-
Bidding for offshore oil: toward an optimal strategy by Keith C. Brown. Southern Methodist University Press c1969
HD9560.5.B75 ECOL

BROWN, KEITH CATES, 1933- ed.
Regulation of the natural gas producing industry. 1972
HD9581.U5R45 ECOL

BROWN, LESLIE.
The life of the African plains. McGraw-Hill, published in cooperation with the World Book Encyclopedia 1972 (Our living world of nature)
QH541.5.P7B76 ECOL

BROWN, LESTER RUSSELL, 1934-
Man and his environment: food by Lester R. Brown and Gail W. Finsterbusch. Harper & Row 1972 (Man and his environment series)
S439.B76 ECOL

Seeds of change; the green revolution and development in the 1970's by Lester R. Brown. Foreword by Eugene R. Black. Published for the Overseas Development Council by Praeger 1970
HD9000.5.B73 ECOL

The social impact of the Green revolution by Lester R. Brown. With comments by L. K. Jha, Sterling Wortman, and Stanley Please. Carnegie Endowment for International Peace 1971. (International conciliation, no. 581)
HD1417.B7 ECOL

World without borders by Lester R. Brown. Random House 1972
HC59.B765 1972b ECOL

BROWN, MARTIN, 1946- ed.
The Social responsibility of the scientist. 1971
Q125.S714 ECOL

BROWN, ROBERT E.
Techniques for teaching conservation education by Robert E. Brown and G. W. Mouser. Burgess Pub. Co. 1964 (Burgess education series)
S946.B7 ECOL

BROWN, ROBERT MEREDITH, 1914- ed.
Use of systems techniques in environmental quality management. 1970.
RA565.A1N38no.7 ECOL

BROWN, ROBERT P., jt. auth.
Smith, David D.
Ocean disposal of barge-delivered liquid and solid wastes from United States coastal cities. 1971.
TD796.7.O25S4 ECOL

BROWN, ROGER JAMES EVAN, 1931-
Permafrost in Canada; its influence on Northern development by Roger J. E. Brown. University of Toronto Press 1970 (Canadian Building series, 4)
TA713.B76 ECOL

BROWN, TOM, 1941-
Oil on ice; Alaskan wilderness at the crossroads, by Tom Brown. Edited, with an introd., by Richard Pollak. Sierra Club 1971 (A Sierra Club battlebook)
HC107.A47E53 ECOL

BROWN, VINSON, 1912-
Knowing the outdoors in the dark. With many illus. by Phyllis Thompson. Stackpole Books 1972
QH81.B856 ECOL

Reading the woods; seeing more in nature's familiar faces. Stackpole Books 1969 **QH541.5.F6B73 ECOL**

BROWN, WILLIAM EDWARD, 1930-
Islands of hope; parks and recreation in environmental crisis, by William E. Brown. National Recreation and Park Association, c1971
HC110.E5B75 ECOL

Watkins, Tom H.
The Grand Colorado. 1969 **fF788.W33 ECOL**

BROWNRIGG, J. T.
United States. Environmental Protection Agency. Office of Research and Monitoring.
Identification of polychlorinated biphenyls in the presence of DDT-type compounds. 1972.
SB951.U52 ECOL

BRUBAKER, STERLING.
To live on earth; man and his environment in perspective. Published for Resources for the Future by Johns Hopkins Press 1972 **QH541.B76 ECOL**

Trends in the world aluminum industry. Published for Resources for the Future by the Johns Hopkins Press c1967 **HD9539.A6B7 ECOL**

BRUNER, HOWARD D., ed.
Northern Colorado Outdoor Nature Center.
K — 12 curriculum guide for environmental education. n.d. **fS946.N6 ECOL**

BRUNNER, DIRK R.
Sanitary landfill design and operation, by Dirk R. Brunner and Daniel J. Keller. U.S. Environmental Protection Agency U.S. Govt. Print. Off. 1972. (Solid waste management series) **TD795.7.B7 ECOL**

BRUNSON, E. EVAN.
Improving water quality management planning in nonmetropolitan areas. Prepared for Office of Air and Water Programs, U.S. Environmental Protection Agency, 1973. **fTD365.B78 ECOL**

BRYCE, ARNOLD J.
General Electric Company. Re-entry and Environmental Systems Division.
Watercraft waste treatment system: development and demonstration report. 1971. **fTD745.G4 ECOL**

BUCHSBAUM, MILDRED, jt. auth.
Buchsbaum, Ralph Morris.
Basic ecology. 1970,c1957 **QH541.B79 ECOL**

BUCHSBAUM, RALPH MORRIS, 1907-
Basic ecology by R. M. Buchsbaum and Mildred Buchsbaum. Boxwood Press 1970,c1957
QH541.B79 ECOL

BUCKMAN, HARRY OLIVER, 1883-
The nature and properties of soils by Harry O. Buckman and Nyle C. Brady. Rev. by Nyle C. Brady. 7th ed. Macmillan 1969 **S591.B88 1969 ECOL**

BUCKMANN, CAROL A.
The first 50; the story of the Iowa Division, Izaak Walton League of America, 1923-1973. Graphic Publishing Co., c1973 **S932.I8B8 ECOL**

BUDHRAJA, VIKRAM S., jt. auth.
Dracup, John A.
Applications of systems analysis techniques to water resources. 1972. **fTC409.D7 ECOL**

BUEL, RONALD A.
Dead end: the automobile in mass transportation by Ronald A. Buel. Prentice-Hall 1972
HE5623.B82 ECOL

BUGGIE, FREDERICK D.
Toward effective and equitable pollution control regulation by Frederick D. Buggie and Richard Gurman. American Management Association 1972 (An AMA Research report) **fHC110.P55B8 ECOL**

BUHRER, EMIL MARTIN, 1913-
Dossenbach, Hans D.
The family life of birds. 1971
QL675.D6613 ECOL

BUNCE, ARTHUR CYRIL, 1901-
The economics of soil conservation. Univ. of Nebraska Press 1950,c1942
HD1411.B96 1950 ECOL

BUNNELL, FRED, ed. and tr.
Ziswiler, Vinzenz.
Extinct and vanishing animals. Rev. English ed. by Fred and Pille Bunnell. 1967. **QL88.Z513 ECOL**

BUNNELL, PILLE, ed. and tr.
Ziswiler, Vinzenz.
Extinct and vanishing animals. Rev. English ed. by Fred and Pille Bunnell. 1967. **QL88.Z513 ECOL**

BUNTS, JAMES H., jt. auth.
Boen, Doyle F.
Study of reutilization of wastewater recycled through groundwater. 1971. **fTD429.B6 ECOL**

BURAS, NATHAN.
Scientific allocation of water resources; water resources development and utilization—a rational approach. American Elsevier Pub. Co. 1972 (Environmental science series) **TC409.B87 ECOL**

BURCH, J. B.
Freshwater sphaeriacean clams (Mollusca: Pelecypoda) of North America. Environmental Protection Agency, 1972. (Biota of freshwater ecosystems, identification manual, no.3.)
fQH96.A2B5no.3 ECOL

BURCH, WILLIAM R., 1933-
Daydreams and nightmares; a sociological essay on the American environment by William R. Burch, Jr. Harper & Row 1971 (Harper & Row monograph series in sociology) **HM206.B83 ECOL**

Social behavior, natural resources, and the environment Editors: William R. Burch, Jr., Neil H. Cheek, Jr. and Lee Taylor. Harper & Row 1972
HM206.B84 ECOL

BUREAU OF MUNICIPAL RESEARCH, TORONTO.
Urban open space: parks, people and planning. 1971. (its Civic affairs, Summer 1971) **GV56.T6B8 ECOL**

BUREAU OF NATIONAL AFFAIRS, WASHINGTON, D.C.
Energy users report. **REF fHD9540.1.E5 ECOL**

Energy users report. Current reports.
REF fHD9540.1.E5 Suppl. ECOL

Environment reporter.
REF fHC110.E5E49 ECOL

Environment reporter. 1970-
REF fKF3775.A6E49 Suppl. ECOL

BURG, NAN C.
Abandoned vehicles: a selected bibliography. Original bibliography (# 192, May 1971) Comp. by Mary Z. Kessler. Rev. and supplemented by Nan C. Burg. Council of Planning Librarians 1972 (Council of Planning Librarians. Exchange bibliography, no. 296)
Ref fHD9975.B87 ECOL

BURG, NAN C., jt. auth.
Powell, David R.
New towns bibliography. 1972.
REF fZ5942.P6 ECOL

BURHOE, RALPH W., 1911- jt. ed.
Hoagland, Hudson.
Evolution and man's progress. 1962.
HM106.H6 ECOL

BURK, JANET L., jt. auth.
Kiraldi, Louis.
Pollution. 1971. **REF fZ7171.K55 ECOL**

BURKE, JACQUELYN M.
The realities of recycling; staff report, by Jacquelyn M. Burke and Weston A. Fisher. Minnesota Pollution Control Agency 1973 v. **REF fTP995.B8 ECOL**

BURKETT, DAVID WARREN.
Writing science news for the mass media. 2d ed., rev. Gulf Pub. Co., 1973. **PN4784.T3B8 1973 ECOL**

BURKHEAD, CARL E., jt. auth.
Kansas. University. Center for Research, Inc.
Oxygen consumption in continuous biological culture. 1971. **fTD755.K3 ECOL**

BURKS, GORDON E., jt. auth.
Robinson, Carmelita Klipple.
Life in a pond. 1967. **fPZ10.R56Li ECOL**

BURLEIGH, THOMAS DEARBORN, 1895- jt. auth.
Peters, Harold Seymour.
The birds of Newfoundland. 1951.
QL654.P47 ECOL

BURNESS, GORDON.
How to watch wildlife. Studio Vista/Van Nostrand Reinhold co. 1972 (A Studio Vista/Van Nostrand Reinhold how-to book) **QL60.B87 ECOL**

BURNET, FRANK MACFARLANE, SIR, 1899-
Dominant mammal; the biology of human destiny by Sir Macfarlane Burnet. St. Martin's Press 1972, c1971
QH331.B887 1972 ECOL

BURNS AND ROE.
Process design manual for suspended solids removal, by Burns and Roe, Inc. for Environmental Protection Agency, Technology Transfer. U.S. Govt. Print. Off. 1971. 1v. **REF fTD745.B8 ECOL**

BURNS, WILLIAM.
Snow, snowshoes, and nature: the white dimension of environment; an interdisciplinary approach. Developed by William Burns and others. Wadena Public Schools? 1972? **fLB1047.B8 ECOL**

BURNS, WILLIAM, 1909-
Noise and man. Lippincott c1968
RA772.N7B8 ECOL

BURT, WILFORD W., jt. auth.
Tucker, L. Scott.
Metropolitan industrial water use. 1972.
fTD223.T8 ECOL

BURTON, IAN, ed.
Readings in resource management and conservation, ed. with introductions by Ian Burton and Robert W. Kates. With the assistance of Lydia Burton. Univ. of Chicago Press 1970,c1965 **S938.B86 ECOL**

BURTON, JANE.
Animals of the African year; the ecology of East Africa. Photos. by Jane Burton. 1st American ed. Holt, Rinehart & Winston 1972 **fQL336.B87 1972 ECOL**

BURTON, MAURICE, 1898- ed.
The world encyclopedia of animals. World Publishing c1972 **fQL9.B8 ECOL**

BUSH-BROWN, LOUISE (CARTER) 1897-
Garden blocks for urban America by Louise Bush-Brown. Scribner 1969 **NA9052.B78 ECOL**

BUSINESS WEEK (NEW YORK).
Osborne, Philip B.
The war that business must win. 1970
HD60.5.U5O8 ECOL

BUTCHER, SAMUEL S., 1936-
An introduction to air chemistry, by S. S. Butcher and Robert J. Charlson. Academic Press 1972
QD163.B87 1972 ECOL

BUTRICO, FRANK A., ed.
Resource management in the Great Lakes Basin. 1971 **HD1694.A2 1971 ECOL**

BUYUKMIHCI, HOPE SAWYER.
Hour of the beaver. Rand McNally 1971
QL795.B5B8 ECOL

BYER, CURTIS O., jt. auth.
Jones, Kenneth Lester.
Environmental health. 1971. **RA565.J65 ECOL**

BYERS, GORDON L., jt. auth.
Hall, Francis R.
The influence of a New England wetland on water quantity and quality. 1972. **fTD224.N4H3 ECOL**

C

CABOT, JAMES ELLIOT, 1821-1903.
Agassiz, Louis.
Lake Superior. 1970, c1850
QH104.5.G7A35 1970 ECOL

CAILLIET, GREG M.
Everyman's guide to ecological living by Greg M. Cailliet, Paulette Y. Setzer and Milton S. Love. Macmillan 1971 **GF75.C33 ECOL**

CAIN, STANLEY ADAIR, 1902-
Manual of vegetation analysis by Stanley A. Cain and G. M. de Oliveira Castro. Hafner Pub. Co., 1971 ,c1959
QK911.C3 1959a ECOL

CALDECOTT, RICHARD S., ed.
Symposium on Radioisotopes in the Biosphere, University of Minnesota, 1959.
A Symposium on Radioisotopes in the Biosphere. 1960. **QH652.S9 1959 ECOL**

CALDER, NIGEL.
The restless Earth: a report on the new geology. Viking Press 1972 **QE26.2.C34 ECOL**
Technopolis; social control of the uses of science. Simon 1970 **HM221.C35 1970 ECOL**

CALDER, NIGEL, ed.
The New scientist.
The world in 1984. 1965,c1964
Q171.N5 1965 ECOL

CALDWELL, D. E., jt. auth.
Benson, Ferris B.
Indoor-outdoor air pollution relationships: a literature review. 1972. **TD890.B4 ECOL**

CALDWELL, LYNTON KEITH, 1913-
Environment: a challenge for modern society. Published for the American Museum of Natural History by the Natural History Press, 1970.
HC110.E5C33 ECOL
In defense of earth: international protection of the biosphere by Lynton K. Caldwell. Indiana University Press 1972 **HC79.E5C34 ECOL**

CALGARY, ALTA. UNIVERSITY.
Banff Conference on Pollution, 1st, 1968.
Man and his environment. 1st ed. 1970-
TD172.5.B3 1968 ECOL

CALHOUN, ALEX ed.
Inland fisheries management. Dept. of Fish and Game, 1966. **fSH222.C2C3 ECOL**

CALIFORNIA ASSOCIATION FOR OUTDOOR EDUCATION.
Teaching conservation and natural science in the outdoors; a handbook for teachers, camp leaders, counselors and youth leaders in preparing and carrying out programs in outdoor education. State of California, Office of Conservation Education, 1968.
fS946.C3 1968 ECOL

CALIFORNIA CONTINUING EDUCATION OF THE BAR.
Brecher, Joseph J.
Environmental law handbook. 1970
REF KF3775.B7 ECOL
National Conference on Environmental Law, San Francisco, 1970.
Transcripts of the speeches. 1971
REF KF3775.A75N3 1970 ECOL

CALIFORNIA. DEPT. OF EDUCATION.
Guide to conservation education: films, filmstrips, and picture sets. 1972. **REF fS946.C24 ECOL**

CALIFORNIA. DEPT. OF EDUCATION.
Atkisson, Jean. Evaluated bibliography of free and inexpensive conservation publications. 1972
REF fZ7164.N3A8 ECOL

CALIFORNIA. DEPT. OF FISH AND GAME.
Calhoun, Alex.
Inland fisheries management. 1966.
fSH222.C2C3 ECOL

CALIFORNIA. DEPT. OF PUBLIC HEALTH.
California solid waste management study (1968) and plan (1970). U.S. Environmental Protection Agency, Solid Waste Management Office, 1971.
TD788.4.C3A45 ECOL

CALIFORNIA. DEPT. OF WATER RESOURCES.
Removal of nitrate by an algal system, phase II. Author: James F. Arthur U.S. Govt. Print. Off., 1971. (Water pollution control research series) (Bioengineering aspects of agricultural drainage, San Joaquin Valley, California) **fTD475.C342 ECOL**

CALIFORNIA INSTITUTE OF TECHNOLOGY, PASADENA.
Are our descendants doomed? 1972
HB849.A74 1972 ECOL

CALIFORNIA INSTITUTE OF TECHNOLOGY, PASADENA. ENVIRONMENTAL QUALITY LABORATORY.
People, power and pollution: environmental and public interest aspects of electric power plant siting, by Peter Borrelli. 1971. (California Institute of Technology. Environmental Quality Laboratory. EQL report no.1) **fTK1193.U5C3 ECOL**

CALIFORNIA. LAWS, STATUTES, ETC.
Laws relating to the protection of environmental quality, 1970. Compiled by George H. Murphy, Legislative Counsel. State of California, Dept. of General Services 1971 **REF KFC610.A3 1970 ECOL**

CALIFORNIA. OFFICE OF CONSERVATION EDUCATION.
California Association for Outdoor Education.
Teaching conservation and natural science in the outdoors. 1968. **fS946.C3 1968 ECOL**

THE CALIFORNIA TOMORROW PLAN.
Edited by Alfred Heller. Rev. ed. W. Kaufmann 1972
HT393.C3C35 1972 ECOL

CALIFORNIA. UNIVERSITY.
Flow into a stratified reservoir. Authors: Antonio A. Zuluaga-Angel, Rufus Benton Darden, Hugo B. Fischer Prepared for Office of Research and Monitoring, U.S. Environmental Protection Agency, 1972. (Environmental protection technology series)
TC167.C3 ECOL

CALIFORNIA. UNIVERSITY, DAVIS, SCHOOL OF LAW.
Legal control of water pollution. 1969
KF3786.A32L4 ECOL

CALIFORNIA. UNIVERSITY. HASTINGS COLLEGE OF THE LAW, SAN FRANCISCO.
National Conference on Environmental Law, San Francisco, 1970.
Transcripts of the speeches. 1971
REF KF3775.A75N3 1970 ECOL

CALIFORNIA. UNIVERSITY. INSTITUTE OF MARINE RESOURCES.
Eutrophication in coastal waters: nitrogen as a controlling factor by Richard W. Eppley. Prepared for the Environmental Protection Agency. U.S. Environmental Protection Agency; for sale by the Supt. of Docs., U.S. Govt. Print. Off., 1971. (Water pollution control research series) **fQH96.8.E9C34 ECOL**

CALIFORNIA. UNIVERSITY. SANITARY ENGINEERING RESEARCH LABORATORY.
Optimization of ammonia removal by ion exchange using clinoptilolite, by Sanitary Engineering Research Laboratory, College of Engineering, and School of Public Health, University of California. Authors: John H. Koon and Warren J. Kaufman U.S. Environmental Protection Agency U.S. Govt. Print. Off., 1971 i.e. 1972 (Water pollution control research series)
fTD757.5.C35 ECOL

CALIFORNIA. UNIVERSITY, SANTA BARBARA. DEPT. OF BIOLOGICAL SCIENCES.
Santa Barbara oil spill: short-term analysis of macroplankton and fish. Prepared for the Office of Water Quality Research, Environmental Protection Agency by A. W. Ebeling and others. Environmental Protection Agency, Water Quality Office; for sale by the Supt. of Docs., U.S. Govt. Print. Off., 1971. (Water pollution control research series)
fTD427.P4C34 ECOL

CALIFORNIA. UNIVERSITY. SCHOOL OF PUBLIC HEALTH.
California. University. Sanitary Engineering Research Laboratory.
Optimization of ammonia removal by ion exchange using clinoptilolite. 1971 i.e. 1972
fTD757.5.C35 ECOL

CALIFORNIA. UNIVERSITY. UNIVERSITY AT LOS ANGELES. GRADUATE SCHOOL OF BUSINESS ADMINISTRATION.
Extensions of mathematical programming for regional water quality management. Prepared for the Office of Research and Monitoring, Environmental Protection Agency. Author: Glenn Graves. U.S. Govt. Print. Off., 1972. (Water pollution control research series) **fTD365,C3 ECOL**

CALIFORNIA. UNIVERSITY. UNIVERSITY EXTENSION.
National Conference on Environmental Law, San Francisco, 1970.
Transcripts of the speeches. 1971
REF KF3775.A75N3 1970 ECOL

CALIFORNIA. UNIVERSITY. WATER RESOURCES CENTER. ARCHIVES.
Dictionary catalog of the Water Resources Center Archives, University of California, Berkeley. G. K. Hall, 1970. 5 v. **REF fZ7935.C32 ECOL**

CALIFORNIA WATER; a study in resource management.
Edited by David Seckler. University of California Press, 1971. **HD1694.C2C35 ECOL**

CALLIHAN, CLAYTON DALE.
Construction of a chemical-microbial pilot plant for production of single-cell protein from cellulosic wastes, by C. D. Callihan and C. E. Dunlap. U.S. Environmental Protection Agency; for sale by the Supt. of Docs., U.S. Govt. Print. Off., 1971. **TP996.B3C3 ECOL**

CALLISON, CHARLES H., ed.
America's natural resources. Ed. for the Natural Resources Council of America, by Charles H. Callison. Rev. print. Ronald Press Co. 1967
S930.C3 1967 ECOL

CAMERON, JENKS, 1879-1957.
The development of governmental forest control in the United States. Da Capo Press, 1972.
SD565.C3 1972 ECOL

CAMPBELL, CATHERINE C., ed.
Symposium on Engineering Geology in the Urban Environment, San Francisco, 1969.
Environmental planning and geology. 1971
TA705.S95 1969 ECOL

CAMPBELL, GEORGE R., jt. auth.
Manufacturing Chemists' Association.
The effect of chlorination on selected organic chemicals. 1972. **fTD462.M3 ECOL**

CAMPBELL, J. F.
Analysis of the injection of a heated turbulent jet into a moving mainstream, with emphasis on a thermal discharge in a waterway by J. F. Campbell and J. A. Schetz. Aerospace Engineering Dept., Virginia Polytechnic Institute and State University, 1972.
fTD427.H4C3 ECOL

CAMPBELL, REX R., comp.
Society and environment: the coming collision by Rex R. Campbell and Jerry L. Wade. Allyn and Bacon 1972 **HC110.E5C35 ECOL**

CANADA.
Agricultural pollution of the Great Lakes Basin; combined report by Canada and the United States. Environmental Protection Agency, Water Quality Office 1971. **fTD223.C25 ECOL**

CANADA CENTRE FOR INLAND WATERS.
Collected reprints. vol. 4- , 1971- , pt. 1- v. **TD226.C3 ECOL**

CANADA. FISHERIES RESEARCH BOARD.
Review. 1965/66- v. **SH223.C3 ECOL**

CANADIAN SOCIETY OF ZOOLOGISTS.
Dunbar, Maxwell John.
Environment and good sense. 1971.
TD182.D85 ECOL

CARAS, ROGER A.
Last chance on earth; a requiem for wildlife, by Roger A. Caras. Illus. by Charles Frace. New preface by the author. Schocken Books 1972 (Schocken SB352)
QL88.C3 1972 ECOL

CARBONATED BEVERAGE CONTAINER MANUFACTURERS ASSOCIATION, INC.
Midwest Regional Seminar on Horizons in Resource Recovery, University of Chicago, 1972.
Horizons in resource recovery: presentations and discussions of a seminar held Feb. 23, 1972. 1972.
fTP995.A1M5 1972 ECOL

CARCICH, ITALO G.
A pressure sewer system demonstration, by I. G. Carcich, Leo J. Hetling, and R. P. Farrell. Prepared for Office of Research and Monitoring, U.S. Environmental Protection Agency. U.S. Gov't Print. Off., 1972. (Environmental protection technology series)
TD670.C3 ECOL

CARDER, MICHAEL, jt. auth.
Symonds, Richard.
The United Nations and the population question, 1945-1970. 1973 **HQ766.S888 ECOL**

CAREFOOT, G. L.
Famine on the wind; man's battle against plant disease, by G. L. Carefoot and E. R. Sprott. Rand McNally 1967 **SB732.C37 ECOL**

CARLSON, BERNICE (WELLS) jt. auth.
Carlson, Carl Walter.
Water fit to use. 1966 **TD348.C3 ECOL**

CARLSON, CARL WALTER, 1907-
Water fit to use by Carl Walter Carlson and Bernice Wells Carlson. Illustrated with photos. and with drawings by Aline Hansens. John Day Co. 1966
TD348.C3 ECOL

CARLSON, CLARENCE A., ed.
International Symposium on River Ecology and the Impact of Man, University of Massachusetts, 1971.
River ecology and man. 1972.
GB1205.I5 1971 ECOL

CARNEGIE ENDOWMENT FOR INTERNATIONAL PEACE.
Conference on Legal and Institutional Responses to Problems of the Global Envirnoment, Arden House, 1971.
Law, institutions, and the global environment. 1972.
KF3775.A75C6 1971 ECOL

Environment and development; the Founex report on development and environment, with commentaries by Miguel Ozorio de Almeida, Wilfred Beckerman, Ignacy Sachs, and Gamani Corea. 1972c1971 (International Conciliation, no. 586) **HC68.C3 1972 ECOL**

CARNEGIE-MELLON UNIVERSITY. TRANSPORTATION RESEARCH INSTITUTE.
International Conference on Urban Transportation, 5th, Pittsburgh, 1971.
Mobility: the fifth freedom. 1971? **fHE148.I5 1971 ECOL**

CAROLINA POPULATION CENTER.
The 99th hour. 1967 **HB3505.N5 ECOL**

CAROVILLANO, ROBERT L., 1932- ed.
Science and the future of man. c1970
CB151.S37 ECOL

CARR, DONALD EATON, 1903-
The breath of life by Donald E. Carr. Norton 1965
TD883.C35 ECOL
Death of the sweet waters by Donald E. Carr. 1st ed. Norton 1966 **TD223.C3 ECOL**

CARRICK, CAROL.
Swamp spring, by Carol and Donald Carrick. Macmillan 1969 **PZ10.C3297Sw ECOL**

CARRICK, DONALD, illus.
Carrick, Carol.
Swamp spring. 1969 **PZ10.C3297Sw ECOL**

CARRIGHAR, SALLY.
Home to the wilderness. Illus. with photographs. Houghton, 1973. **QH31.C3A3 ECOL**
One day at Teton Marsh; illus. by George and Patritia Mattson. Knopf, 1947. **QL215.C3 ECOL**
Wild heritage. With illus. by Rachel S. Horne. Houghton Mifflin, 1965. **QL751.C36 ECOL**

CARROLL, DONALD D., jt. auth.
Borchert, John R.
Minnesota settlement and land use 1985. 1970.
HD111.B6 ECOL

CARSON, GERALD.
Men, beasts, and gods; a history of cruelty and kindness to animals. Scribner 1972
HV4764.C35 ECOL

CARSON, RACHEL LOUISE.
The sea around us. Rev. ed. Oxford University Press, 1961. **GC21.C3 1961 ECOL**
The sense of wonder by Rachel Carson. Photos. by Charles Pratt and others. Harper & Row 1965,c1956
QH51.C35 ECOL
Silent spring. Drawings by Lois and Louis Darling. Houghton Mifflin 1962 **SB959.C3 ECOL**
Under the sea-wind; a naturalist's picture of ocean life. New ed. with corrections Oxford Univ. Press, 1952c1941 **QH92.C3 1952 ECOL**

CARSON, RACHEL LOUISE. SELECTIONS. 1972.
Brooks, Paul.
The house of life: Rachel Carson at work. 1972.
QH31.C33B7 ECOL

CARSTENSEN, VERNON ROSCO, 1907- ed.
The public lands; studies in the history of the public domain. General ed. Univ. of Wisconsin Press 1968,c1962 **HD216.C3 1968 ECOL**

CARTER, ROBERT L., 1917- , ed.
American Nuclear Society.
Nuclear methods in environmental research. 1971
fTD172.5.A4 ECOL

CARVAJAL, JOAN.
Conservation education; a selected bibliography, compiled by Joan Carvajal and Martha E. Munzer. Interstate Printers & Publishers 1968 v. (Conservation Education Association: Education: key to conservation)
REF Z7164.N3C3 ECOL

CARVELL, FRED J., comp.
It's not too late comp. by Fred Carvell and Max Tadlock. Glencoe Press 1971 **HC110.E5C36 ECOL**

CASARETT, ALISON P.
Radiation biology by Alison P. Casarett. Prentice-Hall 1968 **QH652.C3 ECOL**

CASE, MARSHAL T.
Look what I found! Photographs by the author; drawings by Mary Lee Herbster. Chatham Press; dist. by the Viking Press c1971 **S962.C38 ECOL**

CASTRO, G. M. DE OLIVEIRA, jt. auth.
Cain, Stanley Adair.
Manual of vegetation analysis. 1971 ,c1959
QK911.C3 1959a ECOL

CASWELL AND ASSOCIATES, INC., OSSEO, MINN.
The comprehensive sanitary sewer study for the Village of Maple Grove, Minnesota. 1969.
fTD525.M28C3 ECOL

CATE, WILLIAM, ed.
Directory of environmental consultants. Directory Press, c1972. **REF fS920.C3 ECOL**

CAUDILL, HARRY M., 1922-
My land is dying by Harry M. Caudill. 1st ed. E. P. Dutton, 1971. **TN291.C37 1971 ECOL**

CAULFIELD, PATRICIA.
Everglades. Selections from the writings of Peter Matthiessen. Essay by John G. Mitchell. Ed., with an introd. by Paul Brooks. Designed by Kathleen Haven and Patricia Maka. Sierra Club, 1970 (Sierra Club exhibit format series no.21) **QH105.F6C36 ECOL**

CAVAGNARO, DAVID.
Braun, Ernest.
Living water. 1971 **fQH46.B7 ECOL**
This living earth. Words and photos. by David Cavagnaro. American West Pub. Co. 1972
fQH541.5.M4C38 ECOL

CAVENDER, JAMES H.
United States. Environmental Protection Agency. Air Pollution Control Office.
Interstate surveillance project: measurement of air pollution using static monitors. 1971.
TD890.U45 ECOL

CCM INFORMATION CORPORATION.
Environmental pollution; a guide to current research. Produced from data gathered by Science Information Exchange Smithsonian Institution, Washington, D.C. 1971. **REF fTD178.5.C2 ECOL**

CECIL, E. JAMES, jt. auth.
Baron, Norman J.
A survey of attitudes towards the Mississippi River as a total resource in Minnesota. 1972.
GB701.M554no.55 ECOL

CENTER FOR CALIFORNIA PUBLIC AFFAIRS.
Environmental networks; state and regional environmental centers and councils in the United States. Preliminary ed. 1973. **REF fS920.C4 ECOL**

CENTER FOR CURRICULUM DESIGN, EVANSTON, ILL.
McInnis, Noel.
You are an environment: teaching/learning environmental attitudes. c1972 **QH541.2.M4 ECOL**

CENTER FOR THE BIOLOGY OF NATURAL SYSTEMS.
Conference on the Ecological Aspects of International Development, Airlie House, 1968.
The careless technology: ecology and international development. 1st ed. 1972. **QH540.C65 1968 ECOL**

CENTER FOR THE STUDY OF DEMOCRATIC INSTITUTIONS.
Fadiman, Clifton.
Ecocide—and thoughts toward survival. 1971
HC110.E5F32 ECOL

CENTRAL INSTITUTE FOR THE DEAF.
Miller, James D.
Effects of noise on people. 1971. **RA772.N7M5 ECOL**

CENTRE D'ETUDES DE PREVENTION.
United States. Atomic Energy Commission. Division of Technical Information.
Safety manual for use of operators dealing with radiography and industrial gammagraphy. 1968?
TA417.25.U5 ECOL

CENTURY RESEARCH CORPORATION.
Social aspects of urban water conservation; final report. Prepared for Office of Water Resources Research, U.S. Dept. of the Interior. Principal investigators: Henry E. Abbott, Kenneth G. Cook and Robert B. Sleight. 1972. **fTD388.5.C4 ECOL**

CHA, C. Y.
Photochemical methods for purifying water, by C. Y. Cha and J. M. Smith. Prepared for Office of Research and Monitoring, U.S. Environmental Protection Agency. U.S. Govt. Print. Off., 1972. (Environmental protection technology series) **TD459.C4 ECOL**

CHALLENGE FOR SURVIVAL: LAND, AIR, AND WATER FOR MAN IN MEGALOPOLIS.
Edited by Pierre Dansereau, with the assistance of Virginia A. Weadock. Columbia University Press, 1970.
HM206.C4 ECOL

CHALMERS, BRUCE.
Energy. Academic Press 1963 **TJ153.C43 ECOL**

CHALUPNIK, JAMES D., ed.
Transportation noises: a symposium on acceptability criteria. 1970 **TA365.T68 ECOL**

CHAMBER OF COMMERCE OF THE UNITED STATES OF AMERICA.
National Association of Manufacturers of the United States.
Water in industry. 1965. **fTD223.N3 1965 ECOL**

CHAMBERLAIN, STANLEY G., jt. auth.
Beckers, Charles V.
Quantitative methods for preliminary design of water quality surveillance systems. 1972.
TD365.B4 ECOL

CHAMPLIN, ROBERT L.
Supplementary aeration of lagoons in rigorous climate areas, by Robert L. Champlin. Prepared for the Environmental Protection Agency. U.S. Environmental Protection Agency; for sale by the Supt. of Docs., U.S. Govt. Print. Off., 1971. (Water pollution control research series) **fTD746.5.C45 ECOL**

CHANT, DONALD A., 1928-
Pollution Probe, edited by Donald A. Chant. New Press 1970 **TD174.C43 ECOL**

CHAPIN, FRANCIS STUART, 1888-
Urban land use planning, by F. Stuart Chapin, Jr. 2d ed. Univ. of Ill. Press, 1965.
NA9108.C53 1965 ECOL

CHAPMAN, FRANK MICHLER, 1864-
Handbook of birds of eastern North America; with introductory chapters on the study of birds in nature. With full-page plates in colors and black and white by Louis Agassiz Fuertes and text-cuts by Tappan Adney and Ernest Thompson Seton. Rev. ed. Appleton, 1912.
REF QL681.C46 1912 ECOL

CHARLSON, ROBERT J., jt. auth.
Butcher, Samuel S.
An introduction to air chemistry. 1972
QD163.B87 1972 ECOL

CHASAN, DANIEL JACK.
Klondike '70; the Alaskan oil boom. Praeger 1971
TN872.A7C47 ECOL

CHASE, EDITH B., jt. auth.
Rima, Donald R.
Subsurface waste disposal by means of wells—a selective annotated bibliography. 1971.
REF Z5853.S22R55 ECOL

CHASE, STUART, 1888-
Rich land, poor land; a study of waste in the natural resources of America. Maps, diagrams by Henry Billings. AMS Press 1969 **S930.C5 1969 ECOL**

CHEEK, NEIL H., jt. auth.
Burch, William R.
Social behavior, natural resources, and the environment. 1972 **HM206.B84 ECOL**

CHEMICAL ECOLOGY.
Edited by Ernest Sondheimer and John B. Simeone. Academic Press, 1970. (Contributors: John Tyler Bonner and others) **QH345.C435 ECOL**

CHEMICAL ENGINEERING.
Environmental engineering, deskbook issue, 1971- McGraw-Hill. v. **fTA170.C5 ECOL**

CHEMICAL FALLOUT; current research on persistent pesticides.
Edited by Morton W. Miller and George G. Berg. With a foreword by Aser Rothstein. Thomas 1969
SB959.C45 ECOL

CHEMICALS CONTROLLING INSECT BEHAVIOR.
Ed. by Morton Beroza. Foreword by F. F. Knipling. Academic Press, 1970. **QL461.S88 1969 ECOL**

CHERONIS, NICHOLAS DIMITRIUS, 1896-
The study of the physical world by Nicholas D. Cheronis, James B. Parson and Conrad E. Ronneberg. 3d ed. Houghton 1958 **Q160.C34 1958 ECOL**

CHESHER, RICHARD H.
Biological impact of a large-scale desalination plant at Key West. Environmental Protection Agency, Office of Research and Monitoring, 1971. (Water pollution control research series) **fTD478.5.F5C48 ECOL**

CHICAGO. UNIV.
Midwest Regional Seminar on Horizons in Resource Recovery, University of Chicago, 1972.
Horizons in resource recovery: presentations and discussions of a seminar held Feb. 23, 1972. 1972.
fTP995.A1M5 1972 ECOL

CHICAGO. UNIVERSITY. DEPT. OF GEOGRAPHY. RESEARCH PAPER NO. 135.
Johnson, James Francis.
Renovated waste water. 1971. **TD429.J6 ECOL**

CHINERY, MICHAEL.
Concise color encyclopedia of nature. Crowell 1972
fQH309.C46 1972 ECOL

CHISHOLM, ANNE.
Philosophers of the earth; conversations with ecologists. Dutton c1972 **GF75.C4 ECOL**

CHITTENDEN, HIRAM MARTIN, 1858-1917.
The Yellowstone National Park. Edited and with an introd. by Richard A. Bartlett. University of Oklahoma Press 1964 **F722.C54 1964 ECOL**

CHRISTY, FRANCIS T.
Resources for the Future.
Trends in natural resource commodities. 1962.
REF fHF1051.R43 ECOL

CHURCH SOCIETY FOR COLLEGE WORK.
Ecology: crisis and new vision. c1971
GF80.E25 ECOL

CHUTE, ROBERT M., comp.
Environmental insight; readings and comment on human and nonhuman nature by Robert M. Chute. Harper & Row 1971 **GF75.C48 ECOL**

CIACCIO. LEONARD L., 1924- ed.
Water and water pollution handbook. 1971-
TD380.W322 ECOL

CIRCLE OF THE WORLD; readings in ecology.
Benziger, Inc. c1971- v.1- (A Benziger web of life books) **QH541.2.C5 ECOL**

CIRCLE OF THE WORLD. Supplement: Teachers guide.
Benziger, Inc. **QH541.2.C5 Suppl. ECOL**

CISSELL, CHARLES A., jt. auth.
Major, James M.
Environmental education: objectives and field activities. 4th ed. 1971. **fLB1047.M3 ECOL**

CITIZENS LEAGUE, MINNEAPOLIS COMMITTEE ON ENVIRONMENT.
Citizens League report. Needed: better ways of making environmental choices. Recommendations on improving the environmental decision-making framework in Minnesota. Citizens League, 1971.
fHC110.E5C5 ECOL

CLAIBORNE, ROBERT.
Climate, man, and history. Norton 1970
GF71.C55 ECOL

CLARK, B. W.
Description of the environmental monitoring program for the Monticello nuclear generating plant near Monticello, Minnesota. Rev. ed. Northern States Power Co., 1969. **fTK1377.M6C6 1969 ECOL**
Description of the environmental monitoring program for the Prairie Island Nuclear Generating Plant near Red Wing, Minnesota. Northern States Power Co., 1970. **fTK1377.P7C7 ECOL**

CLARK, COLIN, 1905-
Population growth and land use. St. Martin's P., 1968. **HB871.C58 1968 ECOL**

CLARK, JOHN WILLIAM.
Water supply and pollution control by John W. Clark, Warren Viessman, Jr. and Mark J. Hammer. 2d ed. International Textbook Co. 1971 (International series in civil engineering) **TD145.C55 1971 ECOL**

CLARK, ROBERT BERNARD.
Synopsis of animal classification, by R. B. Clark and A. L. Panchen. Chapman and Hall, 1971.
REF QL352.C53 ECOL

CLARKE, GEORGE LEONARD, 1905-
Elements of ecology by George L. Clarke. 1st ed. rev. print., with subject guide to new references. Wiley 1965, c1954 **QH541.C47 1965 ECOL**

CLARKE, JAMES.
Man is the prey. Stein and Day 1969
QL758.C54 ECOL

CLAWSON, MARION, 1905-
America's land and its uses. Published for Resources for the Future by the Johns Hopkins Press 1972
HD205 1972 .C55 ECOL

The Bureau of Land Management. Praeger Publishers 1971 (Praeger library of U.S. Government departments and agencies, no. 27) **HD181.G8C57 ECOL**

Economics of outdoor recreation, by Marion Clawson and Jack L. Knetsch. Published for Resources for the Future by Johns Hopkins Press c1966
GV182.2.C55 ECOL

The Federal lands since 1956; recent trends in the use and management. Resources for the Future; Dist. by the Johns Hopkins Press, 1967 **HD216.C53 ECOL**

The federal lands: their use and management, by Marion Clawson and Burnell Held. Published for Resources for the Future by the Johns Hopkins Press 1966,1957 **HD216.C54 1966 ECOL**

Land and water for recreation; opportunities, problems, and policies. Rand McNally c1963 (Policy background series) **HD205 1963.C53 ECOL**

The land system of the United States; an introduction to the history and practice of land use and land tenure. Univ. of Nebraska Press 1968 **HD191.C53 ECOL**

Man and land in the United States. Univ. of Nebraska Press, 1964. **HD191.C55 ECOL**

Policy directions for U.S. agriculture; long-range choices in farming and rural living. Published for Resources for the Future, by Johns Hopkins Press 1968
HD1761.C54 ECOL

Resources for the Future.
Land for the future. 1960 **HD205 1960.R4 ECOL**

Resources for the Future. Committee on Land Use Statistics.
Land use information. 1969, c1965
HD205 1969.R4 ECOL

Suburban land conversion in the United States: an economic and governmental process. Published for Resources for the Future by the Johns Hopkins Press 1971 **HD259.C55 ECOL**

CLAWSON, MARION, 1905- comp.
Desalting seawater; achievements and prospects by Marion Clawson and Hans H. Landsberg. Gordon and Breach 1972 (Ocean sciences, 2)
TD479.C53 1972 ECOL

CLAWSON, MARION, 1905- ed.
Natural resources and international development; essays by D. Gale Johnson and others. Published for Resources for the Future by the Johns Hopkins Press 1964 **HC55.C57 ECOL**

CLAWSON, MARION, 1905- jt. auth.
Held, R. Burnell.
Soil conservation in perspective. 1965
S624.A1H4 ECOL

CLAWSON, MARION, 1905- **THE FEDERAL LANDS: THEIR USE AND MANAGEMENT.**
Clawson, Marion.
The Federal lands since 1956. 1967
HD216.C53 ECOL

CLEAN AIR AND WATER NEWS. V.3- JAN. 8, 1971-
Commerce Clearing House. v.
REF TD180.C54 ECOL

CLEAVELAND, FREDERIC N.
Congress and urban problems, a casebook on the legislative process, by F. N. Cleaveland and associates. Brookings Institution 1969 **HT334.U5C665 ECOL**

CLEM, ROBERT VERITY, illus.
Stout, Gardner D.
The shorebirds of North America. 1967
fQL681.S78 ECOL

CLEMENT, THOMAS M., JR.
Engineering a victory for our environment: a citizen's guide to the U.S. Army Corps of Engineers. c1972.
fTC423.E5 ECOL

CLEMSON UNIVERSITY. DEPT. OF TEXTILES.
State of the art of textile waste treatment; a study conducted for Water Quality Office, Environmental Protection Agency. Author: John J. Porter Washington Environmental Protection Agency, Water Quality Office; for sale by the Supt. of Docs., U.S. Govt. Print. Off., 1971. (Water pollution control research series)
fTD899.T4C45 ECOL

CLEPPER, HENRY EDWARD, 1901-
Professional forestry in the United States by Henry Clepper. Published for Resources for the Future by the Johns Hopkins Press 1971 **SD143.C56 ECOL**

The world of the forest by Henry Clepper and Arthur B. Meyer. Prepared in cooperation with the Society of American Foresters. (Science resource series)
SD131.C55 ECOL

CLEPPER, HENRY EDWARD, 1901- ed.
Careers in conservation; opportunities in natural resources. Ed. for the Natural Resources Council of America. Ronald Press Co. 1963 (Ronald science library) **S494.5.C57 ECOL**

Origins of American conservation. Ed. for the Natural Resources Council of America by Henry Clepper. Ronald Press 1966 **S930.C57 ECOL**

CLOUD, PRESTON ERCELLE, 1912-
National Research Council. Committee on Resources and Man.
Resources and man. 1969 **HC68.N36 ECOL**

CLUBB, JEROME M.
Ecological data in comparative research; report on a first International Data Confrontation Seminar, by Jerome M. Clubb. Unesco 1970 (Reports and papers in the social sciences, no. 25) (United Nations Educational, Scientific and Cultural Organization. Document) **H62.C6 ECOL**

COASTAL ZONE RESOURCE MANAGEMENT.
Edited by James C. Hite and James M. Stepp. Praeger Publishers 1971 (Praeger special studies in U.S. economic and social development)
HC110.E5C6 ECOL

COATES, DONALD ROBERT, 1922- ed.
Environmental Geomorphology Symposium.
Environmental geomorphology.
GB400.E58 ECOL

COBLENTZ, STANTON ARTHUR, 1896-
The challenge to man's survival by Stanton A. Coblentz. A. S. Barnes 1972 **GF41.C55 ECOL**

COCA-COLA COMPANY. FOODS DIVISION.
Treatment of citrus processing wastes. U.S. Environmental Protection Agency, Water Quality Office, 1970. (Water pollution control research series)
fTD899.F7C6 ECOL

COCHRANE, WILLARD WESLEY, 1914-
The world food problem; a guardedly optimistic view by Willard W. Cochrane. Crowell 1969 (The Crowell economics series) **HD9000.5.C59 ECOL**

COHEN, MARTIN.
A handbook on environmental information programs for public libraries. School of Librarianship, Western Michigan University, 1973. **fZ670.A3C6 ECOL**

COKER, ROBERT ERVIN, 1876-
Streams, lakes, ponds. Univ. of North Carolina Press 1954 **QH96.C6 ECOL**

COLEMAN, D. J.
Highways and the environment: a bibliography of the effects of highways on the physical, biological, recreational and aesthetic environments and of techniques for the analysis of these impacts. 1973. (Council of Planning Librarians. Exchange bibliography, 394.) **fZ7295.C6 ECOL**

COLINVAUX, PAUL ALFRED, 1930-
The environment of crowded men, ed. by Paul A. Colinvaux. MSS Educational Pub. Co. 1970
GF8.C8 ECOL

COLLIER, BOYD.
Dynamic ecology. 1973 **QH541.D9 ECOL**
Measurement and environmental deterioration. Bureau of Business Research, University of Texas at Austin 1971 **HC79.I5C63 ECOL**

COLLINS, DON, illus.
Schlichting, Harold E.
Ecology. 1971 **PZ10.S3713Ec ECOL**

COLLINS, HENRY HILL, 1905-1961.
Complete field guide to American wildlife: East, Central, and North ... Illus. by Russell Francis Peterson, Lloyd Sandford, Nina L. Williams, and John Cameron Yrizarry. Harper & Row c1959 **QL151.C6 ECOL**

COLLINS, LAWRENCE.
Only a little planet. 1972
fPS3553.O4749O5 ECOL

COLLINS, PATRICIA.
Chain of life; a story of a forest food cycle. Written and illustrated by Patricia Collins. 1st ed. Doubleday 1972 **QH541.5.F6C64 ECOL**

COLLINS, RALPH P.
Characterization of taste and odors in water supplies, by Ralph P. Collins for the Office of Research and Monitoring, Environmental Protection Agency. U.S. Environmental Protection Agency U.S. Govt. Print. Off., 1971. (Water pollution control research series)
fTD384.C64 ECOL

COLORADO COMMITTEE FOR ENVIRONMENTAL INFORMATION.
Nuclear explosives in peacetime. 1970
fQC792.N8 ECOL

COLORADO. SCHOOL OF MINES, GOLDEN.
Western Resources Conference, 8th, Colorado School of Mines, 1966.
Natural gas, coal, ground water. 1967
HC103.7.W45 1966 ECOL

COLORADO. STATE UNIVERSITY, FORT COLLINS.
Northern Colorado Outdoor Nature Center. K 12 curriculum guide for environmental education. n.d. **fS946.N6 ECOL**

Water pollution potential of spent oil shale residues. Environmental Protection Agency, Research and Monitoring; for sale by the Supt. of Docs., U. S. Govt. Print. Off., 1971. (Water pollution control research series) **fTD899.P4C65 ECOL**

Western Resources Conference. 7th, Colorado State University, 1965.
Water research. c1966 **REF TD355.W4 1965 ECOL**

COLORADO. STATE UNIVERSITY, FORT COLLINS ENVIRONMENTAL RESOURCES CENTER.
The mechanism of waste treatment at low temperature. Part A- 1972- **fTD745.C58 ECOL**

COLORADO. STATE UNIVERSITY, FORT COLLINS. WILDLIFE CONSERVATION MANUAL COMMITTEE.
A Manual of wildlife conservation. 1971. **fSK353.M35 ECOL**

COLUMBIA UNIVERSITY. INSTITUTE FOR THE STUDY OF SCIENCE IN HUMAN AFFAIRS.
Dubos, Rene Jules.
Reason awake: science for man. 1970. **Q125.D814 ECOL**

COLUMBIA UNIVERSITY. INSTITUTE OF URBAN ENVIRONMENT.
Grava, Sigurd.
Urban planning aspects of water pollution control. 1969. **TD420.G67 ECOL**

COLUMBIA UNIVERSITY. LEGISLATIVE DRAFTING RESEARCH FUND.
Grad, Frank P.
Environmental control: priorities, policies, and the law. 1971. **HC110.E5G7 ECOL**

COLWELL, JIM.
World view. Univ. of Minnesota, 1971. (Secondary environmental education development) **GF75.C6 ECOL**

COMAN, DALE REX, 1906-
The endless adventure. H. Regnery Co. 1972 **QH81.C67 ECOL**

COMAR, CYRIL LEWIS, 1914-
Fallout from nuclear tests. U.S. Atomic Energy Commission, Division of Technical Information 1963 (Understanding the atom) **UF767.C64 ECOL**

Fallout from nuclear tests. Rev. U.S. Atomic Energy Commission, Division of Technical Information 1966 (Understanding the atom) **UF767.C64 1966 ECOL**

COMBINED SOILS, FERTILIZER & AGRICULTURAL PESTICIDES, SHORT COURSE, DEC. 15-17, 1970, MINNEAPOLIS AUDITORIUM. **fSB951.C76 ECOL**

COMBUSTION-GENERATED AIR POLLUTION.
Edited by Ernest S. Starkman. Plenum Press, 1971. **TD883.C575 1971 ECOL**

COMISION FEDERAL DE ELECTRICIDAD, NUCLEAR SECTION, MEXICO CITY.
Stanford Research Institute. Decision Analysis Group.
Decision analysis of nuclear plants in electrical system expansion: final report. **fTK1078.S7 ECOL**

COMMERCE CLEARING HOUSE.
Clean air and water news. v.3- Jan. 8, 1971- **REF TD180.C54 ECOL**

Energy management. c1973. 1v. **Ref KF2120.A6C6 ECOL**

COMMISSION TO STUDY THE ORGANIZATION OF PEACE.
The United Nations and the human environment. Twenty-second report of the Commission to Study the Organization of Peace. 1972 (its Report, 22) **HC68.C62 ECOL**

COMMITTEE FOR ENVIRONMENTAL INFORMATION.
Nuclear explosives in peacetime. 1970 **fQC792.N8 ECOL**

COMMITTEE ON INSTITUTIONAL COOPERATION. CONFERENCE GROUP ON ENVIRONMENTAL STUDIES.
Ragland, Kenneth W.
Environmental studies at the CIC universities—a survey. 1971. **REF fQH541.2.R3 ECOL**

COMMITTEE ON TAXATION, RESOURCES AND ECONOMIC DEVELOPMENT.
Extractive resources and taxation: proceedings. 1967. **HC106.5.E93 ECOL**

COMMONER, BARRY, 1917-
The closing circle; nature, man, and technology. 1st ed. Knopf, 1971. **GF75.C65 ECOL**

Science and survival Viking Press c1966 **Q125.C56 ECOL**

COMMONWEALTH ASSOCIATES, INC.
Northern States Power Company, Minnesota: fossil fueled power plant siting study. 1972. 3v. **REF fTK1331.N6C6 ECOL**

COMPOSTING OF MUNICIPAL SOLID WASTES IN THE UNITED STATES.
Prepared by members of the Federal solid waste management research staff under the direction of Andrew W. Breidenbach. U.S. Environmental Protection Agency; for sale by the Supt. of Docs., U.S. Govt. Print. Off. 1971. **TD796.5.C64 ECOL**

CONARD, DAVID.
Science Curriculum Improvement Study.
Life cycles. c1970 **LB1585.S32 ECOL**

THE CONDENSED CHEMICAL DICTIONARY.
Rev. by Gessner G. Hawley. 8th ed. Van Nostrand Reinhold Co. 1971 **REF QD5.C5 1971 ECOL**

CONFERENCE IN THE MATTER OF POLLUTION OF LAKE MICHIGAN AND ITS TRIBUTARY BASIN IN THE STATES OF WISCONSIN, ILLINOIS, INDIANA, AND MICHIGAN, 3RD, CHICAGO, MAR. 23-25, 1971.
Reconvening of the 3rd session; Proceedings. U.S. Environmental Protection Agency. Water Quality Office 1971- v.1- **fTD223.3.C595 1971 ECOL**

CONFERENCE IN THE MATTER OF POLLUTION OF LAKE MICHIGAN AND ITS TRIBUTARY BASINS, 3D, CHICAGO, SEPT. 28-30, OCT. 1-2, 1970.
Workshop session for the third session (reconvened). Federal Water Quality Administration 1970. v. **fTD223.3.C595 1970a ECOL**

CONFERENCE IN THE MATTER OF POLLUTION OF LAKE SUPERIOR AND ITS TRIBUTARY BASIN IN THE STATES OF MINNESOTA, WISCONSIN, AND MICHIGAN, DULUTH, MAY 13-15, 1969.
Proceedings. U.S. Federal Water Pollution Control Administration 1970 4 v. **fTD223.3.C59 1969 ECOL**

Reconvening of second sessions; transcript of proceedings. U.S. Federal Water Quality Administration, 1971 v.1- **fTD223.3.C59 1970b ECOL**

Second meeting second session (reconvened); proceedings. U.S. Environmental Protection Agency. Water Quality Office 1971. 2v. **fTD223.3.C59 1971 ECOL**

Transcript of proceedings. Federal Water Quality Administration, 1970 2v. **fTD223.3.C59 1970 ECOL**

CONFERENCE IN THE MATTER OF POLLUTION OF THE INTERSTATE AND INTRASTATE WATERS OF THE UPPER MISSISSIPPI RIVER AND ITS TRIBUTARIES—WISCONSIN—MINNESOTA, MINNEAPOLIS, 1968.
Proceedings of progress evaluation meeting held April 30, 1968. Federal Water Pollution Control Administration, 1968. **fTD223.4.A45C6 ECOL**

Proceedings of the second session Minneapolis, Minnesota, Feb. 28, March 1 & 20, 1967. U.S. Dept. of the Interior, Federal Water Pollution Control Administration, 1967. 3v. **TD223.4.A43C6 ECOL**

CONFERENCE IN THE MATTER OF POLLUTION OF THE INTERSTATE WATERS OF THE LOWER MISSISSIPPI RIVER, NEW ORLEANS, 1964.
Proceedings. U.S., Dept. of Health, Education, and Welfare, 1964? 4v. **REF fTD225.M64C6 1964 ECOL**

CONFERENCE IN THE MATTER OF POLLUTION OF THE INTERSTATE WATERS OF THE RED RIVER OF THE NORTH, NORTH DAKOTA—MINNESOTA, FARGO, N.D., 1965.
Proceedings. U.S. Dept. of Health, Education and Welfare v. **fTD225.R34C6 1965 ECOL**

CONFERENCE IN THE MATTER OF POLLUTION OF THE INTERSTATE WATERS OF THE UPPER MISSISSIPPI RIVER, ST. PAUL, 1964.
Conference in the Matter of Pollution of the Interstate Waters of the Upper Mississippi River, St. Paul Minnesota, February 8, 1964. U.S. Dept. of Health, Education and Welfare 196-? v.1- **fTD223.4.C67 1964 ECOL**

CONFERENCE ON AGRICULTURE'S ROLE IN ENVIRONMENTAL QUALITY. UNIVERSITY OF ILLINOIS, URBANA—CHAMPAIGN, 1970.
Agriculture's role in environmental quality. Proceedings of the First Allerton Conference. 1971 (Illinois. University. College of Agriculture. Special Publication 21) **fHC68.C6 1970 ECOL**

CONFERENCE ON CHEMICAL AND BIOLOGICAL WARFARE, LONDON, 1968.
CBW: chemical and biological warfare. Ed. by Steven Rose with the assistance of David Pavett. Beacon Press 1969,c1968 **UG447.C655 1968 ECOL**

CONFERENCE ON ENERGY, ECONOMICS AND THE ENVIRONMENT, CHICAGO, ILL., 1968.
Energy, economics and the environment: proceedings of a conference sponsored by the Committee on Environment, Edison Electric Institute. Edison Electric Institute, 1969. **fHD9540.1.C6 1968 ECOL**

CONFERENCE ON ENVIRONMENTAL IMPACT ANALYSIS, GREEN BAY, WIS., 1972.
Environmental impact analysis: philosophy & methods. Ed. by Robert B. Ditton and Thomas L. Goodale. Univ. of Wisconsin, Sea Grant Program, 1972 (Sea Grant publication WIS - SG - 72 - 111) **HC110.E5C65 1972 ECOL**

CONFERENCE ON ENVIRONMENTAL QUALITY AND AGRICULTURE. UNIVERSITY OF ILLINOIS, URBANA-CHAMPAIGN, 1971.
Environmental quality and agriculture: what are the options? Proceedings of the Second Allerton Conference. 1972 (Illinois. University. College of Agriculture. Special Publication 26) **fHC68.C6 1971 ECOL**

CONFERENCE ON FLOOD PLAIN MANAGEMENT, IOWA STATE UNIVERSITY, 1968.
Flood plain management, Iowa's experience. Papers presented at the Conference on Flood Plain Management, sixth Water Resources Design Conference, Iowa State University. Edited by Merwin D. Dougal. 1st ed. Iowa State University Press 1969 **TC424.I8C6 1968 ECOL**

CONFERENCE ON LAW AND THE ENVIRONMENT, WARRENTON, VA., 1969.
Papers. The Conservation Foundation, n.d. v. **fKF3775.A75C58 1969 ECOL**

CONFERENCE ON LEGAL AND INSTITUTIONAL RESPONSES TO PROBLEMS OF THE GLOBAL ENVIRONMENT, ARDEN HOUSE, 1971.
Law, institutions, and the global environment; papers and analysis of the proceedings. Edited by John Lawrence Hargrove. Oceana Publications, 1972. **KF3775.A75C6 1971 ECOL**

CONFERENCE ON NOISE AS A PUBLIC HEALTH HAZARD, WASH., D.C., 1968.
Noise as a public health hazard; proceedings of the conference ... held in Wash., D.C., June 13-14, 1968. Dixon Ward and James E. Fricke, editors. American Speech and Hearing Ass'n., 1969. (American Speech and Hearing Association. Reports, 4) **RA772.N7C6 ECOL**

CONFERENCE ON SNOWMOBILES AND ALL-TERRAIN VECHICLES, LONDON, ONTARIO, 1971.
Proceedings. Ontario Faculty of Law, University of Western Ontario 1972 **fGV857.S6C6 1971 ECOL**

CONFERENCE ON THE ECOLOGICAL ASPECTS OF INTERNATIONAL DEVELOPMENT, AIRLIE HOUSE, 1968.
The careless technology: ecology and international development; the record. Edited by M. Taghi Farvar and John P. Milton. 1st ed. Natural History Press, 1972. **QH540.C65 1968 ECOL**

CONFERENCE ON THE ECOLOGICAL ASPECTS OF INTERNATIONAL DEVELOPMENT PROGRAMS, WARRENTON, VA., 1968.
The Unforseen international ecologic boomerang. 1969 **fQH541.U5 ECOL**

CONFERENCE ON TOWARD A STATEWIDE GROUND WATER QUALITY INFORMATION SYSTEM, ST. PAUL, MINN., 1972.
Proceedings of conference on toward a statewide ground water quality information system and report of Ground Water Quality Subcommittee Citizens Advisory Committee, Governors Environmental Quality Council. Water Resources Research Center, Univ. of Minnesota, Graduate School, 1973. **fTD224.M6C6 1972 ECOL**

CONFERENCE ON UNDERGRADUATE EDUCATION IN THE BIOLOGICAL SCIENCES FOR STUDENTS IN AGRICULTURE AND NATURAL RESOURCES, WASHINGTON, D.C., 1966.
Undergraduate education in the biological sciences for students in agriculture and natural resources; proceedings. 1967. (National Academy of Sciences. Publication 1495) **S533.C755 1966 ECOL**

CONFERENCE ON WATER AND RELATED LAND RESOURCES PLANNING IN MINNESOTA, ST. PAUL, MINN., 1967.
Papers presented during Conference on Water and Related Land Resources Planning in Minnesota. Water Resources Coordinating Committee, State Planning Agency, 1967. (WRRC Bulletin No. 1) **fHD1694.M6A54 1967 ECOL**

CONGRESS AND THE ENVIRONMENT.
Edited by Richard A. Cooley and Geoffrey Wandesforde-Smith. University of Washington Press 1970 **KF5505.A75C6 ECOL**

CONGRESSIONAL QUARTERLY SERVICE, WASHINGTON, D. C.
Man's control of the environment; to determine his survival or to lay waste his planet. 1970.
fTD180.C65 ECOL

CONNELL, CECIL HARDEE, 1903-
Texas. University. Medical Branch, Galveston.
Phosphorus removal and disposal from municipal wastewater. 1971. **fTD745.T43 ECOL**

CONNELL, JOSEPH H., comp.
Readings in ecology and ecological genetics. Edited by J. H. Connell, David B. Mertz, and William W. Murdoch. Harper 1970 **QH541.C65 ECOL**

CONNELL, JOSEPH H., jt. auth.
MacArthur, Robert H.
The biology of populations. 1966
QL752.M2 ECOL

CONRAD, DAVID.
Science Curriculum Improvement Study.
Populations. c1969 **fLB1585.S35 ECOL**

CONSERVATION & ENVIRONMENTAL STUDIES CENTER, BROWNS MILLS, N.J.
Bonvie, Carolyn.
Art & design in the environment. 1971
fLB1047.B6 ECOL

Hiros, John E.
Inviting involvement with history. 1969
fLB1047.H5 ECOL

Jackson, John Y.
Land use: concern, challenge, commitment. c1969
HD110.J3 ECOL

CONSERVATION AND PRODUCTIVITY OF NATURAL WATERS; the proceedings of a symposium organized jointly by the British Ecological Society and the Zoological Society of London, held at the Zoological Society of London on 22 and 23 October, 1970.
Edited by R. W. Edwards and D. J. Garrod. Published for the Zoological Society of London by Academic Press, 1972.(Symposia of the Zoological Society of London, no. 29) **QL1.Z733no.29 ECOL**

CONSERVATION AND RESEARCH FOUNDATION, NEW LONDON, CONN.
Law and the environment. 1970
KF5505.A75L38 ECOL

CONSERVATION DIRECTORY.
National Wildlife Federation. v. **fS920.C64 ECOL**

CONSERVATION EDUCATION ASSOCIATION.
Conservation quickies; conservation teaching aids. Ed. and illus. by Clifford E. and Virginia Emanuelson. Interstate Printers & Publishers, 1966 1v.
fS946.C57 ECOL

Critical index of films on man and his environment, comp. as of June 1971. Interstate Printers and Publishers c1972 **fS946.C65 1972 ECOL**

CONSERVATION FOUNDATION.
Berlin, Roisman & Kessler.
Law and taxation. 1970 **KF6449.Z9B4 ECOL**
Conference on Law and the Environment, Warrenton, Va., 1969.
Papers. n.d. **fKF3775.A75C58 1969 ECOL**
Conference on the Ecological Aspects of International Development, Airlie House, 1968.
The careless technology: ecology and international development. 1st ed. 1972. **QH540.C65 1968 ECOL**

A Conversation on population, environment, and human well-being. 1971 **HB875.C63 ECOL**

Darling, Frank Fraser.
Future environments of North America. 1966.
HC95.D33 ECOL

Harvard University. Landscape Architecture Research Office.
Three approaches to environmental resource analysis. 1967. **fTA170.H3 ECOL**

Law and the environment. 1970
KF5505.A75L38 ECOL

Munzer, Martha E.
Planning our town. 1964 **NA9108.M8 ECOL**

Munzer, Martha E.
Pockets of hope. 1967 **HC103.7.M78 ECOL**

National parks for the future; an appraisal of the national parks as they begin their second century in a changing America. 1972 **SB482.A4C67 ECOL**

Pollution by pesticides; some not very well calculated risks and some alternatives for better regulation. 1969.
QH545.P4C6 ECOL

Rookery Bay area project; a demonstration study in conservation and development, Naples, Florida. 1968.
QH77.U6C66 ECOL

CONSOLIDATION COAL COMPANY. RESEARCH DIVISION.
Pilot-scale development of the CSF Process. Period: July 1, 1968-Dec. 31, 1970. 1971. 1v. (R & D Report no.39-v.3, book 3) **fTN805.A395no.39 ECOL**

CONTINENTAL OIL COMPANY. RESEARCH AND DEVELOPMENT DEPT.
Microbiological treatment of acid mine drainage waters. Authors: Louis B. Whitesell, Robert L. Huddleston, and Ray C. Allred. Prepared for the Environmental Protection Agency. Environmental Protection Agency, Research and Monitoring; for sale by the Supt. of Docs., U.S. Govt. Print. Off., 1971. (Water pollution control research series)
fTD899.M5C65 ECOL

CONTINUATION OF STUDIES ON THE HYDROLOGY OF PONDS AND SMALL LAKES.
by E.R. Allred and others. Agricultural Experiment Station, University of Minnesota, 1971. (Minnesota. Agricultural Experiment Station, St. Anthony Park Technical bulletin 274) **fGB1825.M6C6ECOL**

A CONVERSATION ON POPULATION, ENVIRONMENT, AND HUMAN WELL-BEING, at Belmont House, Elkridge, Maryland, May 20 and May 21, 1969.
Reported by F. Fraser Darling and Raymond F. Dasmann. Conservation Foundation 1971
HB875.C63 ECOL

CONWAY, JOHN E., jt. auth.
MacDonald, James B.
Environmental litigation. 1972.
KF3775.M3 ECOL

CONWAY RESEARCH, INC., ATLANTA. PUBLICATIONS DIVISION.
Industrial Development.
Site selection handbook, vol.2. 1972.
REF fHC68.I5 1972 ECOL

COOK, DAVID I.
Trees and shrubs for noise abatement, by David I. Cook and David F. Van Haverbeke. United States Forest Service, 1971. (United States. Forest Service. Research bulletin 246) **TD893.C6 ECOL**

COOK, KENNETH G.
Century Research Corporation.
Social aspects of urban water conservation. 1972.
fTD388.5.C4 ECOL

COOK, RAY LEWIS.
Soil management for conservation and production. Wiley c1962 **S591.C7 ECOL**

COOK, ROBERT CARTER, 1898-
People! An introduction to the study of population by Robert C. Cook and Jane Lecht. Population Reference Bureau. Columbia Books 1968 **HB871.C7 ECOL**

COOK, THEODORE D., 1924- ed.
Symposium on Underground Waste Management and Environmental Implications, Houston, Tex., 1971.
Underground waste management and environmental implications; proceedings. 1972.
TD761.S95 1971 ECOL

COOLEY, RICHARD A.
Alaska; a challenge in conservation by Richard A. Cooley. Univ. of Wisconsin Press, 1967.
HC107.A45C6 ECOL

COOLEY, RICHARD A., ed.
Congress and the environment. 1970
KF5505.A75C6 ECOL

COON, NELSON.
Using wayside plants. 4th rev. ed. Hearthside Press 1969 **SB108.U6N7 1969 ECOL**

COOPER, BRYAN.
Alaska: the last frontier. Morrow, 1973.
HD9567.A4C66 ECOL

COOPER, ELIZABETH K.
Science in your own back yard, by Elizabeth K. Cooper, with illus. by the author. Harcourt 1970
QH81.C75 1970 ECOL

A tree is something wonderful. By Elizabeth K. Cooper and Padraic Cooper. Photographs by Padraic Cooper. Golden Gate Junior Books c1972
PZ10.C779Tr ECOL

COOPER, HAL B. H.
Source testing for air pollution control, by Hal B. H. Cooper, Jr. and August T. Rossano, Jr. Environmental Science Services Division, Environmental Research & Applications 1971 **fTD890.C57 ECOL**

COOTNER, PAUL H.
Water demand for steam electric generation; an economic projection model, by Paul H. Cootner and George O. G. Lof. Resources for the Future; distributed by Johns Hopkins Press, 1966,c1965
TK1051.C6 ECOL

COREY, RICHARD CLARKE.
Principles and practices of incineration. Edited by Richard C. Corey. Wiley-Interscience 1969 (Environmental science and technology)
TD803.C66 ECOL

CORLISS, WILLIAM R.
Direct conversion of energy. Atomic Energy Commission, Division of Technical Information 1964 (Understanding the atom) **TK2896.C6 ECOL**

Nuclear Propulsion for space by William R. Corliss. U. S. Atomic Energy Commission, Division of Technical Information 1967 (Understanding the atom)
TL783.5.C62 ECOL

Power reactors in small packages by William R. Corliss. U.S. Atomic Energy Commission, Division of Technical Information 1968 (Understanding the atom)
TK1078.C6 1968 ECOL

SNAP nuclear space reactors by William R. Corliss. U.S. Atomic Energy Commission, Div. of Technical Information 1966 (Understanding the atom)
TL1102.N8C6 ECOL

Space radiation by William R. Corliss. Atomic Energy Commission, Division of Technical Information 1968 (Understanding the atom) **QC485.C613 ECOL**

CORLISS, WILLIAM R., jt. auth.
Mead, Robert L.
Power from radioisotopes. Rev. 1966
TK1078.M38 ECOL

Seaborg, Glenn Theodore.
Man and atom. 1st ed. 1971.
TK9145.S4 1971 ECOL

CORMACK, MARIBELLE, 1902-
First book of trees; pictures by Helene Carter. Watts c1951 **QK475.C59 ECOL**

CORNELIUS, WALTER, ed.
Symposium on Emissions from Continuous Combustion Systems, General Motors Research Laboratories, 1971.
Emissions from continuous combustion systems. 1972. **TD881.S86 1971 ECOL**

CORNELL AERONAUTICAL LABORATORY, INC., BUFFALO.
Research on the physical aspects of thermal pollution. Authors: T. R. Sundaram and others. Prepared for the Water Quality Office, Environmental Protection Agency. Environmental Protection Agency, Water Quality Office; for sale by the Supt. of Docs., U.S. Govt. Print. Off., 1971. (Water pollution control research series) **fTD427.H4C67 ECOL**

CORNELL, JAMES, comp.
Smithsonian Institution. Center for Shortlived Phenomena.
The pulse of the planet. c1972 **fQ225.P8 ECOL**

CORNELL UNIVERSITY. LABORATORY OF ORNITHOLOGY.
The Living bird. 6th- 1967-
REF QL671.L57 ECOL

CORNELL UNIVERSITY. WATER RESOURCES AND MARINE SCIENCES CENTER.
Raney, Edward Cowden.
Heated effluents and effects on aquatic life with emphasis on fishes. 3rd ed. 1969.
REF Z7173.W3R3 1969 ECOL

CORRELL, DONOVAN STEWART, 1908-
Aquatic and wetland plants of southwestern United States, by Donovan S. Correll and Helen B. Correll. For the Environmental Protection Agency. Environmental Protection Agency, Office of Research and Monitoring, 1972. (Water pollution control research series)
QK142.C6 ECOL

CORRELL, HELEN B., jt. auth.
Correll, Donovan Stewart.
Aquatic and wetland plants of southwestern United States. 1972. **QK142.C6 ECOL**

COSTELLO, DAVID FRANCIS, 1904-
The desert world by David F. Costello. Crowell 1972 **QH88.C67 ECOL**

The prairie world. With photos. by the author. Crowell 1969 **QH541.5.P7C6 ECOL**

COTTAM, WALTER PACE, 1894-
Our renewable wild lands, a challenge. Univ. of Utah Press, 1961. **QK941.U8C6 ECOL**

COTTRELL, DOROTHY.
Novick, Sheldon.
Our world in peril. 1971 **HC110.P55N67 ECOL**

COUCH, ROBERT E., jt. auth.
Gunn, Clare A.
Cultural benefits from metropolitan river recreation—San Antonio prototype. 1972. **fHD1694.T4G8 ECOL**

COUCHMAN, J. KENNETH.
Mini-climates. By J. K. Couchman and others Mine Publications c1971 (Examining your environment) **QC863.C68 ECOL**

Snow and ice. By J. K. Couchman and others Mine Publications c1971 (Examining your environment) **QC929.S7C6 ECOL**

COULTER, MERLE CROWE, 1894-1958.
The story of the plant kingdom. Rev. by Howard J. Dittmer. 3d ed. Univ. of Chicago Press 1964 **QK47.C893 1964 ECOL**

COUNCIL OF STATE GOVERNMENTS.
Council of State Governments. Committee of State Officials on Suggested State Legislation.
Suggested state legislation; 1973- v.32- **JK2431.C6 ECOL**

The states' role in land resource management. 1972 **HD205.C6 1972 ECOL**

COUNCIL OF STATE GOVERNMENTS. COMMITTEE OF STATE OFFICIALS ON SUGGESTED STATE LEGISLATION.
Suggested state legislation; 1973- v.32- v. **JK2431.C6 ECOL**

COUNCIL ON ECONOMIC PRIORITIES.
Paper profits: pollution in the pulp and paper industry. Researched and written by Leslie Allen, Eileen Kaufman, and Joanna Underwood. MIT Press c1972 **TD899.W65C65 1972 ECOL**

Paper profits: pollution in the pulp and paper industry. Researched and written by Leslie Allen, Eileen Kaufman, and Joanna Underwood. 1971 1 v. **REF fTD888.P8C6 ECOL**

COUNCIL ON ENVIRONMENTAL QUALITY.
Midwest Research Institute, Kansas City, Missouri.
Resource recovery. 1973. **fTP995.M5 ECOL**

COURTENAY, BOOTH.
Wildflowers and weeds, a guide in full color by Booth Courtenay and James Hall Zimmerman. Van Nostrand 1972? **QK141.C6 ECOL**

COUSTEAU, JACQUES YVES.
The whale, mighty monarch of the sea by Jacques-Yves Cousteau and Philippe Diole. Translated from the French by J. F. Bernard. 1st ed. in U.S. Doubleday, 1972. (The Undersea discoveries of Jacques-Yves Cousteau) **QL737.C4C6913 ECOL**

COUSTEAU, JACQUES YVES, 1909-
Oasis in space: the ocean world of Jacques Cousteau. World Publishing c1972 **fQH91.C64 ECOL**

COWAN, EDWARD, 1933-
Oil and water; the Torrey Canyon disaster. Lippincott 1968 **VK1255.T65C6 ECOL**

COX, DONALD WILLIAM.
Pioneers of ecology, by Donald W. Cox. Portrait illus. by Ted Lewin. Hammond 1971 **QH26.C68 ECOL**

COX, GEORGE W., 1935- comp.
Readings in conservation ecology. Ed. by George W. Cox. Appleton 1969 **S942.C6 ECOL**

COYLE, DAVID CUSHMAN, 1887-
Conservation, an American story of conflict and accomplishment. Rutgers Univ. Press, 1957. **HC103.7.C68 ECOL**

CRAMOND, MICHAEL.
Hunting & fishing in North America; with drawings by Olaus J. Murie. Univ. of Okla. Press c1953 **SK40.C67 ECOL**

CRAVEN, CLAUDE JACKSON, 1908-
Our atomic world; the story of atomic energy by C. J. Craven. Rev. U.S. Atomic Energy Commission, Division of Technical Information, 1964. (Understanding the atom) **QC778.C7 1964 ECOL**

CREATIVE RESEARCH SERVICES, INC.
Progress report, biennial program and long-range plan for water pollution control. Prepared for the Minnesota Pollution Control Agency by Creative Research Services, Inc. 1970. 3v. **fTD224.M65C73 ECOL**

Water quality management plan, interim. Minnesota Pollution Control Agency, Division of Water Quality, 1971. 10v. **REF fTD224.M65C7 ECOL**

CRENSON, MATTHEW A., 1943-
The un-politics of air pollution: a study of non-decision-making in the cities by Matthew A. Crenson. Johns Hopkins Press 1971 **HC110.A4C73 ECOL**

CRESA.
Pollution abatement and by-product recovery in shellfish and fisheries processing. By Edwin Lee Johnson and others. Prepared for the Environmental Protection Agency. U.S. Environmental Protection Agency, U.S. Govt. Print. Off., 1971. (Water pollution control research series) **fTD899.F57C73 ECOL**

CRESSEY, ROGER FRANK, 1930-
The genus Argulus (Crustacea: Branchiura) of the United States. Environmental Protection Agency, 1972. (Biota of freshwater ecosystems, Identification manual, no.2.) **fQH96.A2B5no.2 ECOL**

CRICK, FRANCIS, 1916-
Of molecules and men, by Francis Crick. University of Washington Press, 1969,c1966. (The John Danz lectures) **QH331.C9 1969 ECOL**

CRILE, GEORGE, 1907- jt. auth.
Sandburg, Helga.
Above and below. 1st ed. 1969 **QH91.75.U6S35 ECOL**

CRISLER, LOIS.
Arctic wild. Harper 1958 **QL161.C7 ECOL**

CRONK, GENE E.
Montgomery County Sanitary Dept. Montgomery County, Ohio.
Ground water infiltration and internal sealing of sanitary sewers, Montgomery County, Ohio. 1972. **fTD716.M6 ECOL**

CRONQUIST, ARTHUR.
Gleason, Henry Allan.
The natural geography of plants. 1964. **QK101.G57 ECOL**

CROSBY, ALFRED W.
The Columbian exchange; biological and cultural consequences of 1492 by Alfred W. Crosby, Jr. Foreword by Otto von Mering. Greenwood Pub. Co. 1972 (Contributions in American studies, no.2) **E98.D6C7 ECOL**

CROWE, PHILIP KINGSLAND, 1908-
World wildlife: the last stand. With a foreword by H. R. H. Prince Bernard of the Netherlands. Scribner 1970 **S962.C75 ECOL**

CROWN ZELLERBACH CORPORATION. LEBANON DIVISION.
Aerated lagoon treatment of sulfite pulping effluents. U.S. Environmental Protection Agency 1970. (Water pollution control research series) **fTD899.W65C7 ECOL**

CRUICKSHANK, ALLAN D.
Wings in the wilderness. Oxford Univ. Press, 1947. **QL674.C85 ECOL**

CUFFARI, RICHARD, 1925- illus.
Hoke, John.
Ecology: man's effects on his environment and its mechanisms. 1971 **QH541.H58 ECOL**

Perera, Thomas Biddle.
Who will clean the air? 1971 **TD883.13.P47 ECOL**

CULP, RUSSELL L., 1916-
South Tahoe Public Utility District.
Advanced wastewater treatment as practiced at South Tahoe. 1971. **fTD225.T25S6 ECOL**

CUMMING, KENNETH BARNEY, jt. auth.
Virginia Polytechnic Institute and State University.
Stream faunal recovery after manganese strip mine reclamation. 1971. **fTN291.V5 ECOL**

CUNNINGHAM, CHERYL BOND, jt. auth.
Cunningham, Michael C.
A selected bibliography on the relevance of environmental education to secondary school curricula. 1972 **REF fQH541.2.C8 ECOL**

CUNNINGHAM, MICHAEL C.
A selected bibliography on the relevance of environmental education to secondary school curricula, by M. C. Cunningham and Cheryl Bond Cunningham. Council of Planning Librarians 1972 (Council of Planning Librarians. Exchange bibliography, no. 274) **REF fQH541.2.C8 ECOL**

CUNNINGHAM, MICHAEL C., jt. auth.
Ehrenthal, Frank F.
A selected bibliography on uses of the urban street. 1972. **REF fZ7164.T81E3 ECOL**

CURRENT ISSUES CONFERENCE, 1ST, PORTLAND, OR., 1972.
Timber supply and the environment; proceedings. Ed. by Stuart U. Rich. Eugene, Forest Industries Management Center, Univ. of Oregon 1972 **SD144.A13C87 1972 ECOL**

CURRIE, ROBERT J., jt. auth.
Boen, Doyle F.
Study of reutilization of wastewater recycled through groundwater. 1971. **fTD429.B6 ECOL**

CURRY-LINDAHL, KAI.
Conservation for survival; an ecological strategy. Morrow, 1972. **QH541.C87 ECOL**

Let them live; a worldwide survey of animals threatened with extinction. Morrow, 1972. **S962.C87 ECOL**

National parks of the world, by Kai Curry-Lindahl and Jean-Paul Harroy. Under the general editorship of Vera R. Webster. Golden Press 1972 2 v. (A Golden field guide) **SB481.C87 ECOL**

CURTIS, RICHARD.
Perils of the peaceful atom; the myth of safe nuclear power plants, by Richard Curtis and Elizabeth Hogan. Doubleday, 1969. **HD9698.U52C8 ECOL**

CYRUS WM. RICE & COMPANY.
Datagraphics Incorporated.
Inorganic chemicals industry profile (updated). 1971. **fTD899.C5D37 ECOL**

Datagraphics Incorporated.
Projected wastewater treatment costs in the organic chemicals industry (updated). 1971. **fTD899.C5D388 ECOL**

D

DA COSTA, BEVERLY, ed.
Natural wonders of America. 1972 **QH76.N29 ECOL**

DAEDALUS.
American Academy of Arts and Sciences, Boston. Commission on the Year 2000
Toward the year 2000. 1970,c1968 **E169.1.A47192 1970 ECOL**

DAHLSTEN, DONALD L., 1933-
Pesticides. 1970 **fQH545.P4P48 ECOL**

DALES, JOHN HARKNESS, 1920-
Pollution, property and prices; an essay in policy-making and economics by J. H. Dales. University of Toronto Press 1970,c1968 **HC120.P55D3 1970 ECOL**

DALLAS, OR.
Combined treatment of domestic and industrial wastes by activated sludge. Prepared for the Water Quality Office, Environmental Protection Agency. Environmental Protection Agency, Water Quality Office; for sale by the Supt. of Docs., U.S. Govt. Print Off., 1971. (Water pollution control research series) **fTD756.D35 ECOL**

DALRYMPLE, BYRON W., 1914-
Sportsman's guide to game fish, by Byron Dalrymple. Drawings by Douglas Allen. World Pub. Co. 1968 (Outdoor life books) **QL617.D34 ECOL**

DANIELS, FARRINGTON, 1889-
Direct use of the sun's energy. Yale Univ. Press, 1964. (Trends in science, v.5) **TJ810.D28 ECOL**

DANSEREAU, PIERRE MACKAY, 1911- ed.
Challenge for survival: land, air, and water for man in megalopolis. 1970. **HM206.C4 ECOL**

DARDEN, RUFUS BENTON, jt. auth.
California. University.
Flow into a stratified reservoir. 1972. **TC167.C3 ECOL**

D'ARGE, RALPH C., jt. auth.
Kneese, Allen V.
Economics and the environment. 1970 **HC68.K57 ECOL**

DARLING, FRANK FRASER, 1903-
Natural history in the Highlands & islands. With 46 colour photos. by F. Fraser Darling, John Markham and others. Collins 1947 (The New naturalist; a survey of British natural history. [6]) **QH141.D365 ECOL**

Pelican in the wilderness; a naturalist's odyssey in North America. Random House 1956 **QH104.D3 ECOL**

Wilderness and plenty. With an introd. by Paul Brooks. Houghton Mifflin, 1970. (The Reith lectures, 1969) **QH541.13.D36 ECOL**

DARLING, FRANK FRASER, 1903- ed.
A Conversation on population, environment, and human well-being. 1971 **HB875.C63 ECOL**

Future environments of North America; being the record of a conference convened by the Conservation Foundation in April, 1965, at Airlie House, Warrenton, Virginia. Ed. by F. Fraser Darling and John P. Milton. Natural History Press, 1966. **HC95.D33 ECOL**

DARLING, LOIS.
A place in the sun; ecology and the living world. Written and illustrated by Lois and Louis Darling. Morrow 1968 **QH541.D34 ECOL**

DARLING, LOUIS, jt. auth.
Darling, Lois.
A place in the sun. 1968 **QH541.D34 ECOL**

DARMSTADTER, JOEL, 1928-
Energy in the world economy; a statistical review of trends in output, trade, and consumption since 1925, by Joel Darmstadter, with Perry D. Teitelbaum and Jaroslav G. Polach. Published for Resources for the Future by the Johns Hopkins Press 1971
REF fHD9540.4.D37 ECOL

DARNAY, ARSEN.
The role of packaging in solid waste management 1966 to 1976, by Arsen Darnay and William E. Franklin. U.S. Bureau of Solid Waste Management; for sale by the Supt. of Docs., U.S. Govt. Print. Off., 1969. (U.S. Public Health Service publication no. 1855)
TD795.D37 ECOL

Salvage markets for materials in solid wastes, ... written for the Federal Solid Waste Management Program by Arsen Darnay and William E. Franklin, of the Midwest Research Institute. U.S. Environmental Protection Agency, 1972. (Solid waste management series) **TD795.D38 ECOL**

DARNAY, ARSEN, jt. auth.
Franklin, William E.
The role of nonpackaging paper in solid waste management, 1966 to 1976. 1971. **TD795.F7 ECOL**

DARNELL, REZNEAT M.
Organism and environment; a manual of quantitative ecology. Freeman c1971 **fQH541.2.D3 ECOL**

DASMANN, RAYMOND FREDERICK, 1919-
A Conversation on population, environment, and human well-being. 1971 **HB875.C63 ECOL**

A different kind of country by Raymond F. Dasmann. Macmillan 1968 **QH75.D37 ECOL**

Environmental conservation by Raymond F. Dasmann. 3d ed. Wiley 1972 **S936.D3 1972 ECOL**

No further retreat; the fight to save Florida by Raymond F. Dasmann. Drawings by Elizabeth Dasmann. Macmillan 1971 **S932.F6D37 ECOL**

Planet in peril; man and the biosphere today by Raymond F. Dasmann. World Pub. 1972
QH541.D35 1972 ECOL

Wildlife biology by Raymond F. Dasmann. Wiley 1964 **QL752.D3 ECOL**

DASMANN, WILLIAM.
If deer are to survive. Stackpole Books 1971
QL737.U55D37 ECOL

DATAGRAPHICS INCORPORATED.
Inorganic chemicals industry profile (updated), by Datagraphics Incorporated, of an original study by Cyrus Wm. Rice & Company, for Environmental Protection Agency. Research and Monitoring, Environmental Protection Agency; for sale by the Supt. of Docs., U.S. Govt. Print. Off., 1971. (Water pollution control research series) **fTD899.C5D37 ECOL**

Projected wastewater treatment costs in the organic chemicals industry (updated) by Datagraphics Incorporated, of an original study by Cyrus Wm. Rice and Company, for Environmental Protection Agency. Research and Monitoring, Environmental Protection Agency 1971. (Water pollution control research series) **fTD899.C5D388 ECOL**

DAUBENMIRE, REXFORD F., 1909-
Plant communities; a textbook of plant synecology by Rexford Daubenmire. Harper & Row 1968
QK911.D3 ECOL

Plants and environment; a textbook of plant autecology. 2d ed. Wiley c1959
QK901.D3 1959 ECOL

DAVENPORT, SALLY, ed.
INTASA, Inc.
Planning and evaluation of multiple purpose water resource projects in a multiobjective environment. 1972. **fHD1691.I1 ECOL**

DAVIDSON, RAY, 1918-
Peril on the job; a study of hazards in the chemical industries. Public Affairs Press 1970
HD7269.C452U5 ECOL

DAVIDSON, ROBERT L.
Price, Fred C.
McGraw-Hill's 1972 report on business and the environment. c1972 **fTD174.P7 ECOL**

DAVIES, BRIAN.
Savage luxury: the slaughter of the baby seals. Taplinger 1971,c1970 **QL737.P6D33 1971 ECOL**

DAVIES, J. CLARENCE.
The politics of pollution by J. Clarence Davies, III Pegasus 1970 (Studies in contemporary American politics) **HC110.E5D35 ECOL**

DAVIS, EDWARD WILSON, 1888-
Pioneering with taconite, by E. W. Davis. Minnesota Historical Society, 1964. (Publications of the Minnesota Historical Society) **TN403.M6D3 ECOL**

DAVIS, ERNST M.
Bacterial effects of algae on enteric organisms, by Ernst M. Davis and Earnest F. Gloyna. U.S. Federal Water Quality Administration; for sale by the Supt. of Docs., U.S. Govt. Print. Off., 1970. (Water pollution control research series) **fQR48.D38 ECOL**

DAVIS, JOHN WILLIAM, 1917- ed.
Infectious and parasitic diseases of wild birds. 1st ed. 1971 **SF994.4.A115 ECOL**

DAVIS, KENNETH SIDNEY, 1912- jt. auth.
Leopold, Luna Bergere.
Water. Rev. 1970,c1966 **fGB671.L4 1970 ECOL**

DAVIS, KENNETH SYDNEY, 1912-
Water, the mirror of science, by Kenneth S. Davis and John A. Day. Anchor Books, 1961. (Science study series, S18) **QD169.W3D3 ECOL**

DAVIS, ROBERT K.
The range of choice in water management; a study of dissolved oxygen in the Potomac estuary, by Robert K. Davis. With contributions by Robert M. Steinberg, Leo J. Hetling, and Nicholas C. Matalas. Published for Resources for the Future, Inc. by Johns Hopkins Press 1968 **TD225.P74D3 ECOL**

DAVIS, WILLIAM MORRIS, 1850-1934.
The coral reef problem. American Geographical Society, 1928. (American Geographical Society. Special publication, no. 9) **QE565.D3 ECOL**

DAY, ALBERT M., 1897-
Making a living in conservation; a guide to outdoor careers by Albert M. Day. Stackpole Books 1971
S944.D33 ECOL

DAY, JOHN A.
Dimensions of the environmental crisis by John A. Day, Frederic F. Fost and Peter Rose. Wiley 1971
HC79.E5D35 ECOL

DAY, JOHN A., jt. auth.
Davis, Kenneth Sydney.
Water, the mirror of science. 1961.
QD169.W3D3 ECOL

DAYAN, V. H., 1927-
North American Rockwell Corporation. Rocketdyne Division.
Development of a chemical denitrification process. 1970. **fTD433.N67 ECOL**

DE BELL, GARRETT, comp.
The environmental handbook. Prepared for the first national environmental teaching. Ballantine Books 1970
HC110.E5D42 ECOL

DE MICHELE, VINCENZO.
The world of minerals. With a foreword by G. F. Claringbull. Photos. by Carlo Bevilacqua. World Pub. 1972 (The World of nature) **QE372.D3413 ECOL**

DEAL, RICHARD L.
The application of value theory to water resources planning and management, by R. E. Deal and M. H. Halbert. Performed for the Office of Water Resources Research, United States Dept. of the Interior. Institute for the Study of Inquiring Systems, 1971.
fHD1694.A5D4 ECOL

DEBACH, PAUL, ed.
Biological control of insect pests and weeds, edited by Paul DeBach. Assistant editor: Evert I. Schlinger. Reinhold Pub. Corp. 1964 **REF SB975.D4 ECOL**

DEE, SANDRA R.
A basic environmental collection. 1973. (Council of Planning Librarians. Exchange bibliography, 410)
Ref fZ5863.P6D4 ECOL

Corporations and the environment: PR or propaganda? 1973 (Council of Planning Librarians. Exchange bibliography, 411)
Ref fZ5863.P6D41 ECOL

DEEDY, JOHN G., jt. comp.
Nobile, Philip.
The complete ecology fact book. 1st ed. 1972.
TD174.N6 ECOL

DEGLER, STANLEY E.
Federal pollution control programs: water, air, and solid wastes, by Stanley E. Degler. Rev. ed. BNA Books 1971 (BNA's environmental management series)
TD180.D4 1971 ECOL

State air pollution control laws, by Stanley E. Degler. Rev. ed. Bureau of National Affairs, 1970 (BNA's Environmental management series)
KF3812.Z95D4 1970 ECOL

DEHAVEN, ROBERT C.
Synectics Corporation.
A system for industrial waste treatment RD&D project priority assignment. 1971.
fTD897.5.S9 ECOL

DELACOUR, JEAN THEODORE, 1890-
The waterfowl of the world. With plates in colour by Peter Scott. Country Life, 1954- v.
REF QL696.A5D39 ECOL

DELAFONS, JOHN, 1930-
Land-use controls in the United States. 2d ed. M.I.T. Press 1969 **HD205 1969 .D4 ECOL**

DELAWARE RIVER BASIN COMMISSION.
Interstate planning for regional water supply and pollution control. Environmental Protection Agency, Office of Research and Monitoring, 1971. (Water pollution control research series) **fTD420.D4 ECOL**

DENTINO, KRISTIAN A., jt. auth.
Wright, Sydney.
A bibliography of recreational communities and leisure land development. 1973.
fZ7164.L3W7 ECOL

DENVER. MUSEUM OF NATURAL HISTORY.
Bailey, Alfred Marshall.
Birds of Colorado. 1965.
REF fQL684.C6B3 ECOL

DERMID, JACK, 1923- jt. auth.
Hester, F. Eugene.
The world of the wood duck. 1st ed. 1973
QL696.A5H42 ECOL

DERRICK, CHRISTOPHER, 1921-
The delicate creation; towards a theology of the environment. Foreword by Rene Dubos. Introd. by John Cardinal Wright. Devin-Adair c1972
BD581.D47 ECOL

DERSE, PHILIP H., jt. auth.
Morton, Stephen D.
The carbon dioxide system and eutrophication. 1971. **fQH96.8.E9M6 ECOL**

DESIGN METHODS GROUP.
Emerging methods in environmental design and planning. 1970 **TA170.E46 ECOL**

DESIGN OF WATER-RESOURCE SYSTEMS;
new techniques for relating economic objectives, engineering analysis, and governmental planning. by Arthur Maass and others. Harvard University Press 1970,c1962 **TC409.D4 ECOL**

DETROIT METRO WATER DEPT.
Development of phosphate removal processes; development and demonstration of phosphate removal facilities at Detroit using an activated sludge process and steel pickling liquor. Prepared for the Water Quality Office, Environmental Protection Agency, Environmental Protection Agency, Water Quality Office; for sale by the Supt. of Docs., U.S. Govt. Print. Off., 1970. (Water pollution control research series)
fTD756.D47 ECOL

DETWYLER, THOMAS R., 1938-
Urbanization and environment; the physical geography of the city by Thomas R. Detwyler and Melvin G. Marcus, and contributors. Line drawings by Peter Van Dusen. Duxbury Press 1972
HT151.D46 ECOL

DETWYLER, THOMAS R., 1938- comp.
Man's impact on environment compiled by Thomas R. Detwyler. McGraw-Hill 1971 (McGraw-Hill series in geography) **GF75.D48 ECOL**

DEVELOPMENT OF A COAL-BASED SEWAGE-TREATMENT PROCESS; final report. Prepared for Office of Coal Research, Dept. of the Interior. Office of Coal Research; for sale by the Supt. of Docs., U.S. Govt. Print. Off., 1971
fTN805.A395no.55 ECOL

DEWHURST, JAMES FREDERIC, 1895-
Twentieth Century Fund.
America's needs and resources: a new survey. 1969,c1955 **REF HC106.5.T9 1969 ECOL**

DICK, JOHN HENRY, 1919- illus.
Griscom, Ludlow.
The warblers of America. 1957.
REF QL696.P2G85 ECOL

Sprunt, Alexander.
Carolina low country impressions. 1964.
REF QH105.S6S6 ECOL

DICKEY, MIRIAM E.
Beyond the classroom; a guide to the natural history of the city, a who's who of urban America. Illus. by Charles E. Roth. Massachusetts Audubon Society, 1972. **Ref fQH51.D5 ECOL**

Beyond the classroom: using the urban environment as an instructional medium. Trial edition 1972. By Miriam E. Dickey and Charles E. Roth. A development of the Urban Environmental Education Project of the Masachusetts Audubon Society. 1972.
fQH541.2.D52 ECOL

DICKINSON, ALICE.
The first book of plants. Pictures by Paul Wenck. Watts, c1953. (First book series) **QK49.D5 ECOL**

DILLON, ELIZABETH S.
A manual of common beetles of eastern North America, by Elizabeth Dillon and Lawrence S. Dillon. Dover Publications, 1972. 2v.
QL581.D5 1972 ECOL

DILLON, LAWRENCE S., jt. auth.
Dillon, Elizabeth S.
A manual of common beetles of eastern North America. 1972. **QL581.D5 1972 ECOL**

DIMITRIADES, BASIL.
Interpretation of gas chromatographic spectra in routine analysis of exhaust hydrocarbons, by B. Dimitriades, C. J. Raible, and C. A. Wilson. U.S. Dept. of the Interior, Bureau of Mines 1972 (United States Bureau of Mines. Report of Investigations 7700)
TN23.U7no.7700 ECOL

DINMAN, BERTRAM D., ed.
Environmental mercury contamination. 1972
RA1231.M5E58 ECOL

DIOLE, PHILIPPE, jt. auth.
Cousteau, Jacques Yves.
The whale. 1st ed. in U.S. 1972.
QL737.C4C6913 ECOL

DIRECTORY OF GOVERNMENTAL AIR POLLUTION AGENCIES. 1970-
U.S. Environmental Protection Agency. v.
TD882.D5 ECOL

DIRECTORY OF PUBLIC INFORMATION CONTACTS, WASH., D.C., 1972-
Daniel J. Edelman, Inc. [etc.] v.
REF JK849.A353 ECOL

DISCH, ROBERT, comp.
The ecological conscience; values for survival. Prentice 1970 (Spectrum book)
HC110.E5D58 ECOL

DISTRICT OF COLUMBIA.
District of Columbia solid waste management plan; status report, 1970. U. S. Environmental Protection Agency; for sale by the Supt. of Docs., U.S. Govt. Print. Off. 1971. **TD525.W2A43 ECOL**

D'ITRI, FRANK M.
The environmental mercury problem; a report to the Michigan House of Representatives resulting from House Resolution 424, Great Lakes Contamination (Mercury) Committee, prepared by Frank M. D'Itri. Michigan House of Representatives, 1971. (Michigan House of Representatives. Legislative report)
fQH545.M4D57 ECOL

DITTON, ROBERT B.
National environmental policy act of 1969 (P.L. 91-190): bibliography on impact assessment methods and legal considerations. 1973. (Council of Planning Librarians. Exchange bibliography, 415)
Ref fHC110.E5D582 ECOL

DITTON, ROBERT B., jt. auth.
Conference on Environmental Impact Analysis, Green Bay, Wis., 1972.
Environmental impact analysis: philosophy & methods. 1972 **HC110.E5C65 1972 ECOL**

DOBIE, JOHN.
Methods used for investigating productivity of fish-rearing ponds in Minnesota by John Dobie and John B. Moyle. Rev. Minnesota Dept. of Conservation, Division of Game and Fish, Section of Research and Planning, 1962. (Fisheries Research Unit. Special Publication no.5) **SH222.M6D6 1962 ECOL**

DOBZHANSKY, THEODOSIUS GRIGORIEVICH, 1900- jt. auth.
Asimov, Isaac.
The genetic effects of radiation. c1966
QH652.5.A8 ECOL

DODD, EDWARD, 1904-
Careers for the '70s: conservation by Ed Dodd. Foreword by Theodore Roosevelt III. Crowell-Collier 1971 **S944.D6 ECOL**

DODD, JOHN D.
The ecology of diatoms in hard water habitats, by John D. Dodd, for the Environmental Protection Agency. U.S. Environmental Protection Agency; U.S. Govt. Print. Office, 1971. (Water pollution control research series) **fQK569.D54D6 ECOL**

DOERKSEN, HARVEY R.
Columbia River Interstate Compact, politics of negotiation. Washington State Univ., 1972
KF5590.C6D6 ECOL

DOGAN, MATTEI.
Quantitative ecological analysis in the social sciences, ed. by Mattei Dogan and Stein Rokkan. M.I.T. Press 1969 (M.I.T. studies in comparative politics)
HM206.D6 ECOL

DOHERTY, WILLIAM T., comp.
Minerals compiled by William T. Doherty, Jr. Chelsea House Publishers, 1971. (Conservation in the United States; a documentary history)
REF TN153.D58 ECOL

DONALDSON, GEORGE WARREN, 1915- comp.
Perspectives on outdoor education; readings by George W. Donaldson and Oswald Goering. W. C. Brown Co. 1972 **LB1047.D6 ECOL**

DONNELLY, WARREN H.
Nuclear power and merchant shipping. Rev. U.S. Atomic Energy Commission, Div. of Technical Information c1965 (Understanding the atom)
VM317.D6 1965 ECOL

DOOLEY, DAVID.
Summer School guide for education for an improved environment, by David Dooley, Don Becchetti and Jean Voegeli. Working copy. Independent School District 281, Robbinsdale Area Schools, 1971.
fQH541.2.D6 ECOL

DORFMAN, NANCY, jt. comp.
Dorfman, Robert.
Economics of the environment. 1st ed. 1972
HC79.P55D65 ECOL

DORFMAN, ROBERT, comp.
Economics of the environment; selected readings. Edited by Robert Dorfman and Nancy Dorfman. 1st ed. Norton 1972 **HC79.P55D65 ECOL**

DORFMAN, ROBERT, ed.
Models for managing regional water quality. 1972
TD365.M6 ECOL

DORIAN, EDITH M.
Animals that made U.S. history by Edith Dorian and W. N. Wilson. McGraw-Hill c1964
QL155.D6 ECOL

DORR, JOHN A.
Geology of Michigan, by John A. Dorr and Donald F. Eschman. Illus. by Derwin Bell. Univ. of Mich. Press c1970 **REF fQE125.D6 ECOL**

DORST, JEAN, 1924-
Before nature dies. Tr. by C. D. Sherman. With a preface by Prince Bernhard. 1st American ed. Houghton, 1970. **S936.D6613 ECOL**

DOSSENBACH, HANS D., 1936-
The family life of birds. Photos. and text by Hans D. Dossenbach. Conceived and designed by Emil M. Buhrer. Foreword and scientific advisor: Otto Koenig. Translated from the German by Fritz Bauchwitz McGraw-Hill 1971 **QL675.D6613 ECOL**

DOUGAL, MERWIN D., ed.
Conference on Flood Plain Management, Iowa State University, 1968.
Flood plain management, Iowa's experience. 1st ed. 1969 **TC424.I8C6 1968 ECOL**

DOUGLAS, PAUL HOWARD.
Zisch, William E.
The urban environment: how it can be improved. 1969. **HT175.U6Z4 ECOL**

DOUGLAS, WILLIAM ORVILLE, 1898-
Of men and mountains. Harper 1950
F851.7.D68 ECOL

The three hundred year war: a chronicle of ecological disaster, by William O. Douglas. 1st ed. Random House 1972 **QH541.D68 ECOL**

A wilderness bill of rights by William O. Douglas. 1st ed. Little, Brown 1965 **SK361.D6 ECOL**

DOW CHEMICAL COMPANY. FUNCTIONAL PRODUCTS AND SYSTEMS DEPT.
A literature search and critical analysis of biological trickling filter studies. U.S. Environmental Protection Agency, Office of Research and Monitoring, 1971- v.1- (Water pollution control research series)
fTD443.D6 ECOL

DOW CHEMICAL COMPANY. WESTERN DIVISION RESEARCH LABORATORIES.
Nitrate removal from wastewaters by ion exchange. Prepared for the Water Quality Office, Environmental Protection Agency. Water Quality Office, Environmental Protection Agency; for sale by the Supt. of Docs., U.S. Govt. Print. Off., 1971. (Water pollution control research series) **fTD757.5.D68 ECOL**

DOWDEN, ANNE OPHELIA (TODD) 1907-
Wild green things in the city; a book of weeds. Illus. by the author. Crowell 1972
SB611.D675 1972 ECOL

DRACUP, JOHN A.
Applications of systems analysis techniques to water resources, by John A. Dracup, Vikram S. Budhraja and Sharon G. Grant. Prepared for Office of Water Resources Research, United States Dept. of the Interior. Environmental Dynamics, Inc., 1972. v.
fTC409.D7 ECOL

DRAKE, ELLEN T., ed.
Peabody Museum Centennial Symposium, Yale University, 1966.
Evolution and environment. 1968.
QH366.A1P4 1966 ECOL

DRAPER, DIANNE.
Public participation in environmental decision-making. 1973. (Council of Planning Librarians. Exchange bibliography, 396) **fZ5863.P6D7 ECOL**

DRIVER, CHARLES H.
Assessment of the effectiveness and effects of land disposal methodologies of waste water management. 1972. **fTD760.A86 ECOL**

DROBNY, N. L.
Recovery and utilization of municipal solid waste: a summary of available cost and performance characteristics of unit processes and systems, by N. L. Drobny, H. E. Hull and R. F. Testin. U.S. Environmental Protection Agency, Solid Waste Management Office: U.S. Govt. Print. Off., 1971. (Environmental protection publication) (U.S. Public Health Service Pub. No. 1908) **TD793.D76 ECOL**

DU PONT DE NEMOURS & CO., E. I. WILMINGTON, DEL.
Moore, John A.
Science for society: a bibliography. 2nd ed. 1971
fZ7401.M6 1971 ECOL

DUBEY, GEORGE A., jt. auth.
Wiley, Averill J.
Reverse osmosis concentration of dilute pulp and paper effluents. 1972. **fTD899.W65W5 ECOL**

DUBKIN, LEONARD, 1904-
My secret places; one man's love affair with nature in the city. McKay 1972 **QH105.I3D8 ECOL**

DUBOS, RENE JULES, 1901-
A God within by Rene Dubos. Scribner 1972
HM206.D86 ECOL

Man adapting, by Rene Dubos. Yale University Press, 1965. (Yale University. Mrs. Hepsa Ely Silliman memorial lectures) **R723.D77 ECOL**

Reason awake: science for man by Rene Dubos. Columbia Univ. Press, 1970. **Q125.D814 ECOL**

So human an animal by Rene Dubos. Scribner 1968
HM206.D87 ECOL

DUBOS, RENE JULES, 1901- jt. auth.
Jackson, Barbara (Ward) Lady.
Only one earth. 1st ed. 1972 **GF41.J3 ECOL**

DUCSIK, DENNIS W., 1946- ed.
Power, pollution, and public policy. c1971
HC107.A113E55 ECOL

DUDDINGTON, C. L.
Beginner's guide to the fungi by C. L. Duddington. Drake Publishers 1972 **REF QK603.D83 ECOL**

DUDLEY, RUTH HUBBELL, 1905-
Partners in nature by Ruth H. Dudley. Illustrated by Eva Cellini. Funk & Wagnalls 1965
QH548.D8 ECOL

DUFFER, H. CASPER, jt. auth.
Ramsey, Ralph H.
Soil systems for municipal effluents. 1972.
fTD760.R24 ECOL

DUFFEY, ERIC.
Conservation of nature. McGraw-Hill 1970
S940.D84 ECOL

DUFRESNE, FRANK.
Alaska's animals & fishes. Illus. by Bob Hines. Barnes c1946 **QL628.A4D8 1946 ECOL**

DUGAN, G. L.
Lake Tahoe Area Council.
Eutrophication of surface waters—Lake Tahoe. 1971 i.e. 1972 **fQH96.8.E9L34 ECOL**

DUGAN, PATRICK R.
Biochemical ecology of water pollution by Patrick R. Dugan. Plenum Press, 1972. **TD423.D83 ECOL**

DUGDALE, VERA.
Album of North American animals. Illus. by Clark Bronson. Rand McNally 1966
fPZ10.D745AL ECOL

DUGMORE, ARTHUR RADCLYFFE, 1870-
The romance of the Newfoundland caribou. An intimate account of the life of the reindeer of North America. Illus. with paintings, drawings and photographs from life by the author. Lippincott, 1913.
fQL737.U5D8 ECOL

DUKE UNIVERSITY, DURHAM, N.C. SCHOOL OF LAW.
Air pollution control. 1968.
KF3812.A75A35 1968 ECOL

River basin development. 1957.
HN64.R589 ECOL

Water resources. 1957. HD1694.A5W3 ECOL

DULUTH, MINNESOTA. BOARD OF EDUCATION.
Minnesota. University. Duluth Branch. Agricultural Extension Service.
Natural resource management lesson plan guide. n.d.
fS946.M55 ECOL

DUMONT, RENE, 1904-
The hungry future by Rene Dumont and Bernard Rosier. Tr. from the French by Rosamund Linell and R. B. Sutcliffe. Foreword by Thomas Balogh. Praeger 1969
HD1445.D823 ECOL

DUNBAR, MAXWELL JOHN.
Environment and good sense; an introd. to environmental damage and control in Canada by M. J. Dunbar. McGill-Queen's University Press, 1971. (Environmental damage and control in Canada, 1)
TD182.D85 ECOL

DUNLAP, C. E., jt. auth.
Callihan, Clayton Dale.
Construction of a chemical-microbial pilot plant for production of single-cell protein from cellulosic wastes. 1971.
TP996.B3C3 ECOL

DUNLAP, WILLIAM J.
Robert S. Kerr Water Research Center.
Investigations concerning probable impact of nitrilotriacetic acid on ground waters. 1971.
fTD427.D4R6 ECOL

DUNN, JAMES TAYLOR.
The St. Croix: Midwest border river. Illus. by Gerald Hazzard. Holt 1965 (Rivers of America)
F612.S2D78 ECOL

DUNNINGTON, TOM, illus.
Hungerford, Harold R.
Ecology: the circle of life. 1971
QH541.14.H8 ECOL

DUPREE, WALTER G.
United States energy through the year 2000, by Walter G. Dupree and James A. West. U.S. Dept. of the Interior, 1972. HD9545.D8 ECOL

DUPREY, R. L., COMPILATION OF AIR POLLUTANT EMISSION FACTORS.
United States. Environmental Protection Office. Office of Air Programs.
Compilation of air pollutant emission factors. Rev. 1972. TD883.1.U494 ECOL

DURDEN, KENT.
Gifts of an eagle. Illus. by Peter Parnall. Simon and Schuster 1972 QL795.B57D87 ECOL

DURNING, MARVIN B., 1929-
Legal control of the environment—3D. 1971
KF3775.L44 ECOL

DURRENBERGER, ROBERT W.
Environment and man; a bibliography by Robert W. Durrenberger. National Press Books 1970
Z5118.A5D86 ECOL

DWORSKY, LEONARD B., comp.
Pollution by Leonard B. Dworsky. With an introd. by Stewart L. Udall. Chelsea House Publishers, 1971. (Conservation in the United States)
REF TD174.D95 ECOL

DYNAMIC ECOLOGY.
by Boyd D. Collier and others Prentice-Hall 1973 (Prentice-Hall biological science series)
QH541.D9 ECOL

DYNAMICS OF NUCLEAR SYSTEMS.
David L. Hetrick, editor. University of Arizona Press 1972 TK9202.D9 ECOL

DYNATECH R/D COMPANY.
A survey of alternate methods for cooling condenser discharge water. Environmental Protection Agency, Water Quality Office; U.S. Govt. Print. Off., 1969-
v. (Water pollution control research series)
fTJ403.D9 ECOL

E

EARTH DAY—THE BEGINNING; a guide for survival.
Comp. and ed. by the national staff of Environmental Action. Bantam Books 1970 (A Bantam extra)
HC110.E5E2 ECOL

EARTH MIGHT BE FAIR; reflections on ethics, religion, and ecology.
Edited by Ian G. Barbour. Prentice-Hall 1972
GF80.E15 ECOL

EASTER, K. WILLIAM, jt. auth.
Howe, Charles W.
Interbasin transfers of water. 1971
HD1695.W4H66 ECOL

EATON, WILLIAM W.
Maryland. Governor's Task Force on Nuclear Power Plants.
Nuclear power plants in Maryland. 1969.
TK1344.M3M3 ECOL

EBELING, ALFRED W., 1931-
California. University, Santa Barbara. Dept. of Biological Sciences.
Santa Barbara oil spill: short-term analysis of macroplankton and fish. 1971. fTD427.P4C34 ECOL

EBER, RONALD.
Handbook. Sierra Club, 1971 HC68.E2 ECOL

EBERHARD, MARY JANE WEST, jt. auth.
Evans, Howard Ensign.
The wasps. 1970 QL568.V5E8 ECOL

EBLING, FRANCIS JOHN GOVIER, 1918- ed.
Biology and ethics. 1969. HM216.B48 ECOL

ECCLESTON, BARTON H.
Effect of fuel front-end and midrange volatility on automobile emissions, by B. H. Eccleston and R. W. Hurn. U.S. Dept. of the Interior, Bureau of Mines 1972? (United States. Bureau of Mines. Report of Investigations 7707) TN23.U7no.7707 ECOL

ECKELBERRY, DONALD R., illus.
Pough, Richard Hooper.
Audubon bird guide; eastern land birds...with illus. in color of every species. 1946. QL681.P68 ECOL

ECKENFELDER, WILLIAM WESLEY, 1926-
Industrial water pollution control by W. Wesley Eckenfelder, Jr. McGraw-Hill c1966 (McGraw-Hill series in sanitary science and water resources engineering) TD897.E2 ECOL

ECKENFELDER, WILLIAM WESLEY, 1926- ed.
Water quality improvement by physical and chemical processes. 1970 TD745.W37 ECOL

ECKERT, ALLAN W.
The great auk. a novel. 1st ed. Little, Brown 1963
Fiction ECOL

Wild season, by Allan W. Eckert. With illus. by Karl E. Karalus. 1st ed. Little, Brown 1967 Fiction ECOL

ECKSTEIN, OTTO.
Resources for the Future.
Multiple purpose river development. 1958
REF HN15.R43 ECOL

THE ECOLOGICAL REGISTER: A DIRECTORY OF GOVERNMENTAL AGENCIES AND PRIVATE ORGANIZATIONS CONCERNED ABOUT ENVIRONMENTAL DESTRUCTION AND POLLUTION IN THE STATE AND IN THE SEVEN-COUNTY METROPOLITAN AREA.
Comp. by the Minnesota Association of Commerce and Industry. 2nd ed. Minnesota Association of Commerce and Industry, 1971.
S920.E24 1971 ECOL

THE ECOLOGICAL REGISTER: A DIRECTORY OF ORGANIZATIONS IN THE SEVEN-COUNTY METROPOLITAN AREA CONCERNED ABOUT ENVIRONMENTAL DESTRUCTION AND POLLUTION (PLUS A SUPPLEMENT PROVIDING BRIEF INFORMATION ON SIMILAR ORGANIZATIONS LOCATED ELSEWHERE).
Comp. by Ronald Campbell and others. Minnesota Association of Commerce and Industry, 1970.
fS920.E24 ECOL

ECOLOGICAL SOCIETY OF AMERICA.
Remote sensing in ecology. 1969
QH541.15.R4R4 ECOL

ECOLOGICAL STUDIES OF THE TIMBER WOLF IN NORTHEASTERN MINNESOTA.
L. David Mech and L. D. Frenzel, Jr., editors. U.S. North Central Forest Experiment Station, 1971(USDA Forest Service research paper NC52)
SD11.A45476no.52 ECOL

THE ECOLOGIST.
Blueprint for survival. 1972. S936.B5 1972 ECOL

ECOLOGY AND PHYSIOLOGY OF PARASITES; a symposium held at University of Toronto 19 and 20 February 1970.
Edited by A. M. Fallis. University of Toronto Press 1971 QL757.E26 ECOL

ECOLOGY: CRISIS AND NEW VISION.
Edited by Richard E. Sherrell. John Knox Press c1971 GF80.E25 ECOL

ECOLOGY FORUM. ENVIRONMENT INFORMATION CENTER.
The Environment index: a guide to the key environmental literature of the year. 1971-
REF fZ7171.E6 ECOL

THE ECOLOGY SEA IN SONG AND BALLAD,.
by Bernie Griff and friends. (Phonodisc) Century Records 41194 1973? Phonodisc GC31.E2 ECOL

ECOLOGY USA; a history of the year's important ecological events, 1971-
Special Reports, Inc. v. REF fS936.S62 ECOL

ECONOMIC AND SOCIAL CONSEQUENCES OF NUCLEAR ENERGY,.
edited by Lord Sherfield. University Press, 1972. (Science and engineering policy series)
HD9698.A3G74 ECOL

THE ECONOMIC IMPACT OF POLLUTION CONTROL; a summary of recent studies.
Prepared for the Council on Environmental Quality, Dept. of Commerce, and Environmental Protection Agency. For sale by the Supt. of Docs., U.S. Govt. Print. Off. 1972. TD180.E25 ECOL

ECONOMICS OF AIR AND WATER POLLUTION.
Edited by William R. Walker. Water Resources Research Center, Virginia Polytechnic Institute, 1969.(Virginia Polytechnic Institute, Blacksburg. Water Resources Research Center.
fTD201.V57no.26 ECOL

ECOTACTICS: THE SIERRA CLUB HANDBOOK FOR ENVIRONMENTAL ACTIVISTS,.
edited by John G. Mitchell, with Constance L. Stallings and with an introd. by Ralph Nader. Pocket Books 1970 HC110.E5E26 ECOL

EDINA, MINNESOTA PUBLIC SCHOOLS.
Berry, Marcia.
Environment study. 1971. QH541.2.B4 ECOL

EDISON ELECTRIC INSTITUTE. COMMITTEE ON ENVIRONMENT.
Conference on Energy, Economics and the Environment, Chicago, Ill., 1968.
Energy, economics and the environment: proceedings of a conference sponsored by the Committee on Environment, Edison Electric Institute. 1969.
fHD9540.1.C6 1968 ECOL

EDISON WATER QUALITY LABORATORY. STORM AND COMBINED SEWER OVERFLOWS SECTION.
Environmental impact of highway deicing. Author: Ed Struzeski Environmental Protection Agency, Water Quality Office; for sale by the Supt. of Docs., U.S. Govt. Print. Off., 1971. (Water pollution control research series) fTE220.E35 ECOL

EDLIN, HERBERT LEESON.
Plants and man; the story of our basic food, by H. L. Edlin. Published for the American Museum of Natural History by the Natural History Press 1969, c1967 (Nature and science library) S519.E3 ECOL

EDUCATION FOR SURVIVAL.
Curriculum guides by the teachers of Madison, New Jersey; Gertrude G. Tempe, curriculum coordinator North Jersey Conservation Foundation 1970-
v.1- QH541.2.E4 ECOL

EDUCATION U. S. A.
Environment and the schools. 1971
fHC110.E5E485 ECOL

EDUCATIONAL FACILITIES LABORATORIES.
Environmental education/facility resources: A Report. Developed in cooperation with the National Education Association and National Park Service, U.S. Dept. of the Interior. c1972 fQH541.2.E48 ECOL

Places and things for experimental schools. A joint report from Educational Facilities Laboratories, Inc. and Experimental Schools. 1972
Ref LB3221.E3 ECOL

EDUCATIONAL MEDIA RESEARCH.
Flowers, William J.
Western cultural tradition and human survival: the role of value orientations in the environmental crisis. c1971 GF80.F5 ECOL

EDWARDS, R. W., ed.
Conservation and productivity of natural waters. 1972. QL1.Z733no.29 ECOL

EDWARDS, R. W., jt. ed.
Goodman, Gordon T.
Ecology and the industrial society. 1965
TD180.G6 ECOL

EDWARDS, WALTER MEAYERS, illus.
Findley, Rowe.
Great American deserts. 1972 F787.F5 ECOL

EFFECTIVE TECHNOLOGY FOR RECYCLING METAL; proceedings of two special workshops.
National Association of Secondary Material Industries 1971 fTS214.E36 ECOL

EHLER, CHARLES N.
Environmental systems planning and management: a preliminary sorting of literature. Council of Planning Librarians 1972 (Council of Planning Librarians. Exchange bibliography, no. 251)
REF fZ5863.P6E38 ECOL

AUTHOR AND MAIN ENTRY CATALOG

ENVIRONMENT AND POLICY

EHLERS, VICTOR MARCUS, 1884-1959.
Municipal and rural sanitation by Victor M. Ehlers and Ernest W. Steel. 6th ed. McGraw-Hill c1965 (McGraw-Hill series in sanitary science and water resources engineering) **REF RA425.E5 1965 ECOL**

EHRENFELD, DAVID W.
Biological conservation by David W. Ehrenfeld. Holt, Rinehart and Winston 1970 (Modern biology series)
QH75.E35 ECOL
Conserving life on earth by David W. Ehrenfeld. Oxford University Press, 1972.
QH75.E35 1972 ECOL

EHRENTHAL, FRANK F.
A selected bibliography on uses of the urban street, by Frank F. Ehrenthal and Michael C. Cunningham. Council of Planning Librarians, 1972. (Council of Planning Librarians. Exchange bibliography, 266)
REF fZ7164.T81E3 ECOL

EHRLICH, ANNE H., jt. auth.
Ehrlich, Paul R.
Population resources environment. 1970
HB871.E35 ECOL
Ehrlich, Paul R.
Population, resources, environment. 2d ed. 1972
HB871.E35 1972 ECOL

EHRLICH, PAUL R.
The population bomb by Paul R. Ehrlich. Ballantine Books 1968 (A Sierra Club-Ballantine book)
HB875.E35 ECOL
Population resources environment; issues in human ecology by Paul R. Ehrlich and Anne H. Ehrlich. Freeman 1970 (A Series of books in biology)
HB871.E35 ECOL
Population, resources, environment; issues in human ecology by Paul R. Ehrlich and Anne H. Ehrlich. 2d ed. W. H. Freeman 1972 (A Series of books in biology)
HB871.E35 1972 ECOL

EHRLICH, PAUL R., comp.
Man and the ecosphere; readings from Scientific American. With commentaries by Paul R. Ehrlich, John P. Holdren and Richard W. Holm. W. H. Freeman 1971 **fGF8.E35 ECOL**

EHRLICH, PAUL R., jt. comp.
Holdren, John P.
Global ecology. 1971 **HC110.E5H64 ECOL**

EIDUSON, SAMUEL.
Biochemistry and behavior by Samuel Eiduson and others. Van Nostrand 1964 **QP521.E5 ECOL**

EILERS, RICHARD G., jt. auth.
Smith, Robert.
Cost to the consumer for collection and treatment of wastewater. 1970 i.e. 1972 **fTD523.S65 ECOL**

EISELEY, LOREN C., 1907-
The firmament of time. Atheneum, 1971 c1960
QH367.E4 1971 ECOL
The immense journey. Random House 1957
QH368.E38 ECOL
The invisible pyramid, by Loren Eiseley. Woodcuts by Walter Ferro. Scribner 1970 **CB19.E38 ECOL**
The unexpected universe, by Loren Eiseley. Harcourt, Brace & World 1969 **Q171.E39 ECOL**

EISENBUD, MERRIL.
Environmental radioactivity. McGraw-Hill 1963
RA569.E5 ECOL

EISNER, SIMON, jt. auth.
Gallion, Arthur B.
The urban pattern. 2d ed. 1963
NA9031.G3 1963 ECOL

EITEL, MICHAEL JOHANN, 1929- jt. auth.
Hulbert, Samuel F.
Design of a water-disposable glass packaging container. 1971. **TD799.H8 ECOL**

EKIRCH, ARTHUR ALPHONSE, 1915-
Man and nature in America. Columbia University Press, 1963. **GF503.E46 ECOL**

ELDER, FREDERICK.
Crisis in Eden; a religious study of man and environment. Abingdon Press 1970 **GF80.E4 ECOL**

ELDREDGE, HANFORD WENTWORTH, 1909- comp.
Taming megalopolis, ed., with a pref. and headnotes, by H. Wentworth Eldredge. Anchor Books, 1967. 2v.
HT151.E4 ECOL

ELECTROCHEMISTRY OF CLEANER ENVIRONMENTS.
Edited by John O'M. Bockris. Plenum Press, 1972.
TP256.E43 1972 ECOL

ELEMENTAL COMPOSITION OF SURFICIAL MATERIALS IN THE CONTERMINOUS UNITED STATES: AN ACCOUNT OF THE AMOUNTS OF CERTAIN CHEMICAL ELEMENTS,.
by Hansford T. Shacklette and others. U.S. Govt. Print. Off., 1971. (Geological survey Professional paper 574-D) **REF fQE75.P9no.574-D ECOL**

ELIOT, WILLARD AYRES.
Forest trees of the Pacific coast; including a brief account of the outstanding characters, distribution and habitat of the trees native to Alaska, British Columbia, Washington and Oregon; most of which are also found in Idaho and northern California and eastward to the western slopes of the Rocky Mountains. By Willard Ayres Eliot assisted by G. B. McLean; illus. principally from original photographs by George C. Stephenson. Putnam's Sons, 1938. **QK482.E5 ECOL**

ELLIOTT, RALPH D.
The effects of sewer surcharges on the level of industrial wastes and the use of water by industry, by Ralph D. Elliott and J. A. Seagraves. Water Resources Research Institute of the Univ. of North Carolina 1972. (North Carolina. University. Water Resources Research Institute. Report, no.70) **TD897.5.E4 ECOL**

ELLIOTT, SARAH M.
Our dirty air, by Sarah M. Elliott. Messner 1971
TD883.13.E44 ECOL

ELLIS, MELVIN RICHARD, 1912-
Flight of the white wolf, by Mel Ellis. Holt 1970
Fiction ECOL

ELTRINGHAM, STEWART KEITH.
Life in mud and sand by S. K. Eltringham. Crane 1971
QH541.5.S35E45 ECOL

ELY, NORTHCUTT, 1903-
Summary of mining and petroleum laws of the world. Rev. U.S. Bureau of Mines, U.S. Govt. Print. Off., 1970- v. (United States Bureau of Mines. Information circular 8514) **TN295.U4no.8514 ECOL**

ELY, RICHARD THEODORE, 1854-1943.
Land economics by Richard T. Ely and George S. Wehrwein. Univ. of Wisconsin Press, 1964.
HD111.E37 1964 ECOL

EMANUELSON, CLIFFORD E., ed.
Conservation Education Association.
Conservation quickies. 1966 **fS946.C57 ECOL**

EMANUELSON VIRGINIA, ed.
Conservation Education Association.
Conservation quickies. 1966 **fS946.C57 ECOL**

EMERGING METHODS IN ENVIRONMENTAL DESIGN AND PLANNING; proceedings of the Design Methods Group first international conference, Cambridge, Mass., June 1968. Edited by Gary T. Moore. MIT Press 1970
TA170.E46 ECOL

EMMEL, THOMAS C.
An introduction to ecology and population biology by Thomas C. Emmel. Norton, 1973
QH541.E45 1973 ECOL

EMMEL, THOMAS C., comp.
Behavior and ecology; a book of readings by Thomas C. Emmel. Kendall/Hunt Pub. Co. 1973
QH541.E44 ECOL

EMMONS, WILLIAM HARVEY, 1876-
Geology: principles and processes by William H. Emmons and others. 5th ed. McGraw-Hill, 1960.
QE26.E6 1960 ECOL

ENCYCLOPEDIA OF SCIENCE AND TECHNOLOGY.
McGraw-Hill encyclopedia of science and technology. 3d ed. 1971
REF fQ121.M3 1971 ECOL

ENERGY AND POWER.
W. H. Freeman c1971 **TJ153.E478 ECOL**

ENERGY, ECONOMIC GROWTH, AND THE ENVIRONMENT; papers presented at a forum conducted by Resources for the Future Inc. in Washington, D.C., 20-21 April 1971. Edited by Sam H. Schurr. Published for Resources for the Future, by the Johns Hopkins University Press 1972
HD9545.E6 ECOL

ENERGY USERS REPORT. Current reports, no. 1- August 16, 1973-
Bureau of National Affairs v.
REF fHD9540.1.E5 ECOL

ENERGY USERS REPORT. CURRENT REPORTS. Supplement; Reference file. c1973-
Bureau of National Affairs v.
REF fHD9540.1.E5 Suppl. ECOL

ENGEL, LEONARD, 1916-1964.
The sea, by Leonard Engel and the editors of Life. Time-Life Books c1969 (Life nature library)
fGC21.E5 1969 ECOL

ENGINEERING A VICTORY FOR OUR ENVIRONMENT: A CITIZEN'S GUIDE TO THE U.S. ARMY CORPS OF ENGINEERS.
by Thomas M. Clement Jr. and others. Project director: Charles M. Clusen. United States Environmental Protection Agency, c1972. 1v.
fTC423.E5 ECOL

ENGINEERING FOR THE BENEFIT OF MANKIND; a symposium held at the third autumn meeting of the National Academy of Engineering.
National Academy of Engineering, 1970.
TA5.E52 ECOL

ENGINEERING INSTITUTE OF CANADA.
Banff Conference on Pollution, 1st, 1968.
Man and his environment. 1st ed. 1970-
TD172.5.B3 1968 ECOL

ENGINEERING-SCIENCE, INC.
Annotated bibliography on hydrology and sedimentation, 1966-68, United States and Canada. Comp. and ed. under the auspices of the Hydrology and Sedimentation Committees, Water Resources Council by Engineering-Science, Inc. 1970
REF Z7935.E5 1970 ECOL
Males, Richard Michael.
Decision processes in water quality management. 1971. **fTD365.M3 ECOL**

ENGSTROM, PAUL H., jt. auth.
Jones, Claire.
Pollution: the air we breathe. 1971
TD883.13.J65 1971 ECOL
Jones, Claire.
Pollution: the balance of nature. 1972
QH541.14.J65 ECOL
Jones, Claire.
Pollution: the dangerous atom. 1972
TD880.J65 1972 ECOL
Jones, Claire.
Pollution: the food we eat. 1972
TX533.J65 ECOL
Jones, Claire.
Pollution: the land we live on. 1971
TD176.J65 1971 ECOL
Jones, Claire.
Pollution: the noise we hear. 1972
TD892.J65 1972 ECOL
Jones, Claire.
Pollution: the population explosion. 1972
HB871.J58 ECOL
Jones, Claire.
Pollution: the waters of the earth. 1971
TD422.J65 ECOL

ENVIRO CONTROL, INC.
Systems analysis for water quality management—survey and abstracts. Prepared for the Water Quality Office, Environmental Protection Agency. U.S. Govt. Print. Off. 1971. v.
fTD365.E5 ECOL

ENVIROGENICS COMPANY.
Investigation of a new phosphate removal process. Prepared for the Water Quality Office, Environmental Protection Agency by L. M. Soffer and others. U.S. Govt. Print. Off., 1970. (Water pollution control research series) **fTD745.E5 ECOL**
Reverse osmosis renovation of primary sewage. U.S. Environmental Protection Agency; for sale by the Supt. of Docs., U.S. Govt. Print. Off., 1971. (Water pollution control research series) **fTD754.E58 ECOL**

ENVIROMETRICS, INC., WASH., D.C.
The river basin model. Environmental Protection Agency, Office of Research and Monitoring, 1971-
v.1- (Water pollution control research series)
fTC409.E5 ECOL
The river basin model: computer output. Environmental Protection Agency, Office of Research and Monitoring, 1971. (Water pollution control research series) **fTC409.E51 ECOL**
The river basin model: municipal services department. Environmental Protection Agency, Office of Research and Monitoring, 1971. (Water pollution control research series) **fTC409.E5 ECOL**

THE ENVIRONMENT; a national mission for the seventies,.
by the editors of Fortune. Harper 1970 (Perennial library, P189) **TD176.7.E45 ECOL**

ENVIRONMENT ACTION BULLETIN. 1973
The Organic guide to colleges and universities.
S946.O73 ECOL

ENVIRONMENT AND CHANGE; the next fifty years.
Commissioned and ed. by William R. Ewald, Jr., on behalf of the American Institute of Planners' fiftieth year consultation. Indiana Univ. Press 1970, c1968
HT167.E46 ECOL

ENVIRONMENT AND POLICY; the next fifty years.
Commissioned and ed. by William R. Ewald, Jr. Indiana Univ. Press 1968 **HT167.E48 ECOL**

19

ENVIRONMENT AND THE SCHOOLS; pioneer programs set the pace for States and districts.
National School Public Relations Association 1971(Education U. S. A. special report)
fHC110.E5E485 ECOL

THE ENVIRONMENT CRISIS; a basic overview of the problem of pollution.
by Daniel M. Rohrer and others. National Textbook Co. 1970 (Contemporary issues series)
TD178.6.E58 ECOL

THE ENVIRONMENT FILM REVIEW: A CRITICAL GUIDE TO ECOLOGY FILMS.
V.1- 1972-
Environment Information Center, Inc., Film Reference Dept. v. **fZ5322.E2E5 ECOL**

ENVIRONMENT FOR MAN; the next fifty years.
Ed. by William R. Ewald, Jr. Indiana Univ. Press 1967 **HT167.E5 1967 ECOL**

THE ENVIRONMENT INDEX: A GUIDE TO THE KEY ENVIRONMENTAL LITERATURE OF THE YEAR. 1971-
Environment Information Center of Ecology Forum
V. **REF fZ7171.E6 ECOL**

ENVIRONMENT INFORMATION CENTER, INC.
The Environment film review: a critical guide to ecology films. v.1- 1972-
fZ5322.E2E5 ECOL

ENVIRONMENT LAW REVIEW. 1970-
Sage Hill Publishers. v. **REF KF3790.A2E5 ECOL**

ENVIRONMENT REPORTER.
Bureau of National Affairs 1970- v.
REF fKF3775.A6E49 ECOL

ENVIRONMENT REPORTER. Cases.
Bureau of National Affairs 1970- v.
REF fKF3775.A6E49 Suppl. ECOL

ENVIRONMENT REPORTER. Current developments. v.1- May 1, 1970-
Bureau of National Affairs. v.
REF fHC110.E5E49 ECOL

ENVIRONMENT, THE UNIVERSITY, & THE WELFARE OF MAN.
Edited by Billy Ray Wilson. Lippincott 1969
LC191.E55 ECOL

ENVIRONMENTAL ACTION (ASSOCIATION).
Earth Day—the beginning. 1970
HC110.E5E2 ECOL

Earth tool kit; a field manual for citizen activists. Prepared by Environmental Action. Editor: Sam Love. Assistant editors: Peter Harnik and Avery Taylor. Pocket Books 1971 **HC110.E5E498 ECOL**

THE ENVIRONMENTAL AND ECOLOGICAL FORUM, 1970-1971.
Forum coordinator: A. Burt Kline, Jr. U.S. Atomic Energy Commission, Office of Information Services; available from National Technical Information Service, U.S. Dept. of Commerce, 1972. **TD898.E58 ECOL**

ENVIRONMENTAL CONTROL: EVERYONE'S CONCERN.
Rex Chainbelt Inc., 1971 1v.
REF fHC68.E5 ECOL

ENVIRONMENTAL CONTROL SEMINAR PROCEEDINGS, Rotterdam, Warsaw, Bucharest, May 25-June 4, 1971.
Bureau of International Commerce; for sale by the Supt. of Docs., U.S. Govt. Print. Off., 1971.
fTD172.5.E26 ECOL

ENVIRONMENTAL CONTROL SYMPOSIUM, SAN FRANCISCO, 1972.
Environmental control; proceedings of symposium, 101st AIME annual meeting. Ed. by Carl Rampacek. Metallurgical Society of AIME, 1972
TD888.M4E58 1972 ECOL

THE ENVIRONMENTAL CRISIS.
Ed. by Harold W. Helfrich, Jr. Yale Univ. Press, 1970; c1970-71 2v. **TD176.7.E472 ECOL**

ENVIRONMENTAL DYNAMICS, INC.
Dracup, John A.
Applications of systems analysis techniques to water resources. 1972. **fTC409.D7 ECOL**

ENVIRONMENTAL EDUCATION MATERIALS.
Educational Products Information Exchange, 1971. (Educational product report, no. 33/34)
REF Z7164.N3E6 ECOL

ENVIRONMENTAL EDUCATION 1970.
Scientists' Institute for Public Information, 1970 (A Scientists' Institute for Public Information workbook)
fS946.E55 ECOL

ENVIRONMENTAL EFFECTS OF WEAPONS TECHNOLOGY.
Comp. by Michael McClintock and others. Scientists' Institute for Public Information, 1970 (A Scientists' Institute for Public Information workbook)
fUG447.8.E57 ECOL

ENVIRONMENTAL FACTORS IN RESPIRATORY DISEASE.
Scientific/editor: Douglas H. K. Lee. Academic Press, 1972.(Environmental sciences)(Fogarty International Center. Proceedings, no. 11)
RC732.E59 ECOL

ENVIRONMENTAL GEOMORPHOLOGY SYMPOSIUM.
Environmental geomorphology; a proceedings volume of the Geomorphology symposia series. 1st- 1970- State Univ., of New York. v. (Publications in geomorphology) **GB400.E58 ECOL**

ENVIRONMENTAL LAW.
Edited by Charles M. Hassett. Institute of Continuing Legal Education 1971 **KF3775.A75E54 ECOL**

Edited by Research and Development Corporation. Research and Development Corp. 1971, c1970 (Radco collections) **KF3775.A75E55 ECOL**

ENVIRONMENTAL LAW INSTITUTE.
Environmental law reporter. v.1- Jan. 1971-
REF fKF3775.A6E5 ECOL.

ENVIRONMENTAL LAW REPORTER.
V.1- JAN. 1971-
Environmental Law Institute. v.
REF fKF3775.A6E5 ECOL.

ENVIRONMENTAL MEASUREMENTS, INC.
Monitoring mercury vapor near pollution sites by Anders F. Jepsen and Lee Langan For the Office of Research and Monitoring Environmental Protection Agency. U.S. Govt. Print. Off., 1971. (Water pollution control research series) **fTD427.M4E5 ECOL**

ENVIRONMENTAL MERCURY CONTAMINATION.
Rolf Hartung and Bertram D. Dinman, editors. Ann Arbor Science Publishers 1972
RA1231.M5E58 ECOL

ENVIRONMENTAL MONITORING PROGRAM
Clark, B. W.
Description of the environmental monitoring program for the Monticello nuclear generating plant near Monticello, Minnesota. Rev. ed. 1969.
fTK1377.M6C6 1969 ECOL

ENVIRONMENTAL PERCEPTION AND BEHAVIOR.
David Lowenthal, editor. Dept. of Geography, University of Chicago 1967. (University of Chicago, Dept. of Geography. Research paper, no. 109)
GF51.E5 ECOL

ENVIRONMENTAL PROBLEMS; pesticides, thermal pollution & environmental synergisms.
Ed. by Billy Ray Wilson. Lippincott 1968
TD180.E48 ECOL

ENVIRONMENTAL QUALITY AND SOCIAL RESPONSIBILITY.
Edited by Ravindra S. Khare, James W. Kolka and Carol A. Pollis. University of Wisconsin-Green Bay 1972 **HC110.P55E57 ECOL**

ENVIRONMENTAL QUALITY FORUM, EAST TENNESSEE STATE UNIVERSITY, 1970.
The Nation's environment—problems and action. Research Advisory Council, East Tennessee State University c1971 **TD172.5.E58 1970 ECOL**

ENVIRONMENTAL REQUIREMENTS OF BLUE-GREEN ALGAE; proceedings of a symposium jointly sponsored by University of Washington and Federal Water Pollution Control Administration, Pacific Northwest Water Laboratory, September 23-24, 1966.
Pacific Northwest Water Laboratory, 1967.
QK569.C96E56 ECOL

ENVIRONMENTAL RESEARCH AND APPLICATIONS, INC.
Concentrated mine drainage disposal into sewage treatment systems; the disposal of acid brines from acid mine drainage in municipal wastewater treatment. Environmental Protection Agency, Research and Monitoring 1971. (Water pollution control research series) **fTD899.M5E58 ECOL**

ENVIRONMENTAL SCIENCE & TECHNOLOGY.
Pollution control directory. 1971/72- American Chemical Society. v. **REF fTD180.E52 ECOL**

ENVIRONMENTAL SIDE EFFECTS OF RISING INDUSTRIAL OUTPUT.
Ed. by Alfred J. Van Tassel. Heath Lexington Books 1970 **TD174.E58 ECOL**

ENVIRONMENTAL STUDIES.
Rev. ed.? American Geological Institute 1971,c1970 **LB1027.E6 1971 ECOL**

ENVIRONMENTAL STUDIES BOARD.
Jamaica Bay Environmental Study Group.
Jamaica Bay and Kennedy Airport: a multidisciplinary environmental study. 1971.
fTL725.3.P5J3 ECOL

ENVIRONMENTAL STUDIES BOARD. COMMITTEE FOR INTERNATIONAL ENVIRONMENTAL PROGRAMS.
Institutional arrangements for international environmental cooperation; a report to the Department of State. National Academy of Sciences, 1972.
HC79.E5E6 ECOL

ENVIRONMENTAL SURVEILLANCE IN THE VICINITY OF NUCLEAR FACILITIES; proceedings of a symposium, sponsored by the Health Physics Society.
Ed. by William C. Reinig. Thomas 1970
REF TD887.R3E58 ECOL

ENVIRONMENTAL SYSTEMS CORPORATION.
Development and demonstration of low-level drift instrumentation. Authors: Frederick M. Shofner and Carl O. Thomas. Prepared for Environmental Protection Agency. U.S. Environmental Protection Agency., U.S. Govt. Print. Off. 1971. (Water pollution control research series) **fTD884.5.E58 ECOL**

EPIDEMIOLOGICAL RESEARCH.
Toxicologic and epidemiologic bases for air quality criteria. 1969 **REF fTD890.T6 ECOL**

EPPLEY, RICHARD W.
California. University. Institute of Marine Resources.
Eutrophication in coastal waters: nitrogen as a controlling factor. 1971. **fQH96.8.E9C34 ECOL**

EPSTEIN, MICHAEL M., jt. auth.
Widman, Michael U.
Polymer film overlay system for mercury contaminated sludge—Phase I. 1972.
fTD427.M4W5 ECOL

EPSTEIN, SAMUEL S.
Toxicologic and epidemiologic bases for air quality criteria. 1969 **REF fTD890.T6 ECOL**

EPSTEIN, SAMUEL S., ed.
The Mutagenicity of pesticides: concepts and evaluation. 1971 **RA1270.P4M87 ECOL**

ERIC *see* UNITED STATES. EDUCATIONAL RESOURCES INFORMATION CENTER.

ERIC INFORMATION ANALYSIS CENTER FOR SCIENCE, MATHEMATICS AND ENVIRONMENTAL EDUCATION.
Roth, Robert E.
A review of research related to environmental education. 1972. **QH541.2.R6 ECOL**

ERRINGTON, PAUL LESTER, 1902-
Of men and marshes. Illus. with drawings by H. Albert Hochbaum. Macmillan, 1957.
QH87.3.E7 ECOL

ESCARCEGA, E. D., jt. auth.
Bouwer, Herman.
Renovating secondary sewage by ground water recharge with infiltration basins. 1972.
fTD765.B6 ECOL

ESCHMAN, DONALD F., jt. auth.
Dorr, John A.
Geology of Michigan. c1970
REF fQE125.D6 ECOL

ESKEW, GARNETT LAIDLAW, 1894-
Of land and men; the birth and growth of an idea by Garnett Laidlaw Eskew, assisted by John R. MacDonald Urban Land Institute c1959
NA9000.U715 ECOL

ESPEY, WILLIAM H.
Tracor, Inc.
Estuarine modeling: an assessment. 1971.
fTD370.T73 ECOL

ESPOSITO, JOHN C., 1940-
Vanishing air. 1970. **TD883.2.V35 ECOL**

ESTRIDGE, R. B.
Georgia Kraft Company. Research and Development Center.
Treatment of selected internal kraft mill wastes in a cooling tower. 1971. **fTD899.W65G46 ECOL**

EVANS, DAVID R.
South Tahoe Public Utility District.
Advanced wastewater treatment as practiced at South Tahoe. 1971. **fTD225.T25S6 ECOL**

EVANS, FRANCIS L.
Ozone in water and wastewater treatment. Francis L. Evans III, editor. Ann Arbor Science Publishers 1972
TD461.E93 ECOL

EVANS, HOWARD ENSIGN.
The wasps, by Howard E. Evans and Mary Jane West Eberhard. Drawings by Sarah Landry. University of Michigan Press 1970 (Ann Arbor science library)
QL568.V5E8 ECOL

EVANS, ROBERT GAGE, 1934- jt. auth.
Humphrey, Clifford C.
What's ecology? 1971 **QH541.13.H84 ECOL**

EVERHART, WILLIAM C.
The National Park Service by William C. Everhart. Foreword by George B. Hartzog, Jr. Praeger Publishers c1972 (Praeger library of U.S. Government departments and agencies, no. 31)
SB482.A4E95 ECOL

EVERS, ROBERT AUGUST, 1912-
Poisonous plants of the Midwest & their effects on livestock, by Robert A. Evers & Roger P. Link. Distributed by University of Illinois Press 1972 (University of Illinois at Urbana-Champaign, College of Agriculture. Special publication 24) **SB617.E9 ECOL**

EWALD, WILLIAM R.
McCue, Gerald M.
Creating the human environment. 1970
HN59.M22 ECOL

EWALD, WILLIAM R., ed.
Environment and change. 1970, c1968
HT167.E46 ECOL

Environment and policy. 1968 **HT167.E48 ECOL**

Environment for man. 1967
HT167.E5 1967 ECOL

EWER, R. F.
The carnivores by R. F. Ewer. Cornell University Press 1973 **QL737.C2E93 ECOL**

EXCERPTA MEDICA.
Excerpta Medica Foundations.
Poisoning and intoxication by trace elements in children: an abstract review of the world-wide medical literature 1966-1971. 1973 **RA1211.E9 ECOL**

EXCERPTA MEDICA FOUNDATIONS.
Poisoning and intoxication by trace elements in children: an abstract review of the world-wide medical literature 1966-1971. Prepared by Excerpta Medica Health Services and Mental Health Administration, Division of Community Injury Control 1973
RA1211.E9 ECOL

EXTRACTIVE RESOURCES AND TAXATION: PROCEEDINGS.
Ed. by Mason Gaffney. Univ. of Wisconsin Press, 1967. **HC106.5.E93 ECOL**

F

FABER, H. A., jt. auth.
American Water Works Association Research Foundation, New York
Information resource: water pollution control in the water utility industry. 1971. **REF fTD429.A4 ECOL**

FABRICANT, NEIL, 1937-
Toward a rational power policy: energy, politics, and pollution; a report by the Environmental Protection Administration of the City of New York. Prepared and written by Neil Fabricant and Robert Marshall Hallman. G. Braziller 1971 **HD9685.U5F32 ECOL**

FABUN, DON.
Dimensions of change, by Don Fabun, assisted by Kathy Hyland and Robert Conover, art director. Glencoe Press 1971 **fHM221.F32 ECOL**

The dynamics of change, by Don Fabun, assisted by Niels Sundermeyer. Art director: Bob Conover Prentice-Hall 1967 1 v. **fCB427.F25 ECOL**

FADIMAN, CLIFTON, 1904- comp.
Ecocide—and thoughts toward survival. Edited by Clifton Fadiman and Jean White. Center for the Study of Democratic Institutions 1971
HC110.E5F32 ECOL

FAIN, CHARLES CLIFFORD, jt. auth.
Hulbert, Samuel F.
Design of a water-disposable glass packaging container. 1971. **TD799.H8 ECOL**

FAIR, GORDON MASKEW, 1894-
Water and wastewater engineering by Gordon Maskew Fair, John Charles Geyer and Daniel Alexander Okun. With chapters on information analysis and optimization techniques by Myron Bernard Fiering. Wiley 1966-1968 2v. **REF TD145.F32 ECOL**

FAIRBRIDGE, RHODES WHITMORE, 1914-
The encyclopedia of geochemistry and environmental sciences. Edited by Rhodes W. Fairbridge. Van Nostrand Reinhold Co. 1972 (Encyclopedia of earth sciences series, v. 4A) **REF QE515.F24 ECOL**

FAIRBROTHER, NAN.
New lives, new landscapes; planning for the 21st century. With a foreword by Walter Muir Whitehill. 1st American ed. Knopf, 1970.
HT395.G7F3 1970 ECOL

FAIRCHILD, DAVID GRANDISON, 1869-1954.
Garden islands of the great East; collecting seeds from the Philippines and Netherlands India in the junk "Cheng ho." Scribner, 1943. **SB109.F185 ECOL**

FAITH, WILLIAM LAWRENCE, 1907-
Air pollution by W. L. Faith and Arthur A. Atkisson, Jr. 2d ed. Wiley-Interscience 1972 (Environmental science and technology) **TD883.F23 1972 ECOL**

FALK, RICHARD A.
This endangered planet; prospects and proposals for human survival by Richard A. Falk. 1st ed. Random House 1971 **HC79.E5F27 ECOL**

FALLIS, A. M., ed.
Ecology and physiology of parasites. 1971
QL757.E26 ECOL

FALTERMAYER, EDMUND K.
Redoing America; a nationwide report on how to make our cities and suburbs livable, by Edmund K. Faltermayer. Harper 1968 **HT123.F3 ECOL**

FAN, CHI-YAUN, jt. auth.
Nebolsine, Ross.
High rate filtration of combined sewer overflows. 1972. **fTD662.N4 ECOL**

FANNING, ODOM.
Opportunities in environmental careers. Vocational Guidance Manuals, Universal Pub. and Distributing Corp. c1971 **S944.F3 ECOL**

FARB, PETER.
Ecology, by Peter Farb and the editors of Time-Life Books. Time-Life Books c1970 (Life nature library)
fQH541.F3 1970 ECOL

Face of North America; the natural history of a continent. Introd. by S. L. Udall. Illus. by Bob Hines and Jerome Connolly. Young readers' ed. Harper 1964
QH104.F32 ECOL

Living earth. Photos. by Roman Vishniac. Drawings by Louise Katz. Harper 1959 **QH84.8.F3 ECOL**

FARB, PETER, jt. auth.
Hay, John.
The Atlantic shore. 1969,c1966.
QH95.7.H3 ECOL

FARRELL, R. PAUL, jt. auth.
Carcich, Italo G.
A pressure sewer system demonstration. 1972.
TD670.C3 ECOL

FARVAR, M. TAGHI, ed.
Conference on the Ecological Aspects of International Development, Airlie House, 1968.
The careless technology: ecology and international development. 1st ed. 1972. **QH540.C65 1968 ECOL**

The Unforseen international ecologic boomerang. 1969 **fQH541.U5 ECOL**

FARVOLDEN, R. N., 1928- jt. auth.
Hughes, George Muggah.
Hydrogeology of solid waste disposal sites in northeastern Illinois. 1971 **TD795.7.H84 ECOL**

FASHINGBAUER, BERNARD A.
Big game in Minnesota. 1965.
SH11.M64no.9 ECOL

FAST, ARLO WADE.
The effects of artificial aeration on lake ecology. Prepared for the Environmental Protection Agency. U.S. Environmental Protection Agency; for sale by the Supt. of Docs., U.S. Govt. Print. Off., 1971 i.e.1972 (Water pollution control research series)
fTD458.F38 ECOL

FAUL, HENRY.
Nuclear clocks. Rev. U.S. Atomic Energy Commission, Division of Technical Information 1968 (United States Atomic Energy Commission. Understanding the atom) **QC798.D3F37 1968 ECOL**

FAULKNER, EDWARD HUBERT, 1886-
Plowman's folly, by Edward H. Faulkner. Univ. of Oklahoma Press 1963,c1943 **S603.F36 1963 ECOL**

Soil development. Univ. of Okla. Press 1952
S603.F37 ECOL

FEDER, BERNARD, 1924-
A matter of life and breath: the politics of pollution. American Book Company c1973
HC110.E5F4 ECOL

FEDERAL CONSTRUCTION COUNCIL. TASK GROUP T-65.
Impact of air pollution regulations on fuel selection for federal facilities. National Academy of Sciences, 1970. (Federal Construction Council. Technical report no. 57) **fKF3812.F4 ECOL**

FEDERAL INTERAGENCY WATER DATA HANDLING WORK GROUP.
Design characteristics for a national system to store, retrieve, and disseminate water data. U.S. Office of Water Data Coordination, 1971. **TD211.F4 ECOL**

FEDERAL INTERAGENCY WORK GROUP ON DESIGNATION OF STANDARDS FOR WATER DATA ACQUISITION.
Recommended methods for water data acquisition. Preliminary report of the Federal Interagency Work Group on Designation of Standards for Water Data Acquisition, impaneled by the U.S. Dept. of the Interior, Geological Survey, Off. of Water Data Coordination. 1972. v. **TD211.F44 ECOL**

FEGELY, THOMAS.
The Organic classroom. c1973 **fS946.O7 ECOL**

FEICK, GEORGE.
Control of mercury contamination in freshwater sediments, by George Feick, Edward E. Johanson and Donald S. Yeaple. Prepared for Office of Research and Monitoring, U.S. Environmental Protection Agency. U.S. Govt. Print. Off., 1972. (Environmental protection technology series) **TD427.M4F4 ECOL**

FEIN, ALBERT.
Frederick Law Olmsted and the American environmental tradition. Braziller c1972
SB470.O5F4 ECOL

FEININGER, ANDREAS, 1906-
Trees. Viking Press 1968 (Studio book)
fQK475.F4 ECOL

FELLMETH, ROBERT C.
Politics of land: Ralph Nader's study group report on land use in California. Grossman, 1973.
HD211.C2F45 ECOL

FENTON, CARROLL LANE, 1900-
Trees and their world, by Carroll Lane Fenton and Dorothy Constance Pallas. Illus. by Carroll Lane Fenton. Day Co. 1957 **QK482.F4 ECOL**

FERKISS, VICTOR C.
Technological man: the myth and the reality by Victor C. Ferkiss. Braziller 1969 **HM221.F39 ECOL**

FINCK, MYRON J. jt. auth.
Flowers, William J.
Western cultural tradition and human survival: the role of value orientations in the environmental crisis. c1971 **GF80.F5 ECOL**

FINDLEY, ROWE.
Great American deserts. Photographed by Walter Meayers Edwards. Foreword by Edmund C. Jaeger. Prepared by the Special Publications Division, National Geographic Society. National Geographic Society, 1972 **F787.F5 ECOL**

FINSTEIN, MELVIN S.
Pollution microbiology; a laboratory manual. Marcel Dekker, 1972. **QR48.F5 ECOL**

FINSTERBUSCH, GAIL W., jt. auth.
Brown, Lester Russell.
Man and his environment: food. 1972
S439.B76 ECOL

FIRSKEY, MARGARET, 1901-
The true book of air around us. Pictures by Katherine Evans. Children's Press 1953 (A true book)
QC863.F846 ECOL

FIRTH, FRANK E.
The encyclopedia of marine resources. Edited by Frank E. Firth. Van Nostrand Reinhold Co. 1969
REF SH201.F56 ECOL

FISCHER, HUGO B., jt. auth.
California. University.
Flow into a stratified reservoir. 1972.
TC167.C3 ECOL

FISH, RICHARD G., illus.
Teal, John.
Life and death of the salt marsh. 1969
QH541.5.S24T4 ECOL

FISHER, JAMES, 1912-
Philip, Duke of Edinburg.
Wildlife crisis. 1st American ed. 1970
S962.P55 ECOL

Wildlife in danger, by James Fisher, Noel Simon, Jack Vincent, and members and correspondents of the Survival Service Commission of the International Union for Conservation of Nature and Natural Resources. Foreword by Harold J. Coolidge and Peter Scott. Pref. by Joseph Wood Krutch. Viking Press 1969 (A Studio book) **REF QL88.F48 ECOL**

FISHER, JAMES, 1912- jt. auth.
Peterson, Roger Tory.
Wild America. 1955. **QH102.P38 ECOL**

FISHER, JOSEPH LYMAN.
World prospects for natural resources; some projections of demand and indicators of supply to the year 2000, by Joseph L. Fisher and Neal Potter. Resources for the Future; dist. by John Hopkins Press, 1964 **HC54.F54 ECOL**

FISHER, TADD.
Our overcrowded world. Parents' Magazine Press 1969 (Background series) **HB871.F53 ECOL**

FISHER, WES comp.
Minnesota environmental education areas, comp. by Wes Fisher and Nancy Gruchow. Ed. by Charles Wechsler. Dept. of Natural Resources, Bureau of Information and Education 1972 **fS946.F5 ECOL**

21

FISHER, WESTON A., jt. auth.
Burke, Jacquelyn M.
The realities of recycling. 1973
REF fTP995.B8 ECOL

FITCH, EDWIN M.
The Bureau of Outdoor Recreation. By Edwin M. Fitch and John F. Shanklin. Foreword by Stewart L. Udall. Praeger 1970 (Praeger library of U.S. government departments and agencies) GV53.F5 ECOL

FITCH, STEVEN VAL.
Air. University of Minnesota, 1971. (Secondary environmental education development) TD883.F5 ECOL

FITNESS FOR LIVING.
The Organic guide to colleges and universities. 1973
S946.O73 ECOL

THE FITNESS OF MAN'S ENVIRONMENT.
With an introd. by Jennie Lee. Smithsonian Institution Press 1968 (Smithsonian annual, 2)
HT166.F53 ECOL

FITTER, RICHARD SIDNEY RICHMOND.
Vanishing wild animals of the world, by Richard Fitter. With 43 paintings by John Leigh-Pemberton. Foreword by HRH the Duke of Edinburgh. Introd. by Peter Scott. F. Watts 1968 fQL88.F5 ECOL

FITTER, RICHARD SIDNEY RICHMOND, jt. auth.
Heinzel, Hermann.
The birds of Britain and Europe with North Africa and Middle East. 1972 QL690.A1H44 ECOL

FITZGERALD, GEORGE PATRICK, 1922-
Nutrient sources for algae and their control, by George P. Fitzgerald. U.S. Environmental Protection Agency; for sale by the Supt. of Docs., U.S. Govt. Print. Off. 1971 i.e.1972 (Water pollution control research series) fQH96.8.E9F58 ECOL

FITZPATRICK GEORGE, 1904- jt. auth.
Tucker, Edwin A.
Men who matched the mountains. 1972
SD143.T8 ECOL

FLACK, JOHN ERNEST, 1929- ed.
Western Resources Conference, 9th, University of Colorado, 1967.
Man and the quality of his environment. 1968
TD180.W4 1967 ECOL

FLANDERS, DAVID.
Circle of the world. QH541.2.C5 Suppl. ECOL

Circle of the world. c1971-
QH541.2.C5 ECOL

FLAWN, PETER TYRELL.
Environmental geology: conservation, land-use planning, and resource management. Harper 1970 (Harper's geoscience series) QE33.F5 ECOL

Mineral resources: geology, engineering, economics, politics, law, by Peter T. Flawn. Rand McNally 1966 (Rand McNally geology series)
HD9506.A2F55 ECOL

FLEAGLE, ROBERT GUTHRIE, 1918- ed.
Weather modification. 1969 QC928.W38 ECOL

FLETCHER, COLIN.
The man who walked through time. With photos. taken en route by the author. Knopf, 1967 i.e. 1968
F788.F55 ECOL

FLETCHER, SANDRA.
Science Curriculum Improvement Study.
Life cycles. c1970 LB1585.S32 ECOL

Science Curriculum Improvement Study.
Organisms. c1970 LB1585.S34 ECOL

FLORIDA OCEAN SCIENCES INSTITUTE.
Limitations and effects of waste disposal on an ocean shelf. U.S. Environmental Protection Agency; for sale by the Supt. of Docs., U.S. Govt. Print. Off. 1971 i.e.1972 (Water pollution control research series)
fTD763.F56 ECOL

FLORIDA. UNIVERSITY, GAINESVILLE.
Metcalf and Eddy, Boston.
Storm water management model. 1971.
fGB665.M4 ECOL

FLOWERS, WILLIAM J.
Western cultural tradition and human survival: the role of value orientations in the environmental crisis; a resource unit, by William J. Flowers, Ronald E. Hagberg and Myron F. Finck. Educational Media Research c1971 GF80.F5 ECOL

FOGG, GORDON ELLIOTT.
Algal cultures and phytoplankton ecology by G. E. Fogg. University of Wisconsin Press, 1966, c1965
QK565.F58 ECOL

FOLSOM, PAUL.
And thou shalt die in a polluted land; an approach to Christian ecology. Liguorian Pamphlets & Books 1971
GF80.F6 ECOL

FOOD AND AGRICULTURE ORGANIZATION OF THE UNITED NATIONS.
Atlas of the living resources of the seas. Atlas des resources biologiques des mers. Atlas de los recursos vivos del mar. Prepared by the FAO Dept. of Fisheries. 1972. 1v. REF fGC1015.F6 ECOL

FORBES, ALEXANDER, 1882-
Northernmost Labrador, mapped from the air, by Alexander Forbes, with contributions from O. M. Miller, N. E. Odell and Ernst C. Abbe. American Geographical Society, 1938. (American Geographical Society. Special publication no. 22) F1136.F67 ECOL

FORBES, ROBERT JAMES.
The conquest of nature; technology and its consequences by R. J. Forbes. Praeger 1968 (Britannica perspective) CB478.F57 ECOL

FORBUSH, EDWARD HOWE, 1858-1929.
Birds of Massachusetts and other New England states. Illus. with colored plates from drawings by Louis Agassiz Fuertes and figures and cuts from drawings and photographs by the legislature. Printed by Berwick & Smith, 1925-29 3v. REF QL684.M4F65 ECOL

FORD, RICHARD F., comp.
Readings in aquatic ecology. Edited by Richard F. Ford and William E. Hazen. Saunders, 1972.
QH541.5.W3F67 ECOL

FOREIGN POLICY ASSOCIATION.
Toward the year 2018. c1968 CB161.T6 ECOL

FOREMAN, HARRY, 1915- ed.
Nuclear power and the public. 1970
TK1078.N83 ECOL

FOREST RECREATION SYMPOSIUM, SYRACUSE, N.Y., 1971 Proceedings.
Northeastern Forest Experiment Station, 1971.
SD426.F6 1971 ECOL

FORRESTER, JAY WRIGHT.
World dynamics by Jay W. Forrester. Wright-Allen Press 1971 HD82.F63 ECOL

FORTUNE.
The Environment. 1970 TD176.7.E45 ECOL

The exploding metropolis. Doubleday Anchor Books c1958 HT123.F69 1958 ECOL

FOSS, PHILLIP O., comp.
Politics and ecology. Edited by Phillip O., Foss Duxbury Press 1972 HC110.E5F66 ECOL

Recreation by Phillip O. Foss. Chelsea House Publishers, 1971. (Conservation in the United States; a documentary history) REF GV53.F6 ECOL

FOST, FREDERIC F., 1933- jt. comp.
Day, John A.
Dimensions of the environmental crisis. 1971
HC79.E5D35 ECOL

FOSTER, CATHARINE OSGOOD, 1907-
The organic gardener. Vintage Books 1972
S605.5.F67 1972 ECOL

FOSTER, NANCY.
Freshwater polychaetes (Annelida) of North America. Environmental Protection Agency, 1972. (Biota of freshwater ecosystems, Identification manual, no.4.) fQH96.A2B5no.4 ECOL

FOWLER, JOHN M., ed.
Environmental education 1970. 1970
fS946.E55 ECOL

FOX, CHARLES H.
Radioactive wastes by Charles H. Fox. U.S. Atomic Energy Commission, Division of Technical Information c1965 (Understanding the atom) TD898.F6 ECOL

FOX, CHARLES H. nuclear physicist.
Radioactive wastes. Rev. U.S. Atomic Energy Commission, Division of Technical Information, 1969. (Understanding the atom) TD898.F6 1969 ECOL

FOX, JACKSON L.
The ecology of periphyton in Western Lake Superior, part I—taxonomy and distribution; by Jackson L. Fox, Theron O. Odlaug, Theodore A. Olson. Water Resources Research Center, Univ. of Minn., 1969. (WRRC bulletin no.14) GB701.M554no.14 ECOL

FOX, MATTHEW H., jt. auth.
Barker, Carol M.
Classified files: the yellowing pages. 1972.
JK468.S4B35ECOL

FOX, MICHAEL W., 1937-
Behaviour of wolves, dogs, and related canids, by Michael W. Fox. 1st U.S. ed. Harper & Row 1972, c1971 QL737.C22F69 1972 ECOL

FOX, SIR CYRIL SANKEY, 1886-
Water; a study of its properties, its constitution, its circulation on the earth, and its utilization by man, by Sir Cyril S. Fox. Greenwood Press 1972
GB661.F65 1972 ECOL

FRAM CORPORATION.
Bio-regenerated activated carbon treatment of textile dye wastewater by Fram Corporation on behalf of C. H. Masland & Sons for the Environmental Protection Agency, Water Quality Office. Authors: Clarke A. Rodman and Edward L. Shunney. Environmental Protection Agency, Water Quality Office 1971. (Water pollution control research series)
fTD899.T4F7 ECOL

FRANKEL, LILLIAN BERSON.
This crowded world; an introduction to the study of population by Lillian B. Frankel, Population Reference Bureau, Inc. Columbia Books 1970 HB883.F7 ECOL

FRANKENBERG, ROBERT C. illus.
Heady, Eleanor B.
The soil that feeds us. 1972 PZ10.H42So ECOL

FRANKLIN INSTITUTE, PHILADELPHIA. RESEARCH LABORATORIES.
Investigation of porous pavements for urban runoff control. 1972. fTE215.I58 ECOL

FRANKLIN INSTITUTE, PHILADELPHIA. SCIENCE INFORMATION SERVICE.
Selected urban storm water runoff abstracts, July 1970-June 1971. Prepared for the Environmental Protection Agency, Water Quality Research. U.S. Govt. Print. Off., 1971. (Water pollution control research series) fTD653.F7 ECOL

FRANKLIN, W. E., jt. auth.
Darnay, Arsen.
The role of packaging in solid waste management 1966 to 1976. 1969. TD795.D37 ECOL

FRANKLIN, WILLIAM E.
Environmental impacts of polystyrene foam and molded pulp meat trays, by William E. Franklin and Robert G. Hunt. Prepared for Mobil Chemical Company, Plastics Division. Midwest Research Institute, 1972. fTP373.F7 ECOL

The role of nonpackaging paper in solid waste management, 1966 to 1976, by William E. Franklin and Arsen Darnay. U.S. Solid Waste Management Office; for sale by the Supt. of Docs., U.S. Govt. Print. Off., 1971. (Environmental protection publication) (U.S. Public Health Service publication no. 2040)
TD795.F7 ECOL

FRANKLIN, WILLIAM E., jt. auth.
Darnay, Arsen.
Salvage markets for materials in solid wastes, ... 1972. TD795.D38 ECOL

FRANZINI, JOSEPH B., jt. auth.
Linsley, Ray K.
Water-resources engineering. 2d ed. 1971,c1972
TC145.L55 1972 ECOL

FRASER, DEAN.
The people problem; what you should know about growing population and vanishing resources. Indiana University Press 1971 HB875.F7 1971 ECOL

FREA, JAMES I.
Washout processes in lake systems by James I. Frea, Ting Y. Li. and Robert M. Sykes. 1972.
fTD764.F74 ECOL

FREEDMAN, RONALD, 1917- ed.
Population: the vital revolution. Anchor Books 1964 (VOA forum series) HB881.F76 ECOL

FREEMAN, EDWARD MONROE, 1875-
Minnesota plant diseases, by E. M. Freeman, PH.D. 1905. (Minnesota. Geological and Natural History Survey. Report of the survey. Botanical series V)
REF QK168.F7 ECOL

FREEMAN, MARGARET C., jt. auth.
Park, Charles Frederick.
Affluence in jeopardy. c1968 HD9506.U62P3 ECOL

FREESE, PAUL V.
Full-scale raw wastewater flocculation with polymers, by P. V. Freese and Edward Hicks. Prepared for the Office of Research and Monitoring, Environmental Protection Agency. U.S. Govt. Print. Off., 1970. (Water pollution control research series) fTD751.F7 ECOL

FREEZE, ALLAN R.
A physics-based approach to hydrologic response modeling: Phase I: model development, completion report. IBM Thomas J. Watson Research Center, 1972.
fGB665.F7 ECOL

FREMLING, CALVIN R., 1929-
Minnesota. State College, Winona.
Mayfly distribution as a water quality index. 1970.
fTD370.M562 ECOL

FRENCH, HERBERT E.
Love of earth. Putnam c1973 S936.F7 ECOL

FRENZEL, LOUIS DANIEL, ed.
Ecological studies of the timber wolf in northeastern Minnesota. 1971 SD11.A45476no.52 ECOL

FRETWELL, STEPHEN D.
Populations in a seasonal environment by Stephen D. Fretwell. Princeton University Press, 1972. (Monographs in population biology, 5)
QL752.F73 ECOL

FREY, DAVID GROVE, 1915- ed.
Limnology in North America. Univ. of Wisconsin Press, 1966 c1963
QH96.F7 ECOL

FREY, DAVID GROVE, 1915- jt. auth.
Smith, Ronald W.
Acid mine pollution effects on lake biology. 1971.
fTD899.M5S6 ECOL

FRICKE, JAMES E., ed.
Conference on Noise as a Public Health Hazard, Wash., D.C., 1968.
Noise as a public health hazard. 1969.
RA772.N7C6 ECOL

FRIEDRICH, HERMANN, 1906-
Marine biology, an introduction to its problems and results. Translated from the German by Gwynne Vevers. University of Washington Press 1969 (Biology series)
QH541.5.S3F713 1969 ECOL

FRIENDLY, NATALIE.
Wildlife teams. Illus. by Edna Miller. Prentice-Hall c1963 (P-H junior research books)
PZ10.F7153Wi ECOL

FRIENDS, SOCIETY OF. AMERICAN FRIENDS SERVICE COMMITTEE.
Who shall live? Man's control over birth and death; a report. Hill & Wang 1970
HQ766.3.F7 ECOL

FRIERY, RODNEY N., jt. auth.
Peterson, John H.
Community organization programs and relationships in watershed development. 1972.
fTC409.P4 ECOL

FROME, MICHAEL.
The Forest Service. Praeger 1971 (Praeger library of U. S. Government departments and agencies, no. 30)
SD565.F7 ECOL

FRUH, E. GUS, jt. auth.
Morgan, W. E.
An investigation of phosphorus removal mechanisms in activated sludge systems. 1972.
TD756.M6 ECOL

FUCHS, ERICH.
What makes a nuclear power plant work? Tr. from the German by Edite Kroll. Delacorte Press, 1972.
fPZ10.F77Wh3 ECOL

FUENTES, VICTOR C.
Soil matric suction changes with time in pressed soil briquettes. Water Resources Research Center, University of Minn. Graduate School, 1971. (WRRC bulletin 33)
GB701.M554no.33 ECOL

FUEST, R. W.
Uniroyal, Inc.
Feasibility study of regenerative fibers for water pollution control. 1970 i.e. 1971
fTD757.5.U55 ECOL

FUHRIMAN, DEAN K.
Ground water pollution in Arizona, California, Nevada & Utah, by Dean K. Fuhriman and James R. Barton for the Office of Research and Monitoring, Environmental Protection Agency. U.S. Environmental Protection Agency, U.S. Govt. Print. Off., 1971 i.e. 1972 (Water pollution control research series)
fTD223.9.F85 ECOL

FULLER, RAYMOND TIFFT, 1889-1960.
Now that we have to walk; exploring the out-of-doors. Books for Libraries Press 1972, c1943 (Essay index reprint series)
QH81.F847 1972 ECOL

FULLER, RICHARD BUCKMINSTER, 1895-
Approaching the benign environment by R. B. Fuller, Eric A. Walker and James R. Killian, Jr. Preface by Taylor Littleton. Pub. for Auburn Univ. by Univ. of Alabama Press 1970
Q171.F96 ECOL

Operating manual for spaceship earth. Simon 1969 (Clarion book)
T14.F84 ECOL

FULLER, WILLIAM ALBERT, 1924-
The life of the far north, by W. A. Fuller and John C. Holmes. Pub. in cooperation with the World Book Encyclopedia. McGraw, 1972. (Our living world of nature)
QH541.5.T8F84 ECOL

FUNGAROLI, A. A.
Pollution of subsurface water by sanitary landfills, by A. A. Fungaroli. U.S. Environmental Protection Agency; for sale by the Supt. of Docs., U.S. Govt. Print. Off., 1971 i.e. 1972- v.
TD403.F85 ECOL

FURLONG, STEWART S., jt. auth.
Wylie, Stephen R.
Key to North American waterfowl. 1972
QL696.A5W46 ECOL

G

GABEL, MARGARET.
Sparrows don't drop candy wrappers. Illustrated by Susan Perl. Dodd, Mead 1971
TD176.G3 ECOL

GABRIELSON, IRA NOEL, 1889-
Wildlife conservation. 2d ed. Macmillan 1970, c1959
SK353.G2 1959 ECOL

Wildlife refuges, by Ira N. Gabrielson. Macmillan Co., 1943.
SK357.G3 ECOL

GADLER, STEVE J., jt. auth.
Jones, Claire.
Pollution: the air we breathe. 1971
TD883.13.J65 1971 ECOL

Jones, Claire.
Pollution: the balance of nature. 1972
QH541.14.J65 ECOL

Jones, Claire.
Pollution: the dangerous atom. 1972
TD880.J65 1972 ECOL

Jones, Claire.
Pollution: the food we eat. 1972
TX533.J65 ECOL

Jones, Claire.
Pollution: the land we live on. 1971
TD176.J65 1971 ECOL

Jones, Claire.
Pollution: the noise we hear. 1972
TD892.J65 1972 ECOL

Jones, Claire.
Pollution: the population explosion. 1972
HB871.J58 ECOL

Jones, Claire.
Pollution: the waters of the earth. 1971
TD422.J65 ECOL

GAFFNEY, MASON, ed.
Extractive resources and taxation: proceedings. 1967.
HC106.5.E93 ECOL

GAINESVILLE, FLA. DEPT. OF PUBLIC UTILITIES.
Magnesium carbonate, a recycled coagulant for water treatment by A. P. Black and C. G. Thompson. Prepared for the Environmental Protection Agency, Office of Research and Monitoring. U.S. Govt. Print. Off., 1971. (Water pollution control research series)
fTD433.G3 ECOL

GALBRAITH, JOHN KENNETH, 1908-
The affluent society. 2d ed., rev. Houghton, 1969.
HC106.5.G32 1969 ECOL

Perspectives on conservation. 1969, c1958
HC103.7.P47 1969 ECOL

GALLION, ARTHUR B.
The urban pattern; city planning and design, by Arthur B. Gallion and Simon Eisner. Chapter title sketches by Anthony Stoner. 2d ed. Van Nostrand 1963
NA9031.G3 1963 ECOL

GALLOB, EDWARD.
City leaves, city trees. Photos. and photograms by the author. Scribner 1972
fQK475.8.G35 ECOL

GALSTER, ROBERT, illus.
Billington, Elizabeth T.
Understanding ecology. 1971
QH541.14.B5 1971 ECOL

GAMMON, JAMES ROBERT, 1930-
The effect of inorganic sediment on stream biota, by James R. Gammon for the Water Quality Office of the Environmental Protection Agency. Environmental Protection Agency, Water Quality Office; for sale by the Supt. of Docs., U.S. Govt. Print. Off., 1970. (Water pollution control research series)
fQH541.5.S7G34 ECOL

GAMOW, GEORGE, 1904-
Matter, earth, and sky. 2d ed. Prentice-Hall 1965
QC171.G3 1965 ECOL

GANGEWERE, ROBERT J., comp.
The exploited Eden; literature on the American environment. Edited by Robert J. Gangewere. Harper & Row 1972
PS507.E3G3 ECOL

GARDNER, JOHN F.
A book of nature activities. Interstate Printers and Publishers, 1967
QH53.G3 ECOL

GARRELS, ROBERT MINARD, 1916- jt. auth.
Hunt, Cynthia.
Water: the web of life. 1972
GB661.H84 ECOL

GARROD, D. J., ed.
Conservation and productivity of natural waters. 1972.
QL1.Z733no.29 ECOL

GARVEY, GERALD, 1935-
Energy, ecology, economy. 1st ed. Norton 1972
HC110.E5G35 ECOL

GATES, RICHARD.
The true book of conservation, written and illus. by Richard Gates. Children's Press 1959
PZ10.G493TR ECOL

GATES, WILLIAM E., jt. auth.
Males, Richard Michael.
Decision processes in water quality management. 1971.
fTD365.M3 ECOL

GAUDY, ANTHONY F.
Biological concepts for design and operation of the activated sludge process, by Anthony F. Gaudy, Jr. and Elizabeth T. Gaudy. Prepared for the Office of Research and Monitoring, Environmental Protection Agency. U.S. Environmental Protection Agency U.S. Govt. Print. Off., 1971 i.e. 1972 (Water pollution control research series)
fTD756.G38 ECOL

GAUDY, ELIZABETH T., jt. auth.
Gaudy, Anthony F.
Biological concepts for design and operation of the activated sludge process. 1971 i.e. 1972
fTD756.G38 ECOL

GEDDES, PATRICK, SIR, 1854-1932.
Patrick Geddes: spokesman for man and the environment; a selection. Edited and with an introd. by Marshall Stalley. Rutgers University Press 1972
HT166.G43 1972 ECOL

GEESEY, A. H.
New safety system design for nuclear power reactors, by A. H. Geesey, Jr. and M. A. Schultz. Pennsylvania State University, College of Engineering. 1971. (Engineering research bulletin B-103)
fTA1.P35no.103 ECOL

GEISEL, THEODOR SEUSS, 1904-
The lorax. Random House c1971
fPZ8.3.G276Lo ECOL

GELHAR, L. W.
Ralph M. Parsons Laboratory for Water Resources and Hydrodynamics.
Density induced mixing in confined aquifers. 1972.
fTC176.R33 ECOL

GENERAL DYNAMICS CORPORATION. ELECTRIC BOAT DIVISION.
Potential environmental effects of an offshore submerged nuclear power plant. Prepared for the Water Quality Research Office, Environmental Protection Agency. U.S. Environmental Protection Agency, Water Quality Office; for sale by the Supt. of Docs., U.S. Govt. Print. Off., 1971- v. (Water pollution control research series)
fQH541.5.S3G45 ECOL

GENERAL ELECTRIC COMPANY. RE-ENTRY AND ENVIRONMENTAL SYSTEMS DIVISION.
Watercraft waste treatment system: development and demonstration report, by Arnold J. Bryce and others. Prepared for the Environmental Protection Agency. Research and Monitoring, Environmental Protection Agency, 1971. (Water pollution control research series)
fTD745.G4 ECOL

GENERAL MILLS CHEMICALS.
Feasibility of liquid ion exchange for extracting phosphate from wastewater. Environmental Protection Agency, Water Quality Office; for sale by the Supt. of Docs., U.S. Govt. Print. Off., 1970. (Water pollution control research series)
fTD757.G45 ECOL

GENERAL MOTORS CORPORATION. RESEARCH LABORATORIES.
Symposium on Emissions from Continuous Combustion Systems, General Motors Research Laboratories, 1971.
Emissions from continuous combustion systems. 1972.
TD881.S86 1971 ECOL

GEOMORPHOLOGY SYMPOSIA SERIES.
Environmental Geomorphology Symposium.
Environmental geomorphology.
GB400.E58 ECOL

GEORGESCU-ROEGEN, NICHOLAS.
The entropy law and the economic process. Harvard University Press, 1971.
HB171.G43 ECOL

GEORGIA. INSTITUTE OF TECHNOLOGY, ATLANTA. ENVIRONMENTAL RESOURCES CENTER.
McClanahan, Mark A.
A study of the effects of island development on lake water quality. 1972.
fTD224.G4M3 ECOL

Willeke, Gene E.
A program for metropolitan water management. 1972.
fTD365.W5 ECOL

GEORGIA. INSTITUTE OF TECHNOLOGY, ATLANTA. GRADUATE CITY PLANNING PROGRAM.
Kelnhofer, Guy J.
Metropolitan planning and river basin planning: some interrelationships. 1968.
TD223.K4 ECOL

GEORGIA. INSTITUTE OF TECHNOLOGY, ATLANTA. SCHOOL OF CIVIL ENGINEERING.
McClanahan, Mark A.
A study of the effects of island development on lake water quality. 1972. **fTD224.G4M3 ECOL**

GEORGIA. INSTITUTE OF TECHNOLOGY, ATLANTA. WATER RESOURCES CENTER OF TECHNOLOGY, ATLANTA.
Kelnhofer, Guy J.
Metropolitan planning and river basin planning: some interrelationships. 1968. **TD223.K4 ECOL**

GEORGIA KRAFT COMPANY. RESEARCH AND DEVELOPMENT CENTER.
Treatment of selected internal kraft mill wastes in a cooling tower. Authors: J. A. McAlister, B. G. Turner, and R. B. Estridge. U.S. Environmental Protection Agency; for sale by the Supt. of Docs., U.S. Govt. Print. Off., 1971. (Water pollution control research series) **fTD899.W65G46 ECOL**

GEOTHERMAL WORLD DIRECTORY, 1972-
Compiled, edited and published by Katherine F. Meadows, Glendora, Calif. v. **fGB1003.G46 ECOL**

GERBER, CARL R.
Plowshare by Carl R. Gerber, Richard Hamburger and E. W. Seabrook Hull. U.S. Atomic Energy Commission, Division of Technical Information 1966 (Understanding the atom) **TK9153.G4 ECOL**

GERKING, SHELBY DELOS, 1918-
Biological systems by Shelby D. Gerking. W. B. Saunders, 1969. **QH308.G44 ECOL**

GERLACH, LUTHER P.
Mobilization and participation of citizens groups in improving the quality of water resources environments. Univ. of Minn., Water Resources Research Center, 1973. (Minnesota. University. Water Resources Research Center. WRRC bulletin 57)
GB701.M554no.57 ECOL

GEROUDET, PAUL, jt. auth.
Simon, Noel.
Last survivors. 1970 **QL88.S553 ECOL**

GEYER, JOHN CHARLES, 1906-
Fair, Gordon Maskew.
Water and wastewater engineering. 1966-1968 **REF TD145.F32 ECOL**

GHASSEMI, MASOOD.
Phosphate precipitation with ferrous iron, by Masood Ghassemi and Howard L. Recht. U.S. Environmental Protection Agency U.S. Govt. Print. Off., 1971. (Water pollution control research series) **fTD751.G4 ECOL**

GIBBONS, EUELL.
Stalking the blue-eyed scallop. With illus. by C. R. Hammond. McKay Co. 1964 **TX387.G5 ECOL**
Stalking the good life; my love affair with nature. Illustrated by Freda Gibbons. D. McKay Co. 1971
QK98.5.G45 ECOL
Stalking the wild asparagus. With illus. by Margaret D. Schroeder. McKay Co. 1970, c1962
QK98.5.G48 ECOL

GIBBS, K. C., jt. auth.
Reiling, S. D.
Economic benefits from an improvement in water quality. 1973. **fTD370.R45 ECOL**

GIBSON, J. SULLIVAN.
Soils: their nature, classes, distribution, uses, and care, by J. Sullivan Gibson and James W. Batten. University of Alabama Press 1970 **S591.G52 ECOL**

GIBSON, ULRIC P.
Integrating water quality management into total water resources management in Minnesota, by U. P. Gibson, Conrad P. Straub and Richard G. Bond. Water Resources Research Center, Univ. of Minn., Graduate School, 1970. (WRRC bulletin, 23)
GB701.M554no.23 ECOL

GIBSON, WILLIAM LLOYD, 1910- ed.
Symposium on Research Methods, Virginia Polytechnic Institute, 1965.
Methods for land economics research. 1967?,c1966
HD110.S9 1965 ECOL

GIEFER, GERALD J.
Water publications of State agencies; a bibliography of publications on water resources and their management published by the States of the United States. Edited by Gerald J. Giefer and David K. Todd. With the assistance of Mary Louise Quinn. Water Information Center 1972 **REF Z7935.G55 ECOL**

GILBERT, DOUGLAS L.
Natural resources and public relations by Douglas L. Gilbert. Wildlife Society, 1971. **S944.G48 ECOL**

GILLIAM, HAROLD.
For better or for worse; the ecology of an urban area. Chronicle Books 1972 **HC107.C22S363 ECOL**

GLASS, HIRAM BENTLEY, 1906-
Science and ethical values, by Bentley Glass. Univ. of North Carolina Press 1965 (The John Calvin McNair lectures) **Q175.G58 ECOL**
The timely and the timeless; the interrelationships of science, education, and society, by Bentley Glass. Foreword by Ward Madden. Basic Books 1970 (The John Dewey society lecture, No. 11)
Q181.G45 ECOL

GLASSTONE, SAMUEL, 1897-
Atomic energy and your world, by Samuel Glasstone and S. Joe Thomas. U.S. Atomic Energy Commission, Division of Technical Information, 1970 (A World of the atom series booklet) **QC792.G55 ECOL**
Controlled nuclear fusion. Rev. ed. U.S. Atomic Energy Commission, Division of Technical Information 1968 (Understanding the atom)
QC791.G48 1968 ECOL

GLEASON, HENRY ALLAN, 1882-
The natural geography of plants by Henry A. Gleason and Arthur Cronquist. Columbia Univ. Press, 1964. **QK101.G57 ECOL**

GLENN, HAROLD T.
Automotive smog control manual by Harold T. Glenn. Cowles Education Corp. 1968 (A Cowles repair book) **TL152.G545 ECOL**

GLENNY, MICHAEL.
Urban, George R.
Can we survive our future? 1972, c1971
CB428.U7 1972 ECOL

GLOSSARY: WATER AND WASTEWATER CONTROL ENGINEERING.
Prepared by joint editorial board representing American Public Health Association and others. William T. Ingram: chairman. American Public Health Association, 1969. **TD9.G55 ECOL**

GLOYNA, EARNEST F., ed.
Water quality improvement by physical and chemical processes. 1970 **TD745.W37 ECOL**

GLOYNA, EARNEST F., jt. auth.
Davis, Ernst M.
Bacterial effects of algae on enteric organisms. 1970 **fQR48.D38 ECOL**

GLUCKMAN, LILLIAN A., ed.
Symposium of State and Interstate Solid Waste Planning Agencies, St. Louis, 1969.
Planning for solid waste management. 1971
TD523.S94 1969 ECOL

GLYSSON, EUGENE A.
The problem of solid-waste disposal, by Eugene A. Glysson, James R. Packard and Cyril H. Barnes. College of Engineering, Univ. of Mich. 1972. (Ingenor 9)
TD791.G5 ECOL

GODFREY, ARTHUR, 1903- comp.
The Arthur Godfrey environmental reader. Ed., and with an introd. by Arthur Godfrey. Ballantine Books 1970 **QH541.13.G6 ECOL**

GOERING, OSWALD H., 1923- jt. auth.
Van der Smissen, Margaret Elisabeth.
A leader's guide to nature-oriented activities. 2d ed. 1968 **GV182.2.V3 1968 ECOL**

GOERING, OSWALD H., 1923- jt. comp.
Donaldson, George Warren.
Perspectives on outdoor education. 1972
LB1047.D6 ECOL

GOFMAN, JOHN WILLIAM.
Poisoned power; the case against nuclear power plants, by John W. Gofman and Arthur R. Tamplin. With a foreword by Mike Gravel. Rodale Press 1971
TK9152.G57 ECOL

GOFMAN, JOHN WILLIAM, jt. auth.
Tamplin, Arthur R.
Population control through nuclear pollution. 1970
RA569.T35 ECOL

GOLANY, PINHAS.
Effects of channel characteristics on time parameters for small watershed runoff hydrographs, by Pinhas Golany and Curtis L. Larson. Water Resources Research Center University of Minnesota Graduate School, 1971. (WRRC bulletin, no.31)
GB701.M554no.31 ECOL

GOLDBERG, EDWARD D., jt. comp.
Matthews, William Henry.
Man's impact on terrestrial and oceanic ecosystems. 1971 **TD174.M39 ECOL**

GOLDBERG, EVERETT F., jt. auth.
Maryland. University. School of Law.
Legal problems of coal mine reclamation. 1972.
fKF1830.Z95M37 ECOL

GOLDER, FRANK ALFRED, 1877-1929.
Bering's voyage; an account of the efforts of the Russians to determine the relation of Asia and America, by F. A. Golder. American Geographical Society, 1922-25. 2v. (American Geographical Society. Research series no.1-2. W. L. G. Joerg, editor)
G296.B4G6 ECOL

GOLDIN, AUGUSTA R.
Where does your garden grow? By Augusta Goldin. Illus. by Helen Borten. Crowell 1967 (Let's read-and-find-out science books)
PZ10.G564Wh ECOL

GOLDMAN, MARSHALL I.
The spoils of progress: environmental pollution in the Soviet Union by Marshall I. Goldman. M. I. T. Press 1972 **TD187.5.R9G63 ECOL**

GOLDMAN, MARSHALL I. ed.
Controlling pollution; the economics of a cleaner America, ed. by Marshall I. Goldman. Prentice-Hall c1967 (Modern economic issues) **TD180.G58 ECOL**

GOLDSMITH, EDWARD, 1928- ed.
Blueprint for survival. 1972. **S936.B5 1972 ECOL**

GOLDSTEIN, JEROME, 1931-
Garbage as you like it. Illus. by Virginia Howie. Rodale Books 1969 **TD795.G6 ECOL**
How to manage your company ecologically. Illus. by Virginia Howie. Rodale Press; distributed by McKay 1971 **HD69.P6G65 ECOL**

GOLDSTEIN, JON H.
Competition for wetlands in the Midwest; an economic analysis, by Jon H. Goldstein. Resources for the Future; Distributed by the Johns Hopkins Press, 1971 **HD1683.U4G6 ECOL**

GOOD, DOROTHY, jt. ed.
Pratt, Wallace Everett.
World geography of petroleum. 1950.
REF TN870.P73 ECOL

GOODALE, THOMAS L., ed.
Conference on Environmental Impact Analysis, Green Bay, Wis., 1972.
Environmental impact analysis: philosophy & methods. 1972 **HC110.E5C65 1972 ECOL**

GOODALL, J. D.
Las aves de Chile; su Conocimiento y sus costumbres por J. D. Goodall, A. W. Johnson y R. A. Philippi B. Laminas de J. P. Goodall. Platt Establecimientos Graficos, S.A., 1946 v.1-
Ref QL689.C5G6 ECOL

GOODFRIEND (L.S.) ASSOCIATES.
Noise from industrial plants. Prepared for the United States Office of Noise Abatement and Control. United States Environmental Protection Agency, 1971. v.
fTD892.G66 ECOL

GOODIER, J. L.
Little (Arthur D.) Inc.
Spill prevention techniques for hazardous polluting substances: an inventory and survey of hazardous chemical facilities in Charleston, West Virginia; Baltimore, Maryland; Texas City, Texas; and the Suisun Bay-Delta Area, California. 1971.
fT55.3.H3L4 ECOL

GOODMAN, BRIAN L.
Design handbook of wastewater systems: domestic, industrial, commercial by Brian L. Goodman. Technomic Pub. Co. 1971 **REF fTD745.G65 ECOL**
Manual for activated sludge sewage treatment by Brian L. Goodman. Technomic Pub. Co. 1971
REF fTD756.G66 ECOL

GOODMAN, FREDERICK L.
United States. Educational Resources Information Center.
Thesaurus of ERIC descriptors, with a special chapter on The role and function of the thesaurus in education. 1972. **REF fZ695.1.E3U5 1972 ECOL**

GOODMAN, GORDON T., ed.
Ecology and the industrial society; a symposium of the British Ecological Society, Swansea, 13-16 April 1964. Ed. by Gordon T. Goodman, R. W. Edwards, and J. M. Lambert. Wiley 1965 (British Ecological Society. Symposium no.5) **TD180.G6 ECOL**

GOODMAN, ROBERT, 1936-
After the planners. Simon and Schuster 1972, c1971
HT166.G64 ECOL

GORDEN, MARSHA, jt. comp.
Gorden, Morton.
Environmental management. 1972
TD177.G67 ECOL

GORDEN, MORTON, 1933- comp.
Environmental management; science and politics by Morton Gorden and Marsha Gorden. Chapter illus. by Winnie Fitch. Allyn and Bacon 1972
TD177.G67 ECOL

GORZUCHOWSKI, STANISLAW.
Boyd, Louise Arner.
Polish countrysides. 1937. **DK407.B6 ECOL**

GOTTMANN, JEAN. MEGALOPOLIS.
Von Eckardt, Wolf.
The challenge of Megalopolis. 1964.
HT123.5.A12V6 ECOL

GRAD, FRANK P.
Environmental control: priorities, policies, and the law by Frank P. Grad, George W. Rathjens and Albert J. Rosenthal. Columbia University Press, 1971.
HC110.E5G7 ECOL
Environmental law; sources and problems by Frank P. Grad. M. Bender, 1971- 1 v.
REF KF3775.A7G73 ECOL

GRAHAM, ADA.
Puffin Island, by Ada and Frank Graham, Jr. Photographed by Les Line. 1st ed. Cowles Book Co. 1971 **QL676.G68 1971 ECOL**
Wildlife rescue; alternative to extinction, by Ada and Frank Graham, Jr. Cowles 1970 **S962.G68 ECOL**

GRAHAM, FRANK, 1925-
Disaster by default; politics and water pollution. With a foreword by Harry and Bonaro Overstreet. Modern Library 1966 **TD223.G7 1966 ECOL**
Man's dominion; the story of conservation in America. Drawings by John Pimlott. M. Evans; distributed in association with Lippincott, 1971
S930.G7 ECOL
Since Silent spring. Houghton, 1970.
QH75.G68 ECOL

GRAHAM, FRANK, 1925- jt. auth.
Graham, Ada.
Puffin Island. 1st ed. 1971
QL676.G68 1971 ECOL
Graham, Ada.
Wildlife rescue. 1970 **S962.G68 ECOL**

GRAHAM, JOHN, 1933-
Fast reactor safety. Academic Press, 1971. (Nuclear science and technology, a series of monographs and textbooks, 8) **TK9152.G68 ECOL**

GRAND CANYON SYMPOSIUM, 1970.
Environment, man, survival: Grand Canyon Symposium, 1970. L. H. Wullstein, I. B. McNulty and L. Klikoff, editors. Dept. of Biology, University of Utah c1971 **GF8.G7 1970 ECOL**

GRANT, SHARON G., jt. auth.
Dracup, John A.
Applications of systems analysis techniques to water resources. 1972. **fTC409.D7 ECOL**

GRAVA, SIGURD.
Urban planning aspects of water pollution control. Columbia Univ. Press, 1969. **TD420.G67 ECOL**

GRAVES, CHARLES PARLIN, 1911-1972.
John Muir, by Charles P. Graves. Illustrated by Robert Levering. Crowell, 1973 (A Crowell biography) **QH31.M9G66 ECOL**

GRAVES, JOHN, 1920-
Boyle, Robert H.
The water hustlers. 1971 **HD1694.A5B58 ECOL**

GRAVES, QUINTIN B.
Oklahoma. State University of Agriculture and Applied Science, Stillwater. School of Civil Engineering.
Aerobic digestion of organic waste sludge. 1971 i.e. 1972 **fTD769.O35 ECOL**

GRAY, PETER, 1908- ed.
The encyclopedia of the biological sciences. 2d ed. Van Nostrand Reinhold Co. 1970
REF QH13.G7 1970 ECOL

GRAY, ROBERT, 1922-
Cougar; the natural life of a North American mountain lion. Grosset c1972 **QL737.C2G73 ECOL**

GREAT BRITAIN. CENTRAL ADVISORY WATER COMMITTEE.
The future management of water in England and Wales: a report by the Central Advisory Water Committee. H. M. S. O., 1971.
TD257.A5 1971 ECOL

GREAT BRITAIN. DEPT. OF EDUCATION AND SCIENCE.
Keeping animals in schools; a handbook for teachers. H. M. Stationery Off., 1971. **QL51.G7 ECOL**

GREAT BRITAIN. DEPT. OF THE ENVIRONMENT.
Great Britain. Central Advisory Water Committee.
The future management of water in England and Wales: a report. 1971. **TD257.A5 1971 ECOL**

GREAT BRITAIN. WORKING PARTY ON REFUSE DISPOSAL.
Refuse disposal; report. H. M. Stationery Off., 1971.
TD557.A53 ECOL

GREAT LAKES BASIN COMMISSION.
The future of the Great Lakes: a public meeting. 1972 (its Great Lakes basin framework study)
fGB1627.G8G7 ECOL
Hydroscience, Inc.
Limnological systems analysis of the Great Lakes. 1973. **fTC423.3.H9 ECOL**

GREAT LAKES BASIN COMMISSION. FISH WORK GROUP.
Analysis of fishery programs and review of current plans for the management of fishery resources of the Great Lakes. 1969. (its Study memorandum 8-1)
SH36.G76 ECOL

GREAT LAKES BASIN LIBRARY.
Book catalog. Great Lakes Basin Commission, 1969- v. **REF fZ7164.N3G75 ECOL**
An interim bibliography. Great Lakes Commission, 1969- v.1- **REF fZ7164.N3G7 ECOL**

GREAT LAKES FOUNDATION, ANN ARBOR, MICH.
The common law of water, ed. by members of the Illinois Bar. c1971. **KF3790.Z9L4 ECOL**

GREATER PROVIDENCE CHAMBER OF COMMERCE.
North Eastern Regional Antipollution Conference, 4th, University of Rhode Island, 1971.
Recent developments in industrial pollution control. 1971 **fTD896.N67 1971 ECOL**

GREELEY, WILLIAM BUCKHOUT, 1879-
Forests and men. Doubleday, 1951.
SD143.G74 ECOL

GREEN BAY (WIS.) METROPOLITAN SEWERAGE DISTRICT.
Joint treatment of municipal sewage and pulp mill effluents. A report for the Environmental Protection Agency. U.S. Environmental Protection Agency, U.S. Govt. Print. Off. 1970. (Water pollution control research series) **fTD524.W6G74 ECOL**

GREEN GIANT COMPANY.
Pilot plant installation for fungal treatment of vegetable canning wastes. U.S. Environmental Protection Agency; for sale by the Supt. of Docs., U.S. Govt. Print. Off., 1971. (Water pollution control research series) **fTD899.C3G74 ECOL**

GREEN, IVAH.
Wildlife in danger. With introd. by Robert Porter Allen. Coward-McCann 1960 **QL151.G7 ECOL**

GREEN, JAMES L.
Economic ecology; baselines for urban development, by James L. Green. University of Georgia Press c1969 **HT167.G74 ECOL**

GREENBERG, DAVID BENJAMIN, 1892-1968, comp.
Land that our fathers plowed; the settlement of our country as told by the pioneers themselves and their contemporaries. Comp. and ed. by David B. Greenberg. Univ. of Okla. Press 1969 **S521.G83 ECOL**

GREGORY, G. ROBINSON, 1915-
Forest resource economics by G. Robinson Gregory. Ronald Press 1972 **HD9755.G7 ECOL**

GRETHER, DAVID F.
Population type, distribution and density of the flora on the Sherburne County Generating Plant Site, 15 October through 31 December, 1971. Northern States Power Co.?, 1972 1v. **fTK1331.N6G7 ECOL**

GREY, JERRY.
The race for electric power. Westminster Press 1972
TK1001.G73 ECOL

GRIFF, BERNIE.
The Ecology sea in song and ballad. 1973?
Phonodisc GC31.E2 ECOL

GRIFFITH, CHARLES J.
EP—the new conservation, by Charles J. Griffith, Edward Landin and Karen Jostad. Izaak Walton League of America 1971 **HC110.E5G74 ECOL**

GRIFFITHS, JOEL.
Silent slaughter by Joel Griffiths and Richard Ballantine. Regnery 1972 **RA1231.R2G74 ECOL**

GRIMA, ANGELO P.
Residential water demand; alternative choices for management by Angelo P. Grima. Published for the Univ. of Toronto Dept. of Geography by the Univ. of Toronto Press 1972 **TD353.G7 ECOL**

GRIMM, WILLIAM CAREY, 1907-
Home guide to trees, shrubs, and wild flowers. Stackpole Books 1970 **QK482.G734 ECOL**

GRIMSRUD, G. PAUL, jt. auth.
Beckers, Charles V.
Quantitative methods for preliminary design of water quality surveillance systems. 1972.
TD365.B4 ECOL

GRISCOM, LUDLOW, 1890-
The warblers of America; a popular account of the wood warblers as they occur in the Western Hemisphere, by Ludlow Griscom, Alexander Sprunt, Jr., and other ornithologists of note. Illus. by John Henry Dick. Devin-Adair, 1957.
REF QL696.P2G85 ECOL

GROMAN, WILLIAM A.
Forest fertilization (a state-of-the-art review and description of environmental effects). National Environmental Research Center, Office of Research and Monitoring, U.S. Environmental Protection Agency, 1972. (Environmental protection technology series) **SD408.G7 ECOL**

GRONWALD, RONALD F., jt. auth.
Larson, Curtis L.
Predicting peak flow of small watersheds by use of channel characteristics. 1972.
GB701.M554no.52 ECOL

GROSS, BERTRAM MYRON, 1912-
Social intelligence for America's future; explorations in societal problems. Bertram M. Gross, editor. Allyn and Bacon 1969 **HN59.G76 ECOL**

GROSS, PHYLLIS.
Teaching science in an outdoor environment, by Phyllis Gross and Esther P. Railton. Drawings by Lynne and Toni Justino. University of California Press, 1972. (California natural history guides, 30)
QH51.G867 ECOL

GROSSMAN, MARY LOUISE.
Our vanishing wilderness, by Mary Louise and Shelly Grossman and John N. Hamlet. Photos. by Shelly Grossman. Madison Square Press 1969
fQH541.13.G76 ECOL

GROSSMAN, MARY LOUISE, jt. auth.
Grossman, Shelly.
The how and why wonder book of ecology. 1971
fQH541.14.G78 ECOL

GROSSMAN, SHELLY.
The how and why wonder book of ecology written by Shelly and Mary Louise Grossman. Photos. by Shelly Grossman. Grosset & Dunlap 1971
fQH541.14.G78 ECOL
Understanding ecology, written and photographed by Shelly Grossman. Grosset c1967, 1970
QL756.G7 1970 ECOL

GROSSMAN, SHELLY, jt. auth.
Grossman, Mary Louise.
Our vanishing wilderness. 1969
fQH541.13.G76 ECOL

GROUP FOR ENVIRONMENTAL EDUCATION, INC.
Our man-made environment: a collection of experiences, resources and suggested activities. 1971.
fGF75.G76 ECOL

GROWING AGAINST OURSELVES: THE ENERGY-ENVIRONMENT TANGLE. Problems, policies and approaches.
Ed. by S. L. Kwee and J. S. R. Mullender. With contribution from: Francis A. Beer and others Foreword by Frans A. M. Alting von Geusau. English language consultant: Nanette Gilmour. Lexington Books, 1972. (Publications of the John F. Kennedy Institute, Center for International Studies, no. 6)
TD195.E4G76 ECOL

GRUCHOW, NANCY, jt. comp.
Fisher, Wes.
Minnesota environmental education areas. 1972
fS946.F5 ECOL

GRUEN, VICTOR, 1903-
The heart of our cities; the urban crisis: diagnosis and cure. Simon, 1964. **NA9108.G76 ECOL**

GRUMMAN AEROSPACE CORPORATION.
Development of immobilized enzyme systems for enhancement of biological waste treatment processes. Author: Lawrence Slote. Prepared for the Water Quality Office, Environmental Protection Agency. Environmental Protection Agency, Water Quality Office; for sale by the Supt. of Docs., U.S. Govt. Print Off., 1970 (Water pollution control research series)
fTD755.G78 ECOL

GRUNDEEN, GORDON M., jt. auth.
Walton, William Clarence.
Recharge from induced streambed infiltration under varying groundwater-level and stream-stage conditions. 1967. **GB701.M554no.6 ECOL**

GRUNWALD, JOSEPH, 1920-
Natural resources in Latin American development, by Joseph Grunwald and Philip Musgrove. Published for Resources for the Future, inc., by the Johns Hopkins Press 1970 **REF fHC125.G72 ECOL**

GUERNSEY, JAMES LEE.
Parson, Ruben L.
Conserving American resources. 3d ed. 1972
S930.P3 1972 ECOL

GUEST, STEPHEN HADEN, 1902- ed.
A world geography of forest resources, ed. for the American Geographical Society by Stephen Haden-Guest, John K. Wright and Eileen M. Teclaff. Ronald Press 1956 **REF SD131.G8 ECOL**

GUGGISBERG, CHARLES ALBERT WALTER.
Man and wildlife by C. A. W. Guggisberg. Foreword by F. Vollmar. Arco Pub. Co. 1970
REF S962.G84 ECOL

GUITAR, MARY ANNE.
Property power; how to keep the bull-dozer, the power line, and the highwaymen away from your door. 1st ed. Doubleday, 1972. **HD205 1972 .G8 ECOL**

GULF ENVIRONMENTAL SYSTEMS COMPANY.
Acid mine waste treatment using reverse osmosis. Prepared by James H. Sleigh and S. S. Kremen. Environmental Protection Agency, Water Quality Office 1971 (Water pollution control research series)
fTD754.G84 ECOL

GULLION, EDMUND A., ed.
Uses of the seas. 1968 **GC1015.U8 ECOL**

GUMTZ, GARTH D.
Restoration of Beaches contaminated by oil. Prepared for Office of Research and Monitoring, U.S. Environmental Protection Agency. U.S. Govt. Print. Off., 1972. (Environmental protection technology series) **TD427.P4G8 ECOL**

GUNDERLOY, FRANK C., 1931-
North American Rockwell Corporation. Rocketdyne Division.
Development of a chemical denitrification process. 1970. **fTD433.N67 ECOL**

GUNN, CLARE A.
Cultural benefits from metropolitan river recreation—San Antonio prototype by Clare A. Gunn, David J. Reed and Robert E. Couch. Texas Water Resources Institute, 1972. (Texas. A & M University, College Station. Water Resources Institute. Technical report no. 43) **fHD1694.T4G8 ECOL**

GUNSTON, BILL.
Transportation; problems and prospects. Dutton 1972 (The World of science library) **HE151.G85 ECOL**

GUNTER, JOHN D.
The ecological impact of solid waste by J. D. Gunter and William Carl Jameson. 1973. (Council of Planning Librarians. Exchange bibliography, 406)
Ref fZ5863.P6G8 ECOL

Recycling and re-use: the future of solid waste by J. D. Gunter and William Carl Jameson. 1973. (Council of Planning Librarians. Exchange Bibliography, 407)
Ref fTP156.R38G8 ECOL

Solid waste management: economics and operation. By J. D. Gunter and William Carl Jameson. 1973. (Council of Planning Librarians. Exchange bibliography, 395) **Ref fZ5853.S22G8 ECOL**

GUNTER, PETE ADDISON Y., 1936-
The Big Thicket; a challenge for conservation by Pete Gunter. Photography: Roy Hamric. Jenkins Pub. Co.: distributed by Viking Press, 1971 c1972
fF392.H37G8 ECOL

GURMAN, RICHARD, jt. auth.
Buggie, Frederick D.
Toward effective and equitable pollution control regulation. 1972 **fHC110.P55B8 ECOL**

GUTCHO, SIDNEY.
Waste treatment with polyelectrolytes, 1972. Noyes Data Corp. 1972 (Pollution control review no. 8)
TD751.G87 ECOL

GUTHRIE, JOHN ALEXANDER, 1907-
Western forest industry; an economic outlook by John A. Guthrie and George R. Armstrong. Published for Resources for the Future, Inc., by the Johns Hopkins Press 1961 **HD9755.G8 ECOL**

GUYOT, ARNOLD HENRY, 1807-1884.
The earth and man. Arno 1970, c1849 (American environmental studies) **GB59.G8 1970 ECOL**

GWYNNE, FRED.
Ick's ABC. Windmill Books 1971 **FictionECOL**

H

HAAR, CHARLES MONROE, 1921-
Land-use planning; a casebook on the use, misuse, and re-use of urban land, by Charles M. Haar. 2d ed. Little, Brown, 1971. (Law school casebook series)
KF5692.A4H3 1971 ECOL

HAAS, LARRY A.
Sulfur dioxide: its chemistry as related to methods for removing it from waste gases. U.S. Bureau of Mines 1973 (United States Bureau of Mines. Information circular 8608) **TN23.U7no.8608 ECOL**

HACIA, HENRY.
A selected annotated bibliography of the climate of the Great Lakes. U.S. Environmental Data Service, 1972. (NOAA technical memorandum EDS TM-BS-7) (NOAA technical memorandum EDS TM-BS-7)
REF Z6683.C5H33 ECOL

HAFNER, EVERETT M., ed.
Environmental education 1970. 1970
fS946.E55 ECOL

HAGAMAN, ADALINE P.
What is water. Pictures by Gregory Orloff. Benefic Press 1960 (The What is it series)
PZ10.H12Wh ECOL

HAGBERG, RONALD E., jt. auth.
Flowers, William J.
Western cultural tradition and human survival: the role of value orientations in the environmental crisis. c1971 **GF80.F5 ECOL**

HAGEVIK, GEORGE H., jt. auth.
Van Nest, William J.
Air pollution and urban planning: a selective annotated bibliography. 1972
REF fZ5853.P7V3 ECOL

HAIK, RAYMOND A.
Aspects of water resources law in Minnesota, by R. A. Haik, W. C. Walton and D. L. Hills. Water Resources Research Center, Univ. of Minn., Graduate School, 1969. (Minnesota. University. Water Resources Research Center. Bulletin 11)
GB701.M554no.11 ECOL

Minnesota. University. Water Resources Research Center.
Codified and uncodified state laws and municipal ordinances bearing on water and related land resources in Minnesota. 1968. **GB701.M554no.9 ECOL**

HALACY, DANIEL STEPHEN, 1919-
Habitat by D. S. Halacy, Jr. Macrae Smith Co. 1970 (The Nature of man series, 2) **QH541.14.H3 ECOL**

HALBERT, MICHAEL H., jt. auth.
Deal, Richard L.
The application of value theory to water resources planning and management. 1971
fHD1694.A5D4 ECOL

HALE, MARION, tr.
Nordenskjold, Otto.
The geography of the polar regions, consisting of a general characterization of polar nature. 1928.
G587.N6 ECOL

HALL, FRANCIS R.
The influence of a New England wetland on water quantity and quality, by F. R. Hall, Robert J. Rutherford, and Gordon L. Byers. Water Resource Research Center, Univ. of New Hampshire, 1972. (New Hampshire. University. Water Resource Research Center. Research Report, no. 4)
fTD224.N4H3 ECOL

HALL, GUS.
Ecology: can we survive under capitalism? Drawings by Anton Refregier. 1st ed. International Publishers 1972 (Little new world paperbacks, LNW-33)
HC110.E5H3 ECOL

HALL, O. F.
Principles of natural resource management. Univ. of Minnesota School of Forestry, 1951.
fS938.H3 ECOL

HALLMAN, ROBERT MARSHALL, 1940- jt. auth.
Fabricant, Neil.
Toward a rational power policy: energy, politics, and pollution. 1971 **HD9685.U5F32 ECOL**

HALSTEAD, BRUCE W.
A Golden guide to environmental organizations. Compiled by Bruce W. Halstead under the general editorship of Vera R. Webster. Golden Press 1972
REF GF5.H34 ECOL

World Life Research Institute.
Pharmacological testing of blue-green algae for constituents having therapeutic value. 1970.
fRS165.A7W67 ECOL

HAMBLIN, LYNETTE KAYE.
Pollution: the world crisis by Lynette Hamblin. Barnes 1971,c1970 **TD174.H34 ECOL**

HAMBURGER, RICHARD, jt. auth.
Gerber, Carl R.
Plowshare. 1966 **TK9153.G4 ECOL**

HAMER, AUSTIN F.
Milliken, Margaret.
Field study manual for outdoor living. c1968
QH53.M5 ECOL

HAMILTON, MICHAEL POLLOCK, 1927-
This little planet, edited by Michael Hamilton, with an introd. by Edmund S. Muskie. Scribner 1970
GF80.H35 ECOL

HAMLET, JOHN N., jt. auth.
Grossman, Mary Louise.
Our vanishing wilderness. 1969
fQH541.13.G76 ECOL

HAMMER, MARK J., 1931- jt. auth.
Clark, John William.
Water supply and pollution control. 2d ed. 1971
TD145.C55 1971 ECOL

HAMMERMAN, DONALD R.
Teaching in the outdoors, by Donald R. Hammerman and William M. Hammerman. Illustrated by David Bower. Burgess Pub. Co. 1964 (Burgess books in outdoor education) **LB1047.H3 ECOL**

HAMMERMAN, DONALD R., comp.
Outdoor education; a book of readings, compiled by Donald R. Hammerman and William M. Hammerman. Burgess Pub. Co. c1970,c1968 **LB1047.H28 ECOL**

HAMMERMAN, WILLIAM M., jt. auth.
Hammerman, Donald R.
Outdoor education. c1970,c1968
LB1047.H28 ECOL

Hammerman, Donald R.
Teaching in the outdoors. 1964
LB1047.H3 ECOL

HAMMERSLEY, ALAN, jt. auth.
Perry, Gordon Arthur.
Handbook for environmental studies. 2nd rev. ed. 1971 **LB1585.P4 1971 ECOL**

HANDLER, PHILIP, 1917- ed.
Biology and the future of man. 1970.
QH307.2.B56 ECOL

HANN, ROY W.
Mathematical models of water quality parameters for rivers and estuaries. Principal investigators: Roy W. Hann and Paul Jonathan Young. Water Resources Institute, Texas A & M Univ., 1972 (Texas. A & M University, College Station. Water Resources Institute. Technical report, no. 45) **fTD370.H3 ECOL**

HANNON, BRUCE.
System energy and recycling: a study of the beverage industry. 1972. (Illinois. University. Center for Advanced Computation. Document no.23)
fTP659.H3 ECOL

HANSON, ARTHUR J., jt. auth.
Allan, J. David.
Recycle this book! 1972 **GF8.A4 ECOL**

HANSON, HERBERT CHRISTIAN, 1891-
Dictionary of ecology. Philosophical Library 1962
REF QH541.H25 ECOL

HANSON, LOWELL D.
Soils of the Twin Cities Metropolitan area and their relation to urban development, by L. D. Hanson and others. Agricultural Extension Service, Univ. of Minnesota 1967, c1966 (Minnesota. University. Agricultural Extension Service. Extension bulletin, 320)
fS599.M45H3 1967 ECOL

HARDENBERGH, WILLIAM ANDREW, 1888-
Water supply and waste disposal, by W. A. Hardenbergh and Edward R. Rodie. International Textbook Co. 1970,c1960 (International textbooks in civil engineering) **TD145.H33 1970 ECOL**

HARDIN, GARRETT JAMES, 1915-
Exploring new ethics for survival: the voyage of the spaceship Beagle by Garrett Hardin. Viking Press 1972
HB871.H347 ECOL

Nature and man's fate. New American Library 1961 (Mentor book) **QH361.H25 1961 ECOL**

Science, conflict, and society. 1969
fQ125.S434 ECOL

HARDIN, GARRETT JAMES, 1915- ed.
Population, evolution, and birth control; a collage of controversial ideas, assembled by Garret Hardin. 2d ed. W. H. Freeman 1969 (A Series of books in biology)
HB851.H28 1969 ECOL

HARDY, SIR ALISTER CLAVERING.
The living stream; evolution and man, by Alister Hardy. Harper 1967,c1965 **QH367.H2 1967 ECOL**

HARDY, WILLIAM GEORGE, 1896- ed.
Alberta, a natural history. 1st ed. c1967
fQH106.A54 ECOL

HARGROVE, JOHN LAWRENCE, ed.
Conference on Legal and Institutional Responses to Problems of the Global Evnironment, Arden House, 1971.
Law, institutions, and the global environment. 1972.
KF3775.A75C6 1971 ECOL

HARLIN, CURTIS C., jt. auth.
United States. Environmental Protection Agency.
Induced aeration of small mountain lakes. 1970.
fSH167.T86U5 ECOL

HARMER, RUTH MULVEY.
Unfit for human consumption. Prentice 1971
QH545.P4H36 ECOL

HARNED, JOSEPH W., ed.
Managing the environment: international economic cooperation for pollution control. 1971
HC79.E5M35 1971 ECOL

HARRAR, JACOB GEORGE, 1906-
Prospects of the world food supply. 1966.
fS439.P7 1966 ECOL

HARRINGTON, WALTER S., jt. auth.
Morey, Rexford M.
Feasibility study of electromagnetic subsurface profiling. 1972.
QE602.M6 ECOL

HARRIS, DOUGLAS H. 1930-
Assessment of turbidity, color and odor in water. Prepared by Anacapa Sciences, Inc., for Office of Water Resources Research, U.S. Dept. of the Interior. Anacapa Sciences, Inc., 1972. (Technical report, 128)
fTD380.H3 ECOL

HARRIS, LARRY.
Twilight of the animal kingdom; the endangered species. Written and illustrated by Larry Harris. W. Ritchie Press 1972
QL88.H37 ECOL

HARRIS, LORIN E., 1915-
National Research Council. Committee on Animal Nutrition.
Biological energy interrelationships and glossary of energy terms. 1st rev. ed. 1966.
REF SF95.N3 1966 ECOL

HARRIS, MAUREEN I., ed.
Mutagenic effects of environmental contaminants. 1972.
QH431.M958 ECOL

HARRIS, MELVILLE.
Environmental studies. Citation Press, 1971. (Informal schools in Britain today, TX2042)
LB1047.H32 ECOL

HARRIS, REG.
Natural history collecting. Illustrated by Peter Thornley. Grosset & Dunlap 1972 (The Grosset all-color guide series, 42)
QH60.H36 ECOL

HARRISON, ALFRED S., jt. auth.
Thomsen, Arvid L.
Riprap stability on earth embankments tested in large—and small-scale wave tanks. 1972.
TC533.T4 ECOL

HARRISON, C. WILLIAM.
Conservation, the challenge of reclaiming our plundered land. Messner c1968,1963
S940.H33 1968 ECOL

HARRISON, GEORGE RUSSELL, 1898-
The first book of energy. F. Watts 1965
QC73.H3 ECOL

HARRISON, GORDON A.
Earthkeeping; the war with nature and a proposal for peace by Gordon Harrison. Houghton-Mifflin, 1971.
HC110.E5H33 ECOL

HARRISON, JAMES D.
Environmental preferences: relevant studies for urban planning. 1973. (Council of Planning Librarians. Exchange bibliography, 385) Ref fZ5942.H3 ECOL

HARROY, JEAN PAUL.
Curry-Lindahl, Kai.
National parks of the world. 1972
SB481.C87 ECOL

International Commission on National Parks.
United Nations list of national parks and equivalent reserves. 1972. REF SB481.I55 1971 Suppl. ECOL

International Commission on National Parks.
United Nations list of national parks and equivalent reserves. 2nd ed. 1971.
REF SB481.I55 1971 ECOL

HARTE, JOHN, 1939-
Patient earth by John Harte and Robert H. Socolow. Holt, Rinehart and Winston 1971
QH541.H26 ECOL

HARTFELDT, WILL H., ed.
Minnesota. University. Dept. of Continuing Legal Education.
Minnesota environmental law sourcebook. c1973.
REF KFM5754.A45 ECOL

HARTLEY, GILBERT SPENCER.
Chemicals for pest control, by G. S. Hartley and T. F. West. 1st ed. Pergamon Press 1969 (The Commonwealth and international library. Chemical industry)
TP248.P47H3 1969 ECOL

HARTSHORNE, CHARLES, 1897-
Born to sing: an interpretation and world survey of bird song. Indiana University Press 1973
QL698.5.H27 ECOL

HARTUNG, ROLF, 1935- ed.
Environmental mercury contamination. 1972
RA1231.M5E58 ECOL

HARTWELL, MARJORIE, illus.
Robinson, Carmelita Klipple.
Life in a pond. 1967
fPZ10.R56Li ECOL

HARVARD UNIVERSITY. DEPT. OF LANDSCAPE ARCHITECTURE. RESEARCH OFFICE.
Isard, Walter.
Ecologic-economic analysis for regional development. 1972
HT391.I82 ECOL

HARVARD UNIVERSITY. LANDSCAPE ARCHITECTURE RESEARCH OFFICE.
Three approaches to environmental resource analysis, prepared by the Landscape Architecture Research Office, Graduate School of Design, Harvard Univ. Conservation Foundation 1967. fTA170.H3 ECOL

HARVARD WATER PROGRAM.
The economics of water supply and quality. Environmental Protection Agency., Water Quality Office; for sale by the Supt. of Docs., U.S. Govt. Print. Off., 1971. (Water pollution control research series)
fTD223.H34 ECOL

HARVEST OF DEATH; chemical warfare in Vietnam and Cambodia.
by J. B. Neilands and others. With a foreword by Gunnar Myrdal. Free Press 1971,c1972
DS557.A68H35 1972 ECOL

HARVEY, PATRICK J., jt. auth.
Nebolsine, Ross.
High rate filtration of combined sewer overflows. 1972.
fTD662.N4 ECOL

HARZA ENGINEERING COMPANY.
A program for preserving the quality of Lake Minnetonka; a report for State of Minnesota Pollution Control Agency. Prepared by University of Minnesota, Limnological Research Center, Eugene A. Hickok and Associates, Barr Engineering Co. and Harza Engineering Company. 1971 v.
fTD225.M63H3 ECOL

Report on abandonment and transfer of ownership of dams. Prepared by Harza Engineering Co. for State of Minnesota Dept. of Natural Resources. Harza Eng. Co. 1971. 1v.
fTC557.M6H3 ECOL

HASKELL, ELIZABETH H., 1942-
Managing the environment: nine States look for new answers. Elizabeth H. Haskell, project director. Victoria Price, project associate. William Matthews and others. 1971.
fHC110.E5H35 ECOL

HASSETT, CHARLES M., ed.
Environmental law. 1971 KF3775.A75E54 ECOL

HAUSER, PHILIP MORRIS, 1909-
Population perspectives. Rutgers University Press 1961?c1960
HB3505.H3 ECOL

HAUSER, PHILIP MORRIS, 1909- ed.
American Assembly.
The population dilemma. 2d ed. 1969
HB851.A4 1969 ECOL

HAVIGHURST, CLARK C., ed.
Air pollution control. 1969.
KF3812.A75A35 ECOL

HAWKES, ALFRED L.
Songs of the forest. 1964.
Phonodisc QL698.5.S63 ECOL

HAWKINS, MYRON B., jt. auth.
Boyd, Gail B.
Methods of predicting solid waste characteristics. 1971.
TD793.7.B68 ECOL

HAWKINSON, JOHN, 1912-
Our wonderful wayside. Whitman 1966
PZ10.H34Ou ECOL

HAWLEY, AMOS HENRY.
Human ecology; a theory of community structure. Ronald Press Co. 1950 HM51.H38 ECOL

HAWLEY, GESSNER GOODRICH, 1905-
The Condensed chemical dictionary. Rev. by Gessner G. Hawley. 8th ed. 1971
REF QD5.C5 1971 ECOL

HAY, JOHN, 1915-
The Atlantic shore; human and natural history from Long Island to Labrador, by John Hay and Peter Farb. Harper, 1969,c1966.
QH95.7.H3 ECOL

In defense of nature. Little 1969
QH81.H37 ECOL

The primal alliance: earth and ocean. Lines from The Atlantic shore. Photos. of the Big Sur coast by Richard Kauffman. Foreword by David R. Brower. Friends of the Earth, 1971. (Earth's wild places, 4)
fQH95.7.H32 ECOL

HAYAKAWA, N., jt. auth.
Stefan, Heinz.
Surface discharge of heated water. 1971 i.e. 1972
fTD427.H4S64 ECOL

HAYAMI, YUJIRO, 1932-
Agricultural development; an international perspective by Yujiro Hayami and Vernon W. Ruttan. Johns Hopkins Press 1971 HD1415.H318 ECOL

HAZEN, WILLIAM EUGENE, 1925- jt. comp.
Ford, Richard F.
Readings in aquatic ecology. 1972.
QH541.5.W3F67 ECOL

HEADLEY, JOSEPH CHARLES.
The pesticide problem: an economic approach to public policy, by J. C. Headley and J. N. Lewis. Resources for the Future; dist. by Johns Hopkins Press, c1967
SB959.H35 ECOL

HEADSTROM, BIRGER RICHARD, 1902-
Frogs, toads, and salamanders as pets, by Richard Headstrom. I. Washburn 1972 SF459.A45H4 ECOL

Nature in miniature by Richard Headstrom. Knopf, 1968.
QH309.H4 ECOL

HEADY, EARL OREL, 1916-
Agricultural and water policies and the environment: an analysis of national alternatives in natural resource use, food supply capacity and environmental quality, by Earl O. Heady and others. Ames Center for Agricultural and Rural Development, Iowa State Univ., 1972.
fS441.H4 ECOL

HEADY, ELEANOR B.
The soil that feeds us, by Eleanor B. Heady. Illus. by Robert Frankenberg. Parents' Magazine Press 1972 (A Stepping-stone book) PZ10.H42So ECOL

HEALTH PHYSICS SOCIETY.
Environmental surveillance in the vicinity of nuclear facilities. 1970 REF TD887.R3E58 ECOL

HEALTH PHYSICS SOCIETY. BALTIMORE-WASHINGTON CHAPTER.
The Environmental and ecological forum, 1970-1971. 1972.
TD898.E58 ECOL

HEATH, MILTON SIDNEY, 1928-
A comparative study of state water pollution control laws and programs. Water Resources Research Institute, North Carolina State University 1972. (North Carolina. University. Water Resources Research Institute. Report no. 42) fKF3790.Z95H4 ECOL

HEDLUND, DEBORAH, jt. auth.
Ulrich, Stanley.
Superior pollutor: a saga of the struggle to stop pollution of the largest fresh water lake in the world by its most egregious polluter—the Reserve Mining Company. 1972. TD224.M6U6 ECOL

HEILMANN, GERHARD, 1859-
The origin of birds. Two plates in colour and one hundred and forty photographs and text figures from drawings by the author. Appleton, 1927.
QE871.H4 1927 ECOL

HEINZEL, HERMANN.
The birds of Britain and Europe with North Africa and Middle East by Hermann Heinzel, Richard Fitter and John Parslow. Lippincott 1972
QL690.A1H44 ECOL

HELD, R. BURNELL.
Clawson, Marion.
The federal lands: their use and management. 1966,1957
HD216.C54 1966 ECOL

Soil conservation in perspective, by R. Burnell Held and Marion Clawson. Published for Resources for the Future, by the Johns Hopkins Press 1965
S624.A1H4 ECOL

HELFMAN, ELIZABETH S.
Land, people, and history. D. McKay Co., 1967c1962
HD156.H4 1967 ECOL

Rivers and watersheds in America's future, by Elizabeth S. Helfman. McKay Co., 1965.
TC423.H45 ECOL

Water for the world. Illustrated by James MacDonald. 1st ed. McKay 1967,c1960
GB671.H4 ECOL

HELGESON, STANLEY L., jt. auth.
Roth, Robert E.
A review of research related to environmental education. 1972.
QH541.2.R6 ECOL

HELLER, ALFRED E., ed.
The California Tomorrow plan. Rev. ed. 1972
HT393.C3C35 1972 ECOL

HENAGER, CHARLES H.
Concept evaluation: recovery of floating oil using polyurethane foam sorbent, by C. H. Henager and J. D. Smith. Prepared for Office of Research and Monitoring, U.S. Environmental Protection Agency. U.S. Govt. Print. Office, 1972. (Environmental protection technology series)
fTD427.P4H4 ECOL

HENDERSON, GEORGE J.
Pollution: problems, projects and mathematical exercises grades 6-9. Writing Committee: G. L. Henderson and others. Wisconsin Dept. of Public Instruction 1970
fQH541.2.H46 ECOL

HENDERSON, JOHN J., jt. auth.
Benson, Ferris B.
Indoor-outdoor air pollution relationships: a literature review. 1972. **TD890.B4 ECOL**

HENDERSON, LAWRENCE JOSEPH, 1878-1942.
The fitness of the environment; an inquiry into the biological significance of the properties of matter. Introd. by George Wald. P. Smith, 1970 c1913
QH331.H45 1970 ECOL

HENDERSON, MARTHA T.
Environmental education: Social studies sources and approaches. A paper for the ERIC Clearinghouse for Social Science Education. 1970 (ERIC Clearinghouse for Social Science Education. Review series no.1)
Ref fQH541.2.H4 ECOL

HENDRICKS, DAVID W., jt. auth.
Bishop, A. Bruce.
Analysis of water reuse alternatives in an integrated urban and agricultural area. 1971 **fTD429.B5 ECOL**

HENEIN, NAEIM ABDOU, 1927- jt. auth.
Patterson, Donald J.
Emissions from combustion engines and their control. 1972 **TD886.5.P83 ECOL**

HENKIN, HARMON.
The environment, the establishment, and the law by Harmon Henkin, Martin Merta, and James Staples. Houghton 1971 **QH545.P4H4 ECOL**

HENNINGSON, DURHAM & RICHARDSON.
Minnesota: disposal and reuse of abandoned and retired automobiles. A report to the Minnesota Pollution Control Agency, Solid Waste Division. 1970.
REF fTD795.H36 ECOL

Study and investigation of solid waste control for the Minnesota Pollution Control Agency: phase II, final report. 1969. v. **REF fTD788.4.M6H4 ECOL**

HENNINGSON, DURHAM AND RICHARDSON, INC., OMAHA, NEBRASKA.
Annual capital improvements cost estimates schedules for separation and treatment combined sewerage system, South St. Paul, Minnesota. Omaha n.d. **fTD525.S6H4 ECOL**

HENNY, CHARLES J.
An analysis of the population dynamics of selected avian species; with special reference to changes during the modern pesticide era. Bureau of Sport Fisheries and Wildlife; U.S. Govt. Print. Off , 1972 (United States. Bureau of Sport Fisheries and Wildlife. Wildlife research report, 1) **QL785.5.B6H4 ECOL**

HENRY, MARGUERITE, 1902-
Birds at Home. Illus. by Jacob Bates Abbott. Hubbard Press 1972 **fQL676.H52 1972 ECOL**

HENRY, MARYBETH.
Motor vehicle emissions: a bibliography. Council of Planning Librarians 1972 (Council of Planning Librarians. Exchange bibliography, no. 275)
REF fTL214.P6H4 ECOL

HENSHAW, PAUL STEWART, 1902-
This side of yesterday: extinction or Utopia by Paul S. Henshaw. Wiley 1971 **GF41.H45 ECOL**

HENSON, COLLINS M.
Your environment: air, air pollution, and weather by Collins M. Henson. Interstate Printers & Publishers 1971 **QC863.H45 ECOL**

HEPTING, GEORGE H.
Diseases of forest and shade trees of the United States. U.S. Forest Service, 1971. (United States. Dept. of Agriculture. Handbook 386)
REF SB761.H4 ECOL

HERALD, EARL STANNARD.
Fishes of North America by Earl S. Herald. A Chanticleer Press ed. Doubleday 1972 (Animal life of North America series) **QL635.H47 ECOL**

HERBER, LEWIS.
Crisis in our cities. Prentice-Hall c1965
RA566.H4 ECOL

HERBERT, FREDERICK WULLING, 1892-
Careers in natural resource conservation. Walck, 1965. (Careers for tomorrow) **S944.H45 ECOL**

HERFINDAHL, ORRIS CLEMENS, 1918-
Natural resources information for economic development; a study, by Orris C. Herfindahl. Published for Resources for the Future, Inc., by Johns Hopkins Press 1969 **GA51.H47 ECOL**

Quality of the environment: an economic approach to some problems in using land, water, and air, by Orris C. Herfindahl and Allen V. Kneese. Resources for the Future; dist. by Johns Hopkins Press, 1965
TD153.H46 ECOL

HERNDON, BOOTON.
The great land. Weybright and Talley 1971
TN872.A7H4 ECOL

HERRERA, PHILIP.
Holdren, John P.
Energy. c1971 **TJ153.H65 ECOL**

HERSH, SEYMOUR M.
Chemical and biological warfare; America's hidden arsenal. Anchor Books, Doubleday 1969,c1968
UG447.H42 1969 ECOL

HESSE, WALTER H.
The light at the end of the tunnel; a study guide to pollution problems by Walter H. Hesse. Dickenson Pub. Co. 1972 **fTD175.H47 ECOL**

HESTER, F. EUGENE, 1931-
The world of the wood duck. Text and photographs by F. Eugene Hester and Jack Dermid. 1st ed. Lippincott 1973 (Living world books)
QL696.A5H42 ECOL

HETLING, LEO J., jt. auth.
Carcich, Italo G.
A pressure sewer system demonstration. 1972.
TD670.C3 ECOL

HETRICK, DAVID L., ed.
Dynamics of nuclear systems. 1972
TK9202.D9 ECOL

HIBBARD, BENJAMIN HORACE, 1870-
A history of the public land policies. With a foreword by Paul W. Gates. University of Wisconsin Press, 1965.
HD216.H5 1965 ECOL

HICKEL, WALTER J., 1919-
Who owns America? by Walter J. Hickel. Prentice-Hall 1971 **E855.H5 1971 ECOL**

HICKEY, JOSEPH JAMES, 1907- ed.
Peregrine falcon populations. 1969.
QL696.A2P44 ECOL

HICKMAN, HOWARD J.
A study of the environmental impact of polystyrene vs. paper pulp egg cartons and meat trays, by Howard J. Hickman, Richard Lewis and Janet Salomonson. Univ. of Minn., 1972. v. **fTP373.H5 ECOL**

HICKOK, BEVERLY.
Goals, objectives and values: selected references relating to national, state and urban or regional areas, covering general & transportation aspects. Council of Planning Librarians, 1973 (Council of Planning Librarians. Exchange bibliography, no. 391)
fZ7164.O7H49 ECOL

HICKOK (EUGENE A.) AND ASSOCIATES, WAYZATA.
Harza Engineering Company.
A program for preserving the quality of Lake Minnetonka. 1971 **fTD225.M63H3 ECOL**

HICKOK (EUGENE A.) AND ASSOCIATES, WAYZATA, MINN.
Overall plan for water management Minnehaha Creek Watershed District. 1969
fTC424.M6H5 ECOL

HICKS, EDWARD, jt. auth.
Freese, Paul V.
Full-scale raw wastewater flocculation with polymers. 1970. **fTD751.F7 ECOL**

HIGBEE, EDWARD COUNSELMAN, 1910-
American agriculture: geography, resources, conservation. Wiley 1958 **S441.H59 ECOL**

A question of priorities; new strategies for our urbanized world by Edward Higbee. With an introd. by R. Buckminster Fuller. Morrow, 1970.
HN65.H5 ECOL

HIGHSMITH, RICHARD MORGAN, 1920-
Conservation in the United States, by Richard M. Highsmith, Jr., J. Granville Jensen and Robert D. Rudd. 2d ed. Rand McNally 1969 (Rand McNally geography series) **HC103.7.H5 1969 ECOL**

HILADO, CARLOS J.
Handbook of environmental management. Technomic Publishing Co. 1972- v.1-
REF fGF75.H5 ECOL

HILDRETH, ROLAND J., ed.
National Agricultural Policy Conference.
Readings in agricultural policy. 1968
HD1761.N25 ECOL

HILL, A. CLYDE, ed.
Jacobson, Jay S.
Recognition of air pollution injury to vegetation: a pictorial atlas. 1970. **fQK751.J3 ECOL**

HILL, DONLEY M., jt. auth.
Virginia Polytechnic Institute and State University.
Stream faunal recovery after manganese strip mine reclamation. 1971. **fTN291.V5 ECOL**

HILLCOURT, WILLIAM, 1900-
The new field book of nature activities and hobbies. Rev. ed. Putnam 1970 **QH53.H574 1970 ECOL**

HILLS, DAVID L.
Minnesota. University. Water Resources Research Center.
Codified and uncodified state laws and municipal ordinances bearing on water and related land resources in Minnesota. 1968. **GB701.M554no.9 ECOL**

HILLS, DAVID L., jt. auth.
Haik, Raymond A.
Aspects of water resources law in Minnesota. 1969.
GB701.M554no.11 ECOL

Walton, William Clarence.
Interest groups with water and related land resources programs in Minnesota, 1971. 1972.
GB701.M554no.45 ECOL

Walton, William Clarence.
International, regional, federal-state, interstate and federal organizations with water related land resources programs in Minnesota, 1971. 1971.
GB701.M554no.42 ECOL

Walton, William Clarence.
Recharge from induced streambed infiltration under varying groundwater-level and stream-stage conditions. 1967. **GB701.M554no.6 ECOL**

Walton, William Clarence.
Water and related land resources state administration, legislative process and policies in Minnesota, 1970. 1971 **GB701.M554no.27 ECOL**

HINES, NEAL O.
Atoms, nature, and man by Neal O. Hines. U.S. Atomic Energy Commission, Division of Technical Information c1966 (Understanding the atom)
QC778.H54 ECOL

HINES, NORMAN WILLIAM.
Iowa Water Resources Pollution Control and Abatement Seminar, Iowa State University, 1965.
Water pollution: control and abatement proceedings. 1st ed. 1970,c1967 **TD224.I816 1965 ECOL**

HINES, ROBERT W., illus.
Silverberg, Robert.
The world within the ocean wave. 1972
QH91.8.P5S54 ECOL

HIROS, JOHN E.
Inviting involvement with history. Ed. by Norma T. Vivian and V. Eugene Vivian. Conservation and Environmental Studies Center 1969
fLB1047.H5 ECOL

HIRSCH, S. CARL.
Guardians of tomorrow; pioneers in ecology by S. Carl Hirsch. Illus. by William Steinel. Viking Press 1971
QH541.14.H57 1971 ECOL

The living community; a venture into ecology by S. Carl Hirsch. Illus. by William Steinel. Viking Press 1966
QH541.H54 ECOL

HIRSHLEIFER, JACK.
Water supply: economics, technology, and policy by Jack Hirshleifer, James C. DeHaven and Jerome W. Milliman. Univ. of Chicago Press 1960
HD1694.A5H5 1969 ECOL

HISTORY OF MINNESOTA POLLUTION CONTROL AGENCY.
Prepared for Citizen's Advisory Plant Siting Task Force. Northern States Power Co., 1970 1v.
fTD181.M5 ECOL

HISTORY OF THE WISCONSIN DEPARTMENT OF NATURAL RESOURCES AND RELATED RULES, REGULATIONS, CLASSIFICATIONS AND STANDARDS FOR AIR AND WATER QUALITY.
Prepared for Advisory Committee on Plant Siting and Development. Northern States Power Co. 1970 1v.
fS932.W6H5 ECOL

HITCH, ALLEN S.
Conservation and you, by Allen S. Hitch & Marian Sorenson. Van Nostrand 1964 **S930.H5 ECOL**

HITE, JAMES C., 1941- ed.
Coastal zone resource management. 1971
HC110.E5C6 ECOL

HOADLEY, ALFRED W., jt. auth.
McClanahan, Mark A.
A study of the effects of island development on lake water quality. 1972. **fTD224.G4M3 ECOL**

HOAGLAND, HUDSON, 1899- ed.
Evolution and man's progress, edited by Hudson Hoagland and Ralph W. Burhoe. Columbia University Press, 1962. **HM106.H6 ECOL**

HOBBS, HORTON HOLCOMBE, 1914-
Crayfishes (Astacidae) of North and Middle America. Environmental Protection Agency, 1972. (Biota of freshwater ecosystems, Identification manual, no. 9.) **fQH96.A2B5no.9 ECOL**

HOCHBAUM, HANS ALBERT.
Travels and traditions of waterfowl. Univ. of Minn. Press 1955 **QL698.H65 ECOL**

HOFFMANN, RALPH, 1870-
Birds of the Pacific states; containing brief biographies and descriptions of about four hundred species, with especial reference to their appearance in the field ..with ten plates in color and over two hundred illus. in black and white, by Major Allan Brooks. Houghton, 1927. **Ref QL683.H65 ECOL**

HOFMANN, MELITA.
A trip to the pond; an adventure in nature, written and illus. by Melita Hofmann. Doubleday 1966 **fQH48.H56 ECOL**

HOFSTRA UNIVERSITY, HEMPSTEAD, N. Y. SCHOOL OF BUSINESS.
Environmental side effects of rising industrial output. 1970 **TD174.E58 ECOL**

HOGAN, ELIZABETH R., jt. auth.
Curtis, Richard.
Perils of the peaceful atom. 1969. **HD9698.U52C8 ECOL**

HOGAN, WILLIAM T.
Optimum mechanical aeration systems for rivers and ponds, by Wm. T. Hogan, F. Everett Reed and A. W. Starbird. Environmental Protection Agency, Water Quality Office; for sale by the Supt. of Docs., U.S. Govt. Print. Off., 1970. (Water pollution control research series) **fTD458.H64 ECOL**

HOGBERG, RUDOLPH K.
Environmental geology of the Twin Cities Metropolitan area. Illus. by Ann Cross. Minnesota Geological Survey, 1971 (Minnesota. Geological Survey. Educational series no.5) **QE128.T9H6 ECOL**

Guide to fossil collecting in Minnesota by R. K. Hogberg, R. E. Sloan and Sarah Tufford. Illus. by Ann Cross. Rev. ed. University of Minnesota, Minnesota Geological Survey, 1967. (Minnesota. Geological Survey. Educational series, 1) **QE718.H55 1967 ECOL**

Guide to the caves of Minnesota by R. K. Hogberg and T. N. Bayer. Univ. of Minnesota, Minnesota Geological Survey, 1967 (Minnesota. Geological Survey. Educational series, no.4) **GB605.M5H6 ECOL**

HOGERTON, JOHN F.
Atomic fuel. U.S. Atomic Energy Commission, Division of Technical Information 1969 (Understanding the atom) **TK9360.H6 1969 ECOL**

Atomic fuel. Rev. U.S. Atomic Energy Commission, Division of Technical Information, 1964. (Understanding the atom) **TK9360.H6 1964 ECOL**

Atomic power safety by John F. Hogerton. U.S. Atomic Energy Commission, Division of Technical Information c1964 (Understanding the atom) **TK1078.H62 ECOL**

HOKE, JOHN, 1925-
Ecology: man's effects on his environment and its mechanisms. Illus. by Richard Cuffari. Watts 1971 (A First book) **QH541.H58 ECOL**

Terrariums. F. Watts, 1972. (A First book) **QH68.H65 ECOL**

HOLDEN, RAYMOND PECKHAM, 1894-1972.
Wildlife mysteries. Illustrated by Sherry Streeter. Dodd, Mead 1972 **QL49.H68 ECOL**

HOLDREN, JOHN P.
Energy; a crisis in power, by John Holdren and Philip Herrera. Sierra Club c1971 (The Sierra Club battlebook series, 4) **TJ153.H65 ECOL**

HOLDREN, JOHN P., comp.
Global ecology; readings toward a rational strategy for man, edited by John P. Holdren and Paul R. Ehrlich. Harcourt Brace Jovanovich 1971 **HC110.E5H64 ECOL**

HOLDREN, JOHN P., jt. comp.
Ehrlich, Paul R.
Man and the ecosphere. 1971 **fGF8.E35 ECOL**

HOLLAND, WALTER WERNER.
Air pollution and respiratory disease. Editor: W. W. Holland. Technomic Pub. Co. 1972 **fRC732.H64 ECOL**

HOLLAND, WILLIAM JACOB, 1848-
The moth book; a popular guide to a knowledge of the moths of North America...with forty-eight plates in color photography, and numerous illus. in the text, reproducing specimens in the collection of the author, and in various public and private collections. Doubleday, 1905 1903 **Ref QL544.H74 ECOL**

HOLM, RICHARD W., jt. comp.
Ehrlich, Paul R.
Man and the ecosphere. 1971 **fGF8.E35 ECOL**

HOLMES, JAMES G.
Acid mine drainage treatment by ion exchange, by Jim Holmes and Ed Kreusch. Prepared for Office of Research and Monitoring, U.S. Environmental Protection Agency. U.S. Govt. Printing Office, 1972 (Environmental protection technology series) **TD899.M5H6 ECOL**

HOLMES, JOHN C., 1932- jt. auth.
Fuller, William Albert.
The life of the far north. 1972. **QH541.5.T8F84 ECOL**

HOLOBINKO, PAUL, jt. auth.
Rasmussen, Frederick A.
Man and the environment. 1970, c1971 **QH316.5.R35 ECOL**

HOLSINGER, JOHN R.
The freshwater amphipod crustaceans (Gammaridae) of North America. Environmental Protection Agency, 1972. (Biota of freshwater ecosystems, Identification manual, no.5. Water pollution control research series) **fQH96.A2B5no.5 ECOL**

HOMAN, PAUL THOMAS, 1893- jt. auth.
Lovejoy, Wallace Francis.
Economic aspects of oil conservation regulation. 1967 **HD9566.L6 ECOL**

Lovejoy, Wallace Francis.
Methods of estimating reserves of crude oil, natural gas, and natural gas liquids. 1965 **TN870.L68 ECOL**

HOMESTEAD CENTENNIAL SYMPOSIUM, UNIVERSITY OF NEBRASKA, 1962.
Land use policy and problems in the United States. Edited by Howard W. Ottoson. University of Nebraska Press 1964,c1963 **HD205 1962 .H6 ECOL**

HONE, ELIZABETH B.
Teaching elementary science: a sourcebook for elementary science by Elizabeth B. Hone, Alexander Joseph and Edward Victor. Under the general editorship of Paul F. Brandwein. 2d ed. Harcourt 1971 **LB1585.H65 1971 ECOL**

HOOK, ERNEST B., 1936- ed.
Symposium on Monitoring, Birth Defects and Environment, Albany, N. Y., 1970.
Monitoring, birth defects and environment: the problem of surveillance. 1971. **RG627.S94 1970 ECOL**

HOOVER, HELEN.
Animals at my doorstep. Illustrated by Symeon Shimin. Parents' Magazine Press 1966 **PZ10.H7An ECOL**

The gift of the deer. Pen-and-ink drawings from life by Adrian Hoover. Knopf, 1970c1966 **QL795.D3H6 1970 ECOL**

A place in the woods. Pen-and-ink drawings by Adrian Hoover. 1st ed. Knopf, 1972. **QH105.M55H62 1972 ECOL**

The years of the forest. Pen-and-ink drawings by Adrian Hoover. 1st ed. Knopf, 1973. **QH105.M55H64 1973 ECOL**

HOPEMAN, ALAN ROSWELL.
An economic analysis of flood damage reduction alternatives in the Minnesota River Basin. Univ. of Minn., Water Resources Research Center, 1973. (Minnesota. University. Water Resources Research Center. WRRC bulletin 58) **GB701.M554no.58 ECOL**

HOPKINSON, RICHARD A.
Corporate organization for pollution control. National Industrial Conference Board, c1970 (Conference board report no.507) **fHC110.E5H6 ECOL**

HOPWOOD, ALFRED J.
Evaluation of fishes and bottom fauna in the Mississippi River adjacent to the NSP Sherburne County Generating Plant Site, Becker, Minnesota, during October and November, 1971. Northern States Power Co.? 1972 **fTK1331.N6H6 ECOL**

HORIZONS INCORPORATED.
Foam separation of acid mine drainage. U.S. Environmental Protection Agency, U.S. Govt. Print. Off. 1971 (Water pollution control research series) **fTD899.M5H6 ECOL**

HORNADAY, WILLIAM TEMPLE, 1854-1937.
Our vanishing wildlife: its extermination and preservation. Arno 1970,c1913 (American environmental studies.) **SK353.H6 1970 ECOL**

Thirty years war for wild life. Arno 1970, c1931 (American environmental studies) **SK361.H58 1970 ECOL**

HORSFIELD, BRENDA.
The great ocean business by Brenda Horsfield and Peter Bennet Stone. 1st American ed. Coward, McCann & Geoghega 1972 **GC21.H63 1972b ECOL**

HOTCHKISS, NEIL, 1901-
Common marsh, underwater, and floating-leaved plants of the United States and Canada. Dover Publications 1972 **QK115.H67 1972 ECOL**

Underwater and floating-leaved plants of the United States and Canada, 1972
In: Hotchkiss, Neil. Common marsh, underwater, and floating-leaved plants of the United States and Canada. 1972 **QK115.H67 1972 ECOL**

HOTTEL, HOYT CLARKE, 1903-
New energy technology—some facts and assessments by H. C. Hottel and J. B. Howard. MIT Press 1971 **TJ23.H67 ECOL**

HOUCK, JOHN W.
Outdoor advertising; history and regulation, ed. by John W. Houck. Univ. of Notre Dame Press, 1969. **REF HF5843.H57 ECOL**

HOUGH, ROMEYN BECK, 1857-
Handbook of the trees of the northern states and Canada east of the Rocky Mountains. Photo-descriptive. Third and rev. ed. The author, 1924. **REF QK481H8 1924 ECOL**

HOULT, DAVID P., ed.
Oil on the sea. 1969. **GC1080.O36 ECOL**

HOWARD, JACK BENNY, 1937- jt. auth.
Hottel, Hoyt Clarke.
New energy technology—some facts and assessments. 1971 **TJ23.H67 ECOL**

HOWARD, JOHN ANTHONY.
Aerial photo-ecology by John A. Howard. American Elsevier Pub. Co. 1970, i.e. 1971 **SD387.A25H68 1971 ECOL**

HOWARD, NEEDLES, TAMMEN & BERGENDOFF.
Interstate 394 corridor location study; interim report. Prepared for the Minnesota Dept. of Highways, Federal Highway Administration, United States Dept. of Transportation. 1973? **fTE25.T9H6 ECOL**

HOWE, CHARLES W.
Inland waterway transportation. 1969 **HE629.I57 ECOL**

Interbasin transfers of water; economic issues and impacts by Charles W. Howe and K. William Easter. Published for Resources for the Future by Johns Hopkins Press 1971 **HD1695.W4H66 ECOL**

HOWELL, ARTHUR HOLMES, 1872-1940.
Florida bird life.
Sprunt, Alexander.
Florida bird life. 1954 **QL684.F6S65 ECOL**

HOWELLS, DAVID H., jt. auth.
Stewart, James M.
Perception of water resources research, dissemination, and utilization of research findings. 1971. **fHD1694.N8N6no.58 ECOL**

HU, ALAN C. H., jt. auth.
Streebin, Leale E.
Demonstration of a full-scale waste treatment system for a cannery. 1971. **fTD899.C3S87 ECOL**

HUDDLESTON, ELLIS W., jt. auth.
Wells, Dan M.
Potential pollution of the Ogallala by recharging playa lake water—pesticides. 1970. **fTD224.T4W45 ECOL**

HUDSON, NORMAN.
Soil conservation. Cornell University Press 1972, c1971 **S623.H78 1972 ECOL**

HUDSON, WILLIAM HENRY, 1841-1922.
Birds of La Plata. Twenty-two coloured illus. by H. Gronvold. Dutton, 1920. 2v. **REF QL689.A6H8 ECOL**

HUEPER, WILHELM C., 1894-
Occupational and environmental cancers of the urinary system. Yale University Press, 1969. **RC280.G4H8 ECOL**

HUGHES, GEORGE MUGGAH, 1929-
Hydrogeology of solid waste disposal sites in northeastern Illinois; a final report on a solid waste demonstration grant project, prepared by G. M. Hughes, R. A. Landon, and R. N. Farvolden. U.S. Environmental Protection Agency; for sale by the Supt. of Docs., U.S. Govt. Print. Off. 1971 **TD795.7.H84 ECOL**

HUISMAN, L., 1926-
Groundwater recovery, by L. Huisman. Winchester Press 1972 **TD405.H85 ECOL**

HULBERT, SAMUEL F.
Design of a water-disposable glass packaging container. Prepared by Samuel F. Hulbert, C., Clifford Fain and Michael J. Eitel. U.S. Environmental Protection Agency; for sale by the Supt. of Docs., U.S. Govt. Print. Off. 1971. 1 v. **TD799.H8 ECOL**

HULL, ANDREW P.
Sternglass: a case history, by Andrew P. Hull and Ferdinand J. Shore. Brookhaven National Laboratory 1972? **REF fRA569.H8 ECOL**

HULL, E. W. SEABROOK, jt. auth.
Gerber, Carl R.
Plowshare. 1966 **TK9153.G4 ECOL**

HULL, H. E., jt. auth.
Drobny, N. L.
Recovery and utilization of municipal solid waste: a summary of available cost and performance characteristics of unit processes and systems. 1971.
TD793.D76 ECOL

HUMPHREY, CLIFFORD C.
What's ecology? By Clifford C. Humphrey and Robert G. Evans. Hubbard Press, 1971
QH541.13.H84 ECOL

HUNGERFORD, HAROLD R., 1928-
Ecology: the circle of life, by Harold R. Hungerford. Illus. by Tom Dunnington Childrens Press 1971
QH541.14.H8 ECOL

HUNT, CYNTHIA, 1941-
Water: the web of life by Cynthia A. Hunt and Robert M. Garrels. Norton 1972 **GB661.H84 ECOL**

HUNT, ROBERT G., jt. auth.
Franklin, William E.
Environmental impacts of polystyrene foam and molded pulp meat trays. 1972. **fTP373.F7 ECOL**

HUNTER, BEATRICE TRUM.
Gardening without poisons. 2d ed. With illus. by Bob Hines. Houghton, 1971. **SB975.H8 1971 ECOL**

HUNTER, DONALD C., 1898- ed.
Air pollution experiments for junior and senior high school science classes, ed. by Donald C. Hunter and Henry C. Wohlers. Education Committee Mid-Atlantic States Section, Air Pollution Control Association, 1968.
fTD883.2.H8 ECOL

HURD, CLEMENT, 1908- illus.
Hurd, Edith (Thacher).
Wilson's world. 1st ed. 1971 **FictionECOL**

HURD, EDITH (THACHER) 1910-
Wilson's world. Pictures by Clement Hurd. 1st ed. Harper & Row 1971 **FictionECOL**

HURN, RICHARD WILSON, 1919- jt. auth.
Eccleston, Barton H.
Effect of fuel front-end and midrange volatility on automobile emissions. 1972? **TN23.U7no.7707 ECOL**

HUTCHINGS, EDWARD, ed.
Are our descendants doomed? 1972
HB849.A74 1972 ECOL

HUTCHINS, WELLS A.
Water rights laws in the nineteen western states. Completed by Harold H. Ellis and J. Peter De Braal. Natural Resource Economics Division, Economic Research Service, U.S. Dept. of Agriculture 1971- v.1- (United States Dept. of Agriculture. Miscellaneous publication no. 1206)
KF5559.A45H8 ECOL

HUTCHINSON, GEORGE EVELYN, 1903-
The ecological theater and the evolutionary play by G. E. Hutchinson. Yale University Press, 1965.
QH311.H77 ECOL

HUTH, HANS, 1892-
Nature and the American: three centuries of changing attitudes. Univ. of Calif. Press, 1957.
QH77.U6H8 ECOL

HYDE, MARGARET OLDROYD, 1917-
For pollution fighters only by Margaret O. Hyde. Illustrated by Don Lynch. McGraw-Hill 1971
TD175.H9 ECOL
Plants today and tomorrow. Illus. by P. A. Hutchison. Whittlesey House 1960 **QK50.H9 ECOL**
This crowded planet. Illus. by Mildred Waltrip. Whittlesey House 1961 **HB883.H9 ECOL**

HYDE, PHILIP, 1921- illus.
Abbey, Edward.
Slickrock. 1971 **fF830.A62 ECOL**

HYDROSCIENCE, INC.
Limnological systems analysis of the Great Lakes; phase I—preliminary model design. Prepared for the Great Lakes Basin Commission. 1973.
fTC423.3.H9 ECOL

HYLER, NELSON W.
The how and why wonder book of rocks and minerals. Illus. by Kenyon Shannon. Grosset & Dunlap 1970,c1960 (How and why wonder books)
fQE432.H9 1970 ECOL

HYNES, HUGH BERNARD NOEL, 1917-
The biology of polluted waters. With an introd. by F. T. K. Pentelow. Univ. of Toronto Press, 1971c1960
QH96.H9 1971 ECOL
The ecology of running waters by H. B. N. Hynes. University of Toronto Press, 1970.
QH541.5.S7H9 ECOL

I

IIT RESEARCH INSTITUTE. TECHNOLOGY CENTER.
Development of phosphate-free home laundry detergents. Environmental Protection Agency, Water Quality Off. 1970. (Water pollution control research series) **fTP992.5.I2 ECOL**

ILLINOIS. AGRICULTURAL EXPERIMENT STATION, URBANA.
Conference on Agriculture's Role in Environmental Quality. University of Illinois, Urbana—Champaign, 1970.
Agriculture's role in environmental quality. 1971
fHC68.C6 1970 ECOL
Conference on Environmental Quality and Agriculture. University of Illinois, Urbana-Champaign, 1971.
Environmental quality and agriculture: what are the options? 1972 **fHC68.C6 1971 ECOL**

ILLINOIS. NORTHERN ILLINOIS UNIVERSITY, DE KALB. LORADO TAFT FIELD CAMPUS. DEPT. OF OUTDOOR TEACHER EDUCATION.
Tips and tricks in outdoor education; approaches to providing children with educational experiences in the out-of-doors. Prepared by members of the Department of Outdoor Teacher Education, the Lorado Taft Field Campus of Northern Illinois University. Edited by Malcolm D. Swan. Interstate Printers & Publishers 1970
fLB1047.I44 ECOL

ILLINOIS. UNIVERSITY AT URBANA-CHAMPAIGN. COUNCIL ON ENVIRONMENTAL QUALITY.
Conference on Agriculture's Role in Environmental Quality. University of Illinois, Urbana—Champaign, 1970.
Agriculture's role in environmental quality. 1971
fHC68.C6 1970 ECOL
Conference on Environmental Quality and Agriculture. University of Illinois, Urbana-Champaign, 1971.
Environmental quality and agriculture: what are the options? 1972 **fHC68.C6 1971 ECOL**

ILLINOIS. UNIVERSITY. CENTER FOR ADVANCED COMPUTATION.
Hannon, Bruce.
System energy and recycling: a study of the beverage industry. 1972. **fTP659.H3 ECOL**

ILLINOIS. WATER SURVEY.
Research needs on waste heat transfer from large sources into the environment. William C. Ackermann, principal investigator. 1971. **fTD427.H4I4 ECOL**

IMHOFF, KARL, 1876-
Disposal of sewage and other waterborne wastes by Karl Imhoff, W. J. Muller and D. K. B. Thistlethwayte. 2d ed. Ann Arbor Science Publishers, 1971.
TD741.I5813 1971b ECOL

IMSLAND, DONALD.
Celebrate the earth. Augsburg Pub. House 1971
QH541.I45 ECOL

INCINERATOR INSTITUTE OF AMERICA.
Incinerator standards. 1970,1968 1v.
REF fTD796.I5 1970 ECOL
Incinerator testing. 1971 **fTD796.I53 ECOL**
Modern incineration: a solution—not the problem. 1969? **fTD796.I54 ECOL**

INDEPENDENT PETROLEUM ASSOCIATION OF AMERICA.
The oil producing industry in your state. 1972- v.
REF fHD9564.I55 ECOL

INDIANA NATURAL AREAS SURVEY.
Lindsey, Alton A.
Natural areas in Indiana and their preservation. 1969. **QH76.5.I6L5 ECOL**

INDICATORS OF ENVIRONMENTAL QUALITY.
Edited by William A. Thomas. Plenum Press, 1972. (Environmental science research, v. 1)
TD172.5.I5 1972 ECOL

INDUSTRIAL DEVELOPMENT.
Site selection handbook, vol.2; industry's guide to environmental planning. Publications Division of Conway Research, 1972. **REF fHC68.I5 1972 ECOL**

INDUSTRIAL POLLUTION CONTROL HANDBOOK.
Edited by Herbert F. Lund. McGraw-Hill 1971 1 v.
REF TD897.I42 ECOL

INDUSTRY/GOVERNMENT TELECONFERENCE ON POLLUTION CONTROL, 1971.
NAM: a voice for American industry; proceedings, national telecast and local panel sessions, May 26,1971. National Association of Manufacturers 1971
fTD172.5.I53 1971 ECOL

INFECTIOUS AND PARASITIC DISEASES OF WILD BIRDS.
Edited by John W. Davis and others. 1st ed. Iowa State University Press 1971 **SF994.4.A1I5 ECOL**

INFORMATICS INC.
An assessment of noise concern in other nations. U.S. Environmental Protection Agency 1971. 2 v.
fTD892.I55 ECOL

INGENIORSVETENSKAPSAKADEMIEN, STOCKHOLM.
Study of Man's Impact on Climate, Stockholm, 1970.
Inadvertent climate modification. 1971
QC981.S77 1970 ECOL

INGLE, DWIGHT JOYCE, 1907-
Who should have children? An environmental and genetic approach by Dwight J. Ingle. Bobbs-Merrill 1973 **HQ751.I43 ECOL**

INLAND WATERWAY TRANSPORTATION;
studies in public and private management and investment decisions.
by Charles W. Howe and others. Resources for the Future; dist. by Johns Hopkins Press, 1969
HE629.I57 ECOL

INSTITUTE FOR THE STUDY OF INQUIRING SYSTEMS, PHILA., PA.
Deal, Richard L.
The application of value theory to water resources planning and management. 1971.
fHD1694.A5D4 ECOL

INSTITUTE OF BIOLOGY.
Biology and ethics. 1969. **HM216.B48 ECOL**
Lowe-McConnell, R. H.
Man-made lakes. 1966. **GB1601.L6 1965 ECOL**

INSTITUTE OF CONTINUING LEGAL EDUCATION, ANN ARBOR, MICH.
Environmental law. 1971 **KF3775.A75E54 ECOL**

INSTITUTE OF ECOLOGY.
Workshop on Global Ecological Problems, University of Wisconsin, 1971.
Man in the living environment. 1972
GF3.W6 1971 ECOL

INSTITUTE OF SCRAP IRON & STEEL, NEW YORK.
Yearbook. 31st- 1970- Institute of Scrap Iron & Steel, Inc. v. **REF TS200.I64 ECOL**

INTASA, INC.
Planning and evaluation of multiple purpose water resource projects in a multiobjective environment; an overview and post-audit analyses; final report. Prepared for: Office of Water Resources Research, U.S. Dept. of the Interior. Ed. by: Sally Davenport. 1972. v.
fHD1691.I1 ECOL

INTERCOM.
Teaching about spaceship earth, a role-playing experience for the middle grades. Center for War/Peace Studies of the New York Friends Group, c1972 (its no. 71) **S946.I5 ECOL**

INTERDISCIPLINARY ENVIRONMENTAL EDUCATION.
Sources of reference materials & audiovisual aids for environmental education. W. R. Thrasher, editor. 2d rev. ed. Nova High School 1972
Ref fQH541.2.I68 1972 ECOL

INTERNATIONAL ATOMIC ENERGY AGENCY.
Symposium on Environmental Aspects of Nuclear Power Stations, New York, 1970.
Environmental aspects of nuclear power stations. 1971. **REF TK9006.S887 1970 ECOL**
Symposium on Use of Nuclear Techniques in the Measurement and Control of Environmental Pollution, Salzburg, 1970.
Nuclear techniques in environmental pollution. 1971. **REF TD177.S9 1970 ECOL**
Working Group Meeting on Nuclear Power Plant Control and Instrumentation, Vienna, 1971.
Nuclear power plant control and instrumentation. 1972. **TK9006.W58 1971 ECOL**

INTERNATIONAL COMMISSION ON NATIONAL PARKS.
United Nations list of national parks and equivalent reserves. Addendum—Corrigendum to the second edition. Including data received to 30 June 1972. Hayez, 1972. **REF SB481.I55 1971 Suppl. ECOL**
United Nations list of national parks and equivalent reserves. Prepared and published by the IUCN, International Commission on National Parks pursuant to United Nations Economic and Social Council Resolution 810 (XXXI). (List established by Jean-Paul Harroy. Closing date: 31 May 1967). 2nd ed. Publishers Hayez, 1971. **REF SB481.I55 1971 ECOL**

INTERNATIONAL CONFERENCE ON URBAN TRANSPORTATION, 5TH, PITTSBURGH, 1971.
Mobility: the fifth freedom; official proceedings. Sponsored by Pittsburgh Urban Transit Council. Cosponsored by United States Dept. of Transportation and Transportation Research Institute, Carnegie-Mellon University. Host corporation: Gulf Oil Corporation. 1971? **fHE148.I5 1971 ECOL**

INTERNATIONAL COUNCIL OF SCIENTIFIC UNIONS.
United Nations Educational, Scientific and Cultural Organization.
UNISIST: study report on the feasibility of a world science system. 1971. **REF Q223.U5 ECOL**

INTERNATIONAL DATE CONFRONTATION SEMINAR, 1ST, UNIVERSITY OF MICHIGAN, 1969.
Clubb, Jerome M.
Ecological data in comparative research. 1970 **H62.C6 ECOL**

INTERNATIONAL GREAT LAKES LEVELS BOARD.
Regulation of Great Lakes water levels: interim report on Lakes Superior and Ontario regulation, to the International Joint Commission by the International Great Lakes Levels Board. 1973. **fGB1627.G8152 ECOL**

INTERNATIONAL INSTITUTE FOR ENVIRONMENTAL AFFAIRS.
Who speaks for earth? 1st ed. 1973 **GF8.W49 ECOL**

INTERNATIONAL IUPAC CONGRESS OF PESTICIDE CHEMISTRY, 2D, TEL-AVIV, 1971.
Chemical releasers in insects; proceedings. Ed. by A. S. Tahori. Gordon and Breach c1971 (its Pesticide chemistry, v.3) **SB951.I56 1971vol.3 ECOL**
Fate of pesticides in environment; proceedings. Ed. by A. S. Tahori. Gordon and Breach 1972 (its Pesticide chemistry, v.6) **SB951.I56 1971vol.6 ECOL**
Insecticide resistance, synergism, enzyme induction; proceedings. Ed. by A. S. Tahori. Gordon and Breach c1971 (its Pesticide chemistry, v.2) **SB951.I56 1971vol.2 ECOL**

INTERNATIONAL JOINT COMMISSION (UNITED STATES AND CANADA) 1909-
International Great Lakes Levels Board.
Regulation of Great Lakes water levels: interim report on Lakes Superior and Ontario regulation, to the International Joint Commission by the International Great Lakes Levels Board. 1973. **fGB1627.G8152 ECOL**

INTERNATIONAL MINERALS AND CHEMICAL CORPORATION.
Utilization of phosphate slimes. Environmental Protection Agency, Water Quality Office. U.S. Govt. Print. Off., 1971. (Water pollution control research series) **fTD899.M5I57 ECOL**

INTERNATIONAL ORGANIZATION.
Kay, David A.
World eco-crisis: international organizations in response. 1972 **HC79.E5K38 ECOL**

INTERNATIONAL SNOWMOBILE INDUSTRY ASSOCIATION.
Snowmobile and Off the Road Vehicle Research Symposium, Michigan State University, East Lansing, 1971.
Proceedings. 1971. **fGF75.S6 1971 ECOL**

INTERNATIONAL SYMPOSIUM ON EUTROPHICATION, UNIVERSITY OF WISCONSIN, 1967.
Eutrophication: causes, consequences, correctives; proceedings of a symposium. National Academy of Sciences, 1969. **QH96.A1I63 1967 ECOL**

INTERNATIONAL SYMPOSIUM ON FACTORS DETERMINING THE BEHAVIOR OF PLANT PATHOGENS IN SOIL, BERKELEY, CALIF., 1963.
Ecology of soil-borne plant pathogens, prelude to biological control. Edited by Kenneth F. Baker and William C. Snyder with R. R. Baker and others. University of California Press, **fQR111.I55 1963 ECOL**

INTERNATIONAL SYMPOSIUM ON MAN'S ROLE IN CHANGING THE FACE OF THE EARTH, PRINCETON, N.J., 1955.
Man's role in changing the face of the earth. Ed. by William L. Thomas, with the collaboration of Carl O. Sauer, Marston Bates and Lewis Mumford. Pub. for the Wenner-Gren Foundation for Anthropological Research and the National Science Foundation by the University of Chicago Press 1970,c1956 **G56.I63 1955 ECOL**

INTERNATIONAL SYMPOSIUM ON RIVER ECOLOGY AND THE IMPACT OF MAN, UNIVERSITY OF MASSACHUSETTS, 1971.
River ecology and man; Proceedings. Edited by Ray T. Oglesby, Clarence A. Carlson and James A. McCann. Academic Press, 1972. (Environmental sciences) **GB1205.I5 1971 ECOL**

INTERNATIONAL SYMPOSIUM ON STATISTICAL ECOLOGY, NEW HAVEN, 1969.
Statistical ecology; proceedings Edited by G. P. Patil, E. C. Pielou and W. E. Waters. Pennsylvania State University Press 1971 3 v. (The Penn State statistics series) **QH541.15.M315 1969 ECOL**

INTERNATIONAL SYMPOSIUM ON THE EXTRA-AUDITORY PHYSIOLOGICAL EFFECTS OF AUDIBLE SOUND, BOSTON, 1969.
Physiological effects of noise. 1970. **QP82.2.N6P47 ECOL**

INTERNATIONAL SYMPOSIUM ON WATER POLLUTION CONTROL IN COLD CLIMATES, UNIVERSITY OF ALASKA, FAIRBANKS, 1970.
Papers Held at the University of Alaska, July 22-24, 1970. Sponsored by Institute of Water Resources, Univ. of Alaska and Federal Water Quality Administration. Editors: R. Sage Murphy and David Nyquist. Technical editor: Paul W. Neff. U.S. Environmental Protection Agency, Office of Research & Monitoring, 1972 (Water pollution control research series) **TD423.I5 ECOL**

INTERNATIONAL UNION FOR THE CONSERVATION OF NATURE AND NATURAL RESOURCES.
Curry-Lindahl, Kai.
National parks of the world. 1972 **SB481.C87 ECOL**

International Commission on National Parks.
United Nations list of national parks and equivalent reserves. 1972. **REF SB481.I55 1971 Suppl. ECOL**

International Commission on National Parks.
United Nations list of national parks and equivalent reserves. 2nd ed. 1971. **REF SB481.I55 1971 ECOL**

INTERNATIONAL UNION FOR THE CONSERVATION OF NATURE AND NATURAL RESOURCES. SURVIVAL SERVICE COMMISSION.
Fisher, James.
Wildlife in danger. 1969 **REF QL88.F48 ECOL**

INTERNATIONAL WATER QUALITY SYMPOSIUM, 5TH, WASHINGTON, D.C., 1970.
Water pollution and health: proceedings. Sponsored by the Water Quality Research Council. 1970 **fTD423.I6 1970 ECOL**

INTERREGIONAL LAND ECONOMICS RESEARCH COMMITTEE.
Symposium on Research Methods, Virginia Polytechnic Institute, 1965.
Methods for land economics research. 1967?,c1966 **HD110.S9 1965 ECOL**

INVESTIGATION OF POROUS PAVEMENTS FOR URBAN RUNOFF CONTROL.
by Edmund Thelen and others of the Franklin Institute Research Laboratories. U.S. Environmental Protection Agency U.S. Govt. Print. Off., 1972.(Water pollution control research series) **fTE215.I58 ECOL**

IONICS, INC.
The electro-oxidation of ammonia in sewage to nitrogen. Authors: Ljiljana Marincic and Frank B. Leitz. Prepared for the Water Quality Office, Environmental Protection Agency. Environmental Protection Agency, Water Quality Office; for sale by the Supt. of Docs., U. S. Govt. Print. Off., 1970. (Water pollution control research series) **fTD757.I55 ECOL**

IOWA. STATE UNIVERSITY OF SCIENCE AND TECHNOLOGY, AMES.
Agricultural practices and water quality. 1971,c1970 **TD420.A33 ECOL**

IOWA. UNIVERSITY. COLLEGE OF LAW.
Iowa Water Resources Pollution Control and Abatement Seminar, Iowa State University, 1965.
Water pollution: control and abatement proceedings. 1st ed. 1970,c1967 **TD224.I8I6 1965 ECOL**

IOWA WATER RESOURCES POLLUTION CONTROL AND ABATEMENT SEMINAR, IOWA STATE UNIVERSITY, 1965.
Water pollution: control and abatement proceedings Editors: Ted L. Willrich and N. William Hines. 1st ed. Iowa State University Press 1970,c1967 **TD224.I8I6 1965 ECOL**

IS THERE AN OPTIMUM LEVEL OF POPULATION?
Ed. by S. Fred Singer. McGraw-Hill 1971 **HB851.18 ECOL**

ISARD, WALTER.
Ecologic-economic analysis for regional development; some initial explorations with particular reference to recreational resource use and environmental planning by Walter Isard and others. Regional Science and Landscape Analysis Project, Department of Landscape Architecture Research Office, Graduate School of Design. Harvard Univ. Free Press 1972 **HT391.I82 ECOL**

ISE, JOHN, 1885-
Our national park policy; a critical history. Decorative sketches by Kate Lord. Published for Resources for the Future by Johns Hopkins Press c1961 **SB482.A1I75 ECOL**

ITASCA ENGINEERING, INC., MINNEAPOLIS.
The effectiveness of flood control structures of the Lower Minnesota River Watershed District. Cokato-Hopkins, 1970. **fTC424.M6182 ECOL**

The Lower Minnesota River Watershed District, and its overall plan. 1961. **fTC424.M6184 ECOL**

Overall plan of the Lower Minnesota River Watershed District, 1972. **fTC424.M6186 ECOL**

ITS BIBLIOGRAPHY SERIES, WRSIC 73-201.
Water Resources Scientific Information Center. PCB in water. 1973. **Z7173.W3W3 ECOL**

ITS CONSERVATION YEARBOOK NO. 4.
United States. Dept. of the Interior. Man, an endangered species? 1968 **fS914.A53 ECOL**

ITS CONSERVATION YEARBOOK NO. 5.
United States. Dept. of the Interior. It's your world. 1969 **fS930.A45 ECOL**

ITS THE HUMAN ENVIRONMENT, V.1.
Woodrow Wilson International Center for Scholars. A selective, annotated bibliography of reports and documents on international environmental problems. 1972. **fZ7164.N3W6 ECOL**

ITS THE HUMAN ENVIRONMENT, V.2.
Woodrow Wilson International Center for Scholars. Summaries of national reports submitted in preparation for the United Nations Conference on the Human Environment. 1972. **fHC68.W6 ECOL**

ITS UNDERSTANDING THE ATOM.
United States. Atomic Energy Commission. The first reactor. 1967 **QC787.N8U52 ECOL**

United States. Atomic Energy Commission. Nuclear Power and the environment. 1969. **TK1343.A46 ECOL**

ITS WRRC BULLETIN NO. 1.
Minnesota. University. Water Resources Research Center. Federal, state, and local agencies concerned with water resources research in Minnesota. 1965. **GB701.M554no.1 ECOL**

ITS WRRC BULLETIN NO. 5.
Minnesota. University. Water Resources Research Center. Water resources research and educational needs in Minnesota. 1967. **GB701.M554no.5 ECOL**

ITS WRRC BULLETIN 9.
Minnesota. University. Water Resources Research Center. Codified and uncodified state laws and municipal ordinances bearing on water and related land resources in Minnesota. 1968. **GB701.M554no.9 ECOL**

ITS. WRRC BULLETIN 28.
Minnesota. University. Water Resources Research Center. Conference on impact of future electric power requirements in the state of Minnesota: an issue analysis. 1971. **GB701.M554no.28 ECOL**

ITS WRRC BULLETIN 50.
Minnesota. University. Water Resources Research Center. Watershed planning: papers presented at the Seminar on Watershed Planning sponsored by the Metropolitan Council and the Minnesota Association of Watershed Districts on February 15, 1972 at the Sheraton Motor Inn, Bloomington, Minnesota. 1972. **GB701.M554no.50 ECOL**

IVANY, J. W. GEORGE, 1938- comp.
Environment: readings for teachers. Edited by J. W. George Ivany. Addison-Wesley Pub. Co. 1971, c1972 **GF47.I9 ECOL**

IZAAK WALTON LEAGUE OF AMERICA. CONSERVATION EDUCATION COMMITTEE.
Guidelines to conservation education action, prepared under the auspices of the IWLA Conservation Education Committee in cooperation with the Conservation Education Association and the Nature Centers Division, National Audubon Society. Izaak Walton League of America c1966 **S946.I9 ECOL**

**IZAAK WALTON LEAGUE OF AMERICA.
IOWA DIVISION.**
Buckmann, Carol A.
The first 50. c1973   **S932.I8B8 ECOL**

J

JACKER, CORINNE.
The biological revolution; a background book on making a new world. Parents' Magazine Press 1971 (The Background series)   **QH333.J3 ECOL**

JACKSON, BARBARA (WARD) LADY, 1914-
Only one earth; the care and maintenance of a small planet, by Barbara Ward and Rene Dubos. 1st ed. Norton 1972   **GF41.J3 ECOL**

JACKSON, DANIEL F., ed.
Algae, man, and the environment. c1968   **QK564.5.A4 ECOL**

JACKSON, JOHN BRINCKERHOFF, 1909-
Landscapes: selected writings of J. B. Jackson. Ed. by Ervin H. Zube. Univ. of Massachusetts Press, 1970.   **HN57.J245 ECOL**

JACKSON, JOHN Y.
Land use: concern, challenge, commitment. Ed. by: V. Eugene Vivian and Norma T. Vivian. Conservation and Environmental Studies Center c1969 (An Environmental education instruction plan)   **HD110.J3 ECOL**

JACKSON, NORA.
A dictionary of natural resources and their principal uses, by Nora Jackson, and Philip Penn. 2d ed. Pergamon Press 1969 (The Commonwealth and international library. Geography division)   **REF HF1051.J3 1969 ECOL**

JACKSON, WES, comp.
Man and the environment. Foreword by Paul Ehrlich. Brown Co. 1971 (Biology series)   **HC68.J32 ECOL**

JACKSONVILLE, ARK.
Biological treatment of chlorophenolic wastes; the demonstration of a facility for the biological treatment of a complex chlorophenolic waste. Author: Albert E. Sidwell. Prepared for the Water Quality Office, Environmental Protection Agency. Environmental Protection Agency, Water Quality Office; for sale by the Supt. of Docs., U.S. Govt. Print. Off., 1971. (Water pollution control research series)   **fTD755.J3 ECOL**

JACOBS, JANE, 1916-
The death and life of great American cities. Random House c1961   **NA9108.J3 ECOL**

The economy of cities. Random House 1969   **HT321.J32 ECOL**

JACOBS, MORRIS BORIS, 1905-
The chemical analysis of air pollutants. Interscience Publishers, 1960. (Chemical analysis, v.10)   **TD883.J3 ECOL**

JACOBSON, JAY S., ed.
Recognition of air pollution injury to vegetation: a pictorial atlas, ed. by J. S. Jacobson and A. Clyde Hill. Air Pollution Control Association, 1970. v. (Air Pollution Control Association informative report no.1)   **fQK751.J3 ECOL**

JACOBSON, NORMAN HARRY, 1915-   jt. auth.
Martens, Frederick Hilbert.
Research reactors. 1965   **QC787.N8M32 ECOL**

JACOBY, HENRY D., ed.
Models for managing regional water quality. 1972.   **TD365.M6 ECOL**

JACOBY, NEIL HERMAN, 1909-
The polluters: industry or government? Essay 1, N. H. Jacoby, essay 2, F. G. Pennance. Institute of Economic Affairs, 1972. (IEA Occasional paper, 36)   **TD176.7.J3 ECOL**

JAEGER, ELLSWORTH.
Nature crafts. Macmillan 1971,c1950 (Olympic editions)   **TT157.J24 ECOL**

JAGER, K. W.
Aldrin, dieldrin, endrin and telodrin; an epidemiological and toxicological study of long-term occupational exposure by K. W. Jager. Elsevier Pub. Co., 1970.   **RA1270.P4J33 ECOL**

JAKUBOSWKI, CHARLES, illus.
Simon, Seymour.
Science projects in ecology. 1972   **QH541.14.S55 ECOL**

JAMAICA BAY ENVIRONMENTAL STUDY GROUP.
Jamaica Bay and Kennedy Airport: a multidisciplinary environmental study; a report. National Academy of Sciences, 1971. 2 v. in 1.   **fTL725.3.P5J3 ECOL**

JAMES, RONALD W.
Sewage sludge treatment 1972 by Ronald W. James. Noyes Data Corp. 1972 (Pollution control review no. 12)   **REF fTD768.J35 ECOL**

JAMESON, WILLIAM CARL. jt. auth.
Gunter, John D.
The ecological impact of solid waste. 1973.   **Ref fZ5863.P6G8 ECOL**

Gunter, John D.
Recycling and re-use: the future of solid waste. 1973.   **Ref fTP156.R38G8 ECOL**

Gunter, John D.
Solid waste management: economics and operation. 1973.   **Ref fZ5853.S22G8 ECOL**

JAMISON, ANDREW.
The steam-powered automobile; an answer to air pollution. Indiana Univ. Press 1970   **TL200.J34 ECOL**

JANERICH, DWIGHT T., ed.
Symposium on Monitoring, Birth Defects and Environment, Albany, N. Y., 1970.
Monitoring, birth defects and environment: the problem of surveillance. 1971.   **RG627.S94 1970 ECOL**

JAQUES, FLORENCE (PAGE) 1890-
Canoe country, by Florence Page Jaques; illustrations by Francis Lee Jaques. The University of Minnesota Press c1938   **F606.J36 ECOL**

Snowshoe country, by Florence Page Jaques; illustrations by Frances Lee Jaques. The University of Minnesota Press 1944   **F606.J37 ECOL**

JAQUES, FRANCES LEE, 1887-   illus.
Bovey, Martin Koon.
Saga of the waterfowl. 1949.   **REF SK331.B6 ECOL**

JAQUES, FRANCIS LEE, 1887-   illus.
Jaques, Florence (Page).
Canoe country. c1938   **F606.J36 ECOL**

Jaques, Florence (Page).
Snowshoe country. 1944   **F606.J37 ECOL**

Outdoor life.
Outdoor life's Gallery of North American game. 1946   **fSK40.O8 ECOL**

JAQUES, HARRY EDWIN,.
1880- How to know the weeds.
In: Wilkinson, Robert E. How to know the weeds. 2d ed. 1972   **SB612.A2W54 1972 ECOL**

JAQUES, HARRY EDWIN, 1880-   How to know the trees.
Miller, Howard A.
How to know the trees. 2d ed. 1972   **REF QK482.M65 1972 ECOL**

JAQUES, HARRY EDWIN, 1880-   jt. auth.
Wilkinson, Robert E.
How to know the weeds. 2d ed. 1972   **SB612.A2W54 1972 ECOL**

JARMAN, CATHERINE.
Atlas of animal migration, by Cathy Jarman. Illustrated by Peter Warner and Tony Swift. Maps by Geographical Projects, London. Consultant: Michael Boorer. John Day Co. 1972   **fQL754.J37 ECOL**

JARRETT, HENRY, ed.
Perspectives on conservation. 1969, c1958   **HC103.7.P47 1969 ECOL**

Resources for the Future.
Comparisons in resource management. 1961   **REF SD411.R4 ECOL**

Resources for the Future.
Environmental quality in a growing economy. 1968,c1966   **HC103.7.R39 ECOL**

JBF SCIENTIFIC CORPORATION.
Engineering methodology for river and stream reaeration. Authors: Ronald P. Murro and Donald S. Yeaple. U.S. Environmental Protection Agency; for sale by the Supt. of Docs., U. S. Govt. Print. Off. 1971 (Water pollution control research series)   **fTD458.J17 ECOL**

JEFCOAT, ALLURE, comp.
Health and human values: an ecological approach. Wiley 1972   **RA565.J44 ECOL**

JEFFERS, ROBINSON, 1887-1962.
Brower, David Ross.
Not man apart. 1969   **F869.B63B7 1969 ECOL**

JENKINS, FRANCES BRIGGS, 1905-
Science reference sources. 5th ed. M.I.T. Press 1969   **REF Z7401.J4 1969 ECOL**

JENNINGS, BURGESS HILL, 1903-   ed.
Interactions of man and his environment. Edited by Burgess H. Jennings and John E. Murphy. Plenum Press, 1966.   **TD180.J4 ECOL**

JENSEN, JOHN GRANVILLE, 1911-   jt. auth.
Highsmith, Richard Morgan.
Conservation in the United States. 2d ed 1969   **HC103.7.H5 1969 ECOL**

JENSEN, WALTER GODFRIED WILLEM.
Nuclear power by W. G. Jensen. G. T. Foulis & Co. Ltd., 1969.   **TK9145.J44 ECOL**

JENSEN, WILLIAM A.
Botany: an ecological approach by William A. Jensen and Frank B. Salisbury. Wadsworth Pub. Co. 1972   **QK47.J45 ECOL**

JEPSEN, ANDERS, jt. auth.
Environmental Measurements, Inc.
Monitoring mercury vapor near pollution sites. 1971.   **fTD427.M4E5 ECOL**

JEPSEN, STANLEY M.
Trees and forests. Barnes 1969   **SD143.J39 ECOL**

JEROME, JOHN.
The death of the automobile. 1st ed. Norton 1972   **HE5623.J47 ECOL**

JERUSALEM INTERNATIONAL CONFERENCE ON WATER QUALITY AND POLLUTION RESEARCH, 1969.
Developments in water quality research; proceedings. General editor: Hillil I. Shuval. Editorial board: Yehuda Goldshmid, Gedaliahu Shelef and Alberto Wachs. Ann Arbor-Humphrey Science Publishers, 1970   **TD370.J47 1969 ECOL**

JOERG, WOLFGANG LOUIS GOTTFRIED, 1885-
Brief history of polar exploration since the introduction of flying, by W. L. G. Joerg. American Geographical Society, 1930 (American Geographical Society. Special publication no. 11)   **G590.J6 ECOL**

JOERG, WOLFGANG LOUIS GOTTFRIED, 1885-   ed. and tr.
Nordenskjold, Otto.
The geography of the polar regions, consisting of a general characterization of polar nature. 1928.   **G587.N6 ECOL**

JOFFE, JOYCE.
Conservation. Published for the American Museum of Natural History by the Natural History Press 1970,c1969 (Nature and science library)   **S940.J64 ECOL**

JOHANN, D. R., jt. auth.
McNabb, C. D.
A fluorometric technique for sampling in large-river ecosystems. 1971.   **GB701.M554no.34 ECOL**

JOHANSON, EDWARD E., jt. auth.
Feick, George.
Control of mercury contamination in freshwater sediments. 1972.   **TD427.M4F4 ECOL**

JOHN E. FOGARTY INTERNATIONAL CENTER FOR ADVANCED STUDY IN THE HEALTH SCIENCES.
Environmental factors in respiratory disease. 1972.   **RC732.E59 ECOL**

JOHN E. FOGARTY INTERNATIONAL CENTER FOR ADVANCED STUDY IN THE HEALTH SCIENCES. PROCEEDINGS, NO. 10.
Mutagenic effects of environmental contaminants. 1972.   **QH431.M958 ECOL**

JOHN E. FOGARTY INTERNATIONAL CENTER FOR ADVANCED STUDY IN THE HEALTH SCIENCES. PROCEEDINGS, NO. 11.
Environmental factors in respiratory disease. 1972.   **RC732.E59 ECOL**

JOHN F. KENNEDY INSTITUUT.
Growing against ourselves: the energy-environment tangle. 1972.   **TD195.E4G76 ECOL**

JOHNS, GLENN F., comp.
The Basic book of organic gardening. 1971   **S605.5.B37 ECOL**

JOHNSGARD, PAUL A.
Grouse and quails of North America by Paul A. Johnsgard. University of Nebraska 1973   **QL696.G27J63 ECOL**

Waterfowl, their biology and natural history. Introd. by Peter Scott. University of Nebraska Press 1968   **QL696.A5J63 ECOL**

JOHNSON, A. W., jt. auth.
Goodall, J. D.
Las aves de Chile. 1946   **Ref QL689.C5G6 ECOL**

JOHNSON, ARTHUR TYSILIO, 1873-1956.
Plant names simplified; their meanings and pronunciation. With foreword by A. J. Macself. 2d ed. Grand River Books, 1971.   **QK11.J6 1971 ECOL**

JOHNSON, CECIL E., comp.
Eco-crisis by Cecil E. Johnson. Wiley 1970
QH541.J63 ECOL
Human biology: contemporary readings by Cecil E. Johnson. Van Nostrand Reinhold Co. c1970
QH311.J63 ECOL
The natural world: chaos and conservation compiled by Cecil E. Johnson. McGraw-Hill c1972
QH541.145.J63 ECOL
Social and natural biology; selections from contemporary classics. Cecil E. Johnson, editor. Van Nostrand 1968 **QH302.J58 ECOL**

JOHNSON, EDWIN LEE, 1923-
Cresa.
Pollution abatement and by-product recovery in shellfish and fisheries processing. 1971.
fTD899.F57C73 ECOL

JOHNSON, ELINOR M.
The plant hunters, by Elinor M. Johnson. Drawings by Arvis L. Stewart. Addison-Wesley 1969
Fiction ECOL

JOHNSON, GEORGE ROBBINS, 1900-
Peru from the air, by Lieutenant George R. Johnson ... with text and notes by Raye R. Platt. American Geographical Society, 1930. (American Geographical Society. Special publication no. 12)
F3428.J67 ECOL

JOHNSON, HUEY D., ed.
National Conference on UNESCO, 13th, San Francisco, 1969.
No deposit—no return. 1970
GF3.N38 1969 ECOL

JOHNSON, JACK D.
Development of a mathematical model to predict the role of surface runoff and groundwater flow in over fertilization of surface waters, by J. D. Johnson and Conrad P. Straub. Water Resources Research Center, Univ. of Minn. Graduate School, 1971. (WRRC bulletin, no. 35) **GB701.M554no.35 ECOL**

JOHNSON, JAMES FRANCIS, 1941-
Renovated waste water; an alternative source of municipal water supply in the United States by James F. Johnson. University of Chicago, Dept. of Geography, 1971. **TD429.J6 ECOL**

JOHNSON, JAMES RALPH.
Animals and their food. D. Mckay 1972
QL756.5.J64 ECOL
Zoos of today. McKay Co. 1971
QL77.5.J64 ECOL

JOHNSON, JERRY M.
Potential productivity of fresh water environments as determined by an algae bioassay technique. 1970.
GB701.M554no.20

JOHNSON, PHILIP L., 1931- ed.
Remote sensing in ecology. 1969
QH541.15.R4R4 ECOL

JOHNSON, WILLIAM WEBER, 1909-
Baja California, by William Weber Johnson and the editors of Time-Life Books. With photographs by Jay Maisel. (The American wilderness) **F1246.J6 ECOL**

JOHNSSON, KARL OTTO, 1920-
Nuclear Desalination Information Center.
Indexed bibliography of nuclear desalination literature—7- 1972-
REF fZ5853.S22N8 ECOL
Nuclear Desalination Information Center.
Title—author—company index to reports published by the U.S. Dept. of the Interior, Office of Saline Water through July 1971-
REF fZ5853.S22N84 ECOL

JOINT CONFERENCE ON PREVENTION AND CONTROL OF OIL SPILLS, WASHINGTON, D.C., 1971.
Proceedings of Joint Conference on Prevention and Control of Oil Spills held June 15-17, 1971 at the Sheraton Park Hotel. American Petroleum Institute, 1971? **fGC1080.J6 ECOL**

JONES, CLAIRE.
Pollution: the air we breathe by Claire Jones, Steve J. Gadler and Paul H. Engstrom. Lerner Publications Co. 1971 (A Real world book)
TD883.13.J65 1971 ECOL
Pollution: the balance of nature by C. Jones, Steve J. Gadler and Paul H. Engstrom. Lerner Publications 1972 (A Real world book) **QH541.14.J65 ECOL**
Pollution: the dangerous atom by Claire Jones, Steve J. Gadler and Paul H. Engstrom. Lerner Publications Co. 1972 (A Real world book)
TD880.J65 1972 ECOL
Pollution: the food we eat by C. Jones, Steve J. Gadler and Paul H. Engstrom. Lerner Publications 1972 (A Real world book) **TX533.J65 ECOL**
Pollution: the land we live on by Claire Jones, Steve J. Gadler and Paul H. Engstrom. Lerner Publications Co. 1971 (A Real world book)
TD176.J65 1971 ECOL
Pollution: the noise we hear by Claire Jones, Steve J. Gadler and Paul H. Engstrom. Lerner Publications Co. 1972 (A Real world book) **TD892.J65 1972 ECOL**
Pollution: the population explosion by C. Jones, Steve J. Gadler and Paul H. Engstrom. Lerner Publications 1972 (A Real world book) **HB871.J58 ECOL**
Pollution: the waters of the earth by Claire Jones, Steve J. Gadler and Paul H. Engstrom. Lerner Publications Co. 1971 (A Real world book)
TD422.J65 ECOL

JONES, ERIC, jt. auth.
Perry, Gordon Arthur.
Handbook for environmental studies. 2nd rev. ed. 1971 **LB1585.P4 1971 ECOL**

JONES, H. R.
Detergents and pollution; problems and technological solutions, 1972 by H. R. Jones. Noyes Data Corp. 1972 (Pollution control review no. 7)
fTD427.D4J65 ECOL
Mercury pollution control, 1971 by H. R. Jones. Noyes Data Corp. 1971 (Pollution Control review no. 1) **REF fTD427.M4J66 ECOL**

JONES, JAMES R.
Robert S. Kerr Water Research Center.
Denitrification by anaerobic filters and ponds, phase II. 1971. **TD475.R62 ECOL**

JONES, KENNETH LESTER, 1905-
Environmental health by K. L. Jones, Louis W. Shainberg and Curtis O. Byer. Canfield Press, 1971.
RA565.J65 ECOL

JONES, THOMAS C., comp.
The environment of America: present/future/ past; selected articles from a variety of sources. Edited by Thomas C. Jones. Assisted by Harriet B. Helmer. Associate editor Allan B. Carpenter. J. G. Ferguson Pub. Co.; distributed to the book trade by Doubleday 1971 **fQH541.145.J65 ECOL**

JORGENSEN, S. E., ed.
Symposium on Wolf Management in Selected Areas of North America, Chicago, 1970.
Wolf management in selected areas of North America. 1970 **QL737.C22S9 1970 ECOL**

JOSEPH, ALEXANDER, jt. auth.
Hone, Elizabeth B.
Teaching elementary science: a sourcebook for elementary science. 2d ed. 1971
LB1585.H65 1971 ECOL
Morholt, Evelyn.
A sourcebook for the biological sciences. 2d ed. 1966
QH53.M67 1966 ECOL

JOSEPHY, ALVIN M., 1915- ed.
American heritage.
The American heritage book of natural wonders. c1972,1963 **fE169.A496 1972 ECOL**

JOSTAD, KAREN, jt. auth.
Griffith, Charles J.
EP—the new conservation. 1971
HC110.E5G74 ECOL

JUHOLA, A. J.
Mine Safety Appliances Research Corporation.
Optimization of the regeneration procedure for granular activated carbon. 1970.
fTP245.C4M55 ECOL

JUNEJA, NARENDRA.
Wallace, McHarg, Roberts and Todd.
An ecological study of the Twin Cities Metropolitan Area. 1969. **fQH541.W32 ECOL**

K

KAISER NEWS.
Fabun, Don.
Dimensions of change. 1971 **fHM221.F32 ECOL**

KALLARD, THOMAS.
Electret devices for air pollution control. Ed. by Thomas Kallard. Introductory overview: "The electret," by Bernhard Gross. Optosonic Press 1972 (State of the art review, v.6) **fQC585.K28 ECOL**

KANE, HENRY BUGBEE, 1902-
The tale of a meadow, written and illus. by Henry B. Kane. Knopf 1959 (Borzoi nature study books)
QH48.K23 ECOL
The tale of a wood, written and illus. by Henry B. Kane. Knopf 1962 (Borzoi nature study books)
QH86.K3 ECOL

KANSAS. UNIVERSITY. CENTER FOR RESEARCH, INC.
Oxygen consumption in continuous biological culture. by Walter J. O'Brien and Carl E. Burkhead for the Environmental Protection Agency. United States Environmental Protection Agency U.S. Govt. Print. Off., 1971. (Water pollution control research series)
fTD755.K3 ECOL

KANTRUD, HAROLD A., jt. auth.
Stewart, Robert E.
Classification of natural ponds and lakes in the glaciated prairie region. 1971. **S914.A3no.92 ECOL**

KARL R. ROHRER ASSOCIATES.
Underwater storage of combined sewer overflows. U.S. Environmental Protection Agency; for sale by the Supt. of Docs., U.S. Govt. Print. Off., 1971 (Water pollution control research series) **fTD662.K36 ECOL**

KARLEN, ARNO.
Steinhacker, Charles.
Superior. 1971? **fF552.S725 ECOL**

KARNAVAS, JAMES A.
Black, Sivalls and Bryson, inc., Kansas City, Mo. Applied Technology Division
Evaluation of a new acid mine drainage treatment process. 1971. **fTD899.M5B55 ECOL**

KARPLUS, ROBERT.
Science Curriculum Improvement Study.
Interaction and systems. c1970
LB1585.S36 ECOL

KASTNER, JACOB, 1919-
The natural radiation environment. United States Atomic Energy Commission, Division of Technical Information, 1968. (Understanding the atom)
QH652.K35 ECOL

KATES, ROBERT WILLIAM, jt. auth.
Russell, Clifford S.
Drought and water supply. 1970
TD223.R88 ECOL

KATES, ROBERT WILLIAM, jt. ed.
Burton, Ian.
Readings in resource management and conservation. 1970,c1965 **S938.B86 ECOL**

KATZ, ROBERT, 1933-
A giant in the earth. Stein and Day c1973
HD9000.5.K3 ECOL

KAUFFMAN, RICHARD, 1916- illus.
Hay, John.
The primal alliance: earth and ocean. 1971.
fQH95.7.H32 ECOL
Muir, John.
Gentle wilderness. Rev. ed. 1971c1968
F868.S5M88 1971 ECOL

KAUFMAN, DONALD DEVERE, 1933- jt. auth.
Kearney, Philip C.
Degradation of herbicides. 1969.
REF SB951.4.K4 ECOL

KAUFMAN, EILEEN.
Council on Economic Priorities.
Paper profits: pollution in the pulp and paper industry. c1972 **TD899.W65C65 1972 ECOL**
Council on Economic Priorities.
Paper profits: pollution in the pulp and paper industry. 1971 **REF fTD888.P8C6 ECOL**

KAUFMAN, HERBERT, 1922-
The Forest ranger, a study in administrative behavior. Published for Resources for the Future by Johns Hopkins Press 1960 **SD565.K3 ECOL**

KAUFMAN, WARREN J., 1922-
California. University. Sanitary Engineering Research Laboratory.
Optimization of ammonia removal by ion exchange using clinoptilolite. 1971 i.e. 1972
fTD757.5.C35 ECOL

KAUFMAN, WARREN J., 1922- jt. auth.
Stenquist, Richard J.
Initial mixing in coagulation processes. 1972.
TD455.S7 ECOL

KAVALER, LUCY.
Dangerous air. Illus. by Carl Smith. Day c1967
TD883.13.K3 ECOL

KAY, DAVID A.
World eco-crisis: international organizations in response. Edited by David A. Kay and Eugene B. Skolnikoff. With an introd. by Maurice F. Strong. University of Wisconsin Press 1972
HC79.E5K38 ECOL

KAY, KINGSLEY.
Adverse effects of common environmental pollutants. 1972 **RA1270.P4A32 ECOL**

KEARNEY, PHILIP C., 1932-
Degradation of herbicides, edited by P. C. Kearney and D. D. Kaufman. M. Dekker, 1969.
REF SB951.4.K4 ECOL

KEATS, EZRA JACK, illus.
Selsam, Millicent (Ellis).
How to be a nature detective. 1966,c1963
PZ10.S44Hr3 ECOL

KEENE, MELVIN.
The beginners' story of minerals and rocks. Pictures by Harry McNaught. Harper 1966
QE365.K27 ECOL

KEEP AMERICA BEAUTIFUL, INC.
Inventory of litter-prevention and related environmental programs in the United States. 1972- v.
fTD817.K4 ECOL

KEITH, LAWRENCE H., 1938-
Southeast Water Laboratory.
Catalog of pesticide NMR spectra. 1971.
fSB951.S64 ECOL

KELLER, DANIEL J., jt. auth.
Brunner, Dirk R.
Sanitary landfill design and operation. 1972.
TD795.7.B7 ECOL

KELLEY, BEN.
The pavers and the paved. D. W. Brown 1971
HE355.K38 ECOL

KELLY, JAMES.
Pollution—man's crisis: an investigative approach. By James Kelly and Harold Wengert. N.D. Studies c1971
QH541.2.K45 ECOL

KELNER, MILTON, 1917-
Legal control of the environment—3D. 1971
KF3775.L44 ECOL

KELNHOFER, GUY J.
Metropolitan planning and river basin planning: some interrelationships. Published by the Water Resources Center in cooperation with School of Architecture, Program in City Planning. Georgia Institute of Technology, 1968.
TD223.K4 ECOL

Preserving the Great Lakes. Prepared for National Water Commission. U.S. Dept. of Commerce, National Technical Information Service, 1972.
fTC423.3.K4 ECOL

KENAHAN, CHARLES B.
Bureau of Mines research programs on recycling and disposal of mineral-, metal-, and energy-based wastes, by C. B. Kenahan and others. U.S. Bureau of Mines, 1973. (United States. Bureau of Mines. Information circular 8595)
TN23.U7no.8595 ECOL

KENK, ROMAN, 1898-
Freshwater planarians (Turbellaria) of North America. Environmental Protection Agency, 1972. (Biota of freshwater ecosystems, Identification manual, no.1.)
fQH96.A2B5no.1 ECOL

KENNEDY, DAVID.
Report to the Subcommittee on Legal Problems Governor's Advisory Committee on Air Resources, by David Kennedy, Ralph T. Keyes, and Frank J. Knoll. 1966.
fTD883.5.M65K4 ECOL

KENNER, HUGH.
Bucky; a guided tour of Buckminster Fuller. Morrow, 1973.
TA140.F9K46 ECOL

KENTUCKY. DEPT. OF HEALTH.
Kentucky solid waste management plan. Status report 1970. U.S. Environmental Protection Agency. Solid Waste Management Office 1971
TD788.4.K4A45 ECOL

KEPES, GYORGY, 1906-
Arts of the environment. Edited by Gyorgy Kepes. G. Braziller 1972 (Vision & value series)
N72.S6K37 ECOL

KESSLER, MARY.
Burg, Nan C.
Abandoned vehicles: a selected bibliography. 1972
Ref fHD9975.B87 ECOL

KETCHUM, RICHARD M., 1922-
The secret life of the forest by Richard M. Ketchum. Conceived and produced in cooperation with the St. Regis Paper Company. American Heritage Press 1970
fQK938.F6K4 ECOL

KETELLE, MARTHA J.
Problem lakes in the United States, by Martha J. Ketelle and Paul D. Uttormark. Prepared for the Office of Research and Monitoring, Environmental Protection Agency. U.S. Environmental Protection Agency; for sale by the Supt. of Docs., U.S. Govt. Print. Off., 1971. (Water pollution control research series)
fTD223.K47 ECOL

KEYES, RALPH T., jt. auth.
Kennedy, David.
Report to the Subcommittee on Legal Problems Governor's Advisory Committee on Air Resources. 1966.
fTD883.5.M65K4 ECOL

KHARE, RAVINDRA S., ed.
Environmental quality and social responsibility. 1972
HC110.P55E57 ECOL

KHATTAK, MOHAMMED N., jt. auth.
Bongers, Leonard H.
Sand and gravel overlay for control of mercury in sediments. 1972.
fTD427.M4B6 ECOL

KILBOURNE, EDWIN D.
Human ecology and public health, ed. by Edwin D. Kilbourne and Wilson G. Smillie. 4th ed. Macmillan 1969
RA425.K55 1969 ECOL

KILLIAN, JAMES RHYNE, 1904-
Fuller, Richard Buckminster.
Approaching the benign environment. 1970
Q171.F96 ECOL

KINGSLEY, V. VICTOR.
Bacteriology primer in air contamination control, by V. Victor Kingsley. University of Toronto Press 1967
QR101.K55 ECOL

KIRALDI, LOUIS, 1911-
Pollution; a selected bibliography of U.S. Government publications on air, water, and land pollution. Compiled by Louis Kiraldi and Janet L. Burk. Western Michigan University, Institute of Public Affairs, 1971.
REF fZ7171.K55 ECOL

KIRBY, JOHN T.
Minnesota. Pollution Control Agency.
In the matter of the adoption of proposed amendments to Minnesota Regulations APC 1, APC 3, APC 4, APC 11 and APC 15; and the adoption of Minnesota Regulation APC 16; and the proposed adoption of the Minnesota Air Quality Implementation Plan. 1972
REF fKFM5758.A17 1972 ECOL

KIRCHER, HARRY B., jt. auth.
McNall, Preston Essex.
Our natural resources. 3d ed. 1970
S930.M2 1970 ECOL

KIRK, WILLIAM P.
Krypton 85: a review of the literature and an analysis of radiation hazards. Environmental Protection Agency, Office of Research and Monitoring, 1972
QP82.2.R3K5 ECOL

KIRKWOOD, JAMES PUGH, 1807-1877.
A special report on the pollution of river waters by James P. Kirkwood. Reprint ed. Arno 1970 (American environmental studies) (Public documents of Massachusetts, v. 5 no. 30)
REF TD425.K52 1970 ECOL

KITTRELL, F. W.
A practical guide to water quality studies of streams, by F. W. Kittrell. U.S. Federal Water Pollution Control Administration; U.S. Govt. Print. Off. 1969.
TD425.K53 ECOL

KLEE, ALBERT J., jt. auth.
Muhich, Anton J.
Preliminary data analysis. 1968.
TD795.M82 ECOL

KLEMM, DONALD J.
Freshwater leeches (Annelida: Hirudinea) of North America. Environmental Protection Agency, 1972. (Biota of freshwater ecosystems, Identification manual, no.8.)
fQH96.A2B5no.8 ECOL

KLIKOFF, LIONEL G., ed.
Grand Canyon Symposium, 1970.
Environment, man, survival: Grand Canyon Symposium, 1970. c1971
GF8.G7 1970 ECOL

KLINE, A. BURT.
The Environmental and ecological forum, 1970-1971. 1972.
TD898.E58 ECOL

KLOPFER, PETER H.
Habitats and territories; a study of the use of space by animals by Peter H. Klopfer. Basic Books 1969 (Basic topics in comparative psychology)
QL751.K592 ECOL

KLOPFER, PETER H., comp.
Behavioral ecology by Peter H. Klopfer. Dickenson Pub. Co. 1970 (Contemporary thought in ecological science series)
QL751.K5917 ECOL

KLOTS, ALEXANDER BARRETT, 1903-
Insects of North America by Alexander and Elsie Klots. Doubleday 1971 (Animal life of North America series)
QL473.K56 ECOL

KLOTS, ELSIE BROUGHTON, jt. auth.
Klots, Alexander Barrett.
Insects of North America. 1971
QL473.K56 ECOL

KNAPP, CLIFFORD E.
Outdoor activities for environmental studies. The Instructor Publications, Inc. c1971 (Instructor handbook series)
LB1047.K5 ECOL

KNAPP, GEORGE L., ed.
Water Resources Scientific Information Center.
Sanitary landfills. 1972
REF Z5853.S22W38 ECOL

KNAUTH, PERCY, 1914-
The North Woods by Percy Knauth and the editors of Time-Life Books. Time-Life 1972 (The American wilderness)
QH75.K63 ECOL

KNEESE, ALLEN.
Resources for the Future.
Water pollution: economic aspects and research needs. 1962
TD420.R4 ECOL

KNEESE, ALLEN V.
Economics and the environment; a materials balance approach, by Allen V. Kneese, Robert U. Ayres and Ralph C. d'Arge. Resources for the Future; distributed by the Johns Hopkins Press, 1970
HC68.K57 ECOL

Managing water quality: economics, technology, institution, by Allen V. Kneese and Blair T. Bower. Published for Resources for the Future by the Johns Hopkins Press 1968
TD423.K52 ECOL

KNEESE, ALLEN V., ed.
Managing the environment: international economic cooperation for pollution control. 1971
HC79.E5M35 1971 ECOL

Resources for the Future.
Environmental quality analysis. 1972
HC79.E5R46 ECOL

Western Resources Conference. 7th, Colorado State University, 1965.
Water research. c1966
REF TD355.W4 1965 ECOL

KNEESE, ALLEN V., jt. auth.
Herfindahl, Orris Clemens.
Quality of the environment: an economic approach to some problems in using land, water, and air. 1965
TD153.H46 ECOL

KNEESE, ALLEN V. THE ECONOMICS OF REGIONAL ...
Kneese, Allen V.
Managing water quality: economics, technology, institution. 1968
TD423.K52 ECOL

KNETSCH, JACK LOUIS, 1933- jt. auth.
Clawson, Marion.
Economics of outdoor recreation. c1966
GV182.2.C55 ECOL

KNIGHT, CLIFFORD BURNHAM, 1926-
Basic concepts of ecology by Clifford B. Knight. Macmillan 1965
QH541.K5 ECOL

KNIGHT, DAVID C.
The first book of air; a basic guide to the earth's atmosphere. F. Watts 1961 (The First books, 140)
PZ10.K57Fg ECOL

KNOLL, FRANK J., jt. auth.
Kennedy, David.
Report to the Subcommittee on Legal Problems Governor's Advisory Committee on Air Resources. 1966.
fTD883.5.M65K4 ECOL

KNUTSON, KEITH M.
Evaluation of attached algae in the Mississippi River adjacent to the NSP Sherburne County Generating Plant, Becker, Minnesota, during October and November, 1971. Northern States Power Co.?, 1972
fTK1331.N6K5 ECOL

KOENIG, LOUIS.
Alamo Area Council of Governments.
Basin management for water reuse. 1972.
fTD225.S225A65 ECOL

KOENKER, WILLIAM E.
Petroleum resources and production facilities in the Upper Midwest. Univ. of Minnesota 1963.
fHD1773.A3U6no.8 ECOL

KOFORD, CARL B.
The California condor, by Carl B. Koford. Dover Publications 1966,c1953
QL696.A2K64 1966 ECOL

KOHNKE, HELMUT, 1901-
Soil conservation by Helmut Kohnke and Anson R. Bertrand. McGraw-Hill, 1959. (McGraw-Hill publications in the agricultural sciences)
S623.K56 ECOL

KOLKA, JAMES W., ed.
Environmental quality and social responsibility. 1972
HC110.P55E57 ECOL

KOON, JOHN H.
California. University. Sanitary Engineering Research Laboratory.
Optimization of ammonia removal by ion exchange using clinoptilolite. 1971 i.e. 1972
fTD757.5.C35 ECOL

KORDISH, RAYMOND J., jt. auth.
Ashbaugh, Byron L.
Trail planning and layout. 1971 **QH58.A8 ECOL**

KORMONDY, EDWARD JOHN, 1926-
Concepts of ecology by Edward J. Kormondy. Prentice-Hall 1969 (Concepts of modern biology series)
QH541.K59 ECOL

KOTSONIS, HELEN HOCH.
Modern lesson plans in environmental science by Helen Hoch Kotsonis and Bill Baker. Parker Pub. Co. 1972
QH541.2.K68 ECOL

KRAMER, JAMES RICHARD, 1931- jt. auth.
Allen, Herbert Ellis.
Nutrients in natural waters. 1972
        QH96.A48 ECOL

KRAUSKOPF, KONRAD BATES, 1910-
Fundamentals of physical science by Konrad B. Krauskopf and Arthur Beiser. 6th ed. McGraw-Hill 1971   **Q160.2.K7 1971 ECOL**

KREIS, R. DOUGLAS, jt. auth.
Robert S. Kerr Water Research Center.
Characteristics of rainfall run off from a beef cattle feedlot. 1972.   **TD899.F4R6 ECOL**

KREMEN, S. S., 1919-
Gulf Environmental Systems Company.
Acid mine waste treatment using reverse osmosis. 1971   **fTD754.G84 ECOL**

KRENKEL, PETER A., ed.
National Symposium on Thermal Pollution, Portland, Oregon, 1968.
Biological aspects of thermal pollution. 1969
        QH90.N3 1968 ECOL

National Symposium on Thermal Pollution, Vanderbilt University, 1968.
Engineering aspects of thermal pollution. 1969.
        TD427.H4N3 1968 ECOL

KREUSCH, ED.
Wastewater demineralization by ion exchange, by Ed Kreusch and Ken Schmidt, for the Office of Research and Monitoring, Environmental Protection Agency. U.S. Environmental Protection Agency; U.S. Govt. Print. Off., 1971 i.e.1972 (Water pollution control research series)   **fTD757.5.K74 ECOL**

KREUSCH, ED, jt. auth.
Holmes, James G.
Acid mine drainage treatment by ion exchange. 1972
        TD899.M5H6 ECOL

KRIETT, JOLENE.
Biocides. University of Minnesota, 1971. (Secondary environmental education development)
        QH545.P4K7 ECOL

KROECK, F. WILLIAM, jt. auth.
Willeke, Gene E.
A program for metropolitan water management. 1972.   **fTD365.W5 ECOL**

KRUTCH, JOSEPH WOOD, 1893-
The best nature writing of Joseph Wood Krutch. Illus. by Lydia Rosier. Morrow, 1969 c1970
        QH81.K828 ECOL

The great chain of life. With illus. by Paul Landacre. Houghton, 1957 c1956   **QL751.K87 ECOL**

KRUTCHKOFF, RICHARD G., 1933-
Stochastics, Inc., Blacksburg, Va.
Stochastic modeling for water quality management. 1971.   **fTC409.S8 ECOL**

KRUTILLA, JOHN V.
The Columbia River Treaty; the economics of an international river basin development, by John V. Krutilla. Published for Resources For the Future by Johns Hopkins Press c1967 **HD1694.A2 1967 ECOL**

Resources for the Future.
Multiple purpose river development. 1958
        REF HN15.R43 ECOL

KRUTILLA, JOHN V., ed.
Natural environments: studies in theoretical and applied analysis. 1972   **QH76.N28 ECOL**

KRUTILLA, JOHN V., jt. auth.
Brooks, David B.
Peaceful use of nuclear explosives; some economic aspects. 1969   **HD9698.U52B7 ECOL**

KRZNARICH, SUSAN.
Basic ecology. University of Minnesota, 1971. (Secondary environmental education development)
        QH541.2.K7 ECOL

KULSKI, JULIAN EUGENE, 1929-
Land of urban promise: continuing the great tradition; a search for significant urban space in the urbanized Northeast. University of Notre Dame Press, 1967.
        HT167.K8 ECOL

KUPPERMAN, ROBERT H., 1935-
United States.
The potential for energy conservation. 1972.
        TJ153.U43 ECOL

KUSLER, JON A.
Survey: lake protection and rehabilitation legislation in the United States. A report funded by the Inland Lake Renewal and Shoreland Management Demonstration Project, University of Wisconsin. N.P. 1972.
        REF fKF5568.K8 ECOL

KWEE, SWANLIAT, ed.
Growing against ourselves: the energy-environment tangle. 1972.   **TD195.E4G76 ECOL**

L

LACK, DAVID LAMBERT.
Ecological isolation in birds by David Lack. Main illus. by Robert Gillmor. Harvard University Press, 1971.   **QH401.L32 1971 ECOL**

LACY, WILLIAM J.
United States. Federal Water Quality Administration.
Projects: Industrial Pollution Control Branch. 1970.
        fTD897.5.U56 ECOL

LAKE MICHIGAN ENFORCEMENT CONFERENCE. LAKE MICHIGAN INTERSTATE PESTICIDES COMMITTEE.
An evaluation of DDT and dieldrin in Lake Michigan. Author: Lloyd A. Lueschow Prepared for Office of Research and Monitoring, U.S. Environmental Protection Agency. U.S. Govt. Print. Off., 1972. (Ecological research series)   **TD427.P35L3 ECOL**

LAKE TAHOE AREA COUNCIL.
Eutrophication of surface waters—Lake Tahoe. Prepared for the Environmental Protection Agency. Authors: P. H. McGauhey, G. L. Dugan, and D. B. Porcella. U.S. Environmental Protection Agency; for sale by the Supt. of Docs., U.S. Govt. Print. Off., 1971 i.e. 1972 (Water pollution control research series)
        fQH96.8.E9L34 ECOL

Eutrophication of surface waters—Lake Tahoe Indian Creek Reservoir. U.S. Environmental Protection Agency; for sale by the Supt. of Docs., U.S. Govt. Print. Off. 1971. (Water pollution control research series)
        fTD224.C3L32 ECOL

LAMBERT, JOYCE MILDRED, jt. ed.
Goodman, Gordon T.
Ecology and the industrial society. 1965
        TD180.G6 ECOL

LAND EXCHANGE REVIEW SYMPOSIUM, DULUTH, 1970.
Proceedings of the Land Exchange Review Symposium. Sponsored by the Minnesota Land Exchange Review Board and General Extension Division, University of Minnesota. Duluth Arena-Auditorium, April 30, 1970.
        fHD211.L3 ECOL

LAND IN TRANSITION SYMPOSIUM, 1971, ST. PAUL, MINN. Proceedings.
Sponsored by: Association of Metropolitan Soil and Water Conservation Districts. Held March 23, 1971 at the St. Paul Hotel, St. Paul, Minn. Agricultural Extension Service, Univ. of Minn., Office of Special Programs 1971   **fS623.L3 1971 ECOL**

LANDAU, FAY ROBIN, ed.
Widener, Don.
Timetable for disaster. 1970   **TD180.W53 ECOL**

LANDAU, NORMAN J., 1927-
The environmental law handbook; the legal remedies in existence now to stop Government and industry from destroying our environment, by Norman J. Landau and Paul D. Rheingold. With a foreword by Ralph Nader Ballantine Books, 1971   **KF3775.L3 ECOL**

Legal control of the environment—3D. 1971
        KF3775.L44 ECOL

LANDERMAN, A. M.
United Aircraft Corporation. Research Laboratories, East Hartford, Conn.
Advanced nonthermally polluting gas turbines in utility applications. 1971.   **fTJ778.U5 ECOL**

LANDERMAN, NORMAN J.
Community resource; the development-rehabilitation of sand and gravel lands, by Norman J. Landerman, Stephen Schwartz and D. Rodney Tapp. Southern California Rock Products Association, 1972
        TD195.S3L36 ECOL

LANDIN, EDWARD, jt. auth.
Griffith, Charles J.
EP—the new conservation. 1971
        HC110.E5G74 ECOL

LANDON, RONALD ARTHUR, jt. auth.
Hughes, George Muggah.
Hydrogeology of solid waste disposal sites in northeastern Illinois. 1971   **TD795.7.H84 ECOL**

LANDSBERG, HANS H.
Energy in the United States; sources, uses, and policy issues by Hans H. Landsberg and Sam H. Schurr. Random House 1968   **HD9545.L3 ECOL**

Natural resources for U.S. growth; a look ahead to the year 2,000, by Hans H. Landsberg. Published for Resources for the Future by Johns Hopkins Press c1964
        HC103.7.L3 ECOL

Resources for the Future.
Resources in America's future. 1963
        HC106.5.R48 ECOL

LANDSBERG, HANS H., ed.
America's changing environment. 1970.
        HC110.E5A56 ECOL

LANDSBERG, HANS H., jt. comp.
Clawson, Marion.
Desalting seawater. 1972   **TD479.C53 1972 ECOL**

LANDSCAPE; MAGAZINE OF HUMAN GEOGRAPHY.
Jackson, John Brinckerhoff.
Landscapes: selected writings of J. B. Jackson. 1970.
        HN57.J245 ECOL

LANGAN, LEE, jt. auth.
Environmental Measurements, Inc.
Monitoring mercury vapor near pollution sites. 1971.   **fTD427.M4E5 ECOL**

LANGE, GORDON C.
The survival game; hidden profits from waste, by Gordon C. Lange. Plainfield Plan Publications, 1972 (An Insight book)   **TD178.6.L35 ECOL**

LANGER, RICHARD W.
Grow it! The beginner's complete in-harmony-with-nature small farm guide; from vegetable and grain growing to livestock care by Richard W. Langer. Illus. by Susan McNeill. Agricultural consultant: Wayne Stayton. Saturday Review Press 1972   **S501.L27 1972 ECOL**

THE LANGUAGE AND MUSIC OF THE WOLVES.
[Phonodisc]
Narrated by Robert Redford. Script by Ron Holland. Produced by Bob Maxwell. Tonsil Records 003 c1971 2s.   **PhonodiscQL765.L32 ECOL**

LAPP, RALPH E.
A citizen's guide to nuclear power. The New Republic, c1971.   **TK1078.L3 ECOL**

LAROSA, PAUL J.
Black, Sivalls and Bryson, inc., Kansas City, Mo. Applied Technology Division
Evaluation of a new acid mine drainage treatment process. 1971.   **fTD899.M5B55 ECOL**

Black, Sivalls and Bryson, Inc., Kansas City, Mo. Applied Technology Division
Study of sulfur recovery from coal refuse. 1971.
        fTN890.B57 ECOL

LARSEN, RALPH I.
A mathematical model for relating air quality measurements to air quality standards. Research Triangle Park, N.C., Environmental Protection Agency, Office of Air Programs, U.S. Govt. Print. Off., 1971. (Office of Air Programs publication no.AP-89)
        TD890.L3 ECOL

LARSON, CURTIS L.
Numerical routing of flood hydrographs through open channel junctions, by C. L. Larson, Tsong C. Wei, and C. Edward Bowers. Water Resources Research Center, Univ. of Minn., Graduate School, 1971. (WRRC bulletin, no.40)   **GB701.M554no.40 ECOL**

Predicting peak flow of small watersheds by use of channel characteristics, by Curtis L. Larson, Ronald F. Gronwald, and Alfred G. Pennell. Water Resources Research Center, Univ. of Minnesota, 1972. (WRRC bulletin, no.52)   **GB701.M554no.52 ECOL**

LARSON, CURTIS L., jt. auth.
Golany, Pinhas.
Effects of channel characteristics on time parameters for small watershed runoff hydrographs. 1971.
        GB701.M554no.31 ECOL

Mein, Russell G.
Modeling the infiltration component of the rainfall—runoff process. 1971.
        GB701.M554no.43 ECOL

Rice, Charles E.
Methods for routing hydrographs through open channels. 1972.   **GB701.M554no.51 ECOL**

Wei, Tsong C.
Effects of areal and time distribution of rainfall on small watershed runoff hydrographs. 1971.
        GB701.M554no.30 ECOL

LARSON, PEGGY PICKERING, 1931-
Deserts of America. Illus. by Stanley Wyatt. Prentice 1970 (Prentice-Hall series in nature and natural history)
        QH541.5.D4L28 ECOL

LARSON, STEPHEN P., jt. auth.
Bowers, C. Edward.
Computer programs in hydrology. 1972.
        GB665.B6 ECOL

LARSON, STEVEN P., jt. auth.
Bowers, C. Edward.
Computer program for statistical analysis of annual flood data by the log-Pearson Type III method. 1971.
        GB701.M554no.39 ECOL

THE LAST WHOLE EARTH CATALOG.
Portola Institute/Random House, 1971.
REF fTT155.W52 ECOL

LATIN AMERICA INSTITUTE FOR ECONOMIC AND SOCIAL PLANNING.
Herfindahl, Orris Clemens.
Natural resources information for economic development; a study. 1969
GA51.H47 ECOL

LAUWERYS, JOSEPH ALBERT.
Man's impact on nature by J. A. Lauwerys. Published for the American Museum of Natural History Press 1970,c1969 (Nature and science library)
QH368.L38 ECOL

LAVARONI, CHARLES W.
Air pollution. By Charles W. Lavaroni and Patrick A. O'Donnell. Consultants: Milton Feldstein and Lawrence A. Lindberg. Addison-Wesley Pub. Co. c1971
TD883.L28 ECOL

Water pollution. By Charles W. Lavaroni, P. A. O'Donnell and L. A. Lindberg. Consultant: Milton Feldstein. Addison-Wesley Pub. Co. c1971
TD420.L28 ECOL

LAVARONI, CHARLES W., jt. auth.
O'Donnell, Patrick A.
Noise pollution. Teachers' ed. c1971
TD892.O46 ECOL

LAW AND THE ENVIRONMENT.
Ed. by Malcolm F. Baldwin and James K. Page, Jr. Walker 1970
KF5505.A75L38 ECOL

LAW, JAMES P.
National irrigation return flow research and development program, by James P. Law, Jr. Prepared for the Office of Research and Monitoring, Environmental Protection Agency. U.S. Environmental Protection Agency; for sale by the Supt. of Docs., U.S. Govt. Print. Off., 1971. (Water pollution control research series)
fTC809.L38 ECOL

LAW, JAMES P., jt. auth.
Skogerboe, Gaylord V.
Research needs for irrigation return flow quality control. 1971 i.e. 1972
fTD223.S54 ECOL

LAWRENCE, DONALD BUERMANN, 1911-
Ecology: biology 80. Rev. Univ. of Minn., 1967,1966.
fQH541.2.L3 1967 ECOL

LAWSON, CHESTER A.
Science Curriculum Improvement Study.
Life cycles. c1970
LB1585.S32 ECOL
Science Curriculum Improvement Study.
Organisms. c1970
LB1585.S34 ECOL
Science Curriculum Improvement Study.
Populations. c1969
fLB1585.S35 ECOL

LAY, S. HOUSTON, 1912-
The law relating to activities of man in space by S. Houston Lay and Howard J. Taubenfeld. Univ. of Chicago Press 1970
REF fJX5810.L39 ECOL

LAYCOCK, GEORGE.
Air pollution. Grosset & Dunlap 1972
TD883.13.L38 ECOL

Alaska, the embattled frontier. With an introd. by Les Line. Published in cooperation with the National Audubon Society by Houghton Mifflin, 1971. (The Audubon library)
S932.A4L38 ECOL

America's endangered wildlife. Illus. with photographs. Norton c1969
QL88.L39 ECOL

The diligent destroyers. Doubleday, 1970.
HC110.E5L36 ECOL

Water pollution. Grosset & Dunlap 1972
TD422.L38 ECOL

Wild refuge. Published for the American Museum of Natural History by the Natural History Press 1969
S962.L39 ECOL

Wingspread; a world of birds. Four Winds Press 1972
QL676.L35 ECOL

LEACH, LOWELL E., jt. auth.
United States. Environmental Protection Agency.
Induced aeration of small mountain lakes. 1970.
fSH167.T86U5 ECOL

LEAGUE OF CONSERVATION VOTERS.
Rathlesberger, James.
Nixon and the environment. 1972
HC110.E5R37 ECOL

LEAGUE OF WOMEN VOTERS OF THE UNITED STATES. EDUCATION FUND.
The big water fight; trials and triumphs in citizen action on problems of supply, pollution, floods, and planning across the U.S.A. Greene Press, 1966.
HD1694.A5L4 ECOL

LEARY, RAYMOND D.
Milwaukee. Sewerage Commission.
Phosphorus removal with pickle liquor in an activated sludge plant. 1971.
fTD756.M55 ECOL

LEAVITT, ALVAN W.
Synectics Corporation.
A system for industrial waste treatment RD&D project priority assignment. 1971.
fTD897.5.S9 ECOL

LEAVITT, HELEN, 1932-
Superhighway—superhoax. Doubleday, 1970.
HE355.L4 ECOL

LECHT, JANE, jt. auth.
Cook, Robert Carter.
People! 1968
HB871.C7 ECOL

LECOMPTE, ROBERT G.
Atoms at the science fair; exhibiting nuclear projects by Robert G. LeCompte and Burrell L. Wood. Atomic Energy Commission, Division of Technical Information 1968 (Understanding the atom)
Q105.L412 1968 ECOL

LEE, DOUGLAS HARRY KEDGWIN, 1905- ed.
Environmental factors in respiratory disease. 1972.
RC732.E59 ECOL

Metallic contaminants and human health. 1972.
RA565.M47 1972 ECOL

LEE, ERNEST W., jt. auth.
Sale, Larry L.
Environmental education in the elementary school. 1972
QH541.2.S24 ECOL

LEE, FORREST BYRON.
Minnesota. Dept. of Conservation. Division of Game and Fish.
Ducks and land use in Minnesota. 1964.
SH11.M64no.8 ECOL

Minnesota. Dept. of Conservation. Division of Game and Fish.
Waterfowl in Minnesota. 1964.
SH11.M64no.7 ECOL

LEGAL CONTROL OF THE ENVIRONMENT—3D. Marvin B. Durning, Milton Kelner and Norman Landau, chairmen.
Practising Law Institute 1971 (Criminal law and urban problems course handbook series, no.30)
KF3775.L44 ECOL

LEGAL CONTROL OF WATER POLLUTION.
Frank B. Baldwin, III, faculty editor. Staff: Joseph D. Abkin and others. School of Law. University of California, 1969(U. C. D. law review, v. 1)
KF3786.A32L4 ECOL

LEGATOR, MARVIN S., 1926- ed.
The Mutagenicity of pesticides: concepts and evaluation. 1971
RA1270.P4M87 ECOL

LEIBBRAND, KURT.
Transportation and town planning. Translated by Nigel Seymer. M. I. T. Press 1970, c1964
HE333.L3813 1970 ECOL

LEIGH-PEMBERTON, JOHN, 1911- illus.
Fitter, Richard Sidney Richmond.
Vanishing wild animals of the world. 1968
fQL88.F5 ECOL

LEIGHTON, PHILIP ALBERT, 1897-
Photochemistry of air pollution. Academic Press, 1961. (Physical chemistry, v. 9)
RA576.L4 ECOL

LEINWAND, GERALD, comp.
Air and water pollution comp. by Gerald Leinwand, assisted by Gerald Popkin. Washington Square Press 1969 (Problems of American Society)
TD180.L4 ECOL

LEISS, WILLIAM, 1939-
The domination of nature. Braziller c1972
S936.L45 ECOL

LEITHE, WOLFGANG.
The analysis of air pollutants by W. Leithe. Translated by R. Kondor. Ann Arbor Humphrey Science Publishers, 1971,c1970
TD890.L413 ECOL

LEITNER, IRVING A., jt. auth.
Robinson, Carmelita Klipple.
Life in a pond. 1967
fPZ10.R56Li ECOL

LEITZ, F. B.
Ionics, Inc.
The electro-oxidation of ammonia in sewage to nitrogen. 1970.
fTD757.I55 ECOL

LEMMON, ROBERT STELL, 1885-
Our amazing birds; the little-known facts about their private lives. With 102 paintings in black and white by Don R. Eckelberry. American Garden Guild and Doubleday, 1952.
REF QL681.L4 ECOL

LEMPFERT, O. C.
Paw prints; how to identify rare and common mammals by their tracks. 1st ed. Exposition Press 1972 (An Exposition-banner book)
QL768.L37 ECOL

LENNON, J., comp.
Establishing trails on rights-of-way; principally railroad abandonments. U.S. Dept. of the Interior, Bureau of Outdoor Recreation U.S. Govt. Print. Off. n.d.
G504.L4 ECOL

LENORMAND, SERGEI, jt. auth.
Bregman, J. I.
The pollution paradox. c1966
TD180.B7 ECOL

LEONARD, GEORGE BURR, 1923-
The transformation; a guide to the inevitable changes in humankind by George B. Leonard. Delacorte Press 1972
BF311.L43 ECOL

LEONARD, JONATHAN NORTON, 1903-
Atlantic beaches, by Jonathan Norton Leonard and the editors of Time-Life Books. Time-Life Books 1972 (The American wilderness)
GB459.4.L46 ECOL

LEONARD, JUSTIN WILKINSON, jt. auth.
Allen, Shirley Walter.
Conserving natural resources. 3d ed. c1966
HC103.7.A7 1966 ECOL

LEOPOLD, ALDO, 1886-1948.
A Sand County almanac. With other essays on conservation from Round River Illus. by Charles W. Schwartz. Enl. ed. Oxford Univ. Press, 1966.
QH81.L56 1966 ECOL

LEOPOLD, ALDO, 1886-1948. Round River.
Leopold, Aldo.
A Sand County almanac. Enl. ed. 1966.
QH81.L56 1966 ECOL

LEOPOLD, LUNA BERGERE, 1915-
Water, by Luna B. Leopold, Kenneth S. Davis and the editors of Time-Life Books. Rev. Time-Life Books 1970,c1966 (Life science library)
fGB671.L4 1970 ECOL

LEVERING, ROBERT, 1919- illus.
Graves, Charles Parlin.
John Muir. 1973
QH31.M9G66 ECOL

LEVESON, DAVID, 1934-
A sense of the earth. Photos. by the author. Drawings by Meg Leveson. Published for the American Museum of Natural History by the Natural History Press, 1971.
QE31.L48 ECOL

LEVINE, JOSEPH, 1910- jt. auth.
Pine, Tillie S.
Water all around. c1959
PZ10.P57Wat ECOL

LEVINS, PHILIP L.
Little (Arthur D.) Inc.
Characterization and separation of secondary effluent components by molecular weight. 1971.
fTD735.L58 ECOL

LEVINS, RICHARD.
Evolution in changing environments; some theoretical explorations. Princeton Univ. Press, 1968. (Monographs in population biology, no. 2)
QL752.L4 ECOL

LEVITT, JACOB, 1911-
Responses of plants to environmental stresses by J. Levitt. Academic Press, 1972. (Physiological ecology)
QK754.L42 ECOL

LEWIN, TED, illus.
Cox, Donald William.
Pioneers of ecology. 1971
QH26.C68 ECOL

LEWIS, ALFRED, 1912-
Clean the air! Fighting smoke, smog, and smaze across the country. McGraw c1965
TD883.2L4 ECOL

This thirsty world; water supply problems ahead. McGraw-Hill 1964
TD348.L46 ECOL

LEWIS, HOWARD R.
With every breath you take; the poisons of air pollution, how they are injuring our health, and what we must do about them. Preface by R. H. Smart. Foreword by M. B. Jacobs. Crown Publishers 1965
RA576.L5 ECOL

LEWIS, JACK NEVILLE, jt. auth.
Headley, Joseph Charles.
The pesticide problem: an economic approach to public policy. c1967
SB959.H35 ECOL

LEWIS, JAMES C., 1936-
The world of the wild turkey, by James C. Lewis. Illustrated with photos. 1st ed. Lippincott 1973 (Living world books)
QL696.G2L48 ECOL

LEWIS, RICHARD, jt. auth.
Hickman, Howard J.
A study of the environmental impact of polystyrene vs. paper pulp egg cartons and meat trays. 1972.
fTP373.H5 ECOL

LEWIS, RICHARD S.
The energy crisis. Ed. by Richard S. Lewis and Bernard I. Spinrad. Educational Foundation for Nuclear Science, 1972. (A Science and Public Affairs book. Bulletin of the Atomic Scientists)
fHC103.7.L4 ECOL

LEWIS, RICHARD S., 1916-
The nuclear-power rebellion; citizens vs. the atomic industrial establishment by Richard S. Lewis. Viking Press 1972   **HD9698.A3U44 1972 ECOL**

LEWIS, ROBERT CLARK.
The marginal costs of alternative levels of water quality in the Upper Mississippi River. Water Resources Research Center, Univ. of Minnesota Graduate School, 1970. (WRRC bulletin, no. 25)
    GB701.M554no.25 ECOL

LEWIS, TRENT R., jt. auth.
United States. Environmental Protection Agency. National Environmental Research Center.
Toxicology of atmospheric sulfur dioxide decay products. 1972.   **TD885.5.S8U5 ECOL**

LEYDET, FRANCOIS, 1927-
The last redwoods, and the parkland of Redwood Creek. Photos. by James Rose, and others. Introd. by Edgar and Peggy Wayburn. Sierra Club 1969 (A Sierra Club-Ballantine book)   **SD397.R3L4 ECOL**

Time and the river flowing: Grand Canyon. Ed. by David Brower Sierra Club 1968 (A Sierra Club-Ballantine book)   **F788.L482 ECOL**

LI, TING Y., jt. auth.
Frea, James I.
Washout processes in lake systems. 1972.
    fTD764.F74 ECOL

LIBICKI, SAMUEL.
Great Lakes Foundation, Ann Arbor, Mich.
The common law of water. c1971.
    KF3790.Z9L4 ECOL

LIEBENOW, WILBUR R., jt. auth.
United States. Environmental Protection Agency. Office of Research and Monitoring.
Storage and treatment of combined sewer overflows. 1972.   **fTD662.U54 ECOL**

LIESCH, BRUCE A.
Geohydrology of the Jorden aquifer in the Minneapolis-St. Paul area Minnesota. Minnesota Conservation Dept., Division of Waters, 1961. (Technical paper 2)   **fGB705.M6L5 ECOL**

LIFE (CHICAGO).
Engel, Leonard.
The sea. c1969   **fGC21.E5 1969 ECOL**
Went, Frits Warmolt.
The plants. 1969,c1963   **fQK50.W43 1969 ECOL**
Wilson, Mitchell A.
Energy. 1967   **fTJ147.W53 1967 ECOL**

LILIENTHAL, DAVID, ELI, 1899-
TVA; democracy on the march, by David E. Lilienthal, chairman, Tennessee Valley Authority. Harper c1953   **TK1425.M8L53 1953 ECOL**

LILLIE, ROBERT JONES, 1921-
Air pollutants affecting the performance of domestic animals; a literature review, by Robert J. Lillie. Slightly rev. U.S. Agricultural Research Service; U.S. Govt. Print. Off., 1972.   **SF757.5.L54 1972 ECOL**

THE LIMITS TO GROWTH; a report for the Club of Rome's project on the predicament of mankind. By Donella H. Meadows, Dennis L. Meadows, Jorgen Randers, William W. Behrens III. Universe Books c1972   **HC110.E5L5 ECOL**

LIN, SHEN-MAW.
Porosity and pore-size distribution of soil aggregates. Water Resources Research Center, University of Minnesota Graduate School 1971. (WRRC bulletin no. 29)   **GB701.M554no.29 ECOL**

LINCOLN, FREDERICK CHARLES, 1892- jt. auth.
Phillips, John Charles.
American waterfowl. 1930.   **QL696.A5P45 ECOL**

LINDBERG, LAWRENCE H., jt. auth.
Lavaroni, Charles W.
Water pollution. c1971   **TD420.L28 ECOL**

LINDSEY, ALTON A., 1907-
Natural areas in Indiana and their preservation by Alton A. Lindsey, Damian V. Schmelz and Stanley A. Nichols. The report of the Indiana Natural Areas Survey. Indiana Natural Areas Survey, Dept. of Biological Sciences, Purdue University, 1969.
    QH76.5.I6L5 ECOL

LINDSEY-BRAUER AND ASSOCIATES, INC., EDEN PRAIRIE, MINN.
Mayer sewerage plan. 1970   **fTD525.M3L5 ECOL**

LINE, LES, illus.
Graham, Ada.
Puffin Island. 1st ed. 1971
    QL676.G68 1971 ECOL

LINK, ROGER P., jt. auth.
Evers, Robert August.
Poisonous plants of the Midwest & their effects on livestock. 1972   **SB617.E9 ECOL**

LINN, J. G.
Aquatic plants from Minnesota, part 4 — nutrient composition, by J. G. Linn and others. Univ. of Minnesota, Water Resources Research Center, 1973. (Minnesota. University. Water Resources Research Center. WRRC bulletin 56)
    GB701.M554no.56 ECOL

LINSENMAIER, WALTER.
Insects of the world; drawings, photos. and text, by Walter Linsenmaier. Translated from the German by Leigh E. Chadwick. McGraw-Hill 1972
    fQL463.L4615 ECOL

LINSLEY, RAY K.
A manual on collection of hydrologic data for urban drainage design. Hydrocomp, inc., 1973.
    fTD665.L55 ECOL

Water-resources engineering by Ray K. Linsley and Joseph B. Franzini. 2d ed. McGraw-Hill 1971,c1972 (McGraw-Hill series in water resources and environmental engineering) **TC145.L55 1972 ECOL**

LINTON, RON M.
Terracide; America's destruction of her living environment, by Ron M. Linton. Little 1970
    TD180.L56 ECOL

LINVILLE, BILL.
Review of Bureau of Mines energy program, 1970, by Bill Linville and John D. Spencer. U.S. Dept. of Interior, Bureau of Mines 1971 (U.S. Bureau of Mines. Information circular 8526) **TN295.U4no.8526 ECOL**

LIPSETT, CHARLES H.
Industrial wastes and salvage; conservation and utilization. 2d ed. Atlas Pub. Co. 1963
    TP995.L55 1963 ECOL

LITTLE (ARTHUR D.) INC.
Characterization and separation of secondary effluent components by molecular weight. Author: Philip L. Levins. Environmental Protection Agency; for sale by the Supt. of Docs., U.S. Govt. Print. Off., 1971. (Water pollution control research series) **fTD735.L58 ECOL**

Spill prevention techniques for hazardous polluting substances: an inventory and survey of hazardous chemical facilities in Charleston, West Virginia; Baltimore, Maryland; Texas City, Texas; and the Suisun Bay-Delta Area, California. Prepared by J. L. Goodier and others for the Environmental Protection Agency, Division of Oil and Hazardous Materials. U.S. Govt. Print. Off., 1971. (Oil and hazardous materials program series)   **fT55.3.H3L4 ECOL**

LITTLE, CHARLES E.
Challenge of the land, by Charles E. Little. Open Space Action Institute, 1968
    HD205 1968 .L5 ECOL

LITTLE, ELBERT LUTHER, 1907-
Atlas of United States trees. U.S. Dept. of Agriculture, Forest Service, 1971- v.1- (U.S. Dept. of Agriculture. Miscellaneous publication no. 1146)   **REF fS21.A46no.1146 ECOL**

LITTLETON RESEARCH AND ENGINEERING CORPORATION.
An engineering-economic study of cooling pond performance. Authors: W. T. Hogan, A. A. Liepins, and F. E. Reed. Prepared for Environmental Protection Agency. Environmental Protection Agency, Research and Monitoring: for sale by the Supt. of Docs., U.S. Govt. Print. Off., 1970 (Water pollution control research series)   **fTJ403.L57 ECOL**

LITTON SYSTEMS, INC. APPLIED SCIENCE DIVISION.
Minnesota. Pollution Control Agency.
Progress report and long-range plan and program for water pollution control. 1968.
    REF fTD224.M6A53 ECOL

Minnesota. Pollution Control Agency.
Progress report on water pollution control July 1967 through December 1968. 1968.
    fTD224.M6A532 ECOL

THE LIVING BIRD. 6TH- 1967-
Laboratory of Ornithology, Cornell Univ. v.
    REF QL671.L57 ECOL

LOF, GEORGE O. G., jt. auth.
Cootner, Paul H.
Water demand for steam electric generation. 1966,c1965   **TK1051.C6 ECOL**

LOFTAS, TONY.
The last resource; man's exploitation of the oceans. rev. ed. Regnery 1970   **GC1015.L57 1970 ECOL**

LONDON, ONT. UNIVERSITY OF WESTERN ONTARIO.
Conference on Snowmobiles and All-Terrain Vechicles, London, Ontario, 1971.
Proceedings. 1972   **fGV857.S6C6 1971 ECOL**

LONG, TONY.
Mountain animals. 1st U.S. ed. Harper & Row c1971 (Animal life series)   **QL113.L66 1971 ECOL**

LONGGOOD, WILLIAM FRANK, 1917-
The darkening land by William Longgood. Simon and Schuster 1972   **TD175.L66 ECOL**

LORAINE, JOHN ALEXANDER.
The death of tomorrow by John A. Loraine in association with R. D. E. Rumsey. With a foreword by the Duke of Edinburgh. Lippincott 1972
    HC79.P55L67 1972b ECOL

LORBEER, GEORGE C.
Circle of the world.   **QH541.2.C5 Suppl. ECOL**

Circle of the world. c1971-
    QH541.2.C5 ECOL

LOUTIT, JOHN F.
Irradiation of mice and men. University of Chicago Press 1962   **QH652.L63 ECOL**

LOVE, MILTON S., jt. auth.
Cailliet, Greg M.
Everyman's guide to ecological living. 1971
    GF75.C33 ECOL

LOVE, SAM, 1946-
Ecotage, edited by Sam Love and David Obst. With a foreword by Robert Townsend. Pocket Books 1972
    TD175.L68 ECOL

LOVE, SAM, 1946- ed.
Environmental Action (Association).
Earth tool kit. 1971   **HC110.E5E498 ECOL**

LOVEJOY, WALLACE FRANCIS, 1928-
Economic aspects of oil conservation regulation, by Wallace F. Lovejoy and Paul T. Homan. Published for Resources for the Future by Johns Hopkins Press 1967
    HD9566.L6 ECOL

Methods of estimating reserves of crude oil, natural gas, and natural gas liquids, by Wallace F. Lovejoy and Paul T. Homan. Resources for the Future; distributed by Johns Hopkins Press, 1965   **TN870.L68 ECOL**

LOWE-MCCONNELL, R. H., ed.
Man-made lakes; proceedings. Ed. by R. H. Lowe-McConnell. Published for the Institute of Biology by Academic Press, 1966. (Symposia of the Institute of Biology, no. 15)   **GB1601.L6 1965 ECOL**

LOWENTHAL, DAVID, ed.
Environmental perception and behavior. 1967.
    GF51.E5 ECOL

LUBELL, CECIL, jt. auth.
Lubell, Winifred.
Green is for growing. 1964.   **PZ10.L85Gr ECOL**

LUBELL, WINIFRED.
Green is for growing, by Winifred and Cecil Lubell. Rand McNally, 1964.   **PZ10.L85Gr ECOL**

LUDTKE, RICHARD L.
Social and economic considerations for water resources planning in the Park River Subbasin, North Dakota, by Richard L. Ludtke and others Univ. of North Dakota, 1971. (North Dakota. University. Research report no.2)   **HD1694.N9L8 ECOL**

LUDWIG, JAMES P., ed.
Baron, Norman J.
A survey of attitudes towards the Mississippi River as a total resource in Minnesota. 1972.
    GB701.M554no.55 ECOL

LUESCHOW, LLOYD A.
Lake Michigan Enforcement Conference. Lake Michigan Interstate Pesticides Committee.
An evaluation of DDT and dieldrin in Lake Michigan. 1972.   **TD427.P35L3 ECOL**

LUGO, ARIEL E., ed.
Readings on ecological systems: their function and relation to man. Ed. by A. E. Lugo and S. C. Snedaker. MSS Educational Pub. Co., c1971
    QH540.3.L8 ECOL

LUND, HERBERT F., ed.
Industrial pollution control handbook. 1971
    REF TD897.I42 ECOL

LUND, LEONARD.
Industry expenditures for water pollution abatement. Conference Board, 1972 (Conference Board report no. 541)   **fTD223.L8 ECOL**

LUNDGREN, DONALD GEORGE, 1924-
Syracuse University. Dept. of Biology.
Inorganic sulfur oxidation by iron-oxidizing bacteria. 1971.   **fQR84.S95 ECOL**

LUSK, W. D.
Banks, M. E.
New chemical concepts for utilization of waste plastics. 1971.   **TP156.R38B3 ECOL**

LYERLY, RAY L.
Nuclear power plants by Ray L. Lyerly and Walter Mitchell, III. Rev. U.S. Atomic Energy Commission, Division of Technical Information 1969 (Understanding the atom series)   **TK1078.L9 1969 ECOL**

LYMAN, JAMES D.
Nuclear terms, a brief glossary. 2d ed. U.S. Atomic Energy Commission, Division of Technical Information, 1966. (Understanding the atom)
QC772.L9 1966 ECOL

LYNCH, DONALD, illus.
Hyde, Margaret Oldroyd.
For pollution fighters only. 1971
TD175.H9 ECOL

M

MAAGDENBERG, HARRY J.
National Canners Association. Western Research Laboratory.
Dry caustic peeling of tree fruit for liquid waste reduction. 1970.
fTD899.F7N37 ECOL

MAASS, ARTHUR.
Design of water-resource systems. 1970,c1962
TC409.D4 ECOL

MACAN, THOMAS TOWNLEY.
Freshwater ecology. Longmans 1969,c1963
QH541.5.F7M3 1969 ECOL

MACARTHUR, ROBERT H.
The biology of populations by Robert H. MacArthur and Joseph H. Connell. Wiley 1966
QL752.M2 ECOL

MACAULAY, HUGH HOLLEMAN, 1924-
Stepp, James Marvin.
The pollution problem. 1968   TD180.S65 ECOL

MACAVOY, PAUL W.
Large-scale desalting; a study in the engineering economics of regional development, by Paul W. MacAvoy and Dean F. Peterson. Praeger 1969
TD479.3.M3 ECOL

MACBEAN, JOHN C.
Birds By J. C. MacBean and others Mine Publications c1971 (Examining your environment)
QL676.M22 ECOL

MACDONALD, FRANK W., jt. auth.
Mayer, John K.
Sewer bedding and infiltration, Gulf Coast area. 1972.
fTD653.M3 ECOL

MACDONALD, JAMES B., 1919-
Environmental litigation by James B. MacDonald and John E. Conway. Dept. of Law, University of Wisconsin Extension, 1972.
KF3775.M3 ECOL

MACGOWN, RICHARD H.
The school site in environmental education; guidelines for school site planning, development and utilization in environmental education. Prepared by Richard H. MacGown and Dean B. Bennett. Rev. ed. Maine Environmental Education Project, 1972.
fLB3220.M3 1972 ECOL

MACGOWN, RICHARD H., jt. auth.
Bennett, Dean B.
Guidelines for planning and implementing a comprehensive community environmental inventory. Rev. ed. 1972.   fQH541.2.B38 1972 ECOL

MACKAYE, BENTON, 1879-
The new exploration; a philosophy of regional planning. With an introd. by Lewis Mumford. University of Illinois Press, 1962. (Illini books, IB-3)
GF51.M3 1962 ECOL

MADDOCK, ALISON.
Animals at peace. 1st U.S. ed. Harper & Row c1971 (Animal life series)   QL751.M216 1971 ECOL

MADDOX, JOHN ROYDEN, 1925-
The doomsday syndrome by John Maddox. McGraw-Hill 1972   GF47.M3 1972 ECOL

MADERAK, MARION L.
Chemical quality of ground water in the Minneapolis-St. Paul area, Minnesota, by M. L. Maderak. Prepared cooperatively by the Geological Survey, U.S. Dept. of the Interior, and the Division of Waters, Minnesota Conservation Dept. 1965. (Minnesota. Dept. of Conservation. Division of Waters. Bulletin 23)   fTD224.M6A3no.23 ECOL

Quality of waters, Minnesota; a compilation, 1955-62. Prepared cooperatively by the Geological Survey, U.S. Dept. of the Interior, and the Division of Waters, Minnesota Conservation Dept. 1963. (Minnesota. Dept. of Conservation. Division of Waters. Bulletin No. 21)   fTD224.M6A3no.21 ECOL

MADISON. WIS. BOARD OF EDUCATION. DEPT. OF CURRICULUM DEVELOPMENT.
Science and society. Madison 1969. v.
REF fQ181.M3 ECOL

MADISON, WIS. PUBLIC SCHOOLS. CONSERVATION COMMITTEE.
Guide to environmental education: conservation of natural resources, kindergarten — grade six. Madison Public Schools, Dept. of Curriculum Development, 1970. v.
fS946.M3 ECOL

MAGILL, PAUL L., ed.
Air pollution handbook. Ed. by Paul L. Magill, Francis R. Holden and Charles Ackley. Editorial consultant: Frederick G. Sawyer. McGraw-Hill, 1956. 1v.   REF TD883.M35 ECOL

MAHER, JOHN CHARLES, 1914-
Geologic framework and petroleum potential of the Atlantic Coastal Plain and Continental Shelf, by John C. Maher. With a section on stratigraphy by John C. Maher and Esther R. Applin. U.S. Govt. Print. Off., 1971. (Geological Survey professional paper 659)
REF fQE75.P9no.659 ECOL

MAHLOCH, JEROME L.
The effect of organic amendments from garbage grinding on a biological treatment system. Water Resources Research Institute, Mississippi State Univ., 1972.   fTD756.M32 ECOL

MAIER, FRANZ J.
Manual of water fluoridation practice. McGraw-Hill 1963   TD468.M25 ECOL

MAINE ENVIRONMENTAL EDUCATION PROJECT.
Bennett, Dean B.
Guidelines for planning and implementing a comprehensive community environmental inventory. Rev. ed. 1972.   fQH541.2.B38 1972 ECOL

MAJOR, HARRY M.
Activities for the USDA Soil Conservation Service in providing for quality environment for all people in Minnesota. Office of the State Conservationist 1972. v.
HC110.E5M3 ECOL

USDA - soil conservation service in Minnesota. n.p., United States. Dept. of Agriculture, Soil Conservation Service? 1973.   S624.M6M3 ECOL

MAJOR, JAMES M.
Environmental education: objectives and field activities, by J. M. Major and C. A. Cissell and The Paducah Public School, Environmental Education Staff. 4th ed. 1971.   fLB1047.M3 ECOL

MAJOR NSP GENERATING PLANT SITES;
Twin Cities metropolitan area.
Prepared for Advisory Committee on Plant Siting and Development. Northern States Power Co. 1970. 1v.
fTK1191.M3 ECOL

MAKI, LES, jt. auth.
Orning, George W.
Land management information in northwest Minnesota: the beginnings of a statewide system. 1972.
HD211.M6 ECOL

MALDONADO, TOMAS.
Design, nature, and revolution; toward a critical ecology. Translated from the Italian by Mario Domandi. 1st U.S. ed. Harper & Row 1972
GF41.M3413 1972 ECOL

MALES, RICHARD MICHAEL, 1943-
Decision processes in water quality management, by Richard M. Males and William E. Gates. Engineering-Science, Inc., Research and Development Laboratory, Systems/Behavioral Studies Division, 1971. v.   fTD365.M3 ECOL

MALINA, JOSEPH F.
Austin, Texas
Design guides for biological wastewater treatment processes. 1971 i.e.1972   fTD755.A87 ECOL

MALONEY, FRANK EDWARD.
Water law and administration; the Florida experience by Frank E. Maloney, Sheldon J. Plager and Fletcher N. Baldwin, Jr., with the assistance of William Haddad. University of Florida Press, 1968.
REF KFF446.M3 ECOL

MAMANTOV, GLEB, ed.
ACS Symposium on Determination of Air Quality, Los Angeles, 1971.
Determination of air quality. 1972.
TD890.A2 1971 ECOL

MAN AND HIS ENVIRONMENT; an introduction to using environmental study areas.
Association of Classroom Teachers, National Education Association 1970 (New developments in teaching series, no. 1)   L11.N39no.1 ECOL

MAN AND HIS ENVIRONMENT: THE EFFECTS OF POLLUTION ON MAN.
Edited by Tom Rusk Vickery. Syracuse University Press, 1972   TD172.5.M35 ECOL

MANAGING THE ENVIRONMENT: INTERNATIONAL ECONOMIC COOPERATION FOR POLLUTION CONTROL.
Edited by Allen V. Kneese, Sidney E. Rolfe and Joseph W. Harned. Praeger Publishers 1971 (Praeger special studies in international economics and development)   HC79.E5M35 1971 ECOL

MANCY, KHALIL H.
Analysis of industrial wastewaters by K. H. Mancy and W. J. Weber, Jr. Wiley-Interscience 1971
TD735.M35 ECOL

MANDAN REFINERY.
Fluid bed incineration of petroleum refinery wastes. Author: Herbert E. Simons. Prepared for the Water Quality Office, Environmental Protection Agency. Environmental Protection Agency, Water Quality Office; for sale by thh Supt. of Docs., U.S. Govt. Print. Off., 1971. (Water pollution control research series)
fTD899.P4M35 ECOL

MANGAN, GEORGE F., ed.
Water Resources Scientific Information Center.
Urban water planning. 1972.
REF Z7935.W3 ECOL

MANSON, PHILIP W., 1905-
Some aspects of the hydrology of ponds and small lakes by P. W. Manson, G. M. Schwartz, E. R. Allred. Agricultural Experiment Station, University of Minnesota, 1968. (University of Minnesota. Agricultural Experiment Station Technical bulletin 257)   fGB1825.M6M35 ECOL

A MANUAL OF WILDLIFE CONSERVATION.
Edited by Richard D. Teague. Illus. by Charles W. Schwartz, Ralph Oberg and Francis L. Jaques. Wildlife Society, 1971.   fSK353.M35 ECOL

MANUFACTURING CHEMISTS' ASSOCIATION.
The effect of chlorination on selected organic chemicals. Authors: E. L. Barnhart and G. R. Campbell. Prepared for the Office of Research and Monitoring, Environmental Protection Agency. U.S. Govt. Print. Off., 1972. (Water pollution control research series)
fTD462.M3 ECOL

Slack, Archie Vivian.
Defense against famine. 1st ed. 1970.
S633.S627 ECOL

Warner, Arthur J.
Plastics solid waste disposal by incineration or landfill. c1972, 1971.   fTD798.W36 ECOL

Weaver, Elbert C.
Scientific experiments in environmental pollution. 1968   TD178.5.W4 ECOL

MANZEL, BRUCE W., jt. auth.
Raney, Edward Cowden.
Heated effluents and effects on aquatic life with emphasis on fishes. 3rd ed. 1969.
REF Z7173.W3R3 1969 ECOL

MARCEL, GABRIEL, 1887-
Man against mass society. Translated from the French by G. S. Fraser. Foreword by Donald Mackinnon. Regnery, 1971, 1952 (Gateway edition)
B2430.M253H583 1971 ECOL

MARCHANT, RONALD ALBERT.
Man and beast, by R. A. Marchant. Macmillan 1968
QL85.M3 1968 ECOL

MARCUS, MELVIN GERALD, jt. auth.
Detwyler, Thomas R.
Urbanization and environment. 1972
HT151.D46 ECOL

MARGALEF, RAMON.
Perspectives in ecological theory. University of Chicago Press 1968 (Chicago series in biology v. 1)
QH541.M37 ECOL

MARINCIC, LJILJANA.
Ionics, Inc.
The electro-oxidation of ammonia in sewage to nitrogen. 1970.   fTD757.I55 ECOL

MARINE BIOLOGICAL ASSOCIATION OF THE UNITED KINGDOM. LABORATORY, PLYMOUTH.
Moulder, David S.
A bibliography on marine and estuarine oil pollution. 1971.   REF fZ6004.P6M6 ECOL

'Torrey Canyon' pollution and marine life: a report by the Plymouth Laboratory of the Marine Biological Association of the United Kingdom, under the general editorship of J. E. Smith. Published for the Marine Biological Association of the United Kingdom by Cambridge U.P., 1968.   GC1311.M37 ECOL

MARINE, GENE.
America the raped; the engineering mentality and the devastation of a continent. Simon 1969
S942.M33 ECOL

Food pollution; the violation of our inner ecology by Gene Marine and Judith Van Allen. 1st. ed. Holt, Rinehart and Winston 1972   TX533.M37 ECOL

MARKOFSKY, MARK/A PREDICTIVE MODEL FOR THERMAL STRATIFICATION AND WATER QUALITY IN RESERVOIRS.
Ralph M. Parsons Laboratory for Water Resources and Hydrodynamics.
Temperature prediction in stratified water: mathematical model-user's manual (supplement to report 1613ODJH-01/71). 1971.   fTD395.R3 ECOL

MARMELSTEIN, ALLAN D., jt. auth.
Welch, Robin I.
A feasibility demonstration of an aerial surveillance spill prevention system. 1972.
fTD427.P4W45 ECOL

MAROTTA, JUANITA.
Minnesota wild flowers of forest, field and wetland. Illus. by the author. the author 1971.
QK168.M3 ECOL

MARSH, GEORGE PERKINS, 1801-1882.
Man and nature. Edited by David Lowenthal. Belknap Press of Harvard University Press, 1965. (The John Harvard library) **GF31.M35 1965 ECOL**

MARSH, NORMAN F.
Outdoor education on your school grounds; an action approach to better teaching, a manual for elementary and junior high school teachers. Resources Agency, Office of Conservation Education, 1968
LB1047.M29 ECOL

MARSHALL, JAMES, 1933-
Going to waste; where will all the garbage go? Coward, McCann & Geoghegan 1972 (The New conservation) **TD791.M37 ECOL**

MARTENS, FREDERICK HILBERT, 1921-
Research reactors by Frederick H. Martens and Norman H. Jacobson. U.S. Atomic Energy Commission, Division of Technical Information 1965 (United States. Atomic Energy Commission. Understanding the atom) **QC787.N8M32 ECOL**

MARTIN, G. B.
Effects of fuel additives on air pollutant emissions from distillate-oil-fired furnaces, by G. B. Martin, D. W. Pershing, and E. E. Berkau. Research Triangle Park, N. C., U.S. Environmental Protection Agency, Office of Air Programs; for sale by the Supt. of Docs., U.S. Govt. Print. Off., 1971. (Office of Air Programs publication no. AP-87) **TP355.M29 ECOL**

MARX, WESLEY.
The frail ocean. Coward c1967 **GC1018.M3 ECOL**

Man and his environment: waste. Harper & Row 1971 (Man and his environment series)
TD174.M37 ECOL

Oilspill. Sierra Club c1971 (The Sierra Club battlebook series, 5) **GC1085.M3 ECOL**

The protected ocean; how to keep the seas alive. McCann & Geoghegan 1972 (The New conservation) **GC1018.M32 ECOL**

MARYLAND. DEPT. OF WATER RESOURCES.
Guidelines for erosion and sediment control, planning and implementation, by the Dept. of Water Resources, State of Maryland, Annapolis, Maryland and Burton C. Becker and Thomas R. Mills. Prepared for Office of Research and Monitoring, U.S. Environmental Protection Agency. U.S. Govt. Print. Office, 1972. (Environmental protection technology series)
fS624.A1M3 ECOL

MARYLAND. GOVERNOR'S TASK FORCE ON NUCLEAR POWER PLANTS.
Nuclear power plants in Maryland; a report, by the Governor's Task Force on Nuclear Power Plants, William W. Eaton, chairman. 1969. v.
TK1344.M3M3 ECOL

MARYLAND. UNIVERSITY. SCHOOL OF LAW.
Legal problems of coal mine reclamation; a study in Maryland, Ohio, Pennsylvania, and West Virginia. Project directors, Everett F. Goldberg and Garrett Power. Prepared for the Environmental Protection Agency. For sale by the Supt. of Docs., U.S. Govt. Print. Off., 1972. (Water pollution control research series)
fKF1830.Z95M37 ECOL

MARZANI, CARL.
The wounded earth; an environmental survey. Young Scott Books 1972 **QH541.M38 ECOL**

MASINI, GIANCARLO.
S.O.S. save our earth; an ecological message for everyone. Text by Giancarlo Masini. Introd. by William D. Ruckelshaus, administrator, U.S. Environmental Protection Agency. Grosset & Dunlap c1972
fQH541.M382 1972 ECOL

MASLAND & SONS, INC., CARLISLE, PA.
Fram Corporation.
Bio-regenerated activated carbon treatment of textile dye wastewater. 1971. **fTD899.T4F7 ECOL**

MASON, GEORGE FREDERICK, 1904-
Animal homes. Morrow, 1947. **QL756.M3 ECOL**
Animal sounds. Morrow, 1948. **QL765.M3 ECOL**
Animal tracks. Morrow, 1943. **SK282.M3 ECOL**

The wildlife of North America. Illustrated by the author. Hastings House 1966 (The Hastings House world wildlife conservation series)
SK361.M35 ECOL

MASSACHUSETTS AUDUBON SOCIETY.
Dickey, Miriam.
Beyond the classroom. 1972.
Ref fQH51.D5 ECOL

MASSACHUSETTS. DEPT. OF AGRICULTURE.
Forbush, Edward Howe.
Birds of Massachusetts and other New England states. 1925-29 **REF QL684.M4F65 ECOL**

MASSACHUSETTS INSTITUTE OF TECHNOLOGY.
Oil on the sea. 1969. **GC1080.O36 ECOL**

Power, pollution, and public policy. c1971
HC107.A113E55 ECOL

Study of Critical Environmental Problems.
Man's impact on the global environment. 1970
QH541.S73 ECOL

Study of Man's Impact on Climate, Stockholm, 1970.
Inadvertent climate modification. 1971
QC981.S77 1970 ECOL

MASSACHUSETTS INSTITUTE OF TECHNOLOGY. M.I.T. REPORT NO. 24.
Power, pollution, and public policy. c1971
HC107.A113E55 ECOL

MASSACHUSETTS. PUBLIC DOCUMENT, V. 5, NO. 30.
Kirkwood, James Pugh.
A special report on the pollution of river waters. Reprint ed. 1970 **REF TD425.K52 1970 ECOL**

MASSACHUSETTS. STATE BOARD OF HEALTH.
Kirkwood, James Pugh.
A special report on the pollution of river waters. Reprint ed. 1970 **REF TD425.K52 1970 ECOL**

MATHEMATICA, INC., BETHESDA, MD.
The implications of the net fiscal benefits criterion for cost sharing in flood control projects; a report. Prepared for the Center for Economic Studies. Institute for Water Resources, Corps of Engineers, Dept. of the Army. 1971. (IWR report 71-12) **TC530.M3 ECOL**

MATTHEWS, WILLIAM HENRY, 1919-
Introducing the earth; geology, environment, and man by William H. Matthews III. Dodd 1972
QE29.M27 ECOL

MATTHEWS, WILLIAM HENRY, 1942- comp.
Man's impact on terrestrial and oceanic ecosystems. Edited by William H. Matthews, Frederick E. Smith and Edward D. Goldberg. M.I.T. Press, 1971
TD174.M39 ECOL

MATTHIESSEN, PETER.
Caulfield, Patricia.
Everglades. 1970 **QH105.F6C36 ECOL**
Stout, Gardner D.
The shorebirds of North America. 1967
fQL681.S78 ECOL

MATTSON, GEORGE.
Carrighar, Sally.
One day at Teton Marsh. 1947. **QL215.C3 ECOL**

MAUGHAN, PAUL M., jt. auth.
Welch, Robin I.
A feasibility demonstration of an aerial surveillance spill prevention system. 1972.
fTD427.P4W45 ECOL

MAURITZ, MARILYN, 1941-
Library and informational resources in the Twin City Area. James J. Hill Reference Library 1972- 1v.
REF fZ688.A2M3 ECOL

MAXWELL, KENNETH E., 1908- comp.
Chemicals and life. Dickenson Pub. Co. 1970 (Dickenson series in biology) **QP903.M38 ECOL**

MAY, JULIAN.
The big isl.. Illustrated by John Schoenherr. Follett Pub. Co. 1968. **PZ10.M455Bi ECOL**

Blue River. Illus. by Robert Quackenbush. Holidaa House 1971 **TD425.M46 ECOL**

Forests that change color. Creative Educational Society 1972 **SD373.M38 1972 ECOL**

The land is disappearing. Creative Educational Society 1972 **QE571.M38 1972 ECOL**

The living blanket on the land. Creative Educational Society 1972 **S591.3.M39 1972 ECOL**

The mysterious evergreen forest. Creative Educational Society 1972 **QH541.5.F6M39 ECOL**

MAYER, JOHN K.
Sewer bedding and infiltration, Gulf Coast area, by J. K. Mayer, Frank W. MacDonald and Stephen E. Steimle. Prepared for Office of Research and Monitoring Environmental Protection Agency. U.S. Govt. Print. Office, 1972. (Water pollution control research series) **fTD653.M3 ECOL**

MCALISTER, J. ANDREW.
Georgia Kraft Company. Research and Development Center.
Treatment of selected internal kraft mill wastes in a cooling tower. 1971. **fTD899.W65G46 ECOL**

MCCANN, JAMES A., ed.
International Symposium on River Ecology and the Impact of Man, University of Massachusetts, 1971.
River ecology and man. 1972.
GB1205.I5 1971 ECOL

MCCANN, LESTER J.
Time to cry wolf! Problems facing wildlife in America. Graphic Publishing Co. c1972
SK353.M3 ECOL

MCCARTHY, RICHARD D., 1927-
The ultimate folly; war by pestilence, asphyxiation, and defoliation. Vintage Books 1969
UG447.M233 1969 ECOL

MCCLAIN, THOMAS B.
Complete handbook on environmental control; a reference manual for debaters and others interested in the subject, by Thomas B. McClain and David Zarefsky. National Textbook Co. 1970 **Z5853.P7M32 ECOL**

MCCLANAHAN, MARK A.
A study of the effects of island development on lake water quality, by Mark A. McClanahhn and Alfred W. Hoadley. School of Civil Engineering in cooperation with Environmental Resources Center, Georgia Institute of Technology, 1972. **fTD224.G4M3 ECOL**

MCCLELLAN, GRANT S., ed.
Protecting our environment. Wilson, 1970. (Reference shelf v. 42, no. 1) **TD180.M3 ECOL**

MCCLINTOCK, MICHAEL, comp.
Environmental effects of weapons technology. 1970
fUG447,8.E57 ECOL

MCCLUNG, ROBERT M.
Scoop, the last of the brown pelicans by Robert M. McClung. Illustrated by Robert M. McClung and Lloyd Sandford. Morrow, 1972. **PZ10.M115Sb ECOL**

MCCORMICK, JACK.
The life of the forest. McGraw-Hill 1966 (Our living world of nature) **QK938.F6M19 ECOL**

The living forest. With drawings by Matthew Kalmenoff. Published in cooperation with the American Museum of Natural History by Harper c1959
QK938.F6M2 ECOL

MCCOY, ELIZABETH F.
Role of bacteria in the nitrogen cycle in lakes. Prepared for the Office of Research and Monitoring, Environmental Protection Agency. U.S. Govt. Print. Off., 1972. (Water pollution control research series)
fTD433.M3 ECOL

MCCOY, JAMES W.
Chemical analysis of industrial water, by James W. McCoy. Chemical Pub. Co., 1969. **TD380.M3 ECOL**

MCCOY, JOSEPH J., 1917-
Saving our wildlife. Crowell 1970 **S962.M3 ECOL**

MCCUE, GEORGE.
Ecology. Supplement; teacher's guide; teacher instruction materials to accompany Ecology. By C. Richard Tillis. Benziger c1971
QH541.M22 Suppl. ECOL

Ecology: the city. Benziger c1971 (Benziger web of life book) **QH541.5.C6M23 ECOL**

Ecology: the deserts and man. Supplement; teacher's guide; teacher instruction materials to accompany The deserts and man, by C. Richard Tillis. Benziger c1971
QH541.5.D4M22 Suppl. ECOL

Ecology: the farm. Supplement; teacher's guide; teacher instruction materials to accompany The farm. by C. Richard Tillis. Benziger c1971
QH541.5.F3M22 Suppl. ECOL

Ecology: the forests and man. Benziger c1971 (Benziger web of life book) **QH541.5.F6M22 ECOL**

Ecology: the freshwaters and man. Supplement teacher's guide; teacher instruction materials to accompany The freshwaters and man, by C. Richard Tillis. Benziger c1971
QH541.5.F7M22 Suppl. ECOL

Ecology: the grasslands and man. Supplement teacher's guide; teacher instruction materials to accompany The grasslands and man. By C. Richard Tillis. Benziger c1971
QH541.5.P7M22 Suppl. ECOL

Ecology: the mountains and man. Benziger c1971 (Benziger web of life book)
QH541.5.M65M22 ECOL

Ecology: the oceans and man. Benziger c1971 (Benziger web of life book) **QH541.5.S3M22 ECOL**

Ecology: the suburbs. Supplement; teacher's guide; teacher instruction materials to accompany The suburbs. By C. Richard Tillis. Benziger c1971
QH541.5.C6M22 Suppl. ECOL

MCCUE, GERALD M., 1928-
Creating the human environment; a report of the American Institute of Architects, by Gerald M. McCue, William R. Ewald, Jr., and the Midwest Research Institute. Univ. of Illinois Press 1970
HN59.M22 ECOL

MCCUEN, GARY E., ed.
The ecology controversy: opposing viewpoints. Gary E. McCuen and David L. Bender, editors. Greenhaven Press 1971 (Critical issues series, vol. 3)
QH541.M3 ECOL

MCCULLOUGH, DALE R., 1933-
The tule elk; its history, behavior, and ecology, by Dale R. McCullough. Univ. of Calif. Press, 1971c1969 (University of California publications in zoology, v. 88)
QL1.C15vol.88 ECOL

MCDIVITT, JAMES FREDERICK 1921-
Minerals and men; an exploration of the world of minerals and its effect on the world we live in by James F. McDivitt. Published for Resources for the Future, by Johns Hopkins Press 1965 **TN19.M2 ECOL**

MCDONALD, ERNEST C.
Milliken, Margaret.
Field study manual for outdoor living. c1968
QH53.M5 ECOL

MCDONALD, STEPHEN L.
Petroleum conservation in the United States: an economic analysis, by Stephen L. McDonald. Published for Resources for the Future by the Johns Hopkins Press 1971 **HD9566.M3 ECOL**

MCGAUHEY, P. H.
Lake Tahoe Area Council.
Eutrophication of surface waters—Lake Tahoe. 1971 i.e. 1972 **fQH96.8.E9L34 ECOL**

MCGRAW-HILL ENCYCLOPEDIA OF SCIENCE AND TECHNOLOGY; an international reference work.
3d ed. McGraw-Hill 1971 15v.
REF fQ121.M3 1971 ECOL

MCGRIFF, E. CORBIN.
The efficacy of the complete mix activated sludge process in modular mode. Water Resources Research Institute, Mississippi State Univ., 1972.
fTD756.M3 ECOL

MCHALE, JOHN.
The ecological context. G. Braziller 1970
GF41.M3 ECOL

The future of the future. Braziller 1969
CB161.M3 ECOL

The future of the future. Ballantine 1971
CB161.M3 1971 ECOL

MCHARG, IAN L.
Design with nature by Ian L. McHarg. 1st ed. Published for the American Museum of Natural History by the Natural History Press, 1969.
fHC110.E5M33 ECOL

Wallace, McHarg, Roberts and Todd.
An ecological study of the Twin Cities Metropolitan Area. 1969. **fQH541.W32 ECOL**

MCHENRY, ROBERT, comp.
A documentary history of conservation in America. Edited by Robert McHenry, with Charles Van Doren. Introd. by Ioru and Margery Milne. Praeger 1972
S930.M18 ECOL

MCINNIS, NOEL.
You are an environment: teaching/learning environmental attitudes. The Center for Curriculum Design c1972 **QH541.2.M4 ECOL**

MCKAIN, DAVID W., comp.
The whole earth; essays in appreciation, anger, and hope. Edited by David W. McKain. Martin's Press 1972
QH81.M1518 ECOL

MCKEE, ALEXANDER, 1918-
Farming the sea. Crowell 1969
SH333.M27 1969 ECOL

MCKENNA, RICHARD P., jt. auth.
Ayres, Robert U.
Alternatives to the internal combustion engine. 1972
TL210.A96 ECOL

MCKENZIE, LINDA, ed.
The grass roots and water resources management. Washington State Univ., 1972. **fHD1691.M3 ECOL**

MCKEOWN, JAMES E., comp.
The changing metropolis, edited by James E. McKeown and Frederick I. Tietze. 2d ed. Houghton Mifflin 1971 **HT334.U5M321971ECOL**

MCMILLAN, IAN.
Man and the California condor; the embattled history and uncertain future of North America's largest free-living bird. Dutton, 1968. **QL696.A2H24 ECOL**

MCNABB, C. D.
A fluorometric technique for sampling in large-river ecosystems, by C. D. McNabb, E. F. Miller and D. R. Johann. Water Resources Research Center, University of Minnesota Graduate School, 1971. (WRRC bulletin, 34) **GB701.M554no.34 ECOL**

MCNABB, JAMES F., jt. auth.
Robert S. Kerr Water Research Center.
Characteristics of rainfall run off from a beef cattle feedlot. 1972. **TD899.F4R6 ECOL**

MCNALL, PRESTON ESSEX, 1888-
Our natural resources by P. E. McNall and Harry B. Kircher. 3d ed. Interstate Printers & Publishers 1970
S930.M2 1970 ECOL

MCNULTY, FAITH.
Must they die? The strange case of the prairie dog and the black-footed ferret. 1st ed. Doubleday, 1971.
QL737.C25M27 ECOL

MCNULTY, IRVING B., ed.
Grand Canyon Symposium, 1970.
Environment, man, survival: Grand Canyon Symposium, 1970. c1971 **GF8.G7 1970 ECOL**

MCPHEE, JOHN A.
Encounters with the archdruid by John McPhee. Farrar 1971 **S942.M26 ECOL**

The pine Barrens. Farrar 1968
F142.P5M35 1968 ECOL

MCPHERSON, M. B.
Hydrologic effects of urbanization in the United States. American Society of Civil Engineers, 1972. (American Society of Civil Engineers. ASCE Urban Water Resources Research Program. Technical memorandum no. 17) **fGB665.M3 ECOL**

Urban runoff. American Society of Civil Engineers, 1972. (ASCE Urban Water Resources Research Program. Technical memorandum no. 18)
fGB665.M35 ECOL

MCPHERSON, MURRAY BURNS.
Feasibility of the metropolitan water intelligence system concept (Integrated automatic operational control). American Society of Civil Engineers, 1971. (American Society of Civil Engineers. ASCE Urban Water Resources Research Program. Technical memorandum no. 15) **fTD211.M3 ECOL**

Management problems in metropolitan water resource operations. American Society of Civil Engineers, 1971. (American Society of Civil Engineers. ASCE Urban Water Resources Research Program. Technical memorandum no.14) **fTD353.M3 ECOL**

Prospects for metropolitan water management. American Society of Civil Engineers Urban Water Resources Council, 1970. v. **fTD353.M32 ECOL**

MEAD CORPORATION.
Multi-system biological treatment of bleached kraft effluents. Prepared for the Environmental Protection Agency, Industrial Pollution Control. U.S. Environmental Protection Agency; for sale by the Supt. of Docs., U.S. Govt. Print. Off., 1971. (Water pollution control research series) **fTD899.W65M4 ECOL**

MEAD, MARGARET, 1901-
The Teilhard Review.
Change or decay: a symposium on the Blueprint for survival. 1972. **HC68.T4 ECOL**

MEAD, MARGARET, 1901- comp.
Hunger. Scientists' Institute for Public Information, 1970 (A Scientists' Institute for Public Information workbook) **fHD9000.5.M37 ECOL**

MEAD, ROBERT L.
Power from radioisotopes by Robert L. Mead and William R. Corlis. Rev. U.S. Atomic Energy Commission, Division of Technical Information 1966 (Understanding the atom) **TK1078.M38 ECOL**

MEADOWS, DONELLA H.
The Limits to growth. c1972 **HC110.E5L5 ECOL**

MEADOWS, KATHERINE F., ed.
Geothermal world directory, 1972-
fGB1003.G46 ECOL

MECH, L. DAVID.
The wolf: the ecology and behavior of an endangered species, by L. David Mech. Published for the American Museum of Natural History by the Natural History Press 1970 **QL737.C22M4 ECOL**

The wolves of Isle Royale. U.S. Govt. Print. Off. 1966 (Fauna of the National Parks of the United States. Fauna series, 7) **QL155.A45no.7 ECOL**

MECH, L. DAVID, jt. auth.
Ecological studies of the timber wolf in northeastern Minnesota. 1971 **SD11.A45476no.52 ECOL**

MECHALAS, B. J.
A study of nitrification and denitrification, by B. J. Mechalas, P. M. i.e. H. Allen, III and W. W. Matyskiela. Advanced Waste Treatment Research Laboratory; for sale by the Supt. of Docs., U.S. Govt. Print. Off., 1970. (Water pollution control research series)
fTD433.M43 ECOL

MECKING, LUDWIG, 1879-
Nordenskjold, Otto.
The geography of the polar regions, consisting of a general characterization of polar nature. 1928.
G587.N6 ECOL

MEDICAL RESEARCH COUNCIL OF CANADA.
Ecology and physiology of parasites. 1971
QL757.E26 ECOL

MEGARD, ROBERT ORDELL, 1933-
Lake Minnetonka: nutrients, nutrient abatement, and the photosynthetic system of the phytoplankton. Univ. of Minn. Limnological Research Center, 1970. (Minnesota. University. Limnological Research Center. Interim report no. 7) **fTD225.M63M4 ECOL**

MEHTA, ASHISH J., jt. auth.
Partheniades, Emmanuel.
Deposition of fine sediments in turbulent flows. 1971 i.e. 1972 **fTC175.2.P3 ECOL**

MEIN, RUSSELL G.
Modeling the infiltration component of the rainfall—runoff process, by R. G. Mein and Curtis L. Larson. Water Resources Research Center, Univ. of Minn., Graduate School, 1971. (WRRC bulletin, no. 43)
GB701.M554no.43 ECOL

MELLANBY, KENNETH.
Pesticides and pollution. 2nd rev. ed. Collins, 1970. (The New naturalist: a survey of British natural history)
TD186.5.G7M44 1970 ECOL

MENABONI, ATHOS, 1895-
Birds, by Athos and Sara Menaboni. Rinehart 1950
fQL681.M49 ECOL

MENABONI, SARA (ARNOLD).
Menaboni, Athos.
Birds. 1950 **fQL681.M49 ECOL**

MENGEL, J. T.
Geology of the western Lake Superior region; a guide for visitors. Geology Dept., Wisconsin State Univ., 1970. **fQE78.M4 ECOL**

MERCER, THOMAS T., ed.
Rochester International Conference on Environmental Toxicity; 3d, 1970.
Assessment of airborne particles. 1972
QD549.R59 1970 ECOL

MERCER, WALTER ASHBY, 1915-
National Canners Association. Western Research Laboratory.
Dry caustic peeling of tree fruit for liquid waste reduction. 1970. **fTD899.F7N37 ECOL**

National Canners Association. Western Research Laboratory.
Reduction of salt content of food processing liquid waste effluent. 1971. **fTD899.C3N36 ECOL**

MERRILEES, REBECCA A., illus.
Brockman, Christian Frank.
Trees of North America. 1968
QK481.B864 ECOL

MERRILL, SAMUEL, 1855-
The moose book; facts and stories from northern forests, by Samuel Merrill; illus. with reproductions of paintings, drawings, and photographs, by Carl Rungius and others. Dutton & Co. c1916 **SK301.M4 ECOL**

MERRITT, THOMAS W.
Studies on benthic nematode ecology in a small freshwater pond. Water Resources Research Institute, Auburn University, 1973. (Auburn University. Water Resources Research Institute. WRRI bulletin 8)
fTC1.A85no.8 ECOL

MERTA, MARTIN, jt. auth.
Henkin, Harmon.
The environment, the establishment, and the law. 1971 **QH545.P4H4 ECOL**

MERTZ, DAVID B., jt. comp.
Connell, Joseph H.
Readings in ecology and ecological genetics. 1970
QH541.C65 ECOL

MESTHENE, EMMANUEL G.
Technological change: its impact on man and society. Harvard Univ. Press 1970. (Harvard studies in technology and society) **HM221.M47 1970 ECOL**

METALLIC CONTAMINANTS AND HUMAN HEALTH.
Scientific editor. Douglas H. K. Lee. Academic Press, 1972. (Fogarty International Center proceedings no. 9) (Environmental sciences) **RA565.M47 1972 ECOL**

METALLURGICAL SOCIETY OF AIME. EXTRACTIVE METALLURGY DIVISION.
Environmental Control Symposium, San Francisco, 1972.
Environmental control. 1972
TD888.M4E58 1972 ECOL

METCALF AND EDDY, BOSTON.
Sewerage and water planning report. 1968. v.
fTD525.T9M4 ECOL

Storm water management model, by Metcalf and Eddy, University of Florida, and Water Resources Engineers, Inc. Prepared for the Environmental Protection Agency. Water Quality Office, Environmental Protection Agency 1971. 4v. (Water pollution control research series) **fGB665.M4 ECOL**

Wastewater engineering: collection, treatment, disposal by Metcalf and Eddy, Inc. McGraw-Hill 1972 (McGraw-Hill series in water resources and environmental engineering) **TD645.M57 ECOL**

METCALF, ROBERT LEE, jt. ed.
Advances in environmental sciences. v.1-1969- **REF TD180.A38 ECOL**

METRESS, JAMES F., ed.
Man in ecological perspective. MSS Educational Publishing Co. c1971 **GF75.M4 ECOL**

THE METROPOLITAN AREA—AN AIR POLLUTION CONTROL PROGRAM: A REPORT TO THE SUBCOMMITTEE ON METROPOLITAN PROBLEMS, GOVERNOR'S ADVISORY COMMITTEE ON AIR RESOURCES.
1966 **fTD883.5.M65M4 ECOL**

METROPOLITAN OPEN SPACE AND NATURAL PROCESS.
by David A. Wallace and others. Ed. by David A. Wallace. Univ. of Pennsylvania, 1970.
HT394.P5M46 ECOL

METZGER, H. PETER.
The atomic establishment by H. Peter Metzger. Simon and Schuster 1972 **HD9698.U52M47 ECOL**

MEYER, ARTHUR B., jt. auth.
Clepper, Henry Edward.
The world of the forest. **SD131.C55 ECOL**

MEYERS, CHARLES J.
Selected legal and economic aspects of environmental protection, by Charles J. Meyers and A. Dan Tarlock. Foundation Press, 1971. **KF3775.A7M58 ECOL**

MEYERS, CHARLES J. WATER RESOURCE MANAGEMENT.
Meyers, Charles J.
Selected legal and economic aspects of environmental protection. 1971. **KF3775.A7M58 ECOL**

MICHAELS, H. JAMES.
Black, Sivalls and Bryson, Inc., Kansas City, Mo. Applied Technology Division
Study of sulfur recovery from coal refuse. 1971.
fTN890.B57 ECOL

MICHIGAN. BUREAU OF WATER MANAGEMENT.
Chlorinated municipal waste toxicities to rainbow trout and fathead minnows, by Bureau of Water Management, Michigan Dept. of Natural Resources, for the Environmental Protection Agency, 1971. (Water pollution control research series) **fTD763.M5 ECOL**

MICHIGAN. DEPT. OF NATURAL RESOURCES.
Environmental education for intermediate grades; a teacher's manual. Lansing?, **fS946.M45 ECOL**
Michigan. Bureau of Water Management.
Chlorinated municipal waste toxicities to rainbow trout and fathead minnows. 1971.
fTD763.M5 ECOL

MICHIGAN. LEGISLATURE. HOUSE OF REPRESENTATIVES. GREAT LAKES CONTAMINATION (MERCURY) COMMITTEE.
D'Itri, Frank M.
The environmental mercury problem. 1971.
fQH545.M4D57 ECOL

MICHIGAN. STATE UNIVERSITY. EAST LANSING. AGRICULTURAL EXPERIMENT STATION.
Snowmobile and Off the Road Vehicle Research Symposium, Michigan State University, East Lansing, 1971.
Proceedings. 1971. **fGF75.S6 1971 ECOL**

MICHIGAN. STATE UNIVERSITY, EAST LANSING. AGRICULTURAL POLLUTION CONTROL LABORATORY.
Closed system waste management for livestock, by Patrick O. Ngoddy and others. Prepared for the Office of Research and Monitoring, Environmental Protection Agency. U.S. Environmental Protection Agency, U.S. Govt. Print. Off., 1971 i.e. 1972 (Water pollution control research series) **fTD899.F4M5 ECOL**

MICHIGAN. STATE UNIVERSITY. EAST LANSING. COOPERATIVE EXTENSION SERVICES.
Snowmobile and Off the Road Vehicle Research Symposium, Michigan State University, East Lansing, 1971.

Proceedings. 1971. **fGF75.S6 1971 ECOL**

MICHIGAN. UNIVERSITY. ADVISORY COMMITTEE ON PREDATOR CONTROL.
Predator control—1971: report to the Council on Environmental Quality and the Dept. of the Interior. 1972. **fQL758.M5 ECOL**

MICHIGAN. WESTERN MICHIGAN UNIVERSITY, KALAMAZOO. INSTITUTE OF PUBLIC AFFAIRS.
Kiraldi, Louis.
Pollution. 1971. **REF fZ7171.K55 ECOL**

MICHIGAN. WESTERN MICHIGAN UNIVERSITY, KALAMAZOO. INSTITUTE ON ENVIRONMENTAL INFORMATION PROGRAMS FOR PUBLIC LIBRARIES.
Cohen, Martin.
A handbook on environmental information programs for public libraries. 1973. **fZ670.A3C6 ECOL**

MICHIGAN. WESTERN MICHIGAN UNIVERSITY, KALAMAZOO. SCHOOL OF LIBRARIANSHIP.
Cohen, Martin.
A handbook on environmental information programs for public libraries. 1973. **fZ670.A3C6 ECOL**

MID-WEST DEBATE BUREAU, NORMAL, ILLINOIS.
Control of pollution; how can our physical environment best be controlled and developed? 1970
fTD180.M5 ECOL

MIDDLEBROOK, JAMES B., jt. auth.
Suggs, James D.
Mercury pollution control in stream and lake sediments. 1972. **fTD427.M4S9 ECOL**

MIDWEST PLANNING AND RESEARCH, INC.
Anoka County parks and open-space: comprehensive plan. 1969. **fGV54.M6M52 ECOL**
Anoka County parks and open-space: goals, policies, directions and alternatives. 1968
fGV54.M6M5 ECOL

MIDWEST REGIONAL SEMINAR ON HORIZONS IN RESOURCE RECOVERY, UNIVERSITY OF CHICAGO, 1972.
Horizons in resource recovery: presentations and discussions of a seminar held Feb. 23, 1972. Univ. of Chicago, 1972. **fTP995.A1M5 1972 ECOL**

MIDWEST RESEARCH INSTITUTE, KANSAS CITY, MISSOURI.
Resource recovery; the state of technology. Prepared for the Council on Environmental Quality. U.S. Gov't. Print. Off. 1973. **fTP995.M5 ECOL**

MIDWEST RESEARCH INSTITUTE, KANSAS CITY, MO.
Darnay, Arsen.
The role of packaging in solid waste management 1966 to 1976. 1969. **TD795.D37 ECOL**
Darnay, Arsen.
Salvage markets for materials in solid wastes, ... 1972. **TD795.D38 ECOL**
Franklin, William E.
Environmental impacts of polystyrene foam and molded pulp meat trays. 1972. **fTP373.F7 ECOL**
Light-catalyzed chlorine oxidation for treatment of wastewater. Environmental Protection Agency, Water Quality Office; for sale by the Supt. of Docs., U.S. Govt. Print. Off., 1970. (Water pollution control research series) **fTD758.M5 ECOL**
McCue, Gerald M.
Creating the human environment. 1970
HN59.M22 ECOL
Rapid detection system for organophosphates and carbamate insecticides in water. Prepared for Office of Research and Monitoring, U.S. Environmental Protection Agency. U.S. Govt. Print. Off., 1972. (Environmental protection technology series)
TD427.P35M5 ECOL

MIGNON, MOLLY R., comp.
Our polluted planet: a bibliography of government publications on pollution and the environment. 1971.
fZ5322.E2M5 ECOL

MILLAN, JAIME, jt. auth.
Tucker, L. Scott.
Metropolitan industrial water use. 1972.
fTD223.T8 ECOL

MILLARD, REED.
Clean air—clean water for tomorrow's world, by Reed Millard and the editors of Science Book Associates. Messner 1971 (Tomorrow's world series)
HC79.E5M5 ECOL
How will we meet the energy crisis? Power for tomorrow's world, by Reed Millard and the editors of Science Book Associates. J. Messner 1971 (Tomorrow's world series) **TJ153.M54 ECOL**
Natural resources: will we have enough for tomorrow's world? By Reed Millard and the editors of Science Book Associates. J. Messner 1972 (Tomorrow's world series) **HC103.7.M55 ECOL**

MILLER, E. F., jt. auth.
McNabb, C. D.
A fluorometric technique for sampling in large-river ecosystems. 1971. **GB701.M554no.34 ECOL**

MILLER, HOWARD A.
How to know the trees by Howard A. Miller and H. E. Jaques. 2d ed. W. C. Brown Co. 1972 (Pictured-key nature series) **REF QK482.M65 1972 ECOL**

MILLER, JAMES D.
Effects of noise on people. U.S. Environmental Protection Agency, Office of Noise Abatement and Control, 1971. **RA772.N7M5 ECOL**

MILLER, JOHN A.
Conservation: the scientific aspects: a guide to the literature. 1973. (Council of Planning Librarians. Exchange bibliography, 397)
REF fZ7164.N3M5 ECOL

MILLER, KAREN AMBRY, jt. auth.
Bonvie, Carolyn.
Art & design in the environment. 1971
fLB1047.B6 ECOL

MILLER, MORTON W., 1936- ed.
Chemical fallout. 1969 **SB959.C45 ECOL**

MILLER, O. M., 1897-
Forbes, Alexander.
Northernmost Labrador. 1938. **F1136.F67 ECOL**

MILLER, W. A., jt. auth.
Straka, G. C.
Graphs of ground water levels in Minnesota, 1957-1961. 1963. **fTD224.M6A3no.18 ECOL**

MILLIKEN, MARGARET.
Field study manual for outdoor living, by Margaret Milliken, Austin F. Hamer and Ernest C. McDonald. Burgess Publishing Co. c1968 **QH53.M5 ECOL**

MILLS, DEREK HENRY.
Salmon and trout: a resource, its ecology, conservation, and management by Derek Mills. St. Martin's Press 1971 **QL638.S2M5 1971b ECOL**

MILLS, THOMAS R., jt. auth.
Maryland. Dept. of Water Resources.
Guidelines for erosion and sediment control, planning and implementation. 1972. **fS624.A1M3 ECOL**

MILNE, LORUS JOHNSON, 1910-
The arena of life: the dynamics of ecology by Lorus and Margery Milne. Doubleday 1972
QH541.M52 ECOL

The balance of nature by Lorus J. Milne and Margery Milne. Illus. by Olaus J. Murie. Knopf, 1971 1960
QL751.M48 ECOL

The nature of life; earth, plants, animals, man and their effect on each other by Lorus and Margery Milne. Photos. by Emil Javorsky, and others. Crown Publishers 1970 **fQH45.2.M55 ECOL**

Patterns of survival, by L. J. Milne and Margery Milne. Illus. by Stanley Wyatt. Prentice c1967 (Prentice-Hall series in nature and natural history)
QH546.M5 ECOL

MILNE, LORUS JOHNSON, 1912-
The animal in man, by Lorus and Margery Milne. McGraw-Hill 1973 **BF671.M63 ECOL**

MILNE, MARGERY JOAN (GREENE) 1914- jt. auth.
Milne, Lorus Johnson.
The animal in man. 1973 **BF671.M63 ECOL**
Milne, Lorus Johnson.
The arena of life: the dynamics of ecology. 1972
QH541.M52 ECOL
Milne, Lorus Johnson.
The balance of nature. 1971 1960
QL751.M48 ECOL
Milne, Lorus Johnson.
The nature of life. 1970 **fQH45.2.M55 ECOL**
Milne, Lorus Johnson.
Patterns of survival. c1967 **QH546.M5 ECOL**

MILTON, JOHN P., ed.
Conference on the Ecological Aspects of International Development, Airlie House, 1968.
The careless technology: ecology and international development. 1st ed. 1972. **QH540.C65 1968 ECOL**

MILTON, JOHN P., jt. ed.
Darling, Frank Fraser.
Future environments of North America. 1966.
HC95.D33 ECOL

MILWAUKEE. MILWAUKEE RIVER TECHNICAL STUDY COMMITTEE.
The Milwaukee River; an inventory of its problems, an appraisal of its potentials. 1968.
fTD225.M47M6 ECOL

MILWAUKEE. SEWERAGE COMMISSION.
Evaluation of conditioning and dewatering sewage sludge by freezing. Environmental Protection Agency, Research and Monitoring 1971. (Water pollution control research series) **fTD769.7.M54 ECOL**

Phosphorus removal by an activated sludge plant. U.S. Environmental Protection Agency; for sale by the Supt. of Docs., U.S. Govt. Print. Off., 1970. (Water pollution control research series) **fTD756.M54 ECOL**

Phosphorus removal with pickle liquor in an activated sludge plant. Prepared for the Environmental Protection Agency. Environmental Protection Agency, Research and Monitoring; for sale by the Supt. of Docs., U.S. Govt. Print. Off., 1971. (Water pollution control research series) **fTD756.M55 ECOL**

MILWIDSKY, BENJAMIN MAX, 1923-
Practical detergent analyses, by B. M. Milwidsky. 1st ed. MacNair-Dorland Co. 1970 **TP992.5.M5 ECOL**

MINE SAFETY APPLIANCES RESEARCH CORPORATION.
Optimization of the regeneration procedure for granular activated carbon. Author: A J. Juhola. U.S. Environmental Protection Agency; for sale by the Supt. of Docs., U.S. Govt. Print. Off., 1970. (Water pollution control research series) **fTP245.C4M55 ECOL**

MINER, OPAL IRENE (FRAZINE) SEVREY.
The true book of plants we know. Illus. by Irene Miner and Karl Murr. Childrens Press c1953 (A True book) **QK49.M6 ECOL**

MINES, SAMUEL.
The last days of mankind; ecological survival or extinction. Simon and Schuster 1971 **S936.M55 ECOL**

MINN. ASSOCIATION OF COMMERCE AND INDUSTRY.
The Ecological register: a directory of organizations in the seven-county metropolitan area concerned about environmental destruction and pollution (plus a supplement providing brief information on similar organizations located elsewhere). 1970. **fS920.E24 ECOL**

MINN. DIV. OF WATER QUALITY.
Minnesota. Pollution Control Agency.
Progress report on water pollution control July 1967 through December 1968. 1968. **fTD224.M6A532 ECOL**

MINN. UNIV. SCHOOL OF PUBLIC HEALTH.
The Ecological register: a directory of organizations in the seven-county metropolitan area concerned about environmental destruction and pollution (plus a supplement providing brief information on similar organizations located elsewhere). 1970. **fS920.E24 ECOL**

MINN. UNIV. WATER RESOURCES RESEARCH CENTER. WRRC BULLETIN NO.44.
Bowers, C. Edward.
Computer programs in hydrology. 1972. **GB665.B6 ECOL**

MINNEAPOLIS. OFFICE OF THE CITY COORDINATOR.
Regional transit for Minneapolis: interim report. Office of City Coordinator, 1972. **fHE4491.M62 1972 ECOL**

MINNEAPOLIS. PLANNING AND DEVELOPMENT.
1970 profile of Minneapolis communities. Preliminary report 1. 1971. **fHT165.M6A46 ECOL**

MINNEMAST.
Subarsky, Zachariah.
Living things in field and classroom. 2d ed. 1969 **QH51.S9 1969 ECOL**

MINNESOTA. AIR QUALITY DIVISION.
Highlights of implementation plan for sulfur dioxide, particulates, carbon monoxide, hydrocarbons, nitrogen oxides, photochemical oxidant. Minnesota Pollution Control Agency, Air Quality Division, 1971. **REF fTD883.5.M6A42 ECOL**

Implementation plan to achieve carbon monoxide ambient air quality standards. Prepared for U.S. Environmental Protection Agency by John G. Olin. Pollution Control Agency, Division of Air Quality, 1973. v. **REF fTD883.5.M6A422 ECOL**

TRC—The Research Corporation of New England.
Proposal to the State of Minnesota Pollution Control Agency: Highlights of implementation plan for sulfur dioxide, particulates, carbon monoxide, hydrocarbons, nitrogen oxides, photochemical oxidant. 1971. **Ref fTD883.5.M6T15 ECOL**

MINNESOTA AIR QUALITY IMPLEMENTATION PLAN.
Minnesota. Pollution Control Agency.
In the matter of the adoption of proposed amendments to Minnesota Regulations APC 1, APC 3, APC 4, APC 11 and APC 15; and the adoption of Minnesota Regulation APC 16; and the proposed adoption of the Minnesota Air Quality Implementation Plan. 1972 **REF fKFM5758.A17 1972 ECOL**

MINNESOTA ASSOCIATION OF COMMERCE AND INDUSTRY.
Air pollution regulation handbook; a simplified discussion and statement of the Minnesota State Air Pollution control regulations. 1970? **REF fTD883.5.M6M61 ECOL**

The Ecological register: a directory of governmental agencies and private organizations concerned about environmental destruction and pollution in the state and in the seven-county metropolitan area. 2nd ed. 1971. **S920.E24 1971 ECOL**

Water pollution regulation handbook; a simplified discussion and statement of the Minnesota State Water Pollution control regulations. 1970 **REF fTD420.M66 ECOL**

Water quality control glossary; definitions of technical terms frequently used in relation to water quality. 1970 **fTD370.M56 ECOL**

MINNESOTA ASSOCIATION OF SOIL AND WATER CONSERVATION DISTRICTS.
Outdoor recreational development potentials in Washington Soil and Water Conservation District. **fGV54.M6M54 ECOL**

MINNESOTA COMMITTEE FOR ENVIRONMENTAL INFORMATION.
The costs and benefits of nuclear electric power plants. 1969. 1v. **REF fTK1078.M5 ECOL**

MINNESOTA. CONSERVATION, DEPT. OF GAME AND FISH, DIVISION OF.
White-tailed deer of Minnesota. 1961. **SH11.M64no.5 ECOL**

MINNESOTA. CONSERVATION NEEDS COMMITTEE.
Minnesota soil and water conservation needs inventory. 1971 **fHD243.M6A42 ECOL**

MINNESOTA. DEPT. OF ADMINISTRATION. DOCUMENTS DIVISION.
Minnesota directory of manufacturers. **REF fT12.M5 ECOL**

MINNESOTA. DEPT. OF CONSERVATION.
Minnesota outdoor recreation plan. Bureau of Planning, Minnesota Dept. of Conservation, 1968- v. **fGV54.M6A197 ECOL**

United States. Army. Corps of Engineers.
W. Fork Des Moines River and Perkins Creek flood plain information, Windom, Minnesota. 1972. **GB1225.M6A5 ECOL**

MINNESOTA. DEPT. OF CONSERVATION. DIVISION OF GAME AND FISH.
Big game in Minnesota. 1965. **SH11.M64no.9 ECOL**

Ducks and land use in Minnesota; four studies, by Division of Game and Fish, Section and Research and Planning, the Minnesota game research group: Forrest B. Lee and others. Edited by John B. Moyle. 1964. (Minnesota. Dept. of Conservation. Technical bulletin no. 8) **SH11.M64no.8 ECOL**

Waterfowl in Minnesota, by the Minnesota waterfowl research group: Forrest B. Lee and others. Drawings by John M. Idstrom. Ed. by John B. Moyle. 1964. (Minnesota. Dept. of Conservation. Technical bulletin no. 7) **SH11.M64no.7 ECOL**

MINNESOTA. DEPT. OF CONSERVATION. DIVISION OF GAME AND FISH. SECTION OF RESEARCH AND PLANNING.
Dobie, John R.
Methods used for investigating productivity of fish-rearing ponds in Minnesota. Rev. 1962. **SH222.M6D6 1962 ECOL**

MINNESOTA. DEPT. OF CONSERVATION. DIVISION OF LANDS AND FORESTRY see also **MINNESOTA. DIVISION OF LANDS AND FORESTRY**

Minnesota. Laws, statutes, etc.
Forest laws. 1968. **REF KFM5649.A45 1968 ECOL**

MINNESOTA. DEPT. OF CONSERVATION. DIVISION OF WATERS.
Norvitch, Ralph F.
Ground water in alluvial channel deposits, Nobles County, Minnesota. 1960. **fTD224.M6A3no.14 ECOL**

The St. Louis River Watershed unit. 1964. (its Bulletin 22) **fTD224.M6A3no.22 ECOL**

Water resources of Minneapolis-St. Paul metropolitan area. 1961. (its Bulletin, no. 11) **fTD224.M6A3no.11 ECOL**

MINNESOTA. DEPT. OF CONSERVATION. DIVISION OF WATERS. HYDROLOGIC ATLAS OF MINNESOTA.
Minnesota. Dept. of Conservation. Division of Waters.

The St. Louis River Watershed unit. 1964. **fTD224.M6A3no.22 ECOL**

MINNESOTA. DEPT. OF CONSERVATION. DIVISION OF WATERS, SOILS, AND MINERALS.
An inventory of Minnesota lakes. 1968. (its Bulletin no. 25) **TD224.M6A3no.25 ECOL**

United States. Geological Survey. Water Resources Division.
Water resources data for Minnesota, 1968- **REF GB705.M62A32 ECOL**

MINNESOTA. DEPT. OF ECONOMIC DEVELOPMENT.
Minnesota. Dept. of Natural Resources.
Inter-agency task force report on base metal mining impacts. 1973. **fTN24.M6A5 ECOL**

MINNESOTA. DEPT. OF ECONOMIC DEVELOPMENT. RESEARCH DIVISION.
Minnesota directory of manufacturers. **REF fT12.M5 ECOL**

MINNESOTA. DEPT. OF EDUCATION.
Minnesota Elementary Principals' Association.
Guidelines for out-of-the-classroom education experiences: Elementary schools. 1966. **LB1047.M55 ECOL**

MINNESOTA. DEPT. OF EDUCATION. VOCATIONAL-TECHNICAL DIVISION.
Naylon, Michael J.
Natural resources management: suggested teaching units for agricultural education. 1972? **fS946.N3 ECOL**

MINNESOTA. DEPT. OF HEALTH. DIVISION OF ENVIRONMENTAL HEALTH. SECTION OF WATER POLLUTION CONTROL.
Report on application for waste disposal permit, Allen S. King Plant, Northern States Power Company, Oak Park Heights. 1965. v. **fTK1331.N6M6 ECOL**

MINNESOTA. DEPT. OF HEALTH. DIVISION OF ENVIRONMENTAL SANITATION. SECTION OF WATER POLLUTION CONTROL see **MINNESOTA. DIVISION OF WATER QUALITY**

MINNESOTA. DEPT. OF HEALTH. SECTION OF WATER POLLUTION CONTROL.
Thimsen, Donald J.
Biological treatment in aerated lagoons: theory and practice. 1965. **fTD746.5.T5 ECOL**

MINNESOTA. DEPT. OF HIGHWAYS.
Howard, Needles, Tammen & Bergendoff.
Interstate 394 corridor location study. 1973? **fTE25.T9H6 ECOL**

A research progress report on the effects of studded tires, prepared for the Legislature, State of Minnesota. 1970. **fTL270.M5 1970 ECOL**

A research summary report on the effects of studded tires, prepared for the Legislature, State of Minnesota. 1971. **fTL270.M5 1971 ECOL**

MINNESOTA. DEPT. OF IRON RANGE RESOURCES AND REHABILITATION.
Minnesota. Dept. of Natural Resources.
Inter-agency task force report on base metal mining impacts. 1973. **fTN24.M6A5 ECOL**

MINNESOTA. DEPT. OF NATURAL RESOURCES.
Harza Engineering Company.
Report on abandonment and transfer of ownership of dams. 1971. **fTC557.M6H3 ECOL**

Inter-agency task force report on base metal mining impacts. 1973. v. **fTN24.M6A5 ECOL**

Symposium on the White-tailed Deer in Minnesota, St. Paul, Minnesota, 1971.
The white-tailed deer in Minnesota. 1972? **fQL737.U55S9 1971ECOL**

United States. Soil Conservation Service.
Flood hazard analyses: city of Canby and vicinity, Yellow Medicine County, Minnesota. 1973. **GB1225.M6U5 ECOL**

MINNESOTA. DEPT. OF NATURAL RESOURCES. BUREAU OF INFORMATION AND EDUCATION.
Fisher, Wes.
Minnesota environmental education areas. 1972 **fS946.F5 ECOL**

MINNESOTA. DEPT. OF NATURAL RESOURCES. BUREAU OF PLANNING.
Minnesota resource potentials in state outdoor recreation comp. by Dept. of Natural Resources, Bureau of Planning and State Planning Agency, Environmental Planning Section. 1971. (Project 80. Staff report no. 1) **fGV54.M6A53 ECOL**

MINNESOTA. DEPT. OF NATURAL RESOURCES. DIVISION OF WATERS, SOILS AND MINERALS see MINNESOTA. DIVISION OF WATERS, SOILS AND MINERALS

MINNESOTA DIRECTORY OF MANUFACTURERS; a listing of Minnesota-made products and their products and their producers. v. **REF fT12.M5 ECOL**

MINNESOTA. DIVISION OF LANDS AND FORESTRY see also MINNESOTA. DEPT. OF CONSERVATION. DIVISION OF LANDS AND FORESTRY

Land exchange study report. 1969.
fHD211.M6A45 ECOL

MINNESOTA. DIVISION OF WATER QUALITY see also MINNESOTA. WATER POLLUTION CONTROL COMMISSION

Creative Research Services, Inc.
Water quality management plan, interim. 1971.
REF fTD224.M65C7 ECOL

Investigation of water quality and sources of pollution of waters of Minnesota and Iowa: reports and memorandums. 1960- **fTD224.M6A34 ECOL**

Memorandum on mercury pollution in Minnesota. 1970. **fQH545.M4M57 ECOL**

Memorandum on the waste assimilation capacity of the Mississippi River in the Twin Cities Metropolitan Area. 1969. v. **fTD525.T9M6 ECOL**

Minnesota. Pollution Control Agency.
Progress report and long-range plan and program for water pollution control. 1968.
REF fTD224.M6A53 ECOL

Report on investigation of pollution of the Northern Border waters from the mouth of the Pigeon River at Lake Superior westward through the Boundary Waters Canoe Area and Lower Lakes to the outlet of Rainy Lake. 1969 1v. **fTD224.M6A5 ECOL**

Sewage disposal facilities inventory, State of Minnesota, January 1, 1969. 1969
fTD524.M5A44 ECOL

Waste disposal reports and memorandums of industries of Minnesota. 1961-
fTD224.M6A35 ECOL

Wastewater disposal facilities inventory, State of Minnesota. 1971- v. **fTD224.M6A33 ECOL**

Wastewater treatment works studies, surveys, memorandums, reports, etc. of cities and villages of Minnesota. 1964- **fTD224.M6A36 ECOL**

MINNESOTA. DIVISION OF WATERS, SOILS AND MINERALS.

Brice, William C.
Possible environmental impact of base metal mining in Minnesota. 1972 **fTN24.M6B7 ECOL**

Van Voast, Wayne A.
Ground water for irrigation in the Brooten-Belgrade area, west-central Minnesota. 1971.
TC801.U2no.1899-E ECOL

MINNESOTA ELEMENTARY PRINCIPALS' ASSOCIATION.
Guidelines for out-of-the-classroom education experiences: Elementary schools. 1966.
LB1047.M55 ECOL

MINNESOTA. GOVERNOR, 1971-
Securing a quality environment in Minnesota; special message to the 68th session of the legislature of Minnesota, February 14, 1973. 1973?
REF fHC107.M6A35 ECOL

MINNESOTA. GOVERNOR'S COMMITTEE ON AIR RESOURCES. SUBCOMMITTEE ON HEALTH, ECONOMIC AND NUISANCE EFFECTS OF AIR POLLUTION.
Snyder, Edwin F.
Preliminary report for the Subcommittee on Health, Economic and Nuisance Effects of Air Pollution. 1966.
fTD883.5.M65S6 ECOL

MINNESOTA. GOVERNOR'S COMMITTEE ON AIR RESOURCES. SUBCOMMITTEE ON LEGAL PROBLEMS.
Kennedy, David.
Report to the Subcommittee on Legal Problems Governor's Advisory Committee on Air Resources. 1966. **fTD883.5.M65K4 ECOL**

MINNESOTA. GOVERNOR'S COMMITTEE ON AIR RESOURCES. SUBCOMMITTEE ON METROPOLITAN PROBLEMS.
The Metropolitan Area—an air pollution control program: a report to the Subcommittee on Metropolitan Problems, Governor's Advisory Committee on Air Resources. 1966 **fTD883.5.M65M4 ECOL**

MINNESOTA. GOVERNOR'S ENVIRONMENTAL QUALITY COUNCIL.
Minnesota. State Planning Agency.
Energy use in Minnesota. 1973.
fHD9547.M6A5 ECOL

MINNESOTA. GOVERNOR'S ENVIRONMENTAL QUALITY COUNCIL. CITIZEN'S ADVISORY COMMITTEE.
Environmental quality, policies and decision-making in Minnesota - 1972; a report. 1972.
fHC107.M6A37 ECOL

MINNESOTA. GOVERNOR'S ENVIRONMENTAL QUALITY COUNCIL. CITIZENS ADVISORY COMMITTEE, GROUNDWATER QUALITY SUBCOMMITTEE.
Conference on Toward a Statewide Ground Water Quality Information System, St. Paul, Minn., 1972.
Proceedings of conference on toward a statewide ground water quality information system and report of Ground Water Quality Subcommittee Citizens Advisory Committee, Governors Environmental Quality Council. 1973. **fTD224.M6C6 1972 ECOL**

MINNESOTA. LAC QUI PARLE—YELLOW BANK WATERSHED DISTRICT.
United States. Soil Conservation Service.
Flood hazard analyses: city of Canby and vicinity, Yellow Medicine County, Minnesota. 1973.
GB1225.M6U5 ECOL

MINNESOTA. LAKESHORE DEVELOPMENT STUDY.
Minnesota's lakeshore; summary report, John R. Borchert, Director and others. 1970- v.1-
REF GB459.5.M5M5 ECOL

MINNESOTA. LAWS, STATUTES, ETC.
Forest laws. 1968.
REF KFM5649.A45 1968 ECOL

Haik, Raymond A.
Aspects of water resources law in Minnesota. 1969.
GB701.M554no.11 ECOL

Laws relating to game and fish, 1971/72- v.
REF KFM5853.A44 ECOL

Minnesota. University. Water Resources Research Center.
Codified and uncodified state laws and municipal ordinances bearing on water and related land resources in Minnesota. 1968. **GB701.M554no.9 ECOL**

MINNESOTA. LEGISLATURE. OUTDOOR RECREATION RESOURCES COMMISSION.
M.O.R.R.C. report. 1963/65- v.
REF GV54.M6A19 ECOL

M.O.R.R.C. staff report. 1963/65- v.
REF fGV54.M6A192 ECOL

MINNESOTA. LEGISLATURE. OUTDOOR RECREATION RESOURCES COMMISSION. REPORT.
Minnesota. Legislature. Outdoor Recreation Resources Commission.
M.O.R.R.C. report. 1963/65-
REF GV54.M6A19 ECOL

MINNESOTA. LEGISLATURE. OUTDOOR RECREATION RESOURCES COMMISSION. STAFF REPORT.
Minnesota. Legislature. Outdoor Recreation Resources Commission.
M.O.R.R.C. staff report. 1963/65-
REF fGV54.M6A192 ECOL

MINNESOTA. LEGISLATURE. SENATE. OFFICE OF SENATE COUNSEL.
The law of land exchange in Minnesota. Prepared for the Senate Committee on Public Domain. 1969.
fKFM5851.A84 ECOL

MINNESOTA. LEGISLATURE. SENATE. PUBLIC DOMAIN COMMITTEE.
Minnesota. Legislature. Senate. Office of Senate Counsel.
The law of land exchange in Minnesota. 1969.
fKFM5851.A84 ECOL

MINNESOTA. LOWER MINNESOTA RIVER WATERSHED DISTRICT.
Itasca Engineering, Inc., Minneapolis.
The effectiveness of flood control structures of the Lower Minnesota River Watershed District. 1970.
fTC424.M6182 ECOL

Itasca Engineering, inc. Minneapolis.
The Lower Minnesota River Watershed District. 1961. **fTC424.M6184 ECOL**

Itasca Engineering, inc., Minneapolis.
Overall plan of the Lower Minnesota River Watershed District, 1972. **fTC424.M6186 ECOL**

MINNESOTA MATHEMATICS AND SCIENCE TEACHING PROJECT.
Subarsky, Zachariah.
Living things in field and classroom. 2d ed. 1969
QH51.S9 1969 ECOL

MINNESOTA. METROPOLITAN COUNCIL OF THE TWIN CITIES AREA.
Metcalf and Eddy, Boston.
Sewerage and water planning report. 1968.
fTD525.T9M4 ECOL

Metropolitan development guide; a comprehensive development guide for the metropolitan area. 1973- 1v. **REF fHT168.T9A34 ECOL**

Wallace, McHarg, Roberts and Todd.
An ecological study of the Twin Cities Metropolitan Area. 1969. **fQH541.W32 ECOL**

MINNESOTA. METROPOLITAN COUNCIL OF THE TWIN CITIES AREA. OPEN SPACE ADVISORY COMMITTEE.
Proposals for preserving a Metropolitan open space, report of the Open Space Advisory Committee to the Metropolitan Council, January 1969. 1969
fHD1291.U6T9 ECOL

MINNESOTA. MINNEAPOLIS-ST. PAUL SANITARY DISTRICT.
Toltz, King, Duvall, Anderson and Associates, Inc., St. Paul.
Report on the expansion of the sewage treatment plant. 1969. **fTD525.T9T6 ECOL**

MINNESOTA. POLLUTION CONTROL AGENCY see also MINNESOTA. AIR QUALITY DIVISION; MINNESOTA. DIVISION OF WATER QUALITY; MINNESOTA. WATER POLLUTION CONTROL COMMISSION

Air pollution control in Minnesota, Jan. 1969 through Oct. 1970; progress report. 1970
fTD883.5.M6A47 1970 ECOL

Burke, Jacquelyn M.
The realities of recycling. 1973
REF fTP995.B8 ECOL

Census data: sewage disposal facilities, State of Minnesota, January, 1968. 1968
fTD524.M5A56 ECOL

Comprehensive plan for the storage, collection, transportation and disposal of solid waste in the State of Minnesota. 1970. **fTD524.M6A32 ECOL**

Creative Research Services, Inc.
Progress report, biennial program and long-range plan for water pollution control. 1970.
fTD224.M65C73 ECOL

Henningson, Durham & Richardson.
Study and investigation of solid waste control for the Minnesota Pollution Control Agency: phase II, final report. 1969. **REF fTD788.4.M6H4 ECOL**

History of Minnesota Pollution Control Agency. 1970 **fTD181.M5 ECOL**

In the matter of the adoption of proposed amendments to Minnesota Regulations APC 1, APC 3, APC 4, APC 11 and APC 15; and the adoption of Minnesota Regulation APC 16; and the proposed adoption of the Minnesota Air Quality Implementation Plan. Metropolitan Court Reporters 1972 7v.
REF fKFM5758.A17 1972 ECOL

Minnesota. University. Consortium for the Study of Solid Waste Management/Recycling Options.
A report on solid waste management/recycling options. 1972. **fTD793.M6 ECOL**

Pesticide inputs and levels: Minnesota waters-Lake Superior Basin. Prepared for the Environmental Protection Agency. U.S. Environmental Protection Agency; for sale by the Supt. of Docs., U.S. Govt. Print. Off. 1971 i.e. 1972 (Water pollution control research series) **fTD223.3.M55 ECOL**

Progress report and long-range plan and program for water pollution control. 1968. v.
REF fTD224.M6A53 ECOL

Progress report on water pollution control July 1967 through December 1968. 1968. v.
fTD224.M6A532 ECOL

Solid waste education. 1969?
fTD524.M6A3 ECOL

Water quality sampling program: Minnesota lakes and streams, a compilation of Minnesota sampling stations, v.6- 1967/68- v. **TD380.M6 ECOL**

MINNESOTA. POLLUTION CONTROL AGENCY. AIR QUALITY DIVISION see MINNESOTA. AIR QUALITY DIVISION

MINNESOTA. RESOURCES COMMISSION.
Minnesota. Lakeshore Development Study.
Minnesota's lakeshore. 1970-
REF GB459.5.M5M5 ECOL

MINNESOTA. SECRETARY OF STATE.
Minnesota Legislative manual.
REF JK6131.A25 ECOL

MINNESOTA. STATE COLLEGE, WINONA.
Mayfly distribution as a water quality index, by Calvin R. Fremling, Winona State College for the Water Quality Office, Environmental Protection Agency. Environmental Protection Agency, Water Quality Office; U.S. Govt. Print. Off., 1970. (Water pollution control research series) **fTD370.M562 ECOL**

MINNESOTA. STATE DEPT. OF HEALTH VITAL STATISTICS DIVISION.
Minnesota population data book. 1968.
REF fHA453.A53 ECOL

MINNESOTA. STATE PLANNING AGENCY.
Borchert, John R.
Minnesota settlement and land use 1985. 1970.
HD111.B6 ECOL
Energy use in Minnesota. Prepared by State of Minnesota, Governor's Environmental Quality Council. 1973. **fHD9547.M6A5 ECOL**
Environmental decision-making in Minnesota, summary and alternatives. 1973.
fHC107.M6A43 ECOL
Environmental decision-making in Minnesota: an overview, applicability of innovations in other states to Minnesota and alternatives. 1973
fHC 107.M6A43 1973 ECOL
Orning, George W.
Land management information in northwest Minnesota: the beginnings of a statewide system. 1972.
HD211.M6 ECOL
Protecting the Minnesota environment through regulation of private land use. 1972.
fHC107.M6A45 ECOL
St. John's University, Collegeville, Minnesota Center for the Study of Local Government.
The impact of future electrical power requirements on the state of Minnesota—an issue analysis. 1971.
fHD9685.U6M6 ECOL
State of Minnesota narrative report for the 1972 National Transportation Needs Study. Minnesota State Planning Agency 1971. **REF fTA1123.M5 ECOL**

MINNESOTA. STATE PLANNING AGENCY. ENVIRONMENTAL PLANNING SECTION.
Minnesota. Dept. of Natural Resources. Bureau of Planning.
Minnesota resource potentials in state outdoor recreation. 1971. **fGV54.M6A53 ECOL**

MINNESOTA. STATE PLANNING AGENCY. OFFICE OF LOCAL AND URBAN AFFAIRS.
Minnesota planning legislation. 1971
REF KFM5858.A3 1971 ECOL
Regional planning and development in Minnesota—a handbook on Executive order no. 37 and the Regional Development Act of 1969. 1969.
REF JK6131 1969 .A55 ECOL

MINNESOTA. UNIV. AGRICULTURAL EXTENSION SERVICE. OFFICE OF SPECIAL PROGRAMS.
Land in Transition Symposium, 1971, St. Paul, Minn. 1971 **fS623.L3 1971 ECOL**

MINNESOTA. UNIVERSITY.
Nuclear power and the public. 1970
TK1078.N83 ECOL
References and resource guides for the University of Minnesota SEED Project curricula. n.d. (Secondary environmental education development)
fQH541.2.M5 ECOL

MINNESOTA. UNIVERSITY. AGRICULTURAL EXTENSION SERVICE.
Conservation education assistance directories for Minnesota counties. v. **REF fS946.M5 ECOL**
Soils, soil management and fertilizer monographs. 1973. **fS591.M68 ECOL**
Waelti, John J.
Understanding the water quality controversy in Minnesota. 1969 **fTD420.W3 ECOL**

MINNESOTA. UNIVERSITY. CENTER FOR STUDIES OF THE PHYSICAL ENVIRONMENT.
Minnesota. State Planning Agency.
Environmental decision-making in Minnesota. 1973.
fHC107.M6A43 ECOL
Minnesota. State Planning Agency.
Environmental decision-making in Minnesota: an overview. 1973 **fHC 107.M6A43 1973 ECOL**

MINNESOTA. UNIVERSITY. CENTER FOR URBAN AND REGIONAL AFFAIRS.
Orning, George W.
Land management information in northwest Minnesota: the beginnings of a statewide system. 1972.
HD211.M6 ECOL

MINNESOTA. UNIVERSITY. CONSORTIUM FOR THE STUDY OF SOLID WASTE MANAGEMENT/RECYCLING OPTIONS.
A report on solid waste management/recycling options. 1972. v. **fTD793.M6 ECOL**

MINNESOTA. UNIVERSITY. DEPT. OF CONTINUING LEGAL EDUCATION.
Minnesota environmental law sourcebook. c1973. v.
REF KFM5754.A45 ECOL

MINNESOTA. UNIVERSITY. DEPT. OF HORTICULTURAL SCIENCE.
Methods and materials for the maintenance of turf on highway rights-of-way; an annotated bibliography. Comp. by Margaret H. Smithberg and Donald B. White. 1971. (Investigation no. 619. University of Minnesota Agricultural Experiment Station. Miscellaneous report 105) **REF TE178.M6 ECOL**

MINNESOTA. UNIVERSITY. DULUTH BRANCH. AGRICULTURAL EXTENSION SERVICE.
Natural resource management lesson plan guide. Comp. by the St. Louis County Extension Service with the Duluth Board of Education. n.d.
fS946.M55 ECOL

MINNESOTA. UNIVERSITY. GENERAL EXTENSION DIVISION.
Land Exchange Review Symposium, Duluth, 1970. Proceedings of the Land Exchange Review Symposium. 1970. **fHD211.L3 ECOL**

MINNESOTA. UNIVERSITY INSTITUTE OF TECHNOLOGY. CENTER FOR STUDIES OF THE PHYSICAL ENVIRONMENT.
Hickman, Howard J.
A study of the environmental impact of polystyrene vs. paper pulp egg cartons and meat trays. 1972.
fTP373.H5 ECOL

MINNESOTA. UNIVERSITY. LIMNOLOGICAL RESEARCH CENTER.
Harza Engineering Company.
A program for preserving the quality of Lake Minnetonka. 1971 **fTD225.M63H3 ECOL**

MINNESOTA. UNIVERSITY. MINNESOTA LAND INFORMATION STUDY.
Orning, George W.
Land management information in northwest Minnesota: the beginnings of a statewide system. 1972.
HD211.M6 ECOL

MINNESOTA UNIVERSITY. MUSEUM OF NATURAL HISTORY.
Roberts, Thomas Sadler.
The birds of Minnesota. 1932.
fQL684.M6R47 ECOL
Roberts, Thomas Sadler.
Manual for the identification of the birds of Minnesota and neighboring States. Rev. ed. 1955.
QL684.M6R472 1955 ECOL

MINNESOTA. UNIVERSITY. ST. ANTHONY FALLS HYDRAULIC LABORATORY.
Hydraulics of long vertical conduits and associated cavitation. Prepared for the Water Quality Office Environmental Protection Agency. Environmental Protection Agency; for sale by the Supt. of Docs., U.S. Govt. Print. Off., 1971. (Water pollution control research series) **fTC174.M53 ECOL**

MINNESOTA. UNIVERSITY SCHOOL OF FORESTRY.
Hall, O. F.
Principles of natural resource management. 1951.
fS938.H3 ECOL

MINNESOTA. UNIVERSITY. SCHOOL OF PUBLIC HEALTH.
Lake Superior studies, 1956-61. 1957-61 v.
fGB1627.G89M55 ECOL
Lake Superior study, summer of 1956, by Orlando R. Ruschmeyer, Theodore A. Olson and Herbert M. Bosch, of the School of Public Health; with a memorandum and recommendations by A. C. Redfield, and a detailed literature review by T. O. Odlaug. 1957
fGB1627.G89M5 ECOL
Lake Superior study, summer of 1956: summary of report by Orlando R. Ruschmeyer, Theodore A. Olson and Herbert M. Bosch and preliminary limnological study by A. C. Redfield. 1957. v.
fGB1627.G89M53 ECOL
A preliminary investigation of nutrients in western Lake Superior, 1958-1959, by Hugh D. Putnam and Theodore A. Olson; with foreword by Herbert M. Bosch, and a review of research and literature abstracts by Theron O. Odlaug. 1959.
fGB1627.G89M52 ECOL
Studies on the productivity and Plankton of Lake Superior, by Hugh D. Putnam and Theodore A. Olson; with foreword by Herbert M. Bosch and literature abstracts by Theron O. Odlaug, July 1, 1960-June 30, 1961. 1961 **fQK935.M55 ECOL**
Water movements and temperatures of western Lake Superior, by Orlando R. Ruschmeyer and Theodore A. Olson; with foreword by Herbert M. Bosch, and review of 1956 research and literature abstracts by Theron O. Odlaug. 1958. **fGB1627.G89M54 ECOL**

MINNESOTA. UNIVERSITY. WATER RESOURCES RESEARCH CENTER.
Annual report. A report of activities supported by the Graduate School and the Office of Water Resources Research, U.S. Dept. of the Interior as authorized under the Water Resources Research Act of 1964-   v. (WRRC bulletins) **GB701.M554 ECOL**
Arya, Lalit Mohan.
Water flow in soil in presence of soybean root sinks. 1973. **GB701.M554no.60 ECOL**
Baron, Norman J.
A survey of attitudes towards the Mississippi River as a total resource in Minnesota. 1972.
GB701.M554no.55 ECOL
Codified and uncodified state laws and municipal ordinances bearing on water and related land resources in Minnesota, Comp. by William C. Walton, Raymond A. Haik, and David L. Hills. 1968. (its WRRC bulletin 9) **GB701.M554no.9 ECOL**
Conference on impact of future electric power requirements in the state of Minnesota: an issue analysis. 1971. (its. WRRC bulletin 28)
GB701.M554no.28 ECOL
Conference on Toward a Statewide Ground Water Quality Information System, St. Paul, Minn., 1972.
Proceedings of conference on toward a statewide ground water quality information system and report of Ground Water Quality Subcommittee Citizens Advisory Committee, Governors Environmental Quality Council. 1973. **fTD224.M6C6 1972 ECOL**
Federal, state, and local agencies concerned with water resources research in Minnesota. 1965. (its WRRC bulletin no. 1) **GB701.M554no.1 ECOL**
Gerlach, Luther P.
Mobilization and participation of citizens groups in improving the quality of water resources environments. 1973. **GB701.M554no.57 ECOL**
Gibson, Ulric P.
Integrating water quality management into total water resources management in Minnesota. 1970.
GB701.M554no.23 ECOL
Haik, Raymond A.
Aspects of water resources law in Minnesota. 1969.
GB701.M554no.11 ECOL
Hopeman, Alan Roswell.
An economic analysis of flood damage reduction alternatives in the Minnesota River Basin. 1973.
GB701.M554no.58 ECOL
Information concerning water resources research center projects, 1965-70. 1970-
GB701.M554no.19 ECOL
Lake eutrophication—water pollution causes, effects and control. 1970. (WRRC bulletin, 22)
GB701.M554no.22 ECOL
Larson, Curtis L.
Predicting peak flow of small watersheds by use of channel characteristics. 1972.
GB701.M554no.52 ECOL
Lewis, Robert Clark.
The marginal costs of alternative levels of water quality in the Upper Mississippi River. 1970.
GB701.M554no.25 ECOL
Linn, J. G.
Aquatic plants from Minnesota, part 4 — nutrient composition. 1973. **GB701.M554no.56 ECOL**
Nelson, Robert R.
The effects of enrichment on Lake Superior periphyton. 1973. **GB701.M554no.59 ECOL**
Olson, Theodore A.
The continuous plankton recorder: a review of the literature. 1966. **GB701.M554no.3 ECOL**
Parkos, William G.
Water quality studies on the Great Lakes based on carbon fourteen measurements on primary productivity. 1969. **GB701.M554no.17 ECOL**
Potential productivity of fresh water environments as determined by an algae bioassay technique. 1970.
GB701.M554no.20
Proceedings of Conference on Inland Lake Renewal and Shoreland Management. 1972.
GB701.M554no.53 ECOL
Proceedings of conference on ongoing water resources research in Minnesota, March 1970. 1970. (WRRC bulletin, no. 21) **GB701.M554no.21 ECOL**
Publications related to water resources research center projects, 1965-71 abstract-index. Water Resources Research Center, University of Minnesota Graduate School, 1971. (WRRC bulletin 32)
GB701.M554no.32 ECOL
Soil Conservation Society of America. Minnesota Chapter.
Water pollution by nutrients—sources, effects and control. 1969. **GB701.M554no.13 ECOL**
Walton, William Clarence.
Water and related land resources state administration, legislative process and policies in Minnesota, 1970. 1971 **GB701.M554no.27 ECOL**
Water resources research and educational needs in Minnesota. 1967. (its WRRC bulletin no. 5)
GB701.M554no.5 ECOL
Watershed planning: papers presented at the Seminar on Watershed Planning sponsored by the Metropolitan Council and the Minnesota Association of Watershed Districts on February 15, 1972 at the Sheraton Motor Inn, Bloomington, Minnesota. 1972. (its WRRC bulletin 50) **GB701.M554no.50 ECOL**

MINNESOTA. UNIVERSITY. WATER RESOURCES RESEARCH CENTER. ADVISORY COMMITTEE.
Graduate education in water resources at University of Minnesota—1969; a report of a subcommittee of the Center's Advisory Committee. 1969. (Minnesota. University. Water Resources Research Center. Bulletin 15) **GB701.M554no.15 ECOL**

MINNESOTA. UNIVERSITY. WATER RESOURCES RESEARCH CENTER. CONSULTING COUNCIL.
Inventory of water resources research conducted in Minnesota, 1963 through 1968; a report of a task group of the Water Resources Research Center's Consulting Council. 1969. (Minnesota. University. Water Resources Research Center. Bulletin 12) **GB701.M554no.12 ECOL**

MINNESOTA. WATER POLLUTION CONTROL COMMISSION *see also* **MINNESOTA. DIVISION OF WATER QUALITY; MINNESOTA. POLLUTION CONTROL AGENCY**
Long-range water pollution control plan and program, July 1, 1963. **fTD224.M6A56 ECOL**

Minnesota. Dept. of Health. Division of Environmental Health. Section of Water Pollution Control.
Report on application for waste disposal permit. 1965. **fTK1331.N6M6 ECOL**

Report on a comprehensive sewage works plan for the Minneapolis-St. Paul metropolitan area, Dec. 1964. 1965 **fTD525.T8M6 ECOL**

Report on progress—water pollution control, Jan. 1, 1965 to Dec. 31, 1966. 1967 v. **fTD224.M6A562 ECOL**

Report on Progress - water pollution control, July 1, 1963 to Dec. 31, 1964. 1965? v. **fTD224.M6A561 ECOL**

MINNESOTA. WATER RESOURCES COORDINATING COMMITTEE.
Alternative programs and projects for managing Minnesota's water and related land resources through the year 2020. 1971 **fHD1694.M6A5 1971 ECOL**

Conference on Water and Related Land Resources Planning in Minnesota, St. Paul, Minn., 1967.
Papers presented during Conference on Water and Related Land Resources Planning in Minnesota. 1967. **fHD1694.M6A54 1967 ECOL**

Minnesota water and related land resources, first assessment. 1970. **TD224.M6A563 ECOL**

MINNESOTA. YELLOW MEDICINE SOIL AND CONSERVATION DISTRICT.
United States. Soil Conservation Service.
Flood hazard analyses: city of Canby and vicinity, Yellow Medicine County, Minnesota. 1973. **GB1225.M6U5 ECOL**

MISHAN, EDWARD J.
Technology and growth; the price we pay by E. J. Mishan. Praeger 1970,c1969 **HD82.M514 ECOL**

MISSISSIPPI. STATE UNIVERSITY. WATER RESOURCES RESEARCH INSTITUTE.
Mahloch, Jerome L.
The effect of organic amendments from garbage grinding on a biological treatment system. 1972. **fTD756.M32 ECOL**

McGriff, E. Corbin.
The efficacy of the complete mix activated sludge process in modular mode. 1972. **fTD756.M3 ECOL**

Peterson, John H.
Community organization programs and relationships in watershed development. 1972. **fTC409.P4 ECOL**

Shindala, Adnan.
Primary considerations in regional wastewater treatment planning. 1972. **fTD365.S4 ECOL**

MISSOURI BASIN INTER-AGENCY COMMITTEE.
Comprehensive framework study, Missouri River Basin. U.S. Govt. Print. Off. 1971- v. **fHD1695.M5M48 ECOL**

MISSOURI. SOUTHWEST MISSOURI STATE COLLEGE, SPRINGFIELD.
DNA concentration as an estimate of sludge biomass. Prepared for the Water Quality Office, Environmental Protection Agency. Water Quality Office, Environmental Protection Agency; for sale by the Supt. of Docs., U.S. Govt. Print. Off., 1971. (Water pollution control research series) **fTD767.7.M57 ECOL**

MITCHELL, JOHN G.
Caulfield, Patricia.
Everglades. 1970 **QH105.F6C36 ECOL**

MITCHELL, JOHN G., ed.
Ecotactics: the Sierra Club handbook for environmental activists. 1970 **HC110.E5E26 ECOL**

MITCHELL, RALPH.
Water pollution microbiology. Ed. by Ralph Mitchell. Wiley-Interscience 1971,c1972 **QR48.M58 ECOL**

MITCHELL, WALTER, 1930- jt. auth.
Lyerly, Ray L.
Nuclear power plants. Rev. 1969 **TK1078.L9 1969 ECOL**

MITRE CORPORATION, MCLEAN, VA.
Symposium on Energy, Resources and the Environment, McLean, Va., 1972.
Symposium on energy, resources and the environment. 1972. **fHD9540.1.S9 1972 ECOL**

MIZUMURA, KAZUE.
The blue whale. Written and illus. by Kazue Mizumura. Crowell c1971 (Let's read and find out science book) **QL737.C424M59 ECOL**

If I built a village. Crowell 1971 **Fiction ECOL**

MODELS FOR MANAGING REGIONAL WATER QUALITY.
Edited by Robert Dorfman, Henry D. Jacoby, and Harold A. Thomas, Jr. Harvard University Press, 1972. **TD365.M6 ECOL**

MOELLER, GEORGE H.
The landowner and the snowmobiler—problem or profit? Northeastern Forest Experiment Station, 1971. (U.S.D.A. Forest Service research paper NE 206) **GV857.S6M6 ECOL**

MOHN, VIOLA KOHL, illus.
Russell, Helen Ross.
Winter search party. 1st ed. 1971 **QL465.R85 ECOL**

MONSERUD, WILMA.
Common wild flowers of Minnesota. Illus. by Wilma Monserud. Text by Gerald B. Ownbey. c1971 **QK168.M6 ECOL**

MONTAGU, ASHLEY, 1905-
Man observed. Putnam 1968 **H83.M555 ECOL**

MONTAGUE, KATHERINE.
Mercury, by Katherine and Peter Montague. Sierra Club 1971 (Sierra Club battlebook, 2) **QH545.M4M6 ECOL**

MONTAGUE, PETER, jt. auth.
Montague, Katherine.
Mercury. 1971 **QH545.M4M6 ECOL**

MONTGOMERY COUNTY SANITARY DEPT. MONTGOMERY COUNTY, OHIO.
Ground water infiltration and internal sealing of sanitary sewers, Montgomery County, Ohio. Authors: Gene E. Cronk, et al. Prepared for the Office of Research and Monitoring, Environmental Protection Agency. U.S. Govt. Print. Off., 1972. (Water pollution control research series) **fTD716.M6 ECOL**

MONTGOMERY, FREDERICK HOWARD, 1902-
Trees of the northern United States and Canada. Warne 1970 **QK481.M7 ECOL**

MOORCRAFT, COLIN.
Must the seas die? Gambit, 1973. **GC1085.M66 1973 ECOL**

MOORE, ALMA (CHESTNUT).
The friendly forests; illus. by Matthew Kalmenoff. Viking Press 1963 **SD373.M76 1963 ECOL**

MOORE, GARY T., ed.
Emerging methods in environmental design and planning. 1970 **TA170.E46 ECOL**

MOORE, JOHN A.
Science for society: a bibliography. 2nd ed. American Association for the Advancement of Science, Commission on Science Education 1971 **fZ7401.M6 1971 ECOL**

MOORE, WILBERT ELLIS, comp.
Technology and social change. Ed. with an introd. by Wilbert E. Moore. Quadrangle Books 1972 **T14.5.M66 1972 ECOL**

MORELAND, PETER J.
Battelle Memorial Institute, Columbus, Ohio
Corrosion potential of NTA in detergent formulations. 1971. **fTP992.5.B3 ECOL**

MOREY, REXFORD M.
Feasibility study of electromagnetic subsurface profiling, by Rexford M. Morey and Walter S. Harrington. Prepared for Office of Research and Monitoring, U.S. Environmental Protection Agency, 1972. (Environmental protection technology series) **QE602.M6 ECOL**

MORGAN, ARTHUR ERNEST, 1878-
Dams and other disasters; a century of the Army Corps of Engineers in civil works, by Arthur E. Morgan. Sargent 1971 **UG23.M67 ECOL**

MORGAN, R. F.
Environmental biology. Oxford, Pergamon Press; Macmillan 1963- v. (The Commonwealth and international library of science, technology, engineering, and liberal studies. Rural and environmental studies division, v. 3) **QH308.5.M6 ECOL**

MORGAN, W. E.
An investigation of phosphorus removal mechanisms in activated sludge systems, by W. E. Morgan and E. Gus Fruh. Prepared for Office of Research and Monitoring, U.S. Environmental Protection Agency. U.S. Govt. Print. Off., 1972. (Environmental protection technology series) **TD756.M6 ECOL**

MORHOLT, EVELYN.
A sourcebook for the biological sciences by Evelyn Morholt, Paul F. Brandwein and Alexander Joseph. 2d ed. Harcourt, Brace & World 1966 (Teaching science series) **QH53.M67 1966 ECOL**

MORROW, PAUL E., ed.
Rochester International Conference on Environmental Toxicity, 3d, 1970.
Assessment of airborne particles. 1972 **QD549.R59 1970 ECOL**

MORSE, CHANDLER, 1906- jt. auth.
Barnett, Harold J.
Scarcity and growth. 1963 **HC55.B3 ECOL**

MORTH, ARTHUR H.
Pyritic systems: a mathematical model, by Arthur H. Morth, Edwin E. Smith and Kenesaw S. Shumate. Prepared for Office of Research and Monitoring, U.S. Environmental Protection Agency. U.S. Govt. Print. Office, 1972. (Environmental protection technology series) **TD899.M5M6 ECOL**

MORTON, STEPHEN D.
The carbon dioxide system and eutrophication by Stephen D. Morton, Philip H. Derse and Russell C. Sernau, for the Office of Research and Monitoring, Environmental Protection Agency. 1971. (Water pollution control research series) **fQH96.8.E9M6 ECOL**

MOSS, FRANK E., 1911-
The water crisis by Frank E. Moss. Foreword by Paul H. Douglas. Praeger c1967 **HD1694.A5M63 ECOL**

MOULDER, DAVID S.
A bibliography on marine and estuarine oil pollution; compiled by David S. Moulder and Allen Varley. Laboratory of the Marine Biological Association of the United Kingdom, 1971. **REF fZ6004.P6M6 ECOL**

MOUNDS VIEWS, MINN. INDEPENDENT SCHOOL DISTRICT, 621.
Environmental education curriculum, grades 10 12; teacher's resource guide. n.d. **fQH541.2.M6 ECOL**

MOUSER, G. W., jt. auth.
Brown, Robert E.
Techniques for teaching conservation education. 1964 **S946.B7 ECOL**

MOWAT, FARLEY.
Never cry wolf. 1st American ed. Little 1963 **QL795.W8M6 ECOL**

MOWBRAY, A. Q.
Road to ruin by A. Q. Mowbray. Lippincott 1969 **HE355.M66 ECOL**

MOYLE, JOHN BRIGGS, 1909-
Northern non-woody plants; a field key to the more common ferns and flowering plants of Minnesota and adjacent regions, by John B. Moyle. Rev. ed. Burgess Pub. Co. 1964 **fQK168.M68 1964 ECOL**

MOYLE, JOHN BRIGGS, 1909- ed.
Big game in Minnesota. 1965. **SH11.M64no.9 ECOL**

Minnesota. Dept. of Conservation. Division of Game and Fish.
Ducks and land use in Minnesota. 1964. **SH11.M64no.8 ECOL**

Minnesota. Dept. of Conservation. Division of Game and Fish.
Waterfowl in Minnesota. 1964. **SH11.M64no.7 ECOL**

MOYLE, JOHN BRIGGS, 1909- jt. auth.
Dobie, John.
Methods used for investigating productivity of fish-rearing ponds in Minnesota. Rev. 1962. **SH222.M6D6 1962 ECOL**

MUDD, STUART, 1893- ed.
The population crisis and the use of world resources. Associate editors: Hugo Boyko and others. W. Junk, 1964. (World Academy of Art and Science. Publication 2) **HB885.M8 ECOL**

MUHICH, ANTON J.
Preliminary data analysis; 1968 national survey of community solid waste practices by Anton J. Muhich, Albert J. Klee, and Paul W. Britton. U.S. Dept. of Health, Education, and Welfare, Bureau of Solid Waste Management, 1968. (U.S. Public Health Service publication no. 1867) **TD795.M82 ECOL**

MUIR, JOHN, 1838-1914.
Gentle wilderness; the Sierra Nevada. Photos. by Richard Kauffman. Text from John Muir. Edited by David Brower. Rev. ed. Ballentine Books 1971c1968 **F868.S5M88 1971 ECOL**

Our national parks. Houghton, 1901.
E160.M95 ECOL

MULLENDER, J. S. R., ed.
Growing against ourselves: the energy-environment tangle. 1972. **TD195.E4G76 ECOL**

MULLER, WILHELM JOHANN, 1901-
Imhoff, Karl.
Disposal of sewage and other waterborne wastes. 2d ed. 1971. **TD741.I5813 1971b ECOL**

MULLIGAN, PAUL F., jt. auth.
Bingham, Tayler H.
The beverage container problem. 1972.
TD793.B5 ECOL

MUMFORD, LEWIS, 1895-
The city in history: its origins, its transformations, and its prospects. 1st ed. Harcourt, Brace & World 1961 **HT111.M8 ECOL**

The highway and the city. Harcourt 1963 (A Harvest book) **HT111.M83 ECOL**

MUNZER, MARTHA E.
Planning our town by Martha E. Munzer for the Conservation Foundation. Knopf 1964
NA9108.M8 ECOL

Pockets of hope; studies of land and people, by Martha E. Munzer for the Conservation Foundation. Maps by John Bierhorst. Knopf 1967
HC103.7.M78 ECOL

Unusual careers: solar scientist, meteorologist, oceanographer, geologist, ecologist, sanitary engineer, research chemist, city and regional planner. Illustrated by John Kaufmann. 1st ed. Knopf, 1962.
Q147.M8 ECOL

MUNZER, MARTHA E., jt. auth.
Carvajal, Joan.
Conservation education. 1968
REF Z7164.N3C3 ECOL

MURDOCH, WILLIAM W.
Environment; resources, pollution & society. William W. Murdoch, editor. Sinauer Associates 1971
QH541.M95 ECOL

MURDOCH, WILLIAM W., jt. comp.
Connell, Joseph H.
Readings in ecology and ecological genetics. 1970
QH541.C65 ECOL

MURPHY, C. E.
Texas Christian University, Fort Worth. Dept. of Biology.
Industrial wastes: effects on Trinity River ecology, Fort Worth, Texas. 1971 i.e. 1972
fTD224.T4T4 ECOL

MURPHY, EARL FINBAR, 1928-
Governing nature. Quadrangle Books 1967 (Problems of American society) **HC55.M8 ECOL**
Man and his environment: law. Harper, 1971. (Man and his environment series) **KF3775.Z9M8 ECOL**

MURPHY, FRANCIS C.
Regulating flood-plain development. 1958. (University of Chicago. Dept. of Geography. Research paper no. 56) **TC530.M8 ECOL**

MURPHY, GEORGE H.
California. Laws, statutes, etc.
Laws relating to the protection of environmental quality, 1970. **REF KFC610.A3 1970 ECOL**

MURPHY, JOHN E., jt. ed.
Jennings, Burgess Hill.
Interactions of man and his environment. 1966.
TD180.J4 ECOL

MURPHY, R. SAGE, ed.
International Symposium on Water Pollution Control in Cold Climates, University of Alaska, Fairbanks, 1970.
Papers Held at the University of Alaska, July 22-24, 1970. 1972 **TD423.I5 ECOL**

MURPHY, ROBERT CUSHMAN, 1887-
Bird islands of Peru; the record of a sojourn on the west coast. Illus. from photographs by the author. Putnam, 1925. **REF QH128.M8 ECOL**
Land birds of America by R. C. Murphy and Dean Amadon. Photographed by Eliot Porter and others. Published with the cooperation of The American Museum of Natural History. McGraw 1953
fQL681.M85 ECOL

MURPHY, ROBERT WILLIAM, 1902-
Wild sanctuaries; our national wildlife refuges; a heritage restored, by Robert Murphy. Foreword by Stewart L. Udall. Dutton, 1968.
REF fS962.M8 ECOL

MURRO, RONALD P.
JBF Scientific Corporation.
Engineering methodology for river and stream reaeration. 1971 **fTD458.J17 ECOL**

MUSGROVE, PHILIP, jt. auth.
Grunwald, Joseph.
Natural resources in Latin American development. 1970 **REF fHC125.G72 ECOL**

MUSSELMAN, VIRGINIA W.
Learning about nature through crafts by Virginia W. Musselman. Stackpole Books 1969
TT157.M82 ECOL

MUTAGENIC EFFECTS OF ENVIRONMENTAL CONTAMINANTS.
Scientific editors: H. Eldon Sutton and Maureen I. Harris. Academic Press, 1972.(Fogarty International Center proceedings no. 10)(Environmental sciences)
QH431.M958 ECOL

THE MUTAGENICITY OF PESTICIDES: CONCEPTS AND EVALUATION.
Edited by Samuel S. Epstein and Marvin S. Legator. With a foreword by Joshua Lederberg. MIT Press 1971
RA1270.P4M87 ECOL

MYERS, BEVERLY M., jt. auth.
Rima, Donald R.
Subsurface waste disposal by means of wells—a selective annotated bibliography. 1971.
REF Z5853.S22R55 ECOL

MYERS, CHARLES B.
The environmental crisis: will we survive? By Charles B. Myers. Prentice-Hall 1972 (Inquiry into crucial American problems) **HC110.E5M9 ECOL**

N

NADER, RALPH.
Fellmeth, Robert C.
Politics of land: Ralph Nader's study group report on land use in California. 1973. **HD211.C2F45 ECOL**

Page, Joseph A.
Bitter wages: Ralph Nader's study group report on disease and injury on the job. 1973.
RC967.P33 ECOL

Vanishing air. 1970. **TD883.2.V35 ECOL**

Zwick, David.
Water wasteland. 1971. **TD223.Z86 1971ECOL**

NADLER, ALLEN C.
Air pollution. 1970 **fTD883.A47 ECOL**

NAPIER, JOHN RUSSELL.
The roots of mankind by John Napier. Smithsonian Institution Press, 1970. **QH368.N36 ECOL**

NARDOZZI, A. D., jt. auth.
American Water Works Association Research Foundation, New York
Information resource: water pollution control in the water utility industry. 1971. **REF fTD429.A4 ECOL**

NASH, A. E. KEIR, ed.
United States. Commission on Population Growth and the American future.
Governance and population: the governmental implications of population change. 1972.
HB3505.A526 ECOL

NASH, RODERICK.
Wilderness and the American mind. Yale Univ. Press, 1967. **E169.1.N37 ECOL**

NASH, RODERICK, comp.
The American environment; readings in the history of conservation. Addison-Wesley Pub. Co. 1968 (Themes and social forces in American history series)
S930.N36 ECOL

NASMI AIR POLLUTION CONTROL TECHNOLOGY WORKSHOP, CHICAGO, 1970.
Effective technology for recycling metal. 1971
fTS214.E36 ECOL

NATIONAL ACADEMY OF ENGINEERING.
Engineering for the benefit of mankind. 1970.
TA5.E52 ECOL

Science, engineering, and the city. 1967.
HT166.S32 ECOL

NATIONAL ACADEMY OF ENGINEERING. COMMITTEE ON OCEAN ENGINEERING.
Steering Committee on Coastal Wastes Management.
Wastes management concepts for the coastal zone. 1970. **TD763.S7 ECOL**

NATIONAL ACADEMY OF ENGINEERING. COMMITTEE ON POWER PLANT SITING.
Engineering for resolution of the energy-environment dilemma. National Academy of Engineering, 1972.
fTD177.N38 ECOL

NATIONAL ACADEMY OF SCIENCES, WASHINGTON, D.C.
International Symposium on Eutrophication, University of Wisconsin, 1967.
Eutrophication: causes, consequences, correctives. 1969. **QH96.A1I63 1967 ECOL**

Prospects of the world food supply. 1966.
fS439.P7 1966 ECOL

Science, engineering, and the city. 1967.
HT166.S32 ECOL

NATIONAL AGRICULTURAL POLICY CONFERENCE.
Readings in agricultural policy, edited by R. J. Hildreth. University of Nebraska Press 1968
HD1761.N25 ECOL

NATIONAL ASSOCIATION FOR ENVIRONMENTAL EDUCATION.
Man and environment; bibliography. 1970
REF fZ5322.E2N3 ECOL

NATIONAL ASSOCIATION OF BIOLOGY TEACHERS. NATIONAL CONSERVATION COMMITTEE.
Manual for outdoor laboratories; the development and use of schoolgrounds as outdoor laboratories for teaching science and conservation. Richard L. Weaver, editor. Interstate, 1959. **QH51.N3 ECOL**

NATIONAL ASSOCIATION OF COUNTIES RESEARCH FOUNDATION.
Powell, Mel D.
Community action guidebook for soil erosion and sediment control. 1970 **fS624.A1P68 ECOL**

Powell, Mel D.
Digest of selected local solid waste management ordinances. 1972. **TD788.P6 ECOL**

Solid waste management. 1972? 1v.
fTD791.N3 ECOL

Urban soil erosion and sediment control. U.S. Federal Water Quality Administration; for sale by the Supt. Docs., U.S. Govt. Print. Off., 1970. (Water pollution control research series) **fS624.A1N38 ECOL**

NATIONAL ASSOCIATION OF MANUFACTURERS OF THE UNITED STATES.
Water in industry; a survey of water use in industry by the National Association of Manufacturers and the Chamber of Commerce of the United States in cooperation with the National Technical Task Committee on Industrial Wastes. 1965.
fTD223.N3 1965 ECOL

NATIONAL ASSOCIATION OF MANUFACTURERS OF THE UNITED STATES OF AMERICA.
Industry/Government Teleconference on Pollution Control, 1971.
NAM: a voice for American industry. 1971
fTD172.5.I53 1971 ECOL

NATIONAL ASSOCIATION OF SECONDARY MATERIAL INDUSTRIES.
Effective technology for recycling metal. 1971
fTS214.E36 ECOL

Recycling Day Conference, 1st, New York City, 1971.
Proceedings of Recycling Day in New York. 1971
fTP156.R38R4 1971 ECOL

NATIONAL AUDUBON SOCIETY.
Izaak Walton League of America. Conservation Education Committee.
Guidelines to conservation education action. c1966
S946.I9 ECOL

Koford, Carl B.
The California condor. 1966,c1953
QL696.A2K64 1966 ECOL

NATIONAL AUDUBON SOCIETY. NATURE CENTER PLANNING DIVISION.
Directory of nature centers and related environmental education facilities. 1971
REF fQH51.N23 1971 ECOL

Shomon, Joseph James.
Wildlife habitat improvement. 2d print., rev. 1969
SK361.S52 1969 ECOL

NATIONAL AUDUBON SOCIETY. NATURE CENTERS DIVISION.
Shomon, Joseph James.
Manual of outdoor interpretation. 1968
QH51.S5 ECOL

NATIONAL CANNERS ASSOCIATION.
National Symposium on Food Processing Wastes, 2d, Denver, 1971.
Proceedings. 1971 **fTD899.F585N37 1971 ECOL**

National Symposium on Food Processing Wastes, 3d, New Orleans, 1972.
Proceedings. 1972. **fTD899.F585N37 1972 ECOL**

NATIONAL CANNERS ASSOCIATION. WESTERN RESEARCH LABORATORY.
Dry caustic peeling of tree fruit for liquid waste reduction. Authors: Walter A. Mercer, Jack W. Ralls, and Harry J. Maagdenberg. Prepared for the Environmental Protection Agency. U.S. Environmental Protection Agency; for sale by the Supt. of Docs., U.S. Govt. Print. Off., 1970. (Water pollution control research series) **fTD899.F7N37 ECOL**

Liquid wastes from canning and freezing fruits and vegetables. Authors: Walter A. Mercer, Walter W. Rose, and Kenneth G. Weckel. U.S. Environmental Protection Agency; for sale by the Supt. of Docs., U.S. Govt. Print. Off., 1971 i.e. 1972 (Water pollution control research series) **fTD899.C3N354 ECOL**

Reconditioning of food processing brines. Prepared for the Water Quality Office, Environmental Protection Agency. Authors: W. Mercer and J. Ralls. Environmental Protection Agency, Water Quality Office; for sale by the Supt. of Docs., U.S. Govt. Print. Off., 1971. (Water pollution control research series) **fTD899.C3N356 ECOL**

Reduction of salt content of food processing liquid waste effluent. Prepared for the Water Quality Office, Environmental Protection Agency. Authors: W. A. Mercer and J. W. Ralls. Environmental Protection Agency, Water Quality Office; U.S. Govt. Print. Off., 1971. (Water pollution control research series) **fTD899.C3N36 ECOL**

Waste reduction in food canning operations; a study of four methods to improve the quality or reduce the quantity of effluent discharged by a fruit processing plant. U.S. Federal Water Quality Administration; for sale by the Supt. of Docs., U.S. Govt. Print. Off. 1970 i.e. 1971 (Water pollution control research series) **fTD899.C3N37 ECOL**

NATIONAL CENTER FOR EDUCATIONAL COMMUNICATION. EDUCATIONAL MATERIALS CENTER.
Watt, Lois B.
Environmental - ecological education: a bibliography of fiction, nonfiction, and textbooks for elementary and secondary schools. 1971.
REF fQH541.2.W34 ECOL

NATIONAL COAL ASSOCIATION.
Bituminous coal facts. 1970-
REF fHD9544.B47 ECOL

NATIONAL CONFERENCE ON COMPOSTING-WASTE RECYCLING. 1ST, DENVER, 1971.
How to put waste recycling into practice; first national conference on composting-waste recycling May 20-21, 1971. Sponsored by Rodale Press and Keep Colorado Beautiful Inc. Compost Science 1971.
fTD172.5.N3 1971 ECOL

NATIONAL CONFERENCE ON ENVIRONMENTAL LAW, SAN FRANCISCO, 1970.
Transcripts of the speeches. California Continuing Education of the Bar 1971
REF KF3775.A75N3 1970 ECOL

NATIONAL CONFERENCE ON SOIL, WATER, AND SUBURBIA, WASHINGTON, D.C., 1967.
Soil, water, and suburbia; a report of the proceedings. For sale by the Supt. of Docs., U.S. Govt. Print. Off., 1968 **fHT166.N36 1967 ECOL**

NATIONAL CONFERENCE ON UNESCO, 13TH, SAN FRANCISCO, 1969.
No deposit—no return. Man and his environment: a view toward survival. Ed. by Huey D. Johnson. Addison-Wesley Pub. Co. 1970
GF3.N38 1969 ECOL

NATIONAL COUNCIL OF THE CHURCHES OF CHRIST IN THE UNITED STATES OF AMERICA. DEPT. OF HIGHER EDUCATION.
Ecology: crisis and new vision. c1971
GF80.E25 ECOL

NATIONAL EDUCATION ASSOCIATION OF THE UNITED STATES. RESEARCH DIVISION.
Environmental education in the public schools; a pilot study. 1970 **fLB1047.N36 ECOL**

NATIONAL FOUNDATION FOR ENVIRONMENTAL CONTROL.
NFEC directory of environmental information sources. **REF fHC110.E5N4 ECOL**

NATIONAL GEOGRAPHIC SOCIETY, WASHINGTON, D. C. SPECIAL PUBLICATIONS DIVISION.
As we live and breathe. 1971 **GF75.A8 ECOL**

Findley, Rowe.
Great American deserts. 1972 **F787.F5 ECOL**

NATIONAL GROUND WATER QUALITY SYMPOSIUM, DENVER, 1971.
Proceedings. U.S. Environmental Protection Agency. U.S. Govt. Print. Off. 1972 (Water pollution control research series) **fTD223.N37 1971 ECOL**

NATIONAL INDUSTRIAL POLLUTION CONTROL COUNCIL.
Casebook: pollution cleanup actions. 1971?
fTD897.N37 ECOL

NATIONAL INSTITUTE OF ENVIRONMENTAL HEALTH SCIENCES.
Environmental factors in respiratory disease. 1972.
RC732.E59 ECOL

Metallic contaminants and human health. 1972.
RA565.M47 1972 ECOL

NATIONAL MARINE FISHERIES SERVICE.
Our changing fisheries. Sidney Shapiro, editor. For sale by the Supt. of Docs., U.S. Govt. Print. Off., 1971 **REF SH331.N38 ECOL**

NATIONAL OIL RECOVERY CORP., BAYONNE, N.J.
Conversion of crankcase waste oil into useful products. Water Quality Office, Environmental Protection Agency, 1971. (Water pollution control research series) **fTP687.N3 ECOL**

NATIONAL PARK FOUNDATION.
Adventure in environment. 1971
QH48.A25 ECOL

Adventure in environment: national environmental education development. c1971 **fQH48.A24 ECOL**

Adventure in environment: national environmental education development. 1971 **fQH48.A23 ECOL**

NATIONAL PARKS AND CONSERVATION ASSOCIATION.
Preserving wilderness in our national parks. 1971
fQH76.P74 ECOL

Toward an environmental policy. 1971
fHC110.E5T66 ECOL

NATIONAL RECREATION AND PARK ASSOCIATION.
Brown, William Edward.
Islands of hope. c1971 **HC110.E5B75 ECOL**

Guide to new approaches to financing parks & recreation. Ed. by Robert M. Artz and Hubert Bermont. Acropolis Books 1970 **SB482.A4N38 ECOL**

NATIONAL RESEARCH COUNCIL.
Federal Construction Council. Task Group T-65.
Impact of air pollution regulations on fuel selection for federal facilities. 1970. **fKF3812.F4 ECOL**

Scientific aspects of pest control. 1966.
SB951.S38 ECOL

The Use of drugs in animal feeds. 1969.
SF98.M4U8 ECOL

NATIONAL RESEARCH COUNCIL. ADVISORY BOARD ON MILITARY PERSONNEL SUPPLIES.
Radiation preservation of foods. 1965.
TX611.R28 ECOL

NATIONAL RESEARCH COUNCIL. BUILDING RESEARCH ADVISORY BOARD.
Apartment house incinerators (flue fed). Prepared for the National Academy of Sciences. National Academy of Sciences-National Research Council, 1965. (Its Report to the Federal Housing Administration, no. 29) **fTH23.N333no.29 ECOL**

NATIONAL RESEARCH COUNCIL. COMMISSION ON EDUCATION IN AGRICULTURE AND NATIONAL RESOURCES.
Conference on Undergraduate Education in the Biological Sciences for Students in Agriculture and Natural Resources, Washington, D.C., 1966.
Undergraduate education in the biological sciences for students in agriculture and natural resources. 1967. **S533.C755 1966 ECOL**

NATIONAL RESEARCH COUNCIL. COMMITTEE ON ANIMAL NUTRITION.
Biological energy interrelationships and glossary of energy terms; a report. Prepared by Lorin E. Harris. 1st rev. ed. National Academy of Sciences-National Research Council, 1966. (National Research Council. Publication 1411) **REF SF95.N3 1966 ECOL**

NATIONAL RESEARCH COUNCIL. COMMITTEE ON ATMOSPHERIC SCIENCES.
Weather and climate modification problems and prospects; final report of the Panel on Weather and Climate Modification. National Academy of Sciences-National Research Council, 1966. 2v. (National Research Council. Publication no. 1350)
QC928.N36 ECOL

NATIONAL RESEARCH COUNCIL. COMMITTEE ON BIOLOGIC EFFECTS OF ATMOSPHERIC POLLUTANTS.
Lead; airborne lead in perspective. National Academy of Sciences, 1972. **QP913.P3N38 ECOL**

NATIONAL RESEARCH COUNCIL. COMMITTEE ON NITRATE ACCUMULATION.
Accumulation of nitrate. National Academy of Sciences, 1972. **QH545.N5N37 ECOL**

NATIONAL RESEARCH COUNCIL. COMMITTEE ON OCEANOGRAPHY.
Economic benefits from oceanographic research, a special report. National Academy of sciences-National Research Council, 1964. (National Research Council. Publication 1228) **REF GB58.N3 ECOL**

Steering Committee on Coastal Wastes Management. Wastes management concepts for the coastal zone. 1970. **TD763.S7 ECOL**

Vetter, Richard C.
Oceanography information sources/70. 1970.
REF GC10.V47 ECOL

NATIONAL RESEARCH COUNCIL. COMMITTEE ON POLLUTION.
Waste management and control; a report to the Federal Council for Science and Technology. National Academy of Sciences-National Research Council, 1966. (National Research Council Publication 1400)
REF TD180.N3 ECOL

NATIONAL RESEARCH COUNCIL. COMMITTEE ON RESOURCES AND MAN.
Resources and man; a study and recommendations, by the Committee on Resources and Man of the Division of Earth Sciences, National Academy of Sciences-National Research Council, with the cooperation of the Division of Biology and Agriculture. Preston Cloud, chairman. W. H. Freeman 1969 (National Academy of Sciences publication no. 1703)
HC68.N36 ECOL

NATIONAL RESEARCH COUNCIL. COMMITTEE ON TOXICOLOGY.
Principles and procedures for evaluating the toxicity of household substances. Arnold J. Lehman, chairman and others. National Academy of Sciences-National Research Council, 1964. (National Research Council. Publication 1138) **REF RA1221.N3 ECOL**

NATIONAL RESEARCH COUNCIL. COMMITTEE ON WATER.
Alternatives in water management; a report. National Academy of Sciences-National Research Council, 1966. (National Research Council Publication 1408)
HD1694.A5N48 ECOL

NATIONAL RESEARCH COUNCIL. DIVISION OF BIOLOGY AND AGRICULTURE.
National Research Council. Committee on Resources and Man.
Resources and man. 1969 **HC68.N36 ECOL**

NATIONAL RESEARCH COUNCIL. FOOD PROTECTION COMMITTEE.
Chemicals used in food processing. National Academy of Sciences-National Research Council, 1965. (National Research Council. Publication 1274)
REF fTX553.A3N26 ECOL

Toxicants occurring naturally in foods. 1966.
TX531.T6 ECOL

NATIONAL RESEARCH COUNCIL. SURVEY COMMITTEE ON THE LIFE SCIENCES.
Biology and the future of man. 1970.
QH307.2.B56 ECOL

NATIONAL SANITATION FOUNDATION, ANN ARBOR, MICH.
Use of systems techniques in environmental quality management. 1970. **RA565.A1N38no.7 ECOL**

NATIONAL SCHOOL PUBLIC RELATIONS ASSOCIATION.
Environment and the schools. 1971
fHC110.E5E485 ECOL

NATIONAL SCIENCE TEACHERS ASSOCIATION.
Programs in environmental education. 2d ed. 1971.
REF fQH51.N24 1971 ECOL

NATIONAL STEEL CORPORATION. WEIRTON STEEL DIVISION.
Combined steel mill and municipal waste-waters treatment. Authors: William M. Smith and others. U.S. Environmental Protection Agency U.S. Govt. Print. Off., 1972. (Water pollution control research series)
fTD899.S7N37 ECOL

NATIONAL SYMPOSIUM ON FOOD PROCESSING WASTES, 1ST, PORTLAND, OR., 1970.
Proceedings. U.S. Federal Water Quality Administration U.S. Govt. Print. Off. 1971 (Water pollution control research series)
fTD899.F585N37 1970 ECOL

NATIONAL SYMPOSIUM ON FOOD PROCESSING WASTES, 2D, DENVER, 1971.
Proceedings. Environmental Protection Agency, Research and Monitoring; for sale by the Supt. of Docs., U.S. Govt. Print. Off., 1971 (Water pollution control research series)
fTD899.F585N37 1971 ECOL

NATIONAL SYMPOSIUM ON FOOD PROCESSING WASTES, 3D, NEW ORLEANS, 1972.
Proceedings. U.S. Environmental Protection Agency, Office of Research and Monitoring, National Environmental Protection Agency, 1972. (Environmental protection technology series)
fTD899.F585N37 1972 ECOL

NATIONAL SYMPOSIUM ON THERMAL POLLUTION, PORTLAND, OREGON, 1968.
Biological aspects of thermal pollution; proceedings. Ed. by Peter A. Krenkel and Frank L. Parker. Vanderbilt Univ. Press 1969   QH90.N3 1968 ECOL

NATIONAL SYMPOSIUM ON THERMAL POLLUTION, VANDERBILT UNIVERSITY, 1968.
Engineering aspects of thermal pollution; proceedings. Edited by Frank L. Parker and Peter A. Krenkel. Vanderbilt University Press, 1969.
TD427.H4N3 1968 ECOL

NATIONAL TUBERCULOSIS AND RESPIRATORY DISEASE ASSOCIATION.
Air pollution primer. 1969   TD883.N37 ECOL

NATIONAL WATER COMMISSION.
Kelnhofer, Guy J.
Preserving the Great Lakes. 1972.
fTC423.3.K4 ECOL

NATIONAL WATER WELL ASSOCIATION.
Membership directory. 1972/73–   v.
REF TD407.N3 ECOL
National Ground Water Quality Symposium, Denver, 1971.
Proceedings. 1972   fTD223.N37 1971 ECOL

NATIONAL WILDLIFE FEDERATION.
Conservation directory.   fS920.C64 ECOL

NAT'L. RESEARCH COUNCIL. AGRICULTURAL BOARD.
International Symposium on Factors Determining the Behavior of Plant Pathogens in Soil, Berkeley, Calif., 1963.
Ecology of soil-borne plant pathogens.
fQR111.I55 1963 ECOL

NAT'L. RESEARCH COUNCIL. COMM. ON BIOLOGICAL CONTROL OF SOIL-BORNE PLANT PATHOGENS.
International Symposium on Factors Determining the Behavior of Plant Pathogens in Soil, Berkeley, Calif., 1963.
Ecology of soil-borne plant pathogens.
fQR111.I55 1963 ECOL

NATURAL ENVIRONMENTS: STUDIES IN THEORETICAL AND APPLIED ANALYSIS,.
edited by John V. Krutilla. Published for Resources for the Future by Johns Hopkins University Press 1972
QH76.N28 ECOL

NATURAL HISTORICAL SOCIETY OF MINNESOTA.
Sierra Club. North Star Chapter (Minn.).
A wilderness in crisis: the Boundary Waters Canoe Area. c1970   fQH76.5.M6S5 ECOL

NATURAL HISTORY.
The Unforseen international ecologic boomerang. 1969   fQH541.U5 ECOL

NATURAL RESOURCES COUNCIL OF AMERICA.
Callison, Charles H.
America's natural resources. Rev. print. 1967
S930.C3 1967 ECOL
Clepper, Henry Edward.
Origins of American conservation. 1966
S930.C57 ECOL

What's ahead for our public lands? 1970
KF5606.W5 ECOL

NATURAL SCIENCE CENTER CONFERENCE. 8TH, DAYTON, OHIO, 1970.
Leadership to meet our environmental crisis; proceedings of the Natural Science Center Conference, Dayton, Ohio, Oct. 14-17, 1970. Natural Science for Youth Foundation, 1970 1v.
REF fTD178.3.N3 ECOL

NATURAL SCIENCE CENTERS FOR YOUTH.
Directory. 1970/71–   Natural Science for Youth Foundation. v.   REF fQ147.N38 ECOL

NATURAL SCIENCE FOR YOUTH FOUNDATION.
Natural Science Center Conference. 8th, Dayton, Ohio, 1970.
Leadership to meet our environmental crisis. 1970
REF fTD178.3.N3 ECOL
Natural Science centers for youth.
Directory. 1970/71–   REF fQ147.N38 ECOL

NATURAL WONDERS OF AMERICA,.
by the editors of American heritage. Editor in charge, Beverley da Costa. Introd. by Alvin M. Josephy, Jr. American Heritage Pub. Co. 1972 QH76.N29 ECOL

THE NATURALISTS' DIRECTORY: INTERNATIONAL 41 ED.
PCL Publications, Inc.   REF Q145.S4 ECOL

NAUMOV, NIKOLAI PAVLOVICH.
The ecology of animals, by N. P. Naumov. Edited by Norman D. Levine. Translated by Frederick K. Plous, Jr. University of Illinois Press c1972
QL751.N313 ECOL

NAVARRA, JOHN GABRIEL.
Wide world weather. Doubleday 1968
QC863.N34 ECOL

NAYLON, MICHAEL J.
Natural resources management: suggested teaching units for agricultural education; by Michael J. Naylon and Carl E. Vogt. Minnesota Dept. of Education, Division of Vocational-Technical Education 1972?
fS946.N3 ECOL

NAYMAN, JACQUELINE.
Atlas of wildlife. Illustrated by Adrian Williams & David Nockels. Maps by Geographical Projects, London. Consultant: Maurice Burton. John Day Co. 1972   fQL101.N38 1972 ECOL

NEAL, HARRY EDWARD, 1906-
Nature's guardians; your career in conservation. Messner 1966,c1963   SK361.N45 1966 ECOL

NEBOLSINE, ROSS.
High rate filtration of combined sewer overflows, by Ross Nebolsine, Patrick J. Harvey and Chi-Yuan Fan. Prepared for the Office of Research and Monitoring, Environmental Protection Agency. U.S. Govt. Print. Off., 1972. (Water pollution control research series)
fTD662.N4 ECOL

NEBRASKA. UNIVERSITY.
Homestead Centennial Symposium, University of Nebraska, 1962.
Land use policy and problems in the United States. 1964,c1963   HD205 1962 .H6 ECOL

NEBRASKA. UNIVERSITY. AGRICULTURAL EXPERIMENT STATION.
Cook, David I.
Trees and shrubs for noise abatement. 1971.
TD893.C6 ECOL

NEEDHAM, JAMES GEORGE, 1868-
A guide to the study of fresh-water biology, with special reference to aquatic insects and other invertebrate animals, by James G. Needham and Paul R. Needham. The American Viewpoint Society, Inc. 1927
QH96.N38 ECOL

NEEDHAM, PAUL ROBERT, 1902-   jt. auth.
Needham, James George.
A guide to the study of fresh-water biology. 1927
QH96.N38 ECOL

NEELY, W. C.
Biological and photobiological action of pollutants on aquatic microorganisms, by W. C. Neely and others. Water Resources Research Institute, 1973. (Auburn University. Water Resources Research Institute. WRRI bulletin 9)   fTC1.A85no.9 ECOL

NEILANDS, J. B.
Harvest of death. 1971,c1972
DS557.A68H35 1972 ECOL

NELKIN, DOROTHY.
Nuclear power and its critics; the Cayuga Lake controversy. Cornell University Press 1971 (Science, technology, and society)   TK1344.N7N4 ECOL

NELSON, CLARENCE WALFRED, 1924-
An ex ante profitability analysis of capital investment in taconite pellet production facilities in Minnesota circa 1950-51. 1967.   HD9517.M6N4 ECOL

NELSON, GAYLORD, 1916-
What are me and you gonna do? 1971
TD175.W53 ECOL

NELSON, JON P.
Economic aspects of the airport environment: noise, air pollution, and congestion. 1972. (Council of Planning Librarians. Exchange bibliography, 343)
REF fZ5064.A28N4 ECOL

NELSON, MAYNARD M., ed.
Symposium on the White-tailed Deer in Minnesota, St. Paul, Minnesota, 1971.
The white-tailed deer in Minnesota. 1972?
fQL737.U55S9 1971ECOL

NELSON, ROBERT R.
The effects of enrichment on Lake Superior periphyton, by Robert R. Nelson and others. Univ. of Minnesota, Water Resources Research Center, 1973. (Minnesota. University. Water Resources Research Center. WRRC bulletin 59)
GB701.M554no.59 ECOL

NEMEROW, NELSON LEONARD.
Syracuse University. Civil Engineering Dept.
Benefits of water quality enhancement. 1970.
fTD365.S94 ECOL

NESTLE, MANUEL E.
Brecher, Joseph J.
Environmental law handbook. 1970
REF KF3775.B7 ECOL

NETSCHERT, BRUCE CARLTON.
Resources for the Future.
Energy in the American economy, 1850-1975. 1960
HD9545.R45 ECOL

NEUHAUS, RICHARD JOHN.
In defense of people: ecology and the seduction of radicalism by Richard Neuhaus. Macmillan 1971
HM206.N48 ECOL

NEW JERSEY. DEPT. OF COMMUNITY AFFAIRS.
Metropolitan open space and natural process. 1970.
HT394.P5M46 ECOL

NEW MEXICO STATE UNIVERSITY. PHYSICAL SCIENCE LABORATORY.
Floating oil recovery device. Prepared for the Environmental Protection Agency, Water Quality Office. Environmental Protection Agency, Water Quality Office; for sale by the Supt. of Docs., U.S. Govt. Print. Off., 1971 (Water pollution control research series)   fTD427.P4N48 ECOL

NEW REPUBLIC.
Lapp, Ralph E.
A citizen's guide to nuclear power. c1971.
TK1078.L3 ECOL

THE NEW SCIENTIST.
The world in 1984. The complete New scientist series, edited by Nigel Calder. Penguin Books 1965,c1964 v. (Pelican book A720-A721)
Q171.N5 1965 ECOL

NEW YORK BOARD OF TRADE. NATIONAL BUSINESS COUNCIL ON ENVIRONMENT.
Recycling Day Conference, 1st, New York City, 1971.
Proceedings of Recycling Day in New York. 1971
fTP156.R38R4 1971 ECOL

NEW YORK (CITY). BOTANICAL GARDEN.
Challenge for survival: land, air, and water for man in megalopolis. 1970.   HM206.C4 ECOL

NEW YORK (CITY). ENVIRONMENTAL PROTECTION ADMINISTRATION.
Fabricant, Neil.
Toward a rational power policy: energy, politics, and pollution. 1971   HD9685.U5F32 ECOL

NEW YORK (CITY). PRACTISING LAW INSTITUTE.
Legal control of the environment—3D. 1971
KF3775.L44 ECOL

NEW YORK. COLLEGE OF FORESTRY, SYRACUSE.
Forest Recreation Symposium, Syracuse, N.Y., 1971.
1971.   SD426.F6 1971 ECOL

NEW YORK (STATE) DEPT. OF HEALTH.
New York solid waste management plan. Status report 1970. U.S. Environmental Protection Agency Solid Waste Management Office 1971. 1v.
TD788.4.N4A45 ECOL

NEW YORK (STATE). DEPT. OF HEALTH. BIRTH DEFECTS INSTITUTE.
Symposium on Monitoring, Birth Defects and Environment, Albany, N. Y., 1970.
Monitoring, birth defects and environment: the problem of surveillance. 1971.
RG627.S94 1970 ECOL

NEW YORK (STATE) LEGISLATURE. JOINT COMMITTEE ON ENVIRONMENTAL MANAGEMENT AND NATURAL RESOURCES.
The challenge of the seventies; a managed environment for New York State. 1971.
fHC107.N7A25 ECOL
Report. 197 v. fHC107.N7A24 ECOL

NEW YORK (STATE). STATE UNIVERSITY AT BINGHAMTON.
Environmental Geomorphology Symposium.
Environmental geomorphology. GB400.E58 ECOL

NEW YORK (STATE). STATE UNIVERSITY AT BINGHAMTON. DEPT. OF GEOLOGY.
Environmental Geomorphology Symposium.
Environmental geomorphology. GB400.E58 ECOL

NEW YORK (STATE). STATE UNIVERSITY COLLEGE, BUFFALO. GREAT LAKES LABORATORY.
Fish protein concentrate, a review of pertinent literature with an emphasis on production from freshwater fish II; a supplement for Erie County, New York. 1970. (New York (State). State University College, Buffalo. Great Lakes Laboratory. Special report no. 5) fSH333.F5 ECOL

NEW YORK (STATE) UNIVERSITY.
Environmental education instructional activities. 1972. 2v. fQH541.2.N4 ECOL
An environmental experience. 1971.
fQH541.2.N45 ECOL

NEW YORK ZOOLOGICAL SOCIETY.
Beebe, Charles William.
Galapagos, world's end. 1924. QH123.B4 ECOL
Beebe, Charles William.
Pheasants. 1926. REF QL969.G2B26 ECOL

NEWHALL, NANCY (WYNNE) jt. auth.
Adams, Ansel Easton.
This is the American earth. 1960
fHC103.7.A68 ECOL

NFEC DIRECTORY OF ENVIRONMENTAL INFORMATION SOURCES,.
ed. by Charles E. Thibeau and Peter W. Taliaferro. 1972- National Foundation for Environmental Control. v. REF fHC110.E5N4 ECOL

NGODDY, PATRICK O.
Michigan. State University, East Lansing. Agricultural Pollution Control Laboratory.
Closed system waste management for livestock. 1971 i.e. 1972 fTD899.F4M5 ECOL

NICHOLS, DONALD R., ed.
Symposium on Engineering Geology in the Urban Environment, San Francisco, 1969.
Environmental planning and geology. 1971
TA705.S95 1969 ECOL

NICHOLS, STANLEY A., jt. auth.
Lindsey, Alton A.
Natural areas in Indiana and their preservation. 1969. QH76.5.I6L5 ECOL

NICHOLSON, MAX.
The environmental revolution; a guide for the new masters of the world. McGraw-Hill 1970
S936.N5 ECOL

NICKELSBURG, JANET.
Ecology; habitats, niches, and food chains. Helen Hale, editorial consultant. 1st ed. Lippincott 1969 (Introducing modern science) QH541.14.N5 ECOL
Field trips; ecology for youth leaders. Photos. by Helen Nestor. Burgess Pub. Co. 1971,c1966
QH541.N5 ECOL

NICKS, ORAN W., ed.
This island earth. Scientific and Technical Information Division. Office of Technology Utilization, NASA, 1970. fQB631.N5 ECOL

NIEDRACH, ROBERT J., jt. auth.
Bailey, Alfred Marshall.
Birds of Colorado. 1965.
REF fQL684.C6B3 ECOL

NIKOLAIEFF, GEORGE A., comp.
The water crisis. edited by George A. Nikolaieff. H. W. Wilson Co., 1967. (The Reference shelf, v. 38, no. 6)
TD355.N5 ECOL

NOBILE, PHILIP, comp.
The complete ecology fact book. Edited by Philip Nobile and John Deedy. 1st ed. Doubleday, 1972.
TD174.N6 ECOL

NORDENSKJOLD, OTTO, 1869-1928.
The geography of the polar regions, consisting of a general characterization of polar nature, by Otto Nordenskjold, and a regional geography of the Arctic and the Antarctic, by Ludwig Mecking. American Geographical Society, 1928. (American geographical society. Special publication no. 8) G587.N6 ECOL

NORTH AMERICAN ROCKWELL CORPORATION. ROCKETDYNE DIVISION.
Development of a chemical denitrification process, by Rocketdyne Research. Authors: Frank C. Gunderloy, Jr., Ross I. Wagner, and Victor H. Dayan. Environmental Protection Agency, Water Quality Office; for sale by the Supt. of Docs., U.S. Govt. Print. Off., 1970. (Water pollution control research series)
fTD433.N67 ECOL

NORTH AMERICAN WILDLIFE AND NATURAL RESOURCES CONFERENCE, CHICAGO, 1970.
Symposium on Wolf Management in Selected Areas of North America, Chicago, 1970.
Wolf management in selected areas of North America. 1970 QL737.C22S9 1970 ECOL

NORTH CAROLINA. DEPT. OF PUBLIC INSTRUCTION.
North Carolina. Task Force on Environment and Natural Resources.
Teacher's guide for environmental education. 1970.
REF fQH541.2.N88 ECOL

NORTH CAROLINA. STATE UNIVERSITY, RALEIGH. DEPT. OF BIOLOGICAL AND AGRICULTURAL ENGINEERING.
Role of animal wastes in agricultural land runoff. U.S. Environmental Protection Agency; for sale by the Supt. of Docs., U.S. Govt. Print. Off., 1971. (Water pollution control research series) fTD930.N67 ECOL

NORTH CAROLINA. TASK FORCE ON ENVIRONMENT AND NATURAL RESOURCES.
Teacher's guide for environmental education. Prepared by the Task Force on Environment and Natural Resources in cooperation with the North Carolina Dept. of Public Instruction. 1970.
REF fQH541.2.N88 ECOL

NORTH CAROLINA. UNIVERSITY.
The 99th hour. 1967 HB3505.N5 ECOL

NORTH CAROLINA. UNIVERSITY. WATER RESOURCES RESEARCH INSTITUTE.
Elliott, Ralph D.
The effects of sewer surcharges on the level of industrial wastes and the use of water by industry. 1972. TD897.5.E4 ECOL

NORTH EASTERN REGIONAL ANTIPOLLUTION CONFERENCE, 3D, UNIVERSITY OF RHODE ISLAND, 1970.
Reuse and recycle of wastes; proceedings. Technomic Pub. Co. 1971 fTP995.A1N6 1970 ECOL

NORTH EASTERN REGIONAL ANTIPOLLUTION CONFERENCE, 4TH, UNIVERSITY OF RHODE ISLAND, 1971.
Recent developments in industrial pollution control; proceedings. Technomic Pub. Co. 1971
fTD896.N67 1971 ECOL

NORTH JERSEY CONSERVATION FOUNDATION.
Education for survival. 1970-
QH541.2.E4 ECOL

NORTH STAR RESEARCH AND DEVELOPMENT INSTITUTE, MINNEAPOLIS.
New and ultrathin membranes for municipal waste water treatment by reverse osmosis. U.S. Environmental Protection Agency, Water Quality Office, 1970. (Water pollution control research series)
fTD754.N6 ECOL

NORTHEASTERN FOREST INSECT WORK CONFERENCE, 3RD, NEW HAVEN, 1970.
Toward integrated control; proceedings. Northeastern Forest Experiment Station, 1971. (U.S.D.A. Forest Service research paper NE-194)
SD11.A455492no.194 ECOL

NORTHERN COLORADO OUTDOOR NATURE CENTER.
K - 12 curriculum guide for environmental education. Howard D. Bruner, editor. n.d.
fS946.N6 ECOL

NORTHERN STATES POWER CO.
Lake Itasca seminar, the new industrial man: seminar held at Itasca State Park Sept. 26-Oct. 1, 1971. 1972? 1v. REF fHM221.N6 1971 ECOL

NORTHERN STATES POWER CO. ADVISORY COMMITTEE ON PLANT SITING AND DEVELOPMENT.
Major NSP generating plant sites. 1970.
fTK1191.M3 ECOL

NORTHERN STATES POWER CO. ENVIRONMENTAL AFFAIRS DEPT.
Directory of conservation/environmental organizations. 1971- v. fS932.M5N6 ECOL

NORTHERN STATES POWER COMPANY.
Clark, B. W.
Description of the environmental monitoring program for the Monticello nuclear generating plant near Monticello, Minnesota. Rev. ed. 1969.
fTK1377.M6C6 1969 ECOL

Commonwealth Associates, Inc.
Northern States Power Company, Minnesota: fossil fueled power plant siting study. 1972.
REF fTK1331.N6C6 ECOL

History of Minnesota Pollution Control Agency. 1970 fTD181.M5 ECOL

History of the Wisconsin Department of Natural Resources and related rules, regulations, classifications and standards for air and water quality. 1970
fS932.W6H5 ECOL

Lake Itasca seminar, the new industrial man. 1st 1971- v. REF fHM221.N6 ECOL

Major NSP generating plant sites. 1970.
fTK1191.M3 ECOL

NORTHERN STATES POWER COMPANY. ADVISORY COMMITTEE ON PLANT SITING AND DEVELOPMENT.
History of the Wisconsin Department of Natural Resources and related rules, regulations, classifications and standards for air and water quality. 1970
fS932.W6H5 ECOL

NORTHERN STATES POWER COMPANY. CITIZEN'S ADVISORY PLANT SITING TASK FORCE.
History of Minnesota Pollution Control Agency. 1970 fTD181.M5 ECOL

NORTHERN STATES POWER COMPANY. ENGINEERING DEPARTMENT.
Environmental monitoring program; temperature surveys of the St. Croix River 1969-70 for the Allen S. King generating plant, Oak Park Heights, Minnesota. 1970. 1v. REF fTK1331.N6A42 1970 ECOL

NORTHERN STATES POWER COMPANY. ENGINEERING DEPT.
Environmental monitoring program for the Allen S. King generating plant at Oak Park Heights, Minnesota. 1966. fTK1331.N6A4 ECOL

Environmental monitoring program for the Monticello nuclear generating plant, Monticello, Minnesota; annual report. 1971- v.
REF fTK1377.M6N6 ECOL

NORTHERN STATES POWER COMPANY, MINNEAPOLIS.
Environmental monitoring and ecological studies program; annual report for the Prairie Island nuclear generating plant near Red Wing, Minnesota. 1971- v. REF fTK1377.P7N6 ECOL

NORTHERN STATES POWER COMPANY (OF MINNESOTA).
Environmental report; operating license stage of the Prairie Island nuclear generating plants, no. 1 & 2. 1971. 1v. fTD877.5.N6 ECOL

Environmental report; operating license stage of the Prairie Island nuclear generating plants no. 1 & 2. expanded and updated ed. 1971. 2v.
fTD877.5.N62 1971 ECOL

Environmental report: Monticello Nuclear Generating Plant. 1971. 1v. fTD877.5.N64 ECOL

NORTHSHIELD, ROBERT, 1922-
The people's birds. Foreword by David Brinkley. Scribner 1972 QL674.N67 ECOL

NORTHWESTERN UNIVERSITY, EVANSTON, ILL.
Jennings, Burgess Hill.
Interactions of man and his environment. 1966.
TD180.J4 ECOL

NORTON, BOYD.
Snake wilderness. Sierra Club, c1972.
QH105.12N6 ECOL

NORVITCH, RALPH F.
Ground water in alluvial channel deposits, Nobles County, Minnesota. Prepared cooperatively by the Geological Survey, U.S. Dept. of the Interior, and the Division of Waters, Minnesota Dept. of Conservation. 1960. (Minnesota. Dept. of Conservation. Division of Waters. Bulletin no. 14) fTD224.M6A3no.14 ECOL

NOVICK, SHELDON.
The careless atom. Houghton Mifflin c1969
TK9152.N6 ECOL

NOVICK, SHELDON, comp.
Our world in peril; an Environment review. Edited by Sheldon Novick and Dorothy Cottrell. Fawcett Publications 1971 (A Fawcett premier book Q 522)
HC110.P55N67 ECOL

NOYES DATA CORPORATION.
Pollution control companies, United States of America, 1972. 1971, c1972
  REF fTD173.5.N68 ECOL

NUCLEAR DESALINATION INFORMATION CENTER.
Indexed bibliography of nuclear desalination literature—7- 1972- Oak Ridge National Laboratory. v. **REF fZ5853.S22N8 ECOL**

Title—author—company index to reports published by the U.S. Dept. of the Interior, Office of Saline Water through July 1971- Oak Ridge National Laboratory. v. **REF fZ5853.S22N84 ECOL**

NUCLEAR EXPLOSIVES IN PEACETIME.
Scientists' Institute for Public Information, 1970(A Scientists' Institute for Public Information workbook)
  fQC792.N8 ECOL

NUCLEAR NEWS BUYERS GUIDE. 1972-
American Nuclear Society v.
  REF fTK9012.N82 ECOL

NUCLEAR POWER AND THE PUBLIC.
Harry Foreman, editor. University of Minnesota Press 1970 **TK1078.N83 ECOL**

NUS CORPORATION. CYRUS WM. RICE DIVISION.
The effects of various gas atmospheres on the oxidation of coal mine pyrites. Environmental Protection Agency, Water Quality Office, for sale by the Supt. of Docs., U.S. Govt. Print. Off., 1971. (Water pollution control research series)
  fTD899.M5N2 ECOL

NUTE, GRACE LEE, 1895-
The voyageur's highway, Minnesota's border lake land, by Grace Lee Nute. The Minnesota Historical Society, 1965 c1941 **F606.N97 ECOL**

NUTTONSON, MICHAEL Y., 1904- comp.
Air pollution in relation to certain atmospheric and meteorological conditions and some of the methods employed in the survey and analysis of air pollutants. Edited by M. Y. Nuttonson. American Institute of Crop Ecology, 1971. (AICE survey of USSR air pollution literature, v. 6) **fTD883.7.R9N87 ECOL**

Measurements of dispersal and concentration, identification, and sanitary evaluation of various air pollutants, with special reference to the environs of electric power plants and ferrous metallurgical plants. Edited by M. Y. Nuttonson. American Institute of Crop Ecology, 1971. (AICE survey of USSR air pollution literature, v. 7) **fTD883.7.R9N873 ECOL**

NYQUIST, DAVID, ed.
International Symposium on Water Pollution Control in Cold Climates, University of Alaska, Fairbanks, 1970.
Papers Held at the University of Alaska, July 22-24, 1970. 1972 **TD423.I5 ECOL**

O

OAK RIDGE INSTITUTE OF NUCLEAR STUDIES.
Science teachers handbook. n.d. **fQ181.S3 ECOL**

OAKLEY, DONALD T.
Natural radiation exposure in the United States. U.S. Environmental Protection Agency, Office of Radiation Programs, Surveillance and Inspection Division, 1972.
  REF RA569.O15 ECOL

O'BRIEN, MARY-WIN, jt. auth.
Page, Joseph A.
Bitter wages: Ralph Nader's study group report on disease and injury on the job. 1973.
  RC967.P33 ECOL

O'BRIEN, ROBERT, journalist, jt. auth.
Thompson, Philip Duncan.
Weather. 1969 **fQC863.T5 1969 ECOL**

O'BRIEN, WALTER J., ed.
Kansas. University. Center for Research, Inc.
Oxygen consumption in continuous biological culture. 1971. **fTD755.K3 ECOL**

OBST, DAVID, jt. auth.
Love, Sam.
Ecotage. 1972 **TD175.L68 ECOL**

ODELL, N. E.
Forbes, Alexander.
Northernmost Labrador. 1938. **F1136.F67 ECOL**

ODLAUG, THERON O., jt. auth.
Fox, Jackson L.
The ecology of periphyton in Western Lake Superior. 1969. **GB701.M554no.14 ECOL**
Olson, Theodore A.
The continuous plankton recorder: a review of the literature. 1966. **GB701.M554no.3 ECOL**
Stokes, Lee W.
The photosynthetic pigments of Lake Superior periphyton and their relation to primary productivity. 1970. **GB701.M554no.18 ECOL**

ODLAUG, THERON OSWALD, 1911- jt. auth.
Olson, Theodore A.
Lake Superior periphyton in relation to water quality. 1972. **fQK935.O4 ECOL**
Parkos, William G.
Water quality studies on the Great Lakes based on carbon fourteen measurements on primary productivity. 1969. **GB701.M554no.17 ECOL**

O'DONNELL, PATRICK A.
Noise pollution. By P. A. O'Donnell and C. W. Lavaroni. Consultant: Milton Feldstein. Teachers' ed. Addison-Wesley Pub. Co. c1971 **TD892.O46 ECOL**

O'DONNELL, PATRICK A., jt. auth.
Lavaroni, Charles W.
Air pollution. c1971 **TD883.L28 ECOL**

Lavaroni, Charles W.
Water pollution. c1971 **TD420.L28 ECOL**

ODUM, EUGENE PLEASANTS, 1913-
Ecology. Holt, Rinehart and Winston, 1963 (Modern biology series) **QH541.O29 ECOL**

Fundamentals of ecology by Eugene P. Odum. 3d ed. Saunders, 1971. **QH541.O3 1971 ECOL**

ODUM, HOWARD T.
Environment, power, and society by Howard T. Odum. Wiley-Interscience 1970,c1971
  QH541.O33 ECOL

OGBURN, CHARLTON, 1911-
The continent in our hands. Morrow, 1971.
  E169.O2.O3 ECOL

OGDEN, SAMUEL R.
Step-by-step to organic vegetable growing, by Samuel R. Ogden. Rodale Press 1971 **SB321.O343 ECOL**

OGDEN, SAMUEL R., comp.
America the vanishing; rural life and the price of progress, edited by Samuel R. Ogden. Illustrated with nineteenth-century engravings and twentieth-century photos. by David Plowden. Stephen Greene Press, 1969. **S942.O44 ECOL**

OGLESBY, RAY T., ed.
International Symposium on River Ecology and the Impact of Man, University of Massachusetts, 1971.
River ecology and man. 1972.
  GB1205.I5 1971 ECOL

OHIO. STATE UNIVERSITY, COLUMBUS. RESEARCH FOUNDATION.
Pilot scale study of acid mine drainage. U.S. Govt. Print. Off., 1971. (Water pollution control research series) **fTN321.O3 ECOL**

Smith, Edwin Earle.
Sulfide to sulfate reaction mechanism. 1970.
  fTN321.S58 ECOL

OHMANN, LEWIS F.
Wilderness ecology, virgin plant communities of the Boundary Waters Canoe Area by Lewis F. Ohmann and Robert R. Ream. North Central Forest Experiment Station, Forest Service, U.S. Dept. of Agriculture, 1971. (U.S. Forest Service. Research paper NC-63)
  SD11.A45476no.63 ECOL

OIL ON PUGET SOUND; an interdisciplinary study in systems engineering.
Supervised by Juris Vagners. Coordinated by Paul Mar. Distributed by University of Washington Press 1972(Washington sea grant publication)
  fTD427.P4O38 ECOL

OIL ON THE SEA; proceedings of a symposium on the scientific and engineering aspects of oil pollution of the sea.
Edited by David P. Hoult. Plenum Press, 1969. (Ocean technology) **GC1080.O36 ECOL**

OKEY, R. W., jt. auth.
Balakrishnan, S.
State of the art review on sludge incineration practice. 1970. **fTD803.B36 ECOL**

OKLAHOMA. STATE UNIVERSITY OF AGRICULTURE AND APPLIED SCIENCE, STILLWATER. SCHOOL OF CIVIL ENGINEERING.
Aerobic digestion of organic waste sludge, by Oklahoma State University, College of Engineering, School of Civil Engineering. Authors: Q. B. Graves and others. U.S. Environmental Protection Agency; for sale by the Supt. of Docs., U.S. Govt. Print. Off., 1971 i.e. 1972 (Water pollution control research series)
  fTD769.O35 ECOL

OKLAHOMA. UNIVERSITY. RESEARCH INSTITUTE.
Streebin, Leale E.
Demonstration of a full-scale waste treatment system for a cannery. 1971. **fTD899.C3S87 ECOL**

OKUN, DANIEL ALEXANDER.
Fair, Gordon Maskew.
Water and wastewater engineering. 1966-1968
  REF TD145.F32 ECOL

OLIN, JOHN G.
Minnesota. Air Quality Division.
Implementation plan to achieve carbon monoxide ambient air quality standards. 1973.
  REF fTD883.5.M6A422 ECOL

OLMSTED, FREDERICK LAW, 1822-1903.
Civilizing American cities; a selection of Frederick Law Olmsted's writings on city landscapes. Edited by S. B. Sutton. MIT Press 1971 **HT167.O44 ECOL**

OLSEN, JACK.
Slaughter the animals, poison the earth. Drawings by Laszlo Kubinyi. Simon and Schuster 1971
  QL737.C22O47 ECOL

OLSON, SIGURD F.
Listening point. Illus. by Francis Lee Jaques. 1st ed. Knopf, 1958. **QH102.O38 ECOL**

OLSON, SIGURD F., 1899-
The lonely land. Illus. by Francis Lee Jaques. Knopf, 1961. **F1071.O4 ECOL**

Open horizons, by Sigurd F. Olson. Illus. by Leslie Kouba. Knopf, 1969. **QH102.O39 ECOL**

Runes of the North. Knopf 1969, c1963
  F1060.A204 ECOL

Sigurd F. Olson's Wilderness days. 1st ed. Knopf, 1972. **QH81.O67 1972 ECOL**

The singing wilderness. Illus. by Francis Lee Jaques. Knopf, 1956. **QH102.O4 ECOL**

OLSON, THEODORE A.
The continuous plankton recorder: a review of the literature; by Theodore A. Olson, Theron O. Odlaug, Wayland R. Swain. Water Resources Research Center, University of Minnesota, 1966. (WRRC bulletin no. 3)
  GB701.M554no.3 ECOL

Lake Superior periphyton in relation to water quality, by T. A. Olson and T. O. Odlaug. Environmental Protection Agency, Office of Research and Monitoring, 1972. (Water pollution control research series)
  fQK935.O4 ECOL

Minnesota. University. School of Public Health.
A preliminary investigation of nutrients in western Lake Superior, 1958-1959. 1959.
  fGB1627.G89M52 ECOL

Minnesota. University. School of Public Health.
Studies on the productivity and Plankton of Lake Superior. 1961 **fQK935.M55 ECOL**

Minnesota. University. School of Public Health.
Water movements and temperatures of western Lake Superior. 1958. **fGB1627.G89M54 ECOL**

OLSON, THEODORE A., jt. auth.
Fox, Jackson L.
The ecology of periphyton in Western Lake Superior. 1969. **GB701.M554no.14 ECOL**
Parkos, William G.
Water quality studies on the Great Lakes based on carbon fourteen measurements on primary productivity. 1969. **GB701.M554no.17 ECOL**
Stokes, Lee W.
The photosynthetic pigments of Lake Superior periphyton and their relation to primary productivity. 1970. **GB701.M554no.18 ECOL**

OLYMPUS RESEARCH CORPORATION.
Career education in the environment; a handbook. For sale by the Supt. of Docs., U.S. Govt. Print. Off. 1971 or 2 1 v. **fGF21.O4 ECOL**

O'NEILL, EDWARD A.
Rape of the American Virgins. Praeger 1972
  HC157.V6O5 ECOL

ONLY A LITTLE PLANET.
Edited, with a foreword, by David R. Brower. Lines by Lawrence Collins. Photos. by Martin, Schweitzer. Friends of the Earth 1972(Celebrating the earth, 1)
  fPS3553.O474O5 ECOL

ONONDAGA CO., N.Y.
Onondaga Lake study. Environmental Protection Agency, Water Quality Office, U.S. Govt. Print. Off. 1971. (Water pollution control research series)
  fTD224.N7O5 ECOL

ONTARIO INDUSTRIAL WASTE CONFERENCE.
Listing of papers, 1954/70-
  REF fTD897.O6 Suppl. ECOL

Papers presented. 1st- 1954- v.
  REF fTD897.O6 ECOL

OOSTING, HENRY JOHN, 1903-
The study of plant communities; an introduction to plant ecology. 2d ed. Freeman, 1956.
  QK901.O6 1956 ECOL

OPEN CYCLE COAL BURNING MHD POWER GENERATION; an assessment and a plan for action; final report.
Prepared for Office of Coal Research, Dept. of the Interior. Office of Coal Research 1971
fTN805.A395no.64 ECOL

OPEN SPACE ACTION INSTITUTE.
Little, Charles E.
Challenge of the land. 1968
HD205 1968 .L5 ECOL

ORDISH, GEORGE.
The living house; illus. by Graham Oakley. Lippincott, 1960 c1959
QL751.O7 1960 ECOL

ORDWAY, SAMUEL HANSON, 1900-
A conservation handbook. Conservation Foundation, 1949.
HC55.O7 ECOL

OREGON. STATE UNIVERSITY, CORVALLIS.
Oceanography of the nearshore coastal waters of the Pacific Northwest relating to possible pollution. Environmental Protection Agency, Water Quality Office; for sale by the Supt. of Docs., U.S. Govt. Print. Off. 1971- v. (Water pollution control research series)
fGC851.O7 ECOL

OREGON. STATE UNIVERSITY, CORVALLIS. AIR RESOURCES CENTER.
Alexander, Robert M.
Social aspects of environmental pollution. 1971.
fTD177.A4 ECOL

OREGON. STATE UNIVERSITY, CORVALLIS. DEPT. OF MICROBIOLOGY.
Slime growth evaluation of treated pulp mill waste. Authors: A. W. Anderson and G. A. Beierwaltes. U.S. Environmental Protection Agency; for sale by the Supt. of Docs., U.S. Govt. Print. Off., 1971. (Water pollution control research series)
fTD899.W65O73 ECOL

OREGON. STATE UNIVERSITY, CORVALLIS. SCHOOL OF ENGINEERING.
Oregon. State University, Corvallis. School of Forestry.
Studies on effects of watershed practices on streams. 1971 i.e. 1972
fTC409.O74 ECOL

OREGON. STATE UNIVERSITY, CORVALLIS. SCHOOL OF FORESTRY.
Studies on effects of watershed practices on streams, by School of Forestry and School of Engineering, Oregon State University. U.S. Environmental Protection Agency 1971 i.e. 1972 (Water pollution control research series)
fTC409.O74 ECOL

OREGON. STATE UNIVERSITY, CORVALLIS. WATER RESOURCES RESEARCH INSTITUTE.
Brown, George W.
An improved temperature prediction model for small streams. 1972
fQC909.B7 ECOL

Heavy metals in the environment; seminar conducted by Water Resources Research Institute, Oregon State University, Fall Quarter, 1972. 1973.
fTD176.7.O7 ECOL

OREGON. UNIVERSITY FOREST INDUSTRIES MANAGEMENT CENTER.
Current Issues Conference, 1st, Portland, Or., 1972.
Timber supply and the environment. 1972
SD144.A13C87 1972 ECOL

THE ORGANIC CLASSROOM; introduction to environmental education the organic way, an interdisciplinary approach.
Prepared by Thomas Fegely and Bud Souders for Rodale Press Educational Services Division. Ed. by Rita Reemer. Rodale Press c1973 (Organic classroom series, unit no. 1)
fS946.O7 ECOL

ORGANIC GARDENING AND FARMING.
The Basic book of organic gardening. 1971
S605.5.B37 ECOL

The Organic guide to colleges and universities. 1973
S946.O73 ECOL

THE ORGANIC GUIDE TO COLLEGES AND UNIVERSITIES,.
by the staffs of Environment action bulletin, Organic gardening and farming, and Fitness for living. Rodale Press 1973 (A Rodale organic living paperback)
S946.O73 ECOL

ORLOWSKY, WALLACE, 1939- jt. auth.
Perera, Thomas Biddle.
Who will clean the air? 1971
TD883.13.P47 ECOL

ORNING, GEORGE W.
Land management information in northwest Minnesota: the beginnings of a statewide system by George W. Orning and Les Maki. Univ. of Minnesota, 1972. (Minnesota. Land Management Information System Study. Report no. 1)
HD211.M6 ECOL

ORR, ROBERT THOMAS, 1908-
The animal kingdom by Robert T. Orr. Macmillan 1965
QL50.O7 ECOL
Mammals of North America by Robert T. Orr. Doubleday 1971 (Animal life of North America series)
QL715.O77 ECOL

ORTEGA Y GASSET, JOSE, 1883-1955.
Meditations on hunting. Translated by Howard B. Wescott. Introd. by Paul Shepard. Illustrated by Lewis S. Brown. Scribner 1972
SK31.O7813 ECOL

OSBORN, FAIRFIELD, 1887-
Our plundered planet. Pyramid Books 1968
S623.O8 1968 ECOL

OSBORN, FAIRFIELD, 1887- ed.
Our crowded planet, essays on the pressures of population. Sponsored by the Conservation Foundation, 1962
HB851.O8 ECOL

OSBORN, ROBERT CHESLEY, 1904- ed.
Stewart, George Rippey.
Not so rich as you think. c1967
TD180.S68 ECOL

OSBORNE, PHILIP B.
The war that business must win by P. B. Osborne and the editors of Business week. McGraw 1970
HD60.5.U5O8 ECOL

OTTINGER, R. S.
Banks, M. E.
New chemical concepts for utilization of waste plastics. 1971.
TP156.R38B3 ECOL

OTTO, NORMAN E.
Aquatic pests on irrigation systems: identification guide, by N. E. Otto and T. R. Bartley. Illustrated by D. W. Cunningham. U.S. Dept. of the Interior, Bureau of Reclamation; for sale by the Superintendent of Documents, U.S. Govt. Print. Off., 1972,1965 (A water resources technical publication)
QH96.O88 1972 ECOL

OTTOSON, HOWARD W.
Land and people in the Northern Plains transition area by Howard W. Ottoson and others. Univ. of Nebraska Press c1966
HD1773.A3O8 ECOL

OTTOSON, HOWARD W., ed.
Homestead Centennial Symposium, University of Nebraska, 1962.
Land use policy and problems in the United States. 1964,c1963
HD205 1962 .H6 ECOL

OUTDOOR LIFE.
Outdoor life's Gallery of North American game; a brilliant collection of paintings by Francis Lee Jaques... with descriptive text by distinguished authorities on wildlife. Outdoor Life 1946
fSK40.O8 ECOL

OUTPUT SYSTEMS CORP.
Your government and the environment. v.1- 1971-
REF fHC110.E5Y6 ECOL

OVERMAN, MICHAEL.
Water: solutions to a problem of supply and demand. Doubleday, 1969. (Doubleday science series)
TD348.O85 1969 ECOL

OVERSEAS DEVELOPMENT COUNCIL.
Brown, Lester Russell.
Seeds of change. 1970
HD9000.5.B73 ECOL

OWEN, OLIVER S., 1920-
Natural resource conservation; an ecological approach by Oliver S. Owen. Macmillan 1971
S938.O87 ECOL

OWNBEY, GERALD B.
Monserud, Wilma.
Common wild flowers of Minnesota. c1971
QK168.M6 ECOL

P

PABST, ARTHUR F.
Flood forecasting in the Upper Midwest: data assembly and preliminary analysis, by A. F. Pabst, C. Edward Bowers, and Donald G. Baker. St. Anthony Falls Hydraulic Laboratory, 1972.
fGB678.P32 ECOL

PABST, ARTHUR F., jt. auth.
Bowers, C. Edward.
Computer program for statistical analysis of annual flood data by the log-Pearson Type III method. 1971.
GB701.M554no.39 ECOL
Bowers, C. Edward.
Computer programs in hydrology. 1972.
GB665.B6 ECOL
Bowers, C. Edward.
Review and analysis of rainfall and runoff data for selected watersheds in Minnesota. 1968.
GB701.M554no.8 ECOL

PACIFIC NORTHWEST WATER LABORATORY.
see also UNITED STATES. ENVIRONMENTAL PROTECTION AGENCY. PACIFIC NORTHWEST WATER LABORATORY.

Environmental requirements of blue-green algae. 1967.
QK569.C96E56 ECOL
Groman, William A.
Forest fertilization (a state-of-the-art review and description of environmental effects). 1972.
SD408.G7 ECOL
National Symposium on Food Processing Wastes, 1st, Portland, Or., 1970.
Proceedings. 1971
fTD899.F585N37 1970 ECOL
National Symposium on Food Processing Wastes, 3d, New Orleans, 1972.
Proceedings. 1972.
fTD899.F585N37 1972 ECOL

PACKARD, JAMES R., jt. auth.
Glysson, Eugene A.
The problem of solid-waste disposal. 1972.
TD791.G5 ECOL

PADDOCK, PAUL, jt. auth.
Paddock, William.
Famine, 1975! c1967
HD9000.5.P22 ECOL

PADDOCK, WILLIAM.
Famine, 1975! America's decision: Who will survive? By William and Paul Paddock. Little c1967
HD9000.5.P22 ECOL

PADUCAH, KY. PUBLIC SCHOOLS ENVIRONMENTAL EDUCATION STAFF.
Major, James M.
Environmental education: objectives and field activities. 4th ed. 1971.
fLB1047.M3 ECOL

PAGE, JAMES K., ed.
Law and the environment. 1970
KF5505.A75L38 ECOL

PAGE, JAMES K., jt. auth.
Saltonstall, Richard.
Brownout & slow-down. c1972
HC110.E5S33 ECOL

PAGE, JOSEPH A.
Bitter wages: Ralph Nader's study group report on disease and injury on the job, by Joseph A. Page and Mary-Win O'Brien. Grossman Publishers, 1973.
RC967.P33 ECOL

PALLAS, DOROTHY CONSTANCE, 1933- jt. auth.
Fenton, Carroll Lane.
Trees and their world. 1957
QK482.F4 ECOL

PALMER, RALPH SIMON, 1914-
Stout, Gardner D.
The shorebirds of North America. 1967
fQL681.S78 ECOL

PANCHEN, ALEC LEONARD, jt. auth.
Clark, Robert Bernard.
Synopsis of animal classification. 1971.
REF QL352.C53 ECOL

PANGBORN, MARK WHITE.
Ward, Dederick C.
Geologic reference sources. 1972.
REF Z6031.W35 1972 ECOL

PAPANEK, VICTOR J.
Design for the real world; human ecology and social change by Victor Papanek. With an introd. by R. Buckminster Fuller. 1st American ed. Pantheon Books c1971
TS171.4.P37 1971 ECOL

PAPP, CHARLES S., jt. auth.
Swan, Lester A.
The common insects of North America. 1st ed. 1972
QL473.S9 ECOL

PARADIS, ADRIAN A.
Reclaiming the earth; jobs that help improve the environment, by Adrian A. Paradis. McKay 1971
TA170.P37 ECOL

PARK, CHARLES FREDERICK, 1903-
Affluence in jeopardy; minerals and the political economy by Charles F. Park, Jr., in collaboration with Margaret C. Freeman. Freeman, Cooper c1968
HD9506.U62P3 ECOL

PARK RIVER SUBBASIN.
Ludtke, Richard L.
Social and economic considerations for water resources planning in the Park River Subbasin, North Dakota. 1971.
HD1694.N9L8 ECOL

PARKER, CHARLES HENRY, 1906- jt. auth.
Warner, Arthur J.
Plastics solid waste disposal by incineration or landfill. c1972, 1971.
fTD798.W36 ECOL

PARKER, FRANK L., ed.
National Symposium on Thermal Pollution, Vanderbilt University, 1968.
Engineering aspects of thermal pollution. 1969.
TD427.H4N3 1968 ECOL

PARKER, FRANK L., ed.
National Symposium on Thermal Pollution, Portland, Oregon, 1968.
Biological aspects of thermal pollution. 1969
QH90.N3 1968 ECOL

PARKINSON, THOMAS F., ed.
American Nuclear Society.
Nuclear methods in environmental research. 1971
          fTD172.5.A4 ECOL

PARKINSON, THOMAS FRANCIS, 1920-
Protect the earth by Thomas Parkinson. City Lights Books, 1970. **PS3566.A69P7 ECOL**

PARKOS, WILLIAM G.
Water quality studies on the Great Lakes based on carbon fourteen measurements on primary productivity by William G. Parkos, Theodore A. Olson and Theron O. Odlaug. Water Resources Research Center, University of Minnesota, 1969. (Minnesota. University. Water Resources Research Center WRRC bulletin 17)
          GB701.M554no.17 ECOL

PARNALL, PETER.
The mountain. Written and illustrated by Peter Parnall. 1st ed. Doubleday 1971
          PZ10.P2564Mo ECOL

PARSLOW, JOHN LEONARD FREDERICK, jt. auth.
Heinzel, Hermann.
The birds of Britain and Europe with North Africa and Middle East. 1972 **QL690.A1H44 ECOL**

PARSON, RUBEN L.
Conserving American resources. 2d ed. Prentice-Hall 1964 **S930.P3 1964 ECOL**
Conserving American resources by Ruben L. Parson, and associates J. Lee Guernsey and others 3d ed. Prentice-Hall 1972 **S930.P3 1972 ECOL**

PARTHENIADES, EMMANUEL.
Deposition of fine sediments in turbulent flows, by Emmanuel Partheniades and Ashish J. Mehta. Prepared for the Office of Research and Monitoring, Environmental Protection Agency, 1971 i.e. 1972 (water pollution control research series)
          fTC175.2.P3 ECOL

PATIL, GANAPATI P., ed.
International Symposium on Statistical Ecology, New Haven, 1969.
Statistical ecology. 1971
          QH541.15.M3I5 1969 ECOL

PATTERSON, DONALD J.
Emissions from combustion engines and their control by D. J. Patterson and N. A. Henein. Ann Arbor Science Publishers 1972 **TD886.5.P83 ECOL**

PATTERSON, W. L.
Estimating costs and manpower requirements for conventional wastewater treatment facilities, by W. L. Patterson and R. F. Banker. U.S. Environmental Protection Agency U.S. Govt. Print. Off., 1971 i.e. 1972 (Water pollution control research series)
          fTD743.P36 ECOL

PAULSON, MORTON C.
The great land hustle by Morton C. Paulson. Regnery Co. 1972 **HD255.P38 ECOL**

PAVETT, DAVID, ed.
Conference on Chemical and Biological Warfare, London, 1968.
CBW: chemical and biological warfare. 1969,c1968
          UG447.C655 1968 ECOL

PEABODY MUSEUM CENTENNIAL SYMPOSIUM, YALE UNIVERSITY, 1966.
Evolution and environment, a symposium presented on the occasion of the one hundredth anniversary of the foundation of Peabody Museum of Natural History at Yale University. Edited by Ellen T. Drake. Yale University Press, 1968. (Yale University. Mrs. Hepsa Ely Silliman memorial lectures)
          QH366.A1P4 1966 ECOL

PEARL, RICHARD MAXWELL, 1913-
The wonder world of metals, by Richard M. Pearl. Harper 1966 **TN148.P38 ECOL**

PELCZARSKI, EUGENE A.
Black, Sivalls and Bryson, inc., Kansas City, Mo. Applied Technology Division
Evaluation of a new acid mine drainage treatment process. 1971 **fTD899.M5B55 ECOL**

PELL, CLAIBORNE DE B.
Megalopolis unbound; the supercity and the transportation of tomorrow by Claiborne Pell. Praeger c1966 **HE355.P4 ECOL**

PENN, PHILIP, jt. auth.
Jackson, Nora.
A dictionary of natural resources and their principal uses. 2d ed. 1969 **REF HF1051.J3 1969 ECOL**

PENNANCE, F. G.
Jacoby, Neil Herman.
The polluters: industry or government? 1972.
          TD176.7.J3 ECOL

PENNELL, ALFRED G., jt. auth.
Larson, Curtis L.
Predicting peak flow of small watersheds by use of channel characteristics. 1972.
          GB701.M554no.52 ECOL

PENNSYLVANIA. DEPT. OF PUBLIC INSTRUCTION.
Pennsylvania teaching guide to natural resources conservation. 1962, reprinted 1964 (its Curriculum services series, no. 7) **fL194.B527no.7 1964 ECOL**

PENNSYLVANIA. STATE PLANNING BOARD.
Metropolitan open space and natural process. 1970.
          HT394.P5M46 ECOL

PENNSYLVANIA. STATE UNIVERSITY. CENTER FOR AIR ENVIRONMENT STUDIES.
Guide to research in air pollution; projects active in calendar year 1972- Comp. by Center for Air Environment Studies of Pennsylvania State University. 8th- ed. Environmental Protection Agency. Office of Air Quality Planning and Standards. v. (United States. Environmental Protection Agency. Office of Air Programs. Publication no. AP-47-)
        REF TD883.15.P4 ECOL

PEPE, THOMAS F., comp.
Environmental education; a bibliography pertaining to the environment, environmental education, and environmental education programs and materials. Research and Information Services for Education, 1971.
          fZ5322.E2P4 ECOL

PEREGRINE FALCON POPULATIONS; their biology and decline.
Ed. by Joseph J. Hickey. Univ. of Wisconsin Press, 1969. **QL696.A2P44 ECOL**

PERERA, THOMAS BIDDLE, 1938-
Who will clean the air? By Thomas Biddle Perera and Wallace Orlowsky. Illustrated by Richard Cuffari. Coward, McCann & Geoghegan 1971
          TD883.13.P47 ECOL

PERIN, CONSTANCE.
With man in mind; an interdisciplinary prospectus for environmental design. MIT Press 1970.
          HC68.P47 ECOL

PERL, SUSAN, illus.
Gabel, Margaret.
Sparrows don't drop candy wrappers. 1971
          TD176.G3 ECOL

PERLOFF, HARVEY S.
Resources for the Future.
Regions, resources, and economic growth. 1967,c1960 **HC103.R45 1967 ECOL**

PERLOFF, HARVEY S., ed.
The Quality of the urban environment. 1969
          HT169.U5Q33 ECOL

PERRY, GORDON ARTHUR.
Handbook for environmental studies, by G. A. Perry, E. Jones and A. Hammersley. 2nd rev. ed. Blandford Press 1971 (Blandford Approaches to Environmental Studies) **LB1585.P4 1971 ECOL**

PERRY, JOHN, 1914-
Our polluted world; can man survive? Watts 1967
          TD180.P4 ECOL
Our polluted world; can man survive? Rev. ed. Watts, 1972. **TD175.P46 1972 ECOL**

PERRY, RICHARD, 1909-
The unknown ocean. Illustrated by Nancy Lou Gahan. Taplinger 1972 (His The many worlds of wildlife series, v. 1) **QL124.P47 1972 ECOL**

PERSHING, D. W., jt. auth.
Martin, G. B.
Effects of fuel additives on air pollutant emissions from distillate-oil-fired furnaces. 1971.
          TP355.M29 ECOL

PERSPECTIVES ON CONSERVATION; essays on America's natural resources,.
by John Kenneth Galbraith and others Ed. by Henry Jarrett. Published for Resources for the Future by the Johns Hopkins Press 1969, c1958
         HC103.7.P47 1969 ECOL

PESTICIDES,.
by Donald L. Dahlsten and others. Scientists' Institute for Public Information, 1970(A Scientists' Institute for Public Information workbook)
          fQH545.P4P48 ECOL

PETERS, G. T.
United Aircraft Corporation. Research Laboratories, East Hartford, Conn.
Advanced nonthermally polluting gas turbines in utility applications. 1971. **fTJ778.U5 ECOL**

PETERS, HAROLD SEYMOUR, 1902-
The birds of Newfoundland, by H. S. Peters and Thomas D. Burleigh. Illus. by Roger Tory Peterson. Published in association with the Dept. of Natural Resources, Province of Newfoundland by Houghton, 1951. **QL654.P47 ECOL**

PETERS, JAMES LEE, 1889-
Check-list of birds of the world. by James Lee Peters. Harvard Univ. Press, 1931- v.
        REF QL677.P45 ECOL

PETERSEN, DONALD H., jt. auth.
Suggs, James D.
Mercury pollution control in stream and lake sediments. 1972. **fTD427.M4S9 ECOL**

PETERSEN, WILLIAM.
Population. 2d ed. Macmillan 1969
          HB851.P46 1969 ECOL

PETERSON, DEAN F.
MacAvoy, Paul W.
Large-scale desalting. 1969 **TD479.3.M3 ECOL**

PETERSON, JOHN H.
Community organization programs and relationships in watershed development, by John H. Peterson and Rodney N. Friery. Water Resources Research Institute, Mississippi State Univ., 1972. **fTC409.P4 ECOL**

PETERSON, MATTIE DEHAAN.
Interjurisdictional aspects of water resources management in the Minneapolis-St. Paul metropolitan area of Minnesota. 1971.
        REF fTD225.M6P4 1971 ECOL

PETERSON, OTTIS.
Junior science book of water. Illustrated by Dan Koerner. Garrard Pub. Co. 1966 (Junior science books)
          PZ10.P4472Ju ECOL

PETERSON, ROBIN, ed.
Ecology and the market place, ed. by Robin Peterson and William Phillips. MSS Educational Publishing Co. c1971 **HC79.E5P4 ECOL**

PETERSON, ROGER A.
Transportation and the environment. Univ. of Minnesota, 1971. (Secondary environmental education development) **HE192.A1P4 ECOL**

PETERSON, ROGER TORY, 1908-
A field guide to western birds; field marks of all species found in North America west of the 100th meridian, with a section on the birds of the Hawaiian Islands. Text and illus. by Roger Tory Peterson. 2d ed., rev. and enl. Houghton, 1961. (The Peterson field guide series, 2) **QL683.W4P4 1961 ECOL**
Wild America; the record of a 30,000 mile journey around the continent by a distinguished naturalist and his British colleague, by Roger Tory Peterson and James Fisher. Illus. by Roger Tory Peterson. Houghton, 1955.
          QH102.P38 ECOL

PETERSON, ROGER TORY, 1908- illus.
Peters, Harold Seymour.
The birds of Newfoundland. 1951.
          QL654.P47 ECOL

PETRIDES, GEORGE A.
A field guide to trees and shrubs; field marks of all trees, shrubs, and woody vines that grow wild in the Northeastern and North-Central United States and in southeastern and south-central Canada. 2d ed. Illus. by G. A. Petrides (leaf and twig plates) and Roger T. Peterson (flowers, fruits, silhouettes). Houghton, 1972. (Peterson field guide series, 11)
          QK482.P43 1972 ECOL

PETROW, RICHARD.
In the wake of Torrey Canyon. 1st American ed. Mckay Co. 1968 **G530.T72P4 1968 ECOL**

PETTIGREW, GEORGE L.
State and Federal control of health hazards from radioactive materials other than materials regulated under the Atomic energy act of 1954 (as of October 1, 1969) by George L. Pettigrew, Earl W. Robinson and Gail D. Schmidt. U.S. Bureau of Radiological Health; for sale by the Supt. of Docs., U.S. Govt. Print. Off., 1971. (U.S. Bureau of Radiological Health BRH/DMRE 71-4) **RA1231.R2U5125no.71-4 ECOL**

PHELPS, PAT.
Water problems. University of Minnesota, 1971. (Secondary environmental education development)
          TD420.P4 ECOL

PHILADELPHIA ELECTRIC COMPANY.
Raney, Edward Cowden.
Heated effluents and effects on aquatic life with emphasis on fishes. 3rd ed. 1969.
         REF Z7173.W3R3 1969 ECOL

PHILIP, DUKE OF EDINBURG, 1921-
Wildlife crisis by Philip, Duke of Edinburgh, and James Fisher. Forewords by the Prince of the Netherlands and Peter Scott. Epilogue by Stewart L. Udall. Published with the cooperation of the World Wildlife Fund. 1st American ed. Cowles 1970
          S962.P55 ECOL

PHILIPPI BANADOS, RODOLFO A., 1905- jt. auth.
Goodall, J. D.
Las aves de Chile. 1946 **Ref QL689.C5G6 ECOL**

PHILLIPS, JOHN CHARLES, 1876-
American waterfowl; their present situation and the outlook for their future, by J. C. Phillips and Frederick C. Lincoln; with illus. by Allan Brooks and A. L. Ripley. Houghton, 1930. **QL696.A5P45 ECOL**

PHILLIPS, WILLIAM, jt. ed.
Peterson, Robin.
Ecology and the market place. c1971
    HC79.E5P4 ECOL

PHOENIX AREA ELEMENTARY SCHOOL DISTRICTS.
Project Outreach.
Environmental education resource catalog. 1971
    fQH541.2.P76 ECOL

PHOENIX UNION HIGH SCHOOL SYSTEM.
Project Outreach.
Environmental education resource catalog. 1971
    fQH541.2.P76 ECOL

PHYSICIANS FOR SOCIAL RESPONSIBILITY.
Aronow, Saul.
The fallen sky. 1963   **RA569.A7 ECOL**

PHYSIOLOGICAL EFFECTS OF NOISE.
Ed. by Bruce L. Welch and Annemarie S. Welch. Plenum Press, 1970.   **QP82.2.N6P47 ECOL**

PIELOU, E. C., 1924- ed.
International Symposium on Statistical Ecology, New Haven, 1969.
Statistical ecology. 1971
    QH541.15.M3I5 1969 ECOL

PIMENTEL, DAVID, 1925-
Ecological effects of pesticides on non-target species. Office of Science and Technology; for sale by the Supt. of Docs., U.S. Govt. Print. Off., 1971.
    QH545.P4P55 ECOL

PIMLOTT, DOUGLAS HUMPHREYS,
1920- jt. auth.
Rutter, Russell J.
The world of the wolf. 1968.
    QL737.C2R87 ECOL

PINE, TILLIE S.
Water all around, by Tillie S. Pine and Joseph Levine. Illustrated by Bernice Myers. McGraw-Hill c1959
    PZ10.P57Wat ECOL

PINNA, GIOVANNI.
The dawn of life by Giovanni Pinna. With a foreword by Errol White. Photographs by Carlo Bevilacqua. World c1972 (The World of nature)
    fQE714.3.P5 ECOL

PIPER, ARTHUR MAINE, 1898-
Has the United States enough water? By A. M. Piper. U.S. Govt. Print. Off., 1965.
    REF TC801.U2no.1797 ECOL

PIRIE, N. W.
Food resources, conventional and novel. Penguin Books 1969   **S439.P5 ECOL**

PITTS, JAMES N., ed.
Advances in environmental sciences. v.1-
1969-   **REF TD180.A38 ECOL**

PITTSBURGH URBAN TRANSIT COUNCIL.
International Conference on Urban Transportation, 5th, Pittsburgh, 1971.
Mobility: the fifth freedom. 1971?
    fHE148.I5 1971 ECOL

PIVAL, JEAN G., jt. comp.
Adelstein, Michael E.
Ecocide and population. 1971, c1972
    GF75.A35 ECOL

PIZER, VERNON, 1918-
Preserving food with atomic energy. U.S. Atomic Energy Commission, Division of Technical Information, 1970 (A World of the atom series booklet)
    TX611.5.P58 ECOL

PLAGER, SHELDON JAY, jt. auth.
Maloney, Frank Edward.
Water law and administration. 1968.
    REF KFF446.M3 ECOL

PLANNING RESEARCH CORPORATION.
Pollution through land use management. 1969? 2v.
    fGD205 1969 .P6 ECOL

PLANNING RESEARCH FOR RESOURCE DECISIONS.
by Carl H. Stoltenberg and others. 1st ed. Iowa State University Press 1970   **HC55.P55 ECOL**

PLANTS & GARDENS.
Handbook on biological control of plant pests. Contributors: Raimon L. Beard and others. Brooklyn Botanic Garden 1966,1960   **SB932.P5 1966 ECOL**

PLATT, JOHN RADER, 1918-
The step to man. Wiley 1970,c1966
    HM101.P57 ECOL

PLATT, JOHN RADER, 1918- ed.
New views of the nature of man, edited by John R. Platt. University of Chicago Press 1965 (Chicago. University. The Monday lectures, 1965)
    BD450.P55 ECOL

PLATT, RAYE ROBERTS, 1891-
Johnson, George Robbins.
Peru from the air. 1930.   **F3428.J67 ECOL**

PLATT, RUTHERFORD HAYES, 1894-
The great American forest. Illus. by Stanley Wyatt. Prentice-Hall 1971,c1965 (First Prism paperback edition)   **SD140.P55 1971 ECOL**

A pocket guide to trees, by Rutherford Platt. With drawings by Margaret L. Cosgrove. Photos. by the author. Pocket Books 1972,c1952
    QK482.P5 1972 ECOL

Water: the wonder of life by Rutherford Platt. Line drawings by Stanley Wyatt. Prentice-Hall 1971
    QH91.15.P57 ECOL

PLOWDEN, DAVID.
Floor of the sky: the Great Plains. Edited, with an introd., by John G. Mitchell. Designed by Charles Curtis. Sierra Club 1972 (A Landform book)
    fF595.2.P56 ECOL

The hand of man on America. Smithsonian Institution Press; distributed in the U.S. by G. Braziller, 1971. 1 v.   **E169.02.P55 ECOL**

POHL, RICHARD WALTER, 1916-
How to know the grasses; pictured-keys for determining the common and important American grasses with suggestions and aids for their study by Richard W. Pohl. Rev. ed. W. C. Brown Co. 1968 (Pictured-key nature series)
    QK495.G74P73 1968 ECOL

POLACH, JAROSLAV G., jt. auth.
Darmstadter, Joel.
Energy in the world economy. 1971
    REF fHD9540.4.D37 ECOL

POLLARD, SIDNEY.
The idea of progress: history and society. Basic Books 1969?c1968 (Culture and discovery)
    CB155.P55 ECOL

POLLIS, CAROL A., ed.
Environmental quality and social responsibility. 1972   **HC110.P55E57 ECOL**

POLLUTION ABSTRACTS. INDEX.
V.1/2- 1970/71-
v.   **REF fTD172.P65 INDEXECOL**

POMERANTZ, CHARLOTTE.
The day they parachuted cats on Borneo; a drama of ecology. Play by Charlotte Pomeranta; scenery by Jose Aruego. Young Scott Books c1971
    PN6120.A5P75 ECOL

POPKIN, GERALD.
Leinwand, Gerald.
Air and water pollution. 1969   **TD180.L4 ECOL**

POPKIN, ROY.
Desalination; water for the world's future. Foreword by Stewart L. Udall. Praeger 1968   **TD479.P6 ECOL**

POPULATION REFERENCE BUREAU, WASHINGTON, D.C.
Cook, Robert Carter.
People! 1968   **HB871.C7 ECOL**

Frankel, Lillian Berson.
This crowded world. 1970   **HB883.F7 ECOL**

PORCELLA, D. B.
Lake Tahoe Area Council.
Eutrophication of surface waters—Lake Tahoe. 1971 i.e. 1972   **fQH96.8.E9L34 ECOL**

PORTER, ELIOT, 1901-
The place no one knew: Glen Canyon on the Colorado. Edited by David Brower. Sierra Club 1963
    fF832.C7P6 ECOL

Thoreau, Henry David.
In wildness is the preservation of the world. 1971,c1967   **TR660.T5 1971 ECOL**

PORTER IAN H., ed.
Symposium on Monitoring, Birth Defects and Environment, Albany, N. Y., 1970.
Monitoring, birth defects and environment: the problem of surveillance. 1971
    RG627.S94 1970 ECOL

PORTER JOHN J.
Clemson University. Dept. of Textiles.
State of the art of textile waste treatment. 1971.
    fTD899.T4C45 ECOL

PORTLAND, OR. BUREAU OF SANITARY ENGINEERING.
Demonstration of rotary screening for combined sewer overflows. Environmental Protection Agency, Research and Monitoring; for sale by the Supt. of Docs., U.S. Govt. Print. Off., 1971. (Water pollution control research series)   **fTD748.P67 ECOL**

PORTOLA INSTITUTE, INC.
The Last whole earth catalog. 1971.
    REF fTT155.W52 ECOL

POSTMA, ARLIN KEITH.
Review of organic iodide formation under accident conditions in water-cooled reactors, for Directorate of Licensing, Accident Analysis Branch, U.S. Atomic Energy Commission, by A. K. Postma and R. W. Zavadoski. Battelle-Pacific Northwest Laboratories, 1972.   **fTK9152.P6 ECOL**

POTENTIAL PRODUCTIVITY OF FRESH WATER ENVIRONMENTS AS DETERMINED BY AN ALGAE BIOASSAY TECHNIQUE,.
by Jerry M. Johnson and others. Water Resources Research Center, Univ. of Minnesota Graduate School, 1970.(WRRC bulletin 0020)   **GB701.M554no.20**

POTOMAC ASSOCIATES.
The Limits to growth. c1972   **HC110.E5L5 ECOL**

POTTER, NEAL.
Resources for the Future.
Trends in natural resource commodities. 1962.
    REF fHF1051.R43 ECOL

POTTER, NEAL, jt. auth.
Fisher, Joseph Lyman.
World prospects for natural resources. 1964
    HC54.F54 ECOL

POTTER, VAN RENSSELAER, 1911-
Bioethics: bridge to the future. Prentice-Hall 1971 (Prentice-Hall biological science series)
    QH333.P66 ECOL

POUGH, RICHARD HOOPER, 1904-
Audubon bird guide; eastern land birds...with illus. in color of every species, by Don Eckelberry. Sponsored by National Audubon Society. Doubleday, 1946.
    QL681.P68 ECOL

Audubon land bird guide; small land birds of eastern and central North America from southern Texas to central Greenland. With illus. in color of every species by Don Eckelberry. Doubleday c1949
    QL681.P68 1949 ECOL

Audubon water bird guide; water, game and large land birds, eastern and central North America, from southern Texas to central Greenland. Color illus. by Don Eckelberry, line drawings by Earl L. Poole. Doubleday, 1951.   **QL681.P69 ECOL**

Audubon Western bird guide; land, water, and game birds, Western North America, including Alaska, from Mexico to Bering Strait and the Arctic Ocean. Color illus. by Don Eckelberry; line drawings by Terry M. Shortt. Doubleday, 1957.   **QL683.W4P6 ECOL**

POWELL, DAVID R.
New towns bibliography, by David R. Powell and Nan C. Burg. Council of Planning Librarians, 1972. (Council of Planning Librarians. Exchange bibliography, 249)   **REF fZ5942.P6 ECOL**

POWELL, MEL D.
Community action guidebook for soil erosion and sediment control, by Mel D. Powell, William C. Winter and William P. Bodwitch. National Association of Counties Research Foundation 1970
    fS624.A1P68 ECOL

Digest of selected local solid waste management ordinances, by Mel D. Powell, Bruce P. Fiedelman and Myong J. Roe. National Association of Counties Research Foundation, 1972.   **TD788.P6 ECOL**

POWER, GARRETT, jt. auth.
Maryland. University. School of Law.
Legal problems of coal mine reclamation. 1972.
    fKF1830.Z95M37 ECOL

POWER, POLLUTION, AND PUBLIC POLICY; issues in electric power production, shoreline recreation, and air and water pollution facing New England and the nation.
Dennis W. Ducsik, editor. M.I.T. Press c1971(Massachusetts Institute of Technology. Sea Grant Project Office. Report no MITSG 71-8)(M.I.T. report no. 24)   **HC107.A113E55 ECOL**

PRAIRIE ISLAND NUCLEAR GENERATING PLANT, RED WING, MINNESOTA.
Northern States Power Company, Minneapolis.
Environmental monitoring and ecological studies program. 1971-   **REF fTK1377.P7N6 ECOL**

PRATT, CHARLES, illus.
Carson, Rachel Louise.
The sense of wonder. 1965,c1956
    QH51.C35 ECOL

PRATT, P. F.
Nitrate in the unsaturated zone under agricultural lands. Prepared for Office of Research and Monitoring, Environmental Protection Agency. U.S. Govt. Print. Off., 1972. (Water pollution control research series)
    fS651.P7 ECOL

PRATT, WALLACE EVERETT, 1885-
World geography of petroleum; ed. by Wallace E. Pratt and Dorothy Good. Published for the American Geographical Society by Princeton Univ. Press, 1950.
    REF TN870.P73 ECOL

PREHODA, ROBERT W.
Designing the future; the role of technological forrcasting, by Robert W. Prehoda. Foreword by Sir George Thomson. Chilton Book Co. c1967
T20.P68 ECOL

PRESERVING WILDERNESS IN OUR NATIONAL PARKS; a program for preventing overuse of the national parks through regional recreation planning outside the parks. National Parks and Conservation Association 1971
fQH76.P74 ECOL

THE PRESIDENT'S 1972 ENVIRONMENTAL PROGRAM.
Comp. by the Council on Environmental Quality. U.S. Govt. Print. Off. 1972. **HC110.E5P74 ECOL**

PRESTON, EDNA MITCHELL.
Air. Illus. by Joseph Rogers. Follett Pub. Co. 1965 (Follett beginning science books)
PZ10.P668Ai ECOL

PREUSS, ROGER, illus.
Wallo, Olav O.
Twilight over the wilderness. 1971
fS964.U6W3 ECOL

PRICE, ARCHIBALD GRENFELL, 1892-
White settlers in the tropics. Notes by Robert G. Stone. American Geographical Society, 1939. (American Geographical Society. Special publication no. 23) **GF51.P7 ECOL**

PRICE, DANIEL O., ed.
The 99th hour. 1967 **HB3505.N5 ECOL**

PRICE, FRED C., ed.
McGraw-Hill's 1972 report on business and the environment. Ed. by Fred C. Price, Steven Ross, and Robert L. Davidson. McGraw-Hill Publications Co. c1972 v. **fTD174.P7 ECOL**

THE PRICE OF POWER: ELECTRIC UTILITIES AND THE ENVIRONMENT.
by Charles Komanoff and others. Council on Economic Priorities 1972 v. **REF fTJ164.P7 ECOL**

PRICE, VICTORIA, 1943-
Haskell, Elizabeth H.
Managing the environment: nine States look for new answers. 1971. **fHC110.E5H35 ECOL**

PRIESTLEY, MARY, comp.
A book of birds; with 82 wood engravings by C. F. Tunnicliffe. Macmillan, 1938. **PN6110.B6P75 ECOL**

PRINCETON UNIVERSITY. CENTER OF INTERNATIONAL STUDIES.
Sprout, Harold Hance.
The ecological perspective on human affairs. 1965.
JX1251.S49 ECOL

PRINGLE, LAURENCE.
The only earth we have. Macmillan 1969
TD180.P73 ECOL

PRINGLE, LAURENCE P.
Ecology; science of survival, by Laurence Pringle. Macmillan 1971 **QH541.14.P75 ECOL**

From pond to prairie; the changing world of a pond and its life by Laurence Pringle. Illustrated by Karl W. Stuecklen. Macmillan 1972 **PZ10.P669Ft ECOL**

One earth, many people; the challenge of human population growth by Laurence Pringle. Macmillan 1971 **HB851.P75 ECOL**

Wild river. Photos. and text by Laurence Pringle. 1st ed. Lippincott 1972 **fQH541.5.S7P75 ECOL**

PROJECT 80. STAFF REPORT NO. 1.
Minnesota. Dept. of Natural Resources. Bureau of Planning. Minnesota resource potentials in state outdoor recreation. 1971. **fGV54.M6A53 ECOL**

PROJECT OUTREACH.
Environmental education resource catalog. Prepared by Project Outreach in cooperation with Phoenix Union High School System and Phoenix Area Elementary School Districts. 1971 **fQH541.2.P76 ECOL**

PROSPECTS OF THE WORLD FOOD SUPPLY;
proceedings of a symposium convened during the one hundred and third annual meeting of the National Academy of Sciences. National Academy of Sciences, 1966. **fS439.P7 1966 ECOL**

PRYDE, PHILIP R.
Conservation in the Soviet Union by Philip R. Pryde. University Press, 1972. **S934.R9P76 ECOL**

PUBLISHERS' TRADE LIST ANNUAL.
Books in print; an author-title-series index to the Publishers' trade list annual. 1971- Bowker. v.
REF Z1215.P972 ECOL

Books in print supplement: authors, titles, subjects. 1972/73- Bowker. v.
REF fZ1215.P972 Suppl. ECOL

PUSHKAREV, BORIS, jt. auth.
Tunnard, Christopher.
Man-made America: chaos or control? 1963
fNA9108.T82 ECOL

PUTNAM, HUGH D.
Minnesota. University. School of Public Health.
A preliminary investigation of nutrients in western Lake Superior, 1958-1959. 1959.
fGB1627.G89M52 ECOL

Minnesota. University. School of Public Health.
Studies on the productivity and Plankton of Lake Superior. 1961 **fQK935.M55 ECOL**

PYKE, MAGNUS.
Man and food. McGraw-Hill 1970 (World university library) **TX355.P9 ECOL**

PYLES, HAMILTON K., comp.
What's ahead for our public lands? 1970
KF5606.W5 ECOL

PYTER, BERNADETTE.
A bio-bibliography of Sigurd F. Olson. 1972.
REF fZ7404.O4P8 ECOL

Q

QUACKENBUSH, ROBERT M., illus.
May, Julian.
Blue River. 1971 **TD425.M46 ECOL**

THE QUALITY OF THE URBAN ENVIRONMENT; essays on new resources in an urban age.
Edited by Harvey S. Perloff. Resources for the Future; distributed by the Johns Hopkins Press, 1969
HT169.U5Q33 ECOL

QUINN, MARY LOUISE, jt. auth.
Giefer, Gerald J.
Water publications of State agencies. 1972
REF Z7935.G55 ECOL

R

RABIN, EDWARD H., 1937- comp.
The pollution crisis: official documents, edited and arr. by Edward H. Rabin & Mortimer D. Schwartz. Oceana Publications, 1972 c1971 **TD180.R23 ECOL**

RABKIN, JACOB, jt. auth.
Rabkin, Richard.
Fire Island. 1971 **fQH105.N7R3 ECOL**

RABKIN, RICHARD, 1932-
Fire Island; the wonders of a barrier beach, by Richard and Jacob Rabkin. World Pub. Co., 1971
fQH105.N7R3 ECOL

RADIATION PRESERVATION OF FOODS;
proceedings of an international conference, Boston, Massachusetts, Sept. 27-30, 1964.
National Academy of Sciences-National Research Council, 1965.(National Research Council. Publication 1273) **TX611.R28 ECOL**

RADIO FREE EUROPE.
Urban, George R.
Can we survive our future? 1972, c1971
CB428.U7 1972 ECOL

RADOSEVICH, GEORGE E.
Water law and its relationship to environmental quality: a bibliography of source material, by George E. Radosevich and others. Environmental Resources Center, Colorado State Univ., 1973. (Colorado. State University, Fort Collins. Environmental Resources Center. Information series, no. 6)
REF fKF5551.R3 ECOL

RAGLAND, KENNETH W.
Environmental studies at the CIC universities—a survey, by Kenneth W. Ragland and Thomas W. Smith. 1971. **REF fQH541.2.R3 ECOL**

RAIBLE, CLARENCE J., jt. auth.
Dimitriades, Basil.
Interpretation of gas chromatographic spectra in routine analysis of exhaust hydrocarbons. 1972
TN23.U7no.7700 ECOL

RAILTON, ESTHER P., jt. auth.
Gross, Phyllis.
Teaching science in an outdoor environment. 1972.
QH51.G867 ECOL

RALLS, JACK W.
National Canners Association. Western Research Laboratory.
Dry caustic peeling of tree fruit for liquid waste reduction. 1970. **fTD899.F7N37 ECOL**

National Canners Association. Western Research Laboratory.
Reduction of salt content of food processing liquid waste effluent. 1971. **fTD899.C3N36 ECOL**

RALPH M. PARSONS LABORATORY FOR WATER RESOURCES AND HYDRODYNAMICS.
Density induced mixing in confined aquifers, by L. W. Gelhar and others for the Office of Research and Monitoring, Environmental Protection Agency. U.S. Environmental Protection Agency 1972. (Water pollution control research series) **fTC176.R33 ECOL**

Temperature prediction in stratified water: mathematical model-user's manual (supplement to report 16130DJH-01/71). U.S. Environmental Protection Agency U.S. Govt. Print. Off., 1971. (Water pollution control research series) **fTD395.R3 ECOL**

RAMO, SIMON.
Cure for chaos; fresh solutions to social problems through the systems approach. McKay Co. 1969
HN28.R3 ECOL

RAMPACEK, CARL, ed.
Environmental Control Symposium, San Francisco, 1972.
Environmental control. 1972
TD888.M4E58 1972 ECOL

RAMPARTS.
Eco-catastrophe, by the editors of Ramparts. Harper c1970 **TD180.R3 ECOL**

RAMSEY, PAUL.
Fabricated man; the ethics of genetic control. Yale University Press, 1970. (Yale fastback, 6)
HQ751.R33 ECOL

RAMSEY, RALPH H., 1935-
Soil systems for municipal effluents; a workshop and selected references, by Ralph H. Ramsey, C. Rhys Wetherill and H. Casper Duffer for the Office of Research and Monitoring, Environmental Protection Agency. U.S. Environmental Protection Agency, U.S. Govt. Print. Off. 1972. (Water pollution control research series) **fTD760.R24 ECOL**

RAND DEVELOPMENT CORPORATION, CLEVELAND.
Development of a coal-based sewage-treatment process. 1971 **fTN805.A395no.55 ECOL**

RAND MCNALLY AND COMPANY.
The earth and man: a Rand McNally world atlas. c1972 **REF fG1019.R433 ECOL**

RANDLE, JOAN COFFMAN.
Science Curriculum Improvement Study.
Interaction and systems. c1970
LB1585.S36 ECOL

Science Curriculum Improvement Study.
Material objects: teacher's guide. 1971
LB1585.S3 ECOL

RANEY, EDWARD COWDEN, 1909-
Heated effluents and effects on aquatic life with emphasis on fishes; a bibliography, by Edward C. Raney and Bruce W. Menzel. 3rd ed. Cornell Univ. Water Resources and Marine Sciences Center, 1969. (Ichthyological Associates. Bulletin no. 2)
REF Z7173.W3R3 1969 ECOL

RANSOM, ELMER INGLESBY, 1892-1942.
The woodland book, by Elmer Ransom; illus. by Sabra Mallett. Howell, Soskin 1945
QL681.R2 ECOL

RASMUSSEN, BRUCE C., ed.
Problem—emphasis education: an environmental symposium and the consequences of that symposium at Columbia Heights Senior High School District 13, 1969-1970. 1970 **fLB1027.R3 ECOL**

RASMUSSEN, FREDERICK A.
Man and the environment by Frederick A. Rasmussen, Paul Holobinko and Victor M. Showalter. Houghton Mifflin 1970, c1971 (Life science investigations) **QH316.5.R35 ECOL**

RATHJENS, GEORGE W.
Grad, Frank P.
Environmental control: priorities, policies, and the law. 1971. **HC110.E5G7 ECOL**

RATHLESBERGER, JAMES.
Nixon and the environment; the politics of devastation: thirteen essays. Edited by James Rathlesberger. Introd. by Theodore Roosevelt. Taurus Communications 1972 (A League of Conservation Voters report) (A Village voice book)
HC110.E5R37 ECOL

RAWITSCHER-KUNKEL, ERIKA.
Science Curriculum Improvement Study.
Organisms. c1970 **LB1585.S34 ECOL**

READING WISCONSIN'S LANDSCAPE.
Published in the public interest by: State Dept. of Public Instruction and others. 2d ed. State Dept. of Public Instruction 1962, reprinted 1966.
fS946.R4 1966 ECOL

REAM, ROBERT R., jt. auth.
Ohmann, Lewis F.
Wilderness ecology, virgin plant communities of the Boundary Waters Canoe Area. 1971.
SD11.A45476no.63 ECOL

REASKE, CHRISTOPHER RUSSELL, jt. auth.
Arny, Mary (Travis).
Ecology: a writer's handbook. 1st ed. 1972
    QH541.A72 ECOL

RECHT, HOWARD LEONARD, 1927-   jt. auth.
Ghassemi, Masood.
Phosphate precipitation with ferrous iron. 1971.
    fTD751.G4 ECOL

RECYCLING DAY CONFERENCE, 1ST, NEW YORK CITY, 1971.
Proceedings of Recycling Day in New York, held Feb. 2, 1971 at the Waldorf Astoria. 1971
    fTP156.R38R4 1971 ECOL

REDFORD, ROBERT, NARRATOR.
The Language and music of the wolves. c1971
    PhonodiscQL765.L32 ECOL

REED, CHESTER ALBERT, 1876-1912.
Bird guide. Rev. ed. Doubleday, 1916. v.
    QL683.R32 1916 ECOL

REED, DAVID J., jt. auth.
Gunn, Clare A.
Cultural benefits from metropolitan river recreation—San Antonio prototype. 1972.
    fHD1694.T4G8 ECOL

REED, F. EVERETT, 1914-   jt. auth.
Hogan, William T.
Optimum mechanical aeration systems for rivers and ponds. 1970.   **fTD458.H64 ECOL**

REEMER, RITA, ed.
The Organic classroom. c1973   **fS946.O7 ECOL**

REGULATION OF THE NATURAL GAS PRODUCING INDUSTRY; papers presented at a seminar conducted by Resources for the Future, Inc. in Washington, D.C., 15-17 October, 1970. Edited by Keith C. Brown. Resources for the Future; distributed by the Johns Hopkins University Press, 1972
    HD9581.U5R45 ECOL

REID, GEORGE K.
Ecology of inland waters and estuaries. Reinhold 1961 (Reinhold books in the biological sciences)
    QH96.R43 ECOL

REID, GEORGE WILLARD, 1917-   jt. auth.
Streebin, Leale E.
Demonstration of a full-scale waste treatment system for a cannery. 1971.   **fTD899.C3S87 ECOL**

REID, KEITH.
Nature's network. Published for the American Museum of Natural History by the Natural History Press 1970, c1969 (Nature and science library)
    QH541.14.R43 ECOL

REILICH, HELMUT G.
Technical evaluation of phosphate-free home laundry detergents. U.S. Environmental Protection Agency, Office of Research and Monitoring, 1972. (Water pollution control research series) **fTP992.5.R4 ECOL**

REILING, S. D.
Economic benefits from an improvement in water quality, by S. D. Reiling. K. C. Gibbs, and H. H. Stoevener. Prepared for Office of Research and Monitoring, U.S. Environmental Protection Agency. 1973. (Socioeconomic environmental studies series)
    fTD370.R45 ECOL

REINER, THOMAS A., 1931-
The place of the ideal community in urban planning. Univ. of Pennsylvania Press 1968,c1963
    fNA9030.R45 1968 ECOL

REINIG, WILLIAM C., 1924-   ed.
Environmental surveillance in the vicinity of nuclear facilities. 1970   **REF TD887.R3E58 ECOL**

REITZE, ARNOLD W.
Environmental law. 2nd ed. North American International 1972 v.1-   **fKF3775.R4 1972 ECOL**

REKERS, ROBERT G., jt. auth.
Wells, Dan M.
Potential pollution of the Ogallala by recharging playa lake water—pesticides. 1970.
    fTD224.T4W45 ECOL

REMOTE SENSING IN ECOLOGY.
Edited by Philip L. Johnson. University of Georgia Press 1969   **QH541.15.R4R4 ECOL**

RENSSELAER POLYTECHNIC INSTITUTE, TROY, N.Y. BIO-ENVIRONMENTAL ENGINEERING DIVISION.
Control of pollution from outboard engine exhaust: a reconnaissance study. Environmental Protection Agency U.S. Govt. Print. Off., 1971. (Water pollution control research series)   **fTD427.P4R45 ECOL**

RESCHER, NICHOLAS, jt. auth.
Baier, Kurt.
Values and the future. 1969   **HM221.B27 ECOL**

RESEARCH AND DEVELOPMENT CORPORATION.
Environmental law. 1971, c1970
    KF3775.A75E55 ECOL

RESEARCH AND INFORMATION SERVICES FOR EDUCATION.
Pepe, Thomas F.
Environmental education. 1971.
    fZ5322.E2P4 ECOL

RESEARCH INSTITUTE.
Symposium on Mineral Waste Utilization.
Proceedings. 1st-   1968-
    fTP995.A1S9 ECOL

RESOURCE MANAGEMENT IN THE GREAT LAKES BASIN.
Edited by F. A. Butrico, C. J. Touhill and I. L. Whitman. Heath Lexington Books 1971
    HD1694.A2 1971 ECOL

RESOURCES FOR THE FUTURE.
Ayres, Robert U.
Alternatives to the internal combustion engine. 1972
    TL210.A96 ECOL

Brooks, David B.
Low-grade and nonconventional sources of manganese. 1966   **REF TN490.M3B85 ECOL**

Brooks, David B.
Peaceful use of nuclear explosives; some economic aspects. 1969   **HD9698.U52B7 ECOL**

Brooks, David B.
Supply and competition in minor metals. c1965
    REF HD9506.U62B7 ECOL

Brubaker, Sterling.
To live on earth. 1972   **QH541.B76 ECOL**

Brubaker, Sterling.
Trends in the world aluminum industry. c1967
    HD9539.A6B7 ECOL

Cities and space: the future use of urban land; essays from the fourth RFF forum, by Lowdon Wingo, Jr. and others. Ed. by Lowdon Wingo, Jr. Published for Resources for the Future, by the Johns Hopkins Press 1963   **NA9031.R4 ECOL**

Clawson, Marion.
America's land and its uses. 1972
    HD205 1972 .C55 ECOL

Clawson, Marion.
Economics of outdoor recreation. c1966
    GV182.2.C55 ECOL

Clawson, Marion.
The Federal lands since 1956. 1967
    HD216.C53 ECOL

Clawson, Marion.
The federal lands: their use and management. 1966,1957   **HD216.C54 1966 ECOL**

Clawson, Marion.
Policy directions for U.S. agriculture. 1968
    HD1761.C54 ECOL

Clepper, Henry Edward.
Professional forestry in the United States. 1971
    SD143.C56 ECOL

Comparisons in resource management: six notable programs in other countries and their possible United States application. Essays by H. C. Darby and others. Ed. by Henry Jarrett. Published for Resources for the Future, by Johns Hopkins Press, 1961
    REF SD411.R4 ECOL

Cootner, Paul H.
Water demand for steam electric generation. 1966,c1965   **TK1051.C6 ECOL**

Darmstadter, Joel.
Energy in the world economy. 1971
    REF fHD9540.4.D37 ECOL

Davis, Robert K.
The range of choice in water management. 1968
    TD225.P74D3 ECOL

Design for a worldwide study of regional development; a report to the United Nations on a proposed research-training program. A Resources for the Future staff study. Distributed by the Johns Hopkins Press, 1966   **HD82.R43 ECOL**

Energy, economic growth, and the environment. 1972   **HD9545.E6 ECOL**

Energy in the American economy, 1850-1975; an economic study of its history and prospects, by Sam H. Schurr and Bruce C. Netschert, with Vera F. Eliasberg, Joseph Lerner and Hans H. Landsberg. Johns Hopkins Press 1960   **HD9545.R45 ECOL**

Environmental quality analysis; theory and method in the social sciences. Papers from a Resources for the Future conference, edited by Allen V. Kneese and Blair T. Bower. Published for Resources for the Future by the Johns Hopkins Press 1972   **HC79.E5R46 ECOL**

Environmental quality in a growing economy; essays from the Sixth RFF Forum, by Kenneth E. Boulding and others. Ed. by Henry Jarrett. Published for Resources for the Future by the Johns Hopkins Press 1968,c1966   **HC103.7.R39 ECOL**

Fisher, Joseph Lyman.
World prospects for natural resources. 1964
    HC54.F54 ECOL

Forest credit in the United States: a survey of needs and facilities; report of a committee appointed by Resources for the Future, Inc. 1958.
    HG2051.U5R4 ECOL

Held, R. Burnell.
Soil conservation in perspective. 1965
    S624.A1H4 ECOL

Herfindahl, Orris Clemens.
Natural resources information for economic development; a study. 1969   **GA51.H47 ECOL**

Historical statistics of minerals in the United States, comp. and annotated by Sam H. Schurr with the assistance of Elizabeth K. Vogely. Resources for the Future; dist. by John Hopkins Press, 1966, 1960
    fTN23.R4 1966 ECOL

Howe, Charles W.
Interbasin transfers of water. 1971
    HD1695.W4H66 ECOL

Inland waterway transportation. 1969
    HE629.I57 ECOL

Kneese, Allen V.
Managing water quality: economics, technology, institution. 1968   **TD423.K52 ECOL**

Krutilla, John V.
The Columbia River Treaty. c1967
    HD1694.A2 1967 ECOL

Land for the future, by Marion Clawson, R. Burnell Held and Charles H. Stoddard. Published for Resources for the Future by the Johns Hopkins Press 1960
    HD205 1960.R4 ECOL

Lovejoy, Wallace Francis.
Economic aspects of oil conservation regulation. 1967   **HD9566.L6 ECOL**

Lovejoy, Wallace Francis.
Methods of estimating reserves of crude oil, natural gas, and natural gas liquids. 1965 **TN870.L68 ECOL**

McDivitt, James Frederick.
Minerals and men. 1965   **TN19.M2 ECOL**

Multiple purpose river development; studies in applied economic analysis by John V. Krutilla, research associate and Otto Eckstein. Johns Hopkins Press 1958
    REF HN15.R43 ECOL

Natural environments: studies in theoretical and applied analysis. 1972   **QH76.N28 ECOL**

Perspectives on conservation. 1969, c1958
    HC103.7.P47 1969 ECOL

The Quality of the urban environment. 1969
    HT169.U5Q33 ECOL

Regions, resources, and economic growth, by Harvey S. Perloff and others. Univ. of Nebraska Press 1967,c1960   **HC103.R45 1967 ECOL**

Regulation of the natural gas producing industry. 1972   **HD9581.U5R45 ECOL**

Resources in America's future; patterns of requirements and availabilities; 1960-2000, by Hans H. Landsberg, Leonard L. Fischman, and Joseph L. Fisher. Published for Resources for the Future by the Johns Hopkins Press 1963   **HC106.5.R48 ECOL**

Russell, Clifford S.
Drought and water supply. 1970
    TD223.R88 ECOL

Ruttan, Vernon W.
The economic demand for irrigated acreage. 1965
    HD1735.R8 ECOL

Schmid, A. Allan.
Converting land from rural to urban uses. 1968
    REF HD256.S3 ECOL

Trends in natural resource commodities; statistics of prices, output, consumption, foreign trade, and employment in the United States, 1870-1957, by Neal Potter and Francis T. Christy, Jr., research associates. Ed. by Pauline Manning. Published for Resources for the Future by Johns Hopkins Press, 1962.
    REF fHF1051.R43 ECOL

United States energy policies; an agenda for research. Distributed by the Johns Hopkins Press 1969,c1968
    HD9546.R4 1969 ECOL

Water pollution: economic aspects and research needs, by Allen V. Kneese. 1962   **TD420:R4 ECOL**

Western Resources Conference. 7th, Colorado State University, 1965.
Water research. c1966
    REF TD355.W4 1965 ECOL

Wollman, Nathaniel.
The outlook for water. 1971
REF fTD223.W6 ECOL

Zivnuska, John Arthur.
United States timber resources in a world economy. c1967 **HD9750.5.Z5 ECOL**

RESOURCES FOR THE FUTURE. COMMITTEE ON LAND USE STATISTICS.
Land use information; a critical survey of United States statistics, including possibilities for greater uniformity, by Marion Clawson. Resources for the Future; dist. by Johns Hopkins Press, 1969, c1965 **HD205 1969.R4 ECOL**

RESOURCES FOR THE FUTURE. RESOURCES IN AMERICA'S FUTURE.
Landsberg, Hans H.
Natural resources for U.S. growth. c1964
HC103.7.L3 ECOL

REVELLE, ROGER, 1909- ed.
America's changing environment. 1970.
HC110.E5A56 ECOL

REX CHAINBELT INC.
The Environmental and ecological forum, 1970-1971. 1972. **TD898.E58 ECOL**

Environmental Control: everyone's concern. 1971
REF fHC68.E5 ECOL

REY, GEORGE, 1928-
United States. Environmental Protection Agency. Industrial Pollution Control Branch.
Projects of the Industrial Pollution Control Branch. 1971. **fTD897.5.U54 ECOL**

RHEINGOLD, PAUL D., 1933- jt. auth.
Landau, Norman J.
The environmental law handbook. 1971
KF3775.L3 ECOL

RHINE, RICHARD.
Life in a bucket of soil. Illus. by Elsie Wrigley. Lothrop 1972 **QL110.R48 ECOL**

RHODE ISLAND. UNIVERSITY. COLLEGE OF ENGINEERING.
North Eastern Regional Antipollution Conference, 4th, University of Rhode Island, 1971.
Recent developments in industrial pollution control. 1971 **fTD896.N67 1971 ECOL**

RICE, CHARLES E.
Methods for routing hydrographs through open channels by Charles E. Rice and Curtis L. Larson. Water Resources Research Center, Univ. of Minn., 1972. (WRRC Bulletin no. 51)
GB701.M554no.51 ECOL

RICE, R. C., jt. auth.
Bouwer, Herman.
Renovating secondary sewage by ground water recharge with infiltration basins. 1972.
fTD765.B6 ECOL

RICH, STUART U., ed.
Current Issues Conference, 1st, Portland, Or., 1972.
Timber supply and the environment. 1972
SD144.A13C87 1972 ECOL

RICHARDS, PAUL WESTMACOTT.
The life of the jungle by Paul W. Richards. McGraw-Hill 1970 (Our living world of nature)
QH541.5.J8R53 ECOL

RICKETT, HAROLD WILLIAM, 1896-
The new field book of American wild flowers. With 96 illus. in full color and over 700 drawings by the author. Putnam 1963 **QK118.R5 ECOL**

RIDGEWAY, JAMES, 1936-
The last play; the struggle to monopolize the world's energy resources. 1st ed. Dutton, 1973.
HD9540.5.R5 1973 ECOL

The politics of ecology. 1st ed. Dutton, 1970.
HC110.E5R52 ECOL

RIDKER, RONALD GENE, 1931-
Economic costs of air pollution; studies in measurement by Ronald G. Ridker. Praeger 1967 (Praeger special studies in U.S. economic and social development) **HC110.A4R5 ECOL**

RIDKER, RONALD GENE, 1931- ed.
United States. Commission on Population Growth and the American Future.
Population, resources, and the environment. 1972
HB3505.A527 ECOL

RIEDMAN, SARAH REGAL, 1902-
Water for people. Illus. by Bunji Tagawa. Rev. ed. Abelard-Schuman c1960 **TC153.R5 1960 ECOL**

RIEHL, HERBERT, 1915-
Introduction to the atmosphere. 2d ed. McGraw-Hill 1971,c1972 **QC861.2.R5 1971 ECOL**

RIEKE-CARROLL-MULLER ASSOCIATES, INC., HOPKINS, MINN.
Schoell and Madson, Inc., Hopkins, Minn.
Waste treatment plant site study for Southwest suburban municipalities report. 1968.
fTD525.T9S3 ECOL

RIENOW, LEONA TRAIN, jt. auth.
Rienow, Robert.
Moment in the sun. 1967. **S930.R5 ECOL**

RIENOW, ROBERT, 1907-
Moment in the sun; a report on the deteriorating quality of the American enviroment by Robert Reinow and Leona Train Rienow. Dial Press, 1967.
S930.R5 ECOL

RILEY, CHARLES M.
Our mineral resources; an elementary textbook in economic geology. Wiley 1959 **TN23.R56 ECOL**

RIMA, DONALD R.
Subsurface waste disposal by means of wells—a selective annotated bibliography, by Donald R. Rima, Edith B. Chase, and Beverly M. Myers. U.S. Govt. Print. Off., 1971. **REF Z5853.S22R55 ECOL**

RINGWOOD, R. J.
Industrial recycling of urban solid wastes.
In: Western Plant Engineering and Maintenance Conference, San Francisco, 1970 Proceedings. 1970.
fTS184.W4

RIVER BASIN DEVELOPMENT.
School of Law, Duke Univ., 1957.(Law and contemporary problems, v.22, no. 2)
HN64.R589 ECOL

ROBBINS, R. C., jt. auth.
Robinson, Elmer.
Sources, abundance, and fate of gaseous atmospheric pollutants. 1968. **fTD885.R6 ECOL**

Robinson, Elmer.
Sources, abundance, and fate of gaseous atmospheric pollutants: supplement. 1969. **fTD885.R62 ECOL**

ROBBINSDALE, MINNESOTA. INDEPENDENT SCHOOL DISTRICT 281.
Dooley, David.
Summer school guide for education for an improved environment. 1971. **fQH541.2.D6 Suppl. ECOL**

Sako, Marilyn.
Man and his environment. 1971 **fS946.S2 ECOL**

ROBERT S. KERR WATER RESEARCH CENTER.
Characteristics of rainfall run off from a beef cattle feedlot, by R. Douglas Kreis, Marion R. Scalf, and James F. McNabb. U.S. Govt. Print. Office, 1972. (Environmental protection technology series)
TD899.F4R6 ECOL

Denitrification by anaerobic filters and ponds, by Bryan R. Sword. United States. Environmental Protection Agency, Water Quality Office, 1971. (Water pollution control research series) (Bio-Engineering aspects of agricultural drainage, San Joaquin Valley, Calif.) **fTD475.R6 ECOL**

Denitrification by anaerobic filters and ponds, phase II. Author: James R. Jones U.S. Govt. Print. Office, 1971. (Water pollution control research series) (Bio-engineering aspects of agricultural drainage, San Joaquin Valley, California) **TD475.R62 ECOL**

Desalination of agricultural tile drainages. Author: Bryan R. Sword U.S. Govt. Print. Office, 1971. (Water pollution control research series) (Bio-engineering aspects of agricultural drainage, San Joaquin Valley, California) **TD479.R6 ECOL**

Investigations concerning probable impact of nitrilotriacetic acid on ground waters, by William J. Dunlap and others. U.S. Environmental Protection Agency; for sale by the Supt. of Docs., U.S. Govt. Print. Off., 1971. (Water pollution control research series)
fTD897.D4R6 ECOL

United States. Environmental Protection Agency. Office of Research and Monitoring.
Control of mercury pollution in sediments. 1972.
TD427.M4U5 ECOL

United States. Environmental Protection Agency.
Induced aeration of small mountain lakes. 1970.
fSH167.T86U5 ECOL

ROBERTS, AUSTIN, 1883-
Our South African birds (Ons Suid-Afrikaanse voels). With a foreword by John Voelcker, Hon. Secretary and trustee of the South African Bird Book Fund. Cape Times, ltd., 1941 **REF QL692.R62 ECOL**

ROBERTS, THOMAS SADLER, 1858-1946.
The birds of Minnesota, by Thomas S. Roberts. Illustrated with ninety-two color plates by Allan Brooks, George Miksch Sutton, Walter Alois Weber, Francis Lee Jaques, Walter John Breckenridge, including one plate by the late Louis Agassiz Fuertes. The University of Minnesota Press, 1932. 2v.
fQL684.M6R47 ECOL

Manual for the identification of the birds of Minnesota and neighboring States. Rev. ed. University of Minnesota Press, 1955.
QL684.M6R472 1955 ECOL

ROBIDEAU, R. F.
The discharge of submerged bouyant jets into water of finite depth. General Dynamics Corp., Electric Boat Division, 1972. v. **fTD427.H4R6 ECOL**

ROBINETTE, GARY O.
Plants/people/environmental quality; a study of plants and their environmental functions. Text and photography by G. O. Robinette. U.S. Dept. of the Interior, National Park Service U.S. Gov't Print. Off., 1972 **QK901.R6 ECOL**

ROBINS, JOHN D., jt. auth.
Zaval, Frank J.
Revegetation augmentation by reuse of treated active surface mine drainage. 1972. **TD899.M5Z3 ECOL**

ROBINSON, CARMELITA KLIPPLE.
Life in a pond, by Carmelita Klipple Robinson and Gordon E. Burks with Irving A. Leitner. Illustrated by Marjorie Hartwell. M. Vere De Vault, Educational Consultant. Golden Press 1967 1 v.
fPZ10.R56Li ECOL

ROBINSON, EARL W., jt. auth.
Pettigrew, George L.
State and Federal control of health hazards from radioactive materials other than materials regulated under the Atomic energy act of 1954 (as of October 1, 1969). 1971. **RA1231.R2U5125no.71-4 ECOL**

ROBINSON, ELMER.
Sources, abundance, and fate of gaseous atmospheric pollutants; final report by E. Robinson and R. C. Robbins. Stanford Research Institute, 1968.
fTD885.R6 ECOL

Sources, abundance, and fate of gaseous atmospheric pollutants: supplement, by E. Robinson and R. C. Robbins. Prepared for American Petroleum Institute. 1969. **fTD885.R62 ECOL**

ROBINSON, JOHN, 1909-
Highways and our environment. McGraw-Hill 1971
HE355.R6 ECOL

ROCHESTER INTERNATIONAL CONFERENCE ON ENVIRONMENTAL TOXICITY, 3D, 1970.
Assessment of airborne particles; fundamentals, applications, and implications to inhalation toxicity. Edited by Thomas T. Mercer; Paul E. Morrow and Werner Stober. Thomas 1972
QD549.R59 1970 ECOL

ROCHESTER, N. Y. UNIVERSITY. DEPT. OF RADIATION BIOLOGY AND BIOPHYSICS.
Chemical fallout. 1969 **SB959.C45 ECOL**

ROCHESTER, N.Y. UNIVERSITY. DEPT. OF RADIATION BIOLOGY AND BIOPHYSICS.
Rochester International Conference on Environmental Toxicity, 3d, 1970.
Assessment of airborne particles. 1972
QD549.R59 1970 ECOL

ROCK, DAVID M.
American Enka Corporation. Central Engineering Dept.
Zinc precipitation and recovery from viscose rayon waste water. 1971. **fTD899.T4A44 ECOL**

ROCKEFELLER, LAURANCE S., 1910-
United States. Citizens Advisory Committee on Environmental Quality.
Community action for environmental quality. 1970
HC110.E5A5 ECOL

United States. Citizens' Advisory Committee on Environmental Quality.
Report to the President and to the Council on Environmental Quality. 1971.
HC110.E5A514 ECOL

ROCKEFELLER, NELSON ALDRICH, 1908-
Our environment can be saved by Nelson A. Rockefeller. 1st ed. Doubleday, 1970.
HC110.E5R63 ECOL

ROCKS, LAWRENCE.
The energy crisis by Lawrence Rocks and Richard P. Runyon. Crown Publishers 1972 **HD9545.R57 1972**

RODALE, ROBERT.
Sane living in a mad world; a guide to the organic way of life. Rodale Press 1972 **RA776.5.R57 ECOL**

RODALE, ROBERT, ed.
The Basic book of organic gardening. 1971
S605.5.B37 ECOL

RODGERS, WILLIAM H.
Brown-out; the power crisis in America by William Rogers. Stein and Day 1972
HD9684.U62R63 1972 ECOL

RODIE, EDWARD R., jt. auth.
Hardenbergh, William Andrew.
Water supply and waste disposal. 1970,c1960
TD145.H33 1970 ECOL

RODMAN, CLARKE A.
Fram Corporation.
Bio-regenerated activated carbon treatment of textile dye wastewater. 1971. **fTD899.T4F7 ECOL**

ROGERS, GEORGE WILLIAM, 1917- ed.
Alaska Science Conference, 20th, University of Alaska, 1969.
Change in Alaska. 1970
HD9567.A4A64 1969 ECOL

ROHRER, DANIEL M.
The Environment crisis. 1970
TD178.6.E58 ECOL

ROKKAN, STEIN, jt. auth.
Dogan, Mattei.
Quantitative ecological analysis in the social sciences. 1969 **HM206.D6 ECOL**

ROLFE, SIDNEY E., ed.
Managing the environment: international economic cooperation for pollution control. 1971
HC79.E5M35 1971 ECOL

RONDIERE, PIERRE.
Purity or pollution; the struggle for water. 1st ed. Collins, F. Watts 1971 (International Library)
TD348.R65 ECOL

ROOD, RONALD N.
Wild brother, by Ronald Rood. Drawings by Wendell Minor. Trident Press 1970 **QH81.R74 ECOL**

ROOSEVELT, NICHOLAS, 1893-
Conservation: now or never. Dodd 1970
S942.R6 ECOL

ROSE, JAMES, 1927- illus.
Leydet, Francois.
The last redwoods, and the parkland of Redwood Creek. 1969 **SD397.R3L4 ECOL**

ROSE, PETER, jt. comp.
Day, John A.
Dimensions of the environmental crisis. 1971
HC79.E5D35 ECOL

ROSE, STEVEN, 1938- ed.
Conference on Chemical and Biological Warfare, London, 1968.
CBW: chemical and biological warfare. 1969,c1968
UG447.C655 1968 ECOL

ROSEBURY, THEODOR, 1904-
Life on man. Viking Press 1969 **QR56.R59 ECOL**

ROSENDAHL, CARL OTTO, 1875-
Trees and shrubs of the upper Midwest. University of Minnesota Press 1955 **QK481.R67 ECOL**

ROSENTHAL, ALBERT J.
Grad, Frank P.
Environmental control: priorities, policies, and the law. 1971. **HC110.E5G7 ECOL**

ROSIER, BERNARD, jt. auth.
Dumont, Rene.
The hungry future. 1969 **HD1445.D823 ECOL**

ROSS, RICHARD D.
Air pollution and industry, edited by R. D. Ross. Van Nostrand Reinhold Co. 1972 (Van Nostrand Reinhold environmental engineering series) **TD883.R58 ECOL**
Industrial waste disposal. Ed. by R. D. Ross. Reinhold Book Corp. 1968 (Reinhold environmental engineering series) **TD897.R67 ECOL**

ROSS, STEVEN.
Price, Fred C.
McGraw-Hill's 1972 report on business and the environment. c1972 **fTD174.P7 ECOL**

ROSS, WILDA S.
Who lives in this log? Illus. by Elizabeth Schmidt. Coward 1971 (Science is what and why books)
PZ10.R7244Wh ECOL

ROSSANO, AUGUST T., 1916- jt. auth.
Cooper, Hal B. H.
Source testing for air pollution control. 1971
fTD890.C57 ECOL

ROSZAK, THEODORE, 1933-
Where the wasteland ends; politics and transcendence in postindustrial society. Doubleday, 1972. **HN17.5.R62 ECOL**

ROTH, CHARLES E.
The most dangerous animal in the world. Addison-Wesley c1971 **QH541.R68 ECOL**

ROTH, CHARLES E., jt. auth.
Dickey, Miriam E.
Beyond the classroom: using the urban environment as an instructional medium. 1972.
fQH541.2.D52 ECOL

ROTH, ROBERT E.
A review of research related to environmental education, by Robert E. Roth and Stanley L. Helgeson. The Ohio State Univ., ERIC Information Analysis Center for Science, Mathematics, and Environmental Education, 1972. (Environmental education information reports) (Research review series—Environmental education, paper 1)
QH541.2.R6 ECOL

ROUECHE, BERTON, 1911-
What's left; reports on a diminishing America. Little 1969,c1968 **QH77.U6R6 ECOL**

ROUSE, JOHN E.
World cattle. University of Oklahoma Press 1970 2v.
SF197.R68 ECOL

ROY F. WESTON, INC.
Combined sewer overflow abatement alternatives, Wash., D.C. Environmental Protection Agency, Water Quality Off. U.S. Govt. Print. Off., 1970. (Water pollution control research series)
fTD525.W2R68 ECOL

Concept evaluation report: taconite tailings disposal, Reserve Mining Company, Silver Bay, Minnesota. Prepared for Environmental Protection Agency ... by Roy F. Weston. Environmental Scientists and Engineers. 1971 v. **fTD899.T35 ECOL**

Process design manual for upgrading existing wastewater treatment plants, by Roy F. Weston, Inc. for Environmental Protection Agency, Technology Transfer. United States Govt. Print. Off. 1971. 1v.
REF fTD745.R6 ECOL

ROYAL GEOGRAPHICAL SOCIETY, LONDON.
Biology and ethics. 1969. **HM216.B48 ECOL**

ROYAL GEOGRAPHICAL SOCIETY OF LONDON.
Lowe-McConnell, R. H.
Man-made lakes. 1966. **GB1601.L6 1965 ECOL**

RUCH, WALTER E., ed.
Chemical detection of gaseous pollutants, an annotated bibliography. Edited and rev. by Walter E. Ruch. Ann Arbor Science Publishers
REF fZ5524.G24R8 ECOL

RUDD, ROBERT D., 1924- jt. auth.
Highsmith, Richard Morgan.
Conservation in the United States. 2d ed. 1969
HC103.7.H5 1969 ECOL

RUDD, ROBERT L.
Pesticides and the living landscape by Robert L. Rudd. Univ. of Wisconsin Press, 1964. (A Conservation Foundation study) **SB951.R78 ECOL**

RUE, LEONARD LEE.
The world of the beaver; text and photographs by Leonard Lee Rue III. Lippincott, 1964. (A Living world book) **QL737.R6R84 ECOL**

The world of the ruffed grouse, with text and photos. by Leonard Lee Rue, III. 1st ed. Lippincott 1973, c1972 (Living world books) **QL696.G2R83 ECOL**

RUMSEY, R. D. E.
Loraine, John Alexander.
The death of tomorrow. 1972
HC79.P55L67 1972b ECOL

RUNYON, RICHARD P., jt. auth.
Rocks, Lawrence.
The energy crisis. 1972 **HD9545.R57 1972**

RUSCHMEYER, ORLANDO.
Minnesota. University. School of Public Health.
Water movements and temperatures of western Lake Superior. 1958. **fGB1627.G89M54 ECOL**

RUSCHMEYER, ORLANDO R.
Minnesota. University. School of Public Health.
Lake Superior study, summer of 1956. 1957
fGB1627.G89M5 ECOL

Minnesota. University School of Public Health.
Lake Superior study, summer of 1956: summary of report. 1957. **fGB1627.G89M53 ECOL**

RUSSELL, CLIFFORD S.
Drought and water supply; implications of the Massachusetts experience for municipal planning by Clifford S. Russell, David G. Arey and Robert W. Kates, with the assistance of Duane Bauman and Donald J. Volk. Published for Resources for the Future by the Johns Hopkins Press 1970 **TD223.R88 ECOL**

RUSSELL, HELEN ROSS, 1915-
Winter search party; a guide to insects and other invertebrates. Illus. by Viola Kohl Mohn. 1st ed. T. Nelson 1971 **QL465.R85 ECOL**

RUSSELL, WILLIAM MOY STRATTON.
Man, nature, and history; controlling the environment by W. M. S. Russell. Published for the American Museum of Natural History by the Natural History Press 1969,c1967 (Nature and science library)
GF37.R85 ECOL

RUTGERS UNIVERSITY, NEW BRUNSWICK, N. J.
Environmental problems. 1968 **TD180.E48 ECOL**

RUTHERFORD, ROBERT J., jt. auth.
Hall, Francis R.
The influence of a New England wetland on water quantity and quality. 1972. **fTD224.N4H3 ECOL**

RUTTAN, VERNON W.
The economic demand for irrigated acreage; new methodology and some preliminary projections, 1954-1980, by Vernon W. Ruttan. Published for Resources for the Future, by the Johns Hopkins Press 1965 **HD1735.R8 ECOL**

RUTTAN, VERNON W., jt. auth.
Hayami, Yujiro.
Agricultural development. 1971
HD1415.H318 ECOL

RUTTER, RUSSELL J.
The world of the wolf, by Russell J. Rutter and Douglas H. Pimlott. Lippincott, 1968. (Living world books) **QL737.C2R87 ECOL**

RYCKMAN, EDGERLEY, TOMLINSON AND ASSOCIATES.
Development of a case study of the total effect of pesticides in the environment, nonirrigated croplands of the Mid-west. Environmental Protection Agency, Office of Water Programs, Applied Technology Division, Rural Wastes Branch, U.S. Govt. Print. Off. 1972. v. (Pesticide study series, 4)
fQH545.P4R9 ECOL

Pesticide poisoning of Pond Lick Lake, Ohio; investigation and resolution, June 2-July 5, 1971. Prepared for Environmental Protection Agency, Division of Oil and Hazardous Materials. 1971 (Oil and hazardous materials program series)
fTD224.O3R9 ECOL

Von Rumker, Rosmarie.
The use of pesticides in suburban homes and gardens and their impact on the aquatic environment. 1972.
fQH545.P4V66 ECOL

S

SAARINEN, ELIEL, 1873-1950.
The city, its growth, its decay, its future. M.I.T. Press 1943 **NA9030.S2 ECOL**

SACHSEL, GEORGE F., comp.
Solid Waste Resources Conference, Columbus, Ohio, 1971.
Design of consumer containers for re-use or disposal. 1972. **TD785.S6 1971 ECOL**

SADLEIR, R. M. F. S.
The ecology of reproduction in wild and domestic mammals by R. M. F. S. Sadleir. Methuen, 1969.
QP251.S27 ECOL

ST. JOHN'S UNIVERSITY, COLLEGEVILLE, MINNESOTA CENTER FOR THE STUDY OF LOCAL GOVERNMENT.
The impact of future electrical power requirements on the state of Minnesota—an issue analysis. Prepared at the request of the Minnesota State Planning Agency. 1971. **fHD9685.U6M6 ECOL**

ST. LOUIS PARK, MINN. CITY ATTORNEY'S OFFICE.
City attorney's report, re: flood plain management. 1969 **fTC425.S3A5 ECOL**

ST. PAUL. PUBLIC SCHOOLS. CURRICULUM OFFICE.
Belwin outdoor education laboratory project handbook. 1971. (its Publication, no. 384)
fLB1047.S25 ECOL

ST. REGIS PAPER COMPANY.
Ketchum, Richard M.
The secret life of the forest. 1970
fQK938.F6K4 ECOL

SAKO, MARILYN.
Man and his environment; fourth grade social studies. Robbinsdale Area Schools, Independent School District 281, 1971 **fS946.S2 ECOL**

SALE, LARRY L.
Environmental education in the elementary school by Larry L. Sale and Ernest W. Lee. Holt, Rinehart and Winston 1972 **QH541.2.S24 ECOL**

SALISBURY FRANK B., jt. auth.
Jensen, William A.
Botany: an ecological approach. 1972
QK47.J45 ECOL

SALOMONSON, JANET, jt. auth.
Hickman, Howard J.
A study of the environmental impact of polystyrene vs. paper pulp egg cartons and meat trays. 1972.
fTP373.H5 ECOL

SALTONSTALL, RICHARD, 1937-
Brownout & slow-down by Richard Saltonstall, Jr. and James K. Page, Jr. Walker c1972
HC110.E5S33 ECOL

Your environment and what you can do about it. Walker 1970 **HC110.E5S35 ECOL**

SALVATO, JOSEPH A.
Environmental engineering and sanitation by Joseph A. Salvato, Jr. 2d ed. Wiley-Interscience 1972 (Environmental science and technology)
RA565.S3 1972 ECOL

SAND, GEORGE X., 1915-
The Everglades today; endangered wilderness by George X. Sand. Four Winds Press 1971
QH105.F6S24 ECOL

SANDBURG, HELGA.
Above and below; a journey through our national underwater parks, by Helga Sandburg and George Crile, Jr. 1st ed. McGraw-Hill 1969
QH91.75.U6S35 ECOL

SANDERS, NORMAN K.
Stop it! A guide to defense of the environment by Norman K. Sanders Rinehart Press 1972
HC110.E5S36 ECOL

SANDFORD, LLOYD, illus.
McClung, Robert M.
Scoop, last of the brown pelicans. 1972.
PZ10.M115Sb ECOL

SANDOSKI, DOROTHY A.
Selected urban storm water runoff abstracts, July 1971-June 1972. Prepared for the Office of Research and Monitoring, U.S. Environmental Protection Agency. U.S. Govt. Print. Off., 1972. (Environmental protection technology series) **fTD653.S2 ECOL**

SANITATION INDUSTRY YEAR BOOK. 9 ED. 1972-
Solid Wastes Management. v.
REF fTD791.S3 ECOL

SANTMIRE, H. PAUL.
Brother Earth; nature, God, and ecology in time of crisis by H. Paul Santmire. Nelson 1970
BL435.S25 ECOL

SARNOFF, PAUL.
The New York times encyclopedic dictionary of the environment. Quadrangle Books c1971
REF TD173.S27 1971 ECOL

SARTOR, JAMES D.
Water pollution aspects of street surface contaminants, by James D. Sartor and Gail B. Boyd. U.S. Environmental Protection Agency, Office of Research and Monitoring, 1972. (Environmental protection technology series) **fTD665.S2 ECOL**

SAUVY, ALFRED, 1898-
General theory of population. With a foreword by E. A. Wrigley. Translated by Christophe Campos. Basic Books 1970,c1969 **HB871.S25213 ECOL**

SAVAGE, HENRY, 1903-
Lost heritage. W. Morrow, 1970.
QH26.S28 ECOL

SAX, JOSEPH L.
Defending the environment; a strategy for citizen action. Introd. by George McGovern. Knopf, 1971. (A Borzoi book) **HC110.E5S3 ECOL**

Water law, planning & policy; cases and materials by Joseph L. Sax. Bobbs-Merrill 1968 (Contemporary legal education series) **KF5568.S3 1968 ECOL**

SAX, KARL, 1892-
Standing room only; the world's exploding population. New ed. Beacon Press 1969,c1960
HB881.S33 1969 ECOL

SCALF, MARION R., jt. auth.
Robert S. Kerr Water Research Center.
Characteristics of rainfall run off from a beef cattle feedlot. 1972. **TD899.F4R6 ECOL**

SCHAFER, RUDOLPH J. H. jt. auth.
Atkisson, Jean.
Evaluated bibliography of free and inexpensive conservation publications. 1972
REF fZ7164.N3A8 ECOL

SCHALLER, FRIEDRICH.
Soil animals. Univ. of Mich. Press 1968 (Ann Arbor science library) **QL110.S313 ECOL**

SCHEFFER, VICTOR B.
The year of the seal by Victor B. Scheffer. Illus. by Leonard Everett Fisher. Scribner 1970
QL737.P6S32 ECOL

SCHEIB, IDA, illus.
Adler, Irving.
Rocks and minerals and the stories they tell. 1956.
QE432.A35 ECOL

SCHERGER, DALE A., jt. auth.
Barnes, Robert A.
Ammonia removal in a physical-chemical wastewater treatment process. 1972. **TD462.B3 ECOL**

SCHETZ, J. A., jt. auth.
Campbell, J. F.
Analysis of the injection of a heated turbulent jet into a moving mainstream, with emphasis on a thermal discharge in a waterway. 1972.
fTD427.H4C3 ECOL

SCHIEBE, F. R., jt. auth.
Stefan, Heinz.
Surface discharge of heated water. 1971 i.e. 1972
fTD427.H4S64 ECOL

SCHILDHAUER, CAROLE.
Environmental information sources: engineering and industrial applications; a selected annotated bibliography. Special Libraries Association, 1972.
REF fZ5863.E57S34 ECOL

SCHISSLER, GERALD D.
Minnesota. Pollution Control Agency.
In the matter of the adoption of proposed amendments to Minnesota Regulations APC 1, APC 3, APC 4, APC 11 and APC 15; and the adoption of Minnesota Regulation APC 16; and the proposed adoption of the Minnesota Air Quality Implementation Plan. 1972 **REF fKFM5758.A17 1972 ECOL**

SCHLICHTING, HAROLD E., 1926-
Ecology; the study of environment by Harold E. Schlichting, Jr. and Mary Southworth Schlichting. Illus. by Don Collins. Steck-Vaughn Co. 1971 (Wings books)
PZ10.S3713Ec ECOL

SCHLICHTING, MARY SOUTHWORTH, jt. auth.
Schlichting, Harold E.
Ecology. 1971 **PZ10.S3713Ec ECOL**

SCHMANDT, HENRY J., jt. auth.
Bollens, John Constantinus.
The metropolis. 2d ed. 1970
JS422.B6 1970 ECOL

SCHMELZ, DAMIAN V., jt. auth.
Lindsey, Alton A.
Natural areas in Indiana and their preservation. 1969. **QH76.5.I6L5 ECOL**

SCHMID, A. ALLAN.
Converting land from rural to urban uses, by A. Allan Schmid. Resources for the Future; dist. by Johns Hopkins Press, 1968 **REF HD256.S3 ECOL**

SCHMIDT, ELIZABETH, 1915- illus.
Ross, Wilda S.
Who lives in this log? 1971
PZ10.R7244Wh ECOL

SCHMIDT, GAIL D., jt. auth.
Pettigrew, George L.
State and Federal control of health hazards from radioactive materials other than materials regulated under the Atomic energy act of 1954 (as of October 1, 1969). 1971. **RA1231.R2U5125no.71-4 ECOL**

SCHMIDT, KEN, jt. auth.
Kreusch, Ed.
Wastewater demineralization by ion exchange. 1971 i.e.1972 **fTD757.5.K74 ECOL**

SCHNEIDER, G. R., jt. auth.
Unterberg, W.
Computerized design and cost estimation for multiple-hearth sludge incinerators. 1971 i.e. 1972
fTD770.U58 ECOL

SCHNEIDER, KENNETH R.
Autokind vs. mankind; an analysis of tyranny, a proposal for rebellion, a plan for reconstruction by Kenneth R. Schneider. Illustrated by Richard D. Hedman. 1st ed. Norton 1971
HE5623.S35 1971 ECOL

SCHOELL AND MADSON, INC., HOPKINS, MINN.
Report on the municipal water supply, treatment, storage, and distribution system, City of Waconia, Minnesota. 1967. **fTD225.W3S3 ECOL**

Waste treatment plant site study for Southwest suburban municipalities report by Schoell and Madson Inc. and Rieke-Carroll-Muller Associates, Inc. 1968.
fTD525.T9S3 ECOL

SCHOENFELD, CLARENCE ALBERT, 1918-
Everybody's ecology; a field guide to pleasure and perception in the out-of-doors by Clay Schoenfeld. Original photos. by E. William Wollin. Barnes 1971
QH541.13.S36 ECOL

SCHOENFELD, CLARENCE ALBERT, 1918- ed.
Outlines of environmental education. Dembar Educational Research Services 1971
S946.S43 ECOL

SCHOENHERR, JOHN, illus.
May, Julian.
The big island. 1968 **PZ10.M455Bi ECOL**

SCHORGER, ARLIE WILLIAM, 1884-1972.
The passenger pigeon; its natural history and extinction. University of Oklahoma Press 1973
QL696.C6S3 1973 ECOL

SCHROEDER, HENRY ALFRED, 1906-
Pollution, profits & progress, by Henry A. Schroeder. S. Greene Press 1971 **TD175.S37 ECOL**

SCHROEDER, KEITH.
West St. Paul, Minn. Independent School Dist. no. 197. Elementary Science Committee.
Elementary science guide and resource book. n.d.
fLB1585.W4 ECOL

SCHULTZ, MORTIMER A., 1918- jt. auth.
Geesey, A. H.
New safety system design for nuclear power reactors. 1971. **fTA1.P35no.103 ECOL**

SCHURR, SAM H.
Resources for the Future.
Energy in the American economy, 1850-1975. 1960
HD9545.R45 ECOL

Resources for the Future.
Historical statistics of minerals in the United States. 1966, 1960 **fTN23.R4 1966 ECOL**

SCHURR, SAM H., ed.
Energy, economic growth, and the environment. 1972 **HD9545.E6 ECOL**

SCHURR, SAM H., jt. auth.
Landsberg, Hans H.
Energy in the United States. 1968
HD9545.L3 ECOL

SCHURZ, DANIEL H.
Directory of public information contacts, Wash., D.C., 1972- **REF JK849.A353 ECOL**

SCHWARTZ, BERNICE S., jt. auth.
Schwartz, George I.
Life in a log. 1972 **QH541.5.F6S39 ECOL**

SCHWARTZ, CHARLES WALSH, illus.
Leopold, Aldo.
A Sand County almanac. Enl. ed. 1966.
QH81.L56 1966 ECOL

SCHWARTZ, EUGENE S., 1917-
Overskill; the decline of technology in modern civilization, by Eugene S. Schwartz. Quadrangle Books, 1971. **CB478.S38 1971 ECOL**

SCHWARTZ, GEORGE I.
Life in a log by George I. Schwartz and Bernice S. Schwartz. Photos. and drawings by the authors. Published for the American Museum of Natural History by the Natural History Press 1972
QH541.5.F6S39 ECOL

SCHWARTZ, GEORGE MELVIN, 1892-
Minnesota's rocks and waters; a geological story, by George M. Schwartz and George A. Thiel, with the assistance of Peggy Harding Love. Univ. of Minnesota Press 1954 (Minnesota. Geological Survey. Bulletin 37)
QE127.A22no.37 ECOL

Minnesota's rocks and waters; a geological story, by G. M. Schwartz and George A. Thiel, with the assistance of Peggy H. Love. Rev. ed. University of Minnesota Press 1963 **QE127.A22no.37 1963 ECOL**

SCHWARTZ, GEORGE MELVIN, 1892- jt. auth.
Manson, Philip W.
Some aspects of the hydrology of ponds and small lakes. 1968. **fGB1825.M6M35 ECOL**

SCHWARTZ, JULIUS, 1907-
Through the magnifying glass; little things that make a big difference. Pictures by Jeanne Bendick. McGraw 1954 **Q163.S464 ECOL**

SCHWARTZ, MORTIMER D., jt. comp.
Rabin, Edward H.
The pollution crisis: official documents. 1972 c1971
TD180.R23 ECOL

SCHWARTZ, STEPHEN, 1940- jt. auth.
Landerman, Norman J.
Community resource. 1972 **TD195.S3L36 ECOL**

SCHWARTZ, WILLIAM, comp.
Voices for the wilderness. Ballantine Books 1969 (Walden edition) **QH75.S32 ECOL**

SCHWEITZER, MARTIN, illus.
Only a little planet. 1972
fPS3553.O4749O5 ECOL

SCIENCE AND PUBLIC AFFAIRS.
Lewis, Richard S.
The energy crisis. 1972. **fHC103.7.L4 ECOL**

SCIENCE AND THE FUTURE OF MAN.
Editors: Robert L. Carovillano and James W. Skehan. MIT Press c1970 **CB151.S37 ECOL**

SCIENCE BOOK ASSOCIATES.
Millard, Reed.
Clean air—clean water for tomorrow's world. 1971
HC79.E5M5 ECOL

Millard, Reed.
How will we meet the energy crisis? 1971
TJ153.M54 ECOL

Millard, Reed.
Natural resources: will we have enough for tomorrow's world? 1972 **HC103.7.M55 ECOL**

SCIENCE, CONFLICT, AND SOCIETY; readings from Scientific American.
With introductions by Garrett Hardin. W. H. Freeman 1969 **fQ125.S434 ECOL**

SCIENCE CURRICULUM IMPROVEMENT STUDY.
Interaction and systems; teacher's guide. Collaborating authors: Robert Karplus, and Joan Coffman Randle Rand McNally c1970
LB1585.S36 ECOL

Life cycles; teacher's guide. Rand McNally c1970
LB1585.S32 ECOL

Material objects: teacher's guide. Collaborating authors: Joan Coffman Randle and Herbert D. Thier Rand McNally 1971 **LB1585.S3 ECOL**

Organisms; teacher's guide. Collaborating authors: Sandra Fletcher, Chester A. Lawson, Erika Rawitscher-Kunkel Rand McNally c1970
LB1585.S34 ECOL

Populations; teacher's guide. Preliminary ed. Authors: David Conrad, Chester A. Lawson Rand McNally c1969 **fLB1585.S35 ECOL**

Subsystems and variables; teacher's guide. Collaborating authors: Carl F. Berger and others Rand McNally 1971,c1970 **LB1585.S38 1971 ECOL**

SCIENCE, ENGINEERING, AND THE CITY.
A symposium sponsored jointly by the National Academy of Sciences and the National Academy of Engineering. National Academy of Sciences, 1967.(National Research Council Publication 1498)
HT166.S32 ECOL

SCIENCE TEACHERS HANDBOOK.
Prepared by Special Training Division, Oak Ridge Institute of Nuclear Studies, a unit of Oak Ridge Associated Universities. U.S. Atomic Energy Commission, Division of Technical Information, n.d.
fQ181.S3 ECOL

SCIENTIFIC AMERICAN.
Ehrlich, Paul R.
Man and the ecosphere. 1971 **fGF8.E35 ECOL**

Science, conflict, and society. 1969
fQ125.S434 ECOL

SCIENTIFIC ASPECTS OF PEST CONTROL.
National Academy of Sciences-National Research Council, 1966. **SB951.S38 ECOL**

SCOBY, DONALD R.
Environmental ethics; studies of man's self-destruction. Ed. by Donald R. Scoby. Burgess Pub. Co. 1971 **GF80.S35 ECOL**

SCORER, RICHARD SEGAR, 1919-
Pollution in the air: problems, policies and priorities. Routledge and Kegan Paul 1973 **TD883.S3 ECOL**

SCOTT, PETER MARKHAM, 1909-
Key to the wildfowl of the world. Severn Wildfowl Trust n.d. **REF QL696.A5S349 ECOL**

The swans by Peter Scott and the Wildfowl Trust. Houghton, 1972. **QL696.A5S37 ECOL**

SEABORG, GLENN THEODORE, 1912-
Man and atom; building a new world through nuclear technology, by Glenn T. Seaborg and William R. Corliss. 1st ed. E. P. Dutton, 1971.
TK9145.S4 1971 ECOL

SEAGRAVES, JAMES A., jt. auth.
Elliott, Ralph D.
The effects of sewer surcharges on the level of industrial wastes and the use of water by industry. 1972. **TD897.5.E4 ECOL**

SEARS, PAUL BIGELOW, 1891-
Deserts on the march by Paul B. Sears. 3rd ed. rev. Univ. of Okla. Press 1967,c1959
S493.S4 1959 ECOL

Lands beyond the forest, by Paul B. Sears. Illus. by Stanley Wyatt. Prentice-Hall 1969 (Prentice-Hall series in nature and natural history) **QH541.5.P7S4 ECOL**

The living landscape by Paul B. Sears. Basic Books 1966 (Science & discovery) **QH541.S37 1966 ECOL**

This is our world by Paul B. Sears. Rev. ed. University of Oklahoma Press 1971 **QH309.S3 1971 ECOL**

SECKLER, DAVID WILLIAM, 1935- ed.
California water. 1971. **HD1694.C2C35 ECOL**

SEGERBERG, OSBORN.
Where have all the flowers, fishes, birds, trees, water, and air gone? What ecology is all about. McKay 1971
QH541.S39 ECOL

SELECTED STUDIES ON ALKALINE ADDITIVES FOR SULFUR DIOXIDE CONTROL,.
by R. H. Borgwardt and others. Research Triangle Park, North Carolina, Environmental Protection Agency. National Environmental Research Center, 1971.(Office of Air Programs Publication no. APTD-0737) **TD885.5.S8S4 ECOL**

SELEKOF, J. S., jt. auth.
Young, G. K.
The importance of economic factors in urban surface water supply systems. 1972. **fTD353.Y6 ECOL**

SELSAM, MILLICENT (ELLIS) 1912-
How to be a nature detective, by Millicent Selsam. Pictures by Ezra Jack Keats. Harper & Row 1966,c1963
PZ10.S44Hr3 ECOL

See through the lake. Pictures by Winifred Lubell. Harper 1958 **PZ10.S44Sdi ECOL**

SELSAM, MILLICENT (ELLIS) 1912- Nature detective.
Selsam, Millicent (Ellis).
How to be a nature detective. 1966,c1963
PZ10.S44Hr3 ECOL

SEMINAR ON THE ENGINEER AND THE ENVIRONMENT UNIVERSITY OF MINNESOTA, 1970.
The Engineer and the environment. Papers. Sponsored by the Dept. of Conferences and Institutes of the Univ. of Minn. in cooperation with the American Society of Civil Engineers, Northwestern Section, Water Resources Group. 1971. (WRRC bulletin, no. 38)
GB701.M554no.38 ECOL

SERNAU, RUSSELL C., jt. auth.
Morton, Stephen D.
The carbon dioxide system and eutrophication. 1971. **fQH96.8.E9M6 ECOL**

SETON, ERNEST THOMPSON, 1860-1946.
Lives of game animals; an account of those land animals in America, north of the Mexican border, which are considered "game", either because they have held the attention of sportsmen, or received the protection of law... with 50 maps and 1500 illus. by the author. Doubleday, 1929. v. **QL151.S5 1925 ECOL**

SETZER, PAULETTE Y., jt. auth.
Cailliet, Greg M.
Everyman's guide to ecological living. 1971
GF75.C33 ECOL

SEYMOUR WHITNEY NORTH, comp.
Small urban spaces; the philosophy, design, sociology, and politics of vestpocket parks and other small urban open spaces. New York Univ. Press 1969
SB481.S48 ECOL

SHACKLETTE, HANSFORD T.
Elemental composition of surficial materials in the conterminous United States: an account of the amounts of certain chemical elements. 1971.
REF fQE75.P9no.574-D ECOL

SHADDUCK, GREGG.
Energy. University of Minn., 1971. (Secondary environmental education development)
HD9545.S5 ECOL

SHAINBERG, LOUIS W., jt. auth.
Jones, Kenneth Lester.
Environmental health. 1971. **RA565.J65 ECOL**

SHANKLIN, JOHN F., jt. auth.
Fitch, Edwin M.
The Bureau of Outdoor Recreation. 1970
GV53.F5 ECOL

SHANNON, TERRY.
About the land, the rain, and us. Illus. by Charles Payzant. Melmont Publishers 1963 (Look, read, learn)
PZ10.S52Ai ECOL

SHAPIRO, SIDNEY, ed.
National Marine Fisheries Service.
Our changing fisheries. 1971
REF SH331.N38 ECOL

SHAPP, CHARLES, jt. auth.
Shapp, Martha.
Let's find out about air. 1963.
PE1127.S3S417 ECOL

SHAPP, MARTHA.
Let's find out about air, by Martha and Charles Shapp. Pictures by Laszlo Roth. F. Watts, 1963.
PE1127.S3S417 ECOL

SHEAFFER, JOHN RICHARD.
Flood proofing; an element in a flood damage reduction program. 1960. **TC530.S4 ECOL**

SHELFORD, VICTOR ERNEST, 1877-
The ecology of North America. Univ. of Illinois Press, 1963. **QH102.S5 ECOL**

SHELTON, JOHN S.
Geology illustrated by John S. Shelton. Drawings by Hal Shelton. W. H. Freeman 1966 **fQE26.S5 ECOL**

SHERFIELD, ROGER MELLOR MAKINS, BARON, 1904- ed.
Economic and social consequences of nuclear energy. 1972. **HD9698.A3G74 ECOL**

SHERRELL, RICHARD E., ed.
Ecology: crisis and new vision. c1971
GF80.E25 ECOL

SHERROD, H. FLOYD, ed.
Environment law review. 1970-
REF KF3790.A2E5 ECOL

SHERWOOD, ROBERT J., jt. auth.
Unterberg, W.
Computerized design and cost estimation for multiple-hearth sludge incinerators. 1971 i.e. 1972
fTD770.U58 ECOL

SHINDALA, ADNAN.
Primary considerations in regional wastewater treatment planning. State College, Miss., Water Resources Research Institute, Mississippi State Univ., 1972. **fTD365.S4 ECOL**

SHIPLEY, MARGARET COBB, ed.
Western Resources Conference, 9th, University of Colorado, 1967.
Man and the quality of his environment. 1968
TD180.W4 1967 ECOL

SHOFNER, F. M.
Environmental Systems Corporation.
Development and demonstration of low-level drift instrumentation. 1971. **fTD884.5.E58 ECOL**

SHOMON, JOSEPH JAMES, 1914-
Manual of outdoor conservation education. National Audubon Society, Nature Centers Division 1964 (Information-education bulletin no. 3)
S946.S5 ECOL

Manual of outdoor interpretation. Edited by Joseph J. Shomon. National Audubon Society, Nature Centers Division 1968 **QH51.S5 ECOL**

Nature realms across America. American Froestry Association, 1972. **QH102.S54 ECOL**

Open land for urban America; acquisition, safekeeping, and use. Published in cooperation with the National Audubon Society, by Johns Hopkins Press 1971 **HD257.S56 ECOL**

Wildlife habitat improvement. By Joseph J. Shomon, Byron L. Ashbaugh and Con D. Tolman. Sketches by Ned Smith. Diagrs. by Robert F. Holmes. 2d print., rev. National Audubon Society, Nature Center Planning Division 1969 **SK361.S52 1969 ECOL**

SHORE, FERDINAND J., jt. auth.
Hull, Andrew P.
Sternglass: a case history. 1972?
REF fRA569.H8 ECOL

SHORTEN, MONICA, 1923- jt. auth.
Barkalow, Frederick Schenck.
The world of the gray squirrel. 1973
QL737.R68B37 ECOL

SHOWALTER, VICTOR M., jt. auth.
Rasmussen, Frederick A.
Man and the environment. 1970, c1971
QH316.5.R35 ECOL

SHUBB, MICHAEL, ed.
Snowmobile and Off the Road Vehicle Research Symposium, Michigan State University, East Lansing, 1971.
Proceedings. 1971. **fGF75.S6 1971 ECOL**

SHULTS, W. D., 1929- ed.
ACS Symposium on Determination of Air Quality, Los Angeles, 1971.
Determination of air quality. 1972.
TD890.A2 1971 ECOL

SHUMATE, K. S., 1937- jt. auth.
Smith, Edwin Earle.
Sulfide to sulfate reaction mechanism. 1970.
fTN321.S58 ECOL

SHUMATE, KENESAW S., jt. auth.
Morth, Arthur H.
Pyritic systems: a mathematical model. 1972.
TD899.M5M6 ECOL

SHUNNEY, EDWARD L.
Fram Corporation.
Bio-regenerated activated carbon treatment of textile dye wastewater. 1971. **fTD899.T4F7 ECOL**

SHUTTLESWORTH, DOROTHY EDWARDS, 1907-
Clean air, sparkling water; the fight against pollution. Doubleday 1968 **PZ10.S65CL ECOL**

SHUVAL, HILLEL I., 1926- ed.
Jerusalem International Conference on Water Quality and Pollution Research, 1969.
Developments in water quality research. 1970 **TD370.J47 1969 ECOL**

SICHEL, BEATRICE.
Guide to private citizen action environmental groups. School of Librarianship, Western Michigan Univ., 1973. **REF fS920.S53 ECOL**

SICKA, RICHARD W.
United States. Environmental Protection Agency. Office of Research and Monitoring.
Air modulated vacuum oil recovery collection of spilled oil (foams). 1972. **fTD427.P4U5 ECOL**

SIDWELL, ALBERT EDWIN, 1909-
Jacksonville, Ark.
Biological treatment of chlorophenolic wastes. 1971. **fTD755.J3 ECOL**

SIEGAN, BERNARD H.
Land use without zoning by Bernard H. Siegan. Lexington Books 1972 **HT167.S5 ECOL**

SIERRA CLUB.
Eber, Ronald.
Handbook. 1971 **HC68.E2 ECOL**
Norton, Boyd.
Snake wilderness. c1972. **QH105.I2N6 ECOL**
Plowden, David.
Floor of the sky: the Great Plains. 1972 **fF595.2.P56 ECOL**

SIERRA CLUB CONFERENCE ON THE ELECTRIC POWER INDUSTRY, 1ST, JOHNSON CITY, VT., 1972.
Report on the first Sierra Club power conference [papers]. Sierra Club?, 1972? v. **fHD9685.A2S5 1972 ECOL**

SIERRA CLUB. NORTH STAR CHAPTER (MINN.).
A wilderness in crisis: the Boundary Waters Canoe Area; an analysis by the North Star Chapter, the Sierra Club, in cooperation with the Natural History Society. c1970 **fQH76.5.M6S5 ECOL**

SIERRA CLUB, SAN FRANCISCO.
Ecotactics: the Sierra Club handbook for environmental activists. 1970 **HC110.E5E26 ECOL**
Leydet, Francois.
The last redwoods, and the parkland of Redwood Creek. 1969 **SD397.R3L4 ECOL**
Leydet, Francois.
Time and the river flowing: Grand Canyon. 1968 **F788.L482 ECOL**
Porter, Eliot.
The place no one knew: Glen Canyon on the Colorado. 1963 **fF832.C7P6 ECOL**
Schwartz, William.
Voices for the wilderness. 1969 **QH75.S32 ECOL**

SIGLER, WILLIAM F.
Wildlife law enforcement by William F. Sigler. 2d ed. Brown Co. 1972 **KF5640.S55 1972 ECOL**

SILVERBERG, ROBERT.
Rivers, by Lee Sebastian. 1st ed. Holt, Rinehart and Winston 1966 1 v. (A Book to begin on) **PZ10.S66Ri ECOL**
The world within the ocean wave. Illus. by Bob Hines. Weybright and Talley 1972 **QH91.8.P5S54 ECOL**

SIMEONE, JOHN B., ed.
Chemical ecology. 1970. **QH345.C435 ECOL**

SIMMS, DENTON HARPER, 1912-
The Soil Conservation Service by D. Harper Simms. Praeger 1970 (Praeger library of U.S. Government departments and agencies, no. 23) **S622.S44 ECOL**

SIMON, NOEL.
Last survivors; the natural history of animals in danger of extinction by Noel Simon and Paul Geroudet. Illus. by Helmut Diller and Paul Barruel. World Pub. Co. 1970 **QL88.S553 ECOL**

SIMON, NOEL, jt. auth.
Fisher, James.
Wildlife in danger. 1969 **REF QL88.F48 ECOL**

SIMON, SEYMOUR.
Science projects in ecology. Illustrated by Charles Jakubowski. Holiday House 1972 **QH541.14.S55 ECOL**

SIMONS, HERBERT E.
Mandan Refinery.
Fluid bed incineration of petroleum refinery wastes. 1971. **fTD899.P4M35 ECOL**

SIMPSON, GEORGE GAYLORD.
The meaning of evolution; a study of the history of life and its significance for man. Rev. ed. Yale Univ. Press 1969,c1967 **QH366.S58 1969 ECOL**

SIMPSON, GEORGE GAYLORD, 1902-
This view of life; the world of an evolutionist. Harcourt 1964 **QH369.S5 ECOL**

SINGER, SIEGFRIED FRED, 1924- ed.
Is there an optimum level of population? 1971 **HB851.I8 ECOL**
Symposium on the Global Effects of Environmental Pollution, Dallas, 1968.
Global effects of environmental pollution. 1970 **REF TD172.5.S95 1968 ECOL**

SINGLETON, ARTHUR L.
Sources of nuclear fuel by Arthur L. Singleton, Jr. U.S. Atomic Energy Commission, Division of Technical Information 1968 (Understanding the atom) **TN490.U7S52 ECOL**

SINHA, EVELYN.
Coastal/estuarine pollution, an annotated bibliography. Ocean Engineering Information Service 1970 (Ocean engineering information series v. 3) **REF fZ5853.P7S53 ECOL**
Lake and river pollution; an annotated bibliography. Ocean Engineering Information Service 1971 (Ocean engineering information series no. 4) **REF fZ7173.W3S5 ECOL**
Metals as pollutants in air and water; an annotated bibliography. Ocean Engineering Information Service, 1972. (Ocean engineering information series, v. 6) **REF fZ7171.S55 ECOL**
Methods, models & instruments for studies of aquatic pollution; an annotated bibliography. Ocean Engineering Service 1971 (Ocean engineering information series, v. 5) **REF fZ7173.W3S52 ECOL**

SKEHAN, JAMES WILLIAM, 1923- ed.
Science and the future of man. c1970 **CB151.S37 ECOL**

SKOGERBOE, GAYLORD V.
Evaluation of canal lining for salinity control in Grand Valley, by Gaylord V. Skogerboe and Wynn R. Walker. Prepared for Office of Research and Monitoring, U.S. Environmental Protection Agency. U.S. Govt. Print. Off., 1972. (Environmental protection technology series) **TC930.S5 ECOL**
Research needs for irrigation return flow quality control, by Gaylord V. Skogerboe and James P. Law, Jr. Prepared for the Office of Research and Monitoring, Environmental Protection Agency. U.S. Environmental Protection Agency: U.S. Govt. Print. Off., 1971 i.e. 1972 (Water pollution control research series) **fTD223.S54 ECOL**
Selected irrigation return flow; quality abstracts 1968/69- Prepared for Office of Research and Monitoring, U.S. Environmental Protection Agency. U.S. Govt. Print. Office, 1972- v. (Environmental protection technology series) **fTD223.S5 ECOL**

SKOGERBOE, GAYLORD V., jt. auth.
Walker, Wynn R.
Evaluation of urban water management policies in the Denver metropolitan area. 1973. **fTD225.D4W3 ECOL**

SKOLNIKOFF, EUGENE B., jt. auth.
Kay, David A.
World eco-crisis: international organizations in response. 1972 **HC79.E5K38 ECOL**

SLACK, ARCHIE VIVIAN, 1912-
Defense against famine; the role of the fertilizer industry by A. V. Slack. 1st ed. Doubleday, 1970. (Chemistry in action series) **S633.S627 ECOL**

SLATER, SIR WILLIAM KERSHAW, 1893-
Man must eat. Univ. of Chicago Press 1964 **TX355.S63 ECOL**

SLEIGH, J. H.
Gulf Environmental Systems Company.
Acid mine waste treatment using reverse osmosis. 1971 **fTD754.G84 ECOL**

SLEIGHT, ROBERT B.
Century Research Corporation.
Social aspects of urban water conservation. 1972. **fTD388.5.C4 ECOL**

SLOAN, IRVING J.
Environment and the law, by Irving J. Sloan. Oceana Publications, 1971. (Legal almanac series, no. 65) **KF3775.Z9S55 ECOL**

SLOAN, ROBERT EVAN, 1929- jt. auth.
Hogberg, Rudolph K.
Guide to fossil collecting in Minnesota. Rev. ed. 1967. **QE718.H55 1967 ECOL**

SLOSS, GEORGE J.
Environmental aspects of transportation planning (a revision of CPL Exchange bibliography no. 218). Council of Planning Librarians 1972 (Council of Planning Librarians. Exchange bibliography, no. 353) **REF fZ7164.T8S55 ECOL**
Water-related environmental planning. 1973. (Council of Planning Librarians Exchange bibliography, 365) **fZ5862.W3S5 ECOL**

SLOTE, LAWRENCE.
Grumman Aerospace Corporation.
Development of immobilized enzyme systems for enhancement of biological waste treatment processes. 1970 **fTD755.G78 ECOL**

SMALL, GEORGE L.
The blue whale by George L. Small. Columbia University Press, 1971. **QL737.C424S58 ECOL**

SMALL, HYDEE.
Nature's teakettle; geothermal energy for the people. Selected illus. by Marjie Ott. Geothermal Information Services c1973 **GB1003.S6 ECOL**

SMALL, WILLIAM E., 1937-
Third pollution; the national problem of solid waste disposal by William E. Small. Praeger 1971 **TD795.S56 1971 ECOL**

SMILLIE, WILSON GEORGE, 1886- jt. auth.
Kilbourne, Edwin D.
Human ecology and public health. 4th ed. 1969 **RA425.K55 1969 ECOL**

SMILLIE, WILSON GEORGE, 1886- Preventive medicine and public health. Kilbourne, Edwin D.
Human ecology and public health. 4th ed. 1969 **RA425.K55 1969 ECOL**

SMITH, ALEXANDER HANCHETT, 1904-
The mushroom hunter's field guide. Rev. and enl. Univ. of Mich. Press, 1970 c1963 **REF fQK617.S56 1963 ECOL**

SMITH, ALLEN E.
Ecological factors affecting waterfowl production in the Alberta parklands. Bureau of Sport Fisheries and Wildlife; for sale by the Supt. of Docs., U.S. Govt. Print. Off., 1971. (U.S. Bureau of Sport Fisheries and Wildlife. Resource publication 98) **S914.A3no.98 ECOL**

SMITH, DAVID D.
Ocean disposal of barge-delivered liquid and solid wastes from United States coastal cities, by David D. Smith and Robert P. Brown. Solid Waste Management Office, U.S. Environmental Protection Agency, 1971. (Solid waste management series) **TD796.7.O25S4 ECOL**

SMITH, EDWIN EARLE, 1923-
Sulfide to sulfate reaction mechanism; a study of the sulfide to sulfate reaction mechanism as it relates to the formation of acid mine waters by E. E. Smith and K. S. Shumate. U.S. Federal Water Quality Administration; for sale by the Supt. of Docs., U.S. Govt. Print. Off., 1970. (Water pollution control research series) **fTN321.S58 ECOL**

SMITH, EDWIN EARLE, 1923- jt. auth.
Morth, Arthur H.
Pyritic systems: a mathematical model. 1972. **TD899.M5M6 ECOL**

SMITH, FRANCES C., 1901-
The first book of conservation, by Frances C. Smith. Illus. by Mary DeBall Kwitz. 2d rev. ed. Watts, 1972. **S940.S64 1972 ECOL**
The first book of swamps and marshes, by Frances C. Smith. Watts 1968,c1969 **QH541.5.M3S6 ECOL**

SMITH, FRANK ELLIS, 1918-
The politics of conservation, by Frank E. Smith. Pantheon Books c1966 **S930.S56 ECOL**

SMITH, FRANK ELLIS, 1918- comp.
Land and water compiled by Frank E. Smith. Chelsea House Publishers, 1971. 2 v. (Conservation in the United States, a documentary history) **REF S930.S55 ECOL**

SMITH, FRED, 1908-
Man and his urban environment; a manual of specific considerations for the seventies and beyond. With introductions by Laurance S. Rockefeller and by Alexander H. Leighton and Jane M. Murphy. Man and His Urban Environment Project, 1972 **fHT151.S53 ECOL**

SMITH, FREDERICK E., jt. comp.
Matthews, William Henry.
Man's impact on terrestrial and oceanic ecosystems. 1971 **TD174.M39 ECOL**

SMITH, GEORGE EDWARD, 1913- ed.
Agricultural practices and water quality. 1971,c1970 **TD420.A33 ECOL**

SMITH, GUY HAROLD, 1895- ed.
Conservation of natural resources. Contributors: Robert M. Basile and others. 4th ed. Wiley 1971
S938.S58 1971 ECOL

SMITH, IVAN C.
United States. Environmental Protection Agency. Office of Research and Monitoring.
Control of mercury pollution in sediments. 1972.
TD427.M4U5 ECOL

SMITH, J. M., jt. auth.
Cha, C. Y.
Photochemical methods for purifying water. 1972.
TD459.C4 ECOL

SMITH, JAMES ERIC, 1909- , ed.
Marine Biological Association of the United Kingdom. Laboratory, Plymouth.
'Torrey Canyon' pollution and marine life: a report by the Plymouth Laboratory of the Marine Biological Association of the United Kingdom. 1968.
GC1311.M37 ECOL

SMITH, JOHN D., jt. auth.
Henager, Charles H.
Concept evaluation: recovery of floating oil using polyurethane foam sorbent. 1972.
fTD427.P4H4 ECOL

SMITH, JULIAN W.
Outdoor education by Julian W. Smith and others. Prentice-Hall, 1963. **LB1047.S58 1963 ECOL**

SMITH, LYNWOOD.
Washington (State). University. Fisheries Research Institute.
Responses of teleost fish to environmental stress. 1971. **fQL639.1.W3 ECOL**

SMITH, MALCOLM JULES, 1940-
Uniroyal, Inc.
Feasibility study of regenerative fibers for water pollution control. 1970 i.e. 1971
fTD757.5.U55 ECOL

SMITH, ROBERT, 1921-
Cost to the consumer for collection and treatment of wastewater, by Robert Smith and Richard G. Eilers. U.S. Environmental Protection Agency; for sale by the Supt. of Docs., U.S. Govt. Print. Off., 1970 i.e. 1972 (Water pollution control research series)
fTD523.S65 ECOL

SMITH, ROBERT LEO.
Ecology and field biology. Illustrated by Ned Smith. Harper & Row 1966 **QH541.S6 ECOL**

SMITH, ROBERT LEO, comp.
The ecology of man: an ecosystem approach. Harper & Row 1972 **fGF8.S6 ECOL**

SMITH, RONALD W.
Acid mine pollution effects on lake biology, by Ronald W. Smith and David G. Frey. Prepared for the Environmental Protection Agency. U.S. Environmental Protection Agency; for sale by the Supt. of Docs., U.S. Govt. Print. Off., 1971. (Water pollution control research series) **fTD899.M5S6 ECOL**

SMITH, STEPHEN C., ed.
Western Resources Conference. 7th, Colorado State University, 1965.
Water research. c1966
REF TD355.W4 1965 ECOL

SMITH, THOMAS W., jt. auth.
Ragland, Kenneth W.
Environmental studies at the CIC universities—a survey. 1971. **REF fQH541.2.R3 ECOL**

SMITH, WILLIAM MARTIN, 1935-
National Steel Corporation. Weirton Steel Division.
Combined steel mill and municipal waste-waters treatment. 1972. **fTD899.S7N37 ECOL**

SMITHSONIAN INSTITUTION.
The Fitness of man's environment. 1968
HT166.F53 ECOL

SMITHSONIAN INSTITUTION. CENTER FOR SHORT-LIVED PHENOMENA.
National and international environmental monitoring activities; a directory. 1970. **REF fTA171.S6 ECOL**

SMITHSONIAN INSTITUTION. CENTER FOR SHORT-LIVED PHENOMENA.
The pulse of the planet; a state of the earth report from the Smithsonian Institution Center for Short-lived Phenomena. Comp. and ed. by James Cornell and John Surowiecki. Harmony Books c1972 **fQ225.P8 ECOL**

SMITHSONIAN INSTITUTION. SCIENCE INFORMATION EXCHANGE.
CCM Information Corporation.
Environmental pollution. 1971.
REF fTD178.5.C2 ECOL

Water Resources Scientific Information Center.
Water resources thesaurus. 2d ed. 1971
REF Z695.1.W3W3 1971 ECOL

SMYTHE, WILLIAM ELLSWORTH, 1861-1922.
The conquest of arid America. Introd. by Lawrence B. Lee. University of Washington Press 1969,c1905 (American Library) **F591.S662 1969 ECOL**

SNEDAKER, SAMUEL C., jt. ed.
Lugo, Ariel E.
Readings on ecological systems: their function and relation to man. c1971 **QH540.3.L8 ECOL**

SNOWMOBILE AND OFF THE ROAD VEHICLE RESEARCH SYMPOSIUM, MICHIGAN STATE UNIVERSITY, EAST LANSING, 1971.
Proceedings. Sponsored by the Department of Park and Recreation Resources and the Agricultural Experiment Station, Michigan State University, and the Bureau of Outdoor Recreation, Dept. of Interior. Ed. by Michael Chubb. 1971. **fGF75.S6 1971 ECOL**

SNYDER, EDWIN F.
Preliminary report for the Subcommittee on Health, Economic and Nuisance Effects of Air Pollution, Governor's Advisory Committee on Air Resources. 1966. **fTD883.5.M65S6 ECOL**

SNYDER, LEON A., ed.
Symposium on Radioisotopes in the Biosphere, University of Minnesota, 1959.
A Symposium on Radioisotopes in the Biosphere. 1960. **QH652.S9 1959 ECOL**

SNYDER, LORRAINE HIATT.
The environmental challenge and the aging individual. Council of Planning Librarians 1972 (Council of Planning Librarians. Exchange bibliography, no. 254) **REF fZ7164.O4S63 ECOL**

SNYDER, WILLIAM COWPERTHWAITE, 1904- ed.
International Symposium on Factors Determining the Behavior of Plant Pathogens in Soil, Berkeley, Calif., 1963.
Ecology of soil-borne plant pathogens.
fQR111.I55 1963 ECOL

THE SOCIAL RESPONSIBILITY OF THE SCIENTIST.
Edited by Martin Brown. Free Press 1971
Q125.S714 ECOL

SOCIAL SCIENCE RESEARCH COUNCIL.
American Geographical Society of New York
Pioneer settlement. 1932. **GF51.A5 ECOL**

SOCOLOW, ROBERT H., jt. auth.
Harte, John.
Patient earth. 1971 **QH541.H26 ECOL**

SOFFER, L. M., jt. auth.
Envirogenics Company.
Investigation of a new phosphate removal process. 1970. **fTD745.E5 ECOL**

SOHN, LOUIS B.
Commission to Study the Organization of Peace.
The United Nations and the human environment. 1972 **HC68.C62 ECOL**

SOIL CONSERVATION SOCIETY OF AMERICA.
Proceedings of the annual meeting, 1971- v.
fS900.S6 ECOL

SOIL CONSERVATION SOCIETY OF AMERICA. MINNESOTA CHAPTER.
Water pollution by nutrients—sources, effects and control, papers presented at 1969 annual meeting. Water Resources Research Center, Univ. of Minnesota, Graduate School, 1969. (Minnesota. University. Water Resources Research Center. Bulletin 13)
GB701.M554no.13 ECOL

SOLID WASTE MANAGEMENT; abstracts from the literature. 1964-
U.S. Environmental Protection Agency. v.
REF Z5853.S22S6 ECOL

SOLID WASTE RESOURCES CONFERENCE, COLUMBUS, OHIO, 1971.
Design of consumer containers for re-use or disposal, proceedings ... and papers presented at the seminar co-sponsored by Batelle Memorial Institute-Columbus Laboratories and the U.S. Environmental Protection Agency, May 12 and 13, 1971. Comp. by George F. Sachsel. U.S. Environmental Protection Agency, 1972. (Solid waste management series)
TD785.S6 1971 ECOL

SOLID WASTES MANAGEMENT.
Sanitation industry year book. 9 ed. 1972-
REF fTD791.S3 ECOL

SOLLERS, ALLAN A.
Ours is the earth; appraising natural resources and conservation. Holt 1963 (Holt library of science, ser. 1, no. 9) **S930.S6 ECOL**

SOMMER, ROBERT.
Personal space; the behavioral basis of design. Prentice-Hall 1969 (A Spectrum book)
BF469.S64 ECOL

SONDHEIMER, ERNEST, 1923- ed.
Chemical ecology. 1970. **QH345.C435 ECOL**

SONGS OF THE FOREST.
Droll Yankees, 1964.
Phonodisc QL698.5.S63 ECOL

SOPER, TONY.
Arbib, Robert S.
The hungry bird book. 1971
QL676.5.A7 1971 ECOL

The bird table book
In: Arbib, Robert S. The hungry bird book. 1971
QL676.5.A7 1971 ECOL

SORENSON, MARIAN.
Hitch, Allen S.
Conservation and you. 1964 **S930.H5 ECOL**

SOUDERS, BUD.
The Organic classroom. c1973 **fS946.O7 ECOL**

SOUTH AFRICAN BIRD BOOK FUND.
Roberts, Austin.
Our South African birds (Ons Suid-Afrikaanse voels). 1941 **REF QL692.R62 ECOL**

SOUTH TAHOE PUBLIC UTILITY DISTRICT.
Advanced wastewater treatment as practiced at South Tahoe. Authors: Russell L. Culp, David R. Evans, and Jerry C. Wilson. Prepared for the Water Quality Office, Environmental Protection Agency. Environmental Protection Agency, Water Quality Office; for sale by the Supt. of Docs., U.S. Govt. Print. Off., 1971. (Water pollution control research series)
fTD225.T25S6 ECOL

SOUTHEAST WATER LABORATORY.
Catalog of pesticide NMR spectra. Authors: Ann L. Alford and Lawrence H. Keith. Environmental Protection Agency, Research and Monitoring; for sale by the Supt. of Docs., U.S. Govt. Print. Off., 1971. (Water pollution control research series)
fSB951.S64 ECOL

SOUTHERN CONFERENCE ON ENVIRONMENTAL RADIATION PROTECTION FROM NUCLEAR POWER PLANTS, ST. PETERSBURG, FLA., 1971.
Proceedings of Southern Conference on Environmental Radiation Protection from Nuclear Power Plants, April 21-22, 1971. U.S. Environmental Protection Agency. Office of Radiation Programs. Surveillance and Inspection Division, 1972.
TK9152.S6 ECOL

SOUTHERN INTERSTATE NUCLEAR BOARD.
Nuclear power plant safety. 1972? (its Administrator's guide, no. 2) **fTK9152.S62 ECOL**

SOUTHERN RESEARCH INSTITUTE, BIRMINGHAM, ALA.
Demineralization of wastewater by the transport-depletion process. U.S. Environmental Protection Agency; for sale by the Supt. of Docs., U.S. Govt. Print. Off., 1971. (Water pollution control research series) **fTD754.S67 ECOL**

SOWLS, LYLE K.
Prairie ducks; a study of their behavior, ecology, and management. Stacqpole, 1955. **QL696.A5S64 ECOL**

SPARKS, JOHN. BIRD BEHAVIOR.
Ardley, Neil.
How birds behave. 1971 **fQL785.5.B6A7 ECOL**

SPECIAL LIBRARIES ASSOCIATION.
Schildhauer, Carole.
Environmental information sources: engineering and industrial applications. 1972.
REF fZ5863.E57S34 ECOL

SPECIAL REPORT ECOLOGY.
Special Reports Inc., c1971- v.
REF fS936.S6 ECOL

SPECIAL REPORTS, INC.
Who's who in ecology, 1973-
REF fQH26.W46 ECOL

SPEDDING, C. R. W.
Grassland ecology by C. R. W. Spedding. Clarendon Press, 1971. **QH541.5.P7S65 ECOL**

SPENCER, JOHN D., jt. auth.
Linville, Bill.
Review of Bureau of Mines energy program, 1970. 1971 **TN295.U4no.8526 ECOL**

SPINRAD, BERNARD I., ed.
Lewis, Richard S.
The energy crisis. 1972. **fHC103.7.L4 ECOL**

SPOLIN, VIOLA.
Improvisation for the theater; a handbook of teaching and directing techniques. Northwestern University Press 1963 **PN2071.I5S6 ECOL**

SPROTT, E. R., jt. auth.
Carefoot, G. L.
Famine on the wind; man's battle against plant disease. 1967 **SB732.C37 ECOL**

SPROULL, WAYNE TREBER, 1906-
Air pollution and its control. Exposition Press 1970 (An Exposition-banner book) **TD883.S76 ECOL**

Air pollution and its control, by Wayne T. Sproull. 2d ed. rev. and enl. Exposition Press 1972 (An Exposition-banner book) **TD883.S76 1972 ECOL**

SPROUT, HAROLD HANCE, 1901-
The ecological perspective on human affairs, with special reference to international politics, by Harold and Margaret Sprout. Published for the Princeton Center of International Studies by Princeton Univ. Press, 1965. **JX1251.S49 ECOL**

SPROUT, HAROLD HANCE,
1901- Man-milieu relationship hypotheses in the context of international politics.
Sprout, Harold Hance.
The ecological perspective on human affairs. 1965. **JX1251.S49 ECOL**

SPROUT, MARGARET (TUTTLE) 1903- , jt. auth.
Sprout, Harold Hance.
The ecological perspective on human affairs. 1965. **JX1251.S49 ECOL**

SPRUNT, ALEXANDER, 1898-
Carolina low country impressions. Drawings by John Henry Dick. Devin, 1964. **REF QH105.S6S6 ECOL**

Florida bird life. Based upon and supplementary to Florida bird life, by Arthur H. Howell, published in 1932. Color plates from original paintings by Francis Lee Jaques and John Henry Dick. Coward 1954 **QL684.F6S65 ECOL**

Griscom, Ludlow.
The warblers of America. 1957. **REF QL696.P2G85 ECOL**

STABA, E. JOHN, jt. auth.
Su, K. Lee.
Aquatic plants from Minnesota, part 1—chemical survey. 1972. **GB701.M554no.46 ECOL**

Su, K. Lee.
Aquatic plants from Minnesota part 2—toxicity, anti-neoplastic, and coagulent effects. 1972. **GB701.M554no.47 ECOL**

Su, K. Lee.
Aquatic plants from Minnesota part 3—antimicrobial effects. 1972. **GB701.M554no.48 ECOL**

STACKS, JOHN F.
Stripping, by John F. Stacks. With an introd. by Harry M. Caudill. Sierra Club 1972 (A Sierra Club battlebook series, 6) **TN291.S7 ECOL**

STALL, JOHN B.
Storm sewer design—an evaluation of the RRL method, by John B. Stall and Michael L. Terstriep. Prepared for Office of Research and Monitoring, U.S. Environmental Protection Agency. U.S. Govt. Print. Off., 1972. (Environmental protection technology series) **TD665.S7 ECOL**

STALLINGS, JAMES HENRY.
Soil conservation. Foreword by R. B. Alderfer. Prentice-Hall, 1957. (Prentice-Hall field crop production series) **S623.S73 ECOL**

STANFORD ENVIRONMENTAL LAW SOCIETY.
Public land management—a time for change? 1971- v.1- **fHD216.S7 ECOL**

STANFORD RESEARCH INSTITUTE.
Robinson, Elmer.
Sources, abundance, and fate of gaseous atmospheric pollutants. 1968. **fTD885.R6 ECOL**

Robinson, Elmer.
Sources, abundance, and fate of gaseous atmospheric pollutants: supplement. 1969. **fTD885.R62 ECOL**

STANFORD RESEARCH INSTITUTE. DECISION ANALYSIS GROUP.
Decision analysis of nuclear plants in electrical system expansion: final report, by the Decision Analysis Group, Stanford Research Institute, in collaboration with the Nuclear Section of the Comision Federal de Electricidad, Menlo Park, Calif., 1968. **fTK1078.S7 ECOL**

STAPLEDON, SIR REGINALD GEORGE, 1882-1960.
Human ecology, by George Stapledon. 2nd ed.; edited and introduced by Robert Waller. C. Knight, 1971. (Classics of human ecology, v.1) **HM206.S65 1971 ECOL**

STAPLES, JAMES M., jt. auth.
Henkin, Harmon.
The environment, the establishment, and the law. 1971 **QH545.P4H4 ECOL**

STARBIRD, A. W., jt. auth.
Hogan, William T.
Optimum mechanical aeration systems for rivers and ponds. 1970. **fTD458.H64 ECOL**

STARKMAN, ERNEST S., ed.
Combustion-generated air pollution. 1971. **TD883.C575 1971 ECOL**

STATE OF WASHINGTON WATER RESEARCH CENTER.
Doerksen, Harvey R.
Columbia River Interstate Compact, politics of negotiation. 1972 **KF5590.C6D6 ECOL**

McKenzie, Linda.
The grass roots and water resources management. 1972. **fHD1691.M3 ECOL**

STEAR, JAMES R.
Municipal incineration: a review of literature, by James R. Stear. Research Triangle Park, N. C., Environmental Protection Agency, Office of Air Programs; for sale by the Supt. of Docs., U.S. Govt. Print. Off., 1971. (Office of Air Programs publication no. AP-79) **TD803.S82 ECOL**

STEARNS, JEAN PRIDE, 1919- , comp.
A catalog of the duck stamp prints with biographies of the artists. Stanley Stearns, c1967 1v. **REF fHE6185.U52S7 ECOL**

STECHER, ADAM.
Running water. By Adam Stecher and others Mine Publications c1971 (Examining your environment) **QH541.2.S8 ECOL**

STEEL, ERNEST WILLIAM, 1893- jt. auth.
Ehlers, Victor Marcus.
Municipal and rural sanitation. 6th ed. c1965 **REF RA425.E5 1965 ECOL**

STEELE, MARY Q.
The living year; an almanac for my survivors by Mary Q. Steele. Viking Press 1972 **QH81.S855 1972 ECOL**

STEERING COMMITTEE ON COASTAL WASTES MANAGEMENT.
Wastes management concepts for the coastal zone; requirements for research and investigation. National Academy of Sciences, 1970. **TD763.S7 ECOL**

STEFAN, HEINZ.
Surface discharge of heated water, by H. Stefan, N. Hayakawa, and F. R. Schiebe. Prepared for the Office of Research and Monitoring, Environmental Protection Agency. U.S. Govt. Print. Off., 1971 i.e. 1972 v. (Water pollution control research series) **fTD427.H4S64 ECOL**

STEIMLE, STEPHEN E., jt. auth.
Mayer, John K.
Sewer bedding and infiltration, Gulf Coast area. 1972. **fTD653.M3 ECOL**

STEIN, CLARENCE S.
Toward new towns for America. With an introd. by Lewis Mumford. Rev. ed. M.I.T. Press 1971,c1957 **NA9108.S8 1971 ECOL**

STEINHACKER, CHARLES.
Superior. Photographs by Charles Steinhacker with a text drawn from the journals, diaries, and other writings of travelers to Lake Superior from the years 1650 to 1800; assembled and ed. by Arno Karlen. Foreword by Senator Gaylord Nelson. Harper 1971? **fF552.S725 ECOL**

STEINHART, CAROL E.
Blowout; a case study of the Santa Barbara oil spill, by Carol E. Steinhart and John S. Steinhart. With a foreword by Walter J. Hickel. Duxbury Press 1972 **GC1556.S74 ECOL**

STEINHART, JOHN S., jt. auth.
Steinhart, Carol E.
Blowout. 1972. **GC1556.S74 ECOL**

STEJNEGER, LEONHARD HESS, 1851-
Golder, Frank Alfred.
Bering's voyage. 1922-25. **G296.B4G6 ECOL**

STENQUIST, RICHARD J.
Initial mixing in coagulation processes, by Richard J. Stenquist and Warren J. Kaufman. Prepared for Office of Research and Monitoring, U.S. Environmental Protection Agency. U.S. Govt. Print. Off., 1972. (Environmental protection technology series) **TD455.S7 ECOL**

STEPHENSON, ANNE, jt. auth.
Stephenson, Thomas Alan.
Life between tidemarks on rocky shores. 1972 **QH541.5.S3S68 ECOL**

STEPHENSON, THOMAS ALAN.
Life between tidemarks on rocky shores by T. A. Stephenson and Anne Stephenson. With a foreword by C. M. Yonge. W. H. Freeman 1972 **QH541.5.S3S68 ECOL**

STEPP, JAMES MARVIN.
The pollution problem, by J. M. Stepp and H. H. Macaulay. American Enterprise Institute for Public Policy Research 1968 **TD180.S65 ECOL**

STEPP, JAMES MARVIN, ed.
Coastal zone resource management. 1971 **HC110.E5C6 ECOL**

STERN, ARTHUR CECIL.
Air pollution, ed. by Arthur C. Stern. 2d ed. v.1- (Environmental science; an interdisciplinary monograph series) **REF TD883.S83 ECOL**

STERNGLASS, ERNEST.
Hull, Andrew P.
Sternglass: a case history. 1972? **REF fRA569.H8 ECOL**

STERNGLASS, ERNEST J.
Low-level radiation. Ballantine Books c1972. **RA569.S8 ECOL**

STEVENS, LEONARD A.
How a law is made: the story of a bill against air pollution, by Leonard A. Stevens. Illus. by Robert Galster. Crowell 1970 **KF3812.Z9S7 ECOL**

The town that launders its water; how a California town learned to reclaim and reuse its water, by Leonard A. Stevens. Coward, McCann & Geoghegan 1971 (The New conservation series) **TD429.S84 1971 ECOL**

STEVENSON, GORDON MCKAY.
The politics of airport noise by Gordon McKay Stevenson, Jr. Duxbury Press 1971, c1972 (The Duxbury Press series on public policy) **HE9797.4.N6S83 ECOL**

STEWART, ARVIS L., illus.
Johnson, Elinor M.
The plant hunters. 1969 **Fiction ECOL**

Wong, Herbert H.
Animal habitats: where can red-winged blackbirds live? 1970 **PZ10.W748An ECOL**

STEWART, CHARLES LESLIE, 1890-
Resources for the Future. Committee on Land Use Statistics.
Land use information. 1969, c1965 **HD205 1969.R4 ECOL**

STEWART, GEORGE RIPPEY, 1895-
Not so rich as you think by George R. Stewart. With drawings by Robert Osborn. Houghton Mifflin Co., c1967 **TD180.S68 ECOL**

STEWART, JAMES M.
Perception of water resources research, dissemination, and utilization of research findings, by James M. Stewart and David H. Howells. 1971 (North Carolina. University. Water Resources Research Institute. Report no. 58) **fHD1694.N8N6no.58 ECOL**

STEWART, ROBERT E.
Classification of natural ponds and lakes in the glaciated prairie region, by Robert E. Stewart and Harold A. Kantrud. U.S. Bureau of Sport Fisheries and Wildlife; for sale by the Supt. of Docs., U.S. Govt. Print. Off. 1971. (Bureau of Sport Fisheries and Wildlife. Resource publication, 92) **S914.A3no.92 ECOL**

STICHTING TOEKOMSTBEELD DER TECHNIEK.
Growing against ourselves: the energy-environment tangle. 1972. **TD195.E4G76 ECOL**

STILL, HENRY.
The dirty animal. Hawthorn Books c1967 **TD180.S7 ECOL**

In quest of quiet; meeting the menace of noise pollution: call to citizen action. Stackpole Books 1970 **RA772.N7S74 ECOL**

Will the human race survive? 1st ed. Hawthorn Books 1966 **Q125.S745 ECOL**

STOBER, WERNER, ed.
Rochester International Conference on Environmental Toxicity, 3d, 1970.
Assessment of airborne particles. 1972 **QD549.R59 1970 ECOL**

STOCHASTICS, INC., BLACKSBURG, VA.
Stochastic modeling for water quality management by Richard G. Krutchkoff. Prepared for the Environmental Protection Agency. U.S. Govt. Print. Off., 1971. (Water pollution control research series) **fTC409.S8 ECOL**

STOCK, DENNIS, illus.
Wayburn, Peggy.
Edge of life. c1972 **fQH541.5.E8W3 ECOL**

STOCKHOLM AND BEYOND. Report of the Secretary of State's Advisory Committee on ... 1972. **HC110.E5A43 ECOL**

STOEVENER, H. H. jt. auth.
Reiling, S. D.
Economic benefits from an improvement in water quality. 1973. **fTD370.R45 ECOL**

STOKER, DANIEL G., 1945-
Andrews, William A.
A guide to the study of freshwater ecology. 1972 **QH541.5.F7A48 ECOL**

STOKES, LEE W.
The photosynthetic pigments of Lake Superior periphyton and their relation to primary productivity; by Lee W. Stokes, Theodore A. Olson, Theron O. Odlaug. Water Resources Research Center, Univ. of Minn., 1970. (WRRC bulletin no. 18)
GB701.M554no.18 ECOL

STOLTENBERG, CARL H.
Planning research for resource decisions. 1st ed. 1970
HC55.P55 ECOL

STONE, PETER BENNET, 1933- jt. auth.
Horsfield, Brenda.
The great ocean business. 1st American ed. 1972
GC21.H63 1972b ECOL

STONE, ROBERT GRANVILLE, 1907-
Price, Archibald Grenfell.
White settlers in the tropics. 1939.
GF51.P7 ECOL

STONEHOUSE, BERNARD.
Animals of the Antarctic; the ecology of the Far South. 1st American ed. Holt, Rinehart & Winston 1972
fQL106.S76 1972 ECOL
Animals of the Arctic; the ecology of the Far North. 1st American ed. Holt, Rinehart & Winston 1971
fQH199.S83 1971 ECOL

STORER, JOHN HUMPHRIES, 1888-
Man in the web of life; civilization, science, and natural law by John H. Storer. New American Library 1968 (A Signet science library book, Q3664)
HM206.S7 ECOL
The web of life, a first book of ecology. With an introd. by Fairfield Osborn. Devin-Adair, 1953.
QH541.S68 ECOL

STOUDT, JEROME H.
Ecological factors affecting waterfowl production in the Saskatchewan Parklands. Bureau of Sport Fisheries and Wildlife; U.S. Govt. Print. Off., 1971. (United States. Bureau of Sport Fisheries and Wildlife. Resource publication 99)
S914.A3no.99 ECOL

STOUT, GARDNER D.
The shorebirds of North America. Editor and sponsor: Gardner D. Stout. Text by Peter Matthiessen. Paintings by Robert Verity Clem. Species accounts by Ralph S. Palmer. Viking Press 1967
fQL681.S78 ECOL

STRAKA, G. C.
Graphs of ground water levels in Minnesota, 1957-1961, by G. C. Straka and W. A. Miller. Prepared cooperatively by the Geological Survey, U.S. Dept. of the Interior and the Division of Waters, Minnesota Conservation Dept. 1963. (Minnesota. Dept. of Conservation. Division of Water. Bulletin no. 18)
fTD224.M6A3no.18 ECOL

STRAUB, CONRAD P.
Gibson, Ulric P.
Integrating water quality management into total water resources management in Minnesota. 1970.
GB701.M554no.23 ECOL

STRAUB, CONRAD P., jt. auth.
Johnson, Jack D.
Development of a mathematical model to predict the role of surface runoff and groundwater flow in over fertilization of surface waters. 1971.
GB701.M554no.35 ECOL

STRAUSS, WERNER, ed.
Air pollution control.
TD883.A474 ECOL

STREEBIN, LEALE E.
Demonstration of a full-scale waste treatment system for a cannery, by Leale E. Streebin, George W. Reid and Alan C. H. Hu. U.S. Environmental Protection Agency U.S. Govt. Print. Off., 1971. (Water pollution control research series)
fTD899.C3S87 ECOL

STREET, PHILIP, 1915-
Wildlife preservation. Regnery 1971,c1970
S962.S77 1971 ECOL

STREETER, SHERRY, illus.
Holden, Raymond Peckham.
Wildlife mysteries. 1972
QL49.H68 ECOL

STROBBE, MAURICE A., comp.
Understanding environmental pollution, ed. by Maurice A. Strobbe. Mosby Co., 1971.
QH545.A1S7 ECOL

STROBBE, MAURICE A., 1927-
Environmental science laboratory manual. Mosby Co., 1972.
TA171.S8 ECOL

STRONG, ANN LOUISE.
Planned urban environments: Sweden, Finland, Israel, the Netherlands, France. Johns Hopkins Press 1971
fHT166.S73 ECOL

STRUZESKI, ED.
Edison Water Quality Laboratory. Storm and Combined Sewer Overflows Section.
Environmental impact of highway deicing. 1971.
fTE220.E35 ECOL

STUDDARD, GLORIA J., comp.
Common environmental terms: a glossary. U.S. Environmental Protection Agency, 1973.
REF S922.S7 ECOL

STUDY OF CRITICAL ENVIRONMENTAL PROBLEMS.
Man's impact on the global environment; assessment and recommendations for action; MIT Press 1970
QH541.S73 ECOL

STUDY OF MAN'S IMPACT ON CLIMATE, STOCKHOLM, 1970.
Inadvertent climate modification; report. MIT Press 1971
QC981.S77 1970 ECOL

STUECKLEN, KARL W., illus.
Pringle, Laurence P.
From pond to prairie. 1972
PZ10.P669Ft ECOL

STUMP, PATRICIA L., comp.
Symposium on Solid Waste Demonstration Projects, Cincinnati, Ohio, 1971.
Solid waste demonstration projects. 1972.
TD785.A45 1971 ECOL

SU, K. LEE.
Aquatic plants from Minnesota, part 1—chemical survey; by K. Lee Su and E. John Staba. Water Resources Research Center, University of Minnesota, 1972. (WRRC bulletin no. 46)
GB701.M554no.46 ECOL
Aquatic plants from Minnesota part 2—toxicity, anti-neoplastic, and coagulent effects; by K. Lee Su and E. John Staba. Water Resources Research Center, University of Minnesota, 1972. (WRRC bulletin no. 47)
GB701.M554no.47 ECOL
Aquatic plants from Minnesota part 3—antimicrobial effects; by K. Lee Su, E. John Staba and Y. Abul-Hajj. Water Resources Research Center, Univ. of Minn., 1972. (WRRC bulletin no. 48)
GB701.M554no.48 ECOL

SUBARSKY, ZACHARIAH.
Living things in field and classroom; a Minnemast handbook for teachers of early elementary grades, by Zachariah Subarsky and others. 2d ed. Minnesota Mathematics and Science Teaching Project 1969
QH51.S9 1969 ECOL

SUDWORTH, GEORGE BISHOP, 1864-1927.
United States. Forest Service.
Forest trees of the Pacific slope. 1908.
REF QK481.S95 ECOL

SUFFOLK UNIVERSITY LAW REVIEW.
Zimmerman, Joseph Francis.
The role of the state legislature in air pollution abatement. n.d.
fKF3812.Z9Z5 ECOL

SUGGS, JAMES D.
Mercury pollution control in stream and lake sediments, by James D. Suggs, Donald H. Petersen and James B. Middlebrook of the Advanced Technology Center, Inc., Dallas, Texas, for the Office of Research and Monitoring, Environmental Protection Agency. U.S. Govt. Print. Off., 1972. (Water pollution control research series)
fTD427.M4S9 ECOL

SUNDARAM, THIRUKURUNGUDI RANGASAMY, 1937-
Cornell Aeronautical Laboratory, Inc., Buffalo.
Research on the physical aspects of thermal pollution. 1971.
fTD427.H4C67 ECOL

SUNDERMEYER, NIELS.
Fabun, Don.
The dynamics of change. 1967
fCB427.F25 ECOL

SURGEON GENERAL'S CONFERENCE ON SOLID WASTE MANAGEMENT FOR METROPOLITAN WASHINGTON, WASHINGTON, D. C., 1967. Proceedings.
Edited by Leo Weaver. U.S. National Center for Urban and Industrial Health; for sale by the Supt. of Docs., U.S. Govt. Print. Off., 1967.(U.S. Public Health Service publication no. 1729)
TD525.W2S7 1967 ECOL

SUROWIECKI, JOHN, comp.
Smithsonian Institution. Center for Shortlived Phenomena.
The pulse of the planet. c1972
fQ225.P8 ECOL

SUSQUEHANNA CORPORATION. ATLANTIC RESEARCH SYSTEMS DIVISION. MARINE SYSTEMS.
Recovery of floating oil rotating disk type skimmer. Prepared for the Water Quality Office, Environmental Protection Agency. Environmental Protection Agency, Water Quality Office; for sale by the Supt. of Docs., U.S. Govt. Print. Off., 1971. (Water pollution control research series)
fTD427.P4S9 ECOL

SUTTON, ANN.
Yellowstone: a century of the wilderness idea by Ann and Myron Sutton. Photos. by Charles Steinhacker and others. Macmillan, 1972
fQH105.W8S8 ECOL

SUTTON, HARRY ELDON, 1927- ed.
Mutagenic effects of environmental contaminants. 1972.
QH431.M958 ECOL

SUTTON, MYRON, jt. auth.
Sutton, Ann.
Yellowstone: a century of the wilderness idea. 1972
fQH105.W8S8 ECOL

SVENSKA VETENSKAPSAKADEMIEN, STOCKHOLM.
Study of Man's Impact on Climate, Stockholm, 1970.
Inadvertent climate modification. 1971
QC981.S77 1970 ECOL

SWAIN, DONALD C.
Wilderness defender; Horace M. Albright and conservation by Donald C. Swain. University of Chicago Press 1970
SB482.A4S95 ECOL

SWAIN, WAYLAND R.
The ecology of the second trophic level in Lakes Superior, Michigan and Huron by W. R. Swain, Theodore A. Olson and Theron O. Odlaug. Water Resources Research Center, Univ. of Minn., 1970. (Minnesota. University. Water Resources Research Center. WRRC Bulletin 26)
GB701.M554no.26 ECOL

SWAIN, WAYLAND R., jt. auth.
Olson, Theodore A.
The continuous plankton recorder: a review of the literature. 1966.
GB701.M554no.3 ECOL

SWAN, LESTER A.
The common insects of North America, by Lester A. Swan and Charles S. Papp. Foreword by Evert I. Schlinger. Illus. by Charles S. Papp. 1st ed. Harper & Row 1972
QL473.S9 ECOL

SWAN, MALCOLM D., ed.
Illinois. Northern Illinois University, De Kalb. Lorado Taft Field Campus. Dept. of Outdoor Teacher Education.
Tips and tricks in outdoor education. 1970
fLB1047.I44 ECOL

SWATEK, PAUL.
The user's guide to the protection of the environment. Walden edition Friends of the Earth/Ballantine Book 1970
TX335.S93 ECOL

SWEET, DAVID C.
The economic and social importance of estuaries, by David C. Sweet and others. Environmental Protection Agency, Water Quality Office, Technical Support Division, 1971. (Estuarine Pollution Study series—2)
GB454.E8S95 ECOL

SWENSON, HERBERT A., ed.
Water Resources Scientific Information Center.
Urban water planning. 1972.
REF Z7935.W3 ECOL

SWINDELL-DRESSLER COMPANY.
Process design manual for carbon adsorption, by Swindell-Dressler Company for the Environmental Protection Agency, Technology Transfer. U.S. Gov't. Print. Off., 1971. 1v.
REF fTD753.5.S9 ECOL

SWORD, BRYAN R.
Robert S. Kerr Water Research Center.
Denitrification by anaerobic filters and ponds. 1971.
fTD475.R6 ECOL
Robert S. Kerr Water Research Center.
Desalination of agricultural tile drainages. 1971.
TD479.R6 ECOL

SYKES, GODFREY GLENTON, 1861-
The Colorado delta, by Godfrey Sykes. Pub. jointly by Carnegie Institution of Washington and the American Geographical Society of New York, 1937. (American Geographical Society. Special publication no. 19)
F788.S958 ECOL

SYKES, ROBERT M., jt. auth.
Frea, James I.
Washout processes in lake systems. 1972.
fTD764.F74 ECOL

SYMONDS, RICHARD, 1918-
The United Nations and the population question, 1945-1970, by Richard Symonds and Michael Carder. McGraw-Hill 1973
HQ766.S888 ECOL

SYMPOSIUM OF STATE AND INTERSTATE SOLID WASTE PLANNING AGENCIES, ST. LOUIS, 1969.
Planning for solid waste management; proceedings. Edited by Lillian A. Gluckman. U.S. Environmental Protection Agency; for sale by the Supt. of Docs., U.S. Govt. Print. Off., 1971 (U.S. Public Health Service publication no. 2093)
TD523.S94 1969 ECOL

SYMPOSIUM ON CHEMICALS CONTROLLING INSECT BEHAVIOR, MPLS., 1969.
Chemicals controlling insect behavior. 1970.
QL461.S88 1969 ECOL

SYMPOSIUM ON EMISSIONS FROM CONTINUOUS COMBUSTION SYSTEMS, GENERAL MOTORS RESEARCH LABORATORIES, 1971.
Emissions from continuous combustion systems; proceedings. Edited by Walter Cornelius and William G. Agnew. Plenum Press, 1972.
TD881.S86 1971 ECOL

SYMPOSIUM ON ENERGY, RESOURCES AND THE ENVIRONMENT, MCLEAN, VA., 1972.
Symposium on energy, resources and the environment proceedings. Prepared by Mitre Corp. of McLean, Va. Dist. by National Technical Information Service, U.S. Dept. of Commerce, 1972. 3v.
fHD9540.1.S9 1972 ECOL

SYMPOSIUM ON ENGINEERING GEOLOGY IN THE URBAN ENVIRONMENT, SAN FRANCISCO, 1969.
Environmental planning and geology; proceedings. Donald R. Nichols and Catherine C. Campbell, coeditors. Geological Survey; U.S. Govt. Print. Off., 1971
TA705.S95 1969 ECOL

SYMPOSIUM ON ENVIRONMENTAL ASPECTS OF NUCLEAR POWER STATIONS, NEW YORK, 1970.
Environmental aspects of nuclear power stations. Proceedings of a symposium ... held by the International Atomic Energy Agency in co-operation with the United States Atomic Energy Commission in New York, 10-14 Aug. 1970. International Atomic Energy Agency, 1971. (Proceedings series) **REF TK9006.S887 1970 ECOL**

SYMPOSIUM ON MINERAL WASTE UTILIZATION.
Proceedings. 1st- 1968- v.
fTP995.A1S9 ECOL

SYMPOSIUM ON MONITORING, BIRTH DEFECTS AND ENVIRONMENT, ALBANY, N. Y., 1970.
Monitoring, birth defects and environment: the problem of surveillance; proceedings. Edited by Ernest B. Hook, Dwight T. Janerich and Ian H. Porter. Assistant editors: Sally Kelly and Richard G. Skalko. Academic Press, 1971. **RG627.S94 1970 ECOL**

SYMPOSIUM ON RADIOISOTOPES IN THE BIOSPHERE, UNIVERSITY OF MINNESOTA, 1959.
A Symposium on Radioisotopes in the Biosphere. Edited by Richard S. Caldecott and Leon A. Snyder. University of Minnesota, Center for Continuation Study of the General Extension Division, 1960.
QH652.S9 1959 ECOL

SYMPOSIUM ON RESEARCH METHODS, VIRGINIA POLYTECHNIC INSTITUTE, 1965.
Methods for land economics research. Papers ed. by W. L. Gibson, Jr., R. J. Hildreth and Gene Wunderlich. Univ. of Nebraska Press 1967?,c1966
HD110.S9 1965 ECOL

SYMPOSIUM ON SOLID WASTE DEMONSTRATION PROJECTS, CINCINNATI, OHIO, 1971.
Solid waste demonstration projects; proceedings. Comp. by Patricia L. Stump. U.S. Environmental Protection Agency, 1972. (Solid waste management series, SW-4p) **TD785.A45 1971 ECOL**

SYMPOSIUM ON THE GLOBAL EFFECTS OF ENVIRONMENTAL POLLUTION, DALLAS, 1968.
Global effects of environmental pollution; a symposium organized by the American Association for the Advancement of Science, held in Dallas, Texas, December 1968. Edited by S. Fred Singer. D. Reidel Pub. Co. 1970 **REF TD172.5.S95 1968 ECOL**

SYMPOSIUM ON THE WHITE-TAILED DEER IN MINNESOTA, ST. PAUL, MINNESOTA, 1971.
The white-tailed deer in Minnesota; proceedings of a symposium. Sponsored by Wildlife Society, Minnesota Chapter. Ed. by Maynard M. Nelson. (St. Paul?). Section of Game, Minnesota Dept. of Natural Resources 1972? **fQL737.U55S9 1971ECOL**

SYMPOSIUM ON UNDERGROUND WASTE MANAGEMENT AND ENVIRONMENTAL IMPLICATIONS, HOUSTON, TEX., 1971.
Underground waste management and environmental implications; proceedings. Ed. by T. D. Cook. American Association of Petroleum Geologists, 1972. (American Association of Petroleum Geologists. Memoir 18)
TD761.S95 1971 ECOL

SYMPOSIUM ON USE OF NUCLEAR TECHNIQUES IN THE MEASUREMENT AND CONTROL OF ENVIRONMENTAL POLLUTION, SALZBURG, 1970.
Nuclear techniques in environmental pollution. Proceedings of a symposium ... held by the International Atomic Energy Agency in Salzburg 26-30 Oct., 1970. International Atomic Energy Agency, 1971. (IAEA Proceedings series) **REF TD177.S9 1970 ECOL**

SYMPOSIUM ON WOLF MANAGEMENT IN SELECTED AREAS OF NORTH AMERICA, CHICAGO, 1970.
Wolf management in selected areas of North America. Proceedings of a symposium held in conjunction with the thirty-fifth North American Wildlife and Natural Resources Conference, Chicago, Ill., March 24, 1970. Ed. by S. E. Jorgensen and others. U.S. Dept. of the Interior, Bureau of Sport Fisheries and Wildlife 1970 **QL737.C22S9 1970 ECOL**

SYNECTICS CORPORATION.
A system for industrial waste treatment RD&D project priority assignment. Authors: H. C. Bramer, R. C. DeHaven, and A. W. Leavitt. Prepared for the Environmental Protection Agency. Environmental Protection Agency, Water Quality Office. U.S. Govt. Print. Off., 1971. (Water pollution control research series) **fTD897.5.S9 ECOL**

SYRACUSE UNIVERSITY. CIVIL ENGINEERING DEPT.
Benefits of water quality enhancement, by Dept. of Civil Engineering, Syracuse University. Author: Nelson L. Nemerow. Prepared for the Environmental Protection Agency. Environmental Protection Agency, Water Quality Office; for sale by the Supt. of Docs., U.S. Govt. Print. Off., 1970. (Water pollution control research series) **fTD365.S94 ECOL**

SYRACUSE UNIVERSITY. DEPT. OF BIOLOGY.
Inorganic sulfur oxidation by iron-oxidizing bacteria. Author: Donald G. Lundgren. Prepared for the Environmental Protection Agency. Environmental Protection Agency, Water Quality Office; for sale by the Supt. of Docs., U.S. Govt. Print. Off., 1971. (Water pollution control research series) **fQR84.S95 ECOL**

SYRACUSE UNIVERSITY. DIVISION OF THE SUMMER SESSIONS.
Man and his environment: the effects of pollution on man. 1972 **TD172.5.M35 ECOL**

SYRACUSE UNIVERSITY. ENVIRONMENTAL STUDIES INSTITUTE.
Man and his environment: the effects of pollution on man. 1972 **TD172.5.M35 ECOL**

SYRACUSE UNIVERSITY. LIBRARY.
Watkins, Jessie B.
Ecology and environmental quality. 1971.
REF fZ5322.E2W3 ECOL

T

TABERSHAW, IRVING R.
The toxicology of beryllium. U.S. National Institute for Occupational Safety and Health, 1972.
RA1231.B4T3 ECOL

TADLOCK, MAX, jt. comp.
Carvell, Fred J.
It's not too late. 1971 **HC110.E5C36 ECOL**

TAHORI, ALEXANDER SHALOM, 1919- ed.
International IUPAC Congress of Pesticide Chemistry, 2d, Tel-Aviv, 1971.
Chemical releasers in insects. c1971
SB951.I56 1971vol.3 ECOL

International IUPAC Congress of Pesticide Chemistry, 2d, Tel-Aviv, 1971.
Fate of pesticides in environment. 1972
SB951.I56 1971vol.6 ECOL

International IUPAC Congress of Pesticide Chemistry, 2d, Tel-Aviv, 1971.
Insecticide resistance, synergism, enzyme induction. c1971 **SB951.I56 1971vol.2 ECOL**

TALBOT, ALLAN R.
Power along the Hudson; the Storm King case and the birth of environmentalism by Allan R. Talbot. 1st ed. Dutton, 1972. **HD9685.U7C768 ECOL**

TAMPLIN, ARTHUR R.
Population control through nuclear pollution, by Arthur R. Tamplin and John W. Gofman. Foreword by Paul R. Ehrlich. Nelson-Hall Co. 1970
RA569.T35 ECOL

TAMPLIN, ARTHUR R., jt. auth.
Gofman, John William.
Poisoned power. 1971 **TK9152.G57 ECOL**

TAPP, D. RODNEY, jt. auth.
Landerman, Norman J.
Community resource. 1972 **TD195.S3L36 ECOL**

TARLOCK, A. DAN, 1940- jt. auth.
Meyers, Charles J.
Selected legal and economic aspects of environmental protection. 1971. **KF3775.A7M58 ECOL**

TATE, RO.
Desert animals. 1st U.S. ed. Harper & Row c1971 (Animal life series) **QL116.T37 1971 ECOL**

TAUBENFELD, HOWARD JACK, 1924- jt. auth.
Lay, S. Houston.
The law relating to activities of man in space. 1970
REF fJX5810.L39 ECOL

TAVERNER, PERCY ALGERNON, 1875-
Birds of Western Canada. 2d ed. rev. F. A. Acland, 1928. (Canada. National Museum, Ottawa. Bulletin no.41.) **Ref QH1.C13no.41 1928 ECOL**

TAYLOR, GORDON RATTRAY.
The biological time bomb. World Pub. Co. 1968
QH309.T25 1968 ECOL

TAYLOR, JOHN KEENAN, 1912-
Development of method for NTA analysis in raw water, by John K. Taylor and others. Prepared for Office of Research and Monitoring, U.S. Environmental Protection Agency. U.S. Govt. Print. Off., 1972. (Environmental protection technology series)
TP992.5.T3 ECOL

United States. National Bureau of Standards. Analytical Chemistry Division.
Interaction of nitrilotriacetic acid with suspended and bottom material. 1971. **fTD427.D4U64 ECOL**

TAYLOR, MILLER LEE, 1930- jt. auth.
Burch, William R.
Social behavior, natural resources, and the environment. 1972 **HM206.B84 ECOL**

TEAGUE, RICHARD D., ed.
A Manual of wildlife conservation. 1971.
fSK353.M35 ECOL

TEAL, JOHN.
Life and death of the salt marsh, by John and Mildred Teal. Illus. by Richard G. Fish. Little 1969
QH541.5.S24T4 ECOL

TEAL, MILDRED, jt. auth.
Teal, John.
Life and death of the salt marsh. 1969
QH541.5.S24T4 ECOL

TEALE, EDWIN WAY, 1899-
Journey into summer; a naturalist's record of a 19,000 mile journey through the North American summer. With photos. by the author. Dodd, 1960. (The American seasons) **QH104.T39 ECOL**

North with the spring; a naturalist's record of a 17,000 mile journey with the North-American spring. Illus. with photos. by the author. Dodd c1951
QH104.T42 ECOL

Photographs of American nature. Dodd 1972 1v.
fQH46.T4 ECOL

Wandering through winter; a naturalist's record of a 20,000-mile journey through the North American winter. With photos. by the author. Dodd, 1965.
QH104.T43 ECOL

TEBBUTT, T. H. Y.
Principles of water quality control, by T. H. Y. Tebbutt. 1st ed. Pergamon Press 1971 (The Commonwealth and international library of science, technology, engineering, and liberal studies)
TD365.T4 1971 ECOL

TEHON, LEO ROY, 1895-1954. Illinois plants poisonous to livestock.
Evers, Robert August.
Poisonous plants of the Midwest & their effects on livestock. 1972 **SB617.E9 ECOL**

TEILHARD CENTRE FOR THE FUTURE OF MAN.
The Teilhard Review.
Change or decay: a symposium on the Blueprint for survival. 1972. **HC68.T4 ECOL**

THE TEILHARD REVIEW.
Change or decay: a symposium on the Blueprint for survival, with an editorial by Margaret Mead and contributions by Stafford Beer and others. Teilhard Centre for the Future of Man, 1972.
HC68.T4 ECOL

TEITELBAUM, PERRY D., jt. auth.
Darmstadter, Joel.
Energy in the world economy. 1971
REF fHD9540.4.D37 ECOL

TEMPE, GERTRUDE G.
Education for survival. 1970-
QH541.2.E4 ECOL

TENNESSEE. EAST TENNESSEE STATE UNIVERSITY, JOHNSON CITY.
Environmental Quality Forum, East Tennessee State University, 1970.

The Nation's environment—problems and action. c1971 **TD172.5.E58 1970 ECOL**

TENNESSEE. STATE UNIVERSITY, MEMPHIS.
Effects of noise on wildlife and other animals. Prepared for the U.S. Environmental Protection Agency, Office of Noise Abatement and Control. U.S. Govt. Print. Off., 1971. **fQP82.2.N6T4 ECOL**

TERRY, MARK.
Teaching for survival. Foreword by Garrett Hardin. Ballantine Books, 1971 **QH541.2.T47 ECOL**

TERSTRIEP, MICHAEL L., jt. auth.
Stall, John B.
Storm sewer design—an evaluation of the RRL method. 1972. **TD665.S7 ECOL**

TESTIN, R. F., jt. auth.
Drobny, N. L.
Recovery and utilization of municipal solid waste: a summary of available cost and performance characteristics of unit processes and systems. 1971. **TD793.D76 ECOL**

TEXAS CHRISTIAN UNIVERSITY, FORT WORTH. DEPT. OF BIOLOGY.
Industrial wastes: effects on Trinity River ecology, Fort Worth, Texas. Authors: C. E. Murphy, etal. Prepared for the Office of Research and Monitoring, Environmental Protection Agency. U.S. Govt. Printing Office, 1971 i.e. 1972 (Water pollution control research series) **fTD224.T4T4 ECOL**

TEXAS TECH UNIVERSITY. DEPT. OF GEOSCIENCES.
Infiltration rates and groundwater quality beneath cattle feedlots, Texas High Plains. Environmental Protection Agency, Water Quality Office; for sale by the Supt. of Docs., U.S. Govt. Print. Off., 1971 (Water pollution control research series) **fTD899.F4T48 ECOL**

TEXAS TECH UNIVERSITY. WATER RESOURCES CENTER.
Characteristics of wastes from southwestern cattle feedlots. Prepared for the Environmental Protection Agency. U.S. Govt. Print. Off., 1971. (Water pollution control research series) **fTD899.F4T497 ECOL**

TEXAS. UNIV. AT AUSTIN. CENTER FOR RESEARCH IN WATER RESOURCES.
Austin, Texas
Design guides for biological wastewater treatment processes. 1971 i.e.1972 **fTD755.A87 ECOL**

TEXAS. UNIV. AT AUSTIN. ENVIRONMENTAL HEALTH ENGINEERING RESEARCH LABORATORY.
Austin, Texas
Design guides for biological wastewater treatment processes. 1971 i.e.1972 **fTD755.A87 ECOL**

TEXAS. UNIVERSITY AT AUSTIN. BUREAU OF BUSINESS RESEARCH. RESEARCH MONOGRAPH NO. 34.
Collier, Boyd.
Measurement and environmental deterioration. 1971 **HC79.I5C63 ECOL**

TEXAS. UNIVERSITY. MEDICAL BRANCH, GALVESTON.
Phosphorus removal and disposal from municipal wastewater. Prepared by Cecil H. Connell for the Environmental Protection Agency. Office of Research and Monitoring, Environmental Protection Agency; for sale by the Supt. of Docs., U.S. Govt. Print. Off., 1971. (Water pollution control research series) **fTD745.T43 ECOL**

THELEN, EDMUND.
Investigation of porous pavements for urban runoff control. 1972. **fTE215.I58 ECOL**

THEOBALD, ROBERT.
An alternative future for America II; essays and speeches. 2d ed. Swallow Press 1970 **HN65.T44 1970 ECOL**
The economics of abundance; a noninflationary future. Pitman 1970 **HB171.T48 ECOL**
Habit and habitat. Prentice-Hall 1972 **GF47.T45 ECOL**

THEODORSON, GEORGE A., ed.
Studies in human ecology. Harper 1961 **HM206.T48 ECOL**

THIBEAU, CHARLES E., ed.
NFEC directory of environmental information sources. **REF fHC110.E5N4 ECOL**

THIEL, GEORGE ALFRED, 1892- jt. auth.
Schwartz, George Melvin.
Minnesota's rocks and waters. 1954 **QE127.A22no.37 ECOL**
Schwartz, George Melvin.
Minnesota's rocks and waters. Rev. ed. 1963 **QE127.A22no.37 1963 ECOL**

THIER, HERBERT D.
Science Curriculum Improvement Study. Material objects: teacher's guide. 1971 **LB1585.S3 ECOL**

THIMSEN, DONALD J.
Biological treatment in aerated lagoons: theory and practice. Minnesota Dept. of Health, Section of Water Pollution Control, 1965. **fTD746.5.T5 ECOL**

THIRRING, HANS, 1888-
Energy for man; windmills to nuclear power. Greenwood 1968 **TJ147.T48 1968 ECOL**

THISTLETHWAYTE, D. K. B.
Imhoff, Karl.
Disposal of sewage and other waterborne wastes. 2d ed. 1971. **TD741.I5813 1971b ECOL**

THOMAS, AARON JOSHUA, 1918- jt. auth.
Thomas, Ann (Van Wynen).
Legal limits on the use of chemical and biological weapons. 1970 **REF JX5135.C5T55 ECOL**

THOMAS, ANN (VAN WYNEN).
Legal limits on the use of chemical and biological weapons by Ann Van Wynen Thomas & A. J. Thomas, Jr. Foreword by Charles O. Galvin. Southern Methodist University Press 1970 (An SMU Law School study) **REF JX5135.C5T55 ECOL**

THOMAS, CARL O.
Environmental Systems Corporation.
Development and demonstration of low-level drift instrumentation. 1971. **fTD884.5.E58 ECOL**

THOMAS, HAROLD ALLEN, ed.
Models for managing regional water quality. 1972. **TD365.M6 ECOL**

THOMAS, MYRA H., comp.
Watt, Lois B.
Environmental - ecological education: a bibliography of fiction, nonfiction, and textbooks for elementary and secondary schools. 1971. **REF fQH541.2.W34 ECOL**

THOMAS, S. JOE, jt. auth.
Glasstone, Samuel.
Atomic energy and your world. 1970 **QC792.G55 ECOL**

THOMAS, WILLIAM A., 1939- ed.
Indicators of environmental quality. 1972. **TD172.5.I5 1972 ECOL**

THOMAS, WILLIAM L., 1920- ed.
International Symposium on Man's Role in Changing the Face of the Earth, Princeton, N.J., 1955.
Man's role in changing the face of the earth. 1970,c1956 **G56.I63 1955 ECOL**

THOMPSON, C. G., jt. auth.
Gainesville, Fla. Dept. of Public Utilities.
Magnesium carbonate, a recycled coagulant for water treatment. 1971. **fTD433.G3 ECOL**

THOMPSON, DENNIS L., comp.
Politics, policy, and natural resources. Edited by Dennis L. Thompson. Free Press 1972 **HC110.E5T48 ECOL**

THOMPSON, PHILIP DUNCAN.
Weather, by Philip D. Thompson, Robert O'Brien, and the editors of Time-Life Books. Time-Life Books 1969 (Life science library) **fQC863.T5 1969 ECOL**

THOMSEN, ARVID L.
Riprap stability on earth embankments tested in large—and small-scale wave tanks, by Arvid L. Thomsen, Paul E. Wohlt and Alfred S. Harrison. U.S. Army, Corps of Engineers, Coastal Engineering Research Center and Missouri River Division, 1972. (U.S. Coastal Engineering Research Center. Technical memorandum, no. 37) **TC533.T4 ECOL**

THOREAU, HENRY DAVID, 1817-1862.
In wildness is the preservation of the world, from Henry David Thoreau. Selections and photos. by Eliot Porter. Introd. by Joseph Wood Krutch. Ballantine Books, 1971,c1962 **TR660.T5 1971 ECOL**

THORNLEY, PETER, illus.
Harris, Reg.
Natural history collecting. 1972 **QH60.H36 ECOL**

THORNSJO, MARK.
Planning. University of Minnesota, 1971. (Secondary environmental education development) **HT166.T5 ECOL**

THORUD, DAVID B.
Freezing in forest soil as influenced by soil properties, litter, and snow; selections and photos. by David B. Thorud and David A. Anderson. Water Resources Research Center, Univ. of Minnesota, 1969. (WRRC bulletin no. 10) **GB701.M554no.10 ECOL**

THRASHER, W. R., ed.
Interdisciplinary Environmental Education. Sources of reference materials & audiovisual aids for environmental education. 2d rev. ed. 1972 **Ref fQH541.2.I68 1972 ECOL**

THRUSTON, ALFRED D.
Liquid chromatography of carbamate pesticides. Prepared for National Environmental Research Center, Office of Research and Monitoring, U.S. Environmental Protection Agency. U.S. Govt. Print. Off., 1972. (Environmental protection technology series) **SB951.T4 ECOL**

TIDEMAN, PHILIP L., jt. auth.
Baron, Norman J.
A survey of attitudes towards the Mississippi River as a total resource in Minnesota. 1972. **GB701.M554no.55 ECOL**

TIERNEY, G. F., jt. auth.
Young, G. K.
The importance of economic factors in urban surface water supply systems. 1972. **fTD353.Y6 ECOL**

TIETZE, FREDERICK INGLEBRIT, 1916- jt. comp.
McKeown, James E.
The changing metropolis. 2d ed. 1971 **HT334.U5M321971ECOL**

TILDEN, PAUL M.
Toward an environmental policy. 1971 **fHC110.E5T66 ECOL**

TILLIS, C. RICHARD.
McCue, George.
Ecology. c1971 **QH541.M22 Suppl. ECOL**
McCue, George.
Ecology: the city. c1971 **QH541.5.C6M23 ECOL**
McCue, George.
Ecology: the deserts and man. c1971 **QH541.5.D4M22 ECOL**
McCue, George.
Ecology: the farm. c1971 **QH541.5.F3M22 Suppl. ECOL**
McCue, George.
Ecology: the forests and man. c1971 **QH541.5.F6M22 Suppl. ECOL**
McCue, George.
Ecology: the freshwaters and man. c1971 **QH541.5.F7M22 ECOL**
McCue, George.
Ecology: the grasslands and man. c1971 **QH541.5.P7M22 Suppl. ECOL**
McCue, George.
Ecology: the mountains and man. c1971 **QH541.5.M65M22 Suppl. ECOL**
McCue, George.
Ecology: the oceans and man. c1971 **QH541.5.S3M22 ECOL**
McCue, George.
Ecology: the suburbs. c1971 **QH541.5.C6M22 ECOL**

TILLOTSON, DAVID.
Patterns for preservation: a conservation text. Great Northern Pub. Corp. 1969 **fS938.T5 ECOL**

TIME-LIFE BOOKS.
Abbey, Edward.
Cactus country. 1973 **QH88.A2 ECOL**
Bowen, Ezra.
The high Sierra. 1972 **F868.S5B6 ECOL**
Brown, Dale.
Wild Alaska. 1972 **QH105.A4B7 ECOL**
Farb, Peter.
Ecology. c1970 **fQH541.F3 1970 ECOL**
Johnson, William Weber.
Baja California. **F1246.J6 ECOL**
Knauth, Percy.
The North Woods. 1972 **QH75.K63 ECOL**
Leonard, Jonathan Norton.
Atlantic beaches. 1972 **GB459.4.L46 ECOL**
Leopold, Luna Bergere.
Water. Rev. 1970,c1966 **fGB671.L4 1970 ECOL**
Thompson, Philip Duncan.
Weather. 1969 **fQC863.T5 1969 ECOL**
Wallace, Robert.
The Grand Canyon. 1972 **F788.W23 ECOL**

TINBERGEN, NIKOLAAS, 1907-
Curious naturalists. Anchor Books, Doubleday 1968,c1958 (Natural history library N44) **QL751.T55 1968 ECOL**

TODD, DAVID KEITH, 1923-
The water encyclopedia; a compendium of useful information on water resources. Edited by David Keith Todd. Water Information Center 1970 **REF TD351.T63 ECOL**

TODD, DAVID KEITH, 1923- jt. auth.
Giefer, Gerald J.
Water publications of State agencies. 1972 **REF Z7935.G55 ECOL**

TOEPFER, CAROLINE T. comp.
Environmental psychology: selected readings. Edited by Caroline T. Toepfer and others MSS Information Corp. 1972 **HM206.T6 ECOL**

TOERBER, EDWIN D.
Full scale parallel activated sludge process evaluation. Prepared for Office of Research and Monitoring, U.S. Environmental Protection Agency. U.S. Govt. Print. Office, 1972. (Environmental protection technology series) **TD756.T6 ECOL**

TOLMAN, CON D., jt. auth.
Shomon, Joseph James.
Wildlife habitat improvement. 2d print., rev. 1969 **SK361.S52 1969 ECOL**

TOLTZ, KING, DUVALL, ANDERSON AND ASSOCIATES, INC., ST. PAUL.
Report on the expansion of the sewage treatment plant, Minneapolis-St. Paul Sanitary District. 1969. v. **fTD525.T9T6 ECOL**

TORCHIO, MENICO.
The world beneath the sea. With a foreword by Maurice Burton. World Publishing 1972 (The World of nature) **fQH91.17.T6 ECOL**

TORONTO. UNIVERSITY.
Ecology and physiology of parasites. 1971 **QL757.E26 ECOL**

TOSCO, UBERTO.
The flowering wilderness. With a foreword by George Taylor. World Pub. 1972 (The World of nature) **QK50.T6713 ECOL**

TOUHILL, C. J., ed.
Resource management in the Great Lakes Basin. 1971 **HD1694.A2 1971 ECOL**

TOWARD AN ENVIRONMENTAL POLICY; the policy and editorial comment of the National Parks and Conservation Association over the years of the expanded program, 1958-1971.
Compiled by Paul M. Tilden National Parks and Conservation Association 1971 **fHC110.E5T66 ECOL**

TOWARD THE YEAR 2018.
Ed. by the Foreign Policy Association. Cowles Education Corp. c1968 **CB161.T6 ECOL**

TOXICANTS OCCURRING NATURALLY IN FOODS.
National Academy of Sciences, National Research Council, 1966.(National Research Council Publication 1354) **TX531.T6 ECOL**

TOXICOLOGIC AND EPIDEMIOLOGIC BASES FOR AIR QUALITY CRITERIA.
Introd. by Samuel S. Epstein. Air Pollution Control Association, 1969 **REF fTD890.T6 ECOL**

TRACOR, INC.
Estuarine modeling: an assessment; capabilities and limitations for resource management and pollution control, by George H. Ward and William H. Espey, Tracor, Inc. for the Water Quality Office, Environmental Protection Agency. Environmental Protection Agency, Water Quality Office; for sale by the Supt. of Docs., U.S. Govt. Print. Off. 1971. (Water pollution control research series) **fTD370.T73 ECOL**

TRANSPORTATION NOISES: A SYMPOSIUM ON ACCEPTABILITY CRITERIA.
Edited by James D. Chalupnik. University of Washington Press 1970 **TA365.T68 ECOL**

TRATNYEK, JOSEPH P.
Waste wool as a scavenger for mercury pollution in waters. Prepared for the Office of Research and Monitoring, Environmental Protection Agency. U.S. Govt. Print. Off., 1972. (Water pollution control research series) **fTD427.M4T7 ECOL**

TRC—THE RESEARCH CORPORATION OF NEW ENGLAND.
Proposal to the State of Minnesota Pollution Control Agency: Highlights of implementation plan for sulfur dioxide, particulates, carbon monoxide, hydrocarbons, nitrogen oxides, photochemical oxidant. 1971. **Ref fTD883.5.M6T15 ECOL**

TREFETHEN, JAMES B.
Crusade for wildlife; highlights in conservation progress. Color plates by Carl Rungius; drawings by Bob Hines. Stackpole Co., 1961. (A Boone and Crockett Club book) **SK361.T7 ECOL**

Wildlife management and conservation by James B. Trefethen. Illustrated by Bob Hines. Prepared in cooperation with the Wildlife Management Institute. D. C. Heath 1964 (Science resource series) **S962.T7 ECOL**

TRESHOW, MICHAEL.
Environment & plant response. McGraw-Hill 1970 (McGraw-Hill publications in the agricultural sciences) **QK754.T7 ECOL**

TREWARTHA, GLENN THOMAS, 1896-
An introduction to climate by Glenn T. Trewartha. Cartography by Randall D. Sale. 4th ed. McGraw-Hill 1968 (McGraw-Hill series in geography) **QC981.T65 1968 ECOL**

TREZISE, MARILYN, jt. auth.
Winston, Eric V. A.
Directory of urban affairs information and research centers. 1970. **HT110.W5 ECOL**

TROOST, CORNELIUS J., comp.
Environmental education: a sourcebook. Edited by Cornelius J. Troost & Harold Altman. Wiley 1972 **QH541.2.T76 ECOL**

TROY, JOSEPH C.
Oxidation of pyrites in chlorinated solvents, by Joseph C. Troy, Joseph A. Boros and Donald R. Brenneman. Prepared for Office of Research and Monitoring, U.S. Environmental Protection Agency. U.S. Govt. Print. Off., 1972. (Environmental protection technology series) **TD899.M5T7 ECOL**

TSIVOGLOU, E. C.
Characterization of stream reaeration, capacity, by E. C. Tsivoglou and J. R. Wallace. Prepared for Office of Research and Monitoring, U.S. Environmental Protection Agency. U.S. Govt. Print. Off., 1972. (Ecological research series) **fTD458.T7 ECOL**

TUCK, LESLIE M., 1911-
The murres; their distribution, populations and biology; a study of the genus Uria. R. Duhamel, Queen's printer 1960 i.e. 1961 (Canadian wildlife series, 1) **QL696.A3T8 ECOL**

TUCKER, EDWIN A.
Men who matched the mountains; the Forest Service in the Southwest, by Edwin A. Tucker and George Fitzpatrick. U.S. Gov't Print. Off. 1972. **SD143.T8 ECOL**

TUCKER, L. SCOTT.
Metropolitan industrial water use, by L. Scott Tucker, Jaime Millan and Wilford W. Burt. American Society of Civil Engineers, 1972. (American Society of Civil Engineers. ASCE Urban Water Resources Research Program. Technical memorandum no. 16) **fTD223.T8 ECOL**

TUFFORD, SARAH P.
Hogberg, Rudolph K.
Guide to fossil collecting in Minnesota. Rev. ed. 1967. **QE718.H55 1967 ECOL**

TUNNARD, CHRISTOPHER.
Man-made America: chaos or control? An inquiry into selected problems of design in the urbanized landscape, by Christopher Tunnard and Boris Pushkarev in association with Geoffrey Baker and others. With drawings by Philip Lin and Vladimir Pozharsky and photos. by John Reed and Charles R. Schulze. Yale University Press 1963 **fNA9108.T82 ECOL**

TUNNICLIFFE, CHARLES FREDERICK, 1901- illus.
Priestley, Mary.
A book of birds. 1938. **PN6110.B6P75 ECOL**

TUNZI, MILTON G.
United States. Environmental Protection Agency. Office of Research and Monitoring.
The effects of agricultural waste water treatment on algal bioassay response. 1971. **QH96.8.E9U54 ECOL**

TURK, AMOS.
Ecology, pollution, environment by Amos Turk, Jonathan Turk and Janet T. Wittes. Saunders, 1972. (Saunders golden series) **TD174.T87 ECOL**

TURNER, BILLY G.
Georgia Kraft Company. Research and Development Center.
Treatment of selected internal kraft mill wastes in a cooling tower. 1971. **fTD899.W65G46 ECOL**

TURNER, D. BRUCE, 1931-
Workbook of atmospheric dispersion estimates. Environmental Protection Agency, 1970. **fTD890.T8 1970 ECOL**

TURNER, JAMES S.
The chemical feast; the Ralph Nader study group report of food protection and the Food and Drug Administration, by James S. Turner, project director and others. Grossman Publishers, 1970. **HD9000.9.U5T83 ECOL**

TWENTIETH CENTURY FUND.
America's needs and resources: a new survey, by J. Frederic Dewhurst and associates. 1969,c1955 **REF HC106.5.T9 1969 ECOL**

Barker, Carol M.
Classified files: the yellowing pages. 1972. **JK468.S4B35ECOL**

TWIN CITY AREA URBAN CORPS. ENERGY EDUCATION PROJECT.
Overconsumption of energy; a Minnesota crisis, 1971. 1v. **fHD9547.M5T8 ECOL**

TYCO LABORATORIES.
Electrochemical treatment of acid mine waters. Prepared for the Environmental Protection Agency. U.S. Environmental Protection Agency; for sale by the Supt. of Docs., U.S. Govt. Print. Off., 1972. (Water pollution control research series) **fTD899.M5T88 ECOL**

TYLER, HAMILTON A.
Organic gardening without poisons by Hamilton Tyler. Van Nostrand Reinhold 1970 **S605.5.T9 ECOL**

TYLINEK, ERICH, jt. auth.
Ullrich, Wolfgang.
Endangered species. 1972,c1971 **fQL77.5.U45 ECOL**

TYLINEK, ISABELLA, jt. auth.
Ullrich, Wolfgang.
Endangered species. 1972,c1971 **fQL77.5.U45 ECOL**

U

UDALL, STEWART L.
America's natural treasures; national nature monuments and seashores by Stewart L. Udall. Country Beautiful Corp.; dist. by Rand McNally 1971 **fE160.U28 ECOL**

1976: agenda for tomorrow by Stewart L. Udall. 1st ed. Harcourt, Brace & World 1968 **HN65.U3 ECOL**

The quiet crisis. Introd. by John F. Kennedy. 1st ed. Holt, Rinehart and Winston 1963 **S930.U3**

ULLRICH, WOLFGANG.
Endangered species by Wolfgang Ullrich, Erich and Isabella Tylinek. Hart Publishing Co. 1972,c1971 **fQL77.5.U45 ECOL**

ULRICH, STANLEY.
Superior pollutor: a saga of the struggle to stop pollution of the largest fresh water lake in the world by its most egregious polluter—the Reserve Mining Company, by Stanley Ulrich, Timothy J. Berg and Deborah Hedlund. Ed. by Eileen Bannon. Northern Environmental Council, 1972. **TD224.M6U6 ECOL**

UNDERWOOD, JOANNA.
Council on Economic Priorities.
Paper profits: pollution in the pulp and paper industry. c1972 **TD899.W65C65 1972 ECOL**

Council on Economic Priorities.
Paper profits: pollution in the pulp and paper industry. 1971 **REF fTD888.P8C6 ECOL**

THE UNFORSEEN INTERNATIONAL ECOLOGIC BOOMERANG.
Ed. by M. Taghi Farvar [et al] Conservation Foundation, 1969 **fQH541.U5 ECOL**

UNIROYAL, INC.
Feasibility study of regenerative fibers for water pollution control. Authors: R. W. Fuest and M. J. Smith. Prepared for the Environmental Protection Agency. U.S. Environmental Protection Agency; for sale by the Supt. of Docs., U.S. Govt. Print. Off., 1970 i.e. 1971 (Water pollution control research series) **fTD757.5.U55 ECOL**

UNITED AIRCRAFT CORPORATION. RESEARCH LABORATORIES, EAST HARTFORD, CONN.
Advanced nonthermally polluting gas turbines in utility applications. Prepared for the Environmental Protection Agency, Water Quality Office. Authors: F. R. Biancardi, G. T. Peters, and A. M. Landerman. Environmental Protection Agency, Water Quality Office; for sale by the Supt. of Docs., U.S. Govt. Print. Off., 1971. (Water pollution control research series) **fTJ778.U5 ECOL**

UNITED NATIONS.
Resources for the Future.
Design for a worldwide study of regional development. 1966 **HD82.R43 ECOL**

Winton, Harry N. M.
Man and the environment: a bibliography of selected publications of the United Nations system, 1946-1971. 1972. **REF Z5322.E2W56 ECOL**

UNITED NATIONS CONFERENCE OF THE HUMAN ENVIRONMENT, 1972.
Stockholm and beyond. 1972. **HC110.E5A43 ECOL**

UNITED NATIONS CONFERENCE ON THE HUMAN ENVIRONMENT, STOCKHOLM, 1972.
Jackson, Barbara (Ward) Lady.
Only one earth. 1st ed. 1972 **GF41.J3 ECOL**

UNITED NATIONS CONFERENCE ON THE HUMAN ENVIRONMENT, 1972.
Study of Critical Environmental Problems. Man's impact on the global environment. 1970
QH541.S73 ECOL

UNITED NATIONS. ECONOMIC COMMISSION FOR EUROPE.
Problems relating to iron and steel scrap. United Nations, 1971. (United Nations. Document ST/ECE/Steel/33) **fTS214.U6 ECOL**

UNITED NATIONS EDUCATIONAL, SCIENTIFIC AND CULTURAL ORGANIZATION.
UNISIST: study report on the feasibility of a world science system, by the United Nations Educational, Scientific and Cultural Organization and the International Council of Scientific Unions. Unesco; H.M.S.O. 1971. (its Document SC. 70/D.75/A) **REF Q223.U5 ECOL**

UNITED STATES.
Canada.
Agricultural pollution of the Great Lakes Basin. 1971. **fTD223.3.C25 ECOL**

The potential for energy conservation; a staff study. Office of Emergency Preparedness U.S. Govt. Print. Off. 1972. **TJ153.U43 ECOL**

UNITED STATES. AD HOC COMMITTEE ON THE CUMULATIVE REGULATORY EFFECTS ON THE COST OF AUTOMOTIVE TRANSPORTATION.
Cumulative regulatory effects on the cost of automotive transportation (RECAT): final report. 1972. v. **KF2209.A3U5 ECOL**

UNITED STATES. ADVISORY COMMISSION ON INTERGOVERNMENTAL RELATIONS.
The quest for environmental quality; federal and state action, 1969-70, with annotated bibliography. U.S. Govt. Print. Off., 1971. **HC110.E5A41 ECOL**

UNITED STATES. ADVISORY PANEL ON MUTAGENICITY OF PESTICIDES.
The Mutagenicity of pesticides: concepts and evaluation. 1971 **RA1270.P4M87 ECOL**

UNITED STATES. AGRICULTURAL STABILIZATION AND CONSERVATION SERVICE.
Rural environmental assistance program: summary. 1971- 1972- v. **S954.U6A3 ECOL**

UNITED STATES. ARMY. CORPS OF ENGINEERS.
Flood plain information, Red River of the North, Fargo, North Dakota—Moorhead, Minnesota. Prepared for the cities of Fargo—Moorhead. 1972. **GB1227.R4A52 ECOL**

Flood plain information on the Red River of the North in the vicinity of Grand Forks, North Dakota—East Grand Forks, Minnesota. 1971. **GB1227.R4A5 ECOL**

Interim survey report on Blue Earth River, Minnesota, Minnesota River Basin for flood control and related purposes. 1970? 1v. **Ref fTC424.M6A5 ECOL**

Upper Mississippi River comprehensive basin study. 1970- **fHC107.A15U6 ECOL**

W. Fork Des Moines River and Perkins Creek flood plain information, Windom, Minnesota. Prepared for State of Minnesota, Dept. of Conservation. 1972. **GB1225.M6A5 ECOL**

UNITED STATES. ARMY CORPS OF ENGINEERS. MISSOURI RIVER DIVISION.
Thomsen, Arvid L.
Riprap stability on earth embankments tested in large—and small-scale wave tanks. 1972. **TC533.T4 ECOL**

U.S. ARMY NATICK LABORATORIES, NATICK, MASS.
Radiation preservation of foods. 1965. **TX611.R28 ECOL**

UNITED STATES. ATOMIC ENERGY COMMISSION.
Atomic energy in use. For sale by the Supt. of Docs., U.S. Govt. Print. Off., 1965 **TK9146.U55 ECOL**

Casarett, Alison P.
Radiation biology. 1968 **QH652.C3 ECOL**

Compaction of radioactive solid waste; prepared by AEC Working Group on Compaction. 1970. **fTD898.U5 ECOL**

The first reactor. U.S. Atomic Energy Commission, Division of Technical Information 1967 (its Understanding the atom) **QC787.N8U52 ECOL**

Fox, Charles H.
Radioactive wastes. c1965 **TD898.F6 ECOL**

Fox, Charles H.
Radioactive wastes. Rev. 1969. **TD898.F6 1969 ECOL**

Fundamental nuclear energy research. 1971- For sale by the Supt. of Docs., U.S. Govt. Print. Off. v. **QC788.U5 ECOL**

Illustrations of radio-isotopes: definitions and applications. U.S. Atomic Energy Commission, Division of Technical Information 196-? **TK9400.U5 ECOL**

Index to the Understanding the atom series. U.S. Atomic Energy Commission, Division of Technical Information 1970 **REF Z5160.U4915 1970 ECOL**

The new force of atomic energy: its development and use. Prepared by G. Robinson. Office of Public Relations and Public Education. U.S. Govt. Print. Off. n.d. **TK9146.U5 ECOL**

Northern States Power Company (of Minnesota). Environmental report. 1971. **fTD877.5.N6 ECOL**

Northern States Power Company (of Minnesota). Environmental report. expanded and updated ed. 1971. **fTD877.5.N62 1971 ECOL**

Northern States Power Company (of Minnesota). Environmental report: Monticello Nuclear Generating Plant. 1971. **fTD877.5.N64 ECOL**

Nuclear Power and the environment. U.S. Atomic Energy Commission, Division of Technical Information; U.S. Govt. Print. Off., 1969. (Its Understanding the atom) **TK1343.A46 ECOL**

Radiation preservation of foods. 1965. **TX611.R28 ECOL**

Symposium on Environmental Aspects of Nuclear Power Stations, New York, 1970.
Environmental aspects of nuclear power stations. 1971. **REF TK9006.S887 1970 ECOL**

The United States Atomic Energy Commission; what it is, what it does. USAEC, Division of Technical Information Extension, 1965 **HD9698.A2U5 ECOL**

United States. Office of Science and Technology. Considerations affecting steam power plant site selection. 1968 **TK1193.U5A44 ECOL**

UNITED STATES. ATOMIC ENERGY COMMISSION. DIRECTORATE OF LICENSING.
Postma, Arlin Keith.
Review of organic iodide formation under accident conditions in water-cooled reactors. 1972. **fTK9152.P6 ECOL**

UNITED STATES. ATOMIC ENERGY COMMISSION. DIVISION OF INDUSTRIAL PARTICIPATION.
The nuclear industry. 1971- U.S. Govt. Print. Off. v. **TK9023.A35 ECOL**

UNITED STATES. ATOMIC ENERGY COMMISSION. DIVISION OF OPERATIONS AND FORECASTING.
Forecast of growth of nuclear power. Atomic Energy Commission, 1971. **TK9145.U5 ECOL**

UNITED STATES. ATOMIC ENERGY COMMISSION. DIVISION OF REACTOR DEVELOPMENT AND TECHNOLOGY.
Operating history of United States nuclear power reactors. U.S. Govt. Print. Off., 1971. v. **fTK1343.A467 ECOL**

Operating history of U.S. nuclear power reactors. U.S. Govt. Print. Off., 1972. v. **fTK1343.A467 1972 ECOL**

Thermal effects and United States nuclear power stations. for sale by the Supt. of Docs., U.S. Govt. Print. Off., 1971. 1v. **TD427.H4U52 ECOL**

UNITED STATES. ATOMIC ENERGY COMMISSION. DIVISION OF TECHNICAL INFORMATION.
Safety manual for use of operators dealing with radiography and industrial gammagraphy. Tr. from the French by P. S. Baker. Centre d'Etudes de Prevention 1968? **TA417.25.U5 ECOL**

Science teachers handbook. n.d. **fQ181.S3 ECOL**

UNITED STATES. ATOMIC ENERGY COMMISSION. OFFICE OF SAFEGUARDS AND MATERIALS MANAGEMENT.
United States. Brookhaven National Laboratory. Upton, N.Y. Technical Support Organization. Safeguards dictionary. 1971. **JX1974.7.U5 ECOL**

UNITED STATES. BROOKHAVEN NATIONAL LABORATORY. UPTON, N.Y. TECHNICAL SUPPORT ORGANIZATION.
Safeguards dictionary. U.S. Atomic Energy Commission, Office of Safeguards and Materials Management, 1971. **JX1974.7.U5 ECOL**

U.S. BUREAU OF INTERNATIONAL COMMERCE.
Environmental control seminar proceedings. 1971. **fTD172.5.E26 ECOL**

UNITED STATES. BUREAU OF LAND MANAGEMENT.
All around you: an environmental study guide. U.S. Govt. Print. Off. 1971. **S946.U5 ECOL**

UNITED STATES. BUREAU OF MINES.
Automobile disposal; a national problem. Case studies of factors that influence the accumulation of automobile scrap. For sale by the Supt. of Docs., U.S. Govt. Print. Off., 1967 **HD9710.U52A27 ECOL**

Control of sulfur oxide emissions in copper, lead, and zinc smelting, by Staff, Bureau of Mines. U.S. Dept. of the Interior, Bureau of Mines, 1971 **TN295.U4no.8527 ECOL**

Effective technology for recycling metal. 1971 **fTS214.E36 ECOL**

Haas, Larry A.
Sulfur dioxide: its chemistry as related to methods for removing it from waste gases. 1973 **TN23.U7no.8608 ECOL**

Kenahan, Charles B.
Bureau of Mines research programs on recycling and disposal of mineral-, metal-, and energy-based wastes. 1973. **TN23.U7no.8595 ECOL**

List of Bureau of Mines publications and articles, with subject and author index. 1965/1969- U.S. Govt. Print. Off. v. (its Special publication) **REF Z6736.U759 ECOL**

Mineral facts and problems by the Staff of the Bureau of Mines. U.S. Dept. of the Interior, Bureau of Mines, 1970. (its Bulletin 650) **REF TN23.U4no.650 ECOL**

Minerals yearbook. U.S. Govt. Print. Off., 1969- v. **REF TN23.U612 ECOL**

Symposium on Mineral Waste Utilization. Proceedings. 1st- 1968- **fTP995.A1S9 ECOL**

UNITED STATES. BUREAU OF OUTDOOR RECREATION.
Lennon, J.
Establishing trails on rights-of-way. n.d. **G504.L4 ECOL**

The 1965 nationwide inventory of publicly owned recreation areas and an assessment of private recreation enterprises. U.S. Govt. Print. Off., n.d. **fGV53.A47 1965 ECOL**

The 1970 survey of outdoor recreation activities; preliminary report. U.S. Govt. Print. Off., 1972. **GV53.A472 1970 ECOL**

Selected outdoor recreation statistics. For sale by the Supt. of Docs., U.S. Govt. Print. Off., 1971. **fGV53.A47 1971 ECOL**

U.S. BUREAU OF RADIOLOGICAL HEALTH.
Pettigrew, George L.
State and Federal control of health hazards from radioactive materials other than materials regulated under the Atomic energy act of 1954 (as of October 1, 1969). 1971. **RA1231.R2U5125no.71-4 ECOL**

UNITED STATES. BUREAU OF RECLAMATION.
Design of small dams. 2nd ed. U.S. Govt. Print. Off. 1973. (its A Water resources technical publication) **TC540.U615 1973 ECOL**

Summary report of the Commissioner of the Bureau of Reclamation to the Secretary of the Interior for the fiscal year ended June 30, 1970- and statistical and financial appendix. v. **REF TC823.A27 ECOL**

Thesaurus of water resources terms; a collection of water resources and related terms for use in indexing technical information. U.S. Govt. Print. Off. 1971. **REF Z695.1.W3U52 ECOL**

UNITED STATES. BUREAU OF SOLID WASTE MANAGEMENT *see also* UNITED STATES. OFFICE OF SOLID WASTE MANAGEMENT PROGRAMS.; UNITED STATES. SOLID WASTE MANAGEMENT OFFICE.

American Public Works Association. Institute for Solid Wastes.
Municipal refuse disposal. 3d ed. 1970 **TD795.A45 1970 ECOL**

Muhich, Anton J.
Preliminary data analysis. 1968 **TD795.M82 ECOL**

National Association of Counties Research Foundation.
Solid waste management. 1972? **fTD791.N3 ECOL**

UNITED STATES. BUREAU OF SPORT FISHERIES AND WILDLIFE.
National survey of fishing and hunting, 1970- U.S. Govt. Print. Office. v. (its Resource publication 95) **REF S914.A3no.95 ECOL**

UNITED STATES. BUREAU OF SPORT FISHERIES AND WILDLIFE. DIVISION OF WILDLIFE RESEARCH.
Wildlife research: problems programs, progress, 1969. 1971 (U.S. Bureau of Sport Fisheries and Wildlife. Resource publication 94) **S914.A3no.94 ECOL**

UNITED STATES. BUREAU OF SPORT FISHERIES AND WILDLIFE. OFFICE OF ENDANGERED SPECIES AND INTERNATIONAL ACTIVITIES.
Threatened wildlife of the United States. U.S. Govt. Print. Off., 1973. (U.S. Bureau of Sport Fisheries and Wildlife. Resource publication 114) **S914.A3no.114 1973 ECOL**

UNITED STATES. BUREAU OF THE CENSUS.
Environmental quality control; expenditure and employment for selected large governmental units: fiscal 1969/70- U.S. Govt. Print. Off. v. **REF HC110.E5A26 ECOL**

Pocket data book, USA. 1971- U.S. Govt. Print. Off. v. **REF HA195.A54 ECOL**

Statistical abstract of the United States, v.92- 1971- v. **REF HA202.U5 ECOL**

U.S. BUREAU OF VETERINARY MEDICINE.
The Use of drugs in animal feeds. 1969. **SF98.M4U8 ECOL**

UNITED STATES. CITIZENS ADVISORY COMMITTEE ON ENVIRONMENTAL QUALITY.
Community action for environmental quality. For sale by the Supt. of Docs., U.S. Govt. Print. Off., 1970 **HC110.E5A5 ECOL**

Report to the President and to the Council on Environmental Quality. 1971. **HC110.E5A514 ECOL**

UNITED STATES CITIZENS' ADVISORY COMMITTEE ON RECREATION AND NATURAL BEAUTY.
United States. Electric Utility Industry Task Force on Environment.
The electric utility industry and the environment. 1968? **HD9685.U5U5 ECOL**

UNITED STATES. COMMISSION ON POPULATION GROWTH AND THE AMERICAN FUTURE.
Governance and population: the governmental implications of population change. Ed. by A. E. Keir Nash. U.S. Gov't. Print. Off., 1972. (its Research reports, vol. 4.) **HB3505.A526 ECOL**

Population and the American future; the report. U.S. Govt. Print. Off. 1972 **fHB3505.A525 ECOL**

Population, resources, and the environment. Ed. by Ronald G. Ridker. U.S. Govt. Print. Off., 1972 (United States. Commission on Population Growth and the American Future. Research reports, v. 3) **HB3505.A527 ECOL**

UNITED STATES. COMMITTEE ON RARE AND ENDANGERED WILDLIFE SPECIES.
Rare and endangered fish and wildlife of the United States. Rev. ed. For sale by the Supt. of Docs., U.S. Govt. Print. Off., 1968 i.e. 1969 1 v. (United States Bureau of Sport Fisheries and Wildlife. Resource publication 34) **S914.A3no.34 1969 ECOL**

UNITED STATES CONGRESS.
Official congressional directory. U.S., Govt. Print. Off. **REF JK1011.A3 ECOL**

UNITED STATES. CONGRESS. HOUSE. COMMITTEE ON GOVERNMENT OPERATIONS. CONSERVATION AND NATURAL RESOURCES SUBCOMMITTEE.
The environmental decade (action proposals for the 1970's). Hearings, Ninety-first Congress, second session. United States Govt. Print. Off., 1970. **KF27.G636 1970a ECOL**

Public access to reservoirs to meet growing recreation demands. Hearing before a subcommittee of the Committee on Government Operations ... Ninety-second Congress, first session. June 15, 1971. U.S. Govt. Print. Off., 1971. **KF27.G636 1971 ECOL**

UNITED STATES. CONGRESS. HOUSE. COMMITTEE ON INTERIOR AND INSULAR AFFAIRS.
Compilation of federal laws relating to fuel and energy resources. U.S. Gov't. Print. Off., 1972. **KF2120.A25 1972 ECOL**

Fuel and energy resources. Hearings, Ninety-second Congress, second session ... U.S. Govt. Print. Off., 1972 **KF27.I5 1972 ECOL**

United States. Water Resources Council.
Ohio River Basin comprehensive survey—main report and development program formulation. 1971. **HD1695.O5A55 ECOL**

UNITED STATES. CONGRESS. HOUSE COMMITTEE ON PUBLIC WORKS.
United States. President, 1969- (Nixon).
Control of hazardous polluting substances. 1971. **TD365.U53 ECOL**

UNITED STATES. CONGRESS. JOINT COMMITTEE ON ATOMIC ENERGY.
Certain background information for consideration when evaluating the "national energy dilemma". Prepared at the request of Melvin Price, Chairman, Joint Committee on Atomic Energy, by staff of JCAE. U.S. Gov't. Print. Off., 1973. **HD9545.A53 ECOL**

UNITED STATES. CONGRESS. SENATE. COMMITTEE ON INTERIOR AND INSULAR AFFAIRS.
Energy research policy alternatives. Hearings, Ninety-second Congress, second session, on existing federal energy research and development policies and future technological options. June 7, 1972. U.S. Govt. Print. Off., 1972. **KF26.I5 1972 ECOL**

Geothermal energy resources and research. Hearings, pursuant to S. Res. 45, a national fuels and energy policy study, Ninety-second Congress, second session ... June 15 and 22, 1972. U.S. Govt. Print. Off., 1972. **KF26.I5 1972j ECOL**

United States. Library of Congress. Environmental Policy Division.
Congress and the Nation's environment. 1973. **KF3775.A25 1973 ECOL**

UNITED STATES. CONGRESS. SENATE. COMMITTEE ON INTERIOR AND INSULAR AFFAIRS. SUBCOMMITTEE ON PUBLIC LANDS.
Preservation of wilderness areas. Hearing, Ninety-second Congress, second session on S. 2453 and related wilderness bills to designate certain lands as wilderness. May 5, 1972. U.S. Govt. Print. Off., 1972. **KF26.I547 1972 ECOL**

UNITED STATES. COUNCIL ON ENVIRONMENTAL QUALITY.
The Economic impact of pollution control. 1972. **TD180.E25 ECOL**

Environmental quality; annual report. 1st- 1970- U.S. Govt. Print. Off. v. **HC110.E5A52 ECOL**

Integrated pest management, prepared by the Council on Environmental Quality. U.S. Govt. Print. Off. 1972. **SB950.U5 ECOL**

Michigan. University. Advisory Committee on Predator Control.
Predator control—1971: report to the Council on Environmental Quality and the Dept. of the Interior. 1972. **fQL758.M5 ECOL**

Ocean dumping: a national policy; a report to the President. For sale by the Supt. of Docs., U.S. Govt. Print. Off. 1970. **TD763.U55 ECOL**

The President's 1972 environmental program. 1972. **HC110.E5P74 ECOL**

United States. Citizens' Advisory Committee on Environmental Quality.
Report to the President and to the Council on Environmental Quality. 1971. **HC110.E5A514 ECOL**

UNITED STATES. DEPT. OF AGRICULTURE.
Minnesota. University. Agricultural Extension Service.
Soils, soil management and fertilizer monographs. 1973. **fS591.M68 ECOL**

National Conference on Soil, Water, and Suburbia, Washington, D.C., 1967.
Soil, water, and suburbia. 1968 **fHT166.N36 1967 ECOL**

UNITED STATES. DEPT. OF AGRICULTURE. ECONOMIC RESEARCH SERVICE.
United States. Soil Conservation Service.
Big Sioux River Basin and related areas. 1973. **HD1695.B5A5 ECOL**

UNITED STATES. DEPT. OF COMMERCE.
The Economic impact of pollution control. 1972. **TD180.E25 ECOL**

UNITED STATES. DEPT. OF HEALTH, EDUCATION AND WELFARE.
Conference in the Matter of Pollution of the Interstate Waters of the Red River of the North, North Dakota—Minnesota, Fargo, N.D., 1965.
Proceedings. **fTD225.R34C6 1965 ECOL**

UNITED STATES DEPT. OF HOUSING AND URBAN DEVELOPMENT.
Metropolitan open space and natural process. 1970. **HT394.P5M46 ECOL**

National Conference on Soil, Water, and Suburbia, Washington, D.C., 1967.
Soil, water, and suburbia. 1968 **fHT166.N36 1967 ECOL**

U.S. DEPT. OF INTERIOR. BUREAU OF OUTDOOR RECREATION.
Snowmobile and Off the Road Vehicle Research Symposium, Michigan State University, East Lansing, 1971.
Proceedings. 1971. **fGF75.S6 1971 ECOL**

U.S. DEPT. OF INTERIOR. BUREAU OF SPORT FISHERIES, AND WILDLIFE.
Symposium on Wolf Management in Selected Areas of North America, Chicago, 1970.
Wolf management in selected areas of North America. 1970 **QL737.C22S9 1970 ECOL**

UNITED STATES. DEPT. OF STATE.
Environmental Studies Board. Committee for International Environmental Programs.
Institutional arrangements for international environmental cooperation. 1972. **HC79.E5E6 ECOL**

UNITED STATES DEPT. OF THE AIR FORCE.
United States Dept. of the Army.
Herbicide manual for noncropland weeds. 1970. **SB611.U5 ECOL**

UNITED STATES DEPT. OF THE ARMY.
Herbicide manual for noncropland weeds by Dept. of the Army, the Navy and the Air Force. 1970. **SB611.U5 ECOL**

UNITED STATES. DEPT. OF THE INTERIOR.
Dupree, Walter G.
United States energy through the year 2000. 1972 **HD9545.D8 ECOL**

It's your world; the grassroots conservation story. Dept. of the Interior, Office of Information, 1969 (its Conservation yearbook no. 5) **fS930.A45 ECOL**

Man, an endangered species? U.S. Govt. Print. Off., 1968 (its Conservation yearbook no. 4) **fS914.A53 ECOL**

Michigan. University. Advisory Committee on Predator Control.
Predator control—1971: report to the Council on Environmental Quality and the Dept. of the Interior. 1972. **fQL758.M5 ECOL**

Our environment and natural resources ... indivisibly one. 1971? (Conservation yearbook series, no. 8) **fS914.A533 ECOL**

Our living land. For sale by the Supt. of Docs., U.S. Govt. Print. Off., 1971 (Conservation yearbook series, vol. no. 7) **S914.A535 ECOL**

Quest for quality; conservation yearbook. U.S. Dept. of the Interior, Off. of the Secretary; for sale by the Superintendent of Documents, U.S. Govt. Print. Off., 1965 (its Conservation yearbook, no. 1) **fS930.A5 ECOL**

The third wave. For sale by the Supt. of Docs., U.S. Govt. Print. Off., 1966 (Its Conservation yearbook no. 3) **S914.A54 ECOL**

United States. Task Force on Off-Road Recreation Vehicles.
Off road recreation vehicles: ORRV, a Dept. of the Interior Task Force Study. 1971. **TL234.U5 ECOL**

UNITED STATES. DEPT. OF THE INTERIOR. FEDERAL ADVISORY COMMITTE ON WATER DATA.
Federal Interagency Water Data Handling Work Group.
Design characteristics for a national system to store, retrieve, and disseminate water data. 1971. **TD211.F4 ECOL**

UNITED STATES. DEPT. OF THE INTERIOR. LIBRARY.
Dictionary catalog of the department library. G. K. Hall, 1967. 37v. **REF fZ881.U41 ECOL**

UNITED STATES. DEPT. OF TRANSPORTATION.
International Conference on Urban Transportation, 5th, Pittsburgh, 1971.
Mobility: the fifth freedom. 1971? **fHE148.I5 1971 ECOL**

UNITED STATES. DEPT. OF TRANSPORTATION. LIBRARY SERVICES DIVISION.
Aircraft and air pollution: selected readings. Comp. by Dorothy J. Poehlman 1971. (its Bibliographic list no. 7) **Z7173.A4U5 ECOL**

UNITED STATES. DIVISION OF AIR POLLUTION.
United States. Robert A Taft Sanitary Engineering Center, Cincinnati.
A compilation of selected air pollution emission control regulations and ordinances. 1965.
  REF KF3812.A4 1965 ECOL

UNITED STATES. EDUCATIONAL RESOURCES INFORMATION CENTER.
Henderson, Martha T.
Environmental education: Social studies sources and approaches. 1970 Ref fQH541.2.H4 ECOL

National Association for Environmental Education.
Man and environment. 1970
  REF fZ5322.E2N3 ECOL

Pepe, Thomas F.
Environmental education. 1971.
  fZ5322.E2P4 ECOL

Project Outreach.
Environmental education resource catalog. 1971
  fQH541.2.P76 ECOL

Thesaurus of ERIC descriptors, with a special chapter on The role and function of the thesaurus in education, by Frederick Goodman. CCM Information Corp., 1972.
  REF fZ695.1.E3U5 1972 ECOL

Watt, Lois B.
Environmental - ecological education: a bibliography of fiction, nonfiction, and textbooks for elementary and secondary schools. 1971.
  REF fQH541.2.W34 ECOL

UNITED STATES. ELECTRIC UTILITY INDUSTRY TASK FORCE ON ENVIRONMENT.
The electric utility industry and the environment; a report to the Citizens Advisory Committee on Recreation and Natural Beauty. 1968?
  HD9685.U5U5 ECOL

UNITED STATES. ENVIRONMENTAL PROTECTION AGENCY. OFFICE OF RESEARCH AND MONITORING.
Manufacturing Chemists' Association.
The effect of chlorination on selected organic chemicals. 1972. fTD462.M3 ECOL

UNITED STATES. ENVIRONMENTAL PROTECTION AGENCY. OFFICE OF WATER PROGRAMS.
Ryckman, Edgerley, Tomlinson and Associates.
Development of a case study of the total effect of pesticides in the environment, nonirrigated croplands of the Mid-west. 1972. fQH545.P4R9 ECOL

UNITED STATES ENVIRONMENTAL HEALTH ENGINEERING RESEARCH LABORATORY.
Austin, Texas
Design guides for biological wastewater treatment processes. 1971 i.e.1972 fTD755.A87 ECOL

UNITED STATES ENVIRONMENTAL PROTECTION AGENCY.
Abt Associates.
Factors affecting pollution referenda. 1971.
  fGH4952.A6 ECOL

Austin, Texas
Design guides for biological wastewater treatment processes. 1971 i.e.1972 fTD755.A87 ECOL

Battelle Memorial Institute, Columbus, Ohio. Columbus Laboratories
An investigation of techniques for removal of cyanide from electroplating wastes. 1971 i.e. 1972
  fTD899.M45B32 ECOL

Battelle-Northwest.
Inorganic fertilizer and phosphate mining industries—water pollution and control. 1971.
  fTD899.F47B38 ECOL

Beet Sugar Development Foundation, Fort Collins, Colo.
State-of-art, sugarbeet processing waste treatment. 1971. fTD899.S8B43 ECOL

Black & Veatch, Kansas City, Mo.
Process design manual for phosphorus removal. 1971. REF fTD745.B5 ECOL

Brown, Harley P.
Aquatic dryopoid beetles (Coleoptera) of the United States. 1972. fQH96.A2B5no.6 ECOL

Burch, J. B.
Freshwater sphaeriacean clams (Mollusca: Pelecypoda) of North America. 1972.
  fQH96.A2B5no.3 ECOL

Burns and Roe.
Process design manual for suspended solids removal. 1971. REF fTD745.B8 ECOL

California. University. Institute of Marine Resources.
Eutrophication in coastal waters: nitrogen as a controlling factor. 1971. fQH96.8.E9C34 ECOL

California. University. Sanitary Engineering Research Laboratory.
Optimization of ammonia removal by ion exchange using clinoptilolite. 1971 i.e. 1972
  fTD757.5.C35 ECOL

Champlin, Robert L.
Supplementary aeration of lagoons in rigorous climate areas. 1971. fTD746.5.C45 ECOL

Colorado. State University, Fort Collins.
Water pollution potential of spent oil shale residues. 1971. fTD899.P4C65 ECOL

Composting of municipal solid wastes in the United States. 1971. TD796.5.C64 ECOL

Cresa.
Pollution abatement and by-product recovery in shellfish and fisheries processing. 1971.
  fTD899.F57C73 ECOL

Cressey, Roger Frank.
The genus Argulus (Crustacea: Branchiura) of the United States. 1972. fQH96.A2B5no.2 ECOL

Crown Zellerbach Corporation. Lebanon Division.
Aerated lagoon treatment of sulfite pulping effluents. 1970. fTD899.W65C7 ECOL

Darnay, Arsen.
Salvage markets for materials in solid wastes, ... 1972. TD795.D38 ECOL

Datagraphics Incorporated.
Inorganic chemicals industry profile (updated). 1971. fTD899.C5D37 ECOL

Directory of governmental air pollution agencies. 1970- TD882.D5 ECOL

The Economic impact of pollution control. 1972.
  TD180.E25 ECOL

The economics of clean air. 1970- Annual report of the Administrator of the Environmental Protection Agency to the Congress of the United States in compliance with Public Law 90-148 the Clean Air Act as amended. U.S. Govt. Print. Off., 1971- v.
  TD883.2.A24 ECOL

The economics of clean water. annual report of the administrator of the Environmental Protection Agency to the Congress of the United States 1972- v.
  HC110.P55A24 ECOL

Effects of pesticides in water; a report to the states. n.d. REF fTD427.P35U53 ECOL

Engineering a victory for our environment: a citizen's guide to the U.S. Army Corps of Engineers. c1972.
  fTC423.E5 ECOL

Envirogenics Company.
Reverse osmosis renovation of primary sewage. 1971. fTD754.E58 ECOL

Environmental protection agency; a progress report, December 1970/June 1972- U.S. Govt. Print. Off. 1972- v. fHC68.U5A24 ECOL

Environmental Research and Applications, Inc.
Concentrated mine drainage disposal into sewage treatment systems. 1971. fTD899.M5E58 ECOL

Environmental Systems Corporation.
Development and demonstration of low-level drift instrumentation. 1971. fTD884.5.E58 ECOL

Fast, Arlo Wade.
The effects of artificial aeration on lake ecology. 1971 i.e.1972 fTD458.F38 ECOL

Federal air quality control regions. Prepared by the Office of the Assistant Commissioner for Regional Activities. Environmental Protection Agency, Office of Air Programs, 1972. (Office of Air Programs. Publication no. AP-102) REF TD883.2.U42 ECOL

Fitzgerald, George Patrick.
Nutrient sources for algae and their control. 1971 i.e.1972 fQH96.8.E9F58 ECOL

Florida Ocean Sciences Institute.
Limitations and effects of waste disposal on an ocean shelf. 1971 i.e.1972 fTD763.F56 ECOL

Foster, Nancy.
Freshwater polychaetes (Annelida) of North America. 1972. fQH96.A2B5no.4 ECOL

Fungaroli, A. A.
Pollution of subsurface water by sanitary landfills. 1971 i.e. 1972- TD403.F85 ECOL

General Mills Chemicals.
Feasibility of liquid ion exchange for extracting phosphate from wastewater. 1970.
  fTD757.G45 ECOL

Georgia Kraft Company. Research and Development Center.
Treatment of selected internal kraft mill wastes in a cooling tower. 1971. fTD899.W65G46 ECOL

Green Bay (Wis.) Metropolitan Sewerage District.
Joint treatment of municipal sewage and pulp mill effluents. 1970. fTD524.W6G74 ECOL

Green Giant Company.
Pilot plant installation for fungal treatment of vegetable canning wastes. 1971.
  fTD899.C3G74 ECOL

Guide for air pollution episode avoidance. U.S. Govt. Print. Off., 1971. (its Publication no. AP-76)
  TD883.2.A518 ECOL

Guidelines for developing or revising water quality standards under the Federal Water Pollution Control Act Amendments of 1972. Wash., Environmental Protection Agency, Water Planning Division, Planning and Standards Branch. U.S. Govt. Print. Off. 1973.
  fTD370.U5 ECOL

Guidelines for local governments on solid waste management. U.S. Govt. Print. Off. 1971.
  fTD791.U5 ECOL

High-pressure compaction and baling of solid waste: final report on a solid waste management demonstration grant. 1972. (Solid waste management series (SW-32d))
  TD796.7.U65 ECOL

Hobbs, Horton Holcombe.
Crayfishes (Astacidae) of North and Middle America. 1972. fQH96.A2B5no.9 ECOL

Holsinger, John R.
The freshwater amphipod crustaceans (Gammaridae) of North America. 1972. fQH96.A2B5no.5 ECOL

Horizons Incorporated.
Foam separation of acid mine drainage. 1971
  fTD899.M5H67 ECOL

Induced aeration of small mountain lakes by Lowell E. Leach and Curtis C. Harlin. U.S. Environmental Protection Agency, Robert S. Kerr Water Research Center 1970. (Water pollution control research series)
  fSH167.T86U5 ECOL

Initiating a national effort to improve solid waste management; a comprehensive chronicle (SW-14) of activities and accomplishments in solid waste management within the U.S. Department of Health, Education, and Welfare under authority of the Solid waste disposal act of 1965. 1971. (Solid waste management series (SW-14).)
  REF TD788.A45 ECOL

International Minerals and Chemical Corporation.
Utilization of phosphate slimes. 1971.
  fTD899.M5I57 ECOL

JBF Scientific Corporation.
Engineering methodology for river and stream reaeration. 1971. fTD458.J17 ECOL

Kansas. University. Center for Research, Inc.
Oxygen consumption in continuous biological culture. 1971. fTD755.K3 ECOL

Karl R. Rohrer Associates.
Underwater storage of combined sewer overflows. 1971 fTD662.K36 ECOL

Kenk, Roman.
Freshwater planarians (Turbellaria) of North America. 1972. fQH96.A2B5no.1 ECOL

Ketelle, Martha J.
Problem lakes in the United States. 1971.
  fTD223.K47 ECOL

Klemm, Donald J.
Freshwater leeches (Annelida: Hirudinea) of North America. 1972. fQH96.A2B5no.8 ECOL

Lake Tahoe Area Council.
Eutrophication of surface waters—Lake Tahoe. 1971 i.e. 1972 fQH96.8.E9L34 ECOL

Lake Tahoe Area Council.
Eutrophication of surface waters—Lake Tahoe Indian Creek Reservoir. 1971.
  fTD224.C3L32 ECOL

Law, James P.
National irrigation return flow research and development program. 1971. fTC809.L38 ECOL

Little (Arthur D.) Inc.
Characterization and separation of secondary effluent components by molecular weight. 1971.
  fTD735.L58 ECOL

Masini, Giancarlo.
S.O.S. save our earth. c1972
  fQH541.M382 1972 ECOL

Michigan. Bureau of Water Management.
Chlorinated municipal waste toxicities to rainbow trout and fathead minnows. 1971.
  fTD763.M5 ECOL

Milwaukee. Sewerage Commission.
Evaluation of conditioning and dewatering sewage sludge by freezing. 1971. fTD769.7.M54 ECOL

Milwaukee. Sewerage Commission.
Phosphorus removal by an activated sludge plant. 1970. fTD756.M54 ECOL

Milwaukee. Sewerage Commission.
Phosphorus removal with pickle liquor in an activated sludge plant. 1971. **fTD756.M55 ECOL**

Mine Safety Appliances Research Corporation.
Optimization of the regeneration procedure for granular activated carbon. 1970. **fTP245.C4M55 ECOL**

Minnesota. Pollution Control Agency.
Pesticide inputs and levels: Minnesota waters-Lake Superior Basin. 1971 i.e. 1972 **fTD223.3.M55 ECOL**

National Canners Association. Western Research Laboratory.
Dry caustic peeling of tree fruit for liquid waste reduction. 1970. **fTD899.F7N37 ECOL**

National Ground Water Quality Symposium, Denver, 1971.
Proceedings. 1972 **fTD223.N37 1971 ECOL**

North Carolina. State University, Raleigh. Dept. of Biological and Agricultural Engineering.
Role of animal wastes in agricultural land runoff. 1971. **fTD930.N67 ECOL**

NUS Corporation. Cyrus Wm. Rice Division.
The effects of various gas atmospheres on the oxidation of coal mine pyrites. 1971. **fTD899.M5N2 ECOL**

Oregon. State University, Corvallis. School of Forestry.
Studies on effects of watershed practices on streams. 1971 i.e. 1972 **fTC409.O74 ECOL**

Portland, Or. Bureau of Sanitary Engineering.
Demonstration of rotary screening for combined sewer overflows. 1971. **fTD748.P67 ECOL**

Procedures manual for the review of federal actions impacting the environment. 1972 v. **KF5505.U5 ECOL**

Progress in the prevention and control of air pollution. 1970- Annual report of the Administrator of the Environmental Protection Agency to the Congress of the United States. U.S. Govt. Print. Off., 1971- v. **TD883.2.A22 ECOL**

Ralph M. Parsons Laboratory for Water Resources and Hydrodynamics.
Temperature prediction in stratified water: mathematical model-user's manual (supplement to report 1613ODJH-01/71). 1971. **fTD395.R3 ECOL**

Rensselaer Polytechnic Institute, Troy, N.Y. Bio-Environmental Engineering Division.
Control of pollution from outboard engine exhaust: a reconnaissance study. 1971. **fTD427.P4R45 ECOL**

Roy F. Weston, Inc.
Concept evaluation report: taconite tailings disposal, Reserve Mining Company, Silver Bay, Minnesota. 1971 **fTD899.T35 ECOL**

Roy F. Weston, Inc.
Process design manual for upgrading existing wastewater treatment plants. **REF fTD745.R6 ECOL**

Rubber reuse and solid waste management. For sale by the Supt. of Docs., U.S. Govt. Print. Off. 1971- v. **TD899.R8U55 ECOL**

Smith, Ronald W.
Acid mine pollution effects on lake biology. 1971. **fTD899.M5S6 ECOL**

Solid waste handling and disposal in multi-story buildings and hospitals. U.S. Govt. Print. Off. 1972- v.1- (Solid waste management series, SW-34d.1-) **TD788.A3 ECOL**

Solid waste management. **REF Z5853.S22S6 ECOL**

Solid Waste Resources Conference, Columbus, Ohio, 1971.
Design of consumer containers for re-use or disposal. 1972. **TD785.S6 1971 ECOL**

Southern Research Institute, Birmingham, Ala.
Demineralization of wastewater by the transport-depletion process. 1971. **fTD754.S67 ECOL**

Stochastics, Inc., Blacksburg, Va.
Stochastic modeling for water quality management. 1971. **fTC409.S8 ECOL**

Summary, conclusions and recommendations from report to the President and Congress on noise; report of the Administration of the Environmental Protection Agency, in compliance with title IV of Public Law 91-604; the clean air act amendments of 1970. U.S. Govt. Print. Off., 1971. 1 v. **fTD893.A473 ECOL**

Swindell-Dressler Company.
Process design manual for carbon adsorption. 1971. **REF fTD753.5.S9 ECOL**

Symposium on Solid Waste Demonstration Projects, Cincinnati, Ohio, 1971.

Solid waste demonstration projects. 1972. **TD785.A45 1971 ECOL**

Synectics Corporation.
A system for industrial waste treatment RD&D project priority assignment. 1971. **fTD897.5.S9 ECOL**

Syracuse University. Civil Engineering Dept.
Benefits of water quality enhancement. 1970. **fTD365.S94 ECOL**

Syracuse University. Dept. of Biology.
Inorganic sulfur oxidation by iron-oxidizing bacteria. 1971. **fQR84.S95 ECOL**

Texas Tech University. Water Resources Center.
Characteristics of wastes from southwestern cattle feedlots. 1971. **fTD899.F4T497 ECOL**

Texas. University. Medical Branch, Galveston.
Phosphorus removal and disposal from municipal wastewater. 1971. **fTD745.T43 ECOL**

Uniroyal, Inc.
Feasibility study of regenerative fibers for water pollution control. 1970 i.e. 1971 **fTD757.5.U55 ECOL**

United States. National Bureau of Standards. Analytical Chemistry Division.
Interaction of nitrilotriacetic acid with suspended and bottom material. 1971. **fTD427.D4U64 ECOL**

Virginia Polytechnic Institute and State University.
Stream faunal recovery after manganese strip mine reclamation. 1971. **fTN291.V5 ECOL**

Washington (State). University. Institute of Forest Products.
Pollution abatement by fiber modification. 1971. **fTD899.W65W38 ECOL**

Wells, Dan M.
Potential pollution of the Ogallala by recharging playa lake water—pesticides. 1970. **fTD224.T4W45 ECOL**

West Virginia. University. Coal Research Bureau.
Dewatering of mine drainage sludge. 1971. **fTD899.M5W44 ECOL**

West Virginia. University. Coal Research Bureau.
Underground coal mining methods to abate water pollution. 1970. **fTD899.M5W46 ECOL**

Williams, William David.
Freshwater isopods (Asellidae) of North America. 1972. **fQH96.A2B5no.7 ECOL**

UNITED STATES. ENVIRONMENTAL PROTECTION AGENCY. AIR POLLUTION CONTROL OFFICE. see UNITED STATES. ENVIRONMENTAL PROTECTION AGENCY. OFFICE OF AIR PROGRAMS.; UNITED STATES. NATIONAL AIR POLLUTION CONTROL ADMINISTRATION.

UNITED STATES. ENVIRONMENTAL PROTECTION AGENCY. AIR POLLUTION CONTROL OFFICE.
Interstate surveillance project: measurement of air pollution using static monitors, by James H. Cavender and others. 1971. **TD890.U45 ECOL**

UNITED STATES. ENVIRONMENTAL PROTECTION AGENCY. ANNUAL REPORT.
United States. Environmental Protection Agency. The economics of clean water. 1972- **HC110.P55A24 ECOL**

UNITED STATES. ENVIRONMENTAL PROTECTION AGENCY. DIVISION OF ATMOSPHERIC SURVEILLANCE.
Air quality data: directory of air quality monitoring sites, 1971. 1972. (Office of Air Programs publication no. APTD 0979) **REF TD883.2.A43 ECOL**

Air quality data for 1967 from the National Air Surveillance Networks. Rev. Environmental Protection Agency, 1971. (Office of Air Programs publication no. APTD 0741) **TD883.2.A44 1971 ECOL**

U.S. ENVIRONMENTAL PROTECTION AGENCY. DIVISION OF OIL AND HAZARDOUS MATERIALS.
Little (Arthur D.) Inc.
Spill prevention techniques for hazardous polluting substances; an inventory and survey of hazardous chemical facilities in Charleston, West Virginia; Baltimore, Maryland; Texas City, Texas; and the Suisun Bay-Delta Area, California. 1971. **fT55.3.H3L4 ECOL**

Ryckman, Edgerley, Tomlinson and Associates.
Pesticide poisoning of Pond Lick Lake, Ohio. 1971 **fTD224.O3R9 ECOL**

UNITED STATES. ENVIRONMENTAL PROTECTION AGENCY. INDUSTRIAL POLLUTION CONTROL BRANCH.
Mead Corporation.
Multi-system biological treatment of bleached kraft effluents. 1971. **fTD899.W65M4 ECOL**

Projects of the Industrial Pollution Control Branch. George Rey, chief. Applied Science and Technology Branch, Office of Research and Monitoring, Environmental Protection Agency; for sale by the Supt. of Docs., U.S. Govt. Print. Off., 1971. 1 v. (Water pollution control research series) **fTD897.5.U54 ECOL**

UNITED STATES. ENVIRONMENTAL PROTECTION AGENCY. LIBRARY SYSTEMS BRANCH.
Journal holdings report: 1972- v. **REF fZ6945.U534 ECOL**

United States. Environmental Protection Agency. Library Systems Branch.
Journal holdings report: 1972- **REF fZ6945.U534 ECOL**

UNITED STATES ENVIRONMENTAL PROTECTION AGENCY. NATIONAL ENVIRONMENTAL RESEARCH CENTER.
Selected studies on alkaline additives for sulfur dioxide control. 1971. **TD885.5.S8S4 ECOL**

Toxicology of atmospheric sulfur dioxide decay products by Trent R. Lewis and others. 1972. **TD885.5.S8U5 ECOL**

UNITED STATES. ENVIRONMENTAL PROTECTION AGENCY. OFFICE OF AIR PROGRAMS. see also UNITED STATES. ENVIRONMENTAL PROTECTION AGENCY. AIR POLLUTION CONTROL OFFICE.; UNITED STATES. NATIONAL AIR POLLUTION CONTROL ADMINISTRATION.

Brunson, E. Evan.
Improving water quality management planning in nonmetropolitan areas. 1973. **fTD365.B78 ECOL**

Compilation of air pollutant emission factors. Rev. For sale by the Supt. of Docs., U.S. Govt. Print. Off., 1972. 1 v. (Its Publication no. AP-42) **TD883.1.U494 ECOL**

Guide for control of air pollution episodes in medium-sized urban areas. For sale by the Supt. of Docs., U.S. Govt. Print. Off., 1971. v. (Office of Air Programs publication no. AP-77) **TD883.1.U49 ECOL**

Guide for control of air pollution episodes in small urban areas. U.S. Govt. Print. Off., 1971. (Office of Air Programs publication no. AP-78) **TD883.1.U492 ECOL**

Mercury and air pollution: A bibliography with abstracts. 1972. **TD887.M4U5 ECOL**

Odors and air pollution: a bibliography with abstracts. U.S. Govt. Print. Office 1972. (its Publication no. AP-113) **TD886.U5 ECOL**

United States. Environmental Protection Agency.
Federal air quality control regions. 1972. **REF TD883.2.U42 ECOL**

UNITED STATES. ENVIRONMENTAL PROTECTION AGENCY. OFFICE OF AIR PROGRAMS. OFFICE OF RESEARCH GRANTS.
Air pollution control; active research grants for fiscal year 1971- v. (Office of Air Programs publication no. APTD 0740) **REF TD883.2.A23 ECOL**

UNITED STATES. ENVIRONMENTAL PROTECTION AGENCY, OFFICE OF NOISE ABATEMENT AND CONTROL see UNITED STATES. OFFICE OF NOISE ABATEMENT AND CONTROL

UNITED STATES. ENVIRONMENTAL PROTECTION AGENCY. OFFICE OF PUBLIC AFFAIRS.
Current list of water publications, 1965/71- National Environmental Research Center. **REF Z7173.W3U5 ECOL**

Midwest environmental directory, 1972- v. **REF S920.U5 ECOL**

UNITED STATES. ENVIRONMENTAL PROTECTION AGENCY. OFFICE OF RADIATION PROGRAMS. SURVEILLANCE AND INSPECTION DIVISION.
Oakley, Donald T.
Natural radiation exposure in the United States. 1972. **REF RA569.O15 ECOL**

UNITED STATES. ENVIRONMENTAL PROTECTION AGENCY. OFFICE OF RESEARCH AND MONITORING.
Agnew, Robert W.
A free floating endless belt oil skimmer. 1972. **TD899.P4A3 ECOL**

Air modulated vacuum oil recovery collection of spilled oil (foams). Author: Richard W. Sicka. U.S. Govt. Print. Off., 1972. (Environmental protection technology series) **fTD427.P4U5 ECOL**

Alamo Area Council of Governments.
Basin management for water reuse. 1972. **fTD225.S225A65 ECOL**

Atkins, Patrick R.
The pesticide manufacturing industry—current waste treatment and disposal practices. 1972.
fTD899.C5A8 ECOL

Barnes, Robert A.
Ammonia removal in a physical-chemical wastewater treatment process. 1972. **TD462.B3 ECOL**

Bartsch, A. F.
Role of phosphorus in eutrophication. 1972.
QH96.8.E9B3 ECOL

Beckers, Charles V.
Quantitative methods for preliminary design of water quality surveillance systems. 1972.
TD365.B4 ECOL

Beefland International, Inc.
Elimination of water pollution by packing-house animal paunch and blood. 1971.
fTD899.M4B4 ECOL

Bingham, Tayler H.
The beverage container problem. 1972.
TD793.B5 ECOL

Biospherics Incorporated.
Biomass determination—a new technique for activated sludge control. 1972. **fTD756.B5 ECOL**

Boen, Doyle F.
Study of reutilization of wastewater recycled through groundwater. 1971. **fTD429.B6 ECOL**

Bongers, Leonard H.
Sand and gravel overlay for control of mercury in sediments. 1972. **fTD427.M4B6 ECOL**

Bouwer, Herman.
Renovating secondary sewage by ground water recharge with infiltration basins. 1972.
fTD765.B6 ECOL

Boyce Thompson Institute for Plant Research, Yonkers, N.Y.
Interaction of herbicides and soil microorganisms. 1971. **fSB951.4.B68 ECOL**

Brinkhurst, Ralph O.
The role of sludge worms in eutrophication. 1972.
QH96.8.E9B7 ECOL

California. University.
Flow into a stratified reservoir. 1972.
TC167.C3 ECOL

Carcich, Italo G.
A pressure sewer system demonstration. 1972.
TD670.C3 ECOL

Cha, C. Y.
Photochemical methods for purifying water. 1972.
TD459.C4 ECOL

Chesher, Richard H.
Biological impact of a large-scale desalination plant at Key West. 1971. **fTD478.5.F5C48 ECOL**

Collins, Ralph P.
Characterization of taste and odors in water supplies. 1971. **fTD384.C64 ECOL**

Control of mercury pollution in sediments. Author: Ivan C. Smith U.S. Govt. Print. Off., 1972. (Environmental protection technology series)
TD427.M4U5 ECOL

Correll, Donovan Stewart.
Aquatic and wetland plants of southwestern United States. 1972. **QK142.C6 ECOL**

Datagraphics Incorporated.
Projected wastewater treatment costs in the organic chemicals industry (updated). 1971.
fTD899.C5D388 ECOL

Delaware River Basin Commission.
Interstate planning for regional water supply and pollution control. 1971. **fTD420.D4 ECOL**

Dow Chemical Company. Functional Products and Systems Dept.
A literature search and critical analysis of biological trickling filter studies. 1971- **fTD443.D6 ECOL**

The effects of agricultural waste water treatment on algal bioassay response. Author: Milton G. Tunzi U.S. Govt. Print. Off., 1971. (Water pollution control research series) (Bio-engineering aspects of agricultural drainage, San Joaquin Valley, California)
QH96.8.E9U54 ECOL

Envirometrics, Inc., Wash., D.C.
The river basin model. 1971-
fTC409.E5 ECOL

Envirometrics, Inc., Wash., D.C.
The river basin model: computer output. 1971.
fTC409.E51 ECOL

Envirometrics, Inc., Wash., D.C.
The river basin model: municipal services department. 1971. **fTC409.E5 ECOL**

Environmental Measurements, Inc.
Monitoring mercury vapor near pollution sites. 1971. **fTD427.M4E5 ECOL**

Feick, George.
Control of mercury contamination in freshwater sediments. 1972. **TD427.M4F4 ECOL**

Freese, Paul V.
Full-scale raw wastewater flocculation with polymers. 1970. **fTD751.F7 ECOL**

Fuhriman, Dean K.
Ground water pollution in Arizona, California, Nevada & Utah. 1971 i.e. 1972
fTD223.9.F85 ECOL

Gainesville, Fla. Dept. of Public Utilities.
Magnesium carbonate, a recycled coagulant for water treatment. 1971. **fTD433.G3 ECOL**

Gaudy, Anthony F.
Biological concepts for design and operation of the activated sludge process. 1971 i.e. 1972
fTD756.G38 ECOL

General Electric Company. Re-entry and Environmental Systems Division.
Watercraft waste treatment system: development and demonstration report. 1971. **fTD745.G4 ECOL**

Ghassemi, Masood.
Phosphate precipitation with ferrous iron. 1971.
fTD751.G4 ECOL

Groman, William A.
Forest fertilization (a state-of-the-art review and description of environmental effects). 1972.
SD408.G7 ECOL

Gumtz, Garth D.
Restoration of Beaches contaminated by oil. 1972.
TD427.P4G8 ECOL

Henager, Charles H.
Concept evaluation: recovery of floating oil using polyurethane foam sorbent. 1972.
fTD427.P4H4 ECOL

Holmes, James G.
Acid mine drainage treatment by ion exchange. 1972
TD899.M5H6 ECOL

Identification of polychlorinated biphenyls in the presence of DDT-type compounds. Authors: J. T. Brownrigg and others. Prepared for Office of Research and Monitoring, U.S. Environmental Protection Agency. U.S. Govt. Print. Off., 1972. (Environmental protection technology series) **SB951.U52 ECOL**

Investigation of porous pavements for urban runoff control. 1972. **fTE215.I58 ECOL**

Kirk, William P.
Krypton 85: a review of the literature and an analysis of radiation hazards. 1972 **QP82.2.R3K5 ECOL**

Lake Michigan Enforcement Conference. Lake Michigan Interstate Pesticides Committee.
An evaluation of DDT and dieldrin in Lake Michigan. 1972. **TD427.P35L3 ECOL**

McCoy, Elizabeth F.
Role of bacteria in the nitrogen cycle in lakes. 1972.
fTD433.M3 ECOL

Maryland. Dept. of Water Resources.
Guidelines for erosion and sediment control, planning and implementation. 1972. **fS624.A1M3 ECOL**

Mayer, John K.
Sewer bedding and infiltration, Gulf Coast area. 1972. **fTD653.M3 ECOL**

Michigan. State University, East Lansing. Agricultural Pollution Control Laboratory.
Closed system waste management for livestock. 1971 i.e. 1972 **fTD899.F4M5 ECOL**

Midwest Research Institute, Kansas City, Mo.
Rapid detection system for organophosphates and carbamate insecticides in water. 1972.
TD427.P35M5 ECOL

Montgomery County Sanitary Dept. Montgomery County, Ohio.
Ground water infiltration and internal sealing of sanitary sewers, Montgomery County, Ohio. 1972.
fTD716.M6 ECOL

Morey, Rexford M.
Feasibility study of electromagnetic subsurface profiling. 1972. **QE602.M6 ECOL**

Morgan, W. E.
An investigation of phosphorus removal mechanisms in activated sludge systems. 1972.
TD756.M6 ECOL

Morth, Arthur H.
Pyritic systems: a mathematical model. 1972.
TD899.M5M6 ECOL

Morton, Stephen D.
The carbon dioxide system and eutrophication. 1971. **fQH96.8.E9M6 ECOL**

National Steel Corporation. Weirton Steel Division.
Combined steel mill and municipal waste-waters treatment. 1972. **fTD899.S7N37 ECOL**

Nebolsine, Ross.
High rate filtration of combined sewer overflows. 1972. **fTD662.N4 ECOL**

Oklahoma. State University of Agriculture and Applied Science, Stillwater. School of Civil Engineering.
Aerobic digestion of organic waste sludge. 1971 i.e. 1972 **fTD769.O35 ECOL**

Olson, Theodore A.
Lake Superior periphyton in relation to water quality. 1972. **fQK935.O4 ECOL**

Partheniades, Emmanuel.
Deposition of fine sediments in turbulent flows. 1971 i.e. 1972 **fTC175.2.P3 ECOL**

Patterson, W. L.
Estimating costs and manpower requirements for conventional wastewater treatment facilities. 1971 i.e. 1972 **fTD743.P36 ECOL**

Pratt, P. F.
Nitrate in the unsaturated zone under agricultural lands. 1972. **fS651.P7 ECOL**

Projects of the National Water Quality Control Research Program. U.S. Govt. Print. Off. 1971. (Water pollution control research series)
fTD423.U546 ECOL

Ralph M. Parsons Laboratory for Water Resources and Hydrodynamics.
Density induced mixing in confined aquifers. 1972.
fTC176.R33 ECOL

Ramsey, Ralph H.
Soil systems for municipal effluents. 1972.
fTD760.R24 ECOL

Reilich, Helmut G.
Technical evaluation of phosphate-free home laundry detergents. 1972. **fTP992.5.R4 ECOL**

Reiling, S. D.
Economic benefits from an improvement in water quality. 1973. **fTD370.R45 ECOL**

Robert S. Kerr Water Research Center.
Characteristics of rainfall run off from a beef cattle feedlot. 1972. **TD899.F4R6 ECOL**

Sandoski, Dorothy A.
Selected urban storm water runoff abstracts, July 1971-June 1972. 1972. **fTD653.S2 ECOL**

Sartor, James D.
Water pollution aspects of street surface contaminants. 1972. **fTD665.S2 ECOL**

Skogerboe, Gaylord V.
Evaluation of canal lining for salinity control in Grand Valley. 1972. **TC930.S5 ECOL**

Skogerboe, Gaylord V.
Research needs for irrigation return flow quality control. 1971 i.e. 1972 **fTD223.S54 ECOL**

Skogerboe, Gaylord V.
Selected irrigation return flow. 1972-
fTD223.S5 ECOL

Smith, Robert.
Cost to the consumer for collection and treatment of wastewater. 1970 i.e. 1972 **fTD523.S65 ECOL**

Stall, John B.
Storm sewer design—an evaluation of the RRL method. 1972. **TD665.S7 ECOL**

Stefan, Heinz.
Surface discharge of heated water. 1971 i.e. 1972
fTD427.H4S64 ECOL

Stenquist, Richard J.
Initial mixing in coagulation processes. 1972.
TD455.S7 ECOL

Storage and treatment of combined sewer overflows. Authors: Wilbur R. Liebenow and James K. Bieging U.S. Govt. Print. Off., 1972. (Environmental protection technology series) **fTD662.U54 ECOL**

Streebin, Leale E.
Demonstration of a full-scale waste treatment system for a cannery. 1971. **fTD899.C3S87 ECOL**

Suggs, James D.
Mercury pollution control in stream and lake sediments. 1972. **fTD427.M4S9 ECOL**

The swirl concentrator as a combined sewer overflow regulator facility. Author: American Public Works Association. Prepared for Office of Research and Monitoring, U.S. Environmental Protection Agency and the city of Lancaster, Pennsylvania. U.S. Govt. Print. Off., 1972. (Environmental protection technology series) **TD662.U5 ECOL**

Taylor, John Keeman.
Development of method for NTA analysis in raw water. 1972. **TP992.5.T3 ECOL**

Texas Christian University, Fort Worth. Dept. of Biology.
Industrial wastes: effects on Trinity River ecology, Fort Worth, Texas. 1971 i.e. 1972
fTD224.T4T4 ECOL

Thruston, Alfred D.
Liquid chromatography of carbamate pesticides. 1972. **SB951.T4 ECOL**

Tratnyek, Joseph P.
Waste wool as a scavenger for mercury pollution in waters. 1972. **fTD427.M4T7 ECOL**

Troy, Joseph C.
Oxidation of pyrites in chlorinated solvents. 1972. **TD899.M5T7 ECOL**

Tsivoglou, E. C.
Characterization of stream reaeration, capacity. 1972. **fTD458.T7 ECOL**

Unterberg, W.
Computerized design and cost estimation for multiple-hearth sludge incinerators. 1971 i.e. 1972 **fTD770.U58 ECOL**

Vermont. Agency of Environmental Conservation.
Development of a State effluent charge system. 1972. **fTD224.V5A43 ECOL**

Water Pollution Control Federation.
Research supplement to Journal Water Pollution Control Federation. 1971. **fTD423.W3 ECOL**

Widman, Michael U.
Polymer film overlay system for mercury contaminated sludge—Phase I. 1972. **fTD427.M4W5 ECOL**

Wiley, Averill J.
Reverse osmosis concentration of dilute pulp and paper effluents. 1972. **fTD899.W65W5 ECOL**

Wilson, Raymond Harrison.
Toward a philosophy of planning: attitudes of federal water planners. 1973. **HC110.E5W5 ECOL**

Workbook of thermal plume prediction. U.S. Govt. Print. Office, 1972- v.1- **TD427.H4U54 ECOL**

Zaval, Frank J.
Revegetation augmentation by reuse of treated active surface mine drainage. 1972. **TD899.M5Z3 ECOL**

UNITED STATES. ENVIRONMENTAL PROTECTION AGENCY. OFFICE OF RESEARCH MONITORING.
Welch, Robin I.
A feasibility demonstration of an aerial surveillance spill prevention system. 1972. **fTD427.P4W45 ECOL**

UNITED STATES. ENVIRONMENTAL PROTECTION AGENCY. OFFICE OF WATER PROGRAMS. see also UNITED STATES. ENVIRONMENTAL PROTECTION AGENCY. WATER QUALITY OFFICE.; UNITED STATES. FEDERAL WATER POLLUTION CONTROL ADMINISTRATION.; UNITED STATES. FEDERAL WATER QUALITY ADMINISTRATION.

Brunson, E. Evan.
Improving water quality management planning in nonmetropolitan areas. 1973. **fTD365.B78 ECOL**

The movement and impact of pesticides used for vector control on the aquatic environment in the northeastern United States. U.S. Govt. Print. Off., 1972. (Pesticide study series, no. 9) **fTD427.P35U5 ECOL**

Subsurface water pollution; a selective annotated bibliography. U.S. Govt. Print. Off. 1972. 3v. **Z7173.W3U5 ECOL**

Von Rumker, Rosmarie.
The use of pesticides in suburban homes and gardens and their impact on the aquatic environment. 1972. **fQH545.P4V66 ECOL**

UNITED STATES. ENVIRONMENTAL PROTECTION AGENCY. OFFICE OF WATER PROGRAMS. TRAINING GRANTS BRANCH.
A curriculum activities guide to water pollution and environmental studies 1972- v.1- **REF fS946.U56 ECOL**

UNITED STATES. ENVIRONMENTAL PROTECTION AGENCY. OFFICES OF RESEARCH AND MONITORING.
Kreusch, Ed.
Wastewater demineralization by ion exchange. 1971 i.e.1972 **fTD757.5.K74 ECOL**

UNITED STATES. ENVIRONMENTAL PROTECTION AGENCY. PACIFIC NORTHWEST WATER LABORATORY. see PACIFIC NORTHWEST WATER LABORATORY.

UNITED STATES. ENVIRONMENTAL PROTECTION AGENCY PACIFIC NORTHWEST WATER LABORATORY.
A method for predicting the performance of draft cooling towers. U.S. Govt. Print. Off., 1970. (Water pollution control research series) **fTP159.C6U5 ECOL**

U.S. ENVIRONMENTAL PROTECTION AGENCY. RADIATION OFFICE. SURVEILLANCE AND INSPECTION DIVISION.
Southern Conference on Environmental Radiation Protection from Nuclear Power Plants, St. Petersburg, Fla., 1971.
Proceedings of Southern Conference on Environmental Radiation Protection from Nuclear Power Plants, April 21-22, 1971. 1972. **TK9152.S6 ECOL**

UNITED STATES ENVIRONMENTAL PROTECTION AGENCY. SOLID WASTE MANAGEMENT OFFICE.
Smith, David D.
Ocean disposal of barge-delivered liquid and solid wastes from United States coastal cities. 1971. **TD796.7.O25S4 ECOL**

UNITED STATES. ENVIRONMENTAL PROTECTION AGENCY. WATER QUALITY OFFICE see also UNITED STATES. ENVIRONMENTAL PROTECTION AGENCY. OFFICE OF WATER PROGRAMS.; UNITED STATES. FEDERAL WATER POLLUTION CONTROL ADMINISTRATION.; UNITED STATES. FEDERAL WATER QUALITY ADMINISTRATION.

Alpine Geophysical Associates.
Oil pollution incident. 1971. **fGC1221.A4 ECOL**

American Enka Corporation. Central Engineering Dept.
Zinc precipitation and recovery from viscose rayon waste water. 1971. **fTD899.T4A44 ECOL**

American Process Equipment Corporation.
Ultrasonic filtration of combined sewer overflows. 1970. **fTD753.A6 ECOL**

American Public Works Association.
Feasibility of computer control of wastewater treatment. 1970. **fTD746.A43 ECOL**

American Public Works Association.
Prevention and correction of excessive infiltration and inflow into sewer systems. 1971. **fTD678.A44 ECOL**

Armco Steel Corporation.
Limestone treatment of rinse waters from hydrochloric acid pickling of steel. 1971. **fTD899.M45A75 ECOL**

Battelle Memorial Institute, Columbus, Ohio
Corrosion potential of NTA in detergent formulations. 1971. **fTP992.5.B3 ECOL**

Black, Sivalls and Bryson, inc., Kansas City, Mo. Applied Technology Division
Evaluation of a new acid mine drainage treatment process. 1971. **fTD899.M5B55 ECOL**

Black, Sivalls and Bryson, Inc., Kansas City, Mo. Applied Technology Division
Study of sulfur recovery from coal refuse. 1971. **fTN890.B57 ECOL**

California. University, Santa Barbara. Dept. of Biological Sciences.
Santa Barbara oil spill: short-term analysis of macroplankton and fish. 1971. **fTD427.P4C34 ECOL**

Canada.
Agricultural pollution of the Great Lakes Basin. 1971. **fTD223.3.C25 ECOL**

Clemson University. Dept. of Textiles.
State of the art of textile waste treatment. 1971. **fTD899.T4C45 ECOL**

Coca-Cola Company. Foods Division.
Treatment of citrus processing wastes. 1970. **TD899.F7C6 ECOL**

Conference in the Matter of Pollution of Lake Michigan and its Tributary Basin in the States of Wisconsin, Illinois, Indiana, and Michigan, 3rd, Chicago, Mar. 23-25, 1971.
Reconvening of the 3rd session; Proceedings. 1971- **fTD223.3.C595 1971 ECOL**

Conference in the Matter of Pollution of Lake Superior and its Tributary Basin in the States of Minnesota, Wisconsin, and Michigan, 2nd, Duluth, Jan. 14-15, 1971.
Second meeting second session (reconvened). 1971. **fTD223.3.C59 1971 ECOL**

Cornell Aeronautical Laboratory, Inc., Buffalo.
Research on the physical aspects of thermal pollution. 1971. **fTD427.H4C67 ECOL**

Cost of clean water. 1971- v. **TD420.U5 ECOL**

Dallas, Or.
Combined treatment of domestic and industrial wastes by activated sludge. 1971. **fTD756.D35 ECOL**

Detroit Metro Water Dept.
Development of phosphate removal processes. 1970. **fTD756.D47 ECOL**

Digest of State program plans. 1970/71- U.S. Govt. Print. Off. v. **TD223.A2635 ECOL**

Dow Chemical Company. Western Division Research Laboratories.
Nitrate removal from wastewaters by ion exchange. 1971. **fTD757.5.D68 ECOL**

Dynatech R/D Company.
A survey of alternate methods for cooling condenser discharge water. 1969- **fTJ403.D9 ECOL**

Edison Water Quality Laboratory. Storm and Combined Sewer Overflows Section.
Environmental impact of highway deicing. 1971. **fTE220.E35 ECOL**

Enviro Control, Inc.
Systems analysis for water quality management—survey and abstracts. 1971. **fTD365.E5 ECOL**

Envirogenics Company.
Investigation of a new phosphate removal process. 1970. **fTD745.E5 ECOL**

Fram Corporation.
Bio-regenerated activated carbon treatment of textile dye wastewater. 1971. **fTD899.T4F7 ECOL**

Franklin Institute, Philadelphia. Science Information Service.
Selected urban storm water runoff abstracts, July 1970-June 1971. 1971. **fTD653.F7 ECOL**

Gammon, James Robert.
The effect of inorganic sediment on stream biota. 1970. **fQH541.5.S7G34 ECOL**

General Dynamics Corporation. Electric Boat Division.
Potential environmental effects of an offshore submerged nuclear power plant. 1971- **fQH541.5.S3G45 ECOL**

Grumman Aerospace Corporation.
Development of immobilized enzyme systems for enhancement of biological waste treatment processes. 1970 **fTD755.G78 ECOL**

Gulf Environmental Systems Company.
Acid mine waste treatment using reverse osmosis. 1971 **fTD754.G84 ECOL**

Hogan, William T.
Optimum mechanical aeration systems for rivers and ponds. 1970. **fTD458.H64 ECOL**

IIT Research Institute. Technology Center.
Development of phosphate-free home laundry detergents. 1970. **fTP992.5.I2 ECOL**

Ionics, Inc.
The electro-oxidation of ammonia in sewage to nitrogen. 1970. **fTD757.I55 ECOL**

Jacksonville, Ark.
Biological treatment of chlorophenolic wastes. 1971. **fTD755.J3 ECOL**

Mandan Refinery.
Fluid bed incineration of petroleum refinery wastes. 1971. **fTD899.P4M35 ECOL**

Metcalf and Eddy, Boston.
Storm water management model. 1971. **fGB665.M4 ECOL**

Midwest Research Institute, Kansas City, Mo.
Light-catalyzed chlorine oxidation for treatment of wastewater. 1970. **fTD758.M5 ECOL**

Minnesota. State College, Winona.
Mayfly distribution as a water quality index. 1970. **fTD370.M562 ECOL**

Minnesota. University. St. Anthony Falls Hydraulic Laboratory.
Hydraulics of long vertical conduits and associated cavitation. 1971. **fTC174.M53 ECOL**

National Canners Association. Western Research Laboratory.
Reduction of salt content of food processing liquid waste effluent. 1971. **fTD899.C3N36 ECOL**

National Oil Recovery Corp., Bayonne, N.J.
Conversion of crankcase waste oil into useful products. 1971. **fTP687.N3 ECOL**

New Mexico State University. Physical Science Laboratory.
Floating oil recovery device. 1971. **fTD427.P4N48 ECOL**

North American Rockwell Corporation. Rocketdyne Division.
Development of a chemical denitrification process. 1970. **fTD433.N67 ECOL**

North Star Research and Development Institute, Minneapolis.
New and ultrathin membranes for municipal waste water treatment by reverse osmosis. 1970.
fTD754.N6 ECOL

Onondaga Co., N.Y.
Onondaga Lake study. 1971.
fTD224.N7O5 ECOL

Oregon. State University, Corvallis.
Oceanography of the nearshore coastal waters of the Pacific Northwest relating to possible pollution. 1971- fGC851.O7 ECOL

Robert S. Kerr Water Research Center.
Denitrification by anaerobic filters and ponds. 1971.
fTD475.R6 ECOL

Roy F. Weston, Inc.
Combined sewer overflow abatement alternatives, Wash., D.C. 1970. fTD525.W2R68 ECOL

South Tahoe Public Utility District.
Advanced wastewater treatment as practiced at South Tahoe. 1971. fTD225.T25S6 ECOL

Susquehanna Corporation. Atlantic Research Systems Division. Marine Systems.
Recovery of floating oil rotating disk type skimmer. 1971. fTD427.P4S9 ECOL

Sweet, David C.
The economic and social importance of estuaries. 1971. GB454.E8S95 ECOL

Texas Tech University. Dept. of Geosciences.
Infiltration rates and groundwater quality beneath cattle feedlots, Texas High Plains. 1971
fTD899.F4T48 ECOL

Tracor, Inc.
Estuarine modeling: an assessment. 1971.
fTD370.T73 ECOL

Tyco Laboratories.
Electrochemical treatment of acid mine waters. 1972. fTD899.M5T88 ECOL

United Aircraft Corporation. Research Laboratories, East Hartford, Conn.
Advanced nonthermally polluting gas turbines in utility applications. 1971. fTJ778.U5 ECOL

Washington (State). University.
The oxygen uptake demand of resuspended bottom sediments. 1970. fGC380.W3 ECOL

Water quality criteria data book. 1970-
REF fTD370.W394 ECOL

World Life Research Institute.
Pharmacological testing of blue-green algae for constituents having therapeutic value. 1970.
fRS165.A7W67 ECOL

UNITED STATES. ENVIRONMENTAL PROTECTION AGENCY. WATER QUALITY OFFICE. STATE PROGRAM PLANS.
United States. Environmental Protection Agency. Water Quality Office.
Digest of State program plans. 1970/71-
TD223.A2635 ECOL

UNITED STATES. FEDERAL AVIATION ADMINISTRATION.
Planning the metropolitan airport system, prepared by a joint committee of the Federal Aviation Administration and Airport Operators Council International in cooperation with the Dept. of Housing and Urban Development and Federal Highway Administration. Federal Aviation Administration, Airports Service, 1970. TL725.3.P5U525 ECOL

UNITED STATES. FEDERAL COORDINATOR FOR MARINE ENVIRONMENTAL PREDICTION.
Federal plan for marine environmental prediction; fiscal year 1972. For sale by the Supt. of Docs., U.S. Govt. Print. Off. 1971. GC1015.U525 ECOL

UNITED STATES FEDERAL COUNCIL FOR SCIENCE AND TECHNOLOGY.
National Research Council. Committee on Pollution.
Waste management and control. 1966.
REF TD180.N3 ECOL

UNITED STATES. FEDERAL POWER COMMISSION.
Air pollution and the regulated electric power and natural gas industries; staff report. 1968.
TD883.2.A52 ECOL

Steam-electric plant air and water quality control data for the year ended December 31, 1969, based on EPC form no. 67; summary report. U.S. Govt. Print. Off., 1973. fTD195.E4U5 ECOL

UNITED STATES. FEDERAL WATER POLLUTION CONTROL ADMINISTRATION see also UNITED STATES. ENVIRONMENTAL PROTECTION AGENCY. OFFICE OF WATER PROGRAMS.; UNITED STATES.

ENVIRONMENTAL PROTECTION AGENCY. WATER QUALITY OFFICE.; UNITED STATES. FEDERAL WATER QUALITY ADMINISTRATION.
An appraisal of water pollution in the Lake Superior basin. 1969. TD223.3.U5 ECOL

An appraisal of water pollution in the Lake Superior basin. Rev. ed. 1970,1969. TD223.3U5 1970 ECOL

Armco Steel Corporation.
Treatment of waste water-waste oil mixtures. 1970.
fTD455.A7 ECOL

Conference in the Matter of Pollution of Lake Superior and its Tributary Basin in the States of Minnesota, Wisconsin, and Michigan, Duluth, May 13-15, 1969.
Proceedings. 1970 fTD223.3.C59 1969 ECOL

Conference in the Matter of Pollution of the Interstate and Intrastate Waters of the Upper Mississippi River and its Tributaries—Wisconsin—Minnesota, Minneapolis, 1968.
Proceedings of progress evaluation meeting held April 30, 1968. 1968. fTD223.4.A45C6 ECOL

The economics of clean water. v.
HD4477.A53 ECOL

Kittrell, F. W.
A practical guide to water quality studies of streams. 1969. TD425.K53 ECOL

National Symposium on Thermal Pollution, Portland, Oregon, 1968.
Biological aspects of thermal pollution. 1969
QH90.N3 1968 ECOL

National Symposium on Thermal Pollution, Vanderbilt University, 1968.
Engineering aspects of thermal pollution. 1969.
TD427.H4N3 1968 ECOL

Powell, Mel D.
Community action guidebook for soil erosion and sediment control. 1970 fS624.A1P68 ECOL

Smith, Edwin Earle.
Sulfide to sulfate reaction mechanism. 1970.
fTN321.S58 ECOL

UNITED STATES. FEDERAL WATER POLLUTION CONTROL ADMINISTRATION. GREAT LAKES REGION.
A report on pollution of the Upper Mississippi River and major tributaries. 1966. v. TD225.M5U5 ECOL

UNITED STATES. FEDERAL WATER POLLUTION CONTROL ADMINISTRATION. MISSOURI BASIN REGION.
Compendium of animal waste management. U.S. Dept. of Interior, Federal Water Pollution Control Administration, Missouri Basin Region. v.
TD811.U5 ECOL

UNITED STATES. FEDERAL WATER POLLUTION CONTROL ADMINISTRATION. TWIN CITIES UPPER MISSISSIPPI RIVER PROJECT.
Report on water quality investigations of the Mississippi, Minnesota and St. Croix Rivers. 1966
REF fTD225.T9U5 ECOL

UNITED STATES. FEDERAL WATER QUALITY ADMINISTRATION see also UNITED STATES. ENVIRONMENTAL PROTECTION AGENCY. OFFICE OF WATER PROGRAMS.; UNITED STATES. ENVIRONMENTAL PROTECTION AGENCY. WATER QUALITY OFFICE.; UNITED STATES. FEDERAL WATER POLLUTION CONTROL ADMINISTRATION.

Aerojet-General Corporation. Environmental Systems Division.
Reverse osmosis renovation of municipal wastewater. 1970 fTD754.A35 ECOL

American Public Works Association.
Combined sewer regulator overflow facilities; report. 1970. fTD662.A42 ECOL

Balakrishnan, S.
State of the art review on sludge incineration practice. 1970. fTD803.B36 ECOL

Clean water for the 1970's; a status report. 1970.
fTD365.U5 ECOL

Conference in the Matter of Pollution of the Interstate and Intrastate Waters of the Upper Mississippi River and its Tributaries—Minnesota and Wisconsin.
Proceedings of the second session Minneapolis, Minnesota, Feb. 28, March 1 & 20, 1967. 1967.
REF TD223.4.A43C6 ECOL

Conference in the Matter of Pollution of Lake Superior and its Tributary Basin in the States of Minnesota, Wisconsin, and Michigan, 2d session, Duluth, Aug. 12-13, 1970.
Reconvening of second sessions. 1971
fTD223.3.C59 1970b ECOL

Conference in the Matter of Pollution of Lake Superior and its Tributary Basin in the States of Minnesota, Wisconsin, and Michigan, 3d session, Duluth, April 29-30, 1970.
Transcript of proceedings. 1970
fTD223.3.C59 1970 ECOL

Conference in the Matter of Pollution of Lake Michigan and its Tributary Basins, 3d, Chicago, Sept. 28-30, Oct. 1-2, 1970.
Workshop session for the third session (reconvened). 1970. fTD223.3.C595 1970a ECOL

Davis, Ernst M.
Bacterial effects of algae on enteric organisms. 1970.
fQR48.D38 ECOL

National Association of Counties Research Foundation.
Urban soil erosion and sediment control. 1970.
fS624.A1N38 ECOL

National Canners Association. Western Research Laboratory.
Waste reduction in food canning operations. 1970 i.e. 1971 fTD899.C3N37 ECOL

Projects: Industrial Pollution Control Branch. William J. Lacy, chief. Div. of Applied Science and Technology, Office of Research and Development, Federal Water Quality Administration, U.S. Dept. of the Interior, U.S. Govt. Print. Off., 1970. v. (Water pollution control research series)
fTD897.5.U56 ECOL

Washington (State). University. Fisheries Research Institute.
Responses of teleost fish to environmental stress. 1971. fQL639.1.W3 ECOL

UNITED STATES. FISH AND WILDLIFE SERVICE.
Wildlife abstracts; a bibliography and index of the abstracts in Wildlife review. no.1/66- 1935-51-
U.S. Govt. Print. Off. v. REF SK351.U52 ECOL

UNITED STATES. FOREST SERVICE.
Cook, David I.
Trees and shrubs for noise abatement. 1971.
TD893.C6 ECOL

Forest trees of the Pacific slope. By George B. Sudworth. Govt. Print. Off., 1908.
REF QK481.S95 ECOL

Hepting, George H.
Diseases of forest and shade trees of the United States. 1971. REF SB761.H4 ECOL

United States. Soil Conservation Service.
Big Sioux River Basin and related areas. 1973.
HD1695.B5A5 ECOL

UNITED STATES GEOLOGICAL SURVEY.
Maderak, Marion L.
Chemical quality of ground water in the Minneapolis-St. Paul area, Minnesota. 1965.
fTD224.M6A3no.23 ECOL

Norvitch, Ralph F.
Ground water in alluvial channel deposits, Nobles County, Minnesota. 1960.
fTD224.M6A3no.14 ECOL

Publications of the Geological Survey, 1879-1961. U.S. Govt. Print. Off., 1964
REF Z6034.U49U53 ECOL

Surface water supply of the United States. 1961/65- U.S. Govt. Print. Off. v. (its Water-supply paper) TC801.U2 ECOL

Symposium on Underground Waste Management and Environmental Implications, Houston, Tex., 1971.
Underground waste management and environmental implications; proceedings. 1972.
TD761.S95 1971 ECOL

UNITED STATES. GEOLOGICAL SURVEY. WATER RESOURCES DIVISION.
National reference list of water quality stations, water year 1971- 1971- v. REF TD380.U5 ECOL

Water resources data for Minnesota, 1968- v.
REF GB705.M62A32 ECOL

UNITED STATES GREAT LAKES BASIN COMMISSION.
Great Lakes Basin Library.
Book catalog. 1969-
REF fZ7164.N3G75 ECOL

Great Lakes Basin Library.
An interim bibliography. 1969-
REF fZ7164.N3G7 ECOL

UNITED STATES. HEALTH SERVICES AND MENTAL HEALTH ADMINISTRATION. DIVISION OF COMMUNITY INJURY CONTROL.
Excerpta Medica Foundations.
Poisoning and intoxication by trace elements in children: an abstract review of the world-wide medical literature 1966-1971. 1973 RA1211.E9 ECOL

UNITED STATES INTER-AGENCY COMMITTEE ON WATER RESOURCES.
Engineering-Science, Inc.
Annotated bibliography on hydrology and sedimentation, 1966-68, United States and Canada. 1970   **REF Z7935.E5 1970 ECOL**

UNITED STATES LAWS, STATUTES, ETC.
Degler, Stanley E.
Federal pollution control programs: water, air, and solid wastes. Rev. ed. 1971   **TD180.D4 1971 ECOL**

UNITED STATES LAWS, STATUTES, ETC. NATIONAL ENVIRONMENTAL POLICY ACT. 1970.
Brecher, Joseph J.
Environmental law handbook. 1970
    REF KF3775.B7 ECOL

UNITED STATES. LIBRARY OF CONGRESS. ENVIRONMENTAL POLICY DIVISION.
Congress and the Nation's environment; environmental and natural resources affairs of the 92nd Congress. U.S. Govt. Print. Off., 1973.
    KF3775.A25 1973 ECOL
A legislative history of the Water Pollution Control Act Amendments of 1972, together with a section-by-section index. U.S. Gov't. Print. Off., 1973- . v.   **KF3787.1.A16A5 ECOL**

UNITED STATES. LIBRARY OF CONGRESS. NATIONAL REFERRAL CENTER.
A directory of information resources in the United States: biological sciences. Library of Congress., U.S. Govt. Print. Off., 1972.   **REF QH303.U5 ECOL**
A directory of information resources in the United States; physical sciences, engineering. Library of Congress; U.S. Govt. Print. Off. 1971.
    REF Q223.U526 1971 ECOL

UNITED STATES. LIBRARY OF CONGRESS. NATIONAL REFERRAL CENTER FOR SCIENCE AND TECHNOLOGY.
A directory of information resources in the United States: water. U.S. Govt. Print. Off. 1966.
    fTD211.U5 ECOL

UNITED STATES. LIBRARY OF CONGRESS. NATIONAL REFERRAL CENTER FOR SCIENCE AND TECHNOLOGY. A DIRECTORY OF INFORMATION RESOURCES IN THE UNITED STATES: PHYSICAL SCIENCES, BIOLOGICAL SCIENCES, ENGINEERING.
United States. Library of Congress. National Referral Center.
A directory of information resources in the United States; physical sciences, engineering. 1971.
    REF Q223.U526 1971 ECOL

UNITED STATES. LIBRARY OF CONGRESS. NATIONAL REFERRAL CENTER FOR SCIENCE AND TECHNOLOGY./A DIRECTORY OF INFORMATION RESOURCES IN THE UNITED STATES: PHYSICAL SCIENCES, BIOLOGICAL SCIENCES, ENGINEERING.
United States. Library of Congress. National Referral Center.
A directory of information resources in the United States: biological sciences. 1972.
    REF QH303.U5 ECOL

UNITED STATES NATIONAL AERONAUTICS AND SPACE ADMINISTRATION. OFFICE OF TECHNOLOGY UTILIZATION. SCIENTIFIC AND TECHNICAL INFORMATION DIVISION.
Nicks, Oran W.
This island earth. 1970.   **fQB631.N5 ECOL**

UNITED STATES NATIONAL AGRICULTURAL LIBRARY.
Agricultural Sciences Information Network.
Directory of information resources in agriculture and biology. 1971.   **REF QH321.A37 ECOL**

UNITED STATES. NATIONAL AIR POLLUTION CONTROL ADMINISTRATION
see also UNITED STATES. ENVIRONMENTAL PROTECTION AGENCY. AIR POLLUTION CONTROL OFFICE.; UNITED STATES. ENVIRONMENTAL PROTECTION AGENCY. OFFICE OF AIR PROGRAMS.
Nitrogen oxides: an annotated bibliography. U.S. Dept. of Health, Education and Welfare, Public Health Service, Environmental Health Service, National Air Pollution Control Administration, 1970. (National Air Pollution Control Administration. Publication no. AP-72)   **Z7914.C4U5 ECOL**

UNITED STATES. NATIONAL BUREAU OF STANDARDS.
The economic impact of noise. U.S. Office of Noise Abatement and Control, 1971.   **fTD893.A48 ECOL**
The effects of sonic boom and similar impulsive noise on structures. U.S. Environmental Protection Agency 1971.   **TL574.S55U54 ECOL**

Fundamentals of Noise: measurement, rating schemes, and Standards. U.S. Office of Noise Abatement and Control, 1971 i.e. 1972
    fQC243.U55 ECOL
Measures for air quality, annual report. 1970/71- U.S. Govt. Print. Off. v. (NBS technical note)
    REF TD890.U57 ECOL
The social impact of noise. U.S. Environmental Protection Agency 1971.   **TD893.A49 ECOL**

UNITED STATES. NATIONAL BUREAU OF STANDARDS. ANALYTICAL CHEMISTRY DIVISION.
Interaction of nitrilotriacetic acid with suspended and bottom material by John K. Taylor and others, Division of Analytical Chemistry, Institute for Materials Research, National Bureau of Standards. Prepared for the Environmental Protection Agency. U.S. Environmental Protection Agency; for sale by the Supt. of Docs., U.S. Govt. Print. Off., 1971. (Water pollution control research series)   **fTD427.D4U64 ECOL**

UNITED STATES. NATIONAL CENTER FOR EDUCATIONAL COMMUNICATION.
Environmental education: programs and materials, by Stanley L. Helgeson and others. U.S. Govt. Print. Off., 1972 (PREP report, no. 33)   **S946.U58 ECOL**

UNITED STATES NATIONAL CENTER FOR URBAN AND INDUSTRIAL HEALTH.
Surgeon General's Conference on Solid Waste Management for Metropolitan Washington, Washington, D. C., 1967. 1967.
    TD525.W2S7 1967 ECOL

UNITED STATES. NATIONAL INSTITUTE FOR OCCUPATIONAL SAFETY AND HEALTH.
Criteria for a recommended standard... occupational exposure to carbon monoxide. U.S. Gov't. Print. Off., 1972.   **fRA1247.C17U5 ECOL**
Occupational exposure to inorganic lead; criteria for a recommended standard. 1972.
    fRA1231.L4U5 ECOL
Occupational exposure to ultraviolet radiation; criteria for a recommended standard. 1972.
    fRA1231.R2U5 ECOL
Tabershaw, Irving R.
The toxicology of beryllium. 1972.
    RA1231.B4T3 ECOL

UNITED STATES. NATIONAL LABORATORY, OAK RIDGE, TENN.
Nuclear Desalination Information Center.
Indexed bibliography of nuclear desalination literature—7- 1972-
    REF fZ5853.S22N8 ECOL
Nuclear Desalination Information Center.
Title—author—company index to reports published by the U.S. Dept. of the Interior, Office of Saline Water through July 1971-
    REF fZ5853.S22N84 ECOL

UNITED STATES NATIONAL PARK SERVICE.
National Education Association of the United States. Research Division.
Environmental education in the public schools. 1970
    fLB1047.N36 ECOL
The National Park system plan. 1970.
    SB482.A3 1970a ECOL
Proposed Voyageurs National Park, Minnesota. Dept. of the Interior, National Park Service, Midwest Region, 1964.   **fF612.V6A54 ECOL**
Robinette, Gary O.
Plants/people/environmental quality. 1972
    QK901.R6 ECOL

UNITED STATES. NATIONAL SCIENCE FOUNDATION. NATIONAL SCIENCE BOARD.
Environmental science, challenge for the seventies. 1971. (Report of the National Science Board)
    TD145.U5 ECOL

UNITED STATES. NATIONAL TECHNICAL INFORMATION SERVICE.
Symposium on Energy, Resources and the Environment, McLean, Va., 1972.
Symposium on energy, resources and the environment. 1972.   **fHD9540.1.S9 1972 ECOL**

UNITED STATES NAT'L. COMM. FOR THE U.S. EDUC., SCIENTIFIC AND CULTURAL ORGANIZATION.
National Conference on UNESCO, 13th, San Francisco, 1969.
No deposit—no return. 1970
    GF3.N38 1969 ECOL

UNITED STATES. NAVY DEPT.
United States Dept. of the Army.
Herbicide manual for noncropland weeds. 1970.
    SB611.U5 ECOL

UNITED STATES. NORTHEASTERN FOREST EXPERIMENT STATION, UPPER DARBY, PA.
Forest Recreation Symposium, Syracuse, N.Y., 1971. 1971.   **SD426.F6 1971 ECOL**

UNITED STATES. OFFICE OF AIR PROGRAMS
see UNITED STATES. ENVIRONMENTAL PROTECTION AGENCY. AIR POLLUTION CONTROL OFFICE.; UNITED STATES. ENVIRONMENTAL PROTECTION AGENCY. OFFICE OF AIR PROGRAMS.; UNITED STATES. NATIONAL AIR POLLUTION CONTROL ADMINISTRATION.

UNITED STATES OFFICE OF COAL RESEARCH.
Bituminous Coal Research, Inc.
The economics of generating clean fuel gas from coal using an air-blown two-stage gasifier. 1971.
    fTP759.B5 ECOL
Clean energy from coal—a national priority. 1973 annual report, calendar year 1972. Office of Coal Research, United States Dept. of the Interior. U.S. Govt. Print. Off., 1973   **HD9542.A5U5 ECOL**

Development of a coal-based sewage-treatment process. 1971   **fTN805.A395no.55 ECOL**

UNITED STATES OFFICE OF COAL RESEARCH. RESEARCH AND DEVELOPMENT REPORT NO.39.
Consolidation Coal Company. Research Division.
Pilot-scale development of the CSF Process. 1971.
    fTN805.A395no.39 ECOL

UNITED STATES. OFFICE OF EDUCATION. DIVISION OF MANPOWER DEVELOPMENT AND TRAINING.
Vehicle emission control. 1971?
    fTD886.5.V4 ECOL

UNITED STATES. OFFICE OF EDUCATION. DIVISION OF VOCATIONAL AND TECHNICAL EDUCATION.
Olympus Research Corporation.
Career education in the environment. 1971 or 2
    fGF21.O4 ECOL

UNITED STATES. OFFICE OF EDUCATION. EXPERIMENTAL SCHOOLS PROGRAM.
Educational Facilities Laboratories.
Places and things for experimental schools. 1972
    Ref LB3221.E3 ECOL

UNITED STATES. OFFICE OF EMERGENCY PREPAREDNESS.
The potential for energy conservation: substitution for scarce fuels; a staff study. U.S. Govt. Print. Off. 1973.   **fTJ153.U548 ECOL**
United States.
The potential for energy conservation. 1972.
    TJ153.U43 ECOL

UNITED STATES. OFFICE OF NOISE ABATEMENT AND CONTROL.
Bolt, Beranek, and Newman, Inc.
Noise from construction equipment and operations, building equipment, and home appliances. 1971 i.e. 1972   **fTD893.B63 ECOL**
Goodfriend (L.S.) Associates.
Noise from industrial plants. 1971.
    fTD892.G66 ECOL
Informatics Inc.
An assessment of noise concern in other nations. 1971.   **fTD892.I55 ECOL**
Miller, James D.
Effects of noise on people. 1971.
    RA772.N7M5 ECOL
Noise programs of professional/industrial organizations, universities, and colleges. 1971.
    fTD893.A51 ECOL
Public hearings on noise abatement and control. U.S. Environmental Protection Agency; for sale by the Supt. of Docs., U.S. Govt. Print. Off. 1972-   v.
    TD893.A52 ECOL
Summary of noise programs in the federal government. 1971. v.   **TD893.A522 ECOL**
Tennessee. State University, Memphis.
Effects of noise on wildlife and other animals. 1971.
    fQP82.2.N6T4 ECOL
Transportation noises: a symposium on acceptability criteria. 1970   **TA365.T68 ECOL**
United States. National Bureau of Standards.
The economic impact of noise. 1971.
    fTD893.A48 ECOL
United States. National Bureau of Standards.
The effects of sonic boom and similar impulsive noise on structures. 1971.   **TL574.S55U54 ECOL**

United States. National Bureau of Standards.
The social impact of noise. 1971.
TD893.A49 ECOL

Wyle Laboratories.
Community noise. 1971 i.e. 1972
fTD892.W94 ECOL

Wyle Laboratories.
Transportation noise and noise from equipment powered by internal combustion engines. 1971 i.e. 1972
fTD892.W95 ECOL

UNITED STATES. OFFICE OF SALINE WATER.
Nuclear Desalination Information Center.
Title—author—company index to reports published by the U.S. Dept. of the Interior, Office of Saline Water through July 1971-
REF fZ5853.S22N84 ECOL

UNITED STATES. OFFICE OF SCIENCE AND TECHNOLOGY.
Considerations affecting steam power plant site selection; a report. 1968 **TK1193.U5A44 ECOL**

Electric power and the environment; a report sponsored by the Energy Policy Staff, Office of Science and Technology, in cooperation with Atomic Energy Commission and others. For sale by the Supt. of Docs., U.S. Govt. Print. Off., 1970. **TK1193.U5A45 ECOL**

Pimentel, David.
Ecological effects of pesticides on non-target species. 1971. **QH545.P4P55 ECOL**

Resources for the Future.
United States energy policies. 1969,c1968
HD9546.R4 1969 ECOL

United States. Ad Hoc Committee on the Cumulative Regulatory Effects on the Cost of Automotive Transportation.
Cumulative regulatory effects on the cost of automotive transportation (RECAT): final report. 1972. **KF2209.A3U5 ECOL**

United States. President's Science Advisory Committee.
Report on 2, 4, 5-T. 1971. **SB612.A2A52 ECOL**

UNITED STATES. OFFICE OF SOLID WASTE MANAGEMENT PROGRAMS see also UNITED STATES. BUREAU OF SOLID WASTE MANAGEMENT.; UNITED STATES. SOLID WASTE MANAGEMENT OFFICE.

Darnay, Arsen.
Salvage markets for materials in solid wastes, ... 1972. **TD795.D38 ECOL**

UNITED STATES. OFFICE OF WATER DATA COORDINATION.
Federal Interagency Work Group on Designation of Standards for Water Data Acquisition.
Recommended methods for water data acquisition. 1972. **TD211.F44 ECOL**

UNITED STATES. OFFICE OF WATER RESOURCES RESEARCH.
Campbell, J. F.
Analysis of the injection of a heated turbulent jet into a moving mainstream, with emphasis on a thermal discharge in a waterway. 1972.
fTD427.H4C3 ECOL

Century Research Corporation.
Social aspects of urban water conservation. 1972.
fTD388.5.C4 ECOL

Colorado. State University, Fort Collins Environmental Resources Center.
The mechanism of waste treatment at low temperature. Part A- 1972- **fTD745.C58 ECOL**

Deal, Richard L.
The application of value theory to water resources planning and management. 1971.
fHD1694.A5D4 ECOL

Dracup, John A.
Applications of systems analysis techniques to water resources. 1972. **fTC409.D7 ECOL**

Harris, Douglas H.
Assessment of turbidity, color and odor in water. 1972. **fTD380.H3 ECOL**

INTASA, Inc.
Planning and evaluation of multiple purpose water resource projects in a multiobjective environment. 1972. **fHD1691.I1 ECOL**

Itasca Engineering, Inc., Minneapolis.
The effectiveness of flood control structures of the Lower Minnesota River Watershed District. 1970.
fTC424.M6I82 ECOL

Males, Richard Michael.
Decision processes in water quality management. 1971. **fTD365.M3 ECOL**

McPherson, Murray Burns.
Prospects for metropolitan water management. 1970. **fTD353.M32 ECOL**

Robideau, R. F.
The discharge of submerged bouyant jets into water of finite depth. 1972. **fTD427.H4R6 ECOL**

Walker, Wynn R.
Evaluation of urban water management policies in the Denver metropolitan area. 1973.
fTD225.D4W3 ECOL

Young, G. K.
The importance of economic factors in urban surface water supply systems. 1972. **fTD353.Y6 ECOL**

UNITED STATES. PRESIDENT,
1969- (Nixon).
The President's 1972 environmental program. 1972.
HC110.E5P74 ECOL

UNITED STATES. PRESIDENT,
1969- (NIXON).
Control of hazardous polluting substances; message from the President of the United States, transmitting a report on control of hazardous polluting substances, U.S., Govt. Print. Off., 1971. 1v. (92nd Congress, 1st session. House of Representatives. Document no. 92-70) **TD365.U53 ECOL**

UNITED STATES. PRESIDENT'S COUNCIL ON RECREATION AND NATURAL BEAUTY.
From sea to shining sea; a report on the American environment, our natural heritage. For sale by the Supt. of Docs., U.S. Govt. Print. Off. 1968.
HC110.E5A55 ECOL

UNITED STATES. PRESIDENT'S SCIENCE ADVISORY COMMITTEE.
Report on 2, 4, 5-T; a report of the panel on Herbicides of the President's Science Advisory Committee. Executive Office of the President, Office of Science and Technology, 1971. **SB612.A2A52 ECOL**

UNITED STATES PUBLIC HEALTH SERVICE.
Wolozin, Harold.
The economics of air pollution. c1966
HC110.A4W6 ECOL

UNITED STATES. PUBLIC LAND LAW REVIEW COMMISSION.
One third of the Nation's land; a report to the President and to the Congress. U.S. Govt. Print. Off. 1970 **KF5601.A55P8 ECOL**

UNITED STATES. ROBERT A TAFT SANITARY ENGINEERING CENTER, CINCINNATI.
A compilation of selected air pollution emission control regulations and ordinances. Prepared by Technical Assistance Branch, Robert A. Taft Sanitary Engineering Center. U.S. Dept. of Health, Education, and Welfare, Public Health Service, Division of Air Pollution, 1965. **REF KF3812.A4 1965 ECOL**

UNITED STATES SCIENTIFIC LABORATORY, LOS ALAMOS, N.M.
Ruch, Walter E.
Chemical detection of gaseous pollutants.
REF fZ5524.G24R8 ECOL

UNITED STATES. SECRETARY'S COMMISSION ON PESTICIDES AND THEIR RELATIONSHIP TO ENVIRONMENTAL HEALTH.
The Mutagenicity of pesticides: concepts and evaluation. 1971 **RA1270.P4M87 ECOL**

UNITED STATES. SOIL CONSERVATION SERVICE.
Big Sioux River Basin and related areas; South Dakota—Minnesota—Iowa. Prepared by United States Dept. of Agriculture, Soil Conservation Service, Economic Research Service, Forest Service in cooperation with South Dakota Water Resources Commission and others under direction of USDA Field Advisory Committee. 1973. v. **HD1695.B5A5 ECOL**

Drainage of agricultural land. U.S. Dept. of Agriculture, Soil Conservation Service 1971 (its National Engineering Handbook, section 16)
REF TC970.U5 ECOL

Flood hazard analyses: city of Canby and vicinity, Yellow Medicine County, Minnesota. Prepared by U.S. Dept. of Agriculture, Soil Conservation Service assisting the Yellow Medicine Soil and Water Conservation District in cooperation with Minn. Dept. of Natural Resources, the Lac Qui Parle—Yellow Bank Watershed District, and the city of Canby, Minnesota. n.p. 1973. **GB1225.M6U5 ECOL**

Major, Harry M.
Activities of the USDA Soil Conservation Service in providing for quality environment for all people in Minnesota. 1972. **HC110.E5M3 ECOL**

Major, Harry M.
USDA - soil conservation service in Minnesota. 1973. **S624.M6M3 ECOL**

Minnesota Association of Soil and Water Conservation Districts.
Outdoor recreational development potentials in Washington Soil and Water Conservation District.
fGV54.M6M54 ECOL

National handbook of conservation practices. U.S. Dept. of Agriculture, Soil Conservation Service, 1971. 1v. **REF S922.U5 ECOL**

Resource conservation and development projects: handbook. U.S. Dept. of Agriculture. Soil Conservation Service 1972 **S914.A57 1972 ECOL**

Watershed protection handbook. U.S. Dept. of Agriculture, Soil Conservation Service, 1967-
REF TC423.A53 ECOL

UNITED STATES. SOLID WASTE MANAGEMENT OFFICE see also UNITED STATES. BUREAU OF SOLID WASTE MANAGEMENT.; UNITED STATES. OFFICE OF SOLID WASTE MANAGEMENT PROGRAMS.

The automobile cycle: an environmental and resource reclamation problem. U.S. Govt. Print. Off., 1972.
TD793.U5 ECOL

Banks, M. E.
New chemical concepts for utilization of waste plastics. 1971. **TP156.R38B3 ECOL**

California. Dept. of Public Health.
California solid waste management study (1968) and plan (1970). 1971. **TD788.4.C3A45 ECOL**

Drobny, N. L.
Recovery and utilization of municipal solid waste: a summary of available cost and performance characteristics of unit processes and systems. 1971.
TD793.D76 ECOL

Kentucky. Dept. of Health.
Kentucky solid waste management plan. 1971.
TD788.4.K4A45 ECOL

New York (State) Dept. of Health.
New York solid waste management plan. 1971.
TD788.4.N4A45 ECOL

UNITED STATES SOLID WASTE MANAGEMENT OFFICE MIDWEST RESEARCH INSTITUTE, KANSAS CITY, MO.
Franklin, William E.
The role of nonpackaging paper in solid waste management, 1966 to 1976. 1971. **TD795.F7 ECOL**

UNITED STATES. SOLID WASTES PROGRAM
see UNITED STATES. BUREAU OF SOLID WASTE MANAGEMENT.; UNITED STATES. OFFICE OF SOLID WASTE MANAGEMENT PROGRAMS; UNITED STATES. SOLID WASTE MANAGEMENT OFFICE.

UNITED STATES. TASK FORCE ON OFF-ROAD RECREATION VEHICLES.
Off road recreation vehicles: ORRV, a Dept. of the Interior Task Force Study. Govt. Print. Off. 1971.
TL234.U5 ECOL

UNITED STATES. WATER RESOURCES COUNCIL.
Coordination directory for planning studies and reports. 1971- 1v. **TD345.U5 ECOL**

Engineering-Science, Inc.
Annotated bibliography on hydrology and sedimentation, 1966-68, United States and Canada. 1970 **REF Z7935.E5 1970 ECOL**

Ohio River Basin comprehensive survey—main report and development program formulation. Communication from the Chairman, United States Water Resources Council, transmitting the Council's report on a comprehensive program for water and related land use in the Ohio River Basin, pursuant to Public law 89-80. U.S. Govt. Print. Off., 1971. 1 v. (92d Congress, 1st session. House. Document no. 92-148)
HD1695.O5A55 ECOL

Regulation of flood hazard areas to reduce flood losses. U.S. Govt. Print. Off., 1971-
KF5588.A875 ECOL

Summary, analysis; summary and analysis of public response to the proposed principles and standards for planning water and related land resources and draft environmental statement. U.S. Govt. Print. Off. 1972.
TD345.U52 ECOL

UNITED STATES. 92ND CONGRESS, 1ST SESSION, 1971. HOUSE.
United States. President, 1969- (Nixon). Control of hazardous polluting substances. 1971.
TD365.U53 ECOL

UNTERBERG, W.
Computerized design and cost estimation for multiple-hearth sludge incinerators, by W. Unterberg, R. J. Sherwood and G. R. Schneider. U.S. Environmental Protection Agency U.S. Govt. Print. Off., 1971 i.e. 1972 (Water pollution control research series) **fTD770.U58 ECOL**

UPPER GREAT LAKES REGIONAL COMMISSION.
Orning, George W.
Land management information in northwest Minnesota: the beginnings of a statewide system. 1972
HD211.M6 ECOL
Snowmobile and Off the Road Vehicle Research Symposium, Michigan State University, East Lansing, 1971.
Proceedings. 1971. **fGF75.S6 1971 ECOL**

UPPER MISSISSIPPI RIVER COMPREHENSIVE BASIN STUDY.
Prepared under the leadership of the United States Army Corps of Engineers, North Central Division. 1970- v. **fHC107.A15U6 ECOL**

URBAN, GEORGE R.
Can we survive our future? A symposium. Edited and introduced by G. R. Urban, in collaboration with Michael Glenny. St. Martin's Press 1972, c1971
CB428.U7 1972 ECOL

URBAN PLANNING AND DESIGN, INC., MPLS., MINN.
Apple Valley park development program. 1969. v.
fGV54.M6U7 ECOL

URROWS, GRACE M.
Food preservation by irradiation by Grace M. Urrows. U.S. Atomic Energy Commission, Division of Technical Information 1968 (Understanding the atom)
TX611.5.U7 1968 ECOL
Nuclear energy for desalting. Rev. U.S. Atomic Energy Commission, Division of Technical Information 1967 (Understanding the atom)
TD479.6.U7 1967 ECOL

THE USE OF DRUGS IN ANIMAL FEEDS;
proceedings of a symposium.
National Academy of Sciences, 1969.(National Academy of Sciences. Publication 1679)
SF98.M4U8 ECOL

USE OF SYSTEMS TECHNIQUES IN ENVIRONMENTAL QUALITY MANAGEMENT.
Edited by Robert M. Brown. National Sanitation Foundation, 1970.(National Sanitation Foundation, Monograph no. 7) **RA565.A1N38no.7 ECOL**

USES OF THE SEAS.
Ed. by Edmund A. Gullion Prentice-Hall 1968 (A Spectrum book) **GC1015.U8 ECOL**

USINGER, ROBERT LESLIE, 1912-
The life of rivers and streams. Published in cooperation with the World book encyclopedia by McGraw-Hill c1967 (Our living world of nature)
QH97.U8 ECOL

UTAH WATER RESEARCH LABORATORY.
Bishop, A. Bruce.
Analysis of water reuse alternatives in an integrated urban and agricultural area. 1971 **fTD429.B5 ECOL**

UTTORMARK, PAUL D.
Ketelle, Martha J.
Problem lakes in the United States. 1971.
fTD223.K47 ECOL

V

VAGNERS, JURIS.
Oil on Puget Sound. 1972 **fTD427.P4O38 ECOL**

VAN ALLEN, JUDITH, jt. auth.
Marine, Gene.
Food pollution. 1st. ed. 1972 **TX533.M37 ECOL**

VAN DER LEEDEN, FRITS.
Ground water: a selected bibliography. Compiled and edited by Frits van der Leeden. Water Information Center 1971 **REF Z7935.V35 ECOL**

VAN DER SMISSEN, MARGARET ELISABETH, 1927-
A leader's guide to nature-oriented activities by Betty van der Smissen and Oswald H. Goering. Cartoons by Francis Redman. 2d ed. Iowa State Univ. Press 1968
GV182.2.V3 1968 ECOL

VAN DERSAL, WILLIAM RICHARD, 1907-
The land renewed; the story of soil conservation by William R. Van Dersal. Rev. and enl. ed. Walck, 1968.
S624.A1V3 1968 ECOL

VAN DOREN, CHARLES LINCOLN, 1926- jt. comp.
McHenry, Robert.
A documentary history of conservation in America. 1972 **S930.M18 ECOL**

VAN HAVERBEKE, DAVID F.
Cook, David I.
Trees and shrubs for noise abatement. 1971.
TD893.C6 ECOL

VAN NEST, WILLIAM J.
Air pollution and urban planning: a selective annotated bibliography by W. J. Van Nest and George H. Hagevik. Council of Planning Librarians 1972 (Council of Planning Librarians. Exchange bibliography, no. 257) **REF fZ5853.P7V3 ECOL**

VAN TASSEL, ALFRED J., ed.
Environmental side effects of rising industrial output. 1970 **TD174.E58 ECOL**

VAN VOAST, WAYNE A.
Ground water for irrigation in the Brooten-Belgrade area, west-central Minnesota, by Wayne A. Van Voast. U.S. Govt. Print. Off., 1971.
TC801.U2no.1899-E ECOL

VAN WORMER, JOE.
The world of the coyote. Text and photos. by Joe Van Wormer. Lippincott 1964 (A Living world book)
QL737.C2V32 ECOL
The world of the moose. Text and photos. by Joe Van Wormer. Lippincott 1972 (Living world books)
QL737.U55V32 ECOL

VANDERBILT UNIV., NASHVILLE.
National Symposium on Thermal Pollution, Portland, Oregon, 1968.
Biological aspects of thermal pollution. 1969
QH90.N3 1968 ECOL

VANDERBILT UNIVERSITY, NASHVILLE.
National Symposium on Thermal Pollution, Vanderbilt University, 1968.
Engineering aspects of thermal pollution. 1969.
TD427.H4N3 1968 ECOL

VANISHING AIR; the Ralph Nader study group report on air pollution.
John C. Esposito, project director; Larry J. Silverman, associate director. Grossman Publishers, 1970.
TD883.2.V35 ECOL

VARIN, JEAN PHILIPPE, jt. auth.
Baufle, Jean Marie.
Photographing wildlife. 1972
fTR727.B2813 ECOL

VARLEY, ALLEN, jt. auth.
Moulder, David S.
A bibliography on marine and estuarine oil pollution. 1971. **REF fZ6004.P6M6 ECOL**

VAUGHAN-JACKSON, GENEVIEVE, illus.
Venn, Mary Eleanor.
A day and a night in a tide pool. 1972
QH541.5.S35V45 ECOL

VAYDA, ANDREW PETER, comp.
Environment and cultural behavior; ecological studies in cultural anthropology. Ed. by Andrew P. Vayda. Published for American Museum of Natural History by Natural History Press, 1969. (American Museum sourcebooks in anthropology)
GF51.V35 ECOL

VEHICLE EMISSION CONTROL.
U.S. Office of Education, Division of Manpower Development and Training, 1971?
fTD886.5.V4 ECOL

VENN, MARY ELEANOR, 1908-
A day and a night in a tide pool, by Mary Adrian. Illustrated by Genevieve Vaughan-Jackson. Hastings House 1972 (The Balance of nature series)
QH541.5.S35V45 ECOL

VERMONT. AGENCY OF ENVIRONMENTAL CONSERVATION.
Development of a State effluent charge system. Prepared for the Office of Research and Monitoring, Environmental Protection Agency. U.S. Environmental Protection Agency 1972. (Water pollution control research series) **fTD224.V5A43 ECOL**

VERNBERG, F. JOHN, 1925-
The animal and the environment by F. John Vernberg and Winona B. Vernberg. Holt, Rinehart and Winston 1970 **QH541.V45 ECOL**

VERNBERG, WINONA B., 1924- jt. auth.
Vernberg, F. John.
The animal and the environment. 1970
QH541.V45 ECOL

VESSEL, MATTHEW F., jt. auth.
Wong, Herbert H.
Animal habitats: where can red-winged blackbirds live? 1970 **PZ10.W748An ECOL**
Wong, Herbert H.
Pond life: watching animals find food. c1970
PZ10.W748Po ECOL

VETTER, RICHARD C., 1923-
Oceanography information sources/70. A staff report of the Committee on Oceanography, Division of Earth Sciences, National Research Council comp. by Richard C. Vetter. National Academy of Sciences, 1970.
REF GC10.V47 ECOL

VICKERY, TOM RUSK, ed.
Man and his environment: the effects of pollution on man. 1972 **TD172.5.M35 ECOL**

VICTOR, EDWARD, 1914- jt. auth.
Hone, Elizabeth B.
Teaching elementary science: a sourcebook for elementary science. 2d ed. 1971
LB1585.H65 1971 ECOL

VIERTEL, ARTHUR T.
Trees, shrubs and vines; a pictorial guide to the ornamental woody plants of the Northern United States exclusive of conifers by Arthur T. Viertel. Syracuse University Press 1970 1 v. **QK481.V5 ECOL**

VIESSMAN, WARREN, jt. auth.
Clark, John William.
Water supply and pollution control. 2d ed. 1971
TD145.C55 1971 ECOL

VINCENT, JACK, jt. auth.
Fisher, James.
Wildlife in danger. 1969 **REF QL88.F48 ECOL**

VIRGINIA COOPERATIVE FISHERY UNIT.
Virginia Polytechnic Institute and State University.
Stream faunal recovery after manganese strip mine reclamation. 1971. **fTN291.V5 ECOL**

VIRGINIA POLYTECHNIC INSTITUTE AND STATE UNIVERSITY.
Stream faunal recovery after manganese strip mine reclamation by Kenneth B. Cumming and Donley M. Hill. Prepared for the Environmental Protection Agency. U.S. Govt. Print. Off., 1971. (Water pollution control research series) **fTN291.V5 ECOL**

VIRGINIA POLYTECHNIC INSTITUTE AND STATE UNIVERSITY. AEROSPACE ENGINEERING DEPT.
Campbell, J. F.
Analysis of the injection of a heated turbulent jet into a moving mainstream, with emphasis on a thermal discharge in a waterway. 1972. **fTD427.H4C3 ECOL**

VIRGINIA POLYTECHNIC INSTITUTE, BLACKSBURG. WATER RESOURCES RESEARCH CENTER.
Economics of air and water pollution. 1969.
fTD201.V57no.26 ECOL

VIVIAN, NORMA T. ed.
Jackson, John Y.
Land use: concern, challenge, commitment. c1969
HD110.J3 ECOL

VIVIAN, V. EUGENE, ed.
Jackson, John Y.
Land use: concern, challenge, commitment. c1969
HD110.J3 ECOL

VIVIAN, V. EUGENE, jt. auth.
Bonvie, Carolyn.
Art & design in the environment. 1971
fLB1047.B6 ECOL

VOEGELI, JEAN, jt. auth.
Dooley, David.
Summer school guide for education for an improved environment. 1971. **fQH541.2.D6 Suppl. ECOL**

VOGELY, ELIZABETH K.
Resources for the Future.
Historical statistics of minerals in the United States. 1966, 1960 **fTN23.R4 1966 ECOL**

VOGT, CARL E., jt. auth.
Naylon, Michael J.
Natural resources management: suggested teaching units for agricultural education. 1972?
fS946.N3 ECOL

VOGT, JAMES R., ed.
American Nuclear Society.
Nuclear methods in environmental research. 1971
fTD172.5.A4 ECOL

VOLCO BRASS AND COPPER COMPANY.
Brass wire mill process changes and waste abatement, recovery and reuse. Authors: Leslie E. Lancy and Charles A. Forbes. U.S. Environmental Protection Agency; for sale by the Supt. of Docs., U.S. Govt. Print. Off., 1971. (Water pollution control research series)
fTD899.M45V65 ECOL

VON ECKARDT, WOLF.
The challenge of Megalopolis; a graphic presentation of the urbanized northeastern seaboard of the United States. Based on the original study by Jean Gottmann. Macmillan, 1964. **HT123.5.A12V6 ECOL**

VON RUMKER, ROSMARIE, 1926-
The use of pesticides in suburban homes and gardens and their impact on the aquatic environment, by R. V. Rumker, senior author and others. Environmental Protection Agency, Office of Water Programs, Applied Technology Div., Rural Wastes Branch. U.S. Govt. Print. Off., 1972. v. (Pesticide study series, 2)
fQH545.P4V66 ECOL

VOSBURGH, JOHN R., 1911-
Living with your land, by John Vosburgh. Scribner c1968 **QH75.V57 ECOL**

W

WADE, JERRY L., jt. comp.
Campbell, Rex R.
Society and environment: the coming collision. 1972
HC110.E5C35 ECOL

WADENA, MINNESOTA PUBLIC SCHOOLS.
Burns, William.
Snow, snowshoes, and nature: the white dimension of environment. 1972? **fLB1047.B8 ECOL**

WAELTI, JOHN J.
Understanding the water quality controversy in Minnesota. Agricultural Extension Service, Univ. of Minnesota 1969 (Minnesota. University. Agricultural Extension Service. Extension bulletin 359)
fTD420.W3 ECOL

WAGNER, PHILIP LAURENCE, 1921-
Environments and peoples by Philip L. Wagner. Prentice-Hall 1972 (Foundations of cultural geography series) **GF41.W3 ECOL**
The human use of the earth. Free Press 1964,c1960
HM206.W28 1964 ECOL

WAGNER, RICHARD H., 1934-
Environment and man by Richard H. Wagner. 1st ed. Norton 1971 **QH541.13.W34 ECOL**

WAGNER, ROSS I., 1925-
North American Rockwell Corporation. Rocketdyne Division.
Development of a chemical denitrification process. 1970. **fTD433.N67 ECOL**

WALCOTT, MARY MORRIS (VAUX) 1860-1940.
North American wild flowers. The Smithsonian Institution, 1925. 5v. **REF fQK112.W3 ECOL**

WALKER, ERIC ARTHUR, 1910-
Fuller, Richard Buckminster.
Approaching the benign environment. 1970
Q171.F96 ECOL

WALKER, THEODORE J.
Red salmon, brown bear; the story of an Alaskan lake, based on the experiences of Dr. Theodore J. Walker. Created by Alan Landsburg Productions, Inc. World Pub. 1971 (The American Museum of Natural History's The new explorers) **QH105.A4W36 ECOL**

WALKER, WILLIAM R., ed.
Economics of air and water pollution. 1969.
fTD201.V57no.26 ECOL

WALKER, WYNN R.
Evaluation of urban water management policies in the Denver metropolitan area, by Wynn R. Walker, Robert C. Ward and Gaylord V. Skogerboe. Submitted to Office of Water Resources Research, United States Dept. of the Interior. Environmental Resources Center, Colorado State Univ., 1973. (Colorado. State University, Fort Collins. Environmental Resources Center. Completion report series, partial report no. 46)
fTD225.D4W3 ECOL

WALKER, WYNN R., jt. auth.
Skogerboe, Gaylord V.
Evaluation of canal lining for salinity control in Grand Valley. 1972. **TC930.S5 ECOL**

WALKINSHAW, LAWRENCE H.
The sandhill cranes. Cranbrook Institute of Science 1949 (Cranbrook Institute of Science. Bulletin no. 29)
QL696.G8W3 ECOL

WALLACE, DAVID A., ed.
Metropolitan open space and natural process. 1970.
HT394.P5M46 ECOL

WALLACE, J. R., jt. auth.
Tsivoglou, E. C.
Characterization of stream reaeration, capacity. 1972. **fTD458.T7 ECOL**

WALLACE, MCHARG, ROBERTS AND TODD.
An ecological study of the Twin Cities Metropolitan Area; final report. Prepared for the Metropolitan Council of the Twin Cities. Area under the supervision of Ian L. McHarg and Narendra Juneja 1969.
fQH541.W32 ECOL

WALLACE, ROBERT, 1919-
The Grand Canyon, by Robert Wallace and the editors of Time-Life Books. With photos. by Ernst Haas. Time-Life Books 1972 (The American wilderness)
F788.W23 ECOL

WALLER, ROBERT, ed.
Stapledon, Sir Reginald George.
Human ecology. 2nd ed.; edited and introduced by Robert Waller. 1971. **HM206.S65 1971 ECOL**

WALLO, OLAV O., 1898-
Twilight over the wilderness, by Olav Wallo. With 27 full color paintings by Roger Preuss. T. S. Denison 1971
fS964.U6W3 ECOL

WALTON, KENNETH, 1923-
The arid zones. 1st U.S. ed. Aldine Pub. Co. 1969 (University library of geography)
GB611.W3 1969 ECOL

WALTON, WILLIAM CLARENCE.
Groundwater resource evaluation by William C. Walton. McGraw-Hill 1970 (McGraw-Hill series in water resources and environmental engineering)
GB1003.W28 ECOL

Haik, Raymond A.
Aspects of water resources law in Minnesota. 1969.
GB701.M554no.11 ECOL

Interest groups with water and related land resources programs in Minnesota, 1971; by William C. Walton and David L. Hills. Water Resources Research Center, Univ. of Minn., 1972. (WRRC bulletin no. 45)
GB701.M554no.45 ECOL

International, regional, federal-state, interstate and federal organizations with water related land resources programs in Minnesota, 1971, by William C. Walton and David L. Hills. Water Resources Research Center, Univ. of Minnesota Graduate School, 1971. (WRRC bulletin no. 42) **GB701.M554no.42 ECOL**

Lists of references and selected books bearing on water resources in Minnesota. Univ. of Minnesota, Water Resources Research Center, 1966. (WRRC bulletin no. 4) **GB701.M554no.4 ECOL**

Lists of references and selected books bearing on Water resources in Minnesota. Rev. ed. Univ. of Minnesota, Water Resources Research Center, 1972. (WRRC bulletin no. 4 [rev])
GB701.M554no.4 1972 ECOL

Minnesota. University. Water Resources Research Center.
Codified and uncodified state laws and municipal ordinances bearing on water and related land resources in Minnesota. 1968. **GB701.M554no.9 ECOL**

Recharge from induced streambed infiltration under varying groundwater-level and stream-stage conditions; by William C. Walton, David L. Hills, and Gordon M. Grundeen. Water Resources Research Center, Univ. of Minn., 1967. (WRRC bulletin, no. 6)
GB701.M554no.6 ECOL

Water and related land resources state administration, legislative process and policies in Minnesota, 1970 by W. C. Walton and David L. Hills. Water Resources Research Center, Univ. of Minnesota, Graduate School, 1971 (Minnesota. University. Water Resources Research Center. Bulletin 27)
GB701.M554no.27 ECOL

Water resources administration in Minnesota, 1972. Water Resources Research Center, Univ. of Minn. 1972. (WRRC bulletin no. 49)
GB701.M554no.49 ECOL

The world of water by William C. Walton. Taplinger Pub. Co. 1970 **GB661.W26 ECOL**

WANDESFORDE-SMITH, GEOFFREY, ed.
Congress and the environment. 1970
KF5505.A75C6 ECOL

WANEK, WALLACE J.
A study of the impact of snowmobiling on northern Minnesota ecology. Bemidji State College, Center for Environmental Studies 1971 1v. **fTL234.W3 ECOL**

WAPORA INC.
The effect of temperature on aquatic life in the Ohio River: summary, July—December, 1970. 1971
fTD427.H4W3 ECOL

WARD, DEDERICK C.
Geologic reference sources; a subject and regional bibliography to publications and maps in the geological sciences, by Dederick C. Ward and Marjorie W. Wheeler. With a section on geologic maps, by Mark W. Pangborn, Jr. Scarecrow Press, 1972.
REF Z6031.W35 1972 ECOL

WARD, GEORGE H.
Tracor, Inc.
Estuarine modeling: an assessment. 1971.
fTD370.T73 ECOL

WARD, M. A., ed.
Banff Conference on Pollution, 1st, 1968.
Man and his environment. 1st ed. 1970-
TD172.5.B3 1968 ECOL

WARD, ROBERT C., jt. auth.
Walker, Wynn R.
Evaluation of urban water management policies in the Denver metropolitan area. 1973.
fTD225.D4W3 ECOL

WARD, W. DIXON, ed.
Conference on Noise as a Public Health Hazard, Wash., D.C., 1968.
Noise as a public health hazard. 1969.
RA772.N7C6 ECOL

WARNER, ARTHUR J.
Plastics solid waste disposal by incineration or landfill, by A. J. Warner, C. H. Parker, and Bernard Baum. Manufacturing Chemists' Association c1972, 1971. **fTD798.W36 ECOL**

WASHINGTON SEA GRANT PROGRAM.
Oil on Puget Sound. 1972 **fTD427.P4O38 ECOL**

A WASHINGTON SEA GRANT PUBLICATION (UNNUMB.).
Oil on Puget Sound. 1972 **fTD427.P4O38 ECOL**

WASHINGTON (STATE). UNIVERSITY.
Environmental requirements of blue-green algae. 1967. **QK569.C96E56 ECOL**

The oxygen uptake demand of resuspended bottom sediments. Prepared for the Water Quality Office, Environmental Protection Agency by R. H. Berg. Environmental Protection Agency, Water Quality Office; for sale by the Supt. of Docs., U.S. Govt. Print. Off., 1970. (Water pollution control research series)
fGC380.W3 ECOL

WASHINGTON (STATE). UNIVERSITY. FISHERIES RESEARCH INSTITUTE.
Responses of teleost fish to environmental stress, by L. S. Smith and others. Prepared for the Federal Water Quality Administration, Environmental Protection Agency. U.S. Govt. Print. Off., 1971. (Water pollution control research series) **fQL639.1.W3 ECOL**

WASHINGTON (STATE) UNIVERSITY. GRADUATE SCHOOL OF PUBLIC AFFAIRS.
Weather modification. 1969 **QC928.W38 ECOL**

WASHINGTON (STATE). UNIVERSITY. INSTITUTE OF FOREST PRODUCTS.
Pollution abatement by fiber modification. Author: G. G. Allan, A report for the Environmental Protection Agency. Environmental Protection Agency, Research and Monitoring; for sale by the Supt. of Docs., U.S. Govt. Print. Off., 1971. (Water pollution control research series) **fTD899.W65W38 ECOL**

WATER AND WATER POLLUTION HANDBOOK.
Edited by Leonard L. Ciaccio. M. Dekker, 1971-
v. **TD380.W322 ECOL**

WATER INFORMATION CENTER, INC.
Giefer, Gerald J.
Water publications of State agencies. 1972
REF Z7935.G55 ECOL

WATER POLLUTION CONTROL FEDERATION.
Research supplement to Journal Water Pollution Control Federation. Prepared for the Environmental Protection Agency. U.S. Govt. Print. Off., 1971. (Water pollution control research series) **fTD423.W3 ECOL**

WATER POLLUTION CONTROL FEDERATION DIRECTORY. VOL.44— MARCH 1972-
v. **REF TD201.W32 ECOL**

WATER POLLUTION CONTROL FEDERATION. JOURNAL.
Water Pollution Control Federation.
Research supplement to Journal Water Pollution Control Federation. 1971. **fTD423.W3 ECOL**

WATER QUALITY CRITERIA DATA BOOK.
Prepared for the Environmental Protection Agency, Water Quality Office. Environmental Protection Agency, Water Quality Office; for sale by the Supt. of Docs., U.S. Govt. Print. Off., 1970- v.(Water pollution control research series)
REF fTD370.W394 ECOL

WATER QUALITY IMPROVEMENT BY PHYSICAL AND CHEMICAL PROCESSES.
Edited by Ernest F. Gloyna and W. Wesley Eckenfelder, Jr. Published for the Center for Research in Water Resources by the University of Texas Press 1970(Water Resources Symposium, no. 3)
TD745.W37 ECOL

WATER QUALITY RESEARCH COUNCIL.
International Water Quality Symposium, 5th, Washington, D.C., 1970.
Water pollution and health: proceedings. 1970
fTD423.16 1970 ECOL

WATER RESOURCES.
School of Law, Duke Univ., 1957.(Law and contemporary problems, v.22, no. 3)
HD1694.A5W3 ECOL

WATER RESOURCES CENTERS OF THIRTEEN WESTERN STATES. TECHNICAL COMMITTEE.
Water resources planning and social goals: conceptualization toward a new methodology. Final report: Development of techniques for estimating the potential of water resources development in achieving national and regional social goals. Prepared for the Office of Water Resources Research, U.S. Dept. of the Interior. Printed at Utah State Univ., 1971. (Utah Water Research Laboratory. Publication PRWG-94-1)
fHD1691.W3 ECOL

WATER RESOURCES ENGINEERS, INC. WALNUT CREEK, CALIF.
Metcalf and Eddy, Boston.
Storm water management model. 1971.
fGB665.M4 ECOL

WATER RESOURCES SCIENTIFIC INFORMATION CENTER.
Lake Superior, a bibliography. 1972 (its Bibliography series, WRSIC 72-213) **fZ6005.G7W38 ECOL**
PCB in water; a bibliography. 1973. (its Bibliography series, WRSIC 73-201) **Z7173.W3W3 ECOL**
Sanitary landfills, a bibliography. Ed. by George L. Knapp. 1972 **REF Z5853.S22W38 ECOL**
Urban water planning; a bibliography. Ed. by George F. Mangan and Herbert A. Swenson. 1972.
REF Z7935.W3 ECOL
Use of naturally impaired water; a bibliography. 1973.
Z7935.W32 ECOL
Water resources thesaurus; a vocabulary for indexing and retrieving the literature of water resources research and development. 2d ed. U.S. Govt. Print. Off., 1971.
REF Z695.1.W3W3 1971 ECOL
Wengert, Norman.
Institutions for urban-metropolitan water management: essays in social theory, submitted to Water Resources Scientific Information Center. 1972.
fTD353.W4 ECOL
Wengert, Norman.
Urban-metropolitan institutions for water planning, development and management: an analysis of usages of the term "institutions": a state-of-the-art review: final report, submitted to Water Resources Scientific Information Center. 1972. **fTD353.W42 ECOL**

WATERS, WILLIAM E., 1922- ed.
International Symposium on Statistical Ecology, New Haven, 1969.
Statistical ecology. 1971
QH541.15.M3I5 1969 ECOL

WATKINS, JESSIE B.
Ecology and environmental quality; a selected and annotated bibliography for biologists and earth scientists by Jessie B. Watkins. Syracuse University Libraries, 1971. **REF fZ5322.E2W3 ECOL**

WATKINS, TOM H.
Boyle, Robert H.
The water hustlers. 1971 **HD1694.A5B58 ECOL**
The Grand Colorado; the story of a river and its canyons, by T. H. Watkins and contributors: William E. Brown, Jr. and others. With a foreword by Wallace Stegner. Color photography by Philip Hyde. American West Pub. Co. 1969 **fF788.W33 ECOL**

WATSON, GEOFFREY GRAINGE.
Fun with ecology, by G. G. Watson; foreword by Ian McPhail, with 22 photographs and 15 drawings by W. C. Cartner. Winchester 1971,c1967
QH541.2.W3 1971 ECOL

WATSON, PATTY JO, 1932- jt. auth.
Watson, Richard A.
Man and nature. 1969 **GF23.W3 ECOL**

WATSON, RICHARD A., 1931-
Man and nature; an anthropological essay in human ecology by Richard A. Watson and Patty Jo Watson. Harcourt, Brace & World 1969 **GF23.W3 ECOL**

WATT, KENNETH E. F., 1929-
Ecology and resource management; a quantitative approach by Kenneth E. F. Watt. McGraw-Hill 1968 (McGraw-Hill publications in the biological sciences. Series in population biology) **QL752.W38 ECOL**

WATT, KENNETH E. F., 1929- ed.
Systems analysis in ecology, ed. by Kenneth E. F. Watt. Academic Press, 1966. **QH541.W3 ECOL**

WATT, LOIS B., comp.
Environmental - ecological education: a bibliography of fiction, nonfiction, and textbooks for elementary and secondary schools. Comp by Lois B. Watt, and Myra H. Thomas of the Educational Materials Center of the National Center for Educational Communications. ERIC Clearinghouse for Social Studies/Social Science Education, 1971. (ERIC Clearinghouse for Social Studies/Social Science Education. Reference series no.5)
REF fQH541.2.W34 ECOL

WAYBURN, PEGGY.
Edge of life; the world of the estuary. Photographs by Dennis Stock. With an introd. by Paul Brooks. Designed by Charles Curtis. Sierra Club c1972
fQH541.5.E8W3 ECOL

WEATHER MODIFICATION; science and public policy.
Ed. by Robert G. Fleagle. Univ. of Wash. Press 1969(Public policy issued in resource management [v.3]) **QC928.W38 ECOL**

WEAVER, ELBERT C., ed.
Scientific experiments in environmental pollution. Holt, Rinehart and Winston in cooperation with the Manufacturing Chemists' Ass'n. Inc. 1968
TD178.5.W4 ECOL

WEAVER, JOHN ERNEST, 1884-1966.
Prairie plants and their environment; a fifty-year study in the Midwest. Univ. of Nebraska Press 1968
QK938.P7W42 ECOL

WEAVER, LEO, ed.
Surgeon General's Conference on Solid Waste Management for Metropolitan Washington, Washington, D. C., 1967. 1967.
TD525.W2S7 1967 ECOL

WEAVER, ROBERT CLIFTON.
Zisch, William E.
The urban environment: how it can be improved. 1969. **HT175.U6Z4 ECOL**

WEBER, WALTER J., 1934-
Physiochemical processes for water quality control by Walter J. Weber, Jr. With contributions by Jack A. Borchardt and others Wiley-Interscience 1972 (Environmental science and technology)
TD430.W42 ECOL

WEBER, WALTER J., 1934- jt. auth.
Mancy, Khalil H.
Analysis of industrial wastewaters. 1971
TD735.M35 ECOL

WECHSLER, CHARLES, ed.
Fisher, Wes.
Minnesota environmental education areas. 1972
fS946.F5 ECOL

WEHRWEIN, GEORGE SIMON, 1883-1945, jt. auth.
Ely, Richard Theodore.
Land economics. 1964. **HD111.E37 1964 ECOL**

WEI, TSONG C.
Effects of areal and time distribution of rainfall on small watershed runoff hydrographs, by Tsong C. Wei and Curtis L. Larson. Water Resources Research Center, Univ. of Minnesota Graduate School, 1971. (WRRC bulletin no. 30) **GB701.M554no.30 ECOL**

WEI, TSONG C., jt. auth.
Larson, Curtis L.
Numerical routing of flood hydrographs through open channel junctions. 1971.
GB701.M554no.40 ECOL

WEISBERG, BARRY.
Beyond repair; the ecology of capitalism. Beacon Press 1971 **GF75.W45 1971 ECOL**

WEISBERG, BARRY, comp.
Ecocide in Indochina; the ecology of war. Canfield Press 1970 **DS557.A68W43 ECOL**

WELCH, ANNEMARIE S., ed.
Physiological effects of noise. 1970.
QP82.2.N6P47 ECOL

WELCH, BRUCE L., 1931- ed.
Physiological effects of noise. 1970.
QP82.2.N6P47 ECOL

WELCH, ROBIN I.
A feasibility demonstration of an aerial surveillance spill prevention system, by Robin I. Welch, Allan D. Marmelstein and Paul M. Maughan for the Office of Research and Monitoring, Environmental Protection Agency. U.S. Govt. Print. Off. 1972. (Water pollution control research series) **fTD427.P4W45 ECOL**

WELLCOME TRUST, LONDON. V. TORONTO. UNIVERSITY, DEPT. OF PARASITOLOGY.
Ecology and physiology of parasites. 1971
QL757.E26 ECOL

WELLES, CHRIS.
The elusive bonanza; the story of oil shale—America's richest and most neglected natural resource. 1st ed. Dutton, 1970. **HD9565.W47 ECOL**

WELLFORD, HARRISON.
Sowing the wind; a report from Ralph Nader's Center for Study of Responsive Law on food safety and the chemical harvest. Grossman Pub., 1972.
HD9000.9.U5W4 ECOL

WELLS, DAN M., 1926-
Potential pollution of the Ogallala by recharging playa lake water—pesticides, by Dan M. Wells, Ellis W. Huddleston, and Robert G. Rekers. Prepared for the Environmental Protection Agency. Environmental Protection Agency; for sale by the Supt. of Docs., U.S. Govt. Print. Off., 1970. (Water pollution control research series) **fTD224.T4W45 ECOL**

WENGERT, HAROLD, jt. auth.
Kelly, James.
Pollution—man's crisis: an investigative approach. c1971 **QH541.2.K45 ECOL**

WENGERT, NORMAN.
Urban-metropolitan institutions for water planning, development and management: an analysis of usages of the term "institutions": a state-of-the-art review: final report, submitted to Water Resources Scientific Information Center. Environmental Resources Center, Colorado State Univ., 1972. (Colorado. State University, Fort Collins. Environmental Resources Center. Completion report series, no. 36)
fTD353.W42 ECOL

WENGERT, NORMAN, ed.
Institutions for urban-metropolitan water management: essays in social theory, submitted to Water Resources Scientific Information Center. Environmental Resources Center, Colorado State Univ., 1972. (Colorado. State University, Fort Collins. Environmental Resources Center. Completion report series, no.39) **fTD353.W4 ECOL**

WENGERT, NORMAN I.
Natural resources and the political struggle. Random House, 1967,c1955 (Studies in political science)
HC103.7.W4 1967 ECOL

WENKAM, ROBERT, 1920-
Kauai and the park country of Hawaii. Ed. by Kenneth Brower. With a foreword by David Brower. Sierra Club 1967 (Sierra Club exhibit format series, 15)
DU628.K3W4 ECOL

WENSBERG, KATHERINE S.
Experiences with living things; an introduction to ecology for five- to eight-year-olds, by Katherine Wensberg. With drawings by Pat Ken. Beacon Press 1966 **LB1532.W4 ECOL**

WENT, FRITS WARMOLT, 1903-
The plants, by F. W. Went and the editors of Life. Time, Inc. 1969,c1963 (Life nature library)
fQK50.W43 1969 ECOL

WENTWORTH, DANIEL F.
Pollution. By D. F. Wentworth and others Mine Publications c1971 (Examining your environment)
TD175.W46 ECOL

WERNER, WILLIAM ERNEST, 1925- jt. auth.
Benton, Allen H.
Field biology and ecology. 2d ed. 1966
QH318.5.B4 1966 ECOL
Benton, Allen H.
Manual of field biology and ecology. 4th ed. c1965
QH307.B3 1965 ECOL

WEST-CENTRAL MINNESOTA RESOURCE CONSERVATION AND DEVELOPMENT COMMITTEE.
Van Voast, Wayne A.
Ground water for irrigation in the Brooten-Belgrade area, west-central Minnesota. 1971.
TC801.U2no.1899-E ECOL

WEST, JAMES A., jt. auth.
Dupree, Walter G.
United States energy through the year 2000. 1972.
HD9545.D8 ECOL

WEST, RONALD EMMETT, 1933- jt. comp.
Brittin, Wesley Emil.
Air and water pollution. 1972 **TD881.B75 ECOL**

WEST ST. PAUL, MINN. INDEPENDENT SCHOOL DIST. NO. 197. ELEMENTARY SCIENCE COMMITTEE.
Elementary science guide and resource book. Prepared by: Elementary Science Committee, Keith Schroeder, department coordinator. n.d.
fLB1585.W4 ECOL

WEST, TRUSTHAM FREDERICK, jt. auth.
Hartley, Gilbert Spencer.
Chemicals for pest control. 1st ed. 1969
TP248.P47H3 1969 ECOL

WEST VIRGINIA. UNIVERSITY. COAL RESEARCH BUREAU.
Dewatering of mine drainage sludge. U.S. Environmental Protection Agency; for sale by the Supt. of Docs., U.S. Govt. Print. Off., 1971. (Water pollution control research series) **fTD899.M5W44 ECOL**
Underground coal mining methods to abate water pollution; a state of the art literature review. Environmental Protection Agency, Water Quality Office; for sale by the Supt. of Docs., U.S. Govt. Print. Off., 1970. (Water pollution control research series)
fTD899.M5W46 ECOL

WESTERN PLANT ENGINEERING AND MAINTENANCE CONFERENCE, SAN FRANCISCO, 1970 PROCEEDINGS,.
Sponsored by the American Institute of Plant Engineers, 1970. 1v. **fTS184.W4**

WESTERN REGIONAL CONFERENCE ON RESOURCE RECOVERY: INDUSTRY'S APPROACH, UNIVERSITY OF SOUTHERN CALIFORNIA, 1972.
Resource recovery: industry's approach papers presented at a conference held Feb. 10, 1972. Univ. of Southern California, 1972.
fTP995.A1W4 1972 ECOL

WESTERN RESOURCCS CONFERENCE, 9TH, UNIVERSITY OF COLORADO, 1967.
Man and the quality of his environment. Ed. by J. Ernest Flack and Margaret C. Shipley. Univ. of Colorado Press 1968 (Western resources papers, 1967)
TD180.W4 1967 ECOL

WESTERN RESOURCES CONFERENCE. COLORADO SCHOOL OF MINES, SUMMER 1971.
Needs of a progressive society for mineral and energy resources and realistic solutions to environmental problems posed. 1971   REF fTD172.5.W4 ECOL

WESTERN RESOURCES CONFERENCE, 7TH, COLORADO STATE UNIVERSITY, 1965.
Water research; economic analysis, water management, evaluation problems, water reallocation, political and administrative problems, hydrology and engineering, research programs and need. Papers ed. by Allen V. Kneese and Stephen C. Smith. Published for Resources for the Future by the Johns Hopkins Press c1966   REF TD355.W4 1965 ECOL

WESTERN RESOURCES CONFERENCE, 8TH, COLORADO SCHOOL OF MINES, 1966.
Natural gas, coal, ground water; exploring new methods and techniques in resources research. University of Colorado Press 1967 (Western resources papers, 1966)   HC103.7.W45 1966 ECOL

WESTINGHOUSE OCEAN RESEARCH LABORATORY, ANNAPOLIS, MD.
Chesher, Richard H.
Biological impact of a large-scale desalination plant at Key West. 1971.   fTD478.5.F5C48 ECOL

WETHERILL, C. RHYS, jt. auth.
Ramsey, Ralph H.
Soil systems for municipal effluents. 1972.
fTD760.R24 ECOL

WHAT ARE ME AND YOU GONNA DO?
Children's letters to Senator Gaylord Nelson about the environment.
Ballantine Books 1971   TD175.W53 ECOL

WHAT'S AHEAD FOR OUR PUBLIC LANDS? A summary review of the activities and final report of the Public Land Law Review Commission.
Compiled for the Natural Resources Council of America by Hamilton K. Pyles. Natural Resources Council of America 1970   KF5606.W5 ECOL

WHEELER, MARJORIE W., jt. auth.
Ward, Dederick C.
Geologic reference sources. 1972.
REF Z6031.W35 1972 ECOL

"WHERE HAVE ALL THE FLOWERS GONE?"
A reference guide and sourcebook to ecological literature.
Arrow Co. 1970   REF fZ5322.E2W54 ECOL

WHINSTON, A. B.
Economic analyses of optimal water quality management. Purdue Univ., Water Resources Research Center, 1972. (Purdue University, Lafayette, Ind. Water Resources Research Center. Technical Report, no.25)
fTD365.W4 ECOL

WHITE, ANTHONY G.
Lead in the urban environment: a selected bibliography. 1973. (Council of Planning Librarians. Exchange bibliography, 437.)   fZ6679.L4W5 ECOL

WHITE, GILBERT FOWLER, 1911-
Strategies of American water management by Gilbert F. White. Univ. of Michigan Press 1969
HD1694.A5W5 ECOL

WHITE, GILBERT FOWLER, [1911-   ed.
Papers on flood problems by Wallace E. Akin and others. 1961.   TC530.W4 ECOL

WHITE HOUSE CONFERENCE ON NATURAL BEAUTY, WASHINGTON, D.C., 1965.
Beauty for America; proceedings. For sale by the Superintendent of Documents, U.S. Govt. Print. Off., 1965   QH77.U6W5 1965 ECOL

WHITE, JEAN DUNCAN, jt. comp.
Fadiman, Clifton.
Ecocide—and thoughts toward survival. 1971
HC110.E5F32 ECOL

WHITEHEAD, GEORGE KENNETH, 1913-
Deer of the world by G. Kenneth Whitehead. Viking Press 1972 (A Studio book)
QL737.U55W44 1972b ECOL

WHITESIDE, THOMAS, 1918-
The withering rain; America's herbicidal folly. 1st ed. Dutton, 1971.   QH545.P4W48 1971 ECOL

WHITMAN, I. L., ed.
Resource management in the Great Lakes Basin. 1971   HD1694.A2 1971 ECOL

WHITTAKER, ROBERT HARDING, 1920-
Communities and ecosystems by Robert H. Whittaker. Macmillan 1970 (Current concepts in biology series)   QH541.W44 ECOL

WHO SPEAKS FOR EARTH?
by Barbara Ward and others. Edited by Maurice F. Strong. 1st ed. Norton 1973   GF8.W49 ECOL

WHO'S WHO IN ECOLOGY, 1973-
Special Reports, Inc. v.   REF fQH26.W46 ECOL

WHYTE, WILLIAM HOLLINGSWORTH.
Last landscape. Doubleday, 1968.
HT167.W48 ECOL

WIDENER, DON.
Timetable for disaster. Edited by Fay Robin Landau. Nash Pub. 1970   TD180.W53 ECOL

WIDMAN, MICHAEL U.
Polymer film overlay system for mercury contaminated sludge—Phase I, by Michael U. Widman and Michael M. Epstein. Prepared for the Office of Research and Monitoring, Environmental Protection Agency. U.S. Govt. Print. Off., 1972. (Water pollution control research series)   fTD427.M4W5 ECOL

WIENS, HEROLD JACOB, 1912-
Atoll environment and ecology. Yale University Press, 1971,c1962   QH541.5.C7W5 ECOL

WILDERNESS CONFERENCE.
Schwartz, William.
Voices for the wilderness. 1969   QH75.S32 ECOL

WILDFOWL TRUST.
Scott, Peter Markham.
The swans. 1972.   QL696.A5S37 ECOL

WILDLIFE MANAGEMENT INSTITUTE.
Trefethen, James B.
Wildlife management and conservation. 1964
S962.T7 ECOL

WILDLIFE REVIEW.
United States. Fish and Wildlife Service.
Wildlife abstracts.   REF SK351.U52 ECOL

WILEY, AVERILL J.
Reverse osmosis concentration of dilute pulp and paper effluents, by Averill J. Wiley, George A. Dubey and I. K. Bansal. Prepared for the Office of Research and Monitoring Environmental Protection Agency. U.S. Govt. Print. Off., 1972. (Water pollution control research series)   fTD899.W65W5 ECOL

WILKINSON, ROBERT E., 1926-
How to know the weeds by R. E. Wilkinson and H. E. Jaques. 2d ed. W. C. Brown Co. 1972 (Pictured-key nature series)   SB612.A2W54 1972 ECOL

WILLEKE, GENE E., 1934-
A program for metropolitan water management, by Gene E. Willeke and F. William Kroeck. Environmental Resources Center, Georgia Institute of Technology, 1972.   fTD365.W5 ECOL

WILLIAMS, CURTIS ALVIN, 1927-   , ed.
Environmental education 1970. 1970
fS946.E55 ECOL

WILLIAMS, EUGENE RUSSELL, 1909-
The ways of wildfowl, featuring the distinguished paintings and etchings of Richard E. Bishop with text by Russ Williams. Edited by Thomas C. Jones. J. G. Ferguson Pub. Co. 1971 REF fQL696.A5W48 ECOL

WILLIAMS, ROBERT, 1940-   jt. comp.
Brittin, Wesley Emil.
Air and water pollution. 1972   TD881.B75 ECOL

WILLIAMS, WILLIAM DAVID.
Freshwater isopods (Asellidae) of North America. Environmental Protection Agency, 1972. (Biota of freshwater ecosystems Identification manual, no.7.)
fQH96.A2B5no.7 ECOL

WILLIAMSON, D. E., jt. auth.
Balakrishnan, S.
State of the art review on sludge incineration practice. 1970.   fTD803.B36 ECOL

WILLRICH, MASON.
Global politics of nuclear energy. Praeger Publishers 1971 (Praeger special studies in international politics and public affairs)   TK9145.W49 ECOL

WILLRICH, TED. L.
Iowa Water Resources Pollution Control and Abatement Seminar, Iowa State University, 1965.
Water pollution: control and abatement proceedings. 1st ed. 1970,c1967   TD224.I816 1965 ECOL

WILLRICH, TED L., ed.
Agricultural practices and water quality. 1971,c1970
TD420.A33 ECOL

WILSON, BILLY RAY, ed.
Environment, the university, & the welfare of man. 1969   LC191.E55 ECOL

Environmental problems. 1968   TD180.E48 ECOL

WILSON, BRAYTON FULLER, 1934-
The growing tree. University of Massachusetts Press, 1970.   QK731.W46 ECOL

WILSON, CAROL A., jt. auth.
Dimitriades, Basil.
Interpretation of gas chromatographic spectra in routine analysis of exhaust hydrocarbons. 1972
TN23.U7no.7700 ECOL

WILSON, JERRY C.
South Tahoe Public Utility District.
Advanced wastewater treatment as practiced at South Tahoe. 1971.   fTD225.T25S6 ECOL

WILSON, MITCHELL A.
Energy, by Mitchell Wilson and the editors of Life. Time, Inc. 1967 (Life science library)
fTJ147.W53 1967 ECOL

WILSON, RAYMOND HARRISON.
Toward a philosophy of planning: attitudes of federal water planners. Office of Research and Monitoring, Environmental Protection Agency, 1973. (Socioeconomic environmental studies series)
HC110.E5W5 ECOL

WILSON, W. N., jt. auth.
Dorian, Edith M.
Animals that made U.S. history. c1964
QL155.D6 ECOL

WINGO, LOWDON.
Transportation and urban land. Resources for the Future 1968,c1961   HE4211.W5 ECOL

WINGO, LOWDON, ed.
Resources for the Future.
Cities and space: the future use of urban land. 1963
NA9031.R4 ECOL

WINSTON, ERIC V. A.
Directory of urban affairs information and research centers, comp. by Eric V. A. Winston in cooperation with Marilyn Trezise. Scarecrow Press, 1970.
HT110.W5 ECOL

WINTER, RUTH, 1930-
Poisons in your food. With an introd. by Walter Frederick Mondale. Crown 1969
TX533.W55 1969 ECOL

WINTER, WILLIAM C., jt. auth.
Powell, Mel D.
Community action guidebook for soil erosion and sediment control. 1970   fS624.A1P68 ECOL

WINTON, HARRY N. M.
Man and the environment: a bibliography of selected publications of the United Nations system, 1946-1971. Compiled and edited by Harry N. M. Winton. Unipub, 1972.   REF Z5322.E2W56 ECOL

WISCONSIN. DEPT. OF PUBLIC INSTRUCTION.
Reading Wisconsin's landscape. 2d ed. 1962, reprinted 1966.   fS946.R4 1966 ECOL

WISCONSIN. DIVISION OF ENVIRONMENTAL PROTECTION.
Workshop on Hydrologic and Hydraulic Aspects of Flood Plain Construction, Madison, Wisc., 1968. Proceedings. 1968?   fGB1225.W6W6 1968 ECOL

WISCONSIN. UNIVERSITY.
Peregrine falcon populations. 1969.
QL696.A2P44 ECOL

WISCONSIN. UNIVERSITY—GREEN BAY. CONCENTRATION IN MODERNIZATION PROCESSES.
Environmental quality and social responsibility. 1972   HC110.P55E57 ECOL

WISCONSIN. UNIVERSITY. UNIVERSITY EXTENSION DIVISION. LAW DEPT.
MacDonald, James B.
Environmental litigation. 1972.
KF3775.M3 ECOL

WISE, WILLIAM.
Killer smog; the world's worst air pollution disaster. Rand McNally 1968   RA576.W57 ECOL

WOHLERS, HENRY C., ed.
Hunter, Donald E.
Air pollution experiments for junior and senior high school science classes. 1968.   fTD883.2.H8 ECOL

WOHLT, PAUL E., jt. auth.
Thomsen, Arvid L.
Riprap stability on earth embankments tested in large—and small-scale wave tanks. 1972.
TC533.T4 ECOL

WOLLMAN, NATHANIEL.
The outlook for water; quality, quantity, and national growth, by Nathaniel Wollman and Gilbert W. Bonem. Published for Resources for the Future by the Johns Hopkins Press 1971 **REF fTD223.W6 ECOL**

WOLMAN, ABEL, 1892-
Water, health, and society; selected papers. Ed. by Gilbert F. White. indiana Univ. Press 1969 **REF TD355.W6 ECOL**

WOLOZIN, HAROLD, 1920- ed.
The economics of air pollution; papers ed. by Harold Wolozin. Norton c1966 **HC110.A4W6 ECOL**

WONG, HERBERT H.
Animal habitats: where can red-winged blackbirds live? By Herbert H. Wong and Matthew F. Vessel. Illustrated by Arvis L. Stewart. Addison-Wesley 1970 (Science series for the young) **PZ10.W748An ECOL**

Pond life: watching animals find food. By Herbert H. Wong and Matthew F. Vessel. Illus. by Tony Chen. Addison-Wesley c1970 **PZ10.W748Po ECOL**

WOOD, BURRELL L., jt. auth.
LeCompte, Robert G.
Atoms at the science fair. 1968
Q105.L412 1968 ECOL

WOOD, FLORENCE DOROTHY, jt. auth.
Wood, Frances Elizabeth.
Animals in danger. 1968 **QL88.W6 ECOL**

Wood, Frances Elizabeth.
Forests are for people. 1971 **SD565.W66 ECOL**

WOOD, FRANCES ELIZABETH.
Animals in danger; the story of vanishing American wildlife by Frances and Dorothy Wood. Illustrated with photos. Dodd, Mead 1968 **QL88.W6 ECOL**

Forests are for people; the heritage of our national forests by Frances and Dorothy Wood. Dodd, Mead 1971 **SD565.W66 ECOL**

WOOD, JOHN MARTIN, 1938-
Enzymes and the environment by John M. Wood. Bogden & Quigley 1972 (A B & Q general chemistry separate) **fQP601.W74 ECOL**

WOOD, NANCY C.
Clearcut; the deforestation of America by Nancy Wood. Sierra Club c1971 (The Sierra Club battlebook series, 3) **SD538.2.A1W65 ECOL**

WOODROW WILSON INTERNATIONAL CENTER FOR SCHOLARS.
A selective, annotated bibliography of reports and documents on international environmental problems. 1972. (its The Human environment, v.1) **fZ7164.N3W6 ECOL**

Summaries of national reports submitted in preparation for the United Nations Conference on the Human Environment. 1972. (its The Human environment, v.2) **fHC68.W6 ECOL**

WOODS, BARBARA, comp.
Eco-solutions: a casebook for the environmental crisis. Edited with introductions by Barbara Woods. Schenkman Pub. Co.; distributed by General Learning Press 1972 **GF43.W6 ECOL**

WOODS HOLE, MASS. OCEANOGRAPHIC INSTITUTION.
Oil on the sea. 1969. **GC1080.O36 ECOL**

WORKING GROUP MEETING ON NUCLEAR POWER PLANT CONTROL AND INSTRUMENTATION, VIENNA, 1971.
Nuclear power plant control and instrumentation. Proceedings of a working group meeting organized by the International Atomic Energy Agency and held in Vienna, 15-19 March 1971. International Atomic Energy Agency, 1972. (Panel proceedings series)
TK9006.W58 1971 ECOL

WORKSHOP ON GLOBAL ECOLOGICAL PROBLEMS, UNIVERSITY OF WISCONSIN, 1971.
Man in the living environment; report. Published for the Institute of Ecology, by the University of Wisconsin Press 1972 **GF3.W6 1971 ECOL**

WORKSHOP ON HYDROLOGIC AND HYDRAULIC ASPECTS OF FLOOD PLAIN CONSTRUCTION, MADISON, WISC., 1968.
Proceedings. Editor: Amir al-Khafaji. Dept. of Natural Resources, Division of Environmental Protection 1968? **fGB1225.W6W6 1968 ECOL**

THE WORLD BOOK ENCYCLOPEDIA.
Allen, Durward Leon.
The life of prairies and plains. 1967
QH541.5.P7A4 ECOL

Berrill, Norman John.
The life of the ocean. c1966 **QH91.15.B4 ECOL**

Usinger, Robert Leslie.
The life of rivers and streams. c1967
QH97.U8 ECOL

WORLD HEALTH ORGANIZATION.
Health hazards of the human environment. Prepared by 100 specialists in 15 countries. Geneva, 1972.
RA565.W6 ECOL

WORLD LIFE RESEARCH INSTITUTE.
Pharmacological testing of blue-green algae for constituents having therapeutic value. Prepared for the Water Quality Office, Environmental Protection Agency. Author: Bruce W. Halstead Environmental Protection Agency, Water Quality Office; for sale by the Supt. of Docs., U.S. Govt. Print. Off., 1970. (Water pollution control research series)
fRS165.A7W67 ECOL

THE WORLD OF THE ATOM SERIES.
Pizer, Vernon.
Preserving food with atomic energy. 1970
TX611.5.P58 ECOL

WORLD WILDLIFE FUND.
Philip, Duke of Edinburg.
Wildlife crisis. 1st American ed. 1970
S962.P55 ECOL

WORRELL, ALBERT CADWALLADER, 1913-
Principles of forest policy by Albert C. Worrell. McGraw-Hill Book Co. 1970 (American forest series)
SD565.W67 ECOL

WORTH, CHARLES BROOKE, 1908-
Of mosquitoes, moths, and mice by C. Brooke Worth. 1st ed. Norton 1972 **QL475.N5W66 ECOL**

WRIGHT, JAMES CLAUD, 1922-
The coming water famine by Jim Wright. Coward 1966 **TD223.W7 ECOL**

WRIGHT, JOHN KIRTLAND, 1891- ed.
Antevs, Ernst.
Rainfall and tree growth in the Great basin... 1938.
QC925.1.U35 1938 ECOL

WRIGHT, ROBERT HENRY, 1929-
What good is a weed? Ecology in action by Robert H. Wright. Lothropp Lee & Shepard Co. 1972
QK49.W75 ECOL

WRIGHT, SYDNEY.
A bibliography of recreational communities and leisure land development by S. Wright and Kristian A. Dentino. 1973. (Council of Planning Librarians. Exchange bibliography, 426) **fZ7164.L3W7 ECOL**

WRONG, DENNIS HUME, 1923-
Population and society by Dennis H. Wrong. 3d. ed. Random House 1967 (Random House studies in sociology, SS 15) **HB881.W74 1967 ECOL**

WULLSTEIN, LEROY H., ed.
Grand Canyon Symposium, 1970.
Environment, man, survival: Grand Canyon Symposium, 1970. c1971 **GF8.G7 1970 ECOL**

WURMAN, RICHARD SAUL, 1935- ed.
Yellow pages of learning resources. 1972.
Ref fLC215.Y45 ECOL

WYLE LABORATORIES.
Community noise. U.S. Environmental Protection Agency 1971 i.e. 1972 **fTD892.W94 ECOL**

Transportation noise and noise from equipment powered by internal combustion engines. 1971 i.e. 1972 1 v. **fTD892.W95 ECOL**

WYLIE, STEPHEN R.
Key to North American waterfowl, by Stephen R. Wylie and Stewart S. Furlong. Illustrated by Jack R. Schroeder. Livingston Pub.; distributed by the World Pub. Co. 1972 **QL696.A5W46 ECOL**

X

XEROX CORP.
Moore, John A.
Science for society: a bibliography. 2nd ed. 1971
fZ7401.M6 1971 ECOL

Y

YALE UNIVERSITY. PEABODY MUSEUM OF NATURAL HISTORY.
Peabody Museum Centennial Symposium, Yale University, 1966.
Evolution and environment. 1968.
QH366.A1P4 1966 ECOL

YAPP, WILLIAM BRUNSDON.
The life and organization of birds by W. B. Yapp. American Elsevier Pub. Co. 1970 (Series of student texts in contemporary biology) **QL698.Y36 ECOL**

YEAPLE, DONALD S.
JBF Scientific Corporation.
Engineering methodology for river and stream reaeration. 1971 **fTD458.J17 ECOL**

YEAPLE, DONALD S., jt. auth.
Feick, George.
Control of mercury contamination in freshwater sediments. 1972. **TD427.M4F4 ECOL**

YELLOW PAGES OF LEARNING RESOURCES;
resources directory area code 800.
Written by George Borowsky, and others. Ed. by Richard Saul Wurman. MIT Press, 1972.
Ref fLC215.Y45 ECOL

YOUNG, G. K.
The importance of economic factors in urban surface water supply systems; final report. Prepared by G. K. Young, G. F. Tierney, and J. S. Selekof for U.S. Dept. of the Interior, Office of Water Resources Research. Water Resources Engineers, Inc., 1972. v.
fTD353.Y6 ECOL

YOUNG, LOUISE B., comp.
Evolution of man. Prepared by American Foundation for Continuing Education. Edited by Louise B. Young. Oxford University Press, 1970. **QH368.Y68 ECOL**

Population in perspective, ed. by Louise B. Young. Oxford Univ. Press, 1968. **HB851.Y6 ECOL**

YOUNG, PAUL JONATHAN, jt. auth.
Hann, Roy W.
Mathematical models of water quality parameters for rivers and estuaries. 1972 **fTD370.H3 ECOL**

YOUR GOVERNMENT AND THE ENVIRONMENT. V.1- 1971-
Output Systems Corp. v.
REF fHC110.E5Y6 ECOL

Z

ZAJIC, JAMES E., 1928-
Water pollution; disposal and reuse, by J. E. Zajic. M. Dekker, 1971. 2 v. **TD420.Z35 ECOL**

ZAREFSKY, DAVID, jt. auth.
McClain, Thomas B.
Complete handbook on environmental control. 1970
Z5853.P7M32 ECOL

ZAVADOSKI, R. W., jt. auth.
Postma, Arlin Keith.
Review of organic iodide formation under accident conditions in water-cooled reactors. 1972.
fTK9152.P6 ECOL

ZAVAL, FRANK J.
Revegetation augmentation by reuse of treated active surface mine drainage; a feasibility study, by Frank J. Zaval and John D. Robins. Prepared for Office of Research and Monitoring, U.S. Environmental Protection Agency. U.S. Govt. Print. Off., 1972. (Environmental protection technology series)
TD899.M5Z3 ECOL

ZIMMERMAN, JAMES HALL.
Courtenay, Booth.
Wildflowers and weeds. 1972? **QK141.C6 ECOL**

ZIMMERMAN, JOSEPH FRANCIS, 1928-
The role of the state legislature in air pollution abatement. n.p., n.d. **fKF3812.Z9Z5 ECOL**

ZISCH, WILLIAM E.
The urban environment: how it can be improved by W. E. Zisch, Paul H. Douglas and Robert C. Weaver. Univ. Press, 1969. (The Charles C. Moskowitz lectures, no. 9) **HT175.U6Z4 ECOL**

ZISWILER, VINZENZ.
Extinct and vanishing animals; a biology of extinction and survival. Rev. English ed. by Fred and Pille Bunnell. Springer-Verlag, 1967. (Heidelberg science library, v.2)
QL88.Z513 ECOL

ZIVNUSKA, JOHN ARTHUR, 1916-
United States timber resources in a world economy, by John A. Zivnuska. Resources for the Future; dist. by Johns Hopkins Press, c1967 **HD9750.5.Z5 ECOL**

ZOOLOGICAL SOCIETY OF LONDON.
Conservation and productivity of natural waters. 1972. **QL1.Z733no.29 ECOL**

ZUBE, ERVIN H., ed.
Jackson, John Brinckerhoff.
Landscapes: selected writings of J. B. Jackson. 1970.
HN57.J245 ECOL

ZULUAGA-ANGEL, ANTONIO A., jt. auth.
California. University.
Flow into a stratified reservoir. 1972.
TC167.C3 ECOL

ZUMBERGE, JAMES HERBERT.
The lakes of Minnesota, their origin and classification. Univ. of Minnesota Press, 1952. (Minnesota. Geological Survey. Bulletin 35)
REF QE127.A22no.35 ECOL

ZURHORST, CHARLES.
The conservation fraud. Cowles Book Co. 1970
S942.Z8 ECOL

ZWICK, DAVID.
Water wasteland; Ralph Nader's study group report on water pollution, by David Zwick and Marcy Benstock. Grossman Publishers, 1971.
TD223.Z86 1971 ECOL

Subject Catalog

A

ABANDONMENT OF AUTOMOBILES—UNITED STATES—BIBLIOGRAPHY.
Burg, Nan C. Abandoned vehicles: a selected bibliography. 1972   **Ref fHD9975.B87 ECOL**

ABORTION—RELIGIOUS ASPECTS.
Friends, Society of. American Friends Service Committee. Who shall live? 1970
HQ766.3.F7 ECOL

ABSORPTION, ATMOSPHERIC see SOLAR RADIATION

ACCELERATED EROSION see SOIL EROSION

ACCIDENTS—PREVENTION.
Best's environmental control and safety directory. 13th ed.- 1971/72-   **REF fT55.B4 ECOL**

ACID MINE DRAINAGE.
Black, Sivalls and Bryson, inc., Kansas City, Mo. Applied Technology Division Evaluation of a new acid mine drainage treatment process. 1971.
fTD899.M5B55 ECOL
Environmental Research and Applications, Inc. Concentrated mine drainage disposal into sewage treatment systems. 1971.   **fTD899.M5E58 ECOL**
Gulf Environmental Systems Company. Acid mine waste treatment using reverse osmosis. 1971
fTD754.G84 ECOL
Holmes, James G. Acid mine drainage treatment by ion exchange. 1972   **TD899.M5H6 ECOL**
Horizons Incorporated. Foam separation of acid mine drainage. 1971   **fTD899.M5H67 ECOL**
Morth, Arthur H. Pyritic systems: a mathematical model. 1972.   **TD899.M5M6 ECOL**
NUS Corporation. Cyrus Wm. Rice Division. The effects of various gas atmospheres on the oxidation of coal mine pyrites. 1971.   **fTD899.M5N2 ECOL**
Syracuse University. Dept. of Biology. Inorganic sulfur oxidation by iron-oxidizing bacteria. 1971.
fQR84.S95 ECOL
Troy, Joseph C. Oxidation of pyrites in chlorinated solvents. 1972.   **TD899.M5T ECOL**
Tyco Laboratories. Electrochemical treatment of acid mine waters. 1972.   **fTD899.M5T88 ECOL**
West Virginia. University. Coal Research Bureau. Dewatering of mine drainage sludge. 1971.
fTD899.M5W44 ECOL
West Virginia. University. Coal Research Bureau. Underground coal mining methods to abate water pollution. 1970.   **fTD899.M5W46 ECOL**
Zaval, Frank J. Revegetation augmentation by reuse of treated active surface mine drainage. 1972.
TD899.M5Z3 ECOL

ACID MINE DRAINAGE—INDIANA—PIKE CO.
Smith, Ronald W. Acid mine pollution effects on lake biology. 1971.   **fTD899.M5S6 ECOL**

ACTIVATED CARBON see CARBON, ACTIVATED

ACTIVATED CHARCOAL see CARBON, ACTIVATED

ACTIVITY PROGRAMS IN EDUCATION.
Perry, Gordon Arthur. Handbook for environmental studies. 2nd rev. ed. 1971   **LB1585.P4 1971 ECOL**

ADAPTATION (BIOLOGY).
Milne, Lorus Johnson. Patterns of survival. c1967
QH546.M5 ECOL

ADSORPTION.
Envirogenics Company. Investigation of a new phosphate removal process. 1970. **fTD745.E5 ECOL**

ADVERTISING, OUTDOOR.
Houck, John W. Outdoor advertising. 1969.
REF HF5843.H57 ECOL

ADVERTISING, OUTDOOR—UNITED STATES.
Houck, John W. Outdoor advertising. 1969.
REF HF5843.H57 ECOL

AERATION OF RIVERS see RIVERS—AERATION

AERATION OF SEWAGE see SEWAGE—PURIFICATION—AERATION

AERATION OF SOIL see SOIL AERATION

AERIAL PHOTOGRAPHY IN BOTANY.
Howard, John Anthony. Aerial photo-ecology. 1970, i.e. 1971   **SD387.A25H68 1971 ECOL**

AERIAL PHOTOGRAPHY IN FORESTRY.
Howard, John Anthony. Aerial photo-ecology. 1970, i.e. 1971   **SD387.A25H68 1971 ECOL**

AERIAL PHOTOGRAPHY IN GEOGRAPHY.
Howard, John Anthony. Aerial photo-ecology. 1970, i.e. 1971   **SD387.A25H68 1971 ECOL**

AEROLOGY see METEOROLOGY

AERONAUTICS—FLIGHTS.
Joerg, Wolfgang Louis Gottfried. Brief history of polar exploration since the introduction of flying. 1930
G590.J6 ECOL

AEROPLANES—NOISE.
Wyle Laboratories. Transportation noise and noise from equipment powered by internal combustion engines. 1971 i.e. 1972   **fTD892.W95 ECOL**

AEROSOLS—CONGRESSES.
Rochester International Conference on Environmental Toxicity, 3d, 1970. Assessment of airborne particles. 1972   **QD549.R59 1970 ECOL**

AGGREGATES (BUILDING MATERIALS).
International Minerals and Chemical Corporation. Utilization of phosphate slimes. 1971.
fTD899.M5I57 ECOL

AGGRESSIVE BEHAVIOR IN ANIMALS.
Barber, Carolyn. Animals at war. 1st U.S. ed. c1971
QL758.5.B37 1971 ECOL

AGRARIAN QUESTION see AGRICULTURE—ECONOMIC ASPECTS

AGRIBUSINESS see AGRICULTURE—ECONOMIC ASPECTS

AGRICULTURAL CREDIT—UNITED STATES.
Resources for the Future. Forest credit in the United States: a survey of needs and facilities. 1958.
HG2051.U5R4 ECOL

AGRICULTURAL ECOLOGY see AGRICULTURE—ECOLOGY

AGRICULTURAL ECONOMICS see AGRICULTURE—ECONOMIC ASPECTS

AGRICULTURAL EDUCATION—CONGRESSES.
Conference on Undergraduate Education in the Biological Sciences for Students in Agriculture and Natural Resources, Washington, D.C., 1966. Undergraduate education in the biological sciences for students in agriculture and natural resources. 1967.
S533.C755 1966 ECOL

AGRICULTURAL PESTS.
Plants & gardens. Handbook on biological control of plant pests. 1966,1960   **SB932.P5 1966 ECOL**

AGRICULTURAL RESEARCH—UNITED STATES—DIRECTORIES.
Agricultural Sciences Information Network. Directory of information resources in agriculture and biology. 1971.   **REF QH321.A37 ECOL**

AGRICULTURAL WASTES.
Canada. Agricultural pollution of the Great Lakes Basin. 1971.   **fTD223.3.C25 ECOL**

AGRICULTURE.
Agricultural practices and water quality. 1971,c1970
TD420.A33 ECOL
Brown, Lester Russell. Man and his environment: food. 1972   **S439.B76 ECOL**
Edlin, Herbert Leeson. Plants and man. 1969, c1967   **S519.E3 ECOL**
Osborn, Fairfield. Our plundered planet. 1968
S623.O8 1968 ECOL
Pirie, N. W. Food resources, conventional and novel. 1969   **S439.P5 ECOL**

AGRICULTURE—CONGRESSES.
Prospects of the world food supply. 1966.
fS439.P7 1966 ECOL

AGRICULTURE—ECOLOGY.
Conference on Agriculture's Role in Environmental Quality. University of Illinois, Urbana—Champaign, 1970. Agriculture's role in environmental quality. 1971   **fHC68.C6 1970 ECOL**
Conference on Environmental Quality and Agriculture. University of Illinois, Urbana-Champaign, 1971. Environmental quality and agriculture: what are the options? 1972   **fHC68.C6 1971 ECOL**

AGRICULTURE—ECONOMIC ASPECTS.
Brown, Lester Russell. Seeds of change. 1970
HD9000.5.B73 ECOL
Bunce, Arthur Cyril. The economics of soil conservation. 1950,c1942 **HD1411.B96 1950 ECOL**
Hayami, Yujiro. Agricultural development. 1971
HD1415.H318 ECOL
Sears, Paul Bigelow. Deserts on the march. 3rd ed. rev. 1967,c1959   **S493.S4 1959 ECOL**

AGRICULTURE—ECONOMIC ASPECTS—MIDDLE WEST.
Ottoson, Howard W. Land and people in the Northern Plains transition area. c1966
HD1773.A3O8 ECOL

AGRICULTURE—ECONOMIC ASPECTS—UNITED STATES.
Clawson, Marion. Policy directions for U.S. agriculture. 1968   **HD1761.C54 ECOL**

AGRICULTURE—HANDBOOKS, MANUALS, ETC.
Langer, Richard W. Grow it! 1972
S501.L27 1972 ECOL

AGRICULTURE—SOCIAL ASPECTS.
Brown, Lester Russell. The social impact of the Green revolution. 1971.   **HD1417.B7 ECOL**
Katz, Robert. A giant in the earth. c1973
HD9000.5.K3 ECOL

AGRICULTURE—UNDERDEVELOPED AREAS see UNDERDEVELOPED AREAS—AGRICULTURE

AGRICULTURE—UNITED STATES.
Heady, Earl Orel. Agricultural and water policies and the environment: an analysis of national alternatives in natural resource use, food supply capacity and environmental quality. 1972.
fS441.H4 ECOL
Higbee, Edward Counselman. American agriculture: geography, resources, conservation. 1958
S441.H59 ECOL
Sears, Paul Bigelow. Deserts on the march. 3rd ed. rev. 1967,c1959   **S493.S4 1959 ECOL**

AGRICULTURE AND STATE—UNITED STATES.
Clawson, Marion. Policy directions for U.S. agriculture. 1968   **fD1761.C54 ECOL**
National Agricultural Policy Conference. Readings in agricultural policy. 1968   **HD1761.N25 ECOL**
Paddock, William. Famine, 1975! c1967
HD9000.5.P22 ECOL

AIR see also ATMOSPHERE
Adler, Irving. Air. Rev. ed. c1972
PZ10.A3A12 ECOL
Branley, Franklyn Mansfield. Air is all around you. 1962   **PZ10.B65Ai ECOL**
Butcher, Samuel S. An introduction to air chemistry. 1972   **QD163.B87 1972 ECOL**
Firskey, Margaret. The true book of air around us. 1953   **QC863.F846 ECOL**
Henson, Collins M. Your environment: air, air pollution, and weather. 1971   **QC863.H45 ECOL**
Knight, David C. The first book of air. 1961
PZ10.K57Fg ECOL
Preston, Edna Mitchell. Air. 1965
PZ10.P668Ai ECOL

AIR—ANALYSIS.
Leighton, Philip Albert. Photochemistry of air pollution. 1961.   **RA576.L4 ECOL**

AIR—ANALYSIS—CONGRESSES.
ACS Symposium on Determination of Air Quality. Los Angeles, 1971. Determination of air quality. 1972.
TD890.A2 1971 ECOL

AIR—BACTERIOLOGY see AIR—MICROBIOLOGY

AIR—JUVENILE LITERATURE.
Henson, Collins M. Your environment: air, air pollution, and weather. 1971   **QC863.H45 ECOL**

AIR—MICROBIOLOGY.
Kingsley, V. Victor. Bacteriology primer in air contamination control. 1967   **QR101.K55 ECOL**

AIR—POLLUTION see also AUTOMOBILE EXHAUST GAS; ODORS; RADIOACTIVE POLLUTION OF THE ATMOSPHERE; SMOG
Air pollution. 1970   **fTD883.A47 ECOL**
Air pollution control.   **TD883.A474 ECOL**
Air Pollution Control Association. Proceedings digest of the annual meeting. 62nd- 1969-
REF TD884.A55 ECOL
Aylesworth, Thomas G. This vital air, this vital water: man's environment crisis. 1968
TD180.A9 ECOL
Bach, Wilfrid. Atmospheric pollution. 1971, c1972
TD883.B24 ECOL
Bates, David B. A citizen's guide to air pollution. 1972.   **TD883.B23 ECOL**
Battan, Louis J. The unclean sky. 1966.
TD883.B3 ECOL
Bloome, Enid. The air we breathe! 1971.
TD883.13.B56 ECOL
Carr, Donald Eaton. The breath of life. 1965
TD883.C35 ECOL
Chemical engineering. Environmental engineering, deskbook issue, 1971-   **fTA170.C5 ECOL**
Dimitriades, Basil. Interpretation of gas chromatographic spectra in routine analysis of exhaust hydrocarbons. 1972   **TN23.U7no.7700 ECOL**
Dworsky, Leonard B. Pollution. 1971.
REF TD174.D95 ECOL
Eccleston, Barton H. Effect of fuel front-end and midrange volatility on automobile emissions. 1972?
TN23.U7no.7707 ECOL
Elliott, Sarah M. Our dirty air. 1971
TD883.13.E44 ECOL
Faith, William Lawrence. Air pollution. 2d ed. 1972
TD883.F23 1972 ECOL

Henson, Collins M. Your environment: air, air pollution, and weather. 1971 **QC863.H45 ECOL**

Herber, Lewis. Crisis in our cities. c1965 **RA566.H4 ECOL**

Jacobs, Morris Boris. The chemical analysis of air pollutants. 1960. **TD883.J3 ECOL**

Jacobson, Jay S. Recognition of air pollution injury to vegetation: a pictorial atlas. 1970. **fQK751.J3 ECOL**

Jones, Claire. Pollution: the air we breathe. 1971 **TD883.13.J65 1971 ECOL**

Kavaler, Lucy. Dangerous air. c1967 **TD883.13.K3 ECOL**

Kirk, William P. Krypton 85: a review of the literature and an analysis of radiation hazards. 1972 **QP82.2.R3K5 ECOL**

Lavaroni, Charles W. Air pollution. c1971 **TD883.L28 ECOL**

Laycock, George. Air pollution. 1972 **TD883.13.L38 ECOL**

Leighton, Philip Albert. Photochemistry of air pollution. 1961. **RA576.L4 ECOL**

Leinwand, Gerald. Air and water pollution. 1969 **TD180.L4 ECOL**

Magill, Paul L. Air pollution handbook. 1956. **REF TD883.M35 ECOL**

Martin, G. B. Effects of fuel additives on air pollutant emissions from distillate-oil-fired furnaces. 1971. **TP355.M29 ECOL**

National Research Council. Building Research Advisory Board. Apartment house incinerators (flue fed). 1965. **fTH23.N333no.29 ECOL**

National Tuberculosis and Respiratory Disease Association. Air pollution primer. 1969 **TD883.N37 ECOL**

Perera, Thomas Biddle. Who will clean the air? 1971 **TD883.13.P47 ECOL**

The Price of power: electric utilities and the environment. 1972 **REF fTJ164.P7 ECOL**

Robinson, Elmer. Sources, abundance, and fate of gaseous atmospheric pollutants. 1968. **fTD885.R6 ECOL**

Robinson, Elmer. Sources, abundance, and fate of gaseous atmospheric pollutants: supplement. 1969. **fTD885.R62 ECOL**

Ross, Richard D. Air pollution and industry. 1972 **TD883.R58 ECOL**

Scorer, Richard Segar. Pollution in the air: problems, policies and priorities. 1973 **TD883.S3 ECOL**

Selected studies on alkaline additives for sulfur dioxide control. 1971. **TD885.5.S8S4 ECOL**

Southern Conference on Environmental Radiation Protection from Nuclear Power Plants, St. Petersburg, Fla., 1971. Proceedings of Southern Conference on Environmental Radiation Protection from Nuclear Power Plants, April 21-22, 1971. 1972. **TK9152.S6 ECOL**

Sproull, Wayne Treber. Air pollution and its control. 1970 **TD883.S76 ECOL**

Sproull, Wayne Treber. Air pollution and its control. 2d ed. rev. and enl. 1972 **TD883.S76 1972 ECOL**

Stern, Arthur Cecil. Air pollution. **REF TD883.S83 ECOL**

Toxicologic and epidemiologic bases for air quality criteria. 1969 **REF fTD890.T6 ECOL**

United States. Bureau of Mines. Control of sulfur oxide emissions in copper, lead, and zinc smelting. 1971 **TN295.U4no.8527 ECOL**

United States. Environmental Protection Office. Office of Air Programs. Compilation of air pollutant emission factors. Rev. 1972. **TD883.1.U494 ECOL**

United States. Environmental Protection Agency. Office of Air Programs. Guide for control of air pollution episodes in medium-sized urban areas. 1971. **TD883.1.U49 ECOL**

United States. Environmental Protection Agency. Office of Air Programs. Guide for control of air pollution episodes in small urban areas. 1971. **TD883.1.U492 ECOL**

United States. Environmental Protection Agency. National Environmental Research Center. Toxicology of atmospheric sulfur dioxide decay products. 1972. **TD885.5.S8U5 ECOL**

AIR—POLLUTION—ABSTRACTS.
United States. Environmental Protection Agency. Office of Air Programs. Mercury and air pollution: A bibliography with abstracts. 1972. **TD887.M4U5 ECOL**

AIR—POLLUTION—ADDRESSES, ESSAYS, LECTURES.
Combustion-generated air pollution. 1971. **TD883.C575 1971 ECOL**

McCuen, Gary E. The ecology controversy: opposing viewpoints. 1971 **QH541.M3 ECOL**

AIR—POLLUTION—BIBLIOGRAPHY.
Air Pollution Technical Information Center. Air pollution aspects of emission sources: a bibliography with abstracts. 1971- **Z7173.A4A5 ECOL**

Air Pollution Technical Information Center. Air pollution translations: a bibliography with abstracts. **REF TD881.U55no.AP-56 ECOL**

Air Pollution Technical Information Center. Chlorine and air pollution: an annotated bibliography. 1971. **Z7173.A4A513 ECOL**

Air Pollution Technical Information Center. Hydrochloric acid and air pollution: an annotated bibliography. 1971. **Z7173.A4A52 ECOL**

Air Pollution Technical Information Center. Photochemical oxidants and air pollution: an annotated bibliography. 1971. **REF Z7173.A4A53 ECOL**

United States. Dept. of Transportation. Library Services Division. Aircraft and air pollution: selected readings. 1971. **Z7173.A4U5 ECOL**

United States. Environmental Protection Agency. Office of Air Programs. Odors and air pollution: a bibliography with abstracts. 1972. **TD886.U5 ECOL**

United States. National Air Pollution Control Administration. Nitrogen oxides: an annotated bibliography. 1970. **Z7914.C4U5 ECOL**

Van Nest, William J. Air pollution and urban planning: a selective annotated bibliography. 1972 **REF fZ5853.P7V3 ECOL**

AIR—POLLUTION—CASE STUDIES.
National Industrial Pollution Control Council. Casebook: pollution cleanup actions. 1971? **fTD897.N37 ECOL**

AIR—POLLUTION—CONGRESSES.
American Nuclear Society. Nuclear methods in environmental research. 1971 **fTD172.5.A4 ECOL**

Brittin, Wesley Emil. Air and water pollution. 1972 **TD881.B75 ECOL**

Effective technology for recycling metal. 1971 **fTS214.E36 ECOL**

Environmental control seminar proceedings. 1971. **fTD172.5.E26 ECOL**

Environmental Control Symposium, San Francisco, 1972. Environmental control. 1972 **TD888.M4E58 1972 ECOL**

Symposium on Emissions from Continuous Combustion Systems, General Motors Research Laboratories, 1971. Emissions from continuous combustion systems. 1972. **TD881.S86 1971 ECOL**

AIR—POLLUTION—DIRECTORIES.
Directory of governmental air pollution agencies. 1970- **TD882.D5 ECOL**

AIR—POLLUTION—ECONOMIC ASPECTS—UNITED STATES.
Ridker, Ronald Gene. Economic costs of air pollution. 1967 **HC110.A4R5 ECOL**

Wolozin, Harold. The economics of air pollution. c1966 **HC110.A4W6 ECOL**

AIR—POLLUTION—ECONOMIC ASPECTS—UNITED STATES—ADDRESSES, ESSAYS, LECTURES.
Economics of air and water pollution. 1969. **fTD201.V57no.26 ECOL**

AIR—POLLUTION—HANDBOOKS, MANUALS, ETC.
Turner, D. Bruce. Workbook of atmospheric dispersion estimates. 1970. **fTD890.T8 1970 ECOL**

AIR—POLLUTION—JUVENILE LITERATURE.
Henson, Collins M. Your environment: air, air pollution, and weather. 1971 **QC863.H45 ECOL**

AIR—POLLUTION—LAW AND LEGISLATION—ADDRESSES, ESSAYS, LECTURES.
Environment law review. 1970- **REF KF3790.A2E5 ECOL**

AIR—POLLUTION—LAW AND LEGISLATION—MINNESOTA.
Minnesota. Pollution Control Agency. In the matter of the adoption of proposed amendments to Minnesota Regulations APC 1, APC 3, APC 4, APC 11 and APC 15; and the proposed adoption of Minnesota Regulation APC 16; and the proposed adoption of the Minnesota Air Quality Implementation Plan. 1972 **REF fKFM5758.A17 1972 ECOL**

AIR—POLLUTION—LAW AND LEGISLATION—UNITED STATES.
Degler, Stanley E. State air pollution control laws. Rev. ed. 1970 **KF3812.Z95D4 1970 ECOL**

Federal Construction Council. Task Group T-65. Impact of air pollution regulations on fuel selection for federal facilities. 1970. **fKF3812.F4 ECOL**

Stevens, Leonard A. How a law is made: the story of a bill against air pollution. 1970 **KF3812.Z9S7 ECOL**

United States. Federal Power Commission. Air pollution and the regulated electric power and natural gas industries. 1968. **TD883.2.A52 ECOL**

United States. Robert A Taft Sanitary Engineering Center, Cincinnati. A compilation of selected air pollution emission control regulations and ordinances. 1965. **REF KF3812.A4 1965 ECOL**

Zimmerman, Joseph Francis. The role of the state legislature in air pollution abatement. n.d. **fKF3812.Z9Z5 ECOL**

AIR—POLLUTION—LAW AND LEGISLATION—UNITED STATES—ADDRESSES, ESSAYS, LECTURES.
Air pollution control. 1968. **KF3812.A75A35 1968 ECOL**

Air pollution control. 1969. **KF3812.A75A35 ECOL**

AIR—POLLUTION—LAW AND LEGISLATION—WISCONSIN.
History of the Wisconsin Department of Natural Resources and related rules, regulations, classifications and standards for air and water quality. 1970 **fS932.W6H5 ECOL**

AIR—POLLUTION—LONDON.
Wise, William. Killer smog. 1968 **RA576.W57 ECOL**

AIR—POLLUTION—MEASUREMENT.
Benson, Ferris B. Indoor-outdoor air pollution relationships: a literature review. 1972. **TD890.B4 ECOL**

Cooper, Hal B. H. Source testing for air pollution control. 1971 **fTD890.C57 ECOL**

Environmental Systems Corporation. Development and demonstration of low-level drift instrumentation. 1971. **fTD884.5.E58 ECOL**

Larsen, Ralph I. A mathematical model for relating air quality measurements to air quality standards. 1971. **TD890.L3 ECOL**

Leithe, Wolfgang. The analysis of air pollutants. 1971,c1970 **TD890.L413 ECOL**

Toxicologic and epidemiologic bases for air quality criteria. 1969 **REF TD890.T6 ECOL**

United States. Environmental Protection Agency. Division of Atmospheric Surveillance. Air quality data for 1967 from the National Air Surveillance Networks. Rev. 1971. **TD883.2.A44 1971 ECOL**

United States. Environmental Protection Agency. Air Pollution Control Office. Interstate surveillance project: measurement of air pollution using static monitors. 1971. **TD890.U45 ECOL**

AIR—POLLUTION—MEASUREMENT—BIBLIOGRAPHY.
Ruch, Walter E. Chemical detection of gaseous pollutants. **REF fZ5524.G24R8 ECOL**

AIR—POLLUTION—MEASUREMENT—DIRECTORIES.
United States. Environmental Protection Agency. Division of Atmospheric Surveillance. Air quality data: directory of air quality monitoring sites, 1971. 1972. **REF TD883.2.A43 ECOL**

AIR—POLLUTION—MEASUREMENT—STUDY AND TEACHING.
Weaver, Elbert C. Scientific experiments in environmental pollution. 1968 **TD178.5.W4 ECOL**

AIR—POLLUTION—MEASUREMENT—YEARBOOKS.
United States. National Bureau of Standards. Measures for air quality, annual report. 1970/71- **REF TD890.U57 ECOL**

AIR—POLLUTION—MINNESOTA.
Kennedy, David. Report to the Subcommittee on Legal Problems Governor's Advisory Committee on Air Resources. 1966. **fTD883.5.M65K4 ECOL**

The Metropolitan Area—an air pollution control program: a report to the Subcommittee on Metropolitan Problems, Governor's Advisory Committee on Air Resources. 1966 **fTD883.5.M65M4 ECOL**

Minnesota. Air Quality Division. Highlights of implementation plan for sulfur dioxide, particulates, carbon monoxide, hydrocarbons, nitrogen oxides, photochemical oxidant. 1971. **REF fTD883.5.M6A42 ECOL**

Minnesota Association of Commerce and Industry. Air pollution regulation handbook. 1970? **REF fTD883.5.M6M61 ECOL**

Minnesota. Pollution Control Agency. Air pollution control in Minnesota, Jan. 1969 through Oct. 1970. 1970 **fTD883.5.M6A47 1970 ECOL**

Northern States Power Company. Engineering Dept. Environmental monitoring program for the Allen S. King generating plant at Oak Park Heights, Minnesota. 1966. **fTK1331.N6A4 ECOL**

Snyder, Edwin F. Preliminary report for the Subcommittee on Health, Economic and Nuisance Effects of Air Pollution. 1966. **fTD883.5.M65S6 ECOL**

TRC—The Research Corporation of New England. Proposal to the State of Minnesota Pollution Control Agency: Highlights of implementation plan for sulfur dioxide, particulates, carbon monoxide, hydrocarbons, nitrogen oxides, photochemical oxidant. 1971.
Ref fTD883.5.M6T15 ECOL

AIR—POLLUTION—PHYSIOLOGICAL EFFECT.
Environmental factors in respiratory disease. 1972.
RC732.E59 ECOL
Holland, Walter Werner. Air pollution and respiratory disease. 1972 **fRC732.H64 ECOL**
Lillie, Robert Jones. Air pollutants affecting the performance of domestic animals. Slightly rev. 1972.
SF757.5.L54 1972 ECOL
National Research Council. Committee on Biologic Effects of Atmospheric Pollutants. Lead. 1972.
QP913.P3N38 ECOL

AIR—POLLUTION—PHYSIOLOGICAL EFFECT—CONGRESSES.
Rochester International Conference on Environmental Toxicity, 3d, 1970. Assessment of airborne particles. 1972 **QD549.R59 1970 ECOL**

AIR—POLLUTION—RESEARCH.
Air Pollution Control Association. Technical manual no.1- 1963- **REF fTD881.A4 ECOL**
Pennsylvania. State University. Center for Air Environment Studies. Guide to research in air pollution. 8th- ed. **REF TD883.15.P4 ECOL**

AIR—POLLUTION—RUSSIA—COLLECTED WORKS—TRANSLATIONS FROM RUSSIAN.
Nuttonson, Michael Y. Air pollution in relation to certain atmospheric and meteorological conditions and some of the methods employed in the survey and analysis of air pollutants. 1971.
fTD883.7.R9N87 ECOL
Nuttonson, Michael Y. Measurements of dispersal and concentration, identification, and sanitary evaluation of various air pollutants. 1971.
fTD883.7.R9N873 ECOL

AIR—POLLUTION—STANDARDS.
Toxicologic and epidemiologic bases for air quality criteria. 1969 **REF fTD890.T6 ECOL**

AIR—POLLUTION—STANDARDS—MINNESOTA.
Minnesota. Air Quality Division. Implementation plan to achieve carbon monoxide ambient air quality standards. 1973. **REF fTD883.5.M6A422 ECOL**

AIR—POLLUTION—STANDARDS—UNITED STATES.
Larsen, Ralph I. A mathematical model for relating air quality measurements to air quality standards. 1971.
TD890.L3 ECOL

AIR—POLLUTION—STATISTICS.
United States. Environmental Protection Agency. Division of Atmospheric Surveillance. Air quality data for 1967 from the National Air Surveillance Networks. Rev. 1971. **TD883.2.A44 1971 ECOL**

AIR—POLLUTION—STUDY AND TEACHING.
Fitch, Steven Val. Air. 1971. **TD883.F5 ECOL**
Hunter, Donald C. Air pollution experiments for junior and senior high school science classes. 1968.
fTD883.2.H8 ECOL

AIR—POLLUTION—UNITED STATES.
Air Pollution Control Association. Technical manual no.1- 1963- **REF fTD881.A4 ECOL**
American Association for the Advancement of Science. Committee on Science in the Promotion of Human Welfare. Air Conservation Commission. Air conservation; ... report. 1965. **TD883.2.A65 ECOL**
Crenson, Matthew A. The un-politics of air pollution: a study of non-decision-making in the cities. 1971 **HC110.A4C73 ECOL**
Lewis, Alfred. Clean the air! c1965
TD883.2L4 ECOL
Lewis, Howard R. With every breath you take. 1965
RA576.L5 ECOL
United States. Environmental Protection Agency. Division of Atmospheric Surveillance. Air quality data: directory of air quality monitoring sites, 1971. 1972.
REF TD883.2.A43 ECOL
United States. Environmental Protection Agency. Division of Atmospheric Surveillance. Air quality data for 1967 from the National Air Surveillance Networks. Rev. 1971. **TD883.2.A44 1971 ECOL**
United States. Environmental Protection Agency. The economics of clean air. 1970- 1971-
TD883.2.A24 ECOL
United States. Environmental Protection Agency. Federal air quality control regions. 1972.
REF TD883.2.U42 ECOL
United States. Environmental Protection Agency. Guide for air pollution episode avoidance. 1971.
TD883.2.A518 ECOL

United States. Environmental Protection Agency. Progress in the prevention and control of air pollution. 1971- **TD883.2.A22 ECOL**
United States. Federal Power Commission. Air pollution and the regulated electric power and natural gas industries. 1968. **TD883.2.A52 ECOL**
United States. Federal Power Commission. Steam-electric plant air and water quality control data for the year ended December 31, 1969, based on EPC form no. 67. 1973. **fTD195.E4U5 ECOL**
Vanishing air. 1970. **TD883.2.V35 ECOL**

AIR—POLLUTION—UNITED STATES—RESEARCH.
United States. Environmental Protection Agency. Office of Air Programs. Office of Research Grants. Air pollution control. **REF TD883.2.A23 ECOL**

AIR—RADIOACTIVE POLLUTION see RADIOACTIVE POLLUTION OF THE ATMOSPHERE

AIR POLLUTION see AIR—POLLUTION

AIR QUALITY see AIR—POLLUTION

AIR QUALITY—ADDRESSES, ESSAYS, LECTURES.
Indicators of environmental quality. 1972.
TD172.5.I5 1972 ECOL

AIR QUALITY—CONGRESSES.
ACS Symposium on Determination of Air Quality, Los Angeles, 1971. Determination of air quality. 1972.
TD890.A2 1971 ECOL

AIR SAMPLING ANALYSIS.
Environmental Measurements, Inc. Monitoring mercury vapor near pollution sites. 1971.
fTD427.M4E5 ECOL

AIR SAMPLING APPARATUS.
Kingsley, V. Victor. Bacteriology primer in air contamination control. 1967 **QR101.K55 ECOL**

AIRCRAFT EXHAUST EMISSIONS—BIBLIOGRAPHY.
United States. Dept. of Transportation. Library Services Division. Aircraft and air pollution: selected readings. 1971. **Z7173.A4U5 ECOL**

AIRPORT NOISE.
Stevenson, Gordon McKay. The politics of airport noise. 1971, c1972 **HE9797.4.N6S83 ECOL**

AIRPORTS—BIBLIOGRAPHY.
Nelson, Jon P. Economic aspects of the airport environment: noise, air pollution, and congestion. 1972. **REF fZ5064.A28N4 ECOL**

AIRPORTS—UNITED STATES—PLANNING.
United States. Federal Aviation Administration. Planning the metropolitan airport system. 1970.
TL725.3.P5U525 ECOL

ALASKA—DESCRIPTION AND TRAVEL.
Cooper, Bryan. Alaska: the last frontier. 1973.
HD9567.A4C66 ECOL
Crisler, Lois. Arctic wild. 1958 **QL161.C7 ECOL**
Herndon, Booton. The great land. 1971
TN872.A7H4 ECOL
Olson, Sigurd F. Runes of the North. 1969, c1963
F1060.A204 ECOL

ALASKA—DESCRIPTION AND TRAVEL—1959-
Laycock, George. Alaska, the embattled frontier. 1971. **S932.A4L38 ECOL**

ALASKA—ECONOMIC CONDITIONS.
Cooper, Bryan. Alaska: the last frontier. 1973.
HD9567.A4C66 ECOL

ALBRIGHT, HORACE MARDEN, 1890-
Swain, Donald C. Wilderness defender. 1970
SB482.A4S95 ECOL

ALGAE.
Bartsch, A. F. Role of phosphorus in eutrophication. 1972. **QH96.8.E9B3 ECOL**
California. Dept. of Water Resources. Removal of nitrate by an algal system, phase II. 1971.
fTD475.C342 ECOL
Davis, Ernst M. Bacterial effects of algae on enteric organisms. 1970. **fQR48.D38 ECOL**
Morton, Stephen D. The carbon dioxide system and eutrophication. 1971. **fQH96.8.E9M6 ECOL**

ALGAE—ADDRESSES, ESSAYS, LECTURES.
Algae, man, and the environment. c1968
QK564.5.A4 ECOL

ALGAE—CULTURES AND CULTURE MEDIA.
Fogg, Gordon Elliott. Algal cultures and phytoplankton ecology. 1966, c1965
QK565.F58 ECOL

ALGAE—ECONOMIC ASPECTS—ADDRESSES, ESSAYS, LECTURES.
Algae, man, and the environment. c1968
QK564.5.A4 ECOL

ALGAE—MINNESOTA.
Knutson, Keith M. Evaluation of attached algae in the Mississippi River adjacent to the NSP Sherburne County Generating Plant, Becker, Minnesota, during October and November, 1971. 1972
fTK1331.N6K5 ECOL

ALGAL BLOOM see WATER BLOOM

ALLEN RADIATION BELTS see VAN ALLEN RADIATION BELTS

ALLEN S. KING GENERATING PLANT, OAK PARK HEIGHTS, MINNESOTA.
Minnesota. Dept. of Health. Division of Environmental Health. Section of Water Pollution Control. Report on application for waste disposal permit. 1965. **fTK1331.N6M6 ECOL**
Northern States Power Company. Engineering Department. Environmental monitoring program. 1970. **REF fTK1331.N6A42 1970 ECOL**
Northern States Power Company. Engineering Dept. Environmental monitoring program for the Allen S. King generating plant at Oak Park Heights, Minnesota. 1966. **fTK1331.N6A4 ECOL**

ALLUVIUM.
Norvitch, Ralph F. Ground water in alluvial channel deposits, Nobles County, Minnesota. 1960.
fTD224.M6A3no.14 ECOL

ALPINE FAUNA.
Long, Tony. Mountain animals. 1st U.S. ed. c1971
QL113.L66 1971 ECOL

ALUMINUM INDUSTRY AND TRADE.
Brubaker, Sterling. Trends in the world aluminum industry. c1967 **HD9539.A6B7 ECOL**

AMATEUR THEATRICALS.
Spolin, Viola. Improvisation for the theater. 1963
PN2071.I5S6 ECOL

AMERICAN ECOLOGISTS see ECOLOGISTS, AMERICAN

AMERICAN ELK see ELK

AMERICAN LITERATURE—BIBLIOGRAPHY.
Publishers' trade list annual. Books in print.
REF Z1215.P972 ECOL
Publishers' trade list annual. Books in print supplement: authors, titles, subjects. 1972/73-
REF fZ1215.P972 Suppl. ECOL

AMERICAN LITERATURE (COLLECTIONS).
Gangewere, Robert J. The exploited Eden. 1972
PS507.E3G3 ECOL

AMMONIA.
Barnes, Robert A. Ammonia removal in a physical-chemical wastewater treatment process. 1972.
TD462.B3 ECOL
California. University. Sanitary Engineering Research Laboratory. Optimization of ammonia removal by ion exchange using clinoptilolite. 1971 i.e. 1972 **fTD757.5.C35 ECOL**
Ionics, Inc. The electro-oxidation of ammonia in sewage to nitrogen. 1970. **fTD757.I55 ECOL**

AMPHIBIANS AS PETS.
Headstrom, Birger Richard. Frogs, toads, and salamanders as pets. 1972 **SF459.A45H4 ECOL**

ANALYSIS (CHEMISTRY) see CHEMISTRY, ANALYTIC

ANALYTICAL CHEMISTRY see CHEMISTRY, ANALYTIC

ANATIDAE.
Delacour, Jean Theodore. The waterfowl of the world. 1954- **REF QL696.A5D39 ECOL**

ANDERSON LAKE, MINNESOTA.
Barr Engineering Co. Hydrological study of Hyland-Bush-Anderson lakes. 1971.
fTC424.M6B326 ECOL

ANHYDROUS AMMONIA see AMMONIA

ANIMAL COURTSHIP see COURTSHIP OF ANIMALS

ANIMAL MIGRATION.
Berrill, Jacquelyn. Wonders of animal migration. 1964 **QL754.B4 ECOL**
Jarman, Catherine. Atlas of animal migration. 1972
fQL754.J37 ECOL

ANIMAL POPULATIONS see also POPULATION GENETICS
Allison, Anthony. Population control. 1970
QL752.A58 ECOL
Andrewartha, Herbert George. Introduction to the study of animal populations. 2nd ed. 1971
QL752.A63 1971 ECOL
Boughey, Arthur S. Population and environmental biology. 1967 **QH83.B68 ECOL**
Connell, Joseph H. Readings in ecology and ecological genetics. 1970 **QH541.C65 ECOL**
Fretwell, Stephen D. Populations in a seasonal environment. 1972. **QL752.F73 ECOL**

ANIMAL POPULATIONS

Levins, Richard. Evolution in changing environments. 1968. **QL752.L4 ECOL**

MacArthur, Robert H. The biology of populations. 1966 **QL752.M2 ECOL**

Milne, Lorus Johnson. The balance of nature. 1960 **QL751.M48 ECOL**

Watt, Kenneth E. F. Ecology and resource management. 1968 **QL752.W38 ECOL**

ANIMAL SOUNDS.
Hartshorne, Charles. Born to sing: an interpretation and world survey of bird song. 1973 **QL698.5.H27 ECOL**

The Language and music of the wolves. c1971 **PhonodiscQL765.L32 ECOL**

ANIMAL TRACKS.
Lempfert, O. C. Paw prints. 1st ed. 1972 **QL768.L37 ECOL**

ANIMAL WASTE.
Beefland International, Inc. Elimination of water pollution by packing-house animal paunch and blood. 1971. **fTD899.M4B4 ECOL**

North Carolina. State University, Raleigh. Dept. of Biological and Agricultural Engineering. Role of animal wastes in agricultural land runoff. 1971. **fTD930.N67 ECOL**

United States. Federal Water Pollution Control Administration. Missouri Basin Region. Compendium of animal waste management. **TD811.U5 ECOL**

ANIMALS.
Hoover, Helen. Animals at my doorstep. 1966 **PZ10.H7An ECOL**

ANIMALS—IDENTIFICATION.
Dickey, Miriam. Beyond the classroom. 1972. **Ref fQH51.D5 ECOL**

ANIMALS—PICTORIAL WORKS.
Burton, Maurice. The world encyclopedia of animals. c1972 **fQL9.B8 ECOL**

ANIMALS AND CIVILIZATION see also ZOOLOGY, ECONOMIC
Barker, Will. Wildlife in America's history. 1962 **QL155.B3 ECOL**

Marchant, Ronald Albert. Man and beast. 1968 **QL85.M3 1968 ECOL**

ANIMALS, FOOD HABITS OF.
Grossman, Shelly. Understanding ecology. c1967, 1970 **QL756.G7 1970 ECOL**

Johnson, James Ralph. Animals and their food. 1972 **QL756.5.J64 ECOL**

ANIMALS, HABITATIONS OF.
Wong, Herbert H. Animal habitats: where can red-winged blackbirds live? 1970 **PZ10.W748An ECOL**

ANIMALS, HABITS AND BEHAVIOR OF see also AGGRESSIVE BEHAVIOR IN ANIMALS; ANIMAL MIGRATION; ANIMALS, FOOD HABITS OF; ANIMALS, LEGENDS AND STORIES OF

Barker, Will. Familiar animals of America. 1956 **QL715.B25 ECOL**

Bixby, William. Of animals and men. 1968. **QL751.B53 ECOL**

Bourliere, Francois. The natural history of mammals. 1st American ed. 1954. **QL751.B663 ECOL**

Carrighar, Sally. Home to the wilderness. 1973. **QH31.C3A3 ECOL**

Carrighar, Sally. One day at Teton Marsh. 1947. **QL215.C3 ECOL**

Carrighar, Sally. Wild heritage. 1965. **QL751.C36 ECOL**

Clarke, James. Man is the prey. 1969 **QL758.C54 ECOL**

Crisler, Lois. Arctic wild. 1958 **QL161.C7 ECOL**

Klopfer, Peter H. Behavioral ecology. 1970 **QL751.K5917 ECOL**

Klopfer, Peter H. Habitats and territories. 1969 **QL751.K592 ECOL**

Krutch, Joseph Wood. The great chain of life. 1957 c1956 **QL751.K87 ECOL**

Maddock, Alison. Animals at peace. 1st U.S. ed. c1971 **QL751.M216 1971 ECOL**

Mason, George Frederick. Animal homes. 1947. **QL756.M3 ECOL**

Mowat, Farley. Never cry wolf. 1st American ed. 1963 **QL795.W8M6 ECOL**

Ransom, Elmer Inglesby. The woodland book. 1945 **QL681.R2 ECOL**

Seton, Ernest Thompson. Lives of game animals. 1929. **QL151.S5 1925 ECOL**

ANIMALS, HABITS AND BEHAVIOR OF—ADDRESSES, ESSAYS, LECTURES.
Emmel, Thomas C. Behavior and ecology. 1970 **QH541.E44 ECOL**

ANIMALS, LEGENDS AND STORIES OF.
Barker, Will. Wildlife in America's history. 1962 **QL155.B3 ECOL**

ANIMALS, PROTECTION OF see WILDLIFE CONSERVATION

ANIMALS, RARE see RARE ANIMALS

ANIMALS, TREATMENT OF.
Davies, Brian. Savage luxury: the slaughter of the baby seals. 1971,c1970 **QL737.P6D33 1971 ECOL**

ANIMALS, TREATMENT OF—HISTORY.
Carson, Gerald. Men, beasts, and gods. 1972 **HV4764.C35 ECOL**

ANIMALS, TREATMENT OF—UNITED STATES—HISTORY.
Carson, Gerald. Men, beasts, and gods. 1972 **HV4764.C35 ECOL**

ANNELIDA.
Foster, Nancy. Freshwater polychaetes (Annelida) of North America. 1972. **fQH96.A2B5no.4 ECOL**

Klemm, Donald J. Freshwater leeches (Annelida: Hirudinea) of North America. 1972. **fQH96.A2B5no.8 ECOL**

ANTAGONISM (BACTERIA) see ANTIBIOSIS

ANTARCTIC EXPEDITIONS see ANTARCTIC REGIONS

ANTARCTIC REGIONS see also SCIENTIFIC EXPEDITIONS
American Geographical Society of New York. Problems of polar research. 1928. **G576.A6 ECOL**

Joerg, Wolfgang Louis Gottfried. Brief history of polar exploration since the introduction of flying. 1930 **G590.J6 ECOL**

Nordenskjold, Otto. The geography of the polar regions, consisting of a general characterization of polar nature. 1928. **G587.N6 ECOL**

ANTHROPO-GEOGRAPHY see also MAN—INFLUENCE OF CLIMATE; MAN—INFLUENCE OF ENVIRONMENT
Guyot, Arnold Henry. The earth and man. 1970, c1849 **GB59.G8 1970 ECOL**

Russell, William Moy Stratton. Man, nature, and history. 1969,c1967 **GF37.R85 ECOL**

Wagner, Philip Laurence. Environments and peoples. 1972 **GF41.W3 ECOL**

Wagner, Philip Laurence. The human use of the earth. 1964,c1960 **HM206.W28 1964 ECOL**

ANTHROPO-GEOGRAPHY—CONGRESSES.
International Symposium on Man's Role in Changing the Face of the Earth, Princeton, N.J., 1955. Man's role in changing the face of the earth. 1970,c1956 **G56.I63 1955 ECOL**

ANTHROPO-GEOGRAPHY—UNITED STATES.
Atkinson, Justin Brooks. This bright land. 1st ed. 1972. **GF503.A8 ECOL**

Ekirch, Arthur Alphonse. Man and nature in America. 1963. **GF503.E46 ECOL**

ANTIBIOSIS.
Davis, Ernst M. Bacterial effects of algae on enteric organisms. 1972. **fQR48.D38 ECOL**

ANTICOAGULANTS (MEDICINE).
Su, K. Lee. Aquatic plants from Minnesota part 2—toxicity, anti-neoplastic, and coagulent effects. 1972. **GB701.M554no.47 ECOL**

APARTMENT HOUSES.
National Research Council. Building Research Advisory Board. Apartment house incinerators (flue fed). 1965. **fTH23.N333no.29 ECOL**

APHANIZOMENON FLOS-AQUAE—THERAPEUTIC USE.
World Life Research Institute. Pharmacological testing of blue-green algae for constituents having therapeutic value. 1970. **fRS165.A7W67 ECOL**

APPARATUS, ELECTROCHEMICAL see ELECTROCHEMICAL APPARATUS

AQUACULTURE see FISH-CULTURE

AQUATIC BIOLOGY.
Amos, William Hopkins. The infinite river. 1971,c1970 **QH90.A59 ECOL**

AQUATIC BIRDS see WATER-BIRDS

AQUATIC ECOLOGY see also FRESH-WATER ECOLOGY; MARINE ECOLOGY
Conservation and productivity of natural waters. 1972. **QL1.Z733no.29 ECOL**

United States. Environmental Protection Agency. Effects of pesticides in water. n.d. **REF fTD427.P35U53 ECOL**

AQUATIC ECOLOGY—ADDRESSES, ESSAYS, LECTURES.
Ford, Richard F. Readings in aquatic ecology. 1972. **QH541.5.W3F67 ECOL**

AQUATIC ECOLOGY—UNITED STATES.
Von Rumker, Rosmarie. The use of pesticides in suburban homes and gardens and their impact on the aquatic environment. 1972. **fQH545.P4V66 ECOL**

AQUATIC MICROBIOLOGY.
Neely, W. C. Biological and photobiological action of pollutants on aquatic microorganisms. 1973. **fTC1.A85no.9 ECOL**

AQUATIC PESTS.
Otto, Norman E. Aquatic pests on irrigation systems: identification guide. 1972,1965 **QH96.O88 1972 ECOL**

AQUATIC PLANTS.
Correll, Donovan Stewart. Aquatic and wetland plants of southwestern United States. 1972. **QK142.C6 ECOL**

Su, K. Lee. Aquatic plants from Minnesota, part 1—chemical survey. 1972. **GB701.M554no.46 ECOL**

Su, K. Lee. Aquatic plants from Minnesota part 2—toxicity, anti-neoplastic, and coagulent effects. 1972. **GB701.M554no.47 ECOL**

Su, K. Lee. Aquatic plants from Minnesota part 3—antimicrobial effects. 1972. **GB701.M554no.48 ECOL**

AQUATIC PLANTS—MINNESOTA—ECONOMIC ASPECTS.
Linn, J. G. Aquatic plants from Minnesota, part 4 — nutrient composition. 1973. **GB701.M554no.56 ECOL**

AQUATIC RESOURCES see also FISHERIES; MARINE RESOURCES; WETLANDS
Conservation and productivity of natural waters. 1972. **QL1.Z733no.29 ECOL**

ARCHITECTURAL DESIGN—CONGRESSES.
Emerging methods in environmental design and planning. 1970 **TA170.E46 ECOL**

ARCHITECTURE—UNITED STATES.
McCue, Gerald M. Creating the human environment. 1970 **HN59.M22 ECOL**

ARCTIC EXPEDITIONS see ARCTIC REGIONS

ARCTIC REGIONS see also SCIENTIFIC EXPEDITIONS
American Geographical Society of New York. Problems of polar research. 1928. **G576.A6 ECOL**

Joerg, Wolfgang Louis Gottfried. Brief history of polar exploration since the introduction of flying. 1930 **G590.J6 ECOL**

Nordenskjold, Otto. The geography of the polar regions, consisting of a general characterization of polar nature. 1928. **G587.N6 ECOL**

ARID REGIONS see also DESERTS
Smythe, William Ellsworth. The conquest of arid America. 1969,c1905 **F591.S662 1969 ECOL**

Walton, Kenneth. The arid zones. 1st U.S. ed. 1969 **GB611.W3 1969 ECOL**

ART AND SOCIETY.
Kepes, Gyorgy. Arts of the environment. 1972 **N72.S6K37 ECOL**

ARTIFICAL SATELLITES—LAW AND LEGISLATION see SPACE LAW

ASBESTOS—TOXICOLOGY.
Brodeur, Paul. Asbestos and enzymes. 1972 **RA1231.A8B76 ECOL**

ASTRONAUTICS—LAW AND LEGISLATION see SPACE LAW

ATLANTIC COAST—DESCRIPTION AND TRAVEL.
Hay, John. The Atlantic shore. 1969,c1966. **QH95.7.H3 ECOL**

ATLANTIC COAST (UNITED STATES).
Leonard, Jonathan Norton. Atlantic beaches. 1972 **GB459.4.L46 ECOL**

ATLANTIC SALMON.
Mills, Derek Henry. Salmon and trout: a resource, its ecology, conservation, and management. 1971 **QL638.S2M5 1971b ECOL**

ATLASES.
Rand McNally and Company. The earth and man: a Rand McNally world atlas. c1972 **REF fG1019.R433 ECOL**

ATMOSPHERE see also AIR; METEOROLOGY
Knight, David C. The first book of air. 1961 **PZ10.K57Fg ECOL**

Riehl, Herbert. Introduction to the atmosphere. 2d ed. 1971,c1972 **QC861.2.R5 1971 ECOL**

ATMOSPHERE—POLLUTION see AIR—POLLUTION

ATMOSPHERIC ABSORPTION OF SOLAR RADIATION see SOLAR RADIATION

ATOLLS see CORAL REEFS AND ISLANDS

ATOMIC BOMB—PHYSIOLOGICAL EFFECT.
Aronow, Saul. The fallen sky. 1963
  RA569.A7 ECOL

ATOMIC ENERGY see also ATOMIC POWER; NUCLEAR ENGINEERING; NUCLEAR REACTORS; PROJECT PLOWSHARE
Glasstone, Samuel. Atomic energy and your world. 1970   QC792.G55 ECOL
Hines, Neal O. Atoms, nature, and man. c1966
  QC778.H54 ECOL
Nuclear explosives in peacetime. 1970
  fQC792.N8 ECOL
Seaborg, Glenn Theodore. Man and atom. 1st ed. 1971.   TK9145.S4 1971 ECOL
United States. Atomic Energy Commission. The new force of atomic energy: its development and use. n.d.
  TK9146.U5 ECOL

ATOMIC ENERGY—BIBLIOGRAPHY—CATALOGS.
United States. Atomic Energy Commission. Index to the Understanding the atom series. 1970
  REF Z5160.U4915 1970 ECOL

ATOMIC ENERGY—ECONOMIC ASPECTS.
Lewis, Richard S. The energy crisis. 1972.
  fHC103.7.L4 ECOL

ATOMIC ENERGY—ECONOMIC ASPECTS—GREAT BRITAIN—ADDRESSES, ESSAYS, LECTURES.
Economic and social consequences of nuclear energy. 1972.   HD9698.A3G74 ECOL

ATOMIC ENERGY—ECONOMIC ASPECTS—UNITED STATES.
Brooks, David B. Peaceful use of nuclear explosives; some economic aspects. 1969
  HD9698.U52B7 ECOL

ATOMIC ENERGY—POPULAR WORKS.
Craven, Claude Jackson. Our atomic world. Rev. 1964.   QC778.C7 1964 ECOL
United States. Atomic Energy Commission. Atomic energy in use. 1965   TK9146.U55 ECOL

ATOMIC ENERGY—SOCIAL ASPECTS—GREAT BRITAIN—ADDRESSES, ESSAYS, LECTURES.
Economic and social consequences of nuclear energy. 1972.   HD9698.A3G74 ECOL

ATOMIC ENERGY—SOCIAL ASPECTS—UNITED STATES.
Metzger, H. Peter. The atomic establishment. 1972
  HD9698.U52M47 ECOL

ATOMIC ENERGY INDUSTRIES—DIRECTORIES.
Nuclear news buyers guide. 1972-
  REF fTK9012.N82 ECOL

ATOMIC ENERGY INDUSTRIES—UNITED STATES.
Lewis, Richard S. The nuclear-power rebellion. 1972   HD9698.A3U44 1972 ECOL
Metzger, H. Peter. The atomic establishment. 1972
  HD9698.U52M47 ECOL

ATOMIC ENERGY INDUSTRIES—UNITED STATES—YEARBOOKS.
United States. Atomic Energy Commission. Division of Industrial Participation. The nuclear industry. 1971-   TK9023.A35 ECOL

ATOMIC ENERGY RESEARCH—INTERNATIONAL COOPERATION.
Willrich, Mason. Global politics of nuclear energy. 1971   TK9145.W49 ECOL

ATOMIC ENERGY RESEARCH—INTERNATIONAL COOPERATION—DICTIONARIES.
United States. Brookhaven National Laboratory. Upton, N.Y. Technical Support Organization. Safeguards dictionary. 1971.   JX1974.7.U5 ECOL

ATOMIC ENERGY RESEARCH—UNITED STATES—PERIODICALS.
United States. Atomic Energy Commission. Fundamental nuclear energy research. 1971-
  QC788.U5 ECOL

ATOMIC MERCHANT SHIPS.
Donnelly, Warren H. Nuclear power and merchant shipping. Rev. c1965   VM317.D6 1965 ECOL

ATOMIC POWER see also ATOMIC ENERGY; ATOMIC POWER-PLANTS; CONTROLLED FUSION; NUCLEAR ROCKETS
Jensen, Walter Godfried Willem. Nuclear power. 1969.   TK9145.J44 ECOL

United States. Atomic Energy Commission. Division of Operations and Forecasting. Forecast of growth of nuclear power. 1971.   TK9145.U5 ECOL
United States. Atomic Energy Commission. The new force of atomic energy: its development and use. n.d.
  TK9146.U5 ECOL

ATOMIC POWER—LAW AND LEGISLATION—UNITED STATES.
Lewis, Richard S. The nuclear-power rebellion. 1972   HD9698.A3U44 1972 ECOL
Metzger, H. Peter. The atomic establishment. 1972
  HD9698.U52M47 ECOL

ATOMIC POWER INDUSTRY—UNITED STATES.
Curtis, Richard. Perils of the peaceful atom. 1969.
  HD9698.U52C8 ECOL

ATOMIC POWER-PLANTS.
Corliss, William R. Power reactors in small packages. 1968   TK1078.C6 1968 ECOL
Fuchs, Erich. What makes a nuclear power plant work? 1972.   fPZ10.F77Wh3 ECOL
General Dynamics Corporation. Electric Boat Division. Potential environmental effects of an offshore submerged nuclear power plant. 1971-
  fQH541.5.S3G45 ECOL
Lapp, Ralph E. A citizen's guide to nuclear power. c1971.   TK1078.L3 ECOL
Lyerly, Ray L. Nuclear power plants. Rev. 1969
  TK1078.L9 1969 ECOL
Minnesota Committee for Environmental Information. The costs and benefits of nuclear electric power plants. 1969.   REF fTK1078.M5 ECOL
Stanford Research Institute. Decision Analysis Group. Decision analysis of nuclear plants in electrical system expansion: final report.   fTK1078.S7 ECOL
United States. Atomic Energy Commission. Division of Operations and Forecasting. Forecast of growth of nuclear power. 1971.   TK9145.U5 ECOL
United States. Atomic Energy Commission. Nuclear Power and the environment. 1969.
  TK1343.A46 ECOL

ATOMIC POWER PLANTS—ACCIDENTS.
Curtis, Richard. Perils of the peaceful atom. 1969.
  HD9698.U52C8 ECOL

ATOMIC POWER-PLANTS—ADDRESSES, ESSAYS LECTURES.
The Environmental and ecological forum, 1970-1971. 1972.   TD898.E58 ECOL

ATOMIC POWER-PLANTS—AUTOMATION—CONGRESSES.
Working Group Meeting on Nuclear Power Plant Control and Instrumentation, Vienna, 1971. Nuclear power plant control and instrumentation. 1972.
  TK9006.W58 1971 ECOL

ATOMIC POWER-PLANTS—CONGRESSES.
Nuclear power and the public. 1972
  TK1078.N83 ECOL
Symposium on Environmental Aspects of Nuclear Power Stations, New York, 1970. Environmental aspects of nuclear power stations. 1971.
  REF TK9006.S887 1970 ECOL

ATOMIC POWER-PLANTS—MARYLAND.
Maryland. Governor's Task Force on Nuclear Power Plants. Nuclear power plants in Maryland. 1969.
  TK1344.M3M3 ECOL

ATOMIC POWER PLANTS—MINNESOTA.
Northern States Power Company, Minneapolis. Environmental monitoring and ecological studies program. 1971-   REF fTK1377.P7N6 ECOL

ATOMIC POWER-PLANTS—NEW YORK (STATE).
Nelkin, Dorothy. Nuclear power and its critics. 1971   TK1344.N7N4 ECOL

ATOMIC POWER-PLANTS—SAFETY MEASURES.
Gofman, John William. Poisoned power. 1971
  TK9152.G57 ECOL
Hogerton, John F. Atomic power safety. c1964
  TK1078.H62 ECOL

ATOMIC POWER-PLANTS—SAFETY MEASURES—CONGRESSES.
Environmental surveillance in the vicinity of nuclear facilities. 1970   REF TD887.R3E58 ECOL
Southern Conference on Environmental Radiation Protection from Nuclear Power Plants, St. Petersburg, Fla., 1971. Proceedings of Southern Conference on Environmental Radiation Protection from Nuclear Power Plants, April 21-22, 1971. 1972.
  TK9152.S6 ECOL

ATOMIC POWER-PLANTS—UNITED STATES.
Fabricant, Neil. Toward a rational power policy: energy, politics, and pollution. 1971
  HD9685.U5F32 ECOL

United States. Atomic Energy Commission. Division of Reactor Development and Technology. Operating history of United States nuclear power reactors. 1971.
  fTK1343.A467 ECOL
United States. Atomic Energy Commission. Division of Reactor Development and Technology. Operating history of U.S. nuclear power reactors. 1972.
  fTK1343.A467 1972 ECOL
United States. Atomic Energy Commission. Division of Reactor Development and Technology. Thermal effects and United States nuclear power stations. 1971.
  TD427.H4U52 ECOL

ATOMIC WARFARE—ADDRESSES, ESSAYS, LECTURES.
Environmental effects of weapons technology. 1970
  fUG447.8.E57 ECOL

ATOMIC WARFARE—SAFETY MEASURES.
Aronow, Saul. The fallen sky. 1963
  RA569.A7 ECOL

ATOMIC WEAPONS—SAFETY MEASURES—DICTIONARIES.
United States. Brookhaven National Laboratory. Upton, N.Y. Technical Support Organization. Safeguards dictionary. 1971.   JX1974.7.U5 ECOL

ATOMIC WEAPONS—TESTING.
Comar, Cyril Lewis. Fallout from nuclear tests. 1963   UF767.C64 ECOL
Comar, Cyril Lewis. Fallout from nuclear tests. Rev. 1966   UF767.C64 1966 ECOL

ATTITUDE (PSYCHOLOGY).
Wilson, Raymond Harrison. Toward a philosophy of planning: attitudes of federal water planners. 1973.
  HC110.E5W5 ECOL

AUTOMOBILE EXHAUST GAS.
Eccleston, Barton H. Effect of fuel front-end and midrange volatility on automobile emissions. 1972?
  TN23.U7no.7707 ECOL
Henry, Marybeth. Motor vehicle emissions: a bibliography. 1972   REF fTL214.P6H4 ECOL
Patterson, Donald J. Emissions from combustion engines and their control. 1972 TD886.5.P83 ECOL
Vehicle emission control. 1971?
  fTD886.5.V4 ECOL

AUTOMOBILE EXHAUST GAS—ANALYSIS.
Dimitriades, Basil. Interpretation of gas chromatographic spectra in routine analysis of exhaust hydrocarbons. 1972   TN23.U7no.7700 ECOL

AUTOMOBILE GRAVEYARDS.
United States. Bureau of Mines. Automobile disposal. 1967   HD9710.U52A27 ECOL

AUTOMOBILE INDUSTRY AND TRADE—UNITED STATES.
Jerome, John. The death of the automobile. 1st ed. 1972   HE5623.J47 ECOL

AUTOMOBILE WRECKING AND USED PARTS INDUSTRY—MINNESOTA.
Henningson, Durham & Richardson. Minnesota: disposal and reuse of abandoned and retired automobiles. 1970.   REF fTD795.H36 ECOL

AUTOMOBILE WRECKING AND USED PARTS INDUSTRY—UNITED STATES.
United States. Bureau of Mines. Automobile disposal. 1967   HD9710.U52A27 ECOL

AUTOMOBILES.
United States. Solid Waste Management Office. The automobile cycle: an environmental and resource reclamation problem. 1972.   TD793.U5 ECOL

AUTOMOBILES—LAWS AND REGULATIONS—UNITED STATES.
United States. Ad Hoc Committee on the Cumulative Regulatory Effects on the Cost of Automotive Transportation. Cumulative regulatory effects on the cost of automotive transportation (RECAT): final report. 1972.   KF2209.A3U5 ECOL

AUTOMOBILES—MAINTENANCE AND REPAIR.
Glenn, Harold T. Automotive smog control manual. 1968   TL152.G545 ECOL

AUTOMOBILES—SAFETY MEASURES.
Minnesota. Dept. of Highways. A research progress report on the effects of studded tires. 1970.
  fTL270.M5 1970 ECOL
Minnesota. Dept. of Highways. A research summary report on the effects of studded tires. 1971.
  fTL270.M5 1971 ECOL

AUTOMOBILES—SOCIAL ASPECTS—UNITED STATES.
Jerome, John. The death of the automobile. 1st ed. 1972   HE5623.J47 ECOL
Schneider, Kenneth R. Autokind vs. mankind. 1st ed. 1971   HE5623.S35 1971 ECOL

AUTOMOBILES, ELECTRIC.
Ayres, Robert U. Alternatives to the internal combustion engine. 1972   **TL210.A96 ECOL**

AUTOMOBILES, STEAM.
Jamison, Andrew. The steam-powered automobile. 1970   **TL200.J34 ECOL**

B

BACILLARIOPHYTA see DIATOMS
BACILLARIPOHYCEAE see DIATOMS
BACTERIA, ANAEROBIC.
Robert S. Kerr Water Research Center. Denitrification by anaerobic filters and ponds. 1971.   **fTD475.R6 ECOL**

BACTERIA, DENITRIFYING see also NITRIFICATION
McCoy, Elizabeth F. Role of bacteria in the nitrogen cycle in lakes. 1972.   **fTD433.M3 ECOL**

BACTERIA, NITRIFYING see also NITRIFICATION
McCoy, Elizabeth F. Role of bacteria in the nitrogen cycle in lakes. 1972.   **fTD433.M3 ECOL**

BACTERIA, PATHOGENIC—WAR USE see BIOLOGICAL WARFARE
BACTERIAL ANTAGONISM see ANTIBIOSIS
BACTERIOLOGICAL WARFARE see BIOLOGICAL WARFARE
BACTERIOLOGY, SANITARY see SANITARY MICROBIOLOGY

BAGASSE.
Callihan, Clayton Dale. Construction of a chemical-microbial pilot plant for production of single-cell protein from cellulosic wastes. 1971.   **TP996.B3C3 ECOL**

BAJA CALIFORNIA—DESCRIPTION AND TRAVEL.
Johnson, William Weber. Baja California.   **F1246.J6 ECOL**

BARNYARD MANURE see FARM MANURE
BASE FLOW see GROUNDWATER FLOW
BATES LABORATORY ASPIRATOR see SEPARATORS (MACHINES)
BATRACHIA—NORTH AMERICA.
Barker, Will. Familiar animals of America. 1956   **QL715.B25 ECOL**

BEACH BIRDS see SHORE BIRDS
BEAUTIFICATION OF THE LANDSCAPE see LANDSCAPE PROTECTION
BEAVERS.
Rue, Leonard Lee. The world of the beaver. 1964.   **QL737.R6R84 ECOL**

BEAVERS—LEGENDS AND STORIES.
Buyukmihci, Hope Sawyer. Hour of the beaver. 1971   **QL795.B5B8 ECOL**

BEETLES.
Brown, Harley P. Aquatic dryopoid beetles (Coleoptera) of the United States. 1972.   **fQH96.A2B5no.6 ECOL**

BEETLES—NORTH AMERICA—IDENTIFICATION.
Dillon, Elizabeth S. A manual of common beetles of eastern North America. 1972.   **QL581.D5 1972 ECOL**

BEETS AND BEET SUGAR.
Beet Sugar Development Foundation, Fort Collins, Colo. State-of-art, sugarbeet processing waste treatment. 1971.   **fTD899.S8B43 ECOL**

BERING'S EXPEDITION, 1ST, 1725-1730.
Golder, Frank Alfred. Bering's voyage. 1922-25.   **G296.B4G6 ECOL**

BERING'S EXPEDITION, 2D, 1733-1741.
Golder, Frank Alfred. Bering's voyage. 1922-25.   **G296.B4G6 ECOL**

BERYLLIUM—TOXICOLOGY.
Tabershaw, Irving R. The toxicology of beryllium. 1972.   **RA1231.B4T3 ECOL**

BEVERAGES—PACKAGING.
Bingham, Tayler H. The beverage container problem. 1972.   **TD793.B5 ECOL**
Hannon, Bruce. System energy and recycling: a study of the beverage industry. 1972.   **fTP659.H3 ECOL**

BIG SUR, CALIFORNIA.
Brower, David Ross. Not man apart. 1969   **F869.B63B7 1969 ECOL**

BIG THICKET NATIONAL PARK, TEX. (PROPOSED).
Gunter, Pete Addison Y. The Big Thicket. 1971 c1972   **fF392.H37G8 ECOL**

BILLBOARDS—UNITED STATES.
Blake, Peter. God's own junkyard. 1964   **HF5843.5.B55 ECOL**

BIO-GEOGRAPHY see ANTHROPO-GEOGRAPHY; GEOGRAPHICAL DISTRIBUTION OF ANIMALS AND PLANTS

BIOCHEMICAL OXYGEN DEMAND.
JBF Scientific Corporation. Engineering methodology for river and stream reaeration. 1971   **fTD458.J17 ECOL**
Washington (State). University. The oxygen uptake demand of resuspended bottom sediments. 1970.   **fGC380.W3 ECOL**

BIOCHEMISTRY see BIOLOGICAL CHEMISTRY

BIOLOGICAL CHEMISTRY see also MOLECULAR BIOLOGY
Chemical ecology. 1970.   **QH345.C435 ECOL**
Dugan, Patrick R. Biochemical ecology of water pollution. 1972.   **TD423.D83 ECOL**
Eiduson, Samuel. Biochemistry and behavior. 1964   **QP521.E5 ECOL**

BIOLOGICAL CONTROL OF WEEDS see WEED CONTROL—BIOLOGICAL CONTROL

BIOLOGICAL LABORATORIES—UNITED STATES—DIRECTORIES.
Agricultural Sciences Information Network. Directory of information resources in agriculture and biology. 1971.   **REF QH321.A37 ECOL**

BIOLOGICAL OXYGEN DEMAND see BIOCHEMICAL OXYGEN DEMAND

BIOLOGICAL SPECIMENS—COLLECTION AND PRESERVATION.
Harris, Reg. Natural history collecting. 1972   **QH60.H36 ECOL**

BIOLOGICAL WARFARE.
Hersh, Seymour M. Chemical and biological warfare. 1969, c1968   **UG447.H42 1969 ECOL**
McCarthy, Richard D. The ultimate folly. 1969   **UG447.M233 1969 ECOL**
Thomas, Ann (Van Wynen). Legal limits on the use of chemical and biological weapons. 1970   **REF JX5135.C5T55 ECOL**

BIOLOGICAL WARFARE—ADDRESSES, ESSAYS, LECTURES.
Conference on Chemical and Biological Warfare, London, 1968. CBW: chemical and biological warfare. 1969, c1968   **UG447.C655 1968 ECOL**
Environmental effects of weapons technology. 1970   **fUG447.8.E57 ECOL**

BIOLOGY see also ADAPTATION (BIOLOGY); BOTANY; EVOLUTION; LIFE (BIOLOGY); MARINE BIOLOGY; NATURAL HISTORY; REPRODUCTION; ZOOLOGY
Biology and the future of man. 1970.   **QH307.2.B56 ECOL**
Brandwein, Paul Franz. The world of living things. 1964   **QH308.5.B7 1964 ECOL**
Chinery, Michael. Concise color encyclopedia of nature. 1972   **fQH309.C46 1972 ECOL**
Gerking, Shelby Delos. Biological systems. 1969.   **QH308.G44 ECOL**
Morgan, R. F. Environmental biology. 1963-   **QH308.5.M6 ECOL**
Sears, Paul Bigelow. This is our world. Rev. ed. 1971   **QH309.S3 1971 ECOL**
Taylor, Gordon Rattray. The biological time bomb. 1968   **QH309.T25 1968 ECOL**

BIOLOGY—ADDRESSES, ESSAYS, LECTURES.
Hutchinson, George Evelyn. The ecological theater and the evolutionary play. 1965   **QH311.H77 ECOL**

BIOLOGY—CLASSIFICATION.
Boughey, Arthur S. Population and environmental biology. 1967   **QH83.B68 ECOL**

BIOLOGY—COLLECTED WORKS.
Johnson, Cecil E. Social and natural biology. 1968   **QH302.J58 ECOL**

BIOLOGY—DICTIONARIES.
Gray, Peter. The encyclopedia of the biological sciences. 2d ed. 1970   **REF QH13.G7 1970 ECOL**
Hanson, Herbert Christian. Dictionary of ecology. 1962   **REF QH541.H25 ECOL**

BIOLOGY—EXPERIMENTS.
Rasmussen, Frederick A. Man and the environment. 1970, c1971   **QH316.5.R35 ECOL**

BIOLOGY—FIELD WORK.
Benton, Allen H. Field biology and ecology. 2d ed. 1966   **QH318.5.B4 1966 ECOL**
Benton, Allen H. Manual of field biology and ecology. 4th ed. c1965   **QH307.B3 1965 ECOL**

BIOLOGY—INFORMATION SERVICES—DIRECTORIES.
United States. Library of Congress. National Referral Center. A directory of information resources in the United States: biological sciences. 1972.   **REF QH303.U5 ECOL**

BIOLOGY—OUTLINES, SYLLABI, ETC.
Morholt, Evelyn. A sourcebook for the biological sciences. 2d ed. 1966   **QH53.M67 1966 ECOL**

BIOLOGY—PHILOSOPHY.
Burnet, Frank Macfarlane, Sir. Dominant mammal. 1972, c1971   **QH331.B887 1972 ECOL**
Crick, Francis. Of molecules and men. 1969, c1966.   **QH331.C9 1969 ECOL**
Henderson, Lawrence Joseph. The fitness of the environment. 1970 c1913   **QH331.H45 1970 ECOL**

BIOLOGY—POPULAR WORKS.
Headstrom, Birger Richard. Nature in miniature. 1968.   **QH309.H4 ECOL**

BIOLOGY—SOCIAL ASPECTS.
Jacker, Corinne. The biological revolution. 1971   **QH333.J3 ECOL**
Potter, Van Rensselaer. Bioethics: bridge to the future. 1971   **QH333.P66 ECOL**

BIOLOGY—STUDY AND TEACHING.
Morholt, Evelyn. A sourcebook for the biological sciences. 2d ed. 1966   **QH53.M67 1966 ECOL**

BIOLOGY—STUDY AND TEACHING—CONGRESSES.
Conference on Undergraduate Education in the Biological Sciences for Students in Agriculture and Natural Resources, Washington, D.C., 1966. Undergraduate education in the biological sciences for students in agriculture and natural resources. 1967.   **S533.C755 1966 ECOL**

BIOLOGY—UNITED STATES—INFORMATION—SERVICES—DIRECTORIES.
United States. Library of Congress. National Referral Center. A directory of information resources in the United States: biological sciences. 1972.   **REF QH303.U5 ECOL**

BIOMATHEMATICS.
Watt, Kenneth E. F. Systems analysis in ecology. 1966.   **QH541.W3 ECOL**

BIOTIC COMMUNITIES.
Rudd, Robert L. Pesticides and the living landscape. 1964.   **SB951.R78 ECOL**

BIRD POPULATIONS.
Henny, Charles J. An analysis of the population dynamics of selected avian species. 1972   **QL785.5.B6H4 ECOL**
Lack, David Lambert. Ecological isolation in birds. 1971.   **QH401.L32 1971 ECOL**

BIRD-SONG.
Hartshorne, Charles. Born to sing: an interpretation and world survey of bird song. 1973   **QL698.5.H27 ECOL**
Songs of the forest. 1964.   **Phonodisc QL698.5.S63 ECOL**

BIRDS see also FLIGHT; ORNITHOLOGY
Aymar, Gordon Christian. Bird flight. 1935.   **QL698.A9 ECOL**
Baynes, Ernest Harold. Wild bird guests. 1915.   **SK353.B4 ECOL**
Henry, Marguerite. Birds at Home. 1972   **fQL676.H52 1972 ECOL**
Laycock, George. Wingspread. 1972   **QL676.L35 ECOL**
MacBean, John C. Birds. c1971   **QL676.M22 ECOL**
Yapp, William Brunsdon. The life and organization of birds. 1970   **QL698.Y36 ECOL**

BIRDS—AFRICA, NORTH.
Heinzel, Hermann. The birds of Britain and Europe with North Africa and Middle East. 1972   **QL690.A1H44 ECOL**

BIRDS—AFRICA, SOUTH.
Roberts, Austin. Our South African birds (Ons Suid-Afrikaanse voels). 1941   **REF QL692.R62 ECOL**

BIRDS—AMERICA.
Griscom, Ludlow. The warblers of America. 1957.   **REF QL696.P2G85 ECOL**

BIRDS—ANATOMY.
Heilmann, Gerhard. The origin of birds. 1927.   **QE871.H4 1927 ECOL**

BIRDS—ARGENTINE REPUBLIC.
Hudson, William Henry. Birds of La Plata. 1920.   **REF QL689.A6H8 ECOL**

BIRDS—BEHAVIOR.
Ardley, Neil. How birds behave. 1971   **fQL785.5.B6A7 ECOL**
Henny, Charles J. An analysis of the population dynamics of selected avian species. 1972   **QL785.5.B6H4 ECOL**
Koford, Carl B. The California condor. 1966, c1953   **QL696.A2K64 1966 ECOL**

Tinbergen, Nikolaas. Curious naturalists. 1968,c1958 **QL751.T55 1968 ECOL**

BIRDS—CANADA.
Taverner, Percy Algernon. Birds of Western Canada. 2d ed. rev. 1928. **Ref QH1.C13no.41 1928 ECOL**

BIRDS—CHILE.
Goodall, J. D. Las aves de Chile. 1946 **Ref QL689.C5G6 ECOL**

BIRDS—CLASSIFICATION.
Peters, James Lee. Check-list of birds of the world. 1931- **REF QL677.P45 ECOL**

BIRDS—COLORADO.
Bailey, Alfred Marshall. Birds of Colorado. 1965. **REF fQL684.C6B3 ECOL**

BIRDS—DISEASES.
Infectious and parasitic diseases of wild birds. 1st ed. 1971 **SF994.4.A115 ECOL**

BIRDS—EGGS AND NESTS.
Dossenbach, Hans D. The family life of birds. 1971 **QL675.D6613 ECOL**

BIRDS—EGYPT.
Berg, Bengt Magnus Kristoffer. To Africa with the migratory birds. 1930. **QL692.B4 ECOL**

BIRDS—EUROPE.
Heinzel, Hermann. The birds of Britain and Europe with North Africa and Middle East. 1972 **QL690.A1H44 ECOL**

BIRDS—FLORIDA.
Sprunt, Alexander. Florida bird life. 1954 **QL684.F6S65 ECOL**

BIRDS—HABITS AND BEHAVIOR.
Sowls, Lyle K. Prairie ducks. 1955. **QL696.A5S64 ECOL**
Sprunt, Alexander. Florida bird life. 1954 **QL684.F6S65 ECOL**

BIRDS—MASSACHUSETTS.
Forbush, Edward Howe. Birds of Massachusetts and other New England states. 1925-29 **REF QL684.M4F65 ECOL**

BIRDS—MIGRATION.
Berg, Bengt Magnus Kristoffer. To Africa with the migratory birds. 1930. **QL692.B4 ECOL**
Hochbaum, Hans Albert. Travels and traditions of waterfowl. 1955 **QL698.H65 ECOL**

BIRDS—MINNESOTA.
Roberts, Thomas Sadler. The birds of Minnesota. 1932. **fQL684.M6R47 ECOL**
Roberts, Thomas Sadler. Manual for the identification of the birds of Minnesota and neighboring States. Rev. ed. 1955. **QL684.M6R472 1955 ECOL**

BIRDS—MINNESOTA—BIBLIOGRAPHY.
Roberts, Thomas Sadler. The birds of Minnesota. 1932. **fQL684.M6R47 ECOL**

BIRDS—NEAR EAST.
Heinzel, Hermann. The birds of Britain and Europe with North Africa and Middle East. 1972 **QL690.A1H44 ECOL**

BIRDS—NEW ENGLAND.
Forbush, Edward Howe. Birds of Massachusetts and other New England states. 1925-29 **REF QL684.M4F65 ECOL**

BIRDS—NEW YORK (STATE)—LONG ISLAND.
Arbib, Robert S. The Lord's Woods. 1st ed. 1971 **QH76.5.N7A72 ECOL**

BIRDS—NEWFOUNDLAND.
Peters, Harold Seymour. The birds of Newfoundland. 1951. **QL654.P47 ECOL**

BIRDS—NOMENCLATURE.
American Ornithologists' Union. Check-list of North American birds. 4th ed., constituting the "Systema avium" for North America north of Mexico. 1931. **REF QL677.A52 1932 ECOL**

BIRDS—NORTH AMERICA.
American Ornithologists' Union. Check-list of North American birds. 4th ed., constituting the "Systema avium" for North America north of Mexico. 1931. **REF QL677.A52 1932 ECOL**
Chapman, Frank Michler. Handbook of birds of eastern North America. Rev. ed. 1912. **REF QL681.C46 1912 ECOL**
Johnsgard, Paul A. Grouse and quails of North America. 1973 **QL696.G27J63 ECOL**
Laycock, George. Wingspread. 1972 **QL676.L35 ECOL**
Murphy, Robert Cushman. Land birds of America. 1953 **fQL681.M85 ECOL**
Pough, Richard Hooper. Audubon bird guide; eastern land birds...with illus. in color of every species. 1946. **QL681.P68 ECOL**
Pough, Richard Hooper. Audubon land bird guide. c1949 **QL681.P68 1949 ECOL**
Stout, Gardner D. The shorebirds of North America. 1967 **fQL681.S78 ECOL**

BIRDS—PACIFIC COAST.
Hoffmann, Ralph. Birds of the Pacific states. 1927. **Ref QL683.H65 ECOL**

BIRDS—PERU.
Murphy, Robert Cushman. Bird islands of Peru. 1925. **REF QH128.M8 ECOL**

BIRDS—PHYSIOLOGY.
Yapp, William Brunsdon. The life and organization of birds. 1970 **QL698.Y36 ECOL**

BIRDS—PICTORIAL WORKS.
Cruickshank, Allan D. Wings in the wilderness. 1947. **QL674.C85 ECOL**
Johnsgard, Paul A. Waterfowl, their biology and natural history. 1968 **QL696.A5J63 ECOL**
Menaboni, Athos. Birds. 1950 **fQL681.M49 ECOL**
Murphy, Robert Cushman. Land birds of America. 1953 **fQL681.M85 ECOL**
Northshield, Robert. The people's birds. 1972 **QL674.N67 ECOL**

BIRDS—SWEDEN.
Berg, Bengt Magnus Kristoffer. Tavlor av Svenska faglar. c1925 **REF fQL690.S5B46 ECOL**

BIRDS—UNITED STATES.
Cruickshank, Allan D. Wings in the wilderness. 1947. **QL674.C85 ECOL**
Lemmon, Robert Stell. Our amazing birds. 1952. **REF QL681.L4 ECOL**
Menaboni, Athos. Birds. 1950 **fQL681.M49 ECOL**
Pough, Richard Hooper. Audubon water bird guide. 1951. **QL681.P69 ECOL**
Ransom, Elmer Inglesby. The woodland book. 1945 **QL681.R2 ECOL**
Reed, Chester Albert. Bird guide. Rev. ed. 1916. **QL683.R32 1916 ECOL**

BIRDS—THE WEST.
Peterson, Roger Tory. A field guide to western birds. 2d ed., rev. and enl. 1961. **QL683.W4P4 1961 ECOL**
Pough, Richard Hooper. Audubon Western bird guide. 1957. **QL683.W4P6 ECOL**

BIRDS, AQUATIC see WATER-BIRDS

BIRDS, ATTRACTING OF.
Arbib, Robert S. The hungry bird book. 1971 **QL676.5.A7 1971 ECOL**

BIRDS, EXTINCT.
Allen, Robert Porter. On the trail of vanishing birds. 1957 **QL696.G8A4 ECOL**

BIRDS, FOSSIL.
Heilmann, Gerhard. The origin of birds. 1927. **QE871.H4 1927 ECOL**

BIRDS IN LITERATURE.
Priestley, Mary. A book of birds. 1938. **PN6110.B6P75 ECOL**

BIRDS' NESTS see BIRDS—EGGS AND NESTS

BIRDS, PROTECTION OF.
Baynes, Ernest Harold. Wild bird guests. 1915. **SK353.B4 ECOL**
Bovey, Martin Koon. Saga of the waterfowl. 1949. **REF SK331.B6 ECOL**
McMillan, Ian. Man and the California condor. 1968. **QL696.A2H24 ECOL**
Phillips, John Charles. American waterfowl. 1930. **QL696.A5P45 ECOL**

BIRTH CONTROL.
Hardin, Garrett James. Exploring new ethics for survival: the voyage of the spaceship Beagle. 1972 **HB871.H347 ECOL**

BIRTH CONTROL—ADDRESSES, ESSAYS, LECTURES.
Hardin, Garrett James. Population, evolution, and birth control. 2d ed. 1969 **HB851.H28 1969 ECOL**
McCuen, Gary E. The ecology controversy: opposing viewpoints. 1971 **QH541.M3 ECOL**

BIRTH CONTROL—CONGRESSES.
Are our descendants doomed? 1972 **HB849.A74 1972 ECOL**
The Limits to growth. c1972 **HC110.E5L5 ECOL**

BIRTH CONTROL—RELIGIOUS ASPECTS.
Friends, Society of. American Friends Service Committee. Who shall live? 1970 **HQ766.3.F7 ECOL**

BITUMINOUS COAL.
Bituminous coal facts. 1970- **REF fHD9544.B47 ECOL**

BLACK-FOOTED FERRET.
McNulty, Faith. Must they die? 1st ed. 1971. **QL737.C25M27 ECOL**

BLUE EARTH RIVER WATERSHED, MINNESOTA.
United States. Army. Corps of Engineers. Interim survey report on Blue Earth River, Minnesota, Minnesota River Basin for flood control and related purposes. 1970? **Ref fTC424.M6A5 ECOL**

BLUE WHALE.
Mizumura, Kazue. The blue whale. c1971 **QL737.C424M59 ECOL**
Small, George L. The blue whale. 1971. **QL737.C424S58 ECOL**

B.O.D. see BIOCHEMICAL OXYGEN DEMAND

BODY, HUMAN.
Rosebury, Theodor. Life on man. 1969 **QR56.R59 ECOL**

BOILERS—INCRUSTATIONS.
McCoy, James W. Chemical analysis of industrial water. 1969. **TD380.M3 ECOL**

BOTANICAL SURVEYS see VEGETATION SURVEYS

BOTANY see also CLIMBING PLANTS; LEAVES; PLANTS; TREES; WEEDS
Bold, Harold Charles. The plant kingdom. 3d ed. c1970 **QK48.B59 1970 ECOL**
Coulter, Merle Crowe. The story of the plant kingdom. Rev. by Howard J. Dittmer. 3d ed. 1964 **QK47.C893 1964 ECOL**
Dickinson, Alice. The first book of plants. c1953. **QK49.D5 ECOL**
Dowden, Anne Ophelia (Todd). Wild green things in the city. 1972 **SB611.D675 1972 ECOL**
Hyde, Margaret Oldroyd. Plants today and tomorrow. 1960 **QK50.H9 ECOL**
Jensen, William A. Botany: an ecological approach. 1972 **QK47.J45 ECOL**
Miner, Opal Irene (Frazine) Sevrey. The true book of plants we know. c1953 **QK49.M6 ECOL**
Went, Frits Warmolt. The plants. 1969,c1963 **fQK50.W43 1969 ECOL**

BOTANY—ECOLOGY.
Billings, William Dwight. Plants, man, and the ecosystem. 2d ed. 1970 **QK901.B5 1970 ECOL**
Cottam, Walter Pace. Our renewable wild lands, a challenge. 1961. **QK941.U8C6 ECOL**
Daubenmire, Rexford F. Plants and environment. 2d ed. c1959 **QK901.D3 1959 ECOL**
Jensen, William A. Botany: an ecological approach. 1972 **QK47.J45 ECOL**
Levitt, Jacob. Responses of plants to environmental stresses. 1972. **QK754.L42 ECOL**
Ohmann, Lewis F. Wilderness ecology, virgin plant communities of the Boundary Waters Canoe Area. 1971. **SD11.A45476no.63 ECOL**
Oosting, Henry John. The study of plant communities. 2d ed. 1956. **QK901.O6 1956 ECOL**
Robinette, Gary O. Plants/people/environmental quality. 1972 **QK901.R6 ECOL**
Stewart, Robert E. Classification of natural ponds and lakes in the glaciated prairie region. 1971. **S914.A3no.92 ECOL**
Tosco, Uberto. The flowering wilderness. 1972 **QK50.T6713 ECOL**
Treshow, Michael. Environment & plant response. 1970 **QK754.T7 ECOL**
Weaver, John Ernest. Prairie plants and their environment. 1968 **QK938.P7W42 ECOL**
Wright, Robert Henry. What good is a weed? 1972 **QK49.W75 ECOL**

BOTANY—ECOLOGY—CONGRESSES.
Environmental requirements of blue-green algae. 1967. **QK569.C96E56 ECOL**

BOTANY—FICTION.
Johnson, Elinor M. The plant hunters. 1969 **Fiction ECOL**

BOTANY—LABRADOR.
Forbes, Alexander. Northernmost Labrador. 1938. **F1136.F67 ECOL**

BOTANY—MINNESOTA.
Grether, David F. Population type, distribution and density of the flora on the Sherburne County Generating Plant Site, 15 October through 31 December, 1971. 1972 **fTK1331.N6G7 ECOL**
Moyle, John Briggs. Northern non-woody plants. Rev. ed. 1964 **fQK168.M68 1964 ECOL**

BOTANY—NOMENCLATORS.
Johnson, Arthur Tysilio. Plant names simplified. 2d ed. 1971. **QK11.J6 1971 ECOL**

BOTANY—NORTH AMERICA.
Gleason, Henry Allan. The natural geography of plants. 1964. **QK101.G57 ECOL**

BOTANY—NORTHEASTERN STATES.
Coon, Nelson. Using wayside plants. 4th rev. ed. 1969 **SB108.U6N7 1969 ECOL**
BOTANY—PATHOLOGY see PLANT DISEASES
BOTANY—POPULAR WORKS.
Tosco, Uberto. The flowering wilderness. 1972 **QK50.T6713 ECOL**
BOTANY—SOUTHWEST, NEW.
Correll, Donovan Stewart. Aquatic and wetland plants of southwestern United States. 1972. **QK142.C6 ECOL**
BOTANY—SURVEYING see VEGETATION SURVEYS
BOTANY—UTAH.
Cottam, Walter Pace. Our renewable wild lands, a challenge. 1961. **QK941.U8C6 ECOL**
BOTANY, ECONOMIC.
Coon, Nelson. Using wayside plants. 4th rev. ed. 1969 **SB108.U6N7 1969 ECOL**
Edlin, Herbert Leeson. Plants and man. 1969, c1967 **S519.E3 ECOL**
BOTTLING.
Hannon, Bruce. System energy and recycling: a study of the beverage industry. 1972. **fTP659.H3 ECOL**
BOUNDARY WATERS CANOE AREA, MINNESOTA.
Sierra Club. North Star Chapter (Minn.). A wilderness in crisis: the Boundary Waters Canoe Area. c1970 **fQH76.5.M6S5 ECOL**
BROWN PELICAN.
McClung, Robert M. Scoop, last of the brown pelicans. 1972. **PZ10.M115Sb ECOL**
BROWN TROUT.
Mills, Derek Henry. Salmon and trout: a resource, its ecology, conservation, and management. 1971 **QL638.S2M5 1971b ECOL**
BUILDING SITES.
United States. Office of Science and Technology. Electric power and the environment. 1970. **TK1193.U5A45 ECOL**
BUILDINGS—AERODYNAMICS.
United States. National Bureau of Standards. The effects of sonic boom and similar impulsive noise on structures. 1971. **TL574.S55U54 ECOL**
BUSH LAKE, MINNESOTA.
Barr Engineering Co. Hydrological study of Hyland-Bush-Anderson lakes. 1971. **fTC424.M6B326 ECOL**
BUSINESS—SOCIAL ASPECTS see INDUSTRY—SOCIAL ASPECTS

C

CALIFORNIA—DESCRIPTION AND TRAVEL—VIEWS.
Bronson, William. How to kill a Golden State. 1968. **F866.2.B7 ECOL**
CALIFORNIA CONDOR.
Koford, Carl B. The California condor. 1966,c1953 **QL696.A2K64 1966 ECOL**
McMillan, Ian. Man and the California condor. 1968. **QL696.A2H24 ECOL**
CALIFORNIA TOMORROW.
The California Tomorrow plan. Rev. ed. 1972 **HT393.C3C35 1972 ECOL**
CAMP SITES, FACILITIES, ETC.—MINNESOTA.
Minnesota. Dept. of Conservation. Minnesota outdoor recreation plan. 1968- **fGV54.M6A197 ECOL**
CAMPING.
Brower, David Ross. The Sierra Club wilderness handbook. 2nd rev. ed. c1971 **SK601.B845 1971 ECOL**
CANBY CREEK WATERSHED, MINNESOTA.
United States. Soil Conservation Service. Flood hazard analyses: city of Canby and vicinity, Yellow Medicine County, Minnesota. 1973. **GB1225.M6U5 ECOL**
CANIDAE—BEHAVIOR.
Fox, Michael W. Behaviour of wolves, dogs, and related canids. 1st U.S. ed. 1972, c1971 **QL737.C22F69 1972 ECOL**
CANNERIES—WASTE DISPOSAL.
Green Giant Company. Pilot plant installation for fungal treatment of vegetable canning wastes. 1971. **fTD899.C3G74 ECOL**
National Canners Association. Western Research Laboratory. Reduction of salt content of food processing liquid waste effluent. 1971. **fTD899.C3N36 ECOL**
National Canners Association. Western Research Laboratory. Waste reduction in food canning operations. 1970 i.e. 1971 **fTD899.C3N37 ECOL**
Streebin, Leale E. Demonstration of a full-scale waste treatment system for a cannery. 1971. **fTD899.C3S87 ECOL**
CANOES AND CANOEING—MINNESOTA.
Jaques, Florence (Page). Canoe country. c1938 **F606.J36 ECOL**
CAPITAL OUTPUT RATIOS see COST EFFECTIVENESS
CAPITALISM.
Hall, Gus. Ecology: can we survive under capitalism? 1st ed. 1972 **HC110.E5H3 ECOL**
Weisberg, Barry. Beyond repair. 1971 **GF75.W45 1971 ECOL**
CARBON, ACTIVATED.
Fram Corporation. Bio-regenerated activated carbon treatment of textile dye wastewater. 1971. **fTD899.T4F7 ECOL**
Mine Safety Appliances Research Corporation. Optimization of the regeneration procedure for granular activated carbon. 1970. **fTP245.C4M55 ECOL**
Swindell-Dressler Company. Process design manual for carbon adsorption. 1971. **REF fTD753.5.S9 ECOL**
CARBON DIOXIDE.
Morton, Stephen D. The carbon dioxide system and eutrophication. 1971. **fQH96.8.E9M6 ECOL**
CARBON MONOXIDE.
Minnesota. Air Quality Division. Implementation plan to achieve carbon monoxide ambient air quality standards. 1973. **REF fTD883.5.M6A422 ECOL**
CARBON MONOXIDE—TOXICOLOGY.
United States. National Institute for Occupational Safety and Health. Criteria for a recommended standard... occupational exposure to carbon monoxide. 1972. **fRA1247.C17U5 ECOL**
CARCINOGENS.
Hueper, Wilhelm C. Occupational and environmental cancers of the urinary system. 1969. **RC280.G4H8 ECOL**
CAREERS see PROFESSIONS
CARIBOU.
Dugmore, Arthur Radclyffe. The romance of the Newfoundland caribou. 1913. **fQL737.U5D8 ECOL**
CARNIVORA.
Ewer, R. F. The carnivores. 1973 **QL737.C2E93 ECOL**
CARRIGHAR, SALLY.
Carrighar, Sally. Home to the wilderness. 1973. **QH31.C3A3 ECOL**
CARSON, RACHEL L. SILENT SPRING.
Graham, Frank. Since Silent spring. 1970. **QH75.G68 ECOL**
CARSON, RACHEL LOUISE.
Brooks, Paul. The house of life: Rachel Carson at work. 1972. **QH31.C33B7 ECOL**
CASCADE RANGE.
Douglas, William Orville. Of men and mountains. 1950 **F851.7.D68 ECOL**
CATALOGS, PUBLISHERS'—UNITED STATES.
Publishers' trade list annual. Books in print. **REF Z1215.P972 ECOL**
Publishers' trade list annual. Books in print supplement: authors, titles, subjects. 1972/73- **REF fZ1215.P972 Suppl. ECOL**
CATTLE.
Rouse, John E. World cattle. 1970 **SF197.R68 ECOL**
CAVES—MINNESOTA.
Hogberg, Rudolph K. Guide to the caves of Minnesota. 1967 **GB605.M5H6 ECOL**
CAVITATION.
Minnesota. University. St. Anthony Falls Hydraulic Laboratory. Hydraulics of long vertical conduits and associated cavitation. 1971. **fTC174.M53 ECOL**
CBR WARFARE see BIOLOGICAL WARFARE; CHEMICAL WARFARE
CELLULOSE.
Callihan, Clayton Dale. Construction of a chemical-microbial pilot plant for production of single-cell protein from cellulosic wastes. 1971. **TP996.B3C3 ECOL**
CHANGE, SOCIAL see SOCIAL CHANGE
CHANNELS (HYDRAULIC ENGINEERING).
Larson, Curtis L. Numerical routing of flood hydrographs through open channel junctions. 1971. **GB701.M554no.40 ECOL**
CHARCOAL, ACTIVATED see CARBON, ACTIVATED
CHEMICAL INDUSTRIES—HYGIENIC ASPECTS.
Davidson, Ray. Peril on the job. 1970 **HD7269.C452U5 ECOL**
CHEMICAL INDUSTRIES—WASTE DISPOSAL.
Atkins, Patrick R. The pesticide manufacturing industry—current waste treatment and disposal practices. 1972. **fTD899.C5A8 ECOL**
CHEMICAL KINETICS see CHEMICAL REACTION, RATE OF
CHEMICAL MUTAGENESIS.
Mutagenic effects of environmental contaminants. 1972. **QH431.M958 ECOL**
CHEMICAL PLANTS—UNITED STATES—WASTE DISPOSAL.
Datagraphics Incorporated. Inorganic chemicals industry profile (updated). 1971. **fTD899.C5D37 ECOL**
Datagraphics Incorporated. Projected wastewater treatment costs in the organic chemicals industry (updated). 1971. **fTD899.C5D388 ECOL**
CHEMICAL REACTION, RATE OF.
Smith, Edwin Earle. Sulfide to sulfate reaction mechanism. 1970. **fTN321.S58 ECOL**
CHEMICAL RESEARCH.
Su, K. Lee. Aquatic plants from Minnesota, part 1—chemical survey. 1972. **GB701.M554no.46 ECOL**
CHEMICAL WARFARE.
Harvest of death. 1971,c1972 **DS557.A68H35 1972 ECOL**
Hersh, Seymour M. Chemical and biological warfare. 1969,c1968 **UG447.H42 1969 ECOL**
McCarthy, Richard D. The ultimate folly. 1969 **UG447.M233 1969 ECOL**
Thomas, Ann (Van Wynen). Legal limits on the use of chemical and biological weapons. 1970 **REF JX5135.C5T55 ECOL**
CHEMICAL WARFARE—ADDRESSES, ESSAYS, LECTURES.
Conference on Chemical and Biological Warfare, London, 1968. CBW: chemical and biological warfare. 1969,c1968 **UG447.C655 1968 ECOL**
Environmental effects of weapons technology. 1970 **fUG447.8.E57 ECOL**
CHEMICALS—PHYSIOLOGICAL EFFECT—ADDRESSES, ESSAYS, LECTURES.
Maxwell, Kenneth E. Chemicals and life. 1970 **QP903.M38 ECOL**
CHEMICALS—SAFETY MEASURES.
Little (Arthur D.) Inc. Spill prevention techniques for hazardous polluting substances: an inventory and survey of hazardous chemical facilities in Charleston, West Virginia; Baltimore, Maryland; Texas City, Texas; and the Suisun Bay-Delta Area, California. 1971. **fT55.3.H3L4 ECOL**
CHEMISTRY—DICTIONARIES.
The Condensed chemical dictionary. Rev. by Gessner G. Hawley. 8th ed. 1971 **REF QD5.C5 1971 ECOL**
CHEMISTRY, ANALYTIC see also CHROMATOGRAPHIC ANALYSIS
Jacobs, Morris Boris. The chemical analysis of air pollutants. 1960. **TD883.J3 ECOL**
Leithe, Wolfgang. The analysis of air pollutants. 1971,c1970 **TD890.L413 ECOL**
United States. Environmental Protection Agency. Office of Research and Monitoring. Identification of polychlorinated biphenyls in the presence of DDT-type compounds. 1972. **SB951.U52 ECOL**
CHEMISTRY, BIOLOGICAL see BIOLOGICAL CHEMISTRY
CHEMISTRY IN WARFARE see CHEMICAL WARFARE
CHENG HO (JUNK).
Fairchild, David Grandison. Garden islands of the great East. 1943. **SB109.F185 ECOL**
CHLORINATION OF SEWAGE see SEWAGE—PURIFICATION—CHLORINATION
CHLORINE—BIBLIOGRAPHY.
Air Pollution Technical Information Center. Chlorine and air pollution: an annotated bibliography. 1971. **Z7173.A4A513 ECOL**
CHLORINE—PHYSIOLOGICAL EFFECT.
Manufacturing Chemists' Association. The effect of chlorination on selected organic chemicals. 1972. **fTD462.M3 ECOL**
Michigan. Bureau of Water Management. Chlorinated municipal waste toxicities to rainbow trout and fathead minnows. 1971. **fTD763.M5 ECOL**
CHLORINE ORGANIC COMPOUNDS.
Manufacturing Chemists' Association. The effect of chlorination on selected organic chemicals. 1972. **fTD462.M3 ECOL**
CHROMATOGRAPHIC ANALYSIS.
Thruston, Alfred D. Liquid chromatography of carbamate pesticides. 1972. **SB951.T4 ECOL**

CHROMIUM—PLATING.
Battelle Memorial Institute, Columbus, Ohio Columbus Laboratories An investigation of techniques for removal of chromium from electroplating wastes. 1971. **fTD899.M45B3ECOL**

CHURCH RENEWAL.
Roszak, Theodore. Where the wasteland ends. 1972. **HN17.5.R62 ECOL**

CITIES AND TOWNS.
Detwyler, Thomas R. Urbanization and environment. 1972 **HT151.D46 ECOL**
Eldredge, Hanford Wentworth. Taming megalopolis. 1967. **HT151.E4 ECOL**
McCue, George. Ecology: the city. c1971 **QH541.5.C6M23 Suppl. ECOL**
Smith, Fred. Man and his urban environment. 1972. **fHT151.S53 ECOL**

CITIES AND TOWNS—ATLANTIC STATES.
Von Eckardt, Wolf. The challenge of Megalopolis. 1964. **HT123.5.A12V6 ECOL**

CITIES AND TOWNS—GROWTH see also SUBURBS
Advisory Committee to the Department of Housing and Urban Development. Land Use Subcommittee. Urban growth and land development. 1972. **HD205 1972 .A35 ECOL**
Clawson, Marion. Suburban land conversion in the United States: an economic and governmental process. 1971 **HD259.C55 ECOL**
Jacobs, Jane. The economy of cities. 1969 **HT321.J32 ECOL**
Saarinen, Eliel. The city, its growth, its decay, its future. 1943 **NA9030.S2 ECOL**
Von Eckardt, Wolf. The challenge of Megalopolis. 1964. **HT123.5.A12V6 ECOL**

CITIES AND TOWNS—HISTORY.
Mumford, Lewis. The city in history: its origins, its transformations, and its prospects. 1st ed. 1961 **HT111.M8 ECOL**
Mumford, Lewis. The highway and the city. 1963 **HT111.M83 ECOL**

CITIES AND TOWNS—PLANNING see also FLOOD DAMAGE PREVENTION; HOUSING; REGIONAL PLANNING; URBAN RENEWAL
Blumenfeld, Hans. The modern metropolis. 1968,c1967 **HT166.B54 ECOL**
Eldredge, Hanford Wentworth. Taming megalopolis. 1967. **HT151.E4 ECOL**
Gallion, Arthur B. The urban pattern. 2d ed. 1963 **NA9031.G3 1963 ECOL**
Geddes, Patrick, Sir. Patrick Geddes: spokesman for man and the environment. 1972 **HT166.G43 1972 ECOL**
Grava, Sigurd. Urban planning aspects of water pollution control. 1969. **TD420.G67 ECOL**
Harvard University. Landscape Architecture Research Office. Three approaches to environmental resource analysis. 1967. **fTA170.H3 ECOL**
Herfindahl, Orris Clemens. Quality of the environment: an economic approach to some problems in using land, water, and air. 1965 **TD153.H46 ECOL**
Leibbrand, Kurt. Transportation and town planning. 1970, c1964 **HE333.L3813 1970 ECOL**
Perin, Constance. With man in mind. 1970. **HC68.P47 ECOL**
Reiner, Thomas A. The place of the ideal community in urban planning. 1968,c1963 **fNA9030.R45 1968 ECOL**
Saarinen, Eliel. The city, its growth, its decay, its future. 1943 **NA9030.S2 ECOL**
Wingo, Lowdon. Transportation and urban land. 1968,c1961 **HE4211.W5 ECOL**

CITIES AND TOWNS—PLANNING—ADDRESSES, ESSAYS, LECTURES.
The Fitness of man's environment. 1968 **HT166.F53 ECOL**

CITIES AND TOWNS—PLANNING—BIBLIOGRAPHY.
Harrison, James D. Environmental preferences: relevant studies for urban planning. 1973. **Ref fZ5942.H3 ECOL**
Powell, David R. New towns for America. 1972. **REF fZ5942.P6 ECOL**

CITIES AND TOWNS—PLANNING—CONGRESSES.
Emerging methods in environmental design and planning. 1970 **TA170.E46 ECOL**
National Conference on Soil, Water, and Suburbia, Washington, D.C., 1967. Soil, water, and suburbia. 1968 **fHT166.N36 1967 ECOL**

Science, engineering, and the city. 1967. **HT166.S32 ECOL**

CITIES AND TOWNS—PLANNING—EUROPE—CASE STUDIES.
Strong, Ann Louise. Planned urban environments: Sweden, Finland, Israel, the Netherlands, France. 1971 **fHT166.S73 ECOL**

CITIES AND TOWNS—PLANNING—IOWA—CONGRESSES.
Conference on Flood Plain Management, Iowa State University, 1968. Flood plain management, Iowa's experience. 1st ed. 1969 **TC424.I8C6 1968 ECOL**

CITIES AND TOWNS—PLANNING—MINNEAPOLIS.
Minneapolis. Planning and Development. 1970 profile of Minneapolis communities. 1971. **fHT165.M6A46 ECOL**

CITIES AND TOWNS—PLANNING—SAN ANTONIO.
Gunn, Clare A. Cultural benefits from metropolitan river recreation—San Antonio prototype. 1972. **fHD1694.T4G8 ECOL**

CITIES AND TOWNS—PLANNING—STUDY AND TEACHING.
Thornsjo, Mark. Planning. 1971. **HT166.T5 ECOL**

CITIES AND TOWNS—PLANNING—TWIN CITIES METROPOLITAN AREA.
Minnesota. Metropolitan Council of the Twin Cities Area. Metropolitan development guide. 1973- **REF fHT168.T9A34 ECOL**

CITIES AND TOWNS—PLANNING—UNITED STATES.
Chapin, Francis Stuart. Urban land use planning. 2d ed. 1965. **NA9108.C53 1965 ECOL**
Clawson, Marion. Suburban land conversion in the United States: an economic and governmental process. 1971 **HD259.C55 ECOL**
Delafons, John. Land-use controls in the United States. 2d ed. 1969 **HD205 1969 .D4 ECOL**
Environment and change. 1970, c1968 **HT167.E46 ECOL**
Environment for man. 1967 **HT167.E5 1967 ECOL**
Eskew, Garnett Laidlaw. Of land and men. c1959 **NA9000.U715 ECOL**
Green, James L. Economic ecology. c1969 **HT167.G74 ECOL**
Gruen, Victor. The heart of our cities. 1964. **NA9108.G76 ECOL**
Jacobs, Jane. The death and life of great American cities. c1961 **NA9108.J3 ECOL**
Kelnhofer, Guy J. Metropolitan planning and river basin planning: some interrelationships. 1968. **TD223.K4 ECOL**
Kulski, Julian Eugene. Land of urban promise: continuing the great tradition. 1967. **HT167.K8 ECOL**
Munzer, Martha E. Planning our town. 1964 **NA9108.M8 ECOL**
Olmsted, Frederick Law. Civilizing American cities. 1971 **HT167.O44 ECOL**
Shomon, Joseph James. Open land for urban America. 1971 **HD257.S56 ECOL**
Stein, Clarence S. Toward new towns for America. Rev. ed. 1971,c1957 **NA9108.S8 1971 ECOL**
Tunnard, Christopher. Man-made America: chaos or control? 1963 **fNA9108.T82 ECOL**
White House Conference on Natural Beauty, Washington, D.C., 1965. Beauty for America. 1965 **QH77.U6W5 1965 ECOL**
Whyte, William Hollingsworth. Last landscape. 1968. **HT167.W48 ECOL**

CITIES AND TOWNS—PLANNING—UNITED STATES—ADDRESSES, ESSAYS, LECTURES.
Environment and policy. 1968 **HT167.E48 ECOL**
The Quality of the urban environment. 1969 **HT169.U5Q33 ECOL**

CITIES AND TOWNS—PLANNING—UNITED STATES—CONGRESSES.
Symposium on Engineering Geology in the Urban Environment, San Francisco, 1969. Environmental planning and geology. 1971 **TA705.S95 1969 ECOL**

CITIES AND TOWNS—PLANNING—1945-
Goodman, Robert. After the planners. 1972, c1971 **HT166.G64 ECOL**
Kepes, Gyorgy. Arts of the environment. 1972 **N72.S6K37 ECOL**
Resources for the Future. Cities and space: the future use of urban land. 1963 **NA9031.R4 ECOL**

Strong, Ann Louise. Planned urban environments: Sweden, Finland, Israel, the Netherlands, France. 1971 **fHT166.S73 ECOL**

CITIES AND TOWNS—UNITED STATES.
Faltermayer, Edmund K. Redoing America. 1968 **HT123.F3 ECOL**
Fortune. The exploding metropolis. c1958 **HT123.F69 1958 ECOL**

CITIZEN SUITS (CIVIL PROCEDURE)—UNITED STATES.
MacDonald, James B. Environmental litigation. 1972. **KF3775.M3 ECOL**

CITY AND TOWN LIFE.
Herber, Lewis. Crisis in our cities. c1965 **RA566.H4 ECOL**

CITY AND TOWN LIFE—BIBLIOGRAPHY.
Appleyard, Donald. The urban environment: selected bibliography. 1972. **REF fZ7164.U7A6 ECOL**

CITY NOISE.
Wyle Laboratories. Community noise. 1971 i.e. 1972 **fTD892.W94 ECOL**

CITY PLANNING AND REDEVELOPMENT LAW—MINNESOTA.
Minnesota. State Planning Agency. Office of Local and Urban Affairs. Minnesota planning legislation. 1971 **REF KFM5858.A3 1971 ECOL**

CITY PLANNING AND REDEVELOPMENT LAW—UNITED STATES—CASES.
Haar, Charles Monroe. Land-use planning. 2d ed. 1971. **KF5692.A4H3 1971 ECOL**

CITY TRAFFIC—BIBLIOGRAPHY.
Ehrenthal, Frank F. A selected bibliography on uses of the urban street. 1972. **REF fZ7164.T81E3 ECOL**

CITY TRANSIT see LOCAL TRANSIT

CIVIL ENGINEERING—CANADA.
Brown, Roger James Evan. Permafrost in Canada. 1970 **TA713.B76 ECOL**

CIVILIZATION.
Henshaw, Paul Stewart. This side of yesterday: extinction or Utopia. 1971 **GF41.H45 ECOL**

CIVILIZATION—PHILOSOPHY.
Eiseley, Loren C. The invisible pyramid. 1970 **CB19.E38 ECOL**

CIVILIZATION AND MACHINERY see TECHNOLOGY AND CIVILIZATION

CIVILIZATION AND SCIENCE see SCIENCE AND CIVILIZATION

CIVILIZATION AND TECHNOLOGY see TECHNOLOGY AND CIVILIZATION

CIVILIZATION, MODERN—1950-
Fabun, Don. The dynamics of change. 1967 **fCB427.F25 ECOL**
Roszak, Theodore. Where the wasteland ends. 1972. **HN17.5.R62 ECOL**

CIVILIZATION, MODERN—1950- —ADDRESSES, ESSAYS, LECTURES.
Urban, George R. Can we survive our future? 1972, c1971 **CB428.U7 1972 ECOL**

CIVILIZATION, MODERN—20TH CENTURY.
Fabun, Don. Dimensions of change. 1971 **fHM221.F32 ECOL**

CLAMS.
Burch, J. B. Freshwater sphaeriacean clams (Mollusca: Pelecypoda) of North America. 1972. **fQH96.A2B5no.3 ECOL**

CLEAN ROOMS—MICROBIOLOGY.
Kingsley, V. Victor. Bacteriology primer in air contamination control. 1967 **QR101.K55 ECOL**

CLEAR-CUTTING.
Oregon. State University, Corvallis. School of Forestry. Studies on effects of watershed practices on streams. 1971 i.e. 1972 **fTC409.O74 ECOL**

CLEAR-CUTTING—UNITED STATES.
Wood, Nancy C. Clearcut. c1971 **SD538.2.A1W65 ECOL**

CLIMATIC CHANGES.
Study of Man's Impact on Climate, Stockholm, 1970. Inadvertent climate modification. 1971 **QC981.S77 1970 ECOL**

CLIMATOLOGY.
Claiborne, Robert. Climate, man, and history. 1970 **GF71.C55 ECOL**
Trewartha, Glenn Thomas. An introduction to climate. 4th ed. 1968 **QC981.T65 1968 ECOL**

CLIMBING PLANTS.
Petrides, George A. A field guide to trees and shrubs. 1972. **QK482.P43 1972 ECOL**

CLINOPTILOLITE.
California. University. Sanitary Engineering Research Laboratory. Optimization of ammonia removal by ion exchange using clinoptilolite. 1971 i.e. 1972 **fTD757.5.C35 ECOL**

CLOSED CIRCUIT TELEVISION.
Montgomery County Sanitary Dept. Montgomery County, Ohio. Ground water infiltration and internal sealing of sanitary sewers, Montgomery County, Ohio. 1972. **fTD716.M6 ECOL**

CLUSTERING OF PARTICLES see COAGULATION

COAGULATION see also PRECIPITATION (CHEMISTRY)
Stenquist, Richard J. Initial mixing in coagulation processes. 1972. **TD455.S7 ECOL**

COAL.
United States. Office of Coal Research. Clean energy from coal—a national priority. 1973 **HD9542.A5U5 ECOL**

COAL—CARBONIZATION.
Consolidation Coal Company. Research Division. Pilot-scale development of the CSF Process. 1971. **fTN805.A395no.39 ECOL**

COAL GASIFICATION.
Bituminous Coal Research, Inc. The economics of generating clean fuel gas from coal using an air-blown two-stage gasifier. 1971. **fTP759.B5 ECOL**

COAL LIQUEFACTION.
Consolidation Coal Company. Research Division. Pilot-scale development of the CSF Process. 1971. **fTN805.A395no.39 ECOL**

COAL MINE WASTE.
Black, Sivalls and Bryson, Inc., Kansas City, Mo. Applied Technology Division Study of sulfur recovery from coal refuse. 1971. **fTN890.B57 ECOL**
Stacks, John F. Stripping. 1972 **TN291.S7 ECOL**

COAL MINES AND MINING—APPALACHIAN REGION.
Caudill, Harry M. My land is dying. 1st ed. 1971. **TN291.C37 1971 ECOL**

COAL MINES AND MINING—LAW AND LEGISLATION—APPALACHIAN REGION.
Maryland. University. School of Law. Legal problems of coal mine reclamation. 1972. **fKF1830.Z95M37 ECOL**

COAL MINES AND MINING—UNITED STATES.
Bituminous coal facts. 1970- **REF fHD9544.B47 ECOL**

COAL OIL see PETROLEUM

COAL, PULVERIZED.
Development of a coal-based sewage-treatment process. 1971 **fTN805.A395no.55 ECOL**

COAL RESEARCH.
Consolidation Coal Company. Research Division. Pilot-scale development of the CSF Process. 1971. **fTN805.A395no.39 ECOL**
Linville, Bill. Review of Bureau of Mines energy program, 1970. 1971 **TN295.U4no.8526 ECOL**
Open cycle coal burning MHD power generation. 1971 **fTN805.A395no.64 ECOL**

COASTS—LABRADOR.
Forbes, Alexander. Northernmost Labrador. 1938. **F1136.F67 ECOL**

COASTS—TERMINOLOGY.
Allen, Richard H. A glossary of coastal engineering terms. 1972. **REF TC1645.A4 ECOL**

COASTS—UNITED STATES—PICTORIAL WORKS.
The American coast. 1971 **fE169.02.A648 ECOL**

COLLEGE SITES see SCHOOL SITES

COLONIZATION.
American Geographical Society of New York Pioneer settlement. 1932. **GF51.A5 ECOL**

COLOR.
Harris, Douglas H. Assessment of turbidity, color and odor in water. 1972. **fTD380.H3 ECOL**

COLORADO RIVER.
Watkins, Tom H. The Grand Colorado. 1969 **fF788.W33 ECOL**

COLORADO RIVER—DELTA.
Sykes, Godfrey Glenton. The Colorado delta. 1937. **F788.S958 ECOL**

COMBINED SEWERS.
American Public Works Association. Combined sewer regulator overflow facilities; report. 1970. **fTD662.A42 ECOL**
Carcich, Italo G. A pressure sewer system demonstration. 1972. **TD670.C3 ECOL**
Karl R. Rohrer Associates. Underwater storage of combined sewer overflows. 1971 **fTD662.K36 ECOL**
Nebolsine, Ross. High rate filtration of combined sewer overflows. 1972. **fTD662.N4 ECOL**
United States. Environmental Protection Agency. Office of Research and Monitoring. Storage and treatment of combined sewer overflows. 1972. **fTD662.U54 ECOL**
United States. Environmental Protection Agency. Office of Research and Monitoring. The swirl concentrator as a combined sewer overflow regulator facility. 1972. **TD662.U5 ECOL**

COMBINED SEWERS—MINNESOTA—SOUTH ST. PAUL.
Hennington, Durham and Richardson, Inc., Omaha, Nebraska. Annual capital improvements cost estimates schedules for separation and treatment combined sewerage system, South St. Paul, Minnesota. n.d. **fTD525.S6H4 ECOL**

COMBINED SEWERS—MINNESOTA—STILLWATER.
Bannister Engineering Co., St. Paul, Minn. Report on reducing untreated combined wastewater overflows to the St. Croix River. 1970. **fTD525.S7B3 ECOL**

COMBINED SEWERS—WASHINGTON, D.C.
Roy F. Weston, Inc. Combined sewer overflow abatement alternatives, Wash., D.C. 1970. **fTD525.W2R68 ECOL**

COMBUSTION—ADDRESSES, ESSAYS, LECTURES.
Combustion-generated air pollution. 1971. **TD883.C575 1971 ECOL**

COMBUSTION—CONGRESSES.
Symposium on Emissions from Continuous Combustion Systems, General Motors Research Laboratories, 1971. Emissions from continuous combustion systems. 1972. **TD881.S86 1971 ECOL**

COMBUSTION RESEARCH.
Open cycle coal burning MHD power generation. 1971 **fTN805.A395no.64 ECOL**

COMMEMORATIVE POSTAGE STAMP—UNITED STATES—ALBUMS.
Stearns, Jean Pride. A catalog of the duck stamp prints with biographies of the artists. c1967 **REF HE6185.U52S7 ECOL**

COMMERICAL FISHING see FISHERIES

COMMUNICATION AND TRAFFIC see also TRAFFIC ENGINEERING; TRANSPORTATION
Fabun, Don. Dimensions of change. 1971 **fHM221.F32 ECOL**

COMMUNITY AND SCHOOL.
Yellow pages of learning resources. 1972. **Ref fLC215.Y45 ECOL**

COMMUNITY ORGANIZATION.
Guitar, Mary Anne. Property power. 1st ed. 1972. **HD205 1972 .G8 ECOL**

COMMUNITY POWER.
Crenson, Matthew A. The un-politics of air pollution: a study of non-decision-making in the cities. 1971 **HC110.A4C73 ECOL**

COMPOST see also ORGANICULTURE
Composting of municipal solid wastes in the United States. 1971. **TD796.5.C64 ECOL**
Goldstein, Jerome. Garbage as you like it. 1969 **TD795.G6 ECOL**

COMPOST—CONGRESSES.
National Conference on Composting-Waste Recycling. 1st, Denver, 1971. How to put waste recycling into practice. 1971. **fTD172.5.N3 1971 ECOL**

CONIFERAE.
May, Julian. The mysterious evergreen forest. 1972 **QH541.5.F6M39 ECOL**

CONSCIOUSNESS.
Leonard, George Burr. The transformation. 1972 **BF311.L43 ECOL**

CONSERVATION AS A PROFESSION see NATURAL RESOURCES—VOCATIONAL GUIDANCE

CONSERVATION EDUCATION see CONSERVATION OF NATURAL RESOURCES—STUDY AND TEACHING; ECOLOGY—STUDY AND TEACHING; ENVIRONMENTAL POLICY—STUDY AND TEACHING; HUMAN ECOLOGY—STUDY AND TEACHING; NATURAL HISTORY—STUDY AND TEACHING; NATURAL RESOURCES—STUDY AND TEACHING; NATURE STUDY; OUTDOOR EDUCATION; POLLUTION—STUDY AND TEACHING; SCIENCE—STUDY AND TEACHING

CONSERVATION OF NATURAL RESOURCES
see also MARINE RESOURCES CONSERVATION; NATURE CONSERVATION; PETROLEUM CONSERVATION; SOIL CONSERVATION; WATER CONSERVATION; WILDLIFE CONSERVATION
Adams, Alexander B. Eleventh hour. 1970 **S936.A3 ECOL**
Blueprint for survival. 1972. **S936.B5 1972 ECOL**
Brubaker, Sterling. To live on earth. 1972 **QH541.B76 ECOL**
Darling, Frank Fraser. Wilderness and plenty. 1970. **QH541.13.D36 ECOL**
Darling, Lois. A place in the sun. 1968 **QH541.D34 ECOL**
Dasmann, Raymond Frederick. Environmental conservation. 3d ed. 1972 **S936.D3 1972 ECOL**
Dorst, Jean. Before nature dies. 1st American ed. 1970. **S936.D6613 ECOL**
Duffey, Eric. Conservation of nature. 1970 **S940.D84 ECOL**
Flawn, Peter Tyrell. Environmental geology: conservation, land-use planning, and resource management. 1970 **QE33.F5 ECOL**
French, Herbert E. Love of earth. c1973 **S936.F7 ECOL**
Hall, O. F. Principles of natural resource management. 1951. **fS938.H3 ECOL**
Hamilton, Michael Pollock. This little planet. 1970 **GF80.H35 ECOL**
Joffe, Joyce. Conservation. 1970,c1969 **S940.J64 ECOL**
Jones, Claire. Pollution: the land we live on. 1971 **TD176.J65 1971 ECOL**
Marine, Gene. America the raped. 1969 **S942.M33 ECOL**
Masini, Giancarlo. S.O.S. save our earth. c1972 **fQH541.M382 1972 ECOL**
Mines, Samuel. The last days of mankind. 1971 **S936.M55 ECOL**
Nicholson, Max. The environmental revolution. 1970 **S936.N5 ECOL**
Price, Fred C. McGraw-Hill's 1972 report on business and the environment. c1972 **fTD174.P7 ECOL**
Roosevelt, Nicholas. Conservation: now or never. 1970 **S942.R6 ECOL**
Smith, Frances C. The first book of conservation. 2d rev. ed. 1972. **S940.S64 1972 ECOL**
Smithsonian Institution. Center for Shortlived Phenomena. The pulse of the planet. c1972 **fQ225.P8 ECOL**
Special report ecology. c1971- **REF fS936.S6 ECOL**
Tillotson, David. Patterns for preservation: a conservation text. 1969 **fS938.T5 ECOL**
United States. Dept. of the Interior. It's your world. 1969 **fS930.A45 ECOL**
Zurhorst, Charles. The conservation fraud. 1970 **S942.Z8 ECOL**

CONSERVATION OF NATURAL RESOURCES—ADDRESSES, ESSAYS, LECTURES.
Cox, George W. Readings in conservation ecology. 1969 **S942.C6 ECOL**
Godfrey, Arthur. The Arthur Godfrey environmental reader. 1970 **QH541.13.G6 ECOL**
Lewis, Richard S. The energy crisis. 1972. **fHC103.7.L4 ECOL**
Ogden, Samuel R. America the vanishing. 1969. **S942.O44 ECOL**
The Unforseen international ecologic boomerang. 1969 **fQH541.U5 ECOL**
Woods, Barbara. Eco-solutions: a casebook for the environmental crisis. 1972 **GF43.W6 ECOL**

CONSERVATION OF NATURAL RESOURCES—ALASKA.
Laycock, George. Alaska, the embattled frontier. 1971. **S932.A4L38 ECOL**

CONSERVATION OF NATURAL RESOURCES—BIBLIOGRAPHY.
Atkisson, Jean. Evaluated bibliography of free and inexpensive conservation publications. 1972 **REF fZ7164.N3A8 ECOL**
Miller, John A. Conservation: the scientific aspects: a guide to the literature. 1973. **REF fZ7164.N3M5 ECOL**
United States. Environmental Protection Agency. Office of Public Affairs. Current list of water publications, 1965/71- **REF Z7173.W3U5 ECOL**
Woodrow Wilson International Center for Scholars. A selective, annotated bibliography of reports and documents on international environmental problems. 1972. **fZ7164.N3W6 ECOL**

CONSERVATION OF NATURAL RESOURCES—COLLECTED WORKS.
Lugo, Ariel E. Readings on ecological systems: their function and relation to man. c1971 **QH540.3.L8 ECOL**

CONSERVATION OF NATURAL RESOURCES—CONGRESSES.
Sierra Club Conference on the Electric Power Industry, 1st, Johnson City, Vt., 1972. Report on the first Sierra Club power conference [papers]. 1972?
fHD9685.A2S5 1972 ECOL
Symposium on Energy, Resources and the Environment, McLean, Va., 1972. Symposium on energy, resources and the environment. 1972.
fHD9540.1.S9 1972 ECOL
Workshop on Global Ecological Problems, University of Wisconsin, 1971. Man in the living environment. 1972
GF3.W6 1971 ECOL

CONSERVATION OF NATURAL RESOURCES—DICTIONARIES.
Studdard, Gloria J. Common environmental terms: a glossary. 1973.
REF S922.S7 ECOL

CONSERVATION OF NATURAL RESOURCES—DIRECTORIES.
Cate, William. Directory of environmental consultants. c1972.
REF S920.C3 ECOL
Conservation directory.
fS920.C64 ECOL
Halstead, Bruce W. A Golden guide to environmental organizations. 1972
REF GF5.H34 ECOL

CONSERVATION OF NATURAL RESOURCES—FLORIDA.
Dasmann, Raymond Frederick. No further retreat. 1971
S932.F6D37 ECOL

CONSERVATION OF NATURAL RESOURCES—GREAT LAKES REGION—BIBLIOGRAPHY.
Great Lakes Basin Library. Book catalog. 1969-
REF fZ7164.N3G75 ECOL
Great Lakes Basin Library. An interim bibliography. 1969-
REF fZ7164.N3G7 ECOL

CONSERVATION OF NATURAL RESOURCES—IDAHO—SNAKE RIVER WATERSHED.
Norton, Boyd. Snake wilderness. c1972.
QH105.I2N6 ECOL

CONSERVATION OF NATURAL RESOURCES—IOWA—SOCIETIES, ETC.—HISTORY.
Buckmann, Carol A. The first 50. c1973
S932.I8B8 ECOL

CONSERVATION OF NATURAL RESOURCES—LAW AND LEGISLATION—BIBLIOGRAPHY.
Radosevich, George E. Water law and its relationship to environmental quality: a bibliography of source material. 1973.
REF fKF5551.R3 ECOL

CONSERVATION OF NATURAL RESOURCES—LAW AND LEGISLATION—UNITED STATES.
Kusler, Jon A. Survey: lake protection and rehabilitation legislation in the United States. 1972.
REF fKF5568.K8 ECOL
United States. Library of Congress. Environmental Policy Division. Congress and the Nation's environment. 1973.
KF3775.A25 1973 ECOL

CONSERVATION OF NATURAL RESOURCES—MINNESOTA.
Major, Harry M. Activities of the USDA Soil Conservation Service in providing for quality environment for all people in Minnesota. 1972.
HC110.E5M3 ECOL
Minnesota. Governor, 1971- Securing a quality environment in Minnesota. 1973?
REF fHC107.M6A35 ECOL
Minnesota. Governor's Environmental Quality Council. Citizen's Advisory Committee. Environmental quality, policies and decision-making in Minnesota - 1972. 1972.
fHC107.M6A37 ECOL
Minnesota. State Planning Agency. Environmental decision-making in Minnesota: an overview. 1973
fHC 107.M6A43 1973 ECOL
Minnesota. State Planning Agency. Protecing the Minnesota environment through regulation of private land use. 1972.
fHC107.M6A45 ECOL
Minnesota. University. Water Resources Research Center. Watershed planning: papers presented at the Seminar on Watershed Planning sponsored by the Metropolitan Council and the Minnesota Association of Watershed Districts on February 15, 1972 at the Sheraton Motor Inn, Bloomington, Minnesota. 1972.
GB701.M554no.50 ECOL

CONSERVATION OF NATURAL RESOURCES—MISSISSIPPI VALLEY.
Upper Mississippi River comprehensive basin study. 1970-
fHC107.A15U6 ECOL

CONSERVATION OF NATURAL RESOURCES—NEW YORK (STATE).
New York (State) Legislature. Joint Committee on Environmental Management and Natural Resources. The challenge of the seventies. 1971.
fHC107.N7A25 ECOL

New York (State) Legislature. Joint Committee on Environmental Management and Natural Resources. Report. 197.
fHC107.N7A24 ECOL

CONSERVATION OF NATURAL RESOURCES—RUSSIA.
Pryde, Philip R. Conservation in the Soviet Union. 1972.
S934.R9P76 ECOL

CONSERVATION OF NATURAL RESOURCES—SOCIETIES, ETC.
The Ecological register: a directory of governmental agencies and private organizations concerned about environmental destruction and pollution in the state and in the seven-county metropolitan area. 2nd ed. 1971.
S920.E24 1971 ECOL

The Ecological register: a directory of organizations in the seven-county metropolitan area concerned about environmental destruction and pollution (plus a supplement providing brief information on similar organizations located elsewhere). 1970.
fS920.E24 ECOL

Soil Conservation Society of America. Proceedings of the annual meeting, 1971-
fS900.S6 ECOL

CONSERVATION OF NATURAL RESOURCES—SOCIETIES, ETC.—DIRECTORIES.
Center for California Public Affairs. Environmental networks. Preliminary ed. 1973.
REF fS920.C4 ECOL

Northern States Power Co. Environmental Affairs Dept. Directory of conservation/environmental organizations. 1971-
fS932.M5N6 ECOL

Sichel, Beatrice. Guide to private citizen action environmental groups. 1973.
REF S920.S53 ECOL

United States. Environmental Protection Agency. Office of Public Affairs. Midwest environmental directory, 1972-
REF S920.U5 ECOL

CONSERVATION OF NATURAL RESOURCES—STUDY AND TEACHING.
Brainerd, John W. Nature study for conservation. 1971
S946.B68 ECOL

Burns, William. Snow, snowshoes, and nature: the white dimension of environment. 1972?
fLB1047.B8 ECOL

Dooley, David. Summer school guide for education for an improved environment. 1971.
fQH541.2.D6 Suppl. ECOL
Environmental education materials. 1971.
REF Z7164.N3E6 ECOL
Environmental education 1970. 1970
fS946.E55 ECOL
Fisher, Wes. Minnesota environmental education areas. 1972
fS946.F5 ECOL
Izaak Walton League of America. Conservation Education Committee. Guidelines to conservation education action. c1966
S946.I9 ECOL
Knapp, Clifford E. Outdoor activities for environmental studies. c1971
LB1047.K5 ECOL
Madison. Wis. Board of Education. Dept. of Curriculum Development. Science and society. 1969.
REF fQ181.M3 ECOL
Michigan. Dept. of Natural Resources. Environmental education for intermediate grades.
fS946.M45 ECOL

North Carolina. Task Force on Environment and Natural Resources. Teacher's guide for environmental education. 1970.
REF fQH541.2.N88 ECOL
Northern Colorado Outdoor Nature Center. K 12 curriculum guide for environmental education. n.d.
fS946.N6 ECOL
The Organic classroom. c1973
fS946.O7 ECOL
Peterson, Robin. Ecology and the market place. c1971
HC79.E5P4 ECOL
Roth, Robert E. A review of research related to environmental education. 1972.
QH541.2.R6 ECOL
Schoenfeld, Clarence Albert. Outlines of environmental education. 1971
S946.S43 ECOL
United States. Environmental protection Agency. Office of Water Programs. Training Grants Branch. A curriculum activities guide to water pollution and environmental studies. 1972-
REF fS946.U56 ECOL
United States. National Center for Educational Communication. Environmental education: programs and materials. 1972
S946.U58 ECOL

CONSERVATION OF NATURAL RESOURCES—STUDY AND TEACHING—AUDIO-VISUAL AIDS.
California. Dept. of Education. Guide to conservation education: films, filmstrips, and picture sets. 1972.
REF fS946.C24 ECOL

CONSERVATION OF NATURAL RESOURCES—STUDY AND TEACHING—BIBLIOGRAPHY.
Carvajal, Joan. Conservation education. 1968
REF Z7164.N3C3 ECOL
Minnesota. University. References and resource guides for the University of Minnesota SEED Project curricula. n.d.
fQH541.2.M5 ECOL
National Association for Environmental Education. Man and environment. 1970
REF fZ5322.E2N3 ECOL

CONSERVATION OF NATURAL RESOURCES—STUDY AND TEACHING—CALIFORNIA.
California Association for Outdoor Education. Teaching conservation and natural science in the outdoors. 1968.
fS946.C3 1968 ECOL

CONSERVATION OF NATURAL RESOURCES—STUDY AND TEACHING—CONGRESSES.
Conference on Undergraduate Education in the Biological Sciences for Students in Agriculture and Natural Resources, Washington, D.C., 1966. Undergraduate education in the biological sciences for students in agriculture and natural resources. 1967.
S533.C755 1966 ECOL

CONSERVATION OF NATURAL RESOURCES—STUDY AND TEACHING—DIRECTORIES.
National Audubon Society. Nature Center Planning Division. Directory of nature centers and related environmental education facilities. 1971
REF fQH51.N23 1971 ECOL

CONSERVATION OF NATURAL RESOURCES—STUDY AND TEACHING—MINNESOTA.
Naylon, Michael J. Natural resources management: suggested teaching units for agricultural education. 1972?
fS946.N3 ECOL

CONSERVATION OF NATURAL RESOURCES—STUDY AND TEACHING—MINNESOTA—DIRECTORIES.
Minnesota. University. Agricultural Extension Service. Conservation education assistance directories for Minnesota counties.
REF fS946.M5 ECOL

CONSERVATION OF NATURAL RESOURCES—STUDY AND TEACHING—UNITED STATES.
National Science Teachers Association. Programs in environmental education. 2d ed. 1971.
REF fQH51.N24 1971 ECOL

CONSERVATION OF NATURAL RESOURCES—STUDY AND TEACHING (ELEMENTARY).
Madison, Wis. Public Schools. Conservation Committee. Guide to environmental education: conservation of natural resources. 1970.
fS946.M3 ECOL
Minnesota. University. Duluth Branch. Agricultural Extension Service. Natural resource management lesson plan guide. n.d.
fS946.M55 ECOL
Sako, Marilyn. Man and his environment. 1971
fS946.S2 ECOL
West St. Paul, Minn. Independent School Dist. no. 197. Elementary Science Committee. Elementary science guide and resource book. n.d.
fLB1585.W4 ECOL

CONSERVATION OF NATURAL RESOURCES—STUDY AND TEACHING (HIGHER)—UNITED STATES.
The Organic guide to colleges and universities. 1973
S946.O73 ECOL

CONSERVATION OF NATURAL RESOURCES—STUDY AND TEACHING (SECONDARY).
Mounds Views, Minn. Independent School District, 621. Environmental education curriculum, grades 10 12. n.d.
fQH541.2.M6 ECOL
Rasmussen, Bruce C. Problem—emphasis education: an environmental symposium and the consequences of that symposium at Columbia Heights Senior High School District 13, 1969-1970. 1970
fLB1027.R3 ECOL

CONSERVATION OF NATURAL RESOURCES—UNITED STATES.
Gilbert, Douglas L. Natural resources and public relations. 1971.
S944.G48 ECOL
Highsmith, Richard Morgan. Conservation in the United States. 2d ed. 1969
HC103.7.H5 1969 ECOL
McNall, Preston Essex. Our natural resources. 3d ed. 1970
S930.M2 1970 ECOL
Millard, Reed. Natural resources: will we have enough for tomorrow's world? 1972
HC103.7.M55 ECOL

CONSERVATION OF NATURAL RESOURCES—UNITED STATES

Owen, Oliver S. Natural resource conservation. 1971 **S938.O87 ECOL**

Parson, Ruben L. Conserving American resources. 3d ed. 1972 **S930.P3 1972 ECOL**

Perspectives on conservation. 1969, c1958 **HC103.7.P47 1969 ECOL**

Smith, Guy Harold. Conservation of natural resources. 4th ed. 1971 **S938.S58 1971 ECOL**

United States. Congress. Senate. Committee on Interior and Insular Affairs. Subcommittee on Public Lands. Preservation of wilderness areas. 1972. **KF26.I547 1972 ECOL**

United States. Dept. of the Interior. Man, an endangered species? 1968 **fS914.A53 ECOL**

United States. Dept. of the Interior. Our environment and natural resources ... indivisibly one. 1971? **fS914.A533 ECOL**

United States. Dept. of the Interior. Our living land. 1971 **S914.A535 ECOL**

United States. Environmental Protection Agency. Environmental protection agency. 1972- **fHC68.U5A24 ECOL**

CONSERVATION OF NATURAL RESOURCES—UNITED STATES—FILM CATALOGS.

California. Dept. of Education. Guide to conservation education: films, filmstrips, and picture sets. 1972. **REF fS946.C24 ECOL**

Conservation Education Association. Critical index of films on man and his environment. c1972 **fS946.C65 1972 ECOL**

CONSERVATION OF NATURAL RESOURCES—UNITED STATES—HANDBOOKS, MANUALS, ETC.

United States. Soil Conservation Service. Resource conservation and development projects: handbook. 1972 **S914.A57 1972 ECOL**

CONSERVATION OF NATURAL RESOURCES—UNITED STATES—HISTORY.

Graham, Frank. Man's dominion. 1971 **S930.G7 ECOL**

Hirsch, S. Carl. Guardians of tomorrow. 1971 **QH541.14.H57 1971 ECOL**

Nash, Roderick. The American environment. 1968 **S930.N36 ECOL**

CONSERVATION OF NATURAL RESOURCES—UNITED STATES—HISTORY—SOURCES.

McHenry, Robert. A documentary history of conservation in America. 1972 **S930.M18 ECOL**

Smith, Frank Ellis. Land and water. 1971 **REF S930.S55 ECOL**

CONSERVATION OF NATURAL RESOURCES—UNITED STATES—YEARBOOKS.

Ecology USA. **REF fS936.S62 ECOL**

CONSERVATION OF NATURAL RESOURCES—VOCATIONAL GUIDANCE.

Day, Albert M. Making a living in conservation. 1971 **S944.D33 ECOL**

Dodd, Edward. Careers for the '70s: conservation. 1971 **S944.D6 ECOL**

Paradis, Adrian A. Reclaiming the earth. 1971 **TA170.P37 ECOL**

CONSERVATION OF NATURAL RESOURCES—WISCONSIN.

History of the Wisconsin Department of Natural Resources and related rules, regulations, classifications and standards for air and water quality. 1970 **fS932.W6H5 ECOL**

CONSERVATION OF NATURAL RESOURCES—YEARBOOKS.

United States. Dept. of the Interior. The third wave. 1966 **S914.A54 ECOL**

CONSERVATION OF NATURAL RESOURCES AS A PROFESSION see NATURAL RESOURCES—VOCATIONAL GUIDANCE

CONSERVATION OF THE SOIL see SOIL CONSERVATION

CONSERVATION OF WILDLIFE see WILDLIFE CONSERVATION

CONSERVATIONISTS—DIRECTORIES.

Cate, William. Directory of environmental consultants. c1972. **REF fS920.C3 ECOL**

CONSOLIDATED EDISON COMPANY OF NEW YORK, INC.

Talbot, Allan R. Power along the Hudson. 1st ed. 1972. **HD9685.U5C768 ECOL**

CONSTRUCTION EQUIPMENT—NOISE.

Bolt, Beranek, and Newman, Inc. Noise from construction equipment and operations, building equipment, and home appliances. 1971 i.e. 1972 **fTD893.B63 ECOL**

CONSTRUCTION INDUSTRY—UNITED STATES.

McCue, Gerald M. Creating the human environment. 1970 **HN59.M22 ECOL**

CONSUMER EDUCATION.

Swatek, Paul. The user's guide to the protection of the environment. Walden edition 1970 **TX335.S93 ECOL**

CONSUMPTIVE USE see EVAPOTRANSPIRATION

CONTAINERS.

Bingham, Tayler H. The beverage container problem. 1972. **TD793.B5 ECOL**

CONTAINERS—CONGRESSES.

Solid Waste Resources Conference, Columbus, Ohio, 1971. Design of consumer containers for re-use or disposal. 1972. **TD785.S6 1971 ECOL**

CONTRACEPTION see BIRTH CONTROL

CONTROLLED FUSION.

Glasstone, Samuel. Controlled nuclear fusion. Rev. ed. 1968 **QC791.G48 1968 ECOL**

CONVERSION OF WASTE PRODUCTS see SALVAGE (WASTE, ETC.)

COOKERY.

Gibbons, Euell. Stalking the wild asparagus. 1970, c1962 **QK98.5.G48 ECOL**

COOKERY (WILD FOODS).

Gibbons, Euell. Stalking the good life. 1971 **QK98.5.G45 ECOL**

COOLING TOWERS.

Environmental Systems Corporation. Development and demonstration of low-level drift instrumentation. 1971. **fTD884.5.E58 ECOL**

Georgia Kraft Company. Research and Development Center. Treatment of selected internal kraft mill wastes in a cooling tower. 1971. **fTD899.W65G46 ECOL**

United States. Environmental Protection Agency Pacific Northwest Water Laboratory. A method for predicting the performance of draft cooling towers. 1970. **fTP159.C6U5 ECOL**

COPPER.

United States. Bureau of Mines. Control of sulfur oxide emissions in copper, lead, and zinc smelting. 1971 **TN295.U4no.8527 ECOL**

CORAL REEFS AND ISLANDS.

Davis, William Morris. The coral reef problem. 1928. **QE565.D3 ECOL**

Wiens, Herold Jacob. Atoll environment and ecology. 1971,c1962 **QH541.5.C7W5 ECOL**

CORPORATIONS, NONPROFIT—TAXATION—UNITED STATES.

Berlin, Roisman & Kessler. Law and taxation. 1970 **KF6449.Z9B4 ECOL**

CORROSION AND ANTI-CORROSIVES.

Battelle Memorial Institute, Columbus, Ohio Corrosion potential of NTA in detergent formulations. 1971. **fTP992.5.B3 ECOL**

COSMIC RAYS see also VAN ALLEN RADIATION BELTS

Corliss, William R. Space radiation. 1968 **QC485.C613 ECOL**

COSMOGONY.

Gamow, George. Matter, earth, and sky. 2d ed. 1965 **QC171.G3 1965 ECOL**

COST BENEFIT ANALYSIS see COST EFFECTIVENESS

COST EFFECTIVENESS.

Isard, Walter. Ecologic-economic analysis for regional development. 1972 **HT391.I82 ECOL**

COST EFFECTIVENESS—MATHEMATICAL MODELS.

Synectics Corporation. A system for industrial waste treatment RD&D project priority assignment. 1971. **fTD897.5.S9 ECOL**

COUNTRY LIFE—ADDRESSES, ESSAYS, LECTURES.

Ogden, Samuel R. America the vanishing. 1969. **S942.O44 ECOL**

COUNTRY LIFE—NEW JERSEY.

Buyukmihci, Hope Sawyer. Hour of the beaver. 1971 **QL795.B5B8 ECOL**

COUNTRY LIFE—POLAND.

Boyd, Louise Arner. Polish countrysides. 1937. **DK407.B6 ECOL**

COUNTRY LIFE—UNITED STATES.

Angier, Bradford. One acre and security-how to live off the earth without working it. 1972 **S561.A574 ECOL**

COUNTRY LIFE—VERMONT.

Rood, Ronald N. Wild brother. 1970 **QH81.R74 ECOL**

COURTSHIP OF ANIMALS.

Dossenbach, Hans D. The family life of birds. 1971 **QL675.D6613 ECOL**

COYOTES.

Olsen, Jack. Slaughter the animals, poison the earth. 1971 **QL737.C22O47 ECOL**

Van Wormer, Joe. The world of the coyote. 1964 **QL737.C2V32 ECOL**

CRANES (BIRDS).

Berg, Bengt Magnus Kristoffer. To Africa with the migratory birds. 1930. **QL692.B4 ECOL**

Walkinshaw, Lawrence H. The sandhill cranes. 1949 **QL696.G8W3 ECOL**

CRAYFISH.

Hobbs, Horton Holcombe. Crayfishes (Astacidae) of North and Middle America. 1972. **fQH96.A2B5no.9 ECOL**

CRUSTACEA.

Cressey, Roger Frank. The genus Argulus (Crustacea: Branchiura) of the United States. 1972. **fQH96.A2B5no.2 ECOL**

Holsinger, John R. The freshwater amphipod crustaceans (Gammaridae) of North America. 1972. **fQH96.A2B5no.5 ECOL**

CULTURAL EVOLUTION see SOCIAL CHANGE

CULTURE.

Wagner, Philip Laurence. Environments and peoples. 1972 **GF41.W3 ECOL**

CULTURE DIFFUSION.

Wagner, Philip Laurence. Environments and peoples. 1972 **GF41.W3 ECOL**

CURLEWS.

Bodsworth, Fred. Last of the curlews. 1955. **QL696.L7B6 ECOL**

CYANIDES.

Battelle Memorial Institute, Columbus, Ohio. Columbus Laboratories An investigation of techniques for removal of cyanide from electroplating wastes. 1971 i.e. 1972 **fTD899.M45B32 ECOL**

CYANOPHYTA—CONGRESSES.

Environmental requirements of blue-green algae. 1967. **QK569.C96E56 ECOL**

CYCLING—UNITED STATES.

Lennon, J. Establishing trails on rights-of-way. n.d. **G504.L4 ECOL**

CYCLONES (CHEMICAL TECHNOLOGY) see SEPARATORS (MACHINES)

D

THE DAEDALUS LIBRARY, V. 15.

America's changing environment. 1970. **HC110.E5A56 ECOL**

DAMS.

United States. Bureau of Reclamation. Design of small dams. 2nd ed. 1973. **TC540.U615 1973 ECOL**

DAMS—MINNESOTA.

Harza Engineering Company. Report on abandonment and transfer of ownership of dams. 1971. **fTC557.M6H3 ECOL**

DDT (INSECTICIDE).

Henkin, Harmon. The environment, the establishment, and the law. 1971 **QH545.P4H4 ECOL**

Lake Michigan Enforcement Conference. Lake Michigan Interstate Pesticides Committee. An evaluation of DDT and dieldrin in Lake Michigan. 1972. **TD427.P35L3 ECOL**

United States. Environmental Protection Agency. Office of Research and Monitoring. Identification of polychlorinated biphenyls in the presence of DDT-type compounds. 1972. **SB951.U52 ECOL**

DECISION-MAKING.

Stanford Research Institute. Decision Analysis Group. Decision analysis of nuclear plants in electrical system expansion: final report. **fTK1078.S7 ECOL**

DEER.

Dasmann, William. If deer are to survive. 1971 **QL737.U55D37 ECOL**

Whitehead, George Kenneth. Deer of the world. 1972 **QL737.U55W44 1972b ECOL**

DEER—LEGENDS AND STORIES.

Hoover, Helen. The gift of the deer. 1970c1966 **QL795.D3H6 1970 ECOL**

DEER—MINNESOTA.

Ecological studies of the timber wolf in northeastern Minnesota. 1971 **SD11.A45476no.52 ECOL**

Minnesota. Conservation, Dept. of Game and Fish, Division of. White-tailed deer of Minnesota. 1961. **SH11.M64no.5 ECOL**

DEFOLIATION.

Whiteside, Thomas. The withering rain. 1st ed. 1971. **QH545.P4W48 1971 ECOL**

DEFORESTATION see CLEAR-CUTTING

DEFORMITIES—CAUSES AND THEORIES OF CAUSATION—CONGRESSES.
Symposium on Monitoring, Birth Defects and Environment, Albany, N. Y., 1970. Monitoring, birth defects and environment: the problem of surveillance. 1971. **RG627.S94 1970 ECOL**

DEFORMITIES—GENETIC ASPECTS—CONGRESSES.
Symposium on Monitoring, Birth Defects and Environment, Albany, N. Y., 1970. Monitoring, birth defects and environment: the problem of surveillance. 1971. **RG627.S94 1970 ECOL**

DEMOGRAPHY—MATHEMATICAL MODELS.
Forrester, Jay Wright. World dynamics. 1971 **HD82.F63 ECOL**

DENDROLOGY see TREES

DENITRIFICATION see NITRIFICATION

DENSITY MIXING.
Ralph M. Parsons Laboratory for Water Resources and Hydrodynamics. Density induced mixing in confined aquifers. 1972. **fTC176.R33 ECOL**

DEOXYRIBONUCLEIC ACID.
Missouri. Southwest Missouri State College, Springfield. DNA concentration as an estimate of sludge biomass. 1971. **fTD767.7.M57 ECOL**

DEPOSITION AND SEDIMENTATION see SEDIMENTATION AND DEPOSITION

DESERT BIOLOGY—MEXICO.
Costello, David Francis. The desert world. 1972 **QH88.C67 ECOL**

DESERT BIOLOGY—UNITED STATES.
Costello, David Francis. The desert world. 1972 **QH88.C67 ECOL**

DESERT ECOLOGY.
Larson, Peggy Pickering. Deserts of America. 1970 **QH541.5.D4L28 ECOL**

McCue, George. Ecology: the deserts and man. c1971 **QH541.5.D4M22 ECOL**

DESERT FAUNA.
Tate, Ro. Desert animals. 1st U.S. ed. c1971 **QL116.T37 1971 ECOL**

DESERTS.
Findley, Rowe. Great American deserts. 1972 **F787.F5 ECOL**

DESIGN, INDUSTRIAL.
Papanek, Victor J. Design for the real world. 1st American ed. c1971 **TS171.4.P37 1971 ECOL**

DETERGENT POLLUTION OF RIVERS, LAKES, ETC.
Jones, H. R. Detergents and pollution. 1972 **fTD427.D4J65 ECOL**

Reilich, Helmut G. Technical evaluation of phosphate-free home laundry detergents. 1972 **fTP992.5.R4 ECOL**

DETERGENT POLLUTION OF THE SEA.
Marine Biological Association of the United Kingdom. Laboratory, Plymouth. 'Torrey Canyon' pollution and marine life: a report by the Plymouth Laboratory of the Marine Biological Association of the United Kingdom. 1968. **GC1311.M37 ECOL**

DETERGENTS, SYNTHETIC see also
DETERGENT POLLUTION OF RIVERS, LAKES, ETC.; DETERGENT POLLUTION OF THE SEA

Battelle Memorial Institute, Columbus, Ohio Corrosion potential of NTA in detergent formulations. 1971. **fTP992.5.B3 ECOL**

IIT Research Institute. Technology Center. Development of phosphate-free home laundry detergents. 1970. **fTP992.5.I2 ECOL**

Taylor, John Keeman. Development of method for NTA analysis in raw water. 1972. **TP992.5.T3 ECOL**

DETERGENTS, SYNTHETIC—PATENTS.
Jones, H. R. Detergents and pollution. 1972 **fTD427.D4J65 ECOL**

DETERGENTS, SYNTHETIC—QUALITY CONTROL.
Milwidsky, Benjamin Max. Practical detergent analyses. 1st ed. 1970 **TP992.5.M5 ECOL**

Reilich, Helmut G. Technical evaluation of phosphate-free home laundry detergents. 1972 **fTP992.5.R4 ECOL**

DIATOMS.
Dodd, John D. The ecology of diatoms in hard water habitats. 1971. **fQK569.D54D6 ECOL**

Nelson, Robert R. The effects of enrichment on Lake Superior periphyton. 1973. **GB701.M554no.59 ECOL**

Olson, Theodore A. Lake Superior periphyton in relation to water quality. 1972. **fQK935.O4 ECOL**

DIET.
Rodale, Robert. Sane living in a mad world. 1972 **RA776.5.R57 ECOL**

DIGITAL ELECTRONICS.
Geesey, A. H. New safety system design for nuclear power reactors. 1971. **fTA1.P35no.103 ECOL**

DIRECT ENERGY CONVERSION.
Corliss, William R. Direct conversion of energy. 1964 **TK2896.C6 ECOL**

DISASTERS.
Smithsonian Institution. Center for Shortlived Phenomena. The pulse of the planet. c1972 **fQ225.P8 ECOL**

DISEASE WARFARE see BIOLOGICAL WARFARE

DISEASES OF PLANTS see PLANT DISEASES

DISPOSAL OF REFUSE see REFUSE AND REFUSE DISPOSAL

DISTILLATION.
Black, Sivalls and Bryson, inc., Kansas City, Mo. Applied Technology Division Evaluation of a new acid mine drainage treatment process. 1971. **fTD899.M5B55 ECOL**

DO-IT-YOURSELF WORK.
The Last whole earth catalog. 1971. **REF fTT155.W52 ECOL**

DRAINAGE.
Linsley, Ray K. A manual on collection of hydrologic data for urban drainage design. 1973. **fTD665.L55 ECOL**

Seminar on the Engineer and the Environment University of Minnesota, 1970. The Engineer and the environment. 1971. **GB701.M554no.38 ECOL**

United States. Soil Conservation Service. Drainage of agricultural land. 1971 **REF TC970.U5 ECOL**

DRAINAGE—MINNESOTA.
Goldstein, Jon H. Competition for wetlands in the Midwest. 1971 **HD1683.U4G6 ECOL**

DRAINAGE OF MINES see MINE DRAINAGE

DROUGHTS—UNITED STATES.
Russell, Clifford S. Drought and water supply. 1970 **TD223.R88 ECOL**

DUCKS.
Phillips, John Charles. American waterfowl. 1930. **QL696.A5P45 ECOL**

Sowls, Lyle K. Prairie ducks. 1955. **QL696.A5S64 ECOL**

DUCKS—MINNESOTA.
Minnesota. Dept. of Conservation. Division of Game and Fish. Ducks and land use in Minnesota. 1964. **SH11.M64no.8 ECOL**

DUTCH EAST INDIES—DESCRIPTION AND TRAVEL.
Fairchild, David Grandison. Garden islands of the great East. 1943. **SB109.F185 ECOL**

DYES AND DYEING—WASTE DISPOSAL.
Fram Corporation. Bio-regenerated activated carbon treatment of textile dye wastewater. 1971. **fTD899.T4F7 ECOL**

E

EARTH.
French, Herbert E. Love of earth. c1973 **S936.F7 ECOL**

Nicks, Oran W. This island earth. 1970. **fQB631.N5 ECOL**

EAST GRAND FORKS, MINN.—FLOODS.
United States. Army. Corps of Engineers. Flood plain information on the Red River of the North in the vicinity of Grand Forks, North Dakota—East Grand Forks, Minnesota. 1971. **GB1227.R4A5 ECOL**

ECOLOGICAL RESEARCH—DIRECTORIES.
Cate, William. Directory of environmental consultants. c1972. **REF fS920.C3 ECOL**

ECOLOGICAL SUCCESSION.
Pringle, Laurence P. From pond to prairie. 1972 **PZ10.P669Ft ECOL**

ECOLOGISTS.
Cox, Donald William. Pioneers of ecology. 1971 **QH26.C68 ECOL**

ECOLOGISTS, AMERICAN.
Cox, Donald William. Pioneers of ecology. 1971 **QH26.C68 ECOL**

Who's who in ecology, 1973- **REF fQH26.W46 ECOL**

ECOLOGY.
Anderson, Paul K. Omega. 1971 **QH541.A5 ECOL**

Asimov, Isaac. ABC's of ecology. c1972 **fQH541.14.A85 ECOL**

Bates, Marston. The forest and the sea. 1960 **QH541.B3 ECOL**

Behnke, Frances L. The changing world of living things. c1972 **QH541.14.B47 ECOL**

Benthall, Jonathan. Ecology in theory and practice. 1973,c1972 **QH541.B4 1973 ECOL**

Benton, Allen H. Manual of field biology and ecology. 4th ed. c1965 **QH307.B3 1965 ECOL**

Billington, Elizabeth T. Understanding ecology. 1971 **QH541.14.B5 1971 ECOL**

Blueprint for survival. 1972. **S936.B5 1972 ECOL**

Boughey, Arthur S. Ecology of populations. 1968 **QH541.B67 ECOL**

Brock, Thomas D. Principles of microbial ecology. 1966 **QR41.B72 ECOL**

Brubaker, Sterling. To live on earth. 1972 **QH541.B76 ECOL**

Buchsbaum, Ralph Morris. Basic ecology. 1970,c1957 **QH541.B79 ECOL**

Burch, William R. Daydreams and nightmares. 1971 **HM206.B83 ECOL**

Cailliet, Greg M. Everyman's guide to ecological living. 1971 **GF75.C33 ECOL**

Chemical ecology. 1970. **QH345.C435 ECOL**

Chisholm, Anne. Philosophers of the earth. c1972 **GF75.C4 ECOL**

Clarke, George Leonard. Elements of ecology. 1st ed. rev. print., with subject guide to new references. 1965, c1954 **QH541.C47 1965 ECOL**

Connell, Joseph H. Readings in ecology and ecological genetics. 1970 **QH541.C65 ECOL**

Curry-Lindahl, Kai. Conservation for survival. 1972. **QH541.C87 ECOL**

Darling, Frank Fraser. Wilderness and plenty. 1970. **QH541.13.D36 ECOL**

Darling, Lois. A place in the sun. 1968 **QH541.D34 ECOL**

Dasmann, Raymond Frederick. Environmental conservation. 3d ed. 1972 **S936.D3 1972 ECOL**

Dasmann, Raymond Frederick. Planet in peril. 1972 **QH541.D35 1972 ECOL**

Douglas, William Orville. The three hundred year war: a chronicle of ecological disaster. 1st ed. 1972 **QH541.D68 ECOL**

Dugan, Patrick R. Biochemical ecology of water pollution. 1972. **TD423.D83 ECOL**

Dynamic ecology. 1973 **QH541.D9 ECOL**

Ehrenfeld, David W. Conserving life on earth. 1972. **QH75.E35 1972 ECOL**

Emmel, Thomas C. An introduction to ecology and population biology. 1973 **QH541.E45 1973 ECOL**

Falk, Richard A. This endangered planet. 1st ed. 1971 **HC79.E5F27 ECOL**

Farb, Peter. Ecology. c1970 **fQH541.F3 1970 ECOL**

Grossman, Shelly. The how and why wonder book of ecology. 1971 **fQH541.14.G78 ECOL**

Halacy, Daniel Stephen. Habitat. 1970 **QH541.14.H3 ECOL**

Hirsch, S. Carl. The living community. 1966 **QH541.H54 ECOL**

Hoke, John. Ecology: man's effects on his environment and its mechanisms. 1971 **QH541.H58 ECOL**

Humphrey, Clifford C. What's ecology? 1971 **QH541.13.H84 ECOL**

Hungerford, Harold R. Ecology: the circle of life. 1971 **QH541.14.H8 ECOL**

Imsland, Donald. Celebrate the earth. 1971 **QH541.I45 ECOL**

Jones, Claire. Pollution: the balance of nature. 1972 **QH541.14.J65 ECOL**

Jones, Thomas C. The environment of America: present/future/ past. 1971 **fQH541.145.J65 ECOL**

Knight, Clifford Burnham. Basic concepts of ecology. 1965 **QH541.K5 ECOL**

Kormondy, Edward John. Concepts of ecology. 1969 **QH541.K59 ECOL**

Levins, Richard. Evolution in changing environments. 1968. **QL752.L4 ECOL**

Margalef, Ramon. Perspectives in ecological theory. 1968 **QH541.M37 ECOL**

Marzani, Carl. The wounded earth. 1972 **QH541.M38 ECOL**

Masini, Giancarlo. S.O.S. save our earth. c1972 **fQH541.M382 1972 ECOL**

Matthews, William Henry. Man's impact on terrestrial and oceanic ecosystems. 1971 **TD174.M39 ECOL**

McCue, George. Ecology. c1971 **QH541.M22 Suppl. ECOL**

McCue, George. Ecology: the city. c1971 **QH541.5.C6M23 ECOL**

McCue, George. Ecology: the farm. c1971
QH541.5.F3M22 ECOL

McCue, George. Ecology: the suburbs. c1971
QH541.5.C6M22 Suppl. ECOL

Milne, Lorus Johnson. The arena of life: the dynamics of ecology. 1972 **QH541.M52 ECOL**

Milne, Lorus Johnson. The nature of life. 1970
fQH45.2.M55 ECOL

Milne, Lorus Johnson. Patterns of survival. c1967 **QH546.M5 ECOL**

Mines, Samuel. The last days of mankind. 1971
S936.M55 ECOL

Murdoch, William W. Environment; resources, pollution & society. 1971 **QH541.M95 ECOL**

Nickelsburg, Janet. Ecology. 1st ed. 1969
QH541.14.N5 ECOL

Nickelsburg, Janet. Field trips. 1971, c1966
QH541.N5 ECOL

Odum, Eugene Pleasants. Ecology. 1963
QH541.O29 ECOL

Odum, Eugene Pleasants. Fundamentals of ecology. 3d ed. 1971. **QH541.O3 1971 ECOL**

Odum, Howard T. Environment, power, and society. 1970, c1971 **QH541.O33 ECOL**

Pringle, Laurence P. Ecology; science of survival. 1971 **QH541.14.P75 ECOL**

Ramparts. Eco-catastrophe. c1970
TD180.R3 ECOL

Reid, George K. Ecology of inland waters and estuaries. 1961 **QH96.R43 ECOL**

Reid, Keith. Nature's network. 1970, c1969
QH541.14.R43 ECOL

Roth, Charles E. The most dangerous animal in the world. c1971 **QH541.R68 ECOL**

Schlichting, Harold E. Ecology. 1971
PZ10.S3713Ec ECOL

Sears, Paul Bigelow. The living landscape. 1966
QH541.S37 1966 ECOL

Segerberg, Osborn. Where have all the flowers, fishes, birds, trees, water, and air gone? 1971
QH541.S39 ECOL

Smith, Frances C. The first book of conservation. 2d rev. ed. 1972. **S940.S64 1972 ECOL**

Smith, Robert Leo. Ecology and field biology. 1966
QH541.S6 ECOL

Storer, John Humphries. The web of life. 1953.
QH541.S68 ECOL

Turk, Amos. Ecology, pollution, environment. 1972. **TD174.T87 ECOL**

United States. Dept. of the Interior. It's your world. 1969 **fS930.A45 ECOL**

United States. National Science Foundation. National Science Board. Environmental science, challenge for the seventies. 1971. **TD145.U5 ECOL**

Vernberg, F. John. The animal and the environment. 1970 **QH541.V45 ECOL**

Wagner, Richard H. Environment and man. 1st ed. 1971 **QH541.13.W34 ECOL**

Watt, Kenneth E. F. Ecology and resource management. 1968 **QL752.W38 ECOL**

Whittaker, Robert Harding. Communities and ecosystems. 1970 **QH541.W44 ECOL**

ECOLOGY—ADDRESSES, ESSAYS, LECTURES.
Cox, George W. Readings in conservation ecology. 1969 **S942.C6 ECOL**

Emmel, Thomas C. Behavior and ecology. 1970
QH541.E44 ECOL

The Environment. 1970 **TD176.7.E45 ECOL**

Foss, Phillip O. Politics and ecology. 1972
HC110.E5F66 ECOL

Godfrey, Arthur. The Arthur Godfrey environmental reader. 1970 **QH541.13.G6 ECOL**

Goodman, Gordon T. Ecology and the industrial society. 1965 **TD180.G6 ECOL**

Gorden, Morton. Environmental management. 1972 **TD177.G67 ECOL**

Harte, John. Patient earth. 1971
QH541.H26 ECOL

Hutchinson, George Evelyn. The ecological theater and the evolutionary play. 1965.
QH311.H77 ECOL

Johnson, Cecil E. Eco-crisis. 1970
QH541.J63 ECOL

Johnson, Cecil E. The natural world: chaos and conservation. c1972 **QH541.145.J63 ECOL**

Schoenfeld, Clarence Albert. Everybody's ecology. 1971 **QH541.13.S36 ECOL**

Strobbe, Maurice A. Understanding environmental pollution. 1971. **QH545.A1S7 ECOL**

The Unforseen international ecologic boomerang. 1969 **fQH541.U5 ECOL**

ECOLOGY—AFRICA, EAST.
Burton, Jane. Animals of the African year. 1st American ed. 1972 **fQL336.B87 1972 ECOL**

ECOLOGY—ALASKA—ADDRESSES, ESSAYS, LECTURES.
Alaska Science Conference, 20th, University of Alaska, 1969. Change in Alaska. 1970
HD9567.A4A64 1969 ECOL

ECOLOGY—ARCTIC REGIONS.
Stonehouse, Bernard. Animals of the Arctic. 1st American ed. 1971 **fQH199.S83 1971 ECOL**

ECOLOGY—AUTHORSHIP.
Arny, Mary (Travis). Ecology: a writer's handbook. 1st ed. 1972 **QH541.A72 ECOL**

ECOLOGY—BIBLIOGRAPHY.
The Environment film review: a critical guide to ecology films. v.1- 1972-
fZ5322.E2E5 ECOL

Mignon, Molly R. Our polluted planet: a bibliography of government publications on pollution and the environment. 1971. **fZ5322.E2M5 ECOL**

Watkins, Jessie B. Ecology and environmental quality. 1971. **REF fZ5322.E2W3 ECOL**

"Where have all the flowers gone?". 1970
REF fZ5322.E2W54 ECOL

Winton, Harry N. M. Man and the environment: a bibliography of selected publications of the United Nations system, 1946-1971. 1972.
REF Z5322.E2W56 ECOL

ECOLOGY—CALIFORNIA.
Bakker, Elna S. An island called California. 1971.
QH105.C2B3 ECOL

ECOLOGY—COLLECTED WORKS.
Circle of the world. **QH541.2.C5 Suppl. ECOL**
Circle of the world. c1971-
QH541.2.C5 ECOL

Lugo, Ariel E. Readings on ecological systems: their function and relation to man. c1971
QH540.3.L8 ECOL

ECOLOGY—CONGRESSES.
Conference on the Ecological Aspects of International Development, Airlie House, 1968. The careless technology: ecology and international development. 1st ed. 1972. **QH540.C65 1968 ECOL**

International Symposium on River Ecology and the Impact of Man, University of Massachusetts, 1971. River ecology and man. 1972.
GB1205.I5 1971 ECOL

Peabody Museum Centennial Symposium, Yale University, 1966. Evolution and environment. 1968.
QH366.A1P4 1966 ECOL

Study of Critical Environmental Problems. Man's impact on the global environment. 1970
QH541.S73 ECOL

ECOLOGY—DICTIONARIES.
Hanson, Herbert Christian. Dictionary of ecology. 1962 **REF QH541.H25 ECOL**

ECOLOGY—EXPERIMENTS.
Rasmussen, Frederick A. Man and the environment. 1970, c1971 **QH316.5.R35 ECOL**

Simon, Seymour. Science projects in ecology. 1972
QH541.14.S55 ECOL

ECOLOGY—EXPERIMENTS—JUVENILE LITERATURE.
Simon, Seymour. Science projects in ecology. 1972
QH541.14.S55 ECOL

ECOLOGY—FILM CATALOGS.
"Where have all the flowers gone?". 1970
REF fZ5322.E2W54 ECOL

ECOLOGY—FLORIDA—EVERGLADES.
Sand, George X. The Everglades today. 1971
QH105.F6S24 ECOL

ECOLOGY—GREAT PLAINS.
Costello, David Francis. The prairie world. 1969
QH541.5.P7C6 ECOL

ECOLOGY—ISLANDS OF THE PACIFIC.
Wiens, Herold Jacob. Atoll environment and ecology. 1971, c1962 **QH541.5.C7W5 ECOL**

ECOLOGY—JUVENILE LITERATURE.
Simon, Seymour. Science projects in ecology. 1972
QH541.14.S55 ECOL

ECOLOGY—MATHEMATICAL MODELS.
Watt, Kenneth E. F. Systems analysis in ecology. 1966. **QH541.W3 ECOL**

ECOLOGY—MATHEMATICAL MODELS—CONGRESSES.
International Symposium on Statistical Ecology, New Haven, 1969. Statistical ecology. 1971
QH541.15.M3I5 1969 ECOL

ECOLOGY—MINNESOTA.
Grether, David F. Population type, distribution and density of the flora on the Sherburne County Generating Plant Site, 15 October through 31 December, 1971. 1972 **fTK1331.N6G7 ECOL**

Minnesota. Governor, 1971- Securing a quality environment in Minnesota. 1973?
REF fHC107.M6A35 ECOL

Wallace, McHarg, Roberts and Todd. An ecological study of the Twin Cities Metropolitan Area. 1969.
fQH541.W32 ECOL

ECOLOGY—NORTH AMERICA.
Shelford, Victor Ernest. The ecology of North America. 1963. **QH102.S5 ECOL**

ECOLOGY—SOCIETIES, ETC.—DIRECTORIES.
Sichel, Beatrice. Guide to private citizen action environmental groups. 1973. **REF fS920.S53 ECOL**

ECOLOGY—SONGS AND MUSIC.
The Ecology sea in song and ballad. 1973?
Phonodisc GC31.E2 ECOL

ECOLOGY—STUDY AND TEACHING.
Balarat Center for Environmental Studies. Denver Urban environmental studies for grades kindergarten—six. 1971. **QH541.2.B25 ECOL**

Bennett, Dean B. Guidelines for planning and implementing a comprehensive community environmental inventory. Rev. ed. 1972.
fQH541.2.B38 1972 ECOL

Berry, Marcia. Environment study. 1971.
QH541.2.B4 ECOL

Circle of the world. **QH541.2.C5 Suppl. ECOL**
Circle of the world. c1971-
QH541.2.C5 ECOL

Cohen, Martin. A handbook on environmental information programs for public libraries. 1973.
fZ670.A3C6 ECOL

Darnell, Rezneat M. Organism and environment. c1971 **fQH541.2.D3 ECOL**

Dickey, Miriam E. Beyond the classroom: using the urban environment as an instructional medium. 1972. **fQH541.2.D52 ECOL**

Dooley, David. Summer School guide for education for an improved environment. 1971.
fQH541.2.D6 ECOL

Educational Facilities Laboratories. Environmental education/facility resources: A Report. c1972
QH541.2.E48 ECOL

Environmental education materials. 1971.
REF Z7164.N3E6 ECOL

Environmental education 1970. 1970
fS946.E55 ECOL

Henderson, George J. Pollution: problems, projects and mathematical exercises. 1970
fQH541.2.H46 ECOL

Henderson, Martha T. Environmental education: Social studies sources and approaches. 1970
Ref fQH541.2.H4 ECOL

Intercom. Teaching about spaceship earth. c1972
S946.I5 ECOL

Kelly, James. Pollution—man's crisis: an investigative approach. c1971 **QH541.2.K45 ECOL**

Krznarich, Susan. Basic ecology. 1971.
QH541.2.K7 ECOL

Lawrence, Donald Buermann. Ecology: biology 80. Rev. 1967,1966. **fQH541.2.L3 1967 ECOL**

MacGown, Richard H. The school site in environmental education. Rev. ed. 1972.
fLB3220.M3 1972 ECOL

Madison. Wis. Board of Education. Dept. of Curriculum Development. Science and society. 1969. **REF fQ181.M3 ECOL**

Man and his environment. 1970
L11.N39no.1 ECOL

McCuen, Gary E. The ecology controversy: opposing viewpoints. 1971 **QH541.M3 ECOL**

McInnis, Noel. You are an environment: teaching/learning environmental attitudes. c1972
QH541.M4 ECOL

Michigan. Dept. of Natural Resources. Environmental education for intermediate grades.
fS946.M45 ECOL

New York (State) University. Environmental education instructional activities. 1972.
fQH541.2.N4 ECOL

New York (State) University. An environmental experience. 1971. **fQH541.2.N45 ECOL**

North Carolina. Task Force on Environment and Natural Resources. Teacher's guide for environmental education. 1970. **REF fQH541.2.N88 ECOL**

The Organic classroom. c1973 **fS946.O7 ECOL**

Ragland, Kenneth W. Environmental studies at the CIC universities—a survey. 1971.
REF fQH541.2.R3 ECOL

Rasmussen, Bruce C. Problem—emphasis education: an environmental symposium and the consequences of that symposium at Columbia Heights Senior High School District 13, 1969-1970. 1970
fLB1027.R3 ECOL

Roth, Robert E. A review of research related to environmental education. 1972. **QH541.2.R6 ECOL**

Stecher, Adam. Running water. c1971 **QH541.2.S8 ECOL**

Terry, Mark. Teaching for survival. 1971 **QH541.2.T47 ECOL**

United States. National Center for Educational Communication. Environmental education: programs and materials. 1972 **S946.U58 ECOL**

Watson, Geoffrey Grainge. Fun with ecology. 1971.c1967 **QH541.2.W3 1971 ECOL**

ECOLOGY—STUDY AND TEACHING—AUDIO-VISUAL AIDS—BIBLIOGRAPHY.
Interdisciplinary Environmental Education. Sources of reference materials & audiovisual aids for environmental education. 2d rev. ed. 1972 **Ref fQH541.2.I68 1972 ECOL**

Project Outreach. Environmental education resource catalog. 1971 **fQH541.2.P76 ECOL**

ECOLOGY—STUDY AND TEACHING—BIBLIOGRAPHY.
Cunningham, Michael C. A selected bibliography on the relevance of environmental education to secondary school curricula. 1972 **REF fQH541.2.C8 ECOL**

Minnesota. University. References and resource guides for the University of Minnesota SEED Project curricula. n.d. **fQH541.2.M5 ECOL**

National Association for Environmental Education. Man and environment. 1970 **REF fZ5322.E2N3 ECOL**

Pepe, Thomas F. Environmental education. 1971. **fZ5322.E2P4 ECOL**

ECOLOGY—STUDY AND TEACHING—UNITED STATES.
National Science Teachers Association. Programs in environmental education. 2d ed. 1971. **REF fQH51.N24 1971 ECOL**

ECOLOGY—STUDY AND TEACHING (ELEMENTARY).
Education for survival. 1970- **QH541.2.E4 ECOL**

Sako, Marilyn. Man and his environment. 1971 **fS946.S2 ECOL**

Sale, Larry L. Environmental education in the elementary school. 1972 **QH541.2.S24 ECOL**

West St. Paul, Minn. Independent School Dist. no. 197. Elementary Science Committee. Elementary science guide and resource book. n.d. **fLB1585.W4 ECOL**

ECOLOGY—STUDY AND TEACHING (ELEMENTARY)—BIBLIOGRAPHY.
Watt, Lois B. Environmental - ecological education: a bibliography of fiction, nonfiction, and textbooks for elementary and secondary schools. 1971. **REF fQH541.2.W34 ECOL**

ECOLOGY—STUDY AND TEACHING (HIGHER).
Troost, Cornelius J. Environmental education: a sourcebook. 1972 **QH541.2.T76 ECOL**

ECOLOGY—STUDY AND TEACHING (SECONDARY).
Kotsonis, Helen Hoch. Modern lesson plans in environmental science. 1972 **QH541.2.K68 ECOL**

Mounds Views, Minn. Independent School District, 621. Environmental education curriculum, grades 10 - 12. n.d. **fQH541.2.M6 ECOL**

ECOLOGY—STUDY AND TEACHING (SECONDARY)—BIBLIOGRAPHY.
Watt, Lois B. Environmental - ecological education: a bibliography of fiction, nonfiction, and textbooks for elementary and secondary schools. 1971. **REF fQH541.2.W34 ECOL**

ECOLOGY—TECHNIQUE—CONGRESSES.
Remote sensing in ecology. 1969 **QH541.15.R4R4 ECOL**

ECOLOGY—TERMINOLOGY.
Arny, Mary (Travis). Ecology: a writer's handbook. 1st ed. 1972 **QH541.A72 ECOL**

Studdard, Gloria J. Common environmental terms: a glossary. 1973. **REF S922.S7 ECOL**

ECOLOGY—UNITED STATES.
Ecology USA. **REF fS936.S62 ECOL**

Grossman, Mary Louise. Our vanishing wilderness. 1969 **fQH541.13.G76 ECOL**

Owen, Oliver S. Natural resource conservation. 1971 **S938.O87 ECOL**

United States. Dept. of the Interior. Our environment and natural resources ... indivisibly one. 1971? **fS914.A533 ECOL**

ECOLOGY—UNITED STATES—HISTORY.
Cox, Donald William. Pioneers of ecology. 1971 **QH26.C68 ECOL**

Hirsch, S. Carl. Guardians of tomorrow. 1971 **QH541.14.H57 1971 ECOL**

ECOLOGY—UNITED STATES—HISTORY—SOURCES.
McHenry, Robert. A documentary history of conservation in America. 1972 **S930.M18 ECOL**

ECOLOGY—UNITED STATES—STUDY AND TEACHING.
United States. Bureau of Land Management. All around you: an environmental study guide. 1971. **S946.U5 ECOL**

ECOLOGY—VOCATIONAL GUIDANCE.
Fanning, Odom. Opportunities in environmental careers. c1971 **S944.F3 ECOL**

Olympus Research Corporation. Career education in the environment. 1971 or 2 **fGF21.O4 ECOL**

ECOLOGY, HUMAN see HUMAN ECOLOGY
ECOLOGY, SOCIAL see HUMAN ECOLOGY
ECONOMIC DEVELOPMENT.
Carnegie Endowment for International Peace. Environment and development. 1972c1971 **HC68.C3 1972 ECOL**

Clawson, Marion. Natural resources and international development. 1964 **HC55.C57 ECOL**

Jacobs, Jane. The economy of cities. 1969 **HT321.J32 ECOL**

Mishan, Edward J. Technology and growth. 1970,c1969 **HD82.M514 ECOL**

Resources for the Future. Design for a worldwide study of regional development. 1966 **HD82.R43 ECOL**

ECONOMIC GROWTH see ECONOMIC DEVELOPMENT
ECONOMIC HISTORY—1945-
Brown, Lester Russell. World without borders. 1972 **HC59.B765 1972b ECOL**

ECONOMIC HISTORY—20TH CENTURY.
Fisher, Joseph Lyman. World prospects for natural resources. 1964 **HC54.F54 ECOL**

ECONOMIC POISONS see PESTICIDES
ECONOMIC POLICY—MATHEMATICAL MODELS.
Forrester, Jay Wright. World dynamics. 1971 **HD82.F63 ECOL**

ECONOMIC RESEARCH.
Young, G. K. The importance of economic factors in urban surface water supply systems. 1972. **fTD353.Y6 ECOL**

ECONOMICS.
Georgescu-Roegen, Nicholas. The entropy law and the economic process. 1971. **HB171.G43 ECOL**

Theobald, Robert. The economics of abundance. 1970 **HB171.T48 ECOL**

ECONOMICS—HISTORY—UNITED STATES.
Galbraith, John Kenneth. The affluent society. 2d ed., rev. 1969. **HC106.5.G32 1969 ECOL**

EDUCATION—EXPERIMENTAL METHODS.
Educational Facilities Laboratories. Places and things for experimental schools. 1972 **Ref LB3221.E3 ECOL**

EDUCATION, HIGHER—ADDRESSES, ESSAYS, LECTURES.
Environment, the university, & the welfare of man. 1969 **LC191.E55 ECOL**

EDUCATIONAL INNOVATIONS.
Environmental studies. Rev. ed.? 1971,c1970 **LB1027.E6 1971 ECOL**

EDUCATIONAL SOCIOLOGY—ADDRESSES, ESSAYS, LECTURES.
Environment, the university, & the welfare of man. 1969 **LC191.E55 ECOL**

EGGS—PACKING.
Hickman, Howard J. A study of the environmental impact of polystyrene vs. paper pulp egg cartons and meat trays. 1972. **fTP373.H5 ECOL**

ELECTRETS—PATENTS.
Kallard, Thomas. Electret devices for air pollution control. 1972 **fQC585.K28 ECOL**

ELECTRIC POWER.
Grey, Jerry. The race for electric power. 1972 **TK1001.G73 ECOL**

ELECTRIC POWER—MINNESOTA.
St. John's University, Collegeville, Minnesota Center for the Study of Local Government. The impact of future electrical power requirements on the state of Minnesota—an issue analysis. 1971. **fHD9685.U6M6 ECOL**

ELECTRIC POWER—MINNESOTA—ADDRESSES, ESSAYS, LECTURES.
Minnesota. University. Water Resources Research Center. Conference on impact of future electric power requirements in the state of Minnesota: an issue analysis. 1971. **GB701.M554no.28 ECOL**

ELECTRIC POWER—PLANTS—MINNESOTA.
St. John's University, Collegeville, Minnesota Center for the Study of Local Government. The impact of future electrical power requirements on the state of Minnesota- an issue analysis. 1971. **fHD9685.U6M6 ECOL**

ELECTRIC POWER DISTRIBUTION—MINNESOTA.
Minnesota. University. Water Resources Research Center. Conference on impact of future electric power requirements in the state of Minnesota: an issue analysis. 1971. **GB701.M554no.28 ECOL**

St. John's University, Collegeville, Minnesota Center for the Study of Local Government. The impact of future electrical power requirements on the state of Minnesota—an issue analysis. 1971. **fHD9685.U6M6 ECOL**

ELECTRIC POWER-PLANTS.
Black & Veatch, Kansas City, Mo. Environmental report. 1971- **fTK1331.N6B7 ECOL**

Cootner, Paul H. Water demand for steam electric generation. 1966,c1965 **TK1051.C6 ECOL**

United Aircraft Corporation. Research Laboratories, East Hartford, Conn. Advanced nonthermally polluting gas turbines in utility applications. 1971. **fTJ778.U5 ECOL**

United States. Environmental Protection Agency Pacific Northwest Water Laboratory. A method for predicting the performance of draft cooling towers. 1970. **fTP159.C6U5 ECOL**

ELECTRIC POWER-PLANTS—ENVIRONMENTAL ASPECTS.
Growing against ourselves: the energy-environment tangle. 1972. **TD195.E4G76 ECOL**

ELECTRIC POWER-PLANTS—ENVIRONMENTAL ASPECTS—UNITED STATES.
Association of the Bar of the City of New York. Special Committee on Electric Power and the Environment. Electricity and the environment: the reform of legal institutions. 1972. **KF2125.A97 ECOL**

California Institute of Technology, Pasadena. Environmental Quality Laboratory. People, power and pollution: environmental and public interest aspects of electric power plant siting. 1971. **fTK1193.U5C3 ECOL**

United States. Federal Power Commission. Steam-electric plant air and water quality control data for the year ended December 31, 1969, based on EPC form no. 67. 1973. **fTD195.E4U5 ECOL**

ELECTRIC POWER-PLANTS—LOCATION.
National Academy of Engineering. Committee on Power Plant Siting. Engineering for resolution of the energy-environment dilemma. 1972. **fTD177.N38 ECOL**

ELECTRIC POWER PLANTS—MINNESOTA.
Major NSP generating plant sites. 1970. **fTK1191.M3 ECOL**

Minnesota. University. Water Resources Research Center. Conference on impact of future electric power requirements in the state of Minnesota: an issue analysis. 1971. **GB701.M554no.28 ECOL**

ELECTRIC POWER PLANTS—MINNESOTA—LOCATION.
Commonwealth Associates, Inc. Northern States Power Company, Minnesota: fossil fueled power plant siting study. 1972. **REF fTK1331.N6C6 ECOL**

ELECTRIC POWER-PLANTS—UNITED STATES.
Fabricant, Neil. Toward a rational power policy: energy, politics, and pollution. 1971 **HD9685.U5F32 ECOL**

Holdren, John P. Energy. c1971 **TJ153.H65 ECOL**

United States. Federal Power Commission. Air pollution and the regulated electric power and natural gas industries. 1968. **TD883.2.A52 ECOL**

United States. Office of Science and Technology. Electric power and the environment. 1970. **TK1193.U5A45 ECOL**

ELECTRIC POWER-PLANTS—UNITED STATES—LOCATION.
California Institute of Technology, Pasadena. Environmental Quality Laboratory. People, power and pollution: environmental and public interest aspects of electric power plant siting. 1971. **fTK1193.U5C3 ECOL**

United States. Office of Science and Technology. Considerations affecting steam power plant site selection. 1968 **TK1193.U5A44 ECOL**

ELECTRIC POWER PRODUCTION *see also* DIRECTION ENERGY CONVERSION
Abrahamson, Dean E. Environmental cost of electric power. 1970 **fTK1005.A26 ECOL**
Linville, Bill. Review of Bureau of Mines energy program, 1970. 1971 **TN295.U4no.8526 ECOL**
Power, pollution, and public policy. c1971 **HC107.A113E55 ECOL**

ELECTRIC UTILITIES—CONGRESSES.
Sierra Club Conference on the Electric Power Industry, 1st, Johnson City, Vt., 1972. Report on the first Sierra Club power conference [papers]. 1972? **fHD9685.A2S5 1972 ECOL**

ELECTRIC UTILITIES—LAW AND LEGISLATION—UNITED STATES.
Association of the Bar of the City of New York. Special Committee on Electric Power and the Environment. Electricity and the environment: the reform of legal institutions. 1972. **KF2125.A97 ECOL**

ELECTRIC UTILITIES—UNITED STATES.
United States. Electric Utility Industry Task Force on Environment. The electric utility industry and the environment. 1968? **HD9685.U5U5 ECOL**

ELECTROCHEMICAL ANALYSIS.
Taylor, John Keeman. Development of method for NTA analysis in raw water. 1972. **TP992.5.T3 ECOL**

ELECTROCHEMICAL APPARATUS.
Electrochemistry of cleaner environments. 1972. **TP256.E43 1972 ECOL**

ELECTROCHEMISTRY, INDUSTRIAL.
Electrochemistry of cleaner environments. 1972. **TP256.E43 1972 ECOL**

ELECTROLYTIC OXIDATION *see* OXIDATION, ELECTROLYTIC

ELECTROMAGNETIC MEASUREMENTS.
Morey, Rexford M. Feasibility study of electromagnetic subsurface profiling. 1972. **QE602.M6 ECOL**

ELECTRONIC DATA PROCESSING—HYDROLOGY.
Bowers, C. Edward. Computer programs in hydrology. 1972. **GB665.B6 ECOL**

ELECTRONIC DATA PROCESSING—SEWAGE—PURIFICATION.
American Public Works Association. Feasibility of computer control of wastewater treatment. 1970. **fTD746.A43 ECOL**

ELECTRONIC DATE PROCESSING—SOCIAL SCIENCES—CONGRESSES.
Clubb, Jerome M. Ecological data in comparative research. 1970 **H62.C6 ECOL**

ELECTROPLATING *see* METALS—FINISHING

ELECTROPLATING—WASTE DISPOSAL.
Battelle Memorial Institute, Columbus, Ohio. Columbus Laboratories An investigation of techniques for removal of cyanide from electroplating wastes. 1971 i.e. 1972 **fTD899.M45B32 ECOL**
Battelle Memorial Institute. Columbus, Ohio. Columbus Laboratories A state-of-the-art review of metal finishing waste treatment. 1968 i.e.1970 **fTD899.M45B33 ECOL**

ELK *see also* TULE ELK
Merrill, Samuel. The moose book. c1916 **SK301.M4 ECOL**

ELK, EUROPEAN *see* MOOSE

EMBANKMENTS.
Thomsen, Arvid L. Riprap stability on earth embankments tested in large—and small-scale wave tanks. 1972. **TC533.T4 ECOL**

EMINENT DOMAIN—UNITED STATES—CASES.
Haar, Charles Monroe. Land-use planning. 2d ed. 1971. **KF5692.A4H3 1971 ECOL**

ENERGY METABOLISM—TERMINOLOGY.
National Research Council. Committee on Animal Nutrition. Biological energy interrelationships and glossary of energy terms. 1st ed. 1966. **REF SF95.N3 1966 ECOL**

ENERGY RESOURCES *see* POWER RESOURCES

ENGINEERING *see also* DAMS; DRAINAGE; ENVIRONMENTAL ENGINEERING; HYDRAULIC ENGINEERING; MACHINERY; MECHANICAL ENGINEERING; NUCLEAR ENGINEERING; RIVERS; SANITARY ENGINEERING; WATER-SUPPLY ENGINEERING
Allen, Richard H. A glossary of coastal engineering terms. 1972. **REF TC1645.A4 ECOL**
Seminar on the Engineer and the Environment University of Minnesota, 1970. The Engineer and the environment. 1971. **GB701.M554no.38 ECOL**

ENGINEERING—CONGRESSES.
Engineering for the benefit of mankind. 1970. **TA5.E52 ECOL**

ENGINEERING GEOLOGY—CONGRESSES.
Symposium on Engineering Geology in the Urban Environment, San Francisco, 1969. Environmental planning and geology. 1971 **TA705.S95 1969 ECOL**

ENGINEERING, HYDRAULIC *see* HYDRAULIC ENGINEERING

ENGINEERING, SANITARY *see* SANITARY ENGINEERING

ENGINEERING, WATER-SUPPLY *see* WATER SUPPLY ENGINEERING

ENGLISH LITERATURE—BIBLIOGRAPHY.
Publishers' trade list annual. Books in print. **REF Z1215.P972 ECOL**
Publishers' trade list annual. Books in print supplement: authors, titles, subjects. 1972/73- **REF fZ1215.P972 Suppl. ECOL**

ENTEROBACTERIACEAE.
Davis, Ernst M. Bacterial effects of algae on enteric organisms. 1970. **fQR48.D38 ECOL**

ENTROPY.
Georgescu-Roegen, Nicholas. The entropy law and the economic process. 1971. **HB171.G43 ECOL**

ENVIRONMENT *see also* ADAPTATION (BIOLOGY); ANTHROPO-GEOGRAPHY; ECOLOGY; MAN—INFLUENCE OF ENVIRONMENT; MAN—INFLUENCE ON NATURE
Seminar on the Engineer and the Environment University of Minnesota, 1970. The Engineer and the environment. 1971. **GB701.M554no.38 ECOL**

ENVIRONMENT—SOCIETIES, ETC.—DIRECTORIES.
Center for California Public Affairs. Environmental networks. Preliminary ed. 1973. **REF fS920.C4 ECOL**

ENVIRONMENT AND STATE *see* ENVIRONMENTAL POLICY

ENVIRONMENT LAW—BIBLIOGRAPHY.
Radosevich, George E. Water law and its relationship to environmental quality: a bibliography of source material. 1973. **REF fKF5551.R3 ECOL**

ENVIRONMENTAL CONTROL *see* ENVIRONMENTAL POLICY

ENVIRONMENTAL EDUCATION *see* CONSERVATION OF NATURAL RESOURCES—STUDY AND TEACHING; ECOLOGY—STUDY AND TEACHING; HUMAN ECOLOGY—STUDY AND TEACHING

ENVIRONMENTAL ENGINEERING *see also* ENVIRONMENTAL HEALTH; HUMAN ENGINEERING; SANITARY ENGINEERING
American Chemical Society. Committee on Chemistry and Public Welfare. Subcommittee on Environmental Improvement. Cleaning our environment: the chemical basis for action; a report. 1969. **TD180.A4 ECOL**
Black & Veatch, Kansas City, Mo. Environmental report. 1971- **fTK1331.N6B7 ECOL**
Chemical engineering. Environmental engineering, deskbook issue, 1971- **fTA170.C5 ECOL**
Harvard University. Landscape Architecture Research Office. Three approaches to environmental resource analysis. 1967. **fTA170.H3 ECOL**
National Academy of Engineering. Committee on Power Plant Siting. Engineering for resolution of the energy-environment dilemma. 1972. **fTD177.N38 ECOL**
Robinette, Gary O. Plants/people/environmental quality. 1972 . **QK901.R6 ECOL**
Salvato, Joseph A. Environmental engineering and sanitation. 2d ed. 1972 **RA565.S3 1972 ECOL**
Symposium on Environmental Aspects of Nuclear Power Stations, New York, 1970. Environmental aspects of nuclear power stations. 1971. **REF TK9006.S887 1970 ECOL**
United States. Congress. House. Committee on Government Operations. Conservation and Natural Resources Subcommittee. The environmental decade (action proposals for the 1970's). Hearings, Ninety-first Congress, second session. 1970. **KF27.G636 1970a ECOL**

ENVIRONMENTAL ENGINEERING—ADDRESSES, ESSAYS, LECTURES.
The Environmental and ecological forum, 1970-1971. 1972. **TD898.E58 ECOL**
Environmental problems. 1968 **TD180.E48 ECOL**

ENVIRONMENTAL ENGINEERING—BIBLIOGRAPHY.
Schildhauer, Carole. Environmental information sources: engineering and industrial applications. 1972. **REF fZ5863.E57S34 ECOL**

ENVIRONMENTAL ENGINEERING—CONGRESSES.
Emerging methods in environmental design and planning. 1970 **TA170.E46 ECOL**
Environmental control seminar proceedings. 1971. **fTD172.5.E26 ECOL**
Jennings, Burgess Hill. Interactions of man and his environment. 1966. **TD180.J4 ECOL**

ENVIRONMENTAL ENGINEERING—DIRECTORIES.
Environmental Science & Technology. Pollution control directory. 1971/72- **REF fTD180.E52 ECOL**
Halstead, Bruce W. A Golden guide to environmental organizations. 1972 **REF GF5.H34 ECOL**

ENVIRONMENTAL ENGINEERING—STUDY AND TEACHING—UNITED STATES.
The Organic guide to colleges and universities. 1973 **S946.O73 ECOL**

ENVIRONMENTAL ENGINEERING AS A PROFESSION.
Paradis, Adrian A. Reclaiming the earth. 1971 **TA170.P37 ECOL**

ENVIRONMENTAL ENGINEERING (BUILDINGS).
Federal Construction Council. Task Group T-65. Impact of air pollution regulations on fuel selection for federal facilities. 1970. **fKF3812.F4 ECOL**

ENVIRONMENTAL HEALTH *see also* AIR—POLLUTION; ENVIRONMENTAL ENGINEERING; WATER—POLLUTION
Jones, Kenneth Lester. Environmental health. 1971. **RA565.J65 ECOL**
Metallic contaminants and human health. 1972. **RA565.M47 1972 ECOL**
World Health Organization. Health hazards of the human environment. 1972. **RA565.W6 ECOL**

ENVIRONMENTAL HEALTH—ADDRESSES, ESSAYS, LECTURES.
Jefcoat, Allure. Health and human values. 1972 **RA565.J44 ECOL**

ENVIRONMENTAL HEALTH—CONGRESSES.
Environmental mercury contamination. 1972 **RA1231.M5E58 ECOL**
International Water Quality Symposium, 5th, Washington, D.C., 1970. Water pollution and health: proceedings. 1970 **fTD423.I6 1970 ECOL**

ENVIRONMENTAL HEALTH—STUDY AND TEACHING.
Kotsonis, Helen Hoch. Modern lesson plans in environmental science. 1972 **QH541.2.K68 ECOL**

ENVIRONMENTAL HEALTH ENGINEERING *see* SANITARY ENGINEERING

ENVIRONMENTAL LAW *see also* MARINE POLLUTION—LAW AND LEGISLATION
Alexander, Robert M. Social aspects of environmental pollution. 1971. **fTD177.A4 ECOL**
Conference on Legal and Institutional Responses to Problems of the Global Evnironment, Arden House, 1971. Law, institutions, and the global environment. 1972. **KF3775.A75C6 1971 ECOL**

ENVIRONMENTAL LAW—CALIFORNIA.
California. Laws, statutes, etc. Laws relating to the protection of environmental quality, 1970. 1971 **REF KFC610.A3 1970 ECOL**

ENVIRONMENTAL LAW—MINNESOTA.
Minnesota. University. Dept. of Continuing Legal Education. Minnesota environmental law sourcebook. c1973. **REF KFM5754.A45 ECOL**

ENVIRONMENTAL LAW—UNITED STATES.
Association of the Bar of the City of New York. Special Committee on Electric Power and the Environment. Electricity and the environment: the reform of legal institutions. 1972. **KF2125.A97 ECOL**
Brecher, Joseph J. Environmental law handbook. 1970 **REF KF3775.B7 ECOL**
Ditton, Robert B. National environmental policy act of 1969 (P.L. 91-190): bibliography on impact assessment methods and legal considerations. 1973. **Ref fHC110.E5D582 ECOL**
Dworsky, Leonard B. Pollution. 1971. **REF TD174.D95 ECOL**
Environment reporter. 1970- **REF fKF3775.A6E49 ECOL**
Environmental law reporter. v.1- Jan. 1971- **REF fKF3775.A6E5 ECOL.**

Feder, Bernard. A matter of life and breath. c1973 **HC110.E5F4 ECOL**

Grad, Frank P. Environmental control: priorities, policies, and the law. 1971 **HC110.E5G7 ECOL**

Grad, Frank P. Environmental law. 1971- **REF KF3775.A7G73 ECOL**

Landau, Norman J. The environmental law handbook. 1971 **KF3775.L3 ECOL**

Legal control of the environment—3D. 1971 **KF3775.L44 ECOL**

MacDonald, James B. Environmental litigation. 1972. **KF3775.M3 ECOL**

Meyers, Charles J. Selected legal and economic aspects of environmental protection. 1971 **KF3775.A7M58 ECOL**

Murphy, Earl Finbar. Man and his environment: law. 1971. **KF3775.Z9M8 ECOL**

Reitze, Arnold W. Environmental law. 2nd ed. 1972 **fKF3775.R4 1972 ECOL**

Sloan, Irving J. Environment and the law. 1971. **KF3775.Z9S55 ECOL**

United States. Library of Congress. Environmental Policy Division. Congress and the Nation's environment. 1973. **KF3775.A25 1973 ECOL**

ENVIRONMENTAL LAW—UNITED STATES—ADDRESSES, ESSAYS, LECTURES.

Boston College industrial and commercial law review. Recent developments in environmental law. March 1971- **KF3775.A75B6 ECOL**

Conference on Law and the Environment, Warrenton, Va., 1969. Papers. n.d. **fKF3775.A75C58 1969 ECOL**

Environmental law. 1971 **KF3775.A75E54 ECOL**

Environmental law. 1971, c1970 **KF3775.A75E55 ECOL**

National Conference on Environmental Law, San Francisco, 1970. Transcripts of the speeches. 1971 **REF KF3775.A75N3 1970 ECOL**

ENVIRONMENTAL LAW—UNITED STATES—CONGRESSES.

Environmental quality and social responsibility. 1972 **HC110.P55E57 ECOL**

ENVIRONMENTAL MANAGEMENT see ENVIRONMENTAL POLICY

ENVIRONMENTAL POLICY see also
CONSERVATION OF NATURAL RESOURCES; HUMAN ECOLOGY; MAN—INFLUENCE ON NATURE; POLLUTION

Alexander, Robert M. Social aspects of environmental pollution. 1971. **fTD177.A4 ECOL**

Antoniou, Jim. Environmental management planning for traffic. c1971 **fHE333.A57 ECOL**

Ayres, Robert U. Alternatives to the internal combustion engine. 1972 **TL210.A96 ECOL**

Caldwell, Lynton Keith. In defense of earth: international protection of the biosphere. 1972 **HC79.E5C34 ECOL**

Carnegie Endowment for International Peace. Environment and development. 1972c1971 **HC68.C3 1972 ECOL**

Caudill, Harry M. My land is dying. 1st ed. 1971. **TN291.C37 1971 ECOL**

Commission to Study the Organization of Peace. The United Nations and the human environment. 1972 **HC68.C62 ECOL**

Conference on Agriculture's Role in Environmental Quality. University of Illinois, Urbana—Champaign, 1970. Agriculture's role in environmental quality. 1971 **fHC68.C6 1970 ECOL**

Conference on Environmental Quality and Agriculture. University of Illinois, Urbana-Champaign, 1971. Environmental quality and agriculture: what are the options? 1972 **fHC68.C6 1971 ECOL**

Conference on Legal and Institutional Responses to Problems of the Global Evnironment, Arden House, 1971. Law, institutions, and the global environment. 1972. **KF3775.A75C6 1971 ECOL**

Ehler, Charles N. Environmental systems planning and management: a preliminary sorting of literature. 1972 **REF fZ5863.P6E38 ECOL**

Engineering a victory for our environment: a citizen's guide to the U.S. Army Corps of Engineers. c1972. **fTC423.E5 ECOL**

Environmental Control: everyone's concern. 1971 **REF fHC68.E5 ECOL**

Environmental Studies Board. Committee for International Environmental Programs. Institutional arrangements for international environmental cooperation. 1972. **HC79.E5E6 ECOL**

Falk, Richard A. This endangered planet. 1st ed. 1971 **HC79.E5F27 ECOL**

Flowers, William J. Western cultural tradition and human survival: the role of value orientations in the environmental crisis. c1971 **GF80.F5 ECOL**

Gerlach, Luther P. Mobilization and participation of citizens groups in improving the quality of water resources environments. 1973. **GB701.M554no.57 ECOL**

Goldstein, Jerome. How to manage your company ecologically. 1971 **HD69.P6G65 ECOL**

Industrial Development. Site selection handbook, vol.2. 1972. **REF fHC68.I5 1972 ECOL**

INTASA, Inc. Planning and evaluation of multiple purpose water resource projects in a multiobjective environment. 1972. **fHD1691.I1 ECOL**

Isard, Walter. Ecologic-economic analysis for regional development. 1972 **HT391.I82 ECOL**

Jackson, Wes. Man and the environment. 1971 **HC68.J32 ECOL**

Kneese, Allen V. Economics and the environment. 1970 **HC68.K57 ECOL**

Maldonado, Tomas. Design, nature, and revolution. 1st U.S. ed. 1972 **GF41.M3413 1972 ECOL**

Masini, Giancarlo. S.O.S. save our earth. c1972 **fQH541.M382 1972 ECOL**

Millard, Reed. Clean air—clean water for tomorrow's world. 1971 **HC79.E5M5 ECOL**

Murdoch, William W. Environment; resources, pollution & society. 1971 **QH541.M95 ECOL**

National Research Council. Committee on Resources and Man. Resources and man. 1969 **HC68.N36 ECOL**

Perin, Constance. With man in mind. 1970. **HC68.P47 ECOL**

Peterson, Robin. Ecology and the market place. c1971 **HC79.E5P4 ECOL**

Price, Fred C. McGraw-Hill's 1972 report on business and the environment. c1972 **fTD174.P7 ECOL**

Scorer, Richard Segar. Pollution in the air: problems, policies and priorities. 1973 **TD883.S3 ECOL**

Smithsonian Institution. Center for Short-lived Phenomena. National and international environmental monitoring activities. 1970. **REF fTA171.S6 ECOL**

Snowmobile and Off the Road Vehicle Research Symposium, Michigan State University, East Lansing, 1971. Proceedings. 1971. **fGF75.S6 1971 ECOL**

The Teilhard Review. Change or decay: a symposium on the Blueprint for survival. 1972. **HC68.T4 ECOL**

Theobald, Robert. Habit and habitat. 1972 **GF47.T45 ECOL**

Use of systems techniques in environmental quality management. 1970. **RA565.A1N38no.7 ECOL**

Woodrow Wilson International Center for Scholars. Summaries of national reports submitted in preparation for the United Nations Conference on the Human Environment. 1972. **fHC68.W6 ECOL**

ENVIRONMENTAL POLICY—ADDRESSES, ESSAYS, LECTURES.

Carvell, Fred J. It's not too late. 1971 **HC110.E5C36 ECOL**

Day, John A. Dimensions of the environmental crisis. 1971 **HC79.E5D35 ECOL**

Dorfman, Robert. Economics of the environment. 1st ed. 1972 **HC79.P55D65 ECOL**

Gorden, Morton. Environmental management. 1972 **TD177.G67 ECOL**

Jacoby, Neil Herman. The polluters: industry or government? 1972. **TD176.7.J3 ECOL**

Kay, David A. World eco-crisis: international organizations in response. 1972 **HC79.E5K38 ECOL**

Resources for the Future. Environmental quality analysis. 1972 **HC79.E5R46 ECOL**

ENVIRONMENTAL POLICY—ALASKA.
Brown, Tom. Oil on ice. 1971 **HC107.A47E53 ECOL**

ENVIRONMENTAL POLICY—ALASKA—ADDRESSES, ESSAYS, LECTURES.
Alaska Science Conference, 20th, University of Alaska, 1969. Change in Alaska. 1970 **HD9567.A4A64 1969 ECOL**

ENVIRONMENTAL POLICY—BIBLIOGRAPHY.
Dee, Sandra R. A basic environmental collection. 1973. **Ref fZ5863.P6D4 ECOL**

Woodrow Wilson International Center for Scholars. A selective, annotated bibliography of reports and documents on international environmental problems. 1972. **fZ7164.N3W6 ECOL**

ENVIRONMENTAL POLICY—CALIFORNIA.
California. Laws, statutes, etc. Laws relating to the protection of environmental quality, 1970. 1971 **REF KFC610.A3 1970 ECOL**

ENVIRONMENTAL POLICY—CONGRESSES.
A Conversation on population, environment, and human well-being. 1971 **HB875.C63 ECOL**

Environmental side effects of rising industrial output. 1970 **TD174.E58 ECOL**

Managing the environment: international economic cooperation for pollution control. 1971 **HC79.E5M35 1971 ECOL**

Sierra Club Conference on the Electric Power Industry, 1st, Johnson City, Vt., 1972. Report on the first Sierra Club power conference [papers]. 1972? **fHD9685.A2S5 1972 ECOL**

Stockholm and beyond. 1972. **HC110.E5A43 ECOL**

Symposium on Energy, Resources and the Environment, McLean, Va., 1972. Symposium on energy, resources and the environment. 1972. **fHD9540.1.S9 1972 ECOL**

ENVIRONMENTAL POLICY—DELAWARE RIVER BASIN.
Delaware River Basin Commission. Interstate planning for regional water supply and pollution control. 1971. **fTD420.D4 ECOL**

ENVIRONMENTAL POLICY—GREAT BRITAIN.
Arvill, Robert. Man and environment: crisis and the strategy of choice. Revised ed. 1970,c1969 **HC253.5.A7 1970 ECOL**

ENVIRONMENTAL POLICY—HANDBOOKS, MANUALS, ETC.
Hilado, Carlos J. Handbook of environmental management. 1972- **REF fGF75.H5 ECOL**

ENVIRONMENTAL POLICY—HUDSON VALLEY.
Talbot, Allan R. Power along the Hudson. 1st ed. 1972. **HD9685.U7C768 ECOL**

ENVIRONMENTAL POLICY—JAMAICA BAY.
Jamaica Bay Environmental Study Group. Jamaica Bay and Kennedy Airport: a multidisciplinary environmental study. 1971. **fTL725.3.P5J3 ECOL**

ENVIRONMENTAL POLICY—MINNESOTA.
Black & Veatch, Kansas City, Mo. Environmental report. 1971- **fTK1331.N6B7 ECOL**

Brice, William C. Possible environmental impact of base metal mining in Minnesota. 1972 **fTN24.M6B7 ECOL**

Major, Harry M. Activities of the USDA Soil Conservation Service in providing for quality environment for all people in Minnesota. 1972. **HC110.E5M3 ECOL**

Minnesota. Dept. of Natural Resources. Inter-agency task force report on base metal mining impacts. 1973. **fTN24.M6A5 ECOL**

Minnesota. Governor, 1971- Securing a quality environment in Minnesota. 1973? **REF fHC107.M6A35 ECOL**

Minnesota. Governor's Environmental Quality Council. Citizen's Advisory Committee. Environmental quality, policies and decision-making in Minnesota - 1972. 1972. **fHC107.M6A37 ECOL**

Minnesota. State Planning Agency. Environmental decision-making in Minnesota. 1973. **fHC107.M6A43 ECOL**

Minnesota. State Planning Agency. Environmental decision-making in Minnesota: an overview. 1973 **fHC 107.M6A43 1973 ECOL**

Minnesota. State Planning Agency. Protecting the Minnesota environment through regulation of private land use. 1972. **fHC107.M6A45 ECOL**

ENVIRONMENTAL POLICY—NEW ENGLAND.
Power, pollution, and public policy. c1971 **HC107.A113E55 ECOL**

ENVIRONMENTAL POLICY—NEW YORK (STATE).
New York (State) Legislature. Joint Committee on Environmental Management and Natural Resources. The challenge of the seventies. 1971. **fHC107.N7A25 ECOL**

New York (State) Legislature. Joint Committee on Environmental Management and Natural Resources. Report. 197. **fHC107.N7A24 ECOL**

ENVIRONMENTAL POLICY—PERIODICALS.
Environmental Geomorphology Symposium. Environmental geomorphology. **GB400.E58 ECOL**

ENVIRONMENTAL POLICY—RESEARCH see ENVIRONMENTAL POLICY RESEARCH

ENVIRONMENTAL POLICY—SAN FRANCISCO BAY REGION.
Gilliam, Harold. For better or for worse. 1972 **HC107.C22S363 ECOL**

ENVIRONMENTAL POLICY—STUDY AND TEACHING.
McInnis, Noel. You are an environment: teaching/learning environmental attitudes. c1972 **QH541.2.M4 ECOL**

ENVIRONMENTAL POLICY—STUDY AND TEACHING—UNITED STATES.
Environment and the schools. 1971
fHC110.E5E485 ECOL

Thornsjo, Mark. Planning. 1971.
HT166.T5 ECOL

ENVIRONMENTAL POLICY—TWIN CITIES METROPOLITAN AREA.
Minnesota. Metropolitan Council of the Twin Cities Area. Metropolitan development guide. 1973-
REF fHT168.T9A34 ECOL

ENVIRONMENTAL POLICY—UNITED STATES.
Adams, Ruth. Say no! 1971
HC110.E5A63 ECOL

Brown, William Edward. Islands of hope. c1971
HC110.E5B75 ECOL

Caldwell, Lynton Keith. Environment: a challenge for modern society. 1970.
HC110.E5C33 ECOL

Campbell, Rex R. Society and environment: the coming collision. 1972
HC110.E5C35 ECOL

Citizens League, Minneapolis Committee on Environment. Citizens League report. 1971.
fHC110.E5C5 ECOL

Congressional Quarterly Service, Washington, D. C. Man's control of the environment. 1970.
fTD180.C65 ECOL

Council of State Governments. The states' role in land resource management. 1972
HD205.C6 1972 ECOL

Crenson, Matthew A. The un-politics of air pollution: a study of non-decision-making in the cities. 1971
HC110.A4C73 ECOL

Davies, J. Clarence. The politics of pollution. 1970
HC110.E5D35 ECOL

Dworsky, Leonard B. Pollution. 1971.
REF TD174.D95 ECOL

Eber, Ronald. Handbook. 1971 **HC68.E2 ECOL**
The Environment crisis. 1970
TD178.6.E58 ECOL

Environmental Action (Association). Earth tool kit. 1971
HC110.E5E498 ECOL

Fabricant, Neil. Toward a rational power policy: energy, politics, and pollution. 1971
HD9685.U5F32 ECOL

Fadiman, Clifton. Ecocide—and thoughts toward survival. 1971
HC110.E5F32 ECOL

Feder, Bernard. A matter of life and breath. c1973
HC110.E5F4 ECOL

Garvey, Gerald. Energy, ecology, economy. 1st ed. 1972
HC110.E5G35 ECOL

Grad, Frank P. Environmental control: priorities, policies, and the law. 1971.
HC110.E5G7 ECOL

Griffith, Charles J. EP—the new conservation. 1971
HC110.E5G74 ECOL

Guitar, Mary Anne. Property power. 1st ed. 1972.
HD205 1972 .G8 ECOL

Hall, Gus. Ecology: can we survive under capitalism? 1st ed. 1972
HC110.E5H3 ECOL

Harrison, Gordon A. Earthkeeping. 1971.
HC110.E5H33 ECOL

Heady, Earl Orel. Agricultural and water policies and the environment: an analysis of national alternatives in natural resource use, food supply capacity and environmental quality. 1972.
fS441.H4 ECOL

Holdren, John P. Energy. c1971
TJ153.H65 ECOL

Hopkinson, Richard A. Corporate organization for pollution control. c1970
fHC110.E5H6 ECOL

Laycock, George. The diligent destroyers. 1970.
HC110.E5L36 ECOL

McCue, Gerald M. Creating the human environment. 1970
HN59.M22 ECOL

McHarg, Ian L. Design with nature. 1st ed. 1969.
fHC110.E5M33 ECOL

Mid-West Debate Bureau, Normal, Illinois. Control of pollution. 1970
fTD180.M5 ECOL

Myers, Charles B. The environmental crisis: will we survive? 1972
HC110.E5M9 ECOL

Neuhaus, Richard John. In defense of people: ecology and the seduction of radicalism. 1971
HM206.N48 ECOL

The President's 1972 environmental program. 1972.
HC110.E5P74 ECOL

Ridgeway, James. The politics of ecology. 1970.
HC110.E5R52 ECOL

Robinson, John. Highways and our environment. 1971
HE355.R6 ECOL

Rockefeller, Nelson Aldrich. Our environment can be saved. 1st ed. 1970.
HC110.E5R63 ECOL

Rodgers, William H. Brown-out. 1972
HD9684.U62R63 1972 ECOL

Saltonstall, Richard. Your environment and what you can do about it. 1970 **HC110.E5S35 ECOL**

Sanders, Norman K. Stop it! 1972
HC110.E5S36 ECOL

Sax, Joseph L. Defending the environment. 1971.
HC110.E5S3 ECOL

Stacks, John F. Stripping. 1972 **TN291.S7 ECOL**

Stanford Environmental Law Society. Public land management—a time for change? 1971-
fHD216.S7 ECOL

Thompson, Dennis L. Politics, policy, and natural resources. 1972 **HC110.E5T48 ECOL**

Toward an environmental policy. 1971
fHC110.E5T66 ECOL

United States. Advisory Commission on Intergovernmental Relations. The quest for environmental quality. 1971. **HC110.E5A41 ECOL**

United States. Citizens Advisory Committee on Environmental Quality. Community action for environmental quality. 1970 **HC110.E5A5 ECOL**

United States. Citizens' Advisory Committee on Environmental Quality. Report to the President and to the Council on Environmental Quality. 1971.
HC110.E5A514 ECOL

United States. Commission on Population Growth and the American Future. Population, resources, and the environment. 1972 **HB3505.A527 ECOL**

United States. Council on Environmental Quality. Environmental quality. **HC110.E5A52 ECOL**

United States. Environmental Protection Agency. Environmental protection agency. 1972-
fHC68.U5A24 ECOL

United States. National Science Foundation. National Science Board. Environmental science, challenge for the seventies. 1971. **TD185.U5 ECOL**

United States. President's Council on Recreation and Natural Beauty. From sea to shining sea. 1968.
HC110.E5A55 ECOL

United States. Task Force on Off-Road Recreation Vehicles. Off road recreation vehicles: ORRV, a Dept. of the Interior Task Force Study. 1971.
TL234.U5 ECOL

United States. Water Resources Council. Summary, analysis. 1972. **TD345.U52 ECOL**

Wilson, Raymond Harrison. Toward a philosophy of planning: attitudes of federal water planners. 1973.
HC110.E5W5 ECOL

ENVIRONMENTAL POLICY—UNITED STATES—ADDRESSES, ESSAYS, LECTURES.
America's changing environment. 1970.
HC110.E5A56 ECOL

Anderson, Walt. Politics and environment: a reader in ecological crisis. 1970 **HC110.E5A67 ECOL**

Carvell, Fred J. It's not too late. 1971
HC110.E5C36 ECOL

Coastal zone resource management. 1971
HC110.E5C6 ECOL

Congress and the environment. 1970
KF5505.A75C6 ECOL

De Bell, Garrett. The environmental handbook. 1970 **HC110.E5D42 ECOL**

Disch, Robert. The ecological conscience. 1970
HC110.E5D58 ECOL

Earth Day—the beginning. 1970
HC110.E5E2 ECOL

Ecotactics: the Sierra Club handbook for environmental activists. 1970 **HC110.E5E26 ECOL**

Foss, Phillip O. Politics and ecology. 1972
HC110.E5F66 ECOL

Holdren, John P. Global ecology. 1971
HC110.E5H64 ECOL

Novick, Sheldon. Our world in peril. 1971
HC110.P55N67 ECOL

The Quality of the urban environment. 1969
HT169.U5Q33 ECOL

Rathlesberger, James. Nixon and the environment. 1972 **HC110.E5R37 ECOL**

ENVIRONMENTAL POLICY—UNITED STATES—BIBLIOGRAPHY.
Dee, Sandra R. Corporations and the environment: PR or propaganda? 1973 **Ref fZ5863.P6D41 ECOL**

Ditton, Robert B. National environmental policy act of 1969 (P.L. 91-190): bibliography on impact assessment methods and legal considerations. 1973.
Ref fHC110.E5D582 ECOL

Draper, Dianne. Public participation in environmental decision-making. 1973.
fZ5863.P6D7 ECOL

Gunter, John D. The ecological impact of solid waste. 1973. **Ref fZ5863.P6G8 ECOL**

United States. Advisory Commission on Intergovernmental Relations. The quest for environmental quality. 1971. **HC110.E5A41 ECOL**

ENVIRONMENTAL POLICY—UNITED STATES—CONGRESSES.
Conference on Energy, Economics and the Environment, Chicago, Ill., 1968. Energy, economics and the environment: proceedings of a conference sponsored by the Committee on Environment, Edison Electric Institute. 1969. **fHD9540.1.C6 1968 ECOL**

Conference on Environmental Impact Analysis, Green Bay, Wis., 1972. Environmental impact analysis: philosophy & methods. 1972
HC110.E5C65 1972 ECOL

Energy, economic growth, and the environment. 1972 **HD9545.E6 ECOL**

Natural environments: studies in theoretical and applied analysis. 1972 **QH76.N28 ECOL**

Natural Science Center Conference. 8th, Dayton, Ohio, 1970. Leadership to meet our environmental crisis. 1970 **REF fTD178.3.N3 ECOL**

ENVIRONMENTAL POLICY—UNITED STATES—DIRECTORIES.
NFEC directory of environmental information sources. **REF fHC110.E5N4 ECOL**

ENVIRONMENTAL POLICY—UNITED STATES—FINANCE.
United States. Bureau of the Census. Environmental quality control. **REF HC110.E5A26 ECOL**

ENVIRONMENTAL POLICY—UNITED STATES—PERIODICALS.
Energy users report. **REF fHD9540.1.E5 ECOL**

Energy users report. Current reports.
REF fHD9540.1.E5 Suppl. ECOL

Environment reporter.
REF fHC110.E5E49 ECOL

Your government and the environment. v.1- 1971- **REF fHC110.E5Y6 ECOL**

ENVIRONMENTAL POLICY—UNITED STATES—STATES.
Haskell, Elizabeth H. Managing the environment: nine States look for new answers. 1971.
fHC110.E5H35 ECOL

ENVIRONMENTAL POLICY RESEARCH.
Bennett, Dean B. Guidelines for planning and implementing a comprehensive community environmental inventory. Rev. ed. 1972.
fQH541.2.B38 1972 ECOL

ENVIRONMENTAL STUDY AREAS, NATIONAL
see NATIONAL ENVIRONMENTAL STUDY AREAS

ENVIRONMENTAL TESTING.
Ayers, John C. Lake Michigan environmental survey: final report. 1970.
REF fQH543.6.A9 ECOL

Strobbe, Maurice A. Environmental science laboratory manual. 1972. **TA171.S8 ECOL**

ENVIRONMENTAL TESTING—DIRECTORIES.
Smithsonian Institution. Center for Short-lived Phenomena. National and international environmental monitoring activities. 1970. **REF fTA171.S6 ECOL**

ENZYMES.
Wood, John Martin. Enzymes and the environment. 1972 **fQP601.W74 ECOL**

ENZYMES—CONGRESSES.
International IUPAC Congress of Pesticide Chemistry, 2d, Tel-Aviv, 1971. Insecticide resistance, synergism, enzyme induction. c1971
SB951.I56 1971vol.2 ECOL

ENZYMES—TOXICOLOGY.
Brodeur, Paul. Asbestos and enzymes. 1972
RA1231.A8B76 ECOL

EROSION.
Cottam, Walter Pace. Our renewable wild lands, a challenge. 1961. **QK941.U8C6 ECOL**

May, Julian. The land is disappearing. 1972
QE571.M38 1972 ECOL

Osborn, Fairfield. Our plundered planet. 1968
S623.O8 1968 ECOL

EROSION CONTROL see SOIL CONSERVATION

ESTUARIES.
Reid, George K. Ecology of inland waters and estuaries. 1961 **QH96.R43 ECOL**

Stochastics, Inc., Blacksburg, Va. Stochastic modeling for water quality management. 1971.
fTC409.S8 ECOL

Sweet, David C. The economic and social importance of estuaries. 1971. **GB454.E8S95 ECOL**

ESTUARIES—MATHEMATICAL MODELS.
Tracor, Inc. Estuarine modeling: an assessment. 1971. **fTD370.T73 ECOL**

ESTUARINE AREA CONSERVATION.
Wayburn, Peggy. Edge of life. c1972
fQH541.5.E8W3 ECOL

ESTUARINE ECOLOGY.
Steering Committee on Coastal Wastes Management. Wastes management concepts for the coastal zone. 1970. TD763.S7 ECOL
Sweet, David C. The economic and social importance of estuaries. 1971. GB454.E8S95 ECOL
Wayburn, Peggy. Edge of life. c1972
fQH541.5.E8W3 ECOL

ESTUARINE ECOLOGY—BIBLIOGRAPHY.
Sinha, Evelyn. Coastal/estuarine pollution. 1970
REF fZ5853.P7S53 ECOL

ETHICS—ADDRESSES, ESSAYS, LECTURES.
Glass, Hiram Bentley. Science and ethical values. 1965 Q175.G58 ECOL

EUGENICS.
Hardin, Garrett James. Nature and man's fate. 1961
QH361.H25 1961 ECOL
Ingle, Dwight Joyce. Who should have children? 1973 HQ751.I43 ECOL
Ramsey, Paul. Fabricated man. 1970.
HQ751.R33 ECOL

EUTROPHICATION see also WATER—POLLUTION
Allen, Herbert Ellis. Nutrients in natural waters. 1972 QH96.A48 ECOL
Bartsch, A. F. Role of phosphorus in eutrophication. 1972. QH96.8.E9B3 ECOL
Brinkhurst, Ralph O. The role of sludge worms in eutrophication. 1972. QH96.8.E9B7 ECOL
Fitzgerald, George Patrick. Nutrient sources for algae and their control. 1971 i.e.1972
fQH96.8.E9F58 ECOL
Lake Tahoe Area Council. Eutrophication of surface waters—Lake Tahoe Indian Creek Reservoir. 1971.
fTD224.C3L32 ECOL
Morton, Stephen D. The carbon dioxide system and eutrophication. 1971. fQH96.8.E9M6 ECOL
United States. Environmental Protection Agency. Office of Research and Monitoring. The effects of agricultural waste water treatment on algal bioassay response. 1971. QH96.8.E9U54 ECOL

EUTROPHICATION—CALIFORNIA—SANTA CATALINA, GULF OF.
California. University. Institute of Marine Resources. Eutrophication in coastal waters: nitrogen as a controlling factor. 1971. fQH96.8.E9C34 ECOL

EUTROPHICATION—TAHOE, LAKE.
Lake Tahoe Area Council. Eutrophication of surface waters—Lake Tahoe. 1971 i.e. 1972
fQH96.8.E9L34 ECOL

EVA, LAKE, ALASKA—DESCRIPTION AND TRAVEL.
Walker, Theodore J. Red salmon, brown bear. 1971
QH105.A4W36 ECOL

EVAPOTRANSPIRATION.
Arya, Lalit Mohan. Water flow in soil in presence of soybean root sinks. 1973. GB701.M554no.60 ECOL
Hall, Francis R. The influence of a New England wetland on water quantity and quality. 1972.
fTD224.N4H3 ECOL

EVERGLADES, FLORIDA—PICTORIAL WORKS.
Caulfield, Patricia. Everglades. 1970
QH105.F6C36 ECOL

EVERGLADES NATIONAL PARK.
Caulfield, Patricia. Everglades. 1970
QH105.F6C36 ECOL

EVOLUTION.
Eiseley, Loren C. The immense journey. 1957
QH368.E38 ECOL
Krutch, Joseph Wood. The great chain of life. 1957 c1956 QL751.K87 ECOL
Levins, Richard. Evolution in changing environments. 1968. QL752.L4 ECOL
Simpson, George Gaylord. The meaning of evolution. Rev. ed. 1969,c1967
QH366.S58 1969 ECOL
Simpson, George Gaylord. This view of life. 1964
QH369.S5 ECOL

EVOLUTION—ADDRESSES, ESSAYS, LECTURES.
Eiseley, Loren. The firmament of time. 1971 c1960
QH367.E4 1971 ECOL
Hardin, Garrett James. Population, evolution, and birth control. 2d ed. 1969 HB851.H28 1969 ECOL
Hardy, Sir Alister Clavering. The living stream. 1967,c1965 QH367.H2 1967 ECOL
Hoagland, Hudson. Evolution and man's progress. 1962. HM106.H6 ECOL
Hutchinson, George Evelyn. The ecological theater and the evolutionary play. 1965.
QH311.H77 ECOL
Young, Louise B. Evolution of man. 1970.
QH368.Y68 ECOL

EVOLUTION—CONGRESSES.
Peabody Museum Centennial Symposium, Yale University, 1966. Evolution and environment. 1968.
QH366.A1P4 1966 ECOL

EVOLUTION—HISTORY.
Hardin, Garrett James. Nature and man's fate. 1961
QH361.H25 1961 ECOL

EXCHANGE.
Green, James L. Economic ecology. c1969
HT167.G74 ECOL

EXHAUST GAS ANALYSIS see AUTOMOBILE EXHAUST GAS—ANALYSIS

EXPEDITIONS, ANTARCTIC see ANTARCTIC REGIONS

EXPEDITIONS, ARCTIC see ARCTIC REGIONS

EXPERIMENTAL DESIGN.
Bowers, C. Edward. Computer program for statistical analysis of annual flood data by the log-Pearson Type III method. 1971.
GB701.M554no.39 ECOL

EXPRESS HIGHWAYS—DESIGN—TWIN CITIES METROPOLITAN AREA.
Howard, Needles, Tammen & Bergendoff. Interstate 394 corridor location study. 1973?
fTE25.T9H6 ECOL

EXPRESS HIGHWAYS—UNITED STATES.
Leavitt, Helen. Superhighway—superhoax. 1970.
HE355.L4 ECOL
Mowbray, A. Q. Road to ruin. 1969
HE355.M66 ECOL

EXTINCT ANIMALS.
Green, Ivah. Wildlife in danger. 1960
QL151.G7 ECOL
Ziswiler, Vinzenz. Extinct and vanishing animals. Rev. English ed. by Fred and Pille Bunnell. 1967.
QL88.Z513 ECOL

F

FACTORIES—MAINTENANCE AND REPAIR see PLANT MAINTENANCE

FACTORIES—NOISE see INDUSTRIAL NOISE

FACTORY AND TRADE WASTE see also REFUSE AND REFUSE DISPOSAL; WASTE DISPOSAL IN THE OCEAN; WASTE PRODUCTS; WATER—POLLUTION; WATER REUSE
American Foundrymen's Society. Water Pollution Committee. Water pollution from foundry wastes. 1st ed. 1967. fTD899.A45 ECOL
American Public Health Association. Standard methods for the examination of water and waste water, including bottom sediments and sludges. Ed. 13. c1971
REF QD142.A5 1971 ECOL
Armco Steel Corporation. Treatment of waste water-waste oil mixtures. 1970. fTD455.A7 ECOL
Battelle Memorial Institute, Columbus, Ohio Columbus Laboratories An investigation of techniques for removal of chromium from electroplating wastes. 1971. fTD899.M45B3 ECOL
Besselievre, Edmund Bulkley. The treatment of industrial wastes. 1968,c1969
REF TD897.B38 ECOL
Coca-Cola Company. Foods Division. Treatment of citrus processing wastes. 1970. fTD899.F7C6 ECOL
Eckenfelder, William Wesley. Industrial water pollution control. c1966 TD897.E2 ECOL
Industrial pollution control handbook. 1971
REF TD897.I42 ECOL
Kneese, Allen V. Economics and the environment. 1970 HC68.K57 ECOL
Love, Sam. Ecotage. 1972 TD175.L68 ECOL
National Oil Recovery Corp., Bayonne, N.J. Conversion of crankcase waste oil into useful products. 1971. fTP687.N3 ECOL
Ross, Richard D. Industrial waste disposal. 1968
TD897.R67 ECOL
Roy F. Weston, Inc. Concept evaluation report: taconite tailings disposal, Reserve Mining Company, Silver Bay, Minnesota. 1971 fTD899.T35 ECOL
Ulrich, Stanley. Superior pollutor: a saga of the struggle to stop pollution of the largest fresh water lake in the world by its most egregious polluter—the Reserve Mining Company. 1972. TD224.M6U6 ECOL
Western Plant Engineering and Maintenance Conference, San Francisco, 1970 Proceedings. 1970.
fTS184.W4

FACTORY AND TRADE WASTE—CONGRESSES.
Environmental side effects of rising industrial output. 1970 TD174.E58 ECOL
Industry/Government Teleconference on Pollution Control, 1971. NAM: a voice for American industry. 1971 fTD172.5.153 1971 ECOL
North Eastern Regional Antipollution Conference, 4th, University of Rhode Island, 1971. Recent developments in industrial pollution control. 1971
fTD896.N67 1971 ECOL
Ontario Industrial Waste Conference. Listing of papers, 1954/70-
REF fTD897.O6 Suppl. ECOL
Ontario Industrial Waste Conference. Papers presented. 1st- 1954-
REF fTD897.O6 ECOL
Symposium on Mineral Waste Utilization. Proceedings. 1st- 1968-
fTP995.A1S9 ECOL

FACTORY AND TRADE WASTE—MISSISSIPPI RIVER VALLEY.
United States. Federal Water Pollution Control Administration. Great Lakes Region. A report on pollution of the Upper Mississippi River and major tributaries. 1966. TD225.M5U5 ECOL
United States. Federal Water Pollution Control Administration. Twin Cities Upper Mississippi River Project. Report on water quality investigations of the Mississippi, Minnesota and St. Croix Rivers. 1966
REF fTD225.T9U5 ECOL

FACTORY AND TRADE WASTE—RESEARCH.
Gainesville, Fla. Dept. of Public Utilities. Magnesium carbonate, a recycled coagulant for water treatment. 1971. fTD433.G3 ECOL

FACTORY AND TRADE WASTE—RESEARCH—MATHEMATICAL MODELS.
Synectics Corporation. A system for industrial waste treatment RD&D project priority assignment. 1971.
fTD897.5.S9 ECOL

FACTORY AND TRADE WASTE—RESEARCH—UNITED STATES.
Elliott, Ralph D. The effects of sewer surcharges on the level of industrial wastes and the use of water by industry. 1972. TD897.5.E4 ECOL
United States. Environmental Protection Agency. Industrial Pollution Control Branch. Projects of the Industrial Pollution Control Branch. 1971.
fTD897.5.U54 ECOL
United States. Federal Water Quality Administration. Projects: Industrial Pollution Control Branch. 1970. fTD897.5.U56 ECOL

FACTORY AND TRADE WASTE—TEXAS.
Texas Christian University, Fort Worth. Dept. of Biology. Industrial wastes: effects on Trinity River ecology, Fort Worth, Texas. 1971 i.e. 1972
fTD224.T4T4 ECOL

FACTORY AND TRADE WASTE—UNITED STATES.
Buggie, Frederick D. Toward effective and equitable pollution control regulation. 1972
fHC110.P55B8 ECOL
Smith, David D. Ocean disposal of barge-delivered liquid and solid wastes from United States coastal cities. 1971. TD796.7.O25S4 ECOL

FACTORY AND TRADE WASTE—UNITED STATES—CONGRESSES.
National Symposium on Food Processing Wastes, 1st, Portland, Or., 1970. Proceedings. 1971
fTD899.F585N37 1970 ECOL

FACTORY WASTE see FACTORY AND TRADE WASTE

FAMILY PLANNING see BIRTH CONTROL

FARGO, N.D.—FLOODS.
United States. Army. Corps of Engineers. Flood plain information. 1972. GB1227.R4A52 ECOL

FARM LIFE.
Langer, Richard W. Grow it! 1972
S501.L27 1972 ECOL

FARM LIFE—UNITED STATES—HISTORY.
Greenberg, David Benjamin. Land that our fathers plowed. 1969 S521.G83 ECOL

FARM MANAGEMENT—UNITED STATES.
Angier, Bradford. One acre and security-how to live off the earth without ruining it. 1972
S561.A574 ECOL

FARM MANURE.
Michigan. State University, East Lansing. Agricultural Pollution Control Laboratory. Closed system waste management for livestock. 1971 i.e. 1972
fTD899.F4M5 ECOL

FARMS.
McCue, George. Ecology: the farm. c1971
    QH541.5.F3M22 ECOL

FAST REACTOR.
Graham, John. Fast reactor safety. 1971.
    TK9152.G68 ECOL

FEDERAL AID TO TRANSPORTATION—MINNESOTA.
Minnesota. State Planning Agency. State of Minnesota narrative report for the 1972 National Transportation Needs Study. 1971.
    REF fTA1123.M5 ECOL

FEED-WATER PURIFICATION.
McCoy, James W. Chemical analysis of industrial water. 1969.   **TD380.M3 ECOL**

FEEDLOTS.
Robert S. Kerr Water Research Center. Characteristics of rainfall run off from a beef cattle feedlot. 1972.   **TD899.F4R6 ECOL**

FEEDLOTS—SOUTHWEST, NEW.
Texas Tech University. Water Resources Center. Characteristics of wastes from southwestern cattle feedlots. 1971.   **fTD899.F4T497 ECOL**

FEEDLOTS—TEXAS.
Texas Tech University. Dept. of Geosciences. Infiltration rates and groundwater quality beneath cattle feedlots, Texas High Plains. 1971
    fTD899.F4T48 ECOL

FEEDLOTS—WASTE DISPOSAL.
Michigan. State University, East Lansing. Agricultural Pollution Control Laboratory. Closed system waste management for livestock. 1971 i.e. 1972
    fTD899.F4M5 ECOL

FERMENTATION see also ENZYMES
Callihan, Clayton Dale. Construction of a chemical-microbial pilot plant for production of single-cell protein from cellulosic wastes. 1971.
    TP996.B3C3 ECOL

FERROUS SALTS.
Ghassemi, Masood. Phosphate precipitation with ferrous iron. 1971.   **fTD751.G4 ECOL**

FERTILIZER INDUSTRY—WASTE DISPOSAL.
Battelle-Northwest. Inorganic fertilizer and phosphate mining industries—water pollution and control. 1971.   **fTD899.F47B38 ECOL**

FERTILIZERS AND MANURES.
Johnson, Jack D. Development of a mathematical model to predict the role of surface runoff and groundwater flow in over fertilization of surface waters. 1971.   **GB701.M554no.35 ECOL**

Minnesota. University. Agricultural Extension Service. Soils, soil management and fertilizer monographs. 1973.   **fS591.M68 ECOL**

Pratt, P. F. Nitrate in the unsaturated zone under agricultural lands. 1972.   **fS651.P7 ECOL**

Slack, Archie Vivian. Defense against famine. 1st ed. 1970.   **S633.S627 ECOL**

FERTILIZERS AND MANURES IN FORESTRY
see FOREST SOILS—FERTILIZATION

FETUS, EFFECT OF RADIATION ON.
Hull, Andrew P. Sternglass: a case history. 1972?
    REF fRA569.H8 ECOL

FIBERS.
Uniroyal, Inc. Feasibility study of regenerative fibers for water pollution control. 1970 i.e. 1971
    fTD757.5.U55 ECOL

FIELD CROPS.
Faulkner, Edward Hubert. Soil development. 1952
    S603.F37 ECOL

FILLS, SANITARY see SANITARY LANDFILLS

FILTERS AND FILTRATION.
Dow Chemical Company. Functional Products and Systems Dept. A literature search and critical analysis of biological trickling filter studies. 1971-
    fTD443.D6 ECOL

FIRE ISLAND, NEW YORK.
Rabkin, Richard. Fire Island. 1971
    fQH105.N7R3 ECOL

FISH CONTROL—GREAT LAKES.
Great Lakes Basin Commission. Fish Work Group. Analysis of fishery programs and review of current plans for the management of fishery resources of the Great Lakes. 1969.   **SH36.G76 ECOL**

FISH CULTURE.
New York (State). State University College, Buffalo. Great Lakes Laboratory. Fish protein concentrate. 1970.   **fSH333.F5 ECOL**

United States. Environmental Protection Agency. Induced aeration of small mountain lakes. 1970.
    fSH167.T86U5 ECOL

FISH FLOUR see FISH PROTEIN CONCENTRATE

FISH PROTEIN CONCENTRATE.
New York (State). State University College, Buffalo. Great Lakes Laboratory. Fish protein concentrate. 1970.   **fSH333.F5 ECOL**

FISHERIES see also FISH CULTURE; FISHERY MANAGEMENT; FISHES
National Marine Fisheries Service. Our changing fisheries. 1971   **REF SH331.N38 ECOL**

FISHERIES—BY-PRODUCTS.
Cresa. Pollution abatement and by-product recovery in shellfish and fisheries processing. 1971.
    fTD899.F57C73 ECOL

FISHERIES—CALIFORNIA—HANDBOOKS, MANUALS, ETC.
Calhoun, Alex. Inland fisheries management. 1966.
    fSH222.C2C3 ECOL

FISHERIES—DICTIONARIES.
Firth, Frank E. The encyclopedia of marine resources. 1969   **REF SH201.F56 ECOL**

FISHERIES—MINNESOTA.
Dobie, John. Methods used for investigating productivity of fish-rearing ponds in Minnesota. Rev. 1962.   **SH222.M6D6 1962 ECOL**

FISHERIES—RESEARCH.
National Marine Fisheries Service. Our changing fisheries. 1971   **REF SH331.N38 ECOL**

FISHERIES—RESEARCH—CANADA.
Canada. Fisheries Research Board. Review. 1965/66-   **SH223.C3 ECOL**

FISHERIES—UNITED STATES.
Neal, Harry Edward. Nature's guardians. 1966,c1963   **SK361.N45 1966 ECOL**

FISHERY LAW AND LEGISLATION—MINNESOTA.
Minnesota. Laws, statutes, etc. Laws relating to game and fish, 1971/72-
    REF KFM5853.A44 ECOL

FISHERY MANAGEMENT.
Mills, Derek Henry. Salmon and trout: a resource, its ecology, conservation, and management. 1971
    QL638.S2M5 1971b ECOL

FISHERY MANAGEMENT—GREAT LAKES.
Great Lakes Basin Commission. Fish Work Group. Analysis of fishery programs and review of current plans for the management of fishery resources of the Great Lakes. 1969.   **SH36.G76 ECOL**

FISHERY PROCESSING INDUSTRIES—WASTE DISPOSAL.
Cresa. Pollution abatement and by-product recovery in shellfish and fisheries processing. 1971.
    fTD899.F57C73 ECOL

FISHES.
Dalrymple, Byron W. Sportsman's guide to game fish. 1968   **QL617.D34 ECOL**

Michigan. Bureau of Water Management. Chlorinated municipal waste toxicities to rainbow trout and fathead minnows. 1971.   **fTD763.M5 ECOL**

FISHES—ALASKA.
Dufresne, Frank. Alaska's animals & fishes. c1946
    QL628.A4D8 1946 ECOL

FISHES—MIGRATION.
Washington (State). University. Fisheries Research Institute. Responses of teleost fish to environmental stress. 1971.   **fQL639.1.W3 ECOL**

FISHES—NORTH AMERICA.
Herald, Earl Stannard. Fishes of North America. A Chanticleer Press ed. 1972   **QL635.H47 ECOL**

FISHES—PHYSIOLOGY.
Washington (State). University. Fisheries Research Institute. Responses of teleost fish to environmental stress. 1971.   **fQL639.1.W3 ECOL**

FISHES, EFFECT OF WATER POLLUTION ON
see also WATER—POLLUTION
California. University, Santa Barbara. Dept. of Biological Sciences. Santa Barbara oil spill: short-term analysis of macroplankton and fish. 1971.
    fTD427.P4C34 ECOL

Chesher, Richard H. Biological impact of a large-scale desalination plant at Key West. 1971.
    fTD478.5.F5C48 ECOL

FISHING.
Dalrymple, Byron W. Sportsman's guide to game fish. 1968   **QL617.D34 ECOL**

FISHING—NORTH AMERICA.
Cramond, Michael. Hunting & fishing in North America. c1953   **SK40.C67 ECOL**

FISHING—UNITED STATES.
Brings, Lawrence Martin. Outdoor horizons. c1957
    fSK33.B83 ECOL

FISHING—UNITED STATES—STATISTICS.
United States. Bureau of Sport Fisheries and Wildlife. National survey of fishing and hunting, 1970-
    REF S914.A3no.95 ECOL

FISSIONABLE MATERIALS see RADIOACTIVE SUBSTANCES

FLAMINGOS.
Allen, Robert Porter. On the trail of vanishing birds. 1957   **QL696.G8A4 ECOL**

FLATS see APARTMENT HOUSES

FLIGHT.
Aymar, Gordon Christian. Bird flight. 1935.
    QL698.A9 ECOL

FLOCCULATION see also COAGULATION
Freese, Paul V. Full-scale raw wastewater flocculation with polymers. 1970. **fTD751.F7 ECOL**

Stenquist, Richard J. Initial mixing in coagulation processes. 1972.   **TD455.S7 ECOL**

FLOCCULATION—PATENTS.
Gutcho, Sidney. Waste treatment with polyelectrolytes, 1972.   **TD751.G87 ECOL**

FLOOD CONTROL see FLOOD DAMAGE PREVENTION; RIVERS—REGULATION

FLOOD CONTROL—FINANCE.
Hopeman, Alan Roswell. An economic analysis of flood damage reduction alternatives in the Minnesota River Basin. 1973.   **GB701.M554no.58 ECOL**

Mathematica, Inc., Bethesda, Md. The implications of the net fiscal benefits criterion for cost sharing in flood control projects. 1971.   **TC530.M3 ECOL**

FLOOD CONTROL—LAW AND LEGISLATION—UNITED STATES.
United States. Water Resources Council. Regulation of flood hazard areas to reduce flood losses. 1971-
    KF5588.A875 ECOL

FLOOD CONTROL—MINNESOTA—BLUE EARTH RIVER WATERSHED.
United States. Army. Corps of Engineers. Interim survey report on Blue Earth River, Minnesota, Minnesota River Basin for flood control and related purposes. 1970?   **Ref fTC424.M6A5 ECOL**

FLOOD CONTROL—MINNESOTA—CANBY CREEK WATERSHED.
United States. Soil Conservation Service. Flood hazard analyses: city of Canby and vicinity, Yellow Medicine County, Minnesota. 1973.
    GB1225.M6U5 ECOL

FLOOD CONTROL—MINNESOTA—MINNESOTA RIVER WATERSHED.
Itasca Engineering, Inc., Minneapolis. The effectiveness of flood control structures of the Lower Minnesota River Watershed District. 1970.
    fTC424.M6I82 ECOL

FLOOD CONTROL—MINNESOTA—NINE MILE CREEK WATERSHED.
Barr, Douglas W. Over-all plan for Nine Mile Creek Watershed District. 1961.   **fTC424.M6B36 ECOL**

Barr Engineering Co. Feasibility study: Mt. Normandale Lake and Marsh Lake, for City of Bloomington and Nine Mile Creek Watershed District. 1967.   **fTC424.M6B32 ECOL**

Barr Engineering Company. Nine Mile Creek Watershed District. 1973.   **fTC424.M6B362 ECOL**

FLOOD CONTROL—UNITED STATES.
Murphy, Francis C. Regulating flood-plain development. 1958.   **TC530.M8 ECOL**

FLOOD DAMAGE PREVENTION.
Sheaffer, John Richard. Flood proofing. 1960.
    TC530.S4 ECOL

FLOOD DAMAGE PREVENTION—IOWA—CONGRESSES.
Conference on Flood Plain Management, Iowa State University, 1968. Flood plain management, Iowa's experience. 1st ed. 1969   **TC424.I8C6 1968 ECOL**

FLOOD DAMAGE PREVENTION—MINNESOTA.
Pabst, Arthur F. Flood forecasting in the Upper Midwest: data assembly and preliminary analysis. 1972.   **fGB678.P32 ECOL**

FLOOD DAMAGE PREVENTION—MINNESOTA RIVER BASIN.
Hopeman, Alan Roswell. An economic analysis of flood damage reduction alternatives in the Minnesota River Basin. 1973.   **GB701.M554no.58 ECOL**

FLOOD FORECASTING.
Pabst, Arthur F. Flood forecasting in the Upper Midwest: data assembly and preliminary analysis. 1972.   **fGB678.P32 ECOL**

Rice, Charles E. Methods for routing hydrographs through open channels. 1972.
    GB701.M554no.51 ECOL

FLOODPLAINS—MINNESOTA—ST. LOUIS PARK.
St. Louis Park, Minn. City Attorney's Office. City attorney's report, re: flood plain management. 1969
    fTC425.S3A5 ECOL

FLOODPLAINS—MINNESOTA—WINDOM.
United States. Army. Corps of Engineers. W. Fork Des Moines River and Perkins Creek flood plain information, Windom, Minnesota. 1972.
GB1225.M6A5 ECOL

FLOODPLAINS—RED RIVER OF THE NORTH WATERSHED.
United States. Army. Corps of Engineers. Flood plain information. 1972. GB1227.R4A52 ECOL
United States. Army. Corps of Engineers. Flood plain information on the Red River of the North in the vicinity of Grand Forks, North Dakota—East Grand Forks, Minnesota. 1971. GB1227.R4A5 ECOL

FLOODPLAINS—WISCONSIN.
Workshop on Hydrologic and Hydraulic Aspects of Flood Plain Construction, Madison, Wisc., 1968. Proceedings. 1968? fGB1225.W6W6 1968 ECOL

FLOODS.
Bowers, C. Edward. Computer program for statistical analysis of annual flood data by the log-Pearson Type III method. 1971.
GB701.M554no.39 ECOL

FLOODS—ADDRESSES, ESSAYS, LECTURES.
White, Gilbert Fowler. Papers on flood problems. 1961. TC530.W4 ECOL

FLOODS—MINNESOTA.
Pabst, Arthur F. Flood forecasting in the Upper Midwest: data assembly and preliminary analysis. 1972. fGB678.P32 ECOL

FLOODS—MINNESOTA—YELLOW MEDICINE COUNTY.
United States. Soil Conservation Service. Flood hazard analyses: city of Canby and vicinity, Yellow Medicine County, Minnesota. 1973.
GB1225.M6U5 ECOL

FLOODS—VIRGINIA—BEAVER CREEK WATERSHED.
Sheaffer, John Richard. Flood proofing. 1960.
TC530.S4 ECOL

FLOW, GROUNDWATER *see* GROUNDWATER FLOW

FLOW MEASUREMENT *see* FLOW METERS

FLOW METERS.
Battelle Memorial Institute. Columbus, Ohio. Columbus Laboratories Multidirectional turbulence probe development. fTC177.B3 ECOL

FLUID BED PROCESSES *see* FLUIDIZATION

FLUID MECHANICS.
California. University. Flow into a stratified reservoir. 1972. TC167.C3 ECOL
Campbell, J. F. Analysis of the injection of a heated turbulent jet into a moving mainstream, with emphasis on a thermal discharge in a waterway. 1972.
fTD427.H4C3 ECOL

FLUID METERS *see* FLOW METERS

FLUIDIZATION.
Mandan Refinery. Fluid bed incineration of petroleum refinery wastes. 1971.
fTD899.P4M35 ECOL

FLUVIAL SEDIMENT TRANSPORT *see* SEDIMENT TRANSPORT

FOAM FRACTIONATION (WATER PURIFICATION) *see* WATER—PURIFICATION—FOAM FRACTIONATION

FOOD.
Pyke, Magnus. Man and food. 1970
TX355.P9 ECOL

FOOD—IRRADIATION *see* RADIATION PRESERVATION OF FOOD

FOOD ADDITIVES.
National Research Council. Food Protection Committee. Chemicals used in food processing. 1965.
REF fTX553.A3N26 ECOL

FOOD ADDITIVES—UNITED STATES.
Wellford, Harrison. Sowing the wind. 1972.
HD9000.9.U5W4 ECOL

FOOD ADULTERATION AND INSPECTION.
Jones, Claire. Pollution: the food we eat. 1972
TX533.J65 ECOL
Marine, Gene. Food pollution. 1st. ed. 1972
TX533.M37 ECOL
Winter, Ruth. Poisons in your food. 1969
TX533.W55 1969 ECOL

FOOD ADULTERATION AND INSPECTION—UNITED STATES.
Turner, James S. The chemical feast. 1970.
HD9000.9.U5T83 ECOL
Wellford, Harrison. Sowing the wind. 1972.
HD9000.9.U5W4 ECOL

FOOD CONTAMINATION.
Jones, Claire. Pollution: the food we eat. 1972
TX533.J65 ECOL

Marine, Gene. Food pollution. 1st. ed. 1972
TX533.M37 ECOL
Toxicants occurring naturally in foods. 1966.
TX531.T6 ECOL
Winter, Ruth. Poisons in your food. 1969
TX533.W55 1969 ECOL

FOOD CONTROL *see* FOOD SUPPLY

FOOD INDUSTRY AND TRADE *see also* FOOD ADDITIVES; FOOD SUPPLY
Pyke, Magnus. Man and food. 1970
TX355.P9 ECOL

FOOD INDUSTRY AND TRADE—GREAT BRITAIN.
Barr, John. The assaults on our senses. 1970.
QH77.G7B29 ECOL

FOOD INDUSTRY AND TRADE—UNITED STATES—CONGRESSES.
National Symposium on Food Processing Wastes, 1st, Portland, Or., 1970. Proceedings. 1971
fTD899.F585N37 1970 ECOL

FOOD INDUSTRY AND TRADE—WASTE DISPOSAL—CONGRESSES.
National Symposium on Food Processing Wastes, 2d, Denver, 1971. Proceedings. 1971
fTD899.F585N37 1971 ECOL
National Symposium on Food Processing Wastes, 3d, New Orleans, 1972. Proceedings. 1972.
fTD899.F585N37 1972 ECOL

FOOD POISONING.
Toxicants occurring naturally in foods. 1966.
TX531.T6 ECOL

FOOD SUPPLY *see also* FOOD INDUSTRY AND TRADE
Borgstrom, George. Harvesting the earth. 1973
HD9000.5.B56 1973 ECOL
Borgstrom, George. The hungry planet. Rev. ed. 1967 HD9000.5.B54 1967 ECOL
Borgstrom, George. The hungry planet. 2nd rev. ed. 1972 HD9000.5.B54 1972 ECOL
Brown, Lester Russell. Man and his environment: food. 1972 S439.B76 ECOL
Brown, Lester Russell. Seeds of change. 1970
HD9000.5.B73 ECOL
Cochrane, Willard Wesley. The world food problem. 1969 HD9000.5.C59 ECOL
Dumont, Rene. The hungry future. 1969
HD1445.D823 ECOL
Jones, Claire. Pollution: the population explosion. 1972 HB871.J58 ECOL
Katz, Robert. A giant in the earth. c1973
HD9000.5.K3 ECOL
Paddock, William. Famine, 1975! c1967
HD9000.5.P22 ECOL
Pirie, N. W. Food resources, conventional and novel. 1969 S439.P5 ECOL
Sax, Karl. Standing room only. New ed. 1969,c1960
HB881.S33 1969 ECOL

FOOD SUPPLY—ADDRESSES, ESSAYS, LECTURES.
Mead, Margaret. Hunger. 1970
fHD9000.5.M37 ECOL
Slater, Sir William Kershaw. Man must eat. 1964
TX355.S63 ECOL

FOOD SUPPLY—CONGRESSES.
Prospects of the world food supply. 1966.
fS439.P7 1966 ECOL

FOOD SUPPLY—UNITED STATES.
Heady, Earl Orel. Agricultural and water policies and the environment: an analysis of national alternatives in natural resource use, food supply capacity and environmental quality. 1972.
fS441.H4 ECOL

FOOD TRADE *see* FOOD INDUSTRY AND TRADE

FORCE AND ENERGY.
Harrison, George Russell. The first book of energy. 1965 QC73.H3 ECOL
Odum, Howard T. Environment, power, and society. 1970,c1971 QH541.O33 ECOL

FORCE AND ENERGY—ADDRESSES, ESSAYS, LECTURES.
Energy and power. c1971 TJ153.E478 ECOL

FOREST CLEARCUTTING *see* CLEAR-CUTTING

FOREST CONSERVATION *see* FOREST RESERVES

FOREST CONSERVATION—CALIFORNIA.
Leydet, Francois. The last redwoods, and the parkland of Redwood Creek. 1969
SD397.R3L4 ECOL

FOREST CONSERVATION—NORTHWEST, PACIFIC—CONGRESSES.
Current Issues Conference, 1st, Portland, Or., 1972. Timber supply and the environment. 1972
SD144.A13C87 1972 ECOL

FOREST CONSERVATION—UNITED STATES.
Frome, Michael. The Forest Service. 1971
SD565.F7 ECOL

FOREST ECOLOGY.
Brown, Vinson. Reading the woods. 1969
QH541.5.F6B73 ECOL
Collins, Patricia. Chain of life. 1st ed. 1972
QH541.5.F6C64 ECOL
Kane, Henry Bugbee. The tale of a wood. 1962
QH86.K3 ECOL
Ketchum, Richard M. The secret life of the forest. 1970 fQK938.F6K4 ECOL
May, Julian. The mysterious evergreen forest. 1972
QH541.5.F6M39 ECOL
McCormick, Jack. The life of the forest. 1966
QK938.F6M19 ECOL
McCormick, Jack. The living forest. c1959
QK938.F6M2 ECOL
McCue, George. Ecology: the forests and man. c1971 QH541.5.F6M22 ECOL
Ohmann, Lewis F. Wilderness ecology, virgin plant communities of the Boundary Waters Canoe Area. 1971. SD11.A45476no.63 ECOL
Ross, Wilda S. Who lives in this log? 1971
PZ10.R7244Wh ECOL
Schwartz, George I. Life in a log. 1972
QH541.5.F6S39 ECOL

FOREST ECOLOGY—MINNESOTA.
Wanek, Wallace J. A study of the impact of snowmobiling on northern Minnesota ecology. 1971
fTL234.W3 ECOL

FOREST ECOLOGY—NORTH AMERICA.
May, Julian. The mysterious evergreen forest. 1972
QH541.5.F6M39 ECOL

FOREST ECOLOGY—PICTORIAL WORKS.
Atwood, Ann. The kingdom of the forest. 1972
QH541.5.F6A88 ECOL

FOREST FERTILIZATION *see* FOREST SOILS—FERTILIZATION

FOREST FLORA *see* FORESTS AND FORESTRY

FOREST INSECTS—CONTROL—CONGRESSES.
Northeastern Forest Insect Work Conference, 3rd. New Haven, 1970. Toward integrated control. 1971.
SD11.A455492no.194 ECOL

FOREST MANAGEMENT.
Groman, William A. Forest fertilization (a state-of-the-art review and description of environmental effects). 1972. SD408.G7 ECOL
Neal, Harry Edward. Nature's guardians. 1966,c1963 SK361.N45 1966 ECOL

FOREST PLANTING *see* FORESTS AND FORESTRY

FOREST POLICY.
Worrell, Albert Cadwallader. Principles of forest policy. 1970 SD565.W67 ECOL

FOREST PRODUCTS—UNITED STATES.
Gregory, G. Robinson. Forest resource economics. 1972 HD9755.G7 ECOL

FOREST RESERVES *see also* FORESTS AND FORESTRY; NATIONAL PARKS AND RESERVES; WILDERNESS AREAS
Brockman, Christian Frank. Recreational use of wild lands. 1959. SB481.B66 ECOL

FOREST RESERVES—MINNESOTA.
Fisher, Wes. Minnesota environmental education areas. 1972 fS946.F5 ECOL

FOREST RESERVES—UNITED STATES.
Wood, Frances Elizabeth. Forests are for people. 1971 SD565.W66 ECOL

FOREST RESERVES—UNITED STATES—RECREATIONAL USES—CONGRESSES.
Forest Recreation Symposium, Syracuse, N.Y., 1971. 1971. SD426.F6 1971 ECOL

FOREST SOILS.
Thorud, David B. Freezing in forest soil as influenced by soil properties, litter, and snow. 1969.
GB701.M554no.10 ECOL

FOREST SOILS—FERTILIZATION.
Groman, William A. Forest fertilization (a state-of-the-art review and description of environmental effects). 1972. SD408.G7 ECOL

FORESTATION *see* FORESTS AND FORESTRY

FORESTERS—UNITED STATES.
Kaufman, Herbert. The Forest ranger. 1960
SD565.K3 ECOL

FORESTRY AS A PROFESSION—UNITED STATES.
Tucker, Edwin A. Men who matched the mountains. 1972. **SD143.T8 ECOL**

FORESTRY LAW AND LEGISLATION—MINNESOTA.
Minnesota. Laws, statutes, etc. Forest laws. 1968. **REF KFM5649.A45 1968 ECOL**

FORESTS AND FORESTRY see also TREES
Clepper, Henry Edward. The world of the forest. **SD131.C55 ECOL**

Guest, Stephen Haden. A world geography of forest resources. 1956 **REF SD131.G8 ECOL**

May, Julian. Forests that change color. 1972 **SD373.M38 1972 ECOL**

May, Julian. The mysterious evergreen forest. 1972 **QH541.5.F6M39 ECOL**

Moore, Alma (Chestnut). The friendly forests. 1963 **SD373.M76 1963 ECOL**

FORESTS AND FORESTRY—ECONOMIC ASPECTS—NORTHWEST, PACIFIC—CONGRESSES.
Current Issues Conference, 1st, Portland, Or., 1972. Timber supply and the environment. 1972 **SD144.A13C87 1972 ECOL**

FORESTS AND FORESTRY—ECONOMIC ASPECTS—UNITED STATES.
Gregory, G. Robinson. Forest resource economics. 1972 **HD9755.G7 ECOL**

Resources for the Future. Forest credit in the United States: a survey of needs and facilities. 1958. **HG2051.U5R4 ECOL**

FORESTS AND FORESTRY—NORTH AMERICA.
Clepper, Henry Edward. The world of the forest. **SD131.C55 ECOL**

May, Julian. Forests that change color. 1972 **SD373.M38 1972 ECOL**

May, Julian. The mysterious evergreen forest. 1972 **QH541.5.F6M39 ECOL**

Moore, Alma (Chestnut). The friendly forests. 1963 **SD373.M76 1963 ECOL**

Platt, Rutherford Hayes. The great American forest. 1971,c1965 **SD140.P55 1971 ECOL**

FORESTS AND FORESTRY—UNITED STATES.
Cameron, Jenks. The development of governmental forest control in the United States. 1972. **SD565.C3 1972 ECOL**

Greeley, William Buckhout. Forests and men. 1951. **SD143.G74 ECOL**

Jepsen, Stanley M. Trees and forests. 1969 **SD143.J39 ECOL**

Ketchum, Richard M. The secret life of the forest. 1970 **fQK938.F6K4 ECOL**

McCormick, Jack. The life of the forest. 1966 **QK938.F6M19 ECOL**

McCormick, Jack. The living forest. c1959 **QK938.F6M2 ECOL**

FORESTS AND FORESTRY—UNITED STATES—HISTORY.
Clepper, Henry Edward. Professional forestry in the United States. 1971 **SD143.C56 ECOL**

Tucker, Edwin A. Men who matched the mountains. 1972. **SD143.T8 ECOL**

FORESTS AND FORESTRY—THE WEST.
Guthrie, John Alexander. Western forest industry. 1961 **HD9755.G8 ECOL**

FOUNDARIES.
American Foundrymen's Society. Water Pollution Committee. Water pollution from foundry wastes. 1st ed. 1967. **fTD899.A45 ECOL**

FPC see FISH PROTEIN CONCENTRATE

FRAUD—UNITED STATES.
Paulson, Morton C. The great land hustle. 1972 **HD255.P38 ECOL**

FREE SCHOOLS.
Educational Facilities Laboratories. Places and things for experimental schools. 1972 **Ref LB3221.E3 ECOL**

FREEDOM OF INFORMATION—UNITED STATES.
Barker, Carol M. Classified files: the yellowing pages. 1972. **JK468.S4B35ECOL**

FREEZE-DRYING.
Milwaukee. Sewerage Commission. Evaluation of conditioning and dewatering sewage sludge by freezing. 1971. **fTD769.7.M54 ECOL**

FRESH-WATER BIOLOGY.
Coker, Robert Ervin. Streams, lakes, ponds. 1954 **QH96.C6 ECOL**

Hynes, Hugh Bernard Noel. The biology of polluted waters. 1971c1960 **QH96.H9 1971 ECOL**

Hynes, Hugh Bernard Noel. The ecology of running waters. 1970. **QH541.5.S7H9 ECOL**

Needham, James George. A guide to the study of fresh-water biology. 1927 **QH96.N38 ECOL**

Reid, George K. Ecology of inland waters and estuaries. 1961 **QH96.R43 ECOL**

Robinson, Carmelita Klipple. Life in a pond. 1967 **fPZ10.R56Li ECOL**

Usinger, Robert Leslie. The life of rivers and streams. c1967 **QH97.U8 ECOL**

FRESH-WATER BIOLOGY—CONGRESSES.
International Symposium on Eutrophication, University of Wisconsin, 1967. Eutrophication: causes, consequences, correctives. 1969. **QH96.A1I63 1967 ECOL**

Lowe-McConnell, R. H. Man-made lakes. 1966. **GB1601.L6 1965 ECOL**

FRESH-WATER BIOLOGY—SUPERIOR, LAKE.
Minnesota. University. School of Public Health. Studies on the productivity and Plankton of Lake Superior. 1961 **fQK935.M55 ECOL**

FRESH-WATER ECOLOGY.
Amos, William Hopkins. The life of the pond. 1967 **QH541.5.F7A45 ECOL**

Andrews, William A. A guide to the study of freshwater ecology. 1972 **QH541.5.F7A48 ECOL**

Brown, Alison Leadley. Ecology of fresh water. 1971. **QH541.5.F7B7 1971b ECOL**

Fox, Jackson L. The ecology of periphyton in Western Lake Superior. 1969. **GB701.M554no.14 ECOL**

Frea, James I. Washout processes in lake systems. 1972. **fTD764.F74 ECOL**

Macan, Thomas Townley. Freshwater ecology. 1969,c1963 **QH541.5.F7M3 1969 ECOL**

McCue, George. Ecology: the freshwaters and man. c1971 **QH541.5.F7M22 ECOL**

Merritt, Thomas W. Studies on benthic nematode ecology in a small freshwater pond. 1973. **fTC1.A85no.8 ECOL**

FRESH-WATER ECOLOGY—MINNESOTA.
Hopwood, Alfred J. Evaluation of fishes and bottom fauna in the Mississippi River adjacent to the NSP Sherburne County Generating Plant Site, Becker, Minnesota, during October and November, 1971. 1972 **fTK1331.N6H6 ECOL**

FRESH-WATER ECOLOGY—SUPERIOR, LAKE.
Nelson, Robert R. The effects of enrichment on Lake Superior periphyton. 1973. **GB701.M554no.59 ECOL**

Olson, Theodore A. Lake Superior periphyton in relation to water quality. 1972. **fQK935.O4 ECOL**

FRESH-WATER FAUNA.
Virginia Polytechnic Institute and State University. Stream faunal recovery after manganese strip mine reclamation. 1971. **fTN291.V5 ECOL**

FRESH-WATER FAUNA—MINNESOTA.
Hopwood, Alfred J. Evaluation of fishes and bottom fauna in the Mississippi River adjacent to the NSP Sherburne County Generating Plant Site, Becker, Minnesota, during October and November, 1971. 1972 **fTK1331.N6H6 ECOL**

FRESH-WATER FLORA—CANADA—IDENTIFICATION.
Hotchkiss, Neil. Common marsh, underwater, and floating-leaved plants of the United States and Canada. 1972 **QK115.H67 1972 ECOL**

FRESH-WATER FLORA—MINNESOTA.
Linn, J. G. Aquatic plants from Minnesota, part 4 — nutrient composition. 1973. **GB701.M554no.56 ECOL**

FRESH-WATER FLORA—UNITED STATES—IDENTIFICATION.
Hotchkiss, Neil. Common marsh, underwater, and floating-leaved plants of the United States and Canada. 1972 **QK115.H67 1972 ECOL**

FRESHWATER ALGAE.
Fitzgerald, George Patrick. Nutrient sources for algae and their control. 1971 i.e.1972 **fQH96.8.E9F58 ECOL**

Fox, Jackson L. The ecology of periphyton in Western Lake Superior. 1969. **GB701.M554no.14 ECOL**

Stokes, Lee W. The photosynthetic pigments of Lake Superior periphyton and their relation to primary productivity. 1970. **GB701.M554no.18 ECOL**

FRONTIER AND PIONEER LIFE.
American Geographical Society of New York Pioneer settlement. 1932. **GF51.A5 ECOL**

Bowman, Isaiah. The pioneer fringe. 1931. **GF51.B6 ECOL**

FRONTIER AND PIONEER LIFE—UNITED STATES.
Greenberg, David Benjamin. Land that our fathers plowed. 1969 **S521.G83 ECOL**

Nash, Roderick. Wilderness and the American mind. 1967. **E169.1.N37 ECOL**

FROZEN GROUND—CANADA.
Brown, Roger James Evan. Permafrost in Canada. 1970 **TA713.B76 ECOL**

FRUIT PROCESSING—WASTE DISPOSAL.
National Canners Association. Western Research Laboratory. Dry caustic peeling of tree fruit for liquid waste reduction. 1970. **fTD899.F7N37 ECOL**

FUEL.
United States. Congress. House. Committee on Interior and Insular Affairs. Compilation of federal laws relating to fuel and energy resources. 1972. **KF2120.A25 1972 ECOL**

United States. Congress. House. Committee on Interior and Insular Affairs. Fuel and energy resources. 1972 **KF27.I5 1972 ECOL**

United States. Office of Coal Research. Clean energy from coal—a national priority. 1973 **HD9542.A5U5 ECOL**

FUEL—UNITED STATES.
Commerce Clearing House. Energy management. c1973. **Ref KF2120.A6C6 ECOL**

United States. Office of Emergency Preparedness. The potential for energy conservation: substitution for scarce fuels. 1973. **fTJ153.U548 ECOL**

FUEL OIL BURNERS see OIL BURNERS

FUEL RESEARCH.
Linville, Bill. Review of Bureau of Mines energy program, 1970. 1971 **TN295.U4no.8526 ECOL**

FULLER, RICHARD BUCKMINSTER, 1895-
Kenner, Hugh. Bucky. 1973. **TA140.F9K46 ECOL**

FUNGI.
Duddington, C. L. Beginner's guide to the fungi. 1972 **REF QK603.D83 ECOL**

G

GALAPAGOS ISLANDS—DESCRIPTION AND TRAVEL.
Beebe, Charles William. Galapagos, world's end. 1924. **QH123.B4 ECOL**

GAME AND GAME-BIRDS see also HUNTING; SHORE BIRDS; WATER-BIRDS
Scott, Peter Markham. Key to the wildfowl of the world. n.d. **REF QL696.A5S349 ECOL**

GAME AND GAME-BIRDS—DISEASES.
Infectious and parasitic diseases of wild birds. 1st ed. 1971 **SF994.4.A1I5 ECOL**

GAME AND GAME-BIRDS—MINNESOTA.
Big game in Minnesota. 1965. **SH11.M64no.9 ECOL**

Minnesota. Dept. of Conservation. Division of Game and Fish. Waterfowl in Minnesota. 1964. **SH11.M64no.7 ECOL**

GAME AND GAME BIRDS—NORTH AMERICA.
Outdoor life. Outdoor life's Gallery of North American game. 1946 **fSK40.O8 ECOL**

Phillips, John Charles. American waterfowl. 1930. **QL696.A5P45 ECOL**

Seton, Ernest Thompson. Lives of game animals. 1929. **QL151.S5 1925 ECOL**

GAME AND GAME BIRDS—PICTORIAL WORKS.
Outdoor life. Outdoor life's Gallery of North American game. 1946 **fSK40.O8 ECOL**

GAME AND GAME-BIRDS—UNITED STATES.
Bovey, Martin Koon. Saga of the waterfowl. 1949. **REF SK331.B6 ECOL**

GAME-LAWS—MINNESOTA.
Minnesota. Laws, statutes, etc. Laws relating to game and fish, 1971/72- **REF KFM5853.A44 ECOL**

GAME-LAWS—UNITED STATES.
Hornaday, William Temple. Our vanishing wildlife: its extermination and preservation. 1970,c1913 **SK353.H6 1970 ECOL**

Hornaday, William Temple. Thirty years war for wild life. 1970, c1931 **SK361.H58 1970 ECOL**

Sigler, William F. Wildlife law enforcement. 2d ed. 1972 **KF5640.S55 1972 ECOL**

GAME-PRESERVES.
Gabrielson, Ira Noel. Wildlife refuges. 1943. **SK357.G3 ECOL**

GAME PROTECTION—UNITED STATES.
Hornaday, William Temple. Thirty years war for wild life. 1970, c1931 **SK361.H58 1970 ECOL**

Neal, Harry Edward. Nature's guardians. 1966,c1963 **SK361.N45 1966 ECOL**

GARBAGE *see* REFUSE AND REFUSE DISPOSAL

GARDEN CITIES—UNITED STATES.
Stein, Clarence S. Toward new towns for America. Rev. ed. 1971,c1957 **NA9108.S8 1971 ECOL**

GARDEN PESTS.
Hunter, Beatrice Trum. Gardening without poisons. 2d ed. 1971. **SB975.H8 1971 ECOL**
Plants & gardens. Handbook on biological control of plant pests. 1966,1960 **SB932.P5 1966 ECOL**

GARDENING.
Baker, Jerry. Jerry Baker's Back to nature almanac. 1973- **SB455.B257 ECOL**

GAS AND OIL ENGINES.
Ayres, Robert U. Alternatives to the internal combustion engine. 1972 **TL210.A96 ECOL**

GAS CHROMATOGRAPHY.
Dimitriades, Basil. Interpretation of gas chromatographic spectra in routine analysis of exhaust hydrocarbons. 1972 **TN23.U7no.7700 ECOL**
Taylor, John Keenan. Development of method for NTA analysis in raw water. 1972. **TP992.5.T3 ECOL**

GAS INDUSTRY—UNITED STATES.
United States. Federal Power Commission. Air pollution and the regulated electric power and natural gas industries. 1968. **TD883.2.A52 ECOL**

GAS INDUSTRY—UNITED STATES—CONGRESSES.
Regulation of the natural gas producing industry. 1972 **HD9581.U5R45 ECOL**

GAS, NATURAL.
Lovejoy, Wallace Francis. Methods of estimating reserves of crude oil, natural gas, and natural gas liquids. 1965 **TN870.L68 ECOL**

GAS, NATURAL—CONGRESSES.
Regulation of the natural gas producing industry. 1972 **HD9581.U5R45 ECOL**

GAS RESEARCH.
Linville, Bill. Review of Bureau of Mines energy program, 1970. 1971 **TN295.U4no.8526 ECOL**

GAS-TURBINES.
United Aircraft Corporation. Research Laboratories, East Hartford, Conn. Advanced nonthermally polluting gas turbines in utility applications. 1971. **fTJ778.U5 ECOL**

GASES.
Robinson, Elmer. Sources, abundance, and fate of gaseous atmospheric pollutants. 1968. **fTD885.R6 ECOL**
Robinson, Elmer. Sources, abundance, and fate of gaseous atmospheric pollutants: supplement. 1969. **fTD885.R62 ECOL**

GASES—ANALYSIS—BIBLIOGRAPHY.
Ruch, Walter E. Chemical detection of gaseous pollutants. **REF fZ5524.G24R8 ECOL**

GASES, ASPHYXIATING AND POISONOUS.
Harvest of death. 1971,c1972 **DS557.A68H35 1972 ECOL**

GASIFICATION OF COAL *see* COAL GASIFICATION

GEESE.
Phillips, John Charles. American waterfowl. 1930. **QL696.A5P45 ECOL**

GENITO-URINARY ORGANS—TUMORS.
Hueper, Wilhelm C. Occupational and environmental cancers of the urinary system. 1969. **RC280.G4H8 ECOL**

GEOCHEMISTRY.
Elemental composition of surficial materials in the conterminous United States: an account of the amounts of certain chemical elements. 1971. **REF fQE75.P9no.574-D ECOL**

GEOCHEMISTRY—DICTIONARIES.
Fairbridge, Rhodes Whitmore. The encyclopedia of geochemistry and environmental sciences. 1972 **REF QE515.F24 ECOL**

GEOGRAPHICAL DISTRIBUTION OF ANIMALS AND PLANTS.
Crosby, Alfred W. The Columbian exchange. 1972 **E98.D6C7 ECOL**

GEOGRAPHICAL DISTRIBUTION OF MAN *see* ANTHROPO-GEOGRAPHY

GEOGRAPHY, PHYSICAL *see* PHYSICAL GEOGRAPHY

GEOGRAPHY, SOCIAL *see* ANTHROPO-GEOGRAPHY

GEOLOGICAL SPECIMENS—COLLECTION AND PRESERVATION.
Harris, Reg. Natural history collecting. 1972 **QH60.H36 ECOL**

GEOLOGY *see also* EARTH; EROSION; MINERALOGY; PHYSICAL GEOGRAPHY; SEDIMENTATION AND DEPOSITION
Calder, Nigel. The restless Earth: a report on the new geology. 1972 **QE26.2.C34 ECOL**
Emmons, William Harvey. Geology: principles and processes. 5th ed. 1960. **QE26.E6 1960 ECOL**
Flawn, Peter Tyrell. Environmental geology: conservation, land-use planning, and resource management. 1970 **QE33.F5 ECOL**
Leveson, David. A sense of the earth. 1971. **QE31.L48 ECOL**
Matthews, William Henry. Introducing the earth. 1972 **QE29.M27 ECOL**
Shelton, John S. Geology illustrated. 1966 **fQE26.S5 ECOL**

GEOLOGY—BIBLIOGRAPHY.
Ward, Dederick C. Geologic reference sources. 1972. **REF Z6031.W35 1972 ECOL**

GEOLOGY—MICHIGAN.
Dorr, John A. Geology of Michigan. c1970 **REF fQE125.D6 ECOL**
Mengel, J. T. Geology of the western Lake Superior region. 1970. **fQE78.M4 ECOL**

GEOLOGY—MINNESOTA.
Mengel, J. T. Geology of the western Lake Superior region. 1970. **fQE78.M4 ECOL**
Schwartz, George Melvin. Minnesota's rocks and waters. 1954 **QE127.A22no.37 ECOL**
Schwartz, George Melvin. Minnesota's rocks and waters. Rev. ed. 1963 **QE127.A22no.37 1963 ECOL**

GEOLOGY—SUPERIOR, LAKE—MAPS.
Mengel, J. T. Geology of the western Lake Superior region. 1970. **fQE78.M4 ECOL**

GEOLOGY—TWIN CITIES METROPOLITAN AREA.
Hogberg, Rudolph K. Environmental geology of the Twin Cities Metropolitan area. 1971 **QE128.T9H6 ECOL**

GEOLOGY—UNITED STATES—BIBLIOGRAPHY.
United States. Geological Survey Publications of the Geological Survey, 1879-1961. 1964 **REF Z6034.U49U53 ECOL**
—— Supplement, 1962-1970. 1972. **REF Z6034.U49U53 Suppl. ECOL**

GEOLOGY—WISCONSIN.
Mengel, J. T. Geology of the western Lake Superior region. 1970. **fQE78.M4 ECOL**

GEOLOGY, STRUCTURAL.
Morey, Rexford M. Feasibility study of electromagnetic subsurface profiling. 1972. **QE602.M6 ECOL**

GEOMORPHOLOGY—PERIODICALS.
Environmental Geomorphology Symposium. Environmental geomorphology. **GB400.E58 ECOL**

GEOTHERMAL ENGINEERING.
Small, HyDee. Nature's teakettle. c1973 **GB1003.S6 ECOL**

GEOTHERMAL RESOURCES.
Small, HyDee. Nature's teakettle. c1973 **GB1003.S6 ECOL**

GEOTHERMAL RESOURCES—DIRECTORIES.
Geothermal world directory, 1972- **fGB1003.G46 ECOL**

GEOTHERMAL RESOURCES—UNITED STATES.
United States. Congress. Senate. Committee on Interior and Insular Affairs. Geothermal energy resources and research. 1972. **KF26.I5 1972j ECOL**

GERM WARFARE *see* BIOLOGICAL WARFARE

GERMS *see* MICRO-ORGANISMS

GLASS CONTAINERS.
Hulbert, Samuel F. Design of a water-disposable glass packaging container. 1971. **TD799.H8 ECOL**

GLASS, SOLUBLE *see* SOLUBLE GLASS

GLEN CANYON.
Porter, Eliot. The place no one knew: Glen Canyon on the Colorado. 1963 **fF832.C7P6 ECOL**

GOLDEN EAGLE—LEGENDS AND STORIES.
Durden, Kent. Gifts of an eagle. 1972 **QL795.B57D87 ECOL**

GOVERNMENT OWNERSHIP—UNITED STATES.
Bonbright, James Cummings. Public utilities and the national power policies. 1972, c1940 **HD2766.B57 1972**

GOVERNMENT PUBLICATIONS—BIBLIOGRAPHY.
Mignon, Molly R. Our polluted planet: a bibliography of government publications on pollution and the environment. 1971. **fZ5322.E2M5 ECOL**

GOVERNMENT PUBLICITY—UNITED STATES—DIRECTORIES.
Directory of public information contacts, Wash., D.C., 1972- **REF JK849.A353 ECOL**

GRAND CANYON.
Fletcher, Colin. The man who walked through time. 1967 i.e. 1968 **F788.F55 ECOL**
Leydet, Francois. Time and the river flowing: Grand Canyon. 1968 **F788.L482 ECOL**
Wallace, Robert. The Grand Canyon. 1972 **F788.W23 ECOL**

GRAND FORKS, N.D.—FLOODS.
United States. Army. Corps of Engineers. Flood plain information on the Red River of the North in the vicinity of Grand Forks, North Dakota—East Grand Forks, Minnesota. 1971. **GB1227.R4A5 ECOL**

GRASSES—IDENTIFICATION.
Pohl, Richard Walter. How to know the grasses. Rev. ed. 1968 **QK495.G74P73 1968 ECOL**

GRASSES—UNITED STATES.
Pohl, Richard Walter. How to know the grasses. Rev. ed. 1968 **QK495.G74P73 1968 ECOL**

GRASSLAND ECOLOGY.
McCue, George. Ecology: the grasslands and man. c1971 **QH541.5.P7M22 ECOL**
Sears, Paul Bigelow. Lands beyond the forest. 1969 **QH541.5.P7S4 ECOL**
Spedding, C. R. W. Grassland ecology. 1971. **QH541.5.P7S65 ECOL**

GRASSLAND ECOLOGY—AFRICA.
Brown, Leslie. The life of the African plains. 1972 **QH541.5.P7B76 ECOL**

GRAY SQUIRREL.
Barkalow, Frederick Schenck. The world of the gray squirrel. 1973 **QL737.R68B37 ECOL**

GREAT BRITAIN—ECONOMIC POLICY—1945-
Mishan, Edward J. Technology and growth. 1970,c1969 **HD82.M514 ECOL**

GREAT BRITAIN—SOCIAL POLICY.
Mishan, Edward J. Technology and growth. 1970,c1969 **HD82.M514 ECOL**

GREAT LAKES.
Great Lakes Basin Commission. The future of the Great Lakes: a public meeting. 1972 **fGB1627.G8G7 ECOL**
Swain, Wayland R. The ecology of the second trophic level in Lakes Superior, Michigan and Huron. 1970. **GB701.M554no.26 ECOL**

GREAT LAKES—CLIMATE—BIBLIOGRAPHY.
Hacia, Henry. A selected annotated bibliography of the climate of the Great Lakes. 1972. **REF Z6683.C5H33 ECOL**

GREAT LAKES—DESCRIPTION AND TRAVEL.
Barry, James P. The fate of the lakes. 1972 **F551.B37 ECOL**

GREAT LAKES—LEVEL *see* GREAT LAKES—WATER LEVEL

GREAT LAKES—WATER-LEVEL.
International Great Lakes Levels Board. Regulation of Great Lakes water levels: interim report on Lakes Superior and Ontario regulation, to the International Joint Commission by the International Great Lakes Levels Board. 1973. **fGB1627.G8152 ECOL**

GREAT LAKES REGION—BIBLIOGRAPHY.
Great Lakes Basin Library. Book catalog. 1969- **REF fZ7164.N3G75 ECOL**
Great Lakes Basin Library. An interim bibliography. 1969- **REF fZ7164.N3G7 ECOL**

GREAT LAKES REGION—ECONOMIC CONDITIONS.
Great Lakes Basin Commission. The future of the Great Lakes: a public meeting. 1972 **fGB1627.G8G7 ECOL**

GREAT PLAINS—DESCRIPTION AND TRAVEL—1945-
Plowden, David. Floor of the sky: the Great Plains. 1972 **fF595.2.P56 ECOL**

GREENBELTS—UNITED STATES.
Little, Charles E. Challenge of the land. 1968 **HD205 1968 .L5 ECOL**
Whyte, William Hollingsworth. Last landscape. 1968. **HT167.W48 ECOL**

GROUND WATER *see* WATER, UNDERGROUND

GROUNDWATER FLOW.
Huisman, L. Groundwater recovery. 1972 **TD405.H85 ECOL**
Liesch, Bruce A. Geohydrology of the Jorden aquifer in the Minneapolis-St. Paul area Minnesota. 1961. **fGB705.M6L5 ECOL**
Ralph M. Parsons Laboratory for Water Resources and Hydrodynamics. Density induced mixing in confined aquifers. 1972. **fTC176.R33 ECOL**

GROUSE.
Johnsgard, Paul A. Grouse and quails of North America. 1973 **QL696.G27J63 ECOL**

GROWTH (PLANTS).
Antevs, Ernst. Rainfall and tree growth in the Great basin... 1938. **QC925.1.U35 1938 ECOL**

Lubell, Winifred. Green is for growing. 1964. **PZ10.L85Gr ECOL**

GUANO.
Murphy, Robert Cushman. Bird islands of Peru. 1925. **REF QH128.M8 ECOL**

GUILLEMOTS see MURRES

H

HANDICRAFT.
Jaeger, Ellsworth. Nature crafts. 1971, c1950 **TT157.J24 ECOL**

Musselman, Virginia W. Learning about nature through crafts. 1969 **TT157.M82 ECOL**

Van der Smissen, Margaret Elisabeth. A leader's guide to nature-oriented activities. 2d ed. 1968 **GV182.2.V3 1968 ECOL**

HARDINESS OF PLANTS see PLANTS—HARDINESS

HARP SEAL.
Davies, Brian. Savage luxury: the slaughter of the baby seals. 1971, c1970 **QL737.P6D33 1971 ECOL**

HAZARDOUS SUBSTANCES.
Little (Arthur D.) Inc. Spill prevention techniques for hazardous polluting substances: an inventory and survey of hazardous chemical facilities in Charleston, West Virginia; Baltimore, Maryland; Texas City, Texas; and the Suisun Bay-Delta Area, California. 1971. **fT55.3.H3L4 ECOL**

HAZARDOUS SUBSTANCES—UNITED STATES.
United States. President, 1969- (Nixon). Control of hazardous polluting substances. 1971. **TD365.U53 ECOL**

HEAT POLLUTION OF RIVERS, LAKES, ETC. see THERMAL POLLUTION OF RIVERS, LAKES, ETC.

HERBICIDES.
Kearney, Philip C. Degradation of herbicides. 1969. **REF SB951.4.K4 ECOL**

United States. President's Science Advisory Committee. Report on 2, 4, 5-T. 1971. **SB612.A2A52 ECOL**

HERBICIDES—BIODETERIORATION.
Boyce Thompson Institute for Plant Research, Yonkers, N.Y. Interaction of herbicides and soil microorganisms. 1971. **fSB951.4.B68 ECOL**

HERBICIDES—HANDBOOKS, MANUALS, ETC.
United States Dept. of the Army. Herbicide manual for noncropland weeds. 1970. **SB611.U5 ECOL**

HERBICIDES—TOXICOLOGY.
Whiteside, Thomas. The withering rain. 1st ed. 1971. **QH545.P4W48 1971 ECOL**

HIGHWAY RESEARCH—BIBLIOGRAPHY.
Coleman, D. J. Highways and the environment: a bibliography of the effects of highways on the physical, biological, recreational and aesthetic environments and of techniques for the analysis of these impacts. 1973. **fZ7295.C6 ECOL**

HIKING—UNITED STATES.
Lennon, J. Establishing trails on rights-of-way. n.d. **G504.L4 ECOL**

HISTORY AND SCIENCE see SCIENCE AND CIVILIZATION

HISTORY, NATURAL see NATURAL HISTORY

HOME ECONOMICS.
Bay Laurel, Alicia. Living on the earth. 1971, c1970 **fS605.5.B3 ECOL**

The Last whole earth catalog. 1971. **REF fTT155.W52 ECOL**

HOSPITALS—HYGIENE.
United States. Environmental Protection Agency. Solid waste handling and disposal in multi-story buildings and hospitals. 1972. **TD788.A3 ECOL**

HOT WATER DISCHARGES INTO RIVERS, LAKES, ETC., see THERMAL POLLUTION OF RIVERS, LAKES, ETC.

HOUSEHOLD APPLIANCES, ELECTRIC—NOISE.
Bolt, Beranek, and Newman, Inc. Noise from construction equipment and operations, building equipment, and home appliances. 1971 i.e. 1972 **fTD893.B63 ECOL**

HOUSES, APARTMENT see APARTMENT HOUSES

HOUSING.
Goodman, Robert. After the planners. 1972, c1971 **HT166.G64 ECOL**

HUDSON RIVER.
Boyle, Robert H. The Hudson River. 1st ed. 1969 **QH105.N7B68 ECOL**

HUMAN BEHAVIOR.
Henshaw, Paul Stewart. This side of yesterday: extinction or Utopia. 1971 **GF41.H45 ECOL**

HUMAN BIOLOGY see HUMAN BEHAVIOR; HUMAN ECOLOGY; PSYCHOLOGY

HUMAN BIOLOGY—ADDRESSES, ESSAYS, LECTURES.
Johnson, Cecil E. Human biology: contemporary readings. c1970 **QH311.J63 ECOL**

HUMAN ECOLOGY see also ANTHROPO-GEOGRAPHY; CONSERVATION OF NATURAL RESOURCES; MAN—INFLUENCE OF ENVIRONMENT; MAN—INFLUENCE ON NATURE

Benthall, Jonathan. Ecology in theory and practice. 1973, c1972 **QH541.B4 1973 ECOL**

Boughey, Arthur S. Man and the environment. 1971 **GF43.B68 ECOL**

Bresler, Jack Barry. Human ecology. 1966 **GF31.B65 ECOL**

Brubaker, Sterling. To live on earth. 1972 **QH541.B76 ECOL**

Burnet, Frank Macfarlane, Sir. Dominant mammal. 1972, c1971 **QH331.B887 1972 ECOL**

Chisholm, Anne. Philosophers of the earth. c1972 **GF75.C4 ECOL**

Coblentz, Stanton Arthur. The challenge to man's survival. 1972 **GF41.C55 ECOL**

Dasmann, Raymond Frederick. A different kind of country. 1968 **QH75.D37 ECOL**

Dubos, Rene Jules. A God within. 1972 **HM206.D86 ECOL**

Dubos, Rene Jules. So human an animal. 1968 **HM206.D87 ECOL**

Ehrlich, Paul R. Population resources environment. 1970 **HB871.E35 ECOL**

Ehrlich, Paul R. Population, resources, environment. 2d ed. 1972 **HB871.E35 1972 ECOL**

Hardin, Garrett James. Exploring new ethics for survival: the voyage of the spaceship Beagle. 1972 **HB871.H347 ECOL**

Hawley, Amos Henry. Human ecology. 1950 **HM51.H38 ECOL**

Henshaw, Paul Stewart. This side of yesterday: extinction or Utopia. 1971 **GF41.H45 ECOL**

Ivany, J. W. George. Environment: readings for teachers. 1971, c1972 **GF47.I9 ECOL**

Jackson, Barbara (Ward) Lady. Only one earth. 1st ed. 1972 **GF41.J3 ECOL**

Katz, Robert. A giant in the earth. c1973 **HD9000.5.K3 ECOL**

Kepes, Gyorgy. Arts of the environment. 1972 **N72.S6K37 ECOL**

Kilbourne, Edwin D. Human ecology and public health. 4th ed. 1969 **RA425.K55 1969 ECOL**

Leiss, William. The domination of nature. c1972 **S936.L45 ECOL**

Maddox, John Royden. The doomsday syndrome. 1972 **GF47.M3 1972 ECOL**

Maldonado, Tomas. Design, nature, and revolution. 1st U.S. ed. 1972 **GF41.M3413 1972 ECOL**

McHale, John. The ecological context. 1970 **GF41.M3 ECOL**

McHarg, Ian L. Design with nature. 1st ed. 1969. **fHC110.E5M33 ECOL**

Metress, James F. Man in ecological perspective. c1971 **GF75.M4 ECOL**

Nobile, Philip. The complete ecology fact book. 1st ed. 1972. **TD174.N6 ECOL**

Odum, Howard T. Environment, power, and society. 1970, c1971 **QH541.O33 ECOL**

Rienow, Robert. Moment in the sun. 1967. **S930.R5 ECOL**

Russell, William Moy Stratton. Man, nature, and history. 1969, c1967 **GF37.R85 ECOL**

Saltonstall, Richard. Brownout & slow-down. c1972 **HC110.E5S33 ECOL**

Segerberg, Osborn. Where have all the flowers, fishes, birds, trees, water, and air gone? 1971 **QH541.S39 ECOL**

Sprout, Harold Hance. The ecological perspective on human affairs. 1971 **JX1251.S49 ECOL**

Storer, John Humphries. Man in the web of life. 1968 **HM206.S7 ECOL**

Theobald, Robert. Habit and habitat. 1972 **GF47.T45 ECOL**

Udall, Stewart L. 1976: agenda for tomorrow. 1st ed. 1968 **HN65.U3 ECOL**

Vayda, Andrew Peter. Environment and cultural behavior. 1969. **GF51.V35 ECOL**

Wagner, Philip Laurence. The human use of the earth. 1964, c1960 **HM206.W28 1964 ECOL**

Watson, Richard A. Man and nature. 1969 **GF23.W3 ECOL**

HUMAN ECOLOGY—ADDRESSES, ESSAYS, LECTURES.
Allan, J. David. Recycle this book! 1972 **GF8.A4 ECOL**

Burch, William R. Social behavior, natural resources, and the environment. 1972 **HM206.B84 ECOL**

Challenge for survival: land, air, and water for man in megalopolis. 1970. **HM206.C4 ECOL**

Colinvaux, Paul Alfred. The environment of crowded men. 1970 **GF8.C8 ECOL**

Dogan, Mattei. Quantitative ecological analysis in the social sciences. 1969 **HM206.D6 ECOL**

The Fitness of man's environment. 1968 **HT166.F53 ECOL**

Grand Canyon Symposium, 1970. Environment, man, survival: Grand Canyon Symposium, 1970. c1971 **GF8.G7 1970 ECOL**

Resources for the Future. Environmental quality analysis. 1972 **HC79.E5R46 ECOL**

Scoby, Donald R. Environmental ethics. 1971 **GF80.S35 ECOL**

Smith, Robert Leo. The ecology of man: an ecosystem approach. 1972 **fGF8.S6 ECOL**

Stapledon, Sir Reginald George. Human ecology. 2nd ed.; edited and introduced by Robert Waller. 1971. **HM206.S65 1971 ECOL**

Toepfer, Caroline T. Environmental psychology: selected readings. 1972 **HM206.T6 ECOL**

Who speaks for earth? 1st ed. 1973 **GF8.W49 ECOL**

Woods, Barbara. Eco-solutions: a casebook for the environmental crisis. 1972 **GF43.W6 ECOL**

HUMAN ECOLOGY—BIBLIOGRAPHY.
Durrenberger, Robert W. Environment and man. 1970 **Z5118.A5D86 ECOL**

Olympus Research Corporation. Career education in the environment. 1971 or 2 **fGF21.O4 ECOL**

Winton, Harry N. M. Man and the environment: a bibliography of selected publications of the United Nations system, 1946-1971. 1972. **REF Z5322.E2W56 ECOL**

HUMAN ECOLOGY—COLLECTIONS.
As we live and breath. 1971 **GF75.A8 ECOL**

Ehrlich, Paul R. Man and the ecosphere. 1971 **fGF8.E35 ECOL**

Theodorson, George A. Studies in human ecology. 1961 **HM206.T48 ECOL**

HUMAN ECOLOGY—CONGRESSES.
Clubb, Jerome M. Ecological data in comparative research. 1970 **H62.C6 ECOL**

Environmental Quality Forum, East Tennessee State University, 1970. The Nation's environment—problems and action. c1971 **TD172.5.E58 1970 ECOL**

National Conference on UNESCO, 13th, San Francisco, 1969. No deposit—no return. 1970 **GF3.N38 1969 ECOL**

Stockholm and beyond. 1972. **HC110.E5A43 ECOL**

Workshop on Global Ecological Problems, University of Wisconsin, 1971. Man in the living environment. 1972 **GF3.W6 1971 ECOL**

HUMAN ECOLOGY—DIRECTORIES.
Halstead, Bruce W. A Golden guide to environmental organizations. 1972 **REF GF5.H34 ECOL**

HUMAN ECOLOGY—LITERARY COLLECTIONS.
Gangewere, Robert J. The exploited Eden. 1972 **PS507.E3G3 ECOL**

HUMAN ECOLOGY—MORAL AND RELIGIOUS ASPECTS.
Allsopp, Bruce. The garden Earth. 1972 **GF80.A4 1972b ECOL**

Barbour, Ian G. Western man and environmental ethics. 1973 **GF80.B37 ECOL**

Barnette, Henlee H. The church and the ecological crisis. 1972 **BT695.5.B37 ECOL**

Black, John N. The dominion of man. 1970. **GF80.B55 ECOL**

Earth might be fair. 1972 **GF80.E15 ECOL**

Elder, Frederick. Crisis in Eden. 1970 **GF80.E4 ECOL**

Flowers, William J. Western cultural tradition and human survival: the role of value orientations in the environmental crisis. c1971 **GF80.F5 ECOL**

Folsom, Paul. And thou shalt die in a polluted land. 1971 **GF80.F6 ECOL**

Hamilton, Michael Pollock. This little planet. 1970 **GF80.H35 ECOL**

Neuhaus, Richard John. In defense of people: ecology and the seduction of radicalism. 1971 **HM206.N48 ECOL**

Santmire, H. Paul. Brother Earth. 1970 **BL435.S25 ECOL**

HUMAN ECOLOGY—MORAL AND RELIGIOUS ASPECTS—ADDRESSES, ESSAYS, LECTURES.
Ecology: crisis and new vision. c1971 **GF80.E25 ECOL**

HUMAN ECOLOGY—STUDY AND TEACHING.
Bennett, Dean B. Guidelines for planning and implementing a comprehensive community environmental inventory. Rev. ed. 1972. **fQH541.2.B38 1972 ECOL**
Environmental studies. Rev. ed.? 1971,c1970 **LB1027.E6 1971 ECOL**
Harris, Melville. Environmental studies. 1971. **LB1047.H32 ECOL**
Henderson, Martha T. Environmental education: Social studies sources and approaches. 1971 **Ref fQH541.2.H4 ECOL**
Intercom. Teaching about spaceship earth. c1972 **S946.I5 ECOL**
National Education Association of the United States. Research Division. Environmental education in the public schools. 1970 **fLB1047.N36 ECOL**

HUMAN ECOLOGY—STUDY AND TEACHING—BIBLIOGRAPHY.
National Association for Environmental Education. Man and environment. 1970 **REF fZ5322.E2N3 ECOL**

HUMAN ECOLOGY—STUDY AND TEACHING (ELEMENTARY).
Sako, Marilyn. Man and his environment. 1971 **fS946.S2 ECOL**

HUMAN ECOLOGY—STUDY AND TEACHING (HIGHER)—UNITED STATES.
The Organic guide to colleges and universities. 1973 **S946.O73 ECOL**

HUMAN ECOLOGY—STUDY AND TEACHING (SECONDARY).
Mounds Views, Minn. Independent School District, 621. Environmental education curriculum, grades 10 - 12. n.d. **fQH541.2.M6 ECOL**

HUMAN ECOLOGY—STUDY AND TEACHING (SECONDARY)—UNITED STATES.
Olympus Research Corporation. Career education in the environment. 1971 or 2 **fGF21.O4 ECOL**

HUMAN ENGINEERING.
Papanek, Victor J. Design for the real world. 1st American ed. c1971 **TS171.4.P37 1971 ECOL**

HUMAN EVOLUTION.
Lauwerys, Joseph Albert. Man's impact on nature. 1970,c1969 **QH368.L38 ECOL**

HUMAN EVOLUTION—ADDRESSES, ESSAYS, LECTURES.
Young, Louise B. Evolution of man. 1970. **QH368.Y68 ECOL**

HUMAN GEOGRAPHY *see* ANTHROPO-GEOGRAPHY

HUNTING.
Ortega y Gasset, Jose. Meditations on hunting. 1972 **SK31.O7813 ECOL**

HUNTING—NORTH AMERICA.
Cramond, Michael. Hunting & fishing in North America. c1953 **SK40.C67 ECOL**

HUNTING—SPAIN.
Ortega y Gasset, Jose. Meditations on hunting. 1972 **SK31.O7813 ECOL**

HUNTING—UNITED STATES.
Brings, Lawrence Martin. Outdoor horizons. c1957 **fSK33.B83 ECOL**
Wallo. Olav O. Twilight over the wilderness. 1971 **fS964.U6W3 ECOL**

HUNTING—UNITED STATES—STATISTICS.
United States. Bureau of Sport Fisheries and Wildlife. National survey of fishing and hunting, 1970- **REF S914.A3no.95 ECOL**

HYDRAULIC *see* RIVERS; WATER SUPPLY ENGINEERING; WELLS

HYDRAULIC CYCLE.
McNabb, C. D. A fluorometric technique for sampling in large-river ecosystems. 1971. **GB701.M554no.34 ECOL**

HYDRAULIC ENGINEERING *see also* DRAINAGE; ENGINEERING; HYDRAULIC MACHINERY
Design of water-resource systems. 1970,c1962 **TC409.D4 ECOL**

Linsley, Ray K. Water-resources engineering. 2d ed. 1971,c1972 **TC145.L55 1972 ECOL**

HYDRAULIC MACHINERY.
Battelle Memorial Institute, Columbus, Ohio. Pacific Northwest Laboratory, Richland, Wash. Concept development of a hydraulic skimmer system for recovery of floating oil. 1971. **fTD427.P4B29 ECOL**

HYDRAULIC MEASUREMENTS *see also* FLOW METERS; STREAM MEASUREMENTS
Battelle Memorial Institute. Columbus, Ohio. Columbus Laboratories Multidirectional turbulence probe development. **fTC177.B3 ECOL**

HYDROCHLORIC ACID.
Armco Steel Corporation. Limestone treatment of rinse waters from hydrochloric acid pickling of steel. 1971. **fTD899.M45A75 ECOL**

HYDROCHLORIC ACID—BIBLIOGRAPHY.
Air Pollution Technical Information Center. Hydrochloric acid and air pollution: an annotated bibliography. 1971. **Z7173.A4A52 ECOL**

HYDROCYCLONES *see* SEPARATORS (MACHINES)

HYDROLOGIC CYCLE.
Amos, William Hopkins. The infinite river. 1971,c1970 **QH90.A59 ECOL**

HYDROLOGY *see also* WATER
Fox, Sir Cyril Sankey. Water. 1972 **GB661.F65 1972 ECOL**
Helfman, Elizabeth S. Water for the world. 1st ed. 1967,c1960 **GB671.H4 ECOL**

HYDROLOGY—BIBLIOGRAPHY.
Engineering-Science, Inc. Annotated bibliography on hydrology and sedimentation, 1966-68, United States and Canada. 1970 **REF Z7935.E5 1970 ECOL**

HYDROLOGY—MINNESOTA.
Bowers, C. Edward. Computer programs in hydrology. 1972. **GB665.B6 ECOL**
Liesch, Bruce A. Geohydrology of the Jorden aquifer in the Minneapolis-St. Paul area Minnesota. 1961. **fGB705.M6L5 ECOL**
Rice, Charles E. Methods for routing hydrographs through open channels. 1972. **GB701.M554no.51 ECOL**

HYDROLOGY—MINNESOTA—ST. LOUIS RIVER WATERSHED.
Minnesota. Dept. of Conservation. Division of Waters. The St. Louis River Watershed unit. 1964. **fTD224.M6A3no.22 ECOL**

HYDROLOGY—RESEARCH.
Freeze, Allan R. A physics-based approach to hydrologic response modeling: Phase I: model development, completion report. 1972. **fGB665.F7 ECOL**

HYDROLOGY—SOCIETIES, ETC.—DIRECTORIES.
National Water Well Association. Membership directory. 1972/73- **REF TD407.N3 ECOL**

HYDROLOGY—STATISTICAL METHODS.
Linsley, Ray K. A manual on collection of hydrologic data for urban drainage design. 1972. **fTD665.L55 ECOL**

HYDROLOGY—TABLES, CALCULATIONS, ETC.
Todd, David Keith. The water encyclopedia. 1970 **REF TD351.T63 ECOL**

HYDROLOGY—UNITED STATES.
McPherson, M. B. Hydrologic effects of urbanization in the United States. 1972. **fGB665.M3 ECOL**

HYDROLOGY—WISCONSIN.
Workshop on Hydrologic and Hydraulic Aspects of Flood Plain Construction, Madison, Wisc., 1968. Proceedings. 1968? **fGB1225.W6W6 1968 ECOL**

HYGIENE.
Rodale, Robert. Sane living in a mad world. 1972 **RA776.5.R57 ECOL**
Rosebury, Theodor. Life on man. 1969 **QR56.R59 ECOL**

HYGIENE—ADDRESSES, ESSAYS, LECTURES.
Jefcoat, Allure. Health and human values. 1972 **RA565.J44 ECOL**

HYGIENE, PUBLIC.
Ehlers, Victor Marcus. Municipal and rural sanitation. 6th ed. c1965 **REF RA425.E5 1965 ECOL**
Kilbourne, Edwin D. Human ecology and public health. 4th ed. 1969 **RA425.K55 1969 ECOL**
World Health Organization. Health hazards of the human environment. 1972. **RA565.W6 ECOL**

HYGIENE, RURAL.
Ehlers, Victor Marcus. Municipal and rural sanitation. 6th ed. c1965 **REF RA425.E5 1965 ECOL**

HYLAND LAKE, MINNESOTA.
Barr Engineering Co. Hydrological study of Hyland-Bush-Anderson lakes. 1971. **fTC424.M6B326 ECOL**

I

ICE.
Couchman, J. Kenneth. Snow and ice. c1971 **QC929.S7C6 ECOL**

IMPROVISATION (ACTING).
Spolin, Viola. Improvisation for the theater. 1963 **PN2071.I5S6 ECOL**

INCINERATION.
Mandan Refinery. Fluid bed incineration of petroleum refinery wastes. 1971. **fTD899.P4M35 ECOL**

INCINERATION—UNITED STATES.
Stear, James R. Municipal incineration: a review of literature. 1971. **TD803.S82 ECOL**

INCINERATORS.
Balakrishnan, S. State of the art review on sludge incineration practice. 1970. **fTD803.B36 ECOL**
Corey, Richard Clarke. Principles and practices of incineration. 1969 **TD803.C66 ECOL**
Incinerator Institute of America. Incinerator standards. 1970,1968 **REF fTD796.I5 1970 ECOL**
Incinerator Institute of America. Incinerator testing. 1971 **fTD796.I53 ECOL**
Incinerator Institute of America. Modern incineration: a solution—not the problem. 1969? **fTD796.I54 ECOL**
National Research Council. Building Research Advisory Board. Apartment house incinerators (flue fed). 1965. **fTH23.N333no.29 ECOL**
Stear, James R. Municipal incineration: a review of literature. 1971. **TD803.S82 ECOL**
Warner, Arthur J. Plastics solid waste disposal by incineration or landfill. c1972, 1971. **fTD798.W36 ECOL**

INCINERATORS—MATHEMATICAL MODELS.
Unterberg, W. Computerized design and cost estimation for multiple-hearth sludge incinerators. 1971 i.e. 1972 **fTD770.U58 ECOL**

INDIANS—AGRICULTURE.
Crosby, Alfred W. The Columbian exchange. 1972 **E98.D6C7 ECOL**

INDIANS—DISEASES.
Crosby, Alfred W. The Columbian exchange. 1972 **E98.D6C7 ECOL**

INDIVIDUALITY.
Marcel, Gabriel. Man against mass society. 1971, 1952 **B2430.M253H583 1971 ECOL**

INDUSTRIAL HYGIENE.
Page, Joseph A. Bitter wages: Ralph Nader's study group report on disease and injury on the job. 1973. **RC967.P33 ECOL**

INDUSTRIAL MANAGEMENT.
Goldstein, Jerome. How to manage your company ecologically. 1971 **HD69.P6G65 ECOL**

INDUSTRIAL MANAGEMENT—CASE STUDIES.
Kaufman, Herbert. The Forest ranger. 1960 **SD565.K3 ECOL**

INDUSTRIAL NOISE.
Goodfriend (L.S.) Associates. Noise from industrial plants. 1971. **fTD892.G66 ECOL**

INDUSTRIAL SAFETY—HANDBOOKS, MANUALS, ETC.
Best's environmental control and safety directory. 13th ed.- 1971/72- **REF fT55.B4 ECOL**

INDUSTRIAL SAFETY—STANDARDS.
United States. National Institute for Occupational Safety and Health. Criteria for a recommended standard... occupational exposure to carbon monoxide. 1972. **fRA1247.C17U5 ECOL**
United States. National Institute for Occupational Safety and Health. Occupational exposure to inorganic lead. 1972. **fRA1231.L4U5 ECOL**
United States. National Institute for Occupational Saffaety and Health. Occupational exposure to ultraviolet radiation. 1972. **fRA1231.R2U5 ECOL**

INDUSTRIAL WASTES *see* FACTORY AND TRADE WASTE

INDUSTRIES, LOCATION OF.
Industrial Development. Site selection handbook, vol.2. 1972. **REF fHC68.I5 1972 ECOL**

INDUSTRY—SOCIAL ASPECTS.
Jacobs, Jane. The economy of cities. 1969 **HT321.J32 ECOL**

Price, Fred C. McGraw-Hill's 1972 report on business and the environment. c1972
fTD174.P7 ECOL

INDUSTRY—SOCIAL ASPECTS—UNITED STATES.
Osborne, Philip B. The war that business must win. 1970 **HD60.5.U5O8 ECOL**

INFLUENCE OF ENVIRONMENT.
Benarde, Melvin A. Our precarious habitat. 1st ed. 1970 **TD180.B45 ECOL**

INFORMATION SERVICES.
Cohen, Martin. A handbook on environmental information programs for public libraries. 1973.
fZ670.A3C6 ECOL

INFORMATION SERVICES—UNITED STATES—DIRECTORIES.
Sichel, Beatrice. Guide to private citizen action environmental groups. 1973. **REF fS920.S53 ECOL**

INFORMATION SERVICES—WASHINGTON, D.C.—DIRECTORIES.
Directory of public information contacts, Wash., D.C., 1972- **REF JK849.A353 ECOL**

INLAND WATER TRANSPORTATION—UNITED STATES.
Inland waterway transportation. 1969
HE629.I57 ECOL

INSECT BAITS AND REPELLENTS—CONGRESSES.
Chemicals controlling insect behavior. 1970.
QL461.S88 1969 ECOL

INSECT CONTROL OF WEEDS see WEED CONTROL—BIOLOGICAL CONTROL

INSECT HORMONES—CONGRESSES.
International IUPAC Congress of Pesticide Chemistry, 2d, Tel-Aviv, 1971. Chemical releasers in insects. c1971 **SB951.I56 1971vol.3 ECOL**

INSECT VENOM—CONGRESSES.
International IUPAC Congress of Pesticide Chemistry, 2d, Tel-Aviv, 1971. Chemical releasers in insects. c1971 **SB951.I56 1971vol.3 ECOL**

INSECTICIDES.
Midwest Research Institute, Kansas City, Mo. Rapid detection system for organophosphates and carbamate insectides in water. 1972. **TD427.P35M5 ECOL**

INSECTICIDES—PHYSIOLOGICAL EFFECT—CONGRESSES.
International IUPAC Congress of Pesticide Chemistry, 2d, Tel-Aviv, 1971. Insecticide resistance, synergism, enzyme induction. c1971
SB951.I56 1971vol.2 ECOL

INSECTICIDES—TOXICOLOGY.
Jager, K. W. Aldrin, dieldrin, endrin and telodrin. 1970. **RA1270.P4J33 ECOL**

INSECTS.
Linsenmaier, Walter. Insects of the world. 1972
fQL463.L4615 ECOL

INSECTS—BIOLOGY.
Tinbergen, Nikolaas. Curious naturalists. 1968,c1958 **QL751.T55 1968 ECOL**

INSECTS—COLLECTION AND PRESERVATION.
Russell, Helen Ross. Winter search party. 1st ed. 1971 **QL465.R85 ECOL**

INSECTS—NEW JERSEY.
Worth, Charles Brooke. Of mosquitoes, moths, and mice. 1st ed. 1972 **QL475.N5W66 ECOL**

INSECTS—NORTH AMERICA.
Klots, Alexander Barrett. Insects of North America. 1971 **QL473.K56 ECOL**
Swan, Lester A. The common insects of North America. 1st ed. 1972 **QL473.S9 ECOL**

INSECTS—NORTH AMERICA—IDENTIFICATION.
Swan, Lester A. The common insects of North America. 1st ed. 1972 **QL473.S9 ECOL**

INSECTS, AQUATIC.
Needham, James George. A guide to the study of fresh-water biology. 1927 **QH96.N38 ECOL**

INSECTS, INJURIOUS AND BENEFICIAL—BIOLOGICAL CONTROL.
Carson, Rachel Louise. Silent spring. 1962
SB959.C3 ECOL
DeBach, Paul. Biological control of insect pests and weeds. 1964 **REF SB975.D4 ECOL**
Hunter, Beatrice Trum. Gardening without poisons. 2d ed. 1971 **SB975.H8 1971 ECOL**
Plants & gardens. Handbook on biological control of plant pests. 1966,1960 **SB932.P5 1966 ECOL**

INTERNATIONAL AGENCIES.
Conference on Legal and Institutional Responses to Problems of the Global Evnironment, Arden House, 1971. Law, institutions, and the global environment. 1972. **KF3775.A75C6 1971 ECOL**

INTERNATIONAL AGENCIES—ADDRESSES, ESSAYS, LECTURES.
Kay, David A. World eco-crisis: international organizations in response. 1972
HC79.E5K38 ECOL

INTERNATIONAL COOPERATION.
Environmental Studies Board. Committee for International Environmental Programs. Institutional arrangements for international environmental cooperation. 1972. **HC79.E5E6 ECOL**

INTERNATIONAL RELATIONS.
Sprout, Harold Hance. The ecological perspective on human affairs. 1965. **JX1251.S49 ECOL**

INTERTIDAL ZONATION.
Stephenson, Thomas Alan. Life between tidemarks on rocky shores. 1972 **QH541.5.S3S68 ECOL**

IODIDES.
Postma, Arlin Keith. Review of organic iodide formation under accident conditions in water-cooled reactors. 1972. **fTK9152.P6 ECOL**

ION EXCHANGE RESINS.
Uniroyal, Inc. Feasibility study of regenerative fibers for water pollution control. 1970 i.e. 1971
fTD757.5.U55 ECOL

IRON—METALLURGY.
Davis, Edward Wilson. Pioneering with taconite. 1964. **TN403.M6D3 ECOL**

IRON AND STEEL INDUSTRY.
United Nations. Economic Commission for Europe. Problems relating to iron and steel scrap. 1971.
fTS214.U6 ECOL

IRON INDUSTRY AND TRADE—MINNESOTA.
Nelson, Clarence Walfred. An ex ante profitability analysis of capital investment in taconite pellet production facilities in Minnesota circa 1950-51. 1967.
HD9517.M6N4 ECOL

IRRIGATION—BIBLIOGRAPHY.
Water Resources Scientific Information Center. Use of naturally impaired water. 1973.
Z7935.W32 ECOL

IRRIGATION—THE WEST.
Smythe, William Ellsworth. The conquest of arid America. 1969,c1905 **F591.S662 1969 ECOL**

IRRIGATION—UNITED STATES.
Ruttan, Vernon W. The economic demand for irrigated acreage. 1965 **HD1735.R8 ECOL**

IRRIGATION CANALS AND FLUMES—LININGS.
Skogerboe, Gaylord V. Evaluation of canal lining for salinity control in Grand Valley. 1972.
TC930.S5 ECOL

IRRIGATION WATER.
Law, James P. National irrigation return flow research and development program. 1971.
fTC809.L38 ECOL
Otto, Norman E. Aquatic pests on irrigation systems: identification guide. 1972,1965
QH96.O88 1972 ECOL
Skogerboe, Gaylord V. Research needs for irrigation return flow quality control. 1971 i.e. 1972
fTD223.S54 ECOL
Van Voast, Wayne A. Ground water for irrigation in the Brooten-Belgrade area, west-central Minnesota. 1971. **TC801.U2no.1899-E ECOL**

IRRIGATION WATER—ABSTRACTS.
Skogerboe, Gaylord V. Selected irrigation return flow. 1972- **fTD223.S5 ECOL**

ISLE ROYALE NATIONAL PARK.
May, Julian. The big island. 1968
PZ10.M455Bi ECOL

ISOLATING MECHANISMS.
Lack, David Lambert. Ecological isolation in birds. 1971. **QH401.L32 1971 ECOL**

ISOPODA.
Williams, William David. Freshwater isopods (Asellidae) of North America. 1972.
fQH96.A2B5no.7 ECOL

J

JOHN F. KENNEDY INTERNATIONAL AIRPORT, IDLEWILD, N.Y.
Jamaica Bay Environmental Study Group. Jamaica Bay and Kennedy Airport: a multidisciplinary environmental study. 1971. **fTL725.3.P5J3 ECOL**

JOURNALISM, SCIENTIFIC.
Burkett, David Warren. Writing science news for the mass media. 2d ed., rev. 1973.
PN4784.T3B8 1973 ECOL

JUNGLE ECOLOGY.
Richards, Paul Westmacott. The life of the jungle. 1970 **QH541.5.J8R53 ECOL**

K

KAUAI.
Wenkam, Robert. Kauai and the park country of Hawaii. 1967 **DU628.K3W4 ECOL**

L

LABRADOR—DESCRIPTION AND TRAVEL—MAPS.
Forbes, Alexander. Northernmost Labrador. 1938.
F1136.F67 ECOL

LAKES see also LIMNOLOGY
Frea, James I. Washout processes in lake systems. 1972. **fTD764.F74 ECOL**

LAKES—CONGRESSES.
Lowe-McConnell, R. H. Man-made lakes. 1966.
GB1601.L6 1965 ECOL

LAKES—GREAT PLAINS.
Stewart, Robert E. Classification of natural ponds and lakes in the glaciated prairie region. 1971.
S914.A3no.92 ECOL

LAKES—MINNESOTA.
Continuation of studies on the hydrology of ponds and small lakes. 1971. **fGB1825.M6C6ECOL**
Jaques, Florence (Page). Canoe country. c1938
F606.J36 ECOL
Manson, Philip W. Some aspects of the hydrology of ponds and small lakes. 1968.
fGB1825.M6M35 ECOL
Minnesota. Dept. of Conservation. Division of Waters, Soils, and Minerals. An inventory of Minnesota lakes. 1968. **TD224.M6A3no.25 ECOL**
Minnesota. Lakeshore Development Study. Minnesota's lakeshore. 1970-
REF GB459.5.M5M5 ECOL
Nute, Grace Lee. The voyageur's highway. 1965 c1941 **F606.N97 ECOL**
Zumberge, James Herbert. The lakes of Minnesota, their origin and classification. 1952.
REF QE127.A22no.35 ECOL

LAKES—MINNESOTA—MAPS.
Minnesota. Dept. of Conservation. Division of Waters, Soils, and Minerals. An inventory of Minnesota lakes. 1968. **TD224.M6A3no.25 ECOL**

LAKES—TEMPERATURE.
Minnesota. University. School of Public Health. Water movements and temperatures of western Lake Superior. 1958. **fGB1627.G89M54 ECOL**

LAKES—UNITED STATES.
Ketelle, Martha J. Problem lakes in the United States. 1971. **fTD223.K47 ECOL**
Kusler, Jon A. Survey: lake protection and rehabilitation legislation in the United States. 1972.
REF fKF5568.K8 ECOL

LAND see also AGRICULTURE; AGRICULTURE—ECONOMIC ASPECTS; FARMS; REGIONAL PLANNING
Ely, Richard Theodore. Land economics. 1964.
HD111.E37 1964 ECOL
Helfman, Elizabeth S. Land, people, and history. 1967c1962 **HD156.H4 1967 ECOL**

LAND—ALASKA.
Cooley, Richard A. Alaska. 1967.
HC107.A45C6 ECOL

LAND—BIBLIOGRAPHY.
Wright, Sydney. A bibliography of recreational communities and leisure land development. 1973.
fZ7164.L3W7 ECOL

LAND—CALIFORNIA.
Fellmeth, Robert C. Politics of land: Ralph Nader's study group report on land use in California. 1973.
HD211.C2F45 ECOL

LAND—CLASSIFICATION.
Resources for the Future. Committee on Land Use Statistics. Land use information. 1969, c1965
HD205 1969.R4 ECOL

LAND—CLASSIFICATION—MINNESOTA.
Land Exchange Review Symposium, Duluth, 1970. Proceedings of the Land Exchange Review Symposium. 1970. **fHD211.L3 ECOL**

LAND—INFORMATION SERVICES—MINNESOTA.
Walton, William Clarence. Interest groups with water and related land resources programs in Minnesota, 1971. 1972. **GB701.M554no.45 ECOL**
Walton, William Clarence. International, regional, federal-state, interstate and federal organizations with water related land resources programs in Minnesota, 1971. 1971. **GB701.M554no.42 ECOL**

LAND—MINNESOTA.
Borchert, John R. Minnesota settlement and land use 1985. 1970. **HD111.B6 ECOL**
Minnesota. Conservation Needs Committee. Minnesota soil and water conservation needs inventory. 1971 **fHD243.M6A42 ECOL**

Minnesota. Division of Lands and Forestry. Land exchange study report. 1969. **fHD211.M6A45 ECOL**

Minnesota. State Planning Agency. Protecting the Minnesota environment through regulation of private land use. 1972. **fHC107.M6A45 ECOL**

Orning, George W. Land management information in northwest Minnesota: the beginnings of a statewide system. 1972. **HD211.M6 ECOL**

Planning Research Corporation. Pollution through land use management. 1969? **fGD205 1969 .P6 ECOL**

LAND—TWIN CITIES METROPOLITAN AREA.
Minnesota. Metropolitan Council of the Twin Cities Area. Open Space Advisory Committee. Proposals for preserving a Metropolitan open space. 1969 **fHD1291.U6T9 ECOL**

LAND—UNITED STATES.
Advisory Committee to the Department of Housing and Urban Development. Land Use Subcommittee. Urban growth and land development. 1972. **HD205 1972 .A35 ECOL**

Clawson, Marion. America's land and its uses. 1972 **HD205 1972 .C55 ECOL**

Clawson, Marion. The land system of the United States. 1968 **HD191.C53 ECOL**

Clawson, Marion. Suburban land conversion in the United States: an economic and governmental process. 1971 **HD259.C55 ECOL**

Council of State Governments. The states' role in land resource management. 1972 **HD205.C6 1972 ECOL**

Delafons, John. Land-use controls in the United States. 2d ed. 1969 **HD205 1969 .D4 ECOL**

Guitar, Mary Anne. Property power. 1st ed. 1972. **HD205 1972 .G8 ECOL**

Homestead Centennial Symposium, University of Nebraska, 1962. Land use policy and problems in the United States. 1964,c1963 **HD205 1962 .H6 ECOL**

Little, Charles E. Challenge of the land. 1968 **HD205 1968 .L5 ECOL**

Resources for the Future. Land for the future. 1960 **HD205 1960.R4 ECOL**

Resources for the Future. Committee on Land Use Statistics. Land use information. 1969, c1965 **HD205 1969.R4 ECOL**

Schmid, A. Allan. Converting land from rural to urban uses. 1968 **REF HD256.S3 ECOL**

Shomon, Joseph James. Open land for urban America. 1971 **HD257.S56 ECOL**

LAND—UNITED STATES—HISTORY.
Clawson, Marion. Man and land in the United States. 1964. **HD191.C55 ECOL**

LAND—UNITED STATES—STUDY AND TEACHING.
Jackson, John Y. Land use: concern, challenge, commitment. c1969 **HD110.J3 ECOL**

LAND RESEARCH.
Symposium on Research Methods, Virginia Polytechnic Institute, 1965. Methods for land economics research. 1967?,c1966 **HD110.S9 1965 ECOL**

LAND TENURE—UNITED STATES.
Clawson, Marion. The land system of the United States. 1968 **HD191.C53 ECOL**

Hibbard, Benjamin Horace. A history of the public land policies. 1965. **HD216.H5 1965 ECOL**

LANDSCAPE PROTECTION see also REGIONAL PLANNING

Robinette, Gary O. Plants/people/environmental quality. 1972 **QK901.R6 ECOL**

LANDSCAPE PROTECTION—GREAT BRITAIN.
Barr, John. The assaults on our senses. 1970. **QH77.G7B29 ECOL**

LANDSCAPE PROTECTION—UNITED STATES.
White House Conference on Natural Beauty, Washington, D.C., 1965. Beauty for America. 1965 **QH77.U6W5 1965 ECOL**

LASERS.
Environmental Systems Corporation. Development and demonstration of low-level drift instrumentation. 1971. **fTD884.5.E58 ECOL**

LATIN AMERICA—ECONOMIC CONDITIONS—1945-
Grunwald, Joseph. Natural resources in Latin American development. 1970 **REF fHC125.G72 ECOL**

LAW REPORTS, DIGESTS, ETC.—MINNESOTA.
Minnesota. Pollution Control Agency. In the matter of the adoption of proposed amendments to Minnesota Regulations APC 1, APC 3, APC 4, APC 11 and APC 15; and the adoption of Minnesota Regulation APC 16; and the proposed adoption of the Minnesota Air Quality Implementation Plan. 1972 **REF fKFM5758.A17 1972 ECOL**

LEAD.
United States. Bureau of Mines. Control of sulfur oxide emissions in copper, lead, and zinc smelting. 1971 **TN295.U4no.8527 ECOL**

LEAD—PHYSIOLOGICAL EFFECT.
National Research Council. Committee on Biologic Effects of Atmospheric Pollutants. Lead. 1972. **QP913.P3N38 ECOL**

United States. National Institute for Occupational Safety and Health. Occupational exposure to inorganic lead. 1972. **fRA1231.L4U5 ECOL**

LEAD-POISONING.
National Research Council. Committee on Biologic Effects of Atmospheric Pollutants. Lead. 1972. **QP913.P3N38 ECOL**

United States. National Institute for Occupational Safety and Health. Occupational exposure to inorganic lead. 1972. **fRA1231.L4U5 ECOL**

LEAD POISONING—BIBLIOGRAPHY.
White, Anthony G. Lead in the urban environment: a selected bibliography. 1973. **fZ6679.L4W5 ECOL**

LEAR, WILLIAM POWELL, 1902-
Boesen, Victor. They said it couldn't be done: the incredible story of Bill Lear. 1st ed. 1971. **TL540.L364B64 ECOL**

LEAVES.
Gallob, Edward. City leaves, city trees. 1972 **fQK475.8.G35 ECOL**

LEECHES.
Klemm, Donald J. Freshwater leeches (Annelida: Hirudinea) of North America. 1972. **fQH96.A2B5no.8 ECOL**

LEGISLATION—UNITED STATES—STATES.
Council of State Governments. Committee of State Officials on Suggested State Legislation. Suggested state legislation; 1973- v.32- **JK2431.C6 ECOL**

LENSES.
Schwartz, Julius. Through the magnifying glass. 1954 **Q163.S464 ECOL**

LIBRARIES—SPECIAL COLLECTIONS—DIRECTORIES.
Mauritz, Marilyn. Library and informational resources in the Twin City Area. 1972- **REF fZ688.A2M3 ECOL**

LIBRARIES—UNITED STATES.
United States. Environmental Protection Agency. Library Systems Branch. Journal holdings report: 1972- **REF fZ6945.U534 ECOL**

LIBRARY CATALOGS.
United States. Dept. of the Interior. Library. Dictionary catalog of the department library. 1967. **REF fZ881.U41 ECOL**

LIFE—ORIGIN.
Henderson, Lawrence Joseph. The fitness of the environment. 1970 c1913 **QH331.H45 1970 ECOL**

LIFE (BIOLOGY).
Crick, Francis. Of molecules and men. 1969,c1966. **QH331.C9 1969 ECOL**

Henderson, Lawrence Joseph. The fitness of the environment. 1970 c1913 **QH331.H45 1970 ECOL**

Science Curriculum Improvement Study. Life cycles. c1970 **LB1585.S32 ECOL**

LIMESTONE.
Armco Steel Corporation. Limestone treatment of rinse waters from hydrochloric acid pickling of steel. 1971. **fTD899.M45A75 ECOL**

LIMNOLOGY.
Allen, Herbert Ellis. Nutrients in natural waters. 1972 **QH96.A48 ECOL**

Coker, Robert Ervin. Streams, lakes, ponds. 1954 **QH96.C6 ECOL**

Fast, Arlo Wade. The effects of artificial aeration on lake ecology. 1971 i.e.1972 **fTD458.F38 ECOL**

Hynes, Hugh Bernard Noel. The ecology of running waters. 1970. **QH541.5.S7H9 ECOL**

LIMNOLOGY—CONGRESSES.
International Symposium on Eutrophication, University of Wisconsin, 1967. Eutrophication: causes, consequences, correctives. 1969. **QH96.A1I63 1967 ECOL**

LIMNOLOGY—GREAT LAKES.
Hydroscience, Inc. Limnological systems analysis of the Great Lakes. 1973. **fTC423.3.H9 ECOL**

LIMNOLOGY—INDIAN CREEK RESERVOIR. CALIF.
Lake Tahoe Area Council. Eutrophication of surface waters—Lake Tahoe Indian Creek Reservoir. 1971. **fTD224.C3L32 ECOL**

LIMNOLOGY—NORTH AMERICA—COLLECTED WORKS.
Frey, David Grove. Limnology in North America. 1966 c1963 **QH96.F7 ECOL**

LIMNOLOGY—ONONDAGA LAKE, N.Y.
Onondaga Co., N.Y. Onondaga Lake study. 1971. **fTD224.N7O5 ECOL**

LIMNOLOGY—PIKE CO., INDIANA.
Smith, Ronald W. Acid mine pollution effects on lake biology. 1971. **fTD899.M5S6 ECOL**

LITTER (TRASH)—UNITED STATES—DIRECTORIES.
Keep America Beautiful, Inc. Inventory of litter-prevention and related environmental programs in the United States. 1972- **fTD817.K4 ECOL**

LOCAL GOVERNMENT—NEW ENGLAND.
American Geographical Society of New York New England's prospect: 1933. 1933. **HC107.A11A82 ECOL**

LOCAL TRANSIT.
Wingo, Lowdon. Transportation and urban land. 1968,c1961 **HE4211.W5 ECOL**

LOCAL TRANSIT—CONGRESSES.
International Conference on Urban Transportation, 5th, Pittsburgh, 1971. Mobility: the fifth freedom. 1971? **fHE148.I5 1971 ECOL**

LOCAL TRANSIT—MINNESOTA—MINNEAPOLIS.
Minneapolis. Office of the City Coordinator. Regional transit for Minneapolis: interim report. 1972. **fHE4491.M62 1972 ECOL**

LOCAL TRANSIT—UNITED STATES.
Pell, Claiborne de B. Megalopolis unbound. c1966 **HE355.P4 ECOL**

LOWER MINNESOTA RIVER WATERSHED, MINNESOTA.
Itasca Engineering, inc. Minneapolis. The Lower Minnesota River Watershed District. 1961. **fTC424.M6I84 ECOL**

Itasca Engineering, inc., Minneapolis. Overall plan of the Lower Minnesota River Watershed District, 1972. **fTC424.M6I86 ECOL**

LUMBER TRADE.
Zivnuska, John Arthur. United States timber resources in a world economy. c1967 **HD9750.5.Z5 ECOL**

M

MACHINERY.
Blackwood, Paul Everett. Push and pull. Rev. ed. 1966 **TJ147.B52 1966 ECOL**

MAGNETOHYDRODYNAMIC GENERATORS.
Open cycle coal burning MHD power generation. 1971 **fTN805.A395no.64 ECOL**

MALTHUSIANISM.
The Limits to growth. c1972 **HC110.E5L5 ECOL**

MAMMALS.
Allen, Gertrude E. Everyday animals. 1961. **PZ10.A478Ev ECOL**

Bourliere, Francois. The natural history of mammals. 1st American ed. 1954. **QL751.B663 ECOL**

Bridges, William. Wild animals of the world. 1948 **fQL706.B89 ECOL**

Fitter, Richard Sidney Richmond. Vanishing wild animals of the world. 1968 **fQL88.F5 ECOL**

MAMMALS—ALASKA.
Dufresne, Frank. Alaska's animals & fishes. c1946 **QL628.A4D8 1946 ECOL**

MAMMALS—BEHAVIOR.
Rutter, Russell J. The world of the wolf. 1968. **QL737.C2R87 ECOL**

MAMMALS—COLLECTION AND PRESERVATION.
Booth, Ernest Sheldon. How to know the mammals. 3d ed. 1972, c1971 **QL715.B66 1972 ECOL**

MAMMALS—IDENTIFICATION.
Booth, Ernest Sheldon. How to know the mammals. 3d ed. 1972, c1971 **QL715.B66 1972 ECOL**

Lempfert, O. C. Paw prints. 1st ed. 1972 **QL768.L37 ECOL**

MAMMALS—ISLE ROYALE NATIONAL PARK.
May, Julian. The big island. 1968 **PZ10.M455Bi ECOL**

Mech, L. David. The wolves of Isle Royale. 1966 **QL155.A45no.7 ECOL**

MAMMALS—NORTH AMERICA.
Barker, Will. Familiar animals of America. 1956 **QL715.B25 ECOL**

Dugdale, Vera. Album of North American animals. 1966 **fPZ10.D745AL ECOL**

Orr, Robert Thomas. Mammals of North America. 1971 **QL715.O77 ECOL**

MAMMALS—NORTH AMERICA—IDENTIFICATION.
Booth, Ernest Sheldon. How to know the mammals. 3d ed. 1972, c1971 **QL715.B66 1972 ECOL**

MAMMALS—PHYSIOLOGY.
Sadleir, R. M. F. S. The ecology of reproduction in wild and domestic mammals. 1969.
    QP251.S27 ECOL

MAMMALS—UNITED STATES.
Ransom, Elmer Inglesby. The woodland book. 1945
    QL681.R2 ECOL

MAN.
Burnet, Frank Macfarlane, Sir. Dominant mammal. 1972, c1971   **QH331.B887 1972 ECOL**

Sears, Paul Bigelow. This is our world. Rev. ed. 1971
    QH309.S3 1971 ECOL

MAN—INFLUENCE OF CLIMATE.
Auliciems, Andris. The atmospheric environment. 1972   **QP82.2.T4A9 ECOL**

Claiborne, Robert. Climate, man, and history. 1970
    GF71.C55 ECOL

MAN—INFLUENCE OF ENVIRONMENT.
Bresler, Jack Barry. Human ecology. 1966
    GF31.B65 ECOL

Dubos, Rene Jules. A God within. 1972
    HM206.D86 ECOL

Dubos, Rene Jules. Man adapting. 1965.
    R723.D77 ECOL

Dubos, Rene Jules. So human an animal. 1968
    HM206.D87 ECOL

Environment for man. 1967
    HT167.E5 1967 ECOL

Hueper, Wilhelm C. Occupational and environmental cancers of the urinary system. 1969.
    RC280.G4H8 ECOL

Leiss, William. The domination of nature. c1972
    S936.L45 ECOL

Vayda, Andrew Peter. Environment and cultural behavior. 1969.   **GF51.V35 ECOL**

MAN—INFLUENCE OF ENVIRONMENT—ADDRESSES, ESSAYS, LECTURES.
Burch, William R. Social behavior, natural resources, and the environment. 1972   **HM206.B84 ECOL**

Environmental perception and behavior. 1967.
    GF51.E5 ECOL

Toepfer, Caroline T. Environmental psychology: selected readings. 1972   **HM206.T6 ECOL**

MAN—INFLUENCE OF ENVIRONMENT—BIBLIOGRAPHY.
Appleyard, Donald. The urban environment: selected bibliography. 1972.
    REF fZ7164.U7A6 ECOL

MAN—INFLUENCE OF ENVIRONMENT—CONGRESSES.
A Conversation on population, environment, and human well-being. 1971   **HB875.C63 ECOL**

Jennings, Burgess Hill. Interactions of man and his environment. 1966.   **TD180.J4 ECOL**

MAN—INFLUENCE ON NATURE.
Abrahamson, Dean E. Environmental cost of electric power. 1970   **fTK1005.A26 ECOL**

Adams, Ruth. Say no! 1971
    HC110.E5A63 ECOL

Adelstein, Michael E. Ecocide and population. 1971, c1972   **GF75.A35 ECOL**

Anderson, Paul K. Omega. 1971
    QH541.A5 ECOL

Arbib, Robert S. The Lord's Woods. 1st ed. 1971
    QH76.5.N7A72 ECOL

Atkinson, Justin Brooks. This bright land. 1st ed. 1972.   **GF503.A8 ECOL**

Benarde, Melvin A. Our precarious habitat. 1st ed. 1970   **TD180.B45 ECOL**

Benthall, Jonathan. Ecology in theory and practice. 1973,c1972   **QH541.B4 1973 ECOL**

Black, John N. The dominion of man. 1970.
    GF80.B55 ECOL

Blueprint for survival. 1972. **S936.B5 1972 ECOL**

Bock, Alan. The ecology action guide. c1971
    GF75.B6 ECOL

Brown, Lester Russell. Man and his environment: food. 1972   **S439.B76 ECOL**

Burch, William R. Daydreams and nightmares. 1971   **HM206.B83 ECOL**

Chisholm, Anne. Philosophers of the earth. c1972
    GF75.C4 ECOL

Chute, Robert M. Environmental insight. 1971
    GF75.C48 ECOL

Colwell, Jim. World view. 1971. **GF75.C6 ECOL**

Commoner, Barry. The closing circle. 1st ed. 1971.
    GF75.C65 ECOL

Darling, Frank Fraser. Future environments of North America. 1966.   **HC95.D33 ECOL**

Darling, Frank Fraser. Wilderness and plenty. 1970.
    QH541.13.D36 ECOL

Dasmann, Raymond Frederick. No further retreat. 1971   **S932.F6D37 ECOL**

Dasmann, Raymond Frederick. Planet in peril. 1972   **QH541.D35 1972 ECOL**

Detwyler, Thomas R. Man's impact on environment. 1971   **GF75.D48 ECOL**

Dorst, Jean. Before nature dies. 1st American ed. 1970.   **S936.D6613 ECOL**

Douglas, William Orville. The three hundred year war: a chronicle of ecological disaster. 1st ed. 1972
    QH541.D68 ECOL

Ekirch, Arthur Alphonse. Man and nature in America. 1963.   **GF503.E46 ECOL**

Emmel, Thomas C. An introduction to ecology and population biology. 1973   **QH541.E45 1973 ECOL**

Group for Environmental Education, inc. Our man-made environment: a collection of experiences, resources and suggested activities. 1971.
    fGF75.G76 ECOL

Hall, Gus. Ecology: can we survive under capitalism? 1st ed. 1972   **HC110.E5H3 ECOL**

Harrison, Gordon A. Earthkeeping. 1971.
    HC110.E5H33 ECOL

Hoke, John. Ecology: man's effects on his environment and its mechanisms. 1971
    QH541.H58 ECOL

Imsland, Donald. Celebrate the earth. 1971
    QH541.I45 ECOL

Jones, Claire. Pollution: the balance of nature. 1972
    QH541.14.J65 ECOL

Katz, Robert. A giant in the earth. c1973
    HD9000.5.K3 ECOL

Lauwerys, Joseph Albert. Man's impact on nature. 1970,c1969   **QH368.L38 ECOL**

Leiss, William. The domination of nature. c1972
    S936.L45 ECOL

Linton, Ron M. Terracide. 1970
    TD180.L56 ECOL

Marsh, George Perkins. Man and nature. 1965.
    GF31.M35 1965 ECOL

Marzani, Carl. The wounded earth. 1972
    QH541.M38 ECOL

Masini, Giancarlo. S.O.S. save our earth. c1972
    fQH541.M382 1972 ECOL

Matthews, William Henry. Man's impact on terrestrial and oceanic ecosystems. 1971
    TD174.M39 ECOL

McClellan, Grant S. Protecting our environment. 1970.   **TD180.M3 ECOL**

McHarg, Ian L. Design with nature. 1st ed. 1969.
    fHC110.E5M33 ECOL

Metress, James F. Man in ecological perspective. c1971   **GF75.M4 ECOL**

Myers, Charles B. The environmental crisis: will we survive? 1972   **HC110.E5M9 ECOL**

Nicholson, Max. The environmental revolution. 1970   **S936.N5 ECOL**

Nobile, Philip. The complete ecology fact book. 1st ed. 1972.   **TD174.N6 ECOL**

Ramparts. Eco-catastrophe. c1970
    TD180.R3 ECOL

Resources for the Future. Environmental quality in a growing economy. 1968,c1966
    HC103.7.R39 ECOL

Ridgeway, James. The politics of ecology. 1st ed. 1970.   **HC110.E5R52 ECOL**

Snowmobile and Off the Road Vehicle Research Symposium, Michigan State University, East Lansing, 1971. Proceedings. **fGF75.S6 1971 ECOL**

Study of Man's Impact on Climate, Stockholm, 1970. Inadvertent climate modification. 1971
    QC981.S77 1970 ECOL

The Teilhard Review. Change or decay: a symposium on the Blueprint for survival. 1972.
    HC68.T4 ECOL

Wagner, Richard H. Environment and man. 1st ed. 1971   **QH541.13.W34 ECOL**

Weather modification. 1969   **QC928.W38 ECOL**

Weisberg, Barry. Beyond repair. 1971
    GF75.W45 1971 ECOL

MAN—INFLUENCE ON NATURE—ADDRESSES, ESSAYS, LECTURES.
Burch, William R. Social behavior, natural resources, and the environment. 1972   **HM206.B84 ECOL**

Day, John A. Dimensions of the environmental crisis. 1971   **HC79.E5D35 ECOL**

Disch, Robert. The ecological conscience. 1970
    HC110.E5D58 ECOL

Johnson, Cecil E. The natural world: chaos and conservation. c1972   **QH541.145.J63 ECOL**

McKain, David W. The whole earth. 1972
    QH81.M1518 ECOL

Novick, Sheldon. Our world in peril. 1971
    HC110.P55N67 ECOL

MAN—INFLUENCE ON NATURE—BIBLIOGRAPHY.
Winton, Harry N. M. Man and the environment: a bibliography of selected publications of the United Nations system, 1946-1971. 1972.
    REF Z5322.E2W56 ECOL

MAN—INFLUENCE ON NATURE—COLLECTIONS.
As we live and breath. 1971   **GF75.A8 ECOL**

MAN—INFLUENCE ON NATURE—CONGRESSES.
Conference on the Ecological Aspects of International Development, Airlie House, 1968. The careless technology: ecology and international development. 1st ed. 1972. **QH540.C65 1968 ECOL**

Environmental quality and social responsibility. 1972   **HC110.P55E57 ECOL**

The Limits to growth. c1972   **HC110.E5L5 ECOL**

Natural Science Center Conference. 8th, Dayton, Ohio, 1970. Leadership to meet our environmental crisis. 1970   **REF fTD178.3.N3 ECOL**

Stockholm and beyond. 1972.
    HC110.E5A43 ECOL

Study of Critical Environmental Problems. Man's impact on the global environment. 1970
    QH541.S73 ECOL

Western Resources Conference. Colorado School of Mines, summer 1971. Needs of a progressive society for mineral and energy resources and realistic solutions to environmental problems posed. 1971
    REF fTD172.5.W4 ECOL

MAN—INFLUENCE ON NATURE—HANDBOOKS, MANUALS, ETC.
Hilado, Carlos J. Handbook of environmental management. 1972-   **REF fGF75.H5 ECOL**

MAN—INFLUENCE ON NATURE—STUDY AND TEACHING.
Kelly, James. Pollution—man's crisis: an investigative approach. c1971 **QH541.2.K45 ECOL**

MAN—ORIGIN.
Eiseley, Loren C. The immense journey. 1957
    QH368.E38 ECOL

Napier, John Russell. The roots of mankind. 1970.
    QH368.N36 ECOL

MANAGEMENT—MINNESOTA.
Creative Research Services, Inc. Water quality management plan, interim. 1971.
    REF fTD224.M65C7 ECOL

MANGANESE MINES AND MINING.
Virginia Polytechnic Institute and State University. Stream faunal recovery after manganese strip mine reclamation. 1971.   **fTN291.V5 ECOL**

MANGANESE ORES.
Brooks, David B. Low-grade and nonconventional sources of manganese. 1966
    REF TN490.M3B85 ECOL

MANHOLES.
Mayer, John K. Sewer bedding and infiltration, Gulf Coast area. 1972.   **fTD653.M3 ECOL**

MANUFACTURERS—MINNESOTA—DIRECTORIES.
Minnesota directory of manufacturers.
    REF fT12.M5 ECOL

MARINE BIOLOGY.
Berrill, Norman John. The life of the ocean. c1966
    QH91.15.B4 ECOL

Engel, Leonard. The sea. c1969
    fGC21.E5 1969 ECOL

Platt, Rutherford Hayes. Water: the wonder of life. 1971   **QH91.15.P57 ECOL**

Sandburg, Helga. Above and below. 1st ed. 1969
    QH91.75.U6S35 ECOL

MARINE BIOLOGY—ATLANTIC OCEAN.
Carson, Rachel Louise. Under the sea-wind. New ed. with corrections 1952c1941
    QH92.C3 1952 ECOL

MARINE BIOLOGY—PICTORIAL WORKS.
Cousteau, Jacques Yves. Oasis in space: the ocean world of Jacques Cousteau. c1972
    fQH91.C64 ECOL

Torchio, Menico. The world beneath the sea. 1972
    fQH91.17.T6 ECOL

MARINE ECOLOGY.
Friedrich, Hermann. Marine biology. 1969
    QH541.5.S3F713 1969 ECOL

General Dynamics Corporation. Electric Boat Division. Potential environmental effects of an offshore submerged nuclear power plant. 1971-
    fQH541.5.S3G45 ECOL

Perry, Richard. The unknown ocean. 1972
QL124.P47 1972 ECOL
Silverberg, Robert. The world within the ocean wave. 1972 **QH91.8.P5S54 ECOL**
MARINE FAUNA.
Perry, Richard. The unknown ocean. 1972
QL124.P47 1972 ECOL
Selsam, Millicent (Ellis). See through the lake. 1958
PZ10.S44Sdi ECOL
MARINE FLORA.
Selsam, Millicent (Ellis). See through the lake. 1958
PZ10.S44Sdi ECOL
MARINE PARKS AND RESERVES—UNITED STATES.
Sandburg, Helga. Above and below. 1st ed. 1969
QH91.75.U6S35 ECOL
MARINE PLANKTON.
Silverberg, Robert. The world within the ocean wave. 1972 **QH91.8.P5S54 ECOL**
MARINE POLLUTION.
Marx, Wesley. The protected ocean. 1972
GC1018.M32 ECOL
Moorcraft, Colin. Must the seas die? 1973.
GC1085.M66 1973 ECOL
MARINE POLLUTION—BIBLIOGRAPHY.
Sinha, Evelyn. Coastal/estuarine pollution. 1970
REF fZ5853.P7S53 ECOL
MARINE POLLUTION—ECONOMIC ASPECTS.
Sweet, David C. The economic and social importance of estuaries. 1971. **GB454.E8S95 ECOL**
MARINE POLLUTION—ENGLISH CHANNEL.
Marine Biological Association of the United Kingdom. Laboratory, Plymouth. 'Torrey Canyon' pollution and marine life: a report by the Plymouth Laboratory of the Marine Biological Association of the United Kingdom. 1968. **GC1311.M37 ECOL**
MARINE POLLUTION—LAW AND LEGISLATION.
Brown, Edward Duncan. The legal regime of hydrospace. 1971. **JX4411.B73 ECOL**
MARINE POLLUTION—PACIFIC COAST (NORTH AMERICA).
Oregon. State University, Corvallis. Oceanography of the nearshore coastal waters of the Pacific Northwest relating to possible pollution. 1971-
fGC851.O7 ECOL
MARINE POLLUTION—UNITED STATES.
United States. Council on Environmental Quality. Ocean dumping: a national policy. 1970.
TD763.U55 ECOL
MARINE RADIOECOLOGY.
Ayers, John C. Lake Michigan environmental survey: final report. 1970.
REF fQH543.6.A9 ECOL
MARINE RESOURCES.
Loftas, Tony. The last resource. rev. ed. 1970
GC1015.L57 1970 ECOL
McKee, Alexander. Farming the sea. 1969
SH333.M27 1969 ECOL
National Research Council. Committee on Oceanography. Economic benefits from oceanographic research. 1964. **REF GB58.N3 ECOL**
Uses of the seas. 1968 **GC1015.U8 ECOL**
MARINE RESOURCES—ATLASES.
Food and Agriculture Organization of the United Nations. Atlas of the living resources of the seas. 1972.
REF fGC1015.F6 ECOL
MARINE RESOURCES—DICTIONARIES.
Firth, Frank E. The encyclopedia of marine resources. 1969 **REF SH201.F56 ECOL**
MARINE RESOURCES—LAW AND LEGISLATION.
Uses of the seas. 1968 **GC1015.U8 ECOL**
MARINE RESOURCES AND STATE—UNITED STATES.
United States. Federal Coordinator for Marine environmental prediction. Federal plan for marine environmental prediction. 1971.
GC1015.U525 ECOL
MARINE RESOURCES CONSERVATION.
Marx, Wesley. The frail ocean. c1967
GC1018.M3 ECOL
Marx, Wesley. The protected ocean. 1972
GC1018.M32 ECOL
MARINE SEDIMENTS.
Washington (State). University. The oxygen uptake demand of resuspended bottom sediments. 1970.
fGC380.W3 ECOL
MARITIME LAW.
Brown, Edward Duncan. The legal regime of hydrospace. 1971. **JX4411.B73 ECOL**

MARSH ECOLOGY.
Teal, John. Life and death of the salt marsh. 1969
QH541.5.S24T4 ECOL
MARSH FLORA—CANADA—IDENTIFICATION.
Hotchkiss, Neil. Common marsh, underwater, and floating-leaved plants of the United States and Canada. 1972 **QK115.H67 1972 ECOL**
MARSH FLORA—UNITED STATES—IDENTIFICATION.
Hotchkiss, Neil. Common marsh, underwater, and floating-leaved plants of the United States and Canada. 1972 **QK115.H67 1972 ECOL**
MARSH LAKE, MINNESOTA.
Barr Engineering Co. Feasibility study: Mt. Normandale Lake and Marsh Lake, for City of Bloomington and Nine Mile Creek Watershed District. 1967. **fTC424.M6B32 ECOL**
MARSHES.
Errington, Paul Lester. Of men and marshes. 1957.
QH87.3.E7 ECOL
MARSHES, TIDE.
Teal, John. Life and death of the salt marsh. 1969
QH541.5.S24T4 ECOL
MASS SOCIETY.
Ferkiss, Victor C. Technological man: the myth and the reality. 1969 **HM221.F39 ECOL**
MATHEMATICS—STUDY AND TEACHING (SECONDARY).
Henderson, George J. Pollution: problems, projects and mathematical exercises. 1970
fQH541.2.H46 ECOL
MATTER—PROPERTIES.
Gamow, George. Matter, earth, and sky. 2d ed. 1965 **QC171.G3 1965 ECOL**
MAY-FLIES.
Minnesota. State College, Winona. Mayfly distribution as a water quality index. 1970.
fTD370.M562 ECOL
MEADOW ECOLOGY—CALIFORNIA.
Cavagnaro, David. This living earth. 1972
fQH541.5.M4C38 ECOL
MECHANICAL ENGINEERING.
Thirring, Hans. Energy for man. 1968
TJ147.T48 1968 ECOL
MEDICAL ETHICS.
Augenstine, Leroy George. Come, let us play God. 1969 **R724.A83 ECOL**
Friends, Society of. American Friends Service Committee. Who shall live? 1970
HQ766.3.F7 ECOL
MEDICAL ETHICS—CONGRESSES.
Biology and ethics. 1969. **HM216.B48 ECOL**
MEDICAL GEOGRAPHY—HISTORY.
Crosby, Alfred W. The Columbian exchange. 1972
E98.D6C7 ECOL
MEDICATED FEEDS—CONGRESSES.
The Use of drugs in animal feeds. 1969.
SF98.M4U8 ECOL
MEDICINE—PHILOSOPHY.
Dubos, Rene Jules. Man adapting. 1965.
R723.D77 ECOL
MEDICINE, PREVENTIVE.
Kilbourne, Edwin D. Human ecology and public health. 4th ed. 1969 **RA425.K55 1969 ECOL**
MERCURY.
Tratnyek, Joseph P. Waste wool as a scavenger for mercury pollution in waters. 1972.
fTD427.M4T7 ECOL
MERCURY—ABSTRACTS.
United States. Environmental Protection Agency. Office of Air Programs. Mercury and air pollution: A bibliography with abstracts. 1972.
TD887.M4U5 ECOL
MERCURY—ANALYSIS.
Environmental Measurements, Inc. Monitoring mercury vapor near pollution sites. 1971.
fTD427.M4E5 ECOL
MERCURY—TOXICOLOGY.
D'Itri, Frank M. The environmental mercury problem. 1971. **fQH545.M4D57 ECOL**
Minnesota. Division of Water Quality. Memorandum on mercury pollution in Minnesota. 1970. **fQH545.M4M57 ECOL**
Montague, Katherine. Mercury. 1971
QH545.M4M6 ECOL
MERCURY—TOXICOLOGY—CONGRESSES.
Environmental mercury contamination. 1972
RA1231.M5E58 ECOL
MERCURY COMPOUNDS.
Bongers, Leonard H. Sand and gravel overlay for control of mercury in sediments. 1972.
fTD427.M4B6 ECOL

Feick, George. Control of mercury contamination in freshwater sediments. 1972. **TD427.M4F4 ECOL**
Jones, H. R. Mercury pollution control, 1971. 1971
REF fTD427.M4J66 ECOL
Suggs, James D. Mercury pollution control in stream and lake sediments. 1972. **fTD427.M4S9 ECOL**
United States. Environmental Protection Agency. Office of Research and Monitoring. Control of mercury pollution in sediments. 1972.
TD427.M4U5 ECOL
Widman, Michael U. Polymer film overlay system for mercury contaminated sludge—Phase I. 1972.
fTD427.M4W5 ECOL
METALLURGICAL PLANTS—CONGRESSES.
Environmental Control Symposium, San Francisco, 1972. Environmental control. 1972
TD888.M4E58 1972 ECOL
METALS.
Pearl, Richard Maxwell. The wonder world of metals. 1966 **TN148.P38 ECOL**
METALS—ANALYSIS.
United States. National Bureau of Standards. Analytical Chemistry Division. Interaction of nitrilotriacetic acid with suspended and bottom material. 1971. **fTD427.D4U64 ECOL**
METALS—BIBLIOGRAPHY.
Sinha, Evelyn. Metals as pollutants in air and water. 1972. **REF fZ7171.S55 ECOL**
METALS—FINISHING.
Battelle Memorial Institute, Columbus, Ohio Columbus Laboratories An investigation of techniques for removal of chromium from electroplating wastes. 1971. **fTD899.M45B3ECOL**
METALS—FINISHING—WASTE DISPOSAL.
Battelle Memorial Institute. Columbus, Ohio. Columbus Laboratories A state-of-the-art review of metal finishing waste treatment. 1968 i.e.1970
fTD899.M45B33 ECOL
METALS—PICKLING—BY-PRODUCTS.
Detroit Metro Water Dept. Development of phosphate removal processes. 1970.
fTD756.D47 ECOL
Milwaukee. Sewerage Commission. Phosphorus removal with pickle liquor in an activated sludge plant. 1971. **fTD756.M55 ECOL**
METALS—PICKLING—WASTE DISPOSAL.
Armco Steel Corporation. Limestone treatment of rinse waters from hydrochloric acid pickling of steel. 1971. **fTD899.M45A75 ECOL**
METALS—TOXICOLOGY.
Metallic contaminants and human health. 1972.
RA565.M47 1972 ECOL
Oregon. State University, Corvallis. Water Resources Research Institute. Heavy metals in the environment. 1973. **fTD176.7.O7 ECOL**
METEOROLOGY see also AIR; ATMOSPHERE; CLIMATOLOGY; FLOODS; RAIN AND RAINFALL; SNOW; SOLAR RADIATION; WEATHER
Blumenstock, David Irving. The Ocean of air. 1959.
QC863.B55 ECOL
Firskey, Margaret. The true book of air around us. 1953 **QC863.F846 ECOL**
Navarra, John Gabriel. Wide world weather. 1968
QC863.N34 ECOL
Thompson, Philip Duncan. Weather. 1969
fQC863.T5 1969 ECOL
METERS, FLOW see FLOW METERS
METROPOLITAN AREAS see SUBURBS; URBAN RENEWAL
METROPOLITAN AREAS—ATLANTIC STATES.
Von Eckardt, Wolf. The challenge of Megalopolis. 1964. **HT123.5.A12V6 ECOL**
METROPOLITAN AREAS—UNITED STATES.
Bollens, John Constantinus. The metropolis. 2d ed. 1970 **JS422.B6 1970 ECOL**
Cleaveland, Frederic N. Congress and urban problems. 1969 **HT334.U5C665 ECOL**
Kelnhofer, Guy J. Metropolitan planning and river basin planning: some interrelationships. 1968.
TD223.K4 ECOL
Whyte, William Hollingsworth. Last landscape. 1968. **HT167.W48 ECOL**
METROPOLITAN AREAS—UNITED STATES—ADDRESSES, ESSAYS, LECTURES.
McKeown, James E. The changing metropolis. 2d ed. 1971 **HT334.U5M321971ECOL**
METROPOLITAN GOVERNMENT—UNITED STATES.
Bollens, John Constantinus. The metropolis. 2d ed. 1970 **JS422.B6 1970 ECOL**

MICRO-ORGANISMS.
Brock, Thomas D. Principles of microbial ecology. 1966 **QR41.B72 ECOL**

Rosebury, Theodor. Life on man. 1969 **QR56.R59 ECOL**

Su, K. Lee. Aquatic plants from Minnesota part 3—antimicrobial effects. 1972. **GB701.M554no.48 ECOL**

MICROBES see MICRO-ORGANISMS

MICROBIOLOGY, SANITARY see SANITARY MICROBIOLOGY

MICROSCOPIC ORGANISMS see MICRO-ORGANISMS

MIGRATION, INTERNAL—UNITED STATES.
McKeown, James E. The changing metropolis. 2d ed. 1971 **HT334.U5M321971ECOL**

MILLIKAN RAYS see COSMIC RAYS

MILWAUKEE RIVER.
Milwaukee. Milwaukee River Technical Study Committee. The Milwaukee River. 1968. **fTD225.M47M6 ECOL**

MINE DRAINAGE see also ACID MINE DRAINAGE
Ohio. State University, Columbus. Research Foundation. Pilot scale study of acid mine drainage. 1971. **fTN321.O3 ECOL**

Smith, Edwin Earle. Sulfide to sulfate reaction mechanism. 1970. **fTN321.S58 ECOL**

MINERAL INDUSTRIES.
Flawn, Peter Tyrell. Mineral resources: geology, engineering, economics, politics, law. 1966 **HD9506.A2F55 ECOL**

Park, Charles Frederick. Affluence in jeopardy. c1968 **HD9506.U62P3 ECOL**

MINERAL INDUSTRIES—BIBLIOGRAPHY.
United States. Bureau of Mines. List of Bureau of Mines publications and articles, with subject and author index. 1965/1969- **REF Z6736.U759 ECOL**

MINERAL INDUSTRIES—MINNESOTA.
Brice, William C. Possible environmental impact of base metal mining in Minnesota. 1972 **fTN24.M6B7 ECOL**

Minnesota. Dept. of Natural Resources. Inter-agency task force report on base metal mining impacts. 1973. **fTN24.M6A5 ECOL**

MINERAL INDUSTRIES—UNITED STATES.
Brooks, David B. Supply and competition in minor metals. c1965 **REF HD9506.U62B7 ECOL**

United States. Bureau of Mines. Mineral facts and problems. 1970. **REF TN23.U4no.650 ECOL**

United States. Bureau of Mines. Minerals yearbook. 1969- **REF TN23.U612 ECOL**

MINERAL LANDS see MINING LAW

MINERAL RESOURCES CONSERVATION see also PETROLEUM CONSERVATION

MINERAL RESOURCES CONSERVATION—CONGRESSES.
Symposium on Mineral Waste Utilization. Proceedings. 1st- 1968- **fTP995.A1S9 ECOL**

MINERAL RESOURCES CONSERVATION—UNITED STATES—HISTORY.
Doherty, William T. Minerals. 1971. **REF TN153.D58 ECOL**

MINERALOGY.
Adler, Irving. Rocks and minerals and the stories they tell. 1956. **QE432.A35 ECOL**

De Michele, Vincenzo. The world of minerals. 1972 **QE372.D3413 ECOL**

Hyler, Nelson W. The how and why wonder book of rocks and minerals. 1970,c1960 **fQE432.H9 1970 ECOL**

Keene, Melvin. The beginners' story of minerals and rocks. 1966 **QE365.K27 ECOL**

MINERALS, RADIOACTIVE see RADIOACTIVE SUBSTANCES

MINES AND MINERAL RESOURCES.
Flawn, Peter Tyrell. Mineral resources: geology, engineering, economics, politics, law. 1966 **HD9506.A2F55 ECOL**

McDivitt, James Frederick. Minerals and men. 1965 **TN19.M2 ECOL**

Park, Charles Frederick. Affluence in jeopardy. c1968 **HD9506.U62P3 ECOL**

MINES AND MINERAL RESOURCES—LAW see MINING LAW

MINES AND MINERAL RESOURCES—UNITED STATES.
Riley, Charles M. Our mineral resources. 1959 **TN23.R56 ECOL**

United States. Bureau of Mines. Mineral facts and problems. 1970. **REF TN23.U4no.650 ECOL**

United States. Bureau of Mines. Minerals yearbook. 1969- **REF TN23.U612 ECOL**

MINES AND MINERAL RESOURCES—UNITED STATES—CONGRESSES.
Western Resources Conference. Colorado School of Mines, summer 1971. Needs of a progressive society for mineral and energy resources and realistic solutions to environmental problems posed. 1971 **REF fTD172.5.W4 ECOL**

MINES AND MINERAL RESOURCES—UNITED STATES—STATISTICS.
Resources for the Future. Historical statistics of minerals in the United States. 1966, 1960 **REF TN23.R4 1966 ECOL**

MINING LAW see also PETROLEUM LAW AND LEGISLATION
Ely, Northcutt. Summary of mining and petroleum laws of the world. Rev. 1970- **TN295.U4no.8514 ECOL**

MINNEAPOLIS—SEWERAGE.
Toltz, King, Duvall, Anderson and Associates, Inc., St. Paul. Report on the expansion of the sewage treatment plant. 1969. **fTD525.T9T6 ECOL**

MINNEHAHA CREEK WATERSHED, MINNESOTA.
Hickok (Eugene A.) and Associates, Wayzata, Minn. Overall plan for water management Minnehaha Creek Watershed District. 1969 **fTC424.M6H5 ECOL**

MINNESOTA—DESCRIPTION AND TRAVEL.
Jaques, Florence (Page). Canoe country. c1938 **F606.J36 ECOL**

Jaques, Florence (Page). Snowshoe country. 1944 **F606.J37 ECOL**

MINNESOTA—HISTORY.
Nute, Grace Lee. The voyageur's highway. 1965 c1941 **F606.N97 ECOL**

MINNESOTA—INDUSTRIES—DIRECTORIES.
Minnesota directory of manufacturers. **REF fT12.M5 ECOL**

MINNESOTA—MANUFACTURERS—DIRECTORIES.
Minnesota directory of manufacturers. **REF fT12.M5 ECOL**

MINNESOTA—POLITICS AND GOVERNMENT.
Minnesota. Secretary of State. Minnesota Legislative manual. **REF JK6131.A25 ECOL**

MINNESOTA—POLITICS AND GOVERNMENT—HANDBOOKS, MANUALS, ETC.
Minnesota. State Planning Agency. Office of Local and Urban Affairs. Regional planning and development in Minnesota—a handbook on Executive order no. 37 and the Regional Development Act of 1969. 1969. **REF JK6131 1969 .A55 ECOL**

MINNESOTA—POPULATION.
Minnesota. State Dept. of Health Vital Statistics Division. Minnesota population data book. 1968. **REF fHA453.A53 ECOL**

MINNESOTA—PUBLIC LANDS.
Minnesota. Division of Lands and Forestry. Land exchange study report. 1969. **fHD211.M6A45 ECOL**

Minnesota. Legislature. Senate. Office of Senate Counsel. The law of land exchange in Minnesota. 1969. **fKFM5851.A84 ECOL**

MINNESOTA—REGISTERS.
Minnesota. Secretary of State. Minnesota Legislative manual. **REF JK6131.A25 ECOL**

MINNESOTA. METROPOLITAN SEWER BOARD OF THE TWIN CITIES METROPOLITAN AREA.
Black & Veatch, Kansas City, Mo. Metropolitan sewer board. 1970. **fTD525.T9B5 ECOL**

MINNESOTA RIVER.
United States. Army. Corps of Engineers. Interim survey report on Blue Earth River, Minnesota, Minnesota River Basin for flood control and related purposes. 1970? **Ref fTC424.M6A5 ECOL**

MINNESOTA RIVER—FLOODS.
Itasca Engineering, Inc., Minneapolis. The effectiveness of flood control structures of the Lower Minnesota River Watershed District. 1970. **fTC424.M6I82 ECOL**

MINNESOTA. UNIVERSITY. WATER RESOURCES RESEARCH CENTER—BIBLIOGRAPHY.
Minnesota. University. Water Resources Research Center. Publications related to water resources research center projects, 1965-71 abstract-index. 1971. **GB701.M554no.32 ECOL**

MISSISSIPPI RIVER.
Baron, Norman J. A survey of attitudes towards the Mississippi River as a total resource in Minnesota. 1972. **GB701.M554no.55 ECOL**

MISSISSIPPI VALLEY—ECONOMIC CONDITIONS.
Upper Mississippi River comprehensive basin study. 1970- **fHC107.A15U6 ECOL**

MIXING.
Stenquist, Richard J. Initial mixing in coagulation processes. 1972. **TD455.S7 ECOL**

MOLECULAR BIOLOGY.
Crick, Francis. Of molecules and men. 1969,c1966. **QH331.C9 1969 ECOL**

MOLLUSKS.
Burch, J. B. Freshwater sphaeriacean clams (Mollusca: Pelecypoda) of North America. 1972. **fQH96.A2B5no.3 ECOL**

MONTICELLO NUCLEAR GENERATING PLANT, MONTICELLO, MINNESOTA.
Clark, B. W. Description of the environmental monitoring program for the Monticello nuclear generating plant near Monticello, Minnesota. Rev. ed. 1969. **fTK1377.M6C6 1969 ECOL**

Northern States Power Company. Engineering Dept. Environmental monitoring program for the Monticello nuclear generating plant, Monticello, Minnesota. **REF fTK1377.M6N6 ECOL**

Northern States Power Company (of Minnesota). Environmental report: Monticello Nuclear Generating Plant. 1971. **fTD877.5.N64 ECOL**

MOORHEAD, MINNESOTA—FLOODS.
United States. Army. Corps of Engineers. Flood plain information. 1972. **GB1227.R4A52 ECOL**

MOOSE.
Mech, L. David. The wolves of Isle Royale. 1966 **QL155.A45no.7 ECOL**

Merrill, Samuel. The moose book. c1916 **SK301.M4 ECOL**

Van Wormer, Joe. The world of the moose. 1972 **QL737.U55V32 ECOL**

MOOSE HUNTING.
Merrill, Samuel. The moose book. c1916 **SK301.M4 ECOL**

MOTHS.
Holland, William Jacob. The moth book. 1905 1903 **Ref QL544.H74 ECOL**

MOTOR VEHICLES—MOTORS.
Ayres, Robert U. Alternatives to the internal combustion engine. 1972 **TL210.A96 ECOL**

MOTOR VEHICLES—MOTORS—NOISE.
Wyle Laboratories. Transportation noise and noise from equipment powered by internal combustion engines. 1971 i.e. 1972 **fTD892.W95 ECOL**

MOTOR VEHICLES—POLLUTION CONTROL DEVICES.
Patterson, Donald J. Emissions from combustion engines and their control. 1972 **TD886.5.P83 ECOL**

MOTOR VEHICLES—POLLUTION CONTROL DEVICES—BIBLIOGRAPHY.
Henry, Marybeth. Motor vehicle emissions: a bibliography. 1972 **REF fTL214.P6H4 ECOL**

MOUNTAIN ECOLOGY.
Brooks, Maurice Graham. The life of the mountains. 1967 **QH541.5.M65B7 ECOL**

McCue, George. Ecology: the mountains and man. c1971 **QH541.5.M65M22 ECOL**

MOVING-PICTURES—BIBLIOGRAPHY.
The Environment film review: a critical guide to ecology films. v.1- 1972- **fZ5322.E2E5 ECOL**

MT. NORMANDALE LAKE, MINNESOTA.
Barr Engineering Co. Feasibility study: Mt. Normandale Lake and Marsh Lake, for City of Bloomington and Nine Mile Creek Watershed District. 1967. **fTC424.M6B32 ECOL**

MUD LAKE, MINNESOTA.
Barr Engineering Co. Feasibility study of Mud Lake improvement. 1966. **fTC424.M6B322 ECOL**

Barr Engineering Co. Mud Lake hydrologic study. 1972. **fTC424.M6B34 ECOL**

MUIR, JOHN, 1838-1914.
Graves, Charles Parlin. John Muir. 1973 **QH31.M9G66 ECOL**

MUNICIPAL BONDS—UNITED STATES.
Abt Associates. Factors affecting pollution referenda. 1971. **fGH4952.A6 ECOL**

MUNICIPAL ENGINEERING—MINNEAPOLIS-ST. PAUL.
Peterson, Mattie deHaan. Interjurisdictional aspects of water resources management in the Minneapolis-St. Paul metropolitan area of Minnesota. 1971. **REF fTD225.M6P4 1971 ECOL**

MUNICIPAL RESEARCH—UNITED STATES—DIRECTORIES.
Winston, Eric V. A. Directory of urban affairs information and research centers. 1970.
HT110.W5 ECOL

MUNICIPAL SERVICES—MATHEMATICAL MODELS.
Envirometrics, Inc., Wash., D.C. The river basin model. 1971- **fTC409.E5 ECOL**
Envirometrics, Inc., Wash., D.C. The river basin model: computer output. 1971. **fTC409.E51 ECOL**
Envirometrics, Inc., Wash., D.C. The river basin model: municipal services department. 1971.
fTC409.E5 ECOL

MUNICIPAL TRANSIT see LOCAL TRANSIT

MURRES.
Tuck, Leslie M. The murres. 1960 i.e. 1961
QL696.A3T8 ECOL

MUSHROOMS, EDIBLE—UNITED STATES.
Smith, Alexander Hanchett. The mushroom hunter's field guide. Rev. and enl. 1970 c1963
REF fQK617.S56 1963 ECOL

MUSHROOMS, POISONOUS—UNITED STATES.
Smith, Alexander Hanchett. The mushroom hunter's field guide. Rev. and enl. 1970 c1963
REF fQK617.S56 1963 ECOL

MUTAGENESIS see also RADIOGENETICS
The Mutagenicity of pesticides: concepts and evaluation. 1971 **RA1270.P4M87 ECOL**

MUTATION (BIOLOGY).
Mutagenic effects of environmental contaminants. 1972. **QH431.M958 ECOL**

N

NATIONAL ENVIRONMENTAL STUDY AREAS.
Man and his environment. 1970
L11.N39no.1 ECOL

NATIONAL INCOME—ACCOUNTING.
Collier, Boyd. Measurement and environmental deterioration. 1971 **HC79.I5C63 ECOL**

NATIONAL PARKS AND RESERVES.
Brockman, Christian Frank. Recreational use of wild lands. 1959. **SB481.B66 ECOL**
Curry-Lindahl, Kai. National parks of the world. 1972 **SB481.C87 ECOL**
Guggisberg, Charles Albert Walter. Man and wildlife. 1970 **REF S962.G84 ECOL**
International Commission on National Parks. United Nations list of national parks and equivalent reserves. 1972. **REF SB481.I55 1971 Suppl. ECOL**
International Commission on National Parks. United Nations list of national parks and equivalent reserves. 2nd ed. 1971.
REF SB481.I55 1971 ECOL
Resources for the Future. Comparisons in resource management. 1961 **REF SD411.R4 ECOL**

NATIONAL PARKS AND RESERVES—UNITED STATES.
Adams, Ansel Easton. This is the American earth. 1960 **fHC103.7.A68 ECOL**
Brooks, Maurice Graham. The life of the mountains. 1967 **QH541.5.M65B7 ECOL**
Conservation Foundation. National parks for the future. 1972 **SB482.A4C67 ECOL**
Everhart, William C. The National Park Service. c1972 **SB482.A4E95 ECOL**
Ise, John. Our national park policy. c1961
SB482.A1175 ECOL
Muir, John. Our national parks. 1901.
E160.M95 ECOL
Natural wonders of America. 1972
QH76.N29 ECOL
Preserving wilderness in our national parks. 1971
fQH76.P74 ECOL
Swain, Donald C. Wilderness defender. 1970
SB482.A4S95 ECOL
Udall, Stewart L. America's natural treasures. 1971
fE160.U28 ECOL
United States. National Park Service. The National Park system plan. 1970. **SB482.A3 1970a ECOL**

NATIONAL RESOURCES see NATURAL RESOURCES

NATURAL AREAS see also NATIONAL ENVIRONMENTAL STUDY AREAS; NATIONAL PARKS AND RESERVES; WILDERNESS AREAS

NATURAL AREAS—GREAT BRITAIN.
Baron, William Michael Muir. Nature conservation. 1971 **QH77.G7B28 ECOL**

NATURAL AREAS—INDIANA.
Lindsey, Alton A. Natural areas in Indiana and their preservation. 1969. **QH76.5.I6L5 ECOL**

NATURAL AREAS—RUSSIA.
Pryde, Philip R. Conservation in the Soviet Union. 1972. **S934.R9P76 ECOL**

NATURAL BEAUTY CONSERVATION see LANDSCAPE PROTECTION

NATURAL GAS see GAS, NATURAL

NATURAL HISTORY see also BIOLOGY; BOTANY; GEOGRAPHICAL DISTRIBUTION OF ANIMALS AND PLANTS; GEOLOGY; MARINE BIOLOGY; MINERALOGY; SOIL BIOLOGY; ZOOLOGY

Adventure in environment. 1971
QH48.A25 ECOL
Adventure in environment: national environmental education development. c1971 **fQH48.A24 ECOL**
Adventure in environment: national environmental education development. 1971 **fQH48.A23 ECOL**
Braun, Ernest. Living water. 1971
fQH46.B7 ECOL
French, Herbert E. Love of earth. c1973
S936.F7 ECOL
Harris, Reg. Natural history collecting. 1972
QH60.H36 ECOL
Hawkinson, John. Our wonderful wayside. 1966
PZ10.H34Ou ECOL
Hofmann, Melita. A trip to the pond. 1966
fQH48.H56 ECOL
Kane, Henry Bugbee. The tale of a meadow. 1959
QH48.K23 ECOL
Milne, Lorus Johnson. The nature of life. 1970
fQH45.2.M55 ECOL
Rood, Ronald N. Wild brother. 1970
QH81.R74 ECOL
Sears, Paul Bigelow. Lands beyond the forest. 1969
QH541.5.P7S4 ECOL

NATURAL HISTORY—ADDRESSES, ESSAYS, LECTURES.
Krutch, Joseph Wood. The best nature writing of Joseph Wood Krutch. 1969 c1970
QH81.K828 ECOL

NATURAL HISTORY—AFRICA.
Brown, Leslie. The life of the African plains. 1972
QH541.5.P7B76 ECOL

NATURAL HISTORY—ALASKA.
Brown, Dale. Wild Alaska. 1972
QH105.A4B7 ECOL

NATURAL HISTORY—ALASKA—BARANOF ISLAND.
Walker, Theodore J. Red salmon, brown bear. 1971
QH105.A4W36 ECOL

NATURAL HISTORY—ALBERTA.
Alberta, a natural history. 1st ed. c1967
fQH106.A54 ECOL

NATURAL HISTORY—AMERICA.
Shomon, Joseph James. Nature realms across America. 1972. **QH102.S54 ECOL**

NATURAL HISTORY—ANTARCTIC REGIONS.
Stonehouse, Bernard. Animals of the Antarctic. 1st American ed. 1972 **fQL106.S76 1972 ECOL**

NATURAL HISTORY—ARCTIC REGIONS.
Fuller, William Albert. The life of the far north. 1972. **QH541.5.T8F84 ECOL**
Stonehouse, Bernard. Animals of the Arctic. 1st American ed. 1971 **fQH199.S83 1971 ECOL**

NATURAL HISTORY—BAJA CALIFORNIA.
Johnson, William Weber. Baja California.
F1246.J6 ECOL

NATURAL HISTORY—BIO-BIBLIOGRAPHY.
Pyter, Bernadette. A bio-bibliography of Sigurd F. Olson. 1972. **REF fZ7404.O4P8 ECOL**

NATURAL HISTORY—CALIFORNIA.
Bakker, Elna S. An island called California. 1971.
QH105.C2B3 ECOL

NATURAL HISTORY—FLORIDA—EVERGLADES.
Caulfield, Patricia. Everglades. 1970
QH105.F6C36 ECOL
Sand, George X. The Everglades today. 1971
QH105.F6S24 ECOL

NATURAL HISTORY—GALAPAGOS ISLANDS.
Beebe, Charles William. Galapagos, world's end. 1924. **QH123.B4 ECOL**

NATURAL HISTORY—GREAT PLAINS.
Allen, Durward Leon. The life of prairies and plains. 1967 **QH541.5.P7A4 ECOL**
Costello, David Francis. The prairie world. 1969
QH541.5.P7C6 ECOL

NATURAL HISTORY—HUDSON RIVER.
Boyle, Robert H. The Hudson River. 1st ed. 1969
QH105.N7B68 ECOL

NATURAL HISTORY—IDAHO—SNAKE RIVER WATERSHED.
Norton, Boyd. Snake wilderness. c1972.
QH105.12N6 ECOL

NATURAL HISTORY—ILLINOIS—CHICAGO.
Dubkin, Leonard. My secret places. 1972
QH105.I3D8 ECOL

NATURAL HISTORY—MACHIAS SEAL ISLAND.
Graham, Ada. Puffin Island. 1st ed. 1971
QL676.G68 1971 ECOL

NATURAL HISTORY—MINNESOTA.
Hoover, Helen. A place in the woods. 1st ed. 1972.
QH105.M55H62 1972 ECOL
Hoover, Helen. The years of the forest. 1st ed. 1973.
QH105.M55H64 1973 ECOL
Olson, Sigurd F. Listening point. 1st ed. 1958.
QH102.O38 ECOL

NATURAL HISTORY—MINNESOTA—SUPERIOR NATIONAL FOREST.
Olson, Sigurd F. The singing wilderness. 1956.
QH102.O4 ECOL

NATURAL HISTORY—NEW ENGLAND.
Coman, Dale Rex. The endless adventure. 1972
QH81.C67 ECOL

NATURAL HISTORY—NEW YORK (STATE)—FIRE ISLAND.
Rabkin, Richard. Fire Island. 1971
fQH105.N7R3 ECOL

NATURAL HISTORY—NORTH AMERICA.
Errington, Paul Lester. Of men and marshes. 1957.
QH87.3.E7 ECOL
Olson, Sigurd F. Open horizons. 1969.
QH102.O39 ECOL
Peterson, Roger Tory. Wild America. 1955.
QH102.P38 ECOL

NATURAL HISTORY—NORTHEASTERN STATES.
Leonard, Jonathan Norton. Atlantic beaches. 1972
GB459.4.L46 ECOL

NATURAL HISTORY—ONTARIO—OUTDOOR BOOKS.
Olson, Sigurd F. The singing wilderness. 1956.
QH102.O4 ECOL

NATURAL HISTORY—OUTDOOR BOOKS see also PHENOLOGY
Brown, Vinson. Knowing the outdoors in the dark. 1972 **QH81.B856 ECOL**
Fuller, Raymond Tifft. Now that we have to walk. 1972, c1943 **QH81.F847 1972 ECOL**
Gardner, John F. A book of nature activities. 1967
QH53.G3 ECOL
Hay, John. In defense of nature. 1969
QH81.H37 ECOL
Leopold, Aldo. A Sand County almanac. Enl. ed. 1966. **QH81.L56 1966 ECOL**
Olson, Sigurd F. Listening point. 1st ed. 1958.
QH102.O38 ECOL
Olson, Sigurd F. Open horizons. 1969.
QH102.O39 ECOL
Olson, Sigurd F. Sigurd F. Olson's Wilderness days. 1st ed. 1972. **QH81.O67 1972 ECOL**
Teale, Edwin Way. Journey into summer. 1960.
QH104.T39 ECOL
Teale, Edwin Way. North with the spring. c1951
QH104.T42 ECOL
Teale, Edwin Way. Wandering through winter. 1965. **QH104.T43 ECOL**

NATURAL HISTORY—PERU.
Murphy, Robert Cushman. Bird islands of Peru. 1925. **REF QH128.M8 ECOL**

NATURAL HISTORY—PICTORIAL WORKS.
Cavagnaro, David. This living earth. 1972
fQH541.5.M4C38 ECOL
Hay, John. The primal alliance: earth and ocean. 1971. **fQH95.7.H32 ECOL**
Teale, Edwin Way. Photographs of American nature. 1972 **fQH46.T4 ECOL**

NATURAL HISTORY—RED WING REGION, MINNESOTA.
Northern States Power Company (of Minnesota). Environmental report. 1971. **fTD877.5.N6 ECOL**
Northern States Power Company (of Minnesota). Environmental report. expanded and updated ed. 1971.
fTD877.5.N62 1971 ECOL

NATURAL HISTORY—SCOTLAND.
Darling, Frank Fraser. Natural history in the Highlands & islands. 1947 **QH141.D365 ECOL**

NATURAL HISTORY—SONORAN DESERT.
Abbey, Edward. Cactus country. 1973
QH88.A2 ECOL

NATURAL HISTORY—SOUTH CAROLINA.
Sprunt, Alexander. Carolina low country impressions. 1964. **REF QH105.S6S6 ECOL**

NATURAL HISTORY—STUDY AND TEACHING
see also NATURE STUDY

Adventure in environment: national environmental education development. 1971 **fQH48.A23 ECOL**

Brown, Robert E. Techniques for teaching conservation education. 1964 **S946.B7 ECOL**

Dickey, Miriam. Beyond the classroom. 1972.
Ref fQH51.D5 ECOL

National Association of Biology Teachers. National Conservation Committee. Manual for outdoor laboratories. 1959. **QH51.N3 ECOL**

NATURAL HISTORY—STUDY AND TEACHING—DIRECTORIES.
National Audubon Society. Nature Center Planning Division. Directory of nature centers and related environmental education facilities. 1971
REF fQH51.N23 1971 ECOL

NATURAL HISTORY—STUDY AND TEACHING—UNITED STATES.
National Science Teachers Association. Programs in environmental education. 2d ed. 1971.
REF fQH51.N24 1971 ECOL

NATURAL HISTORY—STUDY AND TEACHING (ELEMENTARY).
Gross, Phyllis. Teaching science in an outdoor environment. 1972. **QH51.G867 ECOL**

NATURAL HISTORY—STUDY AND TEACHING (SECONDARY).
Gross, Phyllis. Teaching science in an outdoor environment. 1972. **QH51.G867 ECOL**

NATURAL HISTORY—SUPERIOR, LAKE.
Agassiz, Louis. Lake Superior. 1970, c1850
QH104.5.G7A35 1970 ECOL

NATURAL HISTORY—TECHNIQUE.
Hillcourt, William. The new field book of nature activities and hobbies. Rev. ed. 1970
QH53.H574 1970 ECOL

NATURAL HISTORY—TENNESSEE—SIGNAL MOUNTAIN.
Steele, Mary Q. The living year. 1972
QH81.S855 1972 ECOL

NATURAL HISTORY—TEXAS—BIG THICKET NATIONAL PARK (PROPOSED).
Gunter, Pete Addison Y. The Big Thicket. 1971 c1972 **fF392.H37G8 ECOL**

NATURAL HISTORY—UNITED STATES.
Darling, Frank Fraser. Pelican in the wilderness. 1956 **QH104.D3 ECOL**

Farb, Peter. Face of North America. Young readers' ed. 1964 **QH104.F32 ECOL**

Grossman, Mary Louise. Our vanishing wilderness. 1969 **fQH541.15.G76 ECOL**

Leopold, Aldo. A Sand County almanac. Enl. ed 1966. **QH81.L56 1966 ECOL**

Savage, Henry. Lost heritage. 1970.
QH26.S28 ECOL

Teale, Edwin Way. Journey into summer. 1960.
QH104.T39 ECOL

Teale, Edwin Way. North with the spring. c1951
QH104.T42 ECOL

Teale, Edwin Way. Wandering through winter. 1965. **QH104.T43 ECOL**

United States. National Park Service. The National Park system plan. 1970. **SB482.A3 1970a ECOL**

NATURAL HISTORY—YELLOWSTONE NATIONAL PARK.
Sutton, Ann. Yellowstone: a century of the wilderness idea. 1972 **fQH105.W8S8 ECOL**

NATURAL MONUMENTS—UNITED STATES.
American heritage. The American heritage book of natural wonders. c1972,1963
fE169.A496 1972 ECOL

Blake, Peter. God's own junkyard. 1964
HF5843.5.B55 ECOL

Natural wonders of America. 1972
QH76.N29 ECOL

NATURAL PURIFICATION OF STREAMS see STREAM SELF-PURIFICATION

NATURAL RESOURCES see also
CONSERVATION OF NATURAL RESOURCES; FISHERIES; FORESTS AND FORESTRY; MARINE RESOURCES; MINES AND MINERAL RESOURCES; PETROLEUM CONSERVATION; POWER RESOURCES; WATER RESOURCES DEVELOPMENT; WATER-SUPPLY

Barnett, Harold J. Scarcity and growth. 1963
HC55.B3 ECOL

Brown, Harrison Scott. The next hundred years: man's natural and technological resources. 1970,c1963
HC55.B7 1970 ECOL

Clawson, Marion. Natural resources and international development. 1964 **HC55.C57 ECOL**

Fisher, Joseph Lyman. World prospects for natural resources. 1964 **HC54.F54 ECOL**

Gates, Richard. The true book of conservation. 1959 **PZ10.G493TR ECOL**

Harvard University. Landscape Architecture Research Office. Three approaches to environmental resource analysis. 1967. **fTA170.H3 ECOL**

Herfindahl, Orris Clemens. Natural resources information for economic development; a study. 1969
GA51.H47 ECOL

Hyde, Margaret Oldroyd. This crowded planet. 1961 **HB883.H9 ECOL**

Loraine, John Alexander. The death of tomorrow. 1972 **HC79.P55L67 1972b ECOL**

Marsh, George Perkins. Man and nature. 1965.
GF31.M35 1965 ECOL

McClellan, Grant S. Protecting our environment. 1970. **TD180.M3 ECOL**

Murdoch, William W. Environment; resources, pollution & society. 1971 **QH541.M95 ECOL**

National Research Council. Committee on Resources and Man. Resources and man. 1969
HC68.N36 ECOL

Ordway, Samuel Hanson. A conservation handbook. 1949. **HC55.O7 ECOL**

Pringle, Laurence. The only earth we have. 1969
TD180.P73 ECOL

Sax, Karl. Standing room only. New ed. 1969,c1960
HB881.S33 1969 ECOL

Sears, Paul Bigelow. Deserts on the march. 3rd ed. rev. 1967,c1959 **S493.S4 1959 ECOL**

Sears, Paul Bigelow. The living landscape. 1966
QH541.S37 1966 ECOL

NATURAL RESOURCES—ADDRESSES, ESSAYS, LECTURES.
Burton, Ian. Readings in resource management and conservation. 1970,c1965 **S938.B86 ECOL**

Mudd, Stuart. The population crisis and the use of world resources. 1964 **HB885.M8 ECOL**

NATURAL RESOURCES—ALASKA.
Cooley, Richard A. Alaska. 1967.
HC107.A45C6 ECOL

NATURAL RESOURCES—BIBLIOGRAPHY.
The Environment index: a guide to the key environmental literature of the year. 1971-
REF fZ7171.E6 ECOL

Winton, Harry N. M. Man and the environment: a bibliography of selected publications of the United Nations system, 1946-1971. 1972.
REF Z5322.E2W56 ECOL

NATURAL RESOURCES—DICTIONARIES.
Jackson, Nora. A dictionary of natural resources and their principal uses. 2d ed. 1969
REF HF1051.J3 1969 ECOL

NATURAL RESOURCES—GREAT BRITAIN.
Arvill, Robert. Man and environment: crisis and the strategy of choice. Revised ed. 1970,c1969
HC253.5.A7 1970 ECOL

NATURAL RESOURCES—INDEXES.
The Environment index: a guide to the key environmental literature of the year. 1971-
REF fZ7171.E6 ECOL

NATURAL RESOURCES—LATIN AMERICA.
Grunwald, Joseph. Natural resources in Latin American development. 1970
REF fHC125.G72 ECOL

NATURAL RESOURCES—LAW AND LEGISLATION—UNITED STATES—ADDRESSES, ESSAYS, LECTURES.
Congress and the environment. 1970
KF5505.A75C6 ECOL

Environment law review. 1970-
REF KF3790.A2E5 ECOL

Law and the environment. 1970
KF5505.A75L38 ECOL

NATURAL RESOURCES—NORTH AMERICA.
Darling, Frank Fraser. Future environments of North America. 1966. **HC95.D33 ECOL**

NATURAL RESOURCES—PENNSYLVANIA.
Pennsylvania. Dept. of Public Instruction. Pennsylvania teaching guide to natural resources conservation. 1962, reprinted 1964
fL194.B527no.7 1964 ECOL

NATURAL RESOURCES—RESEARCH.
Planning research for resource decisions. 1st ed. 1970 **HC55.P55 ECOL**

NATURAL RESOURCES—STUDY AND TEACHING.
Brown, Robert E. Techniques for teaching conservation education. 1964 **S946.B7 ECOL**

Conservation Education Association. Conservation quickies. 1966 **fS946.C57 ECOL**

Hiros, John E. Inviting involvement with history. 1969 **fLB1047.H5 ECOL**

Milliken, Margaret. Field study manual for outdoor living. c1968 **QH53.M5 ECOL**

Pennsylvania. Dept. of Public Instruction. Pennsylvania teaching guide to natural resources conservation. 1962, reprinted 1964
fL194.B527no.7 1964 ECOL

Shomon, Joseph James. Manual of outdoor conservation education. 1964 **S946.S5 ECOL**

United States. Bureau of Land Management. All around you: an environmental study guide. 1971.
S946.U5 ECOL

NATURAL RESOURCES—TAXATION—UNITED STATES.
Extractive resources and taxation: proceedings. 1967. **HC106.5.E93 ECOL**

NATURAL RESOURCES—UNITED STATES.
Adams, Ansel Easton. This is the American earth. 1960 **fHC103.7.A68 ECOL**

Allen, Shirley Walter. Conserving natural resources. 3d ed. c1966 **HC103.7.A7 1966 ECOL**

Callison, Charles H. America's natural resources. Rev. print. 1967 **S930.C3 1967 ECOL**

Chase, Stuart. Rich land, poor land. 1969
S930.C5 1969 ECOL

Clepper, Henry Edward. Origins of American conservation. 1966 **S930.C57 ECOL**

Coyle, David Cushman. Conservation, an American story of conflict and accomplishment. 1957.
HC103.7.C68 ECOL

Ekirch, Arthur Alphonse. Man and nature in America. 1963. **GF503.E46 ECOL**

Harrison, C. William. Conservation, the challenge of reclaiming our plundered land. c1968,1963
S940.H33 1968 ECOL

Highsmith, Richard Morgan. Conservation in the United States. 2d ed. 1969
HC103.7.H5 1969 ECOL

Hitch, Allen S. Conservation and you. 1964
S930.H5 ECOL

Huth, Hans. Nature and the American: three centuries of changing attitudes. 1957.
QH77.U6H8 ECOL

Landsberg, Hans H. Natural resources for U.S. growth. c1964 **HC103.7.L3 ECOL**

Millard, Reed. Natural resources: will we have enough for tomorrow's world? 1972
HC103.7.M55 ECOL

Parson, Ruben L. Conserving American resources. 2d ed. 1964 **S930.P3 1964 ECOL**

Resources for the Future. Environmental quality in a growing economy. 1968,c1966
HC103.7.R39 ECOL

Resources for the Future. Resources in America's future. 1963 **HC106.5.R48 ECOL**

Resources for the Future. Trends in natural resource commodities. 1962. **REF fHF1051.R43 ECOL**

Rienow, Robert. Moment in the sun. 1967.
S930.R5 ECOL

Sollers, Allan A. Ours is the earth. 1963
S930.S6 ECOL

Thompson, Dennis L. Politics, policy, and natural resources. 1972 **HC110.E5T48 ECOL**

United States. Commission on Population Growth and the American Future. Population, resources, and the environment. 1972 **HB3505.A527 ECOL**

United States. Dept. of the Interior. Quest for quality. 1965 **fS930.A5 ECOL**

Wengert, Norman I. Natural resources and the political struggle. 1967,c1955
HC103.7.W4 1967 ECOL

NATURAL RESOURCES—UNITED STATES—ADDRESSES, ESSAYS, LECTURES.
Western Resources Conference, 8th, Colorado School of Mines, 1966. Natural gas, coal, ground water. 1967 **HC103.7.W45 1966 ECOL**

NATURAL RESOURCES—UNITED STATES—BIBLIOGRAPHY.
U.S. Dept. of the Interior. Library. Dictionary catalog of the department library. 1967.
REF fZ881.U41 ECOL

NATURAL RESOURCES—UNITED STATES—CASE STUDIES.
Munzer, Martha E. Pockets of hope. 1967
  HC103.7.M78 ECOL

NATURAL RESOURCES—UNITED STATES—HISTORY.
Smith, Frank Ellis. The politics of conservation. c1966 S930.S56 ECOL
Udall, Stewart L. The quiet crisis. 1st ed. 1963
  S930.U3

NATURAL RESOURCES—UNITED STATES—STUDY AND TEACHING.
Bachert, Russel E., Jr. Directory of degree programs, related to conservation, ecology, environmental education, environmental science, outdoor education & natural resources. 1971 fS946.B3 ECOL

NATURAL RESOURCES—UTAH.
Cottam, Walter Pace. Our renewable wild lands, a challenge. 1961. QK941.U8C6 ECOL

NATURAL RESOURCES—VOCATIONAL GUIDANCE.
Clepper, Henry Edward. Careers in conservation. 1963 S494.5.C57 ECOL
Herbert, Frederick Wulling. Careers in natural resource conservation. 1965. S944.H45 ECOL

NATURAL RESOURCES—WISCONSIN—STUDY AND TEACHING.
Reading Wisconsin's landscape. 2d ed. 1962, reprinted 1966. fS946.R4 1966 ECOL

NATURAL SCIENCE *see* NATURAL HISTORY

NATURALISTS.
Graves, Charles Parlin. John Muir. 1973
  QH31.M9G66 ECOL
Hirsch, S. Carl. Guardians of tomorrow. 1971
  QH541.14.H57 1971 ECOL
Savage, Henry. Lost heritage. 1970.
  QH26.S28 ECOL

NATURALISTS—BIOGRAPHY.
Adams, Alexander B. Eternal quest: the story of the great naturalists. 1969 QH26.A3 ECOL

NATURALISTS, AMERICAN—BIOGRAPHY.
Carrighar, Sally. Home to the wilderness. 1973.
  QH31.C3A3 ECOL

NATURE *see also* MAN—INFLUENCE ON NATURE
Braun, Ernest. Living water. 1971
  fQH46.B7 ECOL
Coman, Dale Rex. The endless adventure. 1972
  QH81.C67 ECOL
Olson, Sigurd F. Sigurd F. Olson's Wilderness days. 1st ed. 1972. QH81.O67 1972 ECOL
Steele, Mary Q. The living year. 1972
  QH81.S855 1972 ECOL

NATURE—ADDRESSES, ESSAYS, LECTURES.
Krutch, Joseph Wood. The best nature writing of Joseph Wood Krutch. 1969 c1970
  QH81.K828 ECOL
McKain, David W. The whole earth. 1972
  QH81.M1518 ECOL

NATURE—RELIGIOUS INTERPRETATIONS.
Santmire, H. Paul. Brother Earth. 1970
  BL435.S25 ECOL

NATURE (AESTHETICS).
Bonvie, Carolyn. Art & design in the environment. 1971 fLB1047.B6 ECOL
Huth, Hans. Nature and the American: three centuries of changing attitudes. 1957.
  QH77.U6H8 ECOL

NATURE AND SCIENCE.
Smithsonian Institution. Center for Shortlived Phenomena. The pulse of the planet. c1972
  fQ225.P8 ECOL

NATURE CONSERVATION.
Brooks, Paul. The pursuit of wilderness. 1971.
  QH75.B73 ECOL
Curry-Lindahl, Kai. Conservation for survival. 1972. QH541.C87 ECOL
Dasmann, Raymond Frederick. Planet in peril. 1972 QH541.D35 1972 ECOL
Ehrenfeld, David W. Biological conservation. 1970
  QH75.E35 ECOL
Ehrenfeld, David W. Conserving life on earth. 1972.
  QH75.E35 1972 ECOL
Marine, Gene. America the raped. 1969
  S942.M33 ECOL
Parnall, Peter. The mountain. 1st ed. 1971
  PZ10.P2564Mo ECOL
Vosburgh, John R. Living with your land. c1968
  QH75.V57 ECOL

NATURE CONSERVATION—ADDRESSES, ESSAYS, LECTURES.
Western Resources Conference, 9th, University of Colorado, 1967. Man and the quality of his environment. 1968 TD180.W4 1967 ECOL

NATURE CONSERVATION—BIBLIOGRAPHY.
Winton, Harry N. M. Man and the environment: a bibliography of selected publications of the United Nations system, 1946-1971. 1972.
  REF Z5322.E2W56 ECOL

NATURE CONSERVATION—CALIFORNIA.
Bronson, William. How to kill a Golden State. 1968.
  F866.2.B7 ECOL

NATURE CONSERVATION—CONGRESSES.
Conference on the Ecological Aspects of International Development, Airlie House, 1968. The careless technology: ecology and international development. 1st ed. 1972. QH540.C65 1968 ECOL

NATURE CONSERVATION—ECONOMIC ASPECTS—UNITED STATES—CONGRESSES.
Natural environments: studies in theoretical and applied analysis. 1972 QH76.N28 ECOL

NATURE CONSERVATION—FLORIDA.
Conservation Foundation. Rookery Bay area project. 1968. QH77.U6C66 ECOL

NATURE CONSERVATION—FLORIDA—EVERGLADES.
Sand, George X. The Everglades today. 1971
  QH105.F6S24 ECOL

NATURE CONSERVATION—GREAT BRITAIN.
Baron, William Michael Muir. Nature conservation. 1971 QH77.G7B28 ECOL

NATURE CONSERVATION—HANDBOOKS, MANUALS, ETC.
United States. Soil Conservation Service. National handbook of conservation practices. 1971.
  REF S922.U5 ECOL

NATURE CONSERVATION—MINNESOTA.
Sierra Club. North Star Chapter (Minn.). A wilderness in crisis: the Boundary Waters Canoe Area. c1970 fQH76.5.M6S5 ECOL

NATURE CONSERVATION—NEW YORK (STATE)—LONG ISLAND.
Arbib, Robert S. The Lord's Woods. 1st ed. 1971
  QH76.5.N7A72 ECOL

NATURE CONSERVATION—UNITED STATES.
Roueche, Berton. What's left. 1969,c1968
  QH77.U6R6 ECOL

NATURE CONSERVATION—UNITED STATES—HISTORY.
Baldwin, Donald N. The quiet revolution: grass roots of today's wilderness preservation movement. 1st ed. c1972 QH76.B35 ECOL

NATURE IN LITERATURE.
Huth, Hans. Nature and the American: three centuries of changing attitudes. 1957.
  QH77.U6H8 ECOL

NATURE PHOTOGRAPHY.
Thoreau, Henry David. In wildness is the preservation of the world. 1971,c1967
  TR660.T5 1971 ECOL

NATURE STORIES.
Hoover, Helen. The years of the forest. 1st ed. 1973.
  QH105.M55H64 1973 ECOL

NATURE STUDY.
Carson, Rachel Louise. The sense of wonder. 1965,c1956 QH51.C35 ECOL
Cooper, Elizabeth K. Science in your own back yard. 1970 QH81.C75 1970 ECOL
Gardner, John F. A book of nature activities. 1967
  QH53.G3 ECOL
Hillcourt, William. The new field book of nature activities and hobbies. Rev. ed. 1970
  QH53.H574 1970 ECOL
Milliken, Margaret. Field study manual for outdoor living. c1968 QH53.M5 ECOL
Musselman, Virginia W. Learning about nature through crafts. 1969 TT157.M82 ECOL
Schwartz, Julius. Through the magnifying glass. 1954 Q163.S464 ECOL
Selsam, Millicent (Ellis). How to be a nature detective. 1966,c1963 PZ10.S44Hr3 ECOL
Shomon, Joseph James. Manual of outdoor interpretation. 1968 QH51.S5 ECOL
Subarsky, Zachariah. Living things in field and classroom. 2d ed. 1969 QH51.S9 1969 ECOL
Watson, Geoffrey Grainge. Fun with ecology. 1971,c1967 QH541.2.W3 1971 ECOL
Wensberg, Katherine S. Experiences with living things. 1966 LB1532.W4 ECOL

NATURE (THEOLOGY).
Barnette, Henlee H. The church and the ecological crisis. 1972 BT695.5.B37 ECOL
Earth might be fair. 1972 GF80.E15 ECOL

NATURE TRAILS.
Ashbaugh, Byron L. Trail planning and layout. 1971
  QH58.A8 ECOL

NEIGHBORHOOD GARDEN ASSOCIATION.
Bush-Brown, Louise (Carter). Garden blocks for urban America. 1969 NA9052.B78 ECOL

NEMATODA.
Merritt, Thomas W. Studies on benthic nematode ecology in a small freshwater pond. 1973.
  fTC1.A85no.8 ECOL

NESTS OF BIRDS *see* BIRDS—EGGS AND NESTS

NEUROCHEMISTRY.
Eiduson, Samuel. Biochemistry and behavior. 1964
  QP521.E5 ECOL

NEW ENGLAND—DESCRIPTION AND TRAVEL.
American Geographical Society of New York New England's prospect: 1933. 1933.
  HC107.A11A82 ECOL

NEW ENGLAND—ECONOMIC CONDITIONS.
American Geographical Society of New York New England's prospect: 1933. 1933.
  HC107.A11A82 ECOL

NEW ENGLAND—SOCIAL CONDITIONS.
American Geographical Society of New York New England's prospect: 1933. 1933.
  HC107.A11A82 ECOL

NIDOLOGY *see* BIRDS—EGGS AND NESTS

NINE MILE CREEK WATERSHED, MINNESOTA.
Barr, Douglas W. Over-all plan for Nine Mile Creek Watershed District. 1961. fTC424.M6B36 ECOL
Barr Engineering Co. Feasibility study: Mt. Normandale Lake and Marsh Lake, for City of Bloomington and Nine Mile Creek Watershed District. 1967. fTC424.M6B32 ECOL
Barr Engineering Co. Feasibility study of Mud Lake improvement. 1966. fTC424.M6B322 ECOL
Barr Engineering Co. Hydrological study of Hyland-Bush-Anderson lakes. 1971.
  fTC424.M6B326 ECOL
Barr Engineering Co. Mud Lake hydrologic study. 1972. fTC424.M6B34 ECOL
Barr Engineering Co. Report to the Board of Managers, Nine Mile Creek Watershed District.
  fTC424.M6B3 ECOL
Barr Engineering Company. Nine Mile Creek Watershed District. 1973. fTC424.M6B362 ECOL

NITRATES *see also* NITRIFICATION
California. Dept. of Water Resources. Removal of nitrate by an algal system, phase II. 1971.
  fTD475.C342 ECOL
Dow Chemical Company. Western Division Research Laboratories. Nitrate removal from wastewaters by ion exchange. 1971.
  fTD757.5.D68 ECOL
North American Rockwell Corporation. Rocketdyne Division. Development of a chemical denitrification process. 1970. fTD433.N67 ECOL
Robert S. Kerr Water Research Center. Denitrification by anaerobic filters and ponds, phase II. 1971. TD475.R62 ECOL

NITRATES—PHYSIOLOGICAL EFFECT.
National Research Council. Committee on Nitrate Accumulation. Accumulation of nitrate. 1972.
  QH545.N5N37 ECOL

NITRIFICATION.
McCoy, Elizabeth F. Role of bacteria in the nitrogen cycle in lakes. 1972. fTD433.M3 ECOL
Pratt, P. F. Nitrate in the unsaturated zone under agricultural lands. 1972. fS651.P7 ECOL
Robert S. Kerr Water Research Center. Denitrification by anaerobic filters and ponds. 1971.
  fTD475.R6 ECOL

NITRILOTRIACETIC ACID.
Battelle Memorial Institute, Columbus, Ohio. Corrosion potential of NTA in detergent formulations. 1971. fTP992.5.B3 ECOL
Robert S. Kerr Water Research Center. Investigations concerning probable impact of nitrilotriacetic acid on ground waters. 1971.
  fTD427.D4R6 ECOL
Taylor, John Keenan. Development of method for NTA analysis in raw water. 1972.
  TP992.5.T3 ECOL
United States. National Bureau of Standards. Analytical Chemistry Division. Interaction of nitrilotriacetic acid with suspended and bottom material. 1971. fTD427.D4U64 ECOL

NITROGEN COMPOUNDS—TOXICOLOGY.
National Research Council. Committee on Nitrate Accumulation. Accumulation of nitrate. 1972.
QH545.N5N37 ECOL

NITROGEN OXIDES—BIBLIOGRAPHY.
United States. National Air Pollution Control Administration. Nitrogen oxides: an annotated bibliography. 1970. **Z7914.C4U5 ECOL**

NOISE.
United States. National Bureau of Standards. Fundamentals of Noise: measurement, rating schemes, and Standards. 1971 i.e. 1972 **fQC243.U55 ECOL**

NOISE—MEASUREMENT.
Miller, James D. Effects of noise on people. 1971.
RA772.N7M5 ECOL

NOISE—MEASUREMENT—CONGRESSES.
Transportation noises: a symposium on acceptability criteria. 1970 **TA365.T68 ECOL**

NOISE—PHYSIOLOGICAL EFFECT.
Burns, William. Noise and man. c1968
RA772.N7B8 ECOL
Conference on Noise as a Public Health Hazard, Wash., D.C., 1968. Noise as a public health hazard. 1969. **RA772.N7C6 ECOL**
Miller, James D. Effects of noise on people. 1971.
RA772.N7M5 ECOL
Still, Henry. In quest of quiet. 1970
RA772.N7S74 ECOL
Tennessee. State University, Memphis. Effects of noise on wildlife and other animals. 1971.
fQP82.2.N6T4 ECOL

NOISE—PHYSIOLOGICAL EFFECT—ADDRESSES, ESSAYS, LECTURES.
Adverse effects of common environmental pollutants. 1972 **RA1270.P4A32 ECOL**

NOISE—PHYSIOLOGICAL EFFECT—CONGRESSES.
Physiological effects of noise. 1970.
QP82.2.N6P47 ECOL

NOISE—POLLUTION.
O'Donnell, Patrick A. Noise pollution. Teachers' ed. c1971 **TD892.O46 ECOL**

NOISE CONTROL.
Aylesworth, Thomas G. This vital air, this vital water: man's environment crisis. 1968
TD180.A9 ECOL
Cook, David I. Trees and shrubs for noise abatement. 1971. **TD893.C6 ECOL**
Informatics Inc. An assessment of noise concern in other nations. 1971. **fTD892.I55 ECOL**
O'Donnell, Patrick A. Noise pollution. Teachers' ed. c1971 **TD892.O46 ECOL**

NOISE CONTROL—CONGRESSES.
Transportation noises: a symposium on acceptability criteria. 1970 **TA365.T68 ECOL**

NOISE CONTROL—UNITED STATES.
Bolt, Beranek, and Newman, Inc. Noise from construction equipment and operations, building equipment, and home appliances. 1971 i.e. 1972
fTD893.B63 ECOL
United States. Environmental Protection Agency. Summary, conclusions and recommendations from report to the President and Congress on noise. 1971.
fTD893.A473 ECOL
United States. Office of Noise Abatement and Control. Public hearings on noise abatement and control. 1972- **TD893.A52 ECOL**

NOISE CONTROL—UNITED STATES—DIRECTORIES.
United States. Office of Noise Abatement and Control. Noise programs of professional/industrial organizations, universities, and colleges. 1971.
fTD893.A51 ECOL
United States. Office of Noise Abatement and Control. Summary of noise programs in the federal government. 1971. **TD893.A522 ECOL**

NOISE POLLUTION.
Baron, Robert Alex. The tyranny of noise. 1970
TD892.B37 ECOL
Bragdon, Clifford R. Noise pollution: the unquiet crisis. c1971 **TD892.B69 ECOL**
Conference on Noise as a Public Health Hazard, Wash., D.C., 1968. Noise as a public health hazard. 1969. **RA772.N7C6 ECOL**
Informatics Inc. An assessment of noise concern in other nations. 1971. **fTD892.I55 ECOL**
Jones, Claire. Pollution: the noise we hear. 1972
TD892.J65 1972 ECOL
Miller, James D. Effects of noise on people. 1971.
RA772.N7M5 ECOL
Tennessee. State University, Memphis. Effects of noise on wildlife and other animals. 1971.
fQP82.2.N6T4 ECOL

Wyle Laboratories. Community noise. 1971 i.e. 1972 **fTD892.W94 ECOL**

NOISE POLLUTION—UNITED STATES.
United States. Environmental Protection Agency. Summary, conclusions and recommendations from report to the President and Congress on noise. 1971.
fTD893.A473 ECOL
United States. National Bureau of Standards. The economic impact of noise. 1971. **fTD893.A48 ECOL**
United States. National Bureau of Standards. The social impact of noise. 1971. **TD893.A49 ECOL**
United States. Office of Noise Abatement and Control. Public hearings on noise abatement and control. 1972- **TD893.A52 ECOL**

NOISE POLLUTION—UNITED STATES—DIRECTORIES.
United States. Office of Noise Abatement and Control. Noise programs of professional/industrial organizations, universities, and colleges. 1971.
fTD893.A51 ECOL
United States. Office of Noise Abatement and Control. Summary of noise programs in the federal government. 1971. **TD893.A522 ECOL**

NOISE PREVENTION see NOISE CONTROL

NON-DESTRUCTIVE TESTING.
Berger, Harold. Nondestructive testing. 1965
TA417.2.B4 ECOL

NORTHERN STATES POWER COMPANY.
Black & Veatch, Kansas City, Mo. Environmental report. 1971- **fTK1331.N6B7 ECOL**

NORTHWEST, CANADIAN—DESCIRPTION AND TRAVEL.
Olson, Sigurd F. Runes of the North. 1969, c1963
F1060.A204 ECOL

NUCLEAR ENERGY see also ATOMIC ENERGY
Hines, Neal O. Atoms, nature, and man. c1966
QC778.H54 ECOL

NUCLEAR ENGINEERING.
Seaborg, Glenn Theodore. Man and atom. 1st ed. 1971. **TK9145.S4 1971 ECOL**
Willrich, Mason. Global politics of nuclear energy. 1971 **TK9145.W49 ECOL**

NUCLEAR FUELS.
Hogerton, John F. Atomic fuel. 1969
TK9360.H6 1969 ECOL
Hogerton, John F. Atomic fuel. Rev. 1964.
TK9360.H6 1964 ECOL

NUCLEAR PHYSICS—DICTIONARIES.
Lyman, James D. Nuclear terms. 2d ed. 1966.
QC772.L9 1966 ECOL

NUCLEAR PHYSICS—EXHIBITIONS.
LeCompte, Robert G. Atoms at the science fair. 1968 **Q105.L412 1968 ECOL**

NUCLEAR PHYSICS—POPULAR WORKS.
United States. Atomic Energy Commission. The first reactor. 1967 **QC787.N8U52 ECOL**

NUCLEAR REACTOR KINETICS—CONGRESSES.
Dynamics of nuclear systems. 1972
TK9202.D9 ECOL

NUCLEAR REACTORS.
Martens, Frederick Hilbert. Research reactors. 1965 **QC787.N8M32 ECOL**
Minnesota Committee for Environmental Information. The costs and benefits of nuclear electric power plants. 1969. **REF fTK1078.M5 ECOL**

NUCLEAR REACTORS—ACCIDENTS.
Novick, Sheldon. The careless atom. c1969
TK9152.N6 ECOL

NUCLEAR REACTORS—ADDRESSES, ESSAYS, LECTURES.
United States. Atomic Energy Commission. The first reactor. 1967 **QC787.N8U52 ECOL**

NUCLEAR REACTORS—CONTAINMENT.
American National Standards Institute. American national standard leakage-rate testing of containment structures for nuclear reactors. 1972
REF fTK9211.A4 ECOL

NUCLEAR REACTORS—CONTROL.
Hull, Andrew P. Sternglass: a case history. 1972?
REF fRA569.H8 ECOL

NUCLEAR REACTORS—CONTROL—CONGRESSES.
Working Group Meeting on Nuclear Power Plant Control and Instrumentation, Vienna, 1971. Nuclear power plant control and instrumentation. 1972.
TK9006.W58 1971 ECOL

NUCLEAR REACTORS—CONTROL-CONGRESSES.
Dynamics of nuclear systems. 1972
TK9202.D9 ECOL

NUCLEAR REACTORS—SAFETY MEASURES.
Geesey, A. H. New safety system design for nuclear power reactors. 1971. **fTA1.P35no.103 ECOL**
Graham, John. Fast reactor safety. 1971.
TK9152.G68 ECOL
Postma, Arlin Keith. Review of organic iodide formation under accident conditions in water-cooled reactors. 1972. **fTK9152.P6 ECOL**
Southern Interstate Nuclear Board. Nuclear power plant safety. 1972? **fTK9152.S62 ECOL**

NUCLEAR REACTORS—TESTING.
American National Standards Institute. American national standard leakage-rate testing of containment structures for nuclear reactors. 1972
REF fTK9211.A4 ECOL

NUCLEAR REACTORS—UNITED STATES.
United States. Atomic Energy Commission. Division of Reactor Development and Technology. Operating history of United States nuclear power reactors. 1971. **fTK1343.A467 ECOL**
United States. Atomic Energy Commission. Division of Reactor Development and Technology. Operating history of U.S. nuclear power reactors. 1972.
fTK1343.A467 1972 ECOL

NUCLEAR ROCKETS.
Corliss, William R. Nuclear Propulsion for space. 1967 **TL783.5.C62 ECOL**

NUCLEAR SALINE WATER CONVERSION PLANTS.
Urrows, Grace M. Nuclear energy for desalting. Rev. 1967 **TD479.6.U7 1967 ECOL**

NUCLEAR SALINE WATER CONVERSION PLANTS—BIBLIOGRAPHY.
Nuclear Desalination Information Center. Indexed bibliography of nuclear desalination literature—7- 1972-
REF fZ5853.S22N8 ECOL

NUTRITION.
Pyke, Magnus. Man and food. 1970
TX355.P9 ECOL

NUTRITION—ADDRESSES, ESSAYS, LECTURES.
Mead, Margaret. Hunger. 1970
fHD9000.5.M37 ECOL

NUTRITION—STUDY AND TEACHING—UNITED STATES.
The Organic guide to colleges and universities. 1973
S946.O73 ECOL

NUTRITION—TERMINOLOGY.
National Research Council. Committee on Animal Nutrition. Biological energy interrelationships and glossary of energy terms. 1st rev. ed. 1966.
REF SF95.N3 1966 ECOL

O

OCCUPATIONAL DISEASES.
Page, Joseph A. Bitter wages: Ralph Nader's study group report on disease and injury on the job. 1973.
RC967.P33 ECOL

OCEAN.
Carson, Rachel Louise. The sea around us. Rev. ed. 1961. **GC21.C3 1961 ECOL**
Engel, Leonard. The sea. c1969
fGC21.E5 1969 ECOL

OCEAN—PICTORIAL WORKS.
Cousteau, Jacques Yves. Oasis in space: the ocean world of Jacques Cousteau. c1972
fQH91.C64 ECOL

OCEANOGRAPHIC RESEARCH—UNITED STATES.
National Research Council. Committee on Oceanography. Economic benefits from oceanographic research. 1964. **REF GB58.N3 ECOL**

OCEANOGRAPHY—BIBLIOGRAPHY.
Vetter, Richard C. Oceanography information sources/70. 1970. **REF GC10.V47 ECOL**

OCEANOGRAPHY—DIRECTORIES.
Vetter, Richard C. Oceanography information sources/70. 1970. **REF GC10.V47 ECOL**

OCEANOGRAPHY—PACIFIC COAST (NORTH AMERICA).
Oregon. State University, Corvallis. Oceanography of the nearshore coastal waters of the Pacific Northwest relating to possible pollution. 1971-
fGC851.O7 ECOL

OCEANOGRAPHY—POPULAR WORKS.
Briggs, Peter. Water: the vital essence. c1967
GC21.B83 ECOL
Horsfield, Brenda. The great ocean business. 1st American ed. 1972 **GC21.H63 1972b ECOL**

OCEANOGRAPHY—STUDY AND TEACHING.
The Ecology sea in song and ballad. 1973?
Phonodisc GC31.E2 ECOL

ODORS.
Collins, Ralph P. Characterization of taste and odors in water supplies. 1971. fTD384.C64 ECOL

Harris, Douglas H. Assessment of turbidity, color and odor in water. 1972. fTD380.H3 ECOL

United States. Environmental Protection Agency. Office of Air Programs. Odors and air pollution: a bibliography with abstracts. 1972. TD886.U5 ECOL

OHIO RIVER.
Wapora Inc. The effect of temperature on aquatic life in the Ohio River: summary, July—December, 1970. 1971 fTD427.H4W3 ECOL

OIL see PETROLEUM

OIL AND GAS LEASES.
Brown, Keith Cates. Bidding for offshore oil: toward an optimal strategy. c1969 HD9560.5.B75 ECOL

OIL AND GAS LEASES—ALASKA.
Brown, Tom. Oil on ice. 1971 HC107.A47E53 ECOL

OIL BURNERS.
Martin, G. B. Effects of fuel additives on air pollutant emissions from distillate-oil-fired furnaces. 1971. TP355.M29 ECOL

OIL POLLUTION OF RIVERS, HARBORS, ETC.
Agnew, Robert W. A free floating endless belt oil skimmer. 1972. TD899.P4A3 ECOL

Battelle Memorial Institute, Columbus, Ohio. Pacific Northwest Laboratory, Richland, Wash. Concept development of a hydraulic skimmer system for recovery of floating oil. 1971. fTD427.P4B29 ECOL

Gumtz, Garth D. Restoration of Beaches contaminated by oil. 1972. TD427.P4G8 ECOL

Henager, Charles H. Concept evaluation: recovery of floating oil using polyurethane foam sorbent. 1972. fTD427.P4H4 ECOL

Marine Biological Association of the United Kingdom. Laboratory, Plymouth. 'Torrey Canyon' pollution and marine life: a report by the Plymouth Laboratory of the Marine Biological Association of the United Kingdom. 1968. GC1311.M37 ECOL

Marx, Wesley. Oilspill. c1971 GC1085.M3 ECOL

National Oil Recovery Corp., Bayonne, N.J. Conversion of crankcase waste oil into useful products. 1971. fTP687.N3 ECOL

New Mexico State University. Physical Science Laboratory. Floating oil recovery device. 1971. fTD427.P4N48 ECOL

Petrow, Richard. In the wake of Torrey Canyon. 1st American ed. 1968 G530.T72P4 1968 ECOL

Rensselaer Polytechnic Institute, Troy, N.Y. Bio-Environmental Engineering Division. Control of pollution from outboard engine exhaust: a reconnaissance study. 1971. fTD427.P4R45 ECOL

Susquehanna Corporation. Atlantic Research Systems Division. Marine Systems. Recovery of floating oil rotating disk type skimmer. 1971. fTD427.P4S9 ECOL

United States. Environmental Protection Agency. Office of Research and Monitoring. Air modulated vacuum oil recovery collection of spilled oil (foams). 1972. fTD427.P4U5 ECOL

Welch, Robin I. A feasibility demonstration of an aerial surveillance spill prevention system. 1972. fTD427.P4W45 ECOL

OIL POLLUTION OF RIVERS, HARBORS, ETC.—BIBLIOGRAPHY.
Moulder, David S. A bibliography on marine and estuarine oil pollution. 1971. REF fZ6004.P6M6 ECOL

OIL POLLUTION OF RIVERS, HARBORS, ETC.—CONGRESSES.
Joint Conference on Prevention and Control of Oil Spills, Washington, D.C., 1971. Proceedings of Joint Conference on Prevention and Control of Oil Spills held June 15-17, 1971 at the Sheraton Park Hotel. 1971? fGG1080.J6 ECOL

Oil on the sea. 1969. GC1080.O36 ECOL

OIL POLLUTION OF RIVERS, HARBORS, ETC.—LOUISIANA.
Alpine Geophysical Associates. Oil pollution incident. 1971. fGC1221.A4 ECOL

OIL POLLUTION OF RIVERS, HARBORS, ETC.—PUGET SOUND.
Oil on Puget Sound. 1972 fTD427.P4O38 ECOL

OIL POLLUTION OF RIVERS, HARBORS, ETC.—SANTA BARBARA, CALIFORNIA.
California. University, Santa Barbara. Dept. of Biological Sciences. Santa Barbara oil spill: short-term analysis of macroplankton and fish. 1971. fTD427.P4C34 ECOL

OIL POLLUTION OF RIVERS, HARBORS, ETC.—SANTA BARBARA CHANNEL.
Steinhart, Carol E. Blowout. 1972 GC1556.S74 ECOL

OIL RECLAMATION.
National Oil Recovery Corp., Bayonne, N.J. Conversion of crankcase waste oil into useful products. 1971. fTP687.N3 ECOL

OIL-SHALE INDUSTRY—UNITED STATES.
Welles, Chris. The elusive bonanza. 1st ed. 1970. HD9565.W47 ECOL

OIL-SHALE INDUSTRY—WASTE DISPOSAL.
Colorado. State University, Fort Collins. Water pollution potential of spent oil shale residues. 1971. fTD899.P4C65 ECOL

OLD AGE—BIBLIOGRAPHY.
Snyder, Lorraine Hiatt. The environmental challenge and the aging individual. 1972 REF fZ7164.O4S63 ECOL

OLMSTED, FREDERICK LAW, 1822-1903.
Fein, Albert. Frederick Law Olmsted and the American environmental tradition. c1972 SB470.O5F4 ECOL

OLSON, SIGURD F., 1899- BIO-BIBLIOGRAPHY.
Pyter, Bernadette. A bio-bibliography of Sigurd F. Olson. 1972. REF fZ7404.O4P8 ECOL

ONONDAGA LAKE, NEW YORK.
Syracuse University. Civil Engineering Dept. Benefits of water quality enhancement. 1970. fTD365.S94 ECOL

ONTARIO—DESCRIPTION AND TRAVEL.
Ogburn, Charlton. The continent in our hands. 1971. E169.02.O3 ECOL

ONTARIO—HISTORY.
Nute, Grace Lee. The voyageur's highway. 1965 c1941 F606.N97 ECOL

ONTARIO, LAKE.
International Great Lakes Levels Board. Regulation of Great Lakes water levels: interim report on Lakes Superior and Ontario regulation, to the International Joint Commission by the International Great Lakes Levels Board. 1973. fGB1627.G8I52 ECOL

OOLOGY see BIRDS—EGGS AND NESTS

OPERATIONS RESEARCH.
Buras, Nathan. Scientific allocation of water resources. 1972 TC409.B87 ECOL

ORGANIC FARMING.
Rodale, Robert. Sane living in a mad world. 1972 RA776.5.R57 ECOL

ORGANIC FARMING—STUDY AND TEACHING (HIGHER)—UNITED STATES.
The Organic guide to colleges and universities. 1973 S946.O73 ECOL

ORGANIC WATER POLLUTANTS.
Washington (State). University. Institute of Forest Products. Pollution abatement by fiber modification. 1971. fTD427.W65W38 ECOL

ORGANICULTURE see also COMPOST
The Basic book of organic gardening. 1971 S605.5.B37 ECOL

Bay Laurel, Alicia. Living on the earth. 1971, c1970 fS605.5.B3 ECOL

Foster, Catharine Osgood. The organic gardener. 1972 S605.5.F67 1972 ECOL

Langer, Richard W. Grow it! 1972 S501.L27 1972 ECOL

The Last whole earth catalog. 1971. REF fTT155.W52 ECOL

Ogden, Samuel R. Step-by-step to organic vegetable growing. 1971 SB321.O343 ECOL

Tyler, Hamilton A. Organic gardening without poisons. 1970 S605.5.T9 ECOL

ORGANICULTURE—STUDY AND TEACHING.
The Organic classroom. c1973 fS946.O7 ECOL

ORGANOPHOSPHORUS COMPOUNDS.
Midwest Research Institute, Kansas City, Mo. Rapid detection system for organophosphates and carbamate insecticles in water. 1972. TD427.P35M5 ECOL

ORNITHOLOGY.
Berger, Andrew John. Bird study. 1971, c1961 QL673.B47 1971 ECOL

ORNITHOLOGY—PERIODICALS.
The Living bird. 6th- 1967- REF QL671.L57 ECOL

OUTBOARD MOTORS.
Rensselaer Polytechnic Institute, Troy, N.Y. Bio-Environmental Engineering Division. Control of pollution from outboard engine exhaust: a reconnaissance study. 1971. fTD427.P4R45 ECOL

OUTDOOR EDUCATION see also CAMPING; NATURAL HISTORY—OUTDOOR BOOKS

Blomberg, Karin. Direct experience teaching in the out-of-doors. 1967. fLB1047.B56 ECOL

Bonvie, Carolyn. Art & design in the environment. 1971 fLB1047.B6 ECOL

Burns, William. Snow, snowshoes, and nature: the white dimension of environment. 1972? fLB1047.B8 ECOL

Hammerman, Donald R. Teaching in the outdoors. 1964 LB1047.H3 ECOL

Harris, Melville. Environmental studies. 1971 LB1047.H32 ECOL

Hiros, John E. Inviting involvement with history. 1969 fLB1047.H5 ECOL

Illinois. Northern Illinois University, De Kalb. Lorado Taft Field Campus. Dept. of Outdoor Teacher Education. Tips and tricks in outdoor education. 1970 fLB1047.I44 ECOL

Knapp, Clifford E. Outdoor activities for environmental studies. c1971 LB1047.K5 ECOL

Major, James M. Environmental education: objectives and field activities. 4th ed. 1971. fLB1047.M3 ECOL

Marsh, Norman F. Outdoor education on your school grounds. 1968 LB1047.M29 ECOL

Minnesota Elementary Principals' Association. Guidelines for out-of-the-classroom education experiences: Elementary schools. 1966. LB1047.M55 ECOL

National Education Association of the United States. Research Division. Environmental education in the public schools. 1970 fLB1047.N36 ECOL

St. Paul. Public Schools. Curriculum Office. Belwin outdoor education laboratory project handbook. 1971. fLB1047.S25 ECOL

Smith, Julian W. Outdoor education. 1963. LB1047.S58 1963 ECOL

OUTDOOR EDUCATION—ADDRESSES, ESSAYS, LECTURES.
Donaldson, George Warren. Perspectives on outdoor education. 1972 LB1047.D6 ECOL

Hammerman, Donald R. Outdoor education. c1970,c1968 LB1047.H28 ECOL

OUTDOOR LIFE.
Angier, Bradford. One acre and security-how to live off the earth without ruining it. 1972 S561.A574 ECOL

Bay Laurel, Alicia. Living on the earth. 1971, c1970 fS605.5.B3 ECOL

The Last whole earth catalog. 1971. REF fTT155.W52 ECOL

Olson, Sigurd F. Sigurd F. Olson's Wilderness days. 1st ed. 1972. QH81.O67 1972 ECOL

Van der Smissen, Margaret Elisabeth. A leader's guide to nature-oriented activities. 2d ed. 1968 GV182.2.V3 1968 ECOL

OUTDOOR LIFE—SAFETY MEASURES.
Brown, Vinson. Knowing the outdoors in the dark. 1972 QH81.B856 ECOL

OUTDOOR PLANNING—MINNESOTA.
Minnesota. Dept. of Conservation. Minnesota outdoor recreation plan. 1968- fGV54.M6A197 ECOL

OUTDOOR RECREATION.
Van der Smissen, Margaret Elisabeth. A leader's guide to nature-oriented activities. 2d ed. 1968 GV182.2.V3 1968 ECOL

OUTDOOR RECREATION—ADDRESSES, ESSAYS, LECTURES.
Schoenfeld, Clarence Albert. Everybody's ecology. 1971 QH541.13.S36 ECOL

OUTDOOR RECREATION—ECONOMIC ASPECTS.
Clawson, Marion. Economics of outdoor recreation. c1966 GV182.2.C55 ECOL

OUTDOOR RECREATION—ECONOMIC ASPECTS—UNITED STATES.
United States. Bureau of Outdoor Recreation. The 1965 nationwide inventory of publicly owned recreation areas and an assessment of private recreation enterprises. n.d. fGV53.A47 1965 ECOL

OUTDOOR RECREATION—FINANCE.
National Recreation and Park Association. Guide to new approaches to financing parks & recreation. 1970 SB482.A4N38 ECOL

OUTDOOR RECREATION—MINNESOTA.
Minnesota. Dept. of Natural Resources. Bureau of Planning. Minnesota resource potentials in state outdoor recreation. 1971. fGV54.M6A53 ECOL

Minnesota. Legislature. Outdoor Recreation Resources Commission. M.O.R.R.C. report. 1963/65- REF GV54.M6A19 ECOL

Minnesota. Legislature. Outdoor Recreation Resources Commission. M.O.R.R.C. staff report. 1963/65- REF fGV54.M6A192 ECOL

OUTDOOR RECREATION—MINNESOTA—ANOKA COUNTY.
Midwest Planning and Research, Inc. Anoka County parks and open-space: comprehensive plan. 1969.
fGV54.M6M52 ECOL

Midwest Planning and Research, Inc. Anoka County parks and open-space: goals, policies, directions and alternatives. 1968. fGV54.M6M5 ECOL

OUTDOOR RECREATION—MINNESOTA—WASHINGTON COUNTY.
Minnesota Association of Soil and Water Conservation Districts. Outdoor recreational development potentials in Washington Soil and Water Conservation District. fGV54.M6M54 ECOL

OUTDOOR RECREATION—TEXAS.
Gunn, Clare A. Cultural benefits from metropolitan river recreation—San Antonio prototype. 1972.
fHD1694.T4G8 ECOL

OUTDOOR RECREATION—UNITED STATES.
Clawson, Marion. Land and water for recreation. c1963 HD205 1963.C53 ECOL

Forest Recreation Symposium, Syracuse, N.Y., 1971. 1971. SD426.F6 1971 ECOL

Foss, Phillip O. Recreation. 1971.
REF GV53.F6 ECOL

Shomon, Joseph James. Open land for urban America. 1971 HD257.S56 ECOL

Snowmobile and Off the Road Vehicle Research Symposium, Michigan State University, East Lansing, 1971. Proceedings. 1971. fGF75.S6 1971 ECOL

OUTDOOR RECREATION—UNITED STATES—STATISTICS.
United States. Bureau of Outdoor Recreation. Selected outdoor recreation statistics. 1971.
fGV53.A47 1971 ECOL

United States. Bureau of Outdoor Recreation. The 1965 nationwide inventory of publicly owned recreation areas and an assessment of private recreation enterprises. n.d. fGV53.A47 1965 ECOL

United States. Bureau of Outdoor Recreation. The 1970 survey of outdoor recreation activities. 1972.
GV53.A472 1970 ECOL

OXIDATION.
NUS Corporation. Cyrus Wm. Rice Division. The effects of various gas atmospheres on the oxidation of coal mine pyrites. 1971. fTD899.M5N2 ECOL

OXIDATION—REDUCTION REACTION.
North American Rockwell Corporation. Rocketdyne Division. Development of a chemical denitrification process. 1970. fTD433.N67 ECOL

OXIDATION, ELECTROLYTIC.
Ionics, Inc. The electro-oxidation of ammonia in sewage to nitrogen. 1970. fTD757.I55 ECOL

Tyco Laboratories. Electrochemical treatment of acid mine waters. 1972. fTD899.M5T88 ECOL

OXIDIZING AGENTS—BIBLIOGRAPHY.
Air Pollution Technical Information Center. Photochemical oxidants and air pollution: an annotated bibliography. 1971. REF Z7173.A4A53 ECOL

P

PACKAGING see also CONTAINERS
Darnay, Arsen. The role of packaging in solid waste management 1966 to 1976. 1969.
TD795.D37 ECOL

PACKAGING—CONGRESSES.
Solid Waste Resources Conference, Columbus, Ohio, 1971. Design of consumer containers for re-use or disposal. 1972. TD785.S6 1971 ECOL

PACKAGING RESEARCH.
Franklin, William E. Environmental impacts of polystyrene foam and molded pulp meat trays. 1972.
fTP373.F7 ECOL

Hickman, Howard J. A study of the environmental impact of polystyrene vs. paper pulp egg cartons and meat trays. 1972. fTP373.H5 ECOL

PACKING-HOUSES.
Beefland International, Inc. Elimination of water pollution by packing-house animal paunch and blood. 1971. fTD899.M4B4 ECOL

PALEONTOLOGY—MINNESOTA—COLLECTING OF SPECIMENS.
Hogberg, Rudolph K. Guide to fossil collecting in Minnesota. Rev. ed. 1967. QE718.H55 1967 ECOL

PALEONTOLOGY—PICTORIAL WORKS.
Pinna, Giovanni. The dawn of life. c1972
fQE714.3.P5 ECOL

PAPER MAKING AND TRADE—WASTE DISPOSAL.
Mead Corporation. Multi-system biological treatment of bleached kraft effluents. 1971.
fTD899.W65M4 ECOL

PAPER RECYCLING.
Burke, Jacquelyn M. The realities of recycling. 1973
REF fTP995.B8 ECOL

PARASITOLOGY see AGRICULTURAL PESTS

PARASITOLOGY—CONGRESSES.
Ecology and physiology of parasites. 1971
QL757.E26 ECOL

PARKS see also NATIONAL PARKS AND RESERVES; PLAYGROUNDS; ZOOLOGICAL GARDENS
Seymour Whitney North. Small urban spaces. 1969
SB481.S48 ECOL

PARKS—FINANCE.
National Recreation and Park Association. Guide to new approaches to financing parks & recreation. 1970
SB482.A4N38 ECOL

PARKS—MINNESOTA—APPLE VALLEY.
Urban Planning and Design, Inc., Mpls., Minn. Apple Valley park development program. 1969.
fGV54.M6U7 ECOL

PARKS—MINNESOTA—NEW BRIGHTON.
Brauer and Associates, inc., Edina, Minn. A study of parks and recreation for the village of New Brighton. 1967 fGV54.M6B7 ECOL

PARKS—UNITED STATES.
Brown, William Edward. Islands of hope. c1971
HC110.E5B75 ECOL

Natural wonders of America. 1972
QH76.N29 ECOL

Olmsted, Frederick Law. Civilizing American cities. 1971 HT167.O44 ECOL

PARTICLE SIZE DETERMINATION—CONGRESSES.
Rochester International Conference on Environmental Toxicity, 3d, 1970. Assessment of airborne particles. 1972 QD549.R59 1970 ECOL

PASSENGER PIGEONS.
Schorger, Arlie William. The passenger pigeon. 1973 QL696.C6S3 1973 ECOL

PAVEMENTS—TESTING.
Minnesota. Dept. of Highways. A research progress report on the effects of studded tires. 1970.
fTL270.M5 1970 ECOL

Minnesota. Dept. of Highways. A research summary report on the effects of studded tires. 1971.
fTL270.M5 1971 ECOL

PAVEMENTS, ASPHALT CONCRETE.
Investigation of porous pavements for urban runoff control. 1972. fTE215.I58 ECOL

PEDOLOGY (SOIL SCIENCE) see SOIL SCIENCE

PERCEPTION see CONSCIOUSNESS

PERCEPTION—ADDRESSES, ESSAYS, LECTURES.
Environmental perception and behavior. 1967.
GF51.E5 ECOL

PEREGRINE FALCON—CONGRESSES.
Peregrine falcon populations. 1969.
QL696.A2P44 ECOL

PERIODICALS—BIBLIOGRAPHY—UNION LISTS.
United States. Environmental Protection Agency. Library Systems Branch. Journal holdings report: 1972- REF fZ6945.U534 ECOL

PERSONAL SPACE.
Sommer, Robert. Personal space. 1969
BF469.S64 ECOL

PERU—DESCRIPTION AND TRAVEL.
Johnson, George Robbins. Peru from the air. 1930.
F3428.J67 ECOL

Murphy, Robert Cushman. Bird islands of Peru. 1925. REF QH128.M8 ECOL

PERU—DESCRIPTION AND TRAVEL—VIEWS.
Johnson, George Robbins. Peru from the air. 1930.
F3428.J67 ECOL

PEST CONTROL—BIOLOGICAL CONTROL—UNITED STATES.
United States. Council on Environmental Quality. Integrated pest management. 1972.
SB950.U5 ECOL

PEST CONTROL—UNITED STATES.
United States. Council on Environmental Quality. Integrated pest management. 1972.
SB950.U5 ECOL

PESTICIDE RESIDUES.
Midwest Research Institute, Kansas City, Mo. Rapid detection system for organophosphates and carbamate insecticides in water. 1972. TD427.P35M5 ECOL

Neely, W. C. Biological and photobiological action of pollutants on aquatic microorganisms. 1973.
fTC1.A85no.9 ECOL

United States. Environmental Protection Agency. Effects of pesticides in water. n.d.
REF fTD427.P35U53 ECOL

PESTICIDE RESIDUES—BIBLIOGRAPHY.
Water Resources Scientific Information Center. PCB in water. 1973. Z7173.W3W3 ECOL

PESTICIDE RESIDUES—CONGRESSES.
International IUPAC Congress of Pesticide Chemistry, 2d, Tel-Aviv, 1971. Fate of pesticides in environment. 1972 SB951.I56 1971vol.6 ECOL

PESTICIDES see also HERBICIDES; INSECTICIDES
Combined soils, fertilizer & agricultural pesticides, short course, Dec. 15-17, 1970, Minneapolis Auditorium. fSB951.C76 ECOL

Hartley, Gilbert Spencer. Chemicals for pest control. 1st ed. 1969 TP248.P47H3 1969 ECOL

Headley, Joseph Charles. The pesticide problem: an economic approach to public policy. c1967
SB959.H35 ECOL

Mellanby, Kenneth. Pesticides and pollution. 2nd rev. ed. 1970. TD186.5.G7M44 1970 ECOL

Rudd, Robert L. Pesticides and the living landscape. 1964. SB951.R78 ECOL

PESTICIDES—ANALYSIS.
Thruston, Alfred D. Liquid chromatography of carbamate pesticides. 1972. SB951.T4 ECOL

PESTICIDES—EFFECT ON WILDLIFE see PESTICIDES AND WILDLIFE

PESTICIDES—LAW AND LEGISLATION—UNITED STATES.
Von Rumker, Rosmarie. The use of pesticides in suburban homes and gardens and their impact on the aquatic environment. 1972. fQH545.P4V66 ECOL

PESTICIDES—SPECTRA.
Southeast Water Laboratory. Catalog of pesticide NMR spectra. 1971. fSB951.S64 ECOL

United States. Environmental Protection Agency. Office of Research and Monitoring. Identification of polychlorinated biphenyls in the presence of DDT-type compounds. 1972. SB951.U52 ECOL

PESTICIDES—TOXICOLOGY see also PESTICIDES AND WILDLIFE
American Chemical Society. Organic pesticides in the environment; a symposium. 1966.
SB951.A4 ECOL

Carson, Rachel Louise. Silent spring. 1962
SB959.C3 ECOL

Conservation Foundation. Pollution by pesticides. 1969. QH545.P4C6 ECOL

Harmer, Ruth Mulvey. Unfit for human consumption. 1971 QH545.P4H36 ECOL

The Mutagenicity of pesticides: concepts and evaluation. 1971 RA1270.P4M87 ECOL

Pimentel, David. Ecological effects of pesticides on non-target species. 1971. QH545.P4P55 ECOL

PESTICIDES—TOXICOLOGY—ADDRESSES, ESSAYS, LECTURES.
Adverse effects of common environmental pollutants. 1972 RA1270.P4A32 ECOL

Scientific aspects of pest control. 1966.
SB951.S38 ECOL

PESTICIDES—TOXICOLOGY—CONGRESSES.
Chemical fallout. 1969 SB959.C45 ECOL

International IUPAC Congress of Pesticide Chemistry, 2d, Tel-Aviv, 1971. Fate of pesticides in environment. 1972 SB951.I56 1971vol.6 ECOL

PESTICIDES AND THE ENVIRONMENT.
Atkins, Patrick R. The pesticide manufacturing industry—current waste treatment and disposal practices. 1972. fTD899.C5A8 ECOL

Conservation Foundation. Pollution by pesticides. 1969. QH545.P4C6 ECOL

Graham, Frank. Since Silent spring. 1970.
QH75.G68 ECOL

Harmer, Ruth Mulvey. Unfit for human consumption. 1971 QH545.P4H36 ECOL

Henkin, Harmon. The environment, the establishment, and the law. 1971
QH545.P4H4 ECOL

Midwest Research Institute, Kansas City, Mo. Rapid detection system for organophosphates and carbamate insecticides in water. 1972. TD427.P35M5 ECOL

Montague, Katherine. Mercury. 1971
QH545.M4M6 ECOL

United States. Environmental Protection Agency. Effects of pesticides in water. n.d.
REF fTD427.P35U53 ECOL

PESTICIDES AND THE ENVIRONMENT—ADDRESSES, ESSAYS, LECTURES.
Pesticides. 1970 fQH545.P4P48 ECOL

PESTICIDES AND THE ENVIRONMENT—BIBLIOGRAPHY.
Water Resources Scientific Information Center. PCB in water. 1973. Z7173.W3W3 ECOL

PESTICIDES AND THE ENVIRONMENT—CONGRESSES.
Chemical fallout. 1969   **SB959.C45 ECOL**

PESTICIDES AND THE ENVIRONMENT—LAKE MICHIGAN.
Lake Michigan Enforcement Conference. Lake Michigan Interstate Pesticides Committee. An evaluation of DDT and dieldrin in Lake Michigan. 1972.   **TD427.P35L3 ECOL**

PESTICIDES AND THE ENVIRONMENT—LAKE SUPERIOR WATERSHED.
Minnesota. Pollution Control Agency. Pesticide inputs and levels: Minnesota waters-Lake Superior Basin. 1971 i.e. 1972   **fTD223.3.M55 ECOL**

PESTICIDES AND THE ENVIRONMENT—OHIO—POND LICK LAKE.
Ryckman, Edgerley, Tomlinson and Associates. Pesticide poisoning of Pond Lick Lake, Ohio. 1971   **fTD224.O3R9 ECOL**

PESTICIDES AND THE ENVIRONMENT—STUDY AND TEACHING.
Kriett, Jolene. Biocides. 1971.   **QH545.P4K7 ECOL**

PESTICIDES AND THE ENVIRONMENT—UNITED STATES.
Ryckman, Edgerley, Tomlinson and Associates. Development of a case study of the total effect of pesticides in the environment, nonirrigated croplands of the Mid-west. 1972.   **fQH545.P4R9 ECOL**

United States. Council on Environmental Quality. Integrated pest management. 1972.   **SB950.U5 ECOL**

Von Rumker, Rosmarie. The use of pesticides in suburban homes and gardens and their impact on the aquatic environment. 1972.   **fQH545.P4V66 ECOL**

PESTICIDES AND WILDLIFE.
Henny, Charles J. An analysis of the population dynamics of selected avian species. 1972   **QL785.5.B6H4 ECOL**

Pimentel, David. Ecological effects of pesticides on non-target species. 1971.   **QH545.P4P55 ECOL**

United States. Bureau of Sport Fisheries and Wildlife. Division of Wildlife Research. Wildlife research: problems programs, progress, 1969. 1971   **S914.A3no.94 ECOL**

PESTS *see* AGRICULTURAL PESTS; ZOOLOGY, ECONOMIC

PESTS—ADDRESSES, ESSAYS, LECTURES.
Scientific aspects of pest control. 1966.   **SB951.S38 ECOL**

PETROGRAPHY *see* PETROLOGY

PETROLEUM.
Lovejoy, Wallace Francis. Methods of estimating reserves of crude oil, natural gas, and natural gas liquids. 1965   **TN870.L68 ECOL**

Pratt, Wallace Everett. World geography of petroleum. 1950.   **REF TN870.P73 ECOL**

PETROLEUM—ALASKA.
Chasan, Daniel Jack. Klondike '70. 1971   **TN872.A7C47 ECOL**

Herndon, Booton. The great land. 1971   **TN872.A7H4 ECOL**

PETROLEUM—GEOLOGY—ATLANTIC COAST (UNITED STATES).
Maher, John Charles. Geologic framework and petroleum potential of the Atlantic Coastal Plain and Continental Shelf. 1971.   **REF fQE75.P9no.659 ECOL**

PETROLEUM—GEOLOGY—NORTH ATLANTIC OCEAN.
Maher, John Charles. Geologic framework and petroleum potential of the Atlantic Coastal Plain and Continental Shelf. 1971.   **REF fQE75.P9no.659 ECOL**

PETROLEUM—UNITED STATES—HISTORY.
Boatwright, Mody Coggin. Folklore of the oil industry. c1963   **TN872.A5B6 ECOL**

PETROLEUM AS FUEL *see* OIL BURNERS

PETROLEUM AS FUEL—ADDITIVES.
Martin, G. B. Effects of fuel additives on air pollutant emissions from distillate-oil-fired furnaces. 1971.   **TP355.M29 ECOL**

PETROLEUM CONSERVATION.
Lewis, Richard S. The energy crisis. 1972.   **fHC103.7.L4 ECOL**

Lovejoy, Wallace Francis. Economic aspects of oil conservation regulation. 1967   **HD9566.L6 ECOL**

McDonald, Stephen L. Petroleum conservation: an economic analysis. 1971   **HD9566.M3 ECOL**

United States. The potential for energy conservation. 1972.   **TJ153.U43 ECOL**

PETROLEUM INDUSTRY AND TRADE—ALASKA.
Cooper, Bryan. Alaska: the last frontier. 1973.   **HD9567.A4C66 ECOL**

PETROLEUM INDUSTRY AND TRADE—ALASKA—ADDRESSES, ESSAYS, LECTURES.
Alaska Science Conference, 20th, University of Alaska, 1969. Change in Alaska. 1970   **HD9567.A4A64 1969 ECOL**

PETROLEUM INDUSTRY AND TRADE—LAW *see* PETROLEUM LAW AND LEGISLATION

PETROLEUM INDUSTRY AND TRADE—MIDDLE WEST.
Koenker, William E. Petroleum resources and production facilities in the Upper Midwest. 1963.   **fHD1773.A3U6no.8 ECOL**

PETROLEUM INDUSTRY AND TRADE—UNITED STATES.
Independent Petroleum Association of America. The oil producing industry in your state. 1972-   **REF fHD9564.I55 ECOL**

Lovejoy, Wallace Francis. Economic aspects of oil conservation regulation. 1967   **HD9566.L6 ECOL**

McDonald, Stephen L. Petroleum conservation in the United States: an economic analysis. 1971   **HD9566.M3 ECOL**

Welles, Chris. The elusive bonanza. 1st ed. 1970.   **HD9565.W47 ECOL**

PETROLEUM LAW AND LEGISLATION.
Ely, Northcutt. Summary of mining and petroleum laws of the world. Rev. 1970-   **TN295.U4no.8514 ECOL**

PETROLEUM LAW AND LEGISLATION—UNITED STATES.
Lovejoy, Wallace Francis. Economic aspects of oil conservation regulation. 1967   **HD9566.L6 ECOL**

McDonald, Stephen L. Petroleum conservation in the United States: an economic analysis. 1971   **HD9566.M3 ECOL**

PETROLEUM RESEARCH.
Linville, Bill. Review of Bureau of Mines energy program, 1970. 1971   **TN295.U4no.8526 ECOL**

PETROLEUM WASTE.
Mandan Refinery. Fluid bed incineration of petroleum refinery wastes. 1971.   **fTD899.P4M35 ECOL**

National Oil Recovery Corp., Bayonne, N.J. Conversion of crankcase waste oil into useful products. 1971.   **fTP687.N3 ECOL**

PETROLOGY *see also* GEOCHEMISTRY; GEOLOGY; LIMESTONE; MINERALOGY
Adler, Irving. Rocks and minerals and the stories they tell. 1956.   **QE432.A35 ECOL**

Hyler, Nelson W. The how and why wonder book of rocks and minerals. 1970,c1960   **fQE432.H9 1970 ECOL**

PETS.
Great Britain. Dept. of Education and Science. Keeping animals in schools. 1971.   **QL51.G7 ECOL**

PHEASANTS.
Beebe, Charles William. Pheasants. 1926.   **REF QL969.G2B26 ECOL**

PHENOIS.
Jacksonville, Ark. Biological treatment of chlorophenolic wastes. 1971.   **fTD755.J3 ECOL**

PHENOLOGY.
Fretwell, Stephen D. Populations in a seasonal environment. 1972.   **QL752.F73 ECOL**

PHEROMONES—CONGRESSES.
Chemicals controlling insect behavior. 1970.   **QL461.S88 1969 ECOL**

International IUPAC Congress of Pesticide Chemistry, 2d, Tel-Aviv, 1971. Chemical releasers in insects. c1971   **SB951.I56 1971vol.3 ECOL**

PHILIPPINE ISLANDS—DESCRIPTION AND TRAVEL.
Fairchild, David Grandison. Garden islands of the great East. 1943.   **SB109.F185 ECOL**

PHILOSOPHICAL ANTHROPOLOGY—ADDRESSES, ESSAYS, LECTURES.
Platt, John Rader. New views of the nature of man. 1965   **BD450.P55 ECOL**

PHILOSOPHY OF MEDICINE *see* MEDICINE—PHILOSOPHY

PHILOSOPHY OF NATURE.
Derrick, Christopher. The delicate creation. c1972   **BD581.D47 ECOL**

PHOSPHATE MINES AND MINING—WASTE DISPOSAL.
Battelle-Northwest. Inorganic fertilizer and phosphate mining industries—water pollution and control. 1971.   **fTD899.F47B38 ECOL**

International Minerals and Chemical Corporation. Utilization of phosphate slimes. 1971.   **fTD899.M5I57 ECOL**

PHOSPHATES.
Detroit Metro Water Dept. Development of phosphate removal processes. 1970.   **fTD756.D47 ECOL**

Envirogenics Company. Investigation of a new phosphate removal process. 1970.   **fTD745.E5 ECOL**

General Mills Chemicals. Feasibility of liquid ion exchange for extracting phosphate from wastewater. 1970.   **fTD757.G45 ECOL**

Ghassemi, Masood. Phosphate precipitation with ferrous iron. 1971.   **fTD751.G4 ECOL**

PHOSPHORUS.
Bartsch, A. F. Role of phosphorus in eutrophication. 1972.   **QH96.8.E9B3 ECOL**

Black & Veatch, Kansas City, Mo. Process design manual for phosphorus removal. 1971.   **REF fTD745.B5 ECOL**

Milwaukee. Sewerage Commission. Phosphorus removal by an activated sludge plant. 1970.   **fTD756.M54 ECOL**

Milwaukee. Sewerage Commission. Phosphorus removal with pickle liquor in an activated sludge plant. 1971.   **fTD756.M55 ECOL**

Morgan, W. E. An investigation of phosphorus removal mechanisms in activated sludge systems. 1972.   **TD756.M6 ECOL**

Texas. University. Medical Branch, Galveston. Phosphorus removal and disposal from municipal wastewater. 1971.   **fTD745.T43 ECOL**

PHOTOCHEMISTRY.
Leighton, Philip Albert. Photochemistry of air pollution. 1961.   **RA576.L4 ECOL**

PHOTOGEOGRAPHY *see* AERIAL PHOTOGRAPHY IN GEOGRAPHY

PHOTOGRAPHY—EXHIBITIONS.
Adams, Ansel Easton. This is the American earth. 1960   **fHC103.7.A68 ECOL**

PHOTOGRAPHY, AERIAL.
Welch, Robin I. A feasibility demonstration of an aerial surveillance spill prevention system. 1972.   **fTD427.P4W45 ECOL**

PHOTOGRAPHY, ARTISTIC.
Brower, David Ross. Not man apart. 1969   **F869.B63B7 1969 ECOL**

PHOTOGRAPHY OF ANIMALS.
Baufle, Jean Marie. Photographing wildlife. 1972.   **fTR727.B2813 ECOL**

PHOTOGRAPHY OF BIRDS.
Aymar, Gordon Christian. Bird flight. 1935.   **QL698.A9 ECOL**

Berg, Bengt Magnus Kristoffer. To Africa with the migratory birds. 1930.   **QL692.B4 ECOL**

PHOTOGRAPHY, SUBMARINE.
Torchio, Menico. The world beneath the sea. 1972   **fQH91.17.T6 ECOL**

PHOTOSYNTHESIS.
Stokes, Lee W. The photosynthetic pigments of Lake Superior periphyton and their relation to primary productivity. 1970.   **GB701.M554no.18 ECOL**

PHYLOGENY.
Heilmann, Gerhard. The origin of birds. 1927.   **QE871.H4 1927 ECOL**

PHYSICAL GEOGRAPHY *see also* EARTH; EROSION; ICE; METEOROLOGY; WATER, UNDERGROUND
Guyot, Arnold Henry. The earth and man. 1970, c1849   **GB59.G8 1970 ECOL**

PHYSICAL GEOGRAPHY—LABRADOR.
Forbes, Alexander. Northernmost Labrador. 1938.   **F1136.F67 ECOL**

PHYSICAL GEOGRAPHY—PERU.
Johnson, George Robbins. Peru from the air. 1930.   **F3428.J67 ECOL**

PHYSICAL GEOGRAPHY—UNITED STATES.
Farb, Peter. Face of North America. Young readers' ed. 1964   **QH104.F32 ECOL**

PHYSICS.
Barrow, George. Your world in motion. 1956   **QC25.B23 ECOL**

Gamow, George. Matter, earth, and sky. 2d ed. 1965   **QC171.G3 1965 ECOL**

PHYSIOGRAPHY *see* PHYSICAL GEOGRAPHY

PHYSIOLOGICAL PSYCHOLOGY *see* BIOLOGICAL CHEMISTRY

PHYSIOPHILOSOPHY *see* NATURAL HISTORY

PHYTOGEOGRAPHY.
Gleason, Henry Allan. The natural geography of plants. 1964.   **QK101.G57 ECOL**

PHYTOPATHOLOGY *see* PLANT DISEASES

PHYTOPLANKTON *see also* ALGAE; DIATOMS

Fogg, Gordon Elliott. Algal cultures and phytoplankton ecology. 1966, c1965
QK565.F58 ECOL

PHYTOPLANKTON—CALIFORNIA—SANTA CATALINA, GULF OF.

California. University. Institute of Marine Resources. Eutrophication in coastal waters: nitrogen as a controlling factor. 1971. **fQH96.8.E9C34 ECOL**

PHYTOPLANKTON—MINNESOTA.

Brook, Alan J. The phytoplankton of Minnesota lakes—a preliminary survey. 1968
GB701.M554no.36 ECOL

PHYTOPLANKTON—MINNETONKA, LAKE, MINNESOTA.

Megard, Robert Ordell. Lake Minnetonka: nutrients, nutrient abatement, and the photosynthetic system of the phytoplankton. 1970. **fTD225.M63M4 ECOL**

PHYTOPLANKTON BLOOM *see* WATER BLOOM

PHYTOSOCIOLOGY *see also* PLANT COMMUNITIES

Daubenmire, Rexford F. Plant communities. 1968
QK911.D3 ECOL

PINE BARRENS.

McPhee, John A. The pine Barrens. 1968
F142.P5M35 1968 ECOL

PIONEERS.

Bowman, Isaiah. The pioneer fringe. 1931.
GF51.B6 ECOL

PIPE—HYDRODYNAMICS.

Minnesota. University. St. Anthony Falls Hydraulic Laboratory. Hydraulics of long vertical conduits and associated cavitation. 1971. **fTC174.M53 ECOL**

PLANKTON—COLLECTION AND PRESERVATION.

Olson, Theodore A. The continuous plankton recorder: a review of the literature. 1966.
GB701.M554no.3 ECOL

PLANKTON—MISSISSIPPI RIVER.

McNabb, C. D. A fluorometric technique for sampling in large-river ecosystems. 1971.
GB701.M554no.34 ECOL

PLANKTON—SUPERIOR, LAKE.

Fox, Jackson L. The ecology of periphyton in Western Lake Superior. 1969.
GB701.M554no.14 ECOL

Minnesota. University. School of Public Health. Studies on the productivity and Plankton of Lake Superior. 1961 **fQK935.M55 ECOL**

PLANKTON, EFFECT OF WATER POLLUTION ON.

California. University, Santa Barbara. Dept. of Biological Sciences. Santa Barbara oil spill: short-term analysis of macroplankton and fish. 1971.
fTD427.P4C34 ECOL

PLANNED PARENTHOOD *see* BIRTH CONTROL

PLANNING.

INTASA, Inc. Planning and evaluation of multiple purpose water resource projects in a multiobjective environment. 1972. **fHD1691.I1 ECOL**

Maldonado, Tomas. Design, nature, and revolution. 1st U.S. ed. 1972 **GF41.M3413 1972 ECOL**

Wilson, Raymond Harrison. Toward a philosophy of planning: attitudes of federal water planners. 1973.
HC110.E5W5 ECOL

PLANNING, REGIONAL *see* REGIONAL PLANNING

PLANT ASSOCIATIONS *see* PLANT COMMUNITIES

PLANT COMMUNITIES.

Cain, Stanley Adair. Manual of vegetation analysis. 1971, c1959 **QK911.C3 1959a ECOL**

PLANT DISEASES *see also* GARDEN PESTS

Freeman, Edward Monroe. Minnesota plant diseases. 1905. **REF QK168.F7 ECOL**

PLANT DISEASES—CONGRESSES.

International Symposium on Factors Determining the Behavior of Plant Pathogens in Soil, Berkeley, Calif., 1963. Ecology of soil-borne plant pathogens.
fQR111.I55 1963 ECOL

PLANT DISEASES—HISTORY.

Carefoot, G. L. Famine on the wind; man's battle against plant disease. 1967 **SB732.C37 ECOL**

PLANT ENGINEERING *see also* FACTORY AND TRADE WASTE; PLANT MAINTENANCE

Western Plant Engineering and Maintenance Conference, San Francisco, 1970 Proceedings. 1970.
fTS184.W4

PLANT INTRODUCTION.

Fairchild, David Grandison. Garden islands of the great East. 1943. **SB109.F185 ECOL**

PLANT MAINTENANCE.

Western Plant Engineering and Maintenance Conference, San Francisco, 1970 Proceedings. 1970.
fTS184.W4

PLANT PATHOLOGY *see* PLANT DISEASES

PLANT PHYSIOLOGY.

Levitt, Jacob. Responses of plants to environmental stresses. 1972. **QK754.L42 ECOL**

Treshow, Michael. Environment & plant response. 1970 **QK754.T7 ECOL**

PLANT SOCIETIES *see* PLANT COMMUNITIES

PLANTS *see also* BOTANY; CLIMBING PLANTS; GARDENING; PLANT INTRODUCTION; POISONOUS PLANTS; WEEDS

Blough, Glenn Orlando. Discovering plants. 1966
PZ10.B29553Dk ECOL

Robinette, Gary O. Plants/people/environmental quality. 1972 **QK901.R6 ECOL**

PLANTS—DISEASES *see* PLANT DISEASES

PLANTS—HARDINESS.

Levitt, Jacob. Responses of plants to environmental stresses. 1972. **QK754.L42 ECOL**

PLANTS—IDENTIFICATION.

Correll, Donovan Stewart. Aquatic and wetland plants of southwestern United States. 1972.
QK142.C6 ECOL

Dickey, Miriam. Beyond the classroom. 1972.
Ref fQH51.D5 ECOL

PLANTS—PATHOLOGY *see* PLANT DISEASES

PLANTS, EDIBLE.

Gibbons, Euell. Stalking the good life. 1971
QK98.5.G45 ECOL

Gibbons, Euell. Stalking the wild asparagus. 1970, c1962 **QK98.5.G48 ECOL**

PLANTS, EFFECT OF AIR POLLUTION ON.

Jacobson, Jay S. Recognition of air pollution injury to vegetation: a pictorial atlas. 1970.
fQK751.J3 ECOL

PLANTS, EFFECT OF NITRATES ON.

National Research Council. Committee on Nitrate Accumulation. Accumulation of nitrate. 1972.
QK545.N5N37 ECOL

PLANTS, EFFECT OF NITROGEN ON.

California. University. Institute of Marine Resources. Eutrophication in coastal waters: nitrogen as a controlling factor. 1971. **fQH96.8.E9C34 ECOL**

PLANTS, EFFECT OF SALTS ON.

Edison Water Quality Laboratory. Storm and Combined Sewer Overflows Section. Environmental impact of highway deicing. 1971.
fTE220.E35 ECOL

PLANTS, ORNAMENTAL—UNITED STATES.

Viertel, Arthur T. Trees, shrubs and vines. 1970
QK481.V5 ECOL

PLANTS, PROTECTION OF.

Fisher, James. Wildlife in danger. 1969
REF QL88.F48 ECOL

PLANTS, PROTECTION OF— MINNESOTA.

Ohmann, Lewis F. Wilderness ecology, virgin plant communities of the Boundary Waters Canoe Area. 1971. **SD11.A45476no.63 ECOL**

PLASTIC PACKAGING *see* PLASTICS IN PACKAGING

PLASTIC SCRAP.

Warner, Arthur J. Plastics solid waste disposal by incineration or landfill. c1972, 1971.
fTD798.W36 ECOL

PLASTICS—RESEARCH.

Banks, M. E. New chemical concepts for utilization of waste plastics. 1971. **TP156.R38B3 ECOL**

PLASTICS IN PACKAGING.

Franklin, William E. Environmental impacts of polystyrene foam and molded pulp meat trays. 1972.
fTP373.F7 ECOL

Hickman, Howard J. A study of the environmental impact of polystyrene vs. paper pulp egg cartons and meat trays. 1972. **fTP373.H5 ECOL**

PLAYGROUNDS *see also* PARKS

Seymour Whitney North. Small urban spaces. 1969
SB481.S48 ECOL

PLOWING.

Faulkner, Edward H. Plowman's folly. 1963,c1943
S603.F36 1963 ECOL

POISONING—ABSTRACTS.

Excerpta Medica Foundations. Poisoning and intoxication by trace elements in children: an abstract review of the world-wide medical literature 1966-1971. 1973 **RA1211.E9 ECOL**

POISONOUS PLANTS.

Su, K. Lee. Aquatic plants from Minnesota part 2—toxicity, anti-neoplastic, and coagulent effects. 1972. **GB701.M554no.47 ECOL**

POISONS, ECONOMIC *see* PESTICIDES

POLAND—DESCRIPTION & TRAVEL.

Boyd, Louise Arner. Polish countrysides. 1937.
DK407.B6 ECOL

POLAR EXPEDITIONS *see* ANTARCTIC REGIONS; ARCTIC REGIONS; SCIENTIFIC EXPEDITIONS

POLITICAL PARTICIPATION—UNITED STATES.

Engineering a victory for our environment: a citizen's guide to the U.S. Army Corps of Engineers. c1972.
fTC423.E5 ECOL

POLLUTION *see also* AIR—POLLUTION; ENVIRONMENTAL ENGINEERING; MARINE POLLUTION; PESTICIDES AND THE ENVIRONMENT; RADIOACTIVE FALLOUT; WATER—POLLUTION

Abrahamson, Dean E. Environmental cost of electric power. 1970 **fTK1005.A26 ECOL**

Alexander, Robert M. Social aspects of environmental pollution. 1971. **fTD177.A4 ECOL**

American Chemical Society. Committee on Chemistry and Public Welfare. Subcommittee on Environmental Improvement. Cleaning our environment: the chemical basis for action; a report. 1969. **TD180.A4 ECOL**

Anderson, Paul K. Omega. 1971
QH541.A5 ECOL

Andrews, William A. A guide to the study of environmental pollution. 1972 **TD174.A53 ECOL**

Armstrong, Terry R. Why do we still have an ecological crisis? 1972 **TD174.A75 ECOL**

Benarde, Melvin A. Our precarious habitat. 1st ed. 1970 **TD180.B45 ECOL**

Bock, Alan. The ecology action guide. c1971
GF75.B6 ECOL

Bourne, Arthur G. Pollute and be damned. 1972.
TD175.B68 ECOL

Cailliet, Greg M. Everyman's guide to ecological living. 1971 **GF75.C33 ECOL**

Chant, Donald A. Pollution Probe. 1970
TD174.C43 ECOL

Commoner, Barry. The closing circle. 1st ed. 1971.
GF75.C65 ECOL

Commoner, Barry. Science and survival. c1966
Q125.C56 ECOL

Detwyler, Thomas R. Man's impact on environment. 1971 **GF75.D48 ECOL**

Ehrenfeld, David W. Biological conservation. 1970
QH75.E35 ECOL

Ehrlich, Paul R. Population resources environment. 1970 **HB871.E35 ECOL**

Ehrlich, Paul R. Population, resources, environment. 2d ed. 1972 **HB871.E35 1972 ECOL**

Electrochemistry of cleaner environments. 1972.
TP256.E43 1972 ECOL

Feick, George. Control of mercury contamination in freshwater sediments. 1972. **TD427.M4F4 ECOL**

Gabel, Margaret. Sparrows don't drop candy wrappers. 1971 **TD176.G3 ECOL**

Gibbons, Euell. Stalking the good life. 1971
QK98.5.G45 ECOL

Gofman, John William. Poisoned power. 1971
TK9152.G57 ECOL

Goldstein, Jerome. How to manage your company ecologically. 1971 **HD69.P6G65 ECOL**

Grey, Jerry. The race for electric power. 1972
TK1001.G73 ECOL

Hamblin, Lynette Kaye. Pollution: the world crisis. 1971,c1970 **TD174.H34 ECOL**

Hesse, Walter H. The light at the end of the tunnel. 1972 **fTD175.H47 ECOL**

Hyde, Margaret Oldroyd. For pollution fighters only. 1971 **TD175.H9 ECOL**

Industrial pollution control handbook. 1971
REF TD897.I42 ECOL

Jones, Claire. Pollution: the balance of nature. 1972
QH541.14.J65 ECOL

Jones, Claire. Pollution: the land we live on. 1971
TD176.J65 1971 ECOL

Jones, H. R. Mercury pollution control, 1971. 1971
REF fTD427.M4J66 ECOL

Jones, Thomas C. The environment of America: present/future/ past. 1971 **fQH541.145.J65 ECOL**

Linton, Ron M. Terracide. 1970
TD180.L56 ECOL

Longgood, William Frank. The darkening land. 1972 **TD175.L66 ECOL**

Marx, Wesley. Man and his environment: waste. 1971 **TD174.M37 ECOL**

Marzani, Carl. The wounded earth. 1972 **QH541.M38 ECOL**

Matthews, William Henry. Man's impact on terrestrial and oceanic ecosystems. 1971 **TD174.M39 ECOL**

McClellan, Grant S. Protecting our environment. 1970. **TD180.M3 ECOL**

Murdoch, William W. Environment; resources, pollution & society. 1971 **QH541.M95 ECOL**

National Academy of Engineering. Committee on Power Plant Siting. Engineering for resolution of the energy-environment dilemma. 1972. **fTD177.N38 ECOL**

Nobile, Philip. The complete ecology fact book. 1st ed. 1972. **TD174.N6 ECOL**

Perry, John. Our polluted world. 1967 **TD180.P4 ECOL**

Perry, John. Our polluted world. Rev. ed. 1972. **TD175.P46 1972 ECOL**

Pringle, Laurence. The only earth we have. 1969 **TD180.P73 ECOL**

Ramparts. Eco-catastrophe. c1970 **TD180.R3 ECOL**

Robinette, Gary O. Plants/people/environmental quality. 1972 **QK901.R6 ECOL**

Schroeder, Henry Alfred. Pollution, profits & progress. 1971 **TD175.S37 ECOL**

Shuttlesworth, Dorothy Edwards. Clean air, sparkling water. 1968 **PZ10.S65CL ECOL**

Stepp, James Marvin. The pollution problem. 1968 **TD180.S65 ECOL**

Still, Henry. The dirty animal. c1967 **TD180.S7 ECOL**

Turk, Amos. Ecology, pollution, environment. 1972. **TD174.T87 ECOL**

United States. Environmental Protection Agency. Office of Research and Monitoring. Control of mercury pollution in sediments. 1972. **TD427.M4U5 ECOL**

United States. Office of Science and Technology. Electric power and the environment. 1970. **TK1193.U5A45 ECOL**

Use of systems techniques in environmental quality management. 1970. **RA565.A1N38no.7 ECOL**

Wagner, Richard H. Environment and man. 1st ed. 1971 **QH541.13.W34 ECOL**

Weisberg, Barry. Beyond repair. 1971 **GF75.W45 1971 ECOL**

Wentworth, Daniel F. Pollution. c1971 **TD175.W46 ECOL**

What are me and you gonna do? 1971 **TD175.W53 ECOL**

Widener, Don. Timetable for disaster. 1970 **TD180.W53 ECOL**

POLLUTION—ABSTRACTS.
The Environment index: a guide to the key environmental literature of the year. 1971- **REF fZ7171.E6 ECOL**

POLLUTION—ABSTRACTS—INDEXES.
Pollution abstracts. Index. v.1/2- 1970/71- **REF fTD172.P65 INDEXECOL**

POLLUTION—ADDRESSES, ESSAYS, LECTURES.
The Environment. 1970 **TD176.7.E45 ECOL**

Environmental problems. 1968 **TD180.E48 ECOL**

Godfrey, Arthur. The Arthur Godfrey environmental reader. 1970 **QH541.13.G6 ECOL**

Goodman, Gordon T. Ecology and the industrial society. 1965 **TD180.G6 ECOL**

Gorden, Morton. Environmental management. 1972 **TD177.G67 ECOL**

Harte, John. Patient earth. 1971 **QH541.H26 ECOL**

Jacoby, Neil Herman. The polluters: industry or government? 1972. **TD176.7.J3 ECOL**

Oregon. State University, Corvallis. Water Resources Research Institute. Heavy metals in the environment. 1973. **fTD176.7.O7 ECOL**

Resources for the Future. Environmental quality analysis. 1972 **HC79.E5R46 ECOL**

Strobbe, Maurice A. Understanding environmental pollution. 1971. **QH545.A1S7 ECOL**

Western Resources Conference, 9th, University of Colorado, 1967. Man and the quality of his environment. 1968 **TD180.W4 1967 ECOL**

Who speaks for earth? 1st ed. 1973 **GF8.W49 ECOL**

POLLUTION—BIBLIOGRAPHY.
The Environment index: a guide to the key environmental literature of the year. 1971- **REF fZ7171.E6 ECOL**

Kiraldi, Louis. Pollution. 1971. **REF fZ7171.K55 ECOL**

Mignon, Molly R. Our polluted planet: a bibliography of government publications on pollution and the environment. 1971. **fZ5322.E2M5 ECOL**

Sinha, Evelyn. Metals as pollutants in air and water. 1972. **REF fZ7171.S55 ECOL**

"Where have all the flowers gone?". 1970 **REF fZ5322.E2W54 ECOL**

POLLUTION—CANADA.
Dunbar, Maxwell John. Environment and good sense. 1971. **TD182.D85 ECOL**

POLLUTION—COLLECTED WORKS.
Advances in environmental sciences. v.1- 1969- **REF TD180.A38 ECOL**

POLLUTION—CONGRESSES.
American Nuclear Society. Nuclear methods in environmental research. 1971 **fTD172.5.A4 ECOL**

Banff Conference on Pollution, 1st, 1968. Man and his environment. 1st ed. 1970- **TD172.5.B3 1968 ECOL**

Environmental Quality Forum, East Tennessee State University, 1970. The Nation's environment—problems and action. c1971 **TD172.5.E58 1970 ECOL**

Environmental side effects of rising industrial output. 1970 **TD174.E58 ECOL**

Industry/Government Teleconference on Pollution Control, 1971. NAM: a voice for American industry. 1971 **fTD172.5.I53 1971 ECOL**

Jennings, Burgess Hill. Interactions of man and his environment. 1966. **TD180.J4 ECOL**

The Limits to growth. c1972 **HC110.E5L5 ECOL**

Man and his environment: the effects of pollution on man. 1972 **TD172.5.M35 ECOL**

Sierra Club Conference on the Electric Power Industry, 1st, Johnson City, Vt., 1972. Report on the first Sierra Club power conference [papers]. 1972? **fHD9685.A2S5 1972 ECOL**

Symposium on the Global Effects of Environmental Pollution, Dallas, 1968. Global effects of environmental pollution. 1970 **REF TD172.5.S95 1968 ECOL**

POLLUTION—DICTIONARIES.
Fairbridge, Rhodes Whitmore. The encyclopedia of geochemistry and environmental sciences. 1972 **REF QE515.F24 ECOL**

Sarnoff, Paul. The New York times encyclopedic dictionary of the environment. c1971 **REF TD173.S27 1971 ECOL**

POLLUTION—DIRECTORIES.
Environmental Science & Technology. Pollution control directory. 1971/72- **REF fTD180.E52 ECOL**

POLLUTION—ECONOMIC ASPECTS.
Armstrong, Terry R. Why do we still have an ecological crisis? 1972 **TD174.A75 ECOL**

Industrial Development. Site selection handbook, vol.2. 1972. **REF fHC68.I5 1972 ECOL**

Kneese, Allen V. Economics and the environment. 1970 **HC68.K57 ECOL**

Loraine, John Alexander. The death of tomorrow. 1972 **HC79.P55L67 1972b ECOL**

Price, Fred C. McGraw-Hill's 1972 report on business and the environment. c1972 **fTD174.P7 ECOL**

POLLUTION—ECONOMIC ASPECTS—ADDRESSES, ESSAYS, LECTURES.
Auld, D. A. L. Economic thinking and pollution problems. 1972 **HC120.P55A84 ECOL**

Dorfman, Robert. Economics of the environment. 1st ed. 1972 **HC79.P55D65 ECOL**

POLLUTION—ECONOMIC ASPECTS—CANADA.
Dales, John Harkness. Pollution, property and prices. 1970,c1968 **HC120.P55D3 1970 ECOL**

POLLUTION—ECONOMIC ASPECTS—CANADA—ADDRESSES, ESSAYS, LECTURES.
Auld, D. A. L. Economic thinking and pollution problems. 1972 **HC120.P55A84 ECOL**

POLLUTION—ECONOMIC ASPECTS—UNITED STATES.
The Economic impact of pollution control. 1972. **TD180.E25 ECOL**

POLLUTION—FICTION.
Gwynne, Fred. Ick's ABC. 1971 **FictionECOL**

Hurd, Edith (Thacher). Wilson's world. 1st ed. 1971 **FictionECOL**

POLLUTION—GREAT BRITAIN.
Barr, John. The assaults on our senses. 1970. **QH77.G7B29 ECOL**

Mellanby, Kenneth. Pesticides and pollution. 2nd rev. ed. 1970. **TD186.5.G7M44 1970 ECOL**

POLLUTION—HANDBOOKS, MANUALS, ETC.
Best's environmental control and safety directory. 13th ed.- 1971/72- **REF fT55.B4 ECOL**

POLLUTION—LAW AND LEGISLATION—MINNESOTA.
Minnesota. Pollution Control Agency. In the matter of the adoption of proposed amendments to Minnesota Regulations APC 1, APC 3, APC 4, APC 11 and APC 15; and the adoption of Minnesota Regulation APC 16; and the proposed adoption of the Minnesota Air Quality Implementation Plan. 1972 **REF fKFM5758.A17 1972 ECOL**

POLLUTION—LAW AND LEGISLATION—UNITED STATES—HANDBOOKS, MANUALS, ETC.
United States. Environmental Protection Agency. Procedures manual for the review of federal actions impacting the environment. 1972 **KF5505.U5 ECOL**

POLLUTION—MEASUREMENT—ADDRESSES, ESSAYS, LECTURES.
Indicators of environmental quality. 1972. **TD172.5.I5 1972 ECOL**

POLLUTION—MEASUREMENT—CONGRESSES.
Symposium on Use of Nuclear Techniques in the Measurement and Control of Environmental Pollution, Salzburg, 1970. Nuclear techniques in environmental pollution. 1971. **REF TD177.S9 1970 ECOL**

POLLUTION—MINNESOTA.
Brice, William C. Possible environmental impact of base metal mining in Minnesota. 1972 **fTN24.M6B7 ECOL**

History of Minnesota Pollution Control Agency. 1970 **fTD181.M5 ECOL**

Minnesota. Dept. of Natural Resources. Inter-agency task force report on base metal mining impacts. 1973. **fTN24.M6A5 ECOL**

Minnesota. Governor, 1971- Securing a quality environment in Minnesota. 1973? **REF fHC107.M6A35 ECOL**

Planning Research Corporation. Pollution through land use management. 1969? **fGD205 1969 .P6 ECOL**

POLLUTION—NEW ENGLAND.
Power, pollution, and public policy. c1971 **HC107.A113E55 ECOL**

POLLUTION—PERIODICALS.
Clean air and water news. v.3- Jan. 8, 1971- **REF TD180.C54 ECOL**

POLLUTION—RESEARCH—DIRECTORIES.
CCM Information Corporation. Environmental pollution. 1971. **REF fTD178.5.C2 ECOL**

POLLUTION—RUSSIA.
Goldman, Marshall I. The spoils of progress: environmental pollution in the Soviet Union. 1972 **TD187.5.R9G63 ECOL**

POLLUTION—SOCIETIES, ETC.
The Ecological register: a directory of governmental agencies and private organizations concerned about environmental destruction and pollution in the state and in the seven-county metropolitan area. 2nd ed. 1971. **S920.E24 1971 ECOL**

The Ecological register: a directory of organizations in the seven-county metropolitan area concerned about environmental destruction and pollution (plus a supplement providing brief information on similar organizations located elsewhere). 1970. **fS920.E24 ECOL**

POLLUTION—STUDY AND TEACHING.
Kelly, James. Pollution—man's crisis: an investigative approach. c1971 **QH541.2.K45 ECOL**

POLLUTION—STUDY AND TEACHING (HIGHER).
Troost, Cornelius J. Environmental education: a sourcebook. 1972 **QH541.2.T76 ECOL**

POLLUTION—STUDY AND TEACHING (SECONDARY).
Kotsonis, Helen Hoch. Modern lesson plans in environmental science. 1972 **QH541.2.K68 ECOL**

POLLUTION—UNITED STATES.
Bregman, J. I. The pollution paradox. c1966 **TD180.B7 ECOL**

Buggie, Frederick D. Toward effective and equitable pollution control regulation. 1972 **fHC110.P55B8 ECOL**

California Institute of Technology, Pasadena. Environmental Quality Laboratory. People, power and pollution: environmental and public interest aspects of electric power plant siting. 1971. **fTK1193.U5C3 ECOL**

Campbell, Rex R. Society and environment: the coming collision. 1972 **HC110.E5C35 ECOL**

Congressional Quarterly Service, Washington, D. C. Man's control of the environment. 1970. **fTD180.C65 ECOL**

Council on Economic Priorities. Paper profits: pollution in the pulp and paper industry. c1972 **TD899.W65C65 1972 ECOL**

Council on Economic Priorities. Paper profits: pollution in the pulp and paper industry. 1971 **REF fTD888.P8C6 ECOL**

Degler, Stanley E. Federal pollution control programs: water, air, and solid wastes. Rev. ed. 1971 **TD180.D4 1971 ECOL**

The Environment crisis. 1970 **TD178.6.E58 ECOL**

Fadiman, Clifton. Ecocide—and thoughts toward survival. 1971 **HC110.E5F32 ECOL**

Feder, Bernard. A matter of life and breath. c1973 **HC110.E5F4 ECOL**

Garvey, Gerald. Energy, ecology, economy. 1st ed. 1972 **HC110.E5G35 ECOL**

Goldman, Marshall I. Controlling pollution. c1967 **TD180.G58 ECOL**

Hopkinson, Richard A. Corporate organization for pollution control. c1970 **fHC110.E5H6 ECOL**

Lange, Gordon C. The survival game. 1972 **TD178.6.L35 ECOL**

Love, Sam. Ecotage. 1972 **TD175.L68 ECOL**

Mid-West Debate Bureau, Normal, Illinois. Control of pollution. 1970 **fTD180.M5 ECOL**

Myers, Charles B. The environmental crisis: will we survive? 1972 **HC110.E5M9 ECOL**

National Research Council. Committee on Pollution. Waste management and control. 1966. **REF TD180.N3 ECOL**

The President's 1972 environmental program. 1972. **HC110.E5P74 ECOL**

Rabin, Edward H. The pollution crisis: official documents. 1972 c1971 **TD180.R23 ECOL**

Saltonstall, Richard. Your environment and what you can do about it. 1970 **HC110.E5S35 ECOL**

Stepp, James Marvin. The pollution problem. 1968 **TD180.S65 ECOL**

Stewart, George Rippey. Not so rich as you think. c1967 **TD180.S68 ECOL**

Swatek, Paul. The user's guide to the protection of the environment. Walden edition 1970 **TX335.S93 ECOL**

United States. Congress. House. Committee on Government Operations. Conservation and Natural Resources Subcommittee. The environmental decade (action proposals for the 1970's). Hearings, Ninety-first Congress, second session. 1970. **KF27.G636 1970a ECOL**

United States. Council on Environmental Quality. Environmental quality. **HC110.E5A52 ECOL**

United States. Dept. of the Interior. Our environment and natural resources ... indivisibly one. 1971? **fS914.A533 ECOL**

United States. Dept. of the Interior. Our living land. 1971 **S914.A535 ECOL**

POLLUTION—UNITED STATES—ADDRESSES, ESSAYS, LECTURES.
Novick, Sheldon. Our world in peril. 1971 **HC110.P55N67 ECOL**

Rathlesberger, James. Nixon and the environment. 1972 **HC110.E5R37 ECOL**

POLLUTION—UNITED STATES—BIBLIOGRAPHY.
McClain, Thomas B. Complete handbook on environmental control. 1970 **Z5853.P7M32 ECOL**

POLLUTION—UNITED STATES—CONGRESSES.
Environmental quality and social responsibility. 1972 **HC110.P55E57 ECOL**

POLLUTION—UNITED STATES—PERIODICALS.
Your government and the environment. v.1- 1971- **REF fHC110.E5Y6 ECOL**

POLLUTION—UNITED STATES—STUDY AND TEACHING.
Natural Science Center Conference. 8th, Dayton, Ohio, 1970. Leadership to meet our environmental crisis. 1970 **REF fTD178.3.N3 ECOL**

POLLUTION CONTROL EQUIPMENT see also MOTOR VEHICLES—POLLUTION CONTROL DEVICES
National Industrial Pollution Control Council. Casebook: pollution cleanup actions. 1971? **fTD897.N37 ECOL**

POLLUTION CONTROL EQUIPMENT—PATENTS.
Kallard, Thomas. Electret devices for air pollution control. 1972 **fQC585.K28 ECOL**

POLLUTION CONTROL EQUIPMENT—UNITED STATES—DIRECTORIES.
Noyes Data Corporation. Pollution control companies, United States of America, 1972. 1971, c1972 **REF fTD173.5.N68 ECOL**

POLYMERS AND POLYMERIZATION.
Freese, Paul V. Full-scale raw wastewater flocculation with polymers. 1970. **fTD751.F7 ECOL**

POLYMERS AND POLYMERIZATION—PATENTS.
Gutcho, Sidney. Waste treatment with polyelectrolytes, 1972. 1972 **TD751.G87 ECOL**

POND ECOLOGY.
Pringle, Laurence P. From pond to prairie. 1972 **PZ10.P669Ft ECOL**

Wong, Herbert H. Pond life: watching animals find food. c1970 **PZ10.W748Po ECOL**

PONDS—GREAT PLAINS.
Stewart, Robert E. Classification of natural ponds and lakes in the glaciated prairie region. 1971. **S914.A3no.92 ECOL**

PONDS—MINNESOTA.
Continuation of studies on the hydrology of ponds and small lakes. 1971. **fGB1825.M6C6ECOL**

Manson, Philip W. Some aspects of the hydrology of ponds and small lakes. 1968. **fGB1825.M6M35 ECOL**

POPULATION see also ANIMAL POPULATIONS; BIRTH CONTROL; CITIES AND TOWNS—GROWTH; EUGENICS; MALTHUSIANISM
Adelstein, Michael E. Ecocide and population. 1971, c1972 **GF75.A35 ECOL**

Allison, Anthony. Population control. 1970 **QL752.A58 ECOL**

American Assembly. The population dilemma. 2d ed. 1969 **HB851.A4 1969 ECOL**

Anderson, Paul K. Omega. 1971 **QH541.A5 ECOL**

Appleman, Philip. The silent explosion. 1965 **HB851.A48 ECOL**

Brown, Harrison Scott. The next hundred years: man's natural and technological resources. 1970,c1963 **HC55.B7 1970 ECOL**

Clark, Colin. Population growth and land use. 1968. **HB871.C58 1968 ECOL**

Cochrane, Willard Wesley. The world food problem. 1969 **HD9000.5.C59 ECOL**

Cook, Robert Carter. People! 1968 **HB871.C7 ECOL**

Dumont, Rene. The hungry future. 1969 **HD1445.D823 ECOL**

Ehrlich, Paul R. The population bomb. 1968 **HB875.E35 ECOL**

Ehrlich, Paul R. Population resources environment. 1970 **HB871.E35 ECOL**

Ehrlich, Paul R. Population, resources, environment. 2d ed. 1972 **HB871.E35 1972 ECOL**

Emmel, Thomas C. An introduction to ecology and population biology. 1973 **QH541.E45 1973 ECOL**

Fisher, Tadd. Our overcrowded world. 1969 **HB871.F53 ECOL**

Frankel, Lillian Berson. This crowded world. 1970 **HB883.F7 ECOL**

Fraser, Dean. The people problem. 1971 **HB875.F7 1971 ECOL**

Freedman, Ronald. Population: the vital revolution. 1964 **HB881.F76 ECOL**

Hardin, Garrett James. Exploring new ethics for survival: the voyage of the spaceship Beagle. 1972 **HB871.H347 ECOL**

Hauser, Philip Morris. Population perspectives. 1961?c1960 **HB3505.H3 ECOL**

Hyde, Margaret Oldroyd. This crowded planet. 1961 **HB883.H9 ECOL**

Jones, Claire. Pollution: the population explosion. 1972 **HB871.J58 ECOL**

Jones, Thomas C. The environment of America: present/future/ past. 1971 **fQH541.145.J65 ECOL**

Katz, Robert. A giant in the earth. c1973 **HD9000.5.K3 ECOL**

Loraine, John Alexander. The death of tomorrow. 1972 **HC79.P55L67 1972b ECOL**

Petersen, William. Population. 2d ed. 1969 **HB851.P46 1969 ECOL**

Pringle, Laurence P. One earth, many people. 1971 **HB851.P75 ECOL**

Sauvy, Alfred. General theory of population. 1970,c1969 **HB871.S25213 ECOL**

Sax, Karl. Standing room only. New ed. 1969,c1960 **HB881.S33 1969 ECOL**

Turk, Amos. Ecology, pollution, environment. 1972. **TD174.T87 ECOL**

Wagner, Richard H. Environment and man. 1st ed. 1971 **QH541.13.W34 ECOL**

Wrong, Dennis Hume. Population and society. 3d. ed. 1967 **HB881.W74 1967 ECOL**

POPULATION—ADDRESSES, ESSAYS, LECTURES.
Emmel, Thomas C. Behavior and ecology. 1970 **QH541.E44 ECOL**

Hardin, Garrett James. Population, evolution, and birth control. 2d ed. 1969 **HB851.H28 1969 ECOL**

Harte, John. Patient earth. 1971 **QH541.H26 ECOL**

Is there an optimum level of population? 1971 **HB851.18 ECOL**

Mudd, Stuart. The population crisis and the use of world resources. 1964. **HB885.M8 ECOL**

Osborn, Fairfield. Our crowded planet, essays on the pressures of population. 1962 **HB851.O8 ECOL**

Toepfer, Caroline T. Environmental psychology: selected readings. 1972 **HM206.T6 ECOL**

Who speaks for earth? 1st ed. 1973 **GF8.W49 ECOL**

Young, Louise B. Population in perspective. 1968. **HB851.Y6 ECOL**

POPULATION—CONGRESSES.
Are our descendants doomed? 1972 **HB849.A74 1972 ECOL**

A Conversation on population, environment, and human well-being. 1971 **HB875.C63 ECOL**

POPULATION—JUVENILE LITERATURE.
Frankel, Lillian Berson. This crowded world. 1970 **HB883.F7 ECOL**

POPULATION FORECASTING—MINNESOTA.
Borchert, John R. Minnesota settlement and land use 1985. 1970. **HD111.B6 ECOL**

POPULATION GENETICS.
Levins, Richard. Evolution in changing environments. 1968. **QL752.L4 ECOL**

POPULATIONS, ANIMAL see ANIMAL POPULATIONS

POROSITY.
Lin, Shen-maw. Porosity and pore-size distribution of soil aggregates. 1971. **GB701.M554no.29 ECOL**

POWER (MECHANICS).
Barrow, George. Your world in motion. 1956 **QC25.B23 ECOL**

Blackwood, Paul Everett. Push and pull. Rev. ed. 1966 **TJ147.B52 1966 ECOL**

Chalmers, Bruce. Energy. 1963 **TJ153.C43 ECOL**

Wilson, Mitchell A. Energy. 1967 **fTJ147.W53 1967 ECOL**

POWER PLANTS.
The Price of power: electric utilities and the environment. 1972 **REF fTJ164.P7 ECOL**

POWER RESOURCES see also ELECTRIC POWER; FUEL
Chalmers, Bruce. Energy. 1963 **TJ153.C43 ECOL**

Millard, Reed. How will we meet the energy crisis? 1971 **TJ153.M54 ECOL**

Park, Charles Frederick. Affluence in jeopardy. c1968 **HD9506.U62P3 ECOL**

Ridgeway, James. The last play. 1st ed. 1973. **HD9540.5.R5 1973 ECOL**

Thirring, Hans. Energy for man. 1968 **TJ147.T48 1968 ECOL**

United States. Office of Coal Research. Clean energy from coal—a national priority. 1973 **HD9542.A5U5 ECOL**

POWER RESOURCES—ADDRESSES, ESSAYS, LECTURES.
Energy and power. c1971 **TJ153.E478 ECOL**

POWER RESOURCES—CONGRESSES.
Symposium on Energy, Resources and the Environment, McLean, Va., 1972. Symposium on energy, resources and the environment. 1972. **fHD9540.1.S9 1972 ECOL**

POWER RESOURCES—LAW AND LEGISLATION.
United States. Congress. House. Committee on Interior and Insular Affairs. Compilation of federal laws relating to fuel and energy resources. 1972.
    KF2120.A25 1972 ECOL

POWER RESOURCES—MINNESOTA.
Twin City Area Urban Corps. Energy Education Project. Overconsumption of energy.
    fHD9547.M5T8 ECOL

POWER RESOURCES—MINNESOTA—STATISTICS.
Minnesota. State Planning Agency. Energy use in Minnesota. 1973.   **fHD9547.M6A5 ECOL**

POWER RESOURCES—RESEARCH.
United States. Congress. Senate. Committee on Interior and Insular Affairs. Energy research policy alternatives. 1972.   **KF26.I5 1972 ECOL**

POWER RESOURCES—STATISTICS.
Darmstadter, Joel. Energy in the world economy. 1971   **REF fHD9540.4.D37 ECOL**

POWER RESOURCES—STUDY AND TEACHING.
Shadduck, Gregg. Energy. 1971.
    HD9545.S5 ECOL

POWER RESOURCES—UNITED STATES.
Dupree, Walter G. United States energy through the year 2000. 1972.   **HD9545.D8 ECOL**
Garvey, Gerald. Energy, ecology, economy. 1st ed. 1972   **HC110.E5G35 ECOL**
Holdren, John P. Energy. c1971
    TJ153.H65 ECOL
Hottel, Hoyt Clarke. New energy technology—some facts and assessments. 1971 **TJ23.H67 ECOL**
Landsberg, Hans H. Energy in the United States. 1968   **HD9545.L3 ECOL**
Linville, Bill. Review of Bureau of Mines energy program, 1970. 1971 **TN295.U4no.8526 ECOL**
Resources for the Future. Energy in the American economy, 1850-1975. 1960 **HD9545.R45 ECOL**
Resources for the Future. United States energy policies. 1969,c1968 **HD9546.R4 1969 ECOL**
Rocks, Lawrence. The energy crisis. 1972
    HD9545.R57 1972
Rodgers, William H. Brown-out. 1972
    HD9684.U62R63 1972 ECOL
Saltonstall, Richard. Brownout & slow-down. c1972
    HC110.E5S33 ECOL
United States. The potential for energy conservation. 1972.   **TJ153.U43 ECOL**
United States. Congress. Joint Committee on Atomic Energy. Certain background information for consideration when evaluating the "national energy dilemma". 1973. **HD9545.A53 ECOL**
United States. Office of Emergency Preparedness. The potential for energy conservation: substitution for scarce fuels. 1973. **fTJ153.U548 ECOL**

POWER RESOURCES—UNITED STATES—CONGRESSES.
Conference on Energy, Economics and the Environment, Chicago, Ill., 1968. Energy, economics and the environment: proceedings of a conference sponsored by the Committee on Environment, Edison Electric Institute. 1969. **fHD9540.1.C6 1968 ECOL**
Energy, economic growth, and the environment. 1972   **HD9545.E6 ECOL**

POWER RESOURCES—UNITED STATES—LAW AND LEGISLATION.
Commerce Clearing House. Energy management. c1973.   **Ref KF2120.A6C6 ECOL**

POWER RESOURCES—UNITED STATES—PERIODICALS.
Energy users report. **REF fHD9540.1.E5 ECOL**
Energy users report. Current reports.
    REF fHD9540.1.E5 Suppl. ECOL

POWER RESOURCES—UNITED STATES CONSERVATION OF NATURAL RESOURCES—UNITED STATES.
United States. Congress. House. Committee on Interior and Insular Affairs. Fuel and energy resources. 1972   **KF27.I5 1972 ECOL**

POWER SUPPLY see POWER RESOURCES

PRAIRIE-DOGS.
McNulty, Faith. Must they die? 1st ed. 1971.
    QL737.C25M27 ECOL

PRAIRIE ECOLOGY.
Allen, Durward Leon. The life of prairies and plains. 1967   **QH541.5.P7A4 ECOL**

PRAIRIE ISLAND NUCLEAR GENERATING PLANT, RED WING, MINNESOTA.
Northern States Power Company (of Minnesota). Environmental report. 1971. **fTD877.5.N6 ECOL**

Northern States Power Company (of Minnesota). Environmental report. expanded and updated ed. 1971.
    fTD877.5.N62 1971 ECOL

PRAIRIES.
Weaver, John Ernest. Prairie plants and their environment. 1968 **QK938.P7W42 ECOL**

PRECIPITATION (CHEMISTRY).
Ghassemi, Masood. Phosphate precipitation with ferrous iron. 1971.   **fTD751.G4 ECOL**

PREDATION (BIOLOGY).
Clarke, James. Man is the prey. 1969
    QL758.C54 ECOL
Mech, L. David. The wolves of Isle Royale. 1966
    QL155.A45no.7 ECOL
Michigan. University. Advisory Committee on Predator Control. Predator control—1971: report to the Council on Environmental Quality and the Dept. of the Interior. 1972.   **fQL758.M5 ECOL**

PREDATOR CONTROL.
Michigan. University. Advisory Committee on Predator Control. Predator control—1971: report to the Council on Environmental Quality and the Dept. of the Interior. 1972.   **fQL758.M5 ECOL**
Olsen, Jack. Slaughter the animals, poison the earth. 1971   **QL737.C22O47 ECOL**

PREDATORY ANIMALS.
Clarke, James. Man is the prey. 1969
    QL758.C54 ECOL

PRESERVATION OF FORESTS see FORESTS AND FORESTRY; NATURAL RESOURCES

PRESERVATION OF WILDLIFE see WILDLIFE CONSERVATION

PRIMARY PRODUCTIVITY (BIOLOGY)—MEASUREMENT.
Stokes, Lee W. The photosynthetic pigments of Lake Superior periphyton and their relation to primary productivity. 1970. **GB701.M554no.18 ECOL**

PRIMATES.
Napier, John Russell. The roots of mankind. 1970.
    QH368.N36 ECOL

PROBLEM SOLVING.
Rasmussen, Bruce C. Problem—emphasis education: an environmental symposium and the consequences of that symposium at Columbia Heights Senior High School District 13, 1969-1970. 1970
    fLB1027.R3 ECOL

PRODUCTION (ECONOMIC THEORY)—CONGRESSES.
The Limits to growth. c1972 **HC110.E5L5 ECOL**

PROFESSIONS.
Munzer, Martha E. Unusual careers: solar scientist, meteorologist, oceanographer, geologist, ecologist, sanitary engineer, research chemist, city and regional planner. 1st ed. 1962. **Q147.M8 ECOL**

PROGRAMMING (ELECTRONIC COMPUTERS).
Bowers, C. Edward. Computer program for statistical analysis of annual flood data by the log-Pearson Type III method. 1971.
    GB701.M554no.39 ECOL

PROGRESS see also CIVILIZATION; SCIENCE AND CIVILIZATION; SOCIAL CHANGE
Coblentz, Stanton Arthur. The challenge to man's survival. 1972   **GF41.C55 ECOL**
Platt, John Rader. The step to man. 1970,c1966
    HM101.P57 ECOL
Pollard, Sidney. The idea of progress: history and society. 1969?c1968   **CB155.P55 ECOL**

PROJECT PLOWSHARE.
Gerber, Carl R. Plowshare. 1966
    TK9153.G4 ECOL

PROJECT SNAP.
Corliss, William R. SNAP nuclear space reactors. 1966   **TL1102.N8C6 ECOL**

PROTECTION OF WILDLIFE see WILDLIFE CONSERVATION

PROTEIDS see PROTEINS

PROTEINS.
Callihan, Clayton Dale. Construction of a chemical-microbial pilot plant for production of single-cell protein from cellulosic wastes. 1971.
    TP996.B3C3 ECOL

PSYCHOLOGY.
Bixby, William. Of animals and men. 1968.
    QL751.B53 ECOL

PSYCHOLOGY, COMPARATIVE.
Carrighar, Sally. Wild heritage. 1965.
    QL751.C36 ECOL
Milne, Lorus Johnson. The animal in man. 1973
    BF671.M63 ECOL

PSYCHOLOGY, PHYSIOLOGICAL.
Eiduson, Samuel. Biochemistry and behavior. 1964
    QP521.E5 ECOL

PSYCHOPHYSICS see BIOLOGICAL CHEMISTRY

PSYCHOPHYSIOLOGY see PSYCHOLOGY, PHYSIOLOGICAL

PUBLIC ADMINISTRATION.
Great Britain. Central Advisory Water Committee. The future management of water in England and Wales: a report. 1971.   **TD257.A5 1971 ECOL**

PUBLIC LIBRARIES—HANDBOOKS, MANUALS, ETC.
Cohen, Martin. A handbook on environmental information programs for public libraries. 1973.
    fZ670.A3C6 ECOL

PUBLIC UTILITIES—UNITED STATES.
Bonbright, James Cummings. Public utilities and the national power policies. 1972, c1940
    HD2766.B57 1972
Rodgers, William H. Brown-out. 1972
    HD9684.U62R63 1972 ECOL

PULVERIZED COAL see COAL, PULVERIZED

PUMAS.
Gray, Robert. Cougar. c1972
    QL737.C2G73 ECOL

PYRITES.
Morth, Arthur H. Pyritic systems: a mathematical model. 1972.   **TD899.M5M6 ECOL**
NUS Corporation. Cyrus Wm. Rice Division. The effects of various gas atmospheres on the oxidation of coal mine pyrites. 1971. **fTD899.M5N2 ECOL**
Ohio. State University, Columbus. Research Foundation. Pilot scale study of acid mine drainage. 1971.   **fTN321.O3 ECOL**
Troy, Joseph C. Oxidation of pyrites in chlorinated solvents. 1972.   **TD899.M5T7 ECOL**

Q

QUAIL.
Johnsgard, Paul A. Grouse and quails of North America. 1973   **QL696.G27J63 ECOL**

QUALITY OF WATER see WATER QUALITY

QUETICO-SUPERIOR AREA—DESCRIPTION AND TRAVEL.
Olson, Sigurd F. Runes of the North. 1969, c1963
    F1060.A204 ECOL

R

RADIATION—PHYSIOLOGICAL EFFECT.
Kirk, William P. Krypton 85: a review of the literature and an analysis of radiation hazards. 1972
    QP82.2.R3K5 ECOL
Loutit, John F. Irradiation of mice and men. 1962
    QH652.L63 ECOL
Sternglass, Ernest J. Low-level radiation. c1972.
    RA569.S8 ECOL
Tamplin, Arthur R. Population control through nuclear pollution. 1970 **RA569.T35 ECOL**

RADIATION—TOXICOLOGY.
Griffiths, Joel. Silent slaughter. 1972
    RA1231.R2G74 ECOL
Tamplin, Arthur R. Population control through nuclear pollution. 1970 **RA569.T35 ECOL**

RADIATION—UNITED STATES.
Oakley, Donald T. Natural radiation exposure in the United States. 1972. **REF RA569.O15 ECOL**

RADIATION BIOLOGY see RADIOBIOLOGY

RADIATION PRESERVATION OF FOOD.
Pizer, Vernon. Preserving food with atomic energy. 1970   **TX611.5.P58 ECOL**

RADIATION SAFETY.
Northern States Power Company, Minneapolis. Environmental monitoring and surveillance program. 1971- **REF fTK1377.P7N6 ECOL**

RADIATION, SOLAR see SOLAR RADIATION

RADIATION STERILIZATION.
Radiation preservation of foods. 1965.
    TX611.R28 ECOL
Urrows, Grace M. Food preservation by irradiation. 1968   **TX611.5.U7 1968 ECOL**

RADIATION STERILIZATION OF FOOD see RADIATION PRESERVATION OF FOOD

RADIO-ELEMENTS see RADIOACTIVE SUBSTANCES

RADIOACTIVATION ANALYSIS—CONGRESSES.
Symposium on Use of Nuclear Techniques in the Measurement and Control of Environmental Pollution, Salzburg, 1970. Nuclear techniques in environmental pollution. 1971. **REF TD177.S9 1970 ECOL**

RADIOACTIVE DATING.
Faul, Henry. Nuclear clocks. Rev. 1968
    QC798.D3F37 1968 ECOL

RADIOACTIVE FALLOUT.
Comar, Cyril Lewis. Fallout from nuclear tests. 1963 **UF767.C64 ECOL**

Comar, Cyril Lewis. Fallout from nuclear tests. Rev. 1966 **UF767.C64 1966 ECOL**

RADIOACTIVE POLLUTION see also RADIOACTIVE FALLOUT; RADIOACTIVE WASTE DISPOSAL
Jones, Claire. Pollution: the dangerous atom. 1972 **TD880.J65 1972 ECOL**

RADIOACTIVE POLLUTION—ADDRESSES, ESSAYS, LECTURES.
The Environmental and ecological forum, 1970-1971. 1972 **TD898.E58 ECOL**

RADIOACTIVE POLLUTION—MINNESOTA.
Northern States Power Company (of Minnesota). Environmental report: Monticello Nuclear Generating Plant. 1971. **fTD877.5.N64 ECOL**

RADIOACTIVE POLLUTION—RED WING REGION, MINNESOTA.
Northern States Power Company (of Minnesota). Environmental report. 1971. **fTD877.5.N6 ECOL**

Northern States Power Company (of Minnesota). Environmental report. expanded and updated ed. 1971. **fTD877.5.N62 1971 ECOL**

RADIOACTIVE POLLUTION—UNITED STATES.
Lewis, Richard S. The nuclear-power rebellion. 1972 **HD9698.A3U44 1972 ECOL**

Oakley, Donald T. Natural radiation exposure in the United States. 1972. **REF RA569.O15 ECOL**

RADIOACTIVE POLLUTION OF THE ATMOSPHERE.
Curtis, Richard. Perils of the peaceful atom. 1969. **HD9698.U52C8 ECOL**

Lapp, Ralph E. A citizen's guide to nuclear power. c1971. **TK1078.L3 ECOL**

Nuclear explosives in peacetime. 1970 **fQC792.N8 ECOL**

Symposium on Environmental Aspects of Nuclear Power Stations, New York, 1970. Environmental aspects of nuclear power stations. 1971. **REF TK9006.S887 1970 ECOL**

United States. Atomic Energy Commission. Nuclear Power and the environment. 1969. **TK1343.A46 ECOL**

RADIOACTIVE POLLUTION OF THE ATMOSPHERE—CONGRESSES.
Environmental surveillance in the vicinity of nuclear facilities. 1970 **REF TD887.R3E58 ECOL**

RADIOACTIVE POLLUTION OF THE SEA.
General Dynamics Corporation. Electric Boat Division. Potential environmental effects of an offshore submerged nuclear power plant. 1971- **fQH541.5.S3G45 ECOL**

RADIOACTIVE SUBSTANCES see also NUCLEAR FUELS; RADIOACTIVE FALLOUT; RADIOACTIVE POLLUTION OF THE ATMOSPHERE; RADIOACTIVITY; RADIOISOTOPES; URANIUM
Eisenbud, Merril. Environmental radioactivity. 1963 **RA569.E5 ECOL**

Novick, Sheldon. The careless atom. c1969 **TK9152.N6 ECOL**

United States Atomic Energy Commission. Compaction of radioactive solid waste. 1970. **fTD898.U5 ECOL**

RADIOACTIVE SUBSTANCES—SAFETY REGULATIONS—UNITED STATES.
Pettigrew, George L. State and Federal control of health hazards from radioactive materials other than materials regulated under the Atomic energy act of 1954 (as of October 1, 1969). 1971. **RA1231.R2U5125no.71-4 ECOL**

RADIOACTIVE SUBSTANCES—UNITED STATES.
Oakley, Donald T. Natural radiation exposure in the United States. 1972. **REF RA569.O15 ECOL**

RADIOACTIVE WASTE DISPOSAL.
Clark, B. W. Description of the environmental monitoring program for the Monticello nuclear generating plant near Monticello, Minnesota. Rev. ed. 1969. **fTK1377.M6C6 1969 ECOL**

Fox, Charles H. Radioactive wastes. c1965 **TD898.F6 ECOL**

Fox, Charles H. Radioactive wastes. Rev. 1969. **TD898.F6 1969 ECOL**

Northern States Power Company, Minneapolis. Environmental monitoring and ecological studies program. 1971- **REF fTK1377.P7N6 ECOL**

United States Atomic Energy Commission. Compaction of radioactive solid waste. 1970. **fTD898.U5 ECOL**

RADIOACTIVE WASTE DISPOSAL IN RIVERS, LAKES, ETC.
Clark, B. W. Description of the environmental monitoring program for the Monticello nuclear generating plant near Monticello, Minnesota. Rev. ed. 1969. **fTK1377.M6C6 1969 ECOL**

Northern States Power Company, Minneapolis. Environmental monitoring and ecological studies program. 1971- **REF fTK1377.P7N6 ECOL**

Symposium on Environmental Aspects of Nuclear Power Stations, New York, 1970. Environmental aspects of nuclear power stations. 1971. **REF TK9006.S887 1970 ECOL**

RADIOACTIVE WASTE DISPOSAL IN RIVERS, LAKES, ETC.—CONGRESSES.
Environmental surveillance in the vicinity of nuclear facilities. 1970 **REF TD887.R3E58 ECOL**

RADIOACTIVITY.
Gofman, John William. Poisoned power. 1971 **TK9152.G57 ECOL**

RADIOACTIVITY—MEASUREMENT—CONGRESSES.
Environmental surveillance in the vicinity of nuclear facilities. 1970 **REF TD887.R3E58 ECOL**

RADIOACTIVITY—PHYSIOLOGICAL EFFECT see also ATOMIC BOMB—PHYSIOLOGICAL EFFECT
Alexander, Peter. Atomic radiation and life. Completely Rev. ed. 1965 **QH652.A6 1965 ECOL**

RADIOACTIVITY—PHYSIOLOGICAL EFFECT—CONGRESSES.
Nuclear power and the public. 1970 **TK1078.N83 ECOL**

RADIOBIOLOGY.
Alexander, Peter. Atomic radiation and life. Completely Rev. ed. 1965 **QH652.A6 1965 ECOL**

Casarett, Alison P. Radiation biology. 1968 **QH652.C3 ECOL**

Kastner, Jacob. The natural radiation environment. 1968. **QH652.K35 ECOL**

Symposium on Radioisotopes in the Biosphere, University of Minnesota, 1959. A Symposium on Radioisotopes in the Biosphere. 1960. **QH652.S9 1959 ECOL**

RADIOCARBON DATING.
Parkos, William G. Water quality studies on the Great Lakes based on carbon fourteen measurements on primary productivity. 1969. **GB701.M554no.17 ECOL**

RADIOGENETICS.
Asimov, Isaac. The genetic effects of radiation. c1966 **QH652.5.A8 ECOL**

RADIOGRAPHY, INDUSTRIAL—SAFETY MEASURES—HANDBOOKS, MANUALS, ETC.
United States. Atomic Energy Commission. Division of Technical Information. Safety manual for use of operators dealing with radiography and industrial gammagraphy. 1968? **TA417.25.U5 ECOL**

RADIOISOTOPES.
Mead, Robert L. Power from radioisotopes. Rev. 1966 **TK1078.M38 ECOL**

Symposium on Radioisotopes in the Biosphere, University of Minnesota, 1959. A Symposium on Radioisotopes in the Biosphere. 1960. **QH652.S9 1959 ECOL**

United States. Atomic Energy Commission. Illustrations of radio-isotopes: definitions and applications. 196-? **TK9400.U5 ECOL**

RADIOISOTOPES—INDUSTRIAL APPLICATIONS.
Baker, Philip Schaffner. Radioisotopes in industry. c1965 **TK9400.B3 ECOL**

RAILROADS—NOISE.
Wyle Laboratories. Transportation noise and noise from equipment powered by internal combustion engines. 1971 i.e. 1972 **fTD892.W95 ECOL**

RAIN AND RAINFALL see also FLOODS; METEOROLOGY; RUNOFF; SNOW
Mein, Russell G. Modeling the infiltration component of the rainfall—runoff process. 1971. **GB701.M554no.43 ECOL**

Metcalf and Eddy, Boston. Storm water management model. 1971. **fGB665.M4 ECOL**

Stall, John B. Storm sewer design—an evaluation of the RRL method. 1972. **TD665.S7 ECOL**

RAIN AND RAINFALL—GREAT BASIN.
Antevs, Ernst. Rainfall and tree growth in the Great basin... 1938. **QC925.1.U35 1938 ECOL**

RAIN AND RAINFALL—MINNESOTA.
Bowers, C. Edward. Review and analysis of rainfall and runoff data for selected watersheds in Minnesota. 1968. **GB701.M554no.8 ECOL**

RAPID TRANSIT see LOCAL TRANSIT
RARE ANIMALS see also EXTINCT ANIMALS
Caras, Roger A. Last chance on earth. 1972 **QL88.C3 1972 ECOL**

Curry-Lindahl, Kai. Let them live. 1972. **S962.C87 ECOL**

Fisher, James. Wildlife in danger. 1969 **REF QL88.F48 ECOL**

Fitter, Richard Sidney Richmond. Vanishing wild animals of the world. 1968 **fQL88.F5 ECOL**

Holden, Raymond Peckham. Wildlife mysteries. 1972 **QL49.H68 ECOL**

Laycock, George. America's endangered wildlife. c1969 **QL88.L39 ECOL**

Philip, Duke of Edinburg. Wildlife crisis. 1st American ed. 1970 **S962.P55 ECOL**

Simon, Noel. Last survivors. 1970 **QL88.S553 ECOL**

United States. Bureau of Sport Fisheries and Wildlife. Office of Endangered Species and International Activities. Threatened wildlife of the United States. 1973. **S914.A3no.114 1973 ECOL**

United States. Committee on Rare and Endangered Wildlife Species. Rare and endangered fish and wildlife of the United States. Rev. ed. 1968 i.e. 1969 **S914.A3no.34 1969 ECOL**

Wood, Frances Elizabeth. Animals in danger. 1968 **QL88.W6 ECOL**

Ziswiler, Vinzenz. Extinct and vanishing animals. Rev. English ed. by Fred and Pille Bunnell. 1967. **QL88.Z513 ECOL**

RARE ANIMALS—PICTORIAL WORKS.
Harris, Larry. Twilight of the animal kingdom. 1972 **QL88.H37 ECOL**

RAW MATERIALS—DICTIONARIES.
Jackson, Nora. A dictionary of natural resources and their principal uses. 2d ed. 1969 **REF HF1051.J3 1969 ECOL**

RAW MATERIALS—UNITED STATES.
Resources for the Future. Trends in natural resource commodities. 1962. **REF fHF1051.R43 ECOL**

RAYON INDUSTRY AND TRADE.
American Enka Corporation. Central Engineering Dept. Zinc precipitation and recovery from viscose rayon waste water. 1971. **fTD899.T4A44 ECOL**

REACTION RATE (CHEMISTRY) see CHEMICAL REACTION, RATE OF
READERS—SCIENCE.
Shapp, Martha. Let's find out about air. 1963. **PE1127.S3S417 ECOL**

REAL ESTATE BUSINESS—UNITED STATES.
Paulson, Morton C. The great land hustle. 1972 **HD255.P38 ECOL**

REAL ESTATE INVESTMENT—UNITED STATES.
Paulson, Morton C. The great land hustle. 1972 **HD255.P38 ECOL**

REAL PROPERTY—CALIFORNIA.
Fellmeth, Robert C. Politics of land: Ralph Nader's study group report on land use in California. 1973. **HD211.C2F45 ECOL**

REAL PROPERTY, EXCHANGE OF—MINNESOTA.
Minnesota. Legislature. Senate. Office of Senate Counsel. The law of land exchange in Minnesota. 1969. **fKFM5851.A84 ECOL**

RECLAMATION OF LAND—ADDRESSES, ESSAYS, LECTURES.
Goodman, Gordon T. Ecology and the industrial society. 1965 **TD180.G6 ECOL**

RECLAMATION OF LAND—CALIFORNIA.
Landerman, Norman J. Community resource. 1972 **TD195.S3L36 ECOL**

RECLAMATION OF LAND—UNITED STATES.
Chase, Stuart. Rich land, poor land. 1969 **S930.C5 1969 ECOL**

United States. Bureau of Reclamation. Summary report of the Commissioner of the Bureau of Reclamation to the Secretary of the Interior for the fiscal year ended June 30, 1970- and statistical and financial appendix. **REF TC823.A27 ECOL**

RECLAMATION OF WATER see WATER REUSE
RECOVERY OF WASTE PRODUCTS see SALVAGE (WASTE, ETC.)
RECREATION.
Brockman, Christian Frank. Recreational use of wild lands. 1959. **SB481.B66 ECOL**

RECREATION AREAS.
Moeller, George H. The landowner and the snowmobiler—problem or profit? 1971. **GV857.S6M6 ECOL**

RECREATION AREAS—BIBLIOGRAPHY.
Wright, Sydney. A bibliography of recreational communities and leisure land development. 1973.
fZ7164.L3W7 ECOL

RECREATION AREAS—CANADA—TORONTO.
Bureau of Municipal Research, Toronto. Urban open space: parks, people and planning. 1971.
GV56.T6B8 ECOL

RECREATION AREAS—MINNESOTA.
Barr Engineering Co. Mud Lake hydrologic study. 1972. fTC424.M6B34 ECOL
Minnesota. Dept. of Conservation. Minnesota outdoor recreation plan. 1968-
fGV54.M6A197 ECOL

RECREATION AREAS—MINNESOTA—ANOKA COUNTY.
Midwest Planning and Research, Inc. Anoka County parks and open-space: comprehensive plan. 1969.
fGV54.M6M52 ECOL
Midwest Planning and Research, Inc. Anoka County parks and open-space: goals, policies, directions and alternatives. 1968 fGV54.M6M5 ECOL

RECREATION AREAS—MINNESOTA—APPLE VALLEY.
Urban Planning and Design, Inc., Mpls., Minn. Apple Valley park development program. 1969.
fGV54.M6U7 ECOL

RECREATION AREAS—MINNESOTA—NEW BRIGHTON.
Brauer and Associates, inc., Edina, Minn. A study of parks and recreation for the village of New Brighton. 1967 fGV54.M6B7 ECOL

RECREATION AREAS—UNITED STATES.
Brown, William Edward. Islands of hope. c1971
HC110.E5B75 ECOL

RECYCLE OPERATIONS (CHEMICAL TECHNOLOGY) *see also* SALVAGE (WASTE, ETC.)
Banks, M. E. New chemical concepts for utilization of waste plastics. 1971. TP156.R38B3 ECOL
Bingham, Tayler H. The beverage container problem. 1972. TD793.B5 ECOL
Hannon, Bruce. System energy and recycling: a study of the beverage industry. 1972.
fTP659.H3 ECOL
Henningson, Durham & Richardson. Minnesota: disposal and reuse of abandoned and retired automobiles. 1970. REF fTD795.H36 ECOL
Midwest Research Institute, Kansas City, Missouri. Resource recovery. 1973. fTP995.M5 ECOL
Recycling Day Conference, 1st, New York City, 1971. Proceedings of Recycling Day in New York. 1971 fTP156.R38R4 1971 ECOL
United States. Solid Waste Management Office. The automobile cycle: an environmental and resource reclamation problem. 1972. TD793.U5 ECOL

RECYCLE OPERATIONS (CHEMICAL TECHNOLOGY)—BIBLIOGRAPHY.
Gunter, John D. Recycling and re-use: the future of solid waste. 1973. Ref fTP156.R38G8 ECOL

RECYCLE OPERATIONS (CHEMICAL TECHNOLOGY)—CONGRESSES.
Midwest Regional Seminar on Horizons in Resource Recovery, University of Chicago, 1972. Horizons in resource recovery: presentations and discussions of a seminar held Feb. 23, 1972. 1972.
fTP995.A1M5 1972 ECOL

RECYCLING (CHEMICAL TECHNOLOGY).
Minnesota. University. Consortium for the Study of Solid Waste Management/Recycling Options. A report on solid waste management/recycling options. 1972. fTD793.M6 ECOL

RECYCLING OF PAPER *see* PAPER RECYCLING

RECYCLING OF WASTE PRODUCTS *see* SALVAGE (WASTE, ETC.)

RECYCLING (WASTE, ETC.) *see* SALVAGE (WASTE, ETC.)

RED-WINGED BLACKBIRD.
Wong, Herbert H. Animal habitats: where can red-winged blackbirds live? 1970
PZ10.W748An ECOL

REDWOOD.
Leydet, Francois. The last redwoods, and the parkland of Redwood Creek. 1969
SD397.R3L4 ECOL

REFERENDUM—UNITED STATES.
Abt Associates. Factors affecting pollution referenda. 1971. fGH4952.A6 ECOL

REFUSE AND REFUSE DISPOSAL *see also* FACTORY AND TRADE WASTE; RADIOACTIVE WASTE DISPOSAL; SEWAGE DISPOSAL; STREET CLEANING; WASTE PRODUCTS; WATER—POLLUTION
American Public Works Association. Institute for Solid Wastes. Municipal refuse disposal. 3d ed. 1970
TD795.A45 1970 ECOL
Banks, M. E. New chemical concepts for utilization of waste plastics. 1971. TP156.R38B3 ECOL
Boettcher, R. A. Air classification of solid wastes. 1972. TD796.7.B64 ECOL
Brunner, Dirk R. Sanitary landfill design and operation. 1972. TD795.7.B7 ECOL
Composting of municipal solid wastes in the United States. 1971. TD796.5.C64 ECOL
Darnay, Arsen. The role of packaging in solid waste management 1966 to 1976. 1969.
TD795.D37 ECOL
Glysson, Eugene A. The problem of solid-waste disposal. 1972. TD791.G5 ECOL
Goldstein, Jerome. Garbage as you like it. 1969
TD795.G6 ECOL
Incinerator Institute of America. Incinerator standards. 1970,1968 REF fTD796.I5 1970 ECOL
Incinerator Institute of America. Incinerator testing. 1971 fTD796.I53 ECOL
Incinerator Institute of America. Modern incineration: a solution—not the problem. 1969?
fTD796.I54 ECOL
Marshall, James. Going to waste. 1972
TD791.M37 ECOL
Marx, Wesley. Man and his environment: waste. 1971 TD174.M37 ECOL
Midwest Research Institute, Kansas City, Missouri. Resource recovery. 1973. fTP995.M5 ECOL
Minnesota. University. Consortium for the Study of Solid Waste Management/Recycling Options. A report on solid waste management/recycling options. 1972. fTD793.M6 ECOL
National Association of Counties Research Foundation. Solid waste management. 1972?
fTD791.N3 ECOL
Roy F. Weston, Inc. Concept evaluation report: taconite tailings disposal, Reserve Mining Company, Silver Bay, Minnesota. 1971 fTD899.T35 ECOL
United States. Environmental Protection Agency. Guidelines for local governments on solid waste management. 1971. fTD791.U5 ECOL
United States. Environmental Protection Agency. High-pressure compaction and baling of solid waste: final report on a solid waste management demonstration grant. 1972. TD796.7.U65 ECOL
United States. Environmental Protection Agency. Solid waste handling and disposal in multi-story buildings and hospitals. 1972- TD788.A3 ECOL

REFUSE AND REFUSE DISPOSAL—ABSTRACTS.
Solid waste management.
REF Z5853.S22S6 ECOL

REFUSE AND REFUSE DISPOSAL—BIBLIOGRAPHY.
Gunter, John D. Solid waste management: economics and operation. 1973.
Ref fZ5853.S22G8 ECOL
Solid waste management.
REF Z5853.S22S6 ECOL

REFUSE AND REFUSE DISPOSAL—CALIFORNIA.
California. Dept. of Public Health. California solid waste management study (1968) and plan (1970). 1971. TD788.4.C3A45 ECOL

REFUSE AND REFUSE DISPOSAL—CONGRESSES.
Midwest Regional Seminar on Horizons in Resource Recovery, University of Chicago, 1972. Horizons in resource recovery: presentations and discussions of a seminar held Feb. 23, 1972. 1972.
fTP995.A1M5 1972 ECOL
National Conference on Composting-Waste Recycling. 1st, Denver, 1971. How to put waste recycling into practice. 1971.
fTD172.5.N3 1971 ECOL
Symposium on Solid Waste Demonstration Projects, Cincinnati, Ohio, 1971. Solid waste demonstration projects. 1972. TD785.A45 1971 ECOL

REFUSE AND REFUSE DISPOSAL—DISTRICT OF COLUMBIA.
District of Columbia District of Columbia solid waste management plan. 1971.
TD525.W2A43 ECOL

REFUSE AND REFUSE DISPOSAL—GREAT BRITAIN.
Great Britain. Working Party on Refuse Disposal. Refuse disposal. 1971. TD557.A53 ECOL

REFUSE AND REFUSE DISPOSAL—KENTUCKY.
Kentucky. Dept. of Health. Kentucky solid waste management plan. 1971. TD788.4.K4A45 ECOL

REFUSE AND REFUSE DISPOSAL—LAW AND LEGISLATION—UNITED STATES.
Powell, Mel D. Digest of selected local solid waste management ordinances. 1972. TD788.P6 ECOL

REFUSE AND REFUSE DISPOSAL—MATHEMATICAL MODELS.
Boyd, Gail B. Methods of predicting solid waste characteristics. 1971. TD793.7.B68 ECOL

REFUSE AND REFUSE DISPOSAL—MINNESOTA.
Henningson, Durham & Richardson. Minnesota: disposal and reuse of abandoned and retired automobiles. 1970. REF fTD795.H36 ECOL
Henningson, Durham & Richardson. Study and investigation of solid waste control for the Minnesota Pollution Control Agency: phase II, final report. 1969.
REF fTD788.4.M6H4 ECOL
Minnesota. Pollution Control Agency. Comprehensive plan for the storage, collection, transportation and disposal of solid waste in the State of Minnesota. 1970. fTD524.M6A32 ECOL
Minnesota. Pollution Control Agency. Solid waste education. 1969? fTD524.M6A3 ECOL

REFUSE AND REFUSE DISPOSAL—NEW YORK.
New York (State) Dept. of Health. New York solid waste management plan. 1971.
TD788.4.N4A45 ECOL

REFUSE AND REFUSE DISPOSAL—UNITED STATES.
Bingham, Tayler H. The beverage container problem. 1972. TD793.B5 ECOL
Darnay, Arsen. Salvage markets for materials in solid wastes, ... 1972. TD795.D38 ECOL
Franklin, William E. The role of nonpackaging paper in solid waste management, 1966 to 1976. 1971.
TD795.F7 ECOL
Small, William E. Third pollution. 1971
TD795.S56 1971 ECOL
Smith, David D. Ocean disposal of barge-delivered liquid and solid wastes from United States coastal cities. 1971. TD796.7.O25S4 ECOL
Stewart, George Rippey. Not so rich as you think. c1967 TD180.S68 ECOL
United States. Environmental Protection Agency. Initiating a national effort to improve solid waste management. 1971. REF TD788.A45 ECOL
United States. Solid Waste Management Office. The automobile cycle: an environmental and resource reclamation problem. 1972. TD793.U5 ECOL

REFUSE AND REFUSE DISPOSAL—UNITED STATES—CONGRESSES.
Solid Waste Resources Conference, Columbus, Ohio, 1971. Design of consumer containers for re-use or disposal. 1972. TD785.S6 1971 ECOL
Symposium of State and Interstate Solid Waste Planning Agencies, St. Louis, 1969. Planning for solid waste management. 1971 TD523.S94 1969 ECOL

REFUSE AND REFUSE DISPOSAL—UNITED STATES—DIRECTORIES.
Keep America Beautiful, Inc. Inventory of litter-prevention and related environmental programs in the United States. 1972- fTD817.K4 ECOL

REFUSE AND REFUSE DISPOSAL—UNITED STATES—STATISTICS.
Muhich, Anton J. Preliminary data analysis. 1968.
TD795.M82 ECOL

REFUSE AND REFUSE DISPOSAL—WASHINGTON METROPOLITAN AREA—CONGRESSES.
Surgeon General's Conference on Solid Waste Management for Metropolitan Washington, Washington, D. C., 1967. 1967.
TD525.W2S7 1967 ECOL

REFUSE AND REFUSE DISPOSAL—YEARBOOKS.
Sanitation industry year book. 9 ed. 1972-
REF fTD791.S3 ECOL

REGENERATION (BIOLOGY).
Fram Corporation. Bio-regenerated activated carbon treatment of textile dye wastewater. 1971.
fTD899.T4F7 ECOL

REGIONAL PLANNING *see also* CITIES AND TOWNS—PLANNING; LANDSCAPE PROTECTION

REGIONAL PLANNING

Darling, Frank Fraser. Future environments of North America. 1966. **HC95.D33 ECOL**

MacKaye, Benton. The new exploration. 1962. **GF51.M3 1962 ECOL**

Perin, Constance. With man in mind. 1970. **HC68.P47 ECOL**

Resources for the Future. Multiple purpose river development. 1958 **REF HN15.R43 ECOL**

REGIONAL PLANNING—ADDRESSES, ESSAYS, LECTURES.
Western Resources Conference, 9th, University of Colorado, 1967. Man and the quality of his environment. 1968 **TD180.W4 1967 ECOL**

REGIONAL PLANNING—CALIFORNIA.
The California Tomorrow plan. Rev. ed. 1972 **HT393.C3C35 1972 ECOL**

REGIONAL PLANNING—CASE STUDIES.
Isard, Walter. Ecologic-economic analysis for regional development. 1972 **HT391.I82 ECOL**

REGIONAL PLANNING—GREAT BRITAIN.
Fairbrother, Nan. New lives, new landscapes. 1st American ed. 1970. **HT395.G7F3 1970 ECOL**

REGIONAL PLANNING—IOWA—CONGRESSES.
Conference on Flood Plain Management, Iowa State University, 1968. Flood plain management, Iowa's experience. 1st ed. 1969 **TC424.I8C6 1968 ECOL**

REGIONAL PLANNING—LAW AND LEGISLATION—UNITED STATES.
United States. Water Resources Council. Regulation of flood hazard areas to reduce flood losses. 1971- **KF5588.A875 ECOL**

REGIONAL PLANNING—MINNESOTA.
Land Exchange Review Symposium, Duluth, 1970. Proceedings of the Land Exchange Review Symposium. 1970. **fHD211.L3 ECOL**

Minnesota. State Planning Agency. Office of Local and Urban Affairs. Minnesota planning legislation. 1971 **REF KFM5858.A3 1971 ECOL**

Minnesota. State Planning Agency. Protecing the Minnesota environment through regulation of private land use. 1972. **fHC107.M6A45 ECOL**

REGIONAL PLANNING—MINNESOTA—ANOKA COUNTY.
Midwest Planning and Research, Inc. Anoka County parks and open-space: comprehensive plan. 1969. **fGV54.M6M52 ECOL**

Midwest Planning and Research, Inc. Anoka County parks and open-space: goals, policies, directions and alternatives. 1968 **fGV54.M6M5 ECOL**

REGIONAL PLANNING—PHILADELPHIA METROPOLITAN AREA.
Metropolitan open space and natural process. 1970. **HT394.P5M46 ECOL**

REGIONAL PLANNING—STUDY AND TEACHING.
Jackson, John Y. Land use: concern, challenge, commitment. c1969 **HD110.J3 ECOL**

REGIONAL PLANNING—UNITED STATES.
Chapin, Francis Stuart. Urban land use planning. 2d ed. 1965. **NA9108.C53 1965 ECOL**

Council of State Governments. The states' role in land resource management. 1972 **HD205.C6 1972 ECOL**

Resources for the Future. Regions, resources, and economic growth. 1967,c1960 **HC103.R45 1967 ECOL**

River basin development. 1957. **HN64.R589 ECOL**

Tunnard, Christopher. Man-made America: chaos or control? 1963 **fNA9108.T82 ECOL**

REGIONAL PLANNING—UNITED STATES—ADDRESSES, ESSAYS, LECTURES.
Coastal zone resource management. 1971 **HC110.E5C6 ECOL**

REGIONAL PLANNING—UNITED STATES—BIBLIOGRAPHY.
Hickok, Beverly. Goals, objectives and values: selected references relating to national, state and urban or regional areas, covering general & transportation aspects. 1973 **fZ7164.O7H49 ECOL**

REMOTE SENSING SYSTEMS.
Morey, Rexford M. Feasibility study of electromagnetic subsurface profiling. 1972. **QE602.M6 ECOL**

REMOTE SENSING SYSTEMS—CONGRESSES.
Remote sensing in ecology. 1969 **QH541.15.R4R4 ECOL**

RENEWABLE NATURAL RESOURCES.
Murphy, Earl Finbar. Governing nature. 1967 **HC55.M8 ECOL**

RENEWABLE NATURAL RESOURCES—UNITED STATES.
Murphy, Earl Finbar. Governing nature. 1967 **HC55.M8 ECOL**

REPRODUCTION.
Sadleir, R. M. F. S. The ecology of reproduction in wild and domestic mammals. 1969. **QP251.S27 ECOL**

REPTILES—ANATOMY.
Heilmann, Gerhard. The origin of birds. 1927. **QE871.H4 1927 ECOL**

REPTILES—NORTH AMERICA.
Barker, Will. Familiar animals of America. 1956 **QL715.B25 ECOL**

REPTILES, FOSSIL.
Heilmann, Gerhard. The origin of birds. 1927. **QE871.H4 1927 ECOL**

RESERVE MINING CO., SILVER BAY, MINNESOTA.
Roy F. Weston, Inc. Concept evaluation report: taconite tailings disposal, Reserve Mining Company, Silver Bay, Minnesota. 1971 **fTD899.T35 ECOL**

Ulrich, Stanley. Superior pollutor: a saga of the struggle to stop pollution of the largest fresh water lake in the world by its most egregious polluter—the Reserve Mining Company. 1972. **TD224.M6U6 ECOL**

RESERVOIRS *see also* WATER SUPPLY
California. University. Flow into a stratified reservoir. 1972. **TC167.C3 ECOL**

RESERVOIRS—CONGRESSES.
Lowe-McConnell, R. H. Man-made lakes. 1966. **GB1601.L6 1965 ECOL**

RESERVOIRS—MATHEMATICAL MODELS.
Ralph M. Parsons Laboratory for Water Resources and Hydrodynamics. Temperature prediction in stratified water: mathematical model-user's manual (supplement to report 1613ODJH-01/71). 1971. **fTD395.R3 ECOL**

RESERVOIRS—TEMPERATURE.
Ralph M. Parsons Laboratory for Water Resources and Hydrodynamics. Temperature prediction in stratified water: mathematical model-user's manual (supplement to report 1613ODJH-01/71). 1971. **fTD395.R3 ECOL**

RESERVOIRS—UNITED STATES—RECREATIONAL USE.
United States. Congress. House. Committee on Government Operations. Conservation and Natural Resources Subcommittee. Public access to reservoirs to meet growing recreation demands. 1971. **KF27.G636 1971 ECOL**

RESERVOIRS, UNDERGROUND.
Karl R. Rohrer Associates. Underwater storage of combined sewer overflows. 1971 **fTD662.K36 ECOL**

RESISTANCE TO INSECTICIDES—CONGRESSES.
International IUPAC Congress of Pesticide Chemistry, 2d, Tel-Aviv, 1971. Insecticide resistance, synergism, enzyme induction. c1971 **SB951.I56 1971vol.2 ECOL**

RESOURCES, AQUATIC *see* AQUATIC RESOURCES

RESOURCES, NATURAL *see* NATURAL RESOURCES

RESPIRATORY ORGANS—DISEASES.
Environmental factors in respiratory disease. 1972. **RC732.E59 ECOL**

Holland, Walter Werner. Air pollution and respiratory disease. 1972 **fRC732.H64 ECOL**

REUSE OF WATER *see* WATER REUSE

RIGHT OF WAY—UNITED STATES.
Lennon, J. Establishing trails on rights-of-way. n.d. **G504.L4 ECOL**

RIVER CHANNELS.
Walton, William Clarence. Recharge from induced streambed infiltration under varying groundwater-level and stream-stage conditions. 1967. **GB701.M554no.6 ECOL**

RIVER DISPOSAL OF RADIOACTIVE WASTES *see* RADIOACTIVE WASTE DISPOSAL IN RIVERS, LAKES, ETC.

RIVERS *see also* DAMS; EMBANKMENTS; EROSION; FLOODS; HYDRAULIC ENGINEERING; WATER—POLLUTION; WATERSHEDS
Braun, Ernest. Living water. 1971 **fQH46.B7 ECOL**

Coker, Robert Ervin. Streams, lakes, ponds. 1954 **QH96.C6 ECOL**

Silverberg, Robert. Rivers. 1st ed. 1966 **PZ10.S66Ri ECOL**

RIVERS—AERATION.
JBF Scientific Corporation. Engineering methodology for river and stream reaeration. 1971 **fTD458.J17 ECOL**

Tsivoglou, E. C. Characterization of stream reaeration, capacity. 1972. **fTD458.T7 ECOL**

RIVERS—CONGRESSES.
International Symposium on River Ecology and the Impact of Man, University of Massachusetts, 1971. River ecology and man. 1972. **GB1205.I5 1971 ECOL**

RIVERS—GREAT BRITAIN.
Great Britain. Central Advisory Water Committee. The future management of water in England and Wales; a report. 1971. **TD257.A5 1971 ECOL**

RIVERS—REGULATION.
Rice, Charles E. Methods for routing hydrographs through open channels. 1972. **GB701.M554no.51 ECOL**

RIVERS—TEMPERATURE.
Brown, George W. An improved temperature prediction model for small streams. 1972 **fQC909.B7 ECOL**

RIVERS—UNITED STATES.
Helfman, Elizabeth S. Rivers and watersheds in America's future. 1965. **TC423.H45 ECOL**

Kirkwood, James Pugh. A special report on the pollution of river waters. Reprint ed. 1970 **REF TD425.K52 1970 ECOL**

ROAD DRAINAGE.
Investigation of porous pavements for urban runoff control. 1972. **fTE215.I58 ECOL**

ROADS—MINNESOTA.
Minnesota. University. Dept. of Horticultural Science. Methods and materials for the maintenance of turf on highway rights-of-way. 1971. **REF TE178.M6 ECOL**

ROADS—SNOW AND ICE CONTROL.
Edison Water Quality Laboratory. Storm and Combined Sewer Overflows Section. Environmental impact of highway deicing. 1971. **fTE220.E35 ECOL**

ROADS—UNITED STATES.
Mowbray, A. Q. Road to ruin. 1969 **HE355.M66 ECOL**

Robinson, John. Highways and our environment. 1971 **HE355.R6 ECOL**

ROADS—UNITED STATES—FINANCE.
Kelley, Ben. The pavers and the paved. 1971 **HE355.K38 ECOL**

ROADSIDE IMPROVEMENT.
Cook, David I. Trees and shrubs for noise abatement. 1971. **TD893.C6 ECOL**

Minnesota. University. Dept. of Horticultural Science. Methods and materials for the maintenance of turf on highway rights-of-way. 1971. **REF TE178.M6 ECOL**

ROCKS, CARBONATE.
Selected studies on alkaline additives for sulfur dioxide control. 1971. **TD885.5.S8S4 ECOL**

ROOKERY BAY SANCTUARY.
Conservation Foundation. Rookery Bay area project. 1968. **QH77.U6C66 ECOL**

RUBBER, RECLAIMED.
United States. Environmental Protection Agency. Rubber reuse and solid waste management. 1971- **TD899.R8U55 ECOL**

RUBBER INDUSTRY AND TRADE—BY-PRODUCTS.
United States. Environmental Protection Agency. Rubber reuse and solid waste management. 1971- **TD899.R8U55 ECOL**

RUFFED GROUSE.
Rue, Leonard Lee. The world of the ruffed grouse. 1st ed. 1973, c1972 **QL696.G2R83 ECOL**

RUNOFF.
Golany, Pinhas. Effects of channel characteristics on time parameters for small watershed runoff hydrographs. 1971. **GB701.M554no.31 ECOL**

Investigation of porous pavements for urban runoff control. 1972. **fTE215.I58 ECOL**

Johnson, Jack D. Development of a mathematical model to predict the role of surface runoff and groundwater flow in over fertilization of surface waters. 1971. **GB701.M554no.35 ECOL**

Larson, Curtis L. Numerical routing of flood hydrographs through open channel junctions. 1971. **GB701.M554no.40 ECOL**

McPherson, M. B. Urban runoff. 1972. **fGB665.M35 ECOL**

Mein, Russell G. Modeling the infiltration component of the rainfall—runoff process. 1971. **GB701.M554no.43 ECOL**

Robert S. Kerr Water Research Center. Characteristics of rainfall run off from a beef cattle feedlot. 1972. **TD899.F4R6 ECOL**

Sartor, James D. Water pollution aspects of street surface contaminants. 1972. **fTD665.S2 ECOL**

Stall, John B. Storm sewer design—an evaluation of the RRL method. 1972. **TD665.S7 ECOL**

Wei, Tsong C. Effects of areal and time distribution of rainfall on small watershed runoff hydrographs. 1971. **GB701.M554no.30 ECOL**

RUNOFF—ABSTRACTS.
Franklin Institute, Philadelphia. Science Information Service. Selected urban storm water runoff abstracts, July 1970-June 1971. 1971. **fTD653.F7 ECOL**

Sandoski, Dorothy A. Selected urban storm water runoff abstracts, July 1971-June 1972. 1972. **fTD653.S2 ECOL**

RUNOFF—MATHEMATICAL MODELS.
Metcalf and Eddy, Boston. Storm water management model. 1971. **fGB665.M4 ECOL**

RUNOFF—MINNESOTA.
Bowers, C. Edward. Review and analysis of rainfall and runoff data for selected watersheds in Minnesota. 1968. **GB701.M554no.8 ECOL**

RUNOFF—STATISTICAL METHODS.
Larson, Curtis L. Predicting peak flow of small watersheds by use of channel characteristics. 1972. **GB701.M554no.52 ECOL**

RURAL CONDITIONS.
Herfindahl, Orris Clemens. Quality of the environment: an economic approach to some problems in using land, water, and air. 1965 **TD153.H46 ECOL**

S

SAFETY APPLIANCES—DIRECTORIES.
Best's environmental control and safety directory. 13th ed.- 1971/72- **REF fT55.B4 ECOL**

ST. CROIX VALLEY, MINNESOTA AND WISCONSIN—HISTORY.
Dunn, James Taylor. The St. Croix: Midwest border river. 1965 **F612.S2D78 ECOL**

ST. PAUL—SEWERAGE.
Toltz, King, Duvall, Anderson and Associates, Inc., St. Paul. Report on the expansion of the sewage treatment plant. 1969. **fTD525.T9T6 ECOL**

SALINE WATER CONVERSION.
Clawson, Marion. Desalting seawater. 1972 **TD479.C53 1972 ECOL**

Popkin, Roy. Desalination. 1968 **TD479.P6 ECOL**

Robert S. Kerr Water Research Center. Desalination of agricultural tile drainages. 1971. **TD479.R6 ECOL**

SALINE WATER CONVERSION—BIBLIOGRAPHY.
Nuclear Desalination Information Center. Indexed bibliography of nuclear desalination literature—7- 1972- **REF fZ5853.S22N8 ECOL**

Nuclear Desalination Information Center. Title—author—company index to reports published by the U.S. Dept. of the Interior, Office of Saline Water through July 1971- **REF fZ5853.S22N84 ECOL**

SALINE WATER CONVERSION—COSTS.
MacAvoy, Paul W. Large-scale desalting. 1969 **TD479.3.M3 ECOL**

SALINE WATER CONVERSION—ION EXCHANGE PROCESS.
National Canners Association. Western Research Laboratory. Reduction of salt content of food processing liquid waste effluent. 1971. **fTD899.C3N36 ECOL**

SALINE WATER CONVERSION—ISRAEL.
MacAvoy, Paul W. Large-scale desalting. 1969 **TD479.3.M3 ECOL**

SALINE WATER CONVERSION PLANTS—WASTE DISPOSAL.
Chesher, Richard H. Biological impact of a large-scale desalination plant at Key West. 1971. **fTD478.5.F5C48 ECOL**

SALINITY.
Skogerboe, Gaylord V. Evaluation of canal lining for salinity control in Grand Valley. 1972. **TC930.S5 ECOL**

SALVAGE (WASTE, ETC.) see also PAPER RECYCLING; PLASTIC SCRAP; RECYCLE OPERATIONS (CHEMICAL TECHNOLOGY); REFUSE AND REFUSE DISPOSAL; SCRAP METALS; WASTE PRODUCTS; WATER REUSE
Boettcher, R. A. Air classification of solid wastes. 1972. **TD796.7.B64 ECOL**

Burke, Jacquelyn M. The realities of recycling. 1973 **REF fTP995.B8 ECOL**

Darnay, Arsen. Salvage markets for materials in solid wastes, ... 1972. **TD795.D38 ECOL**

Drobny, N. L. Recovery and utilization of municipal solid waste: a summary of available cost and performance characteristics of unit processes and systems. 1971. **TD793.D76 ECOL**

Kenahan, Charles B. Bureau of Mines research programs on recycling and disposal of mineral-, metal-, and energy-based wastes. 1973. **TN23.U7no.8595 ECOL**

Midwest Research Institute, Kansas City, Missouri. Resource recovery. 1973. **fTP995.M5 ECOL**

SALVAGE (WASTE, ETC.)—BIBLIOGRAPHY.
Burg, Nan C. Abandoned vehicles: a selected bibliography. 1972 **Ref fHD9975.B87 ECOL**

SALVAGE (WASTE ETC.)—CONGRESSES.
Midwest Regional Seminar on Horizons in Resource Recovery, University of Chicago, 1972. Horizons in resource recovery: presentations and discussions of a seminar held Feb. 23, 1972. 1972. **fTP995.A1M5 1972 ECOL**

North Eastern Regional Antipollution Conference, 3d, University of Rhode Island, 1970. Reuse and recycle of wastes; proceedings. 1971 **fTP995.A1N6 1970 ECOL**

Symposium on Mineral Waste Utilization. Proceedings. 1st- 1968- **fTP995.A1S9 ECOL**

SAN ANTONIO—WATER CONSUMPTION.
Alamo Area Council of Governments. Basin management for water reuse. 1972. **fTD225.S225A65 ECOL**

SAN ANTONIO—WATER-SUPPLY.
Alamo Area Council of Governments. Basin management for water reuse. 1972. **fTD225.S225A65 ECOL**

SAND AND GRAVEL INDUSTRY—ENVIRONMENTAL ASPECTS—CALIFORNIA.
Landerman, Norman J. Community resource. 1972 **TD195.S3L36 ECOL**

SAND FILTERS see SEWAGE—PURIFICATION—FILTRATION

SANITARY BACTERIOLOGY see SANITARY MICROBIOLOGY

SANITARY CHEMISTRY—DIRECTORIES.
Environmental Science & Technology. Pollution control directory. 1971/72- **REF fTD180.E52 ECOL**

SANITARY ENGINEERING see also DRAINAGE; FILTERS AND FILTRATION; HYGIENE, PUBLIC; POLLUTION; REFUSE AND REFUSE DISPOSAL; SANITATION; SEWERAGE; STREET CLEANING; WATER SUPPLY
Clark, John William. Water supply and pollution control. 2d ed. 1971 **TD145.C55 1971 ECOL**

Ehlers, Victor Marcus. Municipal and rural sanitation. 6th ed. c1965 **REF RA425.E5 1965 ECOL**

SANITARY ENGINEERING—DICTIONARIES.
Glossary: water and wastewater control engineering. 1969. **TD9.G55 ECOL**

SANITARY LANDFILLS see also COMPOST
Brunner, Dirk R. Sanitary landfill design and operation. 1972. **TD795.7.B7 ECOL**

Fungaroli, A. A. Pollution of subsurface water by sanitary landfills. 1971 i.e. 1972- **TD403.F85 ECOL**

Warner, Arthur J. Plastics solid waste disposal by incineration or landfill. c1972, 1971. **fTD798.W36 ECOL**

SANITARY LANDFILLS—BIBLIOGRAPHY.
Water Resources Scientific Information Center. Sanitary landfills. 1972 **REF Z5853.S22W38 ECOL**

SANITARY LANDFILLS—ILLINOIS.
Hughes, George Muggah. Hydrogeology of solid waste disposal sites in northeastern Illinois. 1971 **TD795.7.H84 ECOL**

SANITARY MICROBIOLOGY see also AIR—MICROBIOLOGY
Finstein, Melvin S. Pollution microbiology. 1972. **QR48.F5 ECOL**

Mitchell, Ralph. Water pollution microbiology. 1971,c1972 **QR48.M58 ECOL**

Soil Conservation Society of America. Minnesota Chapter. Water pollution by nutrients—sources, effects and control. 1969. **GB701.M554no.13 ECOL**

SANITATION.
Benarde, Melvin A. Our precarious habitat. 1st ed. 1970 **TD180.B45 ECOL**

Ehlers, Victor Marcus. Municipal and rural sanitation. 6th ed. c1965 **REF RA425.E5 1965 ECOL**

Herfindahl, Orris Clemens. Quality of the environment: an economic approach to some problems in using land, water, and air. 1965 **TD153.H46 ECOL**

Salvato, Joseph A. Environmental engineering and sanitation. 2d ed. 1972 **RA565.S3 1972 ECOL**

SASKATCHEWAN—DESCRIPTION AND TRAVEL.
Olson, Sigurd F. The lonely land. 1961. **F1071.O4 ECOL**

SAVANNAS—AFRICA.
Brown, Leslie. The life of the African plains. 1972 **QH541.5.P7B76 ECOL**

SCATOLOGY.
Rosebury, Theodor. Life on man. 1969 **QR56.R59 ECOL**

SCENIC HUDSON PRESERVATION CONFERENCE.
Talbot, Allan R. Power along the Hudson. 1st ed. 1972. **HD9685.U7C768 ECOL**

SCHMIDT, WALTER SETON, 1885-1957.
Eskew, Garnett Laidlaw. Of land and men. c1959 **NA9000.U715 ECOL**

SCHOOL EXCURSIONS.
National Association of Biology Teachers. National Conservation Committee. Manual for outdoor laboratories. 1959. **QH51.N3 ECOL**

SCHOOL FACILITIES—PLANNING.
Educational Facilities Laboratories. Places and things for experimental schools. 1972 **Ref LB3221.E3 ECOL**

MacGown, Richard H. The school site in environmental education. Rev. ed. 1972. **fLB3220.M3 1972 ECOL**

SCHOOL GROUNDS.
National Association of Biology Teachers. National Conservation Committee. Manual for outdoor laboratories. 1959. **QH51.N3 ECOL**

SCHOOL SITES.
MacGown, Richard H. The school site in environmental education. Rev. ed. 1972. **fLB3220.M3 1972 ECOL**

SCHOOLS—FURNITURE, EQUIPMENT, ETC.
Educational Facilities Laboratories. Places and things for experimental schools. 1972 **Ref LB3221.E3 ECOL**

SCIENCE.
Berrill, Norman John. Inherit the earth. 1966 **Q162.B56 ECOL**

Cheronis, Nicholas Dimitrius. The study of the physical world. 3d ed. 1958 **Q160.C34 1958 ECOL**

Krauskopf, Konrad Bates. Fundamentals of physical science. 6th ed. 1971 **Q160.2.K7 1971 ECOL**

Schwartz, Julius. Through the magnifying glass. 1954 **Q163.S464 ECOL**

SCIENCE—ADDRESSES, ESSAYS, LECTURES.
Eiseley, Loren C. The unexpected universe. 1969 **Q171.E39 ECOL**

Fuller, Richard Buckminster. Approaching the benign environment. 1970 **Q171.F96 ECOL**

The New scientist. The world in 1984. 1965,c1964 **Q171.N5 1965 ECOL**

SCIENCE—BIBLIOGRAPHY.
Jenkins, Frances Briggs. Science reference sources. 5th ed. 1969 **REF Z7401.J4 1969 ECOL**

SCIENCE—DICTIONARIES.
McGraw-Hill encyclopedia of science and technology. 3d ed. 1971 **REF fQ121.M3 1971 ECOL**

SCIENCE—EXHIBITIONS.
LeCompte, Robert G. Atoms at the science fair. 1968 **Q105.L412 1968 ECOL**

SCIENCE—INFORMATION SERVICES.
United Nations Educational, Scientific and Cultural Organization. UNISIST: study report on the feasibility of a world science system. 1971. **REF Q223.U5 ECOL**

SCIENCE—PHILOSOPHY—ADDRESSES, ESSAYS, LECTURES.
Glass, Hiram Bentley. Science and ethical values. 1965 **Q175.G58 ECOL**

SCIENCE—SOCIAL ASPECTS—ADDRESSES, ESSAYS, LECTURES.
Science, conflict, and society. 1969 **fQ125.S434 ECOL**

SCIENCE—SOCIAL ASPECTS—BIBLIOGRAPHY.
Bausum, Howard T. Science for society: a bibliography. 3d ed. 1972. **fZ7401.B3 1972 ECOL**

SCIENCE—STUDY AND TEACHING.
Berry, Marcia. Environment study. 1971.
QH541.2.B4 ECOL
Glass, Hiram Bentley. The timely and the timeless. 1970 **Q181.G45 ECOL**
Madison. Wis. Board of Education. Dept. of Curriculum Development. Science and society. 1969.
REF fQ181.M3 ECOL

SCIENCE—STUDY AND TEACHING—DIRECTORIES.
Natural Science centers for youth. Directory. 1970/71- **REF fQ147.N38 ECOL**

SCIENCE—STUDY AND TEACHING (ELEMENTARY).
Hone, Elizabeth B. Teaching elementary science: a sourcebook for elementary science. 2d ed. 1971
LB1585.H65 1971 ECOL
Science Curriculum Improvement Study. Interaction and systems. c1970 **LB1585.S36 ECOL**
Science Curriculum Improvement Study. Life cycles. c1970 **LB1585.S32 ECOL**
Science Curriculum Improvement Study. Material objects: teacher's guide. 1971 **LB1585.S3 ECOL**
Science Curriculum Improvement Study. Organisms. c1970 **LB1585.S34 ECOL**
Science Curriculum Improvement Study. Populations. c1969 **fLB1585.S35 ECOL**
Science Curriculum Improvement Study. Subsystems and variables. 1971,c1970
LB1585.S38 1971 ECOL
West St. Paul, Minn. Independent School Dist. no. 197. Elementary Science Committee. Elementary science guide and resource book. n.d.
fLB1585.W4 ECOL

SCIENCE—STUDY AND TEACHING (ELEMENTARY)—GREAT BRITAIN.
Perry, Gordon Arthur. Handbook for environmental studies. 2nd rev. ed. 1971 **LB1585.P4 1971 ECOL**

SCIENCE—STUDY AND TEACHING (SECONDARY)—UNITED STATES.
Science teachers handbook. n.d. **fQ181.S3 ECOL**

SCIENCE—UNITED STATES—INFORMATION SERVICES.
United States. Library of Congress. National Referral Center. A directory of information resources in the United States; physical sciences, engineering. 1971.
REF Q223.U526 1971 ECOL

SCIENCE AND CIVILIZATION.
Commoner, Barry. Science and survival. c1966
Q125.C56 ECOL
Dubos, Rene Jules. Reason awake: science for man. 1970. **Q125.D814 ECOL**
Glass, Hiram Bentley. The timely and the timeless. 1970 **Q181.G45 ECOL**
Madison. Wis. Board of Education. Dept. of Curriculum Development. Science and society. 1969.
REF fQ181.M3 ECOL
Still, Henry. Will the human race survive? 1st ed. 1966 **Q125.S745 ECOL**

SCIENCE AND CIVILIZATION—ADDRESSES, ESSAYS, LECTURES.
Science, conflict, and society. 1969
fQ125.S434 ECOL
The Social responsibility of the scientist. 1971
Q125.S714 ECOL

SCIENCE AND CIVILIZATION—BIBLIOGRAPHY.
Moore, John A. Science for society: a bibliography. 2nd ed. 1971 **fZ7401.M6 1971 ECOL**

SCIENCE AND CIVILIZATION—CONGRESSES.
Science and the future of man. c1970
CB151.S37 ECOL

SCIENCE AND STATE—ADDRESSES, ESSAYS, LECTURES.
The Social responsibility of the scientist. 1971
Q125.S714 ECOL

SCIENCE AS A PROFESSION.
Munzer, Martha E. Unusual careers: solar scientist, meteorologist, oceanographer, geologist, ecologist, sanitary engineer, research chemist, city and regional planner. 1st ed. 1962. **Q147.M8 ECOL**
Natural Science centers for youth. Directory. 1970/71- **REF fQ147.N38 ECOL**

SCIENCE NEWS.
Smithsonian Institution. Center for Shortlived Phenomena. The pulse of the planet. c1972
fQ225.P8 ECOL

SCIENCE TEACHERS—HANDBOOKS, MANUALS, ETC.
Science Curriculum Improvement Study. Interaction and systems. c1970 **LB1585.S36 ECOL**
Science Curriculum Improvement Study. Material objects: teacher's guide. 1971 **LB1585.S3 ECOL**
Science Curriculum Improvement Study. Organisms. c1970 **LB1585.S34 ECOL**
Science Curriculum Improvement Study. Populations. c1969 **fLB1585.S35 ECOL**
Science Curriculum Improvement Study. Subsystems and variables. 1971,c1970
LB1585.S38 1971 ECOL
Science teachers handbook. n.d. **fQ181.S3 ECOL**

SCIENTIFIC EXPEDITIONS.
Forbes, Alexander. Northernmost Labrador. 1938.
F1136.F67 ECOL

SCIENTISTS—DIRECTORIES.
The Naturalists' directory: international 41 ed.-
REF Q145.S4 ECOL

SCRAP METAL INDUSTRY.
United Nations. Economic Commission for Europe. Problems relating to iron and steel scrap. 1971.
fTS214.U6 ECOL

SCRAP METAL INDUSTRY—SOCIETIES, ETC.
Institute of Scrap Iron & Steel, New York. Yearbook. 31st- 1970- **REF TS200.I64 ECOL**

SCRAP METALS.
Kenahan, Charles B. Bureau of Mines research programs on recycling and disposal of mineral-, metal-, and energy-based wastes. 1973.
TN23.U7no.8595 ECOL

SCRAP METALS—CONGRESSES.
Effective technology for recycling metal. 1971
fTS214.E36 ECOL

SEA BIRDS.
Graham, Ada. Puffin Island. 1st ed. 1971
QL676.G68 1971 ECOL

SEA FOOD.
Gibbons, Euell. Stalking the blue-eyed scallop. 1964
TX387.G5 ECOL

SEA POLLUTION see MARINE POLLUTION

SEA-POWER.
Uses of the seas. 1968 **GC1015.U8 ECOL**

SEA-WATER, DISTILLATION OF.
MacAvoy, Paul W. Large-scale desalting. 1969
TD479.3.M3 ECOL

SEALING—ST. LAWRENCE, GULF OF.
Davies, Brian. Savage luxury: the slaughter of the baby seals. 1971,c1970 **QL737.P6D33 1971 ECOL**

SEALS (ANIMALS).
Scheffer, Victor B. The year of the seal. 1970
QL737.P6S32 ECOL

SEASHORE BIOLOGY see also SHORE BIRDS
Hay, John. In defense of nature. 1969
QH81.H37 ECOL
McCue, George. Ecology: the oceans and man. c1971 **QH541.5.S3M22 ECOL**

SEASHORE BIOLOGY—ATLANTIC COAST.
Hay, John. The Atlantic shore. 1969,c1966.
QH95.7.H3 ECOL
Hay, John. The primal alliance: earth and ocean. 1971. **fQH95.7.H32 ECOL**

SEASHORE BIOLOGY—UNITED STATES.
Gibbons, Euell. Stalking the blue-eyed scallop. 1964
TX387.G5 ECOL

SEASHORE ECOLOGY.
Eltringham, Stewart Keith. Life in mud and sand. 1971 **QH541.5.S35E45 ECOL**
Stephenson, Thomas Alan. Life between tidemarks on rocky shores. 1972 **QH541.5.S3S68 ECOL**
Venn, Mary Eleanor. A day and a night in a tide pool. 1972 **QH541.5.S35V45 ECOL**

SECONDARY RECOVERY OF OIL.
Agnew, Robert W. A free floating endless belt oil skimmer. 1972. **TD899.P4A3 ECOL**
United States. Environmental Protection Agency. Office of Research and Monitoring. Air modulated vacuum oil recovery collection of spilled oil (foams). 1972. **fTD427.P4U5 ECOL**

SECURITY CLASSIFICATION (GOVERNMENT DOCUMENTS)—UNITED STATES.
Barker, Carol M. Classified files: the yellowing pages. 1972. **JK468.S4B35 ECOL**

SEDIMENT LOAD OF STREAMS see SEDIMENT TRANSPORT

SEDIMENT TRANSPORT see also CHANNELS (HYDRAULIC ENGINEERING)
Partheniades, Emmanuel. Deposition of fine sediments in turbulent flows. 1971 i.e. 1972
fTC175.2.P3 ECOL

SEDIMENTATION AND DEPOSITION see also EROSION; GEOLOGY
Gammon, James Robert. The effect of inorganic sediment on stream biota. 1970.
fQH541.5.S7G34 ECOL
Partheniades, Emmanuel. Deposition of fine sediments in turbulent flows. 1971 i.e. 1972
fTC175.2.P3 ECOL

SEDIMENTATION AND DEPOSITION—BIBLIOGRAPHY.
Engineering-Science, Inc. Annotated bibliography on hydrology and sedimentation, 1966-68, United States and Canada. 1970
REF Z7935.E5 1970 ECOL

SEDIMENTS.
Feick, George. Control of mercury contamination in freshwater sediments. 1972. **TD427.M4F4 ECOL**
Suggs, James D. Mercury pollution control in stream and lake sediments. 1972. **fTD427.M4S9 ECOL**
United States. Environmental Protection Agency. Office of Research and Monitoring. Control of mercury pollution in sediments. 1972.
TD427.M4U5 ECOL

SELF-PURIFICATION OF STREAMS see STREAM SELF-PURIFICATION

SELF-REALIZATION (PSYCHOLOGY).
Leonard, George Burr. The transformation. 1972
BF311.L43 ECOL

SEMIARID REGIONS see ARID REGIONS

SENSING SYSTEMS, REMOTE see REMOTE SENSING SYSTEMS

SEPARATION (TECHNOLOGY) see also ADSORPTION; DISTILLATION; SEPARATORS (MACHINES)
Battelle Memorial Institute, Columbus, Ohio. Pacific Northwest Laboratory, Richland, Wash. Concept development of a hydraulic skimmer system for recovery of floating oil. 1971.
fTD427.P4B29 ECOL
Boettcher, R. A. Air classification of solid wastes. 1972. **TD796.7.B64 ECOL**

SEPARATORS (MACHINES).
Michigan. State University, East Lansing. Agricultural Pollution Control Laboratory. Closed system waste management for livestock. 1971 i.e. 1972 **fTD899.F4M5 ECOL**
New Mexico State University. Physical Science Laboratory. Floating oil recovery device. 1971.
fTD427.P4N48 ECOL
Susquehanna Corporation. Atlantic Research Systems Division. Marine Systems. Recovery of floating oil rotating disk type skimmer. 1971.
fTD427.P4S9 ECOL

SEWAGE see also WATER—POLLUTION

SEWAGE—ANALYSIS.
American Public Health Association. Standard methods for the examination of water and waste water, including bottom sediments and sludges. Ed. 13. c1971
REF QD142.A5 1971 ECOL
Little (Arthur D.) Inc. Characterization and separation of secondary effluent components by molecular weight. 1971. **fTD735.L58 ECOL**
Mancy, Khalil H. Analysis of industrial wastewaters. 1971 **TD735.M35 ECOL**

SEWAGE—CHLORINATION see SEWAGE—PURIFICATION—CHLORINATION

SEWAGE—FILTRATION see SEWAGE—PURIFICATION—FILTRATION

SEWAGE—PURIFICATION see also SEWAGE DISPOSAL PLANTS; WATER REUSE
Battelle Memorial Institute, Columbus, Ohio. Columbus Laboratories A state-of-the-art review of metal finishing waste treatment. 1968 i.e.1970
fTD899.M45B33 ECOL
Besselievre, Edmund Bulkley. The treatment of industrial wastes. 1968,c1969
REF TD897.B38 ECOL
Black & Veatch, Kansas City, Mo. Process design manual for phosphorus removal. 1971.
REF fTD745.B5 ECOL
Burns and Roe. Process design manual for suspended solids removal. 1971. **REF fTD745.B8 ECOL**
Eckenfelder, William Wesley. Industrial water pollution control. c1966 **TD897.E2 ECOL**
Envirogenics Company. Investigation of a new phosphate removal process. 1970. **fTD745.E5 ECOL**
Environmental Research and Applications, Inc. Concentrated mine drainage disposal into sewage treatment systems. 1971. **fTD899.M5E58 ECOL**
Ghassemi, Masood. Phosphate precipitation with ferrous iron. 1971. **fTD751.G4 ECOL**
Goodman, Brian L. Design handbook of wastewater systems: domestic, industrial, commercial. 1971
REF fTD745.G65 ECOL
Imhoff, Karl. Disposal of sewage and other waterborne wastes. 2d ed. 1971.
TD741.I5813 1971b ECOL
Ionics, Inc. The electro-oxidation of ammonia in sewage to nitrogen. 1970. **fTD757.I55 ECOL**
North American Rockwell Corporation. Rocketdyne Division. Development of a chemical denitrification process. 1970. **fTD433.N67 ECOL**

Portland, Or. Bureau of Sanitary Engineering. Demonstration of rotary screening for combined sewer overflows. 1971. **fTD748.P67 ECOL**

Roy F. Weston, Inc. Process design manual for upgrading existing wastewater treatment plants. 1971. **REF fTD745.R6 ECOL**

Texas. University. Medical Branch, Galveston. Phosphorus removal and disposal from municipal wastewater. 1971. **fTD745.T43 ECOL**

United States. Environmental Protection Agency. Office of Research and Monitoring. Storage and treatment of combined sewer overflows. 1972. **fTD662.U54 ECOL**

SEWAGE—PURIFICATION—ACTIVATED SLUDGE PROCESS.

Dallas, Or. Combined treatment of domestic and industrial wastes by activated sludge. 1971. **fTD756.D35 ECOL**

Detroit Metro Water Dept. Development of phosphate removal processes. 1970. **fTD756.D47 ECOL**

Gaudy, Anthony F. Biological concepts for design and operation of the activated sludge process. 1971 i.e. 1972 **fTD756.G38 ECOL**

Goodman, Brian L. Design handbook of wastewater systems: domestic, industrial, commercial. 1971 **REF fTD745.G65 ECOL**

Goodman, Brian L. Manual for activated sludge sewage treatment. 1971 **REF fTD756.G66 ECOL**

Kansas. University. Center for Research, Inc. Oxygen consumption in continuous biological culture. 1971. **fTD755.K3 ECOL**

Mahloch, Jerome L. The effect of organic amendments from garbage grinding on a biological treatment system. 1972. **fTD756.M32 ECOL**

McGriff, E. Corbin. The efficacy of the complete mix activated sludge process in modular mode. 1971. **fTD756.M3 ECOL**

Milwaukee. Sewerage Commission. Phosphorus removal by an activated sludge plant. 1970. **fTD756.M54 ECOL**

Milwaukee. Sewerage Commission. Phosphorus removal with pickle liquor in an activated sludge plant. 1971. **fTD756.M55 ECOL**

Morgan, W. E. An investigation of phosphorus removal mechanisms in activated sludge systems. 1972. **TD756.M6 ECOL**

Streebin, Leale E. Demonstration of a full-scale waste treatment system for a cannery. 1971. **fTD899.C3S87 ECOL**

Toerber, Edwin D. Full scale parallel activated sludge process evaluation. 1972. **fTD756.T6 ECOL**

SEWAGE—PURIFICATION—ADDRESSES, ESSAYS, LECTURES.

Water quality improvement by physical and chemical processes. 1970 **TD745.W37 ECOL**

SEWAGE—PURIFICATION—ADSORPTION.

Swindell-Dressler Company. Process design manual for carbon adsorption. 1971. **REF fTD753.5.S9 ECOL**

SEWAGE—PURIFICATION—AERATION see also WATER—AERATION

Crown Zellerbach Corporation. Lebanon Division. Aerated lagoon treatment of sulfite pulping effluents. 1970. **fTD899.W65C7 ECOL**

Kansas. University. Center for Research, Inc. Oxygen consumption in continuous biological culture. 1971. **fTD755.K3 ECOL**

Mead Corporation. Multi-system biological treatment of bleached kraft effluents. 1971. **fTD899.W65M4 ECOL**

Oklahoma. State University of Agriculture and Applied Science, Stillwater. School of Civil Engineering. Aerobic digestion of organic waste sludge. 1971 i.e. 1972 **fTD769.O35 ECOL**

Thimsen, Donald J. Biological treatment in aerated lagoons: theory and practice. 1965. **fTD746.5.T5 ECOL**

SEWAGE—PURIFICATION—BIOLOGICAL TREATMENT.

Austin, Texas Design guides for biological wastewater treatment processes. 1971 i.e.1972 **fTD755.A87 ECOL**

Davis, Ernst M. Bacterial effects of algae on enteric organisms. 1970. **fQR48.D38 ECOL**

Finstein, Melvin S. Pollution microbiology. 1972. **QR48.F5 ECOL**

Green Giant Company. Pilot plant installation for fungal treatment of vegetable canning wastes. 1971. **fTD899.C3G74 ECOL**

Jacksonville, Ark. Biological treatment of chlorophenolic wastes. 1971. **fTD755.J3 ECOL**

SEWAGE—PURIFICATION—BIOLOGICAL TREATMENT ENZYMES.

Grumman Aerospace Corporation. Development of immobilized enzyme systems for enhancement of biological waste treatment processes. 1970 **fTD755.G78 ECOL**

SEWAGE—PURIFICATION—CHLORINATION.

Barnes, Robert A. Ammonia removal in a physical-chemical wastewater treatment process. 1972. **TD462.B3 ECOL**

Manufacturing Chemists' Association. The effect of chlorination on selected organic chemicals. 1972. **fTD462.M3 ECOL**

Michigan. Bureau of Water Management. Chlorinated municipal waste toxicities to rainbow trout and fathead minnows. 1971. **fTD763.M5 ECOL**

Midwest Research Institute, Kansas City, Mo. Light-catalyzed chlorine oxidation for treatment of wastewater. 1970. **fTD758.M5 ECOL**

Troy, Joseph C. Oxidation of pyrites in chlorinated solvents. 1972. **TD899.M5T7 ECOL**

SEWAGE—PURIFICATION—COLD WEATHER CONDITIONS.

Colorado. State University, Fort Collins Environmental Resources Center. The mechanism of waste treatment at low temperature. Part A- 1972- **fTD745.C58 ECOL**

SEWAGE—PURIFICATION—CONGRESSES.

National Symposium on Food Processing Wastes, 1st, Portland, Or., 1970. Proceedings. 1971 **fTD899.F585N37 1970 ECOL**

SEWAGE—PURIFICATION—ELECTRODIALYSIS PROCESS.

Southern Research Institute, Birmingham, Ala. Demineralization of wastewater by the transport-depletion process. 1971. **fTD754.S67 ECOL**

SEWAGE—PURIFICATION—FILTRATION.

American Process Equipment Corporation. Ultrasonic filtration of combined sewer overflows. 1970. **fTD753.A6 ECOL**

Bouwer, Herman. Renovating secondary sewage by ground water recharge with infiltration basins. 1972. **fTD765.B6 ECOL**

Development of a coal-based sewage-treatment process. 1971 **fTN805.A395no.55 ECOL**

SEWAGE—PURIFICATION—ION EXCHANGE PROCESS.

California. University. Sanitary Engineering Research Laboratory. Optimization of ammonia removal by ion exchange using clinoptilolite. 1971 i.e. 1972 **fTD757.5.C35 ECOL**

Dow Chemical Company. Western Division Research Laboratories. Nitrate removal from wastewaters by ion exchange. 1971. **fTD757.5.D68 ECOL**

General Mills Chemicals. Feasibility of liquid ion exchange for extracting phosphate from wastewater. 1970. **fTD757.5.G45 ECOL**

Kreusch, Ed. Wastewater demineralization by ion exchange. 1971 i.e.1972 **fTD757.5.K74 ECOL**

Uniroyal, Inc. Feasibility study of regenerative fibers for water pollution control. 1970 i.e. 1971 **fTD757.5.U55 ECOL**

SEWAGE—PURIFICATION—OZONIZATION.

Evans, Francis L. Ozone in water and wastewater treatment. 1972 **TD461.E93 ECOL**

SEWAGE—PURIFICATION—PATENTS.

Gutcho, Sidney. Waste treatment with polyelectrolytes, 1972. 1972 **TD751.G87 ECOL**

James, Ronald W. Sewage sludge treatment 1972. 1972 **REF fTD768.J35 ECOL**

SEWAGE—PURIFICATION—REVERSE OSMOSIS PROCESS.

Aerojet-General Corporation. Environmental Systems Division. Reverse osmosis renovation of municipal wastewater. 1970 **fTD754.A35 ECOL**

Envirogenics Company. Reverse osmosis renovation of primary sewage. 1971. **fTD754.E58 ECOL**

Gulf Environmental Systems Company. Acid mine waste treatment using reverse osmosis. 1971 **fTD754.G84 ECOL**

North Star Research and Development Institute, Minneapolis. New and ultrathin membranes for municipal waste water treatment by reverse osmosis. 1970. **fTD754.N6 ECOL**

Wiley, Averill J. Reverse osmosis concentration of dilute pulp and paper effluents. 1972. **fTD899.W65W5 ECOL**

SEWAGE DISPOSAL see also FERTILIZERS AND MANURES; REFUSE AND REFUSE DISPOSAL; WASTE DISPOSAL IN THE OCEAN; WATER—POLLUTION; WATER QUALITY MANAGEMENT

Assessment of the effectiveness and effects of land disposal methodologies of waste water management. 1972. **fTD760.A86 ECOL**

Bouwer, Herman. Renovating secondary sewage by ground water recharge with infiltration basins. 1972. **fTD765.B6 ECOL**

Fair, Gordon Maskew. Water and wastewater engineering. 1966-1968 **REF TD145.F32 ECOL**

Grava, Sigurd. Urban planning aspects of water pollution control. 1969. **TD420.G67 ECOL**

Hardenbergh, William Andrew. Water supply and waste disposal. 1970,c1960 **TD145.H33 1970 ECOL**

Imhoff, Karl. Disposal of sewage and other waterborne wastes. 2d ed. 1971. **TD741.I5813 1971b ECOL**

Metcalf and Eddy, Boston. Wastewater engineering: collection, treatment, disposal. 1972 **TD645.M57 ECOL**

Minnesota. Water Pollution Control Commission. Long-range water pollution control plan and program, July 1, 1963. **fTD224.M6A56 ECOL**

Minnesota. Water Pollution Control Commission. Report on progress—water pollution control, Jan. 1, 1965 to Dec. 31, 1966. 1967 **fTD224.M6A562 ECOL**

SEWAGE DISPOSAL—CONGRESSES.

National Conference on Composting-Waste Recycling. 1st, Denver, 1971. How to put waste recycling into practice. 1971. **fTD172.5.N3 1971 ECOL**

SEWAGE DISPOSAL—GREAT BRITAIN.

Great Britain. Central Advisory Water Committee. The future management of water in England and Wales: a report. 1971. **fTD257.A5 1971 ECOL**

SEWAGE DISPOSAL—LAKE TAHOE REGION, CALIFORNIA AND NEVADA.

South Tahoe Public Utility District. Advanced wastewater treatment as practiced at South Tahoe. 1971. **fTD225.T25S6 ECOL**

SEWAGE DISPOSAL—MINNESOTA.

Minnesota. Division of Water Quality. Investigation of water quality and sources of pollution of waters of Minnesota and Iowa: reports and memorandums. 1960- **fTD224.M6A34 ECOL**

Minnesota. Division of Water Quality. Waste disposal reports and memorandums of industries of Minnesota. 1961- **fTD224.M6A35 ECOL**

Minnesota. Division of Water Quality. Wastewater disposal facilities inventory, State of Minnesota. 1971- **fTD224.M6A33 ECOL**

Minnesota. Division of Water Quality. Wastewater treatment works studies, surveys, memorandums, reports, etc. of cities and villages of Minnesota. 1964- **fTD224.M6A36 ECOL**

Minnesota. Pollution Control Agency. Census data: sewage disposal facilities, State of Minnesota, January, 1968. 1968 **fTD524.M5A56 ECOL**

Minnesota. Water Pollution Control Commission. Report on Progress - water pollution control, July 1, 1963 to Dec. 31, 1964. 1965? **fTD224.M6A561 ECOL**

SEWAGE DISPOSAL—MINNESOTA—BURNSVILLE.

Barr Engineering Co. The drainage plan for Burnsville, Minnesota. 1966. **fTD525.B8B3 ECOL**

SEWAGE DISPOSAL—MINNESOTA—LAKEVILLE.

Bonestroo, Rosene, Anderlik and Associates, inc., St. Paul, Minn. Report on sanitary sewerage facilities Airlake Industrial Park for Lakeville, Minnesota. 1967. **fTD525.L3B6 ECOL**

SEWAGE DISPOSAL—MINNESOTA—STATISTICS.

Minnesota. Division of Water Quality. Sewage disposal facilities inventory, State of Minnesota, January 1, 1969. 1969 **fTD524.M5A44 ECOL**

SEWAGE DISPOSAL—MINNESOTA—TWIN CITIES METROPOLITAN AREA.

Metcalf and Eddy, Boston. Sewerage and water planning report. 1968. **fTD525.T9M4 ECOL**

SEWAGE DISPOSAL—RATES.

Elliott, Ralph D. The effects of sewer surcharges on the level of industrial wastes and the use of water by industry. 1972. **TD897.5.E4 ECOL**

SEWAGE DISPOSAL—TWIN CITIES METROPOLITAN AREA.

Minnesota. Division of Water Quality. Memorandum on the waste assimilation capacity of the Mississippi River in the Twin Cities Metropolitan Area. 1969. **fTD525.T9M6 ECOL**

Minnesota. Water Pollution Control Commission. Report on a comprehensive sewage works plan for the Minneapolis-St. Paul metropolitan area, Dec. 1964. 1965 **fTD525.T8M6 ECOL**

Toltz, King, Duvall, Anderson and Associates, Inc., St. Paul. Report on the expansion of the sewage treatment plant. 1969. **fTD525.T9T6 ECOL**

SEWAGE DISPOSAL—UNITED STATES.
Smith, David D. Ocean disposal of barge-delivered liquid and solid wastes from United States coastal cities. 1971. **TD796.7.O25S4 ECOL**

SEWAGE DISPOSAL—UNITED STATES—FINANCE.
Abt Associates. Factors affecting pollution referenda. 1971. **fGH4952.A6 ECOL**

United States. Federal Water Pollution Control Administration. The economics of clean water. **HD4477.A53 ECOL**

SEWAGE DISPOSAL—UNITED STATES—RATES.
Smith, Robert. Cost to the consumer for collection and treatment of wastewater. 1970 i.e. 1972 **fTD523.S65 ECOL**

SEWAGE DISPOSAL—WASHINGTON, D.C.
Roy F. Weston, Inc. Combined sewer overflow abatement alternatives, Wash., D.C. 1970. **fTD525.W2R68 ECOL**

SEWAGE DISPOSAL—WISCONSIN—GREEN BAY.
Green Bay (Wis.) Metropolitan Sewerage District. Joint treatment of municipal sewage and pulp mill effluents. 1970. **fTD524.W6G74 ECOL**

SEWAGE DISPOSAL PLANTS.
Balakrishnan, S. State of the art review on sludge incineration practice. 1970. **fTD803.B36 ECOL**

SEWAGE DISPOSAL PLANTS—COSTS.
United States. Federal Water Pollution Control Administration. The economics of clean water. **HD4477.A53 ECOL**

SEWAGE DISPOSAL PLANTS—ESTIMATES—UNITED STATES.
Patterson, W. L. Estimating costs and manpower requirements for conventional wastewater treatment facilities. 1971 i.e. 1972 **fTD743.P36 ECOL**

SEWAGE DISPOSAL PLANTS—TWIN CITIES METROPOLITAN AREA.
Schoell and Madson, Inc., Hopkins, Minn. Waste treatment plant site study for Southwest suburban municipalities report. 1968. **fTD525.T9S3 ECOL**

SEWAGE-FARMS see SEWAGE IRRIGATION

SEWAGE IRRIGATION.
Assessment of the effectiveness and effects of land disposal methodologies of waste water management. 1972. **fTD760.A86 ECOL**

SEWAGE IRRIGATION—ABSTRACTS.
Ramsey, Ralph H. Soil systems for municipal effluents. 1972. **fTD760.R24 ECOL**

SEWAGE IRRIGATION—BIBLIOGRAPHY.
Ramsey, Ralph H. Soil systems for municipal effluents. 1972. **fTD760.R24 ECOL**

SEWAGE LAGOONS.
Champlin, Robert L. Supplementary aeration of lagoons in rigorous climate areas. 1971. **fTD746.5.C45 ECOL**

Crown Zellerbach Corporation. Lebanon Division. Aerated lagoon treatment of sulfite pulping effluents. 1970. **fTD899.W65C7 ECOL**

Thimsen, Donald J. Biological treatment in aerated lagoons: theory and practice. 1965. **fTD746.5.T5 ECOL**

SEWAGE-PURIFICATION.
General Electric Company. Re-entry and Environmental Systems Division. Watercraft waste treatment system: development and demonstration report. 1971. **fTD745.G4 ECOL**

SEWAGE PURIFICATION—ACTIVATED SLUDGE PROCESS.
Biospherics Incorporated. Biomass determination—a new technique for activated sludge control. 1972. **fTD756.B5 ECOL**

SEWAGE SLUDGE.
Brinkhurst, Ralph O. The role of sludge worms in eutrophication. 1972. **QH96.8.E9B7 ECOL**

Freese, Paul V. Full-scale raw wastewater flocculation with polymers. 1970. **fTD751.F7 ECOL**

Oklahoma. State University of Agriculture and Applied Science, Stillwater. School of Civil Engineering. Aerobic digestion of organic waste sludge. 1971 i.e. 1972 **fTD769.O35 ECOL**

Unterberg, W. Computerized design and cost estimation for multiple-hearth sludge incinerators. 1971 i.e. 1972 **fTD770.U58 ECOL**

SEWAGE SLUDGE—ANALYSIS.
Missouri. Southwest Missouri State College, Springfield. DNA concentration as an estimate of sludge biomass. 1971. **fTD767.7.M57 ECOL**

SEWAGE SLUDGE—DRYING.
Milwaukee. Sewerage Commission. Evaluation of conditioning and dewatering sewage sludge by freezing. 1971. **fTD769.7.M54 ECOL**

West Virginia. University. Coal Research Bureau. Dewatering of mine drainage sludge. 1971. **fTD899.M5W44 ECOL**

SEWAGE SLUDGE—DRYING—PATENTS.
James, Ronald W. Sewage sludge treatment 1972. 1972 **REF fTD768.J35 ECOL**

SEWERAGE.
Carcich, Italo G. A pressure sewer system demonstration. 1972. **TD670.C3 ECOL**

Metcalf and Eddy, Boston. Wastewater engineering: collection, treatment, disposal. 1972 **TD645.M57 ECOL**

SEWERAGE—ABSTRACTS.
Franklin Institute, Philadelphia. Science Information Service. Selected urban storm water runoff abstracts, July 1970-June 1971. 1971. **fTD653.F7 ECOL**

Sandoski, Dorothy A. Selected urban storm water runoff abstracts, July 1971-June 1972. 1972. **fTD653.S2 ECOL**

SEWERAGE—CORROSION.
Mayer, John K. Sewer bedding and infiltration, Gulf Coast area. 1972. **fTD653.M3 ECOL**

SEWERAGE—MAINTENANCE AND REPAIRS—OHIO.
Montgomery County Sanitary Dept. Montgomery County, Ohio. Ground water infiltration and internal sealing of sanitary sewers, Montgomery County, Ohio. 1972. **fTD716.M6 ECOL**

SEWERAGE—MINNESOTA—LAKEVILLE.
Bonestroo, Rosene, Anderlik and Associates, inc., St. Paul, Minn. Report on sanitary sewerage facilities Airlake Industrial Park for Lakeville, Minnesota. 1967. **fTD525.L3B6 ECOL**

SEWERAGE—MINNESOTA—MAPLE GROVE.
Caswell and Associates, inc., Osseo, Minn. The comprehensive sanitary sewer study for the Village of Maple Grove, Minnesota. 1969. **fTD525.M28C3 ECOL**

SEWERAGE—MINNESOTA—MAYER.
Lindsey-Brauer and Associates, Inc., Eden Prairie, Minn. Mayer sewerage plan. 1970 **fTD525.M3L5 ECOL**

SEWERAGE—MINNESOTA—SOUTH ST. PAUL.
Henningson, Durham and Richardson, Inc., Omaha, Nebraska. Annual capital improvements cost estimates schedules for separation and treatment combined sewerage system, South St. Paul, Minnesota. n.d. **fTD525.S6H4 ECOL**

SEWERAGE—MINNESOTA—TWIN CITIES METROPOLITAN AREA.
Metcalf and Eddy, Boston. Sewerage and water planning report. 1968. **fTD525.T9M4 ECOL**

SEWERAGE—STANDARDS.
Mayer, John K. Sewer bedding and infiltration, Gulf Coast area. 1972. **fTD653.M3 ECOL**

SEWERAGE—UNITED STATES.
American Public Works Association. Water pollution aspects of urban runoff. 1969. **TD420.A4 ECOL**

SEWERS see STORM SEWERS

SHELLFISH.
Gibbons, Euell. Stalking the blue-eyed scallop. 1964 **TX387.G5 ECOL**

SHERBURNE COUNTY GENERATING PLANT, BECKER, MINN.
Grether, David F. Population type, distribution and density of the flora on the Sherburne County Generating Plant Site, 15 October through 31 December, 1971. 1972 **fTK1331.N6G7 ECOL**

Hopwood, Alfred J. Evaluation of fishes and bottom fauna in the Mississippi River adjacent to the NSP Sherburne County Generating Plant Site, Becker, Minnesota, during October and November, 1971. 1972 **fTK1331.N6H6 ECOL**

SHERBURNE COUNTY GENERATING PLANT, BECKER, MINNESOTA.
Black & Veatch, Kansas City, Mo. Environmental report. 1971- **fTK1331.N6B7 ECOL**

Knutson, Keith M. Evaluation of attached algae in the Mississippi River adjacent to the NSP Sherburne County Generating Plant, Becker, Minnesota, during October and November, 1971. 1972 **fTK1331.N6K5 ECOL**

SHORE BIRDS.
Stout, Gardner D. The shorebirds of North America. 1967 **fQL681.S78 ECOL**

SHORE-LINES.
Minnesota. Lakeshore Development Study. Minnesota's lakeshore. 1970- **REF GB459.5.M5M5 ECOL**

SHORE PROTECTION.
Minnesota. University. Water Resources Research Center. Proceedings of Conference on Inland Lake Renewal and Shoreland Management. 1972. **GB701.M554no.53 ECOL**

Thomsen, Arvid L. Riprap stability on earth embankments tested in large—and small-scale wave tanks. 1972. **TC533.T4 ECOL**

SHORE PROTECTION—UNITED STATES—ADDRESSES, ESSAYS, LECTURES.
Coastal zone resource management. 1971 **HC110.E5C6 ECOL**

SHRUBS—MIDDLE WEST.
Rosendahl, Carl Otto. Trees and shrubs of the upper Midwest. 1955 **QK481.R67 ECOL**

SHRUBS—NORTH AMERICA.
Petrides, George A. A field guide to trees and shrubs. 1972. **QK482.P43 1972 ECOL**

SIERRA NEVADA MOUNTAINS.
Bowen, Ezra. The high Sierra. 1972 **F868.S5B6 ECOL**

Muir, John. Gentle wilderness. Rev. ed. 1971c1968 **F868.S5M88 1971 ECOL**

SLAUGHTERING AND SLAUGHTER-HOUSES—WASTE see ANIMAL WASTE

SMELTING.
United States. Bureau of Mines. Control of sulfur oxide emissions in copper, lead, and zinc smelting. 1971 **TN295.U4no.8527 ECOL**

SMOG.
Glenn, Harold T. Automotive smog control manual. 1968 **TL152.G545 ECOL**

SMOG—BIBLIOGRAPHY.
Air Pollution Technical Information Center. Photochemical oxidants and air pollution: an annotated bibliography. 1971. **REF Z7173.A4A53 ECOL**

SMOKE PLUMES—HANDBOOKS, MANUALS, ETC.
Turner, D. Bruce. Workbook of atmospheric dispersion estimates. 1970. **fTD890.T8 1970 ECOL**

SMOKE PREVENTION—SOCIETIES, ETC.
Air Pollution Control Association. Proceedings digest of the annual meeting. 62nd- 1969- **REF TD884.A55 ECOL**

SNOW.
Couchman, J. Kenneth. Snow and ice. c1971 **QC929.S7C6 ECOL**

Thorud, David B. Freezing in forest soil as influenced by soil properties, litter, and snow. 1969. **GB701.M554no.10 ECOL**

SNOW—ST. PAUL.
Baker, Donald G. Snow cover and winter soil temperatures at St. Paul, Minn. 1971. **S594.5.B3 ECOL**

SNOW CAMPING.
Bridge, Raymond. The complete snow camper's guide. 1973 **SK602.6.B74 ECOL**

SNOWMOBILES.
Conference on Snowmobiles and All-Terrain Vechicles, London, Ontario, 1971. Proceedings. 1972 **fGV857.S6C6 1971 ECOL**

Moeller, George H. The landowner and the snowmobiler—problem or profit? 1971. **GV857.S6M6 ECOL**

Snowmobile and Off the Road Vehicle Research Symposium, Michigan State University, East Lansing, 1971. Proceedings. 1971. **fGF75.S6 1971 ECOL**

United States. Task Force on Off-Road Recreation Vehicles. Off road recreation vehicles: ORRV, a Dept. of the Interior Task Force Study. 1971. **TL234.U5 ECOL**

Wanek, Wallace J. A study of the impact of snowmobiling on northern Minnesota ecology. 1971 **fTL234.W3 ECOL**

SNOWSHOES AND SNOWSHOEING.
Burns, William. Snow, snowshoes, and nature: the white dimension of environment. 1972? **fLB1047.B8 ECOL**

SOCIAL BEHAVIOR IN ANIMALS.
Maddock, Alison. Animals at peace. 1st U.S. ed. c1971 **QL751.M216 1971 ECOL**

SOCIAL CHANGE see also INDUSTRY—SOCIAL ASPECTS
Platt, John Rader. The step to man. 1970.c1966 **HM101.P57 ECOL**

SOCIAL ETHICS.
Friends, Society of. American Friends Service Committee. Who shall live? 1970 **HQ766.3.F7 ECOL**

SOCIAL ETHICS—CONGRESSES.
Biology and ethics. 1969. **HM216.B48 ECOL**

SOCIAL HISTORY—1945-
Brown, Lester Russell. World without borders. 1972
    HC59.B765 1972b ECOL
Roszak, Theodore. Where the wasteland ends. 1972.
    HN17.5.R62 ECOL

SOCIAL PROBLEMS.
Ramo, Simon. Cure for chaos. 1969
    HN28.R3 ECOL

SOCIAL PSYCHOLOGY.
Marcel, Gabriel. Man against mass society. 1971, 1952
    B2430.M253H583 1971 ECOL

SOCIAL SCIENCE RESEARCH—CONGRESSES.
Clubb, Jerome M. Ecological data in comparative research. 1970
    H62.C6 ECOL

SOCIAL SCIENCES—ADDRESSES, ESSAYS, LECTURES.
Montagu, Ashley. Man observed. 1968
    H83.M555 ECOL

SOCIAL SCIENCES—STATISTICAL METHODS—ADDRESSES, ESSAYS, LECTURES.
Dogan, Mattei. Quantitative ecological analysis in the social sciences. 1969
    HM206.D6 ECOL

SOCIAL SCIENCES—STUDY AND TEACHING.
Henderson, Martha T. Environmental education: Social studies sources and approaches. 1970
    Ref fQH541.2.H4 ECOL
Intercom. Teaching about spaceship earth. c1972
    S946.I5 ECOL

SOCIAL SCIENCES—STUDY AND TEACHING (ELEMENTARY).
Education for survival. 1970-
    QH541.2.E4 ECOL

SOCIAL VALUES—ADDRESSES, ESSAYS, LECTURES.
Baier, Kurt. Values and the future. 1969
    HM221.B27 ECOL

SOCIOLOGY—ADDRESSES, ESSAYS, LECTURES.
Stapledon, Sir Reginald George. Human ecology. 2nd ed.; edited and introduced by Robert Waller. 1971.
    HM206.S65 1971 ECOL

SOCIOLOGY, URBAN.
McKeown, James E. The changing metropolis. 2d ed. 1971
    HT334.U5M321971ECOL

SOIL ABSORPTION.
Lin, Shen-maw. Porosity and pore-size distribution of soil aggregates. 1971.
    GB701.M554no.29 ECOL
Mein, Russell G. Modeling the infiltration component of the rainfall—runoff process. 1971.
    GB701.M554no.43 ECOL

SOIL AERATION.
Pratt, P. F. Nitrate in the unsaturated zone under agricultural lands. 1972.
    fS651.P7 ECOL

SOIL BIOLOGY.
Farb, Peter. Living earth. 1959
    QH84.8.F3 ECOL

SOIL CONSERVATION see also EROSION; SOIL EROSION
Beasley, Robert Patrick. Erosion and sediment pollution control. 1st ed. 1972 **S623.B33 ECOL**
Bunce, Arthur Cyril. The economics of soil conservation. 1950,c1942 **HD1411.B96 1950 ECOL**
Faulkner, Edward H. Plowman's folly. 1963,c1943
    S603.F36 1963 ECOL
Hudson, Norman. Soil conservation. 1972, c1971
    S623.H78 1972 ECOL
Kohnke, Helmut. Soil conservation. 1959.
    S623.K56 ECOL
Osborn, Fairfield. Our plundered planet. 1968
    S623.O8 1968 ECOL
Resources for the Future. Comparisons in resource management. 1961 **REF SD411.R4 ECOL**
Shannon, Terry. About the land, the rain, and us. 1963 **PZ10.S52Ai ECOL**
Stallings, James Henry. Soil conservation. 1957.
    S623.S73 ECOL

SOIL CONSERVATION—CONGRESSES.
National Conference on Soil, Water, and Suburbia, Washington, D.C., 1967. Soil, water, and suburbia. 1968 **fHT166.N36 1967 ECOL**

SOIL CONSERVATION—HANDBOOKS, MANUALS, ETC.
United States. Soil Conservation Service. National handbook of conservation practices. 1971.
    REF S922.U5 ECOL

SOIL CONSERVATION—MINNESOTA.
Land in Transition Symposium, 1971, St. Paul, Minn. 1971 **fS623.L3 1971 ECOL**
Major, Harry M. USDA - soil conservation service in Minnesota. 1973. **S624.M6M3 ECOL**

SOIL CONSERVATION—RESEARCH—MINNESOTA.
Minnesota. Conservation Needs Committee. Minnesota soil and water conservation needs inventory. 1971 **fHD243.M6A42 ECOL**

SOIL CONSERVATION—SOCIETIES, ETC.
Soil Conservation Society of America. Proceedings of the annual meeting, 1971- **fS900.S6 ECOL**

SOIL CONSERVATION—UNITED STATES.
Archer, Sellers Gambrell. Soil conservation. 1969
    S624.A1A7 1969 ECOL
Cook, Ray Lewis. Soil management for conservation and production. c1962 **S591.C7 ECOL**
Held, R. Burnell. Soil conservation in perspective. 1965 **S624.A1H4 ECOL**
Maryland. Dept. of Water Resources. Guidelines for erosion and sediment control, planning and implementation. 1972. **fS624.A1M3 ECOL**
National Association of Counties Research Foundation. Urban soil erosion and sediment control. 1970. **fS624.A1N38 ECOL**
Neal, Harry Edward. Nature's guardians. 1966,c1963 **SK361.N45 1966 ECOL**
Powell, Mel D. Community action guidebook for soil erosion and sediment control. 1970
    fS624.A1P68 ECOL
Van Dersal, William Richard. The land renewed. Rev. and enl. ed. 1968. **S624.A1V3 1968 ECOL**

SOIL CONSERVATION—UNITED STATES—HANDBOOKS, MANUALS, ETC.
United States. Soil Conservation Service. Resource conservation and development projects: handbook. 1972 **S914.A57 1972 ECOL**

SOIL CONSERVATION—UNITED STATES—PERIODICALS.
United States. Agricultural Stabilization and Conservation Service. Rural environmental assistance program: summary. 1971- 1972-
    S954.U6A3 ECOL

SOIL EROSION see also SOIL CONSERVATION
Beasley, Robert Patrick. Erosion and sediment pollution control. 1st ed. 1972 **S623.B33 ECOL**
Hudson, Norman. Soil conservation. 1972, c1971
    S623.H78 1972 ECOL
Van Dersal, William Richard. The land renewed. Rev. and enl. ed. 1968. **S624.A1V3 1968 ECOL**

SOIL EROSION—UNITED STATES.
Maryland. Dept. of Water Resources. Guidelines for erosion and sediment control, planning and implementation. 1972. **fS624.A1M3 ECOL**
National Association of Counties Research Foundation. Urban soil erosion and sediment control. 1970. **fS624.A1N38 ECOL**
Powell, Mel D. Community action guidebook for soil erosion and sediment control. 1970
    fS624.A1P68 ECOL

SOIL FAUNA.
Rhine, Richard. Life in a bucket of soil. 1972
    QL110.R48 ECOL
Schaller, Friedrich. Soil animals. 1968
    QL110.S313 ECOL

SOIL FERTILITY.
Cook, Ray Lewis. Soil management for conservation and production. c1962 **S591.C7 ECOL**
Minnesota. University. Agricultural Extension Service. Soils, soil management and fertilizer monographs. 1973. **fS591.M68 ECOL**

SOIL FREEZING.
Thorud, David B. Freezing in forest soil as influenced by soil properties, litter, and snow. 1969.
    GB701.M554no.10 ECOL

SOIL MECHANICS.
Hanson, Lowell D. Soils of the Twin Cities Metropolitan area and their relation to urban development. 1967, c1966
    fS599.M45H3 1967 ECOL

SOIL MICRO-ORGANISMS.
Boyce Thompson Institute for Plant Research, Yonkers, N.Y. Interaction of herbicides and soil microorganisms. 1971. **fSB951.4.B68 ECOL**

SOIL MICRO-ORGANISMS—CONGRESSES.
International Symposium on Factors Determining the Behavior of Plant Pathogens in Soil, Berkeley, Calif., 1963. Ecology of soil-borne plant pathogens.
    fQR111.I55 1963 ECOL

SOIL MOISTURE.
Arya, Lalit Mohan. Water flow in soil in presence of soybean root sinks. 1973. **GB701.M554no.60 ECOL**

SOIL PERCOLATION.
Pratt, P. F. Nitrate in the unsaturated zone under agricultural lands. 1972. **fS651.P7 ECOL**

SOIL RESEARCH.
Thorud, David B. Freezing in forest soil as influenced by soil properties, litter, and snow. 1969.
    GB701.M554no.10 ECOL

SOIL SCIENCE.
Berger, Kermit Carl. Sun, soil, and survival. 1972
    S591.B45 1972 ECOL
Bridges, Edwin Michael. World soils. 1970.
    S591.B85 ECOL
Buckman, Harry Oliver. The nature and properties of soils. 7th ed. 1969 **S591.B88 1969 ECOL**
Gibson, J. Sullivan. Soils: their nature, classes, distribution, uses, and care. 1970 **S591.G52 ECOL**
Heady, Eleanor B. The soil that feeds us. 1972
    PZ10.H42So ECOL
May, Julian. The living blanket on the land. 1972
    S591.3.M39 1972 ECOL
Minnesota. University. Agricultural Extension Service. Soils, soil management and fertilizer monographs. 1973. **fS591.M68 ECOL**

SOIL STRUCTURE.
Fuentes, Victor C. Soil matric suction changes with time in pressed soil briquettes. 1971.
    GB701.M554no.33 ECOL
Lin, Shen-maw. Porosity and pore-size distribution of soil aggregates. 1971. **GB701.M554no.29 ECOL**

SOIL TEMPERATURE.
Baker, Donald G. Snow cover and winter soil temperatures at St. Paul, Minn. 1971.
    S594.5.B3 ECOL

SOILS.
Bartlett, Margaret Farrington. Down the mountain. c1963. **PZ10.B1748Do ECOL**
Bear, Firman Edward. Earth, the stuff of life. 1962
    S591.B33 ECOL
Cook, Ray Lewis. Soil management for conservation and production. c1962 **S591.C7 ECOL**
Faulkner, Edward H. Plowman's folly. 1963,c1943
    S603.F36 1963 ECOL
Faulkner, Edward Hubert. Soil development. 1952
    S603.F37 ECOL
Goldin, Augusta R. Where does your garden grow? 1967 **PZ10.G564Wh ECOL**
Heady, Eleanor B. The soil that feeds us. 1972
    PZ10.H42So ECOL
May, Julian. The living blanket on the land. 1972
    S591.3.M39 1972 ECOL

SOILS—MINNESOTA—TWIN CITIES METROPOLITAN AREA.
Hanson, Lowell D. Soils of the Twin Cities Metropolitan area and their relation to urban development. 1967, c1966 **fS599.M45H3 1967 ECOL**

SOILS—UNITED STATES—COMPOSITION.
Elemental composition of surficial materials in the conterminous United States: an account of the amounts of certain chemical elements. 1971.
    REF fQE75.P9no.574-D ECOL

SOLAR RADIATION see also VAN ALLEN RADIATION BELTS
Leighton, Philip Albert. Photochemistry of air pollution. 1961. **RA576.L4 ECOL**

SOLID WASTE MANAGEMENT see SALVAGE (WASTE, ETC.)

SOLUBILITY.
United States. National Bureau of Standards. Analytical Chemistry Division. Interaction of nitrilotriacetic acid with suspended and bottom material. 1971. **fTD427.D4U64 ECOL**

SOLUBLE GLASS.
Hulbert, Samuel F. Design of a water-disposable glass packaging container. 1971. **TD799.H8 ECOL**

SONIC BOOM.
United States. National Bureau of Standards. The effects of sonic boom and similar impulsive noise on structures. 1971. **TL574.S55U54 ECOL**

SOUND PRODUCTION BY ANIMALS.
The Language and music of the wolves. c1971
    PhonodiscQL765.L32 ECOL
Mason, George Frederick. Animal sounds. 1948.
    QL765.M3 ECOL

SOUND-WAVES—PHYSIOLOGICAL EFFECT.
United States. National Bureau of Standards. Fundamentals of Noise: measurement, rating schemes, and Standards. 1971 i.e. 1972 **fQC243.U55 ECOL**

SOUTHWEST, NEW—DESCRIPTION AND TRAVEL.
Findley, Rowe. Great American deserts. 1972
    F787.F5 ECOL

SOYBEAN.
Arya, Lalit Mohan. Water flow in soil in presence of soybean root sinks. 1973. **GB701.M554no.60 ECOL**

SPACE LAW.
Lay, S. Houston. The law relating to activities of man in space. 1970 **REF fJX5810.L39 ECOL**

SPACE VEHICLES—NUCLEAR POWER PLANTS.
Corliss, William R. Nuclear Propulsion for space. 1967 **TL783.5.C62 ECOL**

SPOONBILLS.
Allen, Robert Porter. On the trail of vanishing birds. 1957 **QL696.G8A4 ECOL**

SPORT FISHING RESEARCH see FISHERIES—RESEARCH

SPRING.
Carrick, Carol. Swamp spring. 1969 **PZ10.C3297Sw ECOL**
Teale, Edwin Way. North with the spring. c1951 **QH104.T42 ECOL**

STATE AND ENVIRONMENT see ENVIRONMENTAL POLICY

STATE PLANNING see REGIONAL PLANNING

STATICS AND DYNAMICS (SOCIAL SCIENCES).
Forrester, Jay Wright. World dynamics. 1971 **HD82.F63 ECOL**

STEAM POWER-PLANTS.
Cootner, Paul H. Water demand for steam electric generation. 1966,c1965 **TK1051.C6 ECOL**

STEAM POWER-PLANTS—COOLING.
Dynatech R/D Company. A survey of alternate methods for cooling condenser discharge water. 1969- **fTJ403.D9 ECOL**

STEAM POWER-PLANTS—UNITED STATES.
United States. Federal Power Commission. Steam-electric plant air and water quality control data for the year ended December 31, 1969, based on EPC form no. 67. 1973. **fTD195.E4U5 ECOL**

STEEL-WORKS—WASTE DISPOSAL.
National Steel Corporation. Weirton Steel Division. Combined steel mill and municipal waste-waters treatment. 1972. **fTD899.S7N37 ECOL**

STOCK POISONING PLANTS—MIDDLE WEST.
Evers, Robert August. Poisonous plants of the Midwest & their effects on livestock. 1972 **SB617.E9 ECOL**

STORM SEWERS.
Barr Engineering Co. The drainage plan for Burnsville, Minnesota. 1966. **fTD525.B8B3 ECOL**
Linsley, Ray K. A manual on collection of hydrologic data for urban drainage design. 1973. **fTD665.L55 ECOL**
Minnesota. University. St. Anthony Falls Hydraulic Laboratory. Hydraulics of long vertical conduits and associated cavitation. 1971. **fTC174.M53 ECOL**
Sartor, James D. Water pollution aspects of street surface contaminants. 1972. **fTD665.S2 ECOL**
Stall, John B. Storm sewer design—an evaluation of the RRL method. 1972. **TD665.S7 ECOL**

STREAM ECOLOGY.
Gammon, James Robert. The effect of inorganic sediment on stream biota. 1970. **fQH541.5.S7G34 ECOL**
Hynes, Hugh Bernard Noel. The ecology of running waters. 1970. **QH541.5.S7H9 ECOL**

STREAM ECOLOGY—UNITED STATES.
Pringle, Laurence P. Wild river. 1st ed. 1972 **fQH541.5.S7P75 ECOL**

STREAM MEASUREMENTS.
Battelle Memorial Institute. Columbus, Ohio. Columbus Laboratories Multidirectional turbulence probe development. **fTC177.B3 ECOL**

STREAM MEASUREMENTS—MINNESOTA—YEARBOOKS.
United States. Geological Survey. Water Resources Division. Water resources data for Minnesota, 1968- **REF GB705.M62A32 ECOL**

STREAM MEASUREMENTS—UNITED STATES—PERIODICALS.
United States. Geological Survey. Surface water supply of the United States. 1961/65- **TC801.U2 ECOL**

STREAM SEDIMENT TRANSPORT see SEDIMENT TRANSPORT

STREAM SELF-PURIFICATION.
Frea, James I. Washout processes in lake systems. 1972. **fTD764.F74 ECOL**

STREET CLEANING.
American Public Works Association. Water pollution aspects of urban runoff. 1969. **TD420.A4 ECOL**

STREETS—BIBLIOGRAPHY.
Ehrenthal, Frank F. A selected bibliography on uses of the urban street. 1972. **REF fZ7164.T81E3 ECOL**

STRIP MINING.
Caudill, Harry M. My land is dying. 1st ed. 1971. **TN291.C37 1971 ECOL**
Stacks, John F. Stripping. 1972 **TN291.S7 ECOL**
Virginia Polytechnic Institute and State University. Stream faunal recovery after manganese strip mine reclamation. 1971. **fTN291.V5 ECOL**

STRONTIUM—ISOTOPES.
Loutit, John F. Irradiation of mice and men. 1962 **QH652.L63 ECOL**

STUDDED TIRES.
Minnesota. Dept. of Highways. A research progress report on the effects of studded tires. 1970. **fTL270.M5 1970 ECOL**
Minnesota. Dept. of Highways. A research summary report on the effects of studded tires. 1971. **fTL270.M5 1971 ECOL**

SUBJECT HEADINGS—EDUCATION.
United States. Educational Resources Information Center. Thesaurus of ERIC descriptors, with a special chapter on The role and function of the thesaurus in education. 1972. **REF fZ695.1.E3U5 1972 ECOL**

SUBJECT HEADINGS—HYDROLOGY.
Water Resources Scientific Information Center. Water resources thesaurus. 2d ed. 1971 **REF Z695.1.W3W3 1971 ECOL**

SUBJECT HEADINGS—WATER RESOURCES DEVELOPMENT.
United States. Bureau of Reclamation. Thesaurus of water resources terms. 1971. **REF Z695.1.W3U52 ECOL**
Water Resources Scientific Information Center. Water resources thesaurus. 2d ed. 1971 **REF Z695.1.W3W3 1971 ECOL**

SUBSOIL RIGHTS see MINING LAW

SUBTERRANEAN WATER see WATER, UNDERGROUND

SUBURBS.
McCue, George. Ecology: the suburbs. c1971 **QH541.5.C6M22 Suppl. ECOL**

SUBWAYS—MINNEAPOLIS.
Minneapolis. Office of the City Coordinator. Regional transit for Minneapolis: interim report. 1972. **fHE4491.M62 1972 ECOL**

SUGAR—MANUFACTURE AND REFINING—WASTE DISPOSAL.
Beet Sugar Development Foundation, Fort Collins, Colo. State-of-art, sugarbeet processing waste treatment. 1971. **fTD899.S8B43 ECOL**

SULFUR OXIDES.
United States. Bureau of Mines. Control of sulfur oxide emissions in copper, lead, and zinc smelting. 1971 **TN295.U4no.8527 ECOL**

SULPHATES.
Smith, Edwin Earle. Sulfide to sulfate reaction mechanism. 1970. **fTN321.S58 ECOL**

SULPHIDES.
Smith, Edwin Earle. Sulfide to sulfate reaction mechanism. 1970. **fTN321.S58 ECOL**

SULPHITE PULPING PROCESS.
Crown Zellerbach Corporation. Lebanon Division. Aerated lagoon treatment of sulfite pulping effluents. 1970. **fTD899.W65C7 ECOL**

SULPHUR.
Black, Sivalls and Bryson, Inc., Kansas City, Mo. Applied Technology Division Study of sulfur recovery from coal refuse. 1971. **fTN890.B57 ECOL**

SULPHUR DIOXIDE.
Haas, Larry A. Sulfur dioxide: its chemistry as related to methods for removing it from waste gases. 1973 **TN23.U7no.8608 ECOL**
Selected studies on alkaline additives for sulfur dioxide control. 1971. **TD885.5.S8S4 ECOL**

SULPHUR DIOXIDE—TOXICOLOGY.
United States. Environmental Protection Agency. National Environmental Research Center. Toxicology of atmospheric sulfur dioxide decay products. 1972. **TD885.5.S8U5 ECOL**

SUMMER.
Teale, Edwin Way. Journey into summer. 1960. **QH104.T39 ECOL**

SUN—RADIATION see SOLAR RADIATION

SUPERIOR, LAKE.
Agassiz, Louis. Lake Superior. 1970, c1850 **QH104.5.G7A35 1970 ECOL**
International Great Lakes Levels Board. Regulation of Great Lakes water levels: interim report on Lakes Superior and Ontario regulation, to the International Joint Commission by the International Great Lakes Levels Board. 1973. **fGB1627.G8I52 ECOL**
Mengel, J. T. Geology of the western Lake Superior region. 1970. **fQE78.M4 ECOL**
Minnesota. University. School of Public Health. Lake Superior study, summer of 1956. 1957 **fGB1627.G89M5 ECOL**
Minnesota. University School of Public Health. Lake Superior study, summer of 1956: summary of report. 1957. **fGB1627.G89M53 ECOL**
Minnesota. University. School of Public Health. A preliminary investigation of nutrients in western Lake Superior, 1958-1959. 1959. **fGB1627.G89M52 ECOL**
Minnesota. University. School of Public Health. Water movements and temperatures of western Lake Superior. 1958. **fGB1627.G89M54 ECOL**
Steinhacker, Charles. Superior. 1971? **fF552.S725 ECOL**

SUPERIOR, LAKE—ABSTRACTS.
Water Resources Scientific Information Center. Lake Superior. 1972 **fZ6005.G7W38 ECOL**

SUPERIOR, LAKE—BIBLIOGRAPHY.
Water Resources Scientific Information Center. Lake Superior. 1972 **fZ6005.G7W38 ECOL**

SUPERIOR LAKE—RESEARCH.
Minnesota. University. School of Public Health. Lake Superior studies, 1956-61. 1957-61 **fGB1627.G89M55 ECOL**

SUPERPHOSPHATES see PHOSPHATES

SUPPLY AND DEMAND.
Green, James L. Economic ecology. c1969 **HT167.G74 ECOL**

SURFACE ACTIVE AGENTS see also DETERGENTS, SYNTHETIC

IIT Research Institute. Technology Center. Development of phosphate-free home laundry detergents. 1970. **fTP992.5.I2 ECOL**

SURFACE WATER SEWERS see STORM SEWERS

SURPLUS AGRICULTURAL COMMODITIES, AMERICAN.
Paddock, William. Famine, 1975! c1967 **HD9000.5.P22 ECOL**

SURVEYS.
Bennett, Dean B. Guidelines for planning and implementing a comprehensive community environmental inventory. Rev. ed. 1972. **fQH541.2.B38 1972 ECOL**
Herfindahl, Orris Clemens. Natural resources information for economic development; a study. 1969 **GA51.H47 ECOL**

SUSPENDED LOAD OF STREAMS see SEDIMENT TRANSPORT

SWANS.
Phillips, John Charles. American waterfowl. 1930. **QL696.A5P45 ECOL**
Scott, Peter Markham. The swans. 1972. **QL696.A5S37 ECOL**

SYLVICULTURE see FORESTS AND FORESTRY

SYMBIOSIS.
Dudley, Ruth Hubbell. Partners in nature. 1965 **QH548.D8 ECOL**
Friendly, Natalie. Wildlife teams. c1963 **PZ10.F7153Wi ECOL**

SYNTHETIC DETERGENTS see DETERGENTS, SYNTHETIC

SYSTEM ANALYSIS.
Beckers, Charles V. Quantitative methods for preliminary design of water quality surveillance systems. 1972. **TD365.B4 ECOL**
Bishop, A. Bruce. Analysis of water reuse alternatives in an integrated urban and agricultural area. 1971 **fTD429.B5 ECOL**
Dracup, John A. Applications of systems analysis techniques to water resources. 1972. **fTC409.D7 ECOL**
Hydroscience, Inc. Limnological systems analysis of the Great Lakes. 1973. **fTC423.3.H9 ECOL**
Use of systems techniques in environmental quality management. 1970. **RA565.A1N38no.7 ECOL**

SYSTEM ANALYSIS—ABSTRACTS.
Enviro Control, Inc. Systems analysis for water quality management—survey and abstracts. 1971. **fTD365.E5 ECOL**

SYSTEM THEORY.
Ramo, Simon. Cure for chaos. 1969 **HN28.R3 ECOL**
Science Curriculum Improvement Study. Interaction and systems. c1970 **LB1585.S36 ECOL**

SYSTEMATICS (BIOLOGY) see BIOLOGY—CLASSIFICATION

T

TACONITE.
Davis, Edward Wilson. Pioneering with taconite. 1964. **TN403.M6D3 ECOL**

TACONITE—MINNESOTA.
Nelson, Clarence Walfred. An ex ante profitability analysis of capital investment in taconite pellet production facilities in Minnesota circa 1950-51. 1967. **HD9517.M6N4 ECOL**

TAIGA ECOLOGY—ARCTIC REGIONS.
Fuller, William Albert. The life of the far north. 1972. **QH541.5.T8F84 ECOL**

TALL BUILDINGS.
United States. Environmental Protection Agency. Solid waste handling and disposal in multi-story buildings and hospitals. 1972- **TD788.A3 ECOL**

TASTE.
Collins, Ralph P. Characterization of taste and odors in water supplies. 1971. **fTD384.C64 ECOL**

TAXONOMY (BIOLOGY) see BIOLOGY—CLASSIFICATION

TEACHER-STUDENT RELATIONSHIPS.
Environmental studies. Rev. ed.? 1971,c1970 **LB1027.E6 1971 ECOL**

TECHNICAL WRITING.
Arny, Mary (Travis). Ecology: a writer's handbook. 1st ed. 1972 **QH541.A72 ECOL**

TECHNOLOGICAL FORECASTING.
Ayres, Robert U. Technological forecasting and long-range planning. 1969 **T174.A9 ECOL**

TECHNOLOGY—ADDRESSES, ESSAYS, LECTURES.
Fuller, Richard Buckminster. Approaching the benign environment. 1970 **Q171.F96 ECOL**

TECHNOLOGY—DICTIONARIES.
McGraw-Hill encyclopedia of science and technology. 3d ed. 1971 **REF fQ121.M3 1971 ECOL**

TECHNOLOGY—PHILOSOPHY.
Fuller, Richard Buckminster. Operating manual for spaceship earth. 1969 **T14.F84 ECOL**

TECHNOLOGY—SOCIAL ASPECTS.
Northern States Power Co. Lake Itasca seminar. 1972? **REF fHM221.N6 1971 ECOL**
Northern States Power Company. Lake Itasca seminar. 1st 1971- **REF fHM221.N6 ECOL**

TECHNOLOGY—SOCIAL ASPECTS—ADDRESSES, ESSAYS, LECTURES.
Moore, Wilbert Ellis. Technology and social change. 1972 **T14.5.M66 1972 ECOL**

TECHNOLOGY—SOCIAL ASPECTS—CONGRESSES.
Are our descendants doomed? 1972 **HB849.A74 1972 ECOL**

TECHNOLOGY—UNITED STATES—INFORMATION SERVICES.
United States. Library of Congress. National Referral Center. A directory of information resources in the United States; physical sciences, engineering. 1971. **REF Q223.U526 1971 ECOL**

TECHNOLOGY AND CIVILIZATION see also
SOCIAL PROBLEMS; TECHNOLOGY—PHILOSOPHY; TECHNOLOGY—SOCIAL ASPECTS
Barbour, Ian G. Western man and environmental ethics. 1973 **GF80.B37 ECOL**
Calder, Nigel. Technopolis. 1970 **HM221.C35 1970 ECOL**
Dubos, Rene Jules. A God within. 1972 **HM206.D86 ECOL**
Dubos, Rene Jules. So human an animal. 1968 **HM206.D87 ECOL**
Fabun, Don. Dimensions of change. 1971 **fHM221.F32 ECOL**
Ferkiss, Victor C. Technological man: the myth and the reality. 1969 **HM221.F39 ECOL**
Flowers, William J. Western cultural tradition and human survival: the role of value orientations in the environmental crisis. c1971 **GF80.F5 ECOL**
Forbes, Robert James. The conquest of nature. 1968 **CB478.F57 ECOL**
Fuller, Richard Buckminster. Operating manual for spaceship earth. 1969 **T14.F84 ECOL**
Higbee, Edward Counselman. A question of priorities. 1970. **HN65.H5 ECOL**
McHale, John. The future of the future. 1969 **CB161.M3 ECOL**
McHale, John. The future of the future. 1971 **CB161.M3 1971 ECOL**
Northern States Power Co. Lake Itasca seminar. 1972? **REF fHM221.N6 1971 ECOL**
Northern States Power Company. Lake Itasca seminar. 1st 1971- **REF fHM221.N6 ECOL**
Schwartz, Eugene S. Overskill. 1971. **CB478.S38 1971 ECOL**

TECHNOLOGY AND CIVILIZATION—ADDRESSES, ESSAYS, LECTURES.
Baier, Kurt. Values and the future. 1969 **HM221.B27 ECOL**
Mesthene, Emmanuel G. Technological change: its impact on man and society. 1970. **HM221.M47 1970 ECOL**
Urban, George R. Can we survive our future? 1972, c1971 **CB428.U7 1972 ECOL**

TECHNOLOGY AND CIVILIZATION—CONGRESSES.
Engineering for the benefit of mankind. 1970. **TA5.E52 ECOL**

TEMPERATURE—PHYSIOLOGICAL EFFECT.
Auliciems, Andris. The atmospheric environment. 1972 **QP82.2.T4A9 ECOL**

TENNESSEE VALLEY AUTHORITY.
Lilienthal, David, Eli. TVA; democracy on the march. c1953 **TK1425.M8L53 1953 ECOL**

TERRARIUMS.
Hoke, John. Terrariums. 1972. **QH68.H65 ECOL**

TERRITORIALITY (ZOOLOGY).
Ecological studies of the timber wolf in northeastern Minnesota. 1971 **SD11.A45476no.52 ECOL**

TEXTILE WASTE.
American Enka Corporation. Central Engineering Dept. Zinc precipitation and recovery from viscose rayon waste water. 1971. **fTD899.T4A44 ECOL**
Clemson University. Dept. of Textiles. State of the art of textile waste treatment. 1971. **fTD899.T4C45 ECOL**

THERMAL POLLUTION OF RIVERS, LAKES, ETC.
Cornell Aeronautical Laboratory, Inc., Buffalo. Research on the physical aspects of thermal pollution. 1971. **fTD427.H4C67 ECOL**
Lapp, Ralph E. A citizen's guide to nuclear power. c1971. **TK1078.L3 ECOL**
Minnesota. Dept. of Health. Division of Environmental Health. Section of Water Pollution Control. Report on application for waste disposal permit. 1965. **fTK1331.N6M6 ECOL**
Northern States Power Company. Engineering Department. Environmental monitoring program. 1970. **REF fTK1331.N6A42 1970 ECOL**
Northern States Power Company. Engineering Dept. Environmental monitoring program for the Allen S. King generating plant at Oak Park Heights, Minnesota. 1966. **fTK1331.N6A4 ECOL**
Stefan, Heinz. Surface discharge of heated water. 1971 i.e. 1972 **fTD427.H4S64 ECOL**
United Aircraft Corporation. Research Laboratories, East Hartford, Conn. Advanced nonthermally polluting gas turbines in utility applications. 1971. **fTJ778.U5 ECOL**
United States. Atomic Energy Commission. Nuclear Power and the environment. 1969. **TK1343.A46 ECOL**
United States. Environmental Protection Agency Pacific Northwest Water Laboratory. A method for predicting the performance of draft cooling towers. 1970. **fTP159.C6U5 ECOL**
Wapora Inc. The effect of temperature on aquatic life in the Ohio River: summary, July—December, 1970. 1971 **fTD427.H4W3 ECOL**

THERMAL POLLUTION OF RIVERS, LAKES, ETC.—BIBLIOGRAPHY.
Raney, Edward Cowden. Heated effluents and effects on aquatic life with emphasis on fishes. 3rd ed. 1969. **REF Z7173.W3R3 1969 ECOL**

THERMAL POLLUTION OF RIVERS, LAKES, ETC.—CONGRESSES.
National Symposium on Thermal Pollution, Portland, Oregon, 1968. Biological aspects of thermal pollution. 1969 **QH90.N3 1968 ECOL**
National Symposium on Thermal Pollution, Vanderbilt University, 1968. Engineering aspects of thermal pollution. 1969. **TD427.H4N3 1968 ECOL**

THERMAL POLLUTION OF RIVERS, LAKES, ETC.—MATHEMATICAL MODELS.
Campbell, J. F. Analysis of the injection of a heated turbulent jet into a moving mainstream, with emphasis on a thermal discharge in a waterway. 1972. **fTD427.H4C3 ECOL**
Robideau, R. F. The discharge of submerged bouyant jets into water of finite depth. 1972. **fTD427.H4R6 ECOL**
United States. Environmental Protection Agency. Office of Research and Monitoring. Workbook of thermal plume prediction. 1972- **TD427.H4U54 ECOL**

THERMAL POLLUTION OF RIVERS, LAKES, ETC.—RESEARCH.
Illinois. Water Survey. Research needs on waste heat transfer from large sources into the environment. 1971. **fTD427.H4I4 ECOL**

THERMAL POLLUTION OF RIVERS, LAKES, ETC.—UNITED STATES.
United States. Atomic Energy Commission. Division of Reactor Development and Technology. Thermal effects and United States nuclear power stations. 1971. **TD427.H4U52 ECOL**

THERMAL WATERS see GEOTHERMAL RESOURCES

THIOBACILLUS FERROOXIDANS.
Syracuse University. Dept. of Biology. Inorganic sulfur oxidation by iron-oxidizing bacteria. 1971. **fQR84.S95 ECOL**

TIMBER—NORTHWEST, PACIFIC—CONGRESSES.
Current Issues Conference, 1st, Portland, Or., 1972. Timber supply and the environment. 1972 **SD144.A13C87 1972 ECOL**

TIMBER CLEARCUTTING see CLEAR-CUTTING

TORREY CANYON (SHIP).
Cowan, Edward. Oil and water. 1968 **VK1255.T65C6 ECOL**
Marine Biological Association of the United Kingdom. Laboratory, Plymouth. 'Torrey Canyon' pollution and marine life: a report by the Plymouth Laboratory of the Marine Biological Association of the United Kingdom. 1968. **GC1311.M37 ECOL**
Petrow, Richard. In the wake of Torrey Canyon. 1st American ed. 1968 **G530.T72P4 1968 ECOL**

TOXICOLOGY.
National Research Council. Committee on Toxicology. Principles and procedures for evaluating the toxicity of household substances. 1964. **REF RA1221.N3 ECOL**

TOXICOLOGY—ABSTRACTS.
Excerpta Medica Foundations. Poisoning and intoxication by trace elements in children: an abstract review of the world-wide medical literature 1966-1971. 1973 **RA1211.E9 ECOL**

TRACKING AND TRAILING.
Mason, George Frederick. Animal tracks. 1943. **SK282.M3 ECOL**

TRACKLAYING VEHICLES.
United States. Task Force on Off-Road Recreation Vehicles. Off road recreation vehicles: ORRV, a Dept. of the Interior Task Force Study. 1971. **TL234.U5 ECOL**

TRADES—WASTE see FACTORY AND TRADE WASTE

TRAFFIC see COMMUNICATION AND TRAFFIC

TRAFFIC ENGINEERING.
Antoniou, Jim. Environmental management planning for traffic. c1971 **fHE333.A57 ECOL**
Leibbrand, Kurt. Transportation and town planning. 1970, c1964 **HE333.L3813 1970 ECOL**

TRAFFIC ENGINEERING—BIBLIOGRAPHY.
Hickok, Beverly. Goals, objectives and values: selected references relating to national, state and urban or regional areas, covering general & transportation aspects. 1973 **fZ7164.O7H49 ECOL**

TRAFFIC ENGINEERING—UNITED STATES.
Pell, Claiborne de B. Megalopolis unbound. c1966 **HE355.P4 ECOL**

TRAFFIC NOISE.
Cook, David I. Trees and shrubs for noise abatement. 1971. **TD893.C6 ECOL**

TRAFFIC NOISE—CONGRESSES.
Transportation noises: a symposium on acceptability criteria. 1970 **TA365.T68 ECOL**

TRAILS—UNITED STATES.
Lennon, J. Establishing trails on rights-of-way. n.d. **G504.L4 ECOL**

TRANSIT SYSTEMS see LOCAL TRANSIT

TRANSPORTATION.
Gunston, Bill. Transportation. 1972 **HE151.G85 ECOL**
Minnesota. State Planning Agency. State of Minnesota narrative report for the 1972 National Transportation Needs Study. 1971. **REF fTA1123.M5 ECOL**

TRANSPORTATION—STUDY AND TEACHING.
Peterson, Roger A. Transportation and the environment. 1971. **HE192.A1P4 ECOL**

TRANSPORTATION—UNITED STATES.
Saltonstall, Richard. Brownout & slow-down. c1972 **HC110.E5S33 ECOL**

TRANSPORTATION—UNITED STATES—BIBLIOGRAPHY.
Sloss, George J. Environmental aspects of transportation planning (a revision of CPL Exchange bibliography no. 218). 1972
REF fZ7164.T8S55 ECOL

TRANSPORTATION AND STATE—UNITED STATES.
Robinson, John. Highways and our environment. 1971 **HE355.R6 ECOL**

TRANSPORTATION, AUTOMOTIVE—UNITED STATES.
Buel, Ronald A. Dead end: the automobile in mass transportation. 1972 **HE5623.B82 ECOL**

TRANSPORTATION, AUTOMOTIVE—UNITED STATES—LAWS AND REGULATIONS.
United States. Ad Hoc Committee on the Cumulative Regulatory Effects on the Cost of Automotive Transportation. Cumulative regulatory effects on the cost of automotive transportation (RECAT): final report. 1972. **KF2209.A3U5 ECOL**

TRASH see REFUSE AND REFUSE DISPOSAL

TREES.
Cooper, Elizabeth K. A tree is something wonderful. c1972 **PZ10.C779Tr ECOL**
Cormack, Maribelle. First book of trees. c1951 **QK475.C59 ECOL**
Fenton, Carroll Lane. Trees and their world. 1957 **QK482.F4 ECOL**
Ketchum, Richard M. The secret life of the forest. 1970 **fQK938.F6K4 ECOL**

TREES—CANADA—IDENTIFICATION.
Miller, Howard A. How to know the trees. 2d ed. 1972 **REF QK482.M65 1972 ECOL**
Montgomery, Frederick Howard. Trees of the northern United States and Canada. 1970
QK481.M7 ECOL

TREES—DISEASES AND PESTS see also INSECTICIDES; PLANT DISEASES
Hepting, George H. Diseases of forest and shade trees of the United States. 1971.
REF SB761.H4 ECOL
Schwartz, George I. Life in a log. 1972
QH541.5.F6S39 ECOL

TREES—GREAT BASIN.
Antevs, Ernst. Rainfall and tree growth in the Great basin... 1938. **QC925.1.U35 1938 ECOL**

TREES—GROWTH.
Wilson, Brayton Fuller. The growing tree. 1970.
QK731.W46 ECOL

TREES—IDENTIFICATION.
Gallob, Edward. City leaves, city trees. 1972
fQK475.8.G35 ECOL
Miller, Howard A. How to know the trees. 2d ed. 1972 **REF QK482.M65 1972 ECOL**

TREES—MIDDLE WEST.
Rosendahl, Carl Otto. Trees and shrubs of the upper Midwest. 1955 **QK481.R67 ECOL**

TREES—NORTH AMERICA.
Fenton, Carroll Lane. Trees and their world. 1957
QK482.F4 ECOL
Hough, Romeyn Beck. Handbook of the trees of the northern states and Canada east of the Rocky Mountains. Third and rev. ed. 1924.
REF QK481H8 1924 ECOL
Petrides, George A. A field guide to trees and shrubs. 1972. **QK482.P43 1972 ECOL**

TREES—NORTH AMERICA—IDENTIFICATION.
Brockman, Christian Frank. Trees of North America. 1968 **QK481.B864 ECOL**

TREES—PACIFIC STATES.
United States. Forest Service. Forest trees of the Pacific slope. 1908. **REF QK481.S95 ECOL**

TREES—PICTORIAL WORKS.
Feininger, Andreas. Trees. 1968
fQK475.F4 ECOL

TREES—UNITED STATES.
Platt, Rutherford Hayes. A pocket guide to trees. 1972,c1952 **QK482.P5 1972 ECOL**

TREES—UNITED STATES—ATLASES.
Little, Elbert Luther. Atlas of United States trees. 1971- **REF fS21.A46no.1146 ECOL**

TREES—UNITED STATES—IDENTIFICATION.
Miller, Howard A. How to know the trees. 2d ed. 1972 **REF QK482.M65 1972 ECOL**
Montgomery, Frederick Howard. Trees of the northern United States and Canada. 1970
QK481.M7 ECOL

TRICHLOROPHENOXYACETIC ACID.
United States. President's Science Advisory Committee. Report on 2, 4, 5-T. 1971.
SB612.A2A52 ECOL

Whiteside, Thomas. The withering rain. 1st ed. 1971. **QH545.P4W48 1971 ECOL**

TRICHODERMA.
Green Giant Company. Pilot plant installation for fungal treatment of vegetable canning wastes. 1971.
fTD899.C3G74 ECOL

TROPICAL PLANTS.
Tosco, Uberto. The flowering wilderness. 1972
QK50.T6713 ECOL

TROPICS.
Price, Archibald Grenfell. White settlers in the tropics. 1939. **GF51.P7 ECOL**

TROUT.
United States. Environmental Protection Agency. Induced aeration of small mountain lakes. 1970.
fSH167.T86U5 ECOL

TULE ELK.
McCullough, Dale R. The tule elk. 1971c1969
QL1.C15vol.88 ECOL

TUNDRA ECOLOGY—ARCTIC REGIONS.
Fuller, William Albert. The life of the far north. 1972. **QH541.5.T8F84 ECOL**

TURBELLARIA.
Kenk, Roman. Freshwater planarians (Turbellaria) of North America. 1972. **fQH96.A2B5no.1 ECOL**

TURBULENCE.
Battelle Memorial Institute. Columbus, Ohio. Columbus Laboratories Multidirectional turbulence probe development. **fTC177.B3 ECOL**
Harris, Douglas H. Assessment of turbidity, color and odor in water. 1972. **fTD380.H3 ECOL**

TWENTIETH CENTURY.
Marcel, Gabriel. Man against mass society. 1971, 1952 **B2430.M253H583 1971 ECOL**

TWENTY-FIRST CENTURY—FORECASTS.
American Academy of Arts and Sciences, Boston. Commission on the Year 2000 Toward the year 2000. 1970,c1968 **E169.1.A47192 1970 ECOL**
McHale, John. The ecological context. 1970
GF41.M3 ECOL
McHale, John. The future of the future. 1969
CB161.M3 ECOL
McHale, John. The future of the future. 1971
CB161.M3 1971 ECOL
Toward the year 2018. c1968 **CB161.T6 ECOL**

TWIN CITIES METROPOLITAN AREA—LIBRARIES—DIRECTORIES.
Mauritz, Marilyn. Library and informational resources in the Twin City Area. 1972-
REF fZ688.A2M3 ECOL

U

ULTRA-VIOLET RAYS—PHYSIOLOGICAL EFFECT.
United States. National Institute for Occupational Saffaety and Health. Occupational exposure to ultraviolet radiation. 1972. **fRA1231.R2U5 ECOL**

ULTRASONICS.
American Process Equipment Corporation. Ultrasonic filtration of combined sewer overflows. 1970. **fTD753.A6 ECOL**

UNDERDEVELOPED AREAS—AGRICULTURE.
Brown, Lester Russell. The social impact of the Green revolution. 1971. **HD1417.B7 ECOL**

UNDERDEVELOPED AREAS—BIRTH CONTROL.
Symonds, Richard. The United Nations and the population question, 1945-1970. 1973
HQ766.S888 ECOL

UNDERDEVELOPED AREAS—POPULATION.
Symonds, Richard. The United Nations and the population question, 1945-1970. 1973
HQ766.S888 ECOL

UNDERGROUND RESERVOIRS see RESERVOIRS, UNDERGROUND

UNDERGROUND WATER see WATER, UNDERGROUND

UNITED NATIONS.
Commission to Study the Organization of Peace. The United Nations and the human environment. 1972
HC68.C62 ECOL

UNITED NATIONS—TECHNICAL ASSISTANCE.
Symonds, Richard. The United Nations and the population question, 1945-1970. 1973
HQ766.S888 ECOL

UNITED STATES—BIBLIOGRAPHY.
Publishers' trade list annual. Books in print.
REF Z1215.P972 ECOL
Publishers' trade list annual. Books in print supplement: authors, titles, subjects. 1972/73-
REF fZ1215.P972 Suppl. ECOL

UNITED STATES—BUREAU OF MINES—BIBLIOGRAPHY.
United States. Bureau of Mines. List of Bureau of Mines publications and articles, with subject and author index. 1965/1969- **REF Z6736.U759 ECOL**

UNITED STATES—CIVILIZATION.
Nash, Roderick. Wilderness and the American mind. 1967. **E169.1.N37 ECOL**

UNITED STATES—CIVILIZATION—1970-
Hickel, Walter J. Who owns America? 1971
E855.H5 1971 ECOL

UNITED STATES—DESCRIPTION AND TRAVEL.
American heritage. The American heritage book of natural wonders. c1972,1963
fE169.A496 1972 ECOL

UNITED STATES—DESCRIPTION AND TRAVEL—GUIDE-BOOKS.
Natural wonders of America. 1972
QH76.N29 ECOL

UNITED STATES—DESCRIPTION AND TRAVEL—VIEWS.
The American coast. 1971 **fE169.02.A648 ECOL**
Plowden, David. The hand of man on America. 1971. **E169.02.P55 ECOL**

UNITED STATES—DESCRIPTION AND TRAVEL—1940-
Darling, Frank Fraser. Pelican in the wilderness. 1956 **QH104.D3 ECOL**

UNITED STATES—DESCRIPTION AND TRAVEL—1960-
Ogburn, Charlton. The continent in our hands. 1971. **E169.02.O3 ECOL**

UNITED STATES—ECONOMIC CONDITIONS.
Resources for the Future. Regions, resources, and economic growth. 1967,c1960
HC103.R45 1967 ECOL
Sears, Paul Bigelow. Deserts on the march. 3rd ed. rev. 1967,c1959 **S493.S4 1959 ECOL**
Smith, Guy Harold. Conservation of natural resources. 4th ed. 1971 **S938.S58 1971 ECOL**

UNITED STATES—ECONOMIC CONDITIONS—1918-1945.
Chase, Stuart. Rich land, poor land. 1969
S930.C5 1969 ECOL

UNITED STATES—ECONOMIC CONDITIONS—1945-
Twentieth Century Fund. America's needs and resources: a new survey. 1969,c1955
REF HC106.5.T9 1969 ECOL

UNITED STATES—ECONOMIC CONDITIONS.—1961- —ADDRESSES, ESSAYS, LECTURES.
Theobald, Robert. An alternative future for America II. 2d ed. 1970 **HN65.T44 1970 ECOL**

UNITED STATES—ECONOMIC CONDITIONS—1961- —CONGRESSES.
Conference on Energy, Economics and the Environment, Chicago, Ill., 1968. Energy, economics and the environment: proceedings of a conference sponsored by the Committee on Environment, Edison Electric Institute. 1969. **fHD9540.1.C6 1968 ECOL**
Energy, economic growth, and the environment. 1972 **HD9545.E6 ECOL**

UNITED STATES—ECONOMIC POLICY.
Chase, Stuart. Rich land, poor land. 1969
S930.C5 1969 ECOL

UNITED STATES—ECONOMIC POLICY—1961-
Higbee, Edward Counselman. A question of priorities. 1970. **HN65.H5 ECOL**
Theobald, Robert. The economics of abundance. 1970 **HB171.T48 ECOL**

UNITED STATES—FOREST POLICY.
Cameron, Jenks. The development of governmental forest control in the United States. 1972.
SD565.C3 1972 ECOL

UNITED STATES—GOVERNMENT PUBLICATIONS—BIBLIOGRAPHY.
Kiraldi, Louis. Pollution. 1971.
REF fZ7171.K55 ECOL
——— Supplement, 1962-1970. 1972.
REF Z6034.U49U53 Suppl. ECOL
United States. Geological Survey Publications of the Geological Survey, 1879-1961. 1964
REF Z6034.U49U53 ECOL

UNITED STATES—GOVERNMENT PUBLICATIONS—INDEXES.
Nuclear Desalination Information Center. Title—author—company index to reports published by the U.S. Dept. of the Interior, Office of Saline Water through July 1971-
REF fZ5853.S22N84 ECOL

UNITED STATES—GOVERNMENT PUBLICATIONS (STATE GOVERNMENTS)—BIBLIOGRAPHY.
Giefer, Gerald J. Water publications of State agencies. 1972   **REF Z7935.G55 ECOL**

UNITED STATES—HISTORY—PROPHECIES—ADDRESSES, ESSAYS, LECTURES.
American Academy of Arts and Sciences, Boston. Commission on the Year 2000 Toward the year 2000. 1970,c1968   **E169.1.A47192 1970 ECOL**

UNITED STATES—POLITICS AND GOVERNMENT.
United States. Commission on Population Growth and the American future. Governance and population: the governmental implications of population change. 1972.   **HB3505.A526 ECOL**

Wengert, Norman I. Natural resources and the political struggle. 1967,c1955
  HC103.7.W4 1967 ECOL

UNITED STATES—POLITICS AND GOVERNMENT—1969-
Hickel, Walter J. Who owns America? 1971
  E855.H5 1971 ECOL

UNITED STATES—POPULATION.
Freedman, Ronald. Population: the vital revolution. 1964   **HB881.F76 ECOL**

Hauser, Philip Morris. Population perspectives. 1961?c1960   **HB3505.H3 ECOL**

Ingle, Dwight Joyce. Who should have children? 1973   **HQ751.I43 ECOL**

United States. Commission on Population Growth and the American future. Governance and population: the governmental implications of population change. 1972.   **HB3505.A526 ECOL**

United States. Commission on Population Growth and the American Future. Population and the American future. 1972   **fHB3505.A525 ECOL**

United States. Commission on Population Growth and the American Future. Population, resources, and the environment. 1972   **HB3505.A527 ECOL**

The 99th hour. 1967   **HB3505.N5 ECOL**

UNITED STATES—PUBLIC BUILDINGS.
Federal Construction Council. Task Group T-65. Impact of air pollution regulations on fuel selection for federal facilities. 1970   **fKF3812.F4 ECOL**

UNITED STATES—PUBLIC LANDS.
Carstensen, Vernon Rosco. The public lands. General ed. 1968,c1962   **HD216.C3 1968 ECOL**

Clawson, Marion. The Federal lands since 1956. 1967   **HD216.C53 ECOL**

Clawson, Marion. The federal lands: their use and management. 1966,1957   **HD216.C54 1966 ECOL**

Hibbard, Benjamin Horace. A history of the public land policies. 1965.   **HD216.H5 1965 ECOL**

Stanford Environmental Law Society. Public land management—a time for change? 1971-   **fHD216.S7 ECOL**

United States. Congress. Senate. Committee on Interior and Insular Affairs. Subcommittee on Public Lands. Preservation of wilderness areas. 1972.
  KF26.I547 1972 ECOL

United States. Public Land Law Review Commission. One third of the Nation's land. 1970
  KF5601.A55P8 ECOL

What's ahead for our public lands? 1970
  KF5606.W5 ECOL

UNITED STATES—RACE QUESTION—ADDRESSES, ESSAYS, LECTURES.
Theobald, Robert. An alternative future for America II. 2d ed. 1970   **HN65.T44 1970 ECOL**

UNITED STATES—RURAL CONDITIONS.
Clawson, Marion. Policy directions for U.S. agriculture. 1968   **HD1761.C54 ECOL**

Jackson, John Brinckerhoff. Landscapes: selected writings of J. B. Jackson. 1970.   **HN57.J245 ECOL**

UNITED STATES—SOCIAL CONDITIONS.
Jackson, John Brinckerhoff. Landscapes: selected writings of J. B. Jackson. 1970.   **HN57.J245 ECOL**

UNITED STATES—SOCIAL CONDITIONS—1945-
Rienow, Robert. Moment in the sun. 1967.
  S930.R5 ECOL

Zisch, William E. The urban environment: how it can be improved. 1969.   **HT175.U6Z4 ECOL**

UNITED STATES—SOCIAL CONDITIONS—1945- —ADDRESSES, ESSAYS, LECTURES.
Baier, Kurt. Values and the future. 1969
  HM221.B27 ECOL

UNITED STATES—SOCIAL CONDITIONS—1960-
Gross, Bertram Myron. Social intelligence for America's future. 1969   **HN59.G76 ECOL**

Ingle, Dwight Joyce. Who should have children? 1973   **HQ751.I43 ECOL**

UNITED STATES—SOCIAL CONDITIONS—1960- —ADDRESSES, ESSAYS, LECTURES.
Theobald, Robert. An alternative future for America II. 2d ed. 1970   **HN65.T44 1970 ECOL**

UNITED STATES—SOCIAL POLICY.
Environment and change. 1970, c1968
  HT167.E46 ECOL

Gross, Bertram Myron. Social intelligence for America's future. 1969   **HN59.G76 ECOL**

Higbee, Edward Counselman. A question of priorities. 1970.   **HN65.H5 ECOL**

McCue, Gerald M. Creating the human environment. 1970   **HN59.M22 ECOL**

Udall, Stewart L. 1976: agenda for tomorrow. 1st ed. 1968   **HN65.U3 ECOL**

UNITED STATES—STATISTICS.
United States. Bureau of the Census. Pocket data book, USA. 1971-   **REF HA195.A54 ECOL**

United States. Bureau of the Census. Statistical abstract of the United States, v.92-   1971-
  REF HA202.U5 ECOL

UNITED STATES. ARMY. CORPS OF ENGINEERS.
Engineering a victory for our environment: a citizen's guide to the U.S. Army Corps of Engineers. c1972.
  fTC423.E5 ECOL

UNITED STATES. ARMY. CORPS OF ENGINEERS—CIVIL FUNCTIONS.
Morgan, Arthur Ernest. Dams and other disasters. 1971   **UG23.M67 ECOL**

UNITED STATES BUREAU OF LAND MANAGEMENT.
Clawson, Marion. The Bureau of Land Management. 1971   **HD181.G8C57 ECOL**

UNITED STATES BUREAU OF OUTDOOR RECREATION.
Fitch, Edwin M. The Bureau of Outdoor Recreation. 1970   **GV53.F5 ECOL**

UNITED STATES BUREAU OF SPORT FISHERIES AND WILDLIFE. BRANCH OF PREDATOR AND RODENT CONTROL.
McNulty, Faith. Must they die? 1st ed. 1971.
  QL737.C25M27 ECOL

UNITED STATES CONGRESS.
Cleaveland, Frederic N. Congress and urban problems. 1969   **HT334.U5C665 ECOL**

UNITED STATES CONGRESS—BIOGRAPHY.
United States Congress. Official congressional directory.   **REF JK1011.A3 ECOL**

UNITED STATES CONGRESS—REGISTERS.
United States Congress. Official congressional directory.   **REF JK1011.A3 ECOL**

UNITED STATES. CONGRESS SENATE. COMMITTEE ON PUBLIC WORKS.
United States. Library of Congress. Environmental Policy Division. A legislative history of the Water Pollution Control Act Amendments of 1972, together with a section-by-section index. 1973-
  KF3787.1.A16A5 ECOL

UNITED STATES FOOD AND DRUG ADMINISTRATION.
Turner, James S. The chemical feast. 1970.
  HD9000.9.U5T83 ECOL

UNITED STATES FOREST SERVICE.
Frome, Michael. The Forest Service. 1971
  SD565.F7 ECOL

Kauffman, Herbert. The Forest ranger. 1960
  SD565.K3 ECOL

United States. Soil Conservation Service. Big Sioux River Basin and related areas. 1973.
  HD1695.B5A5 ECOL

Wood, Frances Elizabeth. Forests are for people. 1971   **SD565.W66 ECOL**

UNITED STATES. FOREST SERVICE—CONGRESSES.
Current Issues Conference, 1st, Portland, Or., 1972. Timber supply and the environment. 1972
  SD144.A13C87 1972 ECOL

UNITED STATES FOREST SERVICE—HISTORY.
Tucker, Edwin A. Men who matched the mountains. 1972.   **SD143.T8 ECOL**

UNITED STATES. GEOLOGICAL SURVEY—BIBLIOGRAPHY.
United States. Geological Survey Publications of the Geological Survey, 1879-1961. 1964
  REF Z6034.U49U53 ECOL

—— Supplement, 1962-1970. 1972.
  REF Z6034.U49U53 Suppl. ECOL

UNITED STATES. NATIONAL PARK SERVICE.
Everhart, William C. The National Park Service. c1972   **SB482.A4E95 ECOL**

Swain, Donald C. Wilderness defender. 1970
  SB482.A4S95 ECOL

UNITED STATES. PUBLIC LAND LAW REVIEW COMMISSION.
What's ahead for our public lands? 1970
  KF5606.W5 ECOL

UNITED STATES SOIL CONSERVATION SERVICE.
Simms, Denton Harper. The Soil Conservation Service. 1970   **S622.S44 ECOL**

UNIVERSITIES AND COLLEGES—LOCATION
see SCHOOL SITES

URANIUM.
Singleton, Arthur L. Sources of nuclear fuel. 1968
  TN490.U7S52 ECOL

URBAN BEAUTIFICATION—PHILADELPHIA.
Bush-Brown, Louise (Carter). Garden blocks for urban America. 1969   **NA9052.B78 ECOL**

URBAN CLIMATOLOGY—BIBLIOGRAPHY.
Berlin, G. Lennis. The urban environment: a climatological anomaly. 1972
  REF fQC981.7.U7B47 ECOL

URBAN LAND INSTITUTE.
Eskew, Garnett Laidlaw. Of land and men. c1959
  NA9000.U715 ECOL

URBAN RENEWAL.
Goodman, Robert. After the planners. 1972, c1971
  HT166.G64 ECOL

URBAN RENEWAL—UNITED STATES.
Kulski, Julian Eugene. Land of urban promise: continuing the great tradition. 1967.
  HT167.K8 ECOL

Zisch, William E. The urban environment: how it can be improved. 1969.   **HT175.U6Z4 ECOL**

URBAN TRANSIT see LOCAL TRANSIT

URBAN TRANSPORTATION—CONGRESSES.
International Conference on Urban Transportation, 5th, Pittsburgh, 1971. Mobility: the fifth freedom. 1971?   **fHE148.I5 1971 ECOL**

URBAN TRANSPORTATION—UNITED STATES.
Buel, Ronald A. Dead end: the automobile in mass transportation. 1972   **HE5623.B82 ECOL**

URBANIZATION.
Higbee, Edward Counselman. A question of priorities. 1970.   **HN65.H5 ECOL**

URBANIZATION—ADDRESSES, ESSAYS, LECTURES.
The Fitness of man's environment. 1968
  HT166.F53 ECOL

URBANIZATION—UNITED STATES.
McPherson, M. B. Hydrologic effects of urbanization in the United States. 1972.
  fGB665.M3 ECOL

URIA see MURRES

UTAH—DESCRIPTION AND TRAVEL—1951-
Abbey, Edward. Slickrock. 1971
  fF830.A62 ECOL

UTILIZATION OF WASTE PRODUCTS see SALVAGE (WASTE, ETC.)

V

VAN ALLEN RADIATION BELTS.
Corliss, William R. Space radiation. 1968
  QC485.C613 ECOL

VANISHING ANIMALS see RARE ANIMALS

VEGETABLE GARDENING.
Ogden, Samuel R. Step-by-step to organic vegetable growing. 1971   **SB321.O343 ECOL**

VEGETABLE KINGDOM see PLANTS

VEGETATION SURVEYS.
Cain, Stanley Adair. Manual of vegetation analysis. 1971 ,c1959   **QK911.C3 1959a ECOL**

VELOCITY OF CHEMICAL REACTION see CHEMICAL REACTION, RATE OF

VETERINARY TOXICOLOGY.
Lillie, Robert Jones. Air pollutants affecting the performance of domestic animals. Slightly rev. 1972.
  SF757.5.L54 1972 ECOL

VIETNAMESE CONFLICT,
1961-   —ADDRESSES, SERMONS, ETC.
Weisberg, Barry. Ecocide in Indochina. 1970
DS557.A68W43 ECOL

VIETNAMESE CONFLICT,
1961-   —CHEMISTRY.
Harvest of death. 1971,c1972
DS557.A68H35 1972 ECOL

VIETNAMESE CONFLICT,
1961-   —CHEMISTRY—ADDRESSES,
ESSAYS, LECTURES.
Weisberg, Barry. Ecocide in Indochina. 1970
DS557.A68W43 ECOL

VIETNAMESE CONFLICT,
1961-   —DESTRUCTION AND PILLAGE.
Whiteside, Thomas. The withering rain. 1st ed. 1971.
QH545.P4W48 1971 ECOL

VIRGIN ISLANDS OF THE UNITED
STATES—ECONOMIC CONDITIONS.
O'Neill, Edward A. Rape of the American Virgins. 1972
HC157.V6O5 ECOL

VIRGIN ISLANDS OF THE UNITED
STATES—POLITICS AND GOVERNMENT.
O'Neill, Edward A. Rape of the American Virgins. 1972
HC157.V6O5 ECOL

VOYAGES AND TRAVELS.
Brooks, Paul. Roadless area. 1971,c1964.
QH75.B74 ECOL

VOYAGEURS NATIONAL PARK (PROPOSED).
United States. National Park Service. Proposed Voyageurs National Park, Minnesota. 1964.
fF612.V6A54 ECOL

W

WALKING.
Fuller, Raymond Tifft. Now that we have to walk. 1972, c1943
QH81.F847 1972 ECOL

WALLOWA MOUNTAINS.
Douglas, William Orville. Of men and mountains. 1950
F851.7.D68 ECOL

WARBLERS.
Griscom, Ludlow. The warblers of America. 1957.
REF QL696.P2G85 ECOL

WASPS.
Evans, Howard Ensign. The wasps. 1970
QL568.V5E8 ECOL

WASTE DISPOSAL IN THE
GROUND—BIBLIOGRAPHY.
Rima, Donald R. Subsurface waste disposal by means of wells—a selective annotated bibliography. 1971.
REF Z5853.S22R55 ECOL

WASTE DISPOSAL IN THE
GROUND—CONGRESSES.
National Conference on Composting-Waste Recycling. 1st, Denver, 1971. How to put waste recycling into practice. 1971.
fTD172.5.N3 1971 ECOL
Symposium on Underground Waste Management and Environmental Implications, Houston, Tex., 1971. Underground waste management and environmental implications; proceedings. 1972.
TD761.S95 1971 ECOL

WASTE DISPOSAL IN THE OCEAN.
Smith, David D. Ocean disposal of barge-delivered liquid and solid wastes from United States coastal cities. 1971.
TD796.7.O25S4 ECOL
Steering Committee on Coastal Wastes Management. Wastes management concepts for the coastal zone. 1970.
TD763.S7 ECOL
United States. Council on Environmental Quality. Ocean dumping: a national policy. 1970.
TD763.U55 ECOL

WASTE DISPOSAL IN THE
OCEAN—FLORIDA.
Florida Ocean Sciences Institute. Limitations and effects of waste disposal on an ocean shelf. 1971 i.e.1972
fTD763.F56 ECOL

WASTE, DISPOSAL OF see FACTORY AND TRADE WASTE; REFUSE AND REFUSE DISPOSAL; SEWAGE DISPOSAL

WASTE MANAGEMENT see SALVAGE (WASTE, ETC.)

WASTE PAPER.
Franklin, William E. The role of nonpackaging paper in solid waste management, 1966 to 1976. 1971.
TD795.F7 ECOL

WASTE PRODUCTS.
Darnay, Arsen. Salvage markets for materials in solid wastes, ... 1972.
TD795.D38 ECOL
Kenahan, Charles B. Bureau of Mines research programs on recycling and disposal of mineral-, metal-, and energy-based wastes. 1973.
TN23.U7no.8595 ECOL

Lange, Gordon C. The survival game. 1972
TD178.6.L35 ECOL
Lipsett, Charles H. Industrial wastes and salvage; conservation and utilization. 2d ed. 1963
TP995.L55 1963 ECOL

WASTE PRODUCTS—CONGRESSES.
North Eastern Regional Antipollution Conference, 3d, University of Rhode Island, 1970. Reuse and recycle of wastes; proceedings. 1971
fTP995.A1N6 1970 ECOL

WASTE RECLAMATION see SALVAGE (WASTE, ETC.)

WASTE STABILIZATION LAGOONS see SEWAGE LAGOONS

WASTE WATER RECLAMATION see WATER REUSE

WATER see also EROSION; FLOODS; HYDRAULIC ENGINEERING; ICE; LAKES; OCEAN; RAIN AND RAINFALL; RIVERS; SNOW; WATER CONSERVATION; WATER QUALITY; WATER REUSE; WELLS

Archer, Sellers Gambrell. Rain, rivers, and reservoirs. c1968,c1963
GB671.A7 ECOL
Black, Irma (Simonton). Busy water. c1958.
PZ10.B29525Bu ECOL
Bloome, Enid. The water we drink! 1971.
PZ10.B29545Wat ECOL
Coker, Robert Ervin. Streams, lakes, ponds. 1954
QH96.C6 ECOL
Davis, Kenneth Sydney. Water, the mirror of science. 1961.
QD169.W3D3 ECOL
Hagaman, Adaline P. What is water. 1960
PZ10.H12Wh ECOL
Hunt, Cynthia. Water: the web of life.
GB661.H84 ECOL
Leopold, Luna Bergere. Water. Rev. 1970,c1966
fGB671.L4 1970 ECOL
Overman, Michael. Water: solutions to a problem of supply and demand. 1969.
TD348.O85 1969 ECOL
Peterson, Ottis. Junior science book of water. 1966
PZ10.P4472Ju ECOL
Pine, Tillie S. Water all around. c1959
PZ10.P57Wat ECOL
Platt, Rutherford Hayes. Water: the wonder of life. 1971
QH91.15.P57 ECOL
Stecher, Adam. Running water. c1971
QH541.2.S8 ECOL
Walton, William Clarence. The world of water. 1970
GB661.W26 ECOL

WATER—AERATION.
Champlin, Robert L. Supplementary aeration of lagoons in rigorous climate areas. 1971.
fTD746.5.C45 ECOL
Davis, Robert K. The range of choice in water management. 1968
TD225.P74D3 ECOL
Fast, Arlo Wade. The effects of artificial aeration on lake ecology. 1971 i.e.1972
fTD458.F38 ECOL
Hogan, William T. Optimum mechanical aeration systems for rivers and ponds. 1970.
fTD458.H64 ECOL
Tsivoglou, E. C. Characterization of stream reaeration, capacity. 1972.
fTD458.T7 ECOL
United States. Environmental Protection Agency. Induced aeration of small mountain lakes. 1970.
fSH167.T86U5 ECOL

WATER—AERATION—MATHEMATICAL
MODELS.
Stochastics, Inc., Blacksburg, Va. Stochastic modeling for water quality management. 1971.
fTC409.S8 ECOL

WATER—ANALYSIS.
Allen, Herbert Ellis. Nutrients in natural waters. 1972
QH96.A48 ECOL
American Public Health Association. Standard methods for the examination of water and waste water, including bottom sediments and sludges. Ed. 13. c1971
REF QD142.A5 1971 ECOL
Harris, Douglas H. Assessment of turbidity, color and odor in water. 1972.
fTD380.H3 ECOL
Kittrell, F. W. A practical guide to water quality studies of streams. 1969.
TD425.K53 ECOL
McCoy, James W. Chemical analysis of industrial water. 1969.
TD380.M3 ECOL
Water and water pollution handbook. 1971-
TD380.W322 ECOL

WATER—ANALYSIS—MINNESOTA.
Minnesota. Pollution Control Agency. Water quality sampling program: Minnesota lakes and streams.
TD380.M6 ECOL
Potential productivity of fresh water environments as determined by an algae bioassay technique. 1970.
GB701.M554no.20

WATER—ANALYSIS—MINNETONKA, LAKE,
MINNESOTA.
Megard, Robert Ordell. Lake Minnetonka: nutrients, nutrient abatement, and the photosynthetic system of the phytoplankton. 1970.
fTD225.M63M4 ECOL

WATER—COMPOSITION.
Maderak, Marion L. Chemical quality of ground water in the Minneapolis-St. Paul area, Minnesota. 1965.
fTD224.M6A3no.23 ECOL
Maderak, Marion L. Quality of waters, Minnesota. 1963.
fTD224.M6A3no.21 ECOL
Minnesota. University. School of Public Health. A preliminary investigation of nutrients in western Lake Superior, 1958-1959. 1959.
fGB1627.G89M52 ECOL

WATER—CONSERVATION see WATER CONSERVATION

WATER—FLUORIDATION.
Maier, Franz J. Manual of water fluoridation practice. 1963
TD468.M25 ECOL

WATER—INFORMATION
SERVICES—DIRECTORIES.
United States. Library of Congress. National Referral Center for Science and Technology. A directory of information resources in the United States: water. 1966.
fTD211.U5 ECOL

WATER—LAW AND
LEGISLATION—MINNESOTA.
Minnesota. University. Water Resources Research Center. Codified and uncodified state laws and municipal ordinances bearing on water and related land resources in Minnesota. 1968.
GB701.M554no.9 ECOL

WATER—LAWS AND
LEGISLATION—BIBLIOGRAPHY.
Radosevich, George E. Water law and its relationship to environmental quality: a bibliography of source material. 1973.
REF fKF5551.R3 ECOL

WATER—LAWS AND
LEGISLATION—FLORIDA.
Maloney, Frank Edward. Water law and administration. 1968.
REF KFF446.M3 ECOL

WATER—LAWS AND LEGISLATION—THE
WEST.
Hutchins, Wells A. Water rights laws in the nineteen western states. 1971-
KF5559.A45H8 ECOL

WATER—LAWS AND LEGISLATION—UNITED
STATES.
Kusler, Jon A. Survey: lake protection and rehabilitation legislation in the United States. 1972.
REF fKF5568.K8 ECOL

WATER—LAWS AND LEGISLATION—UNITED
STATES—CASES.
Sax, Joseph L. Water law, planning & policy. 1968
KF5568.S3 1968 ECOL

WATER—MICROBIOLOGY.
Collins, Ralph P. Characterization of taste and odors in water supplies. 1971.
fTD384.C64 ECOL

WATER—POLLUTION.
Agricultural practices and water quality. 1971,c1970
TD420.A33 ECOL
Allen, Herbert Ellis. Nutrients in natural waters. 1972
QH96.A48 ECOL
American Foundrymen's Society. Water Pollution Committee. Water pollution from foundry wastes. 1st ed. 1967.
fTD899.A45 ECOL
Aylesworth, Thomas G. This vital air, this vital water: man's environment crisis. 1968
TD180.A9 ECOL
Battelle Memorial Institute, Columbus, Ohio Columbus Laboratories An investigation of techniques for removal of chromium from electroplating wastes. 1971.
fTD899.M45B3ECOL
Beefland International, Inc. Elimination of water pollution by packing-house animal paunch and blood. 1971.
fTD899.M4B4 ECOL
Berg, George G. Water pollution. 1970
TD420.B46 ECOL
Besselievre, Edmund Bulkley. The treatment of industrial wastes. 1968,c1969
REF TD897.B38 ECOL
Bongers, Leonard H. Sand and gravel overlay for control of mercury in sediments. 1972.
fTD427.M4B6 ECOL
Chemical engineering. Environmental engineering, deskbook issue, 1971-
fTA170.C5 ECOL
Chesher, Richard H. Biological impact of a large-scale desalination plant at Key West. 1971.
fTD478.5.F5C48 ECOL
Dugan, Patrick R. Biochemical ecology of water pollution. 1972.
TD423.D83 ECOL
Dworsky, Leonard B. Pollution. 1971.
REF TD174.D95 ECOL

Edison Water Quality Laboratory. Storm and Combined Sewer Overflows Section. Environmental impact of highway deicing. 1971.
fTE220.E35 ECOL

Environmental Measurements, Inc. Monitoring mercury vapor near pollution sites. 1971.
fTD427.M4E5 ECOL

Finstein, Melvin S. Pollution microbiology. 1972.
QR48.F5 ECOL

Grava, Sigurd. Urban planning aspects of water pollution control. 1969. **TD420.G67 ECOL**

Groman, William A. Forest fertilization (a state-of-the-art review and description of environmental effects). 1972. **SD408.G7 ECOL**

Herber, Lewis. Crisis in our cities. c1965
RA566.H4 ECOL

Hynes, Hugh Bernard Noel. The biology of polluted waters. 1971c1960 **QH96.H9 1971 ECOL**

Jones, Claire. Pollution: the waters of the earth. 1971 **TD422.J65 ECOL**

Lavaroni, Charles W. Water pollution. c1971
TD420.L28 ECOL

Laycock, George. Water pollution. 1972
TD422.L38 ECOL

Leinwand, Gerald. Air and water pollution. 1969
TD180.L4 ECOL

Little (Arthur D.) Inc. Spill prevention techniques for hazardous polluting substances: an inventory and survey of hazardous chemical facilities in Charleston, West Virginia; Baltimore, Maryland; Texas City, Texas; and the Suisun Bay-Delta Area, California. 1971.
fT55.3.H3L4 ECOL

May, Julian. Blue River. 1971
TD425.M46 ECOL

Midwest Research Institute, Kansas City, Mo. Rapid detection system for organophosphates and carbamate insecticides in water. 1972. **TD427.P35M5 ECOL**

Minnesota. Division of Water Quality. Wastewater disposal facilities inventory, State of Minnesota. 1971- **fTD224.M6A33 ECOL**

Mitchell, Ralph. Water pollution microbiology. 1971,c1972 **QR48.M58 ECOL**

Neely, W. C. Biological and photobiological action of pollutants on aquatic microorganisms. 1973.
fTC1.A85no.9 ECOL

North Carolina. State University, Raleigh. Dept. of Biological and Agricultural Engineering. Role of animal wastes in agricultural land runoff. 1971.
fTD930.N67 ECOL

The Price of power: electric utilities and the environment. 1972 **REF fTJ164.P7 ECOL**

Resources for the Future. Water pollution: economic aspects and research needs. 1962 **TD420.R4 ECOL**

Robert S. Kerr Water Research Center. Characteristics of rainfall run off from a beef cattle feedlot. 1972. **TD899.F4R6 ECOL**

Rondiere, Pierre. Purity or pollution. 1st ed. 1971
TD348.R65 ECOL

Sartor, James D. Water pollution aspects of street surface contaminants. 1972. **fTD665.S2 ECOL**

Smith, Edwin Earle. Sulfide to sulfate reaction mechanism. 1970. **fTN321.S58 ECOL**

Southern Conference on Environmental Radiation Protection from Nuclear Power Plants, St. Petersburg, Fla., 1971. Proceedings of Southern Conference on Environmental Radiation Protection from Nuclear Power Plants, April 21-22, 1971. 1972.
TK9152.S6 ECOL

Suggs, James D. Mercury pollution control in stream and lake sediments. 1972. **fTD427.M4S9 ECOL**

Tratnyek, Joseph P. Waste wool as a scavenger for mercury pollution in waters. 1972.
fTD427.M4T7 ECOL

Tsivoglou, E. C. Characterization of stream reaeration, capacity. 1972. **fTD458.T7 ECOL**

United States. Environmental Protection Agency. Office of Research and Monitoring. The effects of agricultural waste water treatment on algal bioassay response. 1971. **QH96.8.E9U54 ECOL**

United States. Environmental Protection Agency. Effects of pesticides in water. n.d.
REF fTD427.P35U53 ECOL

Washington (State). University. Fisheries Research Institute. Responses of teleost fish to environmental stress. 1971. **fQL639.1.W3 ECOL**

Water and water pollution handbook. 1971-
TD380.W322 ECOL

Water quality criteria data book. 1970-
REF fTD370.W394 ECOL

Welch, Robin I. A feasibility demonstration of an aerial surveillance spill prevention system. 1972.
fTD427.P4W45 ECOL

Widman, Michael U. Polymer film overlay system for mercury contaminated sludge—Phase I. 1972.
fTD427.M4W5 ECOL

Zajic, James E. Water pollution. 1971.
TD420.Z35 ECOL

WATER—POLLUTION—ADDRESSES, ESSAYS, LECTURES.
McCuen, Gary E. The ecology controversy: opposing viewpoints. 1971 **QH541.M3 ECOL**

Nikolaieff, George A. The water crisis. 1967.
TD355.N5 ECOL

WATER—POLLUTION—BIBLIOGRAPHY.
Sinha, Evelyn. Lake and river pollution. 1971
REF fZ7173.W3S5 ECOL

Sinha, Evelyn. Methods, models & instruments for studies of aquatic pollution. 1971
REF fZ7173.W3S52 ECOL

United States. Environmental Protection Agency. Office of Public Affairs. Current list of water publications, 1965/71-
REF Z7173.W3U5 ECOL

Water Resources Scientific Information Center. PCB in water. 1973. **Z7173.W3W3 ECOL**

WATER—POLLUTION—BOUNDARY WATERS CANOE AREA.
Minnesota. Division of Water Quality. Report on investigation of pollution of the Northern Border waters from the mouth of the Pigeon River at Lake Superior westward through the Boundary Waters Canoe Area and Lower Lakes to the outlet of Rainy Lake. 1969
fTD224.M6A5 ECOL

WATER—POLLUTION—CANADA.
Canada Centre for Inland Waters. Collected reprints. vol. 4- , 1971- , pt. 1-
TD226.C3 ECOL

WATER—POLLUTION—CASE STUDIES.
National Industrial Pollution Control Council. Casebook: pollution cleanup actions. 1971?
fTD897.N37 ECOL

WATER—POLLUTION—CONGRESSES.
American Nuclear Society. Nuclear methods in environmental research. 1971 **fTD172.5.A4 ECOL**

Brittin, Wesley Emil. Air and water pollution. 1972
TD881.B75 ECOL

Environmental control seminar proceedings. 1971.
fTD172.5.E26 ECOL

Environmental requirements of blue-green algae. 1967. **QK569.C96E56 ECOL**

International Symposium on Eutrophication, University of Wisconsin, 1967. Eutrophication: causes, consequences, correctives. 1969.
QH96.A1I63 1967 ECOL

International Symposium on Water Pollution Control in Cold Climates, University of Alaska, Fairbanks, 1970. Papers Held at the University of Alaska, July 22-24, 1970. 1972 **TD423.I5 ECOL**

International Symposium on River Ecology and the Impact of Man, University of Massachusetts, 1971. River ecology and man. 1972.
GB1205.I5 1971 ECOL

Jerusalem International Conference on Water Quality and Pollution Research, 1969. Developments in water quality research. 1970
TD370.J47 1969 ECOL

Joint Conference on Prevention and Control of Oil Spills, Washington, D.C., 1971. Proceedings of Joint Conference on Prevention and Control of Oil Spills held June 15-17, 1971 at the Sheraton Park Hotel. 1971?
fGC1080.J6 ECOL

WATER—POLLUTION—ECONOMIC ASPECTS.
Kneese, Allen V. Managing water quality: economics, technology, institution. 1968
TD423.K52 ECOL

United States. Environmental Protection Agency. Water Quality Office. Cost of clean water. 1971-
TD420.U5 ECOL

WATER—POLLUTION—ECONOMIC ASPECTS—UNITED STATES.
Lund, Leonard. Industry expenditures for water pollution abatement. 1972 **fTD223.L8 ECOL**

United States. Environmental Protection Agency. The economics of clean water. 1972-
HC110.P55A24 ECOL

WATER—POLLUTION—ECONOMIC ASPECTS—UNITED STATES—ADDRESSES, ESSAYS, LECTURES.
Economics of air and water pollution. 1969.
fTD201.V57no.26 ECOL

WATER—POLLUTION—ECONOMIC ASPECTS—VERMONT.
Vermont. Agency of Environmental Conservation. Development of a State effluent charge system. 1972.
fTD224.V5A43 ECOL

WATER—POLLUTION—GREAT LAKES REGION.
Canada. Agricultural pollution of the Great Lakes Basin. 1971. **fTD223.3.C25 ECOL**

Great Lakes Basin Commission. The future of the Great Lakes: a public meeting. 1972
fGB1627.G8G7 ECOL

Kelnhofer, Guy J. Preserving the Great Lakes. 1972. **fTC423.3.K4 ECOL**

WATER—POLLUTION—IOWA.
Minnesota. Division of Water Quality. Investigation of water quality and sources of pollution of waters of Minnesota and Iowa: reports and memorandums. 1960- **fTD224.M6A34 ECOL**

WATER—POLLUTION—IOWA—CONGRESSES.
Iowa Water Resources Pollution Control and Abatement Seminar, Iowa State University, 1965. Water pollution: control and abatement proceedings. 1st ed. 1970,c1967 **TD224.I8I6 1965 ECOL**

WATER—POLLUTION—LAKE MICHIGAN WATERSHED—CONGRESSES.
Conference in the Matter of Pollution of Lake Michigan and its Tributary Basin in the States of Wisconsin, Illinois, Indiana, and Michigan, 3rd, Chicago, Mar. 23-25, 1971. Reconvening of the 3rd session; Proceedings. 1971-
fTD223.3.C595 1971 ECOL

Conference in the Matter of Pollution of Lake Michigan and its Tributary Basins, 3d, Chicago, Sept. 28-30, Oct. 1-2, 1970. Workshop session for the third session (reconvened). 1970.
fTD223.3.C595 1970a ECOL

WATER—POLLUTION—LAKE SUPERIOR WATERSHED.
Minnesota. Pollution Control Agency. Pesticide inputs and levels: Minnesota waters-Lake Superior Basin. 1971 i.e. 1972 **fTD223.3.M55 ECOL**

Roy F. Weston, Inc. Concept evaluation report: taconite tailings disposal, Reserve Mining Company, Silver Bay, Minnesota. 1971 **fTD899.T35 ECOL**

Ulrich, Stanley. Superior pollutor: a saga of the struggle to stop pollution of the largest fresh water lake in the world by its most egregious polluter—the Reserve Mining Company. 1972. **TD224.M6U6 ECOL**

United States. Federal Water Pollution Control Administration. An appraisal of water pollution in the Lake Superior basin. 1969. **TD223.3.U5 ECOL**

United States. Federal Water Pollution Control Administration. An appraisal of water pollution in the Lake Superior basin. Rev. ed. 1970,1969.
TD223.3U5 1970 ECOL

WATER—POLLUTION—LAKE SUPERIOR WATERSHED—CONGRESSES.
Conference in the Matter of Pollution of Lake Superior and its Tributary Basin in the States of Minnesota, Wisconsin, and Michigan, Duluth, May 13-15, 1969. Proceedings. 1970
fTD223.3.C59 1969 ECOL

Conference in the Matter of Pollution of Lake Superior and its Tributary Basin in the States of Minnesota, Wisconsin, and Michigan, 2d session, Duluth, Aug. 12-13, 1970. Reconvening of second sessions. 1971 **fTD223.3.C59 1970b ECOL**

Conference in the Matter of Pollution of Lake Superior and its Tributary Basin in the States of Minnesota, Wisconsin, and Michigan, 2nd, Duluth, Jan. 14-15, 1971. Second meeting second session (reconvened). 1971. **fTD223.3.C59 1971 ECOL**

Conference in the Matter of Pollution of Lake Superior and its Tributary Basin in the States of Minnesota, Wisconsin, and Michigan, 3d session, Duluth, April 29-30, 1970. Transcript of proceedings. 1970 **fTD223.3.C59 1970 ECOL**

WATER—POLLUTION—LAW AND LEGISLATION—ADDRESSES, ESSAYS, LECTURES.
Environment law review. 1970-
REF KF3790.A2E5 ECOL

WATER—POLLUTION—LAW AND LEGISLATION—APPALACHIAN REGION.
Maryland. University. School of Law. Legal problems of coal mine reclamation. 1972.
fKF1830.Z95M37 ECOL

WATER—POLLUTION—LAW AND LEGISLATION—BIBLIOGRAPHY.
Radosevich, George E. Water law and its relationship to environmental quality: a bibliography of source material. 1973. **REF fKF5551.R3 ECOL**

WATER—POLLUTION—LAW AND LEGISLATION—UNITED STATES.
Great Lakes Foundation, Ann Arbor, Mich. The common law of water. c1971. **KF3790.Z9L4 ECOL**

Heath, Milton Sidney. A comparative study of state water pollution control laws and programs. 1972.
fKF3790.Z95H4 ECOL

Meyers, Charles J. Selected legal and economic aspects of environmental protection. 1971.
KF3775.A7M58 ECOL

United States. Environmental Protection Agency. Guidelines for developing or revising water quality standards under the Federal Water Pollution Control Act Amendments of 1972. 1973. **fTD370.U5 ECOL**

United States. Library of Congress. Environmental Policy Division. A legislative history of the Water Pollution Control Act Amendments of 1972, together with a section-by-section index. 1973-
KF3787.1.A16A5 ECOL

WATER—POLLUTION—LAW AND LEGISLATION—VERMONT.

Vermont. Agency of Environmental Conservation. Development of a State effluent charge system. 1972.
fTD224.V5A43 ECOL

WATER—POLLUTION—LAW AND LEGISLATION—WISCONSIN.

History of the Wisconsin Department of Natural Resources and related rules, regulations, classifications and standards for air and water quality. 1970
fS932.W6H5 ECOL

WATER—POLLUTION—LAW AND LEGISLATION—YEARBOOKS.

Legal control of water pollution. 1969
KF3786.A32L4 ECOL

WATER—POLLUTION—MATHEMATICAL MODELS.

Stochastics, Inc., Blacksburg, Va. Stochastic modeling for water quality management. 1971.
fTC409.S8 ECOL

WATER—POLLUTION—MEASUREMENT.

Coca-Cola Company. Foods Division. Treatment of citrus processing wastes. 1970. **fTD899.F7C6 ECOL**

Syracuse University. Civil Engineering Dept. Benefits of water quality enhancement. 1970.
fTD365.S94 ECOL

United States. Geological Survey. Water Resources Division. National reference list of water quality stations, water year 1971-
REF TD380.U5 ECOL

WATER—POLLUTION—MEASUREMENT—STUDY AND TEACHING.

Weaver, Elbert C. Scientific experiments in environmental pollution. 1968 **TD178.5.W4 ECOL**

WATER—POLLUTION—MILWAUKEE RIVER.

Milwaukee. Milwaukee River Technical Study Committee. The Milwaukee River. 1968.
fTD225.M47M6 ECOL

WATER—POLLUTION—MINNESOTA.

Conference in the Matter of Pollution of the Interstate and Intrastate Waters of the Upper Mississippi River and its Tributaries—Wisconsin—Minnesota, Minneapolis, 1968. Proceedings of progress evaluation meeting held April 30, 1968. 1968. **fTD223.4.A45C6 ECOL**

Conference in the Matter of Pollution of the Interstate and Intrastate Waters of the Upper Mississippi River and its Tributaries—Minnesota and Wisconsin. Proceedings of the second session Minneapolis, Minnesota, Feb. 28, March 1 & 20, 1967. 1967. **REF TD223.4.A43C6 ECOL**

Creative Research Services, Inc. Progress report, biennial program and long-range plan for water pollution control. 1970. **fTD224.M65C73 ECOL**

Minnesota Association of Commerce and Industry. Water pollution regulation handbook. 1970
REF fTD420.M56 ECOL

Minnesota. Division of Water Quality. Investigation of water quality and sources of pollution of waters of Minnesota and Iowa: reports and memorandums, 1960- **fTD224.M6A34 ECOL**

Minnesota. Division of Water Quality. Memorandum on mercury pollution in Minnesota. 1970. **fQH545.M4M57 ECOL**

Minnesota. Division of Water Quality. Waste disposal reports and memorandums of industries of Minnesota. 1961- **fTD224.M6A35 ECOL**

Minnesota. Division of Water Quality. Wastewater treatment works studies, surveys, memorandums, reports, etc. of cities and villages of Minnesota. 1964- **fTD224.M6A36 ECOL**

Minnesota. Pollution Control Agency. Progress report and long-range plan and program for water pollution control. 1968. **REF fTD224.M6A53 ECOL**

Minnesota. Pollution Control Agency. Progress report on water pollution control July 1967 through December 1968. 1968. **fTD224.M6A532 ECOL**

Minnesota. University. Water Resources Research Center. Lake eutrophication—water pollution causes, effects and control. 1970. **GB701.M554no.22 ECOL**

Minnesota. Water Pollution Control Commission. Long-range water pollution control plan and program, July 1, 1963. **fTD224.M6A56 ECOL**

Minnesota. Water Pollution Control Commission. Report on progress—water pollution control, Jan. 1, 1965 to Dec. 31, 1966. 1967
fTD224.M6A562 ECOL

Minnesota. Water Pollution Control Commission. Report on Progress - water pollution control, July 1, 1963 to Dec. 31, 1964. 1965? **fTD224.M6A561 ECOL**

Soil Conservation Society of America. Minnesota Chapter. Water pollution by nutrients—sources, effects and control. 1969. **GB701.M554no.13 ECOL**

United States. Federal Water Pollution Control Administration. Twin Cities Upper Mississippi River Project. Report on water quality investigations of the Mississippi, Minnesota and St. Croix Rivers. 1966
REF fTD225.T9U5 ECOL

Waelti, John J. Understanding the water quality controversy in Minnesota. 1969 **fTD420.W3 ECOL**

WATER—POLLUTION—MINNETONKA, LAKE, MINNESOTA.

Harza Engineering Company. A program for preserving the quality of Lake Minnetonka. 1971
fTD225.M63H3 ECOL

Megard, Robert Ordell. Lake Minnetonka: nutrients, nutrient abatement, and the photosynthetic system of the phytoplankton. 1970. **fTD225.M63M4 ECOL**

WATER—POLLUTION—MISSISSIPPI RIVER.

Lewis, Robert Clark. The marginal costs of alternative levels of water quality in the Upper Mississippi River. 1970. **GB701.M554no.25 ECOL**

Minnesota. Division of Water Quality. Memorandum on the waste assimilation capacity of the Mississippi River in the Twin Cities Metropolitan Area. 1969. **fTD525.T9M6 ECOL**

WATER—POLLUTION—MISSISSIPPI RIVER—CONGRESSES.

Conference in the Matter of Pollution of the Interstate Waters of the Upper Mississippi River, St. Paul, 1964. Conference in the Matter of Pollution of the Interstate Waters of the Upper Mississippi River, St. Paul Minnesota, February 8, 1964. 196-?
fTD223.4.C67 1964 ECOL

WATER—POLLUTION—MISSISSIPPI RIVER WATERSHED.

United States. Federal Water Pollution Control Administration. Great Lakes Region. A report on pollution of the Upper Mississippi River and major tributaries. 1966. **TD225.M5U5 ECOL**

WATER—POLLUTION—MISSISSIPPI RIVER WATERSHED—CONGRESSES.

Conference in the Matter of Pollution of the Interstate Waters of the Lower Mississippi River, New Orleans, 1964. Proceedings. 1964?
REF fTD225.M64C6 1964 ECOL

Conference in the Matter of Pollution of the Interstate and Intrastate Waters of the Upper Mississippi River and its Tributaries—Minnesota and Wisconsin. Proceedings of the second session Minneapolis, Minnesota, Feb. 28, March 1 & 20, 1967. 1967. **REF TD223.4.A43C6 ECOL**

WATER—POLLUTION—OHIO.

Ohio. State University, Columbus. Research Foundation. Pilot scale study of acid mine drainage. 1971. **fTN321.O3 ECOL**

WATER—POLLUTION—PERIODICALS.

Water Pollution Control Federation. Research supplement to Journal Water Pollution Control Federation. 1971. **fTD423.W3 ECOL**

WATER—POLLUTION—POND LICK LAKE, OHIO.

Ryckman, Edgerley, Tomlinson and Associates. Pesticide poisoning of Pond Lick Lake, Ohio. 1971
fTD224.O3R9 ECOL

WATER—POLLUTION—RED RIVER OF THE NORTH—CONGRESSES.

Conference in the Matter of Pollution of the Interstate Waters of the Red River of the North, North Dakota—Minnesota, Fargo, N.D., 1965. Proceedings.
fTD225.R34C6 1965 ECOL

WATER—POLLUTION—RESEARCH.

McClanahan, Mark A. A study of the effects of island development on lake water quality. 1972.
fTD224.G4M3 ECOL

United States. Environmental Protection Agency. Office of Research and Monitoring. Projects of the National Water Quality Control Research Program. 1971. **fTD423.U546 ECOL**

Water Pollution Control Federation. Research supplement to Journal Water Pollution Control Federation. 1971. **fTD423.W3 ECOL**

WATER—POLLUTION—RESEARCH—DELAWARE RIVER BASIN.

Delaware River Basin Commission. Interstate planning for regional water supply and pollution control. 1971. **fTD420.D4 ECOL**

WATER—POLLUTION—ST. CROIX RIVER.

Bannister Engineering Co., St. Paul, Minn. Report on reducing untreated combined wastewater overflows to the St. Croix River. 1970. **fTD525.S7B3 ECOL**

WATER—POLLUTION—SOCIETIES—DIRECTORIES.

Water Pollution Control Federation Directory. vol.44- March 1972-
REF TD201.W32 ECOL

WATER—POLLUTION—SOUTHWEST, NEW.

Texas Tech University. Water Resources Center. Characteristics of wastes from southwestern cattle feedlots. 1971. **fTD899.F4T497 ECOL**

WATER—POLLUTION—STUDY AND TEACHING.

Phelps, Pat. Water problems. 1971.
TD420.P4 ECOL

WATER—POLLUTION—TEXAS.

Texas Tech University. Dept. of Geosciences. Infiltration rates and groundwater quality beneath cattle feedlots, Texas High Plains. 1971
fTD899.F4T48 ECOL

WATER—POLLUTION—TRINITY RIVER.

Texas Christian University, Fort Worth. Dept. of Biology. Industrial wastes: effects on Trinity River ecology, Fort Worth, Texas. 1971 i.e. 1972
fTD224.T4T4 ECOL

WATER—POLLUTION—UNITED STATES.

American Public Works Association. Water pollution aspects of urban runoff. 1969.
TD420.A4 ECOL

Briggs, Peter. Water: the vital essence. c1967
GC21.B83 ECOL

Carr, Donald Eaton. Death of the sweet waters. 1st ed. 1966 **TD223.C3 ECOL**

Graham, Frank. Disaster by default. 1966
TD223.G7 1966 ECOL

Ketelle, Martha J. Problem lakes in the United States. 1971. **fTD223.K47 ECOL**

Kirkwood, James Pugh. A special report on the pollution of river waters. Reprint ed. 1970
REF TD425.K52 1970 ECOL

Kittrell, F. W. A practical guide to water quality studies of streams. 1969. **TD425.K53 ECOL**

League of Women Voters of the United States. Education Fund. The big water fight. 1966.
HD1694.A5L4 ECOL

Maryland. Dept. of Water Resources. Guidelines for erosion and sediment control, planning and implementation. 1972. **fS624.A1M3 ECOL**

National Association of Counties Research Foundation. Urban soil erosion and sediment control. 1970. **fS624.A1N38 ECOL**

United States. Environmental Protection Agency. Water Quality Office. Cost of clean water. 1971-
TD420.U5 ECOL

United States. Federal Power Commission. Steam-electric plant air and water quality control data for the year ended December 31, 1969, based on EPC form no. 67. 1973. **fTD195.E4U5 ECOL**

United States. Federal Water Quality Administration. Clean water for the 1970's. 1970.
fTD365.U5 ECOL

United States. President, 1969- (Nixon). Control of hazardous polluting substances. 1971.
TD365.U53 ECOL

United States. Water Resources Council. Summary, analysis. 1972. **TD345.U52 ECOL**

Wright, James Claud. The coming water famine. 1966 **TD223.W7 ECOL**

Zwick, David. Water wasteland. 1971.
TD223.Z86 1971 ECOL

WATER—POLLUTION—WISCONSIN.

Conference in the Matter of Pollution of the Interstate and Intrastate Waters of the Upper Mississippi River and its Tributaries—Wisconsin—Minnesota, Minneapolis, 1968. Proceedings of progress evaluation meeting held April 30, 1968. 1968. **fTD223.4.A45C6 ECOL**

Conference in the Matter of Pollution of the Interstate and Intrastate Waters of the Upper Mississippi River and its Tributaries—Minnesota and Wisconsin. Proceedings of the second session Minneapolis, Minnesota, Feb. 28, March 1 & 20, 1967. 1967. **REF TD223.4.A43C6 ECOL**

WATER—PURIFICATION see also
FEED-WATER PURIFICATION;
WATER—AERATION; WATER-SUPPLY ENGINEERING

American Water Works Association Research Foundation, New York Information resource: water pollution control in the water utility industry. 1971.
REF fTD429.A4 ECOL

American Water Works Association. Water quality and treatment. 3d ed. 1971 **TD430.A6 1971 ECOL**

Armco Steel Corporation. Treatment of waste water-waste oil mixtures. 1970. **fTD455.A7 ECOL**

Black & Veatch, Kansas City, Mo. Process design manual for phosphorus removal. 1971. **REF fTD745.B5 ECOL**

Burns and Roe. Process design manual for suspended solids removal. 1971. **REF fTD745.B8 ECOL**

Frea, James I. Washout processes in lake systems. 1972. **fTD764.F74 ECOL**

Gainesville, Fla. Dept. of Public Utilities. Magnesium carbonate, a recycled coagulant for water treatment. 1971. **fTD433.G3 ECOL**

North American Rockwell Corporation. Rocketdyne Division. Development of a chemical denitrification process. 1970. **fTD433.N67 ECOL**

Roy F. Weston, Inc. Process design manual for upgrading existing wastewater treatment plants. 1971. **REF fTD745.R6 ECOL**

Shindala, Adnan. Primary considerations in regional wastewater treatment planning. 1972. **fTD365.S4 ECOL**

Stenquist, Richard J. Initial mixing in coagulation processes. 1972. **TD455.S7 ECOL**

Weber, Walter J. Physiochemical processes for water quality control. 1972 **TD430.W42 ECOL**

Zajic, James E. Water pollution. 1971. **TD420.Z35 ECOL**

WATER—PURIFICATION—ADSORPTION.
Swindell-Dressler Company. Process design manual for carbon adsorption. 1971. **REF fTD753.5.S9 ECOL**

Tratnyek, Joseph P. Waste wool as a scavenger for mercury pollution in waters. 1972. **fTD427.M4T7 ECOL**

WATER—PURIFICATION—BIOLOGICAL TREATMENT.
California. Dept. of Water Resources. Removal of nitrate by an algal system, phase II. 1971. **fTD475.C342 ECOL**

Robert S. Kerr Water Research Center. Denitrification by anaerobic filters and ponds. 1971. **fTD475.R6 ECOL**

Robert S. Kerr Water Research Center. Denitrification by anaerobic filters and ponds, phase II. 1971. **TD475.R62 ECOL**

WATER—PURIFICATION—BIOLOGICAL TREATMENT—MINNESOTA.
Potential productivity of fresh water environments as determined by an algae bioassay technique. 1970. **GB701.M554no.20**

WATER—PURIFICATION—CHLORINATION.
Cha, C. Y. Photochemical methods for purifying water. 1972. **TD459.C4 ECOL**

WATER—PURIFICATION—FILTRATION.
Dow Chemical Company. Functional Products and Systems Dept. A literature search and critical analysis of biological trickling filter studies. 1971- **fTD443.D6 ECOL**

Robert S. Kerr Water Research Center. Denitrification by anaerobic filters and ponds, phase II. 1971. **TD475.R62 ECOL**

WATER—PURIFICATION—FOAM FRACTIONATION.
Henager, Charles H. Concept evaluation: recovery of floating oil using polyurethane foam sorbent. 1972. **fTD427.P4H4 ECOL**

Horizons Incorporated. Foam separation of acid mine drainage. 1971 **fTD899.M5H67 ECOL**

United States. Environmental Protection Agency. Office of Research and Monitoring. Air modulated vacuum oil recovery collection of spilled oil (foams). 1972. **fTD427.P4U5 ECOL**

WATER—PURIFICATION—ION EXCHANGE PROCESS.
Holmes, James G. Acid mine drainage treatment by ion exchange. 1972 **TD899.M5H6 ECOL**

WATER—PURIFICATION—OXIDATION.
Cha, C. Y. Photochemical methods for purifying water. 1972. **TD459.C4 ECOL**

WATER—PURIFICATION—OZONIZATION.
Evans, Francis L. Ozone in water and wastewater treatment. 1972 **TD461.E93 ECOL**

WATER—QUALITY see WATER QUALITY

WATER—STANDARDS—MISSISSIPPI RIVER.
Lewis, Robert Clark. The marginal costs of alternative levels of water quality in the Upper Mississippi River. 1970. **GB701.M554no.25 ECOL**

WATER—SUPPLY—RESEARCH.
Young, G. K. The importance of economic factors in urban surface water supply systems. 1972. **fTD353.Y6 ECOL**

WATER-BIRDS see also MURRES; SEA BIRDS; SHORE BIRDS
Alexander, Wilfrid Backhouse. Birds of the ocean. 1928. **QL673.A37 ECOL**

Big game in Minnesota. 1965. **SH11.M64no.9 ECOL**

Bovey, Martin Koon. Saga of the waterfowl. 1949. **REF SK331.B6 ECOL**

Cruickshank, Allan D. Wings in the wilderness. 1947. **QL674.C85 ECOL**

Hochbaum, Hans Albert. Travels and traditions of waterfowl. 1955 **QL698.H65 ECOL**

Minnesota. Dept. of Conservation. Division of Game and Fish. Waterfowl in Minnesota. 1964. **SH11.M64no.7 ECOL**

Phillips, John Charles. American waterfowl. 1930. **QL696.A5P45 ECOL**

Pough, Richard Hooper. Audubon water bird guide. 1951. **QL681.P69 ECOL**

Scott, Peter Markham. Key to the wildfowl of the world. n.d. **REF QL696.A5S349 ECOL**

WATER BLOOM.
Bartsch, A. F. Role of phosphorus in eutrophication. 1972. **QH96.8.E9B3 ECOL**

WATER BLOOM—CALIFORNIA.
United States. Environmental Protection Agency. Office of Research and Monitoring. The effects of agricultural waste water treatment on algal bioassay response. 1971. **QH96.8.E9U54 ECOL**

WATER CONSERVATION see also WATER QUALITY MANAGEMENT; WATER REUSE; WATER-SUPPLY
Archer, Sellers Gambrell. Rain, rivers, and reservoirs. c1968,c1963 **GB671.A7 ECOL**

WATER CONSERVATION—CONGRESSES.
National Conference on Soil, Water, and Suburbia, Washington, D.C., 1967. Soil, water, and suburbia. 1968 **fHT166.N36 1967 ECOL**

WATER CONSERVATION—GREAT LAKES REGION.
International Great Lakes Levels Board. Regulation of Great Lakes water levels: interim report on Lakes Superior and Ontario regulation, to the International Joint Commission by the International Great Lakes Levels Board. 1973. **fGB1627.G8I52 ECOL**

Kelnhofer, Guy J. Preserving the Great Lakes. 1972. **fTC423.3.K4 ECOL**

WATER CONSERVATION—MINNESOTA.
Land in Transition Symposium, 1971, St. Paul, Minn. 1971 **fS623.L3 1971 ECOL**

Minnesota. Conservation Needs Committee. Minnesota soil and water conservation needs inventory. 1971 **fHD243.M6A42 ECOL**

WATER CONSERVATION—MINNESOTA—RESEARCH.
Minnesota. University. Water Resources Research Center. Information concerning water resources research center projects, 1965-70. 1970. **GB701.M554no.19 ECOL**

Minnesota. University. Water Resources Research Center. Proceedings of Conference on Inland Lake Renewal and Shoreland Management. 1972. **GB701.M554no.53 ECOL**

Minnesota. University. Water Resources Research Center. Proceedings of conference on ongoing water resources research in Minnesota, March 1970. 1970. **GB701.M554no.21 ECOL**

Minnesota. University. Water Resources Research Center. Publications related to water resources research center projects, 1965-71 abstract-index. 1971. **GB701.M554no.32 ECOL**

WATER CONSERVATION—SOCIAL ASPECTS—RESEARCH.
Century Research Corporation. Social aspects of urban water conservation. 1972. **fTD388.5.C4 ECOL**

WATER CONSERVATION—UNITED STATES.
Engineering a victory for our environment: a citizen's guide to the U.S. Army Corps of Engineers. c1972. **fTC423.E5 ECOL**

WATER CONSERVATION—UNITED STATES—PERIODICALS.
United States. Agricultural Stabilization and Conservation Service. Rural environmental assistance program: summary. 1971- 1972- **S954.U6A3 ECOL**

WATER CONSUMPTION.
Grima, Angelo P. Residential water demand. 1972 **TD353.G7 ECOL**

WATER CONSUMPTION—UNITED STATES.
Wollman, Nathaniel. The outlook for water. 1971 **REF fTD223.W6 ECOL**

WATER LEVEL OF THE GREAT LAKES see GREAT LAKES—WATER LEVEL

WATER PURIFICATION PLANTS see WATER TREATMENT PLANTS

WATER QUALITY MANAGEMENT—MINNESOTA—MINNETONKA, LAKE.
Harza Engineering Company. A program for preserving the quality of Lake Minnetonka. 1971 **fTD225.M63H3 ECOL**

WATER QUALITY see also WATER—POLLUTION
Creative Research Services, Inc. Water quality management plan, interim. 1971. **REF fTD224.M65C7 ECOL**

Dodd, John D. The ecology of diatoms in hard water habitats. 1971. **fQK569.D54D6 ECOL**

Harris, Douglas H. Assessment of turbidity, color and odor in water. 1972. **fTD380.H3 ECOL**

Oregon. State University, Corvallis. School of Forestry. Studies on effects of watershed practices on streams. 1971 i.e. 1972 **fTC409.O74 ECOL**

Reiling, S. D. Economic benefits from an improvement in water quality. 1973. **fTD370.R45 ECOL**

Water quality criteria data book. 1970- **REF fTD370.W394 ECOL**

WATER QUALITY—ADDRESSES, ESSAYS, LECTURES.
Indicators of environmental quality. 1972. **TD172.5.I5 1972 ECOL**

WATER QUALITY—BIBLIOGRAPHY.
United States. Environmental Protection Agency. Office of Public Affairs. Current list of water publications, 1965/71- **REF Z7173.W3U5 ECOL**

Water Resources Scientific Information Center. Use of naturally impaired water. 1973. **Z7935.W32 ECOL**

WATER QUALITY—CALIFORNIA—INDIAN CREEK RESERVOIR.
Lake Tahoe Area Council. Eutrophication of surface waters—Lake Tahoe Indian Creek Reservoir. 1971. **fTD224.C3L32 ECOL**

WATER QUALITY—CONGRESSES.
International Water Quality Symposium, 5th, Washington, D.C., 1970. Water pollution and health: proceedings. 1970 **fTD423.I6 1970 ECOL**

Jerusalem International Conference on Water Quality and Pollution Research, 1969. Developments in water quality research. 1970 **TD370.J47 1969 ECOL**

WATER QUALITY—DICTIONARIES.
Minnesota Association of Commerce and Industry. Water quality control glossary. 1970 **fTD370.M56 ECOL**

WATER QUALITY—GEORGIA.
McClanahan, Mark A. A study of the effects of island development on lake water quality. 1972. **fTD224.G4M3 ECOL**

WATER QUALITY—GREAT LAKES.
Swain, Wayland R. The ecology of the second trophic level in Lakes Superior, Michigan and Huron. 1970. **GB701.M554no.26 ECOL**

WATER QUALITY—GREAT LAKES REGION.
Parkos, William G. Water quality studies on the Great Lakes based on carbon fourteen measurements on primary productivity. 1969. **GB701.M554no.17 ECOL**

WATER QUALITY—MATHEMATICAL MODELS.
Hann, Roy W. Mathematical models of water quality parameters for rivers and estuaries. 1972 **fTD370.H3 ECOL**

Tracor, Inc. Estuarine modeling: an assessment. 1971. **fTD370.T73 ECOL**

WATER QUALITY—MINNESOTA.
Brook, Alan J. The phytoplankton of Minnesota lakes—a preliminary survey. 1971. **GB701.M554no.36 ECOL**

Minnesota. Pollution Control Agency. Water quality sampling program: Minnesota lakes and streams. **TD380.M6 ECOL**

Waelti, John J. Understanding the water quality controversy in Minnesota. 1969 **fTD420.W3 ECOL**

WATER QUALITY—MINNESOTA—CONGRESSES.
Conference on Toward a Statewide Ground Water Quality Information System, St. Paul, Minn., 1972. Proceedings of conference on toward a statewide ground water quality information system and report of Ground Water Quality Subcommittee Citizens Advisory Committee, Governors Environmental Quality Council. 1973. **fTD224.M6C6 1972 ECOL**

WATER QUALITY—MINNESOTA—YEARBOOKS.
United States. Geological Survey. Water Resources Division. Water resources data for Minnesota, 1968- **REF GB705.M62A32 ECOL**

WATER QUALITY—NEW HAMPSHIRE.
Hall, Francis R. The influence of a New England wetland on water quantity and quality. 1972.
fTD224.N4H3 ECOL

WATER QUALITY—NEW YORK (STATE)—ONONDAGA LAKE.
Onondaga Co., N.Y. Onondaga Lake study. 1971.
fTD224.N7O5 ECOL

WATER QUALITY—STANDARDS.
United States. Environmental Protection Agency. Guidelines for developing or revising water quality standards under the Federal Water Pollution Control Act Amendments of 1972. 1973. **fTD370.U5 ECOL**

WATER QUALITY—STANDARDS—MISSISSIPPI RIVER WATERSHED.
Minnesota. State College, Winona. Mayfly distribution as a water quality index. 1970.
fTD370.M562 ECOL

WATER QUALITY—SUPERIOR, LAKE.
Olson, Theodore A. Lake Superior periphyton in relation to water quality. 1972. **fQK935.O4 ECOL**

WATER QUALITY—TEXAS—TRINITY RIVER.
Texas Christian University, Fort Worth. Dept. of Biology. Industrial wastes: effects on Trinity River ecology, Fort Worth, Texas. 1971 i.e. 1972
fTD224.T4T4 ECOL

WATER QUALITY—UNITED STATES.
Skogerboe, Gaylord V. Research needs for irrigation return flow quality control. 1971 i.e. 1972
fTD223.S54 ECOL
United States. Federal Water Pollution Control Administration. The economics of clean water.
HD4477.A53 ECOL
United States. Geological Survey. Water Resources Division. National reference list of water quality stations, water year 1971- **REF TD380.U5 ECOL**

WATER QUALITY—UNITED STATES—ABSTRACTS.
Skogerboe, Gaylord V. Selected irrigation return flow. 1972- **fTD223.S5 ECOL**

WATER QUALITY—UNITED STATES—CONGRESSES.
National Ground Water Quality Symposium, Denver, 1971. Proceedings. 1972
fTD223.N37 1971 ECOL

WATER QUALITY MANAGEMENT *see also* WATER—PURIFICATION; WATER REUSE
Bongers, Leonard H. Sand and gravel overlay for control of mercury in sediments. 1972.
fTD427.M4B6 ECOL
California. University. Flow into a stratified reservoir. 1972. **TC167.C3 ECOL**
Law, James P. National irrigation return flow research and development program. 1971.
fTC809.L38 ECOL
McPherson, Murray Burns. Management problems in metropolitan water resource operations. 1971.
fTD353.M3 ECOL
McPherson, Murray Burns. Prospects for metropolitan water management. 1970.
fTD353.M32 ECOL
Shindala, Adnan. Primary considerations in regional wastewater treatment planning. 1972.
fTD365.S4 ECOL
Suggs, James D. Mercury pollution control in stream and lake sediments. 1972. **fTD427.M4S9 ECOL**
Syracuse University. Civil Engineering Dept. Benefits of water quality enhancement. 1970.
fTD365.S94 ECOL
Tebbutt, T. H. Y. Principles of water quality control. 1st ed. 1971 **TD365.T4 1971 ECOL**
United States. Environmental Protection Agency. Office of Research and Monitoring. Projects of the National Water Quality Control Research Program. 1971. **fTD423.U546 ECOL**
United States. Federal Water Pollution Control Administration. Twin Cities Upper Mississippi River Project. Report on water quality investigations of the Mississippi, Minnesota and St. Croix Rivers. 1966
REF fTD225.T9U5 ECOL
Widman, Michael U. Polymer film overlay system for mercury contaminated sludge—Phase I. 1972.
fTD427.M4W5 ECOL

WATER QUALITY MANAGEMENT—CANADA.
Canada Centre for Inland Waters. Collected reprints. vol. 4- , 1971- , pt. 1-
TD226.C3 ECOL

WATER QUALITY MANAGEMENT—COLORADO.
Skogerboe, Gaylord V. Evaluation of canal lining for salinity control in Grand Valley. 1972.
TC930.S5 ECOL

WATER QUALITY MANAGEMENT—COLORADO—DENVER.
Walker, Wynn R. Evaluation of urban water management policies in the Denver metropolitan area. 1973. **fTD225.D4W3 ECOL**

WATER QUALITY MANAGEMENT—MATHEMATICAL MODELS.
Beckers, Charles V. Quantitative methods for preliminary design of water quality surveillance systems. 1972. **TD365.B4 ECOL**
Dracup, John A. Applications of systems analysis techniques to water resources. 1972.
fTC409.D7 ECOL
Males, Richard Michael. Decision processes in water quality management. 1971. **fTD365.M3 ECOL**
Models for managing regional water quality. 1972.
TD365.M6 ECOL
Whinston, A. B. Economic analyses of optimal water quality management. 1972. **fTD365.W4 ECOL**

WATER QUALITY MANAGEMENT—MINNESOTA.
Creative Research Services, Inc. Progress report, biennial program and long-range plan for water pollution control. 1970. **fTD224.M65C73 ECOL**

WATER QUALITY MANAGEMENT—MINNESOTA—SUPERIOR, LAKE.
Nelson, Robert R. The effects of enrichment on Lake Superior periphyton. 1973.
GB701.M554no.59 ECOL

WATER QUALITY MANAGEMENT—POTOMAC RIVER ESTUARY.
Davis, Robert K. The range of choice in water management. 1968 **TD225.P74D3 ECOL**

WATER QUALITY MANAGEMENT—SOCIAL ASPECTS.
Wengert, Norman. Institutions for urban-metropolitan water management: essays in social theory, submitted to Water Resources Scientific Information Center. 1972. **fTD353.W4 ECOL**
Wengert, Norman. Urban-metropolitan institutions for water planning, development and management: an analysis of usages of the term "institutions": a state-of-the-art review: final report, submitted to Water Resources Scientific Information Center. 1972.
fTD353.W42 ECOL

WATER QUALITY MANAGEMENT—UNITED STATES.
Brunson, E. Evan. Improving water quality management planning in nonmetropolitan areas. 1973.
fTD365.B78 ECOL
Synectics Corporation. A system for industrial waste treatment RD&D project priority assignment. 1971.
fTD897.5.S9 ECOL
United States. Environmental Protection Agency. Water Quality Office. Digest of State program plans. 1970/71- **TD223.A2635 ECOL**
United States. Federal Water Quality Administration. Clean water for the 1970's. 1970.
fTD365.U5 ECOL
United States. President, 1969- (Nixon). Control of hazardous polluting substances. 1971.
TD365.U53 ECOL
Willeke, Gene E. A program for metropolitan water management. 1972. **fTD365.W5 ECOL**

WATER QUALITY MANAGEMENT—UNITED STATES—ABSTRACTS.
Enviro Control, Inc. Systems analysis for water quality management—survey and abstracts. 1971.
fTD365.E5 ECOL

WATER QUALITY MANAGEMENT—UNITED STATES—CONGRESSES.
McKenzie, Linda. The grass roots and water resources management. 1972. **fHD1691.M3 ECOL**

WATER RECLAMATION *see* WATER REUSE

WATER RENOVATION *see* WATER REUSE

WATER RESEARCH—MINNESOTA.
Walton, William Clarence. International, regional, federal-state, interstate and federal organizations with water related land resources programs in Minnesota, 1971. 1971. **GB701.M554no.42 ECOL**

WATER RESOURCES DEVELOPMENT *see also* WATER SUPPLY
Buras, Nathan. Scientific allocation of water resources. 1972 **TC409.B87 ECOL**
Design of water-resource systems. 1970,c1962
TC409.D4 ECOL
INTASA, Inc. Planning and evaluation of multiple purpose water resource projects in a multiobjective environment. 1972. **fHD1691.I1 ECOL**
Linsley, Ray K. Water-resources engineering. 2d ed. 1971,c1972 **TC145.L55 1972 ECOL**
Resources for the Future. Comparisons in resource management. 1961 **REF SD411.R4 ECOL**
Resources for the Future. Multiple purpose river development. 1958 **REF HN15.R43 ECOL**

WATER RESOURCES DEVELOPMENT—ADDRESSES, ESSAYS, LECTURES.
Nikolaieff, George A. The water crisis. 1967.
TD355.N5 ECOL
Western Resources Conference. 7th, Colorado State University, 1965. Water research. c1966
REF TD355.W4 1965 ECOL

WATER RESOURCES DEVELOPMENT—BIBLIOGRAPHY.
California. University. Water Resources Center. Archives. Dictionary catalog of the Water Resources Center Archives, University of California, Berkeley. 1970. **REF fZ7935.C32 ECOL**
Sloss, George J. Water-related environmental planning. 1973. **fZ5862.W3S5 ECOL**
Water Resources Scientific Information Center. Urban water planning. 1972. REF **Z7935.W3 ECOL**

WATER RESOURCES DEVELOPMENT—BIG SIOUX RIVER WATERSHED.
United States. Soil Conservation Service. Big Sioux River Basin and related areas. 1973.
HD1695.B5A5 ECOL

WATER RESOURCES DEVELOPMENT—CALIFORNIA.
Boyle, Robert H. The water hustlers. 1971
HD1694.A5B58 ECOL

WATER RESOURCES DEVELOPMENT—CALIFORNIA—ADDRESSES, ESSAYS, LECTURES.
California water. 1971. **HD1694.C2C35 ECOL**

WATER RESOURCES DEVELOPMENT—CANADA.
Canada Centre for Inland Waters. Collected reprints. vol. 4- , 1971- , pt. 1-
TD226.C3 ECOL

WATER RESOURCES DEVELOPMENT—COLLECTED WORKS.
Wolman, Abel. Water, health, and society. 1969
REF TD355.W6 ECOL

WATER RESOURCES DEVELOPMENT—COLUMBIA RIVER VALLEY.
Krutilla, John V. The Columbia River Treaty. c1967
HD1694.A2 1967 ECOL

WATER RESOURCES DEVELOPMENT—GREAT LAKES REGION.
Kelnhofer, Guy J. Preserving the Great Lakes. 1972. **fTC423.3.K4 ECOL**
Resource management in the Great Lakes Basin. 1971 **HD1694.A2 1971 ECOL**

WATER RESOURCES DEVELOPMENT—INFORMATION SERVICES—DIRECTORIES.
United States. Library of Congress. National Referral Center for Science and Technology. A directory of information resources in the United States: water. 1966. **fTD211.U5 ECOL**

WATER RESOURCES DEVELOPMENT—INFORMATION SERVICES—NORTH CAROLINA.
Stewart, James M. Perception of water resources research, dissemination, and utilization of research findings. 1971. **fHD1694.N8N6no.58 ECOL**

WATER RESOURCES DEVELOPMENT—INFORMATION SERVICES—UNITED STATES.
Federal Interagency Water Data Handling Work Group. Design characteristics for a national system to store, retrieve, and disseminate water data. 1971.
fTD211.F4 ECOL
Federal Interagency Work Group on Designation of Standards for Water Data Acquisition. Recommended methods for water data acquisition. 1972.
TD211.F44 ECOL

WATER RESOURCES DEVELOPMENT—LAW AND LEGISLATION—COLUMBIA RIVER VALLEY.
Doerksen, Harvey R. Columbia River Interstate Compact, politics of negotiation. 1972
KF5590.C6D6 ECOL

WATER RESOURCES DEVELOPMENT—MATHEMATICAL MODELS.
Bishop, A. Bruce. Analysis of water reuse alternatives in an integrated urban and agricultural area. 1971 **fTD429.B5 ECOL**
Dracup, John A. Applications of systems analysis techniques to water resources. 1972.
fTC409.D7 ECOL

WATER RESOURCES DEVELOPMENT—MATHEMATICAL MODELS—GREAT LAKES REGION.
Hydroscience, Inc. Limnological systems analysis of the Great Lakes. 1973. **fTC423.3.H9 ECOL**

WATER RESOURCES DEVELOPMENT—MINNEHAHA CREEK WATERSHED.
Hickok (Eugene A.) and Associates, Wayzata, Minn. Overall plan for water management Minnehaha Creek Watershed District. 1969 **fTC424.M6H5 ECOL**

WATER RESOURCES DEVELOPMENT—MINNESOTA.
Gibson, Ulric P. Integrating water quality management into total water resources management in Minnesota. 1970. **GB701.M554no.23 ECOL**

Haik, Raymond A. Aspects of water resources law in Minnesota. 1969. **GB701.M554no.11 ECOL**

Minnesota. University. Water Resources Research Center. Codified and uncodified state laws and municipal ordinances bearing on water and related land resources in Minnesota. 1968. **GB701.M554no.9 ECOL**

Minnesota. University. Water Resources Research Center. Federal, state, and local agencies concerned with water resources research in Minnesota. 1965. **GB701.M554no.1 ECOL**

Minnesota. University. Water Resources Research Center. Advisory Committee. Graduate education in water resources at University of Minnesota—1969. 1969. **GB701.M554no.15 ECOL**

Minnesota. University. Water Resources Research Center. Information concerning water resources research center projects, 1965-70. 1970- **GB701.M554no.19 ECOL**

Minnesota. University. Water Resources Research Center. Consulting Council. Inventory of water resources research conducted in Minnesota, 1963 through 1968. 1969. **GB701.M554no.12 ECOL**

Minnesota. University. Water Resources Research Center. Proceedings of conference on ongoing water resources research in Minnesota, March 1970. 1970. **GB701.M554no.21 ECOL**

Minnesota. University. Water Resources Research Center. Water resources research and educational needs in Minnesota. 1967. **GB701.M554no.5 ECOL**

Minnesota. Water Resources Coordinating Committee. Alternative programs and projects for managing Minnesota's water and related land resources through the year 2020. 1971 **fHD1694.M6A5 1971 ECOL**

Minnesota. Water Resources Coordinating Committee. Minnesota water and related land resources, first assessment. 1970. **fTD224.M6A563 ECOL**

Seminar on the Engineer and the Environment University of Minnesota, 1970. The Engineer and the environment. 1971. **GB701.M554no.38 ECOL**

Walton, William Clarence. Interest groups with water and related land resources programs in Minnesota, 1971. 1972. **GB701.M554no.45 ECOL**

Walton, William Clarence. International, regional, federal-state, interstate and federal organizations with water related land resources programs in Minnesota, 1971. 1971. **GB701.M554no.42 ECOL**

Walton, William Clarence. Water and related land resources state administration, legislative process and policies in Minnesota, 1970. 1971 **GB701.M554no.27 ECOL**

Walton, William Clarence. Water resources administration in Minnesota, 1972. 1972. **GB701.M554no.49 ECOL**

WATER RESOURCES DEVELOPMENT—MINNESOTA—BIBLIOGRAPHY.
Walton, William Clarence. Lists of references and selected books bearing on water resources in Minnesota. 1966. **GB701.M554no.4 ECOL**

Walton, William Clarence. Lists of references and selected books bearing on Water resources in Minnesota. Rev. ed. 1972. **GB701.M554no.4 1972 ECOL**

WATER RESOURCES DEVELOPMENT—MINNESOTA—CONGRESSES.
Conference on Water and Related Land Resources Planning in Minnesota, St. Paul, Minn., 1967. Papers presented during Conference on Water and Related Land Resources Planning in Minnesota. 1967. **fHD1694.M6A54 1967 ECOL**

WATER RESOURCES DEVELOPMENT—MISSISSIPPI VALLEY.
Upper Mississippi River comprehensive basin study. 1970- **fHC107.A15U6 ECOL**

WATER RESOURCES DEVELOPMENT—MISSOURI RIVER BASIN.
Missouri Basin Inter-agency Committee. Comprehensive framework study, Missouri River Basin. 1971- **fHD1695.M5M48 ECOL**

WATER RESOURCES DEVELOPMENT—NEW YORK METROPOLITAN AREA.
Boyle, Robert H. The water hustlers. 1971 **HD1694.A5B58 ECOL**

WATER RESOURCES DEVELOPMENT—NORTH DAKOTA—ECONOMIC ASPECTS.
Ludtke, Richard L. Social and economic considerations for water resources planning in the Park River Subbasin, North Dakota. 1971. **HD1694.N9L8 ECOL**

WATER RESOURCES DEVELOPMENT—NORTH DAKOTA—SOCIAL ASPECTS.
Ludtke, Richard L. Social and economic considerations for water resources planning in the Park River Subbasin, North Dakota. 1971. **HD1694.N9L8 ECOL**

WATER RESOURCES DEVELOPMENT—OHIO RIVER WATERSHED.
United States. Water Resources Council. Ohio River Basin comprehensive survey—main report and development program formulation. 1971. **HD1695.O5A55 ECOL**

WATER RESOURCES DEVELOPMENT—PUBLIC OPINION.
Gerlach, Luther P. Mobilization and participation of citizens groups in improving the quality of water resources environments. 1973. **GB701.M554no.57 ECOL**

WATER RESOURCES DEVELOPMENT—RESEARCH—NORTH CAROLINA.
Stewart, James M. Perception of water resources research, dissemination, and utilization of research findings. 1971. **fHD1694.N8N6no.58 ECOL**

WATER RESOURCES DEVELOPMENT—SOCIAL ASPECTS.
Wengert, Norman. Institutions for urban-metropolitan water management: essays in social theory, submitted to Water Resources Scientific Information Center. 1972. **fTD353.W4 ECOL**

Wengert, Norman. Urban-metropolitan institutions for water planning, development and management: an analysis of usages of the term "institutions": a state-of-the-art review: final report, submitted to Water Resources Scientific Information Center. 1972. **fTD353.W42 ECOL**

WATER RESOURCES DEVELOPMENT—TEXAS.
Boyle, Robert H. The water hustlers. 1971 **HD1694.A5B58 ECOL**

Gunn, Clare A. Cultural benefits from metropolitan river recreation—San Antonio prototype. 1972. **fHD1694.T4G8 ECOL**

WATER RESOURCES DEVELOPMENT—UNITED STATES.
Briggs, Peter. Water: the vital essence. c1967 **GC21.B83 ECOL**

Deal, Richard L. The application of value theory to water resources planning and management. 1971. **fHD1694.A5D4 ECOL**

Helfman, Elizabeth S. Rivers and watersheds in America's future. 1965. **TC423.H45 ECOL**

Hirshleifer, Jack. Water supply: economics, technology, and policy. 1960 **HD1694.A5H5 1969 ECOL**

Kelnhofer, Guy J. Metropolitan planning and river basin planning: some interrelationships. 1968. **TD223.K4 ECOL**

League of Women Voters of the United States. Education Fund. The big water fight. 1966. **HD1694.A5L4 ECOL**

Moss, Frank E. The water crisis. c1967 **HD1694.A5M63 ECOL**

National Research Council. Committee on Water. Alternatives in water management. 1966. **HD1694.A5N48 ECOL**

River basin development. 1957. **HN64.R589 ECOL**

United States. Water Resources Council. Summary, analysis. 1972. **TD345.U52 ECOL**

Water resources. 1957. **HD1694.A5W3 ECOL**

White, Gilbert Fowler. Strategies of American water management. 1969 **HD1694.A5W5 ECOL**

Wilson, Raymond Harrison. Toward a philosophy of planning: attitudes of federal water planners. 1973. **HC110.E5W5 ECOL**

WATER RESOURCES DEVELOPMENT—UNITED STATES—CONGRESSES.
McKenzie, Linda. The grass roots and water resources management. 1972. **fHD1691.M3 ECOL**

Western Resources Conference. Colorado School of Mines, summer 1971. Needs of a progressive society for mineral and energy resources and realistic solutions to environmental problems posed. 1971 **REF fTD172.5.W4 ECOL**

WATER RESOURCES DEVELOPMENT—UNITED STATES—DIRECTORIES.
United States. Water Resources Council. Coordination directory for planning studies and reports. 1971- **TD345.U5 ECOL**

WATER RESOURCES DEVELOPMENT—THE WEST.
Howe, Charles W. Interbasin transfers of water. 1971 **HD1695.W4H66 ECOL**

WATER REUSE.
Bishop, A. Bruce. Analysis of water reuse alternatives in an integrated urban and agricultural area. 1971 **fTD429.B5 ECOL**

Boen, Doyle F. Study of reutilization of wastewater recycled through groundwater. 1971. **fTD429.B6 ECOL**

Georgia Kraft Company. Research and Development Center. Treatment of selected internal kraft mill wastes in a cooling tower. 1971. **fTD899.W65G46 ECOL**

United States. Environmental Protection Agency. Office of Research and Monitoring. The effects of agricultural waste water treatment on algal bioassay response. 1971. **QH96.8.E9U54 ECOL**

WATER REUSE—ADDRESSES, ESSAYS, LECTURES.
Water quality improvement by physical and chemical processes. 1970 **TD745.W37 ECOL**

WATER REUSE—BIBLIOGRAPHY.
Water Resources Scientific Information Center. Use of naturally impaired water. 1973. **Z7935.W32 ECOL**

WATER REUSE—CALIFORNIA—SANTEE.
Stevens, Leonard A. The town that launders its water. 1971 **TD429.S84 1971 ECOL**

WATER REUSE—TEXAS—SAN ANTONIO.
Alamo Area Council of Governments. Basin management for water reuse. 1972. **fTD225.S225A65 ECOL**

WATER REUSE—UNITED STATES.
Johnson, James Francis. Renovated waste water. 1971. **TD429.J6 ECOL**

United States. Bureau of Reclamation. Summary report of the Commissioner of the Bureau of Reclamation to the Secretary of the Interior for the fiscal year ended June 30, 1970- and statistical and financial appendix. **REF TC823.A27 ECOL**

WATER-RIGHTS—MINNESOTA.
Gibson, Ulric P. Integrating water quality management into total water resources management in Minnesota. 1970. **GB701.M554no.23 ECOL**

WATER-RIGHTS—UNITED STATES.
Hirshleifer, Jack. Water supply: economics, technology, and policy. 1960 **HD1694.A5H5 1969 ECOL**

WATER RIGHTS—THE WEST.
Hutchins, Wells A. Water rights laws in the nineteen western states. 1971- **KF5559.A45H8 ECOL**

WATER-STORAGE—MINNESOTA—WACONIA.
Schoell and Madson, Inc., Hopkins, Minn. Report on the municipal water supply, treatment, storage, and distribution system, City of Waconia, Minnesota. 1967. **fTD225.W3S3 ECOL**

WATER, SUBTERRANEAN see WATER, UNDERGROUND

WATER-SUPPLY see also DAMS; FORESTS AND FORESTRY; RESERVOIRS; RUNOFF; STREAM MEASUREMENTS; WATER—POLLUTION; WATER—PURIFICATION
Carlson, Carl Walter. Water fit to use. 1966 **TD348.C3 ECOL**

Golany, Pinhas. Effects of channel characteristics on time parameters for small watershed runoff hydrographs. 1971. **GB701.M554no.31 ECOL**

Lewis, Alfred. This thirsty world. 1964 **TD348.L46 ECOL**

McPherson, Murray Burns. Management problems in metropolitan water resource operations. 1971. **fTD353.M3 ECOL**

Peterson, Ottis. Junior science book of water. 1966
PZ10.P4472Ju ECOL

Riedman, Sarah Regal. Water for people. Rev. ed. c1960 **TC153.R5 1960 ECOL**

Rondiere, Pierre. Purity or pollution. 1st ed. 1971
TD348.R65 ECOL

Walton, William Clarence. Groundwater resource evaluation. 1970 **GB1003.W28 ECOL**

WATER-SUPPLY—ADDRESSES, ESSAYS, LECTURES.
Nikolaieff, George A. The water crisis. 1967.
TD355.N5 ECOL

Western Resources Conference. 7th, Colorado State University, 1965. Water research. c1966
REF TD355.W4 1965 ECOL

WATER-SUPPLY—BIBLIOGRAPHY.
California. University. Water Resources Center. Archives. Dictionary catalog of the Water Resources Center Archives, University of California, Berkeley. 1970. **REF fZ7935.C32 ECOL**

Water Resources Scientific Information Center. Urban water planning. 1972. **REF Z7935.W3 ECOL**

Water Resources Scientific Information Center. Use of naturally impaired water. 1973.
Z7935.W32 ECOL

WATER-SUPPLY—CANADA.
Canada Centre for Inland Waters. Collected reprints. vol. 4-   , 1971-   , pt. 1-
TD226.C3 ECOL

WATER-SUPPLY—COLLECTED WORKS.
Wolman, Abel. Water, health, and society. 1969
REF TD355.W6 ECOL

WATER SUPPLY—DELAWARE RIVER BASIN.
Delaware River Basin Commission. Interstate planning for regional water supply and pollution control. 1971. **fTD420.D4 ECOL**

WATER-SUPPLY—GREAT BRITAIN.
Great Britain. Central Advisory Water Committee. The future management of water in England and Wales: a report. 1971. **TD257.A5 1971 ECOL**

WATER-SUPPLY—INFORMATION SERVICES.
McPherson, Murray Burns. Feasibility of the metropolitan water intelligence system concept (Integrated automatic operational control). 1971.
fTD211.M3 ECOL

WATER-SUPPLY—INFORMATION SERVICES—DIRECTORIES.
United States. Library of Congress. National Referral Center for Science and Technology. A directory of information resources in the United States: water. 1966. **fTD211.U5 ECOL**

WATER-SUPPLY—ISRAEL—CONGRESSES.
Jerusalem International Conference on Water Quality and Pollution Research, 1969. Developments in water quality research. 1970
TD370.J47 1969 ECOL

WATER-SUPPLY—MINNEAPOLIS.
Minnesota. Dept. of Conservation. Division of Waters. Water resources of Minneapolis-St. Paul metropolitan area. 1961. **fTD224.M6A3no.11 ECOL**

WATER SUPPLY—MINNEAPOLIS-ST. PAUL.
Peterson, Mattie deHaan. Interjurisdictional aspects of water resources management in the Minneapolis-St. Paul metropolitan area of Minnesota. 1971.
REF fTD225.M6P4 1971 ECOL

WATER SUPPLY—MINNESOTA.
Conference on Water and Related Land Resources Planning in Minnesota, St. Paul, Minn., 1967. Papers presented during Conference on Water and Related Land Resources Planning in Minnesota. 1967.
fHD1694.M6A54 1967 ECOL

Maderak, Marion L. Quality of waters, Minnesota. 1963. **fTD224.M6A3no.21 ECOL**

Minnesota. University. Water Resources Research Center. Annual report. **GB701.M554 ECOL**

Minnesota. University. Water Resources Research Center. Consulting Council. Inventory of water resources research conducted in Minnesota, 1963 through 1968. 1969. **GB701.M554no.12 ECOL**

Minnesota. Water Resources Coordinating Committee. Alternative programs and projects for managing Minnesota's water and related land resources through the year 2020. 1971
fHD1694.M6A5 1971 ECOL

Minnesota. Water Resources Coordinating Committee. Minnesota water and related land resources, first assessment. 1970.
fTD224.M6A563 ECOL

Straka, G. C. Graphs of ground water levels in Minnesota, 1957-1961. 1963.
fTD224.M6A3no.18 ECOL

United States. Geological Survey. Water Resources Division. Water resources data for Minnesota, 1968- **REF GB705.M62A32 ECOL**

WATER-SUPPLY—MINNESOTA—ST. LOUIS RIVER WATERSHED.
Minnesota. Dept. of Conservation. Division of Waters. The St. Louis River Watershed unit. 1964.
fTD224.M6A3no.22 ECOL

WATER-SUPPLY—MINNESOTA—TWIN CITIES METROPOLITAN AREA.
Metcalf and Eddy, Boston. Sewerage and water planning report. 1968. **fTD525.T9M4 ECOL**

WATER-SUPPLY—MINNESOTA—WACONIA.
Schoell and Madson, Inc., Hopkins, Minn. Report on the municipal water supply, treatment, storage, and distribution system, City of Waconia, Minnesota. 1967.
fTD225.W3S3 ECOL

WATER-SUPPLY—ST. PAUL.
Minnesota. Dept. of Conservation. Division of Waters. Water resources of Minneapolis-St. Paul metropolitan area. 1961. **fTD224.M6A3no.11 ECOL**

WATER-SUPPLY—SOCIAL ASPECTS.
Wengert, Norman. Institutions for urban-metropolitan water management: essays in social theory, submitted to Water Resources Scientific Information Center. 1972. **fTD353.W4 ECOL**

Wengert, Norman. Urban-metropolitan institutions for water planning, development and management: an analysis of usages of the term "institutions": a state-of-the-art review: final report, submitted to Water Resources Scientific Information Center. 1972.
fTD353.W42 ECOL

WATER-SUPPLY—TABLES, CALCULATIONS, ETC.
Todd, David Keith. The water encyclopedia. 1970
REF TD351.T63 ECOL

WATER-SUPPLY—UNITED STATES.
American Water Works Association. Water quality and treatment. 3d ed. 1971 **TD430.A6 1971 ECOL**

Carr, Donald Eaton. Death of the sweet waters. 1st ed. 1966 **TD223.C3 ECOL**

Heady, Earl Orel. Agricultural and water policies and the environment: an analysis of national alternatives in natural resource use, food supply capacity and environmental quality. 1972.
fS441.H4 ECOL

Hirshleifer, Jack. Water supply: economics, technology, and policy. 1960
HD1694.A5H5 1969 ECOL

Kelnhofer, Guy J. Metropolitan planning and river basin planning: some interrelationships. 1968.
TD223.K4 ECOL

Moss, Frank E. The water crisis. c1967
HD1694.A5M63 ECOL

Piper, Arthur Maine. Has the United States enough water? 1965. **REF TC801.U2no.1797 ECOL**

Russell, Clifford S. Drought and water supply. 1970
TD223.R88 ECOL

Wollman, Nathaniel. The outlook for water. 1971
REF fTD223.W6 ECOL

Wright, James Claud. The coming water famine. 1966 **TD223.W7 ECOL**

WATER-SUPPLY—UNITED STATES—BIBLIOGRAPHY.
Giefer, Gerald J. Water publications of State agencies. 1972 **REF Z7935.G55 ECOL**

WATER-SUPPLY—UNITED STATES-PERIODICALS.
United States. Geological Survey. Surface water supply of the United States. 1961/65-
TC801.U2 ECOL

WATER SUPPLY ENGINEERING see also WATER-SUPPLY, INDUSTRIAL
Fair, Gordon Maskew. Water and wastewater engineering. 1966-1968 **REF TD145.F32 ECOL**

Hardenbergh, William Andrew. Water supply and waste disposal. 1970,c1960 **TD145.H33 1970 ECOL**

WATER-SUPPLY ENGINEERING—RESEARCH—UNITED STATES.
Harvard Water Program. The economics of water supply and quality. 1971. **fTD223.H34 ECOL**

WATER-SUPPLY, INDUSTRIAL.
Cootner, Paul H. Water demand for steam electric generation. 1966,c1965 **TK1051.C6 ECOL**

Elliott, Ralph D. The effects of sewer surcharges on the level of industrial wastes and the use of water by industry. 1972. **TD897.5.E4 ECOL**

McCoy, James W. Chemical analysis of industrial water. 1969. **TD380.M3 ECOL**

WATER-SUPPLY, INDUSTRIAL—UNITED STATES.
National Association of Manufacturers of the United States. Water in industry. 1965.
TD223.N3 1965 ECOL

Tucker, L. Scott. Metropolitan industrial water use. 1972. **fTD223.T8 ECOL**

WATER TREATMENT PLANTS.
American Water Works Association Research Foundation, New York Information resource: water pollution control in the water utility industry. 1971.
REF fTD429.A4 ECOL

Armco Steel Corporation. Treatment of waste water-waste oil mixtures. 1970. **fTD455.A7 ECOL**

Black & Veatch, Kansas City, Mo. Process design manual for phosphorus removal. 1971.
REF fTD745.B5 ECOL

Burns and Roe. Process design manual for suspended solids removal. 1971. **REF fTD745.B8 ECOL**

Roy F. Weston, Inc. Process design manual for upgrading existing wastewater treatment plants. 1971.
REF fTD745.R6 ECOL

Shindala, Adnan. Primary considerations in regional wastewater treatment planning. 1972.
fTD365.S4 ECOL

Swindell-Dressler Company. Process design manual for carbon adsorption. 1971.
REF fTD753.5.S9 ECOL

WATER TREATMENT PLANTS—MINNESOTA—WACONIA.
Schoell and Madson, Inc., Hopkins, Minn. Report on the municipal water supply, treatment, storage, and distribution system, City of Waconia, Minnesota. 1967.
fTD225.W3S3 ECOL

WATER TREATMENT PLANTS—STUDY AND TEACHING.
Brown, James C. An investigation of curricula materials and methodology for training operators of wastewater treatment plants. 1972.
fHD1694.N8N6no.74 ECOL

WATER, UNDERGROUND see also SOIL MOISTURE; WELLS
Huisman, L. Groundwater recovery. 1972
TD405.H85 ECOL

Johnson, Jack D. Development of a mathematical model to predict the role of surface runoff and groundwater flow in over fertilization of surface waters. 1971. **GB701.M554no.35 ECOL**

Walton, William Clarence. Groundwater resource evaluation. 1970 **GB1003.W28 ECOL**

WATER, UNDERGROUND—ARTIFICIAL RECHARGE.
Boen, Doyle F. Study of reutilization of wastewater recycled through groundwater. 1971.
fTD429.B6 ECOL

Bouwer, Herman. Renovating secondary sewage by ground water recharge with infiltration basins. 1972.
fTD765.B6 ECOL

Ralph M. Parsons Laboratory for Water Resources and Hydrodynamics. Density induced mixing in confined aquifers. 1972. **fTC176.R33 ECOL**

Walton, William Clarence. Recharge from induced streambed infiltration under varying groundwater-level and stream-stage conditions. 1967.
GB701.M554no.6 ECOL

WATER, UNDERGROUND—BIBLIOGRAPHY.
Van der Leeden, Frits. Ground water: a selected bibliography. 1971 **REF Z7935.V35 ECOL**

WATER, UNDERGROUND—ILLINOIS.
Hughes, George Muggah. Hydrogeology of solid waste disposal sites in northeastern Illinois. 1971
TD795.7.H84 ECOL

WATER, UNDERGROUND—MINNESOTA.
Liesch, Bruce A. Geohydrology of the Jorden aquifer in the Minneapolis-St. Paul area Minnesota. 1961.
fGB705.M6L5 ECOL

Maderak, Marion L. Chemical quality of ground water in the Minneapolis-St. Paul area, Minnesota. 1965. **fTD224.M6A3no.23 ECOL**

Straka, G. C. Graphs of ground water levels in Minnesota, 1957-1961. 1963.
fTD224.M6A3no.18 ECOL

Van Voast, Wayne A. Ground water for irrigation in the Brooten-Belgrade area, west-central Minnesota. 1971. **TC801.U2no.1899-E ECOL**

WATER, UNDERGROUND—MINNESOTA—NOBLES COUNTY.
Norvitch, Ralph F. Ground water in alluvial channel deposits, Nobles County, Minnesota. 1960.
fTD224.M6A3no.14 ECOL

WATER, UNDERGROUND—POLLUTION.
Fungaroli, A. A. Pollution of subsurface water by sanitary landfills. 1971 i.e. 1972-
TD403.F85 ECOL

Robert S. Kerr Water Research Center. Investigations concerning probable impact of nitrilotriacetic acid on ground waters. 1971.
fTD427.D4R6 ECOL

WATER, UNDERGROUND—POLLUTION—BIBLIOGRAPHY.
United States. Environmental Protection Agency. Office of Water Programs. Subsurface water pollution. 1972. **Z7173.W3U5 ECOL**

WATER, UNDERGROUND—POLLUTION—LUBBOCK CO., TEXAS.
Wells, Dan M. Potential pollution of the Ogallala by recharging playa lake water—pesticides. 1970. **fTD224.T4W45 ECOL**

WATER, UNDERGROUND—POLLUTION—MINNESOTA—CONGRESSES.
Conference on Toward a Statewide Ground Water Quality Information System, St. Paul, Minn., 1972. Proceedings of conference on toward a statewide ground water quality information system and report of Ground Water Quality Subcommittee Citizens Advisory Committee, Governors Environmental Quality Council. 1973. **fTD224.M6C6 1972 ECOL**

WATER, UNDERGROUND—POLLUTION—SOUTHWEST, NEW.
Fuhriman, Dean K. Ground water pollution in Arizona, California, Nevada & Utah. 1971 i.e. 1972 **fTD223.9.F85 ECOL**

WATER, UNDERGROUND—POLLUTION—UNITED STATES—CONGRESSES.
National Ground Water Quality Symposium, Denver, 1971. Proceedings. 1972 **fTD223.N37 1971 ECOL**

WATER, UNDERGROUND—TEXAS—LUBBOCK CO.—ARTIFICIAL RECHARGE.
Wells, Dan M. Potential pollution of the Ogallala by recharging playa lake water—pesticides. 1970. **fTD224.T4W45 ECOL**

WATER WAVES—RESEARCH.
Thomsen, Arvid L. Riprap stability on earth embankments tested in large—and small-scale wave tanks. 1972. **TC533.T4 ECOL**

WATERFOWL *see also* ANATIDAE; DUCKS; GEESE; WATER-BIRDS
Goldstein, Jon H. Competition for wetlands in the Midwest. 1971 **HD1683.U4G6 ECOL**
Johnsgard, Paul A. Waterfowl, their biology and natural history. 1968 **QL696.A5J63 ECOL**
Smith, Allen E. Ecological factors affecting waterfowl production in the Alberta parklands. 1971. **S914.A3no.98 ECOL**
Stoudt, Jerome H. Ecological factors affecting waterfowl production in the Saskatchewan Parklands. 1971. **S914.A3no.99 ECOL**
Williams, Eugene Russell. The ways of wildfowl. 1971 **REF fQL696.A5W48 ECOL**

WATERFOWL—NORTH AMERICA—IDENTIFICATION.
Wylie, Stephen R. Key to North American waterfowl. 1972 **QL696.A5W46 ECOL**

WATERFOWL MANAGEMENT—ALBERTA.
Smith, Allen E. Ecological factors affecting waterfowl production in the Alberta parklands. 1971. **S914.A3no.98 ECOL**

WATERFOWL MANAGEMENT—MINNESOTA.
Minnesota. Dept. of Conservation. Division of Game and Fish. Ducks and land use in Minnesota. 1964. **SH11.M64no.8 ECOL**

WATERFOWL MANAGEMENT—SASKATCHEWAN.
Stoudt, Jerome H. Ecological factors affecting waterfowl production in the Saskatchewan Parklands. 1971. **S914.A3no.99 ECOL**

WATERFRONTS.
Milwaukee. Milwaukee River Technical Study Committee. The Milwaukee River. 1968. **fTD225.M47M6 ECOL**

WATERSHED DEVELOPMENT *see* WATERSHED MANAGEMENT

WATERSHED MANAGEMENT *see also* FOREST MANAGEMENT
Envirometrics, Inc., Wash., D.C. The river basin model. 1971- **fTC409.E5 ECOL**
Envirometrics, Inc., Wash., D.C. The river basin model: computer output. 1971. **fTC409.E51 ECOL**
Envirometrics, Inc., Wash., D.C. The river basin model: municipal services department. 1971. **fTC409.E5 ECOL**
Oregon. State University, Corvallis. School of Forestry. Studies on effects of watershed practices on streams. 1971 i.e. 1972 **fTC409.O74 ECOL**
Peterson, John H. Community organization programs and relationships in watershed development. 1972. **fTC409.P4 ECOL**

WATERSHED MANAGEMENT—MINNESOTA.
Minnesota. University. Water Resources Research Center. Watershed planning: papers presented at the Seminar on Watershed Planning sponsored by the Metropolitan Council and the Minnesota Association of Watershed Districts on February 15, 1972 at the Sheraton Motor Inn, Bloomington, Minnesota. 1972. **GB701.M554no.50 ECOL**
United States. Army. Corps of Engineers. Interim survey report on Blue Earth River, Minnesota, Minnesota River Basin for flood control and related purposes. 1970? **Ref fTC424.M6A5 ECOL**
United States. Soil Conservation Service. Flood hazard analyses: city of Canby and vicinity, Yellow Medicine County, Minnesota. 1973. **GB1225.M6U5 ECOL**

WATERSHED MANAGEMENT—MINNESOTA—LOWER MINNESOTA RIVER WATERSHED.
Itasca Engineering, inc. Minneapolis. The Lower Minnesota River Watershed District. 1961. **fTC424.M6I84 ECOL**
Itasca Engineering, inc., Minneapolis. Overall plan of the Lower Minnesota River Watershed District, 1972. **fTC424.M6I86 ECOL**

WATERSHED MANAGEMENT—MINNESOTA—MINNEHAHA CREEK WATERSHED.
Hickok (Eugene A.) and Associates, Wayzata, Minn. Overall plan for water management Minnehaha Creek Watershed District. 1969 **fTC424.M6H5 ECOL**

WATERSHED MANAGEMENT—MINNESOTA—NINE MILE CREEK WATERSHED.
Barr, Douglas W. Over-all plan for Nine Mile Creek Watershed District. 1961. **fTC424.M6B36 ECOL**
Barr Engineering Co. Feasibility study: Mt. Normandale Lake and Marsh Lake, for City of Bloomington and Nine Mile Creek Watershed District. 1967. **fTC424.M6B32 ECOL**
Barr Engineering Co. Feasibility study of Mud Lake improvement. 1966. **fTC424.M6B322 ECOL**
Barr Engineering Co. Hydrological study of Hyland-Bush-Anderson lakes. 1971. **fTC424.M6B326 ECOL**
Barr Engineering Co. Mud Lake hydrologic study. 1972. **fTC424.M6B34 ECOL**
Barr Engineering Co. Report to the Board of Managers, Nine Mile Creek Watershed District. **fTC424.M6B3 ECOL**
Barr Engineering Company. Nine Mile Creek Watershed District. 1973. **fTC424.M6B362 ECOL**

WATERSHED MANAGEMENT—MINNESOTA—ST. LOUIS PARK.
St. Louis Park, Minn. City Attorney's Office. City attorney's report, re: flood plain management. 1969 **fTC425.S3A5 ECOL**

WATERSHED RESOURCES DEVELOPMENT—UNITED STATES.
United States. Soil Conservation Service. Watershed protection handbook. 1967- **REF TC423.A53 ECOL**

WATERSHEDS.
Golany, Pinhas. Effects of channel characteristics on time parameters for small watershed runoff hydrographs. 1971. **GB701.M554no.31 ECOL**
Larson, Curtis L. Numerical routing of flood hydrographs through open channel junctions. 1971. **GB701.M554no.40 ECOL**
Wei, Tsong C. Effects of areal and time distribution of rainfall on small watershed runoff hydrographs. 1971. **GB701.M554no.30 ECOL**

WATERSHEDS—MATHEMATICAL MODELS.
Freeze, Allan R. A physics-based approach to hydrologic response modeling: Phase I: model development, completion report. 1972. **fGB665.F7 ECOL**

WATERSHEDS—MINNESOTA.
Barr Engineering Co. Report to the Board of Managers, Nine Mile Creek Watershed District. **fTC424.M6B3 ECOL**
Barr Engineering Company. Nine Mile Creek Watershed District. 1973. **fTC424.M6B35 ECOL**
Bowers, C. Edward. Computer programs in hydrology. 1972. **GB665.B6 ECOL**
Bowers, C. Edward. Review and analysis of rainfall and runoff data for selected watersheds in Minnesota. 1968. **GB701.M554no.8 ECOL**
Peterson, Mattie deHaan. Interjurisdictional aspects of water resources management in the Minneapolis-St. Paul metropolitan area of Minnesota. 1971. **REF fTD225.M6P4 1971 ECOL**

WATERSHEDS—RESEARCH.
Larson, Curtis L. Predicting peak flow of small watersheds by use of channel characteristics. 1972. **GB701.M554no.52 ECOL**

WATERSHEDS—UNITED STATES.
Helfman, Elizabeth S. Rivers and watersheds in America's future. 1965. **TC423.H45 ECOL**
United States. Soil Conservation Service. Watershed protection handbook. 1967- **REF TC423.A53 ECOL**

WATERWORKS—MANAGEMENT.
McPherson, Murray Burns. Management problems in metropolitan water resource operations. 1971. **fTD353.M3 ECOL**
McPherson, Murray Burns. Prospects for metropolitan water management. 1970. **fTD353.M32 ECOL**

WEATHER *see also* CLIMATOLOGY; METEOROLOGY; RAIN AND RAINFALL; SNOW; WEATHER CONTROL
Blumenstock, David Irving. The Ocean of air. 1959. **QC863.B55 ECOL**
Couchman, J. Kenneth. Mini-climates. c1971 **QC863.C68 ECOL**
Henson, Collins M. Your environment: air, air pollution, and weather. 1971 **QC863.H45 ECOL**
Trewartha, Glenn Thomas. An introduction to climate. 4th ed. 1968 **QC981.T65 1968 ECOL**

WEATHER—JUVENILE LITERATURE.
Henson, Collins M. Your environment: air, air pollution, and weather. 1971 **QC863.H45 ECOL**

WEATHER CONTROL.
National Research Council. Committee on Atmospheric Sciences. Weather and climate modification problems and prospects. 1966. **QC928.N36 ECOL**
Study of Man's Impact on Climate, Stockholm, 1970. Inadvertent climate modification. 1971 **QC981.S77 1970 ECOL**
Weather modification. 1969 **QC928.W38 ECOL**

WEED CONTROL—BIOLOGICAL CONTROL.
DeBach, Paul. Biological control of insect pests and weeds. 1964 **REF SB975.D4 ECOL**

WEED KILLERS *see* HERBICIDES

WEEDS.
Dowden, Anne Ophelia (Todd). Wild green things in the city. 1972 **SB611.D675 1972 ECOL**
Wright, Robert Henry. What good is a weed? 1972 **QK49.W75 ECOL**

WEEDS—IDENTIFICATION.
Wilkinson, Robert E. How to know the weeds. 2d ed. 1972 **SB612.A2W54 1972 ECOL**

WEEDS—UNITED STATES.
Dowden, Anne Ophelia (Todd). Wild green things in the city. 1972 **SB611.D675 1972 ECOL**
Wilkinson, Robert E. How to know the weeds. 2d ed. 1972 **SB612.A2W54 1972 ECOL**

WELLS.
Huisman, L. Groundwater recovery. 1972 **TD405.H85 ECOL**

WELLS—SOCIETIES, ETC.—DIRECTORIES.
National Water Well Association. Membership directory. 1972/73- **REF TD407.N3 ECOL**

THE WEST—DESCRIPTION AND TRAVEL.
Smythe, William Ellsworth. The conquest of arid America. 1969,c1905 **F591.S662 1969 ECOL**

WETLANDS.
Smith, Frances C. The first book of swamps and marshes. 1968,c1969 **QH541.5.M3S6 ECOL**

WETLANDS—ECONOMIC ASPECTS—MINNESOTA.
Goldstein, Jon H. Competition for wetlands in the Midwest. 1971 **HD1683.U4G6 ECOL**

WETLANDS—NEW HAMPSHIRE.
Hall, Francis R. The influence of a New England wetland on water quantity and quality. 1972. **fTD224.N4H3 ECOL**

WHALES.
Cousteau, Jacques Yves. The whale. 1st ed. in U.S. 1972. **QL737.C4C6913 ECOL**

WHALING.
Mizumura, Kazue. The blue whale. c1971 **QL737.C424M59 ECOL**
Small, George L. The blue whale. 1971. **QL737.C424S58 ECOL**

WHITE-TAILED DEER—MINNESOTA—CONGRESSES.
Symposium on the White-tailed Deer in Minnesota, St. Paul, Minnesota, 1971. The white-tailed deer in Minnesota. 1972? **fQL737.U55S9 1971 ECOL**

WHOOPING CRANES.
Allen, Robert Porter. On the trail of vanishing birds. 1957 **QL696.G8A4 ECOL**
Allen, Robert Porter. The whooping crane. 1952. **QL696.G8A43 ECOL**

WILD AND SCENIC RIVERS—UNITED STATES.
Pringle, Laurence P. Wild river. 1st ed. 1972 **fQH541.5.S7P75 ECOL**

WILD FLOWERS—MIDDLE WEST.
Courtenay, Booth. Wildflowers and weeds. 1972? **QK141.C6 ECOL**

WILD FLOWERS—MINNESOTA.
Marotta, Juanita. Minnesota wild flowers of forest, field and wetland. 1971. **QK168.M3 ECOL**
Monserud, Wilma. Common wild flowers of Minnesota. c1971 **QK168.M6 ECOL**

WILD FLOWERS—NORTH AMERICA.
Walcott, Mary Morris (Vaux). North American wild flowers. 1925. **REF fQK112.W3 ECOL**

WILD FLOWERS—UNITED STATES.
Grimm, William Carey. Home guide to trees, shrubs, and wild flowers. 1970 **QK482.G734 ECOL**
Rickett, Harold William. The new field book of American wild flowers. 1963 **QK118.R5 ECOL**

WILD-FOWL see GAME AND GAME-BIRDS; WATER-BIRDS

WILD TURKEYS.
Lewis, James C. The world of the wild turkey. 1st ed. 1973 **QL696.G2L48 ECOL**

WILDERNESS AREAS.
Brockman, Christian Frank. Recreational use of wild lands. 1959. **SB481.B66 ECOL**
Brooks, Paul. The pursuit of wilderness. 1971. **QH75.B73 ECOL**
Brooks, Paul. Roadless area. 1971,c1964. **QH75.B74 ECOL**
Dasmann, Raymond Frederick. A different kind of country. 1968 **QH75.D37 ECOL**
Ohmann, Lewis F. Wilderness ecology, virgin plant communities of the Boundary Waters Canoe Area. 1971. **SD11.A45476no.63 ECOL**
Schwartz, William. Voices for the wilderness. 1969 **QH75.S32 ECOL**

WILDERNESS AREAS—CANADA.
Knauth, Percy. The North Woods. 1972 **QH75.K63 ECOL**

WILDERNESS AREAS—MINNESOTA.
Fisher, Wes. Minnesota environmental education areas. 1972 **fS946.F5 ECOL**

WILDERNESS AREAS—UNITED STATES.
Knauth, Percy. The North Woods. 1972 **QH75.K63 ECOL**
Preserving wilderness in our national parks. 1971 **fQH76.P74 ECOL**

WILDERNESS AREAS—UNITED STATES—CONGRESSES.
Natural environments: studies in theoretical and applied analysis. 1972 **QH76.N28 ECOL**

WILDERNESS AREAS—UNITED STATES—HISTORY.
Baldwin, Donald N. The quiet revolution: grass roots of today's wilderness preservation movement. 1st ed. c1972 **QH76.B35 ECOL**

WILDERNESS SURVIVAL.
Angier, Bradford. Survival with style. 1972. **SK606.A54 ECOL**
Gibbons, Euell. Stalking the good life. 1971 **QK98.5.G45 ECOL**

WILDERNESS SURVIVAL—NORTH AMERICA.
Berglund, Berndt. Wilderness survival. 1972 **SK606.B47 ECOL**

WILDLIFE CONSERVATION see also BIRDS, PROTECTION OF; FOREST RESERVES; NATIONAL PARKS AND RESERVES; PESTICIDES AND WILDLIFE; RARE ANIMALS; WETLANDS; WILDLIFE MANAGEMENT
Buyukmihci, Hope Sawyer. Hour of the beaver. 1971 **QL795.B5B8 ECOL**
Caras, Roger A. Last chance on earth. 1972 **QL82.C3 1972 ECOL**
Carson, Rachel Louise. Silent spring. 1962 **SB959.C3 ECOL**
Case, Marshal T. Look what I found! c1971 **S962.C38 ECOL**
Crowe, Philip Kingsland. World wildlife: the last stand. 1970 **S962.C75 ECOL**
Curry-Lindahl, Kai. Let them live. 1972. **S962.C87 ECOL**
Ehrenfeld, David W. Biological conservation. 1970 **QH75.E35 ECOL**

Fisher, James. Wildlife in danger. 1969 **REF QL88.F48 ECOL**
Gabrielson, Ira Noel. Wildlife conservation. 2d ed. 1970, c1959 **SK353.G2 1959 ECOL**
Graham, Ada. Wildlife rescue. 1970 **S962.G68 ECOL**
Guggisberg, Charles Albert Walter. Man and wildlife. 1970 **REF S962.G84 ECOL**
Laycock, George. America's endangered wildlife. c1969 **QL88.L39 ECOL**
Laycock, George. Wild refuge. 1969 **S962.L39 ECOL**
Leopold, Aldo. A Sand County almanac. Enl. ed. 1966. **QH81.L56 1966 ECOL**
McCann, Lester J. Time to cry wolf. c1972 **SK353.M3 ECOL**
Olsen, Jack. Slaughter the animals, poison the earth. 1971 **QL737.C22O47 ECOL**
Philip, Duke of Edinburgh. Wildlife crisis. 1st American ed. 1970 **S962.P55 ECOL**
Street, Philip. Wildlife preservation. 1971,c1970 **S962.S77 1971 ECOL**
Tennessee. State University, Memphis. Effects of noise on wildlife and other animals. 1971. **fQP82.2.N6T4 ECOL**
Trefethen, James B. Wildlife management and conservation. 1964 **S962.T7 ECOL**
United States. Dept. of the Interior. It's your world. 1969 **fS900.A45 ECOL**
Ziswiler, Vinzenz. Extinct and vanishing animals. Rev. English ed. by Fred and Pille Bunnell. 1967. **QL88.Z513 ECOL**

WILDLIFE CONSERVATION—ABSTRACTS.
United States. Fish and Wildlife Service. Wildlife abstracts. **REF SK351.U52 ECOL**

WILDLIFE CONSERVATION—HANDBOOKS, MANUALS, ETC.
United States. Soil Conservation Service. National handbook of conservation practices. 1971. **REF S922.U5 ECOL**

WILDLIFE CONSERVATION—HISTORY.
McCoy, Joseph J. Saving our wildlife. 1970 **S962.M3 ECOL**

WILDLIFE CONSERVATION—LAW AND LEGISLATION—UNITED STATES.
Douglas, William Orville. A wildlife bill of rights. 1st ed. 1965 **SK361.D6 ECOL**

WILDLIFE CONSERVATION—MINNESOTA—CONGRESSES.
Symposium on the White-tailed Deer in Minnesota, St. Paul, Minnesota, 1971. The white-tailed deer in Minnesota. 1972? **fQL737.U55S9 1971ECOL**

WILDLIFE CONSERVATION—NORTH AMERICA.
Gabrielson, Ira Noel. Wildlife refuges. 1943. **SK357.G3 ECOL**
Green, Ivah. Wildlife in danger. 1960 **QL151.G7 ECOL**
Mason, George Frederick. The wildlife of North America. 1966 **SK361.M35 ECOL**

WILDLIFE CONSERVATION—UNITED STATES.
Allen, Durward Leon. Our wildlife legacy. Rev. ed. 1962 **SK361.A66 1962 ECOL**
Black, John David. Biological conservation, with particular emphasis on wildlife. c1954 **SK361.B55 ECOL**
Hornaday, William Temple. Our vanishing wildlife: its extermination and preservation. 1913 **SK353.H6 1970 ECOL**
McNulty, Faith. Must they die? 1st ed. 1971. **QL737.C25M27 ECOL**
Trefethen, James B. Crusade for wildlife. 1961. **SK361.T7 ECOL**
United States. Bureau of Sport Fisheries and Wildlife. Office of Endangered Species and International Activities. Threatened wildlife of the United States. 1973. **S914.A3no.114 1973 ECOL**
Wallo, Olav O. Twilight over the wilderness. 1971 **fS964.U6W3 ECOL**

WILDLIFE CONSERVATION—UNITED STATES—YEARBOOKS.
United States. Bureau of Sport Fisheries and Wildlife. Division of Wildlife Research. Wildlife research: problems programs, progress, 1969. 1971 **S914.A3no.94 ECOL**

WILDLIFE, EFFECT OF PESTICIDES ON see PESTICIDES—TOXICOLOGY

WILDLIFE HABITAT IMPROVEMENT.
Shomon, Joseph James. Wildlife habitat improvement. 2d print., rev. 1969 **SK361.S52 1969 ECOL**

WILDLIFE MANAGEMENT see also FISHERY MANAGEMENT
Dasmann, Raymond Frederick. Wildlife biology. 1964 **QL752.D3 ECOL**
Dasmann, William. If deer are to survive. 1971 **QL737.U55D37 ECOL**
Gilbert, Douglas L. Natural resources and public relations. 1971. **S944.G48 ECOL**
A Manual of wildlife conservation. 1971. **fSK353.M35 ECOL**
Trefethen, James B. Wildlife management and conservation. 1964 **S962.T7 ECOL**

WILDLIFE MANAGEMENT—CALIFORNIA—HANDBOOKS, MANUALS, ETC.
Calhoun, Alex. Inland fisheries management. 1966. **fSH222.C2C3 ECOL**

WILDLIFE MANAGEMENT—UNITED STATES—YEARBOOKS.
United States. Bureau of Sport Fisheries and Wildlife. Division of Wildlife Research. Wildlife research: problems programs, progress, 1969. 1971 **S914.A3no.94 ECOL**

WILDLIFE REFUGES—UNITED STATES.
Laycock, George. Wild refuge. 1969 **S962.L39 ECOL**
Murphy, Robert William. Wild sanctuaries. 1968. **REF fS962.M8 ECOL**

WILDLIFE WATCHING.
Blackmore, Michael. Your book of watching wild life. 1971. **QL60.B55 ECOL**
Burness, Gordon. How to watch wildlife. 1972 **QL60.B87 ECOL**

WINDOM, MINN.—FLOODS.
United States. Army. Corps of Engineers. W. Fork Des Moines River and Perkins Creek flood plain information, Windom, Minnesota. 1972 **GB1225.M6A5 ECOL**

WINTER.
Teale, Edwin Way. Wandering through winter. 1965. **QH104.T43 ECOL**

WIRE SCREENS.
Portland, Or. Bureau of Sanitary Engineering. Demonstration of rotary screening for combined sewer overflows. 1971. **fTD748.P67 ECOL**

WOLF HUNTING.
Symposium on Wolf Management in Selected Areas of North America, Chicago, 1970. Wolf management in selected areas of North America. 1970 **QL737.C22S9 1970 ECOL**

WOLVES.
The Language and music of the wolves. c1971 **PhonodiscQL765.L32 ECOL**
Mech, L. David. The wolf: the ecology and behavior of an endangered species. 1970 **QL737.C22M4 ECOL**
Mech, L. David. The wolves of Isle Royale. 1966 **QL155.A45no.7 ECOL**
Mowat, Farley. Never cry wolf. 1st American ed. 1963 **QL795.W8M6 ECOL**
Rutter, Russell J. The world of the wolf. 1968. **QL737.C2R87 ECOL**

WOLVES—BEHAVIOR.
Ecological studies of the timber wolf in northeastern Minnesota. 1971 **SD11.A45476no.52 ECOL**

WOLVES—CONTROL.
Symposium on Wolf Management in Selected Areas of North America, Chicago, 1970. Wolf management in selected areas of North America. 1970 **QL737.C22S9 1970 ECOL**

WOLVES—LEGENDS AND STORIES.
Ellis, Melvin Richard. Flight of the white wolf. 1970 **Fiction ECOL**

WOLVES—MINNESOTA.
Ecological studies of the timber wolf in northeastern Minnesota. 1971 **SD11.A45476no.52 ECOL**

WOMAN—OCCUPATIONS see PROFESSIONS

WOOD-DUCK.
Hester, F. Eugene. The world of the wood duck. 1st ed. 1973 **QL696.A5H42 ECOL**

WOOD-PULP INDUSTRY—UNITED STATES—WASTE DISPOSAL.
Council on Economic Priorities. Paper profits: pollution in the pulp and paper industry. c1972 **TD899.W65C65 1972 ECOL**
Council on Economic Priorities. Paper profits: pollution in the pulp and paper industry. 1971 **REF fTD888.P8C6 ECOL**

WOOD-PULP INDUSTRY—WASTE DISPOSAL.
Crown Zellerbach Corporation. Lebanon Division. Aerated lagoon treatment of sulfite pulping effluents. 1970. **fTD899.W65C7 ECOL**

Georgia Kraft Company. Research and Development Center. Treatment of selected internal kraft mill wastes in a cooling tower. 1971. **fTD899.W65G46 ECOL**

Green Bay (Wis.) Metropolitan Sewerage District. Joint treatment of municipal sewage and pulp mill effluents. 1970. **fTD524.W6G74 ECOL**

Mead Corporation. Multi-system biological treatment of bleached kraft effluents. **fTD899.W65M4 ECOL**

Washington (State). University. Institute of Forest Products. Pollution abatement by fiber modification. 1971. **fTD899.W65W38 ECOL**

Wiley, Averill J. Reverse osmosis concentration of dilute pulp and paper effluents. 1972. **fTD899.W65W5 ECOL**

WOOD-PULP INDUSTRY—WATER-SUPPLY.
Georgia Kraft Company. Research and Development Center. Treatment of selected internal kraft mill wastes in a cooling tower. 1971. **fTD899.W65G46 ECOL**

WOOD-USING INDUSTRIES—THE WEST.
Guthrie, John Alexander. Western forest industry. 1961 **HD9755.G8 ECOL**

WOOD-USING INDUSTRIES—UNITED STATES.
Jepsen, Stanley M. Trees and forests. 1969 **SD143.J39 ECOL**

WOODY PLANTS—UNITED STATES.
Grimm, William Carey. Home guide to trees, shrubs, and wild flowers. 1970 **QK482.G734 ECOL**
Viertel, Arthur T. Trees, shrubs and vines. 1970 **QK481.V5 ECOL**

Y

YELLOWSTONE NATIONAL PARK.
Chittenden, Hiram Martin. The Yellowstone National Park. 1964 **F722.C54 1964 ECOL**

YOSEMITE NATIONAL PARK.
Muir, John. Our national parks. 1901. **E160.M95 ECOL**

Z

ZINC.
American Enka Corporation. Central Engineering Dept. Zinc precipitation and recovery from viscose rayon waste water. 1971. **fTD899.T4A44 ECOL**
United States. Bureau of Mines. Control of sulfur oxide emissions in copper, lead, and zinc smelting. 1971 **TN295.U4no.8527 ECOL**

ZONING—UNITED STATES.
Babcock, Richard F. The zoning game. 1966. **KF5698.B3 ECOL**
Little, Charles E. Challenge of the land. 1968 **HD205 1968 .L5 ECOL**

Siegan, Bernard H. Land use without zoning. 1972 **HT167.S5 ECOL**

ZONING LAW—ST. LOUIS PARK, MINN.
St. Louis Park, Minn. City Attorney's Office. City attorney's report, re: flood plain management. 1969 **fTC425.S3A5 ECOL**

ZONING LAW—UNITED STATES.
Babcock, Richard F. The zoning game. 1966. **KF5698.B3 ECOL**
Murphy, Francis C. Regulating flood-plain development. 1958. **TC530.M8 ECOL**
United States. Water Resources Council. Regulation of flood hazard areas to reduce flood losses. 1971- **KF5588.A875 ECOL**

ZONING LAW—UNITED STATES—CASES.
Haar, Charles Monroe. Land-use planning. 2d ed. 1971. **KF5692.A4H3 1971 ECOL**

ZOO ANIMALS.
Ullrich, Wolfgang. Endangered species. 1972,c1971 **fQL77.5.U45 ECOL**

ZOO ANIMALS—BEHAVIOR.
Johnson, James Ralph. Zoos of today. 1971 **QL77.5.J64 ECOL**

ZOOGEOGRAPHY.
Nayman, Jacqueline. Atlas of wildlife. 1972 **fQL101.N38 1972 ECOL**

ZOOLOGICAL GARDENS.
Johnson, James Ralph. Zoos of today. 1971 **QL77.5.J64 ECOL**

ZOOLOGY.
Holden, Raymond Peckham. Wildlife mysteries. 1972 **QL49.H68 ECOL**
Orr, Robert Thomas. The animal kingdom. 1965 **QL50.O7 ECOL**

ZOOLOGY—AFRICA, EAST—ECOLOGY.
Burton, Jane. Animals of the African year. 1st American ed. 1972 **fQL336.B87 1972 ECOL**

ZOOLOGY—ALASKA.
Crisler, Lois. Arctic wild. 1958 **QL161.C7 ECOL**

ZOOLOGY—ANTARCTIC REGIONS.
Stonehouse, Bernard. Animals of the Antarctic. 1st American ed. 1972 **fQL106.S76 1972 ECOL**

ZOOLOGY—CLASSIFICATION.
Clark, Robert Bernard. Synopsis of animal classification. 1971. **REF QL352.C53 ECOL**

ZOOLOGY—CURIOSA AND MISCELLANY.
Holden, Raymond Peckham. Wildlife mysteries. 1972 **QL49.H68 ECOL**

ZOOLOGY—DICTIONARIES.
Burton, Maurice. The world encyclopedia of animals. c1972 **fQL9.B8 ECOL**

ZOOLOGY—ECOLOGY.
Allee, Warder Clyde. Principles of animal ecology. 1949 **QL751.A616 ECOL**

Dasmann, Raymond Frederick. Wildlife biology. 1964 **QL752.D3 ECOL**
Henny, Charles J. An analysis of the population dynamics of selected avian species. 1972 **QL785.5.B6H4 ECOL**
Klopfer, Peter H. Habitats and territories. 1969 **QL751.K592 ECOL**
Milne, Lorus Johnson. The balance of nature. 1960 **QL751.M48 ECOL**
Naumov, Nikolai Pavlovich. The ecology of animals. c1972 **QL751.N313 ECOL**
Ordish, George. The living house. **QL751.O7 1960 ECOL**
Sadleir, R. M. F. S. The ecology of reproduction in wild and domestic mammals. 1969 **QP251.S27 ECOL**

ZOOLOGY—IDENTIFICATION *see* **ANIMALS—IDENTIFICATION**

ZOOLOGY—NEW JERSEY.
Worth, Charles Brooke. Of mosquitoes, moths, and mice. 1st ed. 1972 **QL475.N5W66 ECOL**

ZOOLOGY—NORTH AMERICA.
Green, Ivah. Wildlife in danger. 1960 **QL151.G7 ECOL**
Mason, George Frederick. Animal tracks. 1943. **SK282.M3 ECOL**
Seton, Ernest Thompson. Lives of game animals. 1929. **QL151.S5 1925 ECOL**

ZOOLOGY—STUDY AND TEACHING.
Great Britain. Dept. of Education and Science. Keeping animals in schools. 1971. **QL51.G7 ECOL**

ZOOLOGY—UNITED STATES.
Barker, Will. Wildlife in America's history. 1962 **QL155.B3 ECOL**
Black, John David. Biological conservation, with particular emphasis on wildlife. c1954 **SK361.B55 ECOL**
Collins, Henry Hill. Complete field guide to American wildlife: East, Central, and North ... c1959 **QL151.C6 ECOL**
Dorian, Edith M. Animals that made U.S. history. c1964 **QL155.D6 ECOL**

ZOOLOGY—WYOMING—JACKSON'S HOLE.
Carrighar, Sally. One day at Teton Marsh. 1947. **QL215.C3 ECOL**

ZOOLOGY, ECONOMIC.
Black, John David. Biological conservation, with particular emphasis on wildlife. c1954 **SK361.B55 ECOL**

ZOOLOGY, ECONOMIC—GREAT BRITAIN.
Ordish, George. The living house. 1960 c1959 **QL751.O7 1960 ECOL**

ZOOLOGY, ECONOMIC—UNITED STATES.
Dorian, Edith M. Animals that made U.S. history. c1964 **QL155.D6 ECOL**

Title Catalog

A

ABANDONED VEHICLES: A SELECTED BIBLIOGRAPHY.
Burg, Nan C. 1972   Ref fHD9975.B87 ECOL

ABC'S OF ECOLOGY.
Asimov, Isaac. c1972   fQH541.14.A85 ECOL

ABOUT THE LAND, THE RAIN, AND US.
Shannon, Terry. 1963   PZ10.S52Ai ECOL

ABOVE AND BELOW.
Sandburg, Helga. 1st ed. 1969
    QH91.75.U6S35 ECOL

ACCUMULATION OF NITRATE.
National Research Council. Committee on Nitrate Accumulation. 1972.   QH545.N5N37 ECOL

ACID MINE DRAINAGE TREATMENT BY ION EXCHANGE.
Holmes, James G. 1972   TD899.M5H6 ECOL

ACID MINE POLLUTION EFFECTS ON LAKE BIOLOGY.
Smith, Ronald W. 1971.   fTD899.M5S6 ECOL

ACID MINE WASTE TREATMENT USING REVERSE OSMOSIS.
Gulf Environmental Systems Company. 1971
    fTD754.G84 ECOL

ACTIVITIES OF THE USDA SOIL CONSERVATION SERVICE IN PROVIDING FOR QUALITY ENVIRONMENT FOR ALL PEOPLE IN MINNESOTA.
Major, Harry M. 1972.   HC110.E5M3 ECOL

ADVANCED NONTHERMALLY POLLUTING GAS TURBINES IN UTILITY APPLICATIONS.
United Aircraft Corporation. Research Laboratories, East Hartford, Conn. 1971.   fTJ778.U5 ECOL

ADVANCED WASTEWATER TREATMENT AS PRACTICED AT SOUTH TAHOE.
South Tahoe Public Utility District. 1971.
    fTD225.T25S6 ECOL

ADVANCES IN CHEMISTRY SERIES, 60.
American Chemical Society. Organic pesticides in the environment; a symposium. 1966.
    SB951.A4 ECOL

ADVANCES IN ENVIRONMENTAL SCIENCES. V.1-
1969-   REF TD180.A38 ECOL

ADVENTURE IN ENVIRONMENT.
1971   QH48.A25 ECOL

ADVENTURE IN ENVIRONMENT: NATIONAL ENVIRONMENTAL EDUCATION DEVELOPMENT.
c1971   fQH48.A24 ECOL
1971   fQH48.A23 ECOL

ADVERSE EFFECTS OF COMMON ENVIRONMENTAL POLLUTANTS.
1972   RA1270.P4A32 ECOL

AERATED LAGOON TREATMENT OF SULFITE PULPING EFFLUENTS.
Crown Zellerbach Corporation. Lebanon Division. 1970.   fTD899.W65C7 ECOL

AERIAL PHOTO-ECOLOGY.
Howard, John Anthony. 1970, i.e. 1971
    SD387.A25H68 1971 ECOL

AEROBIC DIGESTION OF ORGANIC WASTE SLUDGE.
Oklahoma. State University of Agriculture and Applied Science, Stillwater. School of Civil Engineering. 1971 i.e. 1972   fTD769.O35 ECOL

AFFLUENCE IN JEOPARDY.
Park, Charles Frederick. c1968
    HD9506.U62P3 ECOL

THE AFFLUENT SOCIETY.
Galbraith, John Kenneth. 2d ed., rev. 1969.
    HC106.5.G32 1969 ECOL

AFTER THE PLANNERS.
Goodman, Robert. 1972, c1971
    HT166.G64 ECOL

AGRICULTURAL AND WATER POLICIES AND THE ENVIRONMENT: AN ANALYSIS OF NATIONAL ALTERNATIVES IN NATURAL RESOURCE USE, FOOD SUPPLY CAPACITY AND ENVIRONMENTAL QUALITY.
Heady, Earl Orel. 1972.   fS441.H4 ECOL

AGRICULTURAL DEVELOPMENT.
Hayami, Yujiro. 1971   HD1415.H318 ECOL

AGRICULTURAL POLLUTION OF THE GREAT LAKES BASIN.
Canada. 1971.   fTD223.3.C25 ECOL

AGRICULTURAL PRACTICES AND WATER QUALITY.
1971,c1970   TD420.A33 ECOL

AGRICULTURE'S ROLE IN ENVIRONMENTAL QUALITY.
Conference on Agriculture's Role in Environmental Quality. University of Illinois, Urbana—Champaign, 1970. 1971   fHC68.C6 1970 ECOL

AICE SURVEY OF USSR AIR POLLUTION LITERATURE, V. 6.
Nuttonson, Michael Y. Air pollution in relation to certain atmospheric and meteorological conditions and some of the methods employed in the survey and analysis of air pollutants. 1971.
    fTD883.7.R9N87 ECOL

AICE SURVEY OF USSR AIR POLLUTION LITERATURE, V. 7.
Nuttonson, Michael Y. Measurements of dispersal and concentration, identification, and sanitary evaluation of various air pollutants. 1971.
    fTD883.7.R9N873 ECOL

AIR.
Preston, Edna Mitchell. 1965
    PZ10.P668Ai ECOL

AIR AND WATER POLLUTION.
Brittin, Wesley Emil. 1972   TD881.B75 ECOL
Leinwand, Gerald. 1969   TD180.L4 ECOL

AIR CLASSIFICATION OF SOLID WASTES.
Boettcher, R. A. 1972.   TD796.7.B64 ECOL

AIR CONSERVATION; ... REPORT.
American Association for the Advancement of Science. Committee on Science in the Promotion of Human Welfare. Air Conservation Commission. 1965.   TD883.2.A65 ECOL

AIR IS ALL AROUND YOU.
Branley, Franklyn Mansfield. 1962
    PZ10.B65Ai ECOL

AIR MODULATED VACUUM OIL RECOVERY COLLECTION OF SPILLED OIL (FOAMS).
United States. Environmental Protection Agency. Office of Research and Monitoring. 1972.
    fTD427.P4U5 ECOL

AIR POLLUTANTS.
Jacobs, Morris Boris. The chemical analysis of air pollutants. 1960.   TD883.J3 ECOL

AIR POLLUTANTS AFFECTING THE PERFORMANCE OF DOMESTIC ANIMALS.
Lillie, Robert Jones. Slightly rev. 1972.
    SF757.5.L54 1972 ECOL

AIR POLLUTION.
1970   fTD883.A47 ECOL
Faith, William Lawrence. 2d ed. 1972
    TD883.F23 1972 ECOL
Lavaroni, Charles W. c1971   TD883.L28 ECOL
Laycock, George. 1972   TD883.13.L38 ECOL

AIR POLLUTION AND INDUSTRY.
Ross, Richard D. 1972   TD883.R58 ECOL

AIR POLLUTION AND ITS CONTROL.
Sproull, Wayne Treber. 1970   TD883.S76 ECOL
Sproull, Wayne Treber. 2d ed. rev. and enl. 1972
    TD883.S76 1972 ECOL

AIR POLLUTION AND RESPIRATORY DISEASE.
Holland, Walter Werner. 1972
    fRC732.H64 ECOL

AIR POLLUTION AND THE REGULATED ELECTRIC POWER AND NATURAL GAS INDUSTRIES.
United States. Federal Power Commission. 1968.
    TD883.2.A52 ECOL

AIR POLLUTION AND URBAN PLANNING: A SELECTIVE ANNOTATED BIBLIOGRAPHY.
Van Nest, William J. 1972
    REF fZ5853.P7V3 ECOL

AIR POLLUTION ASPECTS OF EMISSION SOURCES: A BIBLIOGRAPHY WITH ABSTRACTS.
Air Pollution Technical Information Center. 1971-   Z7173.A4A5 ECOL

AIR POLLUTION CONTROL.
    TD883.A474 ECOL
1968.   KF3812.A75A35 1968 ECOL
1969.   KF3812.A75A35 ECOL
United States. Environmental Protection Agency. Office of Air Programs. Office of Research Grants.
    REF TD883.2.A23 ECOL

AIR POLLUTION CONTROL ASSOCIATION. TR-7 AGRICULTURAL COMMITTEE. INFORMATIVE REPORT NO. 1.
Jacobson, Jay S. Recognition of air pollution injury to vegetation: a pictorial atlas. 1970.
    fQK751.J3 ECOL

AIR POLLUTION CONTROL IN MINNESOTA, JAN. 1969 THROUGH OCT. 1970.
Minnesota. Pollution Control Agency. 1970
    fTD883.5.M6A47 1970 ECOL

AIR POLLUTION EMISSION CONTROL REGULATIONS AND ORDINANCES.
United States. Robert A Taft Sanitary Engineering Center, Cincinnati. A compilation of selected air pollution emission control regulations and ordinances. 1965.   REF KF3812.A4 1965 ECOL

AIR POLLUTION EXPERIMENTS FOR JUNIOR AND SENIOR HIGH SCHOOL SCIENCE CLASSES.
Hunter, Donald C. 1968.   fTD883.2.H8 ECOL

AIR POLLUTION HANDBOOK.
Magill, Paul L. 1956.   REF TD883.M35 ECOL

AIR POLLUTION IN RELATION TO CERTAIN ATMOSPHERIC AND METEOROLOGICAL CONDITIONS AND SOME OF THE METHODS EMPLOYED IN THE SURVEY AND ANALYSIS OF AIR POLLUTANTS.
Nuttonson, Michael Y. 1971.
    fTD883.7.R9N87 ECOL

AIR POLLUTION PRIMER.
National Tuberculosis and Respiratory Disease Association. 1969   TD883.N37 ECOL

AIR POLLUTION REGULATION HANDBOOK.
Minnesota Association of Commerce and Industry. 1970?   REF fTD883.5.M6M61 ECOL

AIR POLLUTION TRANSLATIONS: A BIBLIOGRAPHY WITH ABSTRACTS.
Air Pollution Technical Information Center.
    REF TD881.U55no.AP-56 ECOL

AIR QUALITY DATA: DIRECTORY OF AIR QUALITY MONITORING SITES, 1971.
United States. Environmental Protection Agency. Division of Atmospheric Surveillance. 1972.
    REF TD883.2.A43 ECOL

AIR QUALITY DATA FOR 1967 FROM THE NATIONAL AIR SURVEILLANCE NETWORKS.
United States. Environmental Protection Agency. Division of Atmospheric Surveillance. Rev. 1971
    TD883.2.A44 1971 ECOL

THE AIR WE BREATHE!
Bloome, Enid. 1971.   TD883.13.B56 ECOL

ALASKA.
Cooley, Richard A. 1967.   HC107.A45C6 ECOL

ALASKA, THE EMBATTLED FRONTIER.
Laycock, George. 1971.   S932.A4L38 ECOL

ALASKA: THE LAST FRONTIER.
Cooper, Bryan. 1973.   HD9567.A4C66 ECOL

ALASKA'S ANIMALS & FISHES.
Dufresne, Frank. c1946
    QL628.A4D8 1946 ECOL

ALBERTA, A NATURAL HISTORY.
1st ed. c1967   fQH106.A54 ECOL

ALBUM OF NORTH AMERICAN ANIMALS.
Dugdale, Vera. 1966   fPZ10.D745AL ECOL

ALDRIN, DIELDRIN, ENDRIN AND TELODRIN.
Jager, K. W. 1970.   RA1270.P4J33 ECOL

ALGAE, MAN, AND THE ENVIRONMENT.
c1968   QK564.5.A4 ECOL

ALGAL CULTURES AND PHYTOPLANKTON ECOLOGY.
Fogg, Gordon Elliott. 1966, c1965
    QK565.F58 ECOL

ALL AROUND YOU: AN ENVIRONMENTAL STUDY GUIDE.
United States. Bureau of Land Management. 1971.
    S946.U5 ECOL

AN ALTERNATIVE FUTURE FOR AMERICA II.
Theobald, Robert. 2d ed. 1970
    HN65.T44 1970 ECOL

ALTERNATIVE PROGRAMS AND PROJECTS FOR MANAGING MINNESOTA'S WATER AND RELATED LAND RESOURCES THROUGH THE YEAR 2020.
Minnesota. Water Resources Coordinating Committee. 1971   fHD1694.M6A5 1971 ECOL

ALTERNATIVES IN WATER MANAGEMENT.
National Research Council. Committee on Water. 1966.   HD1694.A5N48 ECOL

ALTERNATIVES TO THE INTERNAL COMBUSTION ENGINE.
Ayres, Robert U. 1972   TL210.A96 ECOL

AMERICA THE RAPED.
Marine, Gene. 1969   S942.M33 ECOL

AMERICA THE VANISHING.
Ogden, Samuel R. 1969. **S942.O44 ECOL**

AMERICAN AGRICULTURE: GEOGRAPHY, RESOURCES, CONSERVATION.
Higbee, Edward Counselman. 1958
S441.H59 ECOL

AMERICAN ASSOCIATION FOR THE ADVANCEMENT OF SCIENCE. PUBLICATION NO. 80.
American Association for the Advancement of Science. Committee on Science in the Promotion of Human Welfare. Air Conservation Commission. Air conservation; ... report. 1965. **TD883.2.A65 ECOL**

AMERICAN ASSOCIATION OF PETROLEUM GEOLOGISTS. MEMOIR 18.
Symposium on Underground Waste Management and Environmental Implications, Houston, Tex., 1971. Underground waste management and environmental implications; proceedings. 1972.
TD761.S95 1971 ECOL

THE AMERICAN COAST.
1971 **fE169.02.A648 ECOL**

AMERICAN DESERTS.
Findley, Rowe. Great American deserts. 1972
F787.F5 ECOL

AMERICAN ENTERPRISE INSTITUTE FOR PUBLIC POLICY RESEARCH. LEGISLATIVE AND SPECIAL ANALYSES, 90TH CONG., 2D SESS., NO. 16.
Stepp, James Marvin. The pollution problem. 1968
TD180.S65 ECOL

THE AMERICAN ENVIRONMENT.
Nash, Roderick. 1968 **S930.N36 ECOL**

AMERICAN ENVIRONMENTAL STUDIES.
Kirkwood, James Pugh. A special report on the pollution of river waters. Reprint ed. 1970
REF TD425.K52 1970 ECOL

AMERICAN GEOGRAPHICAL SOCIETY. SPECIAL PUBLICATION NO. 23.
Price, Archibald Grenfell. White settlers in the tropics. 1939. **GF51.P7 ECOL**

AMERICAN HERITAGE.
Natural wonders of America. 1972
QH76.N29 ECOL

THE AMERICAN HERITAGE BOOK OF NATURAL WONDERS.
American heritage. c1972,1963
fE169.A496 1972 ECOL

AMERICAN INSTITUTE OF CROP ECOLOGY. AICE SURVEY OF USSR AIR POLLUTION LITERATURE, V. 6.
Nuttonson, Michael Y. Air pollution in relation to certain atmospheric and meteorological conditions and some of the methods employed in the survey and analysis of air pollutants. 1971.
fTD883.7.R9N87 ECOL

AMERICAN INSTITUTE OF CROP ECOLOGY. AICE SURVEY OF USSR AIR POLLUTION LITERATURE, V. 7.
Nuttonson, Michael Y. Measurements of dispersal and concentration, identification, and sanitary evaluation of various air pollutants. 1971.
fTD883.7.R9N873 ECOL

AMERICAN MUSEUM OF NATURAL HISTORY, NEW YORK. THE NEW EXPLORERS.
Walker, Theodore J. Red salmon, brown bear. 1971
QH105.A4W36 ECOL

THE AMERICAN MUSEUM OF NATURAL HISTORY'S THE NEW EXPLORERS.
Walker, Theodore J. Red salmon, brown bear. 1971
QH105.A4W36 ECOL

AMERICAN MUSEUM SOURCEBOOKS IN ANTHROPOLOGY.
Vayda, Andrew Peter. Environment and cultural behavior. 1969. **GF51.V35 ECOL**

AMERICAN NATIONAL STANDARD LEAKAGE-RATE TESTING OF CONTAINMENT STRUCTURES FOR NUCLEAR REACTORS.
American National Standards Institute. 1972
REF fTK9211.A4 ECOL

AMERICAN SOCIETY OF CIVIL ENGINEERS. ASCE URBAN WATER RESOURCES RESEARCH PROGRAM. TECHNICAL MEMORANDUM NO.14.
McPherson, Murray Burns. Management problems in metropolitan water resource operations. 1971.
fTD353.M3 ECOL

AMERICAN SOCIETY OF CIVIL ENGINEERS. ASCE URBAN WATER RESOURCES RESEARCH PROGRAM. TECHNICAL MEMORANDUM NO. 15.
McPherson, Murray Burns. Feasibility of the metropolitan water intelligence system concept (Integrated automatic operational control). 1971.
fTD211.M3 ECOL

AMERICAN SOCIETY OF CIVIL ENGINEERS. ASCE URBAN WATER RESOURCES RESEARCH PROGRAM. TECHNICAL MEMORANDUM NO. 16.
Tucker, L. Scott. Metropolitan industrial water use. 1972. **fTD223.T8 ECOL**

AMERICAN SOCIETY OF CIVIL ENGINEERS. ASCE URBAN WATER RESOURCES RESEARCH PROGRAM. TECHNICAL MEMORANDUM NO. 17.
McPherson, M. B. Hydrologic effects of urbanization in the United States. 1972.
fGB665.M3 ECOL

AMERICAN SOCIETY OF CIVIL ENGINEERS. ASCE URBAN WATER RESOURCES RESEARCH PROGRAM. TECHNICAL MEMORANDUM NO. 18.
McPherson, M. B. Urban runoff. 1972.
fGB665.M35 ECOL

AMERICAN SPEECH AND HEARING ASSOCIATION. REPORTS, 4.
Conference on Noise as a Public Health Hazard, Wash., D.C., 1968. Noise as a public health hazard. 1969. **RA772.N7C6 ECOL**

AMERICAN WATERFOWL.
Phillips, John Charles. 1930.
QL696.A5P45 ECOL

AMERICAN WILD FLOWERS.
Rickett, Harold William. The new field book of American wild flowers. 1963 **QK118.R5 ECOL**

THE AMERICAN WILDERNESS.
Knauth, Percy. The North Woods. 1972
QH75.K63 ECOL

AMERICA'S CHANGING ENVIRONMENT.
1970. **HC110.E5A56 ECOL**

AMERICA'S ENDANGERED WILDLIFE.
Laycock, George. c1969 **QL88.L39 ECOL**

AMERICA'S LAND AND ITS USES.
Clawson, Marion. 1972 **HD205 1972 .C55 ECOL**

AMERICA'S NATURAL RESOURCES.
Callison, Charles H. Rev. print. 1967
S930.C3 1967 ECOL

AMERICA'S NATURAL TREASURES.
Udall, Stewart L. 1971 **fE160.U28 ECOL**

AMERICA'S NEEDS AND RESOURCES: A NEW SURVEY.
Twentieth Century Fund. 1969,c1955
REF HC106.5.T9 1969 ECOL

AMMONIA REMOVAL IN A PHYSICAL-CHEMICAL WASTEWATER TREATMENT PROCESS.
Barnes, Robert A. 1972. **TD462.B3 ECOL**

THE ANALYSIS OF AIR POLLUTANTS.
Leithe, Wolfgang. 1971,c1970
TD890.L413 ECOL

ANALYSIS OF FISHERY PROGRAMS AND REVIEW OF CURRENT PLANS FOR THE MANAGEMENT OF FISHERY RESOURCES OF THE GREAT LAKES.
Great Lakes Basin Commission. Fish Work Group. 1969. **SH36.G76 ECOL**

ANALYSIS OF INDUSTRIAL WASTEWATERS.
Mancy, Khalil H. 1971 **TD735.M35 ECOL**

ANALYSIS OF THE INJECTION OF A HEATED TURBULENT JET INTO A MOVING MAINSTREAM, WITH EMPHASIS ON A THERMAL DISCHARGE IN A WATERWAY.
Campbell, J. F. 1972. **fTD427.H4C3 ECOL**

AN ANALYSIS OF THE POPULATION DYNAMICS OF SELECTED AVIAN SPECIES.
Henny, Charles J. 1972 **QL785.5.B6H4 ECOL**

ANALYSIS OF WATER REUSE ALTERNATIVES IN AN INTEGRATED URBAN AND AGRICULTURAL AREA.
Bishop, A. Bruce. 1971 **fTD429.B5 ECOL**

AND THOU SHALT DIE IN A POLLUTED LAND.
Folsom, Paul. 1971 **GF80.F6 ECOL**

THE ANIMAL AND THE ENVIRONMENT.
Vernberg, F. John. 1970 **QH541.V45 ECOL**

ANIMAL HABITATS: WHERE CAN RED-WINGED BLACKBIRDS LIVE?
Wong, Herbert H. 1970 **PZ10.W748An ECOL**

ANIMAL HOMES.
Mason, George Frederick. 1947.
QL756.M3 ECOL

THE ANIMAL IN MAN.
Milne, Lorus Johnson. 1973 **BF671.M63 ECOL**

THE ANIMAL KINGDOM.
Orr, Robert Thomas. 1965 **QL50.O7 ECOL**

ANIMAL LIFE SERIES.
Barber, Carolyn. Animals at war. 1st U.S. ed. c1971
QL758.5.B37 1971 ECOL
Long, Tony. Mountain animals. 1st U.S. ed. c1971
QL113.L66 1971 ECOL
Tate, Ro. Desert animals. 1st U.S. ed. c1971
QL116.T37 1971 ECOL

ANIMAL TRACKS.
Mason, George Frederick. 1943.
SK282.M3 ECOL

ANIMALS AND THEIR FOOD.
Johnson, James Ralph. 1972 **QL756.5.J64 ECOL**

ANIMALS AT MY DOORSTEP.
Hoover, Helen. 1966 **PZ10.H7An ECOL**

ANIMALS AT PEACE.
Maddock, Alison. 1st U.S. ed. c1971
QL751.M216 1971 ECOL

ANIMALS AT WAR.
Barber, Carolyn. 1st U.S. ed. c1971
QL758.5.B37 1971 ECOL

ANIMALS IN DANGER.
Wood, Frances Elizabeth. 1968 **QL88.W6 ECOL**

ANIMALS OF THE AFRICAN YEAR.
Burton, Jane. 1st American ed. 1972
fQL336.B87 1972 ECOL

ANIMALS OF THE ANTARCTIC.
Stonehouse, Bernard. 1st American ed. 1972
fQL106.S76 1972 ECOL

ANIMALS OF THE ARCTIC.
Stonehouse, Bernard. 1st American ed. 1971
fQH199.S83 1971 ECOL

ANIMALS THAT MADE U.S. HISTORY.
Dorian, Edith M. c1964 **QL155.D6 ECOL**

ANNOTATED BIBLIOGRAPHY ON HYDROLOGY AND SEDIMENTATION, 1966-68, UNITED STATES AND CANADA.
Engineering-Science, Inc. 1970
REF Z7935.E5 1970 ECOL

ANNUAL CAPITAL IMPROVEMENTS COST ESTIMATES SCHEDULES FOR SEPARATION AND TREATMENT COMBINED SEWERAGE SYSTEM, SOUTH ST. PAUL, MINNESOTA.
Henningson, Durham and Richardson, Inc., Omaha, Nebraska. n.d. **fTD525.S6H4 ECOL**

ANOKA COUNTY PARKS AND OPEN-SPACE: COMPREHENSIVE PLAN.
Midwest Planning and Research, Inc. 1969.
fGV54.M6M52 ECOL

ANOKA COUNTY PARKS AND OPEN-SPACE: GOALS, POLICIES, DIRECTIONS AND ALTERNATIVES.
Midwest Planning and Research, Inc. 1968
fGV54.M6M5 ECOL

APARTMENT HOUSE INCINERATORS (FLUE FED).
National Research Council. Building Research Advisory Board. 1965. **fTH23.N333no.29 ECOL**

APPLE VALLEY PARK DEVELOPMENT PROGRAM.
Urban Planning and Design, Inc., Mpls., Minn. 1969.
fGV54.M6U7 ECOL

THE APPLICATION OF VALUE THEORY TO WATER RESOURCES PLANNING AND MANAGEMENT.
Deal, Richard L. 1971. **fHD1694.A5D4 ECOL**

APPLICATIONS OF SYSTEMS ANALYSIS TECHNIQUES TO WATER RESOURCES.
Dracup, John A. 1972. **fTC409.D7 ECOL**

AN APPRAISAL OF WATER POLLUTION IN THE LAKE SUPERIOR BASIN.
United States. Federal Water Pollution Control Administration. 1969. **TD223.3.U5 ECOL**
United States. Federal Water Pollution Control Administration. Rev. ed. 1970,1969.
TD223.3U5 1970 ECOL

APPROACHING THE BENIGN ENVIRONMENT.
Fuller, Richard Buckminster. 1970
Q171.F96 ECOL

AQUATIC AND WETLAND PLANTS OF SOUTHWESTERN UNITED STATES.
Correll, Donovan Stewart. 1972.
QK142.C6 ECOL

AQUATIC DRYOPOID BEETLES (COLEOPTERA) OF THE UNITED STATES.
Brown, Harley P. 1972. **fQH96.A2B5no.6 ECOL**

AQUATIC PESTS ON IRRIGATION SYSTEMS: IDENTIFICATION GUIDE.
Otto, Norman E. 1972,1965
QH96.O88 1972 ECOL

AQUATIC PLANTS FROM MINNESOTA, PART 1—CHEMICAL SURVEY.
Su, K. Lee. 1972. GB701.M554no.46 ECOL

AQUATIC PLANTS FROM MINNESOTA PART 2—TOXICITY, ANTI-NEOPLASTIC, AND COAGULENT EFFECTS.
Su, K. Lee. 1972. GB701.M554no.47 ECOL

AQUATIC PLANTS FROM MINNESOTA PART 3—ANTIMICROBIAL EFFECTS.
Su, K. Lee. 1972. GB701.M554no.48 ECOL

AQUATIC PLANTS FROM MINNESOTA, PART 4 — NUTRIENT COMPOSITION.
Linn, J. G. 1973. GB701.M554no.56 ECOL

ARCTIC WILD.
Crisler, Lois. 1958 QL161.C7 ECOL

ARE OUR DESCENDANTS DOOMED?
1972 HB849.A74 1972 ECOL

THE ARENA OF LIFE: THE DYNAMICS OF ECOLOGY.
Milne, Lorus Johnson. 1972 QH541.M52 ECOL

ARID LANDS IN PERSPECTIVE.
1969 fS613.A7 ECOL

THE ARID ZONES.
Walton, Kenneth. 1st U.S. ed. 1969
GB611.W3 1969 ECOL

ART & DESIGN IN THE ENVIRONMENT.
Bonvie, Carolyn. 1971 fLB1047.B6 ECOL

THE ARTHUR GODFREY ENVIRONMENTAL READER.
Godfrey, Arthur. 1970 QH541.13.G6 ECOL

ARTS OF THE ENVIRONMENT.
Kepes, Gyorgy. 1972 N72.S6K37 ECOL

AS WE LIVE AND BREATHE.
1971 GF75.A8 ECOL

ASBESTOS AND ENZYMES.
Brodeur, Paul. 1972 RA1231.A8B76 ECOL

ASPECTS OF WATER RESOURCES LAW IN MINNESOTA.
Haik, Raymond A. 1969.
GB701.M554no.11 ECOL

THE ASSAULTS ON OUR SENSES.
Barr, John. 1970. QH77.G7B29 ECOL

ASSESSMENT OF AIRBORNE PARTICLES.
Rochester International Conference on Environmental Toxicity, 3d, 1970. 1972
QD549.R59 1970 ECOL

AN ASSESSMENT OF NOISE CONCERN IN OTHER NATIONS.
Informatics Inc. 1971. fTD892.I55 ECOL

ASSESSMENT OF THE EFFECTIVENESS AND EFFECTS OF LAND DISPOSAL METHODOLOGIES OF WASTE WATER MANAGEMENT.
1972. fTD760.A86 ECOL

ASSESSMENT OF TURBIDITY, COLOR AND ODOR IN WATER.
Harris, Douglas H. 1972. fTD380.H3 ECOL

ATLANTIC BEACHES.
Leonard, Jonathan Norton. 1972
GB459.4.L46 ECOL

THE ATLANTIC SHORE.
Hay, John. 1969,c1966. QH95.7.H3 ECOL

ATLAS OF ANIMAL MIGRATION.
Jarman, Catherine. 1972 fQL754.J37 ECOL

ATLAS OF THE LIVING RESOURCES OF THE SEAS.
Food and Agriculture Organization of the United Nations. 1972. REF fGC1015.F6 ECOL

ATLAS OF UNITED STATES TREES.
Little, Elbert Luther. 1971-
REF fS21.A46no.1146 ECOL

ATLAS OF WILDLIFE.
Nayman, Jacqueline. 1972
fQL101.N38 1972 ECOL

THE ATMOSPHERIC ENVIRONMENT.
Auliciems, Andris. 1972 QP82.2.T4A9 ECOL

ATMOSPHERIC POLLUTION.
Bach, Wilfrid. 1971, c1972 TD883.B24 ECOL

ATOLL ENVIRONMENT AND ECOLOGY.
Wiens, Herold Jacob. 1971,c1962
QH541.5.C7W5 ECOL

ATOMIC ENERGY AND YOUR WORLD.
Glasstone, Samuel. 1970 QC792.G55 ECOL

ATOMIC ENERGY IN USE.
United States. Atomic Energy Commission. 1965
TK9146.U55 ECOL

THE ATOMIC ESTABLISHMENT.
Metzger, H. Peter. 1972
HD9698.U52M47 ECOL

ATOMIC FUEL.
Hogerton, John F. 1969 TK9360.H6 1969 ECOL
Hogerton, John F. Rev. 1964.
TK9360.H6 1964 ECOL

ATOMIC POWER SAFETY.
Hogerton, John F. c1964 TK1078.H62 ECOL

ATOMIC RADIATION AND LIFE.
Alexander, Peter. Completely Rev. ed. 1965
QH652.A6 1965 ECOL

ATOMS AT THE SCIENCE FAIR.
LeCompte, Robert G. 1968
Q105.L412 1968 ECOL

ATOMS, NATURE, AND MAN.
Hines, Neal O. c1966 QC778.H54 ECOL

AUBURN UNIVERSITY. WATER RESOURCES RESEARCH INSTITUTE. WRRI BULLETIN 8.
Merritt, Thomas W. Studies on benthic nematode ecology in a small freshwater pond. 1973.
fTC1.A85no.8 ECOL

AUBURN UNIVERSITY. WATER RESOURCES RESEARCH INSTITUTE. WRRI BULLETIN 9.
Neely, W. C. Biological and photobiological action of pollutants on aquatic microorganisms. 1973.
fTC1.A85no.9 ECOL

AUDUBON BIRD GUIDE; EASTERN LAND BIRDS...WITH ILLUS. IN COLOR OF EVERY SPECIES.
Pough, Richard Hooper. 1946. QL681.P68 ECOL

AUDUBON LAND BIRD GUIDE.
Pough, Richard Hooper. c1949
QL681.P68 1949 ECOL

AUDUBON WATER BIRD GUIDE.
Pough, Richard Hooper. 1951. QL681.P69 ECOL

AUDUBON WESTERN BIRD GUIDE.
Pough, Richard Hooper. 1957.
QL683.W4P6 ECOL

AUTOKIND VS. MANKIND.
Schneider, Kenneth R. 1st ed. 1971
HE5623.S35 1971 ECOL

THE AUTOMOBILE CYCLE: AN ENVIRONMENTAL AND RESOURCE RECLAMATION PROBLEM.
United States. Solid Waste Management Office. 1972. TD793.U5 ECOL

AUTOMOBILE DISPOSAL.
United States. Bureau of Mines. 1967
HD9710.U52A27 ECOL

AUTOMOTIVE SMOG CONTROL MANUAL.
Glenn, Harold T. 1968 TL152.G545 ECOL

B

BACK TO NATURE ALMANAC.
Baker, Jerry. Jerry Baker's Back to nature almanac. 1973- SB455.B257 ECOL

BACTERIAL EFFECTS OF ALGAE ON ENTERIC ORGANISMS.
Davis, Ernst M. 1970. fQR48.D38 ECOL

BACTERIOLOGY PRIMER IN AIR CONTAMINATION CONTROL.
Kingsley, V. Victor. 1967 QR101.K55 ECOL

BAJA CALIFORNIA.
Johnson, William Weber. F1246.J6 ECOL

THE BALANCE OF NATURE.
Milne, Lorus Johnson. 1971 1960
QL751.M48 ECOL

THE BASIC BOOK OF ORGANIC GARDENING.
1971 S605.5.B37 ECOL

BASIC CONCEPTS OF ECOLOGY.
Knight, Clifford Burnham. 1965
QH541.K5 ECOL

BASIC ECOLOGY.
Buchsbaum, Ralph Morris. 1970,c1957
QH541.B79 ECOL
Krznarich, Susan. 1971. QH541.2.K7 ECOL

A BASIC ENVIRONMENTAL COLLECTION.
Dee, Sandra R. 1973. Ref fZ5863.P6D4 ECOL

BASIN MANAGEMENT FOR WATER REUSE.
Alamo Area Council of Governments. 1972.
fTD225.S225A65 ECOL

BEAUTY FOR AMERICA.
White House Conference on Natural Beauty, Washington, D.C., 1965. 1965
QH77.U6W5 1965 ECOL

BEFORE NATURE DIES.
Dorst, Jean. 1st American ed. 1970.
S936.D6613 ECOL

BEGINNER'S GUIDE TO THE FUNGI.
Duddington, C. L. 1972 REF QK603.D83 ECOL

THE BEGINNERS' STORY OF MINERALS AND ROCKS.
Keene, Melvin. 1966 QE365.K27 ECOL

BEHAVIOR AND ECOLOGY.
Emmel, Thomas C. 1970 QH541.E44 ECOL

BEHAVIORAL ECOLOGY.
Klopfer, Peter H. 1970 QL751.K5917 ECOL

BEHAVIOUR OF WOLVES, DOGS, AND RELATED CANIDS.
Fox, Michael W. 1st U.S. ed. 1972, c1971
QL737.C22F69 1972 ECOL

BELWIN OUTDOOR EDUCATION LABORATORY PROJECT HANDBOOK.
St. Paul. Public Schools. Curriculum Office. 1971.
fLB1047.S25 ECOL

BENEFITS OF WATER QUALITY ENHANCEMENT.
Syracuse University. Civil Engineering Dept. 1970.
fTD365.S94 ECOL

BERING'S VOYAGE.
Golder, Frank Alfred. 1922-25.
G296.B4G6 ECOL

THE BEST NATURE WRITING OF JOSEPH WOOD KRUTCH.
Krutch, Joseph Wood. 1969 c1970
QH81.K828 ECOL

BEST'S ENVIRONMENTAL CONTROL AND SAFETY DIRECTORY.
13th ed.- 1971/72- REF fT55.B4 ECOL

THE BEVERAGE CONTAINER PROBLEM.
Bingham, Tayler H. 1972. TD793.B5 ECOL

BEYOND REPAIR.
Weisberg, Barry. 1971 GF75.W45 1971 ECOL

BEYOND THE CLASSROOM.
Dickey, Miriam. 1972. Ref fQH51.D5 ECOL

BEYOND THE CLASSROOM: USING THE URBAN ENVIRONMENT AS AN INSTRUCTIONAL MEDIUM.
Dickey, Miriam E. 1972. fQH541.2.D52 ECOL

A BIBLIOGRAPHY OF RECREATIONAL COMMUNITIES AND LEISURE LAND DEVELOPMENT.
Wright, Sydney. 1973. fZ7164.L3W7 ECOL

A BIBLIOGRAPHY ON MARINE AND ESTUARINE OIL POLLUTION.
Moulder, David S. 1971.
REF fZ6004.P6M6 ECOL

BIDDING FOR OFFSHORE OIL: TOWARD AN OPTIMAL STRATEGY.
Brown, Keith Cates. c1969 HD9560.5.B75 ECOL

BIG GAME IN MINNESOTA.
1965. SH11.M64no.9 ECOL

THE BIG ISLAND.
May, Julian. 1968 PZ10.M455Bi ECOL

BIG SIOUX RIVER BASIN AND RELATED AREAS.
United States. Soil Conservation Service. 1973.
HD1695.B5A5 ECOL

THE BIG THICKET.
Gunter, Pete Addison Y. 1971 c1972
fF392.H37G8 ECOL

THE BIG WATER FIGHT.
League of Women Voters of the United States. Education Fund. 1966. HD1694.A5L4 ECOL

A BIO-BIBLIOGRAPHY OF SIGURD F. OLSON.
Pyter, Bernadette. 1972.
REF fZ7404.O4P8 ECOL

BIO-ENGINEERING ASPECTS OF AGRICULTURAL DRAINAGE, SAN JOAQUIN VALLEY, CALIFORNIA.
California. Dept. of Water Resources. Removal of nitrate by an algal system, phase II. 1971.
fTD475.C342 ECOL
Robert S. Kerr Water Research Center. Denitrification by anaerobic filters and ponds. 1971.
fTD475.R6 ECOL
Robert S. Kerr Water Research Center. Denitrification by anaerobic filters and ponds, phase II. 1971. TD475.R62 ECOL

Robert S. Kerr Water Research Center. Desalination of agricultural tile drainages. 1971.
TD479.R6 ECOL

United States. Environmental Protection Agency. Office of Research and Monitoring. The effects of agricultural waste water treatment on algal bioassay response. 1971. **QH96.8.E9U54 ECOL**

BIO-REGENERATED ACTIVATED CARBON TREATMENT OF TEXTILE DYE WASTEWATER.
Fram Corporation. 1971. **fTD899.T4F7 ECOL**

BIOCHEMICAL ECOLOGY OF WATER POLLUTION.
Dugan, Patrick R. 1972. **TD423.D83 ECOL**

BIOCHEMISTRY AND BEHAVIOR.
Eiduson, Samuel. 1964 **QP521.E5 ECOL**

BIOCIDES.
Kriett, Jolene. 1971. **QH545.P4K7 ECOL**

BIOENGINEERING ASPECTS OF AGRICULTURAL DRAINAGE, SAN JOAQUIN VALLEY, CALIFORNIA.
California. Dept. of Water Resources. Removal of nitrate by an algal system, phase II. 1971.
fTD475.C342 ECOL

BIOETHICS: BRIDGE TO THE FUTURE.
Potter, Van Rensselaer. 1971 **QH333.P66 ECOL**

BIOLOGIC EFFECTS OF ATMOSPHERIC POLLUTANTS.
National Research Council. Committee on Biologic Effects of Atmospheric Pollutants. Lead. 1972.
QP913.P3N38 ECOL

BIOLOGICAL AND PHOTOBIOLOGICAL ACTION OF POLLUTANTS ON AQUATIC MICROORGANISMS.
Neely, W. C. 1973. **fTC1.A85no.9 ECOL**

BIOLOGICAL ASPECTS OF THERMAL POLLUTION.
National Symposium on Thermal Pollution, Portland, Oregon, 1968. 1969 **QH90.N3 1968 ECOL**

BIOLOGICAL CONCEPTS FOR DESIGN AND OPERATION OF THE ACTIVATED SLUDGE PROCESS.
Gaudy, Anthony F. 1971 i.e. 1972
fTD756.G38 ECOL

BIOLOGICAL CONSERVATION.
Ehrenfeld, David W. 1970 **QH75.E35 ECOL**

BIOLOGICAL CONSERVATION, WITH PARTICULAR EMPHASIS ON WILDLIFE.
Black, John David. c1954 **SK361.B55 ECOL**

BIOLOGICAL CONTROL OF INSECT PESTS AND WEEDS.
DeBach, Paul. 1964 **REF SB975.D4 ECOL**

BIOLOGICAL CONTROL OF PLANT PESTS.
Plants & gardens. Handbook on biological control of plant pests. 1966,1960 **SB932.P5 1966 ECOL**

BIOLOGICAL ENERGY INTERRELATIONSHIPS AND GLOSSARY OF ENERGY TERMS.
National Research Council. Committee on Animal Nutrition. 1st rev. ed. 1966.
REF SF95.N3 1966 ECOL

BIOLOGICAL IMPACT OF A LARGE-SCALE DESALINATION PLANT AT KEY WEST.
Chesher, Richard H. 1971.
fTD478.5.F5C48 ECOL

THE BIOLOGICAL REVOLUTION.
Jacker, Corinne. 1971 **QH333.J3 ECOL**

BIOLOGICAL SYSTEMS.
Gerking, Shelby Delos. 1969. **QH308.G44 ECOL**

THE BIOLOGICAL TIME BOMB.
Taylor, Gordon Rattray. 1968
QH309.T25 1968 ECOL

BIOLOGICAL TREATMENT IN AERATED LAGOONS: THEORY AND PRACTICE.
Thimsen, Donald J. 1965. **fTD746.5.T5 ECOL**

BIOLOGICAL TREATMENT OF CHLOROPHENOLIC WASTES.
Jacksonville, Ark. 1971. **fTD755.J3 ECOL**

BIOLOGY AND ETHICS.
1969. **HM216.B48 ECOL**

BIOLOGY AND THE FUTURE OF MAN.
1970. **QH307.2.B56 ECOL**

THE BIOLOGY OF POLLUTED WATERS.
Hynes, Hugh Bernard Noel. 1971c1960
QH96.H9 1971 ECOL

THE BIOLOGY OF POPULATIONS.
MacArthur, Robert H. 1966 **QL752.M2 ECOL**

BIOMASS DETERMINATION—A NEW TECHNIQUE FOR ACTIVATED SLUDGE CONTROL.
Biospherics Incorporated. 1972.
fTD756.B5 ECOL

BIOTA OF FRESHWATER ECOSYSTEMS, IDENTIFICATION MANUAL, NO.1.
Kenk, Roman. Freshwater planarians (Turbellaria) of North America. 1972. **fQH96.A2B5no.1 ECOL**

BIOTA OF FRESHWATER ECOSYSTEMS, IDENTIFICATION MANUAL, NO.2.
Cressey, Roger Frank. The genus Argulus (Crustacea: Branchiura) of the United States. 1972.
fQH96.A2B5no.2 ECOL

BIOTA OF FRESHWATER ECOSYSTEMS, IDENTIFICATION MANUAL, NO.3.
Burch, J. B. Freshwater sphaeriacean clams (Mollusca: Pelecypoda) of North America. 1972.
fQH96.A2B5no.3 ECOL

BIOTA OF FRESHWATER ECOSYSTEMS, IDENTIFICATION MANUAL, NO.4.
Foster, Nancy. Freshwater polychaetes (Annelida) of North America. 1972. **fQH96.A2B5no.4 ECOL**

BIOTA OF FRESHWATER ECOSYSTEMS, IDENTIFICATION MANUAL, NO.5.
Holsinger, John R. The freshwater amphipod crustaceans (Gammaridae) of North America. 1972.
fQH96.A2B5no.5 ECOL

BIOTA OF FRESHWATER ECOSYSTEMS, IDENTIFICATION MANUAL, NO.6.
Brown, Harley P. Aquatic dryopoid beetles (Coleoptera) of the United States. 1972.
fQH96.A2B5no.6 ECOL

BIOTA OF FRESHWATER ECOSYSTEMS IDENTIFICATION MANUAL, NO.7.
Williams, William David. Freshwater isopods (Asellidae) of North America. 1972.
fQH96.A2B5no.7 ECOL

BIOTA OF FRESHWATER ECOSYSTEMS, IDENTIFICATION MANUAL, NO.8.
Klemm, Donald J. Freshwater leeches (Annelida: Hirudinea) of North America. 1972.
fQH96.A2B5no.8 ECOL

BIOTA OF FRESHWATER ECOSYSTEMS, IDENTIFICATION MANUAL, NO. 9.
Hobbs, Horton Holcombe. Crayfishes (Astacidae) of North and Middle America. 1972.
fQH96.A2B5no.9 ECOL

BIRD FLIGHT.
Aymar, Gordon Christian. 1935.
QL698.A9 ECOL

BIRD GUIDE.
Reed, Chester Albert. Rev. ed. 1916.
QL683.R32 1916 ECOL

BIRD ISLANDS OF PERU.
Murphy, Robert Cushman. 1925.
REF QH128.M8 ECOL

BIRD STUDY.
Berger, Andrew John. 1971,c1961
QL673.B47 1971 ECOL

THE BIRD TABLE BOOK.
Soper, Tony.
In: Arbib, Robert S. The hungry bird book. 1971
QL676.5.A7 1971 ECOL

BIRDS.
MacBean, John C. c1971 **QL676.M22 ECOL**

BIRDS AT HOME.
Henry, Marguerite. 1972
fQL676.H52 1972 ECOL

THE BIRDS OF BRITAIN AND EUROPE WITH NORTH AFRICA AND MIDDLE EAST.
Heinzel, Hermann. 1972 **QL690.A1H44 ECOL**

BIRDS OF COLORADO.
Bailey, Alfred Marshall. 1965.
REF fQL684.C6B3 ECOL

BIRDS OF LA PLATA.
Hudson, William Henry. 1920.
REF QL689.A6H8 ECOL

BIRDS OF MASSACHUSETTS AND OTHER NEW ENGLAND STATES.
Forbush, Edward Howe. 1925-29
REF QL684.M4F65 ECOL

BIRDS OF THE OCEAN.
Alexander, Wilfrid Backhouse. 1928.
QL673.A37 ECOL

BIRDS OF THE PACIFIC STATES.
Hoffmann, Ralph. 1927. **Ref QL683.H65 ECOL**

BIRDS OF WESTERN CANADA.
Taverner, Percy Algernon. 2d ed. rev. 1928.
Ref QH1.C13no.41 1928 ECOL

BITTER WAGES: RALPH NADER'S STUDY GROUP REPORT ON DISEASE AND INJURY ON THE JOB.
Page, Joseph A. 1973. **RC967.P33 ECOL**

BITUMINOUS COAL FACTS. 1970-
REF fHD9544.B47 ECOL

BLOWOUT.
Steinhart, Carol E. 1972 **GC1556.S74 ECOL**

BLUE RIVER.
May, Julian. 1971 **TD425.M46 ECOL**

BLUEPRINT FOR SURVIVAL.
1972. **S936.B5 1972 ECOL**

BNA'S ENVIRONMENTAL MANAGEMENT SERIES.
Degler, Stanley E. Federal pollution control programs: water, air, and solid wastes. Rev. ed. 1971
TD180.D4 1971 ECOL

Degler, Stanley E. State air pollution control laws. Rev. ed. 1970 **KF3812.Z95D4 1970 ECOL**

BOOK CATALOG.
Great Lakes Basin Library. 1969-
REF fZ7164.N3G75 ECOL

A BOOK OF BIRDS.
Priestley, Mary. 1938. **PN6110.B6P75 ECOL**

A BOOK OF NATURE ACTIVITIES.
Gardner, John F. 1967 **QH53.G3 ECOL**

BOOKS IN PRINT.
Publishers' trade list annual.
REF Z1215.P972 ECOL

BOOKS IN PRINT SUPPLEMENT: AUTHORS, TITLES, SUBJECTS. 1972/73-
Publishers' trade list annual.
REF fZ1215.P972 Suppl. ECOL

BORN TO SING: AN INTERPRETATION AND WORLD SURVEY OF BIRD SONG.
Hartshorne, Charles. 1973 **QL698.5.H27 ECOL**

BOTANY: AN ECOLOGICAL APPROACH.
Jensen, William A. 1972 **QK47.J45 ECOL**

BOUNDARY WATERS CANOE AREA.
Minnesota. Division of Water Quality. Report on investigation of pollution of the Northern Border waters from the mouth of the Pigeon River at Lake Superior westward through the Boundary Waters Canoe Area and Lower Lakes to the outlet of Rainy Lake. 1969
fTD224.M6A5 ECOL

THE BREATH OF LIFE.
Carr, Donald Eaton. 1965 **TD883.C35 ECOL**

BRIEF HISTORY OF POLAR EXPLORATION SINCE THE INTRODUCTION OF FLYING.
Joerg, Wolfgang Louis Gottfried. 1930
G590.J6 ECOL

BROTHER EARTH.
Santmire, H. Paul. 1970 **BL435.S25 ECOL**

BROWN-OUT.
Rodgers, William H. 1972
HD9684.U62R63 1972 ECOL

BROWNOUT & SLOW-DOWN.
Saltonstall, Richard. c1972 **HC110.E5S33 ECOL**

BUCKY.
Kenner, Hugh. 1973. **TA140.F9K46 ECOL**

THE BUREAU OF LAND MANAGEMENT.
Clawson, Marion. 1971 **HD181.G8C57 ECOL**

BUREAU OF MINES RESEARCH PROGRAMS ON RECYCLING AND DISPOSAL OF MINERAL-, METAL-, AND ENERGY-BASED WASTES.
Kenahan, Charles B. 1973.
TN23.U7no.8595 ECOL

BUREAU OF MUNICIPAL RESEARCH, TORONTO. CIVIC AFFAIRS, SUMMER 1971.
Bureau of Municipal Research, Toronto. Urban open space: parks, people and planning. 1971.
GV56.T6B8 ECOL

BUREAU OF NATIONAL AFFAIRS, WASHINGTON, D.C. BNA'S ENVIRONMENTAL MANAGEMENT SERIES.
Degler, Stanley E. Federal pollution control programs: water, air, and solid wastes. Rev. ed. 1971
TD180.D4 1971 ECOL

Degler, Stanley E. State air pollution control laws. Rev. ed. 1970 **KF3812.Z95D4 1970 ECOL**

THE BUREAU OF OUTDOOR RECREATION.
Fitch, Edwin M. 1970 **GV53.F5 ECOL**

BUSINESS AND THE ENVIRONMENT.
Price, Fred C. McGraw-Hill's 1972 report on business and the environment. c1972
fTD174.P7 ECOL

BUSY WATER.
Black, Irma (Simonton). c1958.
PZ10.B29525Bu ECOL

C

CACTUS COUNTRY.
Abbey, Edward. 1973   **QH88.A2 ECOL**

CALIFORNIA INSTITUTE OF TECHNOLOGY. ENVIRONMENTAL QUALITY LABORATORY. EQL REPORT NO.1.
. California Institute of Technology, Pasadena. Environmental Quality Laboratory. People, power and pollution: environmental and public interest aspects of electric power plant siting. 1971.
fTK1193.U5C3 ECOL

CALIFORNIA NATURAL HISTORY GUIDES, 30.
Gross, Phyllis. Teaching science in an outdoor environment. 1972.   **QH51.G867 ECOL**

CALIFORNIA SOLID WASTE MANAGEMENT STUDY (1968) AND PLAN (1970).
California. Dept. of Public Health. 1971.
TD788.4.C3A45 ECOL

THE CALIFORNIA TOMORROW PLAN.
Rev. ed. 1972   **HT393.C3C35 1972 ECOL**

CALIFORNIA. UNIVERSITY, DAVIS. SCHOOL OF LAW. U. C. D. LAW REVIEW, V. 1.
Legal control of water pollution. 1969
KF3786.A32L4 ECOL

CALIFORNIA. UNIVERSITY. UNIVERSITY OF CALIFORNIA PUBLICATIONS IN ZOOLOGY, V. 88.
McCullough, Dale R. The tule elk. 1971c1969
QL1.C15vol.88 ECOL

CALIFORNIA WATER.
1971.   **HD1694.C2C35 ECOL**

CAN WE SURVIVE OUR FUTURE?
Urban, George R. 1972, c1971
CB428.U7 1972 ECOL

CANADIAN BUILDING SERIES, 4.
Brown, Roger James Evan. Permafrost in Canada. 1970   **TA713.B76 ECOL**

CANADIAN WILDLIFE SERIES, 1.
Tuck, Leslie M. The murres. 1960 i.e. 1961
QL696.A3T8 ECOL

CANOE COUNTRY.
Jaques, Florence (Page). c1938   **F606.J36 ECOL**

THE CARBON DIOXIDE SYSTEM AND EUTROPHICATION.
Morton, Stephen D. 1971. **fQH96.8.E9M6 ECOL**

CAREER EDUCATION IN THE ENVIRONMENT.
Olympus Research Corporation. 1971 or 2
fGF21.O4 ECOL

CAREERS FOR THE '70S: CONSERVATION.
Dodd, Edward. 1971   **S944.D6 ECOL**

CAREERS IN CONSERVATION.
Clepper, Henry Edward. 1963 **S494.5.C57 ECOL**

CAREERS IN NATURAL RESOURCE CONSERVATION.
Herbert, Frederick Wulling. 1965.
S944.H45 ECOL

THE CARELESS ATOM.
Novick, Sheldon. c1969   **TK9152.N6 ECOL**

THE CARELESS TECHNOLOGY: ECOLOGY AND INTERNATIONAL DEVELOPMENT.
Conference on the Ecological Aspects of International Development, Airlie House, 1968. 1st ed. 1972.   **QH540.C65 1968 ECOL**

THE CARNIVORES.
Ewer, R. F. 1973   **QL737.C2E93 ECOL**

CAROLINA LOW COUNTRY IMPRESSIONS.
Sprunt, Alexander. 1964.
REF QH105.S6S6 ECOL

CASEBOOK: POLLUTION CLEANUP ACTIONS.
National Industrial Pollution Control Council. 1971?
fTD897.N37 ECOL

CATALOG OF PESTICIDE NMR SPECTRA.
Southeast Water Laboratory. 1971.
fSB951.S64 ECOL

A CATALOG OF THE DUCK STAMP PRINTS WITH BIOGRAPHIES OF THE ARTISTS.
Stearns, Jean Pride. c1967
REF fHE6185.U52S7 ECOL

CBW: CHEMICAL AND BIOLOGICAL WARFARE.
Conference on Chemical and Biological Warfare, London, 1968. 1969,c1968
UG447.C655 1968 ECOL

CELEBRATE THE EARTH.
Imsland, Donald. 1971   **QH541.I45 ECOL**

CELEBRATING THE EARTH, 1.
Only a little planet. 1972
fPS3553.O4749O5 ECOL

CENSUS DATA: SEWAGE DISPOSAL FACILITIES, STATE OF MINNESOTA, JANUARY, 1968.
Minnesota. Pollution Control Agency. 1968
fTD524.M5A56 ECOL

CERTAIN BACKGROUND INFORMATION FOR CONSIDERATION WHEN EVALUATING THE "NATIONAL ENERGY DILEMMA".
United States. Congress. Joint Committee on Atomic Energy. 1973.   **HD9545.A53 ECOL**

CHAIN OF LIFE.
Collins, Patricia. 1st ed. 1972
QH541.5.F6C64 ECOL

CHALLENGE FOR SURVIVAL: LAND, AIR, AND WATER FOR MAN IN MEGALOPOLIS.
1970.   **HM206.C4 ECOL**

THE CHALLENGE OF MEGALOPOLIS.
Von Eckardt, Wolf. 1964. **HT123.5.A12V6 ECOL**

CHALLENGE OF THE LAND.
Little, Charles E. 1968   **HD205 1968 .L5 ECOL**

THE CHALLENGE OF THE SEVENTIES.
New York (State) Legislature. Joint Committee on Environmental Management and Natural Resources. 1971.   **fHC107.N7A25 ECOL**

THE CHALLENGE TO MAN'S SURVIVAL.
Coblentz, Stanton Arthur. 1972 **GF41.C55 ECOL**

CHANGE IN ALASKA.
Alaska Science Conference, 20th, University of Alaska, 1969. 1970   **HD9567.A4A64 1969 ECOL**

CHANGE OR DECAY: A SYMPOSIUM ON THE BLUEPRINT FOR SURVIVAL.
The Teilhard Review. 1972.   **HC68.T4 ECOL**

THE CHANGING METROPOLIS.
McKeown, James E. 2d ed. 1971
HT334.U5M321971ECOL

THE CHANGING WORLD OF LIVING THINGS.
Behnke, Frances L. c1972 **QH541.14.B47 ECOL**

CHARACTERISTICS OF RAINFALL RUN OFF FROM A BEEF CATTLE FEEDLOT.
Robert S. Kerr Water Research Center. 1972.
TD899.F4R6 ECOL

CHARACTERISTICS OF WASTES FROM SOUTHWESTERN CATTLE FEEDLOTS.
Texas Tech University. Water Resources Center. 1971.   **fTD899.F4T497 ECOL**

CHARACTERIZATION AND SEPARATION OF SECONDARY EFFLUENT COMPONENTS BY MOLECULAR WEIGHT.
Little (Arthur D.) Inc. 1971. **fTD735.L58 ECOL**

CHARACTERIZATION OF STREAM REAERATION, CAPACITY.
Tsivoglou, E. C. 1972.   **fTD458.T7 ECOL**

CHARACTERIZATION OF TASTE AND ODORS IN WATER SUPPLIES.
Collins, Ralph P. 1971.   **fTD384.C64 ECOL**

THE CHARLES C. MOSKOWITZ LECTURES, NO. 9.
Zisch, William E. The urban environment: how it can be improved. 1969.   **HT175.U6Z4 ECOL**

CHECK-LIST OF BIRDS OF THE WORLD.
Peters, James Lee. 1931-
REF QL677.P45 ECOL

CHEMICAL ANALYSIS OF INDUSTRIAL WATER.
McCoy, James W. 1969.   **TD380.M3 ECOL**

CHEMICAL AND BIOLOGICAL WARFARE.
Conference on Chemical and Biological Warfare, London, 1968. CBW: chemical and biological warfare. 1969,c1968   **UG447.C655 1968 ECOL**
Hersh, Seymour M. 1969,c1968
UG447.H42 1969 ECOL

CHEMICAL DETECTION OF GASEOUS POLLUTANTS.
Ruch, Walter E.   **REF fZ5524.G24R8 ECOL**

CHEMICAL ECOLOGY.
1970.   **QH345.C435 ECOL**

CHEMICAL FALLOUT.
1969   **SB959.C45 ECOL**

THE CHEMICAL FEAST.
Turner, James S. 1970. **HD9000.9.U5T83 ECOL**

CHEMICAL RELEASERS IN INSECTS.
International IUPAC Congress of Pesticide Chemistry, 2d, Tel-Ariv, 1971. c1971
SB951.I56 1971vol.3 ECOL

CHEMICALS AND LIFE.
Maxwell, Kenneth E. 1970 **QP903.M38 ECOL**

CHEMICALS CONTROLLING INSECT BEHAVIOR.
1970.   **QL461.S88 1969 ECOL**

CHEMICALS FOR PEST CONTROL.
Hartley, Gilbert Spencer. 1st ed. 1969
TP248.P47H3 1969 ECOL

CHEMICALS USED IN FOOD PROCESSING.
National Research Council. Food Protection Committee. 1965.   **REF fTX553.A3N26 ECOL**

CHICAGO. UNIVERSITY. DEPT. OF GEOGRAPHY. RESEARCH PAPER NO. 70.
White, Gilbert Fowler. Papers on flood problems. 1961.   **TC530.W4 ECOL**

CHICAGO. UNIVERSITY. DEPT. OF GEOGRAPHY. RESEARCH PAPER NO. 109.
Environmental perception and behavior. 1967.
GF51.E5 ECOL

CHICAGO. UNIVERSITY. DEPT. OF GEOGRAPHY. RESEARCH PAPER NO. 56.
Murphy, Francis C. Regulating flood-plain development. 1958.   **TC530.M8 ECOL**

CHICAGO. UNIVERSITY. DEPT. OF GEOGRAPHY. RESEARCH PAPER NO. 65.
Sheaffer, John Richard. Flood proofing. 1960.
TC530.S4 ECOL

CHICAGO. UNIVERSITY. THE MONDAY LECTURES, 1965.
Platt, John Rader. New views of the nature of man. 1965   **BD450.P55 ECOL**

CHLORINATED MUNICIPAL WASTE TOXICITIES TO RAINBOW TROUT AND FATHEAD MINNOWS.
Michigan. Bureau of Water Management. 1971.
fTD763.M5 ECOL

CHLORINE AND AIR POLLUTION: AN ANNOTATED BIBLIOGRAPHY.
Air Pollution Technical Information Center. 1971.
Z7173.A4A513 ECOL

THE CHURCH AND THE ECOLOGICAL CRISIS.
Barnette, Henlee H. 1972   **BT695.5.B37 ECOL**

CIRCLE OF THE WORLD.
QH541.2.C5 Suppl. ECOL
c1971-   **QH541.2.C5 ECOL**

CITIES AND SPACE: THE FUTURE USE OF URBAN LAND.
Resources for the Future. 1963
NA9031.R4 ECOL

A CITIZEN'S GUIDE TO AIR POLLUTION.
Bates, David B. 1972.   **TD883.B23 ECOL**

A CITIZEN'S GUIDE TO NUCLEAR POWER.
Lapp, Ralph E. c1971   **TK1078.L3 ECOL**

THE CITY.
McCue, George. Ecology: the city. c1971
QH541.5.C6M23 ECOL

CITY ATTORNEY'S REPORT, RE: FLOOD PLAIN MANAGEMENT.
St. Louis Park, Minn. City Attorney's Office. 1969
fTC425.S3A5 ECOL

THE CITY IN HISTORY: ITS ORIGINS, ITS TRANSFORMATIONS, AND ITS PROSPECTS.
Mumford, Lewis. 1st ed. 1961 **HT111.M8 ECOL**

THE CITY, ITS GROWTH, ITS DECAY, ITS FUTURE.
Saarinen, Eliel. 1943   **NA9030.S2 ECOL**

CITY LEAVES, CITY TREES.
Gallob, Edward. 1972   **fQK475.8.G35 ECOL**

CIVILIZING AMERICAN CITIES.
Olmsted, Frederick Law. 1971
HT167.O44 ECOL

CLASSICS OF HUMAN ECOLOGY, V.1.
Stapledon, Sir Reginald George. Human ecology. 2nd ed.; edited and introduced by Robert Waller. 1971.
HM206.S65 1971 ECOL

CLASSIFICATION OF NATURAL PONDS AND LAKES IN THE GLACIATED PRAIRIE REGION.
Stewart, Robert E. 1971.   **S914.A3no.92 ECOL**

CLASSIFIED FILES: THE YELLOWING PAGES.
Barker, Carol M. 1972.   **JK468.S4B35ECOL**

CLEAN AIR—CLEAN WATER FOR TOMORROW'S WORLD.
Millard, Reed. 1971   **HC79.E5M5 ECOL**

CLEAN AIR AND WATER NEWS. V.3- JAN. 8, 1971-
REF TD180.C54 ECOL

CLEAN AIR, SPARKLING WATER.
Shuttlesworth, Dorothy Edwards. 1968
PZ10.S65CL ECOL

CLEAN ENERGY FROM COAL—A NATIONAL PRIORITY.
United States. Office of Coal Research. 1973
HD9542.A5U5 ECOL

CLEAN THE AIR / TITLE CATALOG

CLEAN THE AIR!
Lewis, Alfred. c1965 **TD883.2L4 ECOL**

CLEAN WATER FOR THE 1970'S.
United States. Federal Water Quality Administration. 1970. **fTD365.U5 ECOL**

CLEANING OUR ENVIRONMENT: THE CHEMICAL BASIS FOR ACTION; A REPORT.
American Chemical Society. Committee on Chemistry and Public Welfare. Subcommittee on Environmental Improvement. 1969.
TD180.A4 ECOL

CLEARCUT.
Wood, Nancy C. c1971 **SD538.2.A1W65 ECOL**

CLIMATE, MAN, AND HISTORY.
Claiborne, Robert. 1970 **GF71.C55 ECOL**

CLOSED SYSTEM WASTE MANAGEMENT FOR LIVESTOCK.
Michigan. State University, East Lansing. Agricultural Pollution Control Laboratory. 1971 i.e. 1972 **fTD899.F4M5 ECOL**

THE CLOSING CIRCLE.
Commoner, Barry. 1st ed. 1971. **GF75.C65 ECOL**

COASTAL ZONE RESOURCE MANAGEMENT.
1971 **HC110.E5C6 ECOL**

COASTAL/ESTUARINE POLLUTION.
Sinha, Evelyn. 1970 **REF fZ5853.P7S53 ECOL**

CODIFIED AND UNCODIFIED STATE LAWS AND MUNICIPAL ORDINANCES BEARING ON WATER AND RELATED LAND RESOURCES IN MINNESOTA.
Minnesota. University. Water Resources Research Center. 1968. **GB701.M554no.9 ECOL**

COLLECTED REPRINTS. VOL. 4- , 1971- PT. 1-
Canada Centre for Inland Waters.
TD226.C3 ECOL

THE COLORADO DELTA.
Sykes, Godfrey Glenton. 1937. **F788.S958 ECOL**

COLORADO. STATE UNIV., FORT COLLINS. ENVIRONMENTAL RESOURCES CENTER/COMPLETION REPORT SERIES, NO.33-
Colorado. State University, Fort Collins Environmental Resources Center. The mechanism of waste treatment at low temperature. Part A- 1972- **fTD745.C58 ECOL**

COLORADO. STATE UNIVERSITY, FORT COLLINS. ENVIRONMENTAL RESOURCES CENTER. COMPLETION REPORT SERIES, NO. 36.
Wengert, Norman. Urban-metropolitan institutions for water planning, development and management: an analysis of usages of the term "institutions": a state-of-the-art review: final report, submitted to Water Resources Scientific Information Center. 1972.
fTD353.W42 ECOL

COLORADO. STATE UNIVERSITY, FORT COLLINS. ENVIRONMENTAL RESOURCES CENTER. COMPLETION REPORT SERIES, NO.39.
Wengert, Norman. Institutions for urban-metropolitan water management: essays in social theory, submitted to Water Resources Scientific Information Center. 1972. **fTD353.W4 ECOL**

COLORADO. STATE UNIVERSITY, FORT COLLINS. ENVIRONMENTAL RESOURCES CENTER. COMPLETION REPORT SERIES, PARTIAL REPORT NO. 46.
Walker, Wynn R. Evaluation of urban water management policies in the Denver metropolitan area. 1973. **fTD225.D4W3 ECOL**

COLORADO. STATE UNIVERSITY, FORT COLLINS. ENVIRONMENTAL RESOURCES CENTER. INFORMATION SERIES, NO. 6.
Radosevich, George E. Water law and its relationship to environmental quality: a bibliography of source material. 1973. **REF fKF5551.R3 ECOL**

COLUMBIA RIVER INTERSTATE COMPACT, POLITICS OF NEGOTIATION.
Doerksen, Harvey R. 1972 **KF5590.C6D6 ECOL**

THE COLUMBIA RIVER TREATY.
Krutilla, John V. c1967 **HD1694.A2 1967 ECOL**

THE COLUMBIAN EXCHANGE.
Crosby, Alfred W. 1972 **E98.D6C7 ECOL**

COMBINED SEWER OVERFLOW ABATEMENT ALTERNATIVES, WASH., D.C.
Roy F. Weston, Inc. 1970 **fTD525.W2R68 ECOL**

COMBINED SEWER REGULATOR OVERFLOW FACILITIES; REPORT.
American Public Works Association. 1970.
fTD662.A42 ECOL

COMBINED SOILS, FERTILIZER & AGRICULTURAL PESTICIDES, SHORT COURSE, DEC. 15-17, 1970, MINNEAPOLIS AUDITORIUM.
fSB951.C76 ECOL

COMBINED STEEL MILL AND MUNICIPAL WASTE-WATERS TREATMENT.
National Steel Corporation. Weirton Steel Division. 1972. **fTD899.S7N37 ECOL**

COMBINED TREATMENT OF DOMESTIC AND INDUSTRIAL WASTES BY ACTIVATED SLUDGE.
Dallas, Or. 1971. **fTD756.D35 ECOL**

COMBUSTION-GENERATED AIR POLLUTION.
1971. **TD883.C575 1971 ECOL**

COME, LET US PLAY GOD.
Augenstine, Leroy George. 1969
R724.A83 ECOL

THE COMING WATER FAMINE.
Wright, James Claud. 1966 **TD223.W7 ECOL**

COMMON ENVIRONMENTAL TERMS: A GLOSSARY.
Studdard, Gloria J. 1973. **REF S922.S7 ECOL**

THE COMMON INSECTS OF NORTH AMERICA.
Swan, Lester A. 1st ed. 1972 **QL473.S9 ECOL**

THE COMMON LAW OF WATER.
Great Lakes Foundation, Ann Arbor, Mich. c1971.
KF3790.Z9L4 ECOL

COMMON MARSH, UNDERWATER, AND FLOATING-LEAVED PLANTS OF THE UNITED STATES AND CANADA.
Hotchkiss, Neil. 1972 **QK115.H67 1972 ECOL**

COMMON WILD FLOWERS OF MINNESOTA.
Monserud, Wilma. c1971 **QK168.M6 ECOL**

COMMUNITIES AND ECOSYSTEMS.
Whittaker, Robert Harding. 1970
QH541.W44 ECOL

COMMUNITY ACTION FOR ENVIRONMENTAL QUALITY.
United States. Citizens Advisory Committee on Environmental Quality. 1970 **HC110.E5A5 ECOL**

COMMUNITY ACTION GUIDEBOOK FOR SOIL EROSION AND SEDIMENT CONTROL.
Powell, Mel D. 1970 **fS624.A1P68 ECOL**

THE COMMUNITY ENVIRONMENTAL INVENTORY.
Bennett, Dean B. Guidelines for planning and implementing a comprehensive community environmental inventory. Rev. ed. 1972.
fQH541.2.B38 1972 ECOL

COMMUNITY IN URBAN PLANNING.
Reiner, Thomas A. The place of the ideal community in urban planning. 1968,c1963
fNA9030.R45 1968 ECOL

COMMUNITY NOISE.
Wyle Laboratories. 1971 i.e. 1972
fTD892.W94 ECOL

COMMUNITY ORGANIZATION PROGRAMS AND RELATIONSHIPS IN WATERSHED DEVELOPMENT.
Peterson, John H. 1972. **fTC409.P4 ECOL**

COMMUNITY RESOURCE.
Landerman, Norman J. 1972
TD195.S3L36 ECOL

COMPACTION OF RADIOACTIVE SOLID WASTE.
United States Atomic Energy Commission. 1970.
fTD898.U5 ECOL

A COMPARATIVE STUDY OF STATE WATER POLLUTION CONTROL LAWS AND PROGRAMS.
Heath, Milton Sidney. 1972.
fKF3790.Z95H4 ECOL

COMPARISONS IN RESOURCE MANAGEMENT.
Resources for the Future. 1961
REF SD411.R4 ECOL

COMPENDIUM OF ANIMAL WASTE MANAGEMENT.
United States. Federal Water Pollution Control Administration. Missouri Basin Region.
TD811.U5 ECOL

COMPETITION FOR WETLANDS IN THE MIDWEST.
Goldstein, Jon H. 1971 **HD1683.U4G6 ECOL**

COMPILATION OF AIR POLLUTANT EMISSION FACTORS.
United States. Environmental Protection Office. Office of Air Programs. Rev. 1972.
TD883.1.U494 ECOL

COMPILATION OF FEDERAL LAWS RELATING TO FUEL AND ENERGY RESOURCES.
United States. Congress. House. Committee on Interior and Insular Affairs. 1972.
KF2120.A25 1972 ECOL

A COMPILATION OF SELECTED AIR POLLUTION EMISSION CONTROL REGULATIONS AND ORDINANCES.
United States. Robert A Taft Sanitary Engineering Center, Cincinnati. 1965.
REF KF3812.A4 1965 ECOL

THE COMPLETE ECOLOGY FACT BOOK.
Nobile, Philip. 1st ed. 1972. **TD174.N6 ECOL**

COMPLETE FIELD GUIDE TO AMERICAN WILDLIFE: EAST, CENTRAL, AND NORTH ...
Collins, Henry Hill. c1959 **QL151.C6 ECOL**

COMPLETE HANDBOOK ON ENVIRONMENTAL CONTROL.
McClain, Thomas B. 1970 **Z5853.P7M32 ECOL**

THE COMPLETE SNOW CAMPER'S GUIDE.
Bridge, Raymond. 1973 **SK602.6.B74 ECOL**

COMPOSTING OF MUNICIPAL SOLID WASTES IN THE UNITED STATES.
1971. **TD796.5.C64 ECOL**

COMPREHENSIVE FRAMEWORK STUDY, MISSOURI RIVER BASIN.
Missouri Basin Inter-agency Committee. 1971-
fHD1695.M5M48 ECOL

COMPREHENSIVE PLAN FOR THE STORAGE, COLLECTION, TRANSPORTATION AND DISPOSAL OF SOLID WASTE IN THE STATE OF MINNESOTA.
Minnesota. Pollution Control Agency. 1970.
fTD524.M6A32 ECOL

THE COMPREHENSIVE SANITARY SEWER STUDY FOR THE VILLAGE OF MAPLE GROVE, MINNESOTA.
Caswell and Associates, inc., Osseo, Minn. 1969.
fTD525.M28C3 ECOL

COMPUTER PROGRAM FOR STATISTICAL ANALYSIS OF ANNUAL FLOOD DATA BY THE LOG-PEARSON TYPE III METHOD.
Bowers, C. Edward. 1971.
GB701.M554no.39 ECOL

COMPUTER PROGRAMS IN HYDROLOGY.
Bowers, C. Edward. 1972. **GB665.B6 ECOL**

COMPUTERIZED DESIGN AND COST ESTIMATION FOR MULTIPLE-HEARTH SLUDGE INCINERATORS.
Unterberg, W. 1971 i.e. 1972 **fTD770.U58 ECOL**

CONCENTRATED MINE DRAINAGE DISPOSAL INTO SEWAGE TREATMENT SYSTEMS.
Environmental Research and Applications, Inc. 1971. **fTD899.M5E58 ECOL**

CONCEPT DEVELOPMENT OF A HYDRAULIC SKIMMER SYSTEM FOR RECOVERY OF FLOATING OIL.
Battelle Memorial Institute, Columbus, Ohio. Pacific Northwest Laboratory, Richland, Wash. 1971.
fTD427.P4B29 ECOL

CONCEPT EVALUATION: RECOVERY OF FLOATING OIL USING POLYURETHANE FOAM SORBENT.
Henager, Charles H. 1972. **fTD427.P4H4 ECOL**

CONCEPTS OF ECOLOGY.
Kormondy, Edward John. 1969
QH541.K59 ECOL

CONCISE COLOR ENCYCLOPEDIA OF NATURE.
Chinery, Michael. 1972 **fQH309.C46 1972 ECOL**

THE CONDENSED CHEMICAL DICTIONARY.
Rev. by Gessner G. Hawley. 8th ed. 1971
REF QD5.C5 1971 ECOL

THE CONFERENCE BOARD. REPORT NO. 541.
Lund, Leonard. Industry expenditures for water pollution abatement. 1972 **fTD223.L8 ECOL**

CONFERENCE ON IMPACT OF FUTURE ELECTRIC POWER REQUIREMENTS IN THE STATE OF MINNESOTA: AN ISSUE ANALYSIS.
Minnesota. University. Water Resources Research Center. 1971. **GB701.M554no.28 ECOL**

CONFERENCE ON THE ELECTRIC POWER INDUSTRY.
Sierra Club Conference on the Electric Power Industry, 1st, Johnson City, Vt., 1972. Report on the first Sierra Club power conference [papers]. 1972?
fHD9685.A2S5 1972 ECOL

CONGRESS AND THE ENVIRONMENT.
1970 KF5505.A75C6 ECOL

CONGRESS AND THE NATION'S ENVIRONMENT.
United States. Library of Congress. Environmental Policy Division. 1973. KF3775.A25 1973 ECOL

CONGRESS AND URBAN PROBLEMS.
Cleaveland, Frederic N. 1969
HT334.U5C665 ECOL

CONGRESSIONAL DIRECTORY.
United States Congress. Official congressional directory. REF JK1011.A3 ECOL

THE CONQUEST OF ARID AMERICA.
Smythe, William Ellsworth. 1969,c1905
F591.S662 1969 ECOL

THE CONQUEST OF NATURE.
Forbes, Robert James. 1968 CB478.F57 ECOL

CONSERVATION.
Joffe, Joyce. 1970,c1969 S940.J64 ECOL

CONSERVATION, AN AMERICAN STORY OF CONFLICT AND ACCOMPLISHMENT.
Coyle, David Cushman. 1957.
HC103.7.C68 ECOL

CONSERVATION AND PRODUCTIVITY OF NATURAL WATERS.
1972. QL1.Z733no.29 ECOL

CONSERVATION AND YOU.
Hitch, Allen S. 1964 S930.H5 ECOL

CONSERVATION DIRECTORY.
fS920.C64 ECOL

CONSERVATION EDUCATION.
Brown, Robert E. Techniques for teaching conservation education. 1964 S946.B7 ECOL
Carvajal, Joan. 1968 REF Z7164.N3C3 ECOL

CONSERVATION EDUCATION ASSISTANCE DIRECTORIES FOR MINNESOTA COUNTIES.
Minnesota. University. Agricultural Extension Service. REF fS946.M5 ECOL

CONSERVATION EDUCATION ASSOCIATION. EDUCATION: KEY TO CONSERVATION.
Carvajal, Joan. Conservation education. 1968
REF Z7164.N3C3 ECOL

CONSERVATION EDUCATION ASSOCIATION. EDUCATION: KEY TO CONSERVATION, NO.7.
Bachert, Russel E., Jr. Directory of degree programs, related to conservation, ecology, environmental education, environmental science, outdoor education & natural resources. 1971 fS946.B3 ECOL

CONSERVATION FOR SURVIVAL.
Curry-Lindahl, Kai. 1972. QH541.C87 ECOL

A CONSERVATION FOUNDATION STUDY.
Rudd, Robert L. Pesticides and the living landscape. 1964. SB951.R78 ECOL

THE CONSERVATION FRAUD.
Zurhorst, Charles. 1970 S942.Z8 ECOL

A CONSERVATION HANDBOOK.
Ordway, Samuel Hanson. 1949. HC55.O7 ECOL

CONSERVATION IN THE SOVIET UNION.
Pryde, Philip R. 1972. S934.R9P76 ECOL

CONSERVATION IN THE UNITED STATES.
Highsmith, Richard Morgan. 2d ed. 1969
HC103.7.H5 1969 ECOL

CONSERVATION: NOW OR NEVER.
Roosevelt, Nicholas. 1970 S942.R6 ECOL

CONSERVATION OF NATURAL RESOURCES.
Smith, Guy Harold. 4th ed. 1971
S938.S58 1971 ECOL

CONSERVATION OF NATURE.
Duffey, Eric. 1970 S940.D84 ECOL

CONSERVATION QUICKIES.
Conservation Education Association. 1966
fS946.C57 ECOL

CONSERVATION, THE CHALLENGE OF RECLAIMING OUR PLUNDERED LAND.
Harrison, C. William. c1968,1963
S940.H33 1968 ECOL

CONSERVATION: THE SCIENTIFIC ASPECTS: A GUIDE TO THE LITERATURE.
Miller, John A. 1973. REF fZ7164.N3M5 ECOL

CONSERVATION YEARBOOK SERIES, NO. 8.
United States. Dept. of the Interior. Our environment and natural resources ... indivisibly one. 1971? fS914.A533 ECOL

CONSERVATION YEARBOOK SERIES, VOL. NO. 7.
United States. Dept. of the Interior. Our living land. 1971 S914.A535 ECOL

CONSERVING AMERICAN RESOURCES.
Parson, Ruben L. 2d ed. 1964
S930.P3 1964 ECOL
Parson, Ruben L. 3d ed. 1972
S930.P3 1972 ECOL

CONSERVING LIFE ON EARTH.
Ehrenfeld, David W. 1972.
QH75.E35 1972 ECOL

CONSERVING NATURAL RESOURCES.
Allen, Shirley Walter. 3d ed. c1966
HC103.7.A7 1966 ECOL

CONSIDERATIONS AFFECTING STEAM POWER PLANT SITE SELECTION.
United States. Office of Science and Technology. 1968 TK1193.U5A44 ECOL

CONSTRUCTION OF A CHEMICAL-MICROBIAL PILOT PLANT FOR PRODUCTION OF SINGLE-CELL PROTEIN FROM CELLULOSIC WASTES.
Callihan, Clayton Dale. 1971.
TP996.B3C3 ECOL

CONTEMPORARY LEGAL EDUCATION SERIES.
Sax, Joseph L. Water law, planning & policy. 1968
KF5568.S3 1968 ECOL

THE CONTINENT IN OUR HANDS.
Ogburn, Charlton. 1971. E169.02.O3 ECOL

CONTINUATION OF STUDIES ON THE HYDROLOGY OF PONDS AND SMALL LAKES.
1971. fGB1825.M6C6ECOL

THE CONTINUOUS PLANKTON RECORDER: A REVIEW OF THE LITERATURE.
Olson, Theodore A. 1966.
GB701.M554no.3 ECOL

CONTROL OF HAZARDOUS POLLUTING SUBSTANCES.
United States. President, 1969- (Nixon). 1971.
TD365.U53 ECOL

CONTROL OF MERCURY CONTAMINATION IN FRESHWATER SEDIMENTS.
Feick, George. 1972. TD427.M4F4 ECOL

CONTROL OF MERCURY POLLUTION IN SEDIMENTS.
United States. Environmental Protection Agency. Office of Research and Monitoring. 1972.
TD427.M4U5 ECOL

CONTROL OF POLLUTION.
Mid-West Debate Bureau, Normal, Illinois. Control of pollution. 1970 fTD180.M5 ECOL

CONTROL OF POLLUTION FROM OUTBOARD ENGINE EXHAUST: A RECONNAISSANCE STUDY.
Rensselaer Polytechnic Institute, Troy, N.Y. Bio-Environmental Engineering Division. 1971.
fTD427.P4R45 ECOL

CONTROL OF SULFUR OXIDE EMISSIONS IN COPPER, LEAD, AND ZINC SMELTING.
United States. Bureau of Mines. 1971
TN295.U4no.8527 ECOL

CONTROLLED NUCLEAR FUSION.
Glasstone, Samuel. Rev. ed. 1968
QC791.G48 1968 ECOL

CONTROLLING POLLUTION.
Goldman, Marshall I. c1967 TD180.G58 ECOL

A CONVERSATION ON POPULATION, ENVIRONMENT, AND HUMAN WELL-BEING.
1971 HB875.C63 ECOL

CONVERSION OF CRANKCASE WASTE OIL INTO USEFUL PRODUCTS.
National Oil Recovery Corp., Bayonne, N.J. 1971.
fTP687.N3 ECOL

CONVERTING LAND FROM RURAL TO URBAN USES.
Schmid, A. Allan. 1968 REF HD256.S3 ECOL

COORDINATION DIRECTORY FOR PLANNING STUDIES AND REPORTS.
United States. Water Resources Council. 1971-
TD345.U5 ECOL

THE CORAL REEF PROBLEM.
Davis, William Morris. 1928. QE565.D3 ECOL

CORPORATE ORGANIZATION FOR POLLUTION CONTROL.
Hopkinson, Richard A. c1970
fHC110.E5H6 ECOL

CORPORATIONS AND THE ENVIRONMENT: PR OR PROPAGANDA?
Dee, Sandra R. 1973 Ref fZ5863.P6D41 ECOL

CORROSION POTENTIAL OF NTA IN DETERGENT FORMULATIONS.
Battelle Memorial Institute, Columbus, Ohio 1971.
fTP992.5.B3 ECOL

COST OF CLEAN WATER.
United States. Environmental Protection Agency. Water Quality Office. 1971- TD420.U5 ECOL

COST TO THE CONSUMER FOR COLLECTION AND TREATMENT OF WASTEWATER.
Smith, Robert. 1970 i.e. 1972 fTD523.S65 ECOL

THE COSTS AND BENEFITS OF NUCLEAR ELECTRIC POWER PLANTS.
Minnesota Committee for Environmental Information. 1969. REF fTK1078.M5 ECOL

COUGAR.
Gray, Robert. c1972 QL737.C2G73 ECOL

COUNCIL OF PLANNING LIBRARIANS. EXCHANGE BIBLIOGRAPHY, NO. 254.
Snyder, Lorraine Hiatt. The environmental challenge and the aging individual. 1972
REF fZ7164.O4S63 ECOL

COUNCIL OF PLANNING LIBRARIANS. EXCHANGE BIBLIOGRAPHY, NO. 251.
Ehler, Charles N. Environmental systems planning and management: a preliminary sorting of literature. 1972 REF fZ5863.P6E38 ECOL

COUNCIL OF PLANNING LIBRARIANS. EXCHANGE BIBLIOGRAPHY, NO. 257.
Van Nest, William J. Air pollution and urban planning: a selective annotated bibliography. 1972
REF fZ5853.P7V3 ECOL

COUNCIL OF PLANNING LIBRARIANS. EXCHANGE BIBLIOGRAPHY, NO. 274.
Cunningham, Michael C. A selected bibliography on the relevance of environmental education to secondary school curricula. 1972 REF fQH541.2.C8 ECOL

COUNCIL OF PLANNING LIBRARIANS. EXCHANGE BIBLIOGRAPHY, NO. 275.
Henry, Marybeth. Motor vehicle emissions: a bibliography. 1972 REF fTL214.P6H4 ECOL

COUNCIL OF PLANNING LIBRARIANS. EXCHANGE BIBLIOGRAPHY, NO. 292.
Berlin, G. Lennis. The urban environment: a climatological anomaly. 1972
REF fQC981.7.U7B47 ECOL

COUNCIL OF PLANNING LIBRARIANS. EXCHANGE BIBLIOGRAPHY, NO. 296.
Burg, Nan C. Abandoned vehicles: a selected bibliography. 1972 Ref fHD9975.B87 ECOL

COUNCIL OF PLANNING LIBRARIANS. EXCHANGE BIBLIOGRAPHY, NO. 353.
Sloss, George J. Environmental aspects of transportation planning (a revision of CPL Exchange bibliography no. 218). 1972
REF fZ7164.T8S55 ECOL

COUNCIL OF PLANNING LIBRARIANS. EXCHANGE BIBLIOGRAPHY, NO. 391.
Hickok, Beverly. Goals, objectives and values: selected references relating to national, state and urban or regional areas, covering general & transportation aspects. 1973 fZ7164.O7H49 ECOL

COUNCIL OF PLANNING LIBRARIANS. EXCHANGE BIBLIOGRAPHY, 249.
Powell, David R. New towns bibliography. 1972.
REF fZ5942.P6 ECOL

COUNCIL OF PLANNING LIBRARIANS. EXCHANGE BIBLIOGRAPHY, 266.
Ehrenthal, Frank F. A selected bibliography on uses of the urban street. 1972.
REF fZ7164.T81E3 ECOL

COUNCIL OF PLANNING LIBRARIANS. EXCHANGE BIBLIOGRAPHY, 291.
Appleyard, Donald. The urban environment: selected bibliography. 1972.
REF fZ7164.U7A6 ECOL

COUNCIL OF PLANNING LIBRARIANS. EXCHANGE BIBLIOGRAPHY, 343.
Nelson, Jon P. Economic aspects of the airport environment: noise, air pollution, and congestion. 1972. REF fZ5064.A28N4 ECOL

COUNCIL OF PLANNING LIBRARIANS. EXCHANGE BIBLIOGRAPHY, 365.
Sloss, George J. Water-related environmental planning. 1973. fZ5862.W3S5 ECOL

COUNCIL OF PLANNING LIBRARIANS. EXCHANGE BIBLIOGRAPHY, 385.
Harrison, James D. Environmental preferences: relevant studies for urban planning. 1973.
Ref fZ5942.H3 ECOL

COUNCIL OF PLANNING LIBRARIANS. EXCHANGE BIBLIOGRAPHY, 394.
Coleman, D. J. Highways and the environment: a bibliography of the effects of highways on the physical, biological, recreational and aesthetic environments and of techniques for the analysis of these impacts. 1973.
fZ7295.C6 ECOL

COUNCIL OF PLANNING LIBRARIANS. EXCHANGE BIBLIOGRAPHY, 395.
Gunter, John D. Solid waste management: economics and operation. 1973.
Ref fZ5853.S22G8 ECOL

COUNCIL OF PLANNING LIBRARIANS. EXCHANGE BIBLIOGRAPHY, 396.
Draper, Dianne. Public participation in environmental decision-making. 1973.
fZ5863.P6D7 ECOL

COUNCIL OF PLANNING LIBRARIANS. EXCHANGE BIBLIOGRAPHY, 397.
Miller, John A. Conservation: the scientific aspects: a guide to the literature. 1973.
REF fZ7164.N3M5 ECOL

COUNCIL OF PLANNING LIBRARIANS. EXCHANGE BIBLIOGRAPHY, 406.
Gunter, John D. The ecological impact of solid waste. 1973. Ref fZ5863.P6G8 ECOL

COUNCIL OF PLANNING LIBRARIANS. EXCHANGE BIBLIOGRAPHY, 407.
Gunter, John D. Recycling and re-use: the future of solid waste. 1973. Ref fTP156.R38G8 ECOL

COUNCIL OF PLANNING LIBRARIANS. EXCHANGE BIBLIOGRAPHY, 410.
Dee, Sandra R. A basic environmental collection. 1973. Ref fZ5863.P6D4 ECOL

COUNCIL OF PLANNING LIBRARIANS. EXCHANGE BIBLIOGRAPHY, 411.
Dee, Sandra R. Corporations and the environment: PR or propaganda? 1973 Ref fZ5863.P6D41 ECOL

COUNCIL OF PLANNING LIBRARIANS. EXCHANGE BIBLIOGRAPHY, 415.
Ditton, Robert B. National environmental policy act of 1969 (P.L. 91-190): bibliography on impact assessment methods and legal considerations. 1973.
Ref fHC110.E5D582 ECOL

COUNCIL OF PLANNING LIBRARIANS. EXCHANGE BIBLIOGRAPHY, 426.
Wright, Sydney. A bibliography of recreational communities and leisure land development. 1973.
fZ7164.L3W7 ECOL

COUNCIL OF PLANNING LIBRARIANS. EXCHANGE BIBLIOGRAPHY, 437.
White, Anthony G. Lead in the urban environment: a selected bibliography. 1973. fZ6679.L4W5 ECOL

CRANBROOK INSTITUTE OF SCIENCE. BULLETIN NO. 29.
Walkinshaw, Lawrence H. The sandhill cranes. 1949 QL696.G8W3 ECOL

CRAYFISHES (ASTACIDAE) OF NORTH AND MIDDLE AMERICA.
Hobbs, Horton Holcombe. 1972.
fQH96.A2B5no.9 ECOL

CREATING THE HUMAN ENVIRONMENT.
McCue, Gerald M. 1970 HN59.M22 ECOL

CRISIS IN EDEN.
Elder, Frederick. 1970 GF80.E4 ECOL

CRISIS IN OUR CITIES.
Herber, Lewis. c1965 RA566.H4 ECOL

CRITERIA FOR A RECOMMENDED STANDARD... OCCUPATIONAL EXPOSURE TO CARBON MONOXIDE.
United States. National Institute for Occupational Safety and Health. 1972. fRA1247.C17U5 ECOL

CRITICAL INDEX OF FILMS ON MAN AND HIS ENVIRONMENT.
Conservation Education Association. c1972
fS946.C65 1972 ECOL

CRUSADE FOR WILDLIFE.
Trefethen, James B. 1961. SK361.T7 ECOL

CULTURAL BENEFITS FROM METROPOLITAN RIVER RECREATION—SAN ANTONIO PROTOTYPE.
Gunn, Clare A. 1972. fHD1694.T4G8 ECOL

CUMULATIVE REGULATORY EFFECTS ON THE COST OF AUTOMOTIVE TRANSPORTATION (RECAT): FINAL REPORT.
United States. Ad Hoc Committee on the Cumulative Regulatory Effects on the Cost of Automotive Transportation. 1972. KF2209.A3U5 ECOL

CURE FOR CHAOS.
Ramo, Simon. 1969 HN28.R3 ECOL

CURIOUS NATURALISTS.
Tinbergen, Nikolaas. 1968,c1958
QL751.T55 1968 ECOL

CURRENT LIST OF WATER PUBLICATIONS, 1965/71-
United States. Environmental Protection Agency. Office of Public Affairs. REF Z7173.W3U5 ECOL

A CURRICULUM ACTIVITIES GUIDE TO WATER POLLUTION AND ENVIRONMENTAL STUDIES.
United States. Environmental protection Agency. Office of Water Programs. Training Grants Branch. 1972- REF fS946.U56 ECOL

D

THE DAEDALUS LIBRARY, V. 15.
America's changing environment. 1970.
HC110.E5A56 ECOL

DALLAS. SOUTHERN METHODIST UNIVERSITY. SCHOOL OF LAW. AN SMU LAW SCHOOL STUDY.
Thomas, Ann (Van Wynen). Legal limits on the use of chemical and biological weapons. 1970
REF JX5135.C5T55 ECOL

DAMS AND OTHER DISASTERS.
Morgan, Arthur Ernest. 1971 UG23.M67 ECOL

DANGEROUS AIR.
Kavaler, Lucy. c1967 TD883.13.K3 ECOL

THE DARKENING LAND.
Longgood, William Frank. 1972
TD175.L66 ECOL

THE DAWN OF LIFE.
Pinna, Giovanni. c1972 fQE714.3.P5 ECOL

A DAY AND A NIGHT IN A TIDE POOL.
Venn, Mary Eleanor. 1972
QH541.5.S35V45 ECOL

THE DAY THEY PARACHUTED CATS ON BORNEO.
Pomerantz, Charlotte. c1971
PN6120.A5P75 ECOL

DAYDREAMS AND NIGHTMARES.
Burch, William R. 1971 HM206.B83 ECOL

DEAD END: THE AUTOMOBILE IN MASS TRANSPORTATION.
Buel, Ronald A. 1972 HE5623.B82 ECOL

THE DEATH AND LIFE OF GREAT AMERICAN CITIES.
Jacobs, Jane. c1961 NA9108.J3 ECOL

THE DEATH OF THE AUTOMOBILE.
Jerome, John. 1st ed. 1972 HE5623.J47 ECOL

DEATH OF THE SWEET WATERS.
Carr, Donald Eaton. 1st ed. 1966
TD223.C3 ECOL

THE DEATH OF TOMORROW.
Loraine, John Alexander. 1972
HC79.P55L67 1972b ECOL

DECISION ANALYSIS OF NUCLEAR PLANTS IN ELECTRICAL SYSTEM EXPANSION: FINAL REPORT.
Stanford Research Institute. Decision Analysis Group. fTK1078.S7 ECOL

DECISION PROCESSES IN WATER QUALITY MANAGEMENT.
Males, Richard Michael. 1971.
fTD365.M3 ECOL

DEER OF THE WORLD.
Whitehead, George Kenneth. 1972
QL737.U55W44 1972b ECOL

DEFENDING THE ENVIRONMENT.
Sax, Joseph L. 1971. HC110.E5S3 ECOL

DEFENSE AGAINST FAMINE.
Slack, Archie Vivian. 1st ed. 1970.
S633.S627 ECOL

DEGRADATION OF HERBICIDES.
Kearney, Philip C. 1969. REF SB951.4.K4 ECOL

THE DELICATE CREATION.
Derrick, Christopher. c1972 BD581.D47 ECOL

DEMINERALIZATION OF WASTEWATER BY THE TRANSPORT-DEPLETION PROCESS.
Southern Research Institute, Birmingham, Ala. 1971. fTD754.S67 ECOL

DEMONSTRATION OF A FULL-SCALE WASTE TREATMENT SYSTEM FOR A CANNERY.
Streebin, Leale E. 1971. fTD899.C3S87 ECOL

DEMONSTRATION OF ROTARY SCREENING FOR COMBINED SEWER OVERFLOWS.
Portland, Or. Bureau of Sanitary Engineering. 1971.
fTD748.P67 ECOL

DENITRIFICATION BY ANAEROBIC FILTERS AND PONDS, PHASE II.
Robert S. Kerr Water Research Center. 1971.
TD475.R62 ECOL

DENSITY INDUCED MIXING IN CONFINED AQUIFERS.
Ralph M. Parsons Laboratory for Water Resources and Hydrodynamics. 1972. fTC176.R33 ECOL

DENVER URBAN ENVIRONMENTAL STUDIES FOR GRADES KINDERGARTEN—SIX.
Balarat Center for Environmental Studies. 1971.
QH541.2.B25 ECOL

DEPOSITION OF FINE SEDIMENTS IN TURBULENT FLOWS.
Partheniades, Emmanuel. 1971 i.e. 1972
fTC175.2.P3 ECOL

DESALINATION.
Popkin, Roy. 1968 TD479.P6 ECOL

DESALINATION OF AGRICULTURAL TILE DRAINAGES.
Robert S. Kerr Water Research Center. 1971.
TD479.R6 ECOL

DESALTING SEAWATER.
Clawson, Marion. 1972 TD479.C53 1972 ECOL

DESERT ANIMALS.
Tate, Ro. 1st U.S. ed. c1971
QL116.T37 1971 ECOL

THE DESERT WORLD.
Costello, David Francis. 1972 QH88.C67 ECOL

THE DESERTS AND MAN.
McCue, George. Ecology: the deserts and man. c1971 QH541.5.D4M22 ECOL

DESERTS OF AMERICA.
Larson, Peggy Pickering. 1970
QH541.5.D4L28 ECOL

DESERTS ON THE MARCH.
Sears, Paul Bigelow. 3rd ed. rev. 1967,c1959
S493.S4 1959 ECOL

DESIGN CHARACTERISTICS FOR A NATIONAL SYSTEM TO STORE, RETRIEVE, AND DISSEMINATE WATER DATA.
Federal Interagency Water Data Handling Work Group. 1971. TD211.F4 ECOL

DESIGN FOR A WORLDWIDE STUDY OF REGIONAL DEVELOPMENT.
Resources for the Future. 1966 HD82.R43 ECOL

DESIGN FOR THE REAL WORLD.
Papanek, Victor J. 1st American ed. c1971
TS171.4.P37 1971 ECOL

DESIGN GUIDES FOR BIOLOGICAL WASTEWATER TREATMENT PROCESSES.
Austin, Texas 1971 i.e.1972 fTD755.A87 ECOL

DESIGN HANDBOOK OF WASTEWATER SYSTEMS: DOMESTIC, INDUSTRIAL, COMMERCIAL.
Goodman, Brian L. 1971
REF fTD745.G65 ECOL

DESIGN, NATURE, AND REVOLUTION.
Maldonado, Tomas. 1st U.S. ed. 1972
GF41.M3413 1972 ECOL

DESIGN OF A WATER-DISPOSABLE GLASS PACKAGING CONTAINER.
Hulbert, Samuel F. 1971. TD799.H8 ECOL

DESIGN OF CONSUMER CONTAINERS FOR RE-USE OR DISPOSAL.
Solid Waste Resources Conference, Columbus, Ohio, 1971. 1972. TD785.S6 1971 ECOL

DESIGN OF SMALL DAMS.
United States. Bureau of Reclamation. 2nd ed. 1973.
TC540.U615 1973 ECOL

DESIGN OF WATER-RESOURCE SYSTEMS.
1970,c1962 TC409.D4 ECOL

DESIGN WITH NATURE.
McHarg, Ian L. 1st ed. 1969.
fHC110.E5M33 ECOL

DESIGNING THE FUTURE.
Prehoda, Robert W. c1967 T20.P68 ECOL

DETERGENTS AND POLLUTION.
Jones, H. R. 1972 fTD427.D4J65 ECOL

DETERMINATION OF AIR QUALITY.
ACS Symposium on Determination of Air Quality, Los Angeles, 1971. 1972. TD890.A2 1971 ECOL

DEVELOPMENT AND CAPITAL IMPROVEMENT PROGRAM.
Brauer and Associates, inc., Edina, Minn. A study of parks and recreation for the village of New Brighton. 1967 fGV54.M6B7 ECOL

DEVELOPMENT AND DEMONSTRATION OF LOW-LEVEL DRIFT INSTRUMENTATION.
Environmental Systems Corporation. 1971.
fTD884.5.E58 ECOL

DEVELOPMENT OF A CASE STUDY OF THE TOTAL EFFECT OF PESTICIDES IN THE ENVIRONMENT, NONIRRIGATED CROPLANDS OF THE MID-WEST.
Ryckman, Edgerley, Tomlinson and Associates. 1972. fQH545.P4R9 ECOL

DEVELOPMENT OF A COAL-BASED SEWAGE-TREATMENT PROCESS.
1971 fTN805.A395no.55 ECOL

DEVELOPMENT OF A MATHEMATICAL MODEL TO PREDICT THE ROLE OF SURFACE RUNOFF AND GROUNDWATER FLOW IN OVER FERTILIZATION OF SURFACE WATERS.
Johnson, Jack D. 1971. GB701.M554no.35 ECOL

TITLE CATALOG

ECOLOGICAL RESEARCH SERIES

DEVELOPMENT OF A STATE EFFLUENT CHARGE SYSTEM.
Vermont. Agency of Environmental Conservation. 1972. **fTD224.V5A43 ECOL**

THE DEVELOPMENT OF GOVERNMENTAL FOREST CONTROL IN THE UNITED STATES.
Cameron, Jenks. 1972. **SD565.C3 1972 ECOL**

DEVELOPMENT OF IMMOBILIZED ENZYME SYSTEMS FOR ENHANCEMENT OF BIOLOGICAL WASTE TREATMENT PROCESSES.
Grumman Aerospace Corporation. 1970 **fTD755.G78 ECOL**

DEVELOPMENT OF METHOD FOR NTA ANALYSIS IN RAW WATER.
Taylor, John Keenan. 1972. **TP992.5.T3 ECOL**

DEVELOPMENT OF PHOSPHATE-FREE HOME LAUNDRY DETERGENTS.
IIT Research Institute. Technology Center. 1970. **fTP992.5.I2 ECOL**

DEVELOPMENT OF PHOSPHATE REMOVAL PROCESSES.
Detroit Metro Water Dept. 1970. **fTD756.D47 ECOL**

DEVELOPMENTS IN WATER QUALITY RESEARCH.
Jerusalem International Conference on Water Quality and Pollution Research, 1969. 1970 **TD370.J47 1969 ECOL**

DEWATERING OF MINE DRAINAGE SLUDGE.
West Virginia. University. Coal Research Bureau. 1971. **fTD899.M5W44 ECOL**

DICTIONARY CATALOG OF THE DEPARTMENT LIBRARY.
United States. Dept. of the Interior. Library. 1967. **REF fZ881.U41 ECOL**

DICTIONARY CATALOG OF THE WATER RESOURCES CENTER ARCHIVES, UNIVERSITY OF CALIFORNIA, BERKELEY.
California. University. Water Resources Center. Archives. 1970. **REF fZ7935.C32 ECOL**

A DICTIONARY OF NATURAL RESOURCES AND THEIR PRINCIPAL USES.
Jackson, Nora. 2d ed. 1969 **REF HF1051.J3 1969 ECOL**

A DIFFERENT KIND OF COUNTRY.
Dasmann, Raymond Frederick. 1968 **QH75.D37 ECOL**

DIGEST OF SELECTED LOCAL SOLID WASTE MANAGEMENT ORDINANCES.
Powell, Mel D. 1972. **TD788.P6 ECOL**

DIGEST OF STATE PROGRAM PLANS. 1970/71-
United States. Environmental Protection Agency. Water Quality Office. **TD223.A2635 ECOL**

THE DILIGENT DESTROYERS.
Laycock, George. 1970. **HC110.E5L36 ECOL**

DIMENSIONS OF CHANGE.
Fabun, Don. 1971 **fHM221.F32 ECOL**

DIMENSIONS OF THE ENVIRONMENTAL CRISIS.
Day, John A. 1971 **HC79.E5D35 ECOL**

DIRECT CONVERSION OF ENERGY.
Corliss, William R. 1964 **TK2896.C6 ECOL**

DIRECT EXPERIENCE TEACHING IN THE OUT-OF-DOORS.
Blomberg, Karin. 1967. **fLB1047.B56 ECOL**

DIRECT USE OF THE SUN'S ENERGY.
Daniels, Farrington. 1964. **TJ810.D28 ECOL**

DIRECTORY OF CONSERVATION/ENVIRONMENTAL ORGANIZATIONS. 1971-
Northern States Power Co. Environmental Affairs Dept. **fS932.M5N6 ECOL**

DIRECTORY OF DEGREE PROGRAMS, RELATED TO CONSERVATION, ECOLOGY, ENVIRONMENTAL EDUCATION, ENVIRONMENTAL SCIENCE, OUTDOOR EDUCATION & NATURAL RESOURCES.
Bachert, Russel E., Jr. 1971 **fS946.B3 ECOL**

DIRECTORY OF ENVIRONMENTAL CONSULTANTS.
Cate, William. c1972. **REF fS920.C3 ECOL**

DIRECTORY OF GOVERNMENTAL AIR POLLUTION AGENCIES. 1970- **TD882.D5 ECOL**

DIRECTORY OF INFORMATION RESOURCES IN AGRICULTURE AND BIOLOGY.
Agricultural Sciences Information Network. 1971. **REF QH321.A37 ECOL**

A DIRECTORY OF INFORMATION RESOURCES IN THE UNITED STATES: BIOLOGICAL SCIENCES.
United States. Library of Congress. National Referral Center. 1972. **REF QH303.U5 ECOL**

A DIRECTORY OF INFORMATION RESOURCES IN THE UNITED STATES; PHYSICAL SCIENCES, ENGINEERING.
United States. Library of Congress. National Referral Center. 1971. **REF Q223.U526 1971 ECOL**

A DIRECTORY OF INFORMATION RESOURCES IN THE UNITED STATES: WATER.
United States. Library of Congress. National Referral Center for Science and Technology. 1966. **fTD211.U5 ECOL**

DIRECTORY OF NATURE CENTERS AND RELATED ENVIRONMENTAL EDUCATION FACILITIES.
National Audubon Society. Nature Center Planning Division. 1971 **REF fQH51.N23 1971 ECOL**

DIRECTORY OF PUBLIC INFORMATION CONTACTS, WASH., D.C., 1972- **REF JK849.A353 ECOL**

DIRECTORY OF URBAN AFFAIRS INFORMATION AND RESEARCH CENTERS.
Winston, Eric V. A. 1970. **HT110.W5 ECOL**

THE DIRTY ANIMAL.
Still, Henry. c1967 **TD180.S7 ECOL**

DISASTER BY DEFAULT.
Graham, Frank. 1966 **TD223.G7 1966 ECOL**

THE DISCHARGE OF SUBMERGED BOUYANT JETS INTO WATER OF FINITE DEPTH.
Robideau, R. F. 1972. **fTD427.H4R6 ECOL**

DISCOVERING PLANTS.
Blough, Glenn Orlando. 1966 **PZ10.B29553Dk ECOL**

DISPOSAL AND REUSE OF ABANDONED AND RETIRED AUTOMOBILES.
Henningson, Durham & Richardson. Minnesota: disposal and reuse of abandoned and retired automobiles. 1970. **REF fTD795.H36 ECOL**

DISPOSAL OF SEWAGE AND OTHER WATERBORNE WASTES.
Imhoff, Karl. 2d ed. 1971. **TD741.I5813 1971b ECOL**

DISTRICT OF COLUMBIA SOLID WASTE MANAGEMENT PLAN.
District of Columbia 1971. **TD525.W2A43 ECOL**

DNA CONCENTRATION AS AN ESTIMATE OF SLUDGE BIOMASS.
Missouri. Southwest Missouri State College, Springfield. 1971. **fTD767.7.M57 ECOL**

A DOCUMENTARY HISTORY OF CONSERVATION IN AMERICA.
McHenry, Robert. 1972 **S930.M18 ECOL**

DOMINANT MAMMAL.
Burnet, Frank Macfarlane, Sir. 1972, c1971 **QH331.B887 1972 ECOL**

THE DOMINATION OF NATURE.
Leiss, William. c1972 **S936.L45 ECOL**

THE DOMINION OF MAN.
Black, John N. 1970. **GF80.B55 ECOL**

THE DOOMSDAY SYNDROME.
Maddox, John Royden. 1972 **GF47.M3 1972 ECOL**

DOWN THE MOUNTAIN.
Bartlett, Margaret Farrington. c1963. **PZ10.B1748Do ECOL**

DRAINAGE OF AGRICULTURAL LAND.
United States. Soil Conservation Service. 1971 **REF TC970.U5 ECOL**

THE DRAINAGE PLAN FOR BURNSVILLE, MINNESOTA.
Barr Engineering Co. 1966. **fTD525.B8B3 ECOL**

DROUGHT AND WATER SUPPLY.
Russell, Clifford S. 1970 **TD223.R88 ECOL**

DRY CAUSTIC PEELING OF TREE FRUIT FOR LIQUID WASTE REDUCTION.
National Canners Association. Western Research Laboratory. 1970. **fTD899.F7N37 ECOL**

DUCKS AND LAND USE IN MINNESOTA.
Minnesota. Dept. of Conservation. Division of Game and Fish. 1964. **SH11.M64no.8 ECOL**

DYNAMIC ECOLOGY.
1973 **QH541.D9 ECOL**

THE DYNAMICS OF CHANGE.
Fabun, Don. 1967 **fCB427.F25 ECOL**

DYNAMICS OF NUCLEAR SYSTEMS.
1972 **TK9202.D9 ECOL**

E

THE EARTH AND MAN.
Guyot, Arnold Henry. 1970, c1849 **GB59.G8 1970 ECOL**

THE EARTH AND MAN: A RAND MCNALLY WORLD ATLAS.
Rand McNally and Company. c1972 **REF fG1019.R433 ECOL**

EARTH DAY—THE BEGINNING.
1970 **HC110.E5E2 ECOL**

EARTH MIGHT BE FAIR.
1972 **GF80.E15 ECOL**

EARTH, THE STUFF OF LIFE.
Bear, Firman Edward. 1962 **S591.B33 ECOL**

EARTH TOOL KIT.
Environmental Action (Association). 1971 **HC110.E5E498 ECOL**

EARTHKEEPING.
Harrison, Gordon A. 1971. **HC110.E5H33 ECOL**

EARTH'S WILD PLACES, 4.
Hay, John. The primal alliance: earth and ocean. 1971. **fQH95.7.H32 ECOL**

ECO-CATASTROPHE.
Ramparts. c1970 **TD180.R3 ECOL**

ECO-CRISIS.
Johnson, Cecil E. 1970 **QH541.J63 ECOL**

ECO-SOLUTIONS: A CASEBOOK FOR THE ENVIRONMENTAL CRISIS.
Woods, Barbara. 1972. **GF43.W6 ECOL**

ECOCIDE—AND THOUGHTS TOWARD SURVIVAL.
Fadiman, Clifton. 1971 **HC110.E5F32 ECOL**

ECOCIDE AND POPULATION.
Adelstein, Michael E. 1971, c1972 **GF75.A35 ECOL**

ECOCIDE IN INDOCHINA.
Weisberg, Barry. 1970 **DS557.A68W43 ECOL**

ECOLOGIC-ECONOMIC ANALYSIS FOR REGIONAL DEVELOPMENT.
Isard, Walter. 1972 **HT391.I82 ECOL**

THE ECOLOGICAL CONSCIENCE.
Disch, Robert. 1970 **HC110.E5D58 ECOL**

THE ECOLOGICAL CONTEXT.
McHale, John. 1970 **GF41.M3 ECOL**

ECOLOGICAL DATA IN COMPARATIVE RESEARCH.
Clubb, Jerome M. 1970 **H62.C6 ECOL**

ECOLOGICAL EFFECTS OF PESTICIDES ON NON-TARGET SPECIES.
Pimentel, David. 1971. **QH545.P4P55 ECOL**

ECOLOGICAL FACTORS AFFECTING WATERFOWL PRODUCTION IN THE ALBERTA PARKLANDS.
Smith, Allen E. 1971. **S914.A3no.98 ECOL**

ECOLOGICAL FACTORS AFFECTING WATERFOWL PRODUCTION IN THE SASKATCHEWAN PARKLANDS.
Stoudt, Jerome H. 1971. **S914.A3no.99 ECOL**

THE ECOLOGICAL IMPACT OF SOLID WASTE.
Gunter, John D. 1973. **Ref fZ5863.P6G8 ECOL**

ECOLOGICAL ISOLATION IN BIRDS.
Lack, David Lambert. 1971. **QH401.L32 1971 ECOL**

THE ECOLOGICAL PERSPECTIVE ON HUMAN AFFAIRS.
Sprout, Harold Hance. 1965. **JX1251.S49 ECOL**

THE ECOLOGICAL REGISTER: A DIRECTORY OF GOVERNMENTAL AGENCIES AND PRIVATE ORGANIZATIONS CONCERNED ABOUT ENVIRONMENTAL DESTRUCTION AND POLLUTION IN THE STATE AND IN THE SEVEN-COUNTY METROPOLITAN AREA.
2nd ed. 1971. **S920.E24 1971 ECOL**

THE ECOLOGICAL REGISTER: A DIRECTORY OF ORGANIZATIONS IN THE SEVEN-COUNTY METROPOLITAN AREA CONCERNED ABOUT ENVIRONMENTAL DESTRUCTION AND POLLUTION (PLUS A SUPPLEMENT PROVIDING BRIEF INFORMATION ON SIMILAR ORGANIZATIONS LOCATED ELSEWHERE).
1970. **fS920.E24 ECOL**

ECOLOGICAL RESEARCH SERIES.
Bartsch, A. F. Role of phosphorus in eutrophication. 1972. **QH96.8.E9B3 ECOL**
Brinkhurst, Ralph O. The role of sludge worms in eutrophication. 1972. **QH96.8.E9B7 ECOL**
Lake Michigan Enforcement Conference. Lake Michigan Interstate Pesticides Committee. An evaluation of DDT and dieldrin in Lake Michigan. 1972. **TD427.P35L3 ECOL**

ECOLOGICAL RESEARCH SERIES   TITLE CATALOG

Tsivoglou, E. C. Characterization of stream reaeration, capacity. 1972. **fTD458.T7 ECOL**

ECOLOGICAL STUDIES OF THE TIMBER WOLF IN NORTHEASTERN MINNESOTA.
1971 **SD11.A45476no.52 ECOL**

AN ECOLOGICAL STUDY OF THE TWIN CITIES METROPOLITAN AREA.
Wallace, McHarg, Roberts and Todd. 1969. **fQH541.W32 ECOL**

THE ECOLOGICAL THEATER AND THE EVOLUTIONARY PLAY.
Hutchinson, George Evelyn. 1965. **QH311.H77 ECOL**

ECOLOGY.
Special report ecology. c1971- **REF fS936.S6 ECOL**
Grossman, Shelly. The how and why wonder book of ecology. 1971 **fQH541.14.G78 ECOL**
Nickelsburg, Janet. 1st ed. 1969 **QH541.14.N5 ECOL**
Schlichting, Harold E. 1971 **PZ10.S3713Ec ECOL**

ECOLOGY: A WRITER'S HANDBOOK.
Arny, Mary (Travis). 1st ed. 1972 **QH541.A72 ECOL**

THE ECOLOGY ACTION GUIDE.
Bock, Alan. c1971 **GF75.B6 ECOL**

ECOLOGY AND ENVIRONMENTAL QUALITY.
Watkins, Jessie B. 1971. **REF fZ5322.E2W3 ECOL**

ECOLOGY AND FIELD BIOLOGY.
Smith, Robert Leo. 1966 **QH541.S6 ECOL**

ECOLOGY AND PHYSIOLOGY OF PARASITES.
1971 **QL757.E26 ECOL**

ECOLOGY AND RESOURCE MANAGEMENT.
Watt, Kenneth E. F. 1968 **QL752.W38 ECOL**

ECOLOGY AND THE INDUSTRIAL SOCIETY.
Goodman, Gordon T. 1965 **TD180.G6 ECOL**

ECOLOGY AND THE MARKET PLACE.
Peterson, Robin. c1971 **HC79.E5P4 ECOL**

ECOLOGY: BIOLOGY 80.
Lawrence, Donald Buermann. Rev. 1967,1966. **fQH541.2.L3 1967 ECOL**

ECOLOGY: CAN WE SURVIVE UNDER CAPITALISM?
Hall, Gus. 1st ed. 1972 **HC110.E5H3 ECOL**

THE ECOLOGY CONTROVERSY: OPPOSING VIEWPOINTS.
McCuen, Gary E. 1971 **QH541.M3 ECOL**

ECOLOGY: CRISIS AND NEW VISION.
c1971 **GF80.E25 ECOL**

ECOLOGY IN THEORY AND PRACTICE.
Benthall, Jonathan. 1973,c1972 **QH541.B4 1973 ECOL**

ECOLOGY: MAN'S EFFECTS ON HIS ENVIRONMENT AND ITS MECHANISMS.
Hoke, John. 1971 **QH541.H58 ECOL**

THE ECOLOGY OF ANIMALS.
Naumov, Nikolai Pavlovich. c1972 **QL751.N313 ECOL**

THE ECOLOGY OF DIATOMS IN HARD WATER HABITATS.
Dodd, John D. 1971. **fQK569.D54D6 ECOL**

ECOLOGY OF FRESH WATER.
Brown, Alison Leadley. 1971. **QH541.5.F7B7 1971b ECOL**

ECOLOGY OF INLAND WATERS AND ESTUARIES.
Reid, George K. 1961 **QH96.R43 ECOL**

THE ECOLOGY OF MAN: AN ECOSYSTEM APPROACH.
Smith, Robert Leo. 1972 **fGF8.S6 ECOL**

THE ECOLOGY OF NORTH AMERICA.
Shelford, Victor Ernest. 1963. **QH102.S5 ECOL**

THE ECOLOGY OF PERIPHYTON IN WESTERN LAKE SUPERIOR.
Fox, Jackson L. 1969. **GB701.M554no.14 ECOL**

ECOLOGY OF POPULATIONS.
Boughey, Arthur S. 1968 **QH541.B67 ECOL**

THE ECOLOGY OF REPRODUCTION IN WILD AND DOMESTIC MAMMALS.
Sadleir, R. M. F. S. 1969. **QP251.S27 ECOL**

THE ECOLOGY OF RUNNING WATERS.
Hynes, Hugh Bernard Noel. 1970. **QH541.5.S7H9 ECOL**

ECOLOGY OF SOIL-BORNE PLANT PATHOGENS.
International Symposium on Factors Determining the Behavior of Plant Pathogens in Soil, Berkeley, Calif., 1963. **fQR111.I55 1963 ECOL**

THE ECOLOGY OF THE SECOND TROPHIC LEVEL IN LAKES SUPERIOR, MICHIGAN AND HURON.
Swain, Wayland R. 1970. **GB701.M554no.26 ECOL**

ECOLOGY; SCIENCE OF SURVIVAL.
Pringle, Laurence P. 1971 **QH541.14.P75 ECOL**

THE ECOLOGY SEA IN SONG AND BALLAD.
1973? **Phonodisc GC31.E2 ECOL**

ECOLOGY, SOCIETY, AND MAN.
Allan, J. David. Recycle this book! 1972 **GF8.A4 ECOL**

ECOLOGY: THE CIRCLE OF LIFE.
Hungerford, Harold R. 1971 **QH541.14.H8 ECOL**

ECOLOGY: THE CITY.
McCue, George. c1971 **QH541.5.C6M23 Suppl. ECOL**

ECOLOGY: THE DESERTS AND MAN.
McCue, George. c1971 **QH541.5.D4M22 Suppl. ECOL**

ECOLOGY: THE FARM.
McCue, George. c1971 **QH541.5.F3M22 ECOL**

ECOLOGY: THE FORESTS AND MAN.
McCue, George. c1971 **QH541.5.F6M22 Suppl. ECOL**

ECOLOGY: THE FRESHWATERS AND MAN.
McCue, George. c1971 **QH541.5.F7M22 ECOL**

ECOLOGY: THE GRASSLANDS AND MAN.
McCue, George. c1971 **QH541.5.P7M22 Suppl. ECOL**

ECOLOGY: THE MOUNTAINS AND MAN.
McCue, George. c1971 **QH541.5.M65M22 ECOL**

ECOLOGY: THE OCEANS AND MAN.
McCue, George. c1971 **QH541.5.S3M22 ECOL**

ECOLOGY: THE SUBURBS.
McCue, George. c1971 **QH541.5.C6M22 ECOL**

ECOLOGY USA.
REF fS936.S62 ECOL

ECONOMIC ANALYSES OF OPTIMAL WATER QUALITY MANAGEMENT.
Whinston, A. B. 1972. **fTD365.W4 ECOL**

AN ECONOMIC ANALYSIS OF FLOOD DAMAGE REDUCTION ALTERNATIVES IN THE MINNESOTA RIVER BASIN.
Hopeman, Alan Roswell. 1973. **GB701.M554no.58 ECOL**

ECONOMIC AND SOCIAL CONSEQUENCES OF NUCLEAR ENERGY.
1972. **HD9698.A3G74 ECOL**

THE ECONOMIC AND SOCIAL IMPORTANCE OF ESTUARIES.
Sweet, David C. 1971. **GB454.E8S95 ECOL**

ECONOMIC ASPECTS OF OIL CONSERVATION REGULATION.
Lovejoy, Wallace Francis. 1967 **HD9566.L6 ECOL**

ECONOMIC ASPECTS OF THE AIRPORT ENVIRONMENT: NOISE, AIR POLLUTION, AND CONGESTION.
Nelson, Jon P. 1972. **REF fZ5064.A28N4 ECOL**

ECONOMIC BENEFITS FROM AN IMPROVEMENT IN WATER QUALITY.
Reiling, S. D. 1973. **fTD370.R45 ECOL**

ECONOMIC BENEFITS FROM OCEANOGRAPHIC RESEARCH.
National Research Council. Committee on Oceanography. 1964. **REF GB58.N3 ECOL**

ECONOMIC COSTS OF AIR POLLUTION.
Ridker, Ronald Gene. 1967 **HC110.A4R5 ECOL**

THE ECONOMIC DEMAND FOR IRRIGATED ACREAGE.
Ruttan, Vernon W. 1965 **HD1735.R8 ECOL**

ECONOMIC ECOLOGY.
Green, James L. c1969 **HT167.G74 ECOL**

THE ECONOMIC IMPACT OF NOISE.
United States. National Bureau of Standards. 1971. **fTD893.A48 ECOL**

THE ECONOMIC IMPACT OF POLLUTION CONTROL.
1972. **TD180.E25 ECOL**

ECONOMIC THINKING AND POLLUTION PROBLEMS.
Auld, D. A. L. 1972 **HC120.P55A84 ECOL**

ECONOMICS AND THE ENVIRONMENT.
Kneese, Allen V. 1970 **HC68.K57 ECOL**

THE ECONOMICS OF ABUNDANCE.
Theobald, Robert. 1970 **HB171.T48 ECOL**

ECONOMICS OF AIR AND WATER POLLUTION.
1969. **fTD201.V57no.26 ECOL**

THE ECONOMICS OF AIR POLLUTION.
Wolozin, Harold. c1966 **HC110.A4W6 ECOL**

THE ECONOMICS OF CLEAN AIR. 1970-
United States. Environmental Protection Agency. 1971- **TD883.2.A24 ECOL**

THE ECONOMICS OF CLEAN WATER.
United States. Environmental Protection Agency. 1972- **HC110.P55A24 ECOL**
United States. Federal Water Pollution Control Administration. **HD4477.A53 ECOL**

THE ECONOMICS OF GENERATING CLEAN FUEL GAS FROM COAL USING AN AIR-BLOWN TWO-STAGE GASIFIER.
Bituminous Coal Research, Inc. 1971. **fTP759.B5 ECOL**

ECONOMICS OF OUTDOOR RECREATION.
Clawson, Marion. c1966 **GV182.2.C55 ECOL**

THE ECONOMICS OF SOIL CONSERVATION.
Bunce, Arthur Cyril. 1950,c1942 **HD1411.B96 1950 ECOL**

ECONOMICS OF THE ENVIRONMENT.
Dorfman, Robert. 1st ed. 1972 **HC79.P55D65 ECOL**

THE ECONOMICS OF WATER SUPPLY AND QUALITY.
Harvard Water Program. 1971. **fTD223.H34 ECOL**

THE ECONOMY OF CITIES.
Jacobs, Jane. 1969 **HT321.J32 ECOL**

ECOTACTICS: THE SIERRA CLUB HANDBOOK FOR ENVIRONMENTAL ACTIVISTS.
1970 **HC110.E5E26 ECOL**

ECOTAGE.
Love, Sam. 1972 **TD175.L68 ECOL**

EDGE OF LIFE.
Wayburn, Peggy. c1972 **fQH541.5.E8W3 ECOL**

EDUCATION FOR SURVIVAL.
1970- **QH541.2.E4 ECOL**

EDUCATION U. S. A. SPECIAL REPORT.
Environment and the schools. 1971 **fHC110.E5E485 ECOL**

THE EFFECT OF CHLORINATION ON SELECTED ORGANIC CHEMICALS.
Manufacturing Chemists' Association. 1972. **fTD462.M3 ECOL**

EFFECT OF FUEL FRONT-END AND MIDRANGE VOLATILITY ON AUTOMOBILE EMISSIONS.
Eccleston, Barton H. 1972? **TN23.U7no.7707 ECOL**

THE EFFECT OF INORGANIC SEDIMENT ON STREAM BIOTA.
Gammon, James Robert. 1970. **fQH541.5.S7G34 ECOL**

THE EFFECT OF ORGANIC AMENDMENTS FROM GARBAGE GRINDING ON A BIOLOGICAL TREATMENT SYSTEM.
Mahloch, Jerome L. 1972. **fTD756.M32 ECOL**

THE EFFECT OF TEMPERATURE ON AQUATIC LIFE IN THE OHIO RIVER: SUMMARY, JULY—DECEMBER, 1970.
Wapora Inc. 1971 **fTD427.H4W3 ECOL**

EFFECTIVE TECHNOLOGY FOR RECYCLING METAL.
1971 **fTS214.E36 ECOL**

THE EFFECTIVENESS OF FLOOD CONTROL STRUCTURES OF THE LOWER MINNESOTA RIVER WATERSHED DISTRICT.
Itasca Engineering, Inc., Minneapolis. 1970. **fTC424.M6182 ECOL**

THE EFFECTS OF AGRICULTURAL WASTE WATER TREATMENT ON ALGAL BIOASSAY RESPONSE.
United States. Environmental Protection Agency. Office of Research and Monitoring. 1971. **QH96.8.E9U54 ECOL**

EFFECTS OF AREAL AND TIME DISTRIBUTION OF RAINFALL ON SMALL WATERSHED RUNOFF HYDROGRAPHS.
Wei, Tsong C. 1971. **GB701.M554no.30 ECOL**

THE EFFECTS OF ARTIFICIAL AERATION ON LAKE ECOLOGY.
Fast, Arlo Wade. 1971 i.e.1972 **fTD458.F38 ECOL**

EFFECTS OF CHANNEL CHARACTERISTICS ON TIME PARAMETERS FOR SMALL WATERSHED RUNOFF HYDROGRAPHS.
Golany, Pinhas. 1971. **GB701.M554no.31 ECOL**

THE EFFECTS OF ENRICHMENT ON LAKE
SUPERIOR PERIPHYTON.
Nelson, Robert R. 1973.
    GB701.M554no.59 ECOL

EFFECTS OF FUEL ADDITIVES ON AIR
POLLUTANT EMISSIONS FROM
DISTILLATE-OIL-FIRED FURNACES.
Martin, G. B. 1971.   TP355.M29 ECOL

EFFECTS OF ISLAND DEVELOPMENT ON
LAKE WATER QUALITY.
McClanahan, Mark A. A study of the effects of island development on lake water quality. 1972.
    fTD224.G4M3 ECOL

EFFECTS OF NOISE ON PEOPLE.
Miller, James D. 1971.   RA772.N7M5 ECOL

EFFECTS OF NOISE ON WILDLIFE AND
OTHER ANIMALS.
Tennessee. State University, Memphis. 1971.
    fQP82.2.N6T4 ECOL

EFFECTS OF PESTICIDES IN WATER.
United States. Environmental Protection Agency.
n.d.   REF fTD427.P35U53 ECOL

THE EFFECTS OF SEWER SURCHARGES ON
THE LEVEL OF INDUSTRIAL WASTES AND
THE USE OF WATER BY INDUSTRY.
Elliott, Ralph P. 1972.   TD897.5.E4 ECOL

THE EFFECTS OF SONIC BOOM AND
SIMILAR IMPULSIVE NOISE ON
STRUCTURES.
United States. National Bureau of Standards. 1971.
    TL574.S55U54 ECOL

EFFECTS OF STUDDED TIRES.
Minnesota. Dept. of Highways. A research progress report on the effects of studded tires. 1970.
    fTL270.M5 1970 ECOL

Minnesota. Dept. of Highways. A research summary report on the effects of studded tires. 1971.
    fTL270.M5 1971 ECOL

THE EFFECTS OF VARIOUS GAS
ATMOSPHERES ON THE OXIDATION OF
COAL MINE PYRITES.
NUS Corporation. Cyrus Wm. Rice Division. 1971.
    fTD899.M5N2 ECOL

THE EFFICACY OF THE COMPLETE MIX
ACTIVATED SLUDGE PROCESS IN
MODULAR MODE.
McGriff, E. Corbin. 1972.   fTD756.M3 ECOL

ELECTRET DEVICES FOR AIR POLLUTION
CONTROL.
Kallard, Thomas. 1972   fQC585.K28 ECOL

ELECTRIC POWER AND THE
ENVIRONMENT.
United States. Office of Science and Technology.
1970.   TK1193.U5A45 ECOL

THE ELECTRIC UTILITY INDUSTRY AND
THE ENVIRONMENT.
United States. Electric Utility Industry Task Force on Environment. 1968?   HD9685.U5U5 ECOL

ELECTRICITY AND THE ENVIRONMENT:
THE REFORM OF LEGAL INSTITUTIONS.
Association of the Bar of the City of New York. Special Committee on Electric Power and the Environment. 1972.   KF2125.A97 ECOL

THE ELECTRO-OXIDATION OF AMMONIA IN
SEWAGE TO NITROGEN.
Ionics, Inc. 1970.   fTD757.I55 ECOL

ELECTROCHEMICAL TREATMENT OF ACID
MINE WATERS.
Tyco Laboratories. 1972.   fTD899.M5T88 ECOL

ELECTROCHEMISTRY OF CLEANER
ENVIRONMENTS.
1972.   TP256.E43 1972 ECOL

ELEMENTAL COMPOSITION OF SURFICIAL
MATERIALS IN THE CONTERMINOUS
UNITED STATES: AN ACCOUNT OF THE
AMOUNTS OF CERTAIN CHEMICAL
ELEMENTS.
1971.   REF fQE75.P9no.574-D ECOL

ELEMENTARY SCIENCE GUIDE AND
RESOURCE BOOK.
West St. Paul, Minn. Independent School Dist. no. 197. Elementary Science Committee. n.d.
    fLB1585.W4 ECOL

ELEMENTS OF ECOLOGY.
Clarke, George Leonard. 1st ed. rev. print., with subject guide to new references. 1965, c1954
    QH541.C47 1965 ECOL

ELEVENTH HOUR.
Adams, Alexander B. 1970   S936.A3 ECOL

ELIMINATION OF WATER POLLUTION BY
PACKING-HOUSE ANIMAL PAUNCH AND
BLOOD.
Beefland International, Inc. 1971.
    fTD899.M4B4 ECOL

THE ELUSIVE BONANZA.
Welles, Chris. 1st ed. 1970.   HD9565.W47 ECOL

EMERGING METHODS IN ENVIRONMENTAL
DESIGN AND PLANNING.
1970   TA170.E46 ECOL

EMISSIONS FROM COMBUSTION ENGINES
AND THEIR CONTROL.
Patterson, Donald J. 1972   TD886.5.P83 ECOL

EMISSIONS FROM CONTINUOUS
COMBUSTION SYSTEMS.
Symposium on Emissions from Continuous Combustion Systems, General Motors Research Laboratories, 1971. 1972.   TD881.S86 1971 ECOL

ENCOUNTERS WITH THE ARCHDRUID.
McPhee, John A. 1971   S942.M26 ECOL

ENCYCLOPEDIA OF EARTH SCIENCES
SERIES, V. 4A.
Fairbridge, Rhodes Whitmore. The encyclopedia of geochemistry and environmental sciences. 1972
    REF QE515.F24 ECOL

THE ENCYCLOPEDIA OF GEOCHEMISTRY
AND ENVIRONMENTAL SCIENCES.
Fairbridge, Rhodes Whitmore. 1972
    REF QE515.F24 ECOL

THE ENCYCLOPEDIA OF MARINE
RESOURCES.
Firth, Frank E. 1969   REF SH201.F56 ECOL

THE ENCYCLOPEDIA OF THE BIOLOGICAL
SCIENCES.
Gray, Peter. 2d ed. 1970
    REF QH13.G7 1970 ECOL

ENCYCLOPEDIC DICTIONARY OF THE
ENVIRONMENT.
Sarnoff, Paul. The New York times encyclopedic dictionary of the environment. c1971
    REF TD173.S27 1971 ECOL

ENDANGERED SPECIES.
Ullrich, Wolfgang. 1972,c1971
    fQL77.5.U45 ECOL

THE ENDLESS ADVENTURE.
Coman, Dale Rex. 1972   QH81.C67 ECOL

ENERGY.
Chalmers, Bruce. 1963   TJ153.C43 ECOL
Holdren, John P. c1971   TJ153.H65 ECOL
Shadduck, Gregg. 1971.   HD9545.S5 ECOL
Wilson, Mitchell A. 1967
    fTJ147.W53 1967 ECOL

ENERGY AND POWER.
c1971   TJ153.E478 ECOL

THE ENERGY CRISIS.
Lewis, Richard S. 1972.   fHC103.7.L4 ECOL
Millard, Reed. How will we meet the energy crisis?
1971   TJ153.M54 ECOL
Rocks, Lawrence. 1972   HD9545.R57 1972

ENERGY, ECOLOGY, ECONOMY.
Garvey, Gerald. 1st ed. 1972
    HC110.E5G35 ECOL

ENERGY, ECONOMIC GROWTH, AND THE
ENVIRONMENT.
1972   HD9545.E6 ECOL

ENERGY, ECONOMICS AND THE
ENVIRONMENT: PROCEEDINGS OF A
CONFERENCE SPONSORED BY THE
COMMITTEE ON ENVIRONMENT, EDISON
ELECTRIC INSTITUTE.
Conference on Energy, Economics and the Environment, Chicago, Ill., 1968. 1969.
    fHD9540.1.C6 1968 ECOL

ENERGY FOR MAN.
Thirring, Hans. 1968   TJ147.T48 1968 ECOL

ENERGY IN THE AMERICAN ECONOMY,
1850-1975.
Resources for the Future. 1960
    HD9545.R45 ECOL

ENERGY IN THE UNITED STATES.
Landsberg, Hans H. 1968   HD9545.L3 ECOL

ENERGY IN THE WORLD ECONOMY.
Darmstadter, Joel. 1971
    REF fHD9540.4.D37 ECOL

ENERGY MANAGEMENT.
Commerce Clearing House. c1973.
    Ref KF2120.A6C6 ECOL

ENERGY RESEARCH POLICY ALTERNATIVES.
United States. Congress. Senate. Committee on Interior and Insular Affairs. 1972.
    KF26.I5 1972 ECOL

ENERGY USE IN MINNESOTA.
Minnesota. State Planning Agency. 1973.
    fHD9547.M6A5 ECOL

ENERGY USERS REPORT.
    REF fHD9540.1.E5 ECOL

ENERGY USERS REPORT. CURRENT
REPORTS.
    REF fHD9540.1.E5 Suppl. ECOL

THE ENGINEER AND THE ENVIRONMENT.
Seminar on the Engineer and the Environment University of Minnesota, 1970. 1971.
    GB701.M554no.38 ECOL

ENGINEERING A VICTORY FOR OUR
ENVIRONMENT: A CITIZEN'S GUIDE TO
THE U.S. ARMY CORPS OF ENGINEERS.
c1972.   fTC423.E5 ECOL

ENGINEERING ASPECTS OF THERMAL
POLLUTION.
National Symposium on Thermal Pollution, Vanderbilt University, 1968. 1969.
    TD427.H4N3 1968 ECOL

ENGINEERING FOR RESOLUTION OF THE
ENERGY-ENVIRONMENT DILEMMA.
National Academy of Engineering. Committee on Power Plant Siting. 1972.   fTD177.N38 ECOL

ENGINEERING FOR THE BENEFIT OF
MANKIND.
1970.   TA5.E52 ECOL

ENGINEERING METHODOLOGY FOR RIVER
AND STREAM REAERATION.
JBF Scientific Corporation. 1971
    fTD458.J17 ECOL

THE ENTROPY LAW AND THE ECONOMIC
PROCESS.
Georgescu-Roegen, Nicholas. 1971.
    HB171.G43 ECOL

THE ENVIRONMENT.
1970   TD176.7.E45 ECOL
Herfindahl, Orris Clemens. Quality of the environment: an economic approach to some problems in using land, water, and air. 1965
    TD153.H46 ECOL

ENVIRONMENT: A CHALLENGE FOR
MODERN SOCIETY.
Caldwell, Lynton Keith. 1970.
    HC110.E5C33 ECOL

ENVIRONMENT AND CHANGE.
1970, c1968   HT167.E46 ECOL

ENVIRONMENT AND CULTURAL BEHAVIOR.
Vayda, Andrew Peter. 1969.   GF51.V35 ECOL

ENVIRONMENT AND DEVELOPMENT.
Carnegie Endowment for International Peace. 1972c1971   HC68.C3 1972 ECOL

ENVIRONMENT AND GOOD SENSE.
Dunbar, Maxwell John. 1971.   TD182.D85 ECOL

ENVIRONMENT AND MAN.
Durrenberger, Robert W. 1970
    Z5118.A5D86 ECOL
Wagner, Richard H. 1st ed. 1971
    QH541.13.W34 ECOL

ENVIRONMENT & PLANT RESPONSE.
Treshow, Michael. 1970   QK754.T7 ECOL

ENVIRONMENT AND POLICY.
1968   HT167.E48 ECOL

ENVIRONMENT AND THE LAW.
Sloan, Irving J. 1971.   KF3775.Z9S55 ECOL

ENVIRONMENT AND THE SCHOOLS.
1971   fHC110.E5E485 ECOL

THE ENVIRONMENT CRISIS.
1970   TD178.6.E58 ECOL

THE ENVIRONMENT FILM REVIEW: A
CRITICAL GUIDE TO ECOLOGY FILMS.
V.1- 1972-   fZ5322.E2E5 ECOL

ENVIRONMENT FOR MAN.
1967   HT167.E5 1967 ECOL

THE ENVIRONMENT INDEX: A GUIDE TO
THE KEY ENVIRONMENTAL LITERATURE
OF THE YEAR. 1971-
    REF fZ7171.E6 ECOL

ENVIRONMENT LAW REVIEW. 1970-
    REF KF3790.A2E5 ECOL

ENVIRONMENT, MAN, SURVIVAL: GRAND
CANYON SYMPOSIUM, 1970.
Grand Canyon Symposium, 1970. c1971
    GF8.G7 1970 ECOL

THE ENVIRONMENT OF AMERICA:
PRESENT/FUTURE/ PAST.
Jones, Thomas C. 1971   fQH541.145.J65 ECOL

THE ENVIRONMENT OF CROWDED MEN.
Colinvaux, Paul Alfred. 1970   GF8.C8 ECOL

ENVIRONMENT, POWER, AND SOCIETY.
Odum, Howard T. 1970, c1971
QH541.O33 ECOL
ENVIRONMENT: READINGS FOR TEACHERS.
Ivany, J. W. George. 1971, c1972 GF47.I9 ECOL
ENVIRONMENT REPORTER.
1970- REF fKF3775.A6E49 ECOL
ENVIRONMENT REPORTER. CASES.
1970- REF fKF3775.A6E49 Suppl. ECOL
ENVIRONMENT REPORTER. CURRENT DEVELOPMENTS.
1970 REF fHC110.E5E49 ECOL
ENVIRONMENT; RESOURCES, POLLUTION & SOCIETY.
Murdoch, William W. 1971 QH541.M95 ECOL
ENVIRONMENT STUDY.
Berry, Marcia. 1971. QH541.2.B4 ECOL
THE ENVIRONMENT, THE ESTABLISHMENT, AND THE LAW.
Henkin, Harmon. 1971 QH545.P4H4 ECOL
ENVIRONMENT, THE UNIVERSITY, & THE WELFARE OF MAN.
1969 LC191.E55 ECOL
ENVIRONMENTAL - ECOLOGICAL EDUCATION: A BIBLIOGRAPHY OF FICTION, NONFICTION, AND TEXTBOOKS FOR ELEMENTARY AND SECONDARY SCHOOLS.
Watt, Lois B. 1971. REF fQH541.2.W34 ECOL
THE ENVIRONMENTAL AND ECOLOGICAL FORUM, 1970-1971.
1972. TD898.E58 ECOL
ENVIRONMENTAL ASPECTS OF NUCLEAR POWER STATIONS.
Symposium on Environmental Aspects of Nuclear Power Stations, New York, 1970. 1971.
REF TK9006.S887 1970 ECOL
ENVIRONMENTAL ASPECTS OF TRANSPORTATION PLANNING (A REVISION OF CPL EXCHANGE BIBLIOGRAPHY NO. 218).
Sloss, George J. 1972 REF fZ7164.T8S55 ECOL
ENVIRONMENTAL BIOLOGY.
Morgan, R. F. 1963- QH308.5.M6 ECOL
THE ENVIRONMENTAL CHALLENGE AND THE AGING INDIVIDUAL.
Snyder, Lorraine Hiatt. 1972
REF fZ7164.O4S63 ECOL
ENVIRONMENTAL CONSERVATION.
Dasmann, Raymond Frederick. 3d ed. 1972
S936.D3 1972 ECOL
ENVIRONMENTAL CONSULTANTS.
Cate, William. Directory of environmental consultants. c1972. REF fS920.C3 ECOL
ENVIRONMENTAL CONTROL.
Environmental Control Symposium, San Francisco, 1972. 1972 TD888.M4E58 1972 ECOL
McClain, Thomas B. Complete handbook on environmental control. 1970 Z5853.P7M32 ECOL
ENVIRONMENTAL CONTROL: EVERYONE'S CONCERN.
1971 REF fHC68.E5 ECOL
ENVIRONMENTAL CONTROL: PRIORITIES, POLICIES, AND THE LAW.
Grad, Frank P. 1971. HC110.E5G7 ECOL
ENVIRONMENTAL CONTROL SEMINAR PROCEEDINGS.
1971. fTD172.5.E26 ECOL
ENVIRONMENTAL COST OF ELECTRIC POWER.
Abrahamson, Dean E. 1970 fTK1005.A26 ECOL
THE ENVIRONMENTAL CRISIS.
1970; c1970-71 TD176.7.E472 ECOL
THE ENVIRONMENTAL CRISIS: WILL WE SURVIVE?
Myers, Charles B. 1972 HC110.E5M9 ECOL
ENVIRONMENTAL DAMAGE AND CONTROL IN CANADA, 1.
Dunbar, Maxwell John. Environment and good sense. 1971. TD182.D85 ECOL
THE ENVIRONMENTAL DECADE (ACTION PROPOSALS FOR THE 1970'S). HEARINGS, NINETY-FIRST CONGRESS, SECOND SESSION.
United States. Congress. House. Committee on Government Operations. Conservation and Natural Resources Subcommittee. 1970.
KF27.G636 1970a ECOL
ENVIRONMENTAL DECISION-MAKING IN MINNESOTA.
Minnesota. State Planning Agency. 1973
fHC107.M6A43 ECOL

ENVIRONMENTAL DECISION-MAKING IN MINNESOTA: AN OVERVIEW.
Minnesota. State Planning Agency. 1973
fHC 107.M6A43 1973 ECOL
ENVIRONMENTAL EDUCATION.
Pepe, Thomas F. 1971. fZ5322.E2P4 ECOL
ENVIRONMENTAL EDUCATION: A SOURCEBOOK.
Troost, Cornelius J. 1972 QH541.2.T76 ECOL
ENVIRONMENTAL EDUCATION CURRICULUM, GRADES 10 - 12.
Mounds Views, Minn. Independent School District, 621. n.d. fQH541.2.M6 ECOL
ENVIRONMENTAL EDUCATION FOR INTERMEDIATE GRADES.
Michigan. Dept. of Natural Resources.
fS946.M45 ECOL
ENVIRONMENTAL EDUCATION IN THE ELEMENTARY SCHOOL.
Sale, Larry L. 1972 QH541.2.S24 ECOL
ENVIRONMENTAL EDUCATION IN THE PUBLIC SCHOOLS.
National Education Association of the United States. Research Division. 1970 fLB1047.N36 ECOL
ENVIRONMENTAL EDUCATION INFORMATION REPORTS.
Roth, Robert E. A review of research related to environmental education. 1972. QH541.2.R6 ECOL
ENVIRONMENTAL EDUCATION INSTRUCTIONAL ACTIVITIES.
New York (State) University. 1972.
fQH541.2.N4 ECOL
ENVIRONMENTAL EDUCATION MATERIALS.
1971. REF Z7164.N3E6 ECOL
ENVIRONMENTAL EDUCATION: OBJECTIVES AND FIELD ACTIVITIES.
Major, James M. 4th ed. 1971.
fLB1047.M3 ECOL
ENVIRONMENTAL EDUCATION: PROGRAMS AND MATERIALS.
United States. National Center for Educational Communication. 1972 S946.U58 ECOL
ENVIRONMENTAL EDUCATION RESOURCE CATALOG.
Project Outreach. 1971 fQH541.2.P76 ECOL
ENVIRONMENTAL EDUCATION: SOCIAL STUDIES SOURCES AND APPROACHES.
Henderson, Martha T. 1970
Ref fQH541.2.H4 ECOL
ENVIRONMENTAL EDUCATION 1970.
1970 fS946.E55 ECOL
ENVIRONMENTAL EDUCATION/FACILITY RESOURCES: A REPORT.
Educational Facilities Laboratories. c1972
fQH541.2.E48 ECOL
ENVIRONMENTAL EFFECTS OF WEAPONS TECHNOLOGY.
1970 fUG447.8.E57 ECOL
ENVIRONMENTAL ENGINEERING AND SANITATION.
Salvato, Joseph A. 2d ed. 1972
RA565.S3 1972 ECOL
ENVIRONMENTAL ENGINEERING, DESKBOOK ISSUE, 1971-
Chemical engineering. fTA170.C5 ECOL
ENVIRONMENTAL ETHICS.
Scoby, Donald R. 1971 GF80.S35 ECOL
AN ENVIRONMENTAL EXPERIENCE.
New York (State) University. 1971.
fQH541.2.N45 ECOL
ENVIRONMENTAL FACTORS IN RESPIRATORY DISEASE.
1972. RC732.E59 ECOL
ENVIRONMENTAL GEOLOGY: CONSERVATION, LAND-USE PLANNING, AND RESOURCE MANAGEMENT.
Flawn, Peter Tyrell. 1970 QE33.F5 ECOL
ENVIRONMENTAL GEOLOGY OF THE TWIN CITIES METROPOLITAN AREA.
Hogberg, Rudolph K. 1971 QE128.T9H6 ECOL
ENVIRONMENTAL GEOMORPHOLOGY.
Environmental Geomorphology Symposium.
GB400.E58 ECOL
THE ENVIRONMENTAL HANDBOOK.
De Bell, Garrett. 1970 HC110.E5D42 ECOL
ENVIRONMENTAL HEALTH.
Jones, Kenneth Lester. 1971. RA565.J65 ECOL
ENVIRONMENTAL IMPACT ANALYSIS: PHILOSOPHY & METHODS.
Conference on Environmental Impact Analysis, Green Bay, Wis., 1972. 1972
HC110.E5C65 1972 ECOL
ENVIRONMENTAL IMPACT OF HIGHWAY DEICING.
Edison Water Quality Laboratory. Storm and Combined Sewer Overflows Section. 1971.
fTE220.E35 ECOL
ENVIRONMENTAL IMPACTS OF POLYSTYRENE FOAM AND MOLDED PULP MEAT TRAYS.
Franklin, William E. 1972. fTP373.F7 ECOL
ENVIRONMENTAL INFORMATION SOURCES: ENGINEERING AND INDUSTRIAL APPLICATIONS.
Schildhauer, Carole. 1972.
REF fZ5863.E57S34 ECOL
ENVIRONMENTAL INSIGHT.
Chute, Robert M. 1971 GF75.C48 ECOL
ENVIRONMENTAL LAW.
1971 KF3775.A75E54 ECOL
1971, c1970 KF3775.A75E55 ECOL
Grad, Frank P. 1971-
REF KF3775.A7G73 ECOL
Reitze, Arnold W. 2nd ed. 1972
fKF3775.R4 1972 ECOL
ENVIRONMENTAL LAW HANDBOOK.
Brecher, Joseph J. 1970 REF KF3775.B7 ECOL
Landau, Norman J. 1971 KF3775.L3 ECOL
ENVIRONMENTAL LAW REPORTER.
V.1- JAN. 1971-
REF fKF3775.A6E5 ECOL.
ENVIRONMENTAL LITIGATION.
MacDonald, James B. 1972. KF3775.M3 ECOL
ENVIRONMENTAL MANAGEMENT.
Gorden, Morton. 1972 TD177.G67 ECOL
Hilado, Carlos J. Handbook of environmental management. 1972- REF fGF75.H5 ECOL
ENVIRONMENTAL MANAGEMENT PLANNING FOR TRAFFIC.
Antoniou, Jim. c1971 fHE333.A57 ECOL
ENVIRONMENTAL MERCURY CONTAMINATION.
1972 RA1231.M5E58 ECOL
THE ENVIRONMENTAL MERCURY PROBLEM.
D'Itri, Frank M. 1971. fQH545.M4D57 ECOL
ENVIRONMENTAL MONITORING PROGRAM FOR THE ALLEN S. KING GENERATING PLANT AT OAK PARK HEIGHTS, MINNESOTA.
Northern States Power Company. Engineering Dept. 1966. fTK1331.N6A4 ECOL
ENVIRONMENTAL MONITORING PROGRAM FOR THE MONTICELLO NUCLEAR GENERATING PLANT, MONTICELLO, MINNESOTA.
Northern States Power Company. Engineering Dept.
REF fTK1377.M6N6 ECOL
ENVIRONMENTAL MONITORING PROGRAM FOR THE PRAIRIE ISLAND NUCLEAR GENERATING PLANT NEAR RED WING, MINNESOTA.
Northern States Power Co., 1970.
fTK1377.P7C7 ECOL
ENVIRONMENTAL NETWORKS.
Center for California Public Affairs. Preliminary ed. 1973. REF fS920.C4 ECOL
ENVIRONMENTAL ORGANIZATIONS.
Halstead, Bruce W. A Golden guide to environmental organizations. 1972
REF GF5.H34 ECOL
ENVIRONMENTAL PERCEPTION AND BEHAVIOR.
1967. GF51.E5 ECOL
ENVIRONMENTAL PLANNING AND GEOLOGY.
Symposium on Engineering Geology in the Urban Environment, San Francisco, 1969. 1971
TA705.S95 1969 ECOL
ENVIRONMENTAL POLLUTION.
CCM Information Corporation. 1971.
REF fTD178.5.C2 ECOL
ENVIRONMENTAL PRACTICE, THE NEW CONSERVATION.
Griffith, Charles J. EP—the new conservation. 1971
HC110.E5G74 ECOL
ENVIRONMENTAL PREFERENCES: RELEVANT STUDIES FOR URBAN PLANNING.
Harrison, James D. 1973. Ref fZ5942.H3 ECOL
ENVIRONMENTAL PROBLEMS.
1968 TD180.E48 ECOL
ENVIRONMENTAL PROTECTION AGENCY.
United States. Environmental Protection Agency. 1972- fHC68.U5A24 ECOL
ENVIRONMENTAL PROTECTION PUBLICATION.
Drobny, N. L. Recovery and utilization of municipal solid waste: a summary of available cost and performance characteristics of unit processes and systems. 1971. TD793.D76 ECOL

Franklin, William E. The role of nonpackaging paper in solid waste management, 1966 to 1976. 1971.
TD795.F7 ECOL

ENVIRONMENTAL PROTECTION TECHNOLOGY SERIES.
Agnew, Robert W. A free floating endless belt oil skimmer. 1972. **TD899.P4A3 ECOL**

Barnes, Robert A. Ammonia removal in a physical-chemical wastewater treatment process. 1972. **TD462.B3 ECOL**

Bingham, Tayler H. The beverage container problem. 1972. **TD793.B5 ECOL**

California. University. Flow into a stratified reservoir. 1972. **TC167.C3 ECOL**

Carcich, Italo G. A pressure sewer system demonstration. 1972. **TD670.C3 ECOL**

Cha, C. Y. Photochemical methods for purifying water. 1972. **TD459.C4 ECOL**

Feick, George. Control of mercury contamination in freshwater sediments. 1972. **TD427.M4F4 ECOL**

Groman, William A. Forest fertilization (a state-of-the-art review and description of environmental effects). 1972. **SD408.G7 ECOL**

Gumtz, Garth D. Restoration of Beaches contaminated by oil. 1972. **TD427.P4G8 ECOL**

Henager, Charles H. Concept evaluation: recovery of floating oil using polyurethane foam sorbent. 1972. **fTD427.P4H4 ECOL**

Holmes, James G. Acid mine drainage treatment by ion exchange. 1972 **TD899.M5H6 ECOL**

Maryland. Dept. of Water Resources. Guidelines for erosion and sediment control, planning and implementation. 1972. **fS624.A1M3 ECOL**

Midwest Research Institute, Kansas City, Mo. Rapid detection system for organophosphates and carbamate insectides in water. 1972. **TD427.P35M5 ECOL**

Morey, Rexford M. Feasibility study of electromagnetic subsurface profiling. 1972. **QE602.M6 ECOL**

Morgan, W. E. An investigation of phosphorus removal mechanisms in activated sludge systems. 1972. **TD756.M6 ECOL**

Morth, Arthur H. Pyritic systems: a mathematical model. 1972. **TD899.M5M6 ECOL**

National Symposium on Food Processing Wastes, 3d, New Orleans, 1972. Proceedings. 1972. **fTD899.F585N37 1972 ECOL**

Robert S. Kerr Water Research Center. Characteristics of rainfall run off from a beef cattle feedlot. 1972. **TD899.F4R6 ECOL**

Sandoski, Dorothy A. Selected urban storm water runoff abstracts, July 1971-June 1972. 1972. **fTD653.S2 ECOL**

Sartor, James D. Water pollution aspects of street surface contaminants. 1972. **TD665.S2 ECOL**

Skogerboe, Gaylord V. Evaluation of canal lining for salinity control in Grand Valley. 1972. **TC930.S5 ECOL**

Skogerboe, Gaylord V. Selected irrigation return flow. 1972- **fTD223.S5 ECOL**

Stall, John B. Storm sewer design—an evaluation of the RRL method. 1972. **TD665.S7 ECOL**

Stenquist, Richard J. Initial mixing in coagulation processes. 1972. **TD455.S7 ECOL**

Taylor, John Keeman. Development of method for NTA analysis in raw water. 1972. **TP992.5.T3 ECOL**

Thruston, Alfred D. Liquid chromatography of carbamate pesticides. 1972. **SB951.T4 ECOL**

Toerber, Edwin D. Full scale parallel activated sludge process evaluation. 1972. **TD756.T6 ECOL**

Troy, Joseph C. Oxidation of pyrites in chlorinated solvents. 1972. **TD899.M5T7 ECOL**

United States. Environmental Protection Agency. Office of Research and Monitoring. Air modulated vacuum oil recovery collection of spilled oil (foams). 1972. **fTD427.P4U5 ECOL**

United States. Environmental Protection Agency. Office of Research and Monitoring. Control of mercury pollution in sediments. 1972. **TD427.M4U5 ECOL**

United States. Environmental Protection Agency. Office of Research and Monitoring. Identification of polychlorinated biphenyls in the presence of DDT-type compounds. 1972. **SB951.U52 ECOL**

United States. Environmental Protection Agency. Office of Research and Monitoring. Storage and treatment of combined sewer overflows. 1972. **fTD662.U54 ECOL**

United States. Environmental Protection Agency. Office of Research and Monitoring. The swirl concentrator as a combined sewer overflow regulator facility. 1972. **TD662.U5 ECOL**

Zaval, Frank J. Revegetation augmentation by reuse of treated active surface mine drainage. 1972. **TD899.M5Z3 ECOL**

ENVIRONMENTAL PSYCHOLOGY: SELECTED READINGS.
Toepfer, Caroline T. 1972 **HM206.T6 ECOL**

ENVIRONMENTAL QUALITY.
United States. Council on Environmental Quality. **HC110.E5A52 ECOL**

ENVIRONMENTAL QUALITY ANALYSIS.
Resources for the Future. 1972 **HC79.E5R46 ECOL**

ENVIRONMENTAL QUALITY AND AGRICULTURE: WHAT ARE THE OPTIONS?
Conference on Environmental Quality and Agriculture. University of Illinois, Urbana-Champaign, 1971. 1972 **fHC68.C6 1971 ECOL**

ENVIRONMENTAL QUALITY AND SOCIAL RESPONSIBILITY.
1972 **HC110.P55E57 ECOL**

ENVIRONMENTAL QUALITY CONTROL.
United States. Bureau of the Census. **REF HC110.E5A26 ECOL**

ENVIRONMENTAL QUALITY IN A GROWING ECONOMY.
Resources for the Future. 1968,c1966 **HC103.7.R39 ECOL**

ENVIRONMENTAL QUALITY, POLICIES AND DECISION-MAKING IN MINNESOTA - 1972.
Minnesota. Governor's Environmental Quality Council. Citizen's Advisory Committee. 1972. **fHC107.M6A37 ECOL**

ENVIRONMENTAL RADIOACTIVITY.
Eisenbud, Merril. 1963 **RA569.E5 ECOL**

ENVIRONMENTAL READER.
Godfrey, Arthur. The Arthur Godfrey environmental reader. 1970 **QH541.13.G6 ECOL**

ENVIRONMENTAL REPORT.
Black & Veatch, Kansas City, Mo. 1971- **fTK1331.N6B7 ECOL**

Northern States Power Company (of Minnesota). 1971. **fTD877.5.N6 ECOL**

Northern States Power Company (of Minnesota). expanded and updated ed. 1971. **fTD877.5.N62 1971 ECOL**

ENVIRONMENTAL REQUIREMENTS OF BLUE-GREEN ALGAE.
1967. **QK569.C96E56 ECOL**

THE ENVIRONMENTAL REVOLUTION.
Nicholson, Max. 1970 **S936.N5 ECOL**

ENVIRONMENTAL SCIENCE, CHALLENGE FOR THE SEVENTIES.
United States. National Science Foundation. National Science Board. 1971. **TD145.U5 ECOL**

ENVIRONMENTAL SCIENCE LABORATORY MANUAL.
Strobbe, Maurice A. 1972. **TA171.S8 ECOL**

ENVIRONMENTAL SCIENCE SERIES.
Buras, Nathan. Scientific allocation of water resources. 1972 **TC409.B87 ECOL**

ENVIRONMENTAL SCIENCES.
Environmental factors in respiratory disease. 1972. **RC732.E59 ECOL**

Metallic contaminants and human health. 1972. **RA565.M47 1972 ECOL**

Mutagenic effects of environmental contaminants. 1972. **QH431.M958 ECOL**

ENVIRONMENTAL SIDE EFFECTS OF RISING INDUSTRIAL OUTPUT.
1970 **TD174.E58 ECOL**

ENVIRONMENTAL STUDIES.
Rev. ed.? 1971,c1970 **LB1027.E6 1971 ECOL**

Harris, Melville. 1971. **LB1047.H32 ECOL**

ENVIRONMENTAL SURVEILLANCE IN THE VICINITY OF NUCLEAR FACILITIES.
1970 **REF TD887.R3E58 ECOL**

ENVIRONMENTAL SYSTEMS PLANNING AND MANAGEMENT: A PRELIMINARY SORTING OF LITERATURE.
Ehler, Charles N. 1972 **REF fZ5863.P6E38 ECOL**

ENVIRONMENTS AND PEOPLES.
Wagner, Philip Laurence. 1972 **GF41.W3 ECOL**

ENZYMES AND THE ENVIRONMENT.
Wood, John Martin. 1972 **fQP601.W74 ECOL**

EP—THE NEW CONSERVATION.
Griffith, Charles J. 1971 **HC110.E5G74 ECOL**

ERIC CLEARINGHOUSE FOR SOCIAL SCIENCE EDUCATION. REVIEW SERIES NO.1.
Henderson, Martha T. Environmental education: Social studies sources and approaches. 1970 **Ref fQH541.2.H4 ECOL**

ERIC CLEARINGHOUSE FOR SOCIAL STUDIES/SOCIAL SCIENCE EDUCATION. REFERENCE SERIES NO.5.
Watt, Lois B. Environmental - ecological education: a bibliography of fiction, nonfiction, and textbooks for elementary and secondary schools. 1971. **REF fQH541.2.W34 ECOL**

ERIC INFORMATION ANALYSIS CENTER FOR SCIENCE, MATHEMATICS AND ENVIRONMENTAL EDUCATION. RESEARCH REVIEW SERIES—ENVIRONMENTAL EDUCATION, PAPER 1.
Roth, Robert E. A review of research related to environmental education. 1972. **QH541.2.R6 ECOL**

EROSION AND SEDIMENT POLLUTION CONTROL.
Beasley, Robert Patrick. 1st ed. 1972 **S623.B33 ECOL**

ESTABLISHING TRAILS ON RIGHTS-OF-WAY.
Lennon, J. n.d. **G504.L4 ECOL**

ESTIMATING COSTS AND MANPOWER REQUIREMENTS FOR CONVENTIONAL WASTEWATER TREATMENT FACILITIES.
Patterson, W. L. 1971 i.e. 1972 **fTD743.P36 ECOL**

ESTUARINE MODELING: AN ASSESSMENT.
Tracor, Inc. 1971. **fTD370.T73 ECOL**

ETERNAL QUEST: THE STORY OF THE GREAT NATURALISTS.
Adams, Alexander B. 1969 **QH26.A3 ECOL**

EUTROPHICATION: CAUSES, CONSEQUENCES, CORRECTIVES.
International Symposium on Eutrophication, University of Wisconsin, 1967. 1969. **QH96.A1I63 1967 ECOL**

EUTROPHICATION IN COASTAL WATERS: NITROGEN AS A CONTROLLING FACTOR.
California. University. Institute of Marine Resources. 1971. **fQH96.8.E9C34 ECOL**

EUTROPHICATION OF SURFACE WATERS—LAKE TAHOE.
Lake Tahoe Area Council. 1971 i.e. 1972 **fQH96.8.E9L34 ECOL**

EUTROPHICATION OF SURFACE WATERS—LAKE TAHOE INDIAN CREEK RESERVOIR.
Lake Tahoe Area Council. 1971. **fTD224.C3L32 ECOL**

EVALUATED BIBLIOGRAPHY OF FREE AND INEXPENSIVE CONSERVATION PUBLICATIONS.
Atkisson, Jean. 1972 **REF fZ7164.N3A8 ECOL**

EVALUATION OF A NEW ACID MINE DRAINAGE TREATMENT PROCESS.
Black, Sivalls and Bryson, inc., Kansas City, Mo. Applied Technology Division 1971. **fTD899.M5B55 ECOL**

EVALUATION OF ATTACHED ALGAE IN THE MISSISSIPPI RIVER ADJACENT TO THE NSP SHERBURNE COUNTY GENERATING PLANT, BECKER, MINNESOTA, DURING OCTOBER AND NOVEMBER, 1971.
Knutson, Keith M. 1972 **fTK1331.N6K5 ECOL**

EVALUATION OF CANAL LINING FOR SALINITY CONTROL IN GRAND VALLEY.
Skogerboe, Gaylord V. 1972. **TC930.S5 ECOL**

EVALUATION OF CONDITIONING AND DEWATERING SEWAGE SLUDGE BY FREEZING.
Milwaukee. Sewerage Commission. 1971. **fTD769.7.M54 ECOL**

AN EVALUATION OF DDT AND DIELDRIN IN LAKE MICHIGAN.
Lake Michigan Enforcement Conference. Lake Michigan Interstate Pesticides Committee. 1972. **TD427.P35L3 ECOL**

EVALUATION OF FISHES AND BOTTOM FAUNA IN THE MISSISSIPPI RIVER ADJACENT TO THE NSP SHERBURNE COUNTY GENERATING PLANT SITE, BECKER, MINNESOTA, DURING OCTOBER AND NOVEMBER, 1971.
Hopwood, Alfred J. 1972 **fTK1331.N6H6 ECOL**

EVALUATION OF URBAN WATER MANAGEMENT POLICIES IN THE DENVER METROPOLITAN AREA.
Walker, Wynn R. 1973. **fTD225.D4W3 ECOL**

EVERGLADES.
   Caulfield, Patricia. 1970   **QH105.F6C36 ECOL**
THE EVERGLADES TODAY.
   Sand, George X. 1971   **QH105.F6S24 ECOL**
EVERYBODY'S ECOLOGY.
   Schoenfeld, Clarence Albert. 1971
      QH541.13.S36 ECOL
EVERYDAY ANIMALS.
   Allen, Gertrude E. 1961.   **PZ10.A478Ev ECOL**
EVERYMAN'S GUIDE TO ECOLOGICAL LIVING.
   Cailliet, Greg M. 1971   **GF75.C33 ECOL**
EVOLUTION AND ENVIRONMENT.
   Peabody Museum Centennial Symposium, Yale University, 1966. 1968.   **QH366.A1P4 1966 ECOL**
EVOLUTION AND MAN'S PROGRESS.
   Hoagland, Hudson. 1962.   **HM106.H6 ECOL**
EVOLUTION IN CHANGING ENVIRONMENTS.
   Levins, Richard. 1968.   **QL752.L4 ECOL**
EVOLUTION OF MAN.
   Young, Louise B. 1970.   **QH368.Y68 ECOL**
AN EX ANTE PROFITABILITY ANALYSIS OF CAPITAL INVESTMENT IN TACONITE PELLET PRODUCTION FACILITIES IN MINNESOTA CIRCA 1950-51.
   Nelson, Clarence Walfred. 1967.
      HD9517.M6N4 ECOL
EXAMINING YOUR ENVIRONMENT.
   Couchman, J. Kenneth. Mini-climates. c1971
      QC863.C68 ECOL
   Couchman, J. Kenneth. Snow and ice. c1971
      QC929.S7C6 ECOL
   MacBean, John C. Birds. c1971
      QL676.M22 ECOL
   Stecher, Adam. Running water. c1971
      QH541.2.S8 ECOL
   Wentworth, Daniel F. Pollution. c1971
      TD175.W46 ECOL
EXPERIENCES WITH LIVING THINGS.
   Wensberg, Katherine S. 1966   **LB1532.W4 ECOL**
THE EXPLODING METROPOLIS.
   Fortune. c1958   **HT123.F69 1958 ECOL**
THE EXPLOITED EDEN.
   Gangewere, Robert J. 1972   **PS507.E3G3 ECOL**
EXPLORING NEW ETHICS FOR SURVIVAL: THE VOYAGE OF THE SPACESHIP BEAGLE.
   Hardin, Garrett James. 1972   **HB871.H347 ECOL**
EXTINCT AND VANISHING ANIMALS.
   Ziswiler, Vinzenz. Rev. English ed. by Fred and Pille Bunnell. 1967.   **QL88.Z513 ECOL**
EXTRACTIVE RESOURCES AND TAXATION: PROCEEDINGS.
   1967.   **HC106.5.E93 ECOL**

F

FABRICATED MAN.
   Ramsey, Paul. 1970.   **HQ751.R33 ECOL**
FACE OF NORTH AMERICA.
   Farb, Peter. Young readers' ed. 1964
      QH104.F32 ECOL
FACTORS AFFECTING POLLUTION REFERENDA.
   Abt Associates. 1971.   **fGH4952.A6 ECOL**
THE FALLEN SKY.
   Aronow, Saul. 1963   **RA569.A7 ECOL**
FALLOUT FROM NUCLEAR TESTS.
   Comar, Cyril Lewis. 1963   **UF767.C64 ECOL**
   Comar, Cyril Lewis. Rev. 1966
      UF767.C64 1966 ECOL
FAMILIAR ANIMALS OF AMERICA.
   Barker, Will. 1956   **QL715.B25 ECOL**
THE FAMILY LIFE OF BIRDS.
   Dossenbach, Hans D. 1971   **QL675.D6613 ECOL**
FAMINE ON THE WIND; MAN'S BATTLE AGAINST PLANT DISEASE.
   Carefoot, G. L. 1967   **SB732.C37 ECOL**
FAMINE, 1975!
   Paddock, William. c1967   **HD9000.5.P22 ECOL**
THE FARM.
   McCue, George. Ecology: the farm. c1971
      QH541.5.F3M22 ECOL
FARMING THE SEA.
   McKee, Alexander. 1969
      SH333.M27 1969 ECOL
FAST REACTOR SAFETY.
   Graham, John. 1971.   **TK9152.G68 ECOL**

FATE OF PESTICIDES IN ENVIRONMENT.
   International IUPAC Congress of Pesticide Chemistry, 2d, Tel-Aviv, 1971. 1972
      SB951.I56 1971vol.6 ECOL
THE FATE OF THE LAKES.
   Barry, James P. 1972   **F551.B37 ECOL**
FAUNA OF THE NATIONAL PARKS OF THE UNITED STATES. FAUNA SERIES, 7.
   Mech, L. David. The wolves of Isle Royale. 1966
      QL155.A45no.7 ECOL
A FEASIBILITY DEMONSTRATION OF AN AERIAL SURVEILLANCE SPILL PREVENTION SYSTEM.
   Welch, Robin I. 1972.   **fTD427.P4W45 ECOL**
FEASIBILITY OF COMPUTER CONTROL OF WASTEWATER TREATMENT.
   American Public Works Association. 1970.
      fTD746.A43 ECOL
FEASIBILITY OF LIQUID ION EXCHANGE FOR EXTRACTING PHOSPHATE FROM WASTEWATER.
   General Mills Chemicals. 1970.
      fTD757.G45 ECOL
FEASIBILITY OF THE METROPOLITAN WATER INTELLIGENCE SYSTEM CONCEPT (INTEGRATED AUTOMATIC OPERATIONAL CONTROL).
   McPherson, Murray Burns. 1971.
      fTD211.M3 ECOL
FEASIBILITY STUDY: MT. NORMANDALE LAKE AND MARSH LAKE, FOR CITY OF BLOOMINGTON AND NINE MILE CREEK WATERSHED DISTRICT.
   Barr Engineering Co. 1967.
      fTC424.M6B32 ECOL
FEASIBILITY STUDY OF ELECTROMAGNETIC SUBSURFACE PROFILING.
   Morey, Rexford M. 1972.   **QE602.M6 ECOL**
FEASIBILITY STUDY OF MUD LAKE IMPROVEMENT.
   Barr Engineering Co. 1966.
      fTC424.M6B322 ECOL
FEASIBILITY STUDY OF REGENERATIVE FIBERS FOR WATER POLLUTION CONTROL.
   Uniroyal, Inc. 1970 i.e. 1971
      fTD757.5.U55 ECOL
FEDERAL AIR QUALITY CONTROL REGIONS.
   United States. Environmental Protection Agency. 1972.   **REF TD883.2.U42 ECOL**
THE FEDERAL LANDS SINCE 1956.
   Clawson, Marion. 1967   **HD216.C53 ECOL**
THE FEDERAL LANDS: THEIR USE AND MANAGEMENT.
   Clawson, Marion. 1966,1957
      HD216.C54 1966 ECOL
FEDERAL PLAN FOR MARINE ENVIRONMENTAL PREDICTION.
   United States. Federal Coordinator for Marine environmental prediction. 1971.
      GC1015.U525 ECOL
FEDERAL POLLUTION CONTROL PROGRAMS: WATER, AIR, AND SOLID WASTES.
   Degler, Stanley E. Rev. ed. 1971
      TD180.D4 1971 ECOL
FEDERAL, STATE, AND LOCAL AGENCIES CONCERNED WITH WATER RESOURCES RESEARCH IN MINNESOTA.
   Minnesota. University. Water Resources Research Center. 1965.   **GB701.M554no.1 ECOL**
FEDERAL WATER POLLUTION CONTROL ACT AMENDMENTS OF 1972.
   United States. Environmental Protection Agency. Guidelines for developing or revising water quality standards under the Federal Water Pollution Control Act Amendments of 1972. 1973.   **fTD370.U5 ECOL**
FIELD BIOLOGY AND ECOLOGY.
   Benton, Allen H. 2d ed. 1966
      QH318.5.B4 1966 ECOL
A FIELD GUIDE TO TREES AND SHRUBS.
   Petrides, George A. 1972.
      QK482.P43 1972 ECOL
FIELD TRIPS.
   Nickelsburg, Janet. 1971,c1966   **QH541.N5 ECOL**
FIRE ISLAND.
   Rabkin, Richard. 1971   **fQH105.N7R3 ECOL**
THE FIRMAMENT OF TIME.
   Eiseley, Loren. 1971 c1960
      QH367.E4 1971 ECOL

THE FIRST BOOK OF AIR.
   Knight, David C. 1961   **PZ10.K57Fg ECOL**
THE FIRST BOOK OF CONSERVATION.
   Smith, Frances C. 2d rev. ed. 1972.
      S940.S64 1972 ECOL
THE FIRST BOOK OF ENERGY.
   Harrison, George Russell. 1965   **QC73.H3 ECOL**
THE FIRST BOOK OF PLANTS.
   Dickinson, Alice. c1953.   **QK49.D5 ECOL**
THE FIRST BOOK OF SWAMPS AND MARSHES.
   Smith, Frances C. 1968,c1969
      QH541.5.M3S6 ECOL
FIRST BOOK OF TREES.
   Cormack, Maribelle. c1951   **QK475.C59 ECOL**
THE FIRST REACTOR.
   United States. Atomic Energy Commission. 1967
      QC787.N8U52 ECOL
THE FIRST 50.
   Buckmann, Carol A. c1973   **S932.I8B8 ECOL**
FISH PROTEIN CONCENTRATE.
   New York (State). State University College, Buffalo. Great Lakes Laboratory. 1970.   **fSH333.F5 ECOL**
FISHES OF NORTH AMERICA.
   Herald, Earl Stannard. A Chanticleer Press ed. 1972
      QL635.H47 ECOL
THE FITNESS OF MAN'S ENVIRONMENT.
   1968   **HT166.F53 ECOL**
THE FITNESS OF THE ENVIRONMENT.
   Henderson, Lawrence Joseph. 1970 c1913
      QH331.H45 1970 ECOL
FLIGHT OF THE WHITE WOLF.
   Ellis, Melvin Richard. 1970   **Fiction ECOL**
FLOATING OIL RECOVERY DEVICE.
   New Mexico State University. Physical Science Laboratory. 1971.   **fTD427.P4N48 ECOL**
FLOOD FORECASTING IN THE UPPER MIDWEST: DATA ASSEMBLY AND PRELIMINARY ANALYSIS.
   Pabst, Arthur F. 1972.   **fGB678.P32 ECOL**
FLOOD HAZARD ANALYSES: CITY OF CANBY AND VICINITY, YELLOW MEDICINE COUNTY, MINNESOTA.
   United States. Soil Conservation Service. 1973.
      GB1225.M6U5 ECOL
FLOOD HAZARD AREAS.
   United States. Water Resources Council. Regulation of flood hazard areas to reduce flood losses. 1971-
      KF5588.A875 ECOL
FLOOD PLAIN INFORMATION.
   United States. Army. Corps of Engineers. 1972.
      GB1227.R4A52 ECOL
FLOOD PLAIN INFORMATION ON THE RED RIVER OF THE NORTH IN THE VICINITY OF GRAND FORKS, NORTH DAKOTA—EAST GRAND FORKS, MINNESOTA.
   United States. Army. Corps of Engineers. 1971.
      GB1227.R4A5 ECOL
FLOOD PLAIN MANAGEMENT, IOWA'S EXPERIENCE.
   Conference on Flood Plain Management, Iowa State University, 1968. 1st ed. 1969
      TC424.I8C6 1968 ECOL
FLOOD PLAIN ZONING AND FLOOD PLAIN MANAGEMENT.
   St. Louis Park, Minn. City Attorney's Office. City attorney's report, re: flood plain management. 1969
      fTC425.S3A5 ECOL
FLOOD PROBLEMS.
   White, Gilbert Fowler. Papers on flood problems. 1961.   **TC530.W4 ECOL**
FLOOD PROOFING.
   Sheaffer, John Richard. 1960.   **TC530.S4 ECOL**
FLOOR OF THE SKY: THE GREAT PLAINS.
   Plowden, David. 1972   **fF595.2.P56 ECOL**
FLORIDA BIRD LIFE.
   Sprunt, Alexander. 1954   **QL684.F6S65 ECOL**
FLORIDA. UNIVERSITY, GAINESVILLE. WATER RESOURCES RESEARCH CENTER. PUBLICATION NO. 4.
   Maloney, Frank Edward. Water law and administration. 1968.   **REF KFF446.M3 ECOL**
FLOW INTO A STRATIFIED RESERVOIR.
   California. University. 1972.   **TC167.C3 ECOL**
THE FLOWERING WILDERNESS.
   Tosco, Uberto. 1972   **QK50.T6713 ECOL**
FLUID BED INCINERATION OF PETROLEUM REFINERY WASTES.
   Mandan Refinery. 1971.   **fTD899.P4M35 ECOL**

A FLUOROMETRIC TECHNIQUE FOR SAMPLING IN LARGE-RIVER ECOSYSTEMS.
McNabb, C. D. 1971. GB701.M554no.34 ECOL

FOAM SEPARATION OF ACID MINE DRAINAGE.
Horizons Incorporated. 1971
fTD899.M5H67 ECOL

FOGARTY INTERNATIONAL CENTER PROCEEDINGS NO. 10.
Mutagenic effects of environmental contaminants. 1972. QH431.M958 ECOL

FOGARTY INTERNATIONAL CENTER. PROCEEDINGS, NO. 11.
Environmental factors in respiratory disease. 1972. RC732.E59 ECOL

FOLKLORE OF THE OIL INDUSTRY.
Boatwright, Mody Coggin. c1963
TN872.A5B6 ECOL

FOOD POLLUTION.
Marine, Gene. 1st. ed. 1972 TX533.M37 ECOL

FOOD PRESERVATION BY IRRADIATION.
Urrows, Grace M. 1968 TX611.5.U7 1968 ECOL

FOOD RESOURCES, CONVENTIONAL AND NOVEL.
Pirie, N. W. 1969 S439.P5 ECOL

FOR BETTER OR FOR WORSE.
Gilliam, Harold. 1972 HC107.C22S363 ECOL

FOR POLLUTION FIGHTERS ONLY.
Hyde, Margaret Oldroyd. 1971 TD175.H9 ECOL

FORECAST OF GROWTH OF NUCLEAR POWER.
United States. Atomic Energy Commission. Division of Operations and Forecasting. 1971.
TK9145.U5 ECOL

THE FOREST AND THE SEA.
Bates, Marston. 1960 QH541.B3 ECOL

FOREST CREDIT IN THE UNITED STATES: A SURVEY OF NEEDS AND FACILITIES.
Resources for the Future. 1958.
HG2051.U5R4 ECOL

FOREST FERTILIZATION (A STATE-OF-THE-ART REVIEW AND DESCRIPTION OF ENVIRONMENTAL EFFECTS).
Groman, William A. 1972. SD408.G7 ECOL

FOREST LAWS.
Minnesota. Laws, statutes, etc. 1968.
REF KFM5649.A45 1968 ECOL

THE FOREST RANGER.
Kaufman, Herbert. 1960 SD565.K3 ECOL

FOREST RECREATION SYMPOSIUM, SYRACUSE, N.Y., 1971.
1971. SD426.F6 1971 ECOL

FOREST RESOURCE ECONOMICS.
Gregory, G. Robinson. 1972 HD9755.G7 ECOL

THE FOREST SERVICE.
Frome, Michael. 1971 SD565.F7 ECOL

FOREST TREES OF THE PACIFIC SLOPE.
United States. Forest Service. 1908.
REF QK481.S95 ECOL

THE FORESTS AND MAN.
McCue, George. Ecology: the forests and man. c1971 QH541.5.F6M22 Suppl. ECOL

FORESTS AND MEN.
Greeley, William Buckhout. 1951.
SD143.G74 ECOL

FORESTS ARE FOR PEOPLE.
Wood, Frances Elizabeth. 1971
SD565.W66 ECOL

FORESTS THAT CHANGE COLOR.
May, Julian. 1972 SD373.M38 1972 ECOL

THE FRAIL OCEAN.
Marx, Wesley. c1967 GC1018.M3 ECOL

FRANKLIN D. ROOSEVELT AND THE ERA OF THE NEW DEAL.
Bonbright, James Cummings. Public utilities and the national power policies. 1972, c1940
HD2766.B57 1972

A FREE FLOATING ENDLESS BELT OIL SKIMMER.
Agnew, Robert W. 1972. TD899.P4A3 ECOL

FREEZING IN FOREST SOIL AS INFLUENCED BY SOIL PROPERTIES, LITTER, AND SNOW.
Thorud, David B. 1969.
GB701.M554no.10 ECOL

THE FRESHWATER AMPHIPOD CRUSTACEANS (GAMMARIDAE) OF NORTH AMERICA.
Holsinger, John R. 1972.
fQH96.A2B5no.5 ECOL

FRESHWATER ECOLOGY.
Andrews, William A. A guide to the study of freshwater ecology. 1972 QH541.5.F7A48 ECOL

FRESHWATER ISOPODS (ASELLIDAE) OF NORTH AMERICA.
Williams, William David. 1972.
fQH96.A2B5no.7 ECOL

FRESHWATER LEECHES (ANNELIDA: HIRUDINEA) OF NORTH AMERICA.
Klemm, Donald J. 1972. fQH96.A2B5no.8 ECOL

FRESHWATER PLANARIANS (TURBELLARIA) OF NORTH AMERICA.
Kenk, Roman. 1972. fQH96.A2B5no.1 ECOL

FRESHWATER POLYCHAETES (ANNELIDA) OF NORTH AMERICA.
Foster, Nancy. 1972. fQH96.A2B5no.4 ECOL

FRESHWATER SPHAERIACEAN CLAMS (MOLLUSCA: PELECYPODA) OF NORTH AMERICA.
Burch, J. B. 1972. fQH96.A2B5no.3 ECOL

THE FRESHWATERS AND MAN.
McCue, George. Ecology: the freshwaters and man. c1971 QH541.5.F7M22 ECOL

THE FRIENDLY FORESTS.
Moore, Alma (Chestnut). 1963
SD373.M76 1963 ECOL

FROGS, TOADS, AND SALAMANDERS AS PETS.
Headstrom, Birger Richard. 1972
SF459.A45H4 ECOL

FROM POND TO PRAIRIE.
Pringle, Laurence P. 1972 PZ10.P669Ft ECOL

FROM SEA TO SHINING SEA.
United States. President's Council on Recreation and Natural Beauty. 1968. HC110.E5A55 ECOL

FUEL AND ENERGY RESOURCES.
United States. Congress. House. Committee on Interior and Insular Affairs. 1972
KF27.I5 1972 ECOL

FULL SCALE PARALLEL ACTIVATED SLUDGE PROCESS EVALUATION.
Toerber, Edwin D. 1972. TD756.T6 ECOL

FULL-SCALE RAW WASTEWATER FLOCCULATION WITH POLYMERS.
Freese, Paul V. 1970. fTD751.F7 ECOL

FUN WITH ECOLOGY.
Watson, Geoffrey Grainge. 1971,c1967
QH541.2.W3 1971 ECOL

FUNDAMENTAL NUCLEAR ENERGY RESEARCH. 1971-
United States. Atomic Energy Commission.
QC788.U5 ECOL

FUNDAMENTALS OF ECOLOGY.
Odum, Eugene Pleasants. 3d ed. 1971.
QH541.O3 1971 ECOL

FUNDAMENTALS OF NOISE: MEASUREMENT, RATING SCHEMES, AND STANDARDS.
United States. National Bureau of Standards. 1971 i.e. 1972 fQC243.U55 ECOL

FUNDAMENTALS OF PHYSICAL SCIENCE.
Krauskopf, Konrad Bates. 6th ed. 1971
Q160.2.K7 1971 ECOL

FUTURE ENVIRONMENTS OF NORTH AMERICA.
Darling, Frank Fraser. 1966. HC95.D33 ECOL

THE FUTURE MANAGEMENT OF WATER IN ENGLAND AND WALES: A REPORT.
Great Britain. Central Advisory Water Committee. 1971. TD257.A5 1971 ECOL

THE FUTURE OF THE FUTURE.
McHale, John. 1969 CB161.M3 ECOL
McHale, John. 1971 CB161.M3 1971 ECOL

THE FUTURE OF THE GREAT LAKES: A PUBLIC MEETING.
Great Lakes Basin Commission. 1972
fGB1627.G8G7 ECOL

G

GALAPAGOS, WORLD'S END.
Beebe, Charles William. 1924. QH123.B4 ECOL

GALLERY OF NORTH AMERICAN GAME.
Outdoor life. Outdoor life's Gallery of North American game. 1946 fSK40.O8 ECOL

GARBAGE AS YOU LIKE IT.
Goldstein, Jerome. 1969 TD795.G6 ECOL

GARDEN BLOCKS FOR URBAN AMERICA.
Bush-Brown, Louise (Carter). 1969
NA9052.B78 ECOL

THE GARDEN EARTH.
Allsopp, Bruce. 1972 GF80.A4 1972b ECOL

GARDEN ISLANDS OF THE GREAT EAST.
Fairchild, David Grandison. 1943.
SB109.F185 ECOL

GARDENING WITHOUT POISONS. 2D ED.
Hunter, Beatrice Trum. 1971.
SB975.H8 1971 ECOL

GENERAL THEORY OF POPULATION.
Sauvy, Alfred. 1970,c1969 HB871.S25213 ECOL

THE GENETIC EFFECTS OF RADIATION.
Asimov, Isaac. c1966 QH652.5.A8 ECOL

GENTLE WILDERNESS.
Muir, John. Rev. ed. 1971c1968
F868.S5M88 1971 ECOL

THE GENUS ARGULUS (CRUSTACEA: BRANCHIURA) OF THE UNITED STATES.
Cressey, Roger Frank. 1972.
fQH96.A2B5no.2 ECOL

THE GEOGRAPHY OF THE POLAR REGIONS, CONSISTING OF A GENERAL CHARACTERIZATION OF POLAR NATURE.
Nordenskjold, Otto. 1928. G587.N6 ECOL

GEOHYDROLOGY OF THE JORDEN AQUIFER IN THE MINNEAPOLIS-ST. PAUL AREA MINNESOTA.
Liesch, Bruce A. 1961. fGB705.M6L5 ECOL

GEOLOGIC FRAMEWORK AND PETROLEUM POTENTIAL OF THE ATLANTIC COASTAL PLAIN AND CONTINENTAL SHELF.
Maher, John Charles. 1971.
REF fQE75.P9no.659 ECOL

GEOLOGIC REFERENCE SOURCES.
Ward, Dederick C. 1972.
REF Z6031.W35 1972 ECOL

GEOLOGY ILLUSTRATED.
Shelton, John S. 1966 fQE26.S5 ECOL

GEOLOGY OF MICHIGAN.
Dorr, John A. c1970 REF fQE125.D6 ECOL

GEOLOGY OF THE WESTERN LAKE SUPERIOR REGION.
Mengel, J. T. 1970. fQE78.M4 ECOL

GEOTHERMAL ENERGY RESOURCES AND RESEARCH.
United States. Congress. Senate. Committee on Interior and Insular Affairs. 1972.
KF26.I5 1972j ECOL

GEOTHERMAL WORLD DIRECTORY, 1972-
fGB1003.G46 ECOL

A GIANT IN THE EARTH.
Katz, Robert. c1973 HD9000.5.K3 ECOL

THE GIFT OF THE DEER.
Hoover, Helen. 1970c1966
QL795.D3H6 1970 ECOL

GIFTS OF AN EAGLE.
Durden, Kent. 1972 QL795.B57D87 ECOL

GLOBAL ECOLOGY.
Holdren, John P. 1971 HC110.E5H64 ECOL

GLOBAL EFFECTS OF ENVIRONMENTAL POLLUTION.
Symposium on the Global Effects of Environmental Pollution, Dallas, 1968. 1970
REF TD172.5.S95 1968 ECOL

GLOBAL POLITICS OF NUCLEAR ENERGY.
Willrich, Mason. 1971 TK9145.W49 ECOL

A GLOSSARY OF COASTAL ENGINEERING TERMS.
Allen, Richard H. 1972. REF TC1645.A4 ECOL

GLOSSARY: WATER AND WASTEWATER CONTROL ENGINEERING.
1969. TD9.G55 ECOL

GOALS, OBJECTIVES AND VALUES: SELECTED REFERENCES RELATING TO NATIONAL, STATE AND URBAN OR REGIONAL AREAS, COVERING GENERAL & TRANSPORTATION ASPECTS.
Hickok, Beverly. 1973 fZ7164.O7H49 ECOL

A GOD WITHIN.
Dubos, Rene Jules. 1972 HM206.D86 ECOL

GOD'S OWN JUNKYARD.
Blake, Peter. 1964 HF5843.B55 ECOL

GOING TO WASTE.
Marshall, James. 1972 TD791.M37 ECOL

A GOLDEN GUIDE TO ENVIRONMENTAL ORGANIZATIONS.
Halstead, Bruce W. 1972 REF GF5.H34 ECOL

GOVERNANCE AND POPULATION: THE GOVERNMENTAL IMPLICATIONS OF POPULATION CHANGE.
United States. Commission on Population Growth and the American future. 1972.
HB3505.A526 ECOL

GOVERNING NATURE.
Murphy, Earl Finbar. 1967   **HC55.M8 ECOL**

GRADUATE EDUCATION IN WATER RESOURCES AT UNIVERSITY OF MINNESOTA—1969.
Minnesota. University. Water Resources Research Center. Advisory Committee. 1969.
GB701.M554no.15 ECOL

THE GRAND CANYON.
Wallace, Robert. 1972   **F788.W23 ECOL**

THE GRAND COLORADO.
Watkins, Tom H. 1969   **fF788.W33 ECOL**

THE GRASS ROOTS AND WATER RESOURCES MANAGEMENT.
McKenzie, Linda. 1972.   **fHD1691.M3 ECOL**

GRASSLAND ECOLOGY.
Spedding, C. R. W. 1971.   **QH541.5.P7S65 ECOL**

THE GRASSLANDS AND MAN.
McCue, George. Ecology: the grasslands and man. c1971   **QH541.5.P7M22 ECOL**

GREAT AMERICAN DESERTS.
Findley, Rowe. 1972   **F787.F5 ECOL**

THE GREAT AMERICAN FOREST.
Platt, Rutherford Hayes. 1971,c1965
SD140.P55 1971 ECOL

THE GREAT AUK.
Eckert, Allan W. 1st ed. 1963   **Fiction ECOL**

THE GREAT CHAIN OF LIFE.
Krutch, Joseph Wood. 1957 c1956
QL751.K87 ECOL

THE GREAT LAND.
Herndon, Booton. 1971   **TN872.A7H4 ECOL**

THE GREAT LAND HUSTLE.
Paulson, Morton C. 1972   **HD255.P38 ECOL**

THE GREAT OCEAN BUSINESS.
Horsfield, Brenda. 1st American ed. 1972
GC21.H63 1972b ECOL

GREEN IS FOR GROWING.
Lubell, Winifred. 1964.   **PZ10.L85Gr ECOL**

GROUND WATER: A SELECTED BIBLIOGRAPHY.
Van der Leeden, Frits. 1971
REF Z7935.V35 ECOL

GROUND WATER FOR IRRIGATION IN THE BROOTEN-BELGRADE AREA, WEST-CENTRAL MINNESOTA.
Van Voast, Wayne A. 1971.
TC801.U2no.1899-E ECOL

GROUND WATER INFILTRATION AND INTERNAL SEALING OF SANITARY SEWERS, MONTGOMERY COUNTY, OHIO.
Montgomery County Sanitary Dept. Montgomery County, Ohio. 1972.   **fTD716.M6 ECOL**

GROUND WATER POLLUTION IN ARIZONA, CALIFORNIA, NEVADA & UTAH.
Fuhriman, Dean K. 1971 i.e. 1972
fTD223.9.F85 ECOL

GROUNDWATER RECOVERY.
Huisman, L. 1972   **TD405.H85 ECOL**

GROUNDWATER RESOURCE EVALUATION.
Walton, William Clarence. 1970
GB1003.W28 ECOL

GROUSE AND QUAILS OF NORTH AMERICA.
Johnsgard, Paul A. 1973   **QL696.G27J63 ECOL**

GROW IT!
Langer, Richard W. 1972   **S501.L27 1972 ECOL**

GROWING AGAINST OURSELVES: THE ENERGY-ENVIRONMENT TANGLE.
1972.   **TD195.E4G76 ECOL**

THE GROWING TREE.
Wilson, Brayton Fuller. 1970.   **QK731.W46 ECOL**

GUARDIANS OF TOMORROW.
Hirsch, S. Carl. 1971   **QH541.14.H57 1971 ECOL**

GUIDE FOR AIR POLLUTION EPISODE AVOIDANCE.
United States. Environmental Protection Agency. 1971.   **TD883.2.A518 ECOL**

GUIDE FOR CONTROL OF AIR POLLUTION EPISODES IN MEDIUM-SIZED URBAN AREAS.
United States. Environmental Protection Agency. Office of Air Programs. 1971.   **TD883.1.U49 ECOL**

GUIDE FOR CONTROL OF AIR POLLUTION EPISODES IN SMALL URBAN AREAS.
United States. Environmental Protection Agency. Office of Air Programs. 1971.   **TD883.1.U492 ECOL**

GUIDE TO CONSERVATION EDUCATION: FILMS, FILMSTRIPS, AND PICTURE SETS.
California. Dept. of Education. 1972.
REF fS946.C24 ECOL

GUIDE TO ENVIRONMENTAL EDUCATION: CONSERVATION OF NATURAL RESOURCES.
Madison, Wis. Public Schools. Conservation Committee. 1970.   **fS946.M3 ECOL**

GUIDE TO NEW APPROACHES TO FINANCING PARKS & RECREATION.
National Recreation and Park Association. 1970
SB482.A4N38 ECOL

GUIDE TO PRIVATE CITIZEN ACTION ENVIRONMENTAL GROUPS.
Sichel, Beatrice. 1973.   **REF fS920.S53 ECOL**

GUIDE TO RESEARCH IN AIR POLLUTION.
Pennsylvania. State University. Center for Air Environment Studies. 8th- ed.
REF TD883.15.P4 ECOL

GUIDE TO THE CAVES OF MINNESOTA.
Hogberg, Rudolph K. 1967   **GB605.M5H6 ECOL**

A GUIDE TO THE STUDY OF ENVIRONMENTAL POLLUTION.
Andrews, William A. 1972   **TD174.A53 ECOL**

A GUIDE TO THE STUDY OF FRESH-WATER BIOLOGY.
Needham, James George. 1927   **QH96.N38 ECOL**

A GUIDE TO THE STUDY OF FRESHWATER ECOLOGY.
Andrews, William A. 1972
QH541.5.F7A48 ECOL

GUIDELINES FOR DEVELOPING OR REVISING WATER QUALITY STANDARDS UNDER THE FEDERAL WATER POLLUTION CONTROL ACT AMENDMENTS OF 1972.
United States. Environmental Protection Agency. 1973.   **fTD370.U5 ECOL**

GUIDELINES FOR EROSION AND SEDIMENT CONTROL, PLANNING AND IMPLEMENTATION.
Maryland. Dept. of Water Resources. 1972.
fS624.A1M3 ECOL

GUIDELINES FOR LOCAL GOVERNMENTS ON SOLID WASTE MANAGEMENT.
United States. Environmental Protection Agency. 1971.   **fTD791.U5 ECOL**

GUIDELINES FOR OUT-OF-THE-CLASSROOM EDUCATION EXPERIENCES: ELEMENTARY SCHOOLS.
Minnesota Elementary Principals' Association. 1966.   **LB1047.M55 ECOL**

GUIDELINES FOR PLANNING AND IMPLEMENTING A COMPREHENSIVE COMMUNITY ENVIRONMENTAL INVENTORY.
Bennett, Dean B. Rev. ed. 1972.
fQH541.2.B38 1972 ECOL

GUIDELINES FOR SCHOOL SITE PLANNING, DEVELOPMENT AND UTILIZATION IN ENVIRONMENTAL EDUCATION.
MacGown, Richard H. The school site in environmental education. Rev. ed. 1972
fLB3220.M3 1972 ECOL

GUIDELINES TO CONSERVATION EDUCATION ACTION.
Izaak Walton League of America. Conservation Education Committee. c1966   **S946.I9 ECOL**

H

HABIT AND HABITAT.
Theobald, Robert. 1972   **GF47.T45 ECOL**

HABITAT.
Halacy, Daniel Stephen. 1970
QH541.14.H3 ECOL

HABITATS AND TERRITORIES.
Klopfer, Peter H. 1969   **QL751.K592 ECOL**

THE HAND OF MAN ON AMERICA.
Plowden, David. 1971.   **E169.02.P55 ECOL**

HANDBOOK FOR ENVIRONMENTAL STUDIES.
Perry, Gordon Arthur. 2nd rev. ed. 1971
LB1585.P4 1971 ECOL

HANDBOOK OF BIRDS OF EASTERN NORTH AMERICA.
Chapman, Frank Michler. Rev. ed. 1912.
REF QL681.C46 1912 ECOL

HANDBOOK OF ENVIRONMENTAL MANAGEMENT.
Hilado, Carlos J. 1972-
REF fGF75.H5 ECOL

HANDBOOK ON BIOLOGICAL CONTROL OF PLANT PESTS.
Plants & gardens. 1966,1960
SB932.P5 1966 ECOL

A HANDBOOK ON ENVIRONMENTAL INFORMATION PROGRAMS FOR PUBLIC LIBRARIES.
Cohen, Martin. 1973.   **fZ670.A3C6 ECOL**

HARVARD STUDIES IN TECHNOLOGY AND SOCIETY.
Mesthene, Emmanuel G. Technological change: its impact on man and society. 1970.
HM221.M47 1970 ECOL

HARVEST OF DEATH.
1971,c1972   **DS557.A68H35 1972 ECOL**

HARVESTING THE EARTH.
Borgstrom, George. 1973
HD9000.5.B56 1973 ECOL

HAS THE UNITED STATES ENOUGH WATER?
Piper, Arthur Maine. 1965.
REF TC801.U2no.1797 ECOL

HEALTH AND HUMAN VALUES.
Jefcoat, Allure. 1972   **RA565.J44 ECOL**

HEALTH HAZARDS OF THE HUMAN ENVIRONMENT.
World Health Organization. 1972.
RA565.W6 ECOL

THE HEART OF OUR CITIES.
Gruen, Victor. 1964.   **NA9108.G76 ECOL**

HEATED EFFLUENTS AND EFFECTS ON AQUATIC LIFE WITH EMPHASIS ON FISHES.
Raney, Edward Cowden. 3rd ed. 1969.
REF Z7173.W3R3 1969 ECOL

HEAVY METALS IN THE ENVIRONMENT.
Oregon. State University, Corvallis. Water Resources Research Institute. 1973.   **fTD176.7.O7 ECOL**

HEIDELBERG SCIENCE LIBRARY, V.2.
Ziswiler, Vinzenz. Extinct and vanishing animals. Rev. English ed. by Fred and Pille Bunnell. 1967.
QL88.Z513 ECOL

HEPSA ELY SILLIMAN MEMORIAL LECTURES, YALE UNIVERSITY.
Dubos, Rene Jules. Man adapting. 1965.
R723.D77 ECOL
Peabody Museum Centennial Symposium, Yale University, 1966. Evolution and environment. 1968.
QH366.A1P4 1966 ECOL

HERBICIDE MANUAL FOR NONCROPLAND WEEDS.
United States Dept. of the Army. 1970.
SB611.U5 ECOL

HIGH-PRESSURE COMPACTION AND BALING OF SOLID WASTE: FINAL REPORT ON A SOLID WASTE MANAGEMENT DEMONSTRATION GRANT.
United States. Environmental Protection Agency. 1972.   **TD796.7.U65 ECOL**

HIGH RATE FILTRATION OF COMBINED SEWER OVERFLOWS.
Nebolsine, Ross. 1972.   **fTD662.N4 ECOL**

THE HIGH SIERRA.
Bowen, Ezra. 1972   **F868.S5B6 ECOL**

HIGHLIGHTS OF IMPLEMENTATION PLAN FOR SULFUR DIOXIDE, PARTICULATES, CARBON MONOXIDE, HYDROCARBONS, NITROGEN OXIDES, PHOTOCHEMICAL OXIDANT.
Minnesota. Air Quality Division. 1971.
REF fTD883.5.M6A42 ECOL

HIGHTLIGHTS OF IMPLEMENTATION PLAN FOR SULFUR DIOXIDE, PARTICULATES, CARBON MONOXIDE, HYDROCARBONS, NITROGEN OXIDES, PHOTOCHEMICAL OXIDANT.
TRC—The Research Corporation of New England. Proposal to the State of Minnesota Pollution Control Agency: Highlights of implementation plan for sulfur dioxide, particulates, carbon monoxide, hydrocarbons, nitrogen oxides, photochemical oxidant. 1971.
Ref fTD883.5.M6T15 ECOL

THE HIGHWAY AND THE CITY.
Mumford, Lewis. 1963   **HT111.M83 ECOL**

HIGHWAYS AND OUR ENVIRONMENT.
Robinson, John. 1971   **HE355.R6 ECOL**

HIGHWAYS AND THE ENVIRONMENT: A BIBLIOGRAPHY OF THE EFFECTS OF HIGHWAYS ON THE PHYSICAL, BIOLOGICAL, RECREATIONAL AND AESTHETIC ENVIRONMENTS AND OF TECHNIQUES FOR THE ANALYSIS OF THESE IMPACTS.
Coleman, D. J. 1973.   **fZ7295.C6 ECOL**

HISTORY OF MINNESOTA POLLUTION CONTROL AGENCY.
1970   **fTD181.M5 ECOL**

A HISTORY OF THE PUBLIC LAND
POLICIES.
Hibbard, Benjamin Horace. 1965.
HD216.H5 1965 ECOL

HISTORY OF THE WISCONSIN
DEPARTMENT OF NATURAL RESOURCES
AND RELATED RULES, REGULATIONS,
CLASSIFICATIONS AND STANDARDS FOR
AIR AND WATER QUALITY.
1970 fS932.W6H5 ECOL

HOME GUIDE TO TREES, SHRUBS, AND
WILD FLOWERS.
Grimm, William Carey. 1970 QK482.G734 ECOL

HOME TO THE WILDERNESS.
Carrighar, Sally. 1973. QH31.C3A3 ECOL

HORIZONS IN RESOURCE RECOVERY:
PRESENTATIONS AND DISCUSSIONS OF A
SEMINAR HELD FEB. 23, 1972.
Midwest Regional Seminar on Horizons in Resource Recovery, University of Chicago, 1972. 1972.
fTP995.A1M5 1972 ECOL

HOUR OF THE BEAVER.
Buyukmihci, Hope Sawyer. 1971
QL795.B5B8 ECOL

THE HOUSE OF LIFE: RACHEL CARSON AT
WORK.
Brooks, Paul. 1972. QH31.C33B7 ECOL

HOW A LAW IS MADE: THE STORY OF A
BILL AGAINST AIR POLLUTION.
Stevens, Leonard A. 1970 KF3812.Z9S7 ECOL

THE HOW AND WHY WONDER BOOK OF
ECOLOGY.
Grossman, Shelly. 1971 fQH541.14.G78 ECOL

THE HOW AND WHY WONDER BOOK OF
ROCKS AND MINERALS.
Hyler, Nelson W. 1970,c1960
fQE432.H9 1970 ECOL

HOW BIRDS BEHAVE.
Ardley, Neil. 1971 fQL785.5.B6A7 ECOL

HOW TO BE A NATURE DETECTIVE.
Selsam, Millicent (Ellis). 1966,c1963
PZ10.S44Hr3 ECOL

HOW TO KILL A GOLDEN STATE.
Bronson, William. 1968. F866.2.B7 ECOL

HOW TO KNOW THE GRASSES.
Pohl, Richard Walter. Rev. ed. 1968
QK495.G74P73 1968 ECOL

HOW TO KNOW THE MAMMALS.
Booth, Ernest Sheldon. 3d ed. 1972, c1971
QL715.B66 1972 ECOL

HOW TO KNOW THE TREES.
Miller, Howard A. 2d ed. 1972
REF QK482.M65 1972 ECOL

HOW TO KNOW THE WEEDS.
Wilkinson, Robert E. 2d ed. 1972
SB612.A2W54 1972 ECOL

HOW TO MANAGE YOUR COMPANY
ECOLOGICALLY.
Goldstein, Jerome. 1971 HD69.P6G65 ECOL

HOW TO PUT WASTE RECYCLING INTO
PRACTICE.
National Conference on Composting-Waste Recycling. 1st, Denver, 1971. 1971.
fTD172.5.N3 1971 ECOL

HOW TO WATCH WILDLIFE.
Burness, Gordon. 1972 QL60.B87 ECOL

HOW WILL WE MEET THE ENERGY CRISIS?
Millard, Reed. 1971 TJ153.M54 ECOL

THE HUDSON RIVER.
Boyle, Robert H. 1st ed. 1969
QH105.N7B68 ECOL

HUMAN BIOLOGY: CONTEMPORARY
READINGS.
Johnson, Cecil E. c1970 QH311.J63 ECOL

HUMAN ECOLOGY.
Stapledon, Sir Reginald George. 2nd ed.; edited and introduced by Robert Waller. 1971.
HM206.S65 1971 ECOL

HUMAN ECOLOGY AND PUBLIC HEALTH.
Kilbourne, Edwin D. 4th ed. 1969
RA425.K55 1969 ECOL

THE HUMAN USE OF THE EARTH.
Wagner, Philip Laurence. 1964,c1960
HM206.W28 1964 ECOL

HUNGER.
Mead, Margaret. 1970 fHD9000.5.M37 ECOL

THE HUNGRY BIRD BOOK.
Arbib, Robert S. 1971 QL676.5.A7 1971 ECOL

THE HUNGRY FUTURE.
Dumont, Rene. 1969 HD1445.D823 ECOL

THE HUNGRY PLANET.
Borgstrom, George. Rev. ed. 1967
HD9000.5.B54 1967 ECOL
Borgstrom, George. 2nd rev. ed. 1972
HD9000.5.B54 1972 ECOL

HUNTING & FISHING IN NORTH AMERICA.
Cramond, Michael. c1953 SK40.C67 ECOL

HYDRAULICS OF LONG VERTICAL
CONDUITS AND ASSOCIATED
CAVITATION.
Minnesota. University. St. Anthony Falls Hydraulic Laboratory. 1971. fTC174.M53 ECOL

HYDROCHLORIC ACID AND AIR
POLLUTION: AN ANNOTATED
BIBLIOGRAPHY.
Air Pollution Technical Information Center. 1971.
Z7173.A4A52 ECOL

HYDROGEOLOGY OF SOLID WASTE
DISPOSAL SITES IN NORTHEASTERN
ILLINOIS.
Hughes, George Muggah. 1971
TD795.7.H84 ECOL

HYDROLOGIC AND HYDRAULIC ASPECTS
OF FLOOD PLAIN CONSTRUCTION.
Workshop on Hydrologic and Hydraulic Aspects of Flood Plain Construction, Madison, Wisc., 1968. Proceedings. 1968? fGB1225.W6W6 1968 ECOL

HYDROLOGIC EFFECTS OF URBANIZATION
IN THE UNITED STATES.
McPherson, M. B. 1972. fGB665.M3 ECOL

HYDROLOGICAL STUDY OF
HYLAND-BUSH-ANDERSON LAKES.
Barr Engineering Co. 1971.
fTC424.M6B326 ECOL

I

IAEA PROCEEDINGS SERIES.
Symposium on Use of Nuclear Techniques in the Measurement and Control of Environmental Pollution, Salzburg, 1970. Nuclear techniques in environmental pollution. 1971. REF TD177.S9 1970 ECOL

ICHTHYOLOGICAL ASSOCIATES. BULLETIN
NO. 2.
Raney, Edward Cowden. Heated effluents and effects on aquatic life with emphasis on fishes. 3rd ed. 1969. REF Z7173.W3R3 1969 ECOL

ICK'S ABC.
Gwynne, Fred. 1971 FictionECOL

THE IDEA OF PROGRESS: HISTORY AND
SOCIETY.
Pollard, Sidney. 1969?c1968 CB155.P55 ECOL

IDENTIFICATION OF POLYCHLORINATED
BIPHENYLS IN THE PRESENCE OF
DDT-TYPE COMPOUNDS.
United States. Environmental Protection Agency. Office of Research and Monitoring. 1972.
SB951.U52 ECOL

IF DEER ARE TO SURVIVE.
Dasmann, William. 1971 QL737.U55D37 ECOL

IF I BUILT A VILLAGE.
Mizumura, Kazue. 1971 Fiction ECOL

IIT RESEARCH INSTITUTE.
Reilich, Helmut G. Technical evaluation of phosphate-free home laundry detergents. 1972.
fTP992.5.R4 ECOL

ILLINOIS. UNIVERSITY AT
URBANA-CHAMPAIGN. SPECIAL
PUBLICATION 24.
Evers, Robert August. Poisonous plants of the Midwest & their effects on livestock. 1972
SB617.E9 ECOL

ILLUSTRATIONS OF RADIO-ISOTOPES:
DEFINITIONS AND APPLICATIONS.
United States. Atomic Energy Commission. 196-?
TK9400.U5 ECOL

THE IMMENSE JOURNEY.
Eiseley, Loren C. 1957 QH368.E38 ECOL

IMPACT OF AIR POLLUTION REGULATIONS
ON FUEL SELECTION FOR FEDERAL
FACILITIES.
Federal Construction Council. Task Group T-65. 1970. fKF3812.F4 ECOL

THE IMPACT OF FUTURE ELECTRICAL
POWER REQUIREMENTS ON THE STATE
OF MINNESOTA—AN ISSUE ANALYSIS.
St. John's University, Collegeville, Minnesota Center for the Study of Local Government. 1971.
fHD9685.U6M6 ECOL

IMPACT OF SNOWMOBILING ON
NORTHERN MINNESOTA ECOLOGY.
Wanek, Wallace J. A study of the impact of snowmobiling on northern Minnesota ecology. 1971
fTL234.W3 ECOL

IMPLEMENTATION PLAN TO ACHIEVE
CARBON MONOXIDE AMBIENT AIR
QUALITY STANDARDS.
Minnesota. Air Quality Division. 1973.
REF fTD883.5.M6A422 ECOL

THE IMPLICATIONS OF THE NET FISCAL
BENEFITS CRITERION FOR COST
SHARING IN FLOOD CONTROL PROJECTS.
Mathematica, Inc., Bethesda, Md. 1971.
TC530.M3 ECOL

THE IMPORTANCE OF ECONOMIC FACTORS
IN URBAN SURFACE WATER SUPPLY
SYSTEMS.
Young, G. K. 1972. fTD353.Y6 ECOL

AN IMPROVED TEMPERATURE PREDICTION
MODEL FOR SMALL STREAMS.
Brown, George W. 1972 fQC909.B7 ECOL

IMPROVING WATER QUALITY
MANAGEMENT PLANNING IN
NONMETROPOLITAN AREAS.
Brunson, E. Evan. 1973. fTD365.B78 ECOL

IMPROVISATION FOR THE THEATER.
Spolin, Viola. 1963 PN2071.I5S6 ECOL

IN DEFENSE OF EARTH: INTERNATIONAL
PROTECTION OF THE BIOSPHERE.
Caldwell, Lynton Keith. 1972
HC79.E5C34 ECOL

IN DEFENSE OF NATURE.
Hay, John. 1969 QH81.H37 ECOL

IN DEFENSE OF PEOPLE: ECOLOGY AND
THE SEDUCTION OF RADICALISM.
Neuhaus, Richard John. 1971
HM206.N48 ECOL

IN QUEST OF QUIET.
Still, Henry. 1970 RA772.N7S74 ECOL

IN THE WAKE OF TORREY CANYON.
Petrow, Richard. 1st American ed. 1968
G530.T72P4 1968 ECOL

IN WILDNESS IS THE PRESERVATION OF
THE WORLD.
Thoreau, Henry David. 1971,c1967
TR660.T5 1971 ECOL

INADVERTENT CLIMATE MODIFICATION.
Study of Man's Impact on Climate, Stockholm, 1970. 1971 QC981.S77 1970 ECOL

INCINERATOR STANDARDS.
Incinerator Institute of America. 1970,1968
REF fTD796.I5 1970 ECOL

INCINERATOR TESTING.
Incinerator Institute of America. 1971
fTD796.I53 ECOL

INDEX TO THE UNDERSTANDING THE
ATOM SERIES.
United States. Atomic Energy Commission. 1970
REF Z5160.U4915 1970 ECOL

INDEXED BIBLIOGRAPHY OF NUCLEAR
DESALINATION
LITERATURE—7- 1972-
Nuclear Desalination Information Center.
REF fZ5853.S22N8 ECOL

INDICATORS OF ENVIRONMENTAL
QUALITY.
1972. TD172.5.I5 1972 ECOL

INDOOR-OUTDOOR AIR POLLUTION
RELATIONSHIPS: A LITERATURE REVIEW.
Benson, Ferris B. 1972. TD890.B4 ECOL

INDUCED AERATION OF SMALL MOUNTAIN
LAKES.
United States. Environmental Protection Agency. 1970. fSH167.T86U5 ECOL

INDUSTRIAL POLLUTION CONTROL
HANDBOOK.
1971 REF TD897.I42 ECOL

INDUSTRIAL RECYCLING OF URBAN SOLID
WASTES.
Ringwood, R. J.
In: Western Plant Engineering and Maintenance Conference, San Francisco, 1970 Proceedings. 1970.
fTS184.W4

INDUSTRIAL WASTE DISPOSAL.
Ross, Richard D. 1968 TD897.R67 ECOL

INDUSTRIAL WASTES AND SALVAGE;
CONSERVATION AND UTILIZATION.
Lipsett, Charles H. 2d ed. 1963
TP995.L55 1963 ECOL

INDUSTRIAL WASTES: EFFECTS ON TRINITY
RIVER ECOLOGY, FORT WORTH, TEXAS.
Texas Christian University, Fort Worth. Dept. of Biology. 1971 i.e. 1972 fTD224.T4T4 ECOL

INDUSTRIAL WATER POLLUTION CONTROL.
Eckenfelder, William Wesley. c1966
    TD897.E2 ECOL

INDUSTRY EXPENDITURES FOR WATER POLLUTION ABATEMENT.
Lund, Leonard. 1972   **fTD223.L8 ECOL**

INFECTIOUS AND PARASITIC DISEASES OF WILD BIRDS.
1st ed. 1971   **SF994.4.A115 ECOL**

INFILTRATION RATES AND GROUNDWATER QUALITY BENEATH CATTLE FEEDLOTS, TEXAS HIGH PLAINS.
Texas Tech University. Dept. of Geosciences. 1971
    fTD899.F4T48 ECOL

THE INFINITE RIVER.
Amos, William Hopkins. 1971,c1970
    QH90.A59 ECOL

THE INFLUENCE OF A NEW ENGLAND WETLAND ON WATER QUANTITY AND QUALITY.
Hall, Francis R. 1972.   **fTD224.N4H3 ECOL**

INFORMAL SCHOOLS IN BRITAIN TODAY, TX2042.
Harris, Melville. Environmental studies. 1971.
    LB1047.H32 ECOL

INFORMATION CONCERNING WATER RESOURCES RESEARCH CENTER PROJECTS, 1965-70.
Minnesota. University. Water Resources Research Center. 1970-   **GB701.M554no.19 ECOL**

INFORMATION-EDUCATION BULLETIN NO. 3.
Shomon, Joseph James. Manual of outdoor conservation education. 1964   **S946.S5 ECOL**

INFORMATION RESOURCE: WATER POLLUTION CONTROL IN THE WATER UTILITY INDUSTRY.
American Water Works Association Research Foundation, New York 1971.
    REF fTD429.A4 ECOL

INGENOR 9.
Glysson, Eugene A. The problem of solid-waste disposal. 1972.   **TD791.G5 ECOL**

INHERIT THE EARTH.
Berrill, Norman John. 1966   **Q162.B56 ECOL**

INITIAL MIXING IN COAGULATION PROCESSES.
Stenquist, Richard J. 1972.   **TD455.S7 ECOL**

INITIATING A NATIONAL EFFORT TO IMPROVE SOLID WASTE MANAGEMENT.
United States. Environmental Protection Agency. 1971.   **REF TD788.A45 ECOL**

INLAND FISHERIES MANAGEMENT.
Calhoun, Alex. 1966.   **fSH222.C2C3 ECOL**

INLAND WATERWAY TRANSPORTATION.
1969   **HE629.I57 ECOL**

INORGANIC CHEMICALS INDUSTRY PROFILE (UPDATED).
Datagraphics Incorporated. 1971.
    fTD899.C5D37 ECOL

INORGANIC FERTILIZER AND PHOSPHATE MINING INDUSTRIES—WATER POLLUTION AND CONTROL.
Battelle-Northwest. 1971.   **fTD899.F47B38 ECOL**

INORGANIC SULFUR OXIDATION BY IRON-OXIDIZING BACTERIA.
Syracuse University. Dept. of Biology. 1971.
    fQR84.S95 ECOL

INSECTICIDE RESISTANCE, SYNERGISM, ENZYME INDUCTION.
International IUPAC Congress of Pesticide Chemistry, 2d, Tel-Aviv, 1971. c1971
    SB951.I56 1971vol.2 ECOL

INSECTS OF NORTH AMERICA.
Klots, Alexander Barrett. 1971 **QL473.K56 ECOL**

INSECTS OF THE WORLD.
Linsenmaier, Walter. 1972 **fQL463.L4615 ECOL**

INSTITUTE OF BIOLOGY. SYMPOSIA. NO. 15.
Lowe-McConnell, R. H. Man-made lakes. 1966.
    GB1601.L6 1965 ECOL

INSTITUTE OF BIOLOGY. SYMPOSIA, NO. 18.
Biology and ethics. 1969.   **HM216.B48 ECOL**

INSTITUTE OF ECONOMIC AFFAIRS, LONDON. OCCASIONAL PAPER, 36.
Jacoby, Neil Herman. The polluters: industry or government? 1972.   **TD176.7.J3 ECOL**

INSTITUTIONAL ARRANGEMENTS FOR INTERNATIONAL ENVIRONMENTAL COOPERATION.
Environmental Studies Board. Committee for International Environmental Programs. 1972.
    HC79.E5E6 ECOL

INSTITUTIONS FOR URBAN-METROPOLITAN WATER MANAGEMENT: ESSAYS IN SOCIAL THEORY, SUBMITTED TO WATER RESOURCES SCIENTIFIC INFORMATION CENTER.
Wengert, Norman. 1972.   **fTD353.W4 ECOL**

INTEGRATED PEST MANAGEMENT.
United States. Council on Environmental Quality. 1972.   **SB950.U5 ECOL**

INTER-AGENCY TASK FORCE REPORT ON BASE METAL MINING IMPACTS.
Minnesota. Dept. of Natural Resources. 1973.
    fTN24.M6A5 ECOL

INTERACTION AND SYSTEMS.
Science Curriculum Improvement Study. c1970
    LB1585.S36 ECOL

INTERACTION OF HERBICIDES AND SOIL MICROORGANISMS.
Boyce Thompson Institute for Plant Research, Yonkers, N.Y. 1971.   **fSB951.4.B68 ECOL**

INTERACTION OF NITRILOTRIACETIC ACID WITH SUSPENDED AND BOTTOM MATERIAL.
United States. National Bureau of Standards. Analytical Chemistry Division. 1971.
    fTD427.D4U64 ECOL

INTERACTIONS OF MAN AND HIS ENVIRONMENT.
Jennings, Burgess Hill. 1966.   **TD180.J4 ECOL**

INTERBASIN TRANSFERS OF WATER.
Howe, Charles W. 1971   **HD1695.W4H66 ECOL**

INTEREST GROUPS WITH WATER AND RELATED LAND RESOURCES PROGRAMS IN MINNESOTA, 1971.
Walton, William Clarence. 1972.
    GB701.M554no.45 ECOL

AN INTERIM BIBLIOGRAPHY.
Great Lakes Basin Library. 1969-
    REF fZ7164.N3G7 ECOL

INTERIM SURVEY REPORT ON BLUE EARTH RIVER, MINNESOTA, MINNESOTA RIVER BASIN FOR FLOOD CONTROL AND RELATED PURPOSES.
United States. Army. Corps of Engineers. 1970?
    Ref fTC424.M6A5 ECOL

INTERNATIONAL ATOMIC ENERGY AGENCY. PANEL PROCEEDINGS SERIES.
Working Group Meeting on Nuclear Power Plant Control and Instrumentation, Vienna, 1971. Nuclear power plant control and instrumentation. 1972.
    TK9006.W58 1971 ECOL

INTERNATIONAL ATOMIC ENERGY AGENCY. PROCEEDINGS SERIES.
Symposium on Use of Nuclear Techniques in the Measurement and Control of Environmental Pollution, Salzburg, 1970. Nuclear techniques in environmental pollution. 1971.   **REF TD177.S9 1970 ECOL**

INTERNATIONAL ATOMIC ENERGY AGENCY/PROCEEDINGS SERIES.
Symposium on Environmental Aspects of Nuclear Power Stations, New York, 1970. Environmental aspects of nuclear power stations. 1971.
    REF TK9006.S887 1970 ECOL

INTERNATIONAL CONCILIATION, NO. 581.
Brown, Lester Russell. The social impact of the Green revolution. 1971.   **HD1417.B7 ECOL**

INTERNATIONAL, REGIONAL, FEDERAL-STATE, INTERSTATE AND FEDERAL ORGANIZATIONS WITH WATER RELATED LAND RESOURCES PROGRAMS IN MINNESOTA, 1971.
Walton, William Clarence. 1971.
    GB701.M554no.42 ECOL

INTERPRETATION OF GAS CHROMATOGRAPHIC SPECTRA IN ROUTINE ANALYSIS OF EXHAUST HYDROCARBONS.
Dimitriades, Basil. 1972 **TN23.U7no.7700 ECOL**

INTERSTATE PLANNING FOR REGIONAL WATER SUPPLY AND POLLUTION CONTROL.
Delaware River Basin Commission. 1971.
    fTD420.D4 ECOL

INTERSTATE SURVEILLANCE PROJECT: MEASUREMENT OF AIR POLLUTION USING STATIC MONITORS.
United States. Environmental Protection Agency. Air Pollution Control Office. 1971.
    TD890.U45 ECOL

INTERSTATE 394 CORRIDOR LOCATION STUDY.
Howard, Needles, Tammen & Bergendoff. 1973?
    fTE25.T9H6 ECOL

INTRODUCING THE EARTH.
Matthews, William Henry. 1972
    QE29.M27 ECOL

AN INTRODUCTION TO AIR CHEMISTRY.
Butcher, Samuel S. 1972 **QD163.B87 1972 ECOL**

AN INTRODUCTION TO CLIMATE.
Trewartha, Glenn Thomas. 4th ed. 1968
    QC981.T65 1968 ECOL

AN INTRODUCTION TO ECOLOGY AND POPULATION BIOLOGY.
Emmel, Thomas C. 1973
    QH541.E45 1973 ECOL

INTRODUCTION TO THE ATMOSPHERE.
Riehl, Herbert. 2d ed. 1971,c1972
    QC861.2.R5 1971 ECOL

INTRODUCTION TO THE STUDY OF ANIMAL POPULATIONS.
Andrewartha, Herbert George. 2nd ed. 1971
    QL752.A63 1971 ECOL

INVENTORY OF LITTER-PREVENTION AND RELATED ENVIRONMENTAL PROGRAMS IN THE UNITED STATES. 1972-
Keep America Beautiful, Inc.   **fTD817.K4 ECOL**

AN INVENTORY OF MINNESOTA LAKES.
Minnesota. Dept. of Conservation. Division of Waters, Soils, and Minerals. 1968.
    TD224.M6A3no.25 ECOL

INVENTORY OF WATER RESOURCES RESEARCH CONDUCTED IN MINNESOTA, 1963 THROUGH 1968.
Minnesota. University. Water Resources Research Center. Consulting Council. 1969.
    GB701.M554no.12 ECOL

INVESTIGATION OF A NEW PHOSPHATE REMOVAL PROCESS.
Envirogenics Company. 1970. **fTD745.E5 ECOL**

AN INVESTIGATION OF CURRICULA MATERIALS AND METHODOLOGY FOR TRAINING OPERATORS OF WASTEWATER TREATMENT PLANTS.
Brown, James C. 1972.
    fHD1694.N8N6no.74 ECOL

AN INVESTIGATION OF PHOSPHORUS REMOVAL MECHANISMS IN ACTIVATED SLUDGE SYSTEMS.
Morgan, W. E. 1972.   **TD756.M6 ECOL**

INVESTIGATION OF POROUS PAVEMENTS FOR URBAN RUNOFF CONTROL.
1972.   **fTE215.I58 ECOL**

AN INVESTIGATION OF TECHNIQUES FOR REMOVAL OF CHROMIUM FROM ELECTROPLATING WASTES.
Battelle Memorial Institute, Columbus, Ohio Columbus Laboratories 1971. **fTD899.M45B3ECOL**

AN INVESTIGATION OF TECHNIQUES FOR REMOVAL OF CYANIDE FROM ELECTROPLATING WASTES.
Battelle Memorial Institute, Columbus, Ohio. Columbus Laboratories 1971 i.e. 1972
    fTD899.M45B32 ECOL

INVESTIGATION OF WATER QUALITY AND SOURCES OF POLLUTION OF WATERS OF MINNESOTA AND IOWA: REPORTS AND MEMORANDUMS.
Minnesota. Division of Water Quality. 1960-
    fTD224.M6A34 ECOL

INVESTIGATIONS CONCERNING PROBABLE IMPACT OF NITRILOTRIACETIC ACID ON GROUND WATERS.
Robert S. Kerr Water Research Center. 1971.
    fTD427.D4R6 ECOL

THE INVISIBLE PYRAMID.
Eiseley, Loren C. 1970   **CB19.E38 ECOL**

INVITING INVOLVEMENT WITH HISTORY.
Hiros, John E. 1969   **fLB1047.H5 ECOL**

IOWA. STATE UNIVERSITY OF SCIENCE AND TECHNOLOGY, AMES. CENTER FOR AGRICULTURAL AND RURAL DEVELOPMENT. CARD REPORT 40T.
Heady, Earl Orel. Agricultural and water policies and the environment: an analysis of national alternatives in natural resource use, food supply capacity and environmental quality. 1972.
    fS441.H4 ECOL

IRRADIATION OF MICE AND MEN.
Loutit, John F. 1962   **QH652.L63 ECOL**

IS THERE AN OPTIMUM LEVEL OF POPULATION?
1971   **HB851.I8 ECOL**

AN ISLAND CALLED CALIFORNIA.
Bakker, Elna S. 1971.   **QH105.C2B3 ECOL**

ISLANDS OF HOPE.
Brown, William Edward. c1971
HC110.E5B75 ECOL

IT'S NOT TOO LATE.
Carvell, Fred J. 1971   HC110.E5C36 ECOL

IT'S YOUR WORLD.
United States. Dept. of the Interior. 1969
fS930.A45 ECOL

J

JAMAICA BAY AND KENNEDY AIRPORT: A MULTIDISCIPLINARY ENVIRONMENTAL STUDY.
Jamaica Bay Environmental Study Group. 1971.
fTL725.3.P5J3 ECOL

JERRY BAKER'S BACK TO NATURE ALMANAC. 1973-
Baker, Jerry.   SB455.B257 ECOL

THE JOHN CALVIN MCNAIR LECTURES.
Glass, Hiram Bentley. Science and ethical values. 1965   Q175.G58 ECOL

THE JOHN DANZ LECTURES.
Crick, Francis. Of molecules and men. 1969,c1966.
QH331.C9 1969 ECOL

DOCUMENT NO. 92-70.
United States. President, 1969-   (Nixon). Control of hazardous polluting substances. 1971.
TD365.U53 ECOL

THE JOHN DEWEY SOCIETY LECTURESHIP SERIES, NO. 11.
Glass, Hiram Bentley. The timely and the timeless. 1970   Q181.G45 ECOL

JOHN E. FOGARTY INTERNATIONAL CENTER FOR ADVANCED STUDY IN THE HEALTH SCIENCES. PROCEEDINGS, NO. 9.
Metallic contaminants and human health. 1972.
RA565.M47 1972 ECOL

JOHN F. KENNEDY INSTITUUT. CENTER FOR INTERNATIONAL STUDIES.
Growing against ourselves: the energy-environment tangle. 1972.   TD195.E4G76 ECOL

THE JOHN HARVARD LIBRARY.
Marsh, George Perkins. Man and nature. 1965.
GF31.M35 1965 ECOL

JOHN MUIR.
Graves, Charles Parlin. 1973
QH31.M9G66 ECOL

JOINT TREATMENT OF MUNICIPAL SEWAGE AND PULP MILL EFFLUENTS.
Green Bay (Wis.) Metropolitan Sewerage District. 1970.   fTD524.W6G74 ECOL

JOURNEY INTO SUMMER.
Teale, Edwin Way. 1960.   QH104.T39 ECOL

JUNIOR SCIENCE BOOK OF WATER.
Peterson, Ottis. 1966   PZ10.P4472Ju ECOL

K

K - 12 CURRICULUM GUIDE FOR ENVIRONMENTAL EDUCATION.
Northern Colorado Outdoor Nature Center. n.d.
fS946.N6 ECOL

KAUAI AND THE PARK COUNTRY OF HAWAII.
Wenkam, Robert. 1967   DU628.K3W4 ECOL

KEEPING ANIMALS IN SCHOOLS.
Great Britain. Dept. of Education and Science. 1971.
QL51.G7 ECOL

KENTUCKY SOLID WASTE MANAGEMENT PLAN.
Kentucky. Dept. of Health. 1971.
TD788.4.K4A45 ECOL

KEY TO NORTH AMERICAN WATERFOWL.
Wylie, Stephen R. 1972   QL696.A5W46 ECOL

KEY TO THE WILDFOWL OF THE WORLD.
Scott, Peter Markham. n.d.
REF QL696.A5S349 ECOL

KILLER SMOG.
Wise, William. 1968   RA576.W57 ECOL

THE KINGDOM OF THE FOREST.
Atwood, Ann. 1972   QH541.5.F6A88 ECOL

KLONDIKE '70.
Chasan, Daniel Jack. 1971   TN872.A7C47 ECOL

KNOWING THE OUTDOORS IN THE DARK.
Brown, Vinson. 1972   QH81.B856 ECOL

L

LAKE AND RIVER POLLUTION.
Sinha, Evelyn. 1971   REF fZ7173.W3S5 ECOL

LAKE EUTROPHICATION—WATER POLLUTION CAUSES, EFFECTS AND CONTROL.
Minnesota. University. Water Resources Research Center. 1970.   GB701.M554no.22 ECOL

LAKE ITASCA SEMINAR.
Northern States Power Company. 1st 1971-
REF fHM221.N6 ECOL

LAKE MICHIGAN ENVIRONMENTAL SURVEY: FINAL REPORT.
Ayers, John C. 1970.   REF fQH543.6.A9 ECOL

LAKE MINNETONKA: NUTRIENTS, NUTRIENT ABATEMENT, AND THE PHOTOSYNTHETIC SYSTEM OF THE PHYTOPLANKTON.
Megard, Robert Ordell. 1970.
fTD225.M63M4 ECOL

LAKE PROTECTION AND REHABILITATION LEGISLATION IN THE UNITED STATES.
Kusler, Jon A. Survey: lake protection and rehabilitation legislation in the United States. 1972.
REF fKF5568.K8 ECOL

LAKE SUPERIOR.
Agassiz, Louis. 1970, c1850
QH104.5.G7A35 1970 ECOL
Water Resources Scientific Information Center. 1972   fZ6005.G7W38 ECOL

LAKE SUPERIOR PERIPHYTON IN RELATION TO WATER QUALITY.
Olson, Theodore A. 1972.   fQK935.O4 ECOL

LAKE SUPERIOR STUDIES, 1956-61.
Minnesota. University. School of Public Health. 1957-61   fGB1627.G89M55 ECOL

LAKE SUPERIOR STUDY, SUMMER OF 1956: SUMMARY OF REPORT.
Minnesota. University. School of Public Health. 1957.   fGB1627.G89M53 ECOL

LAND AND PEOPLE IN THE NORTHERN PLAINS TRANSITION AREA.
Ottoson, Howard W. c1966
HD1773.A3O8 ECOL

LAND AND WATER.
Smith, Frank Ellis. 1971.   REF S930.S55 ECOL

LAND AND WATER FOR RECREATION.
Clawson, Marion. c1963   HD205 1963.C53 ECOL

LAND BIRDS OF AMERICA.
Murphy, Robert Cushman. 1953
fQL681.M85 ECOL

LAND ECONOMICS.
Ely, Richard Theodore. 1964.
HD111.E37 1964 ECOL

LAND EXCHANGE STUDY REPORT.
Minnesota. Division of Lands and Forestry. 1969.
fHD211.M6A45 ECOL

LAND FOR THE FUTURE.
Resources for the Future. 1960
HD205 1960.R4 ECOL

LAND IN TRANSITION SYMPOSIUM, 1971, ST. PAUL, MINN.
1971   fS623.L3 1971 ECOL

THE LAND IS DISAPPEARING.
May, Julian. 1972   QE571.M38 1972 ECOL

LAND MANAGEMENT INFORMATION IN NORTHWEST MINNESOTA: THE BEGINNINGS OF A STATEWIDE SYSTEM.
Orning, George W. 1972.   HD211.M6 ECOL

LAND OF URBAN PROMISE: CONTINUING THE GREAT TRADITION.
Kulski, Julian Eugene. 1967.   HT167.K8 ECOL

LAND, PEOPLE, AND HISTORY.
Helfman, Elizabeth S. 1967c1962
HD156.H4 1967 ECOL

THE LAND RENEWED.
Van Dersal, William Richard. Rev. and enl. ed. 1968.
S624.A1V3 1968 ECOL

THE LAND SYSTEM OF THE UNITED STATES.
Clawson, Marion. 1968   HD191.C53 ECOL

LAND THAT OUR FATHERS PLOWED.
Greenberg, David Benjamin. 1969
S521.G83 ECOL

LAND USE: CONCERN, CHALLENGE, COMMITMENT.
Jackson, John Y. c1969   HD110.J3 ECOL

LAND-USE CONTROLS IN THE UNITED STATES.
Delafons, John. 2d ed. 1969
HD205 1969 .D4 ECOL

LAND USE INFORMATION.
Resources for the Future. Committee on Land Use Statistics. 1969, c1965   HD205 1969.R4 ECOL

LAND-USE PLANNING.
Haar, Charles Monroe. 2d ed. 1971.
KF5692.A4H3 1971 ECOL

LAND USE POLICY AND PROBLEMS IN THE UNITED STATES.
Homestead Centennial Symposium, University of Nebraska, 1962. 1964,c1963
HD205 1962 .H6 ECOL

LAND USE WITHOUT ZONING.
Siegan, Bernard H. 1972   HT167.S5 ECOL

THE LANDOWNER AND THE SNOWMOBILER—PROBLEM OR PROFIT?
Moeller, George H. 1971.   GV857.S6M6 ECOL

LANDS BEYOND THE FOREST.
Sears, Paul Bigelow. 1969   QH541.5.P7S4 ECOL

THE LANGUAGE AND MUSIC OF THE WOLVES.
c1971   PhonodiscQL765.L32 ECOL

LARGE-SCALE DESALTING.
MacAvoy, Paul W. 1969   TD479.3.M3 ECOL

LAS AVES DE CHILE.
Goodall, J. D. 1946   Ref QL689.C5G6 ECOL

LAST CHANCE ON EARTH.
Caras, Roger A. 1972   QL88.C3 1972 ECOL

THE LAST DAYS OF MANKIND.
Mines, Samuel. 1971   S936.M55 ECOL

LAST LANDSCAPE.
Whyte, William Hollingsworth. 1968.
HT167.W48 ECOL

LAST OF THE CURLEWS.
Bodsworth, Fred. 1955.   QL696.L7B6 ECOL

THE LAST PLAY.
Ridgeway, James. 1st ed. 1973.
HD9540.5.R5 1973 ECOL

THE LAST REDWOODS, AND THE PARKLAND OF REDWOOD CREEK.
Leydet, Francois. 1969   SD397.R3L4 ECOL

THE LAST RESOURCE.
Loftas, Tony. rev. ed. 1970
GC1015.L57 1970 ECOL

LAST SURVIVORS.
Simon, Noel. 1970   QL88.S553 ECOL

THE LAST WHOLE EARTH CATALOG.
1971.   REF fTT155.W52 ECOL

LAW AND CONTEMPORARY PROBLEMS.
Air pollution control. 1969.
KF3812.A75A35 ECOL

LAW AND CONTEMPORARY PROBLEMS, V.22, NO. 2.
River basin development. 1957.
HN64.R589 ECOL

LAW AND CONTEMPORARY PROBLEMS, V.22, NO. 3.
Water resources. 1957.   HD1694.A5W3 ECOL

LAW AND CONTEMPORARY PROBLEMS, V.33, NO.2.
Air pollution control. 1968.
KF3812.A75A35 1968 ECOL

LAW AND TAXATION.
Berlin, Roisman & Kessler. 1970
KF6449.Z9B4 ECOL

LAW AND THE ENVIRONMENT.
1970   KF5505.A75L38 ECOL

LAW, INSTITUTIONS, AND THE GLOBAL ENVIRONMENT.
Conference on Legal and Institutional Responses to Problems of the Global Evnironment, Arden House, 1971. 1972.   KF3775.A75C6 1971 ECOL

THE LAW OF LAND EXCHANGE IN MINNESOTA.
Minnesota. Legislature. Senate. Office of Senate Counsel. 1969.   fKFM5851.A84 ECOL

THE LAW RELATING TO ACTIVITIES OF MAN IN SPACE.
Lay, S. Houston. 1970   REF fJX5810.L39 ECOL

LAWS RELATING TO THE PROTECTION OF ENVIRONMENTAL QUALITY, 1970.
California. Laws, statutes, etc. 1971
REF KFC610.A3 1970 ECOL

LEAD.
National Research Council. Committee on Biologic Effects of Atmospheric Pollutants. 1972.
QP913.P3N38 ECOL

LEAD IN THE URBAN ENVIRONMENT: A SELECTED BIBLIOGRAPHY.
White, Anthony G. 1973.   fZ6679.L4W5 ECOL

A LEADER'S GUIDE TO NATURE-ORIENTED ACTIVITIES.
Van der Smissen, Margaret Elisabeth. 2d ed. 1968
GV182.2.V3 1968 ECOL

LEADERSHIP TO MEET OUR ENVIRONMENTAL CRISIS.
Natural Science Center Conference. 8th, Dayton, Ohio, 1970. 1970   **REF fTD178.3.N3 ECOL**

LEARNING ABOUT NATURE THROUGH CRAFTS.
Musselman, Virginia W. 1969   **TT157.M82 ECOL**

LEGAL CONTROL OF THE ENVIRONMENT—3D.
1971   **KF3775.L44 ECOL**

LEGAL CONTROL OF WATER POLLUTION.
1969   **KF3786.A32L4 ECOL**

LEGAL LIMITS ON THE USE OF CHEMICAL AND BIOLOGICAL WEAPONS.
Thomas, Ann (Van Wynen). 1970   **REF JX5135.C5T55 ECOL**

LEGAL PROBLEMS OF COAL MINE RECLAMATION.
Maryland. University. School of Law. 1972.   **fKF1830.Z95M37 ECOL**

THE LEGAL REGIME OF HYDROSPACE.
Brown, Edward Duncan. 1971.   **JX4411.B73 ECOL**

A LEGISLATIVE HISTORY OF THE WATER POLLUTION CONTROL ACT AMENDMENTS OF 1972, TOGETHER WITH A SECTION-BY-SECTION INDEX.
United States. Library of Congress. Environmental Policy Division. 1973- .   **KF3787.1.A16A5 ECOL**

LET THEM LIVE.
Curry-Lindahl, Kai. 1972.   **S962.C87 ECOL**

LET'S FIND OUT ABOUT AIR.
Shapp, Martha. 1963.   **PE1127.S3S417 ECOL**

LIBRARY AND INFORMATIONAL RESOURCES IN THE TWIN CITY AREA.
Mauritz, Marilyn. 1972-   **REF fZ688.A2M3 ECOL**

THE LIBRARY OF WORLD AFFAIRS, NO. 70.
Brown, Edward Duncan. The legal regime of hydrospace. 1971.   **JX4411.B73 ECOL**

LIFE AND DEATH OF THE SALT MARSH.
Teal, John. 1969   **QH541.5.S24T4 ECOL**

THE LIFE AND ORGANIZATION OF BIRDS.
Yapp, William Brunsdon. 1970   **QL698.Y36 ECOL**

LIFE BETWEEN TIDEMARKS ON ROCKY SHORES.
Stephenson, Thomas Alan. 1972   **QH541.5.S3S68 ECOL**

LIFE CYCLES.
Science Curriculum Improvement Study. c1970   **LB1585.S32 ECOL**

LIFE IN A BUCKET OF SOIL.
Rhine, Richard. 1972   **QL110.R48 ECOL**

LIFE IN A LOG.
Schwartz, George I. 1972   **QH541.5.F6S39 ECOL**

LIFE IN A POND.
Robinson, Carmelita Klipple. 1967   **fPZ10.R56Li ECOL**

LIFE IN MUD AND SAND.
Eltringham, Stewart Keith. 1971   **QH541.5.S35E45 ECOL**

LIFE NATURE LIBRARY.
Farb, Peter. Ecology. c1970   **fQH541.F3 1970 ECOL**

THE LIFE OF PRAIRIES AND PLAINS.
Allen, Durward Leon. 1967   **QH541.5.P7A4 ECOL**

THE LIFE OF RIVERS AND STREAMS.
Usinger, Robert Leslie. c1967   **QH97.U8 ECOL**

THE LIFE OF THE AFRICAN PLAINS.
Brown, Leslie. 1972   **QH541.5.P7B76 ECOL**

THE LIFE OF THE FAR NORTH.
Fuller, William Albert. 1972.   **QH541.5.T8F84 ECOL**

THE LIFE OF THE FOREST.
McCormick, Jack. 1966   **QK938.F6M19 ECOL**

THE LIFE OF THE JUNGLE.
Richards, Paul Westmacott. 1970   **QH541.5.J8R53 ECOL**

THE LIFE OF THE MOUNTAINS.
Brooks, Maurice Graham. 1967   **QH541.5.M65B7 ECOL**

THE LIFE OF THE OCEAN.
Berrill, Norman John. c1966   **QH91.15.B4 ECOL**

THE LIFE OF THE POND.
Amos, William Hopkins. 1967   **QH541.5.F7A45 ECOL**

LIFE ON MAN.
Rosebury, Theodor. 1969   **QR56.R59 ECOL**

LIFE SCIENCE INVESTIGATIONS.
Rasmussen, Frederick A. Man and the environment. 1970, c1971   **QH316.5.R35 ECOL**

LIFE SCIENCE LIBRARY.
Leopold, Luna Bergere. Water. Rev. 1970,c1966   **fGB671.L4 1970 ECOL**

Thompson, Philip Duncan. Weather. 1969   **fQC863.T5 1969 ECOL**

THE LIGHT AT THE END OF THE TUNNEL.
Hesse, Walter H. 1972   **fTD175.H47 ECOL**

LIGHT-CATALYZED CHLORINE OXIDATION FOR TREATMENT OF WASTEWATER.
Midwest Research Institute, Kansas City, Mo. 1970.   **fTD758.M5 ECOL**

LIMESTONE TREATMENT OF RINSE WATERS FROM HYDROCHLORIC ACID PICKLING OF STEEL.
Armco Steel Corporation. 1971.   **fTD899.M45A75 ECOL**

LIMITATIONS AND EFFECTS OF WASTE DISPOSAL ON AN OCEAN SHELF.
Florida Ocean Sciences Institute. 1971 i.e.1972   **fTD763.F56 ECOL**

THE LIMITS TO GROWTH.
c1972   **HC110.E5L5 ECOL**

LIMNOLOGICAL SYSTEMS ANALYSIS OF THE GREAT LAKES.
Hydroscience, Inc. 1973.   **fTC423.3.H9 ECOL**

LIMNOLOGY IN NORTH AMERICA.
Frey, David Grove. 1966 c1963   **QH96.F7 ECOL**

LIQUID CHROMATOGRAPHY OF CARBAMATE PESTICIDES.
Thruston, Alfred D. 1972.   **SB951.T4 ECOL**

LISTENING POINT.
Olson, Sigurd F. 1st ed. 1958.   **QH102.O38 ECOL**

LISTING OF PAPERS, 1954/70-
Ontario Industrial Waste Conference.   **REF fTD897.O6 Suppl. ECOL**

LISTS OF REFERENCES AND SELECTED BOOKS BEARING ON WATER RESOURCES IN MINNESOTA.
Walton, William Clarence. 1966.   **GB701.M554no.4 ECOL**

Walton, William Clarence. Rev. ed. 1972.   **GB701.M554no.4 1972 ECOL**

A LITERATURE SEARCH AND CRITICAL ANALYSIS OF BIOLOGICAL TRICKLING FILTER STUDIES.
Dow Chemical Company. Functional Products and Systems Dept. 1971-   **fTD443.D6 ECOL**

LIVES OF GAME ANIMALS.
Seton, Ernest Thompson. 1929.   **QL151.S5 1925 ECOL**

THE LIVING BIRD. 6TH- 1967-   **REF QL671.L57 ECOL**

THE LIVING BLANKET ON THE LAND.
May, Julian. 1972   **S591.3.M39 1972 ECOL**

THE LIVING COMMUNITY.
Hirsch, S. Carl. 1966   **QH541.H54 ECOL**

LIVING EARTH.
Farb, Peter. 1959   **QH84.8.F3 ECOL**

THE LIVING FOREST.
McCormick, Jack. c1959   **QK938.F6M2 ECOL**

THE LIVING HOUSE.
Ordish, George. 1960 c1959   **QL751.O7 1960 ECOL**

THE LIVING LANDSCAPE.
Sears, Paul Bigelow. 1966   **QH541.S37 1966 ECOL**

LIVING ON THE EARTH.
Bay Laurel, Alicia. 1971, c1970   **fS605.5.B3 ECOL**

LIVING RESOURCES OF THE SEAS.
Food and Agriculture Organization of the United Nations. Atlas of the living resources of the seas. 1972.   **REF fGC1015.F6 ECOL**

THE LIVING STREAM.
Hardy, Sir Alister Clavering. 1967,c1965   **QH367.H2 1967 ECOL**

LIVING THINGS IN FIELD AND CLASSROOM.
Subarsky, Zachariah. 2d ed. 1969   **QH51.S9 1969 ECOL**

LIVING WATER.
Braun, Ernest. 1971   **fQH46.B7 ECOL**

LIVING WITH YOUR LAND.
Vosburgh, John R. c1968   **QH75.V57 ECOL**

THE LIVING YEAR.
Steele, Mary Q. 1972   **QH81.S855 1972 ECOL**

THE LONELY LAND.
Olson, Sigurd F. 1961.   **F1071.O4 ECOL**

LONG-RANGE WATER POLLUTION CONTROL PLAN AND PROGRAM, JULY 1, 1963.
Minnesota. Water Pollution Control Commission.   **fTD224.M6A56 ECOL**

LOOK WHAT I FOUND!
Case, Marshal T. c1971   **S962.C38 ECOL**

THE LORAX.
Geisel, Theodor Seuss. c1971   **fPZ8.3.G276Lo ECOL**

THE LORD'S WOODS.
Arbib, Robert S. 1st ed. 1971   **QH76.5.N7A72 ECOL**

LOST HERITAGE.
Savage, Henry. 1970.   **QH26.S28 ECOL**

LOVE OF EARTH.
French, Herbert E. c1973   **S936.F7 ECOL**

LOW-GRADE AND NONCONVENTIONAL SOURCES OF MANGANESE.
Brooks, David B. 1966   **REF TN490.M3B85 ECOL**

LOW-LEVEL RADIATION.
Sternglass, Ernest J. c1972.   **RA569.S8 ECOL**

THE LOWER MINNESOTA RIVER WATERSHED DISTRICT.
Itasca Engineering, inc. Minneapolis. 1961.   **fTC424.M6I84 ECOL**

M

M.I.T. REPORT NO. 24.
Power, pollution, and public policy. c1971   **HC107.A113E55 ECOL**

M.I.T. STUDIES IN COMPARATIVE POLITICS.
Dogan, Mattei. Quantitative ecological analysis in the social sciences. 1969   **HM206.D6 ECOL**

MAGNESIUM CARBONATE, A RECYCLED COAGULANT FOR WATER TREATMENT.
Gainesville, Fla. Dept. of Public Utilities. 1971.   **fTD433.G3 ECOL**

MAJOR NSP GENERATING PLANT SITES.
1970.   **fTK1191.M3 ECOL**

MAKING A LIVING IN CONSERVATION.
Day, Albert M. 1971   **S944.D33 ECOL**

THE MAMMALS.
Booth, Ernest Sheldon. How to know the mammals. 3d ed. 1972, c1971   **QL715.B66 1972 ECOL**

MAMMALS OF NORTH AMERICA.
Orr, Robert Thomas. 1971   **QL715.O77 ECOL**

MAN ADAPTING.
Dubos, Rene Jules. 1965.   **R723.D77 ECOL**

MAN AGAINST MASS SOCIETY.
Marcel, Gabriel. 1971, 1952   **B2430.M253H583 1971 ECOL**

MAN, AN ENDANGERED SPECIES?
United States. Dept. of the Interior. 1968   **fS914.A53 ECOL**

MAN AND ATOM.
Seaborg, Glenn Theodore. 1st ed. 1971.   **TK9145.S4 1971 ECOL**

MAN AND BEAST.
Marchant, Ronald Albert. 1968   **QL85.M3 1968 ECOL**

MAN AND ENVIRONMENT.
National Association for Environmental Education. 1970   **REF fZ5322.E2N3 ECOL**

MAN AND ENVIRONMENT: CRISIS AND THE STRATEGY OF CHOICE.
Arvill, Robert. Revised ed. 1970,c1969   **HC253.5.A7 1970 ECOL**

MAN AND FOOD.
Pyke, Magnus. 1970   **TX355.P9 ECOL**

MAN AND HIS ENVIRONMENT.
1970   **L11.N39no.1 ECOL**

Banff Conference on Pollution, 1st, 1968. 1st ed. 1970-   **TD172.5.B3 1968 ECOL**

Sako, Marilyn. 1971   **fS946.S2 ECOL**

MAN AND HIS ENVIRONMENT: A VIEW TOWARD SURVIVAL.
National Conference on UNESCO, 13th, San Francisco, 1969. No deposit—no return. 1970   **GF3.N38 1969 ECOL**

MAN AND HIS ENVIRONMENT: FOOD.
Brown, Lester Russell. 1972   **S439.B76 ECOL**

MAN AND HIS ENVIRONMENT: LAW.
Murphy, Earl Finbar. 1971.
KF3775.Z9M8 ECOL

MAN AND HIS ENVIRONMENT: THE EFFECTS OF POLLUTION ON MAN.
1972
TD172.5.M35 ECOL

MAN AND HIS ENVIRONMENT: WASTE.
Marx, Wesley. 1971
TD174.M37 ECOL

MAN AND HIS URBAN ENVIRONMENT.
Smith, Fred. 1972.
fHT151.S53 ECOL

MAN AND LAND IN THE UNITED STATES.
Clawson, Marion. 1964.
HD191.C55 ECOL

MAN AND NATURE.
Marsh, George Perkins. 1965.
GF31.M35 1965 ECOL

Watson, Richard A. 1969
GF23.W3 ECOL

MAN AND NATURE IN AMERICA.
Ekirch, Arthur Alphonse. 1963.
GF503.E46 ECOL

MAN AND THE CALIFORNIA CONDOR.
McMillan, Ian. 1968.
QL696.A2H24 ECOL

MAN AND THE ECOSPHERE.
Ehrlich, Paul R. 1971
fGF8.E35 ECOL

MAN AND THE ENVIRONMENT.
Boughey, Arthur S. 1971
GF43.B68 ECOL

Jackson, Wes. 1971
HC68.J32 ECOL

Rasmussen, Frederick A. 1970, c1971
QH316.5.R35 ECOL

MAN AND THE ENVIRONMENT: A BIBLIOGRAPHY OF SELECTED PUBLICATIONS OF THE UNITED NATIONS SYSTEM, 1946-1971.
Winton, Harry N. M. 1972.
REF Z5322.E2W56 ECOL

MAN AND THE QUALITY OF HIS ENVIRONMENT.
Western Resources Conference, 9th, University of Colorado, 1967. 1968
TD180.W4 1967 ECOL

MAN AND WILDLIFE.
Guggisberg, Charles Albert Walter. 1970
REF S962.G84 ECOL

MAN IN ECOLOGICAL PERSPECTIVE.
Metress, James F. c1971
GF75.M4 ECOL

MAN IN THE LIVING ENVIRONMENT.
Workshop on Global Ecological Problems, University of Wisconsin, 1971. 1972
GF3.W6 1971 ECOL

MAN IN THE WEB OF LIFE.
Storer, John Humphries. 1968
HM206.S7 ECOL

MAN IS THE PREY.
Clarke, James. 1969
QL758.C54 ECOL

MAN-MADE AMERICA: CHAOS OR CONTROL?
Tunnard, Christopher. 1963
fNA9108.T82 ECOL

MAN-MADE LAKES.
Lowe-McConnell, R. H. 1966.
GB1601.L6 1965 ECOL

MAN MUST EAT.
Slater, Sir William Kershaw. 1964
TX355.S63 ECOL

MAN, NATURE, AND HISTORY.
Russell, William Moy Stratton. 1969, c1967
GF37.R85 ECOL

MAN OBSERVED.
Montagu, Ashley. 1968
H83.M555 ECOL

THE MAN WHO WALKED THROUGH TIME.
Fletcher, Colin. 1967 i.e. 1968
F788.F55 ECOL

MANAGEMENT PROBLEMS IN METROPOLITAN WATER RESOURCE OPERATIONS.
McPherson, Murray Burns. 1971.
fTD353.M3 ECOL

MANAGING THE ENVIRONMENT: INTERNATIONAL ECONOMIC COOPERATION FOR POLLUTION CONTROL.
1971
HC79.E5M35 1971 ECOL

MANAGING THE ENVIRONMENT: NINE STATES LOOK FOR NEW ANSWERS.
Haskell, Elizabeth H. 1971.
fHC110.E5H35 ECOL

MANAGING WATER QUALITY: ECONOMICS, TECHNOLOGY, INSTITUTION.
Kneese, Allen V. 1968
TD423.K52 ECOL

MAN'S CONTROL OF THE ENVIRONMENT.
Congressional Quarterly Service, Washington, D. C. 1970.
fTD180.C65 ECOL

MAN'S DOMINION.
Graham, Frank. 1971
S930.G7 ECOL

MAN'S IMPACT ON ENVIRONMENT.
Detwyler, Thomas R. 1971
GF75.D48 ECOL

MAN'S IMPACT ON NATURE.
Lauwerys, Joseph Albert. 1970, c1969
QH368.L38 ECOL

MAN'S IMPACT ON TERRESTRIAL AND OCEANIC ECOSYSTEMS.
Matthews, William Henry. 1971
TD174.M39 ECOL

MAN'S IMPACT ON THE GLOBAL ENVIRONMENT.
Study of Critical Environmental Problems. 1970
QH541.S73 ECOL

MAN'S ROLE IN CHANGING THE FACE OF THE EARTH.
International Symposium on Man's Role in Changing the Face of the Earth, Princeton, N.J., 1955. 1970, c1956
G56.I63 1955 ECOL

MANUAL FOR ACTIVATED SLUDGE SEWAGE TREATMENT.
Goodman, Brian L. 1971
REF fTD756.G66 ECOL

MANUAL FOR OUTDOOR LABORATORIES.
National Association of Biology Teachers. National Conservation Committee. 1959.
QH51.N3 ECOL

A MANUAL OF COMMON BEETLES OF EASTERN NORTH AMERICA.
Dillon, Elizabeth S. 1972.
QL581.D5 1972 ECOL

MANUAL OF FIELD BIOLOGY AND ECOLOGY.
Benton, Allen H. 4th ed. c1965
QH307.B3 1965 ECOL

MANUAL OF OUTDOOR CONSERVATION EDUCATION.
Shomon, Joseph James. 1964
S946.S5 ECOL

MANUAL OF OUTDOOR INTERPRETATION.
Shomon, Joseph James. 1968
QH51.S5 ECOL

MANUAL OF VEGETATION ANALYSIS.
Cain, Stanley Adair. 1971, c1959
QK911.C3 1959a ECOL

A MANUAL OF WILDLIFE CONSERVATION.
1971.
fSK353.M35 ECOL

A MANUAL ON COLLECTION OF HYDROLOGIC DATA FOR URBAN DRAINAGE DESIGN.
Linsley, Ray K. 1973.
fTD665.L55 ECOL

MASSACHUSETTS INSTITUTE OF TECHNOLOGY. SEA GRANT PROJECT OFFICE. REPORT NO. MITSG 71-8.
Power, pollution, and public policy. c1971
HC107.A113E55 ECOL

MATERIAL OBJECTS: TEACHER'S GUIDE.
Science Curriculum Improvement Study. 1971
LB1585.S3 ECOL

A MATHEMATICAL MODEL FOR RELATING AIR QUALITY MEASUREMENTS TO AIR QUALITY STANDARDS.
Larsen, Ralph I. 1971.
TD890.L3 ECOL

MATHEMATICAL MODELS OF WATER QUALITY PARAMETERS FOR RIVERS AND ESTUARIES.
Hann, Roy W. 1972
fTD370.H3 ECOL

MATTER, EARTH, AND SKY.
Gamow, George. 2d ed. 1965
QC171.G3 1965 ECOL

A MATTER OF LIFE AND BREATH.
Feder, Bernard. c1973
HC110.E5F4 ECOL

MAYER SEWERAGE PLAN.
Lindsey-Brauer and Associates, Inc., Eden Prairie, Minn. 1970
fTD525.M3L5 ECOL

MAYFLY DISTRIBUTION AS A WATER QUALITY INDEX.
Minnesota. State College, Winona. 1970.
fTD370.M562 ECOL

MCGRAW-HILL ENCYCLOPEDIA OF SCIENCE AND TECHNOLOGY.
3d ed. 1971
REF fQ121.M3 1971 ECOL

MCGRAW-HILL'S 1972 REPORT ON BUSINESS AND THE ENVIRONMENT.
Price, Frank C. c1972
fTD174.P7 ECOL

THE MEANING OF EVOLUTION.
Simpson, George Gaylord. Rev. ed. 1969, c1967
QH366.S58 1969 ECOL

MEASUREMENT AND ENVIRONMENTAL DETERIORATION.
Collier, Boyd. 1971
HC79.I5C63 ECOL

MEASUREMENTS OF DISPERSAL AND CONCENTRATION, IDENTIFICATION, AND SANITARY EVALUATION OF VARIOUS AIR POLLUTANTS.
Nuttonson, Michael Y. 1971.
fTD883.7.R9N873 ECOL

MEASURES FOR AIR QUALITY, ANNUAL REPORT. 1970/71-
United States. National Bureau of Standards.
REF TD890.U57 ECOL

MEDITATIONS ON HUNTING.
Ortega y Gasset, Jose. 1972
SK31.O7813 ECOL

MEGALOPOLIS UNBOUND.
Pell, Claiborne de B. c1966
HE355.P4 ECOL

MEMBERSHIP DIRECTORY. 1972/73-
National Water Well Association.
REF TD407.N3 ECOL

MEMORANDUM ON MERCURY POLLUTION IN MINNESOTA.
Minnesota. Division of Water Quality. 1970.
fQH545.M4M57 ECOL

MEMORANDUM ON THE WASTE ASSIMILATION CAPACITY OF THE MISSISSIPPI RIVER IN THE TWIN CITIES METROPOLITAN AREA.
Minnesota. Division of Water Quality. 1969.
fTD525.T9M6 ECOL

MEN, BEASTS, AND GODS.
Carson, Gerald. 1972
HV4764.C35 ECOL

MEN WHO MATCHED THE MOUNTAINS.
Tucker, Edwin A. 1972.
SD143.T8 ECOL

MERCURY.
Montague, Katherine. 1971
QH545.M4M6 ECOL

MERCURY AND AIR POLLUTION: A BIBLIOGRAPHY WITH ABSTRACTS.
United States. Environmental Protection Agency. Office of Air Programs. 1972.
TD887.M4U5 ECOL

MERCURY POLLUTION CONTROL IN STREAM AND LAKE SEDIMENTS.
Suggs, James D. 1972.
fTD427.M4S9 ECOL

MERCURY POLLUTION CONTROL, 1971.
Jones, H. R. 1971
REF fTD427.M4J66 ECOL

MERCURY POLLUTION IN MINNESOTA.
Minnesota. Division of Water Quality. Memorandum on mercury pollution in Minnesota. 1970.
fQH545.M4M57 ECOL

METAL FINISHERS FOUNDATION.
Battelle Memorial Institute, Columbus, Ohio Columbus Laboratories An investigation of techniques for removal of chromium from electroplating wastes. 1971.
fTD899.M45B3 ECOL

METALLIC CONTAMINANTS AND HUMAN HEALTH.
1972.
RA565.M47 1972 ECOL

METALS AS POLLUTANTS IN AIR AND WATER.
Sinha, Evelyn. 1972.
REF fZ7171.S55 ECOL

A METHOD FOR PREDICTING THE PERFORMANCE OF DRAFT COOLING TOWERS.
United States. Environmental Protection Agency Pacific Northwest Water Laboratory. 1970.
fTP159.C6U5 ECOL

METHODS AND MATERIALS FOR THE MAINTENANCE OF TURF ON HIGHWAY RIGHTS-OF-WAY.
Minnesota. University. Dept. of Horticultural Science. 1971.
REF TE178.M6 ECOL

METHODS FOR LAND ECONOMICS RESEARCH.
Symposium on Research Methods, Virginia Polytechnic Institute, 1965. 1967?, c1966
HD110.S9 1965 ECOL

METHODS FOR ROUTING HYDROGRAPHS THROUGH OPEN CHANNELS.
Rice, Charles E. 1972.
GB701.M554no.51 ECOL

METHODS, MODELS & INSTRUMENTS FOR STUDIES OF AQUATIC POLLUTION.
Sinha, Evelyn. 1971
REF fZ7173.W3S52 ECOL

METHODS OF ESTIMATING RESERVES OF CRUDE OIL, NATURAL GAS, AND NATURAL GAS LIQUIDS.
Lovejoy, Wallace Francis. 1965
TN870.L68 ECOL

METHODS OF PREDICTING SOLID WASTE CHARACTERISTICS.
Boyd, Gail B. 1971.
TD793.7.B68 ECOL

METHODS USED FOR INVESTIGATING PRODUCTIVITY OF FISH-REARING PONDS IN MINNESOTA.
Dobie, John. Rev. 1962.
SH222.M6D6 1962 ECOL

THE METROPOLIS.
Bollens, John Constantinus. 2d ed. 1970
JS422.B6 1970 ECOL

METROPOLITAN DEVELOPMENT GUIDE   TITLE CATALOG

THE METROPOLITAN AREA—AN AIR POLLUTION CONTROL PROGRAM: A REPORT TO THE SUBCOMMITTEE ON METROPOLITAN PROBLEMS, GOVERNOR'S ADVISORY COMMITTEE ON AIR RESOURCES.
1966   **fTD883.5.M65M4 ECOL**

METROPOLITAN DEVELOPMENT GUIDE.
Minnesota. Metropolitan Council of the Twin Cities Area. 1973-   **REF fHT168.T9A34 ECOL**

METROPOLITAN OPEN SPACE AND NATURAL PROCESS.
1970.   **HT394.P5M46 ECOL**

METROPOLITAN PLANNING AND RIVER BASIN PLANNING: SOME INTERRELATIONSHIPS.
Kelnhofer, Guy J. 1968.   **TD223.K4 ECOL**

METROPOLITAN SEWER BOARD.
Black & Veatch, Kansas City, Mo. 1970.
        fTD525.T9B5 ECOL

METROPOLITAN WATER MANAGEMENT.
Willeke, Gene E. A program for metropolitan water management. 1972.   **fTD365.W5 ECOL**

MICHIGAN HOUSE OF REPRESENTATIVES. LEGISLATIVE REPORT.
D'Itri, Frank M. The environmental mercury problem. 1971.   **fQH545.M4D57 ECOL**

MICHIGAN. LEGISLATURE. HOUSE OF REPRESENTATIVES. LEGISLATIVE REPORT.
D'Itri, Frank M. The environmental mercury problem. 1971.   **fQH545.M4D57 ECOL**

MICHIGAN. UNIVERSITY. GREAT LAKES RESEARCH DIVISION. SPECIAL REPORT NO.49.
Ayers, John C. Lake Michigan environmental survey: final report. 1970.
        REF fQH543.6.A9 ECOL

MIDWEST ENVIRONMENTAL DIRECTORY, 1972-
United States. Environmental Protection Agency. Office of Public Affairs.   **REF S920.U5 ECOL**

THE MILWAUKEE RIVER.
Milwaukee. Milwaukee River Technical Study Committee. 1968.   **fTD225.M47M6 ECOL**

MINERAL FACTS AND PROBLEMS.
United States. Bureau of Mines. 1970.
        REF TN23.U4no.650 ECOL

MINERAL RESOURCES: GEOLOGY, ENGINEERING, ECONOMICS, POLITICS, LAW.
Flawn, Peter Tyrell. 1966   **HD9506.A2F55 ECOL**

MINERAL WASTE UTILIZATION.
Symposium on Mineral Waste Utilization. Proceedings. 1st- 1968-
        fTP995.A1S9 ECOL

MINERALS.
Doherty, William T. 1971.
        REF TN153.D58 ECOL

MINERALS AND MEN.
McDivitt, James Frederick. 1965
        TN19.M2 ECOL

MINERALS IN THE UNITED STATES.
Resources for the Future. Historical statistics of minerals in the United States. 1966, 1960
        fTN23.R4 1966 ECOL

MINERALS YEARBOOK.
United States. Bureau of Mines. 1969-
        REF TN23.U612 ECOL

MINI-CLIMATES.
Couchman, J. Kenneth. c1971   **QC863.C68 ECOL**

MINN. DEPT. OF CONSERVATION. DIV. OF WATERS. TECHNICAL PAPER 2.
Liesch, Bruce A. Geohydrology of the Jorden aquifer in the Minneapolis-St. Paul area Minnesota. 1961.
        fGB705.M6L5 ECOL

MINNESOTA. AGRICULTURAL EXPERIMENT STATION. MISCELLANEOUS REPORT NO. 105.
Minnesota. University. Dept. of Horticultural Science. Methods and materials for the maintenance of turf on highway rights-of-way. 1971.
        REF TE178.M6 ECOL

MINNESOTA. AGRICULTURAL EXPERIMENT STATION, ST. ANTHONY PARK. TECHNICAL BULLETIN 257.
Manson, Philip W. Some aspects of the hydrology of ponds and small lakes. 1968.
        fGB1825.M6M35 ECOL

MINNESOTA DEPT. OF CONSERVATION. DIVISION OF GAME AND FISH. TECHNICAL BULLETIN NO.9.
Big game in Minnesota. 1965.
        SH11.M64no.9 ECOL

MINNESOTA. DEPT. OF CONSERVATION. DIVISION OF WATER. BULLETIN NO. 18.
Straka, G. C. Graphs of ground water levels in Minnesota, 1957-1961. 1963.
        fTD224.M6A3no.18 ECOL

MINNESOTA. DEPT. OF CONSERVATION. DIVISION OF WATERS. BULLETIN NO. 21.
Maderak, Marion L. Quality of waters, Minnesota. 1963.   **fTD224.M6A3no.21 ECOL**

MINNESOTA. DEPT. OF CONSERVATION. DIVISION OF WATERS. BULLETIN NO. 14.
Norvitch, Ralph F. Ground water in alluvial channel deposits, Nobles County, Minnesota. 1960.
        fTD224.M6A3no.14 ECOL

MINNESOTA. DEPT. OF CONSERVATION. DIVISION OF WATERS. BULLETIN 23.
Maderak, Marion L. Chemical quality of ground water in the Minneapolis-St. Paul area, Minnesota. 1965.   **fTD224.M6A3no.23 ECOL**

MINNESOTA. DEPT. OF CONSERVATION. TECHNICAL BULLETIN NO. 7.
Minnesota. Dept. of Conservation. Division of Game and Fish. Waterfowl in Minnesota. 1964.
        SH11.M64no.7 ECOL

MINNESOTA. DEPT. OF CONSERVATION. TECHNICAL BULLETIN NO. 8.
Minnesota. Dept. of Conservation. Division of Game and Fish. Ducks and land use in Minnesota. 1964.
        SH11.M64no.8 ECOL

MINNESOTA DIRECTORY OF MANUFACTURERS.
        REF fT12.M5 ECOL

MINNESOTA ECOLOGICAL REGISTER.
The Ecological register: a directory of governmental agencies and private organizations concerned about environmental destruction and pollution in the state and in the seven-county metropolitan area. 2nd ed. 1971.
        S920.E24 1971 ECOL

The Ecological register: a directory of organizations in the seven-county metropolitan area concerned about environmental destruction and pollution (plus a supplement providing brief information on similar organizations located elsewhere). 1970.
        fS920.E24 ECOL

MINNESOTA ENVIRONMENTAL EDUCATION AREAS.
Fisher, Wes. 1972   **fS946.F5 ECOL**

MINNESOTA. GEOLOGICAL AND NATURAL HISTORY SURVEY. REPORT OF THE SURVEY. BOTANICAL SERIES V.
Freeman, Edward Monroe. Minnesota plant diseases. 1905.   **REF QK168.F7 ECOL**

MINNESOTA. GEOLOGICAL SURVEY. BULLETIN 35.
Zumberge, James Herbert. The lakes of Minnesota, their origin and classification. 1952.
        REF QE127.A22no.35 ECOL

MINNESOTA. GEOLOGICAL SURVEY. BULLETIN 37.
Schwartz, George Melvin. Minnesota's rocks and waters. 1954   **QE127.A22no.37 ECOL**

MINNESOTA. GEOLOGICAL SURVEY. BULLETIN 37.
Schwartz, George Melvin. Minnesota's rocks and waters. Rev. ed. 1963   **QE127.A22no.37 1963 ECOL**

MINNESOTA. GEOLOGICAL SURVEY. EDUCATIONAL SERIES, NO.4.
Hogberg, Rudolph K. Guide to the caves of Minnesota. 1967   **GB605.M5H6 ECOL**

MINNESOTA. GEOLOGICAL SURVEY. EDUCATIONAL SERIES NO.5.
Hogberg, Rudolph K. Environmental geology of the Twin Cities Metropolitan area. 1971
        QE128.T9H6 ECOL

MINNESOTA. GEOLOGICAL SURVEY. EDUCATIONAL SERIES, 1.
Hogberg, Rudolph K. Guide to fossil collecting in Minnesota. Rev. ed. 1967.   **QE718.H55 1967 ECOL**

MINNESOTA HISTORICAL SOCIETY. PUBLICATIONS.
Davis, Edward Wilson. Pioneering with taconite. 1964.   **TN403.M6D3 ECOL**

MINNESOTA. LAND MANAGEMENT INFORMATION SYSTEM STUDY. REPORT NO. 1.
Orning, George W. Land management information in northwest Minnesota: the beginnings of a statewide system. 1972.   **HD211.M6 ECOL**

MINNESOTA LEGISLATIVE MANUAL.
Minnesota. Secretary of State.
        REF JK6131.A25 ECOL

MINNESOTA OUTDOOR RECREATION PLAN.
Minnesota. Dept. of Conservation. 1968-
        fGV54.M6A197 ECOL

MINNESOTA PLANNING LEGISLATION.
Minnesota. State Planning Agency. Office of Local and Urban Affairs. 1971
        REF KFM5858.A3 1971 ECOL

MINNESOTA PLANT DISEASES.
Freeman, Edward Monroe. 1905.
        REF QK168.F7 ECOL

MINNESOTA POLLUTION CONTROL AGENCY.
History of Minnesota Pollution Control Agency. 1970   **fTD181.M5 ECOL**

MINNESOTA POPULATION DATA BOOK.
Minnesota. State Dept. of Health Vital Statistics Division. 1968.   **REF fHA453.A53 ECOL**

MINNESOTA RESOURCE POTENTIALS IN STATE OUTDOOR RECREATION.
Minnesota. Dept. of Natural Resources. Bureau of Planning. 1971.   **fGV54.M6A53 ECOL**

MINNESOTA SETTLEMENT AND LAND USE 1985.
Borchert, John R. 1970.   **HD111.B6 ECOL**

MINNESOTA SOIL AND WATER CONSERVATION NEEDS INVENTORY.
Minnesota. Conservation Needs Committee. 1971
        fHD243.M6A42 ECOL

MINNESOTA. UNIVERSITY. AGRICULTURAL EXTENSION SERVICE. EXTENSION BULLETIN, 320.
Hanson, Lowell D. Soils of the Twin Cities Metropolitan area and their relation to urban development. 1967, c1966
        fS599.M45H3 1967 ECOL

MINNESOTA. UNIVERSITY. AGRICULTURAL EXTENSION SERVICE. EXTENSION BULLETIN 359.
Waelti, John J. Understanding the water quality controversy in Minnesota. 1969   **fTD420.W3 ECOL**

MINNESOTA. UNIVERSITY. LIMNOLOGICAL RESEARCH CENTER. INTERIM REPORT NO. 7.
Megard, Robert Ordell. Lake Minnetonka: nutrients, nutrient abatement, and the photosynthetic system of the phytoplankton. 1970.   **fTD225.M63M4 ECOL**

MINNESOTA. UNIVERSITY. WATER RESOURCES COORDINATING COMMITTEE. WRCC BULLETIN NO. 1.
Conference on Water and Related Land Resources Planning in Minnesota, St. Paul, Minn., 1967. Papers presented during Conference on Water and Related Land Resources Planning in Minnesota. 1967.
        fHD1694.M6A54 1967 ECOL

MINNESOTA. UNIVERSITY. WATER RESOURCES RESEARCH CENTER. BULLETIN 11.
Haik, Raymond A. Aspects of water resources law in Minnesota. 1969.   **GB701.M554no.11 ECOL**

MINNESOTA. UNIVERSITY. WATER RESOURCES RESEARCH CENTER. BULLETIN 13.
Soil Conservation Society of America. Minnesota Chapter. Water pollution by nutrients—sources, effects and control. 1969.   **GB701.M554no.13 ECOL**

MINNESOTA. UNIVERSITY. WATER RESOURCES RESEARCH CENTER. BULLETIN 15.
Minnesota. University. Water Resources Research Center. Advisory Committee. Graduate education in water resources at University of Minnesota—1969. 1969.   **GB701.M554no.15 ECOL**

MINNESOTA. UNIVERSITY. WATER RESOURCES RESEARCH CENTER. BULLETIN 27.
Walton, William Clarence. Water and related land resources state administration, legislative process and policies in Minnesota, 1970. 1971
        GB701.M554no.27 ECOL

MINNESOTA. UNIVERSITY. WATER RESOURCES RESEARCH CENTER. WRRC BULLETIN.
Minnesota. University. Water Resources Research Center. Annual report.   **GB701.M554 ECOL**

MINNESOTA. UNIVERSITY. WATER RESOURCES RESEARCH CENTER. WRRC BULLETIN 4.
Walton, William Clarence. Lists of references and selected books bearing on water resources in Minnesota. 1966.   **GB701.M554no.4 ECOL**

MINNESOTA. UNIVERSITY. WATER RESOURCES RESEARCH CENTER. WRRC BULLETIN 4 [REV.].
Walton, William Clarence. Lists of references and selected books bearing on Water resources in Minnesota. Rev. ed. 1972.
        GB701.M554no.4 1972 ECOL

MINNESOTA. UNIVERSITY. WATER RESOURCES RESEARCH CENTER. WRRC BULLETIN NO. 6.
Walton, William Clarence. Recharge from induced streambed infiltration under varying groundwater-level and stream-stage conditions. 1967.
GB701.M554no.6 ECOL

MINNESOTA. UNIVERSITY. WATER RESOURCES RESEARCH CENTER. WRRC BULLETIN NO.8.
Bowers, C. Edward. Review and analysis of rainfall and runoff data for selected watersheds in Minnesota. 1968.
GB701.M554no.8 ECOL

MINNESOTA. UNIVERSITY. WATER RESOURCES RESEARCH CENTER. WRRC BULLETIN NO. 10.
Thorud, David B. Freezing in forest soil as influenced by soil properties, litter, and snow. 1969.
GB701.M554no.10 ECOL

MINNESOTA. UNIVERSITY. WATER RESOURCES RESEARCH CENTER. WRRC BULLETIN, 12.
Minnesota. University. Water Resources Research Center. Consulting Council. Inventory of water resources research conducted in Minnesota, 1963 through 1968. 1969.
GB701.M554no.12 ECOL

MINNESOTA. UNIVERSITY. WATER RESOURCES RESEARCH CENTER. WRRC BULLETIN NO.14.
Fox, Jackson L. The ecology of periphyton in Western Lake Superior. 1969.
GB701.M554no.14 ECOL

MINNESOTA. UNIVERSITY. WATER RESOURCES RESEARCH CENTER WRRC BULLETIN 17.
Parkos, William G. Water quality studies on the Great Lakes based on carbon fourteen measurements on primary productivity. 1969.
GB701.M554no.17 ECOL

MINNESOTA. UNIVERSITY. WATER RESOURCES RESEARCH CENTER. WRRC BULLETIN NO. 18.
Stokes, Lee W. The photosynthetic pigments of Lake Superior periphyton and their relation to primary productivity. 1970.
GB701.M554no.18 ECOL

MINNESOTA. UNIVERSITY. WATER RESOURCES RESEARCH CENTER. WRRC BULLETIN, NO. 19.
Minnesota. University. Water Resources Research Center. Information concerning water resources research center projects, 1965-70. 1970-
GB701.M554no.19 ECOL

MINNESOTA. UNIVERSITY. WATER RESOURCES RESEARCH CENTER. WRRC BULLETIN, NO. 20.
Potential productivity of fresh water environments as determined by an algae bioassay technique. 1970.
GB701.M554no.20

MINNESOTA. UNIVERSITY. WATER RESOURCES RESEARCH CENTER. WRRC BULLETIN, NO. 21.
Minnesota. University. Water Resources Research Center. Proceedings of conference on ongoing water resources research in Minnesota, March 1970. 1970.
GB701.M554no.21 ECOL

MINNESOTA. UNIVERSITY WATER RESOURCES RESEARCH CENTER. WRRC BULLETIN, NO. 22.
Minnesota. University. Water Resources Research Center. Lake eutrophication—water pollution causes, effects and control. 1970. **GB701.M554no.22 ECOL**

MINNESOTA. UNIVERSITY. WATER RESOURCES RESEARCH CENTER. WRRC BULLETIN, NO. 23.
Gibson, Ulric P. Integrating water quality management into total water resources management in Minnesota. 1970. **GB701.M554no.23 ECOL**

MINNESOTA. UNIVERSITY. WATER RESOURCES RESEARCH CENTER. WRRC BULLETIN, NO. 25.
Lewis, Robert Clark. The marginal costs of alternative levels of water quality in the Upper Mississippi River. 1970. **GB701.M554no.25 ECOL**

MINNESOTA. UNIVERSITY. WATER RESOURCES RESEARCH CENTER. WRRC BULLETIN 26.
Swain, Wayland R. The ecology of the second trophic level in Lakes Superior, Michigan and Huron. 1970. **GB701.M554no.26 ECOL**

MINNESOTA. UNIVERSITY. WATER RESOURCES RESEARCH CENTER. WRRC BULLETIN, NO. 29.
Lin, Shen-maw. Porosity and pore-size distribution of soil aggregates. 1971. **GB701.M554no.29 ECOL**

MINNESOTA. UNIVERSITY. WATER RESOURCES RESEARCH CENTER. WRRC BULLETIN, NO. 30.
Wei, Tsong C. Effects of areal and time distribution of rainfall on small watershed runoff hydrographs. 1971. **GB701.M554no.30 ECOL**

MINNESOTA. UNIVERSITY WATER RESOURCES RESEARCH CENTER. WRRC BULLETIN, NO.31.
Golany, Pinhas. Effects of channel characteristics on time parameters for small watershed runoff hydrographs. 1971. **GB701.M554no.31 ECOL**

MINNESOTA. UNIVERSITY. WATER RESOURCES RESEARCH CENTER. WRRC BULLETIN NO. 32.
Minnesota. University. Water Resources Research Center. Publications related to water resources research center projects, 1965-71 abstract-index. 1971.
GB701.M554no.32 ECOL

MINNESOTA. UNIVERSITY. WATER RESOURCES RESEARCH CENTER. WRRC BULLETIN NO. 33.
Fuentes, Victor C. Soil matric suction changes with time in pressed soil briquettes. 1971.
GB701.M554no.33 ECOL

MINNESOTA. UNIVERSITY. WATER RESOURCES RESEARCH CENTER. WRRC BULLETIN, NO. 34.
McNabb, C. D. A fluorometric technique for sampling in large-river ecosystems. 1971.
GB701.M554no.34 ECOL

MINNESOTA. UNIVERSITY. WATER RESOURCES RESEARCH CENTER. WRRC BULLETIN, NO.35.
Johnson, Jack D. Development of a mathematical model to predict the role of surface runoff and groundwater flow in over fertilization of surface waters. 1971. **GB701.M554no.35 ECOL**

MINNESOTA. UNIVERSITY. WATER RESOURCES RESEARCH CENTER. WRRC BULLETIN, NO.36.
Brook, Alan J. The phytoplankton of Minnesota lakes—a preliminary survey. 1971.
GB701.M554no.36 ECOL

MINNESOTA. UNIVERSITY. WATER RESOURCES RESEARCH CENTER. WRRC BULLETIN, NO.37.
Baker, Donald G. Snow cover and winter soil temperatures at St. Paul, Minn. 1971.
S594.5.B3 ECOL

MINNESOTA. UNIVERSITY. WATER RESOURCES RESEARCH CENTER. WRRC BULLETIN, NO. 38.
Seminar on the Engineer and the Environment University of Minnesota, 1970. The Engineer and the environment. 1971. **GB701.M554no.38 ECOL**

MINNESOTA. UNIVERSITY. WATER RESOURCES RESEARCH CENTER. WRRC BULLETIN, NO.39.
Bowers, C. Edward. Computer program for statistical analysis of annual flood data by the log-Pearson Type III method. 1971.
GB701.M554no.39 ECOL

MINNESOTA. UNIVERSITY. WATER RESOURCES RESEARCH CENTER. WRRC BULLETIN, NO.40.
Larson, Curtis L. Numerical routing of flood hydrographs through open channel junctions. 1971.
GB701.M554no.40 ECOL

MINNESOTA. UNIVERSITY, WATER RESOURCES RESEARCH CENTER. WRRC BULLETIN. NO. 42.
Walton, William Clarence. International, regional, federal-state, interstate and federal organizations with water related land resources programs in Minnesota, 1971. 1971. **GB701.M554no.42 ECOL**

MINNESOTA. UNIVERSITY. WATER RESOURCES RESEARCH CENTER. WRRC BULLETIN, NO. 43.
Mein, Russell G. Modeling the infiltration component of the rainfall—runoff process. 1971.
GB701.M554no.43 ECOL

MINNESOTA. UNIVERSITY. WATER RESOURCES RESEARCH CENTER. WRRC BULLETIN NO. 45.
Walton, William Clarence. Interest groups with water and related land resources programs in Minnesota, 1971. 1972. **GB701.M554no.45 ECOL**

MINNESOTA. UNIVERSITY. WATER RESOURCES RESEARCH CENTER. WRRC BULLETIN NO. 46.
Su, K. Lee. Aquatic plants from Minnesota, part 1—chemical survey. 1972.
GB701.M554no.46 ECOL

MINNESOTA. UNIVERSITY. WATER RESOURCES RESEARCH CENTER. WRRC BULLETIN NO. 47.
Su, K. Lee. Aquatic plants from Minnesota part 2—toxicity, anti-neoplastic, and coagulent effects. 1972. **GB701.M554no.47 ECOL**

MINNESOTA. UNIVERSITY. WATER RESOURCES RESEARCH CENTER. WRRC BULLETIN NO. 48.
Su, K. Lee. Aquatic plants from Minnesota part 3—antimicrobial effects. 1972.
GB701.M554no.48 ECOL

MINNESOTA. UNIVERSITY. WATER RESOURCES RESEARCH CENTER. WRRC BULLETIN NO. 49.
Walton, William Clarence. Water resources administration in Minnesota, 1972. 1972.
GB701.M554no.49 ECOL

MINNESOTA. UNIVERSITY, WATER RESOURCES RESEARCH CENTER. WRRC BULLETIN NO. 51.
Rice, Charles E. Methods for routing hydrographs through open channels. 1972.
GB701.M554no.51 ECOL

MINNESOTA. UNIVERSITY. WATER RESOURCES RESEARCH CENTER. WRRC BULLETIN, NO.52.
Larson, Curtis L. Predicting peak flow of small watersheds by use of channel characteristics. 1972.
GB701.M554no.52 ECOL

MINNESOTA. UNIVERSITY. WATER RESOURCES RESEARCH CENTER. WRRC BULLETIN 55.
Baron, Norman J. A survey of attitudes towards the Mississippi River as a total resource in Minnesota. 1972. **GB701.M554no.55 ECOL**

MINNESOTA. UNIVERSITY. WATER RESOURCES RESEARCH CENTER. WRRC BULLETIN 56.
Linn, J. G. Aquatic plants from Minnesota, part 4 — nutrient composition. 1973.
GB701.M554no.56 ECOL

MINNESOTA. UNIVERSITY. WATER RESOURCES RESEARCH CENTER. WRRC BULLETIN 57.
Gerlach, Luther P. Mobilization and participation of citizens groups in improving the quality of water resources environments. 1973.
GB701.M554no.57 ECOL

MINNESOTA. UNIVERSITY. WATER RESOURCES RESEARCH CENTER. WRRC BULLETIN 58.
Hopeman, Alan Roswell. An economic analysis of flood damage reduction alternatives in the Minnesota River Basin. 1973. **GB701.M554no.58 ECOL**

MINNESOTA. UNIVERSITY. WATER RESOURCES RESEARCH CENTER. WRRC BULLETIN 59.
Nelson, Robert R. The effects of enrichment on Lake Superior periphyton. 1973.
GB701.M554no.59 ECOL

MINNESOTA. UNIVERSITY. WATER RESOURCES RESEARCH CENTER. WRRC BULLETIN 60.
Arya, Lalit Mohan. Water flow in soil in presence of soybean root sinks. 1973. **GB701.M554no.60 ECOL**

MINNESOTA WATER AND RELATED LAND RESOURCES, FIRST ASSESSMENT.
Minnesota. Water Resources Coordinating Committee. 1970. **fTD224.M6A563 ECOL**

MINNESOTA WILD FLOWERS OF FOREST, FIELD AND WETLAND.
Marotta, Juanita. 1971. **QK168.M3 ECOL**

MINNESOTA'S LAKESHORE.
Minnesota. Lakeshore Development Study. 1970- **REF GB459.5.M5M5 ECOL**

MINNESOTA'S ROCKS AND WATERS.
Schwartz, George Melvin. 1954
QE127.A22no.37 ECOL
Schwartz, George Melvin. Rev. ed. 1963
QE127.A22no.37 1963 ECOL

MISSOURI RIVER BASIN.
Missouri Basin Inter-agency Committee. Comprehensive framework study, Missouri River Basin. 1971- **fHD1695.M5M48 ECOL**

MOBILITY: THE FIFTH FREEDOM.
International Conference on Urban Transportation, 5th, Pittsburgh, 1971. 1971? **fHE148.I5 1971 ECOL**

MOBILIZATION AND PARTICIPATION OF CITIZENS GROUPS IN IMPROVING THE QUALITY OF WATER RESOURCES ENVIRONMENTS.
Gerlach, Luther P. 1973.
GB701.M554no.57 ECOL

MODELING THE INFILTRATION COMPONENT OF THE RAINFALL—RUNOFF PROCESS.
Mein, Russell G. 1971. **GB701.M554no.43 ECOL**

MODELS FOR MANAGING REGIONAL WATER QUALITY.
1972. **TD365.M6 ECOL**

MODERN ECONOMIC ISSUES.
Goldman, Marshall I. Controlling pollution. c1967 **TD180.G58 ECOL**

MODERN INCINERATION: A SOLUTION—NOT THE PROBLEM.
Incinerator Institute of America. 1969? **fTD796.I54 ECOL**

MODERN LESSON PLANS IN ENVIRONMENTAL SCIENCE.
Kotsonis, Helen Hoch. 1972 **QH541.2.K68 ECOL**

THE MODERN METROPOLIS.
Blumenfeld, Hans. 1968,c1967 **HT166.B54 ECOL**

MOMENT IN THE SUN.
Rienow, Robert. 1967. **S930.R5 ECOL**

MONITORING, BIRTH DEFECTS AND ENVIRONMENT: THE PROBLEM OF SURVEILLANCE.
Symposium on Monitoring, Birth Defects and Environment, Albany, N. Y., 1970. 1971. **RG627.S94 1970 ECOL**

MONITORING MERCURY VAPOR NEAR POLLUTION SITES.
Environmental Measurements, Inc. 1971. **fTD427.M4E5 ECOL**

MONOGRAPHS IN POPULATION BIOLOGY, NO. 2.
Levins, Richard. Evolution in changing environments. 1968. **QL752.L4 ECOL**

MONOGRAPHS IN POPULATION BIOLOGY, 5.
Fretwell, Stephen D. Populations in a seasonal environment. 1972. **QL752.F73 ECOL**

M.O.R.R.C. REPORT. 1963/65-
Minnesota. Legislature. Outdoor Recreation Resources Commission. **REF GV54.M6A19 ECOL**

M.O.R.R.C. STAFF REPORT. 1963/65-
Minnesota. Legislature. Outdoor Recreation Resources Commission. **REF fGV54.M6A192 ECOL**

THE MOST DANGEROUS ANIMAL IN THE WORLD.
Roth, Charles E. c1971 **QH541.R68 ECOL**

MOTOR VEHICLE EMISSIONS: A BIBLIOGRAPHY.
Henry, Marybeth. 1972 **REF fTL214.P6H4 ECOL**

THE MOUNTAIN.
Parnall, Peter. 1st ed. 1971 **PZ10.P2564Mo ECOL**

MOUNTAIN ANIMALS.
Long, Tony. 1st U.S. ed. c1971 **QL113.L66 1971 ECOL**

THE MOUNTAINS AND MAN.
McCue, George. Ecology: the mountains and man. c1971 **QH541.5.M65M22 ECOL**

MUD LAKE HYDROLOGIC STUDY.
Barr Engineering Co. 1972 **fTC424.M6B34 ECOL**

MULTI-SYSTEM BIOLOGICAL TREATMENT OF BLEACHED KRAFT EFFLUENTS.
Mead Corporation. 1971. **fTD899.W65M4 ECOL**

MULTIDIRECTIONAL TURBULENCE PROBE DEVELOPMENT.
Battelle Memorial Institute. Columbus, Ohio. Columbus Laboratories **fTC177.B3 ECOL**

MULTIPLE PURPOSE RIVER DEVELOPMENT.
Resources for the Future. 1958 **REF HN15.R43 ECOL**

MUNICIPAL AND RURAL SANITATION.
Ehlers, Victor Marcus. 6th ed. c1965 **REF RA425.E5 1965 ECOL**

MUNICIPAL INCINERATION: A REVIEW OF LITERATURE.
Stear, James R. 1971. **TD803.S82 ECOL**

MUNICIPAL REFUSE DISPOSAL.
American Public Works Association. Institute for Solid Wastes. 3d ed. 1970 **TD795.A45 1970 ECOL**

MUNICIPAL WATER SUPPLY, TREATMENT, STORAGE, AND DISTRIBUTION SYSTEM, CITY OF WACONIA, MINNESOTA.
Schoell and Madson, Inc., Hopkins, Minn. Report on the municipal water supply, treatment, storage, and distribution system, City of Waconia, Minnesota. 1967. **fTD225.W3S3 ECOL**

THE MUSHROOM HUNTER'S FIELD GUIDE.
Smith, Alexander Hanchett. Rev. and enl. 1970 c1963 **REF fQK617.S56 1963 ECOL**

MUST THE SEAS DIE?
Moorcraft, Colin. 1973. **GC1085.M66 1973 ECOL**

MUST THEY DIE?
McNulty, Faith. 1st ed. 1971. **QL737.C25M27 ECOL**

MUTAGENIC EFFECTS OF ENVIRONMENTAL CONTAMINANTS.
1972. **QH431.M958 ECOL**

THE MUTAGENICITY OF PESTICIDES: CONCEPTS AND EVALUATION.
1971 **RA1270.P4M87 ECOL**

MY LAND IS DYING.
Caudill, Harry M. 1st ed. 1971. **TN291.C37 1971 ECOL**

MY SECRET PLACES.
Dubkin, Leonard. 1972 **QH105.I3D8 ECOL**

THE MYSTERIOUS EVERGREEN FOREST.
May, Julian. 1972 **QH541.5.F6M39 ECOL**

N

THE NADER REPORT: BITTER WAGES.
Page, Joseph A. Bitter wages: Ralph Nader's study group report on disease and injury on the job. 1973. **RC967.P33 ECOL**

NAM: A VOICE FOR AMERICAN INDUSTRY.
Industry/Government Teleconference on Pollution Control, 1971. 1971 **fTD172.5.I53 1971 ECOL**

NATIONAL ACADEMY OF SCIENCES PUBLICATION NO. 1703.
National Research Council. Committee on Resources and Man. Resources and man. 1969 **HC68.N36 ECOL**

NATIONAL ACADEMY OF SCIENCES, WASHINGTON, D.C. PUBLICATION 1495.
Conference on Undergraduate Education in the Biological Sciences for Students in Agriculture and Natural Resources, Washington, D.C., 1966. Undergraduate education in the biological sciences for students in agriculture and natural resources. 1967. **S533.C755 1966 ECOL**

NATIONAL ACADEMY OF SCIENCES, WASHINGTON, D.C. PUBLICATION 1679.
The Use of drugs in animal feeds. 1969. **SF98.M4U8 ECOL**

NATIONAL AUDUBON SOCIETY. NATURE CENTERS DIVISION. INFORMATION-EDUCATION BULLETIN NO. 3.
Shomon, Joseph James. Manual of outdoor conservation education. 1964 **S946.S5 ECOL**

NATIONAL AUDUBON SOCIETY. RESEARCH REPORT NO.3.
Allen, Robert Porter. The whooping crane. 1952. **QL696.G8A43 ECOL**

NATIONAL ENVIRONMENTAL POLICY ACT OF 1969 (P.L. 91-190): BIBLIOGRAPHY ON IMPACT ASSESSMENT METHODS AND LEGAL CONSIDERATIONS.
Ditton, Robert B. 1973. **Ref fHC110.E5D582 ECOL**

NATIONAL HANDBOOK OF CONSERVATION PRACTICES.
United States. Soil Conservation Service. 1971. **REF S922.U5 ECOL**

NATIONAL IRRIGATION RETURN FLOW RESEARCH AND DEVELOPMENT PROGRAM.
Law, James P. 1971. **fTC809.L38 ECOL**

THE NATIONAL PARK SERVICE.
Everhart, William C. c1972 **SB482.A4E95 ECOL**

THE NATIONAL PARK SYSTEM PLAN.
United States. National Park Service. 1970. **SB482.A3 1970a ECOL**

NATIONAL PARKS FOR THE FUTURE.
Conservation Foundation. 1972 **SB482.A4C67 ECOL**

NATIONAL PARKS OF THE WORLD.
Curry-Lindahl, Kai. 1972 **SB481.C87 ECOL**

NATIONAL REFERENCE LIST OF WATER QUALITY STATIONS, WATER YEAR 1971-
United States. Geological Survey. Water Resources Division. **REF TD380.U5 ECOL**

NATIONAL RESEARCH COUNCIL. PUBLICATION NO. 1350.
National Research Council. Committee on Atmospheric Sciences. Weather and climate modification problems and prospects. 1966. **QC928.N36 ECOL**

NATIONAL RESEARCH COUNCIL. PUBLICATION 1138.
National Research Council. Committee on Toxicology. Principles and procedures for evaluating the toxicity of household substances. 1964. **REF RA1221.N3 ECOL**

NATIONAL RESEARCH COUNCIL. PUBLICATION 1228.
National Research Council. Committee on Oceanography. Economic benefits from oceanographic research. 1964. **REF GB58.N3 ECOL**

NATIONAL RESEARCH COUNCIL. PUBLICATION 1273.
Radiation preservation of foods. 1965. **TX611.R28 ECOL**

NATIONAL RESEARCH COUNCIL. PUBLICATION 1274.
National Research Council. Food Protection Committee. Chemicals used in food processing. 1965. **REF fTX553.A3N26 ECOL**

NATIONAL RESEARCH COUNCIL. PUBLICATION 1280.
National Research Council. Building Research Advisory Board. Apartment house incinerators (flue fed). 1965. **fTH23.N333no.29 ECOL**

NATIONAL RESEARCH COUNCIL PUBLICATION 1354.
Toxicants occurring naturally in foods. 1966. **TX531.T6 ECOL**

NATIONAL RESEARCH COUNCIL PUBLICATION 1400.
National Research Council. Committee on Pollution. Waste management and control. 1966. **REF TD180.N3 ECOL**

NATIONAL RESEARCH COUNCIL. PUBLICATION 1402.
Scientific aspects of pest control. 1966. **SB951.S38 ECOL**

NATIONAL RESEARCH COUNCIL PUBLICATION 1408.
National Research Council. Committee on Water. Alternatives in water management. 1966. **HD1694.A5N48 ECOL**

NATIONAL RESEARCH COUNCIL. PUBLICATION 1411.
National Research Council. Committee on Animal Nutrition. Biological energy interrelationships and glossary of energy terms. 1st rev. ed. 1966. **REF SF95.N3 1966 ECOL**

NATIONAL RESEARCH COUNCIL PUBLICATION 1498.
Science, engineering, and the city. 1967. **HT166.S32 ECOL**

NATIONAL SANITATION FOUNDATION, ANN ARBOR, MICH. MONOGRAPH NO. 7.
Use of systems techniques in environmental quality management. 1970. **RA565.A1N38no.7 ECOL**

NATIONAL SANITATION FOUNDATION, MONOGRAPH NO. 7.
Use of systems techniques in environmental quality management. 1970. **RA565.A1N38no.7 ECOL**

NATIONAL SURVEY OF FISHING AND HUNTING, 1970-
United States. Bureau of Sport Fisheries and Wildlife. **REF S914.A3no.95 ECOL**

THE NATION'S ENVIRONMENT—PROBLEMS AND ACTION.
Environmental Quality Forum, East Tennessee State University, 1970. c1971 **TD172.5.E58 1970 ECOL**

NATIONWIDE INVENTORY OF PUBLICLY OWNED RECREATION AREAS AND AN ASSESSMENT OF PRIVATE RECREATION ENTERPRISES.
United States. Bureau of Outdoor Recreation. The 1965 nationwide inventory of publicly owned recreation areas and an assessment of private recreation enterprises. n.d. **fGV53.A47 1965 ECOL**

NATURAL AREAS IN INDIANA AND THEIR PRESERVATION.
Lindsey, Alton A. 1969. **QH76.5.I6L5 ECOL**

NATURAL ENVIRONMENTS: STUDIES IN THEORETICAL AND APPLIED ANALYSIS.
1972 **QH76.N28 ECOL**

NATURAL GAS, COAL, GROUND WATER.
Western Resources Conference, 8th, Colorado School of Mines, 1966. 1967 **HC103.7.W45 1966 ECOL**

THE NATURAL GEOGRAPHY OF PLANTS.
Gleason, Henry Allan. 1964. **QK101.G57 ECOL**

NATURAL HISTORY COLLECTING.
Harris, Reg. 1972 **QH60.H36 ECOL**

THE NATURAL HISTORY OF MAMMALS.
Bourliere, Francois. 1st American ed. 1954.
QL751.B663 ECOL

THE NATURAL RADIATION ENVIRONMENT.
Kastner, Jacob. 1968. **QH652.K35 ECOL**

NATURAL RADIATION EXPOSURE IN THE UNITED STATES.
Oakley, Donald T. 1972. **REF RA569.O15 ECOL**

NATURAL RESOURCE CONSERVATION.
Owen, Oliver S. 1971 **S938.O87 ECOL**

NATURAL RESOURCE MANAGEMENT.
Hall, O. F. Principles of natural resource management. 1951. **fS938.H3 ECOL**

NATURAL RESOURCE MANAGEMENT LESSON PLAN GUIDE.
Minnesota. University. Duluth Branch. Agricultural Extension Service. n.d. **fS946.M55 ECOL**

NATURAL RESOURCES AND INTERNATIONAL DEVELOPMENT.
Clawson, Marion. 1964 **HC55.C57 ECOL**

NATURAL RESOURCES AND PUBLIC RELATIONS.
Gilbert, Douglas L. 1971. **S944.G48 ECOL**

NATURAL RESOURCES AND THE POLITICAL STRUGGLE.
Wengert, Norman I. 1967,c1955
HC103.7.W4 1967 ECOL

NATURAL RESOURCES FOR U.S. GROWTH.
Landsberg, Hans H. c1964 **HC103.7.L3 ECOL**

NATURAL RESOURCES IN LATIN AMERICAN DEVELOPMENT.
Grunwald, Joseph. 1970 **REF fHC125.G72 ECOL**

NATURAL RESOURCES INFORMATION FOR ECONOMIC DEVELOPMENT; A STUDY.
Herfindahl, Orris Clemens. 1969
GA51.H47 ECOL

NATURAL RESOURCES MANAGEMENT: SUGGESTED TEACHING UNITS FOR AGRICULTURAL EDUCATION.
Naylon, Michael J. 1972? **fS946.N3 ECOL**

NATURAL RESOURCES: WILL WE HAVE ENOUGH FOR TOMORROW'S WORLD?
Millard, Reed. 1972 **HC103.7.M55 ECOL**

NATURAL WONDERS.
American heritage. The American heritage book of natural wonders. c1972,1963
fE169.A496 1972 ECOL

NATURAL WONDERS OF AMERICA.
1972 **QH76.N29 ECOL**

THE NATURAL WORLD: CHAOS AND CONSERVATION.
Johnson, Cecil E. c1972 **QH541.145.J63 ECOL**

THE NATURALISTS' DIRECTORY: INTERNATIONAL 41 ED.-
REF Q145.S4 ECOL

NATURE ACTIVITIES.
Gardner, John F. A book of nature activities. 1967
QH53.G3 ECOL

NATURE AND MAN'S FATE.
Hardin, Garrett James. 1961
QH361.H25 1961 ECOL

THE NATURE AND PROPERTIES OF SOILS.
Buckman, Harry Oliver. 7th ed. 1969
S591.B88 1969 ECOL

NATURE AND THE AMERICAN: THREE CENTURIES OF CHANGING ATTITUDES.
Huth, Hans. 1957. **QH77.U6H8 ECOL**

NATURE CONSERVATION.
Baron, William Michael Muir. 1971
QH77.G7B28 ECOL

NATURE CRAFTS.
Jaeger, Ellsworth. 1971,c1950 **TT157.J24 ECOL**

NATURE IN MINIATURE.
Headstrom, Birger Richard. 1968.
QH309.H4 ECOL

THE NATURE OF LIFE.
Milne, Lorus Johnson. 1970 **fQH45.2.M55 ECOL**

NATURE-ORIENTED ACTIVITIES.
Van der Smissen, Margaret Elisabeth. A leader's guide to nature-oriented activities. 2d ed. 1968
GV182.2.V3 1968 ECOL

NATURE REALMS ACROSS AMERICA.
Shomon, Joseph James. 1972. **QH102.S54 ECOL**

NATURE STUDY FOR CONSERVATION.
Brainerd, John W. 1971 **S946.B68 ECOL**

NATURE'S GUARDIANS.
Neal, Harry Edward. 1966,c1963
SK361.N45 1966 ECOL

NATURE'S NETWORK.
Reid, Keith. 1970, c1969 **QH541.14.R43 ECOL**

NATURE'S TEAKETTLE.
Small, HyDee. c1973 **GB1003.S6 ECOL**

NEEDED: BETTER WAYS OF MAKING ENVIRONMENTAL CHOICES.
Citizens League, Minneapolis Committee on Environment. Citizens League report. 1971.
fHC110.E5C5 ECOL

NEEDS OF A PROGRESSIVE SOCIETY FOR MINERAL AND ENERGY RESOURCES AND REALISTIC SOLUTIONS TO ENVIRONMENTAL PROBLEMS POSED.
Western Resources Conference. Colorado School of Mines, summer 1971. 1971
REF fTD172.5.W4 ECOL

NEVER CRY WOLF.
Mowat, Farley. 1st American ed. 1963
QL795.W8M6 ECOL

NEW AND ULTRATHIN MEMBRANES FOR MUNICIPAL WASTE WATER TREATMENT BY REVERSE OSMOSIS.
North Star Research and Development Institute, Minneapolis. 1970. **fTD754.N6 ECOL**

NEW APPROACHES TO FINANCING PARKS & RECREATION.
National Recreation and Park Association. Guide to new approaches to financing parks & recreation. 1970
SB482.A4N38 ECOL

NEW CHEMICAL CONCEPTS FOR UTILIZATION OF WASTE PLASTICS.
Banks, M. E. 1971. **TP156.R38B3 ECOL**

NEW ENERGY TECHNOLOGY—SOME FACTS AND ASSESSMENTS.
Hottel, Hoyt Clarke. 1971 **TJ23.H67 ECOL**

NEW ENGLAND'S PROSPECT: 1933.
American Geographical Society of New York 1933.
HC107.A11A82 ECOL

THE NEW EXPLORATION.
MacKaye, Benton. 1962. **GF51.M3 1962 ECOL**

THE NEW FIELD BOOK OF NATURE ACTIVITIES AND HOBBIES.
Hillcourt, William. Rev. ed. 1970
QH53.H574 1970 ECOL

THE NEW FORCE OF ATOMIC ENERGY: ITS DEVELOPMENT AND USE.
United States. Atomic Energy Commission. n.d.
TK9146.U5 ECOL

NEW HAMPSHIRE. UNIVERSITY. WATER RESOURCE RESEARCH CENTER. RESEARCH REPORT, NO. 4.
Hall, Francis R. The influence of a New England wetland on water quantity and quality. 1972.
fTD224.N4H3 ECOL

NEW INDUSTRIAL MAN.
Northern States Power Co. Lake Itasca seminar. 1972? **REF fHM221.N6 1971 ECOL**

Northern States Power Company. Lake Itasca seminar. 1st 1971- **REF fHM221.N6 ECOL**

NEW LIVES, NEW LANDSCAPES.
Fairbrother, Nan. 1st American ed. 1970.
HT395.G7F3 1970 ECOL

THE NEW NATURALIST: A SURVEY OF BRITISH NATURAL HISTORY.
Mellanby, Kenneth. Pesticides and pollution. 2nd rev. ed. 1970. **TD186.5.G7M44 1970 ECOL**

THE NEW NATURALIST; A SURVEY OF BRITISH NATURAL HISTORY. [6].
Darling, Frank Fraser. Natural history in the Highlands & islands. 1947 **QH141.D365 ECOL**

NEW SAFETY SYSTEM DESIGN FOR NUCLEAR POWER REACTORS.
Geesey, A. H. 1971. **fTA1.P35no.103 ECOL**

NEW VIEWS OF THE NATURE OF MAN.
Platt, John Rader. 1965 **BD450.P55 ECOL**

NEW YORK SOLID WASTE MANAGEMENT PLAN.
New York (State) Dept. of Health. 1971.
TD788.4.N4A45 ECOL

NEW YORK (STATE). STATE UNIVERSITY COLLEGE, BUFFALO. GREAT LAKES LABORATORY. SPECIAL REPORT NO. 5.
New York (State). State University College, Buffalo. Great Lakes Laboratory. Fish protein concentrate. 1970. **fSH333.F5 ECOL**

THE NEW YORK TIMES ENCYCLOPEDIC DICTIONARY OF THE ENVIRONMENT.
Sarnoff, Paul. c1971
REF TD173.S27 1971 ECOL

THE NEXT FIFTY YEARS.
Environment and change. 1970, c1968
HT167.E46 ECOL
Environment and policy. 1968 **HT167.E48 ECOL**
Environment for man. 1967
HT167.E5 1967 ECOL

THE NEXT HUNDRED YEARS: MAN'S NATURAL AND TECHNOLOGICAL RESOURCES.
Brown, Harrison Scott. 1970,c1963
HC55.B7 1970 ECOL

NFEC DIRECTORY OF ENVIRONMENTAL INFORMATION SOURCES.
REF fHC110.E5N4 ECOL

NINE MILE CREEK WATERSHED DISTRICT.
Barr Engineering Company. 1973.
fTC424.M6B35 ECOL

1970 PROFILE OF MINNEAPOLIS COMMUNITIES.
Minneapolis. Planning and Development. 1971.
fHT165.M6A46 ECOL

1976: AGENDA FOR TOMORROW.
Udall, Stewart L. 1st ed. 1968 **HN65.U3 ECOL**

NITRATE IN THE UNSATURATED ZONE UNDER AGRICULTURAL LANDS.
Pratt, P. F. 1972. **fS651.P7 ECOL**

NITRATE REMOVAL FROM WASTEWATERS BY ION EXCHANGE.
Dow Chemical Company. Western Division Research Laboratories. 1971. **fTD757.5.D68 ECOL**

NIXON AND THE ENVIRONMENT.
Rathlesberger, James. 1972 **HC110.E5R37 ECOL**

NO DEPOSIT—NO RETURN.
National Conference on UNESCO, 13th, San Francisco, 1969. 1970 **GF3.N38 1969 ECOL**

NO FURTHER RETREAT.
Dasmann, Raymond Frederick. 1971
S932.F6D37 ECOL

NOAA TECHNICAL MEMORANDUM EDS TM-BS-7.
Hacia, Henry. A selected annotated bibliography of the climate of the Great Lakes. 1972.
REF Z6683.C5H33 ECOL

NOISE ABATEMENT AND CONTROL.
United States. Office of Noise Abatement and Control. Public hearings on noise abatement and control. 1972- **TD893.A52 ECOL**

NOISE AND MAN.
Burns, William. c1968 **RA772.N7B8 ECOL**

NOISE AS A PUBLIC HEALTH HAZARD.
Conference on Noise as a Public Health Hazard, Wash., D.C., 1968. 1969. **RA772.N7C6 ECOL**

NOISE FROM CONSTRUCTION EQUIPMENT AND OPERATIONS, BUILDING EQUIPMENT, AND HOME APPLIANCES.
Bolt, Beranek, and Newman, Inc. 1971 i.e. 1972
fTD893.B63 ECOL

NOISE FROM INDUSTRIAL PLANTS.
Goodfriend (L.S.) Associates. 1971.
fTD892.G66 ECOL

NOISE POLLUTION.
O'Donnell, Patrick A. Teachers' ed. c1971
TD892.O46 ECOL

NOISE POLLUTION: THE UNQUIET CRISIS.
Bragdon, Clifford R. c1971 **TD892.B69 ECOL**

NOISE PROGRAMS OF PROFESSIONAL/INDUSTRIAL ORGANIZATIONS, UNIVERSITIES, AND COLLEGES.
United States. Office of Noise Abatement and Control. 1971. **fTD893.A51 ECOL**

NORTH AMERICAN WILD FLOWERS.
Walcott, Mary Morris (Vaux). 1925.
REF fQK112.W3 ECOL

NORTH CAROLINA. UNIVERSITY. WATER RESOURCES RESEARCH INSTITUTE. REPORT NO. 42.
Heath, Milton Sidney. A comparative study of state water pollution control laws and programs. 1972.
fKF3790.Z95H4 ECOL

NORTH CAROLINA. UNIVERSITY. WATER RESOURCES RESEARCH INSTITUTE. REPORT, NO.70.
Elliott, Ralph D. The effects of sewer surcharges on the level of industrial wastes and the use of water by industry. 1972. **TD897.5.E4 ECOL**

NORTH CAROLINA. UNIVERSITY. WATER RESOURCES RESEARCH INSTITUTE. REPORT NO. 74.
Brown, James C. An investigation of curricula materials and methodology for training operators of wastewater treatment plants. 1972.
fHD1694.N8N6no.74 ECOL

NORTH CAROLINA. UNIVERSITY. WATER RESOURCES RESEARCH INSTITUTE. REPORT NO. 58.
Stewart, James M. Perception of water resources research, dissemination, and utilization of research findings. 1971. fHD1694.N8N6no.58 ECOL

NORTH DAKOTA. UNIVERSITY. RESEARCH REPORT NO.2.
Ludtke, Richard L. Social and economic considerations for water resources planning in the Park River Subbasin, North Dakota. 1971.
HD1694.N9L8 ECOL

NORTH WITH THE SPRING.
Teale, Edwin Way. c1951   QH104.T42 ECOL

NORTHERN NON-WOODY PLANTS.
Moyle, John Briggs. Rev. ed. 1964
fQK168.M68 1964 ECOL

NORTHERN STATES POWER COMPANY, MINNESOTA: FOSSIL FUELED POWER PLANT SITING STUDY.
Commonwealth Associates, Inc. 1972.
REF fTK1331.N6C6 ECOL

NORTHERNMOST LABRADOR.
Forbes, Alexander. 1938.   F1136.F67 ECOL

NOT MAN APART.
Brower, David Ross. 1969
F869.B63B7 1969 ECOL

NOT SO RICH AS YOU THINK.
Stewart, George Rippey. c1967
TD180.S68 ECOL

NOW THAT WE HAVE TO WALK.
Fuller, Raymond Tifft. 1972, c1943
QH81.F847 1972 ECOL

NUCLEAR CLOCKS.
Faul, Henry. Rev. 1968
QC798.D3F37 1968 ECOL

NUCLEAR ENERGY FOR DESALTING.
Urrows, Grace M. Rev. 1967
TD479.6.U7 1967 ECOL

NUCLEAR EXPLOSIVES IN PEACETIME.
1970   fQC792.N8 ECOL

THE NUCLEAR INDUSTRY. 1971-
United States. Atomic Energy Commission. Division of Industrial Participation.   TK9023.A35 ECOL

NUCLEAR METHODS IN ENVIRONMENTAL RESEARCH.
American Nuclear Society. 1971
fTD172.5.A4 ECOL

NUCLEAR NEWS BUYERS GUIDE. 1972-
REF fTK9012.N82 ECOL

NUCLEAR POWER AND ITS CRITICS.
Nelkin, Dorothy. 1971   TK1344.N7N4 ECOL

NUCLEAR POWER AND MERCHANT SHIPPING.
Donnelly, Warren H. Rev. c1965
VM317.D6 1965 ECOL

NUCLEAR POWER AND THE ENVIRONMENT.
United States. Atomic Energy Commission. 1969.
TK1343.A46 ECOL

NUCLEAR POWER AND THE PUBLIC.
1970   TK1078.N83 ECOL

NUCLEAR POWER PLANT CONTROL AND INSTRUMENTATION.
Working Group Meeting on Nuclear Power Plant Control and Instrumentation, Vienna, 1971. 1972.
TK9006.W58 1971 ECOL

NUCLEAR POWER PLANT SAFETY.
Southern Interstate Nuclear Board. 1972?
fTK9152.S62 ECOL

NUCLEAR POWER PLANTS.
Lyerly, Ray L. Rev. 1969
TK1078.L9 1969 ECOL

NUCLEAR POWER PLANTS IN MARYLAND.
Maryland. Governor's Task Force on Nuclear Power Plants. 1969.   TK1344.M3M3 ECOL

THE NUCLEAR-POWER REBELLION.
Lewis, Richard S. 1972
HD9698.A3U44 1972 ECOL

NUCLEAR PROPULSION FOR SPACE.
Corliss, William R. 1967   TL783.5.C62 ECOL

NUCLEAR TECHNIQUES IN ENVIRONMENTAL POLLUTION.
Symposium on Use of Nuclear Techniques in the Measurement and Control of Environmental Pollution, Salzburg, 1970. 1971.   REF TD177.S9 1970 ECOL

NUCLEAR TERMS.
Lyman, James D. 2d ed. 1966.
QC772.L9 1966 ECOL

NUMERICAL ROUTING OF FLOOD HYDROGRAPHS THROUGH OPEN CHANNEL JUNCTIONS.
Larson, Curtis L. 1971. GB701.M554no.40 ECOL

NUTRIENT REQUIREMENTS OF DOMESTIC ANIMALS.
National Research Council. Committee on Animal Nutrition. Biological energy interrelationships and glossary of energy terms. 1st rev. ed. 1966.
REF SF95.N3 1966 ECOL

NUTRIENT SOURCES FOR ALGAE AND THEIR CONTROL.
Fitzgerald, George Patrick. 1971 i.e.1972
fQH96.8.E9F58 ECOL

NUTRIENTS IN NATURAL WATERS.
Allen, Herbert Ellis. 1972   QH96.A48 ECOL

NUTRIENTS IN WESTERN LAKE SUPERIOR.
Minnesota. University. School of Public Health. A preliminary investigation of nutrients in western Lake Superior, 1958-1959. 1959.
fGB1627.G89M52 ECOL

O

OASIS IN SPACE: THE OCEAN WORLD OF JACQUES COUSTEAU.
Cousteau, Jacques Yves. c1972
fQH91.C64 ECOL

OCCUPATIONAL AND ENVIRONMENTAL CANCERS OF THE URINARY SYSTEM.
Hueper, Wilhelm C. 1969.   RC280.G4H8 ECOL

OCCUPATIONAL EXPOSURE TO INORGANIC LEAD.
United States. National Institute for Occupational Safety and Health. 1972.   fRA1231.L4U5 ECOL

OCCUPATIONAL EXPOSURE TO ULTRAVIOLET RADIATION.
United States. National Institute for Occupational Saffaety and Health. 1972.   fRA1231.R2U5 ECOL

OCEAN DISPOSAL OF BARGE-DELIVERED LIQUID AND SOLID WASTES FROM UNITED STATES COASTAL CITIES.
Smith, David D. 1971.   TD796.7.O25S4 ECOL

OCEAN DUMPING: A NATIONAL POLICY.
United States. Council on Environmental Quality. 1970.   TD763.U55 ECOL

OCEAN ENGINEERING INFORMATION SERIES NO. 4.
Sinha, Evelyn. Lake and river pollution. 1971
REF fZ7173.W3S5 ECOL

OCEAN ENGINEERING INFORMATION SERIES V. 3.
Sinha, Evelyn. Coastal/estuarine pollution. 1970
REF fZ5853.P7S53 ECOL

OCEAN ENGINEERING INFORMATION SERIES, V. 5.
Sinha, Evelyn. Methods, models & instruments for studies of aquatic pollution. 1971
REF fZ7173.W3S52 ECOL

OCEAN ENGINEERING INFORMATION SERIES, V. 6.
Sinha, Evelyn. Metals as pollutants in air and water. 1972.   REF fZ7171.S55 ECOL

THE OCEAN OF AIR.
Blumenstock, David Irving. 1959.
QC863.B55 ECOL

OCEANOGRAPHY INFORMATION SOURCES/70.
Vetter, Richard C. 1970. REF GC10.V47 ECOL

OCEANOGRAPHY OF THE NEARSHORE COASTAL WATERS OF THE PACIFIC NORTHWEST RELATING TO POSSIBLE POLLUTION.
Oregon. State University, Corvallis. 1971-
fGC851.O7 ECOL

THE OCEANS AND MAN.
McCue, George. Ecology: the oceans and man. c1971   QH541.5.S3M22 ECOL

ODORS AND AIR POLLUTION: A BIBLIOGRAPHY WITH ABSTRACTS.
United States. Environmental Protection Agency. Office of Air Programs. 1972.   TD886.U5 ECOL

OF ANIMALS AND MEN.
Bixby, William. 1968.   QL751.B53 ECOL

OF LAND AND MEN.
Eskew, Garnett Laidlaw. c1959
NA9000.U715 ECOL

OF MEN AND MARSHES.
Errington, Paul Lester. 1957.   QH87.3.E7 ECOL

OF MEN AND MOUNTAINS.
Douglas, William Orville. 1950
F851.7.D68 ECOL

OF MOLECULES AND MEN.
Crick, Francis. 1969,c1966.
QH331.C9 1969 ECOL

OF MOSQUITOES, MOTHS, AND MICE.
Worth, Charles Brooke. 1st ed. 1972
QL475.N5W66 ECOL

OFF ROAD RECREATION VEHICLES: ORRV, A DEPT. OF THE INTERIOR TASK FORCE STUDY.
United States. Task Force on Off-Road Recreation Vehicles. 1971.   TL234.U5 ECOL

OFFICE OF AIR PROGRAMS PUBLICATION NO. AP-77.
United States. Environmental Protection Agency. Office of Air Programs. Guide for control of air pollution episodes in medium-sized urban areas. 1971.
TD883.1.U49 ECOL

OFFICE OF AIR PROGRAMS PUBLICATION NO. AP-78.
United States. Environmental Protection Agency. Office of Air Programs. Guide for control of air pollution episodes in small urban areas. 1971.
TD883.1.U492 ECOL

OFFICE OF AIR PROGRAMS PUBLICATION NO. AP-79.
Stear, James R. Municipal incineration: a review of literature. 1971.   TD803.S82 ECOL

OFFICE OF AIR PROGRAMS PUBLICATION NO. APTD-0737.
Selected studies on alkaline additives for sulfur dioxide control. 1971.   TD885.5.S8S4 ECOL

OFFICE OF AIR PROGRAMS PUBLICATION NO. APTD 0740.
United States. Environmental Protection Agency. Office of Air Programs. Office of Research Grants. Air pollution control.   REF TD883.2.A23 ECOL

OFFICE OF AIR PROGRAMS PUBLICATION NO.AP-89.
Larsen, Ralph I. A mathematical model for relating air quality measurements to air quality standards. 1971.
TD890.L3 ECOL

OFFICE OF AIR PROGRAMS PUBLICATION NO.AP-99.
Air Pollution Technical Information Center. Chlorine and air pollution: an annotated bibliography. 1971.   Z7173.A4A513 ECOL

OFFICE OF AIR PROGRAMS PUBLICATION NO.AP-100.
Air Pollution Technical Information Center. Hydrochloric acid and air pollution: an annotated bibliography. 1971.   Z7173.A4A52 ECOL

OFFICIAL CONGRESSIONAL DIRECTORY.
United States Congress.   REF JK1011.A3 ECOL

OHIO RIVER BASIN COMPREHENSIVE SURVEY—MAIN REPORT AND DEVELOPMENT PROGRAM FORMULATION.
United States. Water Resources Council. 1971.
HD1695.O5A55 ECOL

OIL AND HAZARDOUS MATERIALS PROGRAM SERIES.
Little (Arthur D.) Inc. Spill prevention techniques for hazardous polluting substances: an inventory and survey of hazardous chemical facilities in Charleston, West Virginia; Baltimore, Maryland; Texas City, Texas; and the Suisun Bay-Delta Area, California. 1971.
fT55.3.H3L4 ECOL

Ryckman, Edgerley, Tomlinson and Associates. Pesticide poisoning of Pond Lick Lake, Ohio. 1971
fTD224.O3R9 ECOL

OIL AND WATER.
Cowan, Edward. 1968   VK1255.T65C6 ECOL

OIL ON ICE.
Brown, Tom. 1971   HC107.A47E53 ECOL

OIL ON PUGET SOUND.
1972   fTD427.P4O38 ECOL

OIL ON THE SEA.
1969.   GC1080.O36 ECOL

OIL POLLUTION INCIDENT.
Alpine Geophysical Associates. 1971.
fGC1221.A4 ECOL

THE OIL PRODUCING INDUSTRY IN YOUR STATE. 1972-
Independent Petroleum Association of America.
REF fHD9564.I55 ECOL

OILSPILL.
Marx, Wesley. c1971   GC1085.M3 ECOL

OMEGA.
Anderson, Paul K. 1971   QH541.A5 ECOL

ON THE TRAIL OF VANISHING BIRDS.
Allen, Robert Porter. 1957   QL696.G8A4 ECOL

ONE ACRE AND SECURITY-HOW TO LIVE OFF THE EARTH WITHOUT RUINING IT.
Angier, Bradford. 1972   S561.A574 ECOL

ONE DAY AT TETON MARSH.
Carrighar, Sally. 1947. QL215.C3 ECOL

ONE EARTH, MANY PEOPLE.
Pringle, Laurence P. 1971 HB851.P75 ECOL

ONE THIRD OF THE NATION'S LAND.
United States. Public Land Law Review Commission. 1970 KF5601.A55P8 ECOL

ONLY A LITTLE PLANET.
1972 fPS3553.O474905 ECOL

THE ONLY EARTH WE HAVE.
Pringle, Laurence. 1969 TD180.P73 ECOL

ONLY ONE EARTH.
Jackson, Barbara (Ward) Lady. 1st ed. 1972 GF41.J3 ECOL

ONONDAGA LAKE STUDY.
Onondaga Co., N.Y. 1971. fTD224.N7O5 ECOL

OPEN CYCLE COAL BURNING MHD POWER GENERATION.
1971 fTN805.A395no.64 ECOL

OPEN HORIZONS.
Olson, Sigurd F. 1969. QH102.O39 ECOL

OPEN LAND FOR URBAN AMERICA.
Shomon, Joseph James. 1971 HD257.S56 ECOL

OPERATING HISTORY OF UNITED STATES NUCLEAR POWER REACTORS.
United States. Atomic Energy Commission. Division of Reactor Development and Technology. 1971. fTK1343.A467 ECOL
United States. Atomic Energy Commission. Division of Reactor Development and Technology. 1972. fTK1343.A467 1972 ECOL

OPERATING MANUAL FOR SPACESHIP EARTH.
Fuller, Richard Buckminster. 1969 T14.F84 ECOL

OPPORTUNITIES IN ENVIRONMENTAL CAREERS.
Fanning, Odom. c1971 S944.F3 ECOL

OPTIMIZATION OF AMMONIA REMOVAL BY ION EXCHANGE USING CLINOPTILOLITE.
California. University. Sanitary Engineering Research Laboratory. 1971 i.e. 1972
fTD757.5.C35 ECOL

OPTIMIZATION OF THE REGENERATION PROCEDURE FOR GRANULAR ACTIVATED CARBON.
Mine Safety Appliances Research Corporation. 1970. fTP245.C4M55 ECOL

OPTIMUM MECHANICAL AERATION SYSTEMS FOR RIVERS AND PONDS.
Hogan, William T. 1970. fTD458.H64 ECOL

OREGON. STATE UNIVERSITY, CORVALLIS. WATER RESOURCES RESEARCH INSTITUTE. WRRI-7.
Alexander, Robert M. Social aspects of environmental pollution. 1971. fTD177.A4 ECOL

THE ORGANIC CLASSROOM.
c1973 fS946.O7 ECOL

THE ORGANIC GARDENER.
Foster, Catharine Osgood. 1972
S605.5.F67 1972 ECOL

ORGANIC GARDENING WITHOUT POISONS.
Tyler, Hamilton A. 1970 S605.5.T9 ECOL

THE ORGANIC GUIDE TO COLLEGES AND UNIVERSITIES.
1973 S946.O73 ECOL

ORGANIC PESTICIDES IN THE ENVIRONMENT; A SYMPOSIUM.
American Chemical Society. 1966. SB951.A4 ECOL

ORGANISM AND ENVIRONMENT.
Darnell, Reznear M. c1971 fQH541.2.D3 ECOL

ORGANISMS.
Science Curriculum Improvement Study. c1970 LB1585.S34 ECOL

THE ORIGIN OF BIRDS.
Heilmann, Gerhard. 1927. QE871.H4 1927 ECOL

ORIGINS OF AMERICAN CONSERVATION.
Clepper, Henry Edward. 1966 S930.C57 ECOL

OUR AMAZING BIRDS.
Lemmon, Robert Stell. 1952. REF QL681.L4 ECOL

OUR ATOMIC WORLD.
Craven, Claude Jackson. Rev. 1964. QC778.C7 1964 ECOL

OUR CHANGING FISHERIES.
National Marine Fisheries Service. 1971 REF SH331.N38 ECOL

OUR CROWDED PLANET, ESSAYS ON THE PRESSURES OF POPULATION.
Osborn, Fairfield. 1962 HB851.O8 ECOL

OUR DIRTY AIR.
Elliott, Sarah M. 1971 TD883.13.E44 ECOL

OUR ENVIRONMENT AND NATURAL RESOURCES ... INDIVISIBLY ONE.
United States. Dept. of the Interior. 1971?
fS914.A533 ECOL

OUR ENVIRONMENT CAN BE SAVED.
Rockefeller, Nelson Aldrich. 1st ed. 1970.
HC110.E5R63 ECOL

OUR LIVING LAND.
United States. Dept. of the Interior. 1971
S914.A535 ECOL

OUR MAN-MADE ENVIRONMENT: A COLLECTION OF EXPERIENCES, RESOURCES AND SUGGESTED ACTIVITIES.
Group for Environmental Education, inc. 1971.
fGF75.G76 ECOL

OUR MINERAL RESOURCES.
Riley, Charles M. 1959 TN23.R56 ECOL

OUR NATIONAL PARK POLICY.
Ise, John. c1961 SB482.A1175 ECOL

OUR NATIONAL PARKS.
Muir, John. 1901. E160.M95 ECOL

OUR NATURAL RESOURCES.
McNall, Preston Essex. 3d ed. 1970
S930.M2 1970 ECOL

OUR OVERCROWDED WORLD.
Fisher, Tadd. 1969 HB871.F53 ECOL

OUR PLUNDERED PLANET.
Osborn, Fairfield. 1968 S623.O8 1968 ECOL

OUR POLLUTED PLANET: A BIBLIOGRAPHY OF GOVERNMENT PUBLICATIONS ON POLLUTION AND THE ENVIRONMENT.
Mignon, Molly R. 1971. fZ5322.E2M5 ECOL

OUR POLLUTED WORLD.
Perry, John. 1967 TD180.P4 ECOL
Perry, John. Rev. ed. 1972.
TD175.P46 1972 ECOL

OUR PRECARIOUS HABITAT.
Benarde, Melvin A. 1st ed. 1970
TD180.B45 ECOL

OUR RENEWABLE WILD LANDS, A CHALLENGE.
Cottam, Walter Pace. 1961. QK941.U8C6 ECOL

OUR SOUTH AFRICAN BIRDS (ONS SUID-AFRIKAANSE VOELS).
Roberts, Austin. 1941 REF QL692.R62 ECOL

OUR VANISHING WILDERNESS.
Grossman, Mary Louise. 1969
fQH541.13.G76 ECOL

OUR VANISHING WILDLIFE: ITS EXTERMINATION AND PRESERVATION.
Hornaday, William Temple. 1970,c1913
SK353.H6 1970 ECOL

OUR WILDLIFE LEGACY.
Allen, Durward Leon. Rev. ed. 1962
SK361.A66 1962 ECOL

OUR WONDERFUL WAYSIDE.
Hawkinson, John. 1966 PZ10.H34Ou ECOL

OUR WORLD IN PERIL.
Novick, Sheldon. 1971 HC110.P55N67 ECOL

OURS IS THE EARTH.
Sollers, Allan A. 1963 S930.S6 ECOL

OUT-OF-THE CLASSROOM EDUCATION EXPERIENCES.
Minnesota Elementary Principals' Association. Guidelines for out-of-the-classroom education experiences: Elementary schools. 1966.
LB1047.M55 ECOL

OUTDOOR ACTIVITIES FOR ENVIRONMENTAL STUDIES.
Knapp, Clifford E. c1971 LB1047.K5 ECOL

OUTDOOR ADVERTISING.
Houck, John W. 1969. REF HF5843.H57 ECOL

OUTDOOR EDUCATION LABORATORY PROJECT HANDBOOK.
St. Paul. Public Schools. Curriculum Office. Belwin outdoor education laboratory project handbook. 1971.
fLB1047.S25 ECOL

OUTDOOR EDUCATION ON YOUR SCHOOL GROUNDS.
Marsh, Norman F. 1968 LB1047.M29 ECOL

OUTDOOR HORIZONS.
Brings, Lawrence Martin. c1957
fSK33.B83 ECOL

OUTDOOR LABORATORIES.
National Association of Biology Teachers. National Conservation Committee. Manual for outdoor laboratories. 1959. QH51.N3 ECOL

OUTDOOR RECREATIONAL DEVELOPMENT POTENTIALS IN WASHINGTON SOIL AND WATER CONSERVATION DISTRICT.
Minnesota Association of Soil and Water Conservation Districts. fGV54.M6M54 ECOL

OUTLINES OF ENVIRONMENTAL EDUCATION.
Schoenfeld, Clarence Albert. 1971
S946.S43 ECOL

THE OUTLOOK FOR WATER.
Wollman, Nathaniel. 1971
REF fTD223.W6 ECOL

OVER-ALL PLAN FOR NINE MILE CREEK WATERSHED DISTRICT.
Barr, Douglas W. 1961. fTC424.M6B36 ECOL

OVERALL PLAN FOR WATER MANAGEMENT MINNEHAHA CREEK WATERSHED DISTRICT.
Hickok (Eugene A.) and Associates, Wayzata, Minn. 1969 fTC424.M6H5 ECOL

OVERALL PLAN OF THE LOWER MINNESOTA RIVER WATERSHED DISTRICT, 1972.
Itasca Engineering, inc., Minneapolis.
fTC424.M6I86 ECOL

OVERCONSUMPTION OF ENERGY.
Twin City Area Urban Corps. Energy Education Project. fHD9547.M5T8 ECOL

OVERSKILL.
Schwartz, Eugene S. 1971.
CB478.S38 1971 ECOL

OXIDATION OF PYRITES IN CHLORINATED SOLVENTS.
Troy, Joseph C. 1972. TD899.M5T7 ECOL

OXYGEN CONSUMPTION IN CONTINUOUS BIOLOGICAL CULTURE.
Kansas. University. Center for Research, Inc. 1971.
fTD755.K3 ECOL

THE OXYGEN UPTAKE DEMAND OF RESUSPENDED BOTTOM SEDIMENTS.
Washington (State). University. 1970.
fGC380.W3 ECOL

OZONE IN WATER AND WASTEWATER TREATMENT.
Evans, Francis L. 1972 TD461.E93 ECOL

P

PANEL PROCEEDINGS SERIES.
Working Group Meeting on Nuclear Power Plant Control and Instrumentation, Vienna, 1971. Nuclear power plant control and instrumentation. 1972.
TK9006.W58 1971 ECOL

PAPER PROFITS: POLLUTION IN THE PULP AND PAPER INDUSTRY.
Council on Economic Priorities. c1972
TD899.W65C65 1972 ECOL
Council on Economic Priorities. 1971
REF fTD888.P8C6 ECOL

PAPERS.
Conference on Law and the Environment, Warrenton, Va., 1969. n.d.
fKF3775.A75C58 1969 ECOL

PAPERS HELD AT THE UNIVERSITY OF ALASKA, JULY 22-24, 1970.
International Symposium on Water Pollution Control in Cold Climates, University of Alaska, Fairbanks, 1970. 1972 TD423.I5 ECOL

PAPERS PRESENTED DURING CONFERENCE ON WATER AND RELATED LAND RESOURCES PLANNING IN MINNESOTA.
Conference on Water and Related Land Resources Planning in Minnesota, St. Paul, Minn., 1967. 1967.
fHD1694.M6A54 1967 ECOL

PARTNERS IN NATURE.
Dudley, Ruth Hubbell. 1965 QH548.D8 ECOL

THE PASSENGER PIGEON.
Schorger, Arlie William. 1973
QL696.C6S3 1973 ECOL

PATIENT EARTH.
Harte, John. 1971 QH541.H26 ECOL

PATRICK GEDDES: SPOKESMAN FOR MAN AND THE ENVIRONMENT.
Geddes, Patrick, Sir. 1972
HT166.G43 1972 ECOL

PATTERNS FOR PRESERVATION: A CONSERVATION TEXT.
Tillotson, David. 1969 fS938.T5 ECOL

PATTERNS OF SURVIVAL.
Milne, Lorus Johnson. c1967 **QH546.M5 ECOL**

THE PAVERS AND THE PAVED.
Kelley, Ben. 1971 **HE355.K38 ECOL**

PAW PRINTS.
Lempfert, O. C. 1st ed. 1972 **QL768.L37 ECOL**

PCB IN WATER.
Water Resources Scientific Information Center. 1973. **Z7173.W3W3 ECOL**

PEACEFUL USE OF NUCLEAR EXPLOSIVES; SOME ECONOMIC ASPECTS.
Brooks, David B. 1969 **HD9698.U52B7 ECOL**

PELICAN IN THE WILDERNESS.
Darling, Frank Fraser. 1956 **QH104.D3 ECOL**

THE PENN STATE STATISTICS SERIES.
International Symposium on Statistical Ecology, New Haven, 1969. Statistical ecology. 1971 **QH541.15.M315 1969 ECOL**

PENNSYLVANIA. STATE UNIVERSITY. COLLEGE OF ENGINEERING. ENGINEERING RESEARCH BULLETIN B-103.
Geesey, A. H. New safety system design for nuclear power reactors. 1971. **fTA1.P35no.103 ECOL**

PENNSYLVANIA TEACHING GUIDE TO NATURAL RESOURCES CONSERVATION.
Pennsylvania. Dept. of Public Instruction. 1962, reprinted 1964 **fL194.B527no.7 1964 ECOL**

PEOPLE!
Cook, Robert Carter. 1968 **HB871.C7 ECOL**

PEOPLE, POWER AND POLLUTION: ENVIRONMENTAL AND PUBLIC INTEREST ASPECTS OF ELECTRIC POWER PLANT SITING.
California Institute of Technology. Pasadena. Environmental Quality Laboratory. 1971. **fTK1193.U5C3 ECOL**

THE PEOPLE PROBLEM.
Fraser, Dean. 1971 **HB875.F7 1971 ECOL**

THE PEOPLE'S BIRDS.
Northshield, Robert. 1972 **QL674.N67 ECOL**

PERCEPTION OF WATER RESOURCES RESEARCH, DISSEMINATION, AND UTILIZATION OF RESEARCH FINDINGS.
Stewart, James M. 1971. **fHD1694.N8N6no.58 ECOL**

PEREGRINE FALCON POPULATIONS.
1969. **QL696.A2P44 ECOL**

PERIL ON THE JOB.
Davidson, Ray. 1970 **HD7269.C452U5 ECOL**

PERILS OF THE PEACEFUL ATOM.
Curtis, Richard. 1969. **HD9698.U52C8 ECOL**

PERMAFROST IN CANADA.
Brown, Roger James Evan. 1970 **TA713.B76 ECOL**

PERSPECTIVES IN ECOLOGICAL THEORY.
Margalef, Ramon. 1968 **QH541.M37 ECOL**

PERSPECTIVES ON CONSERVATION.
1969, c1958 **HC103.7.P47 1969 ECOL**

PERSPECTIVES ON OUTDOOR EDUCATION.
Donaldson, George Warren. 1972 **LB1047.D6 ECOL**

PERU FROM THE AIR.
Johnson, George Robbins. 1930. **F3428.J67 ECOL**

PESTICIDE INPUTS AND LEVELS: MINNESOTA WATERS-LAKE SUPERIOR BASIN.
Minnesota. Pollution Control Agency. 1971 i.e. 1972 **fTD223.3.M55 ECOL**

THE PESTICIDE MANUFACTURING INDUSTRY—CURRENT WASTE TREATMENT AND DISPOSAL PRACTICES.
Atkins, Patrick R. 1972. **fTD899.C5A8 ECOL**

PESTICIDE POISONING OF POND LICK LAKE, OHIO.
Ryckman, Edgerley, Tomlinson and Associates. 1971 **fTD224.O3R9 ECOL**

THE PESTICIDE PROBLEM: AN ECONOMIC APPROACH TO PUBLIC POLICY.
Headley, Joseph Charles. c1967 **SB959.H35 ECOL**

PESTICIDE STUDY SERIES, 2.
Von Rumker, Rosmarie. The use of pesticides in suburban homes and gardens and their impact on the aquatic environment. 1972. **fQH545.P4V66 ECOL**

PESTICIDE STUDY SERIES, 4.
Ryckman, Edgerley, Tomlinson and Associates. Development of a case study of the total effect of pesticides in the environment, nonirrigated croplands of the Mid-west. 1972. **fQH545.P4R9 ECOL**

PESTICIDES.
1970 **fQH545.P4P48 ECOL**

PESTICIDES AND POLLUTION.
Mellanby, Kenneth. 2nd rev. ed. 1970. **TD186.5.G7M44 1970 ECOL**

PESTICIDES AND THE LIVING LANDSCAPE.
Rudd, Robert L. 1964. **SB951.R78 ECOL**

PETROLEUM CONSERVATION IN THE UNITED STATES: AN ECONOMIC ANALYSIS.
McDonald, Stephen L. 1971 **HD9566.M3 ECOL**

PETROLEUM RESOURCES AND PRODUCTION FACILITIES IN THE UPPER MIDWEST.
Koenker, William E. 1963. **fHD1773.A3U6no.8 ECOL**

PHARMACOLOGICAL TESTING OF BLUE-GREEN ALGAE FOR CONSTITUENTS HAVING THERAPEUTIC VALUE.
World Life Research Institute. 1970. **fRS165.A7W67 ECOL**

PHEASANTS.
Beebe, Charles William. 1926. **REF QL969.G2B26 ECOL**

PHILOSOPHERS OF THE EARTH.
Chisholm, Anne. c1972 **GF75.C4 ECOL**

PHOSPHATE PRECIPITATION WITH FERROUS IRON.
Ghassemi, Masood. 1971. **fTD751.G4 ECOL**

PHOSPHATE SLIMES.
International Minerals and Chemical Corporation. Utilization of phosphate slimes. 1971. **fTD899.M5157 ECOL**

PHOSPHORUS REMOVAL AND DISPOSAL FROM MUNICIPAL WASTEWATER.
Texas. University. Medical Branch, Galveston. 1971. **fTD745.T43 ECOL**

PHOSPHORUS REMOVAL BY AN ACTIVATED SLUDGE PLANT.
Milwaukee. Sewerage Commission. 1970. **fTD756.M54 ECOL**

PHOSPHORUS REMOVAL WITH PICKLE LIQUOR IN AN ACTIVATED SLUDGE PLANT.
Milwaukee. Sewerage Commission. 1971. **fTD756.M55 ECOL**

PHOTOCHEMICAL METHODS FOR PURIFYING WATER.
Cha, C. Y. 1972. **TD459.C4 ECOL**

PHOTOCHEMICAL OXIDANTS AND AIR POLLUTION: AN ANNOTATED BIBLIOGRAPHY.
Air Pollution Technical Information Center. 1971. **REF Z7173.A4A53 ECOL**

PHOTOGRAPHING WILDLIFE.
Baufle, Jean Marie. 1972. **fTR727.B2813 ECOL**

PHOTOGRAPHS OF AMERICAN NATURE.
Teale, Edwin Way. 1972 **fQH46.T4 ECOL**

THE PHOTOSYNTHETIC PIGMENTS OF LAKE SUPERIOR PERIPHYTON AND THEIR RELATION TO PRIMARY PRODUCTIVITY.
Stokes, Lee W. 1970. **GB701.M554no.18 ECOL**

A PHYSICS-BASED APPROACH TO HYDROLOGIC RESPONSE MODELING: PHASE I: MODEL DEVELOPMENT, COMPLETION REPORT.
Freeze, Allan R. 1972. **fGB665.F7 ECOL**

PHYSIOCHEMICAL PROCESSES FOR WATER QUALITY CONTROL.
Weber, Walter J. 1972 **TD430.W42 ECOL**

PHYSIOLOGICAL EFFECTS OF NOISE.
1970. **QP82.2.N6P47 ECOL**

THE PHYTOPLANKTON OF MINNESOTA LAKES—A PRELIMINARY SURVEY.
Brook, Alan J. 1971. **GB701.M554no.36 ECOL**

PILOT PLANT INSTALLATION FOR FUNGAL TREATMENT OF VEGETABLE CANNING WASTES.
Green Giant Company. 1971. **fTD899.C3G74 ECOL**

PILOT-SCALE DEVELOPMENT OF THE CSF PROCESS.
Consolidation Coal Company. Research Division. 1971. **fTN805.A395no.39 ECOL**

PILOT SCALE STUDY OF ACID MINE DRAINAGE.
Ohio. State University, Columbus. Research Foundation. 1971. **fTN321.O3 ECOL**

THE PIONEER FRINGE.
Bowman, Isaiah. 1931. **GF51.B6 ECOL**

PIONEER SETTLEMENT.
American Geographical Society of New York 1932. **GF51.A5 ECOL**

PIONEERING WITH TACONITE.
Davis, Edward Wilson. 1964. **TN403.M6D3 ECOL**

PIONEERS OF ECOLOGY.
Cox, Donald William. 1971 **QH26.C68 ECOL**

A PLACE IN THE SUN.
Darling, Lois. 1968 **QH541.D34 ECOL**

A PLACE IN THE WOODS.
Hoover, Helen. 1st ed. 1972. **QH105.M55H62 1972 ECOL**

THE PLACE NO ONE KNEW: GLEN CANYON ON THE COLORADO.
Porter, Eliot. 1963 **fF832.C7P6 ECOL**

THE PLACE OF THE IDEAL COMMUNITY IN URBAN PLANNING.
Reiner, Thomas A. 1968,c1963 **fNA9030.R45 1968 ECOL**

PLACES AND THINGS FOR EXPERIMENTAL SCHOOLS.
Educational Facilities Laboratories. 1972 **Ref LB3221.E3 ECOL**

PLANET IN PERIL.
Dasmann, Raymond Frederick. 1972 **QH541.D35 1972 ECOL**

PLANNED URBAN ENVIRONMENTS: SWEDEN, FINLAND, ISRAEL, THE NETHERLANDS, FRANCE.
Strong, Ann Louise. 1971 **fHT166.S73 ECOL**

PLANNING AND EVALUATION OF MULTIPLE PURPOSE WATER RESOURCE PROJECTS IN A MULTIOBJECTIVE ENVIRONMENT.
INTASA, Inc. 1972. **fHD1691.I1 ECOL**

PLANNING FOR SOLID WASTE MANAGEMENT.
Symposium of State and Interstate Solid Waste Planning Agencies, St. Louis, 1969. 1971 **TD523.S94 1969 ECOL**

PLANNING OUR TOWN.
Munzer, Martha E. 1964 **NA9108.M8 ECOL**

PLANNING RESEARCH FOR RESOURCE DECISIONS.
1st ed. 1970 **HC55.P55 ECOL**

PLANNING THE METROPOLITAN AIRPORT SYSTEM.
United States. Federal Aviation Administration. 1970. **TL725.3.P5U525 ECOL**

PLANT COMMUNITIES.
Daubenmire, Rexford F. 1968 **QK911.D3 ECOL**
Oosting, Henry John. The study of plant communities. 2d ed. 1956. **QK901.O6 1956 ECOL**

THE PLANT HUNTERS.
Johnson, Elinor M. 1969 **Fiction ECOL**

THE PLANT KINGDOM.
Bold, Harold Charles. 3d ed. c1970 **QK48.B59 1970 ECOL**
Coulter, Merle Crowe. The story of the plant kingdom. Rev. by Howard J. Dittmer. 3d ed. 1964 **QK47.C893 1964 ECOL**

PLANT NAMES SIMPLIFIED.
Johnson, Arthur Tysilio. 2d ed. 1971. **QK11.J6 1971 ECOL**

THE PLANTS.
Went, Frits Warmolt. 1969,c1963 **fQK50.W43 1969 ECOL**

PLANTS AND ENVIRONMENT.
Daubenmire, Rexford F. 2d ed. c1959 **QK901.D3 1959 ECOL**

PLANTS AND MAN.
Edlin, Herbert Leeson. 1969, c1967 **S519.E3 ECOL**

PLANTS, MAN, AND THE ECOSYSTEM.
Billings, William Dwight. 2d ed. 1970 **QK901.B5 1970 ECOL**

PLANTS TODAY AND TOMORROW.
Hyde, Margaret Oldroyd. 1960 **QK50.H9 ECOL**

PLANTS/PEOPLE/ENVIRONMENTAL QUALITY.
Robinette, Gary O. 1972 **QK901.R6 ECOL**

PLASTICS SOLID WASTE DISPOSAL BY INCINERATION OR LANDFILL.
Warner, Arthur J. c1972, 1971. **fTD798.W36 ECOL**

PLOWMAN'S FOLLY.
Faulkner, Edward H. 1963,c1943 **S603.F36 1963 ECOL**

PLOWSHARE.
Gerber, Carl R. 1966 **TK9153.G4 ECOL**

POCKET DATA BOOK, USA. 1971-
United States. Bureau of the Census.
REF HA195.A54 ECOL

A POCKET GUIDE TO TREES.
Platt, Rutherford Hayes. 1972,c1952
QK482.P5 1972 ECOL

POCKETS OF HOPE.
Munzer, Martha E. 1967 HC103.7.M78 ECOL

POISONED POWER.
Gofman, John William. 1971 TK9152.G57 ECOL

POISONING AND INTOXICATION BY TRACE ELEMENTS IN CHILDREN: AN ABSTRACT REVIEW OF THE WORLD-WIDE MEDICAL LITERATURE 1966-1971.
Excerpta Medica Foundations. 1973
RA1211.E9 ECOL

POISONOUS PLANTS OF THE MIDWEST & THEIR EFFECTS ON LIVESTOCK.
Evers, Robert August. 1972 SB617.E9 ECOL

POISONS IN YOUR FOOD.
Winter, Ruth. 1969 TX533.W55 1969 ECOL

POLAR.
American Geographical Society of New York Problems of polar research. 1928. G576.A6 ECOL

POLAR EXPLORATIONS SINCE THE INTRODUCTION OF FLYING.
Joerg, Wolfgang Louis Gottfried. Brief history of polar exploration since the introduction of flying. 1930
G590.J6 ECOL

POLICY DIRECTIONS FOR U.S. AGRICULTURE.
Clawson, Marion. 1968 HD1761.C54 ECOL

POLISH COUNTRYSIDES.
Boyd, Louise Arner. 1937. DK407.B6 ECOL

POLITICS AND ECOLOGY.
Foss, Phillip O. 1972 HC110.E5F66 ECOL

POLITICS AND ENVIRONMENT: A READER IN ECOLOGICAL CRISIS.
Anderson, Walt. 1970 HC110.E5A67 ECOL

THE POLITICS OF AIRPORT NOISE.
Stevenson, Gordon McKay. 1971, c1972
HE9797.4.N6S83 ECOL

THE POLITICS OF CONSERVATION.
Smith, Frank Ellis. c1966 S930.S56 ECOL

THE POLITICS OF ECOLOGY.
Ridgeway, James. 1st ed. 1970.
HC110.E5R52 ECOL

POLITICS OF LAND: RALPH NADER'S STUDY GROUP REPORT ON LAND USE IN CALIFORNIA.
Fellmeth, Robert C. 1973. HD211.C2F45 ECOL

THE POLITICS OF POLLUTION.
Davies, J. Clarence. 1970 HC110.E5D35 ECOL

POLITICS, POLICY, AND NATURAL RESOURCES.
Thompson, Dennis L. 1972 HC110.E5T48 ECOL

POLLUTE AND BE DAMNED.
Bourne, Arthur G. 1972 TD175.B68 ECOL

THE POLLUTERS: INDUSTRY OR GOVERNMENT?
Jacoby, Neil Herman. 1972. TD176.7.J3 ECOL

POLLUTION.
Dworsky, Leonard B. 1971.
REF TD174.D95 ECOL
Kiraldi, Louis. 1971. REF fZ7171.K55 ECOL

POLLUTION—MAN'S CRISIS: AN INVESTIGATIVE APPROACH.
Kelly, James. c1971 QH541.2.K45 ECOL

POLLUTION ABATEMENT AND BY-PRODUCT RECOVERY IN SHELLFISH AND FISHERIES PROCESSING.
Cresa. 1971. fTD899.F57C73 ECOL

POLLUTION ABATEMENT BY FIBER MODIFICATION.
Washington (State). University. Institute of Forest Products. 1971. fTD899.W65W38 ECOL

POLLUTION ABSTRACTS. INDEX.
V.1/2- 1970/71-
REF fTD172.P65 INDEXECOL

POLLUTION BY PESTICIDES.
Conservation Foundation. 1969.
QH545.P4C6 ECOL

POLLUTION CONTROL COMPANIES, UNITED STATES OF AMERICA, 1972.
Noyes Data Corporation. 1971, c1972
REF fTD173.5.N68 ECOL

POLLUTION CONTROL DIRECTORY. 1971/72-
Environmental Science & Technology.
REF fTD180.E52 ECOL

POLLUTION CONTROL REVIEW NO. 1.
Jones, H. R. Mercury pollution control, 1971. 1971
REF fTD427.M4J66 ECOL

POLLUTION CONTROL REVIEW NO. 7.
Jones, H. R. Detergents and pollution. 1972
fTD427.D4J65 ECOL

POLLUTION CONTROL REVIEW NO. 8.
Gutcho, Sidney. Waste treatment with polyelectrolytes, 1972. 1972 TD751.G87 ECOL

POLLUTION CONTROL REVIEW NO. 12.
James, Ronald W. Sewage sludge treatment 1972. 1972 REF fTD768.J35 ECOL

THE POLLUTION CRISIS: OFFICIAL DOCUMENTS.
Rabin, Edward H. 1972 c1971 TD180.R23 ECOL

POLLUTION IN THE AIR: PROBLEMS, POLICIES AND PRIORITIES.
Scorer, Richard Segar. 1973 TD883.S3 ECOL

POLLUTION MICROBIOLOGY.
Finstein, Melvin S. 1972. QR48.F5 ECOL

POLLUTION OF SUBSURFACE WATER BY SANITARY LANDFILLS.
Fungaroli, A. A. 1971 i.e. 1972-
TD403.F85 ECOL

THE POLLUTION PARADOX.
Bregman, J. I. c1966 TD180.B7 ECOL

THE POLLUTION PROBLEM.
Stepp, James Marvin. 1968 TD180.S65 ECOL

POLLUTION: PROBLEMS, PROJECTS AND MATHEMATICAL EXERCISES.
Henderson, George J. 1970
fQH541.2.H46 ECOL

POLLUTION, PROFITS & PROGRESS.
Schroeder, Henry Alfred. 1971 TD175.S37 ECOL

POLLUTION, PROPERTY AND PRICES.
Dales, John Harkness. 1970,c1968
HC120.P55D3 1970 ECOL

POLLUTION: THE AIR WE BREATHE.
Jones, Claire. 1971 TD883.13.J65 1971 ECOL

POLLUTION: THE BALANCE OF NATURE.
Jones, Claire. 1972 QH541.14.J65 ECOL

POLLUTION: THE DANGEROUS ATOM.
Jones, Claire. 1972 TD880.J65 1972 ECOL

POLLUTION: THE FOOD WE EAT.
Jones, Claire. 1972 TX533.J65 ECOL

POLLUTION: THE LAND WE LIVE ON.
Jones, Claire. 1971 TD176.J65 1971 ECOL

POLLUTION: THE NOISE WE HEAR.
Jones, Claire. 1972 TD892.J65 1972 ECOL

POLLUTION: THE POPULATION EXPLOSION.
Jones, Claire. 1972 HB871.J58 ECOL

POLLUTION: THE WATERS OF THE EARTH.
Jones, Claire. 1971 TD422.J65 ECOL

POLLUTION: THE WORLD CRISIS.
Hamblin, Lynette Kaye. 1971,c1970
TD174.H34 ECOL

POLLUTION THROUGH LAND USE MANAGEMENT.
Planning Research Corporation. 1969?
fGD205 1969 .P6 ECOL

POLYMER FILM OVERLAY SYSTEM FOR MERCURY CONTAMINATED SLUDGE—PHASE I.
Widman, Michael U. 1972. fTD427.M4W5 ECOL

THE POND.
Amos, William Hopkins. The life of the pond. 1967
QH541.5.F7A45 ECOL

POND LIFE: WATCHING ANIMALS FIND FOOD.
Wong, Herbert H. c1970 PZ10.W748Po ECOL

POPULATION AND ENVIRONMENTAL BIOLOGY.
Boughey, Arthur S. 1967 QH83.B68 ECOL

POPULATION AND SOCIETY.
Wrong, Dennis Hume. 3d. ed. 1967
HB881.W74 1967 ECOL

POPULATION AND THE AMERICAN FUTURE.
United States. Commission on Population Growth and the American Future. 1972
fHB3505.A525 ECOL

THE POPULATION BOMB.
Ehrlich, Paul R. 1968 HB875.E35 ECOL

POPULATION CONTROL.
Allison, Anthony. 1970 QL752.A58 ECOL

POPULATION CONTROL THROUGH NUCLEAR POLLUTION.
Tamplin, Arthur R. 1970 RA569.T35 ECOL

THE POPULATION CRISIS AND THE USE OF WORLD RESOURCES.
Mudd, Stuart. 1964. HB885.M8 ECOL

THE POPULATION DILEMMA.
American Assembly. 2d ed. 1969
HB851.A4 1969 ECOL

POPULATION, EVOLUTION, AND BIRTH CONTROL.
Hardin, Garrett James. 2d ed. 1969
HB851.H28 1969 ECOL

POPULATION GROWTH AND LAND USE.
Clark, Colin. 1968. HB871.C58 1968 ECOL

POPULATION IN PERSPECTIVE.
Young, Louise B. 1968. HB851.Y6 ECOL

POPULATION PERSPECTIVES.
Hauser, Philip Morris. 1961?c1960
HB3505.H3 ECOL

POPULATION, RESOURCES, AND THE ENVIRONMENT.
United States. Commission on Population Growth and the American Future. 1972
HB3505.A527 ECOL

POPULATION RESOURCES ENVIRONMENT.
Ehrlich, Paul R. 1970 HB871.E35 ECOL
Ehrlich, Paul R. 2d ed. 1972
HB871.E35 1972 ECOL

POPULATION: THE VITAL REVOLUTION.
Freedman, Ronald. 1964 HB881.F76 ECOL

POPULATION TYPE, DISTRIBUTION AND DENSITY OF THE FLORA ON THE SHERBURNE COUNTY GENERATING PLANT SITE, 15 OCTOBER THROUGH 31 DECEMBER, 1971.
Grether, David F. 1972 fTK1331.N6G7 ECOL

POPULATIONS.
Science Curriculum Improvement Study. c1969
fLB1585.S35 ECOL

POPULATIONS IN A SEASONAL ENVIRONMENT.
Fretwell, Stephen D. 1972. QL752.F73 ECOL

POROSITY AND PORE-SIZE DISTRIBUTION OF SOIL AGGREGATES.
Lin, Shen-maw. 1971. GB701.M554no.29 ECOL

POSSIBLE ENVIRONMENTAL IMPACT OF BASE METAL MINING IN MINNESOTA.
Brice, William C. 1972 fTN24.M6B7 ECOL

POTENTIAL ENVIRONMENTAL EFFECTS OF AN OFFSHORE SUBMERGED NUCLEAR POWER PLANT.
General Dynamics Corporation. Electric Boat Division. 1971- fQH541.5.S3G45 ECOL

THE POTENTIAL FOR ENERGY CONSERVATION.
United States. 1972. TJ153.U43 ECOL

THE POTENTIAL FOR ENERGY CONSERVATION: SUBSTITUTION FOR SCARCE FUELS.
United States. Office of Emergency Preparedness. 1973. fTJ153.U548 ECOL

POTENTIAL POLLUTION OF THE OGALLALA BY RECHARGING PLAYA LAKE WATER—PESTICIDES.
Wells, Dan M. 1970. fTD224.T4W45 ECOL

POTENTIAL PRODUCTIVITY OF FRESH WATER ENVIRONMENTS AS DETERMINED BY AN ALGAE BIOASSAY TECHNIQUE.
1970. GB701.M554no.20

POWER ALONG THE HUDSON.
Talbot, Allan R. 1st ed. 1972.
HD9685.U7C768 ECOL

POWER FROM RADIOISOTOPES.
Mead, Robert L. Rev. 1966 TK1078.M38 ECOL

POWER, POLLUTION, AND PUBLIC POLICY.
c1971 HC107.A113E55 ECOL

POWER REACTORS IN SMALL PACKAGES.
Corliss, William R. 1968 TK1078.C6 1968 ECOL

PRACTICAL DETERGENT ANALYSES.
Milwidsky, Benjamin Max. 1st ed. 1970
TP992.5.M5 ECOL

A PRACTICAL GUIDE TO WATER QUALITY STUDIES OF STREAMS.
Kittrell, F. W. 1969. TD425.K53 ECOL

PRAIRIE DUCKS.
Sowls, Lyle K. 1955. QL696.A5S64 ECOL

PRAIRIE PLANTS AND THEIR ENVIRONMENT.
Weaver, John Ernest. 1968 QK938.P7W42 ECOL

THE PRAIRIE WORLD.
Costello, David Francis. 1969
QH541.5.P7C6 ECOL

PREDATOR CONTROL—1971: REPORT TO THE COUNCIL ON ENVIRONMENTAL QUALITY AND THE DEPT. OF THE INTERIOR.
Michigan. University. Advisory Committee on Predator Control. 1972. fQL758.M5 ECOL

177

PREDICTING PEAK FLOW OF SMALL WATERSHEDS BY USE OF CHANNEL CHARACTERISTICS.
Larson, Curtis L. 1972. **GB701.M554no.52 ECOL**

PRELIMINARY DATA ANALYSIS.
Muhich, Anton J. 1968. **TD795.M82 ECOL**

PRELIMINARY REPORT FOR THE SUBCOMMITTEE ON HEALTH, ECONOMIC AND NUISANCE EFFECTS OF AIR POLLUTION.
Snyder, Edwin F. 1966. **fTD883.5.M65S6 ECOL**

PRESERVATION OF WILDERNESS AREAS.
United States. Congress. Senate. Committee on Interior and Insular Affairs. Subcommittee on Public Lands. 1972. **KF26.I547 1972 ECOL**

PRESERVING FOOD WITH ATOMIC ENERGY.
Pizer, Vernon. 1970 **TX611.5.P58 ECOL**

PRESERVING THE GREAT LAKES.
Kelnhofer, Guy J. 1972. **fTC423.3.K4 ECOL**

PRESERVING WILDERNESS IN OUR NATIONAL PARKS.
1971 **fQH76.P74 ECOL**

THE PRESIDENT'S 1972 ENVIRONMENTAL PROGRAM.
1972. **HC110.E5P74 ECOL**

A PRESSURE SEWER SYSTEM DEMONSTRATION.
Carcich, Italo G. 1972. **TD670.C3 ECOL**

PREVENTION AND CORRECTION OF EXCESSIVE INFILTRATION AND INFLOW INTO SEWER SYSTEMS.
American Public Works Association. 1971. **fTD678.A44 ECOL**

THE PRICE OF POWER: ELECTRIC UTILITIES AND THE ENVIRONMENT.
1972 **REF fTJ164.P7 ECOL**

THE PRIMAL ALLIANCE: EARTH AND OCEAN.
Hay, John. 1971. **fQH95.7.H32 ECOL**

PRIMARY CONSIDERATIONS IN REGIONAL WASTEWATER TREATMENT PLANNING.
Shindala, Adnan. 1972. **fTD365.S4 ECOL**

PRINCIPLES AND PRACTICES OF INCINERATION.
Corey, Richard Clarke. 1969 **TD803.C66 ECOL**

PRINCIPLES AND PROCEDURES FOR EVALUATING THE TOXICITY OF HOUSEHOLD SUBSTANCES.
National Research Council. Committee on Toxicology. 1964. **REF RA1221.N3 ECOL**

PRINCIPLES OF FOREST POLICY.
Worrell, Albert Cadwallader. 1970 **SD565.W67 ECOL**

PRINCIPLES OF MICROBIAL ECOLOGY.
Brock, Thomas D. 1966 **QR41.B72 ECOL**

PRINCIPLES OF WATER QUALITY CONTROL.
Tebbutt, T. H. Y. 1st ed. 1971 **TD365.T4 1971 ECOL**

PROBLEM—EMPHASIS EDUCATION: AN ENVIRONMENTAL SYMPOSIUM AND THE CONSEQUENCES OF THAT SYMPOSIUM AT COLUMBIA HEIGHTS SENIOR HIGH SCHOOL DISTRICT 13, 1969-1970.
Rasmussen, Bruce C. 1970 **fLB1027.R3 ECOL**

PROBLEM LAKES IN THE UNITED STATES.
Ketelle, Martha J. 1971. **fTD223.K47 ECOL**

THE PROBLEM OF SOLID-WASTE DISPOSAL.
Glysson, Eugene A. 1972. **TD791.G5 ECOL**

PROBLEMS OF POLAR RESEARCH.
American Geographical Society of New York 1928. **G576.A6 ECOL**

PROBLEMS RELATING TO IRON AND STEEL SCRAP.
United Nations. Economic Commission for Europe. 1971. **fTS214.U6 ECOL**

PROCEDURES MANUAL FOR THE REVIEW OF FEDERAL ACTIONS IMPACTING THE ENVIRONMENT.
United States. Environmental Protection Agency. 1972 **KF5505.U5 ECOL**

PROCEEDINGS.
Conference in the Matter of Pollution of the Interstate Waters of the Lower Mississippi River, New Orleans, 1964. 1964? **REF fTD225.M64C6 1964 ECOL**
Conference in the Matter of Pollution of Lake Superior and its Tributary Basin in the States of Minnesota, Wisconsin, and Michigan, Duluth, May 13-15, 1969. 1970 **fTD223.3.C59 1969 ECOL**
Conference on Snowmobiles and All-Terrain Vehicles, London, Ontario, 1971. 1972 **fGV857.S6C6 1971 ECOL**

PROCEEDINGS DIGEST OF THE ANNUAL MEETING. 62ND-
Air Pollution Control Association. 1969- **REF TD884.A55 ECOL**

PROCEEDINGS OF CONFERENCE ON INLAND LAKE RENEWAL AND SHORELAND MANAGEMENT.
Minnesota. University. Water Resources Research Center. 1972. **GB701.M554no.53 ECOL**

PROCEEDINGS OF CONFERENCE ON ONGOING WATER RESOURCES RESEARCH IN MINNESOTA, MARCH 1970.
Minnesota. University. Water Resources Research Center. 1970. **GB701.M554no.21 ECOL**

PROCEEDINGS OF CONFERENCE ON TOWARD A STATEWIDE GROUND WATER QUALITY INFORMATION SYSTEM AND REPORT OF GROUND WATER QUALITY SUBCOMMITTEE CITIZENS ADVISORY COMMITTEE, GOVERNORS ENVIRONMENTAL QUALITY COUNCIL.
Conference on Toward a Statewide Ground Water Quality Information System, St. Paul, Minn., 1972. 1973. **fTD224.M6C6 1972 ECOL**

PROCEEDINGS OF PROGRESS EVALUATION MEETING HELD APRIL 30, 1968.
Conference in the Matter of Pollution of the Interstate and Intrastate Waters of the Upper Mississippi River and its Tributaries—Wisconsin—Minnesota, Minneapolis, 1968. 1968. **fTD223.4.A45C6 ECOL**

PROCEEDINGS OF THE SECOND SESSION MINNEAPOLIS, MINNESOTA, FEB. 28, MARCH 1 & 20, 1967.
Conference in the Matter of Pollution of the Interstate and Intrastate Waters of the Upper Mississippi River and its Tributaries—Minnesota and Wisconsin. 1967. **REF TD223.4.A43C6 ECOL**

PROCEEDINGS SERIES.
Symposium on Environmental Aspects of Nuclear Power Stations, New York, 1970. Environmental aspects of nuclear power stations. 1971. **REF TK9006.S887 1970 ECOL**

PROCEEDINGS. 1ST- 1968-
Symposium on Mineral Waste Utilization. **fTP995.A1S9 ECOL**

PROCESS DESIGN MANUAL FOR CARBON ADSORPTION.
Swindell-Dressler Company. 1971. **REF fTD753.5.S9 ECOL**

PROCESS DESIGN MANUAL FOR PHOSPHORUS REMOVAL.
Black & Veatch, Kansas City, Mo. 1971. **REF fTD745.B5 ECOL**

PROCESS DESIGN MANUAL FOR SUSPENDED SOLIDS REMOVAL.
Burns and Roe. 1971. **REF fTD745.B8 ECOL**

PROCESS DESIGN MANUAL FOR UPGRADING EXISTING WASTEWATER TREATMENT PLANTS.
Roy F. Weston, Inc. 1971. **REF fTD745.R6 ECOL**

PRODUCTIVITY AND PLANKTON OF LAKE SUPERIOR.
Minnesota. University. School of Public Health. Studies on the productivity and Plankton of Lake Superior. 1961 **fQK935.M55 ECOL**

PROFESSIONAL FORESTRY IN THE UNITED STATES.
Clepper, Henry Edward. 1971 **SD143.C56 ECOL**

A PROGRAM FOR METROPOLITAN WATER MANAGEMENT.
Willeke, Gene E. 1972. **fTD365.W5 ECOL**

A PROGRAM FOR PRESERVING THE QUALITY OF LAKE MINNETONKA.
Harza Engineering Company. 1971 **fTD225.M63H3 ECOL**

PROGRAMS IN ENVIRONMENTAL EDUCATION.
National Science Teachers Association. 2d ed. 1971. **REF fQH51.N24 1971 ECOL**

PROGRESS IN THE PREVENTION AND CONTROL OF AIR POLLUTION.
United States. Environmental Protection Agency. 1971- **TD883.2.A22 ECOL**

PROGRESS REPORT AND LONG-RANGE PLAN AND PROGRAM FOR WATER POLLUTION CONTROL.
Minnesota. Pollution Control Agency. 1968. **REF fTD224.M6A53 ECOL**

PROGRESS REPORT, BIENNIAL PROGRAM AND LONG-RANGE PLAN FOR WATER POLLUTION CONTROL.
Creative Research Services, Inc. 1970. **fTD224.M65C73 ECOL**

PROGRESS REPORT ON WATER POLLUTION CONTROL JULY 1967 THROUGH DECEMBER 1968.
Minnesota. Pollution Control Agency. 1968. **fTD224.M6A532 ECOL**

PROJECTED WASTEWATER TREATMENT COSTS IN THE ORGANIC CHEMICALS INDUSTRY (UPDATED).
Datagraphics Incorporated. 1971. **fTD899.C5D388 ECOL**

PROJECTS OF THE NATIONAL WATER QUALITY CONTROL RESEARCH PROGRAM.
United States. Environmental Protection Agency. Office of Research and Monitoring. 1971. **fTD423.U546 ECOL**

PROPERTY POWER.
Guitar, Mary Anne. 1st ed. 1972. **HD205 1972 .G8 ECOL**

PROPOSAL TO THE STATE OF MINNESOTA POLLUTION CONTROL AGENCY: HIGHLIGHTS OF IMPLEMENTATION PLAN FOR SULFUR DIOXIDE, PARTICULATES, CARBON MONOXIDE, HYDROCARBONS, NITROGEN OXIDES, PHOTOCHEMICAL OXIDANT.
TRC—The Research Corporation of New England. 1971. **Ref fTD883.5.M6T15 ECOL**

PROPOSALS FOR PRESERVING A METROPOLITAN OPEN SPACE.
Minnesota. Metropolitan Council of the Twin Cities Area. Open Space Advisory Committee. 1969 **fHD1291.U6T9 ECOL**

PROPOSED VOYAGEURS NATIONAL PARK, MINNESOTA.
United States. National Park Service. 1964. **fF612.V6A54 ECOL**

PROSPECTS FOR METROPOLITAN WATER MANAGEMENT.
McPherson, Murray Burns. 1970. **fTD353.M32 ECOL**

PROSPECTS OF THE WORLD FOOD SUPPLY.
1966. **fS439.P7 1966 ECOL**

PROTECT THE EARTH.
Parkinson, Thomas Francis. 1970. **PS3566.A69P7 ECOL**

THE PROTECTED OCEAN.
Marx, Wesley. 1972. **GC1018.M32 ECOL**

PROTECTING OUR ENVIRONMENT.
McClellan, Grant S. 1970. **TD180.M3 ECOL**

PROTECTING THE MINNESOTA ENVIRONMENT THROUGH REGULATION OF PRIVATE LAND USE.
Minnesota. State Planning Agency. 1972. **fHC107.M6A45 ECOL**

PUBLIC ACCESS TO RESERVOIRS TO MEET GROWING RECREATION DEMANDS.
United States. Congress. House. Committee on Government Operations. Conservation and Natural Resources Subcommittee. 1971. **KF27.G636 1971 ECOL**

PUBLIC DOCUMENTS OF MASSACHUSETTS, V. 5 NO. 30.
Kirkwood, James Pugh. A special report on the pollution of river waters. Reprint ed. 1970 **REF TD425.K52 1970 ECOL**

PUBLIC HEARINGS ON NOISE ABATEMENT AND CONTROL.
United States. Office of Noise Abatement and Control. 1972- **TD893.A52 ECOL**

PUBLIC LAND MANAGEMENT—A TIME FOR CHANGE?
Stanford Environmental Law Society. 1971- **fHD216.S7 ECOL**

THE PUBLIC LANDS.
Carstensen, Vernon Rosco. General ed. 1968,c1962 **HD216.C3 1968 ECOL**

PUBLIC PARTICIPATION IN ENVIRONMENTAL DECISION-MAKING.
Draper, Dianne. 1973. **fZ5863.P6D7 ECOL**

PUBLIC POLICY ISSUED IN RESOURCE MANAGEMENT [V.3].
Weather modification. 1969 **QC928.W38 ECOL**

PUBLIC UTILITIES AND THE NATIONAL POWER POLICIES.
Bonbright, James Cummings. 1972, c1940 **HD2766.B57 1972**

PUBLICATION NO. AP-112.
Benson, Ferris B. Indoor-outdoor air pollution relationships: a literature review. 1972. **TD890.B4 ECOL**

P (cont.)

PUBLICATION OF AMERICAN ASSOCIATION FOR THE ADVANCEMENT OF SCIENCE, NO. 80.
American Association for the Advancement of Science. Committee on Science in the Promotion of Human Welfare. Air Conservation Commission. Air conservation; ... report. 1965. **TD883.2.A65 ECOL**

PUBLICATIONS OF THE GEOLOGICAL SURVEY, 1879-1961.
United States. Geological Survey 1964 **REF Z6034.U49U53 ECOL**

PUBLICATIONS OF THE MINNESOTA HISTORICAL SOCIETY.
Davis, Edward Wilson. Pioneering with taconite. 1964. **TN403.M6D3 ECOL**

PUBLICATIONS RELATED TO WATER RESOURCES RESEARCH CENTER PROJECTS, 1965-71 ABSTRACT-INDEX.
Minnesota. University. Water Resources Research Center. 1971. **GB701.M554no.32 ECOL**

PUFFIN ISLAND.
Graham, Ada. 1st ed. 1971 **QL676.G68 1971 ECOL**

THE PULSE OF THE PLANET.
Smithsonian Institution. Center for Shortlived Phenomena. c1972 **fQ225.P8 ECOL**

PURDUE UNIVERSITY, LAFAYETTE, IND. WATER RESOURCES RESEARCH CENTER. TECHNICAL REPORT, NO.25.
Whinston, A. B. Economic analyses of optimal water quality management. 1972. **fTD365.W4 ECOL**

PURITY OR POLLUTION.
Rondiere, Pierre. 1st ed. 1971 **TD348.R65 ECOL**

THE PURSUIT OF WILDERNESS.
Brooks, Paul. 1971. **QH75.B73 ECOL**

PUSH AND PULL.
Blackwood, Paul Everett. Rev. ed. 1966 **TJ147.B52 1966 ECOL**

PYRITIC SYSTEMS: A MATHEMATICAL MODEL.
Morth, Arthur H. 1972. **TD899.M5M6 ECOL**

Q

QUALITY OF THE ENVIRONMENT: AN ECONOMIC APPROACH TO SOME PROBLEMS IN USING LAND, WATER, AND AIR.
Herfindahl, Orris Clemens. 1965 **TD153.H46 ECOL**

THE QUALITY OF THE URBAN ENVIRONMENT.
1969 **HT169.U5Q33 ECOL**

QUANTITATIVE ECOLOGICAL ANALYSIS IN THE SOCIAL SCIENCES.
Dogan, Mattei. 1969 **HM206.D6 ECOL**

QUANTITATIVE METHODS FOR PRELIMINARY DESIGN OF WATER QUALITY SURVEILLANCE SYSTEMS.
Beckers, Charles V. 1972. **TD365.B4 ECOL**

THE QUEST FOR ENVIRONMENTAL QUALITY.
United States. Advisory Commission on Intergovernmental Relations. 1971. **HC110.E5A41 ECOL**

QUEST FOR QUALITY.
United States. Dept. of the Interior. 1965 **fS930.A5 ECOL**

A QUESTION OF PRIORITIES.
Higbee, Edward Counselman. 1970. **HN65.H5 ECOL**

THE QUIET CRISIS.
Udall, Stewart L. 1st ed. 1963 **S930.U3**

THE QUIET REVOLUTION: GRASS ROOTS OF TODAY'S WILDERNESS PRESERVATION MOVEMENT.
Baldwin, Donald N. 1st ed. c1972 **QH76.B35 ECOL**

R

THE RACE FOR ELECTRIC POWER.
Grey, Jerry. 1972 **TK1001.G73 ECOL**

RADIATION PRESERVATION OF FOODS.
1965. **TX611.R28 ECOL**

RADIOACTIVE WASTES.
Fox, Charles H. c1965 **TD898.F6 ECOL**
Fox, Charles H. Rev. 1969. **TD898.F6 1969 ECOL**

RADIOISOTOPES IN INDUSTRY.
Baker, Philip Schaffner. c1965 **TK9400.B3 ECOL**

RAIN, RIVERS, AND RESERVOIRS.
Archer, Sellers Gambrell. c1968,c1963 **GB671.A7 ECOL**

RAINFALL AND TREE GROWTH IN THE GREAT BASIN...
Antevs, Ernst. 1938. **QC925.1.U35 1938 ECOL**

THE RALPH NADER STUDY GROUP REPORT ON FOOD PROTECTION AND THE FOOD AND DRUG ADMINISTRATION.
Turner, James S. The chemical feast. 1970. **HD9000.9.U5T83 ECOL**

RALPH NADER'S STUDY GROUP REPORT ON WATER POLLUTION.
Zwick, David. Water wasteland. 1971. **TD223.Z86 1971 ECOL**

THE RANGE OF CHOICE IN WATER MANAGEMENT.
Davis, Robert K. 1968 **TD225.P74D3 ECOL**

RAPE OF THE AMERICAN VIRGINS.
O'Neill, Edward A. 1972 **HC157.V6O5 ECOL**

RAPID DETECTION SYSTEM FOR ORGANOPHOSPHATES AND CARBAMATE INSECTICES IN WATER.
Midwest Research Institute, Kansas City, Mo. 1972. **TD427.P35M5 ECOL**

RARE AND ENDANGERED FISH AND WILDLIFE OF THE UNITED STATES.
United States. Committee on Rare and Endangered Wildlife Species. Rev. ed. 1968 i.e. 1969 **S914.A3no.34 1969 ECOL**

READING THE WOODS.
Brown, Vinson. 1969 **QH541.5.F6B73 ECOL**

READING WISCONSIN'S LANDSCAPE.
2d ed. 1962, reprinted 1966. **fS946.R4 1966 ECOL**

READINGS IN AGRICULTURAL POLICY.
National Agricultural Policy Conference. 1968 **HD1761.N25 ECOL**

READINGS IN AQUATIC ECOLOGY.
Ford, Richard F. 1972. **QH541.5.W3F67 ECOL**

READINGS IN CONSERVATION ECOLOGY.
Cox, George W. 1969 **S942.C6 ECOL**

READINGS IN ECOLOGY AND ECOLOGICAL GENETICS.
Connell, Joseph H. 1970 **QH541.C65 ECOL**

READINGS IN RESOURCE MANAGEMENT AND CONSERVATION.
Burton, Ian. 1970,c1965 **S938.B86 ECOL**

READINGS ON ECOLOGICAL SYSTEMS: THEIR FUNCTION AND RELATION TO MAN.
Lugo, Ariel E. c1971 **QH540.3.L8 ECOL**

THE REALITIES OF RECYCLING.
Burke, Jacquelyn M. 1973 **REF fTP995.B8 ECOL**

REASON AWAKE: SCIENCE FOR MAN.
Dubos, Rene Jules. 1970. **Q125.D814 ECOL**

RECENT DEVELOPMENTS IN ENVIRONMENTAL LAW. MARCH 1971-
Boston College industrial and commercial law review. **KF3775.A75B6 ECOL**

RECENT DEVELOPMENTS IN INDUSTRIAL POLLUTION CONTROL.
North Eastern Regional Antipollution Conference, 4th, University of Rhode Island, 1971. 1971 **fTD896.N67 1971 ECOL**

RECHARGE FROM INDUCED STREAMBED INFILTRATION UNDER VARYING GROUNDWATER-LEVEL AND STREAM-STAGE CONDITIONS.
Walton, William Clarence. 1967. **GB701.M554no.6 ECOL**

RECLAIMING THE EARTH.
Paradis, Adrian A. 1971 **TA170.P37 ECOL**

RECOGNITION OF AIR POLLUTION INJURY TO VEGETATION: A PICTORIAL ATLAS.
Jacobson, Jay S. 1970. **fQK751.J3 ECOL**

RECOMMENDED METHODS FOR WATER DATA ACQUISITION.
Federal Interagency Work Group on Designation of Standards for Water Data Acquisition. 1972. **TD211.F44 ECOL**

RECONVENING OF SECOND SESSIONS.
Conference in the Matter of Pollution of Lake Superior and its Tributary Basin in the States of Minnesota, Wisconsin, and Michigan, 2d session, Duluth, Aug. 12-13, 1970. 1971 **fTD223.3.C59 1970b ECOL**

RECONVENING OF THE 3RD SESSION; PROCEEDINGS.
Conference in the Matter of Pollution of Lake Michigan and its Tributary Basin in the States of Wisconsin, Illinois, Indiana, and Michigan, 3rd, Chicago, Mar. 23-25, 1971. 1971- **fTD223.3.C595 1971 ECOL**

RECOVERY AND UTILIZATION OF MUNICIPAL SOLID WASTE: A SUMMARY OF AVAILABLE COST AND PERFORMANCE CHARACTERISTICS OF UNIT PROCESSES AND SYSTEMS.
Drobny, N. L. 1971. **TD793.D76 ECOL**

RECOVERY OF FLOATING OIL ROTATING DISK TYPE SKIMMER.
Susquehanna Corporation. Atlantic Research Systems Division. Marine Systems. 1971. **fTD427.P4S9 ECOL**

RECREATION.
Foss, Phillip O. 1971. **REF GV53.F6 ECOL**

RECREATIONAL USE OF WILD LANDS.
Brockman, Christian Frank. 1959. **SB481.B66 ECOL**

RECYCLE THIS BOOK!
Allan, J. David. 1972 **GF8.A4 ECOL**

RECYCLING AND RE-USE: THE FUTURE OF SOLID WASTE.
Gunter, John D. 1973. **Ref fTP156.R38G8 ECOL**

RED SALMON, BROWN BEAR.
Walker, Theodore J. 1971 **QH105.A4W36 ECOL**

REDOING AMERICA.
Faltermayer, Edmund K. 1968 **HT123.F3 ECOL**

REDUCTION OF SALT CONTENT OF FOOD PROCESSING LIQUID WASTE EFFLUENT.
National Canners Association. Western Research Laboratory. 1971. **fTD899.C3N36 ECOL**

REFERENCE SHELF V. 42, NO. 1.
McClellan, Grant S. Protecting our environment. 1970. **TD180.M3 ECOL**

THE REFERENCE SHELF, V. 38, NO. 6.
Nikolaieff, George A. The water crisis. 1967. **TD355.N5 ECOL**

REFERENCES AND RESOURCE GUIDES FOR THE UNIVERSITY OF MINNESOTA SEED PROJECT CURRICULA.
Minnesota. University. n.d. **fQH541.2.M5 ECOL**

REFUSE DISPOSAL.
Great Britain. Working Party on Refuse Disposal. 1971. **TD557.A53 ECOL**

REGENERATION PROCEDURE FOR GRANULAR ACTIVATED CARBON.
Mine Safety Appliances Research Corporation. Optimization of the regeneration procedure for granular activated carbon. 1970. **fTP245.C4M55 ECOL**

REGIONAL DEVELOPMENT ACT OF 1969.
Minnesota. State Planning Agency. Office of Local and Urban Affairs. Regional planning and development in Minnesota—a handbook on Executive order no. 37 and the Regional Development Act of 1969. 1969. **REF JK6131 1969 .A55 ECOL**

REGIONAL PLANNING AND DEVELOPMENT IN MINNESOTA—A HANDBOOK ON EXECUTIVE ORDER NO. 37 AND THE REGIONAL DEVELOPMENT ACT OF 1969.
Minnesota. State Planning Agency. Office of Local and Urban Affairs. 1969. **REF JK6131 1969 .A55 ECOL**

REGIONAL TRANSIT FOR MINNEAPOLIS: INTERIM REPORT.
Minneapolis. Office of the City Coordinator. 1972. **fHE4491.M62 1972 ECOL**

REGIONS, RESOURCES, AND ECONOMIC GROWTH.
Resources for the Future. 1967,c1960 **HC103.R45 1967 ECOL**

REGULATING FLOOD-PLAIN DEVELOPMENT.
Murphy, Francis C. 1958. **TC530.M8 ECOL**

REGULATION OF FLOOD HAZARD AREAS TO REDUCE FLOOD LOSSES.
United States. Water Resources Council. 1971- **KF5588.A875 ECOL**

REGULATION OF GREAT LAKES WATER LEVELS: INTERIM REPORT ON LAKES SUPERIOR AND ONTARIO REGULATION, TO THE INTERNATIONAL JOINT COMMISSION BY THE INTERNATIONAL GREAT LAKES LEVELS BOARD.
International Great Lakes Levels Board. 1973. **fGB1627.G8152 ECOL**

REGULATION OF THE NATURAL GAS PRODUCING INDUSTRY.
1972 **HD9581.U5R45 ECOL**

THE REITH LECTURES, 1969.
Darling, Frank Fraser. Wilderness and plenty. 1970. **QH541.13.D36 ECOL**

REMOTE SENSING IN ECOLOGY.
1969 **QH541.15.R4R4 ECOL**

REMOVAL OF NITRATE BY AN ALGAL SYSTEM, PHASE II.
California. Dept. of Water Resources. 1971.
fTD475.C342 ECOL

RENOVATED WASTE WATER.
Johnson, James Francis. 1971. TD429.J6 ECOL

RENOVATING SECONDARY SEWAGE BY GROUND WATER RECHARGE WITH INFILTRATION BASINS.
Bouwer, Herman. 1972. fTD765.B6 ECOL

A REPORT FROM RALPH NADER'S CENTER FOR STUDY OF RESPONSIVE LAW
Wellford, Harrison. Sowing the wind. 1972.
HD9000.9.U5W4 ECOL

REPORT ON A COMPREHENSIVE SEWAGE WORKS PLAN FOR THE MINNEAPOLIS-ST. PAUL METROPOLITAN AREA, DEC. 1964.
Minnesota. Water Pollution Control Commission. 1965 fTD525.T8M6 ECOL

REPORT ON ABANDONMENT AND TRANSFER OF OWNERSHIP OF DAMS.
Harza Engineering Company. 1971.
fTC557.M6H3 ECOL

REPORT ON APPLICATION FOR WASTE DISPOSAL PERMIT.
Minnesota. Dept. of Health. Division of Environmental Health. Section of Water Pollution Control. 1965. fTK1331.N6M6 ECOL

REPORT ON INVESTIGATION OF POLLUTION OF THE NORTHERN BORDER WATERS FROM THE MOUTH OF THE PIGEON RIVER AT LAKE SUPERIOR WESTWARD THROUGH THE BOUNDARY WATERS CANOE AREA AND LOWER LAKES TO THE OUTLET OF RAINY LAKE.
Minnesota. Division of Water Quality. 1969
fTD224.M6A5 ECOL

A REPORT ON POLLUTION OF THE UPPER MISSISSIPPI RIVER AND MAJOR TRIBUTARIES.
United States. Federal Water Pollution Control Administration. Great Lakes Region. 1966.
TD225.M5U5 ECOL

REPORT ON PROGRESS—WATER POLLUTION CONTROL, JAN. 1, 1965 TO DEC. 31, 1966.
Minnesota. Water Pollution Control Commission. 1967 fTD224.M6A562 ECOL

REPORT ON PROGRESS - WATER POLLUTION CONTROL, JULY 1, 1963 TO DEC. 31, 1964.
Minnesota. Water Pollution Control Commission. 1965? fTD224.M6A561 ECOL

REPORT ON REDUCING UNTREATED COMBINED WASTEWATER OVERFLOWS TO THE ST. CROIX RIVER.
Bannister Engineering Co., St. Paul, Minn. 1970.
fTD525.S7B3 ECOL

REPORT ON SANITARY SEWERAGE FACILITIES AIRLAKE INDUSTRIAL PARK FOR LAKEVILLE, MINNESOTA.
Bonestroo, Rosene, Anderlik and Associates, inc., St. Paul, Minn. 1967. fTD525.L3B6 ECOL

A REPORT ON SOLID WASTE MANAGEMENT/RECYCLING OPTIONS.
Minnesota. University. Consortium for the Study of Solid Waste Management/Recycling Options. 1972.
fTD793.M6 ECOL

REPORT ON THE EXPANSION OF THE SEWAGE TREATMENT PLANT.
Toltz, King, Duvall, Anderson and Associates, Inc., St. Paul. 1969. fTD525.T9T6 ECOL

REPORT ON THE FIRST SIERRA CLUB POWER CONFERENCE [PAPERS].
Sierra Club Conference on the Electric Power Industry, 1st, Johnson City, Vt., 1972. 1972?
fHD9685.A2S5 1972 ECOL

REPORT ON THE MUNICIPAL WATER SUPPLY, TREATMENT, STORAGE, AND DISTRIBUTION SYSTEM, CITY OF WACONIA, MINNESOTA.
Schoell and Madson, Inc., Hopkins, Minn. 1967.
fTD225.W3S3 ECOL

REPORT ON WATER QUALITY INVESTIGATIONS OF THE MISSISSIPPI, MINNESOTA AND ST. CROIX RIVERS.
United States. Federal Water Pollution Control Administration. Twin Cities Upper Mississippi River Project. 1966 REF fTD225.T9U5 ECOL

REPORT ON 2, 4, 5-T.
United States. President's Science Advisory Committee. 1971. SB612.A2A52 ECOL

REPORT TO THE BOARD OF MANAGERS, NINE MILE CREEK WATERSHED DISTRICT.
Barr Engineering Co. fTC424.M6B3 ECOL

REPORT TO THE PRESIDENT AND TO THE COUNCIL ON ENVIRONMENTAL QUALITY.
United States. Citizens' Advisory Committee on Environmental Quality. 1971.
HC110.E5A514 ECOL

REPORTS AND PAPERS IN THE SOCIAL SCIENCES, NO. 25.
Clubb, Jerome M. Ecological data in comparative research. 1970 H62.C6 ECOL

RESEARCH AND DEVELOPMENT CORPORATION. RADCO COLLECTIONS.
Environmental law. 1971, c1970
KF3775.A75E55 ECOL

RESEARCH NEEDS FOR IRRIGATION RETURN FLOW QUALITY CONTROL.
Skogerboe, Gaylord V. 1971 i.e. 1972
fTD223.S54 ECOL

RESEARCH NEEDS ON WASTE HEAT TRANSFER FROM LARGE SOURCES INTO THE ENVIRONMENT.
Illinois. Water Survey. 1971. fTD427.H414 ECOL

RESEARCH ON THE PHYSICAL ASPECTS OF THERMAL POLLUTION.
Cornell Aeronautical Laboratory, Inc., Buffalo. 1971. fTD427.H4C67 ECOL

RESEARCH PROGRAMS ON RECYCLING AND DISPOSAL OF MINERAL-, METAL-, AND ENERGY-BASED WASTES.
Kenahan, Charles B. Bureau of Mines research programs on recycling and disposal of mineral-, metal- and energy-based wastes. 1973.
TN23.U7no.8595 ECOL

A RESEARCH PROGRESS REPORT ON THE EFFECTS OF STUDDED TIRES.
Minnesota. Dept. of Highways. 1970.
fTL270.M5 1970 ECOL

RESEARCH REACTORS.
Martens, Frederick Hilbert. 1965
QC787.N8M32 ECOL

RESEARCH REPORT OF THE NATIONAL AUDUBON SOCIETY, NO.3.
Allen, Robert Porter. The whooping crane. 1952.
QL696.G8A43 ECOL

RESEARCH REVIEW SERIES—ENVIRONMENTAL EDUCATION, PAPER 1.
Roth, Robert E. A review of research related to environmental education. 1972. QH541.2.R6 ECOL

A RESEARCH SUMMARY REPORT ON THE EFFECTS OF STUDDED TIRES.
Minnesota. Dept. of Highways. 1971.
fTL270.M5 1971 ECOL

RESEARCH SUPPLEMENT TO JOURNAL WATER POLLUTION CONTROL FEDERATION.
Water Pollution Control Federation. 1971.
fTD423.W3 ECOL

RESIDENTIAL WATER DEMAND.
Grima, Angelo P. 1972 TD353.G7 ECOL

RESOURCE CONSERVATION AND DEVELOPMENT PROJECTS: HANDBOOK.
United States. Soil Conservation Service. 1972
S914.A57 1972 ECOL

RESOURCE MANAGEMENT IN THE GREAT LAKES BASIN.
1971 HD1694.A2 1971 ECOL

RESOURCE RECOVERY.
Midwest Research Institute, Kansas City, Missouri. 1973. fTP995.M5 ECOL

RESOURCE RECOVERY: INDUSTRY'S APPROACH.
Western Regional Conference on Resource Recovery: Industry's Approach, University of Southern California, 1972. 1972. fTP995.A1W4 1972 ECOL

RESOURCES AND MAN.
National Research Council. Committee on Resources and Man. 1969 HC68.N36 ECOL

RESOURCES IN AMERICA'S FUTURE.
Resources for the Future. 1963
HC106.5.R48 ECOL

RESPONSES OF PLANTS TO ENVIRONMENTAL STRESSES.
Levitt, Jacob. 1972. QK754.L42 ECOL

RESPONSES OF TELEOST FISH TO ENVIRONMENTAL STRESS.
Washington (State). University. Fisheries Research Institute. 1971. fQL639.1.W3 ECOL

THE RESTLESS EARTH: A REPORT ON THE NEW GEOLOGY.
Calder, Nigel. 1972 QE26.2.C34 ECOL

RESTORATION OF BEACHES CONTAMINATED BY OIL.
Gumtz, Garth D. 1972. TD427.P4G8 ECOL

REUSE AND RECYCLE OF WASTES; PROCEEDINGS.
North Eastern Regional Antipollution Conference, 3d, University of Rhode Island, 1970. 1971
fTP995.A1N6 1970 ECOL

REVEGETATION AUGMENTATION BY REUSE OF TREATED ACTIVE SURFACE MINE DRAINAGE.
Zaval, Frank J. 1972. TD899.M5Z3 ECOL

REVERSE OSMOSIS CONCENTRATION OF DILUTE PULP AND PAPER EFFLUENTS.
Wiley, Averill J. 1972. TD899.W65W5 ECOL

REVERSE OSMOSIS RENOVATION OF MUNICIPAL WASTEWATER.
Aerojet-General Corporation. Environmental Systems Division. 1970 fTD754.A35 ECOL

REVERSE OSMOSIS RENOVATION OF PRIMARY SEWAGE.
Envirogenics Company. 1971. fTD754.E58 ECOL

REVIEW AND ANALYSIS OF RAINFALL AND RUNOFF DATA FOR SELECTED WATERSHEDS IN MINNESOTA.
Bowers, C. Edward. 1968.
GB701.M554no.8 ECOL

REVIEW OF BUREAU OF MINES ENERGY PROGRAM, 1970.
Linville, Bill. 1971 TN295.U4no.8526 ECOL

REVIEW OF ORGANIC IODIDE FORMATION UNDER ACCIDENT CONDITIONS IN WATER-COOLED REACTORS.
Postma, Arlin Keith. 1972. fTK9152.P6 ECOL

A REVIEW OF RESEARCH RELATED TO ENVIRONMENTAL EDUCATION.
Roth, Robert E. 1972. QH541.2.R6 ECOL

REVIEW. 1965/66-
Canada. Fisheries Research Board.
SH223.C3 ECOL

RICH LAND, POOR LAND.
Chase, Stuart. 1969 S930.C5 1969 ECOL

RIPRAP STABILITY ON EARTH EMBANKMENTS TESTED IN LARGE—AND SMALL-SCALE WAVE TANKS.
Thomsen, Arvid L. 1972. TC533.T4 ECOL

RIVER BASIN DEVELOPMENT.
1957. HN64.R589 ECOL

THE RIVER BASIN MODEL.
Envirometrics, Inc., Wash., D.C. 1971-
fTC409.E5 ECOL

THE RIVER BASIN MODEL: COMPUTER OUTPUT.
Envirometrics, Inc., Wash., D.C. 1971.
fTC409.E51 ECOL

THE RIVER BASIN MODEL: MUNICIPAL SERVICES DEPARTMENT.
Envirometrics, Inc., Wash., D.C. 1971.
fTC409.E5 ECOL

RIVER ECOLOGY AND MAN.
International Symposium on River Ecology and the Impact of Man, University of Massachusetts, 1971. 1972. GB1205.I5 1971 ECOL

RIVERS AND WATERSHEDS IN AMERICA'S FUTURE.
Helfman, Elizabeth S. 1965. TC423.H45 ECOL

RIVERS OF AMERICA.
Dunn, James Taylor. The St. Croix: Midwest border river. 1965 F612.S2D78 ECOL

ROAD TO RUIN.
Mowbray, A. Q. 1969 HE355.M66 ECOL

ROADLESS AREA.
Brooks, Paul. 1971,c1964. QH75.B74 ECOL

ROCKS AND MINERALS AND THE STORIES THEY TELL.
Adler, Irving. 1956. QE432.A35 ECOL

ROLE OF ANIMAL WASTES IN AGRICULTURAL LAND RUNOFF.
North Carolina. State University, Raleigh. Dept. of Biological and Agricultural Engineering. 1971.
fTD930.N67 ECOL

ROLE OF BACTERIA IN THE NITROGEN CYCLE IN LAKES.
McCoy, Elizabeth F. 1972. fTD433.M3 ECOL

THE ROLE OF NONPACKAGING PAPER IN SOLID WASTE MANAGEMENT, 1966 TO 1976.
Franklin, William E. 1971. TD795.F7 ECOL

THE ROLE OF PACKAGING IN SOLID WASTE
MANAGEMENT 1966 TO 1976.
Darnay, Arsen. 1969.　　　TD795.D37 ECOL

ROLE OF PHOSPHORUS IN
EUTROPHICATION.
Bartsch, A. F. 1972.　　　QH96.8.E9B3 ECOL

THE ROLE OF SLUDGE WORMS IN
EUTROPHICATION.
Brinkhurst, Ralph O. 1972.　　　QH96.8.E9B7 ECOL

THE ROLE OF THE STATE LEGISLATURE IN
AIR POLLUTION ABATEMENT.
Zimmerman, Joseph Francis. n.d.
　　　fKF3812.Z9Z5 ECOL

THE ROMANCE OF THE NEWFOUNDLAND
CARIBOU.
Dugmore, Arthur Radclyffe. 1913.
　　　fQL737.U5D8 ECOL

ROOKERY BAY AREA PROJECT.
Conservation Foundation. 1968.
　　　QH77.U6C66 ECOL

THE ROOTS OF MANKIND.
Napier, John Russell. 1970.　　　QH368.N36 ECOL

RUBBER REUSE AND SOLID WASTE
MANAGEMENT.
United States. Environmental Protection Agency.
1971-　　　TD899.R8U55 ECOL

RUNES OF THE NORTH.
Olson, Sigurd F. 1969, c1963　　　F1060.A204 ECOL

RUNNING WATER.
Stecher, Adam. c1971　　　QH541.2.S8 ECOL

RURAL ENVIRONMENTAL ASSISTANCE
PROGRAM: SUMMARY. 1971-
United States. Agricultural Stabilization and
Conservation Service. 1972-　　　S954.U6A3 ECOL

S

SAFEGUARDS DICTIONARY.
United States. Brookhaven National Laboratory.
Upton, N.Y. Technical Support Organization. 1971.
　　　JX1974.7.U5 ECOL

SAFETY MANUAL FOR USE OF OPERATORS
DEALING WITH RADIOGRAPHY AND
INDUSTRIAL GAMMAGRAPHY.
United States. Atomic Energy Commission. Division
of Technical Information. 1968?
　　　TA417.25.U5 ECOL

SAGA OF THE WATERFOWL.
Bovey, Martin Koon. 1949.
　　　REF SK331.B6 ECOL

THE ST. CROIX: MIDWEST BORDER RIVER.
Dunn, James Taylor. 1965　　　F612.S2D78 ECOL

SALMON AND TROUT: A RESOURCE, ITS
ECOLOGY, CONSERVATION, AND
MANAGEMENT.
Mills, Derek Henry. 1971
　　　QL638.S2M5 1971b ECOL

SALVAGE MARKETS FOR MATERIALS IN
SOLID WASTES, ...
Darnay, Arsen. 1972.　　　TD795.D38 ECOL

SAND AND GRAVEL OVERLAY FOR
CONTROL OF MERCURY IN SEDIMENTS.
Bongers, Leonard H. 1972.　　fTD427.M4B6 ECOL

A SAND COUNTY ALMANAC.
Leopold, Aldo. Enl. ed. 1966.
　　　QH81.L56 1966 ECOL

SANE LIVING IN A MAD WORLD.
Rodale, Robert. 1972　　　RA776.5.R57 ECOL

SANITARY LANDFILL DESIGN AND
OPERATION.
Brunner, Dirk R. 1972.　　　TD795.7.B7 ECOL

SANITARY LANDFILLS.
Water Resources Scientific Information Center.
1972　　　REF Z5853.S22W38 ECOL

SANITARY SEWER STUDY FOR THE VILLAGE
OF MAPLE GROVE, MINNESOTA.
Caswell and Associates, inc., Osseo, Minn. The
comprehensive sanitary sewer study for the Village of
Maple Grove, Minnesota. 1969.
　　　fTD525.M28C3 ECOL

SANITARY SEWERAGE FACILITIES AIRLAKE
INDUSTRIAL PARK FOR LAKEVILLE,
MINNESOTA.
Bonestroo, Rosene, Anderlik and Associates, inc., St.
Paul, Minn. Report on sanitary sewerage facilities
Airlake Industrial Park for Lakeville, Minnesota. 1967.
　　　fTD525.L3B6 ECOL

SANITATION INDUSTRY YEAR BOOK. 9 ED.
1972-
　　　REF fTD791.S3 ECOL

SANTA BARBARA OIL SPILL: SHORT-TERM
ANALYSIS OF MACROPLANKTON AND
FISH.
California. University, Santa Barbara. Dept. of
Biological Sciences. 1971.　　fTD427.P4C34 ECOL

SAVAGE LUXURY: THE SLAUGHTER OF THE
BABY SEALS.
Davies, Brian. 1971,c1970
　　　QL737.P6D33 1971 ECOL

SAVE OUR EARTH.
Masini, Giancarlo. S.O.S. save our earth. c1972
　　　fQH541.M382 1972 ECOL

SAVING OUR WILDLIFE.
McCoy, Joseph J. 1970　　　S962.M3 ECOL

SAY NO!
Adams, Ruth. 1971　　　HC110.E5A63 ECOL

SCARCITY AND GROWTH.
Barnett, Harold J. 1963　　　HC55.B3 ECOL

THE SCHOOL SITE IN ENVIRONMENTAL
EDUCATION.
MacGown, Richard H. Rev. ed. 1972.
　　　fLB3220.M3 1972 ECOL

SCIENCE AND ETHICAL VALUES.
Glass, Hiram Bentley. 1965　　Q175.G58 ECOL

SCIENCE AND SOCIETY.
Madison. Wis. Board of Education. Dept. of
Curriculum Development. 1969.
　　　REF fQ181.M3 ECOL

SCIENCE AND SURVIVAL.
Commoner, Barry. c1966　　　Q125.C56 ECOL

SCIENCE AND THE FUTURE OF MAN.
c1970　　　CB151.S37 ECOL

SCIENCE, CONFLICT, AND SOCIETY.
1969　　　fQ125.S434 ECOL

SCIENCE, ENGINEERING, AND THE CITY.
1967.　　　HT166.S32 ECOL

SCIENCE FOR SOCIETY: A BIBLIOGRAPHY.
Bausum, Howard T. 3d ed. 1972.
　　　fZ7401.B3 1972 ECOL

SCIENCE IN YOUR OWN BACK YARD.
Cooper, Elizabeth K. 1970
　　　QH81.C75 1970 ECOL

SCIENCE PROJECTS IN ECOLOGY.
Simon, Seymour. 1972　　　QH541.14.S55 ECOL

SCIENCE REFERENCE SOURCES.
Jenkins, Frances Briggs. 5th ed. 1969
　　　REF Z7401.J4 1969 ECOL

SCIENCE STUDY SERIES, S46.
Battan, Louis J. The unclean sky. 1966.
　　　TD883.B3 ECOL

SCIENCE TEACHERS HANDBOOK.
n.d.　　　fQ181.S3 ECOL

SCIENCE, TECHNOLOGY, AND SOCIETY.
Nelkin, Dorothy. Nuclear power and its critics.
1971　　　TK1344.N7N4 ECOL

SCIENTIFIC ALLOCATION OF WATER
RESOURCES.
Buras, Nathan. 1972　　　TC409.B87 ECOL

SCIENTIFIC ASPECTS OF PEST CONTROL.
1966.　　　SB951.S38 ECOL

SCIENTIFIC EXPERIMENTS IN
ENVIRONMENTAL POLLUTION.
Weaver, Elbert C. 1968　　TD178.5.W4 ECOL

SCIENTISTS' INSTITUTE FOR PUBLIC
INFORMATION. A WORKBOOK.
Abrahamson, Dean E. Environmental cost of
electric power. 1970　　　fTK1005.A26 ECOL

Air pollution. 1970　　　fTD883.A47 ECOL

Berg, George G. Water pollution. 1970
　　　fTD420.B46 ECOL

Environmental education 1970. 1970
　　　fS946.E55 ECOL

Environmental effects of weapons technology. 1970
　　　fUG447.8.E57 ECOL

Mead, Margaret. Hunger. 1970
　　　fHD9000.5.M37 ECOL

Nuclear explosives in peacetime. 1970
　　　fQC792.N8 ECOL

Pesticides. 1970　　　fQH545.P4P48 ECOL

SCOOP, LAST OF THE BROWN PELICANS.
McClung, Robert M. 1972.　PZ10.M115Sb ECOL

THE SEA AROUND US.
Carson, Rachel Louise. Rev. ed. 1961.
　　　GC21.C3•1961 ECOL

SECOND MEETING SECOND SESSION
(RECONVENED).
Conference in the Matter of Pollution of Lake
Superior and its Tributary Basin in the States of
Minnesota, Wisconsin, and Michigan, 2nd, Duluth, Jan.
14-15, 1971. 1971.　　fTD223.3.C59 1971 ECOL

SECONDARY ENVIRONMENTAL EDUCATION
DEVELOPMENT.
Colwell, Jim. World view. 1971. GF75.C6 ECOL
Fitch, Steven Val. Air. 1971.　TD883.F5 ECOL
Kriett, Jolene. Biocides. 1971.
　　　QH545.P4K7 ECOL
Krznarich, Susan. Basic ecology. 1971.
　　　QH541.2.K7 ECOL
Minnesota. University. References and resource
guides for the University of Minnesota SEED Project
curricula. n.d.　　　fQH541.2.M5 ECOL
Peterson, Roger A. Transportation and the
environment. 1971.　　HE192.A1P4 ECOL
Phelps, Pat. Water problems. 1971.
　　　TD420.P4 ECOL
Shadduck, Gregg. Energy. 1971.
　　　HD9545.S5 ECOL
Thornsjo, Mark. Planning. 1971.
　　　HT166.T5 ECOL

THE SECRET LIFE OF THE FOREST.
Ketchum, Richard M. 1970　fQK938.F6K4 ECOL

SECURING A QUALITY ENVIRONMENT IN
MINNESOTA.
Minnesota. Governor, 1971-　1973?
　　　REF fHC107.M6A35 ECOL

SEE THROUGH THE LAKE.
Selsam, Millicent (Ellis). 1958
　　　PZ10.S44Sdi ECOL

SEEDS OF CHANGE.
Brown, Lester Russell. 1970
　　　HD9000.5.B73 ECOL

A SELECTED ANNOTATED BIBLIOGRAPHY
OF THE CLIMATE OF THE GREAT LAKES.
Hacia, Henry. 1972.　REF Z6683.C5H33 ECOL

A SELECTED BIBLIOGRAPHY ON THE
RELEVANCE OF ENVIRONMENTAL
EDUCATION TO SECONDARY SCHOOL
CURRICULA.
Cunningham, Michael C. 1972
　　　REF fQH541.2.C8 ECOL

A SELECTED BIBLIOGRAPHY ON USES OF
THE URBAN STREET.
Ehrenthal, Frank F. 1972.
　　　REF fZ7164.T81E3 ECOL

SELECTED IRRIGATION RETURN FLOW.
Skogerboe, Gaylord V. 1972-
　　　fTD223.S5 ECOL

SELECTED LEGAL AND ECONOMIC ASPECTS
OF ENVIRONMENTAL PROTECTION.
Meyers, Charles J. 1971.　KF3775.A7M58 ECOL

SELECTED OUTDOOR RECREATION
STATISTICS.
United States. Bureau of Outdoor Recreation. 1971.
　　　fGV53.A47 1971 ECOL

SELECTED STUDIES ON ALKALINE
ADDITIVES FOR SULFUR DIOXIDE
CONTROL.
1971.　　　TD885.5.S8S4 ECOL

SELECTED URBAN STORM WATER RUNOFF
ABSTRACTS, JULY 1970-JUNE 1971.
Franklin Institute, Philadelphia. Science Information
Service. 1971.　　　fTD653.F7 ECOL

SELECTED URBAN STORM WATER RUNOFF
ABSTRACTS, JULY 1971-JUNE 1972.
Sandoski, Dorothy A. 1972.　fTD653.S2 ECOL

A SELECTIVE, ANNOTATED BIBLIOGRAPHY
OF REPORTS AND DOCUMENTS ON
INTERNATIONAL ENVIRONMENTAL
PROBLEMS.
Woodrow Wilson International Center for Scholars.
1972.　　　fZ7164.N3W6 ECOL

A SENSE OF THE EARTH.
Leveson, David. 1971.　　　QE31.L48 ECOL

THE SENSE OF WONDER.
Carson, Rachel Louise. 1965,c1956
　　　QH51.C35 ECOL

SEWAGE DISPOSAL FACILITIES INVENTORY,
STATE OF MINNESOTA, JANUARY 1, 1969.
Minnesota. Division of Water Quality. 1969
　　　fTD524.M5A44 ECOL

SEWAGE SLUDGE TREATMENT 1972.
James, Ronald W. 1972 **REF fTD768.J35 ECOL**

SEWER BEDDING AND INFILTRATION, GULF COAST AREA.
Mayer, John K. 1972. **fTD653.M3 ECOL**

SEWERAGE AND WATER PLANNING REPORT.
Metcalf and Eddy, Boston. 1968. **fTD525.T9M4 ECOL**

SEWERAGE REPORT, VILLAGE OF MAYER, MARCH, 1970.
Lindsey-Brauer and Associates, Inc., Eden Prairie, Minn. Mayer sewerage plan. 1970 **fTD525.M3L5 ECOL**

THE SHOREBIRDS OF NORTH AMERICA.
Stout, Gardner D. 1967 **fQL681.S78 ECOL**

SIERRA CLUB EXHIBIT FORMAT SERIES NO.21.
Caulfield, Patricia. Everglades. 1970 **QH105.F6C36 ECOL**

SIERRA CLUB EXHIBIT FORMAT SERIES, 15.
Wenkam, Robert. Kauai and the park country of Hawaii. 1967 **DU628.K3W4 ECOL**

THE SIERRA CLUB WILDERNESS HANDBOOK.
Brower, David Ross. 2nd rev. ed. c1971 **SK601.B845 1971 ECOL**

SIGURD F. OLSON'S WILDERNESS DAYS.
Olson, Sigurd F. 1st ed. 1972. **QH81.O67 1972 ECOL**

THE SILENT EXPLOSION.
Appleman, Philip. 1965 **HB851.A48 ECOL**

SILENT SLAUGHTER.
Griffiths, Joel. 1972 **RA1231.R2G74 ECOL**

SILENT SPRING.
Carson, Rachel Louise. 1962 **SB959.C3 ECOL**

SINCE SILENT SPRING.
Graham, Frank. 1970. **QH75.G68 ECOL**

THE SINGING WILDERNESS.
Olson, Sigurd F. 1956. **QH102.O4 ECOL**

SITE SELECTION HANDBOOK, VOL.2.
Industrial Development. 1972. **REF fHC68.I5 1972 ECOL**

SLAUGHTER THE ANIMALS, POISON THE EARTH.
Olsen, Jack. 1971 **QL737.C22O47 ECOL**

SLICKROCK.
Abbey, Edward. 1971 **fF830.A62 ECOL**

SMALL URBAN SPACES.
Seymour Whitney North. 1969 **SB481.S48 ECOL**

SMITHSONIAN ANNUAL, 2.
The Fitness of man's environment. 1968 **HT166.F53 ECOL**

AN SMU LAW SCHOOL STUDY.
Thomas, Ann (Van Wynen). Legal limits on the use of chemical and biological weapons. 1970 **REF JX5135.C5T55 ECOL**

SNAKE WILDERNESS.
Norton, Boyd. c1972. **QH105.I2N6 ECOL**

SNOW AND ICE.
Couchman, J. Kenneth. c1971 **QC929.S7C6 ECOL**

SNOW CAMPER'S GUIDE.
Bridge, Raymond. The complete snow camper's guide. 1973 **SK602.6.B74 ECOL**

SNOW COVER AND WINTER SOIL TEMPERATURES AT ST. PAUL, MINN.
Baker, Donald G. 1971. **S594.5.B3 ECOL**

SNOW, SNOWSHOES, AND NATURE: THE WHITE DIMENSION OF ENVIRONMENT.
Burns, William. 1972? **fLB1047.B8 ECOL**

SNOWSHOE COUNTRY.
Jaques, Florence (Page). 1944 **F606.J37 ECOL**

SO HUMAN AN ANIMAL.
Dubos, Rene Jules. 1968 **HM206.D87 ECOL**

SOCIAL AND ECONOMIC CONSIDERATIONS FOR WATER RESOURCES PLANNING IN THE PARK RIVER SUBBASIN, NORTH DAKOTA.
Ludtke, Richard L. 1971. **HD1694.N9L8 ECOL**

SOCIAL AND NATURAL BIOLOGY.
Johnson, Cecil E. 1968 **QH302.J58 ECOL**

SOCIAL ASPECTS OF ENVIRONMENTAL POLLUTION.
Alexander, Robert M. 1971. **fTD177.A4 ECOL**

SOCIAL ASPECTS OF URBAN WATER CONSERVATION.
Century Research Corporation. 1972. **fTD388.5.C4 ECOL**

SOCIAL BEHAVIOR, NATURAL RESOURCES, AND THE ENVIRONMENT.
Burch, William R. 1972 **HM206.B84 ECOL**

THE SOCIAL IMPACT OF NOISE.
United States. National Bureau of Standards. 1971. **TD893.A49 ECOL**

THE SOCIAL IMPACT OF THE GREEN REVOLUTION.
Brown, Lester Russell. 1971 **HD1417.B7 ECOL**

SOCIAL INTELLIGENCE FOR AMERICA'S FUTURE.
Gross, Bertram Myron. 1969 **HN59.G76 ECOL**

THE SOCIAL RESPONSIBILITY OF THE SCIENTIST.
1971 **Q125.S714 ECOL**

SOCIETY AND ENVIRONMENT: THE COMING COLLISION.
Campbell, Rex R. 1972 **HC110.E5C35 ECOL**

SOCIOECONOMIC ENVIRONMENTAL STUDIES SERIES.
Beckers, Charles V. Quantitative methods for preliminary design of water quality surveillance systems. 1972. **TD365.B4 ECOL**
Wilson, Raymond Harrison. Toward a philosophy of planning: attitudes of federal water planners. 1973. **HC110.E5W5 ECOL**

SOIL ANIMALS.
Schaller, Friedrich. 1968 **QL110.S313 ECOL**

SOIL CONSERVATION.
Hudson, Norman. 1972, c1971 **S623.H78 1972 ECOL**

SOIL CONSERVATION IN PERSPECTIVE.
Held, R. Burnell. 1965 **S624.A1H4 ECOL**

THE SOIL CONSERVATION SERVICE.
Simms, Denton Harper. 1970 **S622.S44 ECOL**

SOIL DEVELOPMENT.
Faulkner, Edward Hubert. 1952 **S603.F37 ECOL**

SOIL MANAGEMENT FOR CONSERVATION AND PRODUCTION.
Cook, Ray Lewis. c1962 **S591.C7 ECOL**

SOIL MATRIC SUCTION CHANGES WITH TIME IN PRESSED SOIL BRIQUETTES.
Fuentes, Victor C. 1971. **GB701.M554no.33 ECOL**

SOIL SYSTEMS FOR MUNICIPAL EFFLUENTS.
Ramsey, Ralph H. 1972. **fTD760.R24 ECOL**

THE SOIL THAT FEEDS US.
Heady, Eleanor B. 1972 **PZ10.H42So ECOL**

SOIL, WATER, AND SUBURBIA.
National Conference on Soil, Water, and Suburbia, Washington, D.C., 1967. 1968 **fHT166.N36 1967 ECOL**

SOILS OF THE TWIN CITIES METROPOLITAN AREA AND THEIR RELATION TO URBAN DEVELOPMENT.
Hanson, Lowell D. 1967, c1966 **fS599.M45H3 1967 ECOL**

SOILS, SOIL MANAGEMENT AND FERTILIZER MONOGRAPHS.
Minnesota. University. Agricultural Extension Service. 1973. **fS591.M68 ECOL**

SOILS: THEIR NATURE, CLASSES, DISTRIBUTION, USES, AND CARE.
Gibson, J. Sullivan. 1970 **S591.G52 ECOL**

SOLID WASTE DEMONSTRATION PROJECTS.
Symposium on Solid Waste Demonstration Projects, Cincinnati, Ohio, 1971. 1972. **TD785.A45 1971 ECOL**

SOLID WASTE EDUCATION.
Minnesota. Pollution Control Agency. 1969? **fTD524.M6A3 ECOL**

SOLID WASTE HANDLING AND DISPOSAL IN MULTI-STORY BUILDINGS AND HOSPITALS.
United States. Environmental Protection Agency. 1972- **TD788.A3 ECOL**

SOLID WASTE MANAGEMENT. **REF Z5853.S22S6 ECOL**
National Association of Counties Research Foundation. 1972? **fTD791.N3 ECOL**

SOLID WASTE MANAGEMENT: ECONOMICS AND OPERATION.
Gunter, John D. 1973. **Ref fZ5853.S22G8 ECOL**

SOLID WASTE MANAGEMENT PLAN, DISTRICT OF COLUMBIA.
District of Columbia District of Columbia solid waste management plan. 1971. **TD525.W2A43 ECOL**

SOLID WASTE MANAGEMENT SERIES.
Banks, M. E. New chemical concepts for utilization of waste plastics. 1971. **TP156.R38B3 ECOL**
Brunner, Dirk R. Sanitary landfill design and operation. 1972. **TD795.7.B7 ECOL**
Darnay, Arsen. Salvage markets for materials in solid wastes, ... 1972. **TD795.D38 ECOL**
Smith, David D. Ocean disposal of barge-delivered liquid and solid wastes from United States coastal cities. 1971. **TD796.7.O25S4 ECOL**

SOLID WASTE MANAGEMENT SERIES, SW-34D.1-
United States. Environmental Protection Agency. Solid waste handling and disposal in multi-story buildings and hospitals. 1972- **TD788.A3 ECOL**

SOLID WASTE MANAGEMENT SERIES, SW-4P.
Symposium on Solid Waste Demonstration Projects, Cincinnati, Ohio, 1971. Solid waste demonstration projects. 1972. **TD785.A45 1971 ECOL**

SOLID WASTE MANAGEMENT/RECYCLING OPTIONS.
Minnesota. University. Consortium for the Study of Solid Waste Management/Recycling Options. A report on solid waste management/recycling options. 1972. **fTD793.M6 ECOL**

SOME ASPECTS OF INVESTMENT IN IRON MINING FACILITIES IN THE LAKE SUPERIOR DISTRICT.
Nelson, Clarence Walfred. An ex ante profitability analysis of capital investment in taconite pellet production facilities in Minnesota circa 1950-51. 1967. **HD9517.M6N4 ECOL**

SOME ASPECTS OF THE HYDROLOGY OF PONDS AND SMALL LAKES.
Manson, Philip W. 1968. **fGB1825.M6M35 ECOL**

SONGS OF THE FOREST.
1964. **Phonodisc QL698.5.S63 ECOL**

S.O.S. SAVE OUR EARTH.
Masini, Giancarlo. c1972 **fQH541.M382 1972 ECOL**

SOURCE TESTING FOR AIR POLLUTION CONTROL.
Cooper, Hal B. H. 1971 **fTD890.C57 ECOL**

A SOURCEBOOK FOR ELEMENTARY SCIENCE.
Hone, Elizabeth B. Teaching elementary science: a sourcebook for elementary science. 2d ed. 1971 **LB1585.H65 1971 ECOL**

A SOURCEBOOK FOR THE BIOLOGICAL SCIENCES.
Morholt, Evelyn. 2d ed. 1966 **QH53.M67 1966 ECOL**

SOURCES, ABUNDANCE, AND FATE OF GASEOUS ATMOSPHERIC POLLUTANTS.
Robinson, Elmer. 1968. **fTD885.R6 ECOL**

SOURCES, ABUNDANCE, AND FATE OF GASEOUS ATMOSPHERIC POLLUTANTS: SUPPLEMENT.
Robinson, Elmer. 1969. **fTD885.R62 ECOL**

SOURCES OF NUCLEAR FUEL.
Singleton, Arthur L. 1968 **TN490.U7S52 ECOL**

SOURCES OF REFERENCE MATERIALS & AUDIOVISUAL AIDS FOR ENVIRONMENTAL EDUCATION.
Interdisciplinary Environmental Education. 2d rev. ed. 1972 **Ref fQH541.2.I68 1972 ECOL**

SOWING THE WIND.
Wellford, Harrison. 1972. **HD9000.9.U5W4 ECOL**

SPACE RADIATION.
Corliss, William R. 1968 **QC485.C613 ECOL**

SPARROWS DON'T DROP CANDY WRAPPERS.
Gabel, Margaret. 1971 **TD176.G3 ECOL**

SPECIAL REPORT ECOLOGY.
c1971- **REF fS936.S6 ECOL**

A SPECIAL REPORT ON THE POLLUTION OF RIVER WATERS.
Kirkwood, James Pugh. Reprint ed. 1970 **REF TD425.K52 1970 ECOL**

SPILL PREVENTION TECHNIQUES FOR HAZARDOUS POLLUTING SUBSTANCES: AN INVENTORY AND SURVEY OF HAZARDOUS CHEMICAL FACILITIES IN CHARLESTON, WEST VIRGINIA; BALTIMORE, MARYLAND; TEXAS CITY, TEXAS; AND THE SUISUN BAY-DELTA AREA, CALIFORNIA.
Little (Arthur D.) Inc. 1971. **fT55.3.H3L4 ECOL**

THE SPOILS OF PROGRESS: ENVIRONMENTAL POLLUTION IN THE SOVIET UNION.
Goldman, Marshall I. 1972
    TD187.5.R9G63 ECOL

SPORTSMAN'S GUIDE TO GAME FISH.
Dalrymple, Byron W. 1968   QL617.D34 ECOL

STALKING THE BLUE-EYED SCALLOP.
Gibbons, Euell. 1964   TX387.G5 ECOL

STALKING THE GOOD LIFE.
Gibbons, Euell. 1971   QK98.5.G45 ECOL

STALKING THE WILD ASPARAGUS.
Gibbons, Euell. 1970, c1962   QK98.5.G48 ECOL

STANDARD METHODS FOR THE EXAMINATION OF WATER AND WASTE WATER, INCLUDING BOTTOM SEDIMENTS AND SLUDGES.
American Public Health Association. Ed. 13. c1971
    REF QD142.A5 1971 ECOL

STANDING ROOM ONLY.
Sax, Karl. New ed. 1969,c1960
    HB881.S33 1969 ECOL

STATE AIR POLLUTION CONTROL LAWS.
Degler, Stanley E. Rev. ed. 1970
    KF3812.Z95D4 1970 ECOL

STATE AND FEDERAL CONTROL OF HEALTH HAZARDS FROM RADIOACTIVE MATERIALS OTHER THAN MATERIALS REGULATED UNDER THE ATOMIC ENERGY ACT OF 1954 (AS OF OCTOBER 1, 1969).
Pettigrew, George L. 1971.
    RA1231.R2U5125no.71-4 ECOL

STATE-OF-ART, SUGARBEET PROCESSING WASTE TREATMENT.
Beet Sugar Development Foundation, Fort Collins, Colo. 1971.   fTD899.S8B43 ECOL

STATE OF THE ART OF TEXTILE WASTE TREATMENT.
Clemson University. Dept. of Textiles. 1971.
    fTD899.T4C45 ECOL

A STATE-OF-THE-ART REVIEW OF METAL FINISHING WASTE TREATMENT.
Battelle Memorial Institute. Columbus, Ohio. Columbus Laboratories 1968 i.e.1970
    fTD899.M45B33 ECOL

STATE OF THE ART REVIEW ON SLUDGE INCINERATION PRACTICE.
Balakrishnan, S. 1970.   fTD803.B36 ECOL

A STATE OF THE EARTH REPORT FROM THE SMITHSONIAN INSTITUTION CENTER FOR SHORT-LIVED PHENOMENA.
Smithsonian Institution. Center for Shortlived Phenomena. The pulse of the planet. c1972
    fQ225.P8 ECOL

STATE PROGRAM PLANS.
United States. Environmental Protection Agency. Water Quality Office. Digest of State program plans. 1970/71-   TD223.A2635 ECOL

THE STATES' ROLE IN LAND RESOURCE MANAGEMENT.
Council of State Governments. 1972
    HD205.C6 1972 ECOL

STATISTICAL ABSTRACT OF THE UNITED STATES, V.92-
United States. Bureau of the Census. 1971-
    REF HA202.U5 ECOL

STATISTICAL ECOLOGY.
International Symposium on Statistical Ecology, New Haven, 1969. 1971
    QH541.15.M3I5 1969 ECOL

STEAM-ELECTRIC PLANT AIR AND WATER QUALITY CONTROL DATA FOR THE YEAR ENDED DECEMBER 31, 1969, BASED ON EPC FORM NO. 67.
United States. Federal Power Commission. 1973.
    fTD195.E4U5 ECOL

THE STEAM-POWERED AUTOMOBILE.
Jamison, Andrew. 1970   TL200.J34 ECOL

STEP-BY-STEP TO ORGANIC VEGETABLE GROWING.
Ogden, Samuel R. 1971   SB321.O343 ECOL

THE STEP TO MAN.
Platt, John Rader. 1970,c1966
    HM101.P57 ECOL

STERNGLASS: A CASE HISTORY.
Hull, Andrew P. 1972?   REF fRA569.H8 ECOL

STOCHASTIC MODELING FOR WATER QUALITY MANAGEMENT.
Stochastics, Inc., Blacksburg, Va. 1971.
    fTC409.S8 ECOL

STOCKHOLM AND BEYOND.
1972.   HC110.E5A43 ECOL

STOP IT!
Sanders, Norman K. 1972 HC110.E5S36 ECOL

STORAGE AND TREATMENT OF COMBINED SEWER OVERFLOWS.
United States. Environmental Protection Agency. Office of Research and Monitoring. 1972.
    fTD662.U54 ECOL

STORM SEWER DESIGN—AN EVALUATION OF THE RRL METHOD.
Stall, John B. 1972.   TD665.S7 ECOL

STORM WATER MANAGEMENT MODEL.
Metcalf and Eddy, Boston. 1971.
    fGB665.M4 ECOL

THE STORY OF THE PLANT KINGDOM.
Coulter, Merle Crowe. Rev. by Howard J. Dittmer. 3d ed. 1964   QK47.C893 1964 ECOL

STRATEGIES OF AMERICAN WATER MANAGEMENT.
White, Gilbert Fowler. 1969
    HD1694.A5W5 ECOL

STREAM FAUNAL RECOVERY AFTER MANGANESE STRIP MINE RECLAMATION.
Virginia Polytechnic Institute and State University. 1971.   fTN291.V5 ECOL

STREAMS, LAKES, PONDS.
Coker, Robert Ervin. 1954   QH96.C6 ECOL

STRIPPING.
Stacks, John F. 1972   TN291.S7 ECOL

STUDIES ON BENTHIC NEMATODE ECOLOGY IN A SMALL FRESHWATER POND.
Merritt, Thomas W. 1973. fTC1.A85no.8 ECOL

STUDIES ON EFFECTS OF WATERSHED PRACTICES ON STREAMS.
Oregon. State University, Corvallis. School of Forestry. 1971 i.e. 1972   fTC409.O74 ECOL

STUDY AND INVESTIGATION OF SOLID WASTE CONTROL FOR THE MINNESOTA POLLUTION CONTROL AGENCY: PHASE II, FINAL REPORT.
Henningson, Durham & Richardson. 1969
    fTD788.4.M6H4 ECOL

A STUDY OF PARKS AND RECREATION FOR THE VILLAGE OF NEW BRIGHTON.
Brauer and Associates, inc., Edina, Minn. 1967
    fGV54.M6B7 ECOL

STUDY OF REUTILIZATION OF WASTEWATER RECYCLED THROUGH GROUNDWATER.
Boen, Doyle F. 1971.   fTD429.B6 ECOL

STUDY OF SULFUR RECOVERY FROM COAL REFUSE.
Black, Sivalls and Bryson, Inc., Kansas City, Mo. Applied Technology Division 1971.
    fTN890.B57 ECOL

A STUDY OF THE EFFECTS OF ISLAND DEVELOPMENT ON LAKE WATER QUALITY.
McClanahan, Mark A. 1972. fTD224.G4M3 ECOL

A STUDY OF THE IMPACT OF SNOWMOBILING ON NORTHERN MINNESOTA ECOLOGY.
Wanek, Wallace J. 1971   fTL234.W3 ECOL

THE STUDY OF THE PHYSICAL WORLD.
Cheronis, Nicholas Dimitrius. 3d ed. 1958
    Q160.C34 1958 ECOL

SUBSURFACE WASTE DISPOSAL BY MEANS OF WELLS—A SELECTIVE ANNOTATED BIBLIOGRAPHY.
Rima, Donald R. 1971.
    REF Z5853.S22R55 ECOL

SUBSURFACE WATER POLLUTION.
United States. Environmental Protection Agency. Office of Water Programs. 1972.
    Z7173.W3U5 ECOL

SUBSYSTEMS AND VARIABLES.
Science Curriculum Improvement Study. 1971,c1970   LB1585.S38 1971 ECOL

SUBURBAN LAND CONVERSION IN THE UNITED STATES: AN ECONOMIC AND GOVERNMENTAL PROCESS.
Clawson, Marion. 1971   HD259.C55 ECOL

SUGGESTED STATE LEGISLATION; 1973- V.32-
Council of State Governments. Committee of State Officials on Suggested State Legislation.
    JK2431.C6 ECOL

SULFIDE TO SULFATE REACTION MECHANISM.
Smith, Edwin Earle. 1970.   fTN321.S58 ECOL

SULFUR DIOXIDE: ITS CHEMISTRY AS RELATED TO METHODS FOR REMOVING IT FROM WASTE GASES.
Haas, Larry A. 1973   TN23.U7no.8608 ECOL

SUMMARIES OF NATIONAL REPORTS SUBMITTED IN PREPARATION FOR THE UNITED NATIONS CONFERENCE ON THE HUMAN ENVIRONMENT.
Woodrow Wilson International Center for Scholars. 1972.   fHC68.W6 ECOL

SUMMARY, ANALYSIS.
United States. Water Resources Council. 1972.
    TD345.U52 ECOL

SUMMARY, CONCLUSIONS AND RECOMMENDATIONS FROM REPORT TO THE PRESIDENT AND CONGRESS ON NOISE.
United States. Environmental Protection Agency. 1971.   fTD893.A473 ECOL

SUMMARY OF MINING AND PETROLEUM LAWS OF THE WORLD.
Ely, Northcutt. Rev. 1970-
    TN295.U4no.8514 ECOL

SUMMER SCHOOL GUIDE FOR EDUCATION FOR AN IMPROVED ENVIRONMENT.
Dooley, David. 1971. fQH541.2.D6 Suppl. ECOL

SUN, SOIL, AND SURVIVAL.
Berger, Kermit Carl. 1972 S591.B45 1972 ECOL

SUPERHIGHWAY—SUPERHOAX.
Leavitt, Helen. 1970.   HE355.L4 ECOL

SUPERIOR POLLUTOR: A SAGA OF THE STRUGGLE TO STOP POLLUTION OF THE LARGEST FRESH WATER LAKE IN THE WORLD BY ITS MOST EGREGIOUS POLLUTER—THE RESERVE MINING COMPANY.
Ulrich, Stanley. 1972.   TD224.M6U6 ECOL

SUPPLEMENTARY AERATION OF LAGOONS IN RIGOROUS CLIMATE AREAS.
Champlin, Robert L. 1971. fTD746.5.C45 ECOL

SUPPLY AND COMPETITION IN MINOR METALS.
Brooks, David B. c1965
    REF HD9506.U62B7 ECOL

SURFACE DISCHARGE OF HEATED WATER.
Stefan, Heinz. 1971 i.e. 1972
    fTD427.H4S64 ECOL

SURFACE WATER SUPPLY OF THE UNITED STATES. 1961/65-
United States. Geological Survey.
    TC801.U2 ECOL

SURGEON GENERAL'S CONFERENCE ON SOLID WASTE MANAGEMENT FOR METROPOLITAN WASHINGTON, WASHINGTON, D. C., 1967.
1967.   TD525.W2S7 1967 ECOL

SURVEY: LAKE PROTECTION AND REHABILITATION LEGISLATION IN THE UNITED STATES.
Kusler, Jon A. 1972. REF fKF5568.K8 ECOL

A SURVEY OF ALTERNATE METHODS FOR COOLING CONDENSER DISCHARGE WATER.
Dynatech R/D Company. 1969-
    fTJ403.D9 ECOL

A SURVEY OF ATTITUDES TOWARDS THE MISSISSIPPI RIVER AS A TOTAL RESOURCE IN MINNESOTA.
Baron, Norman J. 1972.
    GB701.M554no.55 ECOL

THE SURVIVAL GAME.
Lange, Gordon C. 1972   TD178.6.L35 ECOL

SURVIVAL WITH STYLE.
Angier, Bradford. 1972.   SK606.A54 ECOL

SWAMP SPRING.
Carrick, Carol. 1969   PZ10.C3297Sw ECOL

THE SWANS.
Scott, Peter Markham. 1972.
    QL696.A5S37 ECOL

THE SWIRL CONCENTRATOR AS A COMBINED SEWER OVERFLOW REGULATOR FACILITY.
United States. Environmental Protection Agency. Office of Research and Monitoring. 1972.
    TD662.U5 ECOL

SYMPOSIA OF THE INSTITUTE OF BIOLOGY, NO. 15.
Lowe-McConnell, R. H. Man-made lakes. 1966.
GB1601.L6 1965 ECOL

SYMPOSIA OF THE ZOOLOGICAL SOCIETY OF LONDON, NO. 29.
Conservation and productivity of natural waters. 1972. QL1.Z733no.29 ECOL

A SYMPOSIUM ON RADIOISOTOPES IN THE BIOSPHERE.
Symposium on Radioisotopes in the Biosphere, University of Minnesota, 1959. 1960.
QH652.S9 1959 ECOL

SYNOPSIS OF ANIMAL CLASSIFICATION.
Clark, Robert Bernard. 1971.
REF QL352.C53 ECOL

SYSTEM ENERGY AND RECYCLING: A STUDY OF THE BEVERAGE INDUSTRY.
Hannon, Bruce. 1972. fTP659.H3 ECOL

A SYSTEM FOR INDUSTRIAL WASTE TREATMENT RD&D PROJECT PRIORITY ASSIGNMENT.
Synectics Corporation. 1971. fTD897.5.S9 ECOL

SYSTEMS ANALYSIS FOR WATER QUALITY MANAGEMENT—SURVEY AND ABSTRACTS.
Enviro Control, Inc. 1971. fTD365.E5 ECOL

SYSTEMS ANALYSIS IN ECOLOGY.
Watt, Kenneth E. F. 1966. QH541.W3 ECOL

T

TACONITE TAILINGS DISPOSAL.
Roy F. Weston, Inc. Concept evaluation report: taconite tailings disposal, Reserve Mining Company, Silver Bay, Minnesota. 1971 fTD899.T35 ECOL

THE TALE OF A MEADOW.
Kane, Henry Bugbee. 1959 QH48.K23 ECOL

THE TALE OF A WOOD.
Kane, Henry Bugbee. 1962 QH86.K3 ECOL

TAMING MEGALOPOLIS.
Eldredge, Hanford Wentworth. 1967.
HT151.E4 ECOL

TAYLOR AV SVENSKA FAGLAR.
Berg, Bengt Magnus Kristoffer. c1925
REF fQL690.S5B46 ECOL

TEACHER'S GUIDE FOR ENVIRONMENTAL EDUCATION.
North Carolina. Task Force on Environment and Natural Resources. 1970.
REF fQH541.2.N88 ECOL

THE TEACHER'S HANDBOOK TO ENVIRONMENTAL STUDIES.
Perry, Gordon Arthur. Handbook for environmental studies. 2nd rev. ed. 1971 LB1585.P4 1971 ECOL

TEACHING ABOUT SPACESHIP EARTH.
Intercom. c1972 S946.I5 ECOL

TEACHING CONSERVATION AND NATURAL SCIENCE IN THE OUTDOORS.
California Association for Outdoor Education. 1968.
fS946.C3 1968 ECOL

TEACHING ELEMENTARY SCIENCE: A SOURCEBOOK FOR ELEMENTARY SCIENCE.
Hone, Elizabeth B. 2d ed. 1971
LB1585.H65 1971 ECOL

TEACHING FOR SURVIVAL.
Terry, Mark. 1971 QH541.2.T47 ECOL

TEACHING IN THE OUTDOORS.
Hammerman, Donald R. 1964 LB1047.H3 ECOL

TEACHING SCIENCE IN AN OUTDOOR ENVIRONMENT.
Gross, Phyllis. 1972. QH51.G867 ECOL

TECHNICAL EVALUATION OF PHOSPHATE-FREE HOME LAUNDRY DETERGENTS.
Reilich, Helmut G. 1972. fTP992.5.R4 ECOL

TECHNICAL MANUAL NO.1- 1963-
Air Pollution Control Association.
REF fTD881.A4 ECOL

TECHNICAL PAPER 2.
Liesch, Bruce A. Geohydrology of the Jorden aquifer in the Minneapolis-St. Paul area Minnesota. 1961.
fGB705.M6L5 ECOL

TECHNIQUES FOR TEACHING CONSERVATION EDUCATION.
Brown, Robert E. 1964 S946.B7 ECOL

TECHNOLOGICAL CHANGE: ITS IMPACT ON MAN AND SOCIETY.
Mesthene, Emmanuel G. 1970.
HM221.M47 1970 ECOL

TECHNOLOGICAL FORECASTING AND LONG-RANGE PLANNING.
Ayres, Robert U. 1969 T174.A9 ECOL

TECHNOLOGICAL MAN: THE MYTH AND THE REALITY.
Ferkiss, Victor C. 1969 HM221.F39 ECOL

TECHNOLOGY AND GROWTH.
Mishan, Edward J. 1970,c1969
HD82.M514 ECOL

TECHNOLOGY AND SOCIAL CHANGE.
Moore, Wilbert Ellis. 1972
T14.5.M66 1972 ECOL

TECHNOPOLIS.
Calder, Nigel. 1970 HM221.C35 1970 ECOL

TEMPERATURE PREDICTION IN STRATIFIED WATER: MATHEMATICAL MODEL-USER'S MANUAL (SUPPLEMENT TO REPORT 1613ODJH-01/71).
Ralph M. Parsons Laboratory for Water Resources and Hydrodynamics. 1971. fTD395.R3 ECOL

TEMPERATURE SURVEYS OF THE ST. CROIX RIVER.
Northern States Power Company. Engineering Department. Environmental monitoring program. 1970. REF fTK1331.N6A42 1970 ECOL

TERRACIDE.
Linton, Ron M. 1970 TD180.L56 ECOL

TERRARIUMS.
Hoke, John. 1972. QH68.H65 ECOL

TEXAS. A & M UNIVERSITY, COLLEGE STATION. WATER RESOURCES INSTITUTE. TECHNICAL REPORT, NO. 45.
Hann, Roy W. Mathematical models of water quality parameters for rivers and estuaries. 1972
fTD370.H3 ECOL

TEXAS. A & M UNIVERSITY, COLLEGE STATION. WATER RESOURCES INSTITUTE. TECHNICAL REPORT NO. 43.
Gunn, Clare A. Cultural benefits from metropolitan river recreation—San Antonio prototype. 1972.
fHD1694.T4G8 ECOL

THERMAL EFFECTS AND UNITED STATES NUCLEAR POWER STATIONS.
United States. Atomic Energy Commission. Division of Reactor Development and Technology. 1971.
TD427.H4U52 ECOL

THESAURUS OF ERIC DESCRIPTORS, WITH A SPECIAL CHAPTER ON THE ROLE AND FUNCTION OF THE THESAURUS IN EDUCATION.
United States. Educational Resources Information Center. 1972. REF fZ695.1.E3U5 1972 ECOL

THESAURUS OF WATER RESOURCES TERMS.
United States. Bureau of Reclamation. 1971.
REF Z695.1.W3U52 ECOL

THEY SAID IT COULDN'T BE DONE: THE INCREDIBLE STORY OF BILL LEAR.
Boesen, Victor. 1st ed. 1971.
TL540.L364B64 ECOL

THIRD POLLUTION.
Small, William E. 1971 TD795.S56 1971 ECOL

THE THIRD WAVE.
United States. Dept. of the Interior. 1966
S914.A54 ECOL

THIRTY YEARS WAR FOR WILD LIFE.
Hornaday, William Temple. 1970, c1931
SK361.H58 1970 ECOL

THIS BRIGHT LAND.
Atkinson, Justin Brooks. 1st ed. 1972.
GF503.A8 ECOL

THIS CROWDED PLANET.
Hyde, Margaret Oldroyd. 1961 HB883.H9 ECOL

THIS CROWDED WORLD.
Frankel, Lillian Berson. 1970 HB883.F7 ECOL

THIS ENDANGERED PLANET.
Falk, Richard A. 1st ed. 1971
HC79.E5F27 ECOL

THIS IS OUR WORLD.
Sears, Paul Bigelow. Rev. ed. 1971
QH309.S3 1971 ECOL

THIS IS THE AMERICAN EARTH.
Adams, Ansel Easton. 1960 fHC103.7.A68 ECOL

THIS ISLAND EARTH.
Nicks, Oran W. 1970. fQB631.N5 ECOL

THIS LITTLE PLANET.
Hamilton, Michael Pollock. 1970
GF80.H35 ECOL

THIS LIVING EARTH.
Cavagnaro, David. 1972 fQH541.5.M4C38 ECOL

THIS SIDE OF YESTERDAY: EXTINCTION OR UTOPIA.
Henshaw, Paul Stewart. 1971 GF41.H45 ECOL

THIS THIRSTY WORLD.
Lewis, Alfred. 1964 TD348.L46 ECOL

THIS VIEW OF LIFE.
Simpson, George Gaylord. 1964
QH369.S5 ECOL

THIS VITAL AIR, THIS VITAL WATER: MAN'S ENVIRONMENT CRISIS.
Aylesworth, Thomas G. 1968 TD180.A9 ECOL

THREATENED WILDLIFE OF THE UNITED STATES.
United States. Bureau of Sport Fisheries and Wildlife. Office of Endangered Species and International Activities. 1973. S914.A3no.114 1973 ECOL

THREE APPROACHES TO ENVIRONMENTAL RESOURCE ANALYSIS.
Harvard University. Landscape Architecture Research Office. 1967. fTA170.H3 ECOL

THE THREE HUNDRED YEAR WAR: A CHRONICLE OF ECOLOGICAL DISASTER.
Douglas, William Orville. 1st ed. 1972
QH541.D68 ECOL

THROUGH THE MAGNIFYING GLASS.
Schwartz, Julius. 1954 Q163.S464 ECOL

TIMBER SUPPLY AND THE ENVIRONMENT.
Current Issues Conference, 1st, Portland, Or., 1972. 1972 SD144.A13C87 1972 ECOL

TIME AND THE RIVER FLOWING: GRAND CANYON.
Leydet, Francois. 1968 F788.L482 ECOL

TIME TO CRY WOLF!
McCann, Lester J. c1972 SK353.M3 ECOL

THE TIMELY AND THE TIMELESS.
Glass, Hiram Bentley. 1970 Q181.G45 ECOL

TIMETABLE FOR DISASTER.
Widener, Don. 1970 TD180.W53 ECOL

TIPS AND TRICKS IN OUTDOOR EDUCATION.
Illinois. Northern Illinois University, De Kalb. Lorado Taft Field Campus. Dept. of Outdoor Teacher Education. 1970 fLB1047.I44 ECOL

TITLE—AUTHOR—COMPANY INDEX TO REPORTS PUBLISHED BY THE U.S. DEPT. OF THE INTERIOR, OFFICE OF SALINE WATER THROUGH JULY 1971-
Nuclear Desalination Information Center.
REF fZ5853.S22N84 ECOL

TO AFRICA WITH THE MIGRATORY BIRDS.
Berg, Bengt Magnus Kristoffer. 1930.
QL692.B4 ECOL

TO LIVE ON EARTH.
Brubaker, Sterling. 1972 QH541.B76 ECOL

TORONTO. UNIV. DEPT. OF GEOGRAPHY. RESEARCH PUBLICATIONS, 8.
Auliciems, Andris. The atmospheric environment. 1972 QP82.2.T4A9 ECOL

TORONTO. UNIVERSITY. DEPT. OF GEOGRAPHY. RESEARCH PUBLICATIONS, 7.
Grima, Angelo P. Residential water demand. 1972
TD353.G7 ECOL

'TORREY CANYON' POLLUTION AND MARINE LIFE: A REPORT BY THE PLYMOUTH LABORATORY OF THE MARINE BIOLOGICAL ASSOCIATION OF THE UNITED KINGDOM.
Marine Biological Association of the United Kingdom. Laboratory, Plymouth. 1968.
GC1311.M37 ECOL

TOWARD A PHILOSOPHY OF PLANNING: ATTITUDES OF FEDERAL WATER PLANNERS.
Wilson, Raymond Harrison. 1973.
HC110.E5W5 ECOL

TOWARD A RATIONAL POWER POLICY: ENERGY, POLITICS, AND POLLUTION.
Fabricant, Neil. 1971 HD9685.U5F32 ECOL

TOWARD AN ENVIRONMENTAL POLICY.
1971 fHC110.E5T66 ECOL

TOWARD EFFECTIVE AND EQUITABLE POLLUTION CONTROL REGULATION.
Buggie, Frederick D. 1972 fHC110.P55B8 ECOL

TOWARD INTEGRATED CONTROL.
Northeastern Forest Insect Work Conference, 3rd, New Haven, 1970. 1971.
SD11.A455492no.194 ECOL

TITLE CATALOG UNITED NATIONS EDUCATIONAL, SCIENTIFIC AND CULTURAL ORGANIZATION. DOCUMENT

TOWARD NEW TOWNS FOR AMERICA.
Stein, Clarence S. Rev. ed. 1971,c1957
NA9108.S8 1971 ECOL

TOWARD THE YEAR 2000.
American Academy of Arts and Sciences, Boston. Commission on the Year 2000 1970,c1968
E169.1.A47192 1970 ECOL

TOWARD THE YEAR 2018.
c1968 **CB161.T6 ECOL**

THE TOWN THAT LAUNDERS ITS WATER.
Stevens, Leonard A. 1971
TD429.S84 1971 ECOL

TOXICANTS OCCURRING NATURALLY IN FOODS.
1966. **TX531.T6 ECOL**

TOXICOLOGIC AND EPIDEMIOLOGIC BASES FOR AIR QUALITY CRITERIA.
1969 **REF fTD890.T6 ECOL**

TOXICOLOGY OF ATMOSPHERIC SULFUR DIOXIDE DECAY PRODUCTS.
United States. Environmental Protection Agency. National Environmental Research Center. 1972.
TD885.5.S8U5 ECOL

THE TOXICOLOGY OF BERYLLIUM.
Tabershaw, Irving R. 1972. **RA1231.B4T3 ECOL**

TRAIL PLANNING AND LAYOUT.
Ashbaugh, Byron L. 1971 **QH58.A8 ECOL**

TRANSCRIPT OF PROCEEDINGS.
Conference in the Matter of Pollution of Lake Superior and its Tributary Basin in the States of Minnesota, Wisconsin, and Michigan, 3d session, Duluth, April 29-30, 1970. 1970
fTD223.3.C59 1970 ECOL

TRANSCRIPTS OF THE SPEECHES.
National Conference on Environmental Law, San Francisco, 1970. 1971
REF KF3775.A75N3 1970 ECOL

THE TRANSFORMATION.
Leonard, George Burr. 1972 **BF311.L43 ECOL**

TRANSPORTATION.
Gunston, Bill. 1972 **HE151.G85 ECOL**

TRANSPORTATION AND THE ENVIRONMENT.
Peterson, Roger A. 1971. **HE192.A1P4 ECOL**

TRANSPORTATION AND TOWN PLANNING.
Leibbrand, Kurt. 1970, c1964
HE333.L3813 1970 ECOL

TRANSPORTATION AND URBAN LAND.
Wingo, Lowdon. 1968,c1961 **HE4211.W5 ECOL**

TRANSPORTATION NOISE AND NOISE FROM EQUIPMENT POWERED BY INTERNAL COMBUSTION ENGINES.
Wyle Laboratories. 1971 i.e. 1972
fTD892.W95 ECOL

TRANSPORTATION NOISES: A SYMPOSIUM ON ACCEPTABILITY CRITERIA.
1970 **TA365.T68 ECOL**

TRAVELS AND TRADITIONS OF WATERFOWL.
Hochbaum, Hans Albert. 1955
QL698.H65 ECOL

TREATMENT OF CITRUS PROCESSING WASTES.
Coca-Cola Company. Foods Division. 1970.
fTD899.F7C6 ECOL

THE TREATMENT OF INDUSTRIAL WASTES.
Besselievre, Edmund Bulkley. 1968,c1969
REF TD897.B38 ECOL

TREATMENT OF SELECTED INTERNAL KRAFT MILL WASTES IN A COOLING TOWER.
Georgia Kraft Company. Research and Development Center. 1971. **fTD899.W65G46 ECOL**

TREATMENT OF WASTE WATER-WASTE OIL MIXTURES.
Armco Steel Corporation. 1970.
fTD455.A7 ECOL

A TREE IS SOMETHING WONDERFUL.
Cooper, Elizabeth K. c1972 **PZ10.C779Tr ECOL**

TREES AND FORESTS.
Jepsen, Stanley W. 1969 **SD143.J39 ECOL**

TREES AND SHRUBS OF THE UPPER MIDWEST.
Rosendahl, Carl Otto. 1955 **QK481.R67 ECOL**

TREES AND THEIR WORLD.
Fenton, Carroll Lane. 1957 **QK482.F4 ECOL**

TREES OF NORTH AMERICA.
Brockman, Christian Frank. 1968
QK481.B864 ECOL

TREES OF THE NORTHERN UNITED STATES AND CANADA.
Montgomery, Frederick Howard. 1970
QK481.M7 ECOL

TREES, SHRUBS AND VINES.
Viertel, Arthur T. 1970 **QK481.V5 ECOL**

TRENDS IN NATURAL RESOURCE COMMODITIES.
Resources for the Future. 1962.
REF fHF1051.R43 ECOL

TRENDS IN SCIENCE, V.5.
Daniels, Farrington. Direct use of the sun's energy. 1964. **TJ810.D28 ECOL**

TRENDS IN THE WORLD ALUMINUM INDUSTRY.
Brubaker, Sterling. c1967 **HD9539.A6B7 ECOL**

A TRIP TO THE POND.
Hofmann, Melita. 1966 **fQH48.H56 ECOL**

THE TRUE BOOK OF AIR AROUND US.
Firskey, Margaret. 1953 **QC863.F846 ECOL**

THE TRUE BOOK OF CONSERVATION.
Gates, Richard. 1959 **PZ10.G493TR ECOL**

THE TRUE BOOK OF PLANTS WE KNOW.
Miner, Opal Irene (Frazine) Sevrey. c1953
QK49.M6 ECOL

TWILIGHT OF THE ANIMAL KINGDOM.
Harris, Larry. 1972 **QL88.H37 ECOL**

TWILIGHT OVER THE WILDERNESS.
Wallo, Olav O. 1971 **fS964.U6W3 ECOL**

THE TYRANNY OF NOISE.
Baron, Robert Alex. 1970 **TD892.B37 ECOL**

U

U. C. D. LAW REVIEW, V. 1.
Legal control of water pollution. 1969
KF3786.A32L4 ECOL

THE ULTIMATE FOLLY.
McCarthy, Richard D. 1969
UG447.M233 1969 ECOL

ULTRASONIC FILTRATION OF COMBINED SEWER OVERFLOWS.
American Process Equipment Corporation. 1970.
fTD753.A6 ECOL

THE UN-POLITICS OF AIR POLLUTION: A STUDY OF NON-DECISION-MAKING IN THE CITIES.
Crenson, Matthew A. 1971 **HC110.A4C73 ECOL**

THE UNCLEAN SKY.
Battan, Louis J. 1966. **TD883.B3 ECOL**

UNDER THE SEA-WIND.
Carson, Rachel Louise. New ed. with corrections 1952c1941 **QH92.C3 1952 ECOL**

UNDERGRADUATE EDUCATION IN THE BIOLOGICAL SCIENCES FOR STUDENTS IN AGRICULTURE AND NATURAL RESOURCES.
Conference on Undergraduate Education in the Biological Sciences for Students in Agriculture and Natural Resources, Washington, D.C., 1966. 1967.
S533.C755 1966 ECOL

UNDERGROUND COAL MINING METHODS TO ABATE WATER POLLUTION.
West Virginia. University. Coal Research Bureau. 1970. **fTD899.M5W46 ECOL**

UNDERGROUND WASTE MANAGEMENT AND ENVIRONMENTAL IMPLICATIONS; PROCEEDINGS.
Symposium on Underground Waste Management and Environmental Implications, Houston, Tex., 1971. 1972. **TD761.S95 1971 ECOL**

UNDERSTANDING ECOLOGY.
Billington, Elizabeth T. 1971
QH541.14.B5 1971 ECOL
Grossman, Shelly. c1967, 1970
QL756.G7 1970 ECOL

UNDERSTANDING ENVIRONMENTAL POLLUTION.
Strobbe, Maurice A. 1971. **QH545.A1S7 ECOL**

UNDERSTANDING THE ATOM.
Asimov, Isaac. The genetic effects of radiation. c1966 **QH652.5.A8 ECOL**
Baker, Philip Schaffner. Radioisotopes in industry. c1965 **TK9400.B3 ECOL**
Berger, Harold. Nondestructive testing. 1965
TA417.2.B4 ECOL
Comar, Cyril Lewis. Fallout from nuclear tests. 1963 **UF767.C64 ECOL**
Comar, Cyril Lewis. Fallout from nuclear tests. Rev. 1966 **UF767.C64 1966 ECOL**
Corliss, William R. Direct conversion of energy. 1964 **TK2896.C6 ECOL**
Corliss, William R. Nuclear Propulsion for space. 1967 **TL783.5.C62 ECOL**
Corliss, William R. Power reactors in small packages. 1968 **TK1078.C6 1968 ECOL**
Corliss, William R. SNAP nuclear space reactors. 1966 **TL1102.N8C6 ECOL**
Corliss, William R. Space radiation. 1968
QC485.C613 ECOL
Craven, Claude Jackson. Our atomic world. Rev. 1964. **QC778.C7 1964 ECOL**
Donnelly, Warren H. Nuclear power and merchant shipping. Rev. c1965 **VM317.D6 1965 ECOL**
Fox, Charles H. Radioactive wastes. Rev. 1969.
TD898.F6 1969 ECOL
Glasstone, Samuel. Controlled nuclear fusion. Rev. ed. 1968 **QC791.G48 1968 ECOL**
Hines, Neal O. Atoms, nature, and man. c1966
QC778.H54 ECOL
Hogerton, John F. Atomic fuel. 1969
TK9360.H6 1969 ECOL
Hogerton, John F. Atomic fuel. Rev. 1964.
TK9360.H6 1964 ECOL
Hogerton, John F. Atomic power safety. c1964
TK1078.H62 ECOL
Kastner, Jacob. The natural radiation environment. 1968. **QH652.K35 ECOL**
LeCompte, Robert G. Atoms at the science fair. 1968 **Q105.L412 1968 ECOL**
Singleton, Arthur L. Sources of nuclear fuel. 1968
TN490.U7S52 ECOL
Urrows, Grace M. Food preservation by irradiation. 1968 **TX611.5.U7 1968 ECOL**
Urrows, Grace M. Nuclear energy for desalting. Rev. 1967 **TD479.6.U7 1967 ECOL**

UNDERWATER AND FLOATING-LEAVED PLANTS OF THE UNITED STATES AND CANADA, 1972.
Hotchkiss, Neil,
In: Hotchkiss, Neil. Common marsh, underwater, and floating-leaved plants of the United States and Canada. 1972 **QK115.H67 1972 ECOL**

UNDERWATER STORAGE OF COMBINED SEWER OVERFLOWS.
Karl R. Rohrer Associates. 1971
fTD662.K36 ECOL

THE UNEXPECTED UNIVERSE.
Eiseley, Loren C. 1969 **Q171.E39 ECOL**

UNFIT FOR HUMAN CONSUMPTION.
Harmer, Ruth Mulvey. 1971
QH545.P4H36 ECOL

THE UNFORSEEN INTERNATIONAL ECOLOGIC BOOMERANG.
1969 **fQH541.U5 ECOL**

UNIDIRECTIONAL TURBULENCE SENSOR DEVELOPMENT.
Battelle Memorial Institute. Columbus, Ohio. Columbus Laboratories Multidirectional turbulence probe development. **fTC177.B3 ECOL**

UNISIST: STUDY REPORT ON THE FEASIBILITY OF A WORLD SCIENCE SYSTEM.
United Nations Educational, Scientific and Cultural Organization. 1971. **REF Q223.U5 ECOL**

THE UNITED NATIONS AND THE HUMAN ENVIRONMENT.
Commission to Study the Organization of Peace. 1972 **HC68.C62 ECOL**

THE UNITED NATIONS AND THE POPULATION QUESTION, 1945-1970.
Symonds, Richard. 1973 **HQ766.S888 ECOL**

UNITED NATIONS. DOCUMENT ST/ECE/STEEL/33.
United Nations. Economic Commission for Europe. Problems relating to iron and steel scrap. 1971.
fTS214.U6 ECOL

UNITED NATIONS EDUCATIONAL, SCIENTIFIC AND CULTURAL ORGANIZATION. DOCUMENT.
Clubb, Jerome M. Ecological data in comparative research. 1970 **H62.C6 ECOL**

UNITED NATIONS EDUCATIONAL, SCIENTIFIC AND CULTURAL ORGANIZATION. DOCUMENT SC. 70/D.75.
United Nations Educational, Scientific and Cultural Organization. UNISIST: study report on the feasibility of a world science system. 1971.
REF Q223.U5 ECOL

UNITED NATIONS EDUCATIONAL, SCIENTIFIC AND CULTURAL ORGANIZATION. DOCUMENT SHC.70/XV.25.
Clubb, Jerome M. Ecological data in comparative research. 1970 **H62.C6 ECOL**

UNITED NATIONS EDUCATIONAL, SCIENTIFIC AND CULTURAL ORGANIZATION. SOCIAL SCIENCE CLEARING HOUSE. REPORTS AND PAPERS IN THE SOCIAL SCIENCES NO. 25.
Clubb, Jerome M. Ecological data in comparative research. 1970   **H62.C6 ECOL**

UNITED NATIONS LIST OF NATIONAL PARKS AND EQUIVALENT RESERVES.
International Commission on National Parks. 1972.   **REF SB481.I55 1971 Suppl. ECOL**
International Commission on National Parks. 2nd ed. 1971.   **REF SB481.I55 1971 ECOL**

UNITED STATES ARMY CORPS OF ENGINEERS. INSTITUTE FOR WATER RESOURCES. REPORT 71-12.
Mathematica, Inc., Bethesda, Md. The implications of the net fiscal benefits criterion for cost sharing in flood control projects. 1971.   **TC530.M3 ECOL**

THE UNITED STATES ATOMIC ENERGY COMMISSION.
United States. Atomic Energy Commission. 1965   **HD9698.A2U5 ECOL**

UNITED STATES ATOMIC ENERGY COMMISSION. UNDERSTANDING THE ATOM.
Asimov, Isaac. The genetic effects of radiation. c1966   **QH652.5.A8 ECOL**
Baker, Philip Schaffner. Radioisotopes in industry. c1965   **TK9400.B3 ECOL**
Berger, Harold. Nondestructive testing. 1965   **TA417.2.B4 ECOL**
Comar, Cyril Lewis. Fallout from nuclear tests. 1963   **UF767.C64 ECOL**
Comar, Cyril Lewis. Fallout from nuclear tests. Rev. 1966   **UF767.C64 1966 ECOL**
Corliss, William R. Direct conversion of energy. 1964   **TK2896.C6 ECOL**
Corliss, William R. Nuclear Propulsion for space. 1967   **TL783.5.C62 ECOL**
Corliss, William R. Power reactors in small packages. 1968   **TK1078.C6 1968 ECOL**
Corliss, William R. SNAP nuclear space reactors. 1966   **TL1102.N8C6 ECOL**
Corliss, William R. Space radiation. 1968   **QC485.C613 ECOL**
Craven, Claude Jackson. Our atomic world. Rev. 1964.   **QC778.C7 1964 ECOL**
Donnelly, Warren H. Nuclear power and merchant shipping. Rev. c1965   **VM317.D6 1965 ECOL**
Faul, Henry. Nuclear clocks. Rev. 1968   **QC798.D3F37 1968 ECOL**
Fox, Charles H. Radioactive wastes. c1965   **TD898.F6 ECOL**
Fox, Charles H. Radioactive wastes. Rev. 1969.   **TD898.F6 1969 ECOL**
Gerber, Carl R. Plowshare. 1966   **TK9153.G4 ECOL**
Glasstone, Samuel. Controlled nuclear fusion. Rev. ed. 1968   **QC791.G48 1968 ECOL**
Hines, Neal O. Atoms, nature, and man. c1966   **QC778.H54 ECOL**
Hogerton, John F. Atomic fuel. 1969   **TK9360.H6 1969 ECOL**
Hogerton, John F. Atomic fuel. Rev. 1964.   **TK9360.H6 1964 ECOL**
Hogerton, John F. Atomic power safety. c1964   **TK1078.H62 ECOL**
Kastner, Jacob. The natural radiation environment. 1968.   **QH652.K35 ECOL**
LeCompte, Robert G. Atoms at the science fair. 1968   **Q105.L412 1968 ECOL**
Lyerly, Ray L. Nuclear power plants. Rev. 1969   **TK1078.L9 1969 ECOL**
Lyman, James D. Nuclear terms. 2d ed. 1966.   **QC772.L9 1966 ECOL**
Martens, Frederick Hilbert. Research reactors. 1965   **QC787.N8M32 ECOL**
Mead, Robert L. Power from radioisotopes. Rev. 1966   **TK1078.M38 ECOL**
Singleton, Arthur L. Sources of nuclear fuel. 1968   **TN490.U7S52 ECOL**
United States. Atomic Energy Commission. Index to the Understanding the atom series. 1970   **REF Z5160.U4915 1970 ECOL**
Urrows, Grace M. Food preservation by irradiation. 1968   **TX611.5.U7 1968 ECOL**
Urrows, Grace M. Nuclear energy for desalting. Rev. 1967   **TD479.6.U7 1967 ECOL**

UNITED STATES BUREAU OF MINES. INFORMATION CIRCULAR 8514.
Ely, Northcutt. Summary of mining and petroleum laws of the world. Rev. 1970-   **TN295.U4no.8514 ECOL**

U.S. BUREAU OF MINES. INFORMATION CIRCULAR 8526.
Linville, Bill. Review of Bureau of Mines energy program, 1970. 1971   **TN295.U4no.8526 ECOL**

UNITED STATES. BUREAU OF MINES. INFORMATION CIRCULAR 8595.
Kenahan, Charles B. Bureau of Mines research programs on recycling and disposal of mineral-, metal-, and energy-based wastes. 1973.   **TN23.U7no.8595 ECOL**

UNITED STATES BUREAU OF MINES. INFORMATION CIRCULAR 8608.
Haas, Larry A. Sulfur dioxide: its chemistry as related to methods for removing it from waste gases. 1973   **TN23.U7no.8608 ECOL**

UNITED STATES BUREAU OF MINES. REPORT OF INVESTIGATIONS 7700.
Dimitriades, Basil. Interpretation of gas chromatographic spectra in routine analysis of exhaust hydrocarbons. 1972   **TN23.U7no.7700 ECOL**

UNITED STATES. BUREAU OF MINES. REPORT OF INVESTIGATIONS 7707.
Eccleston, Barton H. Effect of fuel front-end and midrange volatility on automobile emissions. 1972?   **TN23.U7no.7707 ECOL**

U.S. BUREAU OF RADIOLOGICAL HEALTH. BRH/DMRE 71-4.
Pettigrew, George L. State and Federal control of health hazards from radioactive materials other than materials regulated under the Atomic energy act of 1954 (as of October 1, 1969). 1971.   **RA1231.R2U5125no.71-4 ECOL**

UNITED STATES BUREAU OF RECLAMATION. A WATER RESOURCES TECHNICAL PUBLICATION.
Otto, Norman E. Aquatic pests on irrigation systems: identification guide. 1972,1965   **QH96.O88 1972 ECOL**

UNITED STATES BUREAU OF SPORT FISHERIES AND WILDLIFE. RESOURCE PUBLICATION 34.
United States. Committee on Rare and Endangered Wildlife Species. Rare and endangered fish and wildlife of the United States. Rev. ed. 1968 i.e. 1969   **S914.A3no.34 1969 ECOL**

UNITED STATES. BUREAU OF SPORT FISHERIES AND WILDLIFE. RESOURCE PUBLICATION 99.
Stoudt, Jerome H. Ecological factors affecting waterfowl production in the Saskatchewan Parklands. 1971.   **S914.A3no.99 ECOL**

U.S. BUREAU OF SPORT FISHERIES AND WILDLIFE. RESOURCE PUBLICATION 114.
United States. Bureau of Sport Fisheries and Wildlife. Office of Endangered Species and International Activities. Threatened wildlife of the United States. 1973.   **S914.A3no.114 1973 ECOL**

UNITED STATES. BUREAU OF SPORT FISHERIES AND WILDLIFE RESOURCE PUBLICATION, 44 (ETC.).
Hotchkiss, Neil. Common marsh, underwater, and floating-leaved plants of the United States and Canada. 1972   **QK115.H67 1972 ECOL**

UNITED STATES BUREAU OF SPORT FISHERIES AND WILDLIFE. RESOURCE PUBLICATION, 92.
Stewart, Robert E. Classification of natural ponds and lakes in the glaciated prairie region. 1971.   **S914.A3no.92 ECOL**

U.S. BUREAU OF SPORT FISHERIES AND WILDLIFE. RESOURCE PUBLICATION 94.
United States. Bureau of Sport Fisheries and Wildlife. Division of Wildlife Research. Wildlife research: problems programs, progress, 1969. 1971   **S914.A3no.94 ECOL**

U.S. BUREAU OF SPORT FISHERIES AND WILDLIFE. RESOURCE PUBLICATION 98.
Smith, Allen E. Ecological factors affecting waterfowl production in the Alberta parklands. 1971.   **S914.A3no.98 ECOL**

UNITED STATES. BUREAU OF SPORT FISHERIES AND WILDLIFE. WILDLIFE RESEARCH REPORT, 1.
Henny, Charles J. An analysis of the population dynamics of selected avian species. 1972   **QL785.5.B6H4 ECOL**

U.S. COASTAL ENGINEERING RESEARCH CENTER. MISCELLANEOUS PAPER 2-72.
Allen, Richard H. A glossary of coastal engineering terms. 1972   **REF TC1645.A4 ECOL**

U.S. COASTAL ENGINEERING RESEARCH CENTER. TECHNICAL MEMORANDUM, NO. 37.
Thomsen, Arvid L. Riprap stability on earth embankments tested in large—and small-scale wave tanks. 1972.   **TC533.T4 ECOL**

UNITED STATES. COMMISSION ON POPULATION GROWTH AND THE AMERICAN FUTURE. RESEARCH REPORTS, V. 3.
United States. Commission on Population Growth and the American Future. Population, resources, and the environment. 1972   **HB3505.A527 ECOL**

UNITED STATES. DEPT. OF AGRICULTURE. AGRICULTURE HANDBOOK NO. 380.
Lillie, Robert Jones. Air pollutants affecting the performance of domestic animals. Slightly rev. 1972.   **SF757.5.L54 1972 ECOL**

U.S. DEPT. OF AGRICULTURE. MISCELLANEOUS PUBLICATION NO. 1146.
Little, Elbert Luther. Atlas of United States trees. 1971-   **REF fS21.A46no.1146 ECOL**

UNITED STATES DEPT. OF AGRICULTURE. MISCELLANEOUS PUBLICATION NO. 1206.
Hutchins, Wells A. Water rights laws in the nineteen western states. 1971-   **KF5559.A45H8 ECOL**

U.S. DEPT. OF HEALTH, EDUCATION, AND WELFARE. DHEW PUBLICATION NO. (FDA) 72-8001.
Pettigrew, George L. State and Federal control of health hazards from radioactive materials other than materials regulated under the Atomic energy act of 1954 (as of October 1, 1969). 1971.   **RA1231.R2U5125no.71-4 ECOL**

UNITED STATES. DEPT. OF STATE. INTERNATIONAL ORGANIZATION AND CONFERENCE SERIES, 101.
Stockholm and beyond. 1972.   **HC110.E5A43 ECOL**

UNITED STATES. DEPT. OF STATE. PUBLICATION 8657.
Stockholm and beyond. 1972.   **HC110.E5A43 ECOL**

UNITED STATES. DEPT. OF THE INTERIOR. CONSERVATION YEARBOOK NO. 8.
United States. Dept. of the Interior. Our environment and natural resources ... indivisibly one. 1971?   **fS914.A533 ECOL**

UNITED STATES ENERGY POLICIES.
Resources for the Future. 1969,c1968   **HD9546.R4 1969 ECOL**

UNITED STATES ENERGY THROUGH THE YEAR 2000.
Dupree, Walter G. 1972.   **HD9545.D8 ECOL**

UNITED STATES ENVIRONMENTAL PROTECTION AGENCY. AIR POLLUTION CONTROL OFFICE. PUB. NO.AP-92-93.
Air Pollution Technical Information Center. Air pollution aspects of emission sources: a bibliography with abstracts. 1971-   **Z7173.A4A5 ECOL**

UNITED STATES ENVIRONMENTAL PROTECTION AGENCY. INDUSTRIAL POLLUTION CONTROL BRANCH.
Battelle Memorial Institute, Columbus, Ohio Columbus Laboratories An investigation of techniques for removal of chromium from electroplating wastes. 1971.   **fTD899.M45B3ECOL**

UNITED STATES ENVIRONMENTAL PROTECTION AGENCY. OFFICE OF AIR PROGRAMS. PUB. NO.AP-94-
Air Pollution Technical Information Center. Air pollution aspects of emission sources: a bibliography with abstracts. 1971-   **Z7173.A4A5 ECOL**

UNITED STATES ENVIRONMENTAL PROTECTION AGENCY. OFFICE OF AIR PROGRAMS. PUBLICATION NO. AP-100.
Air Pollution Technical Information Center. Hydrochloric acid and air pollution: an annotated bibliography. 1971.   **Z7173.A4A52 ECOL**

UNITED STATES. ENVIRONMENTAL PROTECTION AGENCY. OFFICE OF AIR PROGRAMS. PUBLICATION NO. AP-102.
United States. Environmental Protection Agency. Federal air quality control regions. 1972.   **REF TD883.2.U42 ECOL**

UNITED STATES. ENVIRONMENTAL PROTECTION AGENCY. OFFICE OF AIR PROGRAMS. PUBLICATION NO. AP-47-
Pennsylvania. State University. Center for Air Environment Studies. Guide to research in air pollution. 8th- ed.   **REF TD883.15.P4 ECOL**

U.S. FOREST SERVICE. RESEARCH PAPER NC-63.
Ohmann, Lewis F. Wilderness ecology, virgin plant communities of the Boundary Waters Canoe Area. 1971. **SD11.A45476no.63 ECOL**

U.S. PUBLIC HEALTH SERVICE PUB. NO. 1908.
Drobny, N. L. Recovery and utilization of municipal solid waste: a summary of available cost and performance characteristics of unit processes and systems. 1971. **TD793.D76 ECOL**

U.S. PUBLIC HEALTH SERVICE PUBLICATION NO. 1729.
Surgeon General's Conference on Solid Waste Management for Metropolitan Washington, Washington, D. C., 1967. 1967. **TD525.W2S7 1967 ECOL**

U.S. PUBLIC HEALTH SERVICE PUBLICATION NO. 1855.
Darnay, Arsen. The role of packaging in solid waste management 1966 to 1976. 1969. **TD795.D37 ECOL**

U.S. PUBLIC HEALTH SERVICE PUBLICATION NO. 1867.
Muhich, Anton J. Preliminary data analysis. 1968. **TD795.M82 ECOL**

U.S. PUBLIC HEALTH SERVICE PUBLICATION NO. 2040.
Franklin, William E. The role of nonpackaging paper in solid waste management, 1966 to 1976. 1971. **TD795.F7 ECOL**

U.S. PUBLIC HEALTH SERVICE PUBLICATION NO. 2093.
Symposium of State and Interstate Solid Waste Planning Agencies, St. Louis, 1969. Planning for solid waste management. 1971 **TD523.S94 1969 ECOL**

UNITED STATES TIMBER RESOURCES IN A WORLD ECONOMY.
Zivnuska, John Arthur. c1967 **HD9750.5.Z5 ECOL**

THE UNKNOWN OCEAN.
Perry, Richard. 1972 **QL124.P47 1972 ECOL**

UNUSUAL CAREERS: SOLAR SCIENTIST, METEOROLOGIST, OCEANOGRAPHER, GEOLOGIST, ECOLOGIST, SANITARY ENGINEER, RESEARCH CHEMIST, CITY AND REGIONAL PLANNER.
Munzer, Martha E. 1st ed. 1962. **Q147.M8 ECOL**

UPPER MISSISSIPPI RIVER COMPREHENSIVE BASIN STUDY.
1970- **fHC107.A15U6 ECOL**

THE URBAN ENVIRONMENT: A CLIMATOLOGICAL ANOMALY.
Berlin, G. Lennis. 1972 **REF fQC981.7.U7B47 ECOL**

THE URBAN ENVIRONMENT: HOW IT CAN BE IMPROVED.
Zisch, William E. 1969. **HT175.U6Z4 ECOL**

THE URBAN ENVIRONMENT: SELECTED BIBLIOGRAPHY.
Appleyard, Donald. 1972. **REF fZ7164.U7A6 ECOL**

URBAN GROWTH AND LAND DEVELOPMENT.
Advisory Committee to the Department of Housing and Urban Development. Land Use Subcommittee. 1972. **HD205 1972 .A35 ECOL**

URBAN LAND USE PLANNING.
Chapin, Francis Stuart. 2d ed. 1965. **NA9108.C53 1965 ECOL**

URBAN-METROPOLITAN INSTITUTIONS FOR WATER PLANNING, DEVELOPMENT AND MANAGEMENT: AN ANALYSIS OF USAGES OF THE TERM "INSTITUTIONS": A STATE-OF-THE-ART REVIEW: FINAL REPORT, SUBMITTED TO WATER RESOURCES SCIENTIFIC INFORMATION CENTER.
Wengert, Norman. 1972. **fTD353.W42 ECOL**

URBAN OPEN SPACE: PARKS, PEOPLE AND PLANNING.
Bureau of Municipal Research, Toronto. 1971. **GV56.T6B8 ECOL**

THE URBAN PATTERN.
Gallion, Arthur B. 2d ed. 1963 **NA9031.G3 1963 ECOL**

URBAN PLANNING ASPECTS OF WATER POLLUTION CONTROL.
Grava, Sigurd. 1969. **TD420.G67 ECOL**

URBAN RUNOFF.
McPherson, M. B. 1972. **fGB665.M35 ECOL**

URBAN SOIL EROSION AND SEDIMENT CONTROL.
National Association of Counties Research Foundation. 1970. **fS624.A1N38 ECOL**

URBAN WATER PLANNING.
Water Resources Scientific Information Center. 1972. **REF Z7935.W3 ECOL**

URBANIZATION AND ENVIRONMENT.
Detwyler, Thomas R. 1972 **HT151.D46 ECOL**

U.S.A.E.C.; WHAT IT IS, WHAT IT DOES.
United States. Atomic Energy Commission. The United States Atomic Energy Commission. 1965 **HD9698.A2U5 ECOL**

USDA - SOIL CONSERVATION SERVICE IN MINNESOTA.
Major, Harry M. 1973. **S624.M6M3 ECOL**

USDA FOREST SERVICE RESEARCH PAPER NC52.
Ecological studies of the timber wolf in northeastern Minnesota. 1971 **SD11.A45476no.52 ECOL**

U.S.D.A. FOREST SERVICE RESEARCH PAPER NE-194.
Northeastern Forest Insect Work Conference, 3rd, New Haven, 1970. Toward integrated control. 1971 **SD11.A455492no.194 ECOL**

THE USE OF DRUGS IN ANIMAL FEEDS.
1969. **SF98.M4U8 ECOL**

USE OF NATURALLY IMPAIRED WATER.
Water Resources Scientific Information Center. 1973. **Z7935.W32 ECOL**

THE USE OF PESTICIDES IN SUBURBAN HOMES AND GARDENS AND THEIR IMPACT ON THE AQUATIC ENVIRONMENT.
Von Rumker, Rosmarie. 1972. **fQH545.P4V66 ECOL**

USE OF SYSTEMS TECHNIQUES IN ENVIRONMENTAL QUALITY MANAGEMENT.
1970. **RA565.A1N38no.7 ECOL**

THE USER'S GUIDE TO THE PROTECTION OF THE ENVIRONMENT.
Swatek, Paul. Walden edition 1970 **TX335.S93 ECOL**

USES OF THE SEAS.
1968 **GC1015.U8 ECOL**

USING WAYSIDE PLANTS.
Coon, Nelson. 4th rev. ed. 1969 **SB108.U6N7 1969 ECOL**

UTILIZATION OF PHOSPHATE SLIMES.
International Minerals and Chemical Corporation. 1971. **fTD899.M5I57 ECOL**

V

VALUES AND THE FUTURE.
Baier, Kurt. 1969 **HM221.B27 ECOL**

VANISHING AIR.
1970. **TD883.2.V35 ECOL**

VANISHING WILD ANIMALS OF THE WORLD.
Fitter, Richard Sidney Richmond. 1968 **fQL88.F5 ECOL**

VEHICLE EMISSION CONTROL.
1971? **fTD886.5.V4 ECOL**

VIRGINIA POLYTECHNIC INSTITUTE, BLACKSBURG. WATER RESOURCES RESEARCH CENTER. BULLETIN 26.
Economics of air and water pollution. 1969. **fTD201.V57no.26 ECOL**

VOICES FOR THE WILDERNESS.
Schwartz, William. 1969 **QH75.S32 ECOL**

THE VOYAGEUR'S HIGHWAY.
Nute, Grace Lee. 1965 c1941 **F606.N97 ECOL**

W

W. FORK DES MOINES RIVER AND PERKINS CREEK FLOOD PLAIN INFORMATION, WINDOM, MINNESOTA.
United States. Army. Corps of Engineers. 1972. **GB1225.M6A5 ECOL**

WANDERING THROUGH WINTER.
Teale, Edwin Way. 1965. **QH104.T43 ECOL**

THE WAR THAT BUSINESS MUST WIN.
Osborne, Philip B. 1970 **HD60.5.U5O8 ECOL**

THE WARBLERS OF AMERICA.
Griscom, Ludlow. 1957. **REF QL696.P2G85 ECOL**

WASHINGTON SEA GRANT PUBLICATION.
Oil on Puget Sound. 1972 **fTD427.P4O38 ECOL**

WASHOUT PROCESSES IN LAKE SYSTEMS.
Frea, James I. 1972. **fTD764.F74 ECOL**

WASTE ASSIMILATION CAPACITY OF THE MISSISSIPPI RIVER IN THE TWIN CITIES METROPOLITAN AREA.
Minnesota. Division of Water Quality. Memorandum on the waste assimilation capacity of the Mississippi River in the Twin Cities Metropolitan Area. 1969. **fTD525.T9M6 ECOL**

WASTE DISPOSAL REPORTS AND MEMORANDUMS OF INDUSTRIES OF MINNESOTA.
Minnesota. Division of Water Quality. 1961- **fTD224.M6A35 ECOL**

WASTE MANAGEMENT AND CONTROL.
National Research Council. Committee on Pollution. 1966. **REF TD180.N3 ECOL**

WASTE REDUCTION IN FOOD CANNING OPERATIONS.
National Canners Association. Western Research Laboratory. 1970 i.e. 1971 **fTD899.C3N37 ECOL**

WASTE TREATMENT PLANT SITE STUDY FOR SOUTHWEST SUBURBAN MUNICIPALITIES REPORT.
Schoell and Madson, Inc., Hopkins, Minn. 1968. **fTD525.T9S3 ECOL**

WASTE TREATMENT WITH POLYELECTROLYTES, 1972.
Gutcho, Sidney. 1972 **TD751.G87 ECOL**

WASTE WOOL AS A SCAVENGER FOR MERCURY POLLUTION IN WATERS.
Tratnyek, Joseph P. 1972. **fTD427.M4T7 ECOL**

WASTES MANAGEMENT CONCEPTS FOR THE COASTAL ZONE.
Steering Committee on Coastal Wastes Management. 1970. **TD763.S7 ECOL**

WASTEWATER DEMINERALIZATION BY ION EXCHANGE.
Kreusch, Ed. 1971 i.e.1972 **fTD757.5.K74 ECOL**

WASTEWATER DISPOSAL FACILITIES INVENTORY, STATE OF MINNESOTA.
Minnesota. Division of Water Quality. 1971- **fTD224.M6A33 ECOL**

WASTEWATER ENGINEERING: COLLECTION, TREATMENT, DISPOSAL.
Metcalf and Eddy, Boston. 1972 **TD645.M57 ECOL**

WASTEWATER MANAGEMENT REPORT 72-1.
Assessment of the effectiveness and effects of land disposal methodologies of waste water management. 1972. **fTD760.A86 ECOL**

WASTEWATER TREATMENT WORKS STUDIES, SURVEYS, MEMORANDUMS, REPORTS, ETC. OF CITIES AND VILLAGES OF MINNESOTA.
Minnesota. Division of Water Quality. 1964- **fTD224.M6A36 ECOL**

WATCHING ANIMALS.
Wong, Herbert H. Pond life: watching animals find food. c1970 **PZ10.W748Po ECOL**

WATER.
Fox, Sir Cyril Sankey. 1972 **GB661.F65 1972 ECOL**

WATER ALL AROUND.
Pine, Tillie S. c1959 **PZ10.P57Wat ECOL**

WATER AND WASTEWATER CONTROL ENGINEERING.
Glossary: water and wastewater control engineering. 1969. **TD9.G55 ECOL**

WATER AND WASTEWATER ENGINEERING.
Fair, Gordon Maskew. 1966-1968 **REF TD145.F32 ECOL**

WATER AND WATER POLLUTION HANDBOOK.
1971- **TD380.W322 ECOL**

THE WATER CRISIS.
Moss, Frank E. c1967 **HD1694.A5M63 ECOL**
Nikolaieff, George A. 1967. **TD355.N5 ECOL**

WATER DEMAND FOR STEAM ELECTRIC GENERATION.
Cootner, Paul H. 1966,c1965 **TK1051.C6 ECOL**

THE WATER ENCYCLOPEDIA.
Todd, David Keith. 1970 **REF TD351.T63 ECOL**

WATER FIT TO USE.
Carlson, Carl Walter. 1966 **TD348.C3 ECOL**

WATER FLOW IN SOIL IN PRESENCE OF SOYBEAN ROOT SINKS.
Arya, Lalit Mohan. 1973. **GB701.M554no.60 ECOL**

WATER FOR PEOPLE.
Riedman, Sarah Regal. Rev. ed. c1960
TC153.R5 1960 ECOL

WATER FOR THE WORLD.
Helfman, Elizabeth S. 1st ed. 1967,c1960
GB671.H4 ECOL

WATER, HEALTH, AND SOCIETY.
Wolman, Abel. 1969 **REF TD355.W6 ECOL**

THE WATER HUSTLERS.
Boyle, Robert H. 1971 **HD1694.A5B58 ECOL**

WATER IN INDUSTRY.
National Association of Manufacturers of the United States. 1965. **fTD223.N3 1965 ECOL**

WATER LAW AND ADMINISTRATION.
Maloney, Frank Edward. 1968.
REF KFF446.M3 ECOL

WATER LAW AND ITS RELATIONSHIP TO ENVIRONMENTAL QUALITY: A BIBLIOGRAPHY OF SOURCE MATERIAL.
Radosevich, George E. 1973.
REF fKF5551.R3 ECOL

WATER MOVEMENTS AND TEMPERATURES OF WESTERN LAKE SUPERIOR.
Minnesota. University. School of Public Health. 1958. **fGB1627.G89M54 ECOL**

WATER POLLUTION.
Berg, George G. 1970 **fTD420.B46 ECOL**
Lavaroni, Charles W. c1971 **TD420.L28 ECOL**
Laycock, George. 1972 **TD422.L38 ECOL**
Zajic, James E. 1971. **TD420.Z35 ECOL**

WATER POLLUTION AND HEALTH: PROCEEDINGS.
International Water Quality Symposium, 5th, Washington, D.C., 1970. 1970
fTD423.I6 1970 ECOL

WATER POLLUTION ASPECTS OF STREET SURFACE CONTAMINANTS.
Sartor, James D. 1972. **fTD665.S2 ECOL**

WATER POLLUTION ASPECTS OF URBAN RUNOFF.
American Public Works Association. 1969.
TD420.A4 ECOL

WATER POLLUTION BY NUTRIENTS—SOURCES, EFFECTS AND CONTROL.
Soil Conservation Society of America. Minnesota Chapter. 1969. **GB701.M554no.13 ECOL**

WATER POLLUTION: CONTROL AND ABATEMENT PROCEEDINGS.
Iowa Water Resources Pollution Control and Abatement Seminar, Iowa State University, 1965. 1st ed. 1970,c1967 **TD224.I8I6 1965 ECOL**

WATER POLLUTION CONTROL FEDERATION DIRECTORY. VOL.44- MARCH 1972-
REF TD201.W32 ECOL

WATER POLLUTION CONTROL IN THE WATER UTILITY INDUSTRY.
American Water Works Association Research Foundation, New York Information resource: water pollution control in the water utility industry. 1971.
REF fTD429.A4 ECOL

WATER POLLUTION CONTROL RESEARCH SERIES.
Investigation of porous pavements for urban runoff control. 1972. **fTE215.I58 ECOL**
Water quality criteria data book. 1970-
REF fTD370.W394 ECOL
Abt Associates. Factors affecting pollution referenda. 1971. **fGH4952.A6 ECOL**
Aerojet-General Corporation. Environmental Systems Division. Reverse osmosis renovation of municipal wastewater. 1970 **fTD754.A35 ECOL**
Alamo Area Council of Governments. Basin management for water reuse. 1972.
fTD225.S225A65 ECOL
Alpine Geophysical Associates. Oil pollution incident. 1971. **fGC1221.A4 ECOL**
American Enka Corporation. Central Engineering Dept. Zinc precipitation and recovery from viscose rayon waste water. 1971. **fTD899.T4A44 ECOL**
American Process Equipment Corporation. Ultrasonic filtration of combined sewer overflows. 1970. **fTD753.A6 ECOL**
American Public Works Association. Combined sewer regulator overflow facilities; report. 1970.
fTD662.A42 ECOL
American Public Works Association. Feasibility of computer control of wastewater treatment. 1970.
fTD746.A43 ECOL
American Public Works Association. Prevention and correction of excessive infiltration and inflow into sewer systems. 1971. **fTD678.A44 ECOL**
American Public Works Association. Water pollution aspects of urban runoff. 1969.
TD420.A4 ECOL
Armco Steel Corporation. Limestone treatment of rinse waters from hydrochloric acid pickling of steel. 1971. **fTD899.M45A75 ECOL**
Atkins, Patrick R. The pesticide manufacturing industry—current waste treatment and disposal practices. 1972. **fTD899.C5A8 ECOL**
Austin, Texas Design guides for biological wastewater treatment processes. 1971 i.e.1972
fTD755.A87 ECOL
Balakrishnan, S. State of the art review on sludge incineration practice. 1970. **fTD803.B36 ECOL**
Battelle Memorial Institute, Columbus, Ohio. Pacific Northwest Laboratory, Richland, Wash. Concept development of a hydraulic skimmer system for recovery of floating oil. 1971. **fTD427.P4B29 ECOL**
Battelle Memorial Institute, Columbus, Ohio Corrosion potential of NTA in detergent formulations. 1971. **fTP992.5.B3 ECOL**
Battelle Memorial Institute, Columbus, Ohio Columbus Laboratories An investigation of techniques for removal of chromium from electroplating wastes. 1971. **fTD899.M45B3 ECOL**
Battelle Memorial Institute, Columbus, Ohio. Columbus Laboratories An investigation of techniques for removal of cyanide from electroplating wastes. 1971 i.e. 1972 **fTD899.M45B32 ECOL**
Battelle Memorial Institute, Columbus, Ohio. Columbus Laboratories Multidirectional turbulence probe development. 1971. **fTC177.B3 ECOL**
Battelle Memorial Institute, Columbus, Ohio. Columbus Laboratories A state-of-the-art review of metal finishing waste treatment. 1968 i.e.1970
fTD899.M45B33 ECOL
Battelle-Northwest. Inorganic fertilizer and phosphate mining industries—water pollution and control. 1971. **fTD899.F47B38 ECOL**
Beefland International, Inc. Elimination of water pollution by packing-house animal paunch and blood. 1971. **fTD899.M4B4 ECOL**
Beet Sugar Development Foundation, Fort Collins, Colo. State-of-art, sugarbeet processing waste treatment. 1971. **fTD899.S8B43 ECOL**
Biospherics Incorporated. Biomass determination—a new technique for activated sludge control. 1972. **fTD756.B5 ECOL**
Black, Sivalls and Bryson, inc., Kansas City, Mo. Applied Technology Division Evaluation of a new acid mine drainage treatment process. 1971.
fTD899.M5B55 ECOL
Black, Sivalls and Bryson, Inc., Kansas City, Mo. Applied Technology Division Study of sulfur recovery from coal refuse. 1971. **fTN890.B57 ECOL**
Boen, Doyle F. Study of reutilization of wastewater recycled through groundwater. 1971.
fTD429.B6 ECOL
Bongers, Leonard H. Sand and gravel overlay for control of mercury in sediments. 1972.
fTD427.M4B6 ECOL
Bouwer, Herman. Renovating secondary sewage by ground water recharge with infiltration basins. 1972.
fTD765.B6 ECOL
Boyce Thompson Institute for Plant Research, Yonkers, N.Y. Interaction of herbicides and soil microorganisms. 1971. **fSB951.4.B68 ECOL**
California. Dept. of Water Resources. Removal of nitrate by an algal system, phase II. 1971.
fTD475.C342 ECOL
California. University. Institute of Marine Resources. Eutrophication in coastal waters: nitrogen as a controlling factor. 1971. **fQH96.8.E9C34 ECOL**
California. University. Sanitary Engineering Research Laboratory. Optimization of ammonia removal by ion exchange using clinoptilolite. 1971 i.e. 1972 **fTD757.5.C35 ECOL**
California. University, Santa Barbara. Dept. of Biological Sciences. Santa Barbara oil spill: short-term analysis of macroplankton and fish. 1971.
fTD427.P4C34 ECOL
Champlin, Robert L. Supplementary aeration of lagoons in rigorous climate areas. 1971.
fTD746.5.C45 ECOL
Chesher, Richard H. Biological impact of a large-scale desalination plant at Key West. 1971.
fTD478.5.F5C48 ECOL
Clemson University. Dept. of Textiles. State of the art of textile waste treatment. 1971.
fTD899.T4C45 ECOL
Coca-Cola Company. Foods Division. Treatment of citrus processing wastes. 1970 **fTD899.F7C6 ECOL**
Collins, Ralph P. Characterization of taste and odors in water supplies. 1971. **fTD384.C64 ECOL**
Colorado. State University, Fort Collins. Water pollution potential of spent oil shale residues. 1971.
fTD899.P4C65 ECOL
Cornell Aeronautical Laboratory, Inc., Buffalo. Research on the physical aspects of thermal pollution. 1971. **fTD427.H4C67 ECOL**
Correll, Donovan Stewart. Aquatic and wetland plants of southwestern United States. 1972.
QK142.C6 ECOL
Cresa. Pollution abatement and by-product recovery in shellfish and fisheries processing. 1971.
fTD899.F57C73 ECOL
Crown Zellerbach Corporation. Lebanon Division. Aerated lagoon treatment of sulfite pulping effluents. 1970. **fTD899.W65C7 ECOL**
Dallas, Or. Combined treatment of domestic and industrial wastes by activated sludge. 1971.
fTD756.D35 ECOL
Datagraphics Incorporated. Inorganic chemicals industry profile (updated). 1971.
fTD899.C5D37 ECOL
Datagraphics Incorporated. Projected wastewater treatment costs in the organic chemicals industry (updated). 1971. **fTD899.C5D388 ECOL**
Davis, Ernst M. Bacterial effects of algae on enteric organisms. 1970. **fQR48.D38 ECOL**
Delaware River Basin Commission. Interstate planning for regional water supply and pollution control. 1971. **fTD420.D4 ECOL**
Detroit Metro Water Dept. Development of phosphate removal processes. 1970.
fTD756.D47 ECOL
Dodd, John D. The ecology of diatoms in hard water habitats. 1971. **fQK569.D54D6 ECOL**
Dow Chemical Company. Functional Products and Systems Dept. A literature search and critical analysis of biological trickling filter studies. 1971-
fTD443.D6 ECOL
Dow Chemical Company. Western Division Research Laboratories. Nitrate removal from wastewaters by ion exchange. 1971.
fTD757.5.D68 ECOL
Dynatech R/D Company. A survey of alternate methods for cooling condenser discharge water. 1969- **fTJ403.D9 ECOL**
Edison Water Quality Laboratory. Storm and Combined Sewer Overflows Section. Environmental impact of highway deicing. 1971.
fTE220.E35 ECOL
Envirogenics Company. Investigation of a new phosphate removal process. 1970. **fTD745.E5 ECOL**
Envirogenics Company. Reverse osmosis renovation of primary sewage. 1971. **fTD754.E58 ECOL**
Envirometrics, Inc., Wash., D.C. The river basin model. 1971- **fTC409.E5 ECOL**
Envirometrics, Inc., Wash., D.C. The river basin model: computer output. 1971. **fTC409.E51 ECOL**
Envirometrics, Inc., Wash., D.C. The river basin model: municipal services department. 1971.
fTC409.E5 ECOL
Environmental Measurements, Inc. Monitoring mercury vapor near pollution sites. 1971.
fTD427.M4E5 ECOL
Environmental Research and Applications, Inc. Concentrated mine drainage disposal into sewage treatment systems. 1971. **fTD899.M5E58 ECOL**
Environmental Systems Corporation. Development and demonstration of low-level drift instrumentation. 1971. **fTD884.5.E58 ECOL**
Fast, Arlo Wade. The effects of artificial aeration on lake ecology. 1971 i.e.1972 **fTD458.F38 ECOL**
Fitzgerald, George Patrick. Nutrient sources for algae and their control. 1971 i.e.1972
fQH96.8.E9F58 ECOL
Florida Ocean Sciences Institute. Limitations and effects of waste disposal on an ocean shelf. 1971 i.e.1972 **fTD763.F56 ECOL**
Fram Corporation. Bio-regenerated activated carbon treatment of textile dye wastewater. 1971.
fTD899.T4F7 ECOL
Franklin Institute, Philadelphia. Science Information Service. Selected urban storm water runoff abstracts, July 1970-June 1971. 1971. **fTD653.F7 ECOL**
Freese, Paul V. Full-scale raw wastewater flocculation with polymers. 1970. **fTD751.F7 ECOL**
Fuhriman, Dean K. Ground water pollution in Arizona, California, Nevada & Utah. 1971 i.e. 1972
fTD223.9.F85 ECOL
Gainesville, Fla. Dept. of Public Utilities. Magnesium carbonate, a recycled coagulant for water treatment. 1971. **fTD433.G3 ECOL**

TITLE CATALOG

WATER POLLUTION CONTROL RESEARCH SERIES

Gammon, James Robert. The effect of inorganic sediment on stream biota. 1970.
fQH541.5.S7G34 ECOL

Gaudy, Anthony F. Biological concepts for design and operation of the activated sludge process. 1971 i.e. 1972 **fTD756.G38 ECOL**

General Dynamics Corporation. Electric Boat Division. Potential environmental effects of an offshore submerged nuclear power plant. 1971-
fQH541.5.S3G45 ECOL

General Electric Company. Re-entry and Environmental Systems Division. Watercraft waste treatment system: development and demonstration report. 1971. **fTD745.G4 ECOL**

General Mills Chemicals. Feasibility of liquid ion exchange for extracting phosphate from wastewater. 1970. **fTD757.G45 ECOL**

Georgia Kraft Company. Research and Development Center. Treatment of selected internal kraft mill wastes in a cooling tower. 1971. **fTD899.W65G46 ECOL**

Ghassemi, Masood. Phosphate precipitation with ferrous iron. 1971. **fTD751.G4 ECOL**

Green Bay (Wis.) Metropolitan Sewerage District. Joint treatment of municipal sewage and pulp mill effluents. 1970. **fTD524.W6G74 ECOL**

Green Giant Company. Pilot plant installation for fungal treatment of vegetable canning wastes. 1971. **fTD899.C3G74 ECOL**

Grumman Aerospace Corporation. Development of immobilized enzyme systems for enhancement of biological waste treatment processes. 1970
fTD755.G78 ECOL

Gulf Environmental Systems Company. Acid mine waste treatment using reverse osmosis. 1971
fTD754.G84 ECOL

Harvard Water Program. The economics of water supply and quality. 1971. **fTD223.H34 ECOL**

Hogan, William T. Optimum mechanical aeration systems for rivers and ponds. 1970.
fTD458.H64 ECOL

Horizons Incorporated. Foam separation of acid mine drainage. 1971 **fTD899.M5H67 ECOL**

IIT Research Institute. Technology Center. Development of phosphate-free home laundry detergents. 1970. **fTP992.5.I2 ECOL**

International Minerals and Chemical Corporation. Utilization of phosphate slimes. 1971.
fTD899.M5I57 ECOL

International Symposium on Water Pollution Control in Cold Climates, University of Alaska, Fairbanks, 1970. Papers Held at the University of Alaska, July 22-24, 1970. 1972 **TD423.I5 ECOL**

Ionics, Inc. The electro-oxidation of ammonia in sewage to nitrogen. 1970. **fTD757.I55 ECOL**

Jacksonville, Ark. Biological treatment of chlorophenolic wastes. 1971. **fTD755.J3 ECOL**

JBF Scientific Corporation. Engineering methodology for river and stream reaeration. 1971
fTD458.J17 ECOL

Kansas. University. Center for Research, Inc. Oxygen consumption in continuous biological culture. 1971. **fTD755.K3 ECOL**

Karl R. Rohrer Associates. Underwater storage of combined sewer overflows. 1971
fTD662.K36 ECOL

Ketelle, Martha J. Problem lakes in the United States. 1971. **fTD223.K47 ECOL**

Kreusch, Ed. Wastewater demineralization by ion exchange. 1971 i.e.1972 **fTD757.5.K74 ECOL**

Lake Tahoe Area Council. Eutrophication of surface waters—Lake Tahoe. 1971 i.e. 1972
fQH96.8.E9L34 ECOL

Lake Tahoe Area Council. Eutrophication of surface waters—Lake Tahoe Indian Creek Reservoir. 1971.
fTD224.C3L32 ECOL

Law, James P. National irrigation return flow research and development program. 1971.
fTC809.L38 ECOL

Little (Arthur D.) Inc. Characterization and separation of secondary effluent components by molecular weight. 1971. **fTD735.L58 ECOL**

Mandan Refinery. Fluid bed incineration of petroleum refinery wastes. 1971.
fTD899.P4M35 ECOL

Manufacturing Chemists' Association. The effect of chlorination on selected organic chemicals. 1972.
fTD462.M3 ECOL

Maryland. University. School of Law. Legal problems of coal mine reclamation. 1972.
fKF1830.Z95M37 ECOL

Mayer, John K. Sewer bedding and infiltration, Gulf Coast area. 1972. **fTD653.M3 ECOL**

McCoy, Elizabeth F. Role of bacteria in the nitrogen cycle in lakes. 1972. **fTD433.M3 ECOL**

Mead Corporation. Multi-system biological treatment of bleached kraft effluents. 1971.
fTD899.W65M4 ECOL

Metcalf and Eddy, Boston. Storm water management model. 1971. **fGB665.M4 ECOL**

Michigan. State University, East Lansing. Agricultural Pollution Control Laboratory. Closed system waste management for livestock. 1971 i.e. 1972 **fTD899.F4M5 ECOL**

Midwest Research Institute, Kansas City, Mo. Light-catalyzed chlorine oxidation for treatment of wastewater. 1970. **fTD758.M5 ECOL**

Milwaukee. Sewerage Commission. Evaluation of conditioning and dewatering sewage sludge by freezing. 1971. **fTD769.7.M54 ECOL**

Milwaukee. Sewerage Commission. Phosphorus removal by an activated sludge plant. 1970.
fTD756.M54 ECOL

Milwaukee. Sewerage Commission. Phosphorus removal with pickle liquor in an activated sludge plant. 1971. **fTD756.M55 ECOL**

Minnesota. Pollution Control Agency. Pesticide inputs and levels: Minnesota waters-Lake Superior Basin. 1971 i.e. 1972 **fTD223.3.M55 ECOL**

Minnesota. State College, Winona. Mayfly distribution as a water quality index. 1970.
fTD370.M562 ECOL

Minnesota. University. St. Anthony Falls Hydraulic Laboratory. Hydraulics of long vertical conduits and associated cavitation. 1971. **fTC174.M53 ECOL**

Missouri. Southwest Missouri State College, Springfield. DNA concentration as an estimate of sludge biomass. 1971. **fTD767.7.M57 ECOL**

Montgomery County Sanitary Dept. Montgomery County, Ohio. Ground water infiltration and internal sealing of sanitary sewers, Montgomery County, Ohio. 1972. **fTD716.M6 ECOL**

Morton, Stephen D. The carbon dioxide system and eutrophication. 1971. **fQH96.8.E9M6 ECOL**

National Association of Counties Research Foundation. Urban soil erosion and sediment control. 1970. **fS624.A1N38 ECOL**

National Canners Association. Western Research Laboratory. Dry caustic peeling of tree fruit for liquid waste reduction. 1970. **fTD899.F7N37 ECOL**

National Canners Association. Western Research Laboratory. Reduction of salt content of food processing liquid waste effluent. 1971.
fTD899.C3N36 ECOL

National Canners Association. Western Research Laboratory. Waste reduction in food canning operations. 1970 i.e. 1971 **fTD899.C3N37 ECOL**

National Ground Water Quality Symposium, Denver, 1971. Proceedings. 1972
fTD223.N37 1971 ECOL

National Oil Recovery Corp., Bayonne, N.J. Conversion of crankcase waste oil into useful products. 1971. **fTP687.N3 ECOL**

National Steel Corporation. Weirton Steel Division. Combined steel mill and municipal waste-waters treatment. 1972. **fTD899.S7N37 ECOL**

National Symposium on Food Processing Wastes, 2d, Denver, 1971. Proceedings. 1971
fTD899.F585N37 1971 ECOL

Nebolsine, Ross. High rate filtration of combined sewer overflows. 1972. **fTD662.N4 ECOL**

New Mexico State University. Physical Science Laboratory. Floating oil recovery device. 1971.
fTD427.P4N48 ECOL

North American Rockwell Corporation. Rocketdyne Division. Development of a chemical denitrification process. 1970. **fTD433.N67 ECOL**

North Carolina. State University, Raleigh. Dept. of Biological and Agricultural Engineering. Role of animal wastes in agricultural land runoff. 1971.
fTD930.N67 ECOL

North Star Research and Development Institute, Minneapolis. New and ultrathin membranes for municipal waste water treatment by reverse osmosis. 1970. **fTD754.N6 ECOL**

NUS Corporation. Cyrus Wm. Rice Division. The effects of various gas atmospheres on the oxidation of coal mine pyrites. 1971. **fTD899.M5N2 ECOL**

Ohio. State University, Columbus. Research Foundation. Pilot scale study of acid mine drainage. 1971. **fTN321.O3 ECOL**

Oklahoma. State University of Agriculture and Applied Science, Stillwater. School of Civil Engineering. Aerobic digestion of organic waste sludge. 1971 i.e. 1972 **fTD769.O35 ECOL**

Olson, Theodore A. Lake Superior periphyton in relation to water quality. 1972. **fQK935.O4 ECOL**

Onondaga Co., N.Y. Onondaga Lake study. 1971.
fTD224.N7O5 ECOL

Oregon. State University, Corvallis. Oceanography of the nearshore coastal waters of the Pacific Northwest relating to possible pollution. 1971-
fGC851.O7 ECOL

Oregon. State University, Corvallis. School of Forestry. Studies on effects of watershed practices on streams. 1971 i.e. 1972 **fTC409.O74 ECOL**

Partheniades, Emmanuel. Deposition of fine sediments in turbulent flows. 1971 i.e. 1972
fTC175.2.P3 ECOL

Patterson, W. L. Estimating costs and manpower requirements for conventional wastewater treatment facilities. 1971 i.e. 1972 **fTD743.P36 ECOL**

Portland, Or. Bureau of Sanitary Engineering. Demonstration of rotary screening for combined sewer overflows. 1971. **fTD748.P67 ECOL**

Pratt, P. F. Nitrate in the unsaturated zone under agricultural lands. 1972. **fS651.P7 ECOL**

Ralph M. Parsons Laboratory for Water Resources and Hydrodynamics. Density induced mixing in confined aquifers. 1972. **fTC176.R33 ECOL**

Ralph M. Parsons Laboratory for Water Resources and Hydrodynamics. Temperature prediction in stratified water: mathematical model-user's manual (supplement to report 1613ODJH-01/71). 1971.
fTD395.R3 ECOL

Ramsey, Ralph H. Soil systems for municipal effluents. 1972. **fTD760.R24 ECOL**

Reilich, Helmut G. Technical evaluation of phosphate-free home laundry detergents. 1972.
fTP992.5.R4 ECOL

Rensselaer Polytechnic Institute, Troy, N.Y. Bio-Environmental Engineering Division. Control of pollution from outboard engine exhaust: a reconnaissance study. 1971. **fTD427.P4R45 ECOL**

Robert S. Kerr Water Research Center. Denitrification by anaerobic filters and ponds. 1971.
fTD475.R6 ECOL

Robert S. Kerr Water Research Center. Denitrification by anaerobic filters and ponds, phase II. 1971. **TD475.R62 ECOL**

Robert S. Kerr Water Research Center. Desalination of agricultural tile drainages. 1971.
TD479.R6 ECOL

Robert S. Kerr Water Research Center. Investigations concerning probable impact of nitrilotriacetic acid on ground waters. 1971.
fTD427.D4R6 ECOL

Roy F. Weston, Inc. Combined sewer overflow abatement alternatives, Wash., D.C. 1970.
fTD525.W2R68 ECOL

Smith, Edwin Earle. Sulfide to sulfate reaction mechanism. 1970. **fTN321.S58 ECOL**

Smith, Robert. Cost to the consumer for collection and treatment of wastewater. 1970 i.e. 1972
fTD523.S65 ECOL

Smith, Ronald W. Acid mine pollution effects on lake biology. 1971. **fTD899.M5S6 ECOL**

South Tahoe Public Utility District. Advanced wastewater treatment as practiced at South Tahoe. 1971. **fTD225.T25S6 ECOL**

Southeast Water Laboratory. Catalog of pesticide NMR spectra. 1971. **fSB951.S64 ECOL**

Southern Research Institute, Birmingham, Ala. Demineralization of wastewater by the transport-depletion process. 1971.
fTD754.S67 ECOL

Stefan, Heinz. Surface discharge of heated water. 1971 i.e. 1972 **fTD427.H4S64 ECOL**

Stochastics, Inc., Blacksburg, Va. Stochastic modeling for water quality management. 1971.
fTC409.S8 ECOL

Streebin, Leale E. Demonstration of a full-scale waste treatment system for a cannery. 1971.
fTD899.C3S87 ECOL

Suggs, James D. Mercury pollution control in stream and lake sediments. 1972. **fTD427.M4S9 ECOL**

Susquehanna Corporation. Atlantic Research Systems Division. Marine Systems. Recovery of floating oil rotating disk type skimmer. 1971.
fTD427.P4S9 ECOL

Synectics Corporation. A system for industrial waste treatment RD&D project priority assignment. 1971.
fTD897.5.S9 ECOL

Syracuse University. Civil Engineering Dept. Benefits of water quality enhancement. 1970.
fTD365.S94 ECOL

Syracuse University. Dept. of Biology. Inorganic sulfur oxidation by iron-oxidizing bacteria. 1971.
fQR84.S95 ECOL

Texas Christian University, Fort Worth. Dept. of Biology. Industrial wastes: effects on Trinity River ecology, Fort Worth, Texas. 1971 i.e. 1972
fTD224.T4T4 ECOL

Texas Tech University. Dept. of Geosciences. Infiltration rates and groundwater quality beneath cattle feedlots, Texas High Plains. 1971
fTD899.F4T48 ECOL

Texas Tech University. Water Resources Center. Characteristics of wastes from southwestern cattle feedlots. 1971.
fTD899.F4T497 ECOL

Texas. University. Medical Branch, Galveston. Phosphorus removal and disposal from municipal wastewater. 1971.
fTD745.T43 ECOL

Tracor, Inc. Estuarine modeling: an assessment. 1971.
fTD370.T73 ECOL

Tratnyek, Joseph P. Waste wool as a scavenger for mercury pollution in waters. 1972.
fTD427.M4T7 ECOL

Tyco Laboratories. Electrochemical treatment of acid mine waters. 1972.
fTD899.M5T88 ECOL

Uniroyal, Inc. Feasibility study of regenerative fibers for water pollution control. 1970 i.e. 1971
fTD757.5.U55 ECOL

United Aircraft Corporation. Research Laboratories, East Hartford, Conn. Advanced nonthermally polluting gas turbines in utility applications. 1971.
fTJ778.U5 ECOL

United States. Environmental Protection Agency. Induced aeration of small mountain lakes. 1970.
fSH167.T86U5 ECOL

United States. Environmental Protection Agency. Industrial Pollution Control Branch. Projects of the Industrial Pollution Control Branch. 1971.
fTD897.5.U54 ECOL

United States. Environmental Protection Agency. Office of Research and Monitoring. The effects of agricultural waste water treatment on algal bioassay response. 1971.
QH96.8.E9U54 ECOL

United States. Environmental Protection Agency. Office of Research and Monitoring. Projects of the National Water Quality Control Research Program. 1971.
fTD423.U546 ECOL

United States. Environmental Protection Agency Pacific Northwest Water Laboratory. A method for predicting the performance of draft cooling towers. 1970.
fTP159.C6U5 ECOL

United States. Federal Water Quality Administration. Projects: Industrial Pollution Control Branch. 1970.
fTD897.5.U56 ECOL

United States. National Bureau of Standards. Analytical Chemistry Division. Interaction of nitrilotriacetic acid with suspended and bottom material. 1971.
fTD427.D4U64 ECOL

Unterberg, W. Computerized design and cost estimation for multiple-hearth sludge incinerators. 1971 i.e. 1972
fTD770.U58 ECOL

Vermont. Agency of Environmental Conservation. Development of a State effluent charge system. 1972.
fTD224.V5A43 ECOL

Virginia Polytechnic Institute and State University. Stream faunal recovery after manganese strip mine reclamation. 1971.
fTN291.V5 ECOL

Washington (State). University. The oxygen uptake demand of resuspended bottom sediments. 1970.
fGC380.W3 ECOL

Washington (State). University. Fisheries Research Institute. Responses of teleost fish to environmental stress. 1971.
fQL639.1.W3 ECOL

Washington (State). University. Institute of Forest Products. Pollution abatement by fiber modification. 1971.
fTD899.W65W38 ECOL

Water Pollution Control Federation. Research supplement to Journal Water Pollution Control Federation. 1971.
fTD423.W3 ECOL

Welch, Robin I. A feasibility demonstration of an aerial surveillance spill prevention system. 1972.
fTD427.P4W45 ECOL

Wells, Dan M. Potential pollution of the Ogallala by recharging playa lake water—pesticides. 1970.
fTD224.T4W45 ECOL

West Virginia. University. Coal Research Bureau. Dewatering of mine drainage sludge. 1971.
fTD899.M5W44 ECOL

West Virginia. University. Coal Research Bureau. Underground coal mining methods to abate water pollution. 1970.
fTD899.M5W46 ECOL

Widman, Michael U. Polymer film overlay system for mercury contaminated sludge—Phase I. 1972.
fTD427.M4W5 ECOL

Wiley, Averill J. Reverse osmosis concentration of dilute pulp and paper effluents. 1972.
fTD899.W65W5 ECOL

World Life Research Institute. Pharmacological testing of blue-green algae for constituents having therapeutic value. 1970.
fRS165.A7W67 ECOL

WATER POLLUTION FROM FOUNDRY WASTES.
American Foundrymen's Society. Water Pollution Committee. 1st ed. 1967.
fTD899.A45 ECOL

WATER POLLUTION MICROBIOLOGY.
Mitchell, Ralph. 1971,c1972 **QR48.M58 ECOL**

WATER POLLUTION POTENTIAL OF SPENT OIL SHALE RESIDUES.
Colorado. State University, Fort Collins. 1971.
fTD899.P4C65 ECOL

WATER POLLUTION REGULATION HANDBOOK.
Minnesota Association of Commerce and Industry. 1970 **REF fTD420.M66 ECOL**

WATER PROBLEMS.
Phelps, Pat. 1971. **TD420.P4 ECOL**

WATER PUBLICATIONS OF STATE AGENCIES.
Giefer, Gerald J. 1972 **REF Z7935.G55 ECOL**

WATER QUALITY AND TREATMENT.
American Water Works Association. 3d ed. 1971
TD430.A6 1971 ECOL

WATER QUALITY CONTROL GLOSSARY.
Minnesota Association of Commerce and Industry. 1970 **fTD370.M56 ECOL**

WATER QUALITY CRITERIA DATA BOOK.
1970- **REF fTD370.W394 ECOL**

WATER QUALITY IMPROVEMENT BY PHYSICAL AND CHEMICAL PROCESSES.
1970 **TD745.W37 ECOL**

WATER QUALITY SAMPLING PROGRAM: MINNESOTA LAKES AND STREAMS.
Minnesota. Pollution Control Agency.
TD380.M6 ECOL

WATER QUALITY STUDIES ON THE GREAT LAKES BASED ON CARBON FOURTEEN MEASUREMENTS ON PRIMARY PRODUCTIVITY.
Parkos, William G. 1969.
GB701.M554no.17 ECOL

WATER-RELATED ENVIRONMENTAL PLANNING.
Sloss, George J. 1973. **fZ5862.W3S5 ECOL**

WATER RESEARCH.
Western Resources Conference. 7th, Colorado State University, 1965. c1966
REF TD355.W4 1965 ECOL

WATER RESOURCES.
1957. **HD1694.A5W3 ECOL**

WATER RESOURCES ADMINISTRATION IN MINNESOTA, 1972.
Walton, William Clarence. 1972.
GB701.M554no.49 ECOL

WATER RESOURCES DATA FOR MINNESOTA, 1968-
United States. Geological Survey. Water Resources Division. **REF GB705.M62A32 ECOL**

WATER-RESOURCES ENGINEERING.
Linsley, Ray K. 2d ed. 1971,c1972
TC145.L55 1972 ECOL

WATER RESOURCES OF MINNEAPOLIS-ST. PAUL METROPOLITAN AREA.
Minnesota. Dept. of Conservation. Division of Waters. 1961. **fTD224.M6A3no.11 ECOL**

WATER RESOURCES RESEARCH AND EDUCATIONAL NEEDS IN MINNESOTA.
Minnesota. University. Water Resources Research Center. 1967. **GB701.M554no.5 ECOL**

WATER RESOURCES SYMPOSIUM, NO. 3.
Water quality improvement by physical and chemical processes. 1970 **TD745.W37 ECOL**

A WATER RESOURCES TECHNICAL PUBLICATION.
Otto, Norman E. Aquatic pests on irrigation systems: identification guide. 1972,1965
QH96.O88 1972 ECOL

WATER RESOURCES THESAURUS.
Water Resources Scientific Information Center. 2d ed. 1971 **REF Z695.1.W3W3 1971 ECOL**

WATER RIGHTS LAWS IN THE NINETEEN WESTERN STATES.
Hutchins, Wells A. 1971-
KF5559.A45H8 ECOL

WATER: SOLUTIONS TO A PROBLEM OF SUPPLY AND DEMAND.
Overman, Michael. 1969.
TD348.O85 1969 ECOL

WATER SUPPLY AND POLLUTION CONTROL.
Clark, John William. 2d ed. 1971
TD145.C55 1971 ECOL

WATER SUPPLY AND WASTE DISPOSAL.
Hardenbergh, William Andrew. 1970,c1960
TD145.H33 1970 ECOL

WATER, THE MIRROR OF SCIENCE.
Davis, Kenneth Sydney. 1961.
QD169.W3D3 ECOL

WATER: THE VITAL ESSENCE.
Briggs, Peter. c1967 **GC21.B83 ECOL**

WATER: THE WEB OF LIFE.
Hunt, Cynthia. 1972 **GB661.H84 ECOL**

WATER: THE WONDER OF LIFE.
Platt, Rutherford Hayes. 1971
QH91.15.P57 ECOL

WATER WASTELAND.
Zwick, David. 1971. **TD223.Z86 1971ECOL**

THE WATER WE DRINK!
Bloome, Enid. 1971. **PZ10.B29545Wat ECOL**

WATERCRAFT WASTE TREATMENT SYSTEM: DEVELOPMENT AND DEMONSTRATION REPORT.
General Electric Company. Re-entry and Environmental Systems Division. 1971.
fTD745.G4 ECOL

WATERFOWL IN MINNESOTA.
Minnesota. Dept. of Conservation. Division of Game and Fish. 1964. **SH11.M64no.7 ECOL**

THE WATERFOWL OF THE WORLD.
Delacour, Jean Theodore. 1954-
REF QL696.A5D39 ECOL

WATERFOWL, THEIR BIOLOGY AND NATURAL HISTORY.
Johnsgard, Paul A. 1968 **QL696.A5J63 ECOL**

WATERSHED PLANNING: PAPERS PRESENTED AT THE SEMINAR ON WATERSHED PLANNING SPONSORED BY THE METROPOLITAN COUNCIL AND THE MINNESOTA ASSOCIATION OF WATERSHED DISTRICTS ON FEBRUARY 15, 1972 AT THE SHERATON MOTOR INN, BLOOMINGTON, MINNESOTA.
Minnesota. University. Water Resources Research Center. 1972. **GB701.M554no.50 ECOL**

WATERSHED PROTECTION HANDBOOK.
United States. Soil Conservation Service. 1967-
REF TC423.A53 ECOL

THE WAYS OF WILDFOWL.
Williams, Eugene Russell. 1971
REF fQL696.A5W48 ECOL

WEATHER.
Thompson, Philip Duncan. 1969
fQC863.T5 1969 ECOL

WEATHER AND CLIMATE MODIFICATION PROBLEMS AND PROSPECTS.
National Research Council. Committee on Atmospheric Sciences. 1966. **QC928.N36 ECOL**

WEATHER MODIFICATION.
1969 **QC928.W38 ECOL**

THE WEB OF LIFE.
Storer, John Humphries. 1953.
QH541.S68 ECOL

WESTERN CULTURAL TRADITION AND HUMAN SURVIVAL: THE ROLE OF VALUE ORIENTATIONS IN THE ENVIRONMENTAL CRISIS.
Flowers, William J. c1971 **GF80.F5 ECOL**

WESTERN FOREST INDUSTRY.
Guthrie, John Alexander. 1961
HD9755.G8 ECOL

WESTERN MAN AND ENVIRONMENTAL ETHICS.
Barbour, Ian G. 1973. **GF80.B37 ECOL**

WESTERN PLANT ENGINEERING AND MAINTENANCE CONFERENCE, SAN FRANCISCO, 1970 PROCEEDINGS.
1970. **fTS184.W4**

WESTERN RESOURCES PAPERS, 1966.
Western Resources Conference, 8th, Colorado School of Mines, 1966. Natural gas, coal, ground water. 1967 **HC103.7.W45 1966 ECOL**

WESTERN RESOURCES PAPERS, 1967.
Western Resources Conference, 9th, University of Colorado, 1967. Man and the quality of his environment. 1968 **TD180.W4 1967 ECOL**

TITLE CATALOG

THE WESTON REPORT.
Roy F. Weston, Inc. Concept evaluation report: taconite tailings disposal, Reserve Mining Company, Silver Bay, Minnesota. 1971 **fTD899.T35 ECOL**

THE WHALE.
Cousteau, Jacques Yves. 1st ed. in U.S. 1972.
QL737.C4C6913 ECOL

WHAT ARE ME AND YOU GONNA DO?
1971 **TD175.W53 ECOL**

WHAT GOOD IS A WEED?
Wright, Robert Henry. 1972 **QK49.W75 ECOL**

WHAT IS WATER.
Hagaman, Adaline P. 1960 **PZ10.H12Wh ECOL**

WHAT MAKES A NUCLEAR POWER PLANT WORK?
Fuchs, Erich. 1972. **fPZ10.F77Wh3 ECOL**

WHAT'S ECOLOGY?
Humphrey, Clifford C. 1971
QH541.13.H84 ECOL

WHAT'S LEFT.
Roueche, Berton. 1969,c1968 **QH77.U6R6 ECOL**

WHERE CAN RED-WINGED BLACKBIRDS LIVE?
Wong, Herbert H. Animal habitats: where can red-winged blackbirds live? 1970
PZ10.W748An ECOL

WHERE DOES YOUR GARDEN GROW?
Goldin, Augusta R. 1967 **PZ10.G564Wh ECOL**

WHERE HAVE ALL THE FLOWERS, FISHES, BIRDS, TREES, WATER, AND AIR GONE?
Segerberg, Osborn. 1971 **QH541.S39 ECOL**

"WHERE HAVE ALL THE FLOWERS GONE?".
1970 **REF fZ5322.E2W54 ECOL**

WHERE THE WASTELAND ENDS.
Roszak, Theodore. 1972. **HN17.5.R62 ECOL**

WHITE SETTLERS IN THE TROPICS.
Price, Archibald Grenfell. 1939. **GF51.P7 ECOL**

THE WHITE-TAILED DEER IN MINNESOTA.
Symposium on the White-tailed Deer in Minnesota, St. Paul, Minnesota, 1971. 1972?
fQL737.U55S9 1971ECOL

WHITE-TAILED DEER OF MINNESOTA.
Minnesota. Conservation, Dept. of Game and Fish, Division of. 1961. **SH11.M64no.5 ECOL**

WHO LIVES IN THIS LOG?
Ross, Wilda S. 1971 **PZ10.R7244Wh ECOL**

WHO OWNS AMERICA?
Hickel, Walter J. 1971 **E855.H5 1971 ECOL**

WHO SHALL LIVE?
Friends, Society of. American Friends Service Committee. 1970 **HQ766.3.F7 ECOL**

WHO SHOULD HAVE CHILDREN?
Ingle, Dwight Joyce. 1973 **HQ751.I43 ECOL**

WHO WILL CLEAN THE AIR?
Perera, Thomas Biddle. 1971
TD883.13.P47 ECOL

THE WHOLE EARTH.
McKain, David W. 1972 **QH81.M1518 ECOL**

WHO'S WHO IN ECOLOGY, 1973-
REF fQH26.W46 ECOL

WHO'S WHO OF URBAN AMERICA.
Dickey, Miriam. Beyond the classroom. 1972.
Ref fQH51.D5 ECOL

WHY DO WE STILL HAVE AN ECOLOGICAL CRISIS?
Armstrong, Terry R. 1972 **TD174.A75 ECOL**

WIDE WORLD WEATHER.
Navarra, John Gabriel. 1968 **QC863.N34 ECOL**

WILD ALASKA.
Brown, Dale. 1972 **QH105.A4B7 ECOL**

WILD AMERICA.
Peterson, Roger Tory. 1955. **QH102.P38 ECOL**

WILD ANIMALS OF THE WORLD.
Bridges, William. 1948 **fQL706.B89 ECOL**

WILD BIRD GUESTS.
Baynes, Ernest Harold. 1915. **SK353.B4 ECOL**

WILD BROTHER.
Rood, Ronald N. 1970 **QH81.R74 ECOL**

WILD GREEN THINGS IN THE CITY.
Dowden, Anne Ophelia (Todd). 1972
SB611.D675 1972 ECOL

WILD HERITAGE.
Carrighar, Sally. 1965. **QL751.C36 ECOL**

WILD REFUGE.
Laycock, George. 1969 **S962.L39 ECOL**

WILD RIVER.
Pringle, Laurence P. 1st ed. 1972
fQH541.5.S7P75 ECOL

WILD SANCTUARIES.
Murphy, Robert William. 1968.
REF fS962.M8 ECOL

WILD SEASON.
Eckert, Allan W. 1st ed. 1967 **Fiction ECOL**

WILDERNESS AND PLENTY.
Darling, Frank Fraser. 1970.
QH541.13.D36 ECOL

WILDERNESS AND THE AMERICAN MIND.
Nash, Roderick. 1967. **E169.1.N37 ECOL**

A WILDERNESS BILL OF RIGHTS.
Douglas, William Orville. 1st ed. 1965
SK361.D6 ECOL

WILDERNESS DAYS.
Olson, Sigurd F. Sigurd F. Olson's Wilderness days. 1st ed. 1972. **QH81.O67 1972 ECOL**

WILDERNESS DEFENDER.
Swain, Donald C. 1970 **SB482.A4S95 ECOL**

WILDERNESS ECOLOGY, VIRGIN PLANT COMMUNITIES OF THE BOUNDARY WATERS CANOE AREA.
Ohmann, Lewis F. 1971
SD11.A45476no.63 ECOL

WILDERNESS HANDBOOK.
Brower, David Ross. The Sierra Club wilderness handbook. 2nd rev. ed. c1971
SK601.B845 1971 ECOL

A WILDERNESS IN CRISIS: THE BOUNDARY WATERS CANOE AREA.
Sierra Club. North Star Chapter (Minn.). c1970
fQH76.5.M6S5 ECOL

WILDERNESS SURVIVAL.
Berglund, Berndt. 1972 **SK606.B47 ECOL**

WILDFLOWERS AND WEEDS.
Courtenay, Booth. 1972? **QK141.C6 ECOL**

WILDLIFE ABSTRACTS.
United States. Fish and Wildlife Service.
REF SK351.U52 ECOL

WILDLIFE BIOLOGY.
Dasmann, Raymond Frederick. 1964
QL752.D3 ECOL

WILDLIFE CONSERVATION.
Gabrielson, Ira Noel. 2d ed. 1970, c1959
SK353.G2 1959 ECOL

WILDLIFE CRISIS.
Philip, Duke of Edinburgh. 1st American ed. 1970
S962.P55 ECOL

WILDLIFE IN AMERICA'S HISTORY.
Barker, Will. 1962 **QL155.B3 ECOL**

WILDLIFE IN DANGER.
Fisher, James. 1969 **REF QL88.F48 ECOL**

Green, Ivah. 1960 **QL151.G7 ECOL**

WILDLIFE LAW ENFORCEMENT.
Sigler, William F. 2d ed. 1972
KF5640.S55 1972 ECOL

WILDLIFE MANAGEMENT AND CONSERVATION.
Trefethen, James B. 1964 **S962.T7 ECOL**

WILDLIFE MYSTERIES.
Holden, Raymond Peckham. 1972
QL49.H68 ECOL

THE WILDLIFE OF NORTH AMERICA.
Mason, George Frederick. 1966
SK361.M35 ECOL

WILDLIFE PRESERVATION.
Street, Philip. 1971,c1970 **S962.S77 1971 ECOL**

WILDLIFE REFUGES.
Gabrielson, Ira Noel. 1943. **SK357.G3 ECOL**

WILDLIFE RESCUE.
Graham, Ada. 1970 **S962.G68 ECOL**

WILDLIFE RESEARCH: PROBLEMS PROGRAMS, PROGRESS, 1969.
United States. Bureau of Sport Fisheries and Wildlife. Division of Wildlife Research. 1971
S914.A3no.94 ECOL

WILDLIFE TEAMS.
Friendly, Natalie. c1963 **PZ10.F7153Wi ECOL**

WILL THE HUMAN RACE SURVIVE?
Still, Henry. 1st ed. 1966 **Q125.S745 ECOL**

WILSON'S WORLD.
Hurd, Edith (Thacher). 1st ed. 1971
FictionECOL

WINGS IN THE WILDERNESS.
Cruickshank, Allan D. 1947. **QL674.C85 ECOL**

WINGSPREAD.
Laycock, George. 1972 **QL676.L35 ECOL**

WINTER SEARCH PARTY.
Russell, Helen Ross. 1st ed. 1971
QL465.R85 ECOL

WITH EVERY BREATH YOU TAKE.
Lewis, Howard R. 1965 **RA576.L5 ECOL**

WITH MAN IN MIND.
Perin, Constance. 1970. **HC68.P47 ECOL**

THE WITHERING RAIN.
Whiteside, Thomas. 1st ed. 1971.
QH545.P4W48 1971 ECOL

WOLF MANAGEMENT IN SELECTED AREAS OF NORTH AMERICA.
Symposium on Wolf Management in Selected Areas of North America, Chicago, 1970. 1970
QL737.C22S9 1970 ECOL

THE WOLF: THE ECOLOGY AND BEHAVIOR OF AN ENDANGERED SPECIES.
Mech, L. David. 1970 **QL737.C22M4 ECOL**

THE WOLVES OF ISLE ROYALE.
Mech, L. David. 1966 **QL155.A45no.7 ECOL**

THE WONDER WORLD OF METALS.
Pearl, Richard Maxwell. 1966 **TN148.P38 ECOL**

WONDERS OF ANIMAL MIGRATION.
Berrill, Jacquelyn. 1964 **QL754.B4 ECOL**

THE WOODLAND BOOK.
Ransom, Elmer Inglesby. 1945 **QL681.R2 ECOL**

WORKBOOK OF ATMOSPHERIC DISPERSION ESTIMATES.
Turner, D. Bruce. 1970. **fTD890.T8 1970 ECOL**

WORKBOOK OF THERMAL PLUME PREDICTION.
United States. Environmental Protection Agency. Office of Research and Monitoring. 1972-
TD427.H4U54 ECOL

WORKSHOP SESSION FOR THE THIRD SESSION (RECONVENED).
Conference in the Matter of Pollution of Lake Michigan and its Tributary Basins, 3d, Chicago, Sept. 28-30, Oct. 1-2, 1970. 1970.
fTD223.3.C595 1970a ECOL

WORLD ACADEMY OF ART AND SCIENCE. PUBLICATION 2.
Mudd, Stuart. The population crisis and the use of world resources. 1964. **HB885.M8 ECOL**

THE WORLD BENEATH THE SEA.
Torchio, Menico. 1972 **fQH91.17.T6 ECOL**

WORLD CATTLE.
Rouse, John E. 1970 **SF197.R68 ECOL**

WORLD DYNAMICS.
Forrester, Jay Wright. 1971 **HD82.F63 ECOL**

WORLD ECO-CRISIS: INTERNATIONAL ORGANIZATIONS IN RESPONSE.
Kay, David A. 1972 **HC79.E5K38 ECOL**

THE WORLD ENCYCLOPEDIA OF ANIMALS.
Burton, Maurice. c1972 **fQL9.B8 ECOL**

THE WORLD FOOD PROBLEM.
Cochrane, Willard Wesley. 1969
HD9000.5.C59 ECOL

A WORLD GEOGRAPHY OF FOREST RESOURCES.
Guest, Stephen Haden. 1956
REF SD131.G8 ECOL

WORLD GEOGRAPHY OF PETROLEUM.
Pratt, Wallace Everett. 1950.
REF TN870.P73 ECOL

THE WORLD IN 1984.
The New scientist. 1965,c1964
Q171.N5 1965 ECOL

THE WORLD OF LIVING THINGS.
Brandwein, Paul Franz. 1964
QH308.5.B7 1964 ECOL

THE WORLD OF MINERALS.
De Michele, Vincenzo. 1972
QE372.D3413 ECOL

THE WORLD OF THE ATOM SERIES.
Glasstone, Samuel. Atomic energy and your world. 1970 **QC792.G55 ECOL**

A WORLD OF THE ATOM SERIES BOOKLET.
Pizer, Vernon. Preserving food with atomic energy. 1970 **TX611.5.P58 ECOL**

THE WORLD OF THE BEAVER.
Rue, Leonard Lee. 1964. **QL737.R6R84 ECOL**

THE WORLD OF THE COYOTE.
Van Wormer, Joe. 1964 **QL737.C2V32 ECOL**

THE WORLD OF THE FOREST.
Clepper, Henry Edward. **SD131.C55 ECOL**

THE WORLD OF THE GRAY SQUIRREL.
Barkalow, Frederick Schenck. 1972
QL737.R68B37 ECOL

THE WORLD OF THE MOOSE.
Van Wormer, Joe. 1972 **QL737.U55V32 ECOL**

THE WORLD OF THE RUFFED GROUSE.
Rue, Leonard Lee. 1st ed. 1973, c1972
QL696.G2R83 ECOL

THE WORLD OF THE WILD TURKEY.
Lewis, James C. 1st ed. 1973
QL696.G2L48 ECOL

THE WORLD OF THE WOLF.
Rutter, Russell J. 1968. QL737.C2R87 ECOL

THE WORLD OF THE WOOD DUCK.
Hester, F. Eugene. 1st ed. 1973
QL696.A5H42 ECOL

THE WORLD OF WATER.
Walton, William Clarence. 1970
GB661.W26 ECOL

WORLD PROSPECTS FOR NATURAL RESOURCES.
Fisher, Joseph Lyman. 1964 HC54.F54 ECOL

WORLD SOILS.
Bridges, Edwin Michael. 1970. S591.B85 ECOL

WORLD VIEW.
Colwell, Jim. 1971. GF75.C6 ECOL

WORLD WILDLIFE: THE LAST STAND.
Crowe, Philip Kingsland. 1970 S962.C75 ECOL

THE WORLD WITHIN THE OCEAN WAVE.
Silverberg, Robert. 1972 QH91.8.P5S54 ECOL

WORLD WITHOUT BORDERS.
Brown, Lester Russell. 1972
HC59.B765 1972b ECOL

THE WOUNDED EARTH.
Marzani, Carl. 1972 QH541.M38 ECOL

WRITING SCIENCE NEWS FOR THE MASS MEDIA.
Burkett, David Warren. 2d ed., rev. 1973.
PN4784.T3B8 1973 ECOL

WRRC BULLETIN NO. 1.
Conference on Water and Related Land Resources Planning in Minnesota, St. Paul, Minn., 1967. Papers presented during Conference on Water and Related Land Resources Planning in Minnesota. 1967.
fHD1694.M6A54 1967 ECOL

WRRC BULLETIN NO. 4.
Walton, William Clarence. Lists of references and selected books bearing on water resources in Minnesota. 1966. GB701.M554no.4 ECOL

WRRC BULLETIN NO. 4 [REV].
Walton, William Clarence. Lists of references and selected books bearing on Water resources in Minnesota. Rev. ed. 1972.
GB701.M554no.4 1972 ECOL

WRRC BULLETIN, NO. 6.
Walton, William Clarence. Recharge from induced streambed infiltration under varying groundwater-level and stream-stage conditions. 1967.
GB701.M554no.6 ECOL

WRRC BULLETIN NO.8.
Bowers, C. Edward. Review and analysis of rainfall and runoff data for selected watersheds in Minnesota. 1968. GB701.M554no.8 ECOL

WRRC BULLETIN NO. 10.
Thorud, David B. Freezing in forest soil as influenced by soil properties, litter, and snow. 1969.
GB701.M554no.10 ECOL

WRRC BULLETIN NO. 18.
Stokes, Lee W. The photosynthetic pigments of Lake Superior periphyton and their relation to primary productivity. 1970. GB701.M554no.18 ECOL

WRRC BULLETIN 20.
Potential productivity of fresh water environments as determined by an algae bioassay technique. 1970.
GB701.M554no.20

WRRC BULLETIN, NO. 21.
Minnesota. University. Water Resources Research Center. Proceedings of conference on ongoing water resources research in Minnesota, March 1970. 1970.
GB701.M554no.21 ECOL

WRRC BULLETIN, NO. 25.
Lewis, Robert Clark. The marginal costs of alternative levels of water quality in the Upper Mississippi River. 1970. GB701.M554no.25 ECOL

WRRC BULLETIN NO. 29.
Lin, Shen-maw. Porosity and pore-size distribution of soil aggregates. 1971. GB701.M554no.29 ECOL

WRRC BULLETIN NO. 30.
Wei, Tsong C. Effects of areal and time distribution of rainfall on small watershed runoff hydrographs. 1971. GB701.M554no.30 ECOL

WRRC BULLETIN, NO.31.
Golany, Pinhas. Effects of channel characteristics on time parameters for small watershed runoff hydrographs. 1971. GB701.M554no.31 ECOL

WRRC BULLETIN, NO. 35.
Johnson, Jack D. Development of a mathematical model to predict the role of surface runoff and groundwater flow in over fertilization of surface waters. 1971. GB701.M554no.35 ECOL

WRRC BULLETIN, NO.36.
Brook, Alan J. The phytoplankton of Minnesota lakes—a preliminary survey. 1971.
GB701.M554no.36 ECOL

WRRC BULLETIN, NO.37.
Baker, Donald G. Snow cover and winter soil temperatures at St. Paul, Minn. 1971.
S594.5.B3 ECOL

WRRC BULLETIN, NO. 38.
Seminar on the Engineer and the Environment University of Minnesota, 1970. The Engineer and the environment. 1971. GB701.M554no.38 ECOL

WRRC BULLETIN, NO.39.
Bowers, C. Edward. Computer program for statistical analysis of annual flood data by the log-Pearson Type III method. 1971.
GB701.M554no.39 ECOL

WRRC BULLETIN, NO.40.
Larson, Curtis L. Numerical routing of flood hydrographs through open channel juncitions. 1971.
GB701.M554no.40 ECOL

WRRC BULLETIN NO. 42.
Walton, William Clarence. International, regional, federal-state, interstate and federal organizations with water related lands resources programs in Minnesota, 1971. 1971. GB701.M554no.42 ECOL

WRRC BULLETIN NO. 43.
Mein, Russell G. Modeling the infiltration component of the rainfall—runoff process. 1971.
GB701.M554no.43 ECOL

WRRC BULLETIN NO. 45.
Walton, William Clarence. Interest groups with water and related lands resources programs in Minnesota, 1971. 1972. GB701.M554no.45 ECOL

WRRC BULLETIN NO. 46.
Su, K. Lee. Aquatic plants from Minnesota, part 1—chemical survey. 1972.
GB701.M554no.46 ECOL

WRRC BULLETIN NO. 47.
Su, K. Lee. Aquatic plants from Minnesota part 2—toxicity, anti-neoplastic, and coagulent effects. 1972. GB701.M554no.47 ECOL

WRRC BULLETIN NO. 48.
Su, K. Lee. Aquatic plants from Minnesota part 3—antimicrobial effects. 1972.
GB701.M554no.48 ECOL

WRRC BULLETIN NO. 49.
Walton, William Clarence. Water resources administration in Minnesota, 1972. 1972.
GB701.M554no.49 ECOL

WRRC BULLETIN NO. 51.
Rice, Charles E. Methods for routing hydrographs through open channels. 1972.
GB701.M554no.51 ECOL

WRRC BULLETIN, NO.52.
Larson, Curtis L. Predicting peak flow of small watersheds by use of channel characteristics. 1972.
GB701.M554no.52 ECOL

Y

YALE UNIVERSITY. MRS. HEPSA ELY SILLIMAN MEMORIAL LECTURES.
Dubos, Rene Jules. Man adapting. 1965.
R723.D77 ECOL

Peabody Museum Centennial Symposium, Yale University, 1966. Evolution and environment. 1968.
QH366.A1P4 1966 ECOL

THE YEAR OF THE SEAL.
Scheffer, Victor B. 1970 QL737.P6S32 ECOL

THE YEARS OF THE FOREST.
Hoover, Helen. 1st ed. 1973.
QH105.M55H64 1973 ECOL

YELLOW PAGES OF LEARNING RESOURCES.
1972. Ref fLC215.Y45 ECOL

YELLOWSTONE: A CENTURY OF THE WILDERNESS IDEA.
Sutton, Ann. 1972 fQH105.W8S8 ECOL

THE YELLOWSTONE NATIONAL PARK.
Chittenden, Hiram Martin. 1964
F722.C54 1964 ECOL

YOU ARE AN ENVIRONMENT: TEACHING/LEARNING ENVIRONMENTAL ATTITUDES.
McInnis, Noel. c1972 QH541.2.M4 ECOL

YOUR BOOK OF WATCHING WILD LIFE.
Blackmore, Michael. 1971. QL60.B55 ECOL

YOUR ENVIRONMENT: AIR, AIR POLLUTION, AND WEATHER.
Henson, Collins M. 1971 QC863.H45 ECOL

YOUR ENVIRONMENT AND WHAT YOU CAN DO ABOUT IT.
Saltonstall, Richard. 1970 HC110.E5S35 ECOL

YOUR GOVERNMENT AND THE ENVIRONMENT. V.1- 1971-
REF fHC110.E5Y6 ECOL

YOUR WORLD IN MOTION.
Barrow, George. 1956 QC25.B23 ECOL

Z

ZINC PRECIPITATION AND RECOVERY FROM VISCOSE RAYON WASTE WATER.
American Enka Corporation. Central Engineering Dept. 1971. fTD899.T4A44 ECOL

THE ZONING GAME.
Babcock, Richard F. 1966. KF5698.B3 ECOL

ZOOLOGICAL SOCIETY OF LONDON. SYMPOSIA, NO. 29.
Conservation and productivity of natural waters. 1972. QL1.Z733no.29 ECOL

ZOOS OF TODAY.
Johnson, James Ralph. 1971 QL77.5.J64 ECOL

APPENDIX 1

Pamphlet File Subject Headings

Abortion *see* POPULATION
Acid mine drainage *see* MINE DRAINAGE
ACTION
ADVERTISING
AGRICULTURAL EXTENSION SERVICE
Agricultural pollution *see*
   AGRICULTURAL WASTES
AGRICULTURAL WASTES
AGRICULTURE
AIR POLLUTION
AIR POLLUTION—CALIFORNIA
AIR POLLUTION—FOREIGN COUNTRIES
AIR POLLUTION—LAWS AND
   LEGISLATION
AIR POLLUTION—MINNESOTA
AIR POLLUTION CONTROL
AIR POLLUTION CONTROL—ANALYTICAL
   AND TEST METHODS AND TECHNIQUES
AIR POLLUTION CONTROL—MINNESOTA
Air pollution control—Odors *see* ODORS
AIR POLLUTION DAMAGE
AIR POLLUTION EQUIPMENT
AIR PURIFICATION
AIR QUALITY STANDARDS
AIR SAMPLING
AIRPLANE EMISSIONS
AIRPLANES
AIRPORTS
ALASKAN PIPELINE
ALL-TERRAIN VEHICLES
ALUMINUM
ANIMAL WASTES
Anti-pollution ordinances *see* LAW,
   ENVIRONMENTAL; AIR POLLUTION—
   LAWS AND LEGISLATION; WATER
   POLLUTION—LAWS AND LEGISLATION
Army Corps of Engineers *see*
   U.S. ARMY CORPS OF ENGINEERS
ASBESTOS
Atomic power *see* NUCLEAR POWER
AUDUBON SOCIETY
AUTOMOBILE EMISSIONS CONTROL
AUTOMOBILE POLLUTANTS
AUTOMOBILE SCRAP

BACKPACKING
Ban-the-can *see* CONTAINERS
BELL MUSEUM OF NATURAL HISTORY
Bibliographies *see* Separate Bibliography Drawer
BICYCLES
BILLBOARDS
Biocides *see* specific types such as
   PESTICIDES and HERBICIDES
BIRDHOUSES
BIRDS
Birth control *see* POPULATION; ZERO
   POPULATION GROWTH
Birth rate *see* POPULATION
BOATING
Bogs *see* WETLANDS
Bottles *see* GLASS; CONTAINERS;
   RECYCLING
BOUNDARY WATERS CANOE AREA
BROADCASTING TOWERS

CAMPING
CANS
CAREERS
CARTOONS
CHANNELIZATION
CHEMICAL INDUSTRY
Chlorination *see* WATER PURIFICATION
CITIES
CLEARCUTTING
Coal mining *see* STRIP MINING; MINES
   AND MINERAL RESOURCES
COASTLINES
COLORADO OPEN SPACE COUNCIL
COMPOSTING
CONFERENCES AND SYMPOSIA
CONFERENCES AND SYMPOSIA—AGENDAS
CONFERENCES AND SYMPOSIA—
   MINNESOTA
CONSERVATION
CONSERVATION—MINNESOTA
Conservation commissions *see*
   ENVIRONMENTAL COMMISSIONS
CONSERVATION FOUNDATION

CONTAINERS
Copper-nickel mining *see* MINES
   AND MINERALS—MINNESOTA

Dams *see* U.S. BUREAU OF RECLAMA-
   TION: WATER RESOURCES DEVELOP-
   MENT
DDT
Deep well disposal *see* SOLID WASTE
   DISPOSAL—DEEP WELL
DEER
DESIGN, ENVIRONMENTAL
DETERGENTS AND SOAP
DISPLAYS
Drinking water *see* WATER; WATER
   PURIFICATION
Ducks *see* WATERFOWL
Dumps *see* SOLID WASTE DISPOSAL—
   DUMPS
DUTCH ELM DISEASE

EAGLES
EARTH DAY
EARTH WEEK
ECOLOGY
ECOLOGY CENTERS
ECONOMICS AND ENVIRONMENT
EDUCATION, ENVIRONMENTAL
EDUCATION, ENVIRONMENTAL—
   ACTIVITIES
EDUCATION, ENVIRONMENTAL—
   COMMUNITY AND SCHOOL PROJECTS
   AND EXPERIMENTS
EDUCATION, ENVIRONMENTAL—
   MINNESOTA
EDUCATION, ENVIRONMENTAL—
   OUTDOOR
EDUCATION, ENVIRONMENTAL—
   PROPOSALS AND GRANTS
EDUCATION, ENVIRONMENTAL—
   SAMPLE MATERIALS (ELEMENTARY
   LEVEL)
EDUCATION, ENVIRONMENTAL—
   TEACHER'S RESOURCES AND

Appendix 1

CURRICULUM GUIDES
ELECTRIC POWER INDUSTRY
ELECTRIC POWER INDUSTRY—MINNESOTA
ENDANGERED SPECIES
ENERGY
ENERGY—ALTERNATIVE SOURCES
ENERGY CONSERVATION
ENERGY RESOURCES
ENVIRONMENT
ENVIRONMENT—CALIFORNIA
ENVIRONMENT—CANADA
ENVIRONMENT—FOREIGN COUNTRIES
ENVIRONMENT—MAINE
ENVIRONMENT—MINNESOTA
ENVIRONMENT—NEW YORK
ENVIRONMENT—NORTH DAKOTA
ENVIRONMENT—RELIGIOUS AND PHILOSOPHICAL INTERPRETATIONS
ENVIRONMENT—SWEDEN
Environmental careers *see* CAREERS
ENVIRONMENTAL COMMISSIONS
ENVIRONMENTAL DEFENSE FUND
Environmental education *see* EDUCATION, ENVIRONMENTAL
Environmental health *see* HEALTH, ENVIRONMENTAL
ENVIRONMENTAL IMPACT STATEMENTS
ENVIRONMENTAL POLICY
ENVIRONMENTAL POLICY—MINNESOTA
Environmental Quality Council *see* MINNESOTA ENVIRONMENTAL QUALITY COUNCIL
Environmental Science Center *see* MINNESOTA ENVIRONMENTAL SCIENCES FOUNDATION, INC.
ENVIRONMENTAL SERVICE BUREAU
EROSION
ESTUARIES
EUTROPHICATION
Extinction *see* ENDANGERED SPECIES; WILDLIFE

Famine *see* FOOD SUPPLY
Farming *see* AGRICULTURE; ORGANIC FARMING AND GARDENING
FERTILIZERS
FILMS—AIR POLLUTION
FILMS—CATALOGS
FILMS—POPULATION
FILMS—SOLID WASTE
FILMS—WILDLIFE
FISH
Floodplain regulations *see* FLOODS AND FLOOD CONTROL
FLOODS AND FLOOD CONTROL
FOOD
FOOD ADDITIVES
FOOD CHAINS
FOOD LABELING AND STANDARDS
FOOD SUPPLY
FOREST FIRES
Forest products *see* WOOD; PAPER
FORESTS

FORESTS—ECONOMIC ASPECTS
FORESTS—HISTORY
FORESTS—MINNESOTA
FORESTS—RESEARCH, STUDIES AND EXPERIMENTS
Fossil fuels *see* PETROLEUM; GAS, NATURAL; MINES AND MINERAL RESOURCES; POWER PRODUCTION; FUEL
FRESHWATER BIOLOGICAL INSTITUTE
FRIENDS OF THE EARTH (FOE)
FUEL
FUSION
FUTURE

GAME BIRDS
GAS, NATURAL
Gasoline *see* PETROLEUM
Geese *see* WATERFOWL
Geothermal energy *see* ENERGY—ALTERNATIVE SOURCES; ENERGY RESOURCES
GLASS
GREAT LAKES

HEALTH, ENVIRONMENTAL
HERBICIDES
Highway beautification *see* VISUAL POLLUTION; BILLBOARDS
HIGHWAYS
HUNTING AND FISHING
HUNTING AND FISHING—MINNESOTA

Incineration *see* SOLID WASTE DISPOSAL—INCINERATION
INDUSTRY
Insecticides *see* PESTICIDES
INSECTS
INTER-ACT
Irrigation *see* WATER RESOURCES DEVELOPMENT; AGRICULTURE
IZAAK WALTON LEAGUE

LAKE MINNETONKA
LAKE SUPERIOR
LAKES
LAND RECLAMATION
LAND USE PLANNING
LAND USE PLANNING—MINNESOTA
Landfill, Sanitary *see* SOLID WASTE DISPOSAL—SANITARY LANDFILLS
LAW, ENVIRONMENTAL
LEAGUE OF WOMEN VOTERS
Legislation *see* LAW, ENVIRONMENTAL; MINNESOTA LEGISLATURE
LIBRARIES AND INFORMATION CENTERS
LITTER
Lumber *see* FORESTS; WOOD

MAPS
Marine disposal *see* SOLID WASTE DISPOSAL—MARINE; MARINE POLLUTION
MARINE POLLUTION
Mass transit *see* TRANSPORTATION

MERCURY
METRO CLEAN AIR COMMITTEE
METROPOLITAN COUNCIL
METROPOLITAN COUNCIL—AGENDAS
METROPOLITAN OPEN SPACE INFORMATION PROJECT (MOSIP)
METROPOLITAN TRANSIT COMMISSION
MINE DRAINAGE
MINES AND MINERAL RESOURCES
MINES AND MINERAL RESOURCES—MINNESOTA
MINNEAPOLIS
MINNEAPOLIS—DEPARTMENT OF WATER WORKS
MINNESOTA
MINNESOTA ACADEMY OF SCIENCE
MINNESOTA ASSOCIATION FOR CONSERVATION EDUCATION (MACE)
MINNESOTA COMMITTEE FOR ENVIRONMENTAL INFORMATION (MCEI)
MINNESOTA CONSERVATION FEDERATION
MINNESOTA DEPARTMENT OF HIGHWAYS
MINNESOTA DEPARTMENT OF IRON RANGE RESOURCES AND REHABILITATION
MINNESOTA DEPARTMENT OF NATURAL RESOURCES
MINNESOTA ENVIRONMENTAL CONTROL CITIZEN'S ASSOCIATION (MECCA)
MINNESOTA ENVIRONMENTAL EDUCATION COUNCIL (MEEC)
MINNESOTA ENVIRONMENTAL QUALITY COUNCIL
MINNESOTA ENVIRONMENTAL QUALITY COUNCIL—AGENDAS
MINNESOTA ENVIRONMENTAL QUALITY COUNCIL—MINUTES
MINNESOTA ENVIRONMENTAL QUALITY COUNCIL—SUMMARIES OF INFORMATION FROM MEETINGS
MINNESOTA ENVIRONMENTAL QUALITY COUNCIL—TASK FORCE ON POWER PLANT SITING
MINNESOTA ENVIRONMENTAL RESOURCES COUNCIL (MERC)
MINNESOTA ENVIRONMENTAL SCIENCES FOUNDATION, INC.
MINNESOTA EXPERIMENTAL CITY
MINNESOTA LEGISLATURE
MINNESOTA LEGISLATURE—HOUSE
MINNESOTA LEGISLATURE—SENATE
MINNESOTA POLLUTION CONTROL AGENCY (MPCA)
MINNESOTA POLLUTION CONTROL AGENCY—AGENDAS
MINNESOTA POLLUTION CONTROL AGENCY—AIR
MINNESOTA POLLUTION CONTROL AGENCY—MEETINGS
MINNESOTA POLLUTION CONTROL AGENCY—REQUESTS FOR VARIANCE
MINNESOTA POLLUTION CONTROL AGENCY—SOLID WASTE

Pamphlet File Subject Headings

MINNESOTA POLLUTION CONTROL AGENCY—WATER
MINNESOTA POLLUTION CONTROL AGENCY—WATER—DISPOSAL SYSTEM PERMIT APPLICATIONS BY INDUSTRIES AND MUNICIPALITIES
MINNESOTA POLLUTION CONTROL AGENCY—WATER—DREDGING PERMIT APPLICATION NOTICES
MINNESOTA POLLUTION CONTROL AGENCY—WATER—LIQUID STORAGE PERMIT APPLICATION NOTICES
MINNESOTA RESOURCES COMMISSION
MINNESOTA-WISCONSIN BOUNDARY AREA COMMISSION
MINNESOTA ZOOLOGICAL GARDEN
Minnetonka, Lake *see* LAKE MINNETONKA
MISSISSIPPI RIVER
MISSISSIPPI RIVER PARKWAY COMMISSION

NATIONAL ADVISORY COMMITTEE ON OCEANS AND ATMOSPHERE
NATIONAL COALITION AGAINST POISONING OF WILDLIFE
National Environmental Research Centers *see* U.S. ENVIRONMENTAL PROTECTION AGENCY
National forests *see* WILDERNESS AREAS
National Park Service *see* NATIONAL PARKS AND MONUMENTS
NATIONAL PARKS AND MONUMENTS
NATIONAL WATER QUALITY LABORATORY
NATIONAL WILDLIFE FEDERATION
National Wildlife Week *see* NATIONAL WILDLIFE FEDERATION
Natural gas *see* GAS, NATURAL
Natural resources *see* CONSERVATION; specific resource such as PETROLEUM
NATURE CENTERS
NATURE CONSERVANCY—MINNESOTA CHAPTER
NINE MILE CREEK CITIZEN'S COMMITTEE
NOISE
NOISE—AIRPLANE
NOISE—MINNESOTA
NOISE—PHYSIOLOGICAL EFFECT
NUCLEAR FUELS
NUCLEAR POLLUTION
NUCLEAR POWER
NUCLEAR POWER—CANADA
NUCLEAR POWER—MINNESOTA
NUCLEAR POWER PLANTS
Nuclear power plants—Minnesota *see* NUCLEAR POWER—MINNESOTA
NUCLEAR POWER PLANTS—SAFETY DEVICES AND MEASURES
NUCLEAR RESEARCH
Nuclear testing *see* NUCLEAR RESEARCH
Nutrition *see* FOOD

Occupational training *see* VOCATIONAL EDUCATION

Ocean dumping *see* SOLID WASTE DISPOSAL—MARINE POLLUTION
OCEANS
ODORS
Oil *see* PETROLEUM
Oil shale *see* ENERGY RESOURCES
OIL SPILLS
Open burning *see* AIR POLLUTION—LAWS AND LEGISLATION; SOLID WASTE MANAGEMENT—MINNESOTA
ORGANIC FARMING AND GARDENING
ORGANIZATIONS
ORGANIZATIONS, LEGAL
ORGANIZATIONS, MINNESOTA

PACKAGING
PAPER
PAPER INDUSTRY—MINNESOTA
PAPER PRODUCTS (RECYCLED)
PAPER RECYCLING
PARKS
PEOPLE
PESTICIDE CONTROLS
PESTICIDE EFFECTS
PESTICIDE RESIDUE
PESTICIDE USAGE
PESTICIDE USAGE—MINNESOTA
Pet population *see* POPULATION
PETROLEUM
Phosphates *see* DETERGENTS AND SOAPS
PICTURES
PLANTS
PLASTICS
POLITICIANS—ENVIRONMENTAL RECORDS
POLLUTION
Pollution—Economic aspects *see* ECONOMICS AND ENVIRONMENT
POLLUTION CONTROL
POPULATION
Posters *see* DISPLAYS
Power plants *see* POWER PRODUCTION; NUCLEAR POWER PLANTS; NUCLEAR POWER—MINNESOTA
PREDATOR CONTROL
PRUNING
Pyrolysis *see* SOLID WASTE DISPOSAL—PYROLYSIS

RADIATION
Radioactive fallout *see* NUCLEAR POLLUTION
Radioactive pollution *see* NUCLEAR POLLUTION
Radioactive waste disposal *see* RADIOACTIVE WASTES
RADIOACTIVE WASTES
RAIL TRANSPORTATION
Railroads *see* RAIL TRANSPORTATION
Rare animals *see* ENDANGERED SPECIES
Reclamation of land *see* LAND RECLAMATION
RECREATION
RECREATION—MINNESOTA

RECREATION PLANNING
RECYCLING
REDWOODS
REGIONAL PLANNING AND DEVELOPMENT
RESERVOIRS
RESOURCE CATALOGS
RIVERS AND WATERWAYS
RIVERS AND WATERWAYS—MINNESOTA
Road salting *see* SALT
RUBBER

ST. CROIX RIVER
SALT
Sanitary landfill *see* SOLID WASTE DISPOSAL—SANITARY LANDFILL
SEWAGE DISPOSAL
SEWAGE TREATMENT
SEWERS
SIERRA CLUB
Smog *see* AIR POLLUTION; AIR POLLUTION—CALIFORNIA
SNOWMOBILES
SOCIETY OF AMERICAN FORESTERS
SOIL CONSERVATION
SOIL CONSERVATION DISTRICTS
Soil erosion *see* EROSION
Solar energy *see* ENERGY—ALTERNATIVE SOURCES; ENERGY RESOURCES
SOLID WASTE
SOLID WASTE—LAWS AND LEGISLATION
SOLID WASTE—RECLAMATION AND REUSE
SOLID WASTE COLLECTION
SOLID WASTE DISPOSAL
Solid waste disposal—Composting *see* COMPOSTING
SOLID WASTE DISPOSAL—DUMPS
SOLID WASTE DISPOSAL—INCINERATION
SOLID WASTE DISPOSAL—MARINE
SOLID WASTE DISPOSAL—PYROLYSIS
SOLID WASTE DISPOSAL—SANITARY LANDFILL
SOLID WASTE MANAGEMENT
SOLID WASTE MANAGEMENT—MINNESOTA
SOUTHERN MINNESOTA RIVER BASIN COMMISSION
Spraying *see* PESTICIDE USAGE
State parks *see* PARKS
STEEL INDUSTRY
Stockholm conference *see* UNITED NATIONS CONFERENCE ON THE HUMAN ENVIRONMENT
STRIP MINING
STUDENT CONSERVATION PROGRAM
Superior, Lake *see* LAKE SUPERIOR
Supersonic transport (SST) *see* NOISE, AIRPLANE; AIRPLANE EXHAUST EMISSIONS
Surface mining *see* STRIP MINING
Swamps *see* WETLANDS

TACONITE
TERRARIUMS

195

Appendix 1

THERMAL POLLUTION
THERMAL POLLUTION—WATER
Tires *see* RUBBER
Towers *see* BROADCASTING TOWERS
TOXIC METALS
TRACKING
TRANSPORTATION
TRANSPORTATION—MINNESOTA
Tree planting *see* TREES
TREES
TREES—DISEASES AND PESTS
TREES—MINNESOTA
TROUT

UNITED NATIONS CONFERENCE ON THE HUMAN ENVIRONMENT
U.S. ARMY CORPS OF ENGINEERS
U.S. ENVIRONMENTAL PROTECTION AGENCY (EPA)
U.S. DEPARTMENT OF THE INTERIOR
U.S. BUREAU OF RECLAMATION
URBAN DESIGN
URBAN PLANNING

VICTOR GRUEN FOUNDATION
VISUAL POLLUTION
VOCATIONAL EDUCATION
VOYAGEURS NATIONAL PARK

Wastewater treatment *see* WATER PURIFICATION (MUNICIPAL); WATER REUSE (INDUSTRIAL); SEWAGE
WATER—MINNESOTA
WATER POLLUTION
WATER POLLUTION—EFFECTS ON LIFE
WATER POLLUTION—LAWS AND LEGISLATION
WATER POLLUTION—MINNESOTA
WATER POLLUTION CONTROL
WATER PURIFICATION
WATER QUALITY STANDARDS
WATER RESOURCES DEVELOPMENT
WATER RESOURCES DEVELOPMENT—MINNESOTA
Water Resources Research Center, University of Minnesota *see* WATER RESOURCES DEVELOPMENT—MINNESOTA

WATER REUSE
WATER SAMPLING
WATER SUPPLY
Water supply—Minneapolis *see* MINNEAPOLIS—DEPARTMENT OF WATER WORKS
WATER SUPPLY—MINNESOTA
WATERFOWL
Watersheds *see* WATER CONSERVATION
WEATHER
Weeds *see* HERBICIDES
WETLANDS
WILDERNESS
WILDERNESS AREAS
WILDERNESS SOCIETY
WILDLIFE
WILDLIFE—MINNESOTA
WILDLIFE CONSERVATION
WILDLIFE MANAGEMENT
WOLVES
WOOD

ZERO POPULATION GROWTH
ZONING
ZOOS

APPENDIX 2

Periodical List

This list includes periodicals and newsletters currently received in the Environmental Conservation Library. For each title the following information is provided: title, founding date, frequency of publication, annual subscription price, publisher or source and address. If a publication is received by ECOL directly from the publisher or organization, rather than through a subscription agent, the word *Direct* appears after the entry.

A few periodicals which have recently ceased publication are included if their contents are indexed in one or more standard indexes and they may still be useful in environmental research. Some titles which are listed as free may have some geographical or other restrictions on their distribution.

Due to the fact that periodical titles, publishers' addresses, and prices change frequently, the reader should check all such data against the current editions of *Ulrich's, Ayer's* and other standard directories.

AIChE Environmental Division Newsletter. Quarterly. Free? American Institute of Chemical Engineers, 345 E. 47th St., New York, NY 10017. Direct.

Air and Water News. 1967. Weekly. $145. 801-7 New Center Bldg., Detroit, MI 48202. Direct.

Air Pollution Control Association. Journal. 1951. Monthly. $25. Air Pollution Control Assn., 4400 Fifth Ave., Pittsburgh, PA 15213.

Air Pollution Notes. 1967. Bimonthly. Free. College of Agriculture and Environmental Science, Rutgers University, New Brunswick, NJ 08903. Direct.

Ambio. 1972. Bimonthly. $13. Universitetsforlaget, PO Box 142, Boston, MA 02113.

American Birds (incorporating *Audubon Field Notes*). 1947. Bimonthly. $6. National Audubon Society, 950 3rd Ave., New York, NY 10028.

American Forests. 1895. Monthly. $7.50. 1319 18th St. NW, Washington, DC 20036.

Archives of Environmental Health. 1954. Monthly. $12. American Medical Association, 535 N. Dearborn St., Chicago, IL 60610.

Audubon Magazine. 1899. Bimonthly. $10. 950 Third Ave., New York, NY 10022.

The Auk. 1884. Quarterly. $12. American Ornithologists Union, Museum of Natural History, Smithsonian Institution, Washington, DC 20560.

Aware; the environmental magazine about the electric industry. 1970. Monthly. $9. Community Performance Publications, 615 N. Sherman Ave., Madison, WI 53704.

Backpacker. 1973. Quarterly. $6. 28 W. 44th St., New York, NY 10036.

The Best Economically and Technologically Feasible Newsletter. 1972. Monthly. Free. Public Information Office, Minnesota Pollution Control Agency, 1935 W. County Road B2, Roseville, MN 55113. Direct.

Biological Conservation. 1968. Quarterly. $20. Applied Science Publishing Ltd., Ripple Road, Barking, Essex, England.

BioScience. 1951. Monthly. $24. American Institute of Biological Sciences, 3900 Wisconsin Ave., NW, Washington, DC 20016.

Bounty News. 1967? Semiannual. Free. Bounty Information Service, c/o Chas. Laun, Stephens College Post Office, Columbia, MO 65201. Direct.

Bulletin of the Atomic Scientists; a journal of science and public affairs. 1945. Monthly. $8.50. Educational Foundation for Nuclear Science, 1020-24 E. 58th St., Chicago, IL 60637.

Camp Natch News. 1968? Monthly Membership $4. Camp Natch Inc., 5148 29th Ave. So., Minneapolis, MN 55417. Direct.

Canadian Whole Earth Almanac. 1970. Quarterly. Ceased publication September 1973. Room 208, 341 Bloor St. West, Toronto 181, Canada.

Catalyst for Environmental Quality. 1971. Quarterly. $5. Circulation Dept., 274 Madison Ave., New York, NY 10016.

Center for Environmental Study News. Bimonthly. Free. Center for Environmental Study, 1447 Lake Drive SE, Grand Rapids, MI 49506.

ChemEcology. 1972. Monthly. Free. Manufacturing Chemists Assn., 1825 Connecticut Ave. NW, Washington, DC 20009.

Clean Air. 1971. Quarterly. $3.50. National Society for Clean Air, 136 North St., Brighton, BNI 1RG, England.

Clean Air; monthly Washington report. 1972. Monthly. $25. The Public Interest Campaign, 1525 New Hampshire Ave. NW, Washington, DC 20036.

Clean Air and Water News. 1967. Weekly. $100. Commerce Clearing House, Inc., 4025 W. Peterson Ave., Chicago, IL 60646. Direct.

Appendix 2

Clear Air Clear Water Unlimited. Newsletter. Irregular. Membership $5. PO Box 311, South St. Paul, MN 55075. Direct.

Clear Creek. 1972. Monthly. Ceased publication March 1973. 617 Mission St. San Francisco, CA 94105.

Clearing the Air. 1969. Monthly. Free. Metro Clean Air Committee, 1829 Portland Ave., Minneapolis, MN 55404. Direct.

Colorado Master Plan for Environmental Education Newsletter. 1972. Irregular. Free. Center for Research and Education, 2010 E. 17th Ave., Denver, CO 80206. Direct.

Colorado Open Space Council Newsletter. Irregular. Membership $10. Colorado Open Space Council, 1325 Delaware St., Denver, CO 80204. Direct.

Communicator. 1970. Monthly. Free. Great Lakes Basin Commission, PO Box 999, 3475 Plymouth Rd., Ann Arbor, MI 48106. Direct.

Compost Science. 1960? Bimonthly. $6. Rodale Press, 33 E. Minor St., Emmaus, PA 18049.

The Concrete Opposition. Irregular. Free. Highway Action Coalition, Room 731, 1346 Connecticut Ave. NW, Washington, DC 20036. Direct.

Conservation Foundation Letter. (formerly *CF Letter*). 1966. Monthly. $6. The Conservation Foundation, 1717 Massachusetts Ave. NW, Washington, DC 20036.

Conservation News. 1935. Biweekly. Free. National Wildlife Federation, 1412 16th St. NW, Washington, DC 20036. Direct.

Conservation Report. Weekly during sessions of Congress. Free. National Wildlife Federation, 1412 16th St. NW, Washington, DC 20036. Direct.

The Conservationist. 1955. Bimonthly. $2. New York State Department of Environmental Conservation, 50 Wolf Rd., Albany, NY 12201.

Critical Reviews in Environmental Control. 1970. Quarterly. $56. The Chemical Rubber Co., 18901 Cranwood Pkwy., Cleveland, OH 44128. Direct.

Cry California. 1965. Quarterly. Membership $12. California Tomorrow, 681 Market St., San Francisco, CA 94105.

Defenders of Wildlife News. 1926? Bimonthly. $5. Defenders of Wildlife, 2000 N. St. NW, Washington, DC 20036.

Down to Earth; a review of agricultural chemical progress. 1945? Quarterly. Free. Dow Chemical Co., Midland, MI 48640. Direct.

Dupont Context (formerly *Better Living*). Semiannual. Free. E. I. Dupont De Nemours and Co., Public Affairs Dept., D-8111, 1007 Market St., Wilmington, DE 19898.

ECOL News. 1972. Quarterly. Free. Environmental Conservation Library. Minneapolis Public Library, 300 Nicollet Mall, Minneapolis, MN 55401.

ELM Newsletter. 1970. Monthly. Free. Environmental Library of Minnesota, 1222 4th St. SE, Minneapolis, MN 55414. Direct.

EPA Bulletin. Monthly. Free. Office of Public Affairs, U.S. Environmental Protection Agency, Washington, DC 20460. Direct.

EPA Citizens Bulletin. Monthly. Free. Office of Public Affairs, U.S. Environmental Protection Agency, Washington, DC 20460. Direct.

Earth, I Care. 1971. Irregular. $5. Earth Awareness Foundation, Suite 209, 1730 Nasa Blvd., Houston, TX 77058.

Earth Journal (formerly *Minnesota Earth Journal*). 1971. Bimonthly. $5. Minnesota Geographic Society, PO Box 6181, Minnehaha Stn., Minneapolis, MN 55406. Direct.

Earth Science. 1946. Bimonthly. $3. Earth Science Publishing Co., Box 1815, Colorado Springs, CO 80901.

Ecolibrium. 1972. Quarterly. Free. Shell Oil Co., PO Box 2463, Rm. 1507, Houston, TX 77001. Direct.

Ecolog. Irregular. Free. Environmental Science Center, 5400 Glenwood Ave., Minneapolis, MN 55422. Direct.

Ecological Monographs. 1931. Quarterly. $14. Duke University Press, Box 6697, College Station, Durham, NC 27708.

The Ecological Society of America Bulletin. 1920. Quarterly. $4. Box 6697 College Station, Durham, NC 27708.

The Ecologist. 1970. Monthly. $9. 73 Molesworth St., Wadebridge, Cornwall PL27 8DS, England.

Ecology. 1920. Bimonthly. $24. Duke University Press, Box 6697, College Station, Durham, NC 27708.

Ecology Placement Service. Placement Bulletin. 1972. Monthly. $48. 1711 Lincoln Ave., St. Paul, MN 55105.

Eco-News; a young people's environmental newsletter. 1970. Monthly. $2. Environmental Action Coalition, 235 E. 49th St., New York, NY 10017.

EcoSystems. 1970. Monthly. Free. Oklahoma Environmental Information and Media Center, East Central State College, Ada, OK 74820. Direct.

Environment (formerly *Scientist and Citizen*). 1958. Monthly. $8.50. Committee for Environmental Information, 438 N. Skinker Blvd., St. Louis, MO 63130.

Environment Action Bulletin. 1970. Weekly. $10. Rodale Press, 33 E. Minor St., Emmaus, PA 18049. Direct.

Environment and Behavior. 1969. Quarterly. $18. Sage Publications, Inc., 275 S. Beverly Dr., Beverly Hills, CA 20212.

Environment Information ACCESS. 1971. Biweekly. $125. Environment Information Center, 124 E. 39th St., New York, NY 10016.

Environment Midwest (formerly *Region V Public Report*). Monthly. Free. Public Affairs Office, Region V EPA, 1 N. Wacker Dr., Chicago, IL 60606.

The Environment Monthly. Monthly. $35. 420 Lexington Ave., New York, NY 10017.

Environment News. Monthly. Free. Environmental Protection Agency, Region I, 2203 JFK Federal Building, Boston, MA 02203.

Environmental Action. 1969. Biweekly. $7.50. Environmental Action, Inc., Rm. 731, 1346 Connecticut Ave. NW, Washington, DC 20036.

Environmental Affairs. 1971. Quarterly. $18. Environmental Law Center, Boston College Law School, Brighton, MA 02135.

Environmental Awareness Reading List. 1969. Biweekly. $16. National Technical Information Service, U.S. Dept. of Commerce, Springfield, VA 22151.

Environmental Comment. 1973. Monthly. $20. Urban Land Institute, 1200 18th St. NW, Washington, DC 20036.

Environmental Letters. 1971. 8 per year. $45. Marcel Dekker Inc., 95 Madison Ave., New York, NY 10016.

Environmental Pollution. 1970. Quarterly. $40. Elsevier Publishing Co. Ltd., Ripple Rd., Barking, Essex, England.

Environmental Pollution and Control. Weekly. $23.50. National Technical Information Service, U.S. Dept. of Commerce, Springfield, VA 22151.

Environmental Quality. 1971. Monthly. Ceased publication Sept. 1973. Environmental Awareness Associates, 10658 Burbank Blvd., North Hollywood, CA 91061.

Environmental Quality Bulletin. 1967. Irregular. Free. Public Relations Dept., American Iron and Steel Institute, 1000 16th St. NW, Washington, DC 20036. Direct.

Environmental Science and Technology. 1967. Monthly. $9. Subscription Service Dept., American Chemical Society,

1115 Sixteenth St. NW, Washington, DC 20036.

Environmental Service Bureau [Newsletter]. 1971. Irregular. $5. 122 W. Franklin Ave., Minneapolis, MN 55404. Direct.

Environmental Spectrum. 1968. Bimonthly. Free. College of Agriculture and Environmental Science, Rutgers Univ., New Brunswick, NJ 08903. Direct.

Environmental Vistas. 1968. Quarterly. Free. Forest Service, U.S. Dept. of Agriculture, 633 West Wisconsin Ave., Milwaukee, WI 53203.

Facets of Freshwater Newsletter. 1970. Quarterly. Free. Freshwater Biological Research Foundation, 2845 Harriet Ave. So., Minneapolis, MN 55408. Direct.

Food and Nutrition News. 1971. Bimonthly. Free. National Live Stock and Meat Board, 36 So. Wabash Ave., Chicago, IL 60603. Direct.

Greater Minnesota. 1964. Bimonthly. $6. Minnesota Assn. of Commerce and Industry, 1600 Pioneer Bldg., St. Paul, MN 55101.

Howl. 1972. Monthly. $10. Canadian and American Wolf Defenders, 68 Panetta Rd., Carmel Valley, CA 93924.

hs popins. 1971. Irregular. Free. Population Institute, 100 Maryland Ave. NE, Washington, DC 20002.

Human Ecology. 1971. Semiannual. $28. Plenum Publishing Corp., 227 West 17th St., New York, NY 10011.

IVL Bulletin. 1972. Semiannual. Free. Institutet Föer Vattenoch Luftvaerdsforskning, Box 5607, S - 11486 Stockholm, Sweden.

Inland Bird Banding News. 1929. Bimonthly. $5. Larry L. Hood, ed., PO Box 478, Laurel, MA 20810.

Institute for Research on Land and Water Resources. Newsletter. 1970. Bimonthly. Free. Institute for Research on Land and Water Resources, Pennsylvania State University, University Park, PA 16802.

Intecol Bulletin. 1969. Annual. $3. Secretary General, Intecol, c/o Institute of Biology, 41 Queen's Gate, London S.W.7, England.

Interchange. 1972. Quarterly. $2. Population Reference Bureau, 1755 Massachusetts Ave. NW, Washington, DC 20036.

International Journal of Environmental Studies. 1970. Quarterly. $41. Gordon and Breach Science Publishers, One Park Ave., New York, NY 10016.

International Wildlife. 1971. Bimonthly. Membership $6.50. National Wildlife Federation, Inc., 1412 16th St. NW, Washington, DC 20036.

Journal of Environmental Education. 1970. Quarterly. $10. Dember Educational Research Services, Box 1605, Madison, WI 53701.

Journal of Environmental Management. 1973. Quarterly. $17. Academic Press, 111 Fifth Ave., New York, NY 10003.

Journal of Environmental Sciences. 1958. Bimonthly. Membership $14. Institute of Environmental Sciences, 940 E. Northwest Hwy., Mt. Prospect, IL 60056.

Journal of Forestry. 1902. Monthly. $18. Society of American Foresters, 1010 16th St. NW, Washington, DC 20036.

Journal of Outdoor Education. Three per year. Free. Box 299, Oregon, IL 61061. Direct.

Journal of Soil and Water Conservation. 1946. Bimonthly. $12.50. Soil Conservation Society of America, 7515 N.E. Ankeny Rd., Ankeny, IA 50051. Direct.

Journal of Wildlife Management. 1937. Quarterly. $20. The Wildlife Society, Suite S-176, 3900 Wisconsin Ave. NW, Washington, DC 20016.

The Kansas School Naturalist. 1954? Quarterly. Free in Kansas; included with subscription to *Nature Study*. Kansas State Teachers College, 1200 Commercial St., Emporia, KS 66801.

Kingfisher. 1950. Monthly. Free. Minneapolis Bird Club, PO Box 566, Minneapolis, MN 55440.

Lake Superior News. 1969. Irregular. Membership $2. Save Lake Superior Association, 1707 - 9th Ave., Two Harbors, MN 55616. Direct.

The Latest Word. Monthly. Free. Division of Game and Fish, Minn. Dept. of Natural Resources, 390 Centennial Bldg., St. Paul, MN 55155. Direct.

Library Reference Service, Federal Aid in Fish and Wildlife Restoration. Newsletter. Quarterly. Free. Denver Public Library, 1357 Broadway, Denver, CO 80203.

Lifestyle! 1973. Bimonthly. $6. PO Box 1, Unionville, OH 44088.

Limnos. Quarterly. 1968. $6. 3750 Nixon Road, Ann Arbor, MI 48105.

Living Wilderness. 1935. Quarterly. $4. The Wilderness Society, 729 15th St. NW, Washington, DC 20005.

The Loon. (formerly *The Flicker*). 1928. Quarterly. $4.50. Minnesota Ornithologists' Union, Museum of Natural History, University of Minnesota, Minneapolis, MN 55455.

MACI Environmental Affairs. (formerly *MACI Environment*). Irregular. Free. Minnesota Assn. of Commerce and Industry, 1600 Pioneer Bldg., St. Paul, MN 55101.

MECCA News. Bimonthly. Membership $10. Minnesota Environmental Control Citizens Assn., Central Manor, 26 E. Exchange St., St. Paul, MN 55101.

MPCA Board REPORT. 1973. Monthly. Free. Public Information Officer, Minn. Pollution Control Agency, 1935 W. County Rd. B2, Roseville, MN 55113.

Maine Environment. Monthly. $6. Natural Resources Council of Maine, 20 Willow St., Augusta, ME 04330.

Man and Resources. 1971. Irregular. Free. Canadian Council of Resources and Environment Ministers, 1170 Beaver Hall Sq., Montreal 111, PQ, Canada.

Marine Pollution Bulletin. 1970. Monthly. $11.17. Macmillan Journals Ltd., Little Essex St., London WC2R 3LF England.

Metropolitan Council Action Briefs. 1970. Biweekly. Free. Community Services Dept., Metropolitan Council, 300 Metro Sq. Bldg., 7th and Robert St., St. Paul, MN 55101. Direct.

Metropolitan Council Newsletter. 1968. Monthly. Free. Community Services Dept., Metropolitan Council, 300 Metro Sq. Bldg., 7th and Robert St., St. Paul, MN 55101.

Metropolitan Open Space Information Project. 1973. Irregular. Free. 111 E. Franklin Ave. So., Minneapolis, MN 55404. Direct.

Minneapolis Star and Tribune Index. 1971. Monthly. $100. Assistant Chief—Subject Depts., Minneapolis Public Library, 300 Nicollet Mall, Minneapolis, MN 55401. Direct.

Minnesota Academy of Science Journal. 1945. Semiannual. Membership $10. 3100 38th Ave. So., Minneapolis, MN 55406. Direct.

Minnesota Academy of Science. News, Notes, and Reminders. 1971. Bimonthly. Free. 3100 38th Ave. So., Minneapolis, MN 55406. Direct.

Minnesota Agricultural Economist. Monthly. Free. Agricultural Extension Service, University of Minnesota, St. Paul, MN 55101. Direct.

Minnesota Assn. for Conservation Education. 1971. Irregu-

Appendix 2

lar. Membership $5. MACE, 5400 Glenwood Ave., Minneapolis, MN 55422. Direct.

Minnesota Dept. of Natural Resources News. 1971. Weekly. Free. Minnesota Dept. of Natural Resources, Rm. 350, Centennial Office Bldg., St. Paul, MN 55101.

Minnesota Horticulturist. 1872. Bimonthly. $3.50. Minnesota State Horticultural Society, St. Paul Campus, University of Minnesota, St. Paul, MN 55101.

Minnesota Nature Center News. 1972. Irregular. $3. Northwoods Audubon Center, Sandstone, MN 55072. Direct.

Minnesota Out-of-Doors. Monthly. $3. Minnesota Conservation Federation, 4313 Shady Oak Rd., Hopkins, MN 55343. Direct.

Minnesota Pest Report. Weekly. Free. State of Minnesota, Dept. of Agriculture, Division of Plant Industry, 670 State Office Bldg., St. Paul, MN 55155. Direct.

Minnesota Science. 1953. Quarterly. Free. University of Minnesota Agricultural Experiment Station, St. Paul, MN 55101. Direct.

Minnesota Science Teachers Association Newsletter. Irregular. $5. Minnesota Academy of Science, 3100 38th Ave. So., Minneapolis, MN 55406. Direct.

Minnesota Volunteer (formerly *Conservation Volunteer*). 1939. Bimonthly. Free. Minnesota Department of Natural Resources, Centennial Bldg., 658 Cedar St., St. Paul, MN 55155. Direct.

Minnesota Waltonian. Irregular. Membership? The Izaak Walton League of America, Minnesota Chapter, 106 Times Bldg., 57 So. 4th St., Minneapolis, MN 55401. Direct.

Minnesota Weather Peek (formerly *Twin Cities Monthly Nature Peek*). 1972. Monthly. Donation. Bruce F. Watson, 2514 Brenner St., Roseville, MN 55113. Direct.

Minnesota Zoological Garden Newsletter. 1969. Irregular. Membership $8. Minnesota Zoological Board, Veterans Service Bldg., St. Paul, MN 55155. Direct.

Mother Earth News. 1970. Bimonthly. $6. PO Box 38, Madison, OH 44057.

NCRR Bulletin. 1971. Quarterly. $5. National Center for Resource Recovery, Inc., 1211 Connecticut Ave. NW, Washington, DC 20036. Direct.

National Coalition Against Poisoning of Wildlife. 1972. Bimonthly. $5. PO Box 14156, San Francisco, CA 94114. Direct.

National Parks and Conservation Magazine. 1919. Monthly. Membership $10. National Parks Assn., 1701 18th St. NW, Washington, DC 20009.

National Wildlife. 1962. Bimonthly. Membership $6.50. National Wildlife Federation, Inc., 1412 16th St. NW, Washington, DC 20036.

Natural History. 1900. Monthly. $8. American Museum of Natural History, Central Park West at 79th Street, New York, NY 10024.

Natural Resources Journal. 1960. Quarterly. $11. School of Law, The University of New Mexico, 1117 Stanford NE, Albuquerque, NM 87106.

Naturalist. 1949. Quarterly. $5. Natural History Society, 315 Medical Arts Bldg., Minneapolis, MN 55402.

Nature and Resources. 1964. Quarterly. $2.50. UNESCO Publications Center, PO Box 433, New York, NY 10016. Direct.

Nature Canada. 1939. Quarterly. $6. Canadian Nature Federation, 46 Elgin St., Ottawa KIP-5K6, Ontario, CAN.

Nature Study. 1946. Quarterly. Membership $5. American Nature Study Society, J. A. Gustafson, RD 1, Homer, NY 13077.

News From MEEC. 1972. Irregular. Free. Minnesota Environmental Education Council, Capital Sq. Bldg., St. Paul, MN 55101. Direct.

Northern Environmental Council Newsletter. Monthly. $6. PO Box 89, Ashland, WI 54806. Direct.

Not Man Apart. 1971. Monthly. Membership $15. Friends of the Earth, 529 Commercial St., San Francisco, CA 94111. Direct.

Nuclear News. 1957. Monthly. $30. American Nuclear Society, 244 East Ogden Ave., Hinsdale, IL 60521.

Nuclear Safety. Bimonthly. $3.50. Superintendent of Documents, Govt. Print. Off., Washington, DC 20402.

Oilletter. 1972. Monthly. Donation. Oil Coalition, 324 C St. SE, Washington, DC 20003. Direct.

102 Monitor. 1971. Monthly. $6.50. Superintendent of Documents, Govt. Print. Off., Washington, DC 20402.

Outdoor America (formerly *The Izaak Walton Magazine*). 1925. Monthly. $5. Izaak Walton League of America, 1800 N. Kent St., Suite 806, Arlington, VA 22209.

Outdoor News Bulletin. 1946. Biweekly. Free. Wildlife Management Institute, 709 Wire Bldg., Washington, DC 20005. Direct.

The Outfall. 1972. Monthly. Free. Metropolitan Sewer Board, 350 Metro Square Bldg., St. Paul, MN 55101. Direct.

PRB Selection. Irregular. Membership $5. Population Reference Bureau, 1755 Massachusetts Ave. NW, Washington, DC 20036. Direct.

Pesticides Monitoring Journal. 1967. Quarterly. $3. Superintendent of Documents, Govt. Print. Off., Washington, DC 20402.

Petroleum Independent. 1930. Bimonthly. $3. Independent Petroleum Assoc. of America, 1101 16th St. NW, Washington, DC 20036.

Phoenix Quarterly. 1969. Quarterly. Free. Institute of Scrap Iron and Steel, Inc., 1729 H Street NW, Washington, DC 20006. Direct.

Pollution Abstracts. 1970. Bimonthly. $80. PO Box 2369, LaJolla, CA 92037.

Pollution Engineering (U.S.). 1969. Monthly. $12. Technical Publishing Co., 35 Mason St., Greenwich, CT 06830.

Population Bulletin. 1944. Bimonthly. $5. Population Reference Bureau, 1755 Massachusetts Ave. NW, Washington, DC 20036.

Power from Oil. Quarterly. Free. Metropolitan Petroleum Co., 380 Madison Ave., New York, NY 10017. Direct.

Public Science (formerly *Science and Public Policy Study Group Newsletter*). 1970. Monthly. Individuals $15, Institutions $30. MIT Press, 28 Careton St., Cambridge, MA 02142.

Public Utilities Fortnightly. 1926. Biweekly. $30. Public Utilities Reports, Inc., Suite 502, 1828 L St. NW, Washington, DC 20036.

Ranger Rick's Nature Magazine. 1967. Monthly. Membership $7. National Wildlife Federation, 1412 16th Street NW, Washington, DC 20036.

Research and Development News. Monthly. Rates on request. Water Information Center, 44 Sintsink Drive East, Port Washington, Long Island, NY 11050.

Reuse/Recycle. 1972. Monthly. $25. Technomic Publishing Co., 265 W. State St., Westport, CT 06880. Direct.

SMEAC Newsletter, Environmental Education. 1970. Irregular. Free. ERIC Information Analysis Center for Science, Mathematics and Environmental Education, 400 Lincoln Tower, Ohio State University, Columbus, OH 43210.

Save Our Bays Association Newsletter. 1972. Quarterly. $1. 2348 Maple St., Seaford, NY 11783. Direct.

Science. 1880. Weekly. $20. American Association for the Advancement of Science, 1515 Massachusetts Ave. NW, Washington, DC 20005.

Science for the People. 1969. Bimonthly. $10. Scientists and Engineers for Social and Political Action, 9 Walden St., Jamaica Plain, MA 02130.

Science World; teacher's edition. 1946. Weekly. Teachers ed. $6. 902 Sylvan Ave., Englewood Cliffs, NJ 08732. Direct.

Scientific American. 1845. Monthly. $10. Scientific American, PO Box 5919, New York, NY 10017.

Selected References on Environmental Quality as it Relates to Health. 1971. Monthly. $7. Superintendent of Documents, Government Printing Office, Washington, DC 20402.

Selected Water Resources Abstracts. 1960. Semimonthly. $22. National Technical Information Service, Springfield, VA 22151.

Sierra Club Bulletin. 1893. Monthly. $5. 1050 Mills Tower, San Francisco, CA 94104.

Sierra North Star. 1964. Monthly. $2.50. Sierra Club, North Star Chapter, PO Box 80004, St. Paul MN 55108. Direct.

Soil Conservation. 1935. Monthly. $3.50. Superintendent of Documents, Government Printing Office, Washington, DC, 20402.

Solid Wastes Management—Refuse Removal Journal. 1958. Monthly. $7. Communication Channels, Inc., 461 8th Ave., New York, NY 10001.

South Dakota Conservation Digest. 1934. Bimonthly. $2. South Dakota Department of Game, Fish and Parks, Box 70, Pierre, SD 57501.

Special Report Ecology. 1971. Weekly. $135. Special Reports, Inc., 8 West 40th Street, New York, NY 10018.

Sport Fishing Institute Bulletin. Monthly. Free. Sport Fishing Institute, 608 13th St. NW, Washington, DC 20005. Direct.

Steel Facts. Quarterly. Free. American Iron and Steel Institute, 1000 16th St. NW, Washington, DC 20036. Direct.

TEEM; teachers' environment enrichment materials. 1972. Monthly Sept.-May. $12.50. T. S. Denison and Company, 5100 West 82nd St., Minneapolis, MN 55437.

Thunder Bay Field Naturalists Club Newsletter. 1947. Quarterly. Free. 226 North Franklin Street, Postal Station "F", Thunder Bay, Ontario. Direct.

Transit News. 1970. Monthly. Free. Twin Cities Area Metropolitan Transit Commission, 330 Metro Square Bldg., St. Paul, MN 55101. Direct.

UNESCO Courier. 1948. Monthly. $5. UNIPUB, Box 433, New York, NY 10016.

Voyageur. 1966. Irregular. $20. Box 7246, Powderhorn Station, Minneapolis, MN 55407. Direct.

Waste Age. 1970. Bimonthly. $10. 6311 Gross Point Road, Niles, IL 60648.

Waste Trade Journal. 1905. Weekly. Ceased publication June 1973. Atlas Publishing Company, 140 West 42nd Street, New York, NY 10036.

Water. Quarterly. Free. Water Resources Research Center, University of Minnesota, Rm. 107, Hubbard Bldg., 2675 University Ave., St. Paul, MN 55114. Direct.

Water, Air and Soil Pollution. 1971. Quarterly. $53.55. Reidel Publishing Co., PO Box 17, Dordrecht, Holland.

Water Newsletter. 1959. Biweekly. $28. Water Information Center, Inc., 44 Sintsink Drive E., Port Washington, NY 11050.

Water Pollution Abstracts. 1927. Monthly. $7.80. British Information Services, 845 Third Ave., New York, NY 10022.

Water Pollution Control Federation Highlights. 1964. Monthly. $2.50. 3900 Wisconsin Ave. NW, Washington, DC. 20016.

Water Pollution Control Federation Journal. 1929. Monthly. $35. 3900 Wisconsin Ave. NW, Washington, DC 20016.

Water Spectrum. 1969. Quarterly. $4.50. Superintendent of Documents, Government Printing Office, Washington, DC 20402.

Wilderness News. 1964. Quarterly. Free. Quetico-Superior Foundation, 2400 First National Bank Bldg., Minneapolis, MN 55402. Direct.

Wilderness Report. 1964. Irregular. Free? Wilderness Society, 729 15th St. NW, Washington, DC 20005.

Wildlife Review. 1935. Irregular. Free. United States. Bureau of Sport Fisheries and Wildlife, Patuxent Wildlife Research Center, Laurel, MD 20810. Direct.

Wilson Bulletin. 1889. Quarterly. $10. Wilson Ornithological Society, 2140 Lewis Drive, Lakewood, OH 44107.

Youth Advisory Board Newsletter. 1971. Irregular. Free. Environmental Protection Agency, 1 North Wacker Drive, Chicago, IL 60606.

Zero Population Growth. Monthly. Membership $15. Twin Cities Chapter ZPG, 111 E. Franklin Ave., Ramar Bldg., Suite 210, Minneapolis, MN 55404. Direct.